Dreamweaver 8

THE MISSING MANUAL

*The book that
should have been
in the box*

OTHER RESOURCES FROM O'REILLY

Related titles

Creating Web Sites: The Missing Manual

FrontPage 2003: The Missing Manual

Flash 8: The Missing Manual

Head First HTML with CSS and XHTML

Photoshop Elements 4: The Missing Manual

eBay: The Missing Manual

Yahoo! Hacks™

Google Hacks™

Web Site Measurement Hacks™

Internet Annoyances

oreilly.com

oreilly.com is more than a complete catalog of O'Reilly books. You'll also find links to news, events, articles, weblogs, sample chapters, and code examples.

oreillynet.com is the essential portal for developers interested in open and emerging technologies, including new platforms, programming languages, and operating systems.

Conferences

O'Reilly brings diverse innovators together to nurture the ideas that spark revolutionary industries. We specialize in documenting the latest tools and systems, translating the innovator's knowledge into useful skills for those in the trenches. Visit *conferences.oreilly.com* for our upcoming events.

Safari Bookshelf (*safari.oreilly.com*) is the premier online reference library for programmers and IT professionals. Conduct searches across more than 1,000 books. Subscribers can zero in on answers to time-critical questions in a matter of seconds. Read the books on your Bookshelf from cover to cover or simply flip to the page you need. Try it today with a free trial.

Dreamweaver 8
THE MISSING MANUAL

David Sawyer McFarland

POGUE PRESS™
O'REILLY®

Beijing · Cambridge · Farnham · Köln · Paris · Sebastopol · Taipei · Tokyo

Dreamweaver 8: The Missing Manual

by David Sawyer McFarland

Published by O'Reilly Media, Inc., 1005 Gravenstein Highway North, Sebastopol, CA 95472.

O'Reilly books may be purchased for educational, business, or sales promotional use. Online editions are also available for most titles (*safari.oreilly.com*). For more information, contact our corporate/institutional sales department: (800) 998-9938 or *corporate@oreilly.com*.

Printing History:

December 2005:   First Edition.

ISBN: 0-596-10056-6
[M]

Table of Contents

Part Four: Building a Web Site

Part Five: Dreamweaver Power

DREAMWEAVER 8: THE MISSING MANUAL

The Missing Credits

About the Author

David Sawyer McFarland is president of Sawyer McFarland Media, Inc., a Web development company in Portland, Oregon. He's been building Web sites since 1995, when he designed his first Web site: an online magazine for communication professionals. He's served as the Webmaster at the University of California at Berkeley and the Berkeley Multimedia Research Center, and he has helped build, design, and program numerous Web sites for clients including Intuit, Macworld.com, and Playlistmag.com, among others.

In addition to building Web sites, David is also a writer, trainer, and instructor. He's taught Dreamweaver at UC Berkeley Graduate School of Journalism, the Center for Electronic Art, the Academy of Art College, Ex'Pressions Center for New Media, and the Art Institute of Portland. He currently teaches in the Multimedia Program at Portland State University. He has written articles about Dreamweaver and the Web for *Macworld* magazine, CreativePro.com, and *MX Developer's Journal*.

David has used Dreamweaver since version 2, and he has acted as a member of Macromedia's Dreamweaver Advisory Council for several years. He welcomes feedback about this book by email: *missing@sawmac.com*. (If you're seeking technical help, however, please refer to the sources listed in Appendix A.)

About the Creative Team

David Pogue (editor) is the weekly computer columnist for the *New York Times*, an Emmy-winning correspondent for *CBS News Sunday Morning*, and the creator of the Missing Manual series. He's the author or co-author of 37 books, including 16 in this series and 6 in the "For Dummies" line (including *Macs*, *Magic*, *Opera*, and *Classical Music*). In his other life, David is a former Broadway show conductor, a magician, and a pianist. News and photos await at *www.davidpogue.com*. He welcomes feedback about his books at *david@pogueman.com*.

Peter Meyers (editor) works as an editor at O'Reilly Media on the Missing Manual series. He lives with his wife in New York City. Email: *peter.meyers@gmail.com*.

Linley Dolby (copy editor) spent several years in the production department at O'Reilly before moving to Martha's Vineyard to pursue a freelance career. She now helps whip technical books into shape for several companies, including O'Reilly and Pogue Press. Email: *linley@gremlinley.com*.

Sohaila Abdulali (copy editor) is a freelance writer and editor. She has published a novel, several children's books, and numerous short stories and articles. She is currently finishing an ethnography of an aboriginal Indian woman. She lives in New York City with her husband and daughter. Web: *www.sohailaink.com*.

Chris Banks (technical reviewer) is a senior software engineer at Macromedia and has worked on Dreamweaver since version 3. He describes the Dreamweaver team as "a great bunch of people and a joy to work with." In his spare time, he takes photos. He's blessed with a great wife, Alice, and his first child, Elizabeth, recently born. Email: *cbank@macromedia.com*.

Murray Summers (technical reviewer), a biochemist by training, has spent the last 20 years working in the computer industry. In 1998, Murray started his Web site production company, Great Web Sights (*www.great-web-sights.com*). He's a Team Macromedia member, a Macromedia Certified Web Site Developer and Dreamweaver Developer, and has contributed chapters and authored books about Web development.

Rose Cassano (cover illustration) has worked as an independent designer and illustrator for 20 years. Assignments have ranged from the nonprofit sector to corporate clientele. She lives in beautiful Southern Oregon, grateful for the miracles of modern technology that make working there a reality. Email: *cassano@uci.net*. Web: *www.rosecassano.com*.

Acknowledgements

Many thanks to all those who helped with this book, including my students, who always help me see technical issues through beginners' eyes, and the readers of previous editions of this book, who have given me great ideas, helped me fix important oversights, and pointed out the occassional typo. Thanks as well to my technical editors: Murray Summers, whose prolific critiques have provided a comfortable safety net to protect me from any embarassing gaffes, and Chris Bank of Macromedia, whose in-depth, insider knowledge of Dreamweaver has helped me understand many of the program's subtleties.

Of course, without the hard work of the Dremaweaver team, this book wouldn't have been possible.

Finally, thanks to David Pogue, whose unflagging enthusiasm and boundless energy never fails to inspire; to my editor, Peter Meyers, who has helped make my words sharper and my writing clearer; to my wife, Scholle, for being such a strong supporter of my writing and a wonderful partner in my life; my mom and Doug; Mary, David, Marisa, and Tessa; Phyllis and Les; and my son, Graham, who has given new meaning to my life and a profound understanding of the importance of sleep.

—David Sawyer McFarland

The Missing Manual series is a joint venture between Pogue Press—the dream team introduced on these pages—and O'Reilly Media, one of the most respected publishers on earth. It's only because Tim O'Reilly and his team had the vision to take a gamble on this concept that this book came into existence.

Thanks, too, to agent David Rogelberg; David Sawyer McFarland, who was not only a dream author but who performed an eleventh-hour "beta read" of his own; Lucie Haskins for her masterful indexing talent; Sanders Kleinfeld for his proof-reading smarts; and the other Pogues—Jennifer, Kelly, Tia, and Jeffrey—who make this series, and everything else, possible.

—David Pogue

The Missing Manual Series

Missing Manuals are witty, superbly written guides to computer products that don't come with printed manuals (which is just about all of them). Each book features a handcrafted index and cross-references to specific page numbers (not just "see Chapter 14").

Recent and upcoming titles include:

Access for Starters: The Missing Manual by Kate Chase and Scott Palmer

AppleScript: The Missing Manual by Adam Goldstein

AppleWorks 6: The Missing Manual by Jim Elferdink and David Reynolds

Creating Web Sites: The Missing Manual by Matthew MacDonald

eBay: The Missing Manual by Nancy Conner

Excel: The Missing Manual by Matthew MacDonald

Excel for Starters: The Missing Manual by Matthew MacDonald

FileMaker Pro 8: The Missing Manual by Geoff Coffey and Susan Prosser

FrontPage 2003: The Missing Manual by Jessica Mantaro

GarageBand 2: The Missing Manual by David Pogue

Google: The Missing Manual, Second Edition by Sarah Milstein and Rael Dornfest

Home Networking: The Missing Manual by Scott Lowe

iLife '05: The Missing Manual by David Pogue

iMovie HD & iDVD 5: The Missing Manual by David Pogue

iPhoto 5: The Missing Manual by David Pogue

iPod & iTunes: The Missing Manual, Third Edition by J.D. Biersdorfer

iWork '05: The Missing Manual by Jim Elferdink

Mac OS X Power Hound, Panther Edition by Rob Griffiths

Mac OS X: The Missing Manual, Tiger Edition by David Pogue

Office 2004 for Macintosh: The Missing Manual by Mark H. Walker and Franklin Tessler

PCs: The Missing Manual by Andy Rathbone

Photoshop Elements 4: The Missing Manual by Barbara Brundage

QuickBooks 2006: The Missing Manual by Bonnie Biafore

Quicken for Starters: The Missing Manual by Bonnie Biafore

Switching to the Mac: The Missing Manual, Tiger Edition by David Pogue and Adam Goldstein

Windows 2000 Pro: The Missing Manual by Sharon Crawford

Windows XP Power Hound by Preston Gralla

Windows XP for Starters: The Missing Manual by David Pogue

Windows XP Home Edition: The Missing Manual, Second Edition by David Pogue

Windows XP Pro: The Missing Manual, Second Edition by David Pogue, Craig Zacker, and Linda Zacker

Introduction

The World Wide Web continues to evolve, growing in scope and complexity, with new technologies popping up every year to make the Web look and work better. Even people building personal Web sites now employ various programming languages and server technologies to dish up content. Throughout its history, Dreamweaver has managed to keep pace with this changing technological landscape with each new version.

Dreamweaver 8 is no exception: It's capable of working with more technologies than any previous version. Whether you're creating database-enabled Active Server Pages, adding your favorite site's XML-based news feeds directly to your home page, using Cascading Style Sheets for cutting-edge design effects, or simply sticking to straightforward HTML pages, Dreamweaver has just about all the tools you need.

Any enterprising designer can create Web pages, Cascading Style Sheets, and even JavaScript programs with a simple text editor. In fact, Dreamweaver 8 provides powerful text-editing abilities for creating basic text files or complex Java server pages. But why go to all that trouble when Dreamweaver's *visual* page-building approach makes your job of creating beautiful and complex Web sites so much easier? Whether you're new to building Web pages or a hard-core, hand-coding HTML jockey, Dreamweaver is a powerful tool that lets you build Web sites quickly and efficiently, without compromising the quality of your code.

What's New in Dreamweaver 8

If you've never used Dreamweaver before, see Chapter 1 for a welcome and the grand tour. If you're upgrading from Dreamweaver MX 2004 or some other version, you'll find that Dreamweaver 8 offers a host of new features aimed at both the novice Web designer and the seasoned HTML guru.

- Dreamweaver 8 adds significant improvements to Dreamweaver's **Cascading Style Sheet** support. The program improves on Dreamweaver MX 2004's already excellent display of complex CSS designs. Now, even as you use cutting-edge CSS techniques to design your pages, Dreamweaver's visual Design view provides near WYSIWYG—what you see is what you get—editing power. In addition, to streamline the process of CSS style creation and editing, Dreamweaver 8 introduces a completely **new CSS Styles panel** that groups editing tools and CSS style inspectors into a unified, easy to use control panel. The program also makes it easy to create and use style sheets for different **media types**—for example, styles for pages you want viewers to print out—and new CSS visualization aids make it easy to see the placement and properties of CSS-positioned elements.

- To aid Web page design and layout, Dreamweaver 8 offers many new tools that have long made life easier for print page-layout veterans. Now you can **zoom** in and out of your page, which helps with pixel-perfect placement of graphics and page elements. **Guides** provide handy alignment aids, which you can freely move around the page to help with placement of page elements.

- You may find that you need different windows open when you work on different Web sites. For example, say you want the Application panel open when working on a database-driven site, but you want to hide it when working on plain old HTML pages. Dreamweaver 8 lets you create and save different **workspace layouts**. So, when switching over to a database-driven Web site, you won't need to waste time arranging the panels to fit your workflow—just turn on your previously created workspace layout and watch Dreamweaver rearrange its panels and inspectors for you.

- One of Dreamweaver's greatest time-savers has always been its FTP tool. When moving a page from your computer to your Web server, you don't have to switch to a different program, and go through a bunch of steps, to simply transfer files; Dreamweaver can get a page to or from your Web server with one simple button. It can even transfer a whole site's worth of files with a single command.

Unfortunately, in previous versions of Dreamweaver, doing this transfer also meant you had to wait and wait and wait while Dreamweaver beamed files across the Internet; you could never do anything else in the program while it was busy with this operation. Well, the wait is over. Dreamweaver 8 includes **background FTP**. Now, even if you move a thousand pages from your home computer to your Web server, you can still work on your Web site as Dreamweaver quietly and dutifully transfers files in the background. In addition, vastly improved **file synchronization** lets you feel confident that Dreamweaver can make sure all of the files on your Web server are up to date.

• For those people who write their HTML code by hand (eeeww), Dreamweaver 8 offers many coding enhancements, including a **coding toolbar** that offers a palette of buttons for common code-editing tasks (even hand coders like to push buttons with their mice). In addition, as you scan a 200-line HTML document, you can neatly hide chunks of HTML using **code collapse**. This feature lets you hide lines of code that you don't need to concentrate on—for example, a part of the page that's complete, or not relevant to the coding task at hand.

• One of Dreamweaver 8's most exciting new features is its visual **XSLT authoring tool**. Using Dreamweaver's visual design tools, you can create documents that display XML data just like a Web page. The program simplifies the creation of XSLT style sheets—a highly technical programming language. If you ever learned to write HTML by hand, writing XSLT code is about 10 times more difficult. Fortunately, Dreamweaver simplifies the process so that it's no more difficult than creating a Web page (in fact, the two procedures feel nearly the same). So now you can include news headlines collected from XML-based Web feeds directly on your site. Imagine adding headline news from CNN, sports news from ESPN, or local weather information from the National Weather Service right on your home page. Dreamweaver's also added support for **PHP 5** and **ColdFusion 7**, so you can use the latest versions of these server-side programming languages in your Dreamweaver sites.

• And if you don't find the answer you're looking for in this book (say it ain't so), you may find it in one of the many new **built-in reference guides** on topics like SQL, XML, and XSLT, provided by one of the most respected technology publishers, O'Reilly Media (which also happens to be the parent of the Missing Manual series).

Note: Macromedia occasionally issues updates to Dreamweaver. To make sure you're using the latest version, visit the Macromedia Web site at *www.macromedia.com/support/dreamweaver/downloads_updaters.html*.

HTML, XHTML, and CSS 101

Underneath the hood of any Web page—whether it's your uncle's "Check out this summer's fishin'" page or the home page of a billion-dollar online retailer—is nothing more than line after line of ordinary typed text. With its use of simple commands called *tags*, HTML (Hypertext Markup Language) is still at the heart of most of the Web.

The HTML code that creates a Web page can be as simple as this:

```
<html>
<head>
<title>Hey, I am the title of this Web page.</title>
```

```
</head>
<body>
<p>Hey, I am some body text on this Web page.</p>
</body>
</html>
```

While it may not be exciting, the HTML shown here is all you need to make an actual Web page.

Of Tags and Properties

In the example above—and, indeed, in the HTML code of any Web page you examine—you'll notice that most commands appear in *pairs* that surround a block of text or other commands.

These bracketed commands constitute the "markup" part of the Hypertext Markup Language and are called *tags*. Sandwiched between brackets, tags are simply instructions that tell a Web browser how to display the Web page.

The starting tag of each pair tells the browser where the instruction begins, and the ending tag tells it where the instruction ends. An ending tag always include a forward slash (/) after the first bracket symbol (<), which tells the browser that it is a closing tag.

Fortunately, Dreamweaver can generate all of these tags *automatically*. There's no need for you to memorize or even type these commands (although many programmers still enjoy doing so for greater control). Behind the scenes, Dreamweaver's all-consuming mission is to convert your visual designs into underlying codes like these:

- The <html> tag appears once at the beginning of a Web page and again (with an added slash) at the end. This tag tells a Web browser that the information contained in this document is written in HTML, as opposed to some other language. All the contents of a page, including other tags, appear between the opening and closing <html> tags.

  If you were to think of a Web page as a tree, the <html> tag would be its trunk. Springing from the trunk are two branches that represent the two main parts of any Web page: the head and the body.

- The *head* of a Web page, surrounded by <head> tags, contains the title of the page. It may also provide other, invisible information (such as search keywords) that browsers and Web search engines can exploit.

  In addition, the head can contain information that the Web browser uses for displaying the Web page and adding interactivity. *Cascading Style Sheet* information, used for formatting text and other elements, may be defined in the head of the document (see Chapter 6). In addition, JavaScript scripts, functions, and variables can be declared in the head of the document. In fact,

---

Dreamweaver Behaviors (Chapter 11) achieve their interactive effects with the help of JavaScript code stored in a page's head.

- The *body* of a Web page, as set apart by its surrounding <**body**> tags, contains all the information that appears inside a browser window—headlines, text, pictures, and so on.

In Dreamweaver, the blank white portion of the document window represents the body area (see Figure I-1). It resembles the blank window of a word processing program.

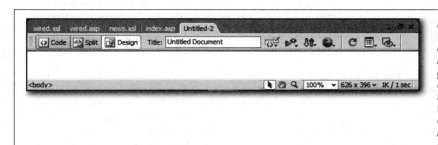

Figure I-1:
The document window displays your page as you build it. You can add text, graphics, and other elements to it, and—thanks to Dreamweaver's visual approach—see a close approximation of how the page will appear in a Web browser.

Most of your work with Dreamweaver involves inserting and formatting text, pictures, and other objects in the body of the document. Many tags commonly used in Web pages appear within the <body> tag. Here are a few:

- You can tell a Web browser where a paragraph of text begins with a <**p**> (opening paragraph tag), and where it ends with a </p> (closing paragraph tag).

- The <**strong**> tag is used to emphasize text. If you surround some text with it and its partner tag, </strong>, you get boldface type. The HTML snippet <strong>Warning!</strong> would tell a Web browser to display the word "Warning!" in bold type on the screen.

- The <**a**> tag, or anchor tag, creates a link (hyperlink) in a Web page. A link, of course, can lead anywhere on the Web. How do you tell the browser where the link should point? Simply give address instructions to the browser inside the <a> tags. For instance, you might type *<a href="http://www.missingmanuals. com/">Click here!</a>*.

The browser knows that when your visitor clicks the words "Click here!" it should go to the Missing Manual Web site. The *href* part of the tag is called, in Dreamweaver, a *property* (you may also hear the term *attribute*), and the URL (the Uniform Resource Locator, or Web address) is the *value*. In this example, *http://www.missingmanuals.com* is the *value* of the *Href* property.

Fortunately, Dreamweaver exempts you from having to type any of these codes and provides an easy-to-use window called the *Property inspector* for adding properties to your tags and other page elements. To create links the Dreamweaver way (read: the easy way), turn to Chapter 4.

XHTML, Too

Like any technology, HTML is showing its age. Although it's served its purpose well, it's always been a somewhat sloppy language. Among other things, it allows uppercase, lowercase, or mixed-case letters in tags (<body> and <BODY> are both correct, for example) and permits unclosed tags (so that you can use a single <p> tag without the closing </p> to create a paragraph). While this flexibility may make page writing easier, it also makes life more difficult for Web browsers, PDAs, and other technologies that must interact with data on the Web. Additionally, HTML doesn't work with one of the hottest up-and-coming Internet languages: XML, or Extensible Markup Language (see page 842 for a quick intro to XML).

To keep pace with the times, an improved version of HTML called XHTML is finding its way into more and more Web sites. Once again, Dreamweaver 8 is right on the cutting edge: it can create and work with XHTML files. If you understand only HTML, don't worry—XHTML isn't a revolutionary new language that takes years to learn. It's basically HTML, but with somewhat stricter guidelines. For example, the HTML page code shown on page 3 would look like *this* in XHTML:

```
<!DOCTYPE html PUBLIC "-//W3C//DTD XHTML 1.0 Transitional//EN"
"http://www.w3.org/TR/xhtml1/DTD/xhtml1-transitional.dtd">
<html xmlns="http://www.w3.org/1999/xhtml">
<head>
<title>Hey, I am the title of this Web page.</title>
<meta http-equiv="Content-Type" content="text/html; charset=iso-
8859-1" />
</head>
<body>
<p>Hey, I am some body text on this Web page.</p>
</body>
</html>
```

Notice that everything below the <head> is *exactly* the same as the HTML page. The information that begins the page, however, is how the page identifies which standards it conforms to. In this case, it merely says that the page is a type of XML document, in particular, an XHTML document. (Don't worry, Dreamweaver automatically writes all of this code when you create a new XHTML page.)

As you can see, the real code used to make the page is much like HTML. To make an XHTML file comply with XML, however, there are a few strict rules to keep in mind:

• **Begin the page with a document-type declaration and a namespace.** That's the first few lines in the code above. They simply state what type of document the page is and point to files on the Web that contain definitions for this type of file.

- **Tags and tag attributes must be lowercase.** Unlike in HTML, typing the tag <BODY> in an XHTML file is incorrect.

- **Quotation marks are required for tag attributes.** For example, a link written like this: <a href=http://www.missingmanual.com> is valid in HTML, but doesn't work in XHTML. You have to enclose the value of the Href property in quotes: <a href="http://www.missingmanual.com">.

- **All tags (even empty tags) must be closed.** To create a paragraph in XHTML, for example, you must begin with <p> and end with </p>. However, some tags don't come in pairs. These tags, called *empty tags,* have no closing tag. The line break tag is one example. To close an empty tag, you must include a backslash at the end of the tag, like this: <br />.

If all this seems a bit confusing, don't worry. All these strict XHTML rules are built into Dreamweaver, so creating an XHTML page using Dreamweaver's visual design tools won't feel one bit different from creating an old-style HTML page. (For more information on creating an XHTML page in Dreamweaver, see page 36.)

Note: Dreamweaver 8 adds support for XHTML 1.0 Strict and XHTML 1.1—two newer versions of XHTML.

Adding Style with Cascading Style Sheets

HTML used to be the only language you needed to know. You could build pages with colorful text and graphics and make words jump out using different sizes, fonts, and colors. But today, you can't add much visual sophistication to a site without Cascading Style Sheets (CSS). CSS is a formatting language used to make text look good, add sophisticated layout to pages, and basically add style to your site.

From now on, think of HTML as merely the language you use to give organization to a page. It helps identify and structure the stuff you want the world to know about. Tags like <h1>, <h2>, and <h3> denote headlines and assign them relative importance: a *heading 1* is more important than a *heading 2.* The <p> tag indicates a basic paragraph of information. Other tags provide further structural clues: for example, a <ul> tag identifies a bulleted list (to make a list of recipe ingredients more intelligible).

Cascading Style Sheets, on the other hand, add design flair to the highly structured HTML content, making it more beautiful and easier to read. In fact, Dreamweaver 8 adds many enhancements to its CSS tools. Essentially, a CSS *style* is just a rule that tells a Web browser how to display a particular element on a page—for example, to make a <h1> tag appear 36 pixels tall, in the Verdana font and the color orange.

But CSS is more powerful than that. You can use it to add borders, change margins, and even control the exact placement of an element on a page.

If you want to be a Web designer, you need to get to know Cascading Style Sheets. You'll learn more about this exciting technology in Chapter 6.

The Very Basics

You'll find very little jargon or nerd terminology in this book. You will, however, encounter a few terms and concepts that you'll encounter frequently in your computing life:

- **Clicking.** This book gives you three kinds of instructions that require you to use your computer's mouse or trackpad. To *click* means to point the arrow cursor at something on the screen and then—without moving the cursor at all—press and release the clicker button on the mouse (or laptop trackpad). To *double-click,* of course, means to click twice in rapid succession, again without moving the cursor at all. And to *drag* means to move the cursor while holding down the button.

- **Keyboard shortcuts.** Every time you take your hand off the keyboard to move the mouse, you lose time and potentially disrupt your creative flow. That's why many experienced computer fans use keystroke combinations instead of menu commands wherever possible. Ctrl+B (⌘-B), for example, is a keyboard shortcut for boldface type in Dreamweaver (and most other programs).

  When you see a shortcut like Ctrl+S (⌘-S), it's telling you to hold down the Ctrl or ⌘ key and, while it's down, type the letter S, and then release both keys. (This command, by the way, saves changes to the current document.)

- **Choice is good.** Dreamweaver frequently gives you several ways to trigger a particular command—by selecting a menu command, *or* by clicking a toolbar button, *or* by pressing a key combination, for example. Some people prefer the speed of keyboard shortcuts; others like the satisfaction of a visual command available in menus or toolbars. This book lists all of the alternatives, but by no means are you expected to memorize all of them.

About This Book

Despite the many improvements in software over the years, one feature has grown consistently worse: documentation. Until version 4, Dreamweaver came with a printed manual. But since MX 2004, all you get is a *Getting Started* booklet. To get any real information, you need to delve into the program's online help screens.

But even if you have no problem reading a help screen in one window as you work in another, something's still missing. At times, the terse electronic help screens assume you already understand the discussion at hand, and hurriedly skip over important topics that require an in-depth presentation. In addition, you don't always get an objective evaluation of the program's features. Engineers often add technically sophisticated features to a program because they *can,* not because you need them. You shouldn't have to waste your time learning features that don't help you get your work done.

The purpose of this book is to serve as the manual that should have been in the box. In this book's pages, you'll find step-by-step instructions for using every Dreamweaver feature, including those you may not even have quite understood, let alone mastered, such as Libraries, Layout view, Behaviors, Dreamweaver's Dynamic Web site tools, and Dreamweaver 8's new XML and XSLT features. In addition, you'll find clear evaluations of each feature that help you determine which ones are useful to you, as well as how and when to use them.

Note: This book periodically recommends *other* books, covering topics that are too specialized or tangential for a manual about using Dreamweaver. Careful readers may notice that not every one of these titles is published by Missing Manual parent O'Reilly Media. While we're happy to mention other Missing Manuals and books in the O'Reilly family, if there's a great book out there that doesn't happen to be published by O'Reilly, we'll still let you know about it.

Dreamweaver 8: The Missing Manual is designed to accommodate readers at every technical level. The primary discussions are written for advanced-beginner or intermediate computer users. But if you're new to building Web pages, special sidebar articles called "Up To Speed" provide the introductory information you need to understand the topic at hand. If you're an advanced user, on the other hand, keep your eye out for similar shaded boxes called "Power Users' Clinic." They offer more technical tips, tricks, and shortcuts for the experienced computer fan.

About → These → Arrows

Throughout this book, and throughout the Missing Manual series, you'll find sentences like this one: "Open the System → Library → Fonts folder." That's shorthand for a much longer instruction that directs you to open three nested folders in sequence, like this: "On your hard drive, you'll find a folder called System. Open that. Inside the System folder window is a folder called Library; double-click it to open it. Inside *that* folder is yet another one called Fonts. Double-click to open it, too."

Similarly, this kind of arrow shorthand helps to simplify the business of choosing commands in menus, as shown in Figure I-2.

Macintosh and Windows

Dreamweaver 8 works almost precisely the same way in its Macintosh and Windows versions. Every button in every dialog box is exactly the same; the software response to every command is identical. In this book, the illustrations have been given even-handed treatment, alternating between the two operating systems where Dreamweaver feels at home (Windows XP and Mac OS X).

One of the biggest differences between Mac and Windows software is the keystrokes, because the Ctrl key in Windows is the equivalent of the Macintosh ⌘ key.

And the key labeled Alt on a PC (and on non-U.S. Macs) is the equivalent of the Option key on American Mac keyboards.

Whenever this book refers to a key combination, therefore, you'll see the Windows keystroke listed first (with + symbols, as is customary in Windows documentation); the Macintosh keystroke follows in parentheses (with - symbols, in time-honored Mac fashion). In other words, you might read, "The keyboard shortcut for saving a file is Ctrl+S (⌘-S)."

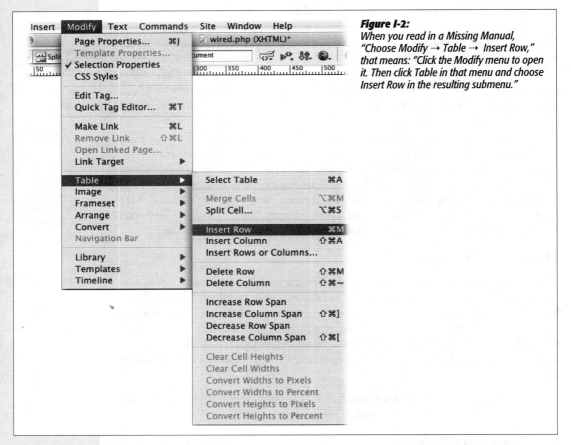

Figure I-2:
When you read in a Missing Manual, "Choose Modify → Table → Insert Row," that means: "Click the Modify menu to open it. Then click Table in that menu and choose Insert Row in the resulting submenu."

About the Outline

Dreamweaver 8: The Missing Manual is divided into six parts, each containing several chapters:

- Part One, **Building a Web Page,** explores Dreamweaver's interface and takes you through the basic steps of building a Web page. It explains how to add text and format it, how to link from one page to another, and how to spice up your designs with graphics.

- Part Two, **Building a Better Web Page,** takes you deeper into Dreamweaver and explains how to gain greater control of the design of a Web page. You'll learn how to use more advanced features, such as tables, layers, and Cascading Style Sheets. In addition, you'll get step-by-step instructions for creating advanced page layouts, as well as on how to view and work with the underlying HTML code of a page.

Note: Previous versions of this book contained a chapter on HTML frames—a method of displaying several Web pages in a single Web browser window. This technique is going the way of the dodo bird. Since Dreamweaver 8 has so many new and exciting features and this book's already bursting at its seams (if we added any more pages, we'd have to issue a medical warning to those with bad backs), the frames chapter has been moved online. You can find it, free of charge, at *www.sawmac.com/dw8/*.

- Part Three, **Bringing Your Pages to Life,** helps you add interactivity to your site. From using forms to collect information from your site's visitors to adding complex JavaScript programs, this section guides you through adding animation, multimedia, and other interactive effects with ease.

- Part Four, **Building a Web Site,** covers the big picture: managing the pages and files in your Web site, testing links and pages, and moving your site onto a Web server connected to the Internet. And since you're not always working solo, this section also covers features that let you work with a team of Web developers.

- Part Five, **Dreamweaver Power,** shows you how to take full advantage of such time-saving features as Libraries, Templates, and History panel automation. It also covers Dreamweaver's Extension Manager, a program that can add hundreds of new free and commercial features to the program.

- Part Six, **Dynamic Dreamweaver,** presents a gentle introduction to the often confusing and complex world of database-driven Web sites. You'll learn what you need to know to build a dynamic Web site; how to connect Dreamweaver to a database; and how to use Dreamweaver to build pages that can display database information as well as add, edit, and delete database records. The last chapter of this section covers Dreamweaver 8's powerful new XSLT tools for converting XML files (including RSS feeds) into browser-ready Web designs.

At the end of the book, two appendixes provide a list of Internet resources for additional Web design help and a menu-by-menu explanation of Dreamweaver 8.

Living Examples

This book is designed to get your work onto the Web faster and more professionally; it's only natural, then, that half the value of this book also lies on the Web.

As you read the book's chapters, you'll encounter a number of *living examples*— step-by-step tutorials that you can build yourself, using raw materials (like graphics and half-completed Web pages) that you can download from *www.sawmac. com/dw8/*. You might not gain very much from simply reading these step-by-step lessons while relaxing in your porch hammock. But if you take the time to work through them at the computer, you'll discover that these tutorials give you unprecedented insight into the way professional designers build Web pages.

You'll also find, in this book's lessons, the URLs of the finished pages, so that you can compare your Dreamweaver work with the final result. In other words, you won't just see pictures of Dreamweaver's output in the pages of the book; you'll find the actual, working Web pages on the Internet.

About MissingManuals.com

At *www.missingmanuals.com*, you'll find articles, tips, and updates to *Dreamweaver 8: The Missing Manual*. In fact, you're invited and encouraged to submit such corrections and updates yourself. In an effort to keep the book as up to date and accurate as possible, each time we print more copies of this book, we'll make any confirmed corrections you've suggested. We'll also note such changes on the Web site, so that you can mark important corrections into your own copy of the book, if you like. (Click the book's name, and then click the Errata link, to see the changes.)

In the meantime, we'd love to hear your own suggestions for new books in the Missing Manual line. There's a place for that on the Web site, too, as well as a place to sign up for free email notification of new titles in the series.

Safari® Enabled

 When you see a Safari® Enabled icon on the cover of your favorite technology book, that means the book is available online through the O'Reilly Network Safari Bookshelf.

Safari offers a solution that's better than e-books. It's a virtual library that lets you easily search thousands of top tech books, cut and paste code samples, download chapters, and find quick answers when you need the most accurate, current information. Try it for free at *http://safari.oreilly.com*.

Part One:
Building a Web Page

1

Dreamweaver 8 Guided Tour

Welcome to Dreamweaver 8

Dreamweaver is a program for producing and managing Web sites. Whether you need a simple five-page Web site to let your friends know about your summer vacation or a thousand-page e-commerce site with database connections and dynamically generated content, Dreamweaver can help. It lets you build Web pages and sites quickly and maintain them with ease. It also lets you add interactive behavior and advanced Web technologies like Cascading Style Sheets, Dynamic HTML, and database connectivity.

What Dreamweaver Is All About

Dreamweaver is a complete Web site production and management tool. It works with Web technologies like HTML, XHTML, CSS, and JavaScript.

The enhancements in the latest version, in fact, make it easier than ever to design and lay out Web sites. In particular, revamped Cascading Style Sheet support lets you access the latest Web techniques for creating fast-loading, easily modified Web page designs. Dreamweaver also includes a multitude of tools for managing Web sites once you've built them. You can check for broken links, use templates to streamline site-wide page changes, and reorganize your site in a flash with the program's site management tools.

Note: Get used to the acronym CSS, which you'll encounter frequently in this book. It stands for Cascading Style Sheets, a formatting language used to design HTML Web pages. Dreamweaver 8 continues the trend started in MX 2004 of integrating advanced CSS creation and editing tools into Dreamweaver.

It's also a serious tool for creating *dynamic* (database-driven) Web sites. You can now turn your company's database of products into a constantly updated online catalog—or turn that cherished recipe collection into an online culinary resource for an adoring public. You can even create Web pages for updating and deleting database records, meanwhile keeping designated areas of your site secure from unauthorized visitors. Best of all, Dreamweaver 8 does the programming for you.

If you've never used Dreamweaver before, but have already built one or more Web sites, you won't have to start from scratch. Dreamweaver happily opens Web pages and Web sites that were created in other programs without destroying any of your carefully handcrafted code. While Dreamweaver has always prided itself on leaving the HTML code you write exactly as you wrote it, Dreamweaver 8 offers more features for hand-coded Web pages.

Why Dreamweaver?

There are other Web design programs—dozens of them, in fact. But Dreamweaver has become one of the leading programs thanks to key benefits like these:

- **Visual page building.** If you've spent any time using a text editor to punch out the HTML code for your Web pages, you know the tedium involved in adding even a simple item like a photograph to a Web page. When your boss asks you to add her photo to the company home page, you launch your trusty text editor and type something like this: *<img src="images/staff/bigcheese.gif" width="100" height="150" alt="The Boss" border="0">*.

  Not only is this approach prone to typos, but it also separates you from what you want the page to *look* like.

  Dreamweaver, on the other hand, takes a *visual* approach to building Web pages. If you put an image on your page, Dreamweaver shows you the picture on the screen. As in a word processor, which displays documents onscreen as they look when printed, Dreamweaver provides a very close approximation of what your Web page will look like in a Web browser.

- **Complex interactivity, simply.** You've probably seen Web pages where a graphic (on a navigation bar, for example) lights up or changes appearance when you move your mouse over it.

  Dynamic effects like this—mouse rollovers, alert boxes, and navigational pop-up menus—usually require programming in JavaScript, a programming language that most Web browsers understand. While JavaScript can do amazing things, it requires time and practice to learn.

  But Dreamweaver relieves you of having to learn JavaScript for these purposes; the program makes it easy to add complex interactivity with just a click of the mouse. Chapter 11 explains how you can use these *behaviors* (ready-made Java-Script programs in Dreamweaver) to bring your pages to life.

• **Roundtrip code.** Every now and then, even in Dreamweaver, you may sometimes want to put aside the WYSIWYG (what you see is what you get) view and look at the underlying HTML code of a page. You may feel more comfortable creating some of your HTML by hand, for example, or you may want to tweak the HTML that Dreamweaver produces.

Macromedia realized that many professional Web developers still do a lot of work "in the trenches," typing HTML code by hand. In Dreamweaver, you can edit the raw HTML to your heart's content. Switching back and forth between the visual mode—called the Design view—and the Code view is seamless and, best of all, nondestructive. Unlike many visual Web page programs, where making a change in the WYSIWYG mode stomps all over the underlying HTML code, Dreamweaver respects hand-typed code and doesn't try to rewrite it (unless you ask it to).

In addition, Dreamweaver can open many other types of files commonly used in Web sites, such as external JavaScript files (.js files), so you don't have to switch to another program to work on them.

Dreamweaver 8 adds a lot more hand-coding power, including tools to make editing and viewing code easier. See Chapter 9 to learn more about how Dreamweaver handles writing and editing code.

UP TO SPEED

Hand Coding vs. WYSIWYG Editors

Creating Web pages in a text editor was long considered the best method of building Web sites. The precise control over HTML available when code is written by hand was (and often still is) seen as the only way to assure quality Web pages.

Hand coding's reputation as the only way to go for pros is fueled by the behavior of many visual page-building programs that add unnecessary code to pages—code that affects how a page appears and how quickly it downloads over the Internet.

But hand coding is time-consuming and error-prone. One typo can render a Web page useless.

Fortunately, Dreamweaver brings solid code writing to a visual environment. Since its earliest incarnation, Macromedia has prided itself on Dreamweaver's ability to produce clean HTML and its tolerance of code created by other programs—including text editors. In fact, Dreamweaver includes a powerful built-in text-editing mode that lets you freely manipulate the HTML of a page—or any other code, including JavaScript, Visual Basic, or ColdFusion Markup Language.

But the real story is that the code produced when working in the visual mode is as solid and well written as hand coding. Knowing this, you should feel free to take advantage of the increased productivity that Dreamweaver's visual-editing mode brings to your day-to-day work with its one-click objects, instant JavaScript, and simplified layout tools. Doing so won't compromise your code, and will certainly let you finish your next Web site in record time.

Besides, no Web design program is really WYSIWYG (what you see is what you get). Because every browser interprets the HTML language slightly differently, Web design is more like WYSIRWYGOAGD: what you see is roughly what you'll get, on a good day.

• **Site management tools.** Rarely will you build just a single Web page. More often, you'll be creating and editing pages that work together to form part of a Web site. Or you may be building an entire Web site from scratch.

Either way, Dreamweaver's site management tools make your job of dealing with site development easier. From managing links, images, pages, and other media to working with a team of people and moving your site onto a Web server, Dreamweaver automates many of the routine tasks every Webmaster faces. Part Four of this book looks at how Dreamweaver can help you build and maintain Web sites.

• **Database-driven Web sites.** Data makes the world go round. Whether you're a human-resource records manager or a high school teacher, you probably keep track of a lot of information. Today, companies and individuals store reams of information in database systems like Microsoft Access or Oracle 10g. Dreamweaver 8 can help you bring that information to life on the Web without having to learn a lot of programming along the way. From accessing information—such as the latest items in your company's product catalog—to updating and editing databases online, Dreamweaver 8 can help you build database-driven Web sites. Part Six of this book offers a gentle introduction to building dynamic Web sites.

• **Have it your way.** As if Dreamweaver didn't have enough going for it, the engineers at Macromedia have created a software product that is completely customizable, or, as they call it, *extensible.* Anyone can add to or change the menus, commands, objects, and windows in the program.

Suppose, for example, that you hardly ever use any of the commands in the Edit menu. By editing one text file in the Dreamweaver Configuration folder, you can get rid of any unwanted menu items—or even add new commands of your creation. This incredible flexibility lets you customize the program to fit your work methods, and even add features that Macromedia's programmers never imagined. Best of all, the Macromedia Exchange Web site includes hundreds of free and commercial extensions to download and add to Dreamweaver. See Chapter 19 for details.

The Dreamweaver 8 Interface

Dreamweaver's windows let you add and modify elements of a Web page. Macromedia refers to most of these windows as *panels,* and Dreamweaver has an almost overwhelming number of them.

Many of these windows are used to assist with specific tasks, like building style sheets, and are described in the relevant chapters. But you'll frequently interact with four main groups of windows: the document window, the Insert bar, the Property inspector, and panel groups.

Note: The look of these windows depends on what kind of computer you're using (Windows or Macintosh) and what changes you've made to the program's preference settings.

Even so, the features and functions generally work identically no matter what your situation. In this book, where the program's operation differs dramatically in one operating system or the other, special boxes and illustrations (labeled "For Macs Only" or "For Windows Only") will let you know.

The Document Window

You build your Web pages in the *document window.* As in a word processor, you can simply click inside the document window and type to add text to the page. You'll work in this window as you build a page, and you'll open new document windows as you add or edit pages for your site.

Several other screen components provide useful information about your document. They may appear in different locations in Windows or on the Mac (see Figures 1-1 and 1-2), but they work the same. For example:

- **Title bar.** The *title bar* shows the name of the file you're currently working on and, in Windows, where the file is located on your computer. In addition, if the Web page is XHTML-compliant (see page 6), then that's indicated in parentheses. For instance, in the example shown in Figure 1-1, the Web page is written in XHTML and is saved as a file named *aries.html* in the folder *horoscopes,* which is nested inside several other folders on the Y: drive. (In Windows, the title bar appears on the top of the screen; on the Mac, it's at the top of the document window, and the location of the file isn't listed.)

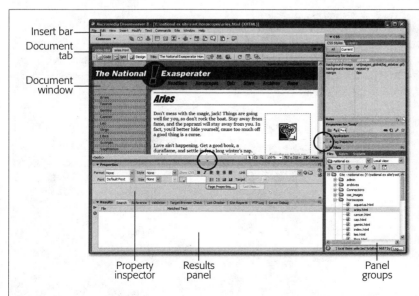

Insert bar
Document tab
Document window

Property inspector
Results panel
Panel groups

Figure 1-1:
Dreamweaver on a Windows PC. You can switch between documents by clicking the tab immediately above theDocument toolbar. Here, clicking the aries.html tab brings that page to the front. (This nifty feature works only if the document window is maximized.) You can also hide the panels in one fell swoop (either the stack of panels on the right edge of the window or the panels at the bottom-left) by clicking either of the Hide Panels buttons (circled). To show the panels, click the button again.

- **Document toolbar.** The *Document toolbar* lets you change the title of a page, switch between Design and Code views, preview the page in different Web browsers, access a context-sensitive reference (help) system, and change the look of the document window. You'll be reading about its various buttons and menus in the relevant chapters of this book. (To make the toolbar visible if it's not already, choose View → Toolbars → Document.)

- **The Standard toolbar.** The *Standard toolbar* includes buttons for frequent file and editing tasks like creating a new page, opening a page, saving one or all open documents, cutting, copying, pasting, and undoing and redoing actions. (This toolbar is hidden until you summon it by choosing View → Toolbars → Standard.)

GEM IN THE ROUGH

The Window Size Pop-Up Menu

Creating pages that look good on different monitors set to a wide range of resolutions is one of the most difficult tasks facing Web designers. After all, not everyone has a 21-inch monitor or views Web sites with the browser window maximized to fill the whole screen. Nothing's more dispiriting than spending a solid week designing the coolest-looking Web page, only to have your client call up to say that your design doesn't fit his 15-inch monitor (a painfully common story).

You can simulate browser windows of different sizes by dragging the resize handle at the lower-right corner of the document window, of course. But Dreamweaver has a better tool for such experiments: the Window Size pop-up menu on the status bar at the bottom of your document window. Clicking the black arrow next to the window-size stats lets you choose a different setting for the document window, as shown here. Use this feature to test how your page will look inside different-size browser windows. The numbers indicate the width and height in pixels.

(Windows note: If your document window is maximized, this feature doesn't work. Choose Window → Cascade to "unlock" the document window from its space on the screen. Now you're free to resize the window and use the Window Size pop-up menu. Note that this gets rid of the nifty document tabs that let you quickly switch between open documents—as pictured in Figure 1-1. To get them back, just click the Maximize window button in the document window.)

The first pair of numbers indicates the amount of usable space in the document window; the numbers in parentheses indicate the resolution of the monitor. The fourth option shown here, in other words, indicates that if someone has an 800×600 monitor and maximizes the browser window, there are 760×420 pixels of space to display a Web page. (Even though a monitor's resolution is, say, 800×600, after you subtract the space required to display the browser's toolbar, location bar, status bar, and other "chrome," 760×420 pixels of space will be visible when a Web page is opened.)

Dreamweaver 8 introduces a new feature—page guides—which also let you identify the viewable space of a page without having to completely resize your document window. See page 224 for more information.

In any case, note that the Window Size pop-up menu doesn't actually set the size of your Web page or add any code to your page; Web pages are usually fluid, and can grow or shrink to the size of each visitor's browser window. For techniques that let you exercise greater control of your page presentation, see Chapter 7.

- **The Style Rendering toolbar.** The *Style Rendering toolbar* lets you preview the effect of different CSS style sheets on your page. As described on page 169, you can use different style sheets for different types of displays and output devices. For example, you can make the page look one way when displayed on a monitor, but completely differently when printed. This tricky use of CSS, as well as how to use this nifty toolbar, is described on page 170. (This toolbar is also hidden until you choose View → Toolbars → Style Rendering.)

- **Head content.** Most of what you put on a Web page winds up in the *body* of the page, but some elements are specific to the region of the page called the *head*. Here you put things like the title of the page, *meta tags* (keywords) that provide information for some search engines and browsers, JavaScript scripts, and Cascading Style Sheet information (Chapter 6).

  None of this information is actually visible on your Web page once it's "live" on the Internet. But while working in Dreamweaver, you can have a look at it by choosing View → Head Content. You'll see a row of icons representing the different bits of information in the head.

- **The status bar** provides useful information about your page. It appears at the bottom of the document.

  The tag selector (shown in Figure 1-2) is also extremely useful. It provides a sneak peek at the HTML that, behind the scenes, composes your Web page. It indicates how tags are nested in the document, based on what you've selected or where the insertion point is.

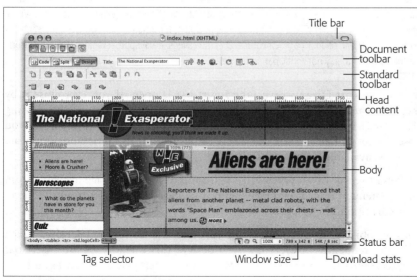

Figure 1-2:
Dreamweaver on the Mac. A document window like this represents each Web page; here's where you add text, graphics, and other objects as you build a page. As of Dreamweaver 8, the Mac version of Dreamweaver also includes tabs for switching between open documents.

You can also use the tag selector to select an HTML tag and all the information nested inside it. For instance, clicking the <p> tag selects the paragraph and everything inside it. This feature is very useful when you want to set *properties* (see "The Property Inspector" on page 24), add *behaviors* (Chapter 11), or precisely control the application of *styles* (Chapter 6).

You'll make good use of the tag selector in the tutorials to come. For experienced Dreamweaver fans, it's one of the program's most popular tools.

Tip: In Design view, clicking the <body> tag in the tag selector is usually the same as pressing Ctrl+A (⌘-A) or choosing Edit → Select All: it selects everything in the document window. However, if you've clicked inside of a table (Chapter 7) or inside of a CSS-positioned element (sometimes called a *layer* [Chapter 8]), you'll select only the contents of a table cell or layer. In this case, you need to press Ctrl+A (⌘-A) several times to select everything on a page. However, after selecting everything this way, you can press the Delete key to instantly get rid of everything in your document.

Careful, though. Pressing Ctrl+A (⌘-A) or choosing Edit → Select All in Code view selects all the code. Deleting *this* gives you an empty file—and an invalid Web page.

The Insert Bar

If the document window is your canvas, the Insert bar holds your brushes and paints, as shown in Figure 1-3. While you can add text to a Web page simply by typing in the document window, adding elements like images, horizontal rules, forms, and multimedia elements is simplified by the click-to-add approach of the Insert bar. Want to put a picture on your Web page? Just click the Image icon.

Note: Adding elements to your Web page this way may feel like magic, but the Insert bar is really just a quick way to add code to a page, whether it's HTML, XHTML, JavaScript, or server-side code like Visual Basic (see Part Six of this book). Clicking the horizontal-rule icon, for instance, simply inserts the <hr> tag into the underlying HTML of your page. Of course, Dreamweaver's visual approach hides that messy code and cheerfully displays a gray horizontal bar on the page.

When you first start Dreamweaver, the Insert bar is open. If you ever close it by mistake, you can open it again by choosing Window → Insert or by pressing Ctrl+F2 (⌘-F2). On the other hand, if space is at a premium on your screen, you can close the Insert bar and use the Insert *menu* instead. Its commands duplicate all the objects available from the Insert bar.

Eight different sets of objects are available from the Insert bar, each available from the pop-up menu at the left end (see Figure 1-3). Select a category from the menu to see the corresponding category of objects worth inserting:

- **Common objects.** In addition to images, tables, and horizontal rules, which you'll use frequently in everyday Web design, this category of the Insert bar offers access to Dreamweaver's *template* features. Templates let you build basic Web page designs that you can use over and over again in your site, speeding up your production process and facilitating easy updates. See Chapter 17 for details.

- **Layout objects.** The objects in this category help you control the layout of a Web page by organizing a page's contents using *HTML tables* or *layers*. In addition, this panel lets you use Dreamweaver's Layout view—a customized approach to building complex table designs that's covered in Chapter 7.

- **Form objects.** Want to get some input from visitors to your Web site? You can use *forms* to receive their comments, collect credit card information for online sales, or gather any other kind of data. The Forms tab lets you add form elements like radio buttons, pull-down menus, and text boxes (see Chapter 10). You'll also use this tab when building the dynamic Web pages discussed in Part Six.

- **Text objects.** For formatting type—making it bold or italic, for instance—you can turn to the Text category. Most of the buttons on this tab aren't technically objects; they don't insert new objects onto the page. Instead, they format text already present on the page. For the most part, the Property inspector offers the same formatting options and is a more common tool for formatting text.

Note: Using the Text objects tab can be disorienting. Some "text objects" create incomplete HTML and actually dump you into the raw HTML of the page, leaving the nice visual Design view behind. In general, the Property inspector and Text menu let you do everything in this tab—more quickly and more safely.

- **HTML objects.** This grab bag inserts elements that appear only in the <head> of a document (like keywords used for search engines); tags used for building tables and frames, and objects to insert JavaScript code; and horizontal rules. Like text objects (above), some of these work only in Code view.

- **Application objects.** Dreamweaver makes connecting your Web pages to databases as easy as clicking a few buttons. (OK, *almost* as easy; see Part Six.) The Application tab adds many powerful tools for building dynamic pages: controls that add records to your database, for example, or that update information already in a database.

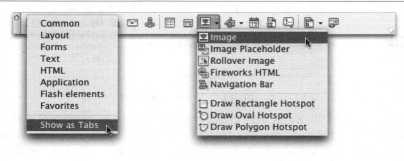

Figure 1-3:
Toolbar buttons are grouped into eight categories (Common, Layout, and so on). When you select a category, the other buttons change. If you prefer the original Dreamweaver MX tabbed style, select Show as Tabs. To leave tabs behind and return to the menu version, right-click any tab and select Show as Menu.

- **Flash elements.** Although nearly empty, this category in Dreamweaver 8 is intended to hold future *Flash elements*—Flash movies that you can customize with Dreamweaver. As of this writing, only one object shows up here—Image Viewer, which lets you build Flash slideshows (see page 452).

- **Favorites.** Perhaps the most useful category, Favorites can be anything you want it to be. That is, after you've discovered which objects you use the most (like the Image command, if you work with a lot of graphics), you can add them to this personal category. You may find that once you've customized this tab, you'll never again need the other categories in the Insert bar. For instructions on adding objects to your Favorites tab, see the box on page 118.

- **ASP, PHP, JSP, .NET, ColdFusion.** If you're building database-driven Web pages, you'll discover yet another category of objects. The exact name of the category depends on the server model you're using (Microsoft's Active Server Page or Macromedia's ColdFusion server, for example), but it always contains frequently used code snippets for that programming language. See Chapters 20 through 24 for more on working with databases.

The Property Inspector

After dropping in an image, table, or anything else from the Insert bar, you can use the Property inspector to fine-tune its appearance and attributes. Suppose, for example, that your boss has decided she wants her picture centered in the middle of the page. After highlighting her picture in the document window, you would then use the Property inspector to change its alignment.

The Property inspector (Figure 1-4) is a chameleon. It's aware of what you're working on in the document window—a table, an image, some text—and displays the appropriate set of properties (that is, options). You'll use the Property inspector extensively in Dreamweaver.

Figure 1-4:
If you don't see the Property inspector, you can reopen it by choosing Window → Properties, or by pressing Ctrl+F3 (⌘-F3).

For now, though, here are two essential tips to get you started:

- Double-click any blank gray area in the Property inspector—or striped area in Mac OS X—to hide or show the bottom half of the palette, where Dreamweaver displays an additional set of advanced options. (It's a good idea to leave the inspector fully expanded most of the time, since you may otherwise miss some useful options.)

- At its heart, the Property inspector is simply a display of the attributes of HTML tags. The *src* (source) attribute of the <img> (image) tag, for instance, tells a Web browser where to look for an image file.

The best way to make sure you're setting the properties of the correct object is to click its tag in the tag selector (see page 21).

Panel Groups

So far, this chapter has described the Insert bar, Property inspector, and document window—but those are just the beginning of Dreamweaver's windows. In Dreamweaver 8, most of the remaining windows—called *panels*—sit in tidy groups on the right edge of your screen.

For example, a panel group named Files harbors panels for working with your Web page files, Web site assets, and code snippets (see Figure 1-5).

Tip: To view the panels in a group, click the expander arrow or the panel group's name; to hide the panels, click the arrow (or name) again.

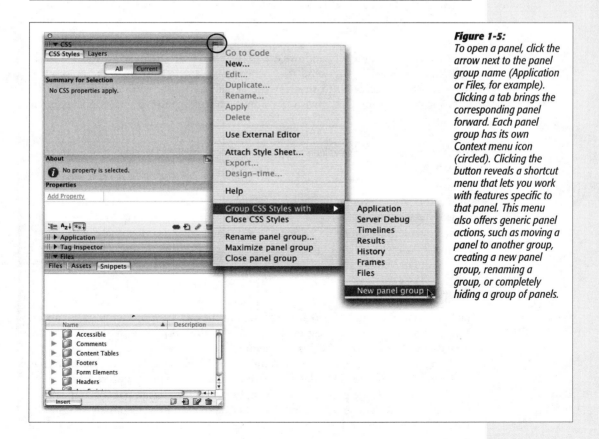

Figure 1-5:
To open a panel, click the arrow next to the panel group name (Application or Files, for example). Clicking a tab brings the corresponding panel forward. Each panel group has its own Context menu icon (circled). Clicking the button reveals a shortcut menu that lets you work with features specific to that panel. This menu also offers generic panel actions, such as moving a panel to another group, creating a new panel group, renaming a group, or completely hiding a group of panels.

The various panels and their uses will come up in relevant sections of this book. But a few tips concerning Dreamweaver's panels are worth noting here:

- You can open a particular panel from the Window menu. For example, to open the Files panel, choose Window → Files.

- Double-click anywhere in a panel group's gray title bar to open that panel group *and* expand it to fill the maximum space available. To give the panel as much space as possible, any open panels are also closed.

  This is really the best way to open a panel group. Not only is the title bar a larger target, but most panels contain a lot of information. You'll want to see as much of it as possible.

- You can even rename a panel group. Maybe the name Code doesn't make sense as the name of a panel group; after all, there are plenty of different kinds of codes involved in building Web sites.

  To rename a group, open its contextual menu, either by clicking the context menu *icon* (see Figure 1-5) or by right-clicking (Windows) or Control-clicking (Mac) the title bar. In the contextual menu, choose Rename Panel Group. Type the new name in the resulting window—*HTML*, in this example—and then click OK.

- If you want to hide all windows *except* for documents, choose Window → Hide Panels or press F4—a useful trick when you want to maximize the amount of your screen dedicated to showing the actual Web page you're working on. To bring back all of Dreamweaver's administrative windows, press F4 again or choose Window → Show Panels.

Tip: Dreamweaver for Windows includes a button for hiding only the panel groups. See Figure 1-1 for this handy trick.

- On the Mac, if you've really made a mess of your screen by dragging Dreamweaver windows all over the place, you can make them snap back into a tidy arrangement by choosing Window → Arrange Panels. (Unfortunately, this command arranges only tool panels and inspector windows. It doesn't arrange your document windows.)

Workspace Layouts

Dreamweaver 8 introduces a wonderful, time-saving productivity enhancer: Workspace Layouts. This feature lets you save the position and size of Dreamweaver's panels and windows as a "layout," which you can return to by simply selecting the layout's name from Window → Workspace Layout. For example, when you're working on a database-driven Web site, you may like to have the Application and Code panel groups open, but close the Design panel group. When working on a design-heavy site, on the other hand, you may absolutely require the Design panel group to be open, but could care less about the Tag Inspector. You can create a different layout for each situation and then simply switch between them.

First, you should organize your workspace the way you want to work:

- Open the panels you work with most frequently. For example, choose Window → Files to open the Files panel.

- Increase or decrease the height of a panel by dragging the empty space to the right of a panel or panel-group name (see Figure 1-6.)

- You can move a panel group to another area of your screen by dragging its gripper (see Figure 1-6). This is especially useful if you have a large monitor, since you can place one group of panels on the right edge of the monitor and another group either next to the first or on the left side of the monitor. If you're lucky enough to have two monitors hooked up to your computer, you can even spread the panels across both monitors.

Figure 1-6:
Resizing a panel is as easy as dragging up or down (circled). If you're lucky enough to have a large monitor, it's often helpful to put the Files panel by itself on either the left or right side of the screen.

- Open the toolbars you'll want to work with most often (see pages 20–21).

- Choose the Insert bar tab containing the objects you use most frequently. (You can collect your favorite objects onto a single tab, as described on page 118.)

To save your layout, select Window → Workspace Layout → Save Current (see Figure 1-7.) The Save Workspace Layout dialog box appears; type the name for the layout and click OK. (If you type the same name as a layout you've already saved, Dreamweaver lets you know it and gives you the option to replace the old layout with this new layout. This is the only way to update a layout you've previously created.) Dreamweaver saves your new layout.

Tip: This feature is also handy if you share your computer with other people. You can create your own Workspace Layout—use your own name when naming the layout—with all the panels and windows exactly where you like them. Then, when you go to use the computer and the bozo before you has rearranged the entire workspace, just select your layout from the Window → Workspace Layouts menu.

To switch to a layout you've already saved, simply select Window → Workspace Layout → The Name of Your Layout (see Figure 1-7). After a brief pause, Dreamweaver switches to the selected layout.

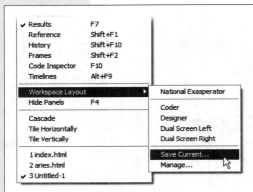

Figure 1-7:
The Windows version of Dreamweaver (shown here) includes three preprogrammed layouts, including one that puts all the panels and other windows on a second monitor, while leaving the first monitor available for just Web page documents. The Mac version has a default and a dual-screen layout.

The Dreamweaver Test Drive

Although reading a book is a good way to learn the ins and outs of a program, nothing beats sitting in front of the computer and taking a program through its paces. Many of this book's chapters, therefore, conclude with hands-on training: step-by-step tutorials that take you through the creation of a real, working, professionally designed Web site for the fictional online magazine the *National Exasperator*.

The rest of this chapter, for example, introduces Dreamweaver by taking you step by step through the process of building a Web page. It shouldn't take more than an hour. When it's over, you'll have learned the basic steps of building any Web page: creating and saving a new document, adding and formatting text, inserting graphics, adding links, and making the program work for you.

If you're already using Dreamweaver and want to jump right into the details of the program, feel free to skip this tutorial. On the other hand, this tutorial identifies some major changes in Dreamweaver 8, so you may want to take a spin, even if you're comfortable with Dreamweaver MX 2004. (And if you're the type who likes to read first and try second, read Chapters 2 through 5 and then return to this chapter to practice what you've just learned.)

Note: The tutorial in this chapter requires the example files from this book's Web site, *www.sawmac. com/missing/dw8/*. Click the Tutorials link to go to the tutorials page. Download the files by clicking the Chapter 1 link. All the tutorial files are stored as ZIP files: a type of file that compresses a lot of different files into one, smaller file.

Windows owners will need a utility to "unzip" or decompress the tutorial files. Many Windows machines include just such a utility, so double-clicking the downloaded file will usually do the trick. But if your computer doesn't have a program to unzip the file, you can download a free and easy-to-use unzip utility here: *http://members.ozemail.com.au/~nulifetv/freezip/freezip.exe*. Mac OS X has built-in ZIP support, so you can just double-click the file to decompress it.

At any rate, after you've downloaded and decompressed the files, you should have a DWTutorial1 folder on your computer, containing the Web pages and graphics needed for this tutorial.

UP TO SPEED

Folders Worth Knowing About

During the tutorial in these pages—and, indeed, everywhere in Dreamweaver—you'll encounter a few terms frequently heard at Web designer luncheons:

- **Root folder.** The first basic rule of Web design is that every piece of the site you're working on—Web page (HTML) documents, graphic images, sound files, and so on—must sit in a single folder on your hard drive. That master folder is the *root* folder for your Web site—in fact, it's the local root folder. (*Local* means on your computer, as opposed to the copies of these Web pages that will ultimately hang on the Internet. *Root* means the master, outer, main folder.) Of course, to help organize your site's files, you can include any number of subfolders inside the root folder.

- **Local site.** The usual routine for creating Web pages goes like this: you first create the page on your own computer, using a program like Dreamweaver; then you upload it to a computer on the Internet called a Web server, where your handiwork becomes available to the masses. In other words, almost every Web site in the universe exists in two places at once. One copy is on the Internet, where everyone can get at it. The other, original copy is on some Web designer's hard drive.

The copy on your own computer is called the *local site*, or the development site. Think of the local site as a sort of staging ground, where you build your site, test it, and modify it. Because the local site isn't on a Web server and can't be accessed by the public, you can freely edit and add to a local site without affecting the pages your visitors are viewing, meanwhile, on the remote site.

- **Remote site.** When you've added or updated a file, you move it from the local site to the remote site. The *remote*, or live, site is a mirror image of the local site. Because you create it by uploading your local site, it has the same organizational folder structure as the local site and contains the same files. Only polished, fully functional pages go online to the remote site; save the half-finished, typo-ridden drafts for your local site. Chapter 15 explains how to use Dreamweaver's FTP features to define and work with a remote site.

(If you're using Dreamweaver's database features, by the way, you'll encounter yet another term: a testing server. You'll find the lowdown on this kind of site, which is used to test database features, on page 689.)

Phase 1: Getting Dreamweaver in Shape

Before you get started working in Dreamweaver, you need to make sure the program's all set up to work for you. In the following steps, you'll double-check a key Dreamweaver preference setting, and you'll organize your workspace using the new Workspace Layout feature.

First, you'll make sure the preferences are all set:

1. **If it isn't already open, start Dreamweaver.**

   Hey, you've got to start with the basics, right?

2. **Choose Edit → Preferences (Windows) or Dreamweaver → Preferences (Mac).**

   The Preferences dialog box opens, listing a dizzying array of categories and options (see Figure 1-8).

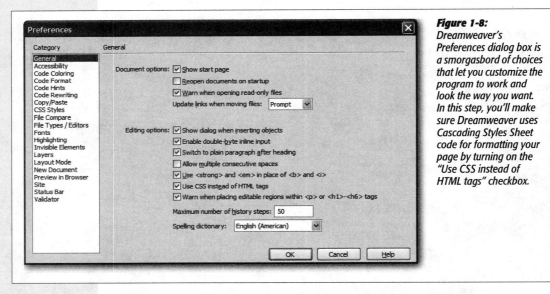

Figure 1-8:
Dreamweaver's Preferences dialog box is a smorgasbord of choices that let you customize the program to work and look the way you want. In this step, you'll make sure Dreamweaver uses Cascading Styles Sheet code for formatting your page by turning on the "Use CSS instead of HTML tags" checkbox.

3. **In the Category list on the left side of the Preferences dialog box, click General. Make sure the checkbox "Use CSS instead of HTML tags" is turned on.**

   The program offers wide support for Cascading Style Sheets, but also still supports outdated HTML tags to add formatting to text, links, and basic properties of a Web page, as described in the note on the next page.

Note: Out of the box, Dreamweaver uses CSS (instead of the outmoded <font> tag) to format text and old-school HTML attributes to format the <body> tag.

You may still want to use old HTML tags in a couple of cases: if you already have a site that uses the <font> tag religiously and you're not ready to undertake the big challenge of converting the entire site to CSS, or if you're using Dreamweaver to create an HTML email. Though many email programs can display emails formatted with CSS, to play it safe and make sure your HTML email looks good in as many email programs as possible, it's a good idea to use the old <font> tags for formatting text. To use these tags, turn off "Use CSS Instead of HTML tags," as pictured in Figure 1-8. But be careful; that approach is *deprecated* (considered obsolete) by the W3C, the main Web standards organization. Future browsers may not understand those tags and attributes.

4. **Click OK.**

   The dialog box closes. You're ready to get your workspace in order. As noted at the beginning of this chapter, Dreamweaver has many different windows that help you build Web pages. For this tutorial, though, you'll need only three: the Insert bar, the document window, and the Property inspector. But, for good measure (and to give you a bit of practice) you'll open a few panels as well.

5. **Make sure the Property inspector and Insert bar are open (see Figure 1-1).**

   If they aren't, choose Window → Property Inspector and Window → Insert Bar, respectively (see Figure 1-9).

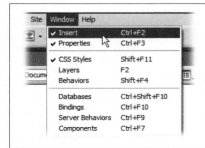

Figure 1-9:
In the Window menu, a checkmark next to the window or panel name lets you know that it's open.

6. **If the CSS styles panel isn't open, choose Window → CSS Styles.**

   This panel lists styles—essentially, formatting instructions for your page—that you've created. You'll use it frequently; it's discussed in greater detail on page 165.

7. **If the Files panel isn't open, choose Window → Files.**

   This is another frequently encountered panel. It lists all the files in your site and provides an easy way to open, delete, and manage your Web pages.

With the most important windows and panels open, you'll clean up your workspace by eliminating a panel group that you won't use for any of these basic tutorials.

8. **Right-click (Control-click on Mac) the empty area to the right of the Application group tab (see Figure 1-10) and from the pop-up menu, select "Close panel group."**

This closes the Application panel, which is used for the advanced, database-driven Web sites described in Part Six of this book. Your workspace is all set up now; next, you'll save this layout, so you can return to this exact same positioning of panels and windows whenever you like.

Note: Don't worry if you make a mess of your workspace, you can always revert back to the original setup by choosing Window → Workspace Layout → Designer (Windows) or Window → Workspace Layout → Default (Mac).

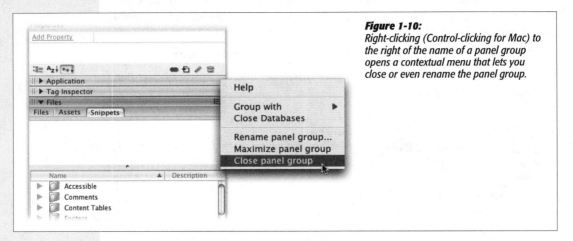

Figure 1-10:
Right-clicking (Control-clicking for Mac) to the right of the name of a panel group opens a contextual menu that lets you close or even rename the panel group.

9. **Choose Window → Workspace Layout → Save Current….**

The Save Workspace Layout window appears, waiting for you to name your new layout.

10. **Type *Tutorial 1* (or any name you like) and click OK.**

You've just created a new workspace layout. To see if it works, you'll switch to Dreamweaver's original layout, see how the screen changes, and then switch back to your new setup.

11. **Choose Window → Workspace Layout → Designer (Default on the Mac).**

This returns the workspace to what you see when you first install Dreamweaver; notice how the Application panel reappears and the CSS Styles panel is closed.

12. **Choose Window → Workspace Layout → Tutorial 1 (or whatever name you gave in step 10).**

Voilà! Dreamweaver sets up everything the way you want it. You can create multiple layouts for different Web sites or different types of sites.

Phase 2: Creating a Web Site

Whenever you build a new Web site or edit an existing one, you must begin by introducing Dreamweaver to it—a process called *defining a site*. This is the most important first step when you start using Dreamweaver, whether you plan to work on a five-page Web site, build a thousand-page online store, or edit an existing Web site.

Whenever you want to use Dreamweaver to create or edit a Web site, your first step is always to show the program where the *root folder* is—the master folder for all your Web site files. You do it like this:

1. **Choose Site → New Site.**

The Site Definition window appears. There's a basic and an advanced method for defining a site. You'll learn the basic method first, so make sure the Basic tab is selected (see Figure 1-11).

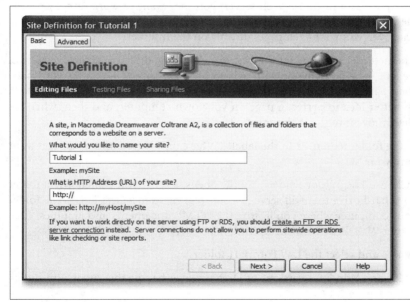

Figure 1-11:
The Basic tab of the Site Definition window takes you step by step through the process of setting up a new site. Each stage of the process—Editing Files, Testing Files, and Sharing Files—is clearly labeled. Depending on the type of site you're building, and which Dreamweaver features you plan on using, you'll be taken through a series of simple questions that help you set up your site.

2. **Type *Tutorial 1* in the Site Name field.**

The name you type here is solely for your own reference, to help you identify the site in Dreamweaver's Site menu. It won't appear on the Web. Dreamweaver also asks for the Web address for your site. On a real site, you'd type an address like *http://www.mysite.com/*, but for this tutorial, there isn't any real Web site, and Dreamweaver works just fine when you leave this blank.

3. **Click Next.**

   In the next step, you'll tell Dreamweaver whether you plan on building (a) regular Web pages or (b) pages that require a special server for creating the dynamic, database-driven Web sites discussed in Part Six of this book.

4. **Click "No, I do not want to use a server technology." Click Next.**

   In this tutorial, you'll be building a basic Web page.

   In the next steps, you'll tell Dreamweaver how you want to work on the files in your site and where you'll store those files. In this example, you'll use the folder you downloaded from this book's Web site (at other times, you'll choose or create a folder of your own).

5. **Click "Edit local copies on my machine."**

   Understanding why you made this choice takes a bit of explanation.

   The most common method of working on the files of a Web site involves having two sets of files: the *local site* on your hard drive and the *remote site* on the Web (see the box on page 29).

   But there are other ways to work on Web sites. For example, if you work at a company with an in-house Web server, you may want to work directly on the online Web files over the corporate network. In fact, there's a third method: you can even edit your Web pages directly on the Internet.

   But the first method is by far the best one. Working directly on the live version of the site—the one anyone with a Web browser can see—exposes your half-finished pages, with their typos and missing pictures, to your audience. It's a much better idea to perfect a page on your own computer, and then, when it's finished, move it to the Web server.

6. **Click the folder icon next to the label, "Where on your computer do you want to store your files?"**

   The Choose Local Root Folder window opens, so that you can choose a folder on your hard drive that will serve as your *local root site folder*. This is the folder on your computer where you'll store the HTML documents and graphics, CSS, and other Web files that make up your Web site.

7. **Browse to and select the DWTutorial1 folder.**

   The Mac and Windows versions of Dreamweaver handle this ritual a bit differently; see Figure 1-12.

   If you were starting a Web site from scratch, you could also create a new empty folder at this point. You would then save your Web pages and graphics into this folder as you built your site.

   For more on root folders and organizing Web sites, see Part Four of this book. For now, the fact to burn into your brain is that all the files that will constitute your Web site must live in the local root folder while you're working on them. (You can have subfolders with Web files *inside* the local root folder. You just can't have any files *outside* this root folder.)

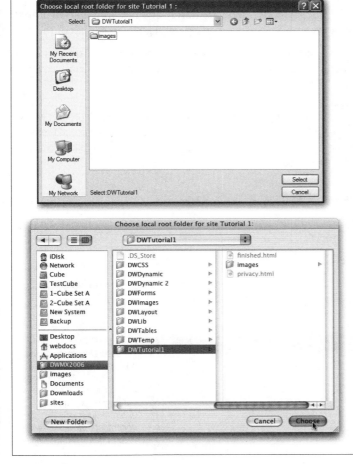

Figure 1-12:
When it comes to selecting a local root folder, the Windows and Mac versions of Dreamweaver differ slightly.

Top: In Windows, the folder name appears in the Select field at the top of the Choose Local Folder window. Click Select to define it as the local root.

Bottom: In Mac OS X 10.3 or later, highlight a folder in the list in the middle of the window and then click Choose to set it as the local root folder.

8. **Click Next.**

    Now Dreamweaver asks how you want to connect to your *remote server*—the computer that will dish up the finished Web files to your adoring public.

9. **From the "How do you connect to your remote server?" menu, choose None; click Next.**

    Dreamweaver can move your files to a Web server automatically, as you'll learn in Chapter 15.

    After clicking Next, you'll see a summary of your settings. If you made a mistake, click Back to return to the appropriate step in the process to make changes.

10. **Click Done.**

After defining the site, Dreamweaver creates a *site cache* for your Web site. That's a small database (cache) that tracks pages, links, images, and other components of your site. The cache helps Dreamweaver's site-management tools avoid breaking links, warn you when you're about to delete important files, and help you reorganize your site quickly. Since there are hardly any files in the DWTutorial1 folder, you may not even notice this happening—it'll go by in a blink of the eye.

Defining a site doesn't actually do anything to your computer; it doesn't create a home page or add a folder, for example. It merely prepares Dreamweaver for working on a site.

Tip: Dreamweaver lets you define *multiple* Web sites, a handy feature if you're a Web designer with several clients, or if your company builds and manages more than one site. To define an additional site, choose Site → New Site and follow the steps starting on page 33. You can then switch from one site to another using the Site List in the Files panel.

Phase 3: Creating and Saving a Web Page

"Enough already! I want to build a Web page," you're probably saying. You'll do so in this phase of the tutorial:

1. **Choose File → New.**

Although you may already have a blank document open, you should get to know the New Document dialog box (see Figure 1-13).

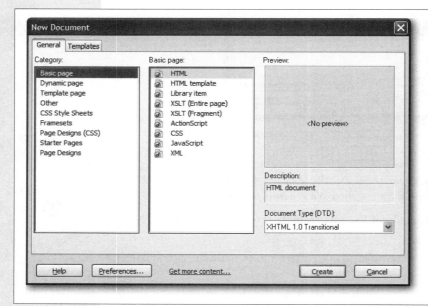

Figure 1-13:
The New Document dialog box appears whenever you choose File → New or press Ctrl+N (⌘-N). It lets you create a whole range of different types of documents, including basic Web pages, dynamic pages (see Part Six), style sheets (Chapter 6), and templates (Chapter 17), to name a few. Furthermore, the categories labeled CSS Style Sheets, Framesets, Page Designs (CSS), Starter Pages, and Page Designs include a bunch of ready-made Web page designs.

Tip: If you don't want to deal with this window every time you create a new page, click Preferences. In the Preferences dialog box, click the New Document category and turn off the "Show New Document Dialog on Control-N" checkbox.

While you're at it, you can also specify what kind of file you want Dreamweaver to make whenever you press Ctrl+N (⌘-N). For example, if you most commonly create plain HTML files, choose HTML. But if you most often create dynamic pages (like the ASP.NET pages described on page 686), choose a different type of file—ASP.NET VB, for example.

With these settings, pressing Ctrl+N (⌘-N) will instantly create a new blank document. (Choosing File → New, however, will still open the New Document window.)

2. **On the General panel, highlight the Basic Page category; in the Basic page list, highlight HTML.**

   You'll do one last thing before finally creating your new Web page: to be truly up to the minute with Web building techniques, you'll also use XHTML to build this page. XHTML, further described on page 6, is the latest incarnation of HTML. The main Web standards organization, the World Wide Web Consortium (W3C), recommends it due to its compatibility with future standards and its cleaner, more logical structure. (In other words, plain-old HTML sites will theoretically become technologically obsolete before XHTML sites.)

3. **Select "XHTML 1.0 Transitional" from the Document Type (DTD) menu in the bottom right of the window.**

   The window should look like Figure 1-13. There are actually several "flavors" of XHTML. The "Transitional" type will keep your pages compatible with older browsers and give you a wider range of HTML tags to work with. If you want to continue to create regular HTML pages, select "HTML 4.01 Transitional" (this is the standard type for previous versions of Dreamweaver) or "HTML 4.01 Strict."

4. **Click Create.**

   Dreamweaver opens a new, blank XHTML page. Even though the underlying code for an XHTML page is different in many ways from that of a plain HTML page, you have nothing to worry about. Dreamweaver manages all that code, so you don't have to.

5. **Choose File → Save.**

   The Save As dialog box opens.

   Always save your pages right away. This habit prevents serious headaches if the power goes out as you finish that beautiful—but unsaved—creation.

6. **Save the page as *advertise.html* in the DWTutorial1 folder.**

   You could also save the page as *advertise.htm*; both .html and .htm are valid.

   Make sure you save this page into the correct folder. In Phase 1, you defined the DWTutorial1 folder as the root of the site: the folder that holds all the pages and files for the site. If you save the page outside of this folder, Dreamweaver will get confused, and its site management features won't work correctly.

Note: Most operating systems let you save files with long names, spaces, and characters like #, $, and &. But some browsers and servers have trouble interpreting anything other than letters and numbers; for example, Netscape 4.x can't "see" any files with spaces in their names. Play it safe: use only letters, numbers, and—if you want a good substitute for a space—the underline or underscore character, like_this (Shift+hyphen).

Furthermore, Web servers rely on file extensions like .htm, .html, .gif, and .jpg to know whether a file is a Web page, graphic, or some other type of file. Dreamweaver for Windows automatically adds the extension to your saved document names. But on the Mac, where you can save files without extensions, make sure the file ends in the suffix .html or .htm when you save a Dreamweaver document.

7. **If the document-window toolbar isn't already open, choose View → Toolbars → Document to display it.**

   The toolbar at the top of the document window provides easy access to a variety of tasks you'll perform frequently, such as titling a page, previewing it in a Web browser, and looking at the HTML source code.

8. **In the Title field in the toolbar, select the text "Untitled Document"; type** *Advertise with the National Exasperator.*

   The Title field lets you set a page's title—the information that appears in the title bar of a Web browser. The page title is also what shows up as the name of your Web page when someone searches the Web using a search engine like Yahoo! or Google.

Note: Try this simple experiment: go to *www.google.com* and search for *Untitled Document.* You'll find that the Web is strewn with thousands upon thousands of Web pages without titles, many of which were created with Dreamweaver.

That's because when you create a new Web page, Dreamweaver assigns it the not-so-glamorous title "Untitled Document," and all too many people forget to change that dummy text to something more meaningful. Not only does "Untitled Document" look very unprofessional on a Web page, but an untitled page looks terrible in the results list of a search engine.

9. **On the Property inspector, click the Page Properties button, or choose Modify → Page Properties.**

   The Page Properties dialog box opens (see Figure 1-14), allowing you to define the basic attributes of each Web page you create. There are five categories of settings that let you control properties like background color, link colors, and page margins.

10. **From the Page font menu, select "Verdana, Arial, Helvetica, sans-serif."**

   This sets a basic font (and three backup fonts, in case your visitor's machine lacks Verdana) that Dreamweaver will automatically use for all text on the page.

As you'll see later in this tutorial, though, you can always specify a different font for selected text.

Next, you'll set a basic text color for the page.

11. **Click the small gray box next to the "Text color" label. From the pop-up color palette, choose a white swatch.**

Unless you intervene, all Web page text starts out black in Dreamweaver. But in the next step, you'll set the background of this page to a darker color, so the text will need to be a light color—white, in this case—to be readable. (Here again, you can override this color on a case-by-case basis, as you'll see later in this tutorial.)

Tip: Alternatively, you could type *#FFFFFF* into the box beside the palette square. That's *hexadecimal* notation, which is familiar to HTML coding gurus. Both the palette and the hexadecimal color-specifying field appear fairly often in Dreamweaver.

12. **Click the small gray box next to the words "Background color." Using the eye-dropper cursor, select the blue-gray square pictured in Figure 1-14.**

The numbers #669999 should appear at the top of the box. You've just changed the page background from white to bluish-gray.

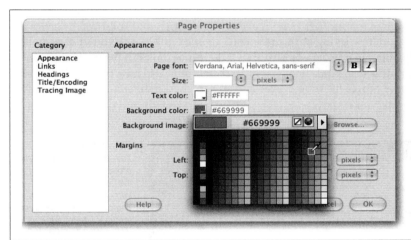

Figure 1-14:
The Page Properties dialog box lets you set general properties of a Web page, like the color of text and links. Clicking a color box opens the color selector, where you can choose from the palette or use the eyedropper to sample a color from anywhere in your document window.

Tip: You can even fill the background of your page with a graphic—to add a subtle pattern for texture or to put the company logo in the background as a "watermark." Be careful with background images, however. If there's a lot of contrast and detail in your background image, it can easily obscure the rest of the content on the page.

To choose a background image, click the Browse button shown in Figure 1-14. A window opens, where you can search for the graphic you want to use.

You can control the placement of a background image—whether it repeats across the entire page, or just along the top or side, and more—using CSS. See page 197 for more detail.

13. **If you want to eliminate margins from the edge of the browser window, type** *0* **into the Left and Top margin boxes.**

    Most browsers put a little bit of space between the contents of your Web page and the top and left sides of the browser window. The size of this margin varies from browser to browser.

    If you like, you can change this setting to make the browser add more space to the top and left side of the page, or eliminate the space altogether. In fact, you can even add a little extra empty space on the *right* side of a page. (The right margin control is especially useful for languages that read from right to left, like Hebrew.)

    Note, however, that the *bottom* margin has no effect on the page display. For this tutorial, you don't need to set any margins, but keep this discussion in mind when you start building your own pages.

14. **Click the Links category and add the following properties: in the Links color field, type** *#FFCC00*; **in the "Visited links" field, type** *#FF9900*; **in the "Roll-over links" field, type** *#FF0000*; **and in the "Active links" color field, type** *FFFFCC* **(see Figure 1-15).**

    These are hexadecimal codes that specify specific Web page colors; more on this notation on page 41.

    Links come in four varieties: regular, visited, active, and rollover. An *active* link is one you're clicking at this moment; a *visited* link is one you've already been to, as noted in a browser's History list. A *regular* link is a plain-old link, unvis-ited, untouched. And, finally, a *rollover* link indicates how the link looks when someone moves his mouse over it. You can choose different colors for each of these link states.

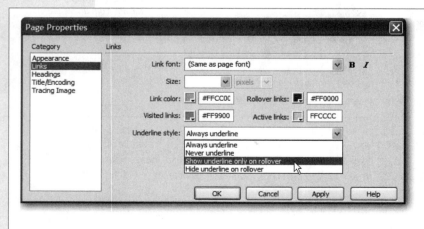

Figure 1-15:
You can set many different properties for links using the Links category of the Page Properties window. You can choose a different font and size for links, as well as specify colors for four different link states. Finally, you can choose whether (or when) links are underlined. Most browsers automatically underline links, but you can override this behavior with the help of this dialog box and Cascading Style Sheets (see Chapter 6).

Note: Although Dreamweaver uses the term *rollover* link, in the world of Cascading Style Sheets, this is called a *hover* link.

UP TO SPEED

Using Dreamweaver's Color Box

The innocent-looking gray box on the Property inspector, the Modify Page Properties window, and in various boxes throughout Dreamweaver is called the color box. You can use it to choose a color for the selected Web page element in any of three ways.

First, you can click one of the colors on the pop-up rainbow palette that appears when you click the box.

Second, you can use the eyedropper cursor that appears when you click the color box. This cursor is "loaded"; you can click any spot on your screen—even outside the dialog box—to select a color, a trick that comes in handy when you want to use a color from a graphic in your document. You can even sample a color from another application (from any visible window, Dreamweaver or not): just move the eyedropper over the color and click. (This click may take you out of Dreamweaver. Just return to Dreamweaver, and you'll see that the color you sampled has been applied.)

Finally, you can click the Color Picker icon, identified here, to launch the Mac or Windows color-picker dialog box, which lets you choose from among millions of possible colors.

If you decide you don't want to add color, or you want to remove a color you've already applied, click the Default Color button. Without a specific color setting, Web browsers will use default colors for the element in question. For instance, text on a Web page is usually black unless you specify otherwise.

Next to the color box in any Dreamweaver dialog box is a blank text field. If you know your Web colors, you can type their *hex codes* into this box, which is sometimes faster and more precise than clicking on the rainbow palette.

In a hex code, a Web color is represented by a six-digit code like this: #FF0000. (Hexadecimal notation is a system computers use for counting. In this system, you count like this: 0, 1, 2, 3, 4, 5, 6, 7, 8, 9, A, B, C, D, E, F. The # tells the computer

that the following sequence is a series of hexadecimal numbers—in this case, three pairs of them.) The best way to learn a color's hex value is to choose the color you want by clicking on it in the palette and then looking at the code that Dreamweaver writes into the text box next to it.

You can choose a different set of rainbow colors (the ones that appear in the palette), too, using the Palette Options menu. You can choose from among five different palettes: Color Cubes, Continuous Tone, Windows OS, Mac OS, and Grayscale. The first two contain the Web-safe color palette (colors that most browsers on most machines will reliably display in the same shades you pick) in different arrangements. The Windows OS and Mac OS palettes display the colors available on those respective operating systems when in 256 color mode. Finally, the Grayscale palette offers 256 somber shades of gray; you'll find them useful primarily when building Ingmar Bergman tribute sites.

Finally, when you use the eyedropper to sample a color, Dreamweaver uses the nearest Web-safe color—one of only 216 colors. When people surfed the Web with old monitors and old video cards, sticking to Web-safe colors was a good idea. Today, however, most computer screens can show thousands or millions of different colors—many more than are available from the Web-safe palette. In short, consider turning off this behavior by turning off the Snap to Web Safe option in the Palette Options menu. You'll have a much wider range of colors to choose from—and all of them, these days, are safe.

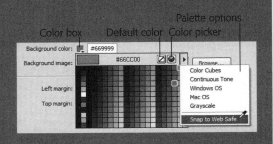

Chapter 1: Dreamweaver 8 Guided Tour

While it may seem a bit like overkill to have four different colors for links, the regular and visited link colors can provide very useful feedback to Web visitors by indicating which links they've already followed and which remain to be checked out. For its part, the rollover link gives instant feedback, changing color as soon as a visitor moves the mouse over it. Since an active link color appears for only the split second someone actually clicks the link, if you never set its color, nobody will notice.

15. **Click OK to close the window and apply these changes to the page.**

    You return to your document window. If you see an asterisk next to the file name at the top of the document window, Dreamweaver is trying to tell you that you've made changes to the page since you last saved it (see Figure 1-16).

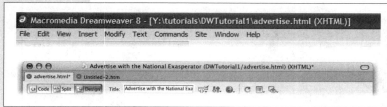

Figure 1-16:
The title of the page appears in the Toolbar and at either the top of the screen (Windows, top) or at the top of the document window (Mac, bottom).

16. **Choose File → Save (or press Ctrl+S [⌘-S]).**

    Save your work frequently. (This isn't a Web technique as much as a computer-always-crashes-when-you-least-expect-it technique.)

Phase 4: Adding Images and Text

Now you'll add the real meat of your Web page: words and pictures.

1. **On the Common tab of the Insert bar, select Image from the Image menu (see Figure 1-17).**

    Alternatively, choose Insert → Image. Either way, the Select Image Source dialog box opens.

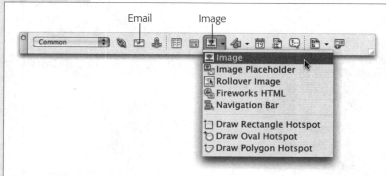

Figure 1-17:
Some of the buttons on Dreamweaver 8's Insert bar do double duty as menus (the buttons with the small, black, down-pointing arrows). Once you select an option from the menu (in this case, the Image object), it becomes the button's current setting. If you want to insert the same object again (in this case, an image), you don't need to use the menu—just click the button.

2. **Browse to the *images* folder in the DWTutorial1 folder; double-click the graphics file called *banner.gif*.**

    The Image Tag Accessibility window appears. Fresh out of the box and onto your computer, Dreamweaver 8 has several accessibility preferences automatically turned on. These preferences are aimed at making your Web pages more accessible to people who use alternative devices for viewing Web sites—for example, people with viewing disabilities who require special Web browser software such as a "screen reader," which literally reads the contents of a Web page out loud. Of course, images aren't words, so they can't be spoken. But you can add what's called an *alt* property. This is a text description of the graphic that's useful not only for screen-reading software, but also for people who deliberately *turn off* pictures in their Web browsers, in exchange for a dramatic speed-up in the appearance of Web pages.

Note: If you don't see this window, type Ctrl+U (⌘-U) to open the Preferences panel, select the Accessibility category, and then turn on the Images checkbox and click OK.

3. **In the Alternate Text box, type *The National Exasperator*. Click OK to add the image to the page.**

    The banner picture appears at the top of the page, as shown in Figure 1-18. A thin border appears around the image, indicating that it's selected. The Property inspector changes to reflect the properties of the image.

Note: You can also add or edit the *alt* text in the Property inspector (Figure 1-18).

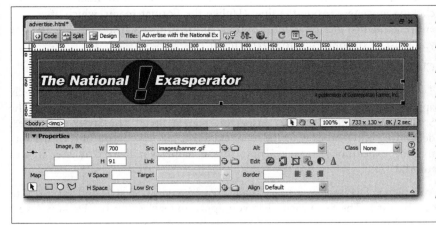

Figure 1-18:
When you select an image in the document window, the Property inspector reveals its dimensions. In the top-left corner, a small thumbnail image appears, as does the word Image (to let you know an image is selected) and the image's file size (in this case, 8 KB). The other image properties are described in Chapter 5.

4. **Deselect the image by clicking anywhere in the document window, or by pressing the right arrow key.**

    Keep the arrow keys in mind—they're a great way to deselect a selected page element *and* move your cursor into place for adding text or more images.

5. **Press Enter to create a new paragraph. Type** *Ad Sizes and Rates.*

   Notice that the text is white and uses the Verdana font; these are the exact properties you set up earlier in the Page Properties window. The Property inspector now displays text-formatting options.

Note: The key called Enter on a Windows keyboard is named Return on most Macintosh keyboards. On the Mac, you can press either Return or Enter.

---

6. **From the Format menu in the Property inspector, choose Heading 1 (see Figure 1-19).**

   The text you just typed becomes big and bold—the default style for Heading 1. This Format pop-up menu offers a number of different paragraph types. Because the text isn't visually bold enough, you'll change its color next.

Paragraph formatting   CSS style menu

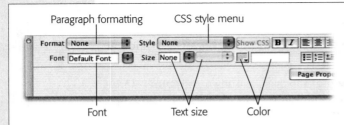

Font   Text size   Color

Figure 1-19:
When you're editing text, the Property inspector offers the relevant formatting controls. You'll notice that both the font and color are already set with the font properties you chose in the Page Properties window (steps 9, 10, and 11 on page 38).

7. **Select the text you just typed.**

   You can do so either by dragging carefully across the entire line or by triple-clicking anywhere inside the line. (Unlike the Format menu, which affects an entire *paragraph* at a time, most options in the Property inspector, like the one you'll use next, apply only to *selected* text.)

8. **Click the color box in the Property inspector and select a black color swatch.**

   Two things happen. First, the color of the text changes to black (it'll actually appear white until you deselect it). Second, a new style name appears in the Style menu on the Property inspector, named Style1 (or Style2, or Style3, depending on whether your independent spirit has led you off into earlier formatting expeditions). Make a note of the name; you'll need it later in this tutorial.

   Meanwhile, Dreamweaver has actually created a new CSS style and applied it to this heading. The Style menu lets you apply any styles you (or Dreamweaver) create. You'll learn plenty about CSS styles in Chapter 6.

9. **Click to the right of the heading text to deselect it. Press Enter to create another new paragraph. Type this:** *The National Exasperator offers three sizes and rates for advertisements.*

This text is smaller than the headline above it. When you press Enter or Return at the end of a headline-formatted paragraph, Dreamweaver automatically formats the next line as a paragraph. (Want proof? Look at the Property inspector's Format menu. It says "paragraph.")

Not only is this new text a bit dull, it also retains the black color of the headline. If you look at the Style menu in the Property inspector, you'll notice that this text is also in Style1, so your next move is to remove this formatting.

10. **From the Property inspector's Style menu, choose None.**

You've just removed the style. Now you'll spice up the text, like this:

11. **Highlight the entire sentence you've most recently typed. From the Font menu in the Property inspector, choose "Georgia, Times New Roman, Times, serif."**

The sentence is now displayed in another font. (Why is more than one font listed for each choice in the Font menu? Turn to page 91 to find out.) In addition, Dreamweaver has created another CSS style (called Style2, or whatever) and listed it in the Style menu on the Property inspector. Again, keep track of the name of this style; you'll need it later in the tutorial.

Next, you'll want to italicize the name of your publication.

12. **Select the words "National Exasperator," and then click the button labeled I in the top row of the Property inspector.**

The I button, of course, means *italics*. Dreamweaver italicizes your selection.

Note: Dreamweaver actually uses the <em> tag (meaning *emphasis*) whenever you apply italics to text. See page 91 for full details.

For added attractiveness, you can now add a horizontal line—a *rule,* as designers call it—underneath the text you've typed so far.

13. **Click at the end of the last sentence to place the cursor there, and press Enter to create a new paragraph. From the Insert bar menu, choose HTML.**

A new set of Object buttons appears on the Insert bar. You'll insert the first object: the horizontal rule.

14. **Click the Horizontal Rule button (the first button on the Insert bar).**

You can also choose Insert → HTML → Horizontal Rule. Either way, Dreamweaver inserts a line across the page. It's highlighted, meaning that the Property inspector is showing its characteristics.

15. **With the horizontal rule still selected, type *700* in the W field of the Property inspector. Press Enter.**

The width of a freshly minted horizontal line is 100 percent—meaning that it spans the entire width of a browser window, no matter how wide the window is. You've just changed your selected line's width to 700 pixels.

16. **From the Align menu in the Property inspector, choose Left.**

    Normally, a horizontal rule is centered in the middle of a page. Now the line is aligned to the left, to match the alignment of the text and graphics on the page.

    Next, you'll add a subhead, a graphic, and a set of bulleted information points to the page.

17. **Click below the horizontal rule and type** *Square Button.* **From the Style menu in the Property inspector, choose None; from the Format menu, choose Heading 2.**

    You've removed the style that was applied to the previous paragraph, and the text for Square Button (one of the online ad sizes your Web site will be offering) changes. It's now bigger and bolder, though smaller than the Heading 1 paragraph at the top of the page. Now apply some additional formatting to this text.

18. **Select the text you just typed, and then click the Color box in the Property inspector. From the pop-up palette, choose a light-yellow color.**

    The text changes to the color you selected. Dreamweaver adds yet another style (Style3) to the Style menu. This is the last time you need to do this, but note the name Dreamweaver uses for this style; you'll need it later on, when you rename the style to something more descriptive.

    A quick way to select this paragraph is to click the <h2> that appears in the lower-left corner of the document window. (This is the tag selector, which lets you quickly and accurately select HTML tags—in this case, the Heading 2 tag.)

19. **Click at the end of the line of text; press Enter.**

    Although the new line is formatted as a "paragraph" and not Heading 2, it still retains the style of the previous paragraph. You don't want that style for this paragraph, so you need to get rid of it.

20. **From the Style menu in the Property inspector, choose None (see Figure 1-20).**

    Doing so removes the style from the text, restoring your original page setting's white Verdana text.

    Now you'll add another image—a sample advertisement—to the page.

Figure 1-20:
The Property inspector's Style menu lists CSS styles, like those created by Dreamweaver in this tutorial or those you'll learn to create in Chapter 3. You can use this menu to apply styles to selected text.

21. On the Common tab of the Insert bar, click the Image button.

Alternatively, choose Insert → Image.

22. Browse to the *images* folder in the DWTutorial1 folder and double-click the file called *square_ad.gif*.

Again, the Image Tag Accessibility window appears (see step 2 on page 43).

23. Type *Square Ad Sample* in the Alternative Text box and then click OK.

A square ad for the *National Exasperator* appears.

Next, you'll add a bulleted list of specifications for this type of ad.

24. Click to the right of the image to deselect it. Press the Enter key to create a new paragraph.

A new paragraph appears just below the graphic. Next, you'll transform it into a bulleted list.

25. Click the Bulleted List button in the Property inspector (see Figure 1-21).

Next, you'll be adding a series of bulleted items that explain the size and cost of a "Square Button" ad in the *National Exasperator*.

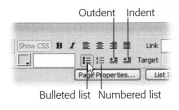

Figure 1-21:
Many of the Property inspector text formatting options are similar to tools you'd find in a word processing program: B for bold, I for italics, text-alignment options, bulleted and numbered lists, and so on.

26. Type *$100 for one month*; hit Enter. Type *Dimensions 125 pixels x 125 pixels* and hit Enter *twice*.

When working in a list, pressing Enter once creates a new list item, but pressing Enter two times ends the list and leaves you with a paragraph. (You can also turn a bulleted item into a regular paragraph by pressing the Bulleted List button again or by clicking the Outdent button.)

You've just added a list with two bulleted items and reset the formatting to a regular paragraph—no indent and no fancy formatting. Next, you'll add another horizontal rule.

27. Choose Insert → HTML → Horizontal Rule.

Alternatively, on the HTML tab of the Insert bar, click the Horizontal Rule button. (For even faster horizontal ruling next time, add this button to the Favorites tab, as described on page 118.)

Dreamweaver inserts a line across the page. This line is highlighted, meaning that it's selected.

28. **Click in the W field of the Property inspector; type *700*. From the Align menu in the Property inspector, choose Left.**

    As you did once before, you just created a horizontal rule of a specified width, aligned against the left edge of the window.

    Your Web page in progress should now look like the one shown in Figure 1-22.

29. **Choose File → Save.**

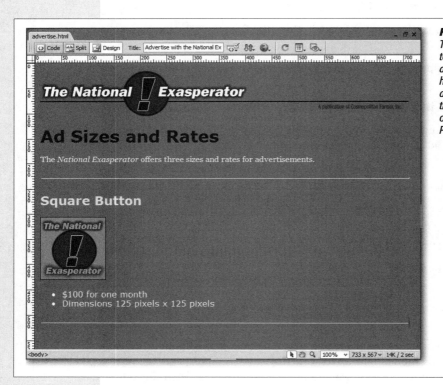

Figure 1-22:
The Web page is starting to come together. You've added graphics, text, and horizontal rules, as well as played with some of the text-formatting options available in the Property inspector.

Phase 5: Preview Your Work

Dreamweaver is as close as a Web design program can be to a WYSIWYG application, meaning that for the most part, What You See (in the document window) Is What You'll Get (on the Web).

At least that's how it's supposed to work. But Dreamweaver may display *more* information than you'll see on the Web (including "invisible" objects, table borders, and other elements that you won't see in a Web browser) and may display *less* (it sometimes has trouble rendering complex designs).

Furthermore, much to the eternal woe of Web designers, different Web browsers display pages differently. Pages viewed in Internet Explorer don't always look the same in more modern browsers like Firefox or Safari. In some cases, the differences may be subtle (for example, text may be slightly larger or smaller). Or they can be dramatic—some of the advanced page-layout techniques described in Chapter 8 look *awful* in older Web browsers. Throughout this book, you'll find tips and techniques to deal with this problem.

Tip: One entrepreneurial company has tackled this problem head-on. Using the services offered by Browsercam (*www.browsercam.com*), you can preview a page through many different browsers and operating systems, letting you test your design without having to set up lots of different computer and browser combinations yourself. Alas, entrepreneurs like to make money, so this service isn't free.

If you're designing Web pages for use on a company intranet and only have to worry about the one Web browser your IT department has put on everyone's computer, you're lucky. But most of us have to deal with the fact that our sites must withstand scrutiny by a wide range of browsers, so it's a good idea to preview your Web pages using whatever browsers you expect visitors to your Web sites to use. Fortunately, Dreamweaver lets you preview a Web page using any browser you have installed on your computer.

Before you can preview a page, you need to set up your list of browsers in the program's preference window, like this:

1. **Choose File → Preview in Browser → Edit Browser List.**

    The Preview in Browser preferences window opens (see Figure 1-23).

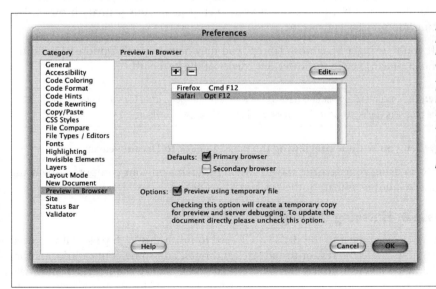

Figure 1-23:
Dreamweaver can launch a Web browser and load a page in it, so you can preview your design. One useful option—"Preview using temporary file"—comes in handy when working with Cascading Style Sheets, as described on page 175.

2. **Click the + button.**

   The Add Browser or Select Browser window opens.

3. **Click the Browse button. Search your hard drive to find the browser program you use most frequently and select it.**

   Dreamweaver inserts the browser's default name in the Name field of the Add Browser window. If you wish to change its name for display purposes within Dreamweaver, select it and type a new name. (But don't do this *before* selecting the browser, since Dreamweaver will erase anything you've typed as soon as you do finally select a browser.)

4. **Turn on the Primary Browser box. Click OK.**

   You've just designated the browser as your *primary* browser while working in Dreamweaver. You can now preview your pages in this browser with a simple keyboard shortcut: F12 (Option-F12 on Mac).

   If you like, you can also choose a secondary browser, which you'll be able to launch by pressing the Ctrl+F12 (⌘-F12) key combination.

   Now you're ready to preview your document in a real, bona fide Web browser. Fortunately, Dreamweaver makes it easy.

5. **Press the F12 key (Option F12 on Mac) (or choose Edit → "Preview in Browser" and select a browser from the menu).**

   The F12 key (Option-F12 on Mac) is the most important keyboard shortcut you'll learn. Macintosh fans: Macromedia has changed the shortcut to Option-F12 in Dreamweaver 8 (so it doesn't interfere with the keyboard shortcut for Dashboard in OS 10.4). It opens your Web page in your primary browser, letting you preview your work.

   If you're using a Macintosh laptop, you may have to press Option-F12 and the function (fn) key in the lower-left corner of the keyboard.

Note: The Document toolbar also has a Preview button—the globe icon. Click it to open a menu listing all the browsers you've set up in the "Preview in Browser" dialog box (Figure 1-23).

---

6. **When you're done previewing the page, go back to Dreamweaver.**

   Do so using your favorite way to switch programs on your computer—by using the Windows taskbar, or the Dock in Mac OS X.

Phase 6: Finishing the Page

You've covered most of the steps you'll need to finish this Web page. All you need to do now is add the rest of the ad sizes and rates, add some contact information, and add a copyright notice. But before that, you'll change the names of the styles Dreamweaver created. As you've seen, when you use the Property inspector to format the color and font of a text, Dreamweaver creates new CSS styles with goofy names like *style1* and *style2*. Sure, they're straightforward, but they're not very descriptive. Fortunately, Dreamweaver makes it easy to change the name of a style.

1. **In the Property inspector's Style menu, select Rename… (see Figure 1-20).**

   This opens the Rename Style dialog box, which lets you select a style from a menu and then rename it by typing a new name.

2. **Make sure *style1* (or whatever style was created in step 8 on page 44) is selected in the Rename Style menu, type *title* in the New Name box, and click OK.**

   Behind the scenes, Dreamweaver does a quick find-and-replace operation; essentially locating every instance of the old style name and replacing it with the new name you just provided. You'll notice that a new panel—the Results panel—pops up at the bottom of the screen. You'll learn more about this on page 649, but for now, just realize it's displaying the results of the behind-the-scenes search Dreamweaver just performed.

3. **Repeat steps 1 and 2 for the style created in step 11 on page 45 (probably *style2*). Rename this style *text*.**

   Using descriptive names for your styles will make them that much easier to identify when you need to edit them.

4. **Repeat steps 1 and 2 to rename the last style (created in step 18 on page 46) *adName*.**

   As you'll learn on page 166, style names can't have spaces, so *ad Name* wouldn't work. Now, you'll finish up the page, by adding the remaining text and graphics.

5. **Click below the last horizontal rule in the document window; type *Full Banner*.**

   Notice that there's no formatting. Since the text is a heading of the same importance as the "Square Button" paragraph heading above it, it would be nice to make it look the same.

Note: If a horizontal rule is the last item on a page, sometimes you'll select the horizontal rule when you click at the bottom of the page. To get a new paragraph *after* the rule, just press the right arrow key (this deselects the horizontal rule) and press Enter.

---

6. **Select Heading 2 from the Format menu on the Property inspector, and select "adName" from the Style menu.**

   This formats the text as a Heading 2, and also applies the style you just renamed.

   Now it's time to add another graphic—a sample full banner ad—and a set of bulleted information points, just as you did for the "Square Button" section of the page.

7. **Click at the end of the paragraph and press Enter to create a new paragraph; choose None from the Property inspector's Style menu.**

Doing so removes the style you applied a moment ago, creating a clean slate for adding and formatting new text or images.

8. **On the Common tab of the Insert bar, click the Image button (or choose Insert → Image).**

The Insert Image dialog box appears.

9. **In the DWTutorial1 → *images* folder, double-click the file *full_banner_ad.gif.***

The Image Tag Accessibility window appears (see step 2 on page 43).

10. **Type *Full Banner Ad Sample* in the Alternative Text box and click OK.**

A full banner ad for the *National Exasperator* appears. Now you need only to add details for this ad.

11. **Click to the right of this image and hit Enter to create a new paragraph; click the Bulleted List button in the Property inspector.**

You've just added a bullet at the beginning of the paragraph.

12. **Type *$560 for one month,* and then press Enter; type *Dimensions: 468 pixels x 60 pixels,* and then press Enter twice to end the list.**

You've just created two bulleted items. To wrap up, you'll insert another horizontal line beneath your ad rates.

13. **Choose Insert → HTML → Horizontal Rule.**

Dreamweaver inserts the line; you'll need to make it look like the other lines on the page.

14. **With the horizontal rule still selected, click in the W field of the Property inspector and type *700.* From the Align menu in the Property inspector, choose Left.**

The line moves to the left edge of the window, just like the other lines you inserted.

15. **Choose File → Save.**

You're now ready to add the last elements to this page and finish this tutorial.

16. **Click below the last horizontal rule in the document window; type *Half Banner.***

17. **Repeat steps 2 through 12 to add and format the final ad size and rates.**

You'll use the graphic called *half_banner_ad.gif* located in the *images* folder. Use the text "Half Banner Ad Sample" for the *alt* property. The two bulleted items of text should read: "$230 for one month" and "Dimensions: 234 pixels x 60 pixels."

18. **Press Enter twice to end the list and create a new paragraph.**

    Next you'll add another horizontal rule by copying and pasting one you added earlier.

19. **Click any of the horizontal rules on the page and choose Edit → Copy.**

    As with most other programs, you can select anything in the document window, copy it, and then paste it.

20. **Click in the empty paragraph at the bottom of the page and choose Edit → Paste.**

    The keyboard shortcut Ctrl+V (⌘-V) is a faster way to paste.

21. **Click to the right of the new rule, and hit Enter.**

    You'll next add some links to the page: an email link for sending email and an external link to another Web site.

22. **Type *Contact Information.* Choose Heading 1 from the Format menu in the Property inspector, and select "title" from the Style menu.**

    You've just created a big, bold heading just like the one at the top of the Web page.

23. **Click to the right of the Heading 1 to deselect it and press the Enter key; choose "None" from the Style menu in the Property inspector.**

24. **Type *The sales staff at the National Exasperator would be happy to take your money. Contact us and we'll make it so. Call us at 555-768-9090 or email our* (don't type a final period).**

    Web pages can contain email links: a link that opens your visitor's email program and automatically adds an email address to a new message. Dreamweaver has a built-in function for adding this type of link.

25. **Click the Insert Email Link button in the Insert bar (see Figure 1-17), or choose Insert → Email Link.**

    The Insert Email Link dialog box opens.

26. **Type *Advertising Department* in the Text field.**

    This is the text that will appear on the Web page.

27. **Type *adsales@nationalexasperator.com* in the E-Mail field, and then click OK.**

    Notice that "Advertising Department" appears on the page underlined and in yellow. This is the formatting for links that you specified earlier in the Page Properties window. The email address *adsales@nationalexasperator.com,* however, is embedded into the link of the page. It may be invisible to your audience, but a Web browser knows it's there.

28. Click at the end of the line and type a period. Press Enter to create a new paragraph.

A blank line appears. You'll add some text and a link to another Web site.

29. Type *For more information on online advertising, visit the Interactive Advertising Bureau.*

30. Select the words "Interactive Advertising Bureau."

You'll turn these words into a link that, when clicked, will send your visitor to another Web site.

31. In the Link field in the Property inspector, type *http://www.iab.net/* and press the Enter key.

You've just added an *external link*. When you preview this page and click that link, you'll be taken to the home page for the Interactive Advertising Bureau.

32. Click at the end of the line; press Enter and add another 700-pixel horizontal rule to the page.

Either insert a new rule as in steps 13 and 14 earlier, or use the copy-and-paste technique in steps 19 and 20. This line, like the other ones you've added, helps break up the page into distinct sections.

33. Click below that last line and type *Copyright 2006, the National Exasperator.*

No page is complete without stamping your legal rights onto it. But that doesn't mean you have to rub it in anyone's face, so you'll make the text a little less noticeable, as follows.

34. Select your copyright notice text; from the Size menu in the Property inspector, choose 12.

You've just set the text to 12 pixels tall. (See page 192 for an explanation of different ways to specify the size of text.) It also creates one last style: Style4. You can choose to rename this (following steps 1 and 2, earlier) to something more meaningful like "copyright." Lastly, you'll add some text and link it to a page already in your site.

35. Click at the end of the copyright notice and type *View our online privacy policy.*

Now for the link.

36. Select the text you just typed. In the Property inspector, click the folder icon that appears to the right of the link field.

The Select File dialog box appears.

37. Navigate to the DWTutorial1 folder and select the file called *privacy.html.*

To apply the link, select the file and click OK, or simply double-click the file name. Either way, the Select File box closes, and you return to your finished Web page.

38. **Choose File → Save. Press the F12 key to preview your work in your browser.**

Test out the links to make sure they work.

Congratulations! You've just built your first Web page in Dreamweaver, complete with graphics, formatted text, and links. If you'd like to compare your work with an actual, Internet-posted version of the same page, visit the tutorial page for this book, *www.sawmac.com/dw8/tutorials*. (The finished page, called *finished.html*, is also in your *DWTutorial1* folder.)

Much of the work of building Web sites will involve using the procedures covered in this tutorial—defining a site, adding links, formatting text, and inserting graphics. The next few chapters cover these basics in greater depth and introduce other important tools, tips, and techniques for using Dreamweaver to build great Web pages.

Adding Text to Your Web Pages

True broadband Internet media like streaming video, audio, and high-quality graphics continue to grab the headlines. After all, it's exciting to speculate about the Web replacing your telephone or tapping your keyboard to get movies on demand.

But the Web is primarily woven with *words*. Sony PlayStation Portable reviews, Brad Pitt gossip, and countless personal blogs about cats still drive people to the Web. As you build Web pages and Web sites, you'll spend a lot of your time adding and formatting *text*. Understanding how Dreamweaver works with text is vital to getting your message across effectively.

This chapter covers the not-always-simple act of getting text *into* your Dreamweaver documents. In Chapter 3, you can read about formatting this text so that it looks professionally designed.

Adding Text in Dreamweaver

In many ways, Dreamweaver works like a word processing program. When you create a new document, the blinking cursor appears at the top of the page, ready for you to begin typing. When you finish a paragraph, you press Enter or Return to start a new one. Text, as well as anything else you add to a Web page, starts at the top of the page and works its way to the bottom.

Adding Special Characters

Many useful special characters—such as copyright or trademark symbols—don't appear on your keyboard, making them difficult or impossible to type. The Text tab of the Insert bar lets you use a variety of symbols and international characters quickly by clicking an icon.

To open this panel:

1. **From the menu on the Insert bar, choose Text.**

   If the Insert bar isn't visible, choose Window → Insert to open it, or use the keyboard shortcut Ctrl+F2 (⌘-F2).

   The palette shown in Figure 2-1 appears. Many of the options let you add common HTML tags like the <b> (bold) and <strong> (strong) tags, most of which you can apply more easily using the Property inspector or keyboard shortcuts, as discussed in the next chapter. This panel also features less frequently used tags like <abbr> (abbreviation) or <dl> (definition list). You can satisfy your curiosity about these tags by using Dreamweaver's HTML reference (see page 353).

   The last option on the bar is actually a menu that offers a wide range of symbols and international characters. Unlike regular Western characters, such as *a* or *z*, these special characters are represented in HTML by a code name or number. For instance, a trademark symbol (™) is written in HTML as ™.

2. **From the menu at the right end of the Insert bar, select the symbol you wish to insert (see Figure 2-1).**

   Dreamweaver inserts the appropriate HTML code into your Web page. (Alternatively, you can select the Other Characters option to bring up the wider-ranging Insert Other Character dialog box shown at bottom in Figure 2-1.)

Note: If you set the encoding of your Web page to anything other than Western in the Page Properties window (by choosing Modify → Page Properties and clicking the Title/Encoding category), you can reliably insert only line breaks and nonbreaking spaces. The other special characters available from the Character category of the Objects panel may not work.

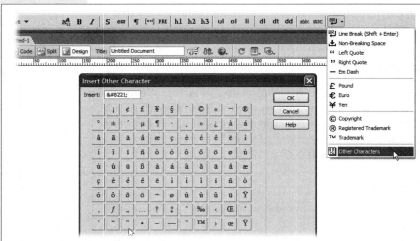

Figure 2-1:
Selecting Other Characters from the Characters menu (top) brings up the Insert Other Character dialog box (bottom). However, there are even more characters in the Western alphabet than are listed in this dialog box. You can find a table listing these characters and their associated entity names and numbers at www. evolt.org/article/A_Simple_Character_Entity_Chart/17/21234/.

Line Breaks

Pressing Enter creates a new paragraph, exactly as in a word processor. Unfortunately, Web browsers automatically insert a blank line's worth of extra space above and below paragraphs—which is a real nuisance if you're trying to create several single-spaced lines of text, like this:

702 A Street
Toadsuck, AR
98789 USA

Here, each part of the address is on its own line, but it's still just a single paragraph (and shares the overall formatting of that paragraph, as you'll learn in the next chapter).

Tip: If you want to *entirely* dispense with the space that browsers insert between paragraphs, don't use line breaks each time. Instead, use CSS to eliminate the top and bottom margins of the <p> tag, as described in the tip in on page 203.

To create this effect, you need to insert a *line break* at the insertion point, using one of these techniques:

- From the Characters menu on the Text tab of the Insert bar, select Line Break (the first menu option at top in Figure 2-1).

- Choose Insert → HTML → Special Characters → Line Break.

- Press Shift+Enter.

Tip: When you place a line break in Dreamweaver, you may get no visual hint that it's even there; after all, a regular paragraph break and a line break both create a new line of text.

This is especially likely if you copy text from applications other than Microsoft Word or Excel. Text from other programs—especially email programs—can be loaded with an infuriating number of line breaks. To add to the confusion, a line break may go unnoticed if it occurs at the end of a long line. Your only hope is to make line breaks visible.

To do so, choose Edit → Preferences (or Dreamweaver → Preferences on the Mac), or press Ctrl+U (⌘-U). Click the Invisible Elements category. Make sure the Line Breaks checkbox is turned on. Now you'll see each line break appear as a small gold shield. (If after doing this, you still don't see the line break character, choose View → Visual Aids and make sure the Invisible Elements checkbox is turned on.)

You can select a line break by clicking the shield, and then delete it like any page element. Better yet, select the shield, and then hit Enter or Return, to eliminate the line break *and* create a new paragraph.

Another way to avoid pasting hidden line breaks—new in Dreamweaver 8—is the Paste Special command (see page 63).

Nonbreaking Spaces

You may've noticed that if you type more than one space in a row, Dreamweaver ignores all but the first space. This isn't a glitch in the program; it's standard HTML. Web browsers ignore any spaces following the first one.

Therefore, a line like "Beware   of   llama," with several spaces between each word, would appear on a Web page like this: "Beware of llama." Not only do Web browsers ignore multiple spaces, but they also ignore any spaces that aren't *between* words. So if you hit the Space bar a couple of times to indent the first line of a paragraph, you're wasting your time. A Web browser won't display any of those spaces.

This feature makes good sense, because it prevents Web pages from being littered with extraneous spaces that many people insert when writing HTML code. (Extra spaces in a page of HTML often make the code easier to read.)

There may be times, however, when you *need* more than one space in a row. Consider the text navigation bar at the bottom of a Web page, a common Web page element that lists the different sections of a Web site. Visitors can click one of the section titles to jump directly to a different area of the site. For clarity, many designers like to add multiple spaces between the text links, like this:

News   Classifieds   Jobs

In all these cases, a *nonbreaking space* can save the day. It looks just like a regular space, but it acts as glue that prevents the words on either side from being split apart at the end of a line. (That's why it's called a nonbreaking space.)

Note: Designers used to use the nonbreaking space to create an indent on the first line of paragraphs. Fortunately, you don't need to resort to such trickery anymore. The *CSS Text-Indent* property, described on page 201, creates the same effect more efficiently.

But when designing Web pages, you'll probably be interested in this fascinating cousin of the regular Space bar for a different reason: it's the only "text spacer" you can use in HTML text.

To insert a nonbreaking space, click where you wish to add the space, and then do one of the following:

- From the Characters menu on the Text tab of the Insert bar, select Non-Breaking Space (the second menu option at top in Figure 2-1).

- Choose Insert → HTML → Special Characters → Non-Breaking Space.

- Press Ctrl+Shift+Space bar (⌘-Shift-Space bar).

Note: If you often add multiple spaces, Dreamweaver offers a shortcut. Choose Edit → Preferences to open Dreamweaver's Preferences window (in Mac OS X, choose Dreamweaver → Preferences instead). Click the General category. Then, under "Editing options," turn on "Allow multiple consecutive spaces." Now, whenever you press the Space bar more than once, Dreamweaver inserts *nonbreaking* spaces.

In fact, Dreamweaver 8 is even smarter than that. It inserts a regular space if you press the Space bar just once, a nonbreaking space followed by a regular space if you hit the Space bar twice, and multiple non-breaking spaces followed by a final *regular* space if you hit the Space bar repeatedly. Since nonbreaking spaces act like glue that keeps words stuck together (see the box below), the extra regular spaces allow the lines to break normally, if necessary.

TROUBLESHOOTING MOMENT

Keeping Headlines Together

You can use nonbreaking spaces as invisible glue that keeps two or more words together on a single line. That's a very useful tactic when you're dealing with headlines, for example, in which a single word, if forced onto its own line, would create unappealing white space and confuse the headline's meaning, as shown here.

Adding a nonbreaking space between the words "Mother" and "Says" in this example ensures that those words won't get split across a line break, and helps clarify the presentation and meaning of this headline. You can use any of the three methods that are described on page 60. There is

also a CSS property called White-space to which you can apply the value "nowrap" [see page 201]. This move prevents words from wrapping to the next line, effectively gluing them together.)

> **Child Not An Alien Mother Says**

> **Child Not An Alien Mother Says**

Adding a Date to Your Page

The Common tab of the Insert bar offers an icon called Date. Clicking this icon (📅) or choosing Insert → Date opens the Insert Date dialog box (Figure 2-2). Either way, Dreamweaver inserts today's date, as your computer understands it, onto your Web page in progress. You can also specify whether to include the day of the week and the current time.

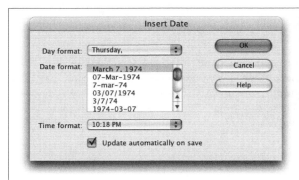

Figure 2-2:
When you insert a Date object (a placeholder for the actual date) onto a Web page, you have several additional options: If you want to add the day of the week, choose the format you want from the "Day format" pop-up menu (top). You may also choose to add the current time in hours and minutes—in either military time (22:18) or regular time (10:18 PM)—from the "Time format" pop-up menu (bottom).

Select the format you wish from the Date Format list. There are 13 different formats to choose from, such as March 7, 1974 or 3/7/74.

You may wonder why Dreamweaver includes an insert-date function anyway. How hard is it to type *Thursday, July 12*?

Actually, the real value of the Insert Date feature lies in the "Update Automatically on Save" checkbox. Choosing this option forces Dreamweaver to *update* the date each time you save the document.

Many designers use this feature to stamp their Web pages with dates that indicate when the contents were last updated. For example, you might type *This page was last revised on:* and then choose Insert → Date and select the "Update automatically on save" option. Now, each time you make a change to the page, Dreamweaver automatically changes the date to reflect when you saved the document. You never again have to worry about it.

Copying and Pasting Text

If you're building Web sites as part of a team or for clients, your writers are likely to send you their copy in the form of word processing documents. If the text comes in a Microsoft Word document or Excel spreadsheet, you're lucky. Dreamweaver 8 includes commands for pasting text from these two types of files. If you're using Windows, you can even import those kinds of files directly into a Web page using File → Import → Word/Excel Document (see page 68).

Simple Copy and Paste

For non–Microsoft-spawned text, you can, of course, still simply copy and paste like generations of Web designers before you.

Open the document in whatever program created it—WordPerfect, AppleWorks, your email program, or whatever. Select the text you want (by dragging through it, for example), or choose Edit → Select All (Ctrl+A [⌘-A]) to highlight all text in the document. Then choose Edit → Copy, or press Ctrl+C (⌘-C), to copy it. Switch to Dreamweaver, click in the document window where you wish the text to go, and then choose Edit → Paste (Ctrl+V [⌘-V]).

This routine pastes the text into place. Unfortunately, you lose all text formatting (font type, size, color, bold, italic, and so on) in the process, as shown in Figure 2-3.

Furthermore, you may find that pasted paragraphs are separated by line break characters, not standard carriage returns. Strangely enough, this means that when you paste in a series of paragraphs, Dreamweaver treats them as though they were one gargantuan paragraph. These line-break characters can pose problems when trying to format what you *think* is a single paragraph. To identify these line breaks, see the note on page 59.

Tip: If you *have* to copy and paste text from other programs, there's a way to get paragraphs (and not just lines separated by the line-break character) when you paste into Dreamweaver: make sure whoever's typing up the original documents inserts an extra paragraph between each paragraph of text. Pressing Enter (or Return) twice at the end of a paragraph inserts an empty paragraph. When you copy and paste, Dreamweaver removes the empty paragraphs *and* pastes the text as regular paragraphs.

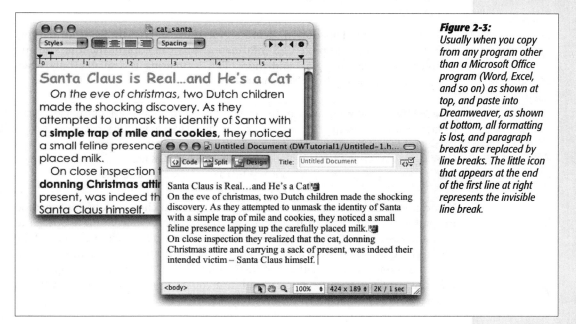

Figure 2-3:
Usually when you copy from any program other than a Microsoft Office program (Word, Excel, and so on) as shown at top, and paste into Dreamweaver, as shown at bottom, all formatting is lost, and paragraph breaks are replaced by line breaks. The little icon that appears at the end of the first line at right represents the invisible line break.

Paste Special

Actually, the previous explanation isn't exactly true. Dreamweaver 8 has added some new text-pasting features, some of which it attempts to use *whenever* it pastes text. Dreamweaver 8 actually supports four different types of paste methods, ranging from plain text to highly formatted HTML:

- **Text only.** This option is the most basic of all. Text is pasted without any formatting whatsoever. Even paragraphs and line breaks are ignored, so you end up with essentially one long sentence. Though you won't want this effect often, it can come in handy when you copy a long paragraph of text from an email program that's added unnecessary line breaks at the end of each line of email text.

- **Text with structure.** Dreamweaver tries to preserve the structure of the text, including paragraphs, headers, bulleted lists, and so on. This option doesn't keep formatting applied to text, such as bold or italics. Most non–Microsoft Office copied text is pasted using this method. In most cases, however,

Dreamweaver ends up preserving only paragraphs and misses bulleted lists and headers.

- **Basic formatting.** When pasting with basic formatting, Dreamweaver includes the same elements as the "Text with structure" option, but also includes text formatting such as bold, italics, and underlining. This is the method Dreamweaver uses when pasting Microsoft Word or Excel information, as described in the next section.

- **Full formatting.** This option includes everything offered by Basic formatting, but also attempts to paste CSS information that can control the font size and color, paragraph margins, and more. Full formatting is available only when copying and pasting from Word or Excel (see page 65).

Note to Windows owners: You can copy an entire page of HTML from Firefox or Internet Explorer and paste it into Dreamweaver. Click inside a Web page, press Ctrl+A to select the entire page, and then press Ctrl+C to copy the HTML. Then, switch to Dreamweaver, click inside an empty page, and press Ctrl+V to paste. All the HTML is copied, and even graphics appear. This text comes in with "full formatting," but note that external style sheets (see page 163) do *not* come along for the ride.

You can override Dreamweaver's default behavior and choose a different method for pasting by using the Paste Special command. Choose Edit → Paste Special to open the Paste Special window (see Figure 2-4). Here, you can choose which of the four techniques you wish to use…sort of. You're limited to what Dreamweaver can paste. For non–Microsoft Office products, you can only use the first two options— the others are grayed out—whereas with text copied from Word or Excel, you can choose from any of the four.

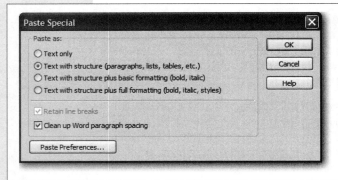

Figure 2-4:
The Paste Special command lets you paste text copied from other programs. If you want Dreamweaver to apply the same setting each time you use the Paste Special command, click the Paste Preferences button. This opens the Preferences window. Select whatever settings– Basic formatting, for example–that you want Dreamweaver to apply every time you use the Paste Special command.

In general, Dreamweaver's default settings are a good place to start for text copied from most programs. For Word or Excel information, there are a few options worth considering, as described next.

Pasting Text from Word: The Basic Method

While text from other applications doesn't retain much beyond paragraph formatting when pasted into Dreamweaver, Dreamweaver 8 includes both basic and advanced methods of copying and pasting Word text. You can even paste spreadsheet information from Excel, complete with rows, columns, and cells.

Frequently, you'll just want to preserve basic formatting like bold or italic text, headlines, and bulleted lists. You won't need (and in most cases, won't want) more extravagant formatting like different fonts, colors, or margin settings. After all, you're the Web designer, and you'll use your own design sense—and Dreamweaver's CSS-based formatting tools—to add beauty to basic text.

Pasting Word text works like any copy/paste action described in the previous section. Just select the text in Word, copy it, switch to Dreamweaver, and then choose Edit → Paste to drop it into a Web page. You don't have to spend a lot of time reformatting the pasted text (see Figure 2-5), since many basic formatting options are preserved:

- Any paragraphs formatted with Word's built-in Heading styles (Heading 1, Heading 2, and so on) get the HTML heading tags <h1> (or heading 1), <h2>, <h3>, and so on.

- Paragraphs remain paragraphs…most of the time. Actually, how Dreamweaver pastes paragraphs depends on both how the paragraphs are formatted in Word and the setting of the Paste Special window's "Clean up Word paragraph spacing" setting (see Figure 2-4). If this option is selected (which it is by default), paragraphs you paste from Word appear as one large paragraph with line break characters at the end of each paragraph. Not the best method. To get Dreamweaver to paste each paragraph as a paragraph, choose Edit → Paste Special, turn off the "Clean up Word paragraph spacing" checkbox, and then click OK.

WORKAROUND WORKSHOP

Pasting HTML

Suppose you've copied some HTML code, maybe out of the Source view of an actual Web page in a Web browser, or from a "How to Write HTML" Web site. You'll notice that when you paste it into Dreamweaver, all the HTML tags appear in the document window, complete with brackets (< >) and other assorted messiness.

Unfortunately, Dreamweaver 8 eliminated the very useful Paste HTML tool, which let you paste HTML code while in Design view. Now you have to go into Code view and paste

the HTML directly into the page's code. Code view is discussed in depth on page 330.

By the way, you don't have to worry about any of this when copying and pasting *within* Dreamweaver. The regular Copy and Paste commands are smart enough to keep all the formatting—and HTML tags—when copying and pasting within a Dreamweaver document. (If you do want to just paste the text and ignore the Dreamweaver formatting, choose Edit → Paste Special and select the "Text only" option.)

Tip: If the Word document you're copying from has an empty line between each paragraph (in other words, an empty paragraph generated by pressing the Enter key twice after each paragraph), then make sure you DO have the "Clean up Word paragraph spacing" setting checkbox turned on. This eliminates those extra empty paragraphs.

- Bold and italic text maintain their look in Dreamweaver. (The actual HTML tags, however, can vary, as described on page 91.)

- Basic alignment options (left, right, and center) remain intact. Justified text, on the other hand, gets pasted as left-aligned text. (You can compensate for this small oversight by using the justified alignment option on the Property inspector, described on page 80.)

- Numbered lists come through as numbered lists in Dreamweaver (see page 82) *if* you used Word's automatic numbered-list feature to create them.

- If you use Word's built-in list-bulleting feature, you end up with a proper HTML bulleted list (see page 82). However, if the bulleted list includes custom bullets like checkmarks or clown faces, Dreamweaver—for whatever bizarre reason—interprets the list as basic paragraphs preceded by bullet characters. That is, you don't wind up with the proper HTML for a bulleted list (which involves the <ul> tag)—you just get plain paragraphs preceded by a bullet text character. This bullet might get deleted, ruining the look of the list, but even worse, you can't then take advantage of CSS's list-formatting properties to change this bullet into a square, hollow circle, or even little graphics (as described on page 206).

- Graphics from Word documents get pasted as graphics. In fact, even if the original graphics aren't in a Web-ready format (if they're BMP, TIFF, or PICT files, for example), Dreamweaver converts them to either the GIF or JPEG formats understood by Web browsers. Dreamweaver even copies the files to your local site root *and* links them correctly to the page. (Chapter 5 covers images in depth.)

Note: There are a couple of caveats with this feature. First, you can't copy and paste more than 300 KB worth of text, so you have to transfer really long documents in pieces (or better yet, spread them out among multiple Web pages). And second, this feature works only with versions of Word later than Office 97 (for Windows) or Office 98 (for Mac).

Pasting Text with Word Formatting

If you simply must keep that three-inch-tall, orange-text, crazy-cartoon-like font, you can turn to the "Full Formatting" option of the Paste Special command. After copying text from Word and returning to Dreamweaver, choose Edit → Paste Special or press Ctrl+Shift+V (⌘-Shift-V). When the Paste Special window appears, choose the "Full Formatting" option and click OK. (If you want this to be the default setting, so that you always paste the full formatting from Word, turn on the "Use these settings…" checkbox *before* clicking OK in the Paste Special window.)

Dreamweaver pastes the text with as much formatting as possible, including margins, fonts, and text colors and sizes (see Figure 2-5). Behind the scenes, Dreamweaver pastes the text *and* adds Cascading Style Sheet code that attempts to approximate the look of the text in Word.

Figure 2-5:
Dreamweaver 8 lets you paste Word text (and graphics)—like the contents of the Word file (top)—into a Web page, while preserving basic formatting options like headlines, italics, paragraphs, and bold (bottom left). The Paste Special command lets you preserve more advanced formatting such as font faces, colors, sizes, and margins (bottom right). But this special treatment comes at a price: the file size of the page on the bottom right is about 10 percent larger than the one on the bottom left.

Unfortunately, all this extra code increases the document's file size and download time and can interfere with future formatting changes. What's worse, most of your visitors won't even be able to *see* some of this formatting—such as uncommon font faces. For these reasons, use this feature with caution.

Pasting Excel Spreadsheet Information

Dreamweaver 8 also lets you paste information from Microsoft Excel. Options include a basic method, using the standard Ctrl+V (⌘-V) or Edit → Paste, and a format-rich method, using the "Full Formatting" option of the Paste Special window: choose Edit → Paste Special (or press Ctrl+Shift+V [⌘-Shift-V]), choose Full Formatting from the Paste Special window, and click OK. Both methods paste spreadsheet information as an HTML table composed of cells, rows, and columns. (See Chapter 7 for more on tables.)

But unlike pasting from Word, the basic Paste command from Excel preserves *no* formatting: it doesn't even hang on to bold and italics.

The Full Formatting option, however, preserves advanced formatting like font, font size, text color, and cell background colors.

Importing Word and Excel Documents (Windows)

Windows fans can also import material directly from a Word or Excel file into any Dreamweaver document. Just place the cursor where you wish to insert the text or spreadsheet, and then choose File → Import → Word Document (or Excel Document). An Open file dialog box appears; find and double-click the Word or Excel document you wish to import.

Dreamweaver captures the information just as if you'd used Edit → Paste. That is, for Word documents, Dreamweaver carries over basic formatting like bold, italics, headlines, and paragraphs, and imports and converts images. The importing process doesn't create style sheets or apply advanced formatting. For Excel documents, you get just an organized table of data—no formatting.

GEM IN THE ROUGH

Clean Up Word

From Word, you can save any document as a Web page, essentially turning a Word doc into HTML. The drawback to this method is that Word produces hideous HTML code. One look at it, and you'd think that your cat fell asleep on the keyboard.

The explanation: So you will be able to reopen the document as a Word file when the time comes, Word injects reams of information that adds to the file size of the page. This is a particular problem with the latest versions of Word, which add loads of XML and Cascading Style Sheet information.

Fortunately, Dreamweaver's Clean Up Word HTML command can strip out most of that unnecessary code and produce leaner Web pages. To use it, open the Word HTML file just as you would any other Web page: by choosing File → Open. Once the file is open, choose Commands → Clean Up Word HTML.

The Clean Up Word HTML dialog box opens; Dreamweaver automatically detects whether the HTML was produced by Word 97/98 or Word 2000/2001/2002/X/XP, and then applies the appropriate rules for cleaning up the HTML.

Selecting Text

After you get text into your Dreamweaver document, you'll undoubtedly need to edit it. You'll delete words and paragraphs, move sentences around, add words, and fix typos.

The first step in any of these procedures is learning how to select text, which works much as it does in word processors. You drag across text to highlight it, or just click where you wish the selection to begin and hold down the Shift key as you click at the end of the selection. You can also use shortcuts like these:

- To select a word, double-click it.

- To select a paragraph, triple-click anywhere in it.

- To select a line of text, move your cursor to the left of the line of text until the cursor changes from an I-beam to an arrow, signaling that you've reached the left-margin selection strip. Click once to highlight one line of text, or drag vertically in this selection strip to select multiple lines.

- While pressing Shift, use the left and right arrow keys to select one letter at a time. Use Ctrl+Shift (⌘-Shift) and the left and right arrow keys to select one *word* at a time.

- Ctrl+A (⌘-A) selects everything in the body of the page—text, graphics, and all. (Well, this isn't 100% true; if you're using tables or layers, Ctrl+A may select just the text within a table or layer; see the notes on pages 248 and 249 for more info about this behavior.)

Once you've selected text, you can cut, copy, or delete it. To move text to another part of the Web page, or even to another Dreamweaver document, use the Cut, Copy, and Paste commands in the Edit menu. You can also move text around by dragging and dropping it, as shown in Figure 2-6.

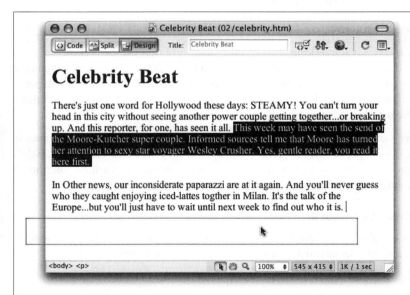

Figure 2-6:
You can move a blob of selected text simply by dragging it to another location in the document window. Point to a spot inside your highlighted selection and the cursor changes from an I-beam to an arrow; you can now drag the selection. Let go of the mouse button to drop your selection at the spot indicated by the vertical bar, as shown here. This technique works with graphics and other objects you've selected in the document window, too. You can even move a copy of the selection by pressing Ctrl (Option) as you drag and drop.

Once copied, the text remains on your Clipboard and can be placed again and again (until you copy something else to the Clipboard, of course). When you cut (or copy) and paste *within* Dreamweaver, all the code affecting that text comes along for the ride. If you copy a paragraph that includes bold text, for example, you'll copy the HTML tags both for creating a paragraph and for producing bold text.

Note: Not *all* the formatting necessarily comes along for the ride. With Dreamweaver 8's support for Cascading Style Sheets, most of your text formatting includes some CSS formatting, and, unfortunately, cutting and pasting text from one document to another does *not* also copy the CSS code. So on some occasions, you may copy text from one document, paste it into another, and find that the formatting disappears. (You'll find more detail about this particular problem on page 173.)

To delete any selection, press Delete or choose Edit → Clear.

Spell Checking

You spend a lot of time perfecting your Web pages, making sure the images look great, that the text is properly formatted, and that everything aligns to make a beautiful visual presentation. But one step is often forgotten, especially given the hyperspeed development process of the Web—making sure your Web pages are free from typos.

Spelling mistakes give an unprofessional impression and imply a lack of attention to detail. Who wants to hire an "illustraightor" or "Web dezyner"? Dreamweaver's spell checking feature can help you.

About Dictionaries

Before you start spell checking, you should make sure that the correct *dictionary* is selected. Dreamweaver comes with 14 dictionaries for 11 different languages, including three English variations and both Iberian and Brazilian Portuguese. When it checks your spelling, the program compares the text in your document against the list of words in one of these dictionaries.

To specify a dictionary, choose Edit → Preferences (Dreamweaver → Preferences in Mac OS X)—or press Ctrl+U (⌘-U)—to open the Preferences dialog box. Select the General category, and then choose a language from the Spelling Dictionary pop-up menu at the bottom of the window.

Performing the Check

Once you've selected a dictionary, open the Web page whose spelling you wish to check. You can check as much or as little text as you like, as follows:

1. **Highlight the text (which can be even a single word).**

   If you want to check the *entire* document, make sure that nothing is selected in the document window. (One good way to make sure nothing is selected is to click in the middle of a paragraph of text.) Like spell checkers in other programs, you must place the cursor at the beginning of the document to begin spell checking from the top of the page.

Note: Unfortunately, Dreamweaver doesn't offer a site-wide spell-checking feature. You must check each page individually.

2. **Choose Text → Check Spelling (or press Shift+F7).**

    The Check Spelling dialog box opens (see Figure 2-7). If the selected word isn't in Dreamweaver's dictionary, it appears in the top field of the box, along with a list of suggested alternative spellings.

    The first suggestion is listed in the "Change to" field.

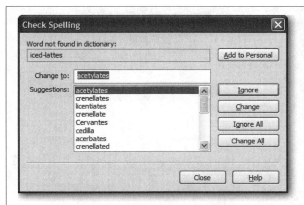

Figure 2-7:
Dreamweaver's spell-checking feature checks only words in the document window. It can't check the spelling of comments, alt tags, or any text that appears in the head of the document with the exception of the page's title. Nor can you spell check an entire Web site's worth of pages with a single command; you need to check each Web page individually.

3. **If the "Change to" field is correct, click Change.**

    If Dreamweaver has correctly flagged the word as misspelled but the correct spelling isn't in the "Change to" field, double-click the correct spelling in the list. If the correct spelling isn't in the list, type it yourself in the "Change to" box.

    Then click the Change button to correct this one instance, or click Change All to replace the misspelled word everywhere it appears in the document.

    Dreamweaver makes the change and moves on to the next questionable spelling.

4. **If the word is actually correctly spelled (but not in Dreamweaver's dictionary), click Ignore, Ignore All, or Add to Personal.**

    If you want Dreamweaver to ignore this word *every* time it appears in the document, rather than just this instance of it, click Ignore All.

    On the other hand, you'll frequently use some words that Dreamweaver doesn't have in its dictionaries. You may, for instance, use a client's name throughout your Web pages. If that name isn't in Dreamweaver's dictionary, Dreamweaver will consistently claim that it's a spelling error.

To teach Dreamweaver the client's name so that the Check Spelling dialog box won't pop up each time you spell check, click Add to Personal. Dreamweaver will add the word to your personal dictionary, which is a special dictionary file that Dreamweaver also consults when checking your spelling.

After you click Ignore or Change, Dreamweaver moves on to the next word it doesn't recognize. Begin again from step 3. If you didn't begin the spell check at the beginning of the document, once Dreamweaver reaches the end of the document, it will ask if you wish to continue spell checking from the beginning.

5. **To end spell checking, click Close.**

FREQUENTLY ASKED QUESTION

Editing Your Personal Dictionary

Oops! I added a word to my personal dictionary by accident! How do I undo that?

If you click Add to Personal accidentally, you'll probably want to fix your mistake—but there's no obvious way to remove words from your Personal dictionary!

Your personal dictionary is a file called Personal Dictionary MX.tlx, and all the Macromedia Studio programs—Fireworks, Flash, and Dreamweaver—make use of it. For Windows 2000, NT, and XP, you'll find this file in your own application-data folder, usually on the C: drive under Documents and Settings → [your name] → Application Data → Macromedia → Common. (Note: The Application Data folder is usually hidden in Windows. If you don't see it, you need to use Folder Options—located in the Control Panel—to reveal hidden folders and files.)

If you use a Mac, look inside your Home → Library → Application Support → Macromedia → Common folder.

Make a backup copy of this file, just in case. Then, open it in Dreamweaver by choosing File → Open and navigating to the .tlx file. Although the file is a text file, the .tlx extension isn't a recognized document type in Dreamweaver. You'll need to select "All files" (NOT "All Documents") from the pop-up menu before you can open the personal dictionary.

Don't touch the first line of the file, which indicates what language the dictionary uses. Each line thereafter lists a word followed by a tab and the letter *i*.

To delete an entry, delete its entire line. You can also add a word by manually typing the word, a tab, and the letter *i*. (Dreamweaver's spell checking engine uses that little *i* for its own purposes.)

Undo, Redo, and the History Panel

One of the great consciousness-altering moments of the 20th century was the introduction of the Undo command. After a long day in front of the computer, the ability to undo any action seems quite natural. (Unfortunately, reaching for the Ctrl+Z keys after spilling grape juice on Grandma's antique tablecloth still doesn't work in the real world.)

Fortunately, most steps you take in Dreamweaver can be reversed with either the Undo command or the History panel.

Undo

Like most computer programs these days, Dreamweaver lets you undo the last step you took by pressing Ctrl+Z (⌘-Z), or by choosing Edit → Undo. (This command changes to reflect your most recent action. If you just deleted some text, for example, it says Edit → Undo Delete.) When you're feeling indecisive, you can *redo* the action you just undid by choosing Edit → Redo or by pressing Ctrl+Y (⌘-Y).

Tip: Jumping back and forth with the Undo/Redo commands is a good way to compare a change you made to a Web page with its previous appearance. For instance, suppose you're having trouble deciding on a background color for a Web page. You could set it to dark blue, then set it to dark purple, and then choose Edit → Undo Set Page Properties to return to the dark blue background. Choose Edit → Redo Set Page Properties to see the purple background again. This before-and-after toggling feature of the Undo/ Redo combo can be a great addition to your Web-building arsenal.

You're not limited to a single undo, either. You can undo multiple steps—up to 50 of them, or whatever number you specify in Preferences. Choose Edit → Preferences (on the Mac, it's Dreamweaver → Preferences) to open this dialog box, click the General category from the Category list, and change the number in the Maximum Number of History Steps box. (Note, however, that the more steps Dreamweaver remembers, the more memory the program needs. If you set this number very high or your computer doesn't have a lot of memory, you may find your computer acting sluggish.)

Note: You can even undo actions *after you have saved* a document (although not after you've closed it). Unlike many programs, Dreamweaver doesn't erase the list of actions you've performed when a page is saved. This means you can feel free to save as often as you want—a wise safeguard against crashes and other mishaps—without losing the ability to undo what you've done.

History Panel

You may wonder why the Preferences setting for the Undo command refers to "History Steps." It's because Dreamweaver creates a *history* for a document as you work on it. Each time you add text, insert a graphic, change the background color of the page, or do anything else to a document, Dreamweaver adds a new step to a list of previous actions.

All of these steps are listed in the History panel (see Figure 2-8). To see it, choose Window → History, or press Shift+F10.

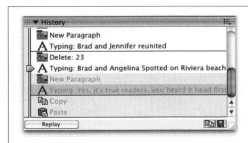

Figure 2-8:
The History panel can do a lot more than undo actions. It can also be used for automating many routine tasks that you perform while building your Web pages. To find out how to use this feature, see Chapter 19.

Each row in the panel represents one action or step, and includes a description. For instance, hitting Return or Enter while typing in the document creates a step called New Paragraph. Steps are listed in the order you perform your actions, with the latest actions at the bottom and earliest action at the top of the list.

But the History panel isn't just a dull document to pore over—it's a living, multiple-step Undo command. Use the History slider to move to any step in the history list. To undo one action, for example, drag the slider up one step. When you do this, you'll notice that the slider's former position step is grayed out. Steps that are dimmed represent future steps, so moving the slider down one step is the equivalent of choosing Edit → Redo.

You can undo or redo multiple steps by moving the slider up or down the list. Alternatively, you can click the track to the left of a step to move the slider to that step.

If you want to eliminate all the history steps for a document—to free up some of your computer's memory, for example—select Clear History from the History panel's context menu. But be careful: this is the one action you can't undo.

Text Formatting

Getting text onto a Web page (Chapter 2) is a good start, but effective communication requires effective design, too. Large, bold headlines help readers scan a page's important topics. Colorful text focuses attention. Bulleted sentences crystallize and summarize ideas. Just as a monotonous, low-key voice puts a crowd to sleep, a vast desert of plain HTML text is sure to turn visitors away from the important message of your site. In fact, text formatting could be the key to making your *Widgets Online 2006 Sale-a-thon* a resounding success instead of an unnoticed disaster.

To help you get your point across, Dreamweaver provides the tools you need to format your text in compelling and eye-catching ways. (See Figure 3-1 for examples of good and bad text formatting.)

Paragraph Formatting

Just as you use paragraphs to help organize your thoughts into clear, well-structured, and cohesive units when you're writing a paper or letter, you organize content on Web pages into blocks of information within HTML tags (see page 4 for more on tags). The most basic block of information is a simple paragraph, indicated in HTML by a paragraph tag, like this:

```
<p>Hello. This is one paragraph on this Web page. </p>
```

To a Web browser, everything between the opening <p> and closing </p> tags is considered part of the same paragraph. Many Dreamweaver formatting options—headlines, lists, indents, and alignment, for example—can apply only to an entire paragraph at a time, as opposed to individual words. In a word processor, you'd call this kind of formatting *paragraph* formatting; in Web design, it's called *block-level* formatting. The idea is exactly the same: these characteristics affect an entire paragraph (that is, a *block* of text, whether that's just one sentence or several sentences) at a time. (*Character-level* formatting, on the other hand, can be applied to individual words or even letters. Bold and italic fall into this category, as described later in this chapter.)

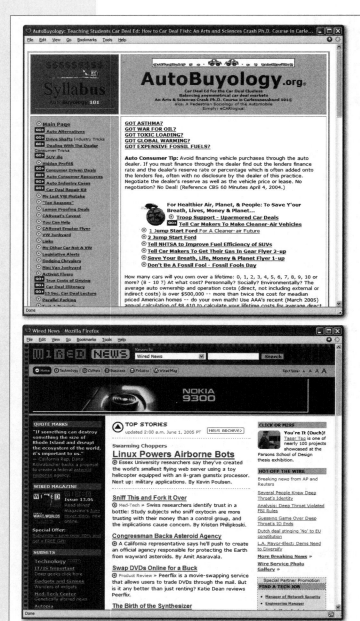

Figure 3-1:
Both these pages use different fonts, colors, and sizes to display text, but the one at bottom uses a consistent arrangement of styles to organize the text and guide the reader through the page. Notice how the headline "Linux Powers Airborne Bots," with its larger type, draws your eye to it immediately. Below that, the supplementary articles and their summaries are easy to identify and read. In the page at top, by contrast, while the name of the site is big and bold, the rest of the text on the page shares similar font sizes and colors. Nothing stands out or grabs your attention.

Paragraphs

When you create a new document in Dreamweaver and start typing, the text you type has no paragraph formatting at all, as indicated by the word None in the Format menu at the left side of the Property inspector. (*None* isn't an HTML tag; it just means that your text isn't surrounded by *any* of the paragraph tags used in this menu—<p>, <h1>, and so on.)

When you press Enter or Return, you create a new paragraph, complete with opening and closing <p> tags, as shown earlier, but your newly born paragraph still has no design applied to it. When your Web site visitors look at it, the font and size of your type are determined by their own Web browser preference settings. It may not look anything like the typography you saw in Dreamweaver.

UP TO SPEED

Separating Structure from Presentation

Formatting isn't just about good looks or fancy design. Some formatting options also give structure to a Web page, providing valuable insight into the organization of content on a page.

For example, the Heading 1 (<h1>) tag indicates a headline of the highest level and, therefore, greatest importance; the smaller Heading 2 (<h2>) tag represents a headline of slightly lower importance: a subhead. You'll see this kind of structure in this book. Each section begins with a headline ("Paragraph Formatting," on page 75, for example), and includes subheads that further divide the content into logical blocks of information.

Structure is more about organizing content than making it look pretty. Whether or not the headlines in this book used different colors and fonts, the fundamental organization—chapter title, main headlines, subheads, bulleted lists, numbered step-by-step instructions, and paragraphs of information—would remain the same.

HTML is actually intended to provide structure to a document, rather than making it look good. In fact, for some types of visitors (people who can't see, computer spiders that crawl Web sites for information, search engines, or text-only browsers, for example), how a Web page looks—its presentation—is irrelevant. What matters are the cues that let the visitor know what the content means.

For a while, HTML did double duty, giving structure through tags like <h1>, <ul> (for bulleted lists), and <p> (for a paragraph of information), and providing visual design with tags like <font> (for setting font types, colors, and sizes).

Today, however, the World Wide Web Consortium (W3C, the main organization for determining the current and future standards for the Web) considers this approach outmoded. It has officially *deprecated* HTML tags that add design to a page, like the <font> tag, which means that future versions of HTML (and possibly future versions of Web browsers) won't recognize them.

Dreamweaver 8 takes the same approach. The program comes with old-style, design-oriented HTML tags turned off. (To turn them back on, see page 30.) Instead, to provide visual design to a page, you should use Cascading Style Sheets, just as professional designers do.

CSS provides much more advanced and beautiful design possibilities than HTML ever did. In other words, let HTML provide the structure; let CSS create the presentation. HTML gives order, while CSS makes everything look good.

Chapter 6 covers CSS in depth, and throughout the book, you'll find notes that indicate when you can use CSS instead of HTML to achieve the same design goals.

You can add the Paragraph format to any block of text. Since this formatting option affects all of the text in the block, you don't need to select any text as a first step. Simply click inside the block of text and do one of the following:

- In the Property inspector (Figure 3-2), choose Paragraph from the Format menu.

- Choose Text → Paragraph Format → Paragraph.

- Press Ctrl+Shift+P (Shift-P).

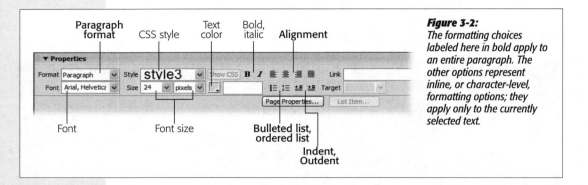

Figure 3-2:
The formatting choices labeled here in bold apply to an entire paragraph. The other options represent inline, or character-level, formatting options; they apply only to the currently selected text.

Note: Much to the chagrin of Web designers, Web browsers display a line's worth of blank space before and after block-level elements like headings and paragraphs. This visual gap is distracting, but unfortunately, you can't get rid of it with regular HTML.

However, many of the formatting limitations of HTML, including this one, go away when you use Cascading Style Sheets. See the Tip on page 203 to fix this problem.

Headlines

Headlines announce information ("The Vote Is In!") and help organize content. Just as this book uses different levels of headings to introduce its topics—from chapter titles all the way down to subsections—the HTML heading tag comes in a variety of sizes used to indicate importance.

Headlines range in size from 1 (largest) to 6 (smallest), as shown in Figure 3-3. They provide organization to a document, much like an outline has headings, sub-heads, and sub-subheads.

To turn a paragraph into a headline, click inside the line, or block, of text and then do one of the following:

- In the Property inspector, select one of the heading levels (Heading 1 through Heading 6) from the Format menu.

- Choose Text → Paragraph Format → Heading 1 (or Heading 2, Heading 3, and so on).

- Press Ctrl+1 (⌘-1), for the Heading 1 style, Ctrl+2 (⌘-2) for Heading 2, and so on.

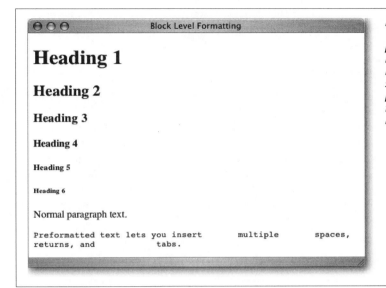

Preformatted Text

Web browsers normally ignore extra spaces, tabs, and other blank space characters in the underlying HTML when displaying a Web page. However, using the Preformatted paragraph format, you can override this behavior. Preformatted paragraphs display *every* text character in a paragraph, including tabs, multiple spaces, and line breaks, so you don't have to resort to multiple nonbreaking space characters (see page 60) to insert more than one space in a row.

The original idea behind the Preformatted format was to display tabular data—as in a spreadsheet—without the use of tables. That's why preformatted paragraphs show up in a *monospaced* font like Courier. In monospaced fonts, each letter of the alphabet, from i to w, is the same width and takes up the same horizontal space on a page, making it easy to align letters in columns. That's also why, when you use this paragraph style, you can use tabs to align text in columns. (When you use any other paragraph format, Web browsers ignore tabs.) These days, however, Dreamweaver's table feature is a much more superior method of creating columns; see Chapter 7.

Nonetheless, the Preformatted format can still be useful—when displaying sample HTML or programming code, for example. You can add the Preformatted format to any block of text. Simply click inside the block of text and then take one of these two steps:

- In the Property inspector, choose Format → Preformatted.

- Choose Text → Paragraph Format → Preformatted Text.

Keep in mind that preformatted text appears exactly as you enter it. Unlike normal paragraph text, lines of preformatted text don't automatically wrap if they're wider than the window. That means if you present your site visitors with a really long line of preformatted text, they'll have to scroll horizontally to see all of it. To end a line of preformatted text and create another, you must press the Enter or Return key to create a manual line break.

Paragraph Alignment

All text in a Web page starts out aligned with the left edge of the page (or, in the case of tables, to the left edge of a table cell). But there are times when you may want to center text in the middle of the page—perhaps an elegantly centered title—or align it to the right side. You can even create nice straight margins on both sides of a paragraph using the justification option. Although justified text looks elegant—simulating the typography of a fine book—the formatting doesn't show up in some browsers (Internet Explorer 4, for example). While there are many ways to align text in Dreamweaver, the Property inspector's word processor–like controls make this a snap (or, rather, a click).

To change a paragraph's alignment, click inside a paragraph and do one of the following:

- In the Property inspector, click one of the alignment icons in the upper-right corner (see Figure 3-2).

- Choose Text → Align → Left, Center, Right, or Justify.

- Use one of the following keyboard shortcuts:

> **Left:** Ctrl+Alt+Shift+L (Shift-Option-⌘-L)
> **Centered:** Ctrl+Alt+Shift+C (Shift-Option-⌘-C)
> **Right:** Ctrl+Alt+Shift+R (Shift-Option-⌘-R)
> **Justify:** Ctrl+Alt+Shift+J (Shift-Option-⌘-J)

UP TO SPEED

Keep Your Pages Lean

Many of the things that contribute to slow Web page downloads—congestion on the Internet, for example—are out of your control. But you can do your part by making sure your pages are as compact as possible. For instance, keep the file size of graphics down and eliminate extraneous lines of HTML code. The more HTML you include in a page, the larger the file, and the slower the download.

An example of a situation in which extraneous HTML code is produced is when aligning text to the left. Text on a Web page aligns to the left of a page by default. You'd be pointlessly bloating your Web page, therefore, by specifying left alignment of your text using a paragraph's alignment property. In fact, when you encounter the phrase "by default" describing an HTML property in this book, it's a safe bet that you can get that effect without adding any HTML.

Other ways to keep your pages lean and fast are highlighted throughout this book, but remember this rule of thumb: the less HTML code you create, the faster your Web page downloads, and the happier your audience is. (A good target for a page's maximum size is 40 to 45 KB.)

After you align a paragraph, the Property inspector displays a depressed button for the alignment option you chose, indicating what kind of alignment you've applied.

Note: Dreamweaver aligns text by adding code to the selected HTML tag. For example, centering a paragraph of text adds *align="center"* to the <p> tag. You can achieve the same effect with the Text-Align CSS property described on page 201.

You can remove an alignment by reapplying the *same* alignment. For instance, if you've right-aligned a paragraph, clicking the right-align button in the Property inspector removes all alignment information and returns that paragraph to its original setting. (This method of resetting the paragraph is a better solution than clicking the left-align button, which adds extra lines of HTML code to do the same thing.)

Indented Paragraphs

Indenting a paragraph can set it apart from the paragraphs before and after it. It's perfect for adding a small amount of space on either side of a paragraph, and it's frequently used to present a long quote or passage from a book or other source. In fact, an indented paragraph is called a *blockquote* in HTML.

To indent a paragraph or block-level element like a heading, click it and do one of the following:

- On the Property inspector, click the Indent button (see Figure 3-2).
- Choose Text → Indent.
- Press Ctrl+Alt+] (Option-]).

Unfortunately, since indenting a paragraph simply nests that paragraph in a basic HTML <blockquote> tag, you don't have any control over how *much* space is added to the margins of the paragraph. Most Web browsers insert about 40 pixels of blank space on the left and right side of a blockquote.

You can add additional space to the margins of a paragraph by applying *another* indent, thus creating a nested set of blockquotes. To do so, click an already indented paragraph and repeat one of the indenting procedures described above. To add multiple indents, continue in this way.

Note: Technically, the <blockquote> is designed to identify quotes on a page, not to indent regular paragraphs of text.

But if you use the CSS *margin* property (see page 203) instead, you get superior formatting choices. For example, you can specify exactly how much indentation you want, right down to the pixel; specify indentation to just the left or right; and even provide independent indentation amounts for each side of the paragraph.

But what if you want to remove indents from a paragraph? Use Dreamweaver to *outdent* it, of course. (Yes, *outdent* is a real word—ever since Microsoft made it up.)

To remove a paragraph's indent formatting—that is, remove a <blockquote> tag—click inside the paragraph and do one of the following:

• On the Property inspector, click the Outdent button (see Figure 3-2).

• Choose Text → Outdent.

• Press Ctrl+Alt+[(Option-[).

You can continue to outdent a paragraph using one of these methods until the paragraph returns to the left edge of the page; at that point, the outdenting commands have no further effect.

Lists

Lists organize the everyday information of our lives: to-do lists, grocery lists, top-10 lists, and so on. On Web pages, lists are indispensable for presenting groups of items such as links, company services or employees, or a series of instructions.

HTML offers formatting options for three basic categories of lists (see Figure 3-4). The two most common types of lists are *bulleted* (called *unordered lists* in the HTML language) and *numbered* (called *ordered* in HTML). The third and lesser-known list type, a *definition* list, comes in handy for creating glossaries or dictionary-like entries.

Bulleted and Numbered Lists

Bulleted and numbered lists share similar formatting. Dreamweaver automatically indents items in either type of list, and automatically precedes each list item by a character—a bullet, number, or letter, for example:

• Unordered or bulleted lists, like this one, are good for groups of items that don't necessarily follow any sequence. They're preceded by a bullet.

• Ordered lists are useful when presenting items that follow a sequence, such as the numbered instructions in the following section. Instead of a bullet, a number or letter precedes each item in an ordered list. Dreamweaver suggests a number (1, 2, 3, and so on), but you can substitute Roman numerals, letters, and other variations.

You can create a list from scratch within Dreamweaver, or add list formatting to text already on a Web page.

Creating a new bulleted or numbered list

When making a new list in Dreamweaver, you start by choosing a list format, and then typing the list items:

1. **In the document window, click where you wish to start a list.**

   See Chapter 2 for full details on adding text to a Web page.

2. **In the Property inspector, click the Ordered or Unordered List button to apply the list format.**

   Alternatively, you can choose Text → List → Unordered List or Ordered List. Either way, the first bullet or number appears in your document automatically.

3. **Type the first list item and then press Enter or Return. Repeat until you've added all items in the list.**

   The text you type appears (*Organic Compost*, for example, in Figure 3-4) after the bullet or number. When you press Return, a new bullet or number appears, ready for your next item. (If you just want to move to the next line *without* creating a new bullet, insert a line break by pressing Shift+Enter [Shift-Return].)

4. **When you've finished the list, press Enter or Return twice.**

   The double carriage return ends the list and creates a new empty paragraph.

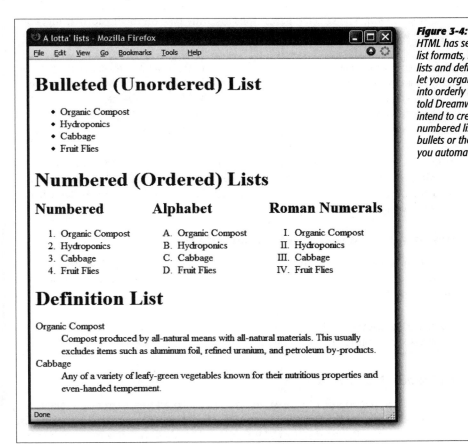

Figure 3-4:
HTML has several predefined list formats, including bulleted lists and definition lists, which let you organize information into orderly units. Once you've told Dreamweaver that you intend to create a bulleted or numbered list, it adds the bullets or the numbering for you automatically.

Formatting existing text as a list

You may have several paragraphs of text that you've already typed or pasted in from another program. It's a simple process to change any such group of paragraphs into a list.

1. **Select the text you wish to turn into a list.**

   The easiest way to select text is to drag from the first list item straight down into the last item of the list. Lists are block-level elements; each paragraph, whether it's a headline or regular paragraph, becomes one bulleted or numbered item in the list. In other words, you don't actually need to select all of the text in either the first or last paragraph.

2. **Apply the list format.**

   As when creating a list from scratch as described above, click either the Unordered or Ordered List button in the Property inspector, or choose from the Text → List submenu. The selected paragraphs instantly take on the list formatting, complete with bullets and automatic numbering.

Note: You may sometimes run into this problem: You select what looks like a handful of paragraphs and apply the list format, but only one bullet (or number) appears. This glitch arises when you've used the line break <br> tag to move text down a line in a paragraph. While doing so visually separates lines in a paragraph into separate blocks, the text is still part of single paragraph, which will appear as only *one* bulleted or numbered item. See page 59 for more on the <br> tag and how to avoid this situation.

Whichever way you started making a list—either by typing from scratch or reformatting existing text—you're not stuck with the results of your early decisions. You can add onto lists, add extra spaces, and even renumber them, as described in the following section.

Reformatting Bulleted and Numbered Lists

HTML tags define lists, just as they define other Web page features. Making changes to an existing list is a matter of changing those tags, using Dreamweaver's menu commands and Property inspector tools.

Note: Web browsers generally display list items one on top of the other. If you want to add a little breathing room between each list item, use the CSS *margin* properties, as described on page 203.

Adding new items to a list

Once you've created a list, it's easy to add items. To add an item at the beginning of a list, click before the first character of the first list item, type the item you wish to add, and press Enter or Return. Dreamweaver makes your newly typed item the first in the list, adding a bullet or number accordingly (and renumbering the other list items, if necessary).

To add an item at the middle or end of a list, click at the end of the *previous* list item and press Enter or Return. The insertion point appears after a new bullet or number; type your list item on this new line.

Changing bullets and numbers

Bulleted and numbered lists aren't limited to just the standard round, black bullet or the numbers 1, 2, and 3. You can choose from two bullet types and a handful of different numbering schemes. Here's how to change their settings:

1. **Click once inside any list item.**

   Strangely enough, you can't change the properties of a list if you've first selected the entire list, an entire single list item, or several list items.

2. **Open the List Properties dialog box (Figure 3-5).**

   To do so, either click the List Item button in the bottom half of the Property inspector or choose Text → List → Properties. (If the list is inside a table cell, your only choice is to use the Text menu. In this situation, the List Item button doesn't appear in the Property inspector.)

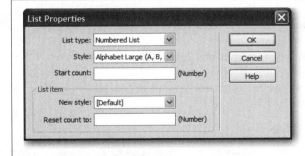

Figure 3-5:
The List Properties dialog box lets you set the type and style of a list. For example, if you select a Numbered List, you can choose from five different styles: Number (1, 2, 3); Roman Small (i, ii, iii); Roman Large (I, II, III); Alphabet Small (a, b, c); and Alphabet Large (A, B, C).

3. **Choose a type from the "List type" pop-up menu.**

   You can turn a numbered list into a bulleted list, or vice versa. You should avoid the two other options in the menu—Directory List and Menu List. These are old list types that won't necessarily work in modern Web browsers.

4. **Choose a bullet or numbering style.**

   Bulleted lists can have three different styles: *default, bullet,* and *square.* In most browsers, the default style is the same as the bullet style (a simple, solid, black circle). As you might guess, the square style uses a solid black square for the bullet character.

   Numbered lists, on the other hand, have a greater variety of style options. Dreamweaver starts you off with a simple numbering scheme (1, 2, 3, and so on), but you can choose from any of five styles for ordered lists, as explained in Figure 3-5.

人

5. **Set the starting number for the list.**

   You don't have to begin a numbered list at 1, A, or the Roman numeral I. You can start it at another number, if you wish—a trick that can come in handy if, for example, you're creating a Web page to explain how to rebuild a car's engine.

   As part of each step, say you want to include a photograph. You create a numbered list, type in the directions for step 1, hit Return, and insert an image (as described in Chapter 5). You hit Return again and type in the text for step 2. Unfortunately, the photo, because it's technically an item in an ordered list, now has the number 2 next to it, and your real step 2 is listed as 3!

   If you remove the list formatting from the photo to get rid of the 2, you create one list above it and another below it (as described on page 88). Step 2, *below* the photo, now thinks it's the beginning of a new list—and starts over with the number 1!

   The solution is to make the list below the photo think it's a *new* list that begins with 2.

   To start the list at something other than 1, type the starting number in the "Start count" field (Figure 3-5). You must enter a number, even if you want the list to use letters. So to begin a list at D instead of A, type *4* in the "Start count" field.

   In fact, you can even change the style of a *single* list item. For instance, you could change the third item in a numeric list from a 3 to the letter C. (Of course, just because you can doesn't mean you should. Dreamweaver is very thorough in supporting the almost overwhelming combination of options available in HTML, but, unless you're building a Dadaist revival site, how often do you want a list that's numbered 1, 2, C, iv, 1?)

6. **Click OK to apply the changes.**

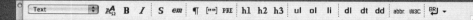

Note: Once again, you can access more advanced formatting options for lists using Cascading Style Sheets. For example, you can use a graphic of your own creation to begin each bulleted list item, instead of choosing from the same boring set of square or circular bullets. See page 206 for the details.

Nested lists

Some complex outlines require multiple *levels* of lists. Legal documents, for instance, may list major clauses with capital letters (A, B, C, and so on) and use roman numerals (i, ii, iii, and so on) for subclauses (see Figure 3-6).

It's easy to create such nested lists in Dreamweaver; Figure 3-6 shows the steps.

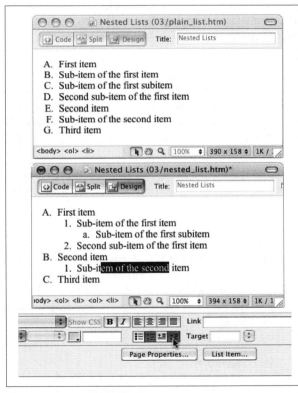

Figure 3-6:
Top: To create a nested list, start with a single list—in this case, a numbered list using capital letters instead of numbers. Select a subtopic and click the Indent button (where the cursor is in the bottom figure) or choose Text → Indent.

Bottom: The item becomes a nested list, indented from the main list and with its own numbering. Notice, too, that the major points have been renumbered—letter E from the first figure is letter B in the second figure—to reflect the new ordering of the list.

Definition Lists

Definition lists can be used to display items in a dictionary or glossary, or whenever you need to present a term and its definition. Each item in a definition list is composed of two parts: a word or term, and a definition.

As you can see in Figure 3-4, definition lists aren't as fancy as they sound. The first item in the list—the word or term—is presented on its own line with no indent, and the second item—the definition—appears directly underneath, indented.

Note: Behind the scenes, Dreamweaver creates an entire definition list using the <dl> tag. Each item in the list is then composed of two tags: <dt> for the definition term or word, and <dd> for the definition itself.

You can't create a definition list using the Property inspector. Instead, start by highlighting the paragraphs that contain the terms and definitions you wish to include in the list, and then choose Text → List → Definition List.

To turn a definition list *back* to regular paragraphs, select it and choose Text → List → None, or click the Outdent button in the Property inspector.

Removing and Deleting List Items

Dreamweaver lets you take items out of a list in two ways: either by removing the list *formatting* from an item or items (and changing them back into normal paragraphs) or by deleting their text outright.

Removing list items

To remove list formatting from one or more list items (or an entire list), highlight the lines in question and then choose Text → List → None (or just click the Outdent button on the Property inspector). You've just removed all list formatting; the text remains on the screen, now formatted as standard paragraphs. (For nested lists, you'll need to click the Outdent button several times.)

If you reformat an item in the middle of a list using this technique, it becomes a regular paragraph. Dreamweaver turns the items above it and below it into separate lists.

Deleting list items

A simple way to delete a list or list item is to use the tag selector in the status bar of the document window (see Figure 3-7). To delete an entire list, click anywhere inside the list, and then click its tag in the tag selector—<ul> for a bulleted list or <ol> for a numbered list—and press Delete. You can also, of course, drag through all the text of the list and then press Delete.

Figure 3-7:
The tag selector is a great way to quickly and accurately select an HTML tag. Clicking the <ol> (ordered list) tag, for instance, selects the entire numbered list.

To delete a single list item, click that item in the document window, click the <li> tag in the tag selector, and then press Delete.

Tip: You can rearrange a list by dragging a list item to another position within the list. If it's an ordered list (1, 2, 3, and so on), Dreamweaver automatically renumbers the list. For example, if you select an item numbered 4 (or D, if it's an alphabetical list) and drag it to the second position in the list, Dreamweaver changes the item to 2 (or B) and renumbers all items that follow.

However, selecting a list item can be tricky. If you simply drag to select the text, you don't actually select the list item itself, with all its formatting and numbering. To be sure you've selected a list item, click the <li> tag in the tag selector in the document window's status bar (see Figure 3-7). Now, when you drag the selection to a new position in the list, the number (or bullet) follows. You can also select a list item in this way, copy or cut it, and paste it back into the list in another position.

Character Formatting

The simple formatting applied by a paragraph format isn't much to write home about, much less to advertise on a résumé. Heading 1, for instance, is generally displayed in black and bold using a large Times New Roman font. As mentioned in the box on page 77, this type of paragraph formatting is intended to provide structure, not good looks.

To make your Web pages stand out, you'll want to apply different fonts, colors, sizes, and styles to your text. Unlike paragraph formatting, which applies to an entire HTML paragraph, you can apply character formatting to any selection of text, whether it's a single word, one sentence, an entire paragraph, or your whole Web page.

In general, you apply character formatting just as you would in a word processor: Select the text (using any of the methods described on page 68) and then apply a format using the Property inspector or Text menu.

Up to this point, you've been using HTML only for structuring your Web page with headlines, paragraphs, lists, and so on. When using the Property inspector to apply formatting like fonts, colors, and text sizes, Dreamweaver is working behind the scenes to create Cascading Style Sheets to format text (see page 98 for an explanation). Professional Web designers—who not only want to keep up with technical trends but who also must build functional Web sites that please the vast audience of Web surfers—have already embraced the more sophisticated typographic controls offered by Cascading Style Sheets.

Note: Cascading Style Sheets aren't just for text, either. You can format any HTML element—images, tables, and so on—with the power of CSS. Read all about it in Chapter 6.

Using the instructions in the rest of this chapter, you'll learn how to apply basic CSS-based formatting to text by using the Property inspector and Text menu. (A wider array of additional CSS formatting options is discussed further in Chapter 6.)

Note: If you don't want to use CSS (perhaps you've built an entire site using the <font> tag and you wish to remain consistent), you can revert to Dreamweaver's old method of formatting text. Press Ctrl+U (⌘-U) to open the Preferences window. Select the General category, turn off the "Use CSS instead of HTML tags" checkbox, and then click OK to close Preferences.

But if you're building a new site, you're better off sticking with CSS, a standard that will last a lot longer than out-of-date HTML tags.

Text Styles

To add emphasis to your words, you can choose from several text styles. You can apply the two most common emphasis effects, bold and italics, from the Property inspector. For less frequently used styles, choose from the Text → Style submenu (see Figure 3-8).

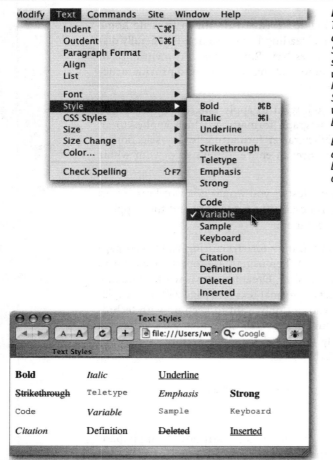

Figure 3-8:
Top: While the Property inspector lets you apply bold and italic styles to text, the Text → Style menu offers a larger selection of text styles. Don't be confused by the term "styles," which, in this case, merely refers to different HTML tags. They're unrelated to Cascading Style Sheet styles and are intended to identify very specific types of text, like citations from a book or magazine.

Bottom: As you can see, the many style options are usually displayed in bold, italics, the browser's monospaced font (usually Courier), or some combination of the three.

To add bold or italic formatting to text, select the word or words you'd like to make bold or italic, and then click the Bold or Italic button on the Property inspector.

Note: Use italics with care. While italics are frequently used in printed material to add *emphasis* or when referencing a book title, they can be difficult to read on a computer screen, especially at small type sizes.

As shown in Figure 3-8, HTML offers a host of different text styles, some of which fulfill obscure purposes. For instance, the Code and Variable styles are intended for formatting the display of programming code, while the Sample style represents the output from a computer program—not exactly styles you'll need often in promoting, say, your *Cheeses of the World* mail-order company.

Unless you intend to include content whose meaning is supported by the tag (for example, you include some sample computer code on a page, so you format it with the Code style), you're better off avoiding such styles. But if you think one of them might come in handy, you can find more about these styles from Dreamweaver's built-in HTML reference; see Chapter 9 for details.

In particular, avoid the underline and strikethrough styles: both have been deprecated (page 77) in the HTML 4 standard and may produce no effect in future browser versions. (You can, however, turn to Cascading Styles Sheets' text-formatting abilities to put lines through and under any text you'd like. See page 195 for more.)

UP TO SPEED

When Bold and Italic Are Neither

You may be confused by the HTML code that Dreamweaver produces when making text bold or italic. Instead of using the <b> tag—the traditional HTML code for bold—Dreamweaver uses the <strong> tag. And instead of <i> for italics, clicking the I button on the Property inspector gets you <em>, or the emphasis tag. That's because Macromedia has decided to follow industry practices rather than stick to an old tradition.

For most purposes, <strong> and <em> behave identically to <b> and <i>. They look the same—bolded or italicized—in most browsers. However, when encountered by screen readers (software or equipment that reads Web pages aloud for the benefit of the visually impaired), the <strong> tag triggers a loud, strong voice. The <em> tag also brings an emphasis to the voice of screen readers, though with less strength than the <strong> tag.

Since most Web browsers simply treat the <strong> tag like the <b> tag, and the <em> tag like the <i> tag, you'll probably never notice the difference. However, if you prefer the simple <b> and <i> tags, choose Edit → Preferences. Select the General category and turn off the checkbox labeled "Use <strong> and <em> in place of <b> and <i>."

Fonts

Formatting fonts for the Web is very much like using fonts in a word processor. Sadly, it carries some of the same drawbacks. For example, if you create some beautiful document in Microsoft Word, using fancy fonts you just bought from a small font company in Nome, Alaska, you're in for a rude surprise when you email the document to your boss. He won't see anything resembling what the memo looked like on *your* screen. Because he doesn't own the same fonts, he'll see some default font on his computer—Times, perhaps. Fonts show up in a distributed document only if each recipient happens to have the same fonts installed.

On the Web, you're in the same predicament. You're free, as a Web designer, to specify any font you want in a Web page, but it won't show up on a viewer's computer unless she's installed the same font on her system. Otherwise, your visitor's Web browser will show your text in a default font, which is usually some version of Times or Courier.

There are several solutions to this dilemma. One is to use Flash text, described on page 150, or to convert your text into graphic images. Another is to specify the font you'd *like* to use; if your viewer's computer has the specified font installed, that's what she'll see. You can specify secondary or tertiary font choices if the preferred font isn't available. In fact, Dreamweaver offers prepackaged lists of such "first choice, second choice, third choice" fonts, as you'll find out in the following section.

Applying font formatting

Dreamweaver's approach to font formatting is straightforward:

1. **Select the text whose font you want to change.**

   As in a word processor, you can also click anywhere in your Web page and then choose a font for text that you're *about* to type. (If you're pasting text from another program, paste first and then select the text and apply a font.)

2. **From the Property inspector or the Text menu, select the font.**

   Choose a font from the Font pop-up menu in the Property inspector, or choose Text → Font and select a font from the submenu.

UP TO SPEED

Knowing Your Font Types

You can find literally tens of thousands of different fonts to express your every thought: from bookish, staid, and classical typefaces to rounded, cartoonish squiggles.

Most fonts are divided into two categories: serif and sans-serif. Serif fonts are best for long passages of text, as it's widely believed that serifs—small decorative strokes ("hands" and "feet") at the end of a letter's main strokes—gently lead the eye from letter to letter, making text easier to read. Examples of serif fonts are Times, Times New Roman, Georgia, and Minion, the font in the main body paragraphs of this book.

Sans-serif fonts, on the other hand, are often used for headlines, thanks to their clean and simple appearance. Examples of sans-serif fonts include Arial, Helvetica, Verdana, and Formata, which you're reading now. Some people believe that you should use only sans-serif fonts on Web pages because they think the delicate decorative strokes of serif fonts don't display well on the coarse resolution of a computer screen. This is an aesthetic judgment, so you should feel free to pick the fonts you think look best.

You'll soon discover that Dreamweaver's font menus aren't quite what you're used to. When you apply a font to text, you have to choose a little *list* of fonts like "Arial, Helvetica, sans-serif." You can't just choose a single font, such as Helvetica.

That's because, as noted on page 91, in order for your viewer's computer to display a font correctly on a Web page, it must have the same font installed. If the font's not there, the browser simply replaces the font specified in the Web page with the browser's default font.

To gain some control over the font-picking process, you can specify a list of fonts that look similar to your first-choice font (Arial, for example). Your visitor's Web browser checks if the first font in the list is installed on the computer. If it is, that's what your visitor sees when viewing your Web page.

But if the first font isn't installed, the browser looks down the list until it finds a font that is. Different operating systems use different fonts, so these lists include one font that's common on Windows and another, similar-looking font that's common on the Mac. Arial, for instance, is found on all Windows machines, while Helvetica is a similar font for Macs.

That's it. You've just applied one of Dreamweaver's preinstalled fonts. If you'd like a greater degree of control of what fonts your page displays, read on.

POWER USERS' CLINIC

Font Convergence

While Mac and Windows used to come with very different sets of preinstalled fonts, there's been some convergence in the past few years. These days, you can count on the average Mac or PC having the following fonts: Arial, Arial Black, Arial Narrow, Comic Sans MS, Courier, Courier New, Georgia, Times New Roman, Trebuchet MS, Verdana, and Webdings.

If your audience includes people running Unix or Linux, all bets are off. In that case, stick to these three fonts: Helvetica (make sure to also specify Arial for Windows owners), Times (Times New Roman for Windows), and Courier (Courier New for Windows).

You can find a list of fonts included with various versions of Mac and Windows operating systems at the following Web sites:

Mac OS X and Windows XP: *www.xvsxp.com/fonts/*. This page not only provides lists of preinstalled fonts for Mac OS

X and Win XP, but also contains useful information on how to use fonts in the two operating systems.

Windows 2000: *www.microsoft.com/typography/fonts/win200.htm*.

And for a concise comparison that lists fonts friendly to both operating systems, check out *www.ampsoft.net/webdesign-l/WindowsMacFonts.html*.

To jump-start your adventures, here are a few font combinations that work relatively well for both Mac and Windows visitors:

- Tahoma, Lucida Grande, sans-serif

- Lucida Console, American Typewriter, monospace

- Marker Felt Wide, Comic Sans MS, fantasy

Creating custom font lists

Dreamweaver comes with six preset "first choice, second choice, third choice" font lists, which incorporate fonts that are standard on both Windows and Macs. But you can easily stray from the pack and create your own font lists for use in your Web pages. If you proceed with the custom approach, make sure you know what fonts your visitors have—easily done if you're designing a corporate intranet and know what computers are used in your company—and always specify one font that you *know* is installed. In this way, your page may not look exactly as you intended, but it'll at least be readable.

Here's how you create a new "first choice, second choice, third choice" font list.

Note: Technically, you can specify any number of fallback fonts in one of these lists, not just first, second, and third choices. Your list can specify only a single font, or a long list arranged in order of preference.

---

1. **Open the Edit Font List dialog box.**

   Choose Edit Font List from the Property inspector's Font menu, or choose Text → Font → Edit Font List. Either way, the Edit Font List dialog box appears (Figure 3-9).

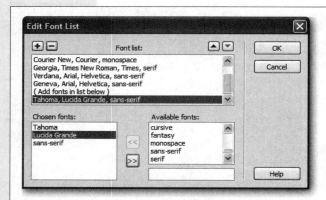

Figure 3-9:
Not only can you create your own font lists, but you can also edit, remove, or reorder the current lists in this dialog box. When you click a list in the "Font list" menu, the "first choice, second choice, third choice" fonts appear in the lower-left corner. To remove a font from that list, click the font name and then click the >> button. To add a font to the list, select a font in the "Available fonts" menu and click the << button. Finally, to reorder the font lists as they appear in the Property inspector or Text → Font menu, click the arrow keys near the upper-right corner of the dialog box.

2. **Select a first-choice font from the list of "Available fonts," or type in the font name.**

   All fonts on your computer are listed in the "Available fonts" menu. Simply click to select the font you wish to add.

   Alternatively, you can type a font's name into the box that appears directly below the list of available fonts—a handy trick if you want to include a font that *isn't* installed on your computer (a Windows font when you're working on a Mac, for example).

3. **Add the font you've just specified to your new, custom font list by clicking the << button (or just double-clicking the font name).**

   Your first-choice font appears in the "Chosen fonts" list.

4. **Repeat steps 2 and 3 for each font you wish to include in your custom list.**

   The order in which you add the fonts is the order they appear in the list. These become the "first choice, second choice, third choice" fonts.

   Unfortunately, there's no way to change the order of the fonts once you've added them. So if you accidentally put the fonts in the wrong order, you must delete the list by clicking the minus (–) button (at the upper-left corner of the dialog box) and start over.

5. **Add a generic font family.**

   This last step isn't strictly necessary, but it's a good idea. If your Web page visitor is some kind of anti-font radical whose PC doesn't have *any* of the fonts you've chosen, his browser will substitute the generic font family you specify here.

   Generic fonts are listed at the bottom of the list of "Available fonts" and include "cursive," "fantasy," "monospace," "sans-serif," and "serif." On most systems, the monospaced font is Courier, the serif font is Times, and the sans-serif font is Arial or Helvetica. Select a generic font that's similar in appearance to the fonts in your list. For instance, choose "sans-serif" if your list consists of sans-serif fonts like Helvetica or Arial; choose "serif" if you specified fonts like Times or Georgia; or choose "monospace" for a font like Courier.

6. **Click OK.**

   Your new font package appears in the Property inspector's Font menu, ready to apply.

Font Size

Varying the sizes of fonts on a Web page is one way to direct a viewer's attention. Large type screams "Read Me!"—excellent for attention-grabbing headlines—while small type fades into the background—perfect for necessary but unexciting legal mumbo jumbo like copyright notices.

Unless you specifically define its size, text in a regular paragraph appears at the default size specified by your visitor's Web browser, such as 12 points. (A *point* is a typographic measurement equal to 1/72 of an inch.)

In theory, 12-point lettering is roughly 1/6 of an inch tall. In practice, however, the resolution of the monitor, the font itself, and the operating system drastically affect the size of type on the screen. To the eternal frustration of Web designers who are used to, say, Adobe InDesign or Quark XPress, text on a Web page viewed in Netscape Navigator for Windows, for instance, appears substantially larger than when viewed in Navigator on a Mac. Add to this the fact that people can change their browsers' default text size to any size they like, and you'll quickly understand that Web design requires a Zen-like acceptance of factors beyond your control.

___

Note: You may notice two options under the Text menu (see Figure 3-8): Size and Size Change. These submenus are used to apply the old-style <font> tag *size* property, which was limited to only seven sizes (1 through 7). Unless you purposely turn off the CSS option (see the note on page 30), these submenus are grayed out, making these properties inaccessible.

___

Dreamweaver has replaced the old <font> tag method of sizing text with CSS, which offers a much wider range of sizes. To specify a text size, first select the text, and then use the Property inspector's Size menu to select a font size (see Figure 3-10). The choices available from the Size menu break down into four groups:

- The **None** option removes any size information that you may have applied to the text. The text returns to its default size.

- The numeric choices—**9 through 36**—indicate how tall you wish to make the text, in pixels. Nine-pixel-tall text is nearly unreadable, while 36 pixels makes a bold statement. One benefit of pixel sizes is that text appears nearly the same across different browsers and different operating systems, overcoming the problems mentioned above.

- The options **xx-small through xx-large** indicate fixed sizes, replacing the sizes 1 through 7 used with the old HTML <font> tag. The *medium* size is usually the same as the default size.

- The last two choices—**smaller and larger**—are relative sizes, meaning that they shrink or enlarge the selected text based on the default size. These choices come in handy when you've defined a base font size for the entire page using the Page Properties window (see Figure 1-15 on page 40).

Suppose the default size of text on a page is 12 pixels. If you apply a "larger" size to a selection of text, it will get bigger (the exact amount varies by Web browser). If, later, you change the base size to 14 pixels (in Page Properties), all of that "larger" text will also increase proportionally.

Figure 3-10:
You can set a dizzying array of font sizes using the Property inspector. Dreamweaver generates CSS styles when formatting text using the Property inspector. In this case, the style is unimaginatively named style3.

To change the size of text, simply select it and choose a new size from the Property inspector (Figure 3-10). If you applied a number (that is, a pixel value), you have an additional option: if you don't like any of the sizes listed, you can type any number you wish. In fact, unlike HTML, CSS can handle humongous text—hundreds of pixels tall, if that's what you're into.

You're not limited to pixels, either. The Units pop-up menu (to the right of the Size menu, shown in Figure 3-10) lets you specify pixels, points, inches, centimeters, millimeters, picas, ems, percentages, or exes (an *ex* is the width of the letter X in the current font). Most of these measurement systems aren't intended for onscreen display. The most popular options are:

- **Pixels** are great for ensuring that text looks the same size across different browsers and operating systems. The downside, however, is that Internet Explorer for Windows doesn't let Web surfers adjust the pixel size. So people who can't see well, or whose monitors are set to very high resolutions, are stuck with your choice of pixel size. Make it too small, and they won't be able to read your text.

- **Ems** are a relative measurement, meaning that the actual point size varies.

  One em is equal to the default font size. So suppose a Web browser's default font size is 14 pixels tall. In that case, 1 em would mean 14 pixels tall, 2 ems would be twice that (28 pixels), and 1.5 ems would be 21 pixels.

  The advantage of ems is that they allow Web visitors to control the size of onscreen text. If it's too small, they can increase the base font size. (In Internet Explorer, you make this adjustment by choosing an option from the View → Text Size menu [View → Text Zoom on the Mac].) Any text measured in ems then changes according to the Web browser's new setting.

  You can use pixels and ems together. You could, for instance, set the base font size on your page to 16 pixels (see Figure 1-15 on page 40) and then use ems for other parts of the page. For example, you could set headlines to 2 ems, making them 32 pixels tall. If you later thought the overall text size of the page was too small or too large, you could simply change the base font size for the page, and the headlines and all other text would resize proportionally.

  Many Web experts advocate the use of ems, because they allow visitors to decide how big text should appear, thus making the site more widely accessible. Many designers, on the other hand, don't like the fact that other people can radically change the design of a page by simply changing a browser setting.

- **Percentages** (%) are another relative size measurement. When applied to text size, they're functionally equivalent to ems. If you're more comfortable with the notion of percentages than the typography-inspired ems, use percentage values instead.

The other measurement options, like inches and millimeters, don't make as much sense as pixels, ems, and percentages, because there's no consistent way to measure them on monitors. For example, Windows is set to 96 pixels to the inch, whereas Mac OS X is set to 72 pixels per inch—but even these settings can be changed, so there's no reliable way to measure an "inch" on a computer screen.

Font Color

Most color formatting in Dreamweaver, whether it's for text or for a table cell, makes use of Dreamweaver's *color box*. For more information on applying color in Dreamweaver and using the color box, see page 41.

To set the color of text, first select it and then take your pick:

- In the Property inspector, click the color well and select a color.

- In the Property inspector, click the Font Color field and type in the *hexadecimal number* (see page 41) of the color you want. (Clearly, this is the option for hard-core HTML geeks. After all, surely you've memorized the hex number of that light shade of blue you always use—#6699FF, isn't it?)

Remember, as part of the properties for a Web page, you can choose a default color for all text on the page—see Figure 1-14 on page 39. Setting this default color provides a useful shortcut for when you want all or most of the text on a page to be a color other than black.

Character Formatting Behind the Scenes

Dreamweaver creates Cascading Style Sheets for most of the character formatting choices you make in the Property inspector. For example, if you select a paragraph of text and then apply a color to it, Dreamweaver creates a CSS style and applies it to the paragraph. You'll learn a lot more about Cascading Style Sheets in Chapter 6, but until then, here are the basics.

A CSS style is a set of instructions telling a Web browser how to display things on a Web page. When you use the Property inspector to change the font, color, or size of text, Dreamweaver creates a new style and places the code for it in the <head> of the document. The new style's name now appears in the Property inspector's CSS Style menu (Figure 3-10) with an unimaginative name like *style1, style2, style3*, and so on. Because these names don't mean much, you should rename them to something more descriptive such as *mainHeadline, bodyText*, and so on. (Renaming styles is discussed on page 100.)

Note: If you already know a thing or two about CSS, you may want to note that Dreamweaver creates these styles using a *class selector.*

Depending on how you select the text, one of two other things happens:

- If you select an entire paragraph, Dreamweaver adds an HTML attribute called *class* to the paragraph. This attribute ties the new CSS style to the paragraph of text and informs the Web browser to apply the style to this particular paragraph.

For example, if you add a dark-blue color to the first paragraph of text on a page, Dreamweaver creates a new style called, say, *style1*. The HTML looks like this: <p class="style1">. All text in the paragraph becomes dark blue, and this new style's name appears in the Property inspector.

The same process takes place when you style other block-level elements, such as headlines.

• If you select just a few words of a paragraph and then apply some character formatting, Dreamweaver behaves slightly differently. It still creates a new style (*style2*, say), which still appears in the Property inspector. But it also injects an HTML tag called span. The <span> tag might look like this: <span class="style2"> [your text here] </span>. This tag wraps around the text you selected, so that the style affects only the text inside the span. (See page 171 for more on spans.)

A good way to determine which method Dreamweaver used is to look at the tag selector (Figure 3-11). If you see something like <p.style4>, then the paragraph as a whole is in *style4*. If you see <span.style6>, then Dreamweaver applied the style to just a portion of the paragraph, headline, or block-level element.

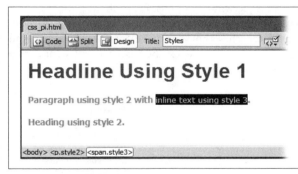

Figure 3-11:
You can apply a style to any text. In this case, style2 is applied to both the middle paragraph (<p> tag) and the bottom headline (<h1> tag). When you apply a style to only part of a paragraph, the <span> tag is used. The tag selector (at bottom) can help you identify and select these (and other) tags.

Character Formatting Styles

Once you've formatted text just the way you want it, you needn't repeat the same steps for formatting other text on a page. Since Dreamweaver has already created a style containing your formatting choices, you can reuse it freely throughout your document via the Property inspector.

Applying styles

To format an entire paragraph, either select the paragraph or click anywhere inside it, and choose from the Property inspector's Style menu (Figure 3-12). To format just a few words, select the text and choose a style name from the Style menu; in this case, Dreamweaver formats just the selected text (wrapping it in a <span> tag as described above).

Removing styles

Removing a style is just as easy. Click anywhere inside the styled text or, using the tag selector, select the paragraph, headline, or range of text whose style you wish to remove, and then select None from the Property inspector's Style menu. This action removes the *class* property (or eliminates the <span> tag) used to apply the style. Note that the style itself—that is, the code placed in the <head> of the Web page—remains. (To remove that code, see page 178.)

Tip: To reuse styles you've created on other Web pages, consider exporting them as an external CSS style sheet. See the Tip on page 167 for details.

Renaming styles

Because Dreamweaver uses generic names—*style1*, *style2*, and so on—for the styles you create using the Property inspector, it's a good idea to rename them using more descriptive titles. For example, if you create a style for formatting a copyright notice, *copyright* is a more descriptive name than *style16*.

To rename a style, choose Rename… from the Styles menu in the Property inspector (see Figure 3-12). The Rename Style window opens. From the top menu, select the style you wish to rename, type the new name, and then click the OK button. Behind the scenes, Dreamweaver searches the Web page for the old name and replaces it with the new name. (That's why you'll see the Search Results panel pop open after renaming a style this way.)

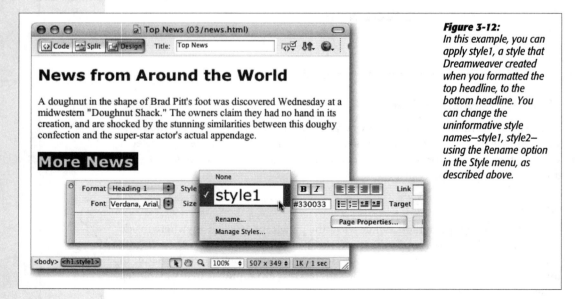

Figure 3-12:
In this example, you can apply style1, a style that Dreamweaver created when you formatted the top headline, to the bottom headline. You can change the uninformative style names—style1, style2—using the Rename option in the Style menu, as described above.

You need to keep a few things in mind when renaming a style. Style renaming is described in greater detail on page 178, but in a nutshell:

- Use only letters and numbers in the name.

- Don't use spaces or any punctuation marks like !, *, &, and so on.

- Always begin the name with a letter: header2005 is good, but 2005header is not.

Editing styles

Editing styles is trickier, and you may find yourself running into some of Dreamweaver's strange antics pretty quickly.

Suppose you've selected a paragraph and applied Arial, Helvetica, sans-serif as the font; colored it red; and changed its size to 36 pixels. Dreamweaver creates a new style—say, *style1*. You decide you don't like the red color, so you immediately change it to a deep orange. Dreamweaver (as you'd expect) updates the *style1* style with a deep orange color. So far, so good.

But now suppose that you apply this style to another headline on the page. Now there are two headlines with the identical *style1* style. However, you've again decided the color is wrong (man, are you picky!). So you select the second headline and change the color to a lovely chartreuse.

Several strange things happen: First, the Property inspector's Style menu now reads *style2*, or something similar like *style3* or *style4*. Second, the first headline *doesn't change color*.

Instead of updating the original style, Dreamweaver created yet another style and applied it to the paragraph (replacing the previously applied style). This approach may seem crazy, but it happened because Dreamweaver had no idea what you wanted. Did you intend to change the color of just that one headline for special emphasis? Or were you trying to change the color of the whole style?

In any case, Dreamweaver's behavior may seem erratic, and it's certainly not helping you edit the style. You have two choices if you want to update the style. First, make sure that *no other text* on the page uses the style. You can then change the color, typeface, and size using the Property inspector, causing Dreamweaver to update the style. Once you're done—really done—then you can use that style elsewhere on the page.

A better choice, if you wish to edit the style itself, is to use Dreamweaver's CSS tools and *not* the Property inspector, as discussed on page 173.

Using the Property inspector to format text is quick, easy, and sometimes quirky: it's great for a single, one-off, "gotta get it down now" type of Web page. But, because editing these styles is tricky, and because the more you use the Property inspector to format text, the more styles (*style3, style5, style1001,* and so on) are added to your page, the Property inspector isn't the best method for formatting an entire Web site. You'll generally want more consistency over your style names and how they're used throughout your site. You'll also want to tap into many more formatting options and harness advanced CSS features that aren't available from the Property inspector. For this, you'll need to learn how to use the CSS Styles panel and Dreamweaver's other CSS tools, as described in Chapter 6.

Links

The humble hyperlink may not raise eyebrows anymore, but the notion that you can navigate a whole sea of information, jumping from one island of content to another with a simple click, is a very recent and powerful invention. Interested in a particular band? Go to Yahoo.com, type in the band's name, *click* to go to its Web site, *click* to go to the page that lists its upcoming gigs, *click* to go to the Web site for the club where the band's currently playing, and *click* to buy tickets.

Although links are a basic part of building pages, and although Dreamweaver, for the most part, shields you from their complexities, they can be tricky to understand. The following section provides a brief overview of links, including some of the technical distinctions between the different types. If you already understand links, or are just eager to start using Dreamweaver, jump to "Adding a Link" on page 108.

Understanding Links

A link is a snippet of computer code that gives a Web browser directions for how to get from one page to another on the Web. What makes links powerful is the fact that the distance those directions cover doesn't matter. A link can just as easily lead to another page on the same site or to a page on a Web server halfway around the globe.

Behind the scenes, a simple HTML tag called the anchor (<a>) tag makes each and every link work. Links come in three different flavors: *absolute, document-relative,* and *root-relative*. See page 106 for some examples of each link type in practice.

Absolute Links

When people need to mail you a letter, they ask for your address. Suppose it's 123 Main St., New York, NY 12001. No matter where in the country your friends are, if they write *123 Main St., New York, NY 12001* on an envelope and mail it, their letters will get to you. That's because your address is unique—just like an absolute link.

Similarly, every Web page has a unique address, called a *URL* (most people pronounce it "you are el"), or Uniform Resource Locator. If you open a Web browser and type *http://www.sawmac.com/dw8/index.html* into the address bar, the home page for this book opens.

This URL is an *absolute link;* it's the complete, unique address for a single page. Absolute links always begin with *http://,* and you'll use them any time you link to a Web page *outside of your own site.* An absolute link always leads to the same page, whether the link to it is on a page in the current site or an entirely different site.

The bottom line: use absolute links when you want to link to a page on another Web site.

Document-Relative Links

Suppose you, the resident of 123 Main Street, drop in on a couple who just moved into the neighborhood. After letting them know about all the great restaurants nearby, you tell them about a party you're having at your place.

When they ask you where you live, you could, of course, say, "I live at 123 Main St., New York, NY 12001," but your neighbors would probably think you needed a little psychiatric help. More likely, you would say something like, "Just go across the street and turn left. I'm the second house on the right." Of course, you can't use these instructions as your mailing address, because they work relative only to your neighbors' house.

When you want to create a link from one Web page to another within the same Web site, you can use similar shorthand: a *document-relative link.* In essence, a document-relative link—like the directions you give your neighbor—simply tells the browser where to find the linked page *relative* to the current page. If two pages are in the same folder, for instance, the path is as simple as "Go to that page over there." In this case, the link is simply the name of the file you wish to link to: *index.html,* for example. You can leave off all that *http://* and *www.sawmac.com* business, because you're already there.

Document-relative links can be finicky, however, because they're completely dependent on the location of the page containing the link. If you move the page to another part of the site—filing it in a different folder, for example—the link won't work. That's why working with document-relative links has traditionally been one of the most troublesome chores for a Web designer, even though this kind of link is ideal for linking from one page to another in the same site.

Fortunately, Dreamweaver makes working with document-relative links so easy, you may forget what all the fuss is about. For example, whenever you save a page into a different folder—a maneuver that would normally shatter all document-relative links on the page—Dreamweaver quietly *rewrites* the links so they still work. Even better, using the program's site management tools, you can cavalierly reorganize your Web site, moving folders and files without harming the delicate connections between your site's files. Dreamweaver's site management features are discussed in depth in Part Four.

Root-Relative Links

Root-relative links describe how to get from one page to another within the same site, just like document-relative links. However, in this case, the path is described relative to the site's *root folder*—the folder that contains the home page and other pages, folders, and files that make up your site. (For a detailed description of the root folder and structuring a Web site, see Chapter 13.)

Imagine you work in a big office building. You need to get to a co-worker's office for a meeting. You call her for directions. Now, she may not know the precise directions from your office to hers, but she can tell you how to get from your building's entrance to her office. Since you both know where your building's front door is, these directions work well. Think of the office building as your site, and its front door as the *root* of your site. Root-relative links always begins with a slash (/). This slash is a stand-in character for the root folder—the front door—of the site. The same root-relative link always leads to the same page, no matter where it is on your Web site.

UP TO SPEED

Parts of a URL

Each chunk of a URL helps a Web browser locate the proper Web page. Take the following URL, for instance: *http://www.sawmac.com/dw8/index.html*.

http. This portion specifies the *protocol*: the method the Web browser must use to communicate with the Web server. HTTP stands for hypertext transfer protocol. For what it's worth, HTTP specifies a connection to a Web page, as opposed to protocols like *ftp* (for transferring files) and *mailto* (for email addresses).

www.sawmac.com. This portion specifies the exact computer that's dishing out the Web site in question—that is, it's

the address of the Web *server*. The www part identifies a Web site within the *domain* sawmac.com. It's possible to have multiple Web sites in a single domain, such as *news.sawmac.com*, *secret.sawmac.com*, and so on.

/dw8/. This is the name of a folder (also called a directory) on the Web server.

index.html. This is the name of the actual document or file that the Web browser is supposed to open—the Web page itself. It's these HTML documents that Dreamweaver creates.

If you use Dreamweaver for all of your Web page development, you probably won't find a need for root-relative links, but they can come in handy. For example, suppose you're asked to create a new page for an existing Web site. Your client gives you text, some graphics, and a list of the other pages on the site that this page must link to. The problem is, your client doesn't know where on the site the new page is supposed to go, and his Webmaster won't return your calls.

You could use root-relative links to get around this dilemma. Since these links work no matter where the page is on your site, you could complete the page and let the client put it where it belongs. The links will still work.

But there's one major drawback to using root-relative links in Dreamweaver: They don't work when you test them on your own computer. Clicking a root-relative link in a Web browser *on your own machine* produces only a "File not found" error. Such links work only after the files that contain them are moved to a Web server. Web servers understand root-relative links, but your personal computer doesn't.

Tip: There's one exception. Dreamweaver 8 provides two ways of previewing a Web page: *with* a temporary file or *without* one. The temporary-file option gives you a couple of advantages: you get to preview a page without having to save it first, and you gain the ability to preview on your local computer any root-relative links you've created. To turn this feature on, open Preferences (Edit → Preferences or, on the Mac, Dreamweaver → Preferences), click the Preview in Browser category, and turn on the Preview Using Temporary File checkbox. Behind the scenes, Dreamweaver secretly rewrites root-relative links as *document-relative* links whenever it creates a temporary file. If you see files in your site with weird names like TMP2zlc3mvs10.htm, those are the temporary files Dreamweaver creates. Feel free to delete them.

It's generally best to stick to document-relative links for your pages, but keep this discussion in mind. You'll see later that Dreamweaver's site management features use root-relative paths to track your site's files behind the scenes.

Note: Previous versions of Dreamweaver also had trouble with root-relative links if the site wasn't located in the Web server root folder. Suppose, for example, that your buddy gives you space on his Web server for your pages. He says that you can put your site in a folder called *my_friend,* so your URL is *www.my_buddy.com/my_friend/.* In this case, your Web pages don't sit at the root of the site–they're in a folder *inside* the root. So a root-relative link to your home page would be */my_friend/index.html.* Before version 8, Dreamweaver would write this file path as */index.html.* Dreamweaver 8 solved this problem, but only if you tell it the correct URL of your site–for example, *http://www.my_buddy/my_friend/*–in either the first screen of the New Site wizard (see step 2 on page 33), or in the HTTP Address box on the Advanced tab of the New Site window (see page 472).

Link Types in Action

Figure 4-1 shows a Web site as it lies on a hard drive: folders filled with HTML documents and graphics. Here's a closer look at some links you might find on the pages there, and how they might work.

Link from the Home page (index.html) to the Contact Us page (contact.html)

The home-page document is usually called *index.html* or *index.htm*. (The exact name depends on the configuration of your Web server. Contact your Web host, or the person in charge of your Web server, to confirm the file name you need to use for your Web server.) You could create the link from it to the *contact.html* page—identified by the number 1 in Figure 4-1—using any of the three link types:

- **Absolute.** *http://www.nationalexasperator.com/contact.html.* What it means: Go to the Web site at *www.nationalexasperator.com* and download the page *contact. html.*

- **Document-Relative.** *contact.html.* What it means: Look in the same Web site and folder as the current page and download the page *contact.html.*

- **Root-Relative.** */contact.html.* What it means: Go to the top-level folder of this site and download *contact.html.*

Tip: If you can write an absolute URL, you can easily create a root-relative URL. Simply strip off the *http://* and the Web server name. In the above example, erasing the *http://www.nationalexasperator.com* in the absolute address leaves */contact.html*—the root-relative path.

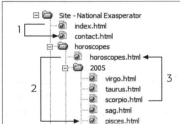

Figure 4-1:
Here are a few examples of links for a fictitious Web site located at www.nationalexasperator.com. The three lines in this example show the connection between the page you're linking from (where each line starts) and the page you're linking to (where each arrow ends).

Link from the Horoscopes page to the Pisces page

Now imagine you're building a Web page and you wish to link it to another page that's inside a subfolder on your site. Here's how you'd use each of the three link types to open a document that's nested in a subfolder (called 2005, in this case), as identified by the number 2 in Figure 4-1:

- **Absolute.** *http://www.nationalexasperator.com/horoscopes/2005/pisces.html.* What it means: Go to the Web site at *www.nationalexasperator.com,* look in the folder *horoscopes,* and then in the folder 2005; download the page *pisces.html.*

- **Document-relative.** *2005/pisces.html.* What it means: From the current page, look in the folder 2005 and download the page *pisces.html.*

- **Root-relative.** */horoscopes/2005/pisces.html.* What it means: Go to the top-level folder of this site, look in the folder *horoscopes,* and then in the folder 2005; download the page *pisces.html.*

Link from the Scorpio page to the Horoscopes page

Now suppose you're building a Web page that's in a deeply nested folder, and you want it to link to a document that's *outside* of its folder, like the link labeled 3 in Figure 4-1:

- **Absolute.** *http://www.nationalexasperator.com/horoscopes/horoscopes.html.* What it means: Go to the Web site at *www.nationalexasperator.com,* look in the folder *horoscopes,* and download the page *horoscopes.html.*

- **Document-Relative.** *../horoscopes.html.* What it means: Go up one level—outside of the current folder—and download the page *horoscopes.html.* In links, a slash / represents a folder or directory. The two dots (..) mean, "Go up one level," into the folder that *contains* the current folder. So to link to a page that's up two levels—for example, to link from the *scorpio.html* page to the home page (*index.html*)—you would use ../ twice, like this: *../../index.html.*

- **Root-Relative.** */horoscopes/horoscopes.html.* What it means: Go to the top-level folder of this site, look in the folder *horoscopes,* and download the page *horoscopes.html.*

Executive Summary

To summarize all of this discussion: use absolute URLs for linking *outside* of your site, use document-relative links for links *within a site,* and avoid using root-relative links altogether.

Adding a Link

If all that talk of links got you confused, don't worry. Links *are* confusing, and that's one of the best reasons to use Dreamweaver. If you can navigate to a document on your own computer or anywhere on the Web, you can create a link to it in Dreamweaver, even if you don't know the first thing about URLs and don't intend to learn the details of how they're configured.

Browsing for a File

To create a link from one page to another on your own Web site, use the Browse for File button on the Property inspector (see Figure 4-2) or its keyboard shortcut, as described in the following steps.

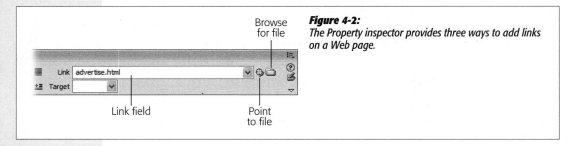

Browse for file

Figure 4-2:
The Property inspector provides three ways to add links on a Web page.

Link field

Point to file

To browse for a file in Dreamweaver, you use the same type of dialog box that you already use to open or save a file, making Browse for File the easiest way to add a link. (To link to a page on another Web site, you'll need to type the Web address into the Property inspector. Turn to page 112 for instructions.)

1. **In the document window, select the text or image you want to use for the link.**

   You can select a single word, a sentence, or an entire paragraph. When this process is over, the selected words will show up blue and underlined (depending on your visitors' Web browser settings), like billions of links before them.

   In addition, you can turn a picture into a link—a great trick for adding attractive navigation buttons.

2. **In the Property inspector, click the folder (Browse for File) icon.**

   Alternatively, choose Modify → Make Link or press Ctrl+L (⌘-L). In any case, the Select File dialog box opens (see Figure 4-3).

3. **Navigate to and select the file you want the link to open.**

   The file should be a Web page that's part of your Web site. In other words, it should be in the local root folder (see page 29), or in a folder therein.

   If you try to link to a file *outside* the root folder, Dreamweaver alerts you to this problem and offers to copy the file into the root folder. Accept the offer. Remember: For a Web site, the root folder is like the edges of the known universe; nothing exists outside it.

4. **Make sure the correct type of link—Document or Site Root—is selected from the "Relative to" menu.**

   As noted earlier in this chapter, document-relative links are the best choice. Root-relative links (which is short for *Site Root–relative links*) don't work when you preview the Web site on your own computer. (They do, however, work once you move them to your Web server.)

Note: Dreamweaver 8 adds a new preference feature, which lets you define what type of links—document-relative or root-relative—you wish to use for most of the links on your site. To set this preference, click the "Change default Link Relative To" link in the Select File dialog box (see the circle in Figure 4-3, bottom). The Site Definition window opens. Click either the Document or Site root radio button next to the text "Links Relative to," and then click OK to close the window and set this preference. As stated before, the Document option is usually your best bet. (You can still change the link-type setting individually for each link as you create it. The preference-setting option just sets up a "default" that Dreamweaver will use unless you specify otherwise.)

---

5. **Click OK (Windows) or Choose (Mac) to apply the link.**

   The text or image now links to another Web page. If you haven't yet saved the other Web page into your site, Dreamweaver doesn't know how to write the document-relative link. Instead, it displays a dialog box saying that it will assign a temporary path for the link until you save the page—see the box on page 116.

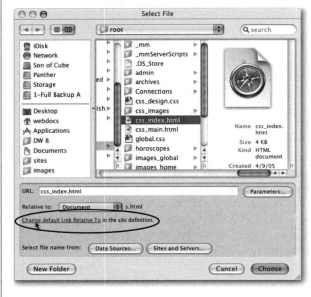

Figure 4-3:
The Select File dialog box looks slightly different in Windows (top) and the Mac (bottom), but either way, it lets you browse your computer to select the file you wish to link to. From the "Relative to" pop-up menu (circled in the top figure), you can choose what type of link to create—Document- or Site Root–relative. Since root-relative links may not work when you preview your pages on your computer, choosing Document from the pop-up menu is almost always your best bet. You can tell Dreamweaver which type of link to use for your site in the Site Definition window, as described in the note on page 109. Short version: just click the link named "Change default Link Relative To" (circled in the bottom figure) and choose from the window that appears. If you find that your links aren't working when you preview your pages, odds are you have the Site Root option set, or you've been selecting Site Root from the "Relative to" pop-up menu.

After you apply a link, graphics don't look any different, but linked text appears underlined and colored (using the color defined by the Page Properties window, which is shown in Figure 1-15). If you want to take the link for a spin, press F12 (Option-F12 on the Mac) to preview the page in your browser, where you can click the link.

Tip: You can also drag a file from the Files panel into the Link box (in the Property inspector) to link to it.

Using the Point-to-File Icon

You can also create links in Dreamweaver by dragging from the Property inspector to the Files panel (shown in Figure 4-4). If your site involves a lot of links, learning to use the Point-to-File tool will save you time and energy.

Figure 4-4:
In this figure, the text "Horoscopes" (circled) is selected in the document window. To link to another page, drag from the Point-to-File icon in the Property inspector to a Web page in the Files panel (right). In this example, Dreamweaver creates a link to the Web page called index.html inside the horoscopes folder. You could also Shift-drag from the text "Horoscopes" to the page index.html in the Files panel to create the same link.

To use this trick effectively, position your document window and Files window side by side, as shown in Figure 4-4.

1. **In the document window, select the text or image you want to turn into a link.**

   Make sure that both the Property inspector and Files window are open. To open the Property inspector if it's not on the screen, choose Window → Properties. To open the Files window, choose Window → Files. (Before using the Files window, you need to create a local site, as described on page 33.)

2. **Drag the Point-to-File icon from the Property inspector onto a Web page in the Files window (see Figure 4-4).**

   Alternatively, you can Shift-drag the selected text or image in the document window to any Web page in the Files panel; this method bypasses the Property inspector altogether.

3. **After dragging over the correct Web page, release the mouse button.**

The selected text or image in your Web page turns into a link to the file you just pointed to.

Typing (or Pasting) the URL or Path

If you need to link to another Web site, or you feel comfortable with how document-relative links work, you can also simply type the URL or path to the page in the Property inspector. Note that this manual insertion is the *only* way to add a link to a page outside of the current Web site.

1. **In the document window, select the text or image you want to make into a link.**

2. **In the Property inspector, type the URL or path to the file in the Link field (see Figure 4-2).**

If the link leads to another Web site, type an absolute URL—that is, a complete Web address, starting with *http://*.

Tip: An easier approach is to copy a complete URL–including the *http://*–from the address bar in your browser window and then paste the address into the Link field.

To link to another page on your own site, type a document-relative link (see page 104 for some examples). You'll be less prone to error if you let Dreamweaver write the correct path using the browsing or point-to-file techniques described above; but typing the path can come in handy when, for instance, you want to create a link to a page you haven't yet created.

Tip: If you're adding an absolute link to a Web site without specifying a Web page, add a final / to the address. For example, to link to Yahoo, type *http://www.yahoo.com/.* The final slash tells the Web server that you're requesting the default page (home page) at Yahoo.com.

Although leaving out the slash works, too (*http://www.yahoo.com*), the server has to do a little extra work to figure out what page to send back, resulting in a slight and unnecessary delay.

Also include the slash when you provide a link to the default page inside a folder on a site, like this: *http:// www.sawmac.com/dwmx2004/.*

FREQUENTLY ASKED QUESTION

Targeting Links

What's the Target menu in the Property inspector for?

The Target menu has nothing to do with the accuracy of your links, nor with shooting ranges. Instead, it deals with how the destination page appears when you click a link.

The new page can appear (a) right in the browser window, just the way most links work; (b) in a new browser window (choose the _blank option); or (c) in a different *frame* on the same page (for details about this increasingly obsolete technology, see the online chapter about frames, which you can find at *www.sawmac.com/dw8/frames.pdf*).

3. **Press Enter (Return) to apply the link.**

   The text or image now links to another Web page.

Using the Hyperlink Object

Dreamweaver provides yet another way to add a link. The Hyperlink object on the Common tab of the Insert bar lets you insert a link with many optional properties.

Unfortunately, not all browsers understand all of these additional properties, and you can only use the Hyperlink object to create a *new* text link. You can't use it to add a link to an image or to text you've already placed on the page.

If you want to give this feature a spin anyway, here's how it works. Start by clicking on the page where you wish to insert a new link. Then:

1. **Choose Insert → Hyperlink or click the icon on the Insert bar.**

   The Hyperlink dialog box opens (see Figure 4-5).

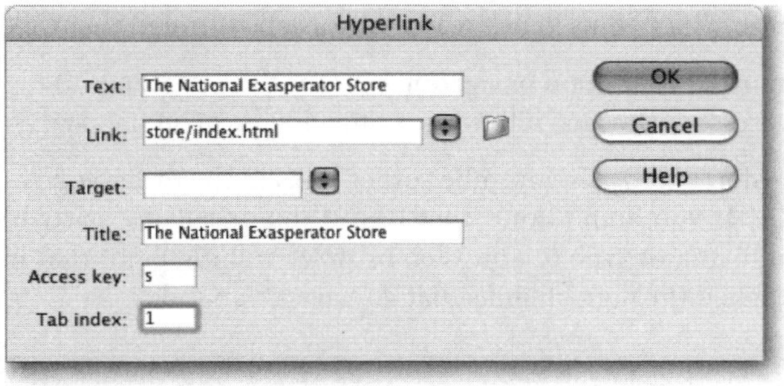

Figure 4-5:
To apply the optional properties in this dialog box to an image or existing text, you have a couple of options. You can always go into Code view (as described in Chapter 9) and hand-edit the HTML, but it's easier to use the Tag inspector to access all the properties available to a particular link. (For details, see page 346.)

2. **Type the text you want to appear in the Text box.**

   Whatever you type here is the text that you'll see on the page, and that your audience will click to follow the link.

3. **Click the folder icon and search for the page you want to link to.**

   Alternatively, you can type a URL in the Link box.

4. **Set the target for the link.**

   If you want the link to open in the same window, like most links, don't select anything; the targeting option will work just like a regular link (see page 112).

   The last three options are more interesting.

5. **Type a title for the page you're linking to.**

   This property is optional. Most Web browsers display this property in a small tooltip window when you move your mouse over the link.

6. **Type a key to define an access key.**

An access key provides a way to trigger a link from the keyboard. Internet Explorer, Netscape 6 and later, Safari, and Firefox understand this property in conjunction with the Alt key (Control key on the Mac). For example, if you type *h* in the Access key box, a visitor to your page could press Alt+H (Control-H) to mouselessly open that link. Of course, unless those who visit your site are psychic, it's a good idea to provide instructions by adding the access-key information next to the link itself: Home Page (Alt+H).

7. **In the "Tab index" box, type a number for the tab order.**

In most newer browsers (Internet Explorer, Mozilla, Safari, and Opera, to name a few), you can press the Tab key (Option-Tab in Safari) to step through the links on a page (and boxes on a form). This feature not only provides useful keyboard control of your Web browser, but it's also important for people who can't use the mouse due to disability.

Normally when you press Tab, the browser highlights links in the order in which they appear in the HTML of the page. The Tab index, by contrast, lets *you* control the order in which links light up as a visitor tabs through them.

For example, you can make your main navigation buttons the first things to highlight when someone presses Tab, even if they aren't the first links on the page.

For the first link in order, type *1* here; number other links in the order you want the Tab key to follow. If you aren't concerned about the order of a particular link, leave this option blank or type *0*. The Web browser will highlight that link after the visitor has tabbed through all links that *do* have a Tab index.

EXTENSION ALERT

QuickLink Is Quick Work

Dreamweaver makes it easy to add innovative commands and tools—including those written by independent, non-Macromedia programmers—to your copy of the program. You can read a lot more about these add-on programs, called *extensions,* in Chapter 19.

When you're working with links, one extension that really comes in handy is called QuickLink. Created by renowned Dreamweaver guru Tom Muck, this extension instantly turns text into either a *mailto* or an *absolute* URL. You can find QuickLink at *www.tom-muck.com/extensions/.*

Once you've installed the extension, here's how it works. Suppose you paste the text, "You can download the free PDF viewer at *www.adobe.com.*" To turn *www.adobe.com* into a real link, you can either select the text and then go to the Property inspector and type *http://www.adobe.com/*—or, with QuickLink, simply select the text and choose Commands → QuickLink. QuickLink writes the proper code in the Property inspector, including the initial (and mandatory) *http://,* even if those characters were missing from the original text.

QuickLink also converts email addresses into proper *mailto* links: just select the email address (*missing@sawmac.com,* say), apply the QuickLink command, and watch as the extension automatically inserts the correct code (*mailto: missing@sawmac.com*) into your page.

For even faster action, create a keyboard shortcut for this command; Shift+Ctrl+L is a good one. (See page 665 for more on keyboard shortcuts.)

Adding an Email Link

Whenever you want to invite your visitors to email you, an *email link* is the perfect solution. When someone clicks an email link, her email program launches automatically, and a new message opens with your email address already in the To field. She can then just type her message and send it off.

An email link looks like this: *mailto:nessie@nationalexasperator.com.* The first part, *mailto:*, indicates the type of link, while the second part (*nessie@nationalexasperator.com*) specifies the email address.

Note: Email links work only if the person who clicks the link has an email program set up and running on his computer. If someone visits your site from a computer at the public library, for example, he might not be able to send email. If this drawback troubles you, you can also collect information using a *form* (as discussed in Chapter 10), a feedback method that has neither the limitations nor the easy setup of an email link.

You can create an email link much the way you'd create any other Dreamweaver link: by selecting some text or an image and typing the mailto address, as shown above, into the Link field in the Property inspector. To simplify this process, Dreamweaver has a quick method of inserting an email link:

1. **On the Common tab of the Insert bar, click the Email link icon, which looks like an envelope (see Figure 4-6).**

   Alternatively, choose Insert → Email link. In either case, if you've already typed the text (*Email me!*) on your Web page, select it first. The Email Link dialog box opens (see Figure 4-7).

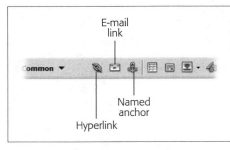

Figure 4-6:
The Common tab of the Insert bar includes three link-related objects: the Hyperlink for adding text links, the Email link for adding links for email addresses, and the Named anchor for adding links within a page.

E-mail link

Named anchor

Hyperlink

Figure 4-7:
The Email Link dialog box lets you specify the text that appears on the Web page and the email address for a mailto link. You can also select some text you've already added to the document and click the Email Link icon on the Objects panel. The text you selected is copied into the Text field in this dialog box.

2. **In the Text field, type the text that you want to appear on the Web page.**

You've just indicated the link's purpose, like *Email the Webmaster.* (If you select text in the document first, it automatically appears in the Text field.)

3. **Type an email address into the E-Mail field.**

This is the address that appears in your visitors' email program when they click the link. (You don't have to type *mailto:*—Dreamweaver adds it automatically.)

4. **Click OK.**

Dreamweaver adds the text to the page, complete with a mailto link.

Linking Within a Web Page

Clicking a link usually loads a Web page into the browser window. But what if you want to link not only to a Web page, but to a specific *spot* on the page? See Figure 4-8 for an example.

Introducing the *named-anchor link,* a special link type that's designed to autoscroll to a particular spot on a particular page.

FREQUENTLY ASKED QUESTION

The Mysterious Triple Slashes

Why do my links start with file:///?

Links that begin with *file:///* (*file:///D:/missingmanual/ book_site/national_ex/subscribe.html*, for example) aren't valid links on the Web. Rather, they're temporary addresses that Dreamweaver creates as placeholders for links to be rewritten later. (A *file:///* path tells Dreamweaver where to look on your computer for the file.) You'll spot these addresses when you add document-relative links to a page that hasn't been saved, or when working with files that are outside of your site's local root folder.

Suppose you're working on a Web page that will contain your company's legal mumbo-jumbo, but you haven't yet saved it. After adding a document-relative link to your home page, you notice that the path displayed in the Property inspector's Link field begins with *file:///*. Since your legal page hasn't yet been saved and therefore doesn't yet have a folder location, Dreamweaver can't create a link telling a browser how to get from it to the home page.

So Dreamweaver creates a temporary link, which helps it keep track of what page to link to. Once you save the page somewhere in the site, Dreamweaver rewrites the link in proper document-relative format, and the *file:///* disappears.

Likewise, when you work with files that are outside of the local root folder, Dreamweaver can't write a proper link. (Any folder outside of the local root folder isn't part of the Web site, and there's no way to write a correct link from nowhere to somewhere.) So, if you save a page *outside* of the local root folder, Dreamweaver writes all document-relative links on that page as file paths beginning with *file:///*. To avoid this invalid link problem, always save your Web pages *inside* the local root folder or a folder inside of the local root folder. To learn more about root folders and Web sites, see Chapter 13.

When you *link to* a page—or add an image (Chapter 5)— that's stored outside of the local root folder, Dreamweaver has the same problem. However, in this instance, Dreamweaver gives you the option of copying the out-of-bounds file to a location of your choosing within the root folder.

Phase 1: Creating a Named Anchor

Creating a named-anchor link is a two-step process: First add and name an anchor on the page that you're linking to, thus identifying the destination for the link; then, add a link that goes to that named anchor. For instance, in the Table of Contents page example shown in Figure 4-8, you would place a named anchor at the beginning of each chapter section.

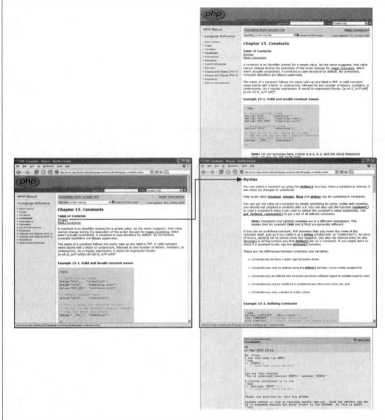

Figure 4-8:
Some pages may have a lot of information that you'd prefer not to break up into several different Web pages. To make it easy for visitors to jump to a location farther down on the page, you might have a list of contents for that page, which, when clicked (left), jumps down the page to the appropriate section (right).

To create a named anchor:

1. **In the document window, click where you want to insert the named anchor.**

   The named anchor is the place where you want the link to jump to.

2. **Insert a named anchor.**

   You can do so using any of three methods: Choose Insert → Named Anchor; press Ctrl+Alt+A (⌘-Option-A); or from the Insert bar, select the Common tab and click the Named Anchor icon (see Figure 4-6).

3. **Type the name of the anchor in the Insert Named Anchor dialog box.**

   Each anchor on a page should have a unique name, something short and easy to remember. No spaces or punctuation marks are allowed. If you violate any of these rules, Dreamweaver will remind you with an error message and strip out any of the offending characters.

4. **Click OK to insert the named anchor.**

   You'll see a gold shield with an anchor on it at the point where you created the anchor. Click this icon to show the name of the anchor in the Property inspector. (If you don't see it, see page 120 for details on hiding and showing anchors.)

The Named Anchor icon (the gold shield) is the key to removing or editing the anchor later: just click the icon and press Delete to get rid of it, or click it and change its name in the Property inspector. (Deleting the name in the Property inspector deletes the anchor from the page.)

FREQUENTLY ASKED QUESTION

Adding Objects to the Favorites Tab

Help! I'm tired of wading through so many tabs to find all my favorite Dreamweaver objects. How can I see all of my most used objects in one place?

Dreamweaver includes a marvelous productivity tool: the Favorites tab. It lets you collect all of your most used objects into a single place, without any interference from HTML tags and objects you never use. Maybe you use the Email link object on the Insert bar all of the time, but never touch the Named anchor object.

To add objects to the Favorites tab, right-click (Control-click) anywhere on the Insert bar. From the shortcut menu, choose Customize Favorites to open the Customize Favorite Objects window. All of the objects available in all of the Insert bar categories appear in the left-hand list. Select an object and click the >> button to add it to your Favorites. (You can view the objects for just one category by selecting the category from the "Available objects" menu.) Repeat with other objects, if you like.

To rearrange the order of the toolbar buttons, click one and then click the up or down arrow to move it left or right on the toolbar. (Buttons at the top of the list appear on the left side of the Insert bar.) You can even use the Add Separator button to insert a thin gray line between buttons on the Insert bar—to separate one group of similar objects (graphic-related objects, say) from another (such as form objects), for example. Unfortunately, you can't group Favorite objects into submenus. Each item you add is a single button on the Insert bar.

To delete a button or separator from the list, select it and then click the Trash icon. Click OK to close the window and create your new list of Favorite objects, which are now available under the Favorites tab of the Insert bar.

After you've created your Favorites tab, you can always add more objects (or delete ones you no longer need) by right-clicking (Control-clicking) the Insert bar and choosing Customize Favorites from the shortcut menu.

Phase 2: Linking to an Anchor

Creating a link to a named anchor isn't all that different from linking to a Web page. Once you've created and named an anchor, you can link to it from within the same Web page, or from a different page.

To link to an anchor on the same page:

1. **In the document window, select the text or image you want to make into a link.**

    For example, drag across some text, or highlight a graphic.

2. **In the Property inspector's Link field, type #, followed by the anchor name. (Alternatively, use the Point-to-File icon, as shown in Figure 4-9.)**

    The # sign indicates that the link goes to a named anchor. In other words, if you wish to link to an anchor named *directions,* the link would be *#directions.*

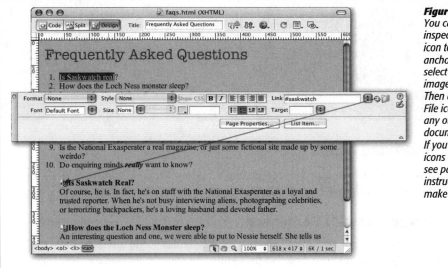

Figure 4-9:
You can use the Property inspector's Point-to-File icon to link to a named anchor on a page. Simply select some text or an image in an open page. Then drag the Point-to-File icon to an anchor on any other open document to set the link. If you can't see the shield icons that mark anchors, see page 120 for instructions on how to make them visible.

You can also link from one Web page to a particular location on another Web page in your site. The process is the same as linking to an anchor on the same page, except that you have to specify both the path to the Web page and the name of the anchor:

1. **In the document window, select the text or image you want to turn into a link. In the Link field of the Property inspector, type or choose the URL or path of the page you wish to link to.**

    You can use any of the methods described above: browsing, point-to-file, or typing the path. Unfortunately, if you browse to select the linked file, Dreamweaver doesn't display any anchors on that page, so you need to perform one extra step.

2. Click at the end of the URL or path. Type #, followed by the anchor name.

The Link field should look something like this: *contact.html#directions.*

Viewing and Hiding Anchors

A named anchor isn't visible in a Web browser; it appears in Dreamweaver as an anchor-on-a-gold-shield icon. Like other invisible elements—line breaks, for instance—you can hide named anchors in Dreamweaver by choosing View → Visual Aids → Invisible Elements, or choosing Visual Aids → Invisible Elements from the Visual Aids menu in the toolbar (see Figure 8-8 on page 306). (If anchors still don't appear, visit the Preferences window, pictured in Figure 1-8, and in the Invisible Elements category, make sure the Anchor box is turned on.)

FREQUENTLY ASKED QUESTION

Anchors Away

When I click a link to an anchor, the Web browser is supposed to go to the page and display the anchor at the top of the browser window. But sometimes the anchor appears in the middle of the browser. What's that about?

Web browsers can't scroll beyond the bottom of a Web page, so an anchor near the bottom of a page sometimes can't move to the top of the browser window. If one of your own Web pages exhibits this problem, the fix is simple: just add a bunch of empty lines—press the Enter key repeatedly—below the last item on the page. You've just added space at the bottom of the page, so the browser can scroll the page all the way to the anchor.

Modifying a Link

At some point, you may need to change or edit a link. Perhaps the URL you were linking to has changed, or you simply no longer need that link.

Changing a Link's Destination

As you'll read in Part Four, Dreamweaver provides some amazing tools for automatically updating your links so that your site stays in working order, even if you move files around your site. But even Dreamweaver isn't smart enough to know when a page on someone *else's* Web site has been moved or deleted. And you may decide you simply need to change a link so that it points to a different page on your own site. In both of these cases, you'll need to change the links on your Web pages by hand:

1. **Select the text link or picture link.**

The existing link path appears in the Link field in the Property inspector.

2. **Use any of the techniques described on page 108 for specifying the link's target.**

For example, click the Browse for File button in the Property inspector and locate a different Web page in your site. The destination of the link changes to the new URL, path, or anchor.

Removing a Link

Sometimes, you want to stop a link from linking—when the Web page you were linking to no longer exists, for example. You want the text or image on your Web page to stay the same, but you want to remove the disabled link. In that case, just select the link text or image and then use one of these tactics:

- Choose Modify → Remove Link, or press Ctrl+Shift+L (⌘-Shift-L).

- Delete the text in the Link field of the Property inspector and press the Enter or Return key.

The text or image remains on your Web page, but it no longer links to anything. If it's a text link, the color changes from your site's link color (see the box called "Link Colors" below) to the normal text color for the page.

Of course, if you're feeling particularly destructive, you can also delete the link text or image itself; doing so gets rid of the link.

FREQUENTLY ASKED QUESTIONS

Link Colors

How can I change the color of my links?

To help Web visitors identify links, Web browsers usually display linked text in a special color (blue, for example). If you'd prefer a different hue, you can control which color the browser uses from the Page Properties dialog box. Choose Modify → Page Properties to open it. Then click the Links category and change the link colors, as described in step 14 on page 40.

While we're on the subject, I'm already using a different color for my links to make them stand out from the other text. Can I get rid of the underline that Dreamweaver automatically puts under links?

Yes, but not with HTML alone. By default, all text links show up with underlines, and no HTML code can change that. However, Cascading Style Sheets provide a lot more formatting control than plain HTML—including, yes, the ability to remove link underlines. To find out how, see the Tip on page 196.

Images

Nobody believes that a picture is worth a thousand words more than today's Web designers, as evidenced by the highly visual nature of the Internet. In fact, it's not difficult to stumble onto a home page these days composed almost entirely of graphics (see Figure 5-1).

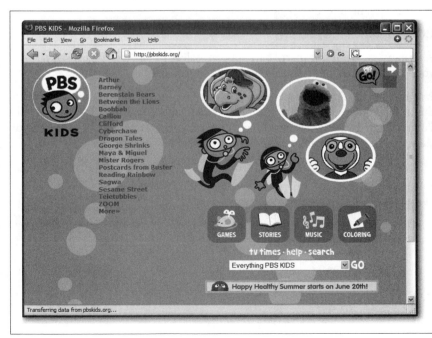

Figure 5-1:
Some Web sites rely almost exclusively on graphics for both looks and function. The home page for the PBS Kids Web site, for instance, uses graphics not just for pictures of their shows' characters, but also for the page's background and navigation buttons.

Even if you don't want to go that far, understanding how to use graphics effectively is invaluable. Whether you want to plop a simple photo onto your page, cover it with clickable "hotspots," or design an interactive set of buttons that light up when the cursor passes over them, Dreamweaver makes the job—and the underlying JavaScript programming—easy.

Adding Images

If you were writing out the HTML instructions for your Web page by hand, you'd insert an image into a Web page using the image tag: <img>. The primary *property* of an image is called the *source* (Src) property, which is the URL or path to the graphics file.

Dreamweaver does all of this coding for you automatically when you insert a picture into your fledgling Web page:

1. **Save the Web page that will contain the image.**

   To insert an image, Dreamweaver must determine the path from your Web page to that image, which could be anywhere on your hard drive. As with links (see page 116), saving the page before you proceed allows Dreamweaver to correctly determine the path from the page you just saved to the image.

2. **In the document window, click where you want to insert the image.**

   You can choose the beginning or end of a paragraph, or within a cell in a table (see Chapter 7). To set a graphic apart from other text, press Enter (Return), creating a blank line, before inserting it.

3. **Choose Insert → Image.**

   Alternatively, from the Insert bar, you can select Image (see Figure 5-2). Or, if you're a keyboard nut, press Ctrl+Alt+I (⌘-Option-I).

   In any case, the Select Image Source dialog box opens. This box is identical to the Select File window that appears when adding a link to a page (see Figure 4-3). The only difference is a Preview Images checkbox—turning it on shows a thumbnail of any selected image in the Preview window.

Figure 5-2:
The Image menu on the Common tab of the Insert bar provides tools for adding graphics to your pages.

4. **Browse to and select the graphics file you wish to add to the page.**

The file must be in one of the formats that work on the Web: GIF, JPEG, or PNG.

The file should be stored somewhere in the local root folder of your site (see page 29) or in one of its subfolders. If it isn't, Dreamweaver can't add the correct path to your Web page.

That's why, if you select a graphic for insertion that's not already in your site folder, Dreamweaver offers to add a *copy* of it there. If you choose Yes, a Copy File As dialog box opens, so that you can save the file in your local root folder, renaming it if you wish. If you choose No, Dreamweaver uses a file-relative path (beginning with *file:///*) for the image's Src property (see page 124). But clicking No is usually a bad idea: while it allows the graphic to be displayed while you work with Dreamweaver on your computer, the graphic won't appear once you move the document to the Web (see the box on page 116).

UP TO SPEED

GIFs, JPEGs, and PNGs: The Graphics of the Web

Computer graphics come in hundreds of different file formats. The assorted acronyms can be mind-numbing: TIFF, PICT, BMP, EPS, Amiga IFF, and so on.

Fortunately, graphics on the Web are a bit simpler. There are only three graphics formats: two established formats and one exciting newcomer. All three provide good *compression*; through clever computer manipulation, they reduce the graphic's file size so it can travel more rapidly across the Internet. They differ only in the details.

GIF (Graphics Interchange Format) files provide good compression for images that have areas of solid color: logos, text, simple banners. GIFs also offer single-color transparency, meaning that one color in the graphic can be made to disappear, permitting the background of a Web page to show through part of the image.

A GIF image can only contain a maximum of 256 shades, however, generally making photos look blotchy. That radiant sunset photo you took with your digital camera won't look so good as a GIF.

JPEG (Joint Photographic Experts Group) graphics, on the other hand, pick up where GIFs leave off. JPEG graphics can contain millions of different colors, making them ideal for photographic images. Not only do JPEGs do a better job on photos, they also compress multicolored images much better than GIFs, because the JPEG compression algorithm considers how the human eye perceives different adjacent color values. When your graphics software saves a JPEG file, it runs a complex color analysis to lower the amount of data required to accurately represent the image. On the downside, JPEG compression makes text and large areas of solid color look blotchy.

Finally, the **PNG** (Portable Network Graphics) format holds great promise for the future. PNG files can be compressed even smaller than those in GIF format, can contain millions of colors, and offer 256 levels of transparency, which means that you could actually see the background of a Web page through a drop shadow on a graphic. Most current Web browsers recognize this format, but Internet Explorer 5 and 6 for Windows don't support PNG's 256 levels of transparency (though IE 5 for Mac does!). (To see this transparency effect in action, visit *www.w3.org/Graphics/PNG/inline-alpha.html* with a browser like Firefox or Safari; to see it NOT work, go to the same page with Windows Internet Explorer 5 or 6.)

---

5. **Confirm the type of path to create: Document or Site Root.**

   When you insert an image into a Web page, you don't actually add the graphics file to the HTML file. Instead, you create a *path* to the image, a coded description of where to find the relevant graphics file, so that a Web browser knows where to look for and download the graphic.

   In general, Document is the best choice. Site Root–relative paths don't always work when previewing a page. (See page 104 for details on the difference between document- and root-relative links.)

6. **Click OK (Windows) or Choose (Mac).**

   Depending on the accessibility preference settings you've chosen, either the image appears on your Web page, or an "Image Tag Accessibility Attributes" window appears (see the box on page 130).

Tip: Dreamweaver also permits several drag-and-drop techniques for quickly adding images to your pages.

Make sure you've defined a site as described on page 33. Then open the Files window (press F8). You can drag any graphics file from that window right into an open Dreamweaver document. You can also drag graphics in from the Assets panel, as described on page 492.

Dreamweaver even lets you drag a graphic from your desktop onto a page. If you do this, Dreamweaver dutifully informs you that you must copy the file into your site folder (and provides a dialog box that lets you specify *which* folder), so that the image will show up properly on the Web page. (You can even define a default images folder for a site, so that when you drag an image onto a page, Dreamweaver automatically copies it into the correct folder; see page 474.)

Adding an Image Placeholder

It's not uncommon to find yourself working on a Web site without all the pieces of the puzzle. You may start building a page, even when your client has yet to give you all the text she wants on the page. Or you may find that a photograph hasn't been shot, but you want to get the page ready for it. Other times, you may be responsible for building the Web pages, for example, while another designer is creating the banners and navigation buttons.

To help out in these kinds of situations, Dreamweaver includes the Image Placeholder button. It lets you insert a placeholder—called an *FPO* (For Placement Only) image in publishing—so that you can stake out space on the page for a graphic that isn't ready yet. This way, you can lay out the basic structure of the page without having to wait for all the graphics to arrive in their final form.

To insert a placeholder, do one of the following:

- Choose Insert → Image Placeholder.

- On the Common tab of the Insert bar, select the Image Placeholder icon from the Image menu (see Figure 5-2).

In the window that appears (see Figure 5-3), type a width and height for the image, which determines how much space the placeholder will take up on the page. The Name and "Alternate text" fields are optional. (If you fill them out, they'll appear in the Name and Alt boxes of the image's Property inspector, as discussed next.)

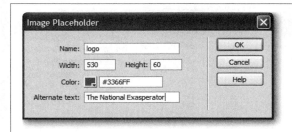

Figure 5-3:
The values you type for Name, Width, Height, and "Alternate text" appear in the Property inspector after you insert an image placeholder. The Color option just lets you choose a color for the placeholder.

The Color box lets you specify a color for the placeholder—presumably to make the placeholder more colorful than the default gray color. The color disappears (as does the code that created it) once you replace the placeholder with a real graphic.

Warning: The name you provide for a placeholder image is also added as an ID attribute to the <img> tag. IDs are used for both JavaScript and Cascading Style Sheets, as described on page 188. If the name you provide for the image placeholder is the same as an ID name for a CSS style you created, you can run into some weird display problems.

Of course, using a placeholder doesn't do you any good if you don't eventually replace it with a real image. Once you've got the image that should finally appear on the page, just double-click the placeholder on the Web page. The Select Image Source window appears. Follow steps 4 through 6 on page 125 to insert the new image.

If you also own Fireworks, Dreamweaver's Web graphics companion program, there's an added benefit to the image placeholder. When an image placeholder is selected in the document window, the Property inspector includes a button called Create. Clicking this button launches Fireworks and opens a new, blank graphics document set to the exact dimensions you specified earlier. You can then create your graphic in Fireworks. After you save the file, Fireworks exports it to whatever folder you specify and automatically inserts it into your document—replacing the placeholder.

Modifying an Image

After inserting a graphic, you can work on it in several ways: attaching a link to the image, aligning it on the page, or adding a border and margin to it, for example. Dreamweaver also includes some basic tools that let you crop, resize, optimize, sharpen, and adjust contrast and brightness (see "Editing Graphics" on page 134).

As with most objects on a Web page, you set *image* properties using the Property inspector (see Figure 5-4).

Figure 5-4:
The Property inspector shows the selected graphic's dimensions, source, alignment, border, and margins. A thumbnail version appears in the upper-left corner—in this case, bearing the logo of Fireworks, which created it.

Naming an Image

Just to the right of an image's thumbnail on the Property inspector is a small field where you can type a name for that image. Most of the time, you'll leave this field blank.

However, if you plan to add interactive effects to it—like the rollover effect discussed on page 144—using Dreamweaver *behaviors* (see Chapter 11) or your own JavaScript programming, you *must* name your picture. Whatever name you choose should use only letters and numbers—no spaces or other punctuation. Furthermore, every graphic's name must be unique on the page. This rule is what allows JavaScript to "talk" to a specific image.

When you add a name, Dreamweaver adds both a Name property and an ID property to the image tag. The name tag is still used by most browsers, but the more recent ID tag is fast becoming the standard way that JavaScript identifies an object on a page. (IDs are also used by Cascading Style Sheets, as described on page 188.)

Note: JavaScript uses the image name or ID that you type in the Image Placeholder box for its own reference; no one actually sees this name in a Web browser. In other words, this box isn't the place to give your graphic a text label that shows up when your reader has graphics turned off. For that purpose, read on.

Adding a Text Description to an Image

Not everyone who visits your Web site gets to see those stunning photos of your last summer vacation. Some people deliberately turn off graphics when they surf, enjoying the Web without the wait, since graphics-free Web pages appear almost instantly. Other people have vision impairments that prevent them from enjoying the visual aspects of the Web. They rely on special software that reads Web page text aloud, including any labels you've given your graphics.

To assist Web surfers in both situations, make a habit of setting the Alt property of the image. Short for *alternative text*, the Alt property is a text description that Web browsers use as a stand-in for the image (see Figure 5-5).

Tip: To have Dreamweaver automatically remind you to add an Alt property each time you add an image to a page, see the box on page 130.

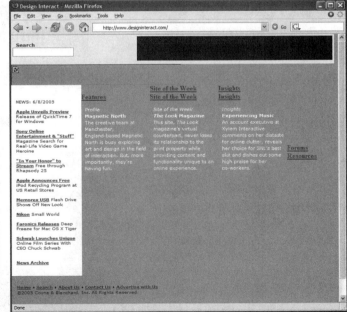

Figure 5-5:
The Alt property is an important aid for people who are surfing but can't see the graphics on your Web page.

Top: Graphics denote the different sections of this site, such as Features, Site of the Week, and Insights.

Bottom: With graphics turned off, that information is still available, thanks to the alt text. In contrast, graphics that don't use the Alt property simply disappear or display the generic label IMAGE. In the case of an important identifying graphic like the site logo (the "design interact" banner in the top figure), a missing Alt property leaves visitors wondering where they are.

To add a text description to an image, type it in the Alt field in the Property inspector. If you're naming graphics that will be navigation buttons, you could just use the same text that appears on the button, such as *Home* or *Products.* For images that carry greater meaning—such as a photo of the product itself—you might use a more detailed description: "Photo of Sasquatch relaxing at his lodge in the Adirondacks."

Tip: In some cases, however, a description is more of a distraction than a help. For example, a common technique in laying out a Web page involves using invisible 1-pixel images, often called *spacer images* (see page 241). Because these images serve as a layout aid and don't convey any meaningful information, a description isn't necessary.

In this instance, you can use the pop-up menu that appears to the right of the Alt field. This menu lets you choose one option: <empty>. Use the <empty> Alt property for any images that don't add meaning to the page, like spacer GIFs. This trick will help your pages meet accessibility requirements without adding distracting and unnecessary descriptions.

POWER USERS' CLINIC

Making Accessible Web Sites

Many people using the Web have disabilities that make reading, seeing, hearing, or using a mouse difficult. Visually impaired people, for example, may be unable to benefit from images on the screen, even though they have software that can read aloud a Web page's text.

Dreamweaver includes a number of features for making your Web sites more accessible. That's good news if you're building a Web site for the federal government or one of the many states that support Section 508 of the Workforce Investment Act. This law requires Web sites built for or funded by the government to offer equal or equivalent access to everyone. Throughout this book, you'll find tips for using Dreamweaver's accessibility features, and on page 525, you'll learn how to use a tool to find out if your site is compliant with Section 508.

The Alt property described on page 128 is an important first step for assisting visually impaired Web surfers. For complex images, such as a graph that plots changes in utility rates over time, you can also supply a more detailed description on a separate Web page. The Longdesc (long description) property of an image lets you specify a link to a page containing a text description of the image. Some Web browsers understand this property, allowing visually impaired visitors to jump to a page with a text description that screen-reading software can read aloud.

While you can't find the Longdesc property in the Property inspector, you can turn on an accessibility option in Dreamweaver that lets you add it every time you insert a graphic. Choose Edit → Preferences (Dreamweaver → Preferences on the Mac) to open the Preferences window, and select the Accessibility category. Turn on the Images checkbox.

Now whenever you insert a graphic, the window shown below appears, so that you can quickly set the Alt text and select an HTML page containing a long description.

Note that you're *not required* by Section 508 to use the long description property when inserting images. It's merely recommended if the image is particularly complex or includes information that can't be explained in the Alt property—for example, graphs or images that include a lot of text information. For an overview of Web accessibility and helpful tips on making accessible sites, visit *www.w3. org/WAI/gettingstarted/*.

Changing the Size of an Image

The Width and Height properties of a graphic do more than determine its screen size; they also help Web browsers load the graphic quickly and efficiently. Since the HTML of a Web page downloads before any graphics do, a Web browser displays the text on the page first, and then adds the images as they arrive. If width and height attributes are missing, the browser doesn't know how much space on the page to give each image, so it has to redraw the page after each image is downloaded. The stuttering appearance of this redrawing is disconcerting, makes Web pages appear slowly, and shatters your reputation as a cool, competent Web designer.

Fortunately, you don't have to worry about specifying the picture's dimensions yourself: whenever Dreamweaver inserts an image into a Web page, it automatically calculates its width and height and enters those values into the W and H fields in the Property inspector (see Figure 5-4).

Note: This cool feature works only in Design view. If you use the Insert Image command to add an image while working in Code view, Dreamweaver adds only the <img> tag with the proper reference to the graphic file; it leaves out the Width and Height properties.

WORKAROUND WORKSHOP

Watch Those Resize Handles!

After you insert an image in the document window, a thin black border appears around it, indicating that it's selected. Three small black squares—the resize handles—appear on the right edge, bottom edge, and lower-right corner, as circled in the illustration.

Dragging these handles changes the width and height of the graphic—or, rather, the Width and Height properties in the Property inspector. Pressing Shift while dragging the corner handle keeps the proportions of the image the same. The graphic file itself remains unchanged.

However, dragging one of these handles to make the picture appear bigger is almost always unsuccessful, resulting in distortion and ugly pixellation.

But those pesky resize handles are far too easy to accidentally grab and drag. In fact, sometimes you may resize a graphic and not even know it. Perhaps you accidentally dragged the left resize handle a few pixels, making the graphic wider, but not enough to notice.

Fortunately, the Property inspector does provides some subtle feedback to let you know if your graphic is distorted.

A boldfaced number in the W or H field tells you that the Width or Height property now differs from the actual dimensions of the graphic.

Clicking the letter W or H in the Property inspector *resets* the Width or Height property back to that of the original graphic file, undoing your little slip of the mouse. Clicking the recycling-symbol icon (also circled) resets both properties.

You can, if you like, shrink a graphic by typing smaller values into the W and H fields, but doing so won't do anything to speed up the download time. You'll make the picture *appear* smaller, but the Web browser will still have to download the entire graphics file. To make your graphic smaller both in appearance and file size, shrink it in an image-editing program like Fireworks, Photoshop, or ImageReady, or use the Resample Image tool described on page 136. Not only will you get an image that's exactly the size you want, but you'll also trim a few bytes off its file size, and maybe even save a second or two in download time.

On the other hand, setting width and height values that are *larger* than the actual dimensions of the graphic merely distorts the image by stretching it, creating an undesirable pixellated effect. If you want a larger image without distortion or pixellation, start with a larger original image. To do so, return to your digital camera or stock photo CD, or recreate the graphic at a larger size in Photoshop or Fireworks.

Aligning an Image

Images, like text, appear in the normal flow of HTML in a page. In other words, a picture can appear in a paragraph by itself, or within a sentence or paragraph of text.

The Property inspector has two sets of alignment controls that affect images (Figure 5-6). Only the Align menu, however, controls alignment specific to an image. (The second set of alignment options applies to the entire paragraph; see page 80.)

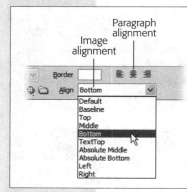

Figure 5-6:
Only the Align menu provides options specific to the image. The Paragraph alignment icons affect the entire paragraph—not just the image. If you just want to center-align a graphic, however, without affecting any text around it, put the image in its own paragraph and click the center paragraph alignment button. Or use the Cascading Style Sheet Text Align property (see page 201).

If you've inserted a graphic into a text paragraph, you can specify exactly how the image relates to the words around it. The Align menu in the Property inspector lets you select 10 different options (see Figure 5-6). However, only six of them work in all browsers. Avoid the other four, as explained in the Note on page 134, which work only in certain browsers.

To set a graphic's vertical alignment, click the image to select it. Then choose one of the options from the Align menu at the right side of the Property inspector. You can see each illustrated in Figure 5-7:

- **Default** means that the graphic sits on the baseline (the bottom of the line of text on which the graphic appears). The effect is identical to choosing **Bottom**.

- **Middle** aligns the text on the current line with the middle of the graphic, but may add an awkward-looking complication. Subsequent lines of text move *below* the graphic—a problem you can solve by using either of the two wrap alignment options (Left or Right), as described below.

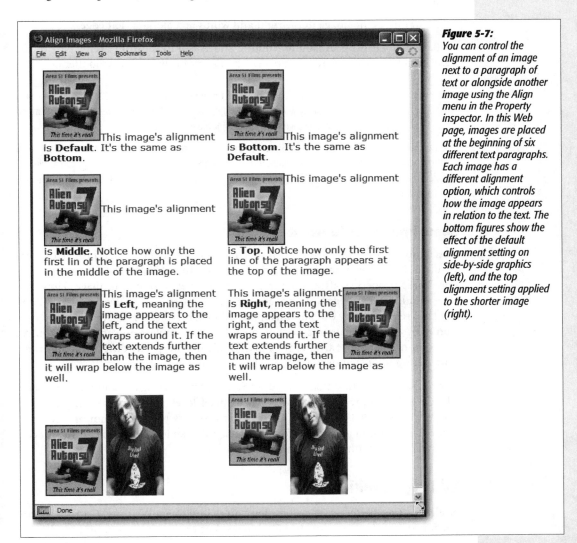

Figure 5-7:
You can control the alignment of an image next to a paragraph of text or alongside another image using the Align menu in the Property inspector. In this Web page, images are placed at the beginning of six different text paragraphs. Each image has a different alignment option, which controls how the image appears in relation to the text. The bottom figures show the effect of the default alignment setting on side-by-side graphics (left), and the top alignment setting applied to the shorter image (right).

- **Top** aligns the image with the top of the line of text in the paragraph. Again, because top alignment can create a gap between the first line and the rest of the text, consider using the Left or Right wrapping options. The Top option is good, however, if you have two graphics of different heights side by side on the same line (see Figure 5-7, bottom). Normally, a browser aligns graphics by their bottom edges, making a kind of city skyscraper skyline (left). The top option aligns the graphics along their top edges, forming a cave-ceiling, stalactite-like effect (right).

- **Left** places an image to the left of any text, which then wraps down the right side of the image.

- **Right** moves the image to the right and wraps text along its left edge.

- **Baseline, TextTop, Absolute Middle,** and **Absolute Bottom** aren't part of the official HTML standard and only work in a few browsers, so avoid them.

Note: Only Top, Bottom, Middle, Left, and Right are considered valid transitional XHTML code. In other words, future Web browsers probably won't understand options like Absolute Middle or TextTop. Furthermore, *strict XHTML* doesn't offer any alignment options for the image tag.

You can, however, use Cascading Style Sheets to provide alignment for images. The CSS left and right Float properties discussed on page 202 work the same as the Left and Right options. You can apply top, middle, or bottom alignment by setting the Vertical Alignment property found in the CSS Block category (see page 200).

Some Properties to Avoid

You'll notice that the Property inspector includes a few other properties (see Figure 5-4) that seem intriguing and possibly useful—V Space, H Space, and Border. These properties affect the margins and borders around an image. However, they should be avoided. Not only are these properties so Web-Design-Circa-1999, but they're on the way out and unsupported in some versions of XHTML. In addition, they offer very anemic design control. For example, you can't easily control the color of the border around the image, nor can you specify different margins for both the right *and* left or bottom *and* top edges of an image.

Fortunately, you'll find that Cascading Style Sheets once again come to the rescue. The CSS Margin property lets you provide pixel-level control over each edge of an image (see page 203), while the CSS Border property (page 205) not only lets you control the color of an image's four borders, but even lets you specify different colors, styles, and widths for each individual border.

Editing Graphics

Nothing's ever perfect, especially when you're building a Web site. Corrections are par for the course—not just to a Web page, but to the pictures on it, as well. Perhaps a picture is a tad too dark, or you'd like to crop out the rowdy co-worker being escorted out by security from your company's holiday party photo.

In the hands of less-capable software, you'd face quite a tedious switching-and-opening task each time you wanted to edit a graphic. You'd have to open Photoshop, Fireworks, or whatever graphics program you prefer; choose File → Open; navigate to your Web site folder; find the graphic that needs touching up (if you can even remember its name); and then open it to make your changes.

Dreamweaver 8 includes tools for performing many basic editing tasks. For more complex work, like changing the text on a button from "Now Firing" to "Now Hiring," you need to switch to a different program. However, Dreamweaver is considerate of your time; it lets you access your favorite graphics program with just a couple of clicks.

The Built-In Editing Tools

Dreamweaver includes four tools for cropping, resizing, sharpening, and adjusting the brightness and contrast of images (see Figure 5-8). Suppose your boss emails you his portrait with instructions to put it on his "Meet the boss" page. Unfortunately, it's too big and too dark. Rather than launch a separate image-editing program, you can simply add the photo to the page and make the corrections within Dreamweaver.

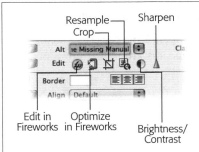

Figure 5-8:
The Property inspector includes tools for editing images directly inside Dreamweaver.

But first, a warning: All of these tools change the *original* GIF, PNG, or JPEG image in your site folder. If you shrink a graphic, and then later change your mind, you may be out of luck. It's a good idea, therefore, to make backups of all of your images before you use these tools.

EASTER EGG HUNT

Meet the Geeks Behind Dreamweaver

Want to see pictures of the engineers behind Dreamweaver? OK, maybe you don't, but you *can*, if you want, find these little snapshots hidden away in the Property inspector. Select an image in the document window. Then, simply Ctrl+double-click (or ⌘-double-click) the thumbnail of the graphic in the left side of the Property inspector. A picture of one of Dreamweaver's programmers appears, along with his name. Ctrl (⌘)-double-click the thumbnail repeatedly to cycle through the names and pictures of other members of the Dreamweaver team.

Furthermore, remember that if you use that same file on other pages, your modifications appear on those pages, too. For instance, if you decide you want to shrink your company logo to a smaller size on one page, you may find that *every* page on your site now has the smaller logo! If you want to change a graphic on only one page, make a copy of it first, insert the *copy* on the page you wish to change, and modify just that image file. That way, the rest of your site keeps the original graphic.

Of course, if you discover right away that you've made a change you don't want, you can choose Edit → Undo or press Ctrl+Z (⌘-Z). Until you close the page, you can continue to undo multiple image changes.

Cropping an image

Dreamweaver's Crop tool can remove extraneous or distracting parts of an image. (You can use it to focus on a face, or to get rid of those teenagers making faces in the corner, for example.)

To do so, select the graphic you wish to crop, and then click the Crop tool on the Property inspector (see Figure 5-8). (Alternatively, choose Modify → Image → Crop.) A rectangular box with eight handles appears inside the image; anything outside the box is cropped out. So just move this box (by dragging it) and resize it (by dragging the handles), until you've got just what you want inside the box.

When you're done, double-click inside the box, or click the Crop tool again on the Property inspector. Dreamweaver crops the image, discarding the unwanted areas of the graphic.

To undo a crop that you don't like, simply press Ctrl+Z (⌘-Z). In fact, you can back out before you've used the Crop tool at all; clicking anywhere on the page outside the image makes the cropping box go away.

Resampling an image

If a photo is just too big to fit on a Web page, you could select the image and use one of the resize handles to alter its dimensions (see page 131). Unfortunately, graphics that you shrink this way give you the worst of both worlds: they look muddier than they were before, yet they still retain all the slow-downloading data of the larger image.

You can, however, use this resizing technique in conjunction with the Image Resample tool to resize the actual graphic file. You'll end up with a trimmed-down file with its appearance intact.

To use the Resample tool, select an image on a page, and then resize it using the resize handles (see page 131). (Shift-drag to prevent distortion.) When you're done, click the Resample button on the Property inspector (see Figure 5-8). Dreamweaver resizes the image file.

You can even make an image *larger* than the original using this technique. The end result isn't perfect—even Dreamweaver can't create image information that was never there—but the program does its best to prevent the image from looking too pixellated. You won't want to enlarge images this way often, but in a pinch, it's a quick way to make a photo just a little bit larger.

Dreamweaver changes the graphic, altering the width and height of the actual file. If you change your mind about resampling the image, your only option is the old undo command, Ctrl+Z (⌘-Z).

Brightness and Contrast

If an image on a page is too light, dark, or washed out, you can use Dreamweaver's Brightness/Contrast dialog box to fix it.

First, select the picture and then, on the Property inspector, click the Brightness/Contrast icon (Figure 5-8) to open the Brightness/Contrast dialog box (Figure 5-9). Move the Brightness slider to the right to lighten the image (great for underexposed interior shots), or to the left to darken the image. The Contrast control works in the same way: right to increase contrast (making dark colors darker and light colors lighter); left to decrease contrast (moving all colors toward gray).

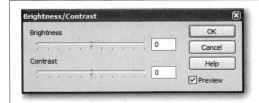

Figure 5-9:
If you've ever used image-editing software like Fireworks or Photoshop Elements, this dialog box should look familiar. Make sure the Preview checkbox is turned on so that you can see your changes right in the document window.

You'll often use the Brightness and Contrast sliders in conjunction. Brightening (lightening) an image also has a fading effect. By increasing contrast, you can restore some punch to a brightened image.

As with the other image-editing controls, if you're unhappy with the changes you've made, choose Edit → Undo or press Ctrl+Z (⌘-Z) to return the image to its previous glory.

Sharpening images

Sometimes graphics, even those from some scanners and digital cameras, look a little fuzzy, especially if you've resampled the image (page 136). Dreamweaver's Sharpen tool on the Property inspector helps restore clarity and make such images "pop." It works like similar tools in graphic-editing programs: it increases the contrast between an image's pixels to create the illusion of sharper, more in-focus graphics. (Insert your own Sharper Image joke here.)

To use this tool, select the graphic and then click the Sharpen icon on the Property inspector (Figure 5-8). The Sharpen window appears, as shown in Figure 5-10. Move the slider to the right to increase the amount of sharpening, or type a number in the box (10 is maximum sharpening; 0 is no change). You probably won't use the maximum setting unless you're going for a special effect, since it tends to highlight "noise" in the image, creating an unappealing halo effect around pixels. Once you've selected a level of sharpening that you like, click OK.

If you're unhappy with the results, just press Ctrl+Z (⌘-Z) or choose Edit → Undo.

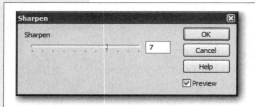

Figure 5-10:
The Sharpen box can make fuzzy pictures "pop." Make sure the Preview checkbox is turned on so you can see the effect on the image as you move the slider.

Setting Up an External Editor

Before you can take advantage of this time-saving feature, you need to tell Dreamweaver which graphics program you want to use.

1. **Choose Edit → Preferences (Dreamweaver → Preferences in Mac OS X).**

   The Preferences dialog box opens, as shown in Figure 5-11.

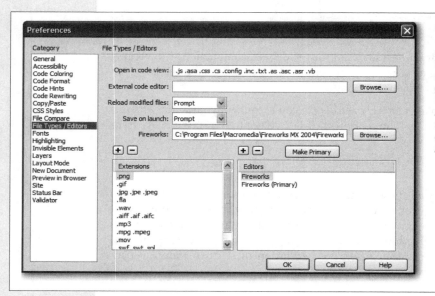

Figure 5-11:
You can select external image-editing programs to use with various types of Web files—including graphics formats such as GIFs, JPEGs, and PNGs—make your selection in the File Types/Editors category of the Preferences dialog box.

2. **In the left pane, click File Types/Editors.**

   The Preferences box now displays your current settings for the editing programs you prefer for editing different types of files. Two columns appear in the bottom half of the box: Extensions and Editors.

3. **From the Extensions list, select a graphic extension.**

   Three types of graphic files are listed: GIFs, JPEGs, and PNGs. You can choose a different editing program for each type of file, if you like. You can add file name extensions for file types not shown by clicking the + button above the Extensions list.

4. **Click the + button above the Editors list.**

   The Select External Editor dialog box opens.

5. **On your hard drive, find the program you wish to assign as an editor for the selected type of graphics file.**

   It can be Photoshop, AppleWorks, ImageReady, or whatever.

6. **If you wish to make this program the primary program for editing this type of file, click Make Primary.**

   This *primary* editor is the one Dreamweaver opens when you choose to edit the graphic. (You can define other, less frequently used editors, as well. See the Tip at the end of this list.)

7. **Repeat steps 3–6 for each type of graphics file that you work with.**

   Dreamweaver treats GIFs, JPEGs, and PNGs as separate file types, so you need to assign an editor to each. Of course, most people choose the same program for all three file types.

8. **Click OK to close the Preferences dialog box.**

   From now on, whenever you need to touch up a graphic on your Web page, just select it and then click Edit on the Property inspector (see Figure 5-4). Alternatively, you can simply double-click the file in the Files panel, or right-click (Control-click) the image on the page and choose Edit With Fireworks (or Edit With Photoshop, if you set that as your primary editor) from the contextual menu. In any case, your graphic now opens in the graphics program that you set as your primary editor in step 4.

   Now you can edit the graphic and save changes to it. When you return to Dreamweaver, the modified image appears on the page. (If you're a Fireworks fan, you're in even better shape; read on.)

Tip: You aren't limited to just one external editor. For instance, if there's a Fireworks feature you need, even though Photoshop is your primary editor, you can still jump to Fireworks directly from Dreamweaver.

The trick is to right-click (Control-click) the image you want to edit, whether it's in the document window or the Site Files window. Choose the Edit With menu. If you've added the other image editor to your preferences (Figure 5-11), that editor is listed in the submenu. Otherwise, select Browse from the contextual menu and choose the editing program you want to use in the resulting dialog box. That program opens automatically, with the graphic you clicked open and ready to be edited.

Editing Images with Fireworks

Fireworks is Dreamweaver's companion graphics program—a powerful image-editing program made specifically to create and optimize Web graphics.

The engineers at Macromedia have made sure that these sibling programs play well together. You can switch back and forth between them with a single click, for example. And instead of simply opening a GIF or JPEG file when you click the Edit button in the Property inspector, Fireworks can open the original Fireworks file from which the Web-ready image was created.

That's good, because most Web graphics don't start life as compressed GIF or JPEG files. Very often, you'll have a higher-quality image in your image editor's native format—.psd for Photoshop or ImageReady, for example, or .png for Fireworks. This source file may contain lots of additional information that doesn't need to be in the final image you use on the Web. For example, in most image-editing programs, text can remain editable, so that it's easy to modify the link description on a button, say. In other words, most often, you'll want to make changes to the original Photoshop or Fireworks file and *then* export it as a GIF or JPEG. If you're using Fireworks, Dreamweaver makes this process easier.

When you export a GIF or JPEG graphic from Fireworks, save it into your Web site folder—into a subfolder called Images, for instance. (See page 468 for strategies to help you organize your site's files.) When you do so, Fireworks creates a folder called _notes in the same folder. This folder contains small files whose names end in .mno—for Macromedia Note—that tell Dreamweaver where to find the original Fireworks PNG file on your computer.

When Dreamweaver opens a Web page, it checks for this folder and any notes that are associated with the graphics on the page. When you select an image created with Fireworks, Dreamweaver displays this information in the Property inspector (see Figure 5-12).

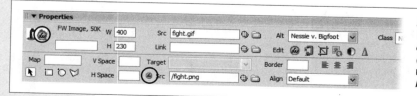

Figure 5-12:
The Property inspector displays special logos (circled) when you're working with a graphic created in Fireworks.

To edit a Fireworks graphic, just click it in the document window, and then click the Fireworks logo (the Edit button) in the Property inspector. Or, if you're in a hurry, just Ctrl (⌘)-double-click the image; or right-click (Control-click) it and choose Edit With Fireworks from the contextual menu. Either way, Dreamweaver launches Fireworks. (You may be prompted to choose whether to open the source file of the exported GIF or JPEG, depending on how you've set up your Fireworks preferences.)

In Fireworks, make any changes you wish to the image. When you're finished, click Done. Fireworks exports the image, closes the file, and returns you to Dreamweaver. The updated graphic appears on your page.

Optimizing an Image with Fireworks

If you have Fireworks, you can also click a button on the Property inspector to open Fireworks' Optimize Image dialog box. This feature offers a quick, easy way to compress an image, making it smaller for quicker download over the Internet.

With JPEG images, you control file size by adjusting the quality setting on a scale of 1 (lowest quality—which is too low for most purposes) to 100 (highest quality, and also the largest file size).

Note: When you click the "Optimize in Fireworks" button, Dreamweaver asks if you wish to edit a Fireworks PNG file. If you used Fireworks to create the image in the first place, editing this Fireworks source file is the best bet. It lets you select and work on the original, high-quality image, rather than the final compressed image file in your Web site. If you didn't create the image in Fireworks or don't have the original PNG file, just click the "Use this file" button, and Fireworks opens the GIF or JPEG file from your site.

A setting of 80 is a good compromise between quality and size. However, you can never make a JPEG image *higher* in quality than its original. In other words, if you take a JPEG image that starts out with a quality setting of 60 and increase the quality to 80, the picture won't look any better, but the file *will* get larger. In fact, Dreamweaver's optimization settings work best on high-quality Photoshop or Fireworks files rather than existing JPEGs. The more times you optimize a JPEG file, the worse it looks, as you lose pixel information with each compression.

The size of a GIF file is mainly controlled by the number of colors in it—the size of its *palette*. Fewer colors means a smaller file size. The "number of colors" menu on the optimize window lets you select from 2 to 256 different colors (256 is the maximum for a GIF image). As with JPEG images, if your GIF image starts out with only 64 colors, choosing 256 won't add colors or quality to the GIF.

Tip: Never convert a JPEG file into a GIF, or vice versa. The image almost always ends up looking worse. If you have a JPEG file that you think should be a GIF instead (see page 125 for some guidelines), it's best to return to the original Photoshop, Fireworks, or Illustrator file, if available, and use that program's Save for Web command (or equivalent) to export the file in the format you want.

Once you've made your optimization changes, click the Update button in the Optimize Image window. Fireworks recompresses the graphic and returns you to Dreamweaver. You can choose Edit → Undo to back out of the change.

Image Maps

As Chapter 4 makes clear, it's easy to turn a graphic into a clickable link. It's also possible to add *multiple* links to a single image.

Suppose your company has offices all over the country, for instance, and you want to provide an easy way for your visitors to locate the nearest state office. One approach would be simply to list all of the state names and link them to separate pages for each state. But that's boring! Instead, you could use a map of the United States—one image—and turn each state's outline into a hotspot that's linked to an appropriate page, listing all of the offices in that state.

The array of invisible link buttons (called *hotspots*) responsible for this magic is called an *image map*. An image map contains one or more hotspots, each leading somewhere else.

Here's how to create an image map:

1. **Select the graphic you wish to make into an image map.**

   The Property inspector displays that image's properties and, in the lower-left corner, the image-map tools, shown at bottom in Figure 5-13. (These appear in the lower half of the Property inspector, which appears only if the Property inspector is fully expanded, as described on page 24.)

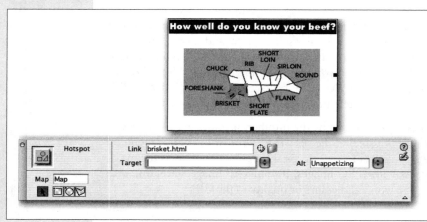

Figure 5-13:
Each link on an image map is called a hotspot. When you select a hotspot, the Property inspector displays its Link, Target, and Alt properties. The lower half of the inspector displays the name of the map as well as tools for selecting and drawing additional hotspots.

2. **In the Map field of the Property inspector, type a name for the map.**

   The name should contain only letters and numbers, and can't begin with a number. If you don't give the map a name, Dreamweaver automatically assigns the map the ingenious name *Map*. If you create additional image maps, Dreamweaver calls them Map2, Map3, and so on.

3. **Select one of the image-map tools.**

   Choose the rectangle tool, the circle tool, or the polygon tool, depending on the shape you have in mind for your hotspot. For instance, in the image in Figure 5-13, the polygon tool was used to draw each of the oddly shaped hotspots.

Note: If you have the images accessibility preference setting turned on (page 130), you'll get a window reminding you to add an Alt property to the hotspot you're about to draw. Each hotspot can have its own Alt description.

---

4. **Draw the hotspot.**

   To use the rectangle and circle tools, click directly on your picture; drag diagonally to form a rectangle or circle. To make a perfect square, press Shift while dragging with the rectangle tool. (The circle tool always creates a perfect circle.)

   To draw an irregularly shaped hotspot using the polygon tool, click once to define one corner of the hotspot. Continue clicking until you've defined each corner of the hotspot. Dreamweaver automatically joins the corners to close the shape.

   Dreamweaver fills the inside of the hotspot with a light blue tint to make it easy to see. (Your Web visitors won't see the blue highlighting.)

   If you need to adjust the hotspot you've just drawn, click the arrow tool on the Property inspector. You can drag the light-blue square handles of your hotspot to reshape or resize the area, or drag inside the hotspot to move the whole thing. If you change your mind about the hotspot, press Delete to get rid of it altogether.

Tip: After you draw a hotspot, the drawing tool is still active so that you can draw additional hotspots. Click the arrow tool in the Property inspector to deselect the hotspot drawing tool.

---

5. **Add a link to the hotspot.**

   After you draw a hotspot, that same hotspot is selected; its properties appear in the Property inspector (see Figure 5-13). Use any of the techniques discussed on page 108 to link this hotspot to another Web page or anchor.

6. **If necessary, set the Target property.**

   Most of the options in the Target pop-up menu are useful only when you're working with frames, as discussed in the online chapter about frames, which you can find at *www.sawmac.com/dw8/frames.pdf*. The "_blank" option, however, is useful any time: It forces your visitor's Web browser to load the linked page into a *new* browser window. The original page remains open, underneath the new window.

7. **Set the Alt property of the hotspot.**

   By typing a label into the Alt box in the Property inspector, you provide a written name for this portion of the graphic. As noted on page 128, *alt* tags are extremely important to people who surf the Web with graphics turned off, or who use text-to-speech reading software.

8. **Repeat steps 2–7 for each hotspot you wish to add to an image.**

   As you work, you can see the light blue hotspots filling in your image map.

Editing a Hotspot's Properties

As noted in step 4, you can change a hotspot's shape by dragging its tiny square handles. But you can also change its other properties—which Web page it links to, for example.

To do so, click to select the image map. Using the black arrow tool—the hotspot selection tool—on the far left side of the Property inspector (see Figure 5-13), click the hotspot you wish to edit. Then use the Property inspector controls to edit the Link, Target, and Alt properties.

If you're having a fit of frustration, you can also press Delete or Backspace to delete the hotspot altogether.

Rollover Images

Rollover images are among the most common interactive elements on the Web, especially when it comes to creating navigation buttons (see Figure 5-14). You've almost certainly seen rollovers in action, when your mouse moves over a button on some Web page and the image lights up, or glows, or turns into a frog.

Figure 5-14:
Rollover graphics appear frequently in navigation bars. Before your cursor touches a rollover button (top), it just sits there blankly. But when your cursor arrives, the button changes appearance (bottom) to indicate that the graphic has a functional purpose—in this case, "I'm a link. Click me."

This simple change in appearance is a powerful way to inform a visitor that the graphic is more than just a pretty picture—it's a button that actually does something. Rollovers are usually used to announce that the image is a link. (Though you can use them for other creative effects, as described on page 428.)

Behind the scenes, you create a rollover by preparing *two different* graphics— "before" and "after." One graphic appears when the Web page first loads, and the other appears when your visitor's mouse moves over the first. If the cursor then rolls away without clicking, the original image pops back into place.

This dynamic effect is achieved by using *JavaScript,* a programming language that most Web browsers use to add interactivity to Web pages. Fortunately, you don't need to be a programmer to take advantage of this exciting technology. Dreamweaver's many prewritten JavaScript programs, called *behaviors,* let you add rollover images and other interactivity to your pages. (You can find more about behaviors in Chapter 11.)

To insert a rollover image, start by using a graphics program to prepare the "before" and "after" button images. Unless you're going for a bizarre distortion effect, both images should be exactly the same size. Store them somewhere in your Web site folder.

Then, in the document window, click where you want to insert the rollover image. Frequently, you'll use a table to lay out your rollover buttons (Chapter 7), and insert one or more buttons within a table cell. If you're using CSS to lay out your pages, as described in Chapter 8, you can place the buttons inside a <div> tag, as described in the CSS layout tutorial on page 314.

Choose Insert → Interactive Images → Rollover Image (or click the Rollover Image button on the Common tab of the Insert bar). Either way, the Insert Rollover Image dialog box appears (see Figure 5-15). Fill in the blanks like this:

• **Image name.** Type a name for the graphic, if you like. JavaScript requires *some* name for the rollover effect. If you leave this blank, Dreamweaver gives the image an unimaginative name—for example, Image2—when you insert a rollover. However, if you plan to later add additional interactive effects (Chapter 11), you may want to change it to something more descriptive, to make it easier to identify the graphic.

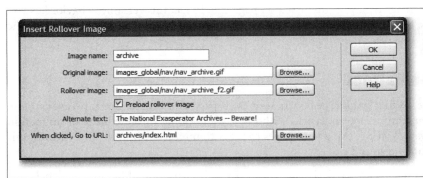

Figure 5-15:
This box lets you specify the name, link, and image files to use for the rollover effect. "Preload rollover image" forces the browser to download the rollover image file along with the rest of the page, avoiding a delay when the mouse moves over the rollover image.

- **Original image.** When you click the top Browse button, a dialog box appears prompting you to choose the graphic you want to use as the "before" button—the one that first appears when the Web page loads. (See page 125 for more on choosing graphics.)

- **Rollover image.** When you click the second Browse button, Dreamweaver prompts you to choose the "after" graphic image—the one that appears when your visitor's mouse rolls over the first one.

- **Alternate text.** You can give a text description for a rollover button just as you would for any graphic, as described on page 128.

- **When clicked, go to URL.** Rollover images are most commonly used for navigation elements that, when clicked, take the surfer to another Web page. In this box, you specify what happens when your visitor actually falls for the animated bait and *clicks* the rollover button. Click the Browse button to select a Web page from your site (see page 108) or, if you wish to link to another Web site, type an absolute URL (see page 112) beginning with *http://*.

When you click OK, you return to your document window, where only the "before" button image appears. You can select it and modify it just as you would any image. In fact, it's just a regular image with a link and a Dreamweaver behavior attached.

To see your rollover in action, preview it in a Web browser by pressing the F12 key (Option-F12 on a Mac) or using the File → Preview in Browser command.

Note: Attention Windows XP owners: If you have Service Pack 2 (Microsoft's operating system update that attempts to fix, among other things, the many security holes that exist in Internet Explorer), you'll have trouble previewing your rollover images. If, when previewing your page, you see a yellow banner with the ominous statement that begins "To help protect your security…," you've got Service Pack 2 installed. Fortunately, this glitch affects only pages viewed locally—off of your hard drive—and won't affect any of the thousands of visitors who come to your live site on the Internet. But if this still drives you crazy, Dreamweaver 8 provides a simple solution: choose Commands → Insert Mark of the Web. Selecting this adds a little code to your page, which stops Internet Explorer from butting into your rollover business.

You can achieve the same effect, with a little more effort, using Dreamweaver's Swap Image behavior, discussed on page 428. In fact this versatile behavior lets you create multiple, simultaneous image swaps where several images change at the same time (see Figure 11-11.)

Flash Buttons

While adding graphic rollovers to a Web page is a breeze, Dreamweaver's *Flash button* feature is even easier. Without any additional image-editing or animation software, you can bring your pages to life with interactive buttons that include animation and sound.

Flash buttons are predesigned buttons to which you can add your own labels and links. They can do much more than just change from a "before" look to an "after" look. For example, they may have *three* different looks (a third being a "pushed down" look that shows up when the button is clicked; see Figure 5-16). They may also play a sound or trigger a little animation.

You can download additional button styles from the Macromedia Exchange, Macromedia's one-stop source for Dreamweaver add-ons. See page 670.

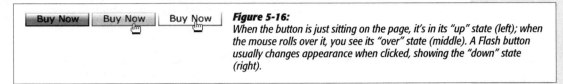

Figure 5-16:
When the button is just sitting on the page, it's in its "up" state (left); when the mouse rolls over it, you see its "over" state (middle). A Flash button usually changes appearance when clicked, showing the "down" state (right).

A Warning about Flash

It's important to understand, however, that Flash buttons (and Flash text, as discussed on page 150) are based on Macromedia's Flash Web-animation technology. Flash is the standard format for Web animation, thanks to its small file size, crisp graphics, and interactive effects. But Flash files (called Flash movies) require special software to view; they won't work on your Web page unless each of your Web site visitors has installed the Flash plug-in.

Most Macintosh and Windows browsers now come with the Flash plug-in already installed, and Macromedia even offers versions for Linux and Solaris. (Macromedia says that over 98 percent of the Web browsers worldwide have at least the Flash 3 plug-in installed—which is fortunate, since Dreamweaver's Flash buttons work with version 3 and above of the Flash plug-in.)

Note: If you're running Windows XP Service Pack 2, you'll have the same difficulties previewing your Flash pages as you do with rollover images. The problem and the fix are described on page 146.

However, to add more confusion to the situation, some new and popular browsers like Firefox, don't have the Flash plug-in installed, so surfers have to make the trip to Macromedia and download and install the plug-in to see your Flash content.

The point is that if you want to ensure that *everyone*, regardless of computer type, can savor your Web site to the same degree (without having to scurry off to another Web site to download the Flash plug-in), steer clear of Flash buttons. Furthermore, Flash movies can pose problems for disabled Web surfers, who won't be able to see (or hear) any text in a Flash button, and some search engines can't follow links embedded in Flash buttons, so the pages in your site may not all get added to a search engine's index.

Adding a Flash Button to a Web Page

If you're undaunted by the fact that not everyone may be able to enjoy Flash buttons (they're kind of fun after all), you're ready to proceed.

When you add a Flash button to a Web page, Dreamweaver creates and inserts a Flash movie file, ending in the extension .swf, into your Web page. You can preview the button within Dreamweaver and edit it at any time.

You perform most of the work in a single dialog box (Figure 5-17), which appears when you choose Insert → Interactive Images → Flash Buttons. You can also click the Flash Button object in the Media menu of the Insert bar (Figure 5-18). Now you can choose the correct settings for the lively button you're about to create.

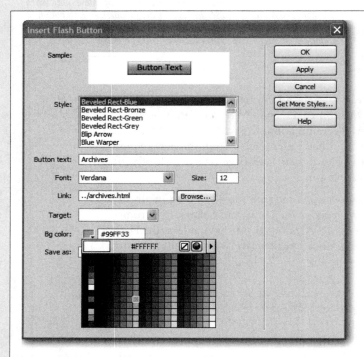

Figure 5-17:
The Insert Flash Button window lets you select a style, set text, and add links and formatting to a Flash button. You can also go onto the Web and collect more button styles by clicking the Get More Styles button. When you do, your Web browser launches and opens the Macromedia Exchange Web site. To go to the section of the Exchange where you can find additional styles, choose Flash Media from the Browse Extensions pop-up menu. See page 670 for more detail on using Macromedia Exchange.

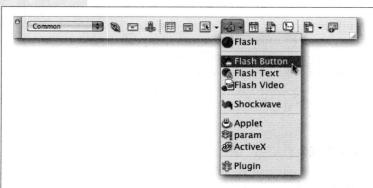

Figure 5-18:
The Flash button and Flash text icons appear in the Common tab of the Insert bar, in the Media menu.

- **Style.** When you click a style name, an interactive sample appears at the top of the window. Try pointing to each sample as well as clicking it (and holding down your mouse button) to see all of its different looks. Stop when you find one you like.

- **Button text.** Most button styles have space for a short piece of text that appears as a label, right on the button. Into this box, type something informative about the button's function (Buy Now!) or its link (Home). Buttons have limited space; Dreamweaver ignores letters that don't fit on the button.

- **Font, Size.** You can select a font from the Font menu and specify a size (in points) in the Size field. You can use any TrueType font you have installed on your computer; unfortunately, Flash buttons can't handle PostScript fonts.

- **Link.** If you want your button to link to another page when clicked, you can add either an absolute link or a document-relative link (see page 104). Type an absolute link starting with *http://* in the Link field. Alternatively, you can click the Browse button and select a page from your site to create a document-relative link.

  One thing to keep in mind about document-relative links in Flash buttons: The link information is embedded inside the Flash file. As a result, if you save the page you're working on to a different folder, the link may not work anymore.

  That's why, if you hope to create one set of Flash navigation buttons and use them over and over on all the pages of your site, you should use *absolute* links. These work regardless of the location of the Flash button file or the Web page the button is on. (*Site root–relative links* [see page 105] don't work at all in Flash movies.)

Warning: Dreamweaver doesn't always update links in a Flash button when you move or rename the page that the button links to. Sometimes you can use Dreamweaver's Link Checker (see page 510) to find the broken links, but this tool doesn't always work either!

- **Target.** If you want the linked page to open into a new browser window when clicked (leaving the current page in the current window), select the "_blank" option. The other choices on the Target menu are useful when working with frames, as described in the online chapter about frames, which you can find at *www.sawmac.com/dw8/frames.pdf.*

- **Bg color.** Use this pop-up palette to choose a background color for your button.

  Flash buttons can't be transparent and, like all Web page graphics, must be only square or rectangular. In other words, if your Flash button is rounded (as most are), some areas around its corners obscure the background of your Web page. What you're specifying here is a color for these exposed corner areas.

  By default, the background of a Flash button is white, but if you plan to use a button on a page with a different colored background, set the button to match the page's own background color.

• **Save as.** Dreamweaver automatically gives the button a file name—something like *button1.swf*—but you can change the name, if you like, by typing it into this box.

Flash button files must end in the extension .swf (the file extension used by Flash movies), even on a Macintosh.

In some browsers, document-relative links don't work in Flash movies unless the Flash movie is in the same folder as the Web page that displays the Flash movie. Because of this, Dreamweaver won't let you save your movie into any folder besides the one that contains the page that you're adding your Flash movie to.

When you click OK, Dreamweaver creates the Flash movie and saves it in the location you specified. Dreamweaver also inserts the movie into the Web page, with all of the appropriate properties set in the HTML of the page.

Editing Flash buttons

Once you've added a button to a Web page, you can edit it by double-clicking it (or by selecting it in the document window and clicking Edit in the Property inspector). The Insert Flash Button dialog box (see Figure 5-17) reappears. Make any changes you wish to the button, and then click OK.

And since Flash buttons are simply Flash movies, you can change any of the *movie* properties—such as height, width, or background color—using the Property inspector (see Chapter 12 for more on using Flash movies in Web pages).

Previewing Flash Buttons

You can see the button in action by previewing the page in a Web browser by pressing F12 (Option-F12). Or, if you just want to see the different looks for the button, you can preview the button without leaving Dreamweaver. The following procedure may sound a little peculiar, but only until you remember that a Flash button is actually a little movie. Select the button and then click Play on the Property inspector. The Flash button is now "playing." You can move your mouse over it, click it, and so on, savoring its animated smarts. To stop the button, click Stop in the Property inspector. (You can't double-click the button to edit it when it's playing.)

Flash Text

As noted in Chapter 3, Web browsers simply don't offer a lot of font choices. Even though it's possible to specify *any* font for your text, unless your visitors have the same font installed on their systems, they won't see the font you intended.

For this reason, Web designers either stick to the handful of fonts that are commonly installed on Windows and Macintosh computers, or they render type *as graphics* and insert them in the page. This workaround has its own downsides, of course: Graphics take longer to download, and you can't edit the text once you've frozen it into a picture. (In addition, search engine "spiders" can't read text inside of Flash creations, so your pages may not get properly indexed by a search engine.)

In an effort to give designers greater choices, Dreamweaver offers Flash text. Based on Macromedia's successful Flash technology, Flash text is a text-only Flash movie on your Web page that maintains the shape and quality of any TrueType font you have installed on your computer. It offers a number of benefits:

- Your visitors see exactly the same fonts you used when you created the Web page, even if they don't have the same fonts on their machines.

- The resulting Flash file is usually much smaller and of higher quality than the same text rendered as a graphics file.

- Since Flash uses *vectors*—mathematical formulas—to describe an image's shape and color, you can resize Flash text without degrading its quality.

Unfortunately, Flash text has a downside, too: Like Flash buttons, Flash text requires the Flash plug-in. As discussed on page 147, some visitors may not be able to enjoy your handiwork.

Note: For a method that works even when the Flash plug-in isn't installed (and also works with screen readers used by visually impaired Web surfers), check out a technique called sIFR 2.0 at *www.mikeindustries.com/sifr/*. Unfortunately, it's not integrated with Dreamweaver (meaning you'll have a little extra learning to do to get it working).

Adding Flash Text to a Web Page

Inserting Flash text is a combination of adding text and creating a Flash movie. Because you have so many choices, working with Flash text takes longer than most Dreamweaver processes, although it's no harder. Once again, it all happens in a single dialog box (Figure 5-19).

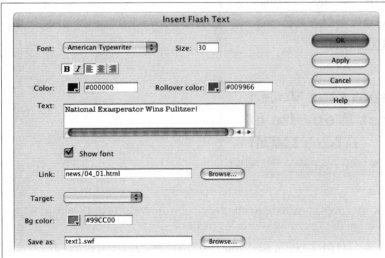

Figure 5-19:
The Flash text tool creates small text-only Flash movies that you can include on your Web pages. As with Flash buttons (see page 146), you can make the Flash text link to another Web page when clicked, either in your site or elsewhere on the Web.

To create Flash text, choose Insert → Interactive Images → Flash Text (or click the Flash Text icon on the Media menu of the Insert bar). Now choose your settings.

- **Font, Size.** You can select any TrueType font you have installed on your computer. As noted earlier, Flash text doesn't work with PostScript fonts. Type a font size, measured in points, in the Size field.

  Unlike text in a Web page, which, thanks to the quirky HTML language, comes only in *relative* font sizes (1, 2, 3, 4, and so on), Flash text uses the traditional typographic units of measurement, *points*. A size of 24 points is good for headlines, but you can specify a much larger one if you like.

- **B, I, alignment.** Using the tools just below the Font menu, you specify type-style attributes. For example, you can apply bold or italics by clicking the B or I buttons. You can also set the alignment of the text—left, right, or centered—by clicking one of the three alignment buttons (see Figure 5-20).

Figure 5-20:
You can align the text within a Flash text file. The alignment you choose here doesn't affect how the text is aligned on your Web page; it determines how the text is aligned inside of the finished Flash movie. If you think of each Flash text file as its own paragraph, the alignment options—shown here with Left, Middle, and Right alignment (from top to bottom, respectively)—make more sense.

- **Color.** Use this pop-up palette to choose a color for your text. (See page 41 for details on using the Dreamweaver color picker.)

- **Rollover color.** Flash text can have one basic dynamic effect: it can change color when a viewer moves her mouse over it. This effect is particularly useful if you wish to use the text as a link, because rollover effects are commonly used to indicate links. Use the "Rollover color" pop-up palette to specify the color the text becomes when the cursor points to it. If you don't want any rollover effect, leave this option blank.

- **Text.** The Text field displays your words in whatever font you've chosen. (If you turn off Show Font, on the other hand, you'll see only some generic font as you edit the text, but the software may feel more responsive as you edit.)

  As you type, you must manually enter a line break—by pressing Enter (Return)—wherever you want a line of text to end and a new line to begin. If you don't, Dreamweaver creates a wide (perhaps very wide, depending on how much text you have) Flash text movie. That's one reason it's usually better to use Flash text for short pieces of text like headlines or links.

- **Link.** You can use Flash text as a navigational element by attaching a link to it. In conjunction with a rollover color, you can use this feature to create simple dynamic navigation. In other words, if your Flash text says *Home*, you can set it up so that it's a button link back to your home page.

- **Target.** If you decide to turn your Flash text into a link, you can choose a *target* for that link using the Target pop-up menu, if appropriate. As noted earlier, select the "_blank" option if you want the link to produce a new browser window when clicked. Otherwise, use this pop-up menu only when working with frames, as described in the online chapter about frames, which you can find at *www.sawmac.com/dw8/frames.pdf*.

- **Bg color.** The Flash text you're creating is a rectangular text block, but the spaces between your lettering and the edge of the block aren't transparent; in fact, they start out white. The result—a bunch of white rectangles—looks pretty goofy if the background of your Web page is, say, fuchsia.

  To make it look like the Flash lettering is sitting directly on your Web page's background (without the white rectangles), choose the background color that matches your Web page's background.

- **Save as.** Type a name for your Flash text movie here. The Flash text tool stores the Flash movie in your site folder, within the folder that contains the Web page it's on. If you wish to save it in some other folder (an Images folder, for example), click the Browse button and navigate to it. If you've added a link to the text, however, save the Flash text movie in the same place as the Web page. If you don't, the link may not work in all browsers.

- **Apply.** The Apply button creates the Flash file and shows you the text on the Web page, while leaving the dialog box open. The advantage here is that you can make adjustments before exiting the dialog box.

When you click OK, Dreamweaver creates a Flash file and inserts it on your Web page.

Editing Flash text

To edit Flash text you've created, open the Insert Flash Text dialog box using any of these procedures:

- Double-click the Flash text block in the document window.

- Select the Flash text and then click the Edit button in the Property inspector.

- Right-click (Control-click) the Flash text and choose Edit from the contextual menu.

Once the dialog box is open, you can make any changes you wish to the settings or text.

Resizing Flash text

You can freely resize Flash text in the document window, without ever worrying that it won't look good at one point size or another. Just select the Flash text block, and then use either of these techniques:

- Type new dimensions into the Width and Height fields in the Property inspector. You can set the size using either pixels or percentages.

- Drag one of the square handles on the edges of the Flash object. To avoid distorting the text as you resize the Flash object, Shift-drag the lower-right handle.

You can always return the Flash object to its original size by clicking the Reset Size button on the Property inspector.

Tutorial: Adding Rollover Images

Adding interactive elements to a Web page can be quite a chore. Unless you're a programmer, learning and using the JavaScript programming language is time consuming and frustrating. Fortunately, Dreamweaver does most of the work for you, with its powerful, yet easy-to-use, *behaviors* (described in detail in Chapter 11).

In this tutorial, you'll add rollover images (page 144) to a page on the *National Exasperator* Web site.

Note: Before you begin, you'll need the tutorial files from *www.sawmac.com/dw8/*. Click the Tutorials link. Then click the Chapter 5: Rollover Tutorials link to download the files to your computer.

After you've downloaded and decompressed the files, you should have a *DWImages* folder on your computer, containing the Web pages and graphics needed for this tutorial. If you're having difficulties, the Web site contains detailed instructions for downloading the files you'll be using with this book:

1. **In Dreamweaver, choose Site → Manage Sites.**

   The Manage Sites window opens.

---

2. **Click the New Button and, from the pop-up menu, select Site.**

   The Site Definition window opens. In the first tutorial, you used Dream-weaver's Site Definition wizard (the Basic tab in this window) to get started. You'll use the Advanced tab this time, so make sure you've selected it. (There's more detail about the Advanced tab in Chapter 13.)

3. **In the Site Name box, type *Rollovers.***

   Dreamweaver will use this name while you're working on this tutorial.

4. **Click the folder icon next to the Local Root Folder field, browse to and select the *DWImages* folder, and then click Choose. Click OK.**

   For a recap on how to select a folder, see Figure 1-12 on page 35. If you see a message that Dreamweaver is about to create a cache for this site, click OK.

5. **Click Done to close the Manage Sites window.**

   You've now defined the site you'll be working on in this tutorial. Defining a site is the most basic and important step in building a Web site with Dreamweaver. Make sure you understand and are comfortable with this procedure; if you aren't, read page 472 if you're still unclear on how it works and why.

   The site's Files window should appear, listing all of the files in the DWImages folder. (If it doesn't, choose Window → Files.)

6. **In the Files window, double-click the file called *story.html.***

   A *National Exasperator* Web page opens. You'll add rollover images to create a navigation bar.

7. **Click in the empty blue-gray space below the "X" in the National Exasperator logo.**

   If you first selected the photo or clicked anywhere inside the main area of the page, you may see some translucent boxes (marked with numbers like "100% 900") covering this empty blue-gray area. These boxes are helpful aids for work-ing with tables (Chapter 7), but they can make it difficult to click inside that space. If you're having trouble, first select an image (like the logo) near the top of the page. Now you should be able to clearly see—and click—in the blue area.

   The insertion point should now be blinking. You've just placed the cursor inside a table cell where you can add other content such as images or text.

8. **Choose Insert → Image Objects → Rollover Image.**

   You may prefer to select Rollover Image from the Image menu on the Com-mon tab of the Insert bar (Figure 5-2). Either way, the Insert Rollover Image dialog box opens (Figure 5-21).

9. **In the Image Name field, type *Headlines.***

   For this effect to work, each button must have its own name, which the Java-Script program uses to communicate with and control the graphic. Dreamweaver gives the graphic a generic name like Image1, but creating a more descriptive name makes it easier for you to edit this effect later on.

10. **Click the top-most Browse button.**

    The Original Image dialog box appears. In the next step, you'll select the image for the button that will appear on the page.

11. **Browse to the DWImages → images_global → nav folder; double-click the graphics file called *nav_headline.gif*.**

    Graphics for just the navigation bar are in a special folder (*nav*) which is, in turn, inside the main images folder (*images_global*). The path to that graphic— *images_ global/nav/nav_headline.gif*—appears in the "Original image" box.

    Next stop: choosing the graphic that appears when a visitor moves the cursor over the button.

12. **Click the second Browse button; this time, double-click the file called *nav_ headline_f2.gif*.**

    Now, you'll make the button more accessible to people who've turned off their graphics, or who are using screen readers to read the page.

13. **In the "Alternate text" box, type *Headlines*.**

    Now all you need to do is add a link to turn the graphic into a navigation button.

14. **Click the third Browse button (next to the "When clicked, Go to URL" box).**

    The On Click, Go to URL dialog box opens, awaiting your selection of a Web page that opens when you click your rollover button.

    In this case, your button links to the main page of the Headlines section of the site.

15. **Browse to the *headlines* folder in the DWImages folder, find and double-click the file *index.html*.**

    At this point, the dialog box should look like Figure 5-21.

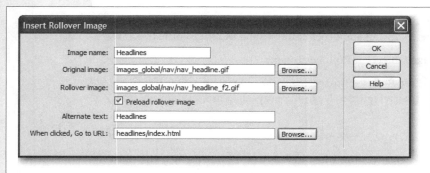

Figure 5-21:
The Insert Rollover Image window lets you define the name, graphics, and link for a rollover. Make sure the "Preload rollover image" checkbox is turned on.

16. **Click OK.**

    You're back at your Web page document, where your new, rectangular button, called Headlines, proudly appears.

    Congratulations! You've made your first rollover. To try it out for yourself, press F12 (Option-F12 on the Mac) to preview the page in your Web browser. When you move your cursor over the button, the text should turn red and pop out at you. When you click the button, it should open the Headlines page.

17. **Return to Dreamweaver.**

    Do so however you switch programs on your computer—by using the Windows taskbar or the Mac OS X Dock, for example.

    Finish up the navigation bar by adding the five other rollover images. Simply click next to the Headlines button, and then repeat steps 8–16 above. Here are the names, graphics and pages you should use:

    - Name: *horoscopes*
      Graphics: *nav_horoscopes.gif* and *nav_horoscopes_f2.gif*
      Alternate Text: *Horoscopes*
      Page to Link to: *horoscopes/index.html*

    - Name: *quiz*
      Graphics: *nav_quiz.gif* and *nav_quiz _f2.gif*
      Alternate Text: *Quiz*
      Page to Link to: *quiz/index.html*

    - Name: *store*
      Graphics: *nav_store.gif* and *nav_store_f2.gif*
      Alternate Text: *Store*
      Page to Link to: *store/index.html*

    - Name: *archives*
      Graphics: *nav_archives.gif* and *nav_archives_f2.gif*
      Alternate Text: *Archives*
      Page to Link to: *archives/index.html*

    - Name: *home*
      Graphics: *nav_home.gif* and *nav_home_f2.gif*
      Alternate Text: *Home*
      Page to Link to: *index.html* (the one inside the DWImages folder)

Note: If you're curious why all of these pages are named *index.html,* see the box on page 472.

When you're finished, choose File → Save, and then preview your new navigation bar (Figure 5-22) in your Web browser. Move your mouse over the buttons to see if they change; click to jump to another page.

Go to the DWImages folder to see a completed version of this page named *finished. html*.

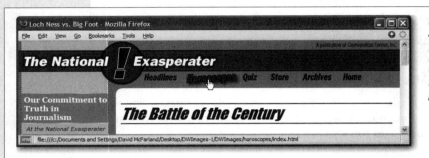

Figure 5-22:
Adding interactivity to your site using Dreamweaver's rollover objects is a breeze. No messy JavaScript programming to learn!

Part Two:
Building a Better Web Page

2

Cascading Style Sheets

When you compare the formatting options HTML provides with the text and styling you see in a magazine, the Web looks like the ugly duckling of the media world. HTML doesn't hold a candle to the typographic and layout control you get when creating a document in even the most basic word processing program.

But not anymore. A technology called Cascading Style Sheets addresses many of these shortcomings of HTML. Cascading Style Sheets (CSS) allow much greater control over the layout and design of Web pages. Using them, you can add margins to paragraphs (just as in a word processor), colorful and stylish borders to images, and even dynamic rollover effects to text links. Best of all, Dreamweaver's streamlined approach lets you combine many of these formats into powerful style sheets with just a few mouse clicks.

Dreamweaver 8 sports many enhancements to Dreamweaver's already powerful CSS tools. If you've created styles in previous versions of Dreamweaver, you'll be pleased at how much easier it is to create, edit, and apply styles.

Note: Cascading Style Sheets can be a difficult Web design concept to grasp. As you read the following pages, resist the temptation to fling your monitor into the hallway until *after* you've followed the tutorial steps at the end of this chapter, which put all of the tech-talk into context.

Cascading Style Sheet Basics

If you've used styles in word processing programs like Microsoft Word or page layout programs like Adobe InDesign, Cascading Style Sheets (CSS) will feel familiar. A *style* is simply a rule describing how to format a particular piece of HTML. (A *style sheet* is a set of these canned styles.)

You can create a single style, for example, that formats text with the font Arial, colored red, and with a left margin of 50 pixels. You can also create styles specifically for working with images; for instance, a style can align an image along the right edge of a Web page, surround the image with a colorful border, and place a 50-pixel margin between the image and the surrounding text.

Once you've created a style, you can apply it to text, images, or other elements on a page. For example, you could select a paragraph of text and apply a style to instantly change the text's size, color, and font. You can also create styles for specific tags, so that all <h1> tags in your site, for example, are displayed in the same style, no matter where they appear.

Why Use CSS?

Although HTML alone provides basic formatting options for text, images, tables, and other Web page elements, Cascading Style Sheets have many advantages that make them a superior choice for most formatting tasks. In fact, the World Wide Web Consortium (W3C), the organization responsible for defining standards for the Web, has already *phased out* the <font> tag from the current HTML standard in favor of CSS. (For a list of other obsolete tags, see *www.codehelp.co.uk/html/ deprecated.html*.)

POWER USERS' CLINIC

Getting to Know (and Love) CSS

Cascading Style Sheets are an exciting—and complex—addition to your Web building toolkit, worthy of entire books and Web sites on this topic alone. For example:

- For an excellent tutorial on CSS, visit W3 Schools' CSS tutorials at *www.w3schools.com/css/*.

- If you want to get help and learn more about CSS, the CSS-Discuss mailing list (*www.css-discuss.org/*) gives you access to a great community of CSS enthusiasts. Just be prepared for an overflowing inbox, and be aware of the list etiquette spelled out on the list's home page.

- You'll also find a helpful collection of wisdom generated from the CSS-Discuss Wiki at *http://css-discuss. incutio.com*. This site provides insider tips, tricks, and resources for solving many common CSS problems.

- For the ultimate source of information, turn to the World Wide Web Consortium's Web site: *www.w3. org/Style/CSS/*. The W3C is the body responsible for

many of the standards that drive the Web—including HTML and CSS. (Beware: This site is the ultimate authority on the matter and reads like a college physics textbook.)

- For a great list of CSS-related sites, visit the Information and Technology Systems and Services Web site at the University of Minnesota, Duluth: *www.d.umn.edu/ itss/support/Training/Online/webdesign/css.html*.

- If you just love to curl up by the fireplace with a good computer book, *Cascading Style Sheets: The Definitive Guide* by Eric Meyer (O'Reilly) can't be beat. Eric's Web site provides a lot of helpful information, too: *http://meyerweb.com/eric/css/*.

- Finally, you don't have to look any further than your own desktop for the ultimate reference to each CSS property. Dreamweaver's built-in Reference window provides instant access to concise information on Cascading Style Sheets (see the box on page 353).

But even if the threat of obsolescence doesn't motivate you to use CSS, consider this: Style sheets offer far more formatting choices than HTML. With CSS, you can format paragraphs as they appear in a book or newspaper (the first line indented and no space between each paragraph, for example) and control the leading (the space between lines of type in a paragraph). When you use CSS to add a background image to a page, you get to decide how (and whether) it tiles (repeats). HTML can't even begin to do any of these things.

Even better, CSS styles take up much less space than HTML's formatting options, such as the much-hated <font> tag. You can usually trim a lot of kilobytes from text-heavy Web pages using CSS while maintaining a high level of formatting control. As a result, your pages look great *and* load faster.

Style sheets also make updating your site easier. You can collect all of your styles into a single external style sheet that's linked to every page in your site. When you edit a style, that change immediately ripples through your site, *wherever* that style is used. You can thus completely change the appearance of a site by simply editing a single style sheet.

Cascading Style Sheets may sound like a cure-all for HTML's anemic formatting powers, but they're tricky to use. For example, CSS support varies from browser to browser, so you need to test your pages thoroughly in a wide variety of browsers. Even modern browsers—like Internet Explorer 6 for Windows; Firefox, Opera, and Safari for the Mac—have their share of weird CSS behavior (see page 203).

Fortunately, Dreamweaver 8 is better than ever at displaying complex CSS-based designs, so you can develop your general design in Dreamweaver, and use the preview feature to fine-tune your designs for different browsers.

Internal vs. External Style Sheets

Each new style you create gets added to a style sheet that is stored either in the Web page itself (in which case it's an *internal style sheet*), or in another file called an *external style sheet*.

Internal style sheets appear in the <head> portion of a Web page and contain styles that apply to that page. An internal style sheet is a good choice when you have a very specific formatting task for a single page. For example, perhaps you want to create styles to format the text and table of a chart that only appears on a single page.

Tip: It's often easier, when creating a new design, to add styles to an internal style sheet. Once you're satisfied with the design, you can then export the styles to an external style sheet—for use by all your site's pages—as described on page 167.

An external style sheet, on the other hand, contains only styles—no HTML—and can be linked to numerous pages. You can create a single style sheet that affects many pages in your site, creating uniform formatting throughout. For instance, you can put a headline style in an external style sheet and link that sheet to every page in the site. Every headline on the site then shares the same look—instant design consistency! Even better, when the boss (or the interior decorator in you) calls up and asks you to change the color of the headlines, you need to edit only a single file—the external style sheet—to update hundreds or even thousands of Web pages.

You can create both types of style sheets easily in Dreamweaver, and you aren't limited to choosing one or the other. A single Web page can have both an external style sheet (for styles that apply to the whole site) and an internal style sheet (for page-specific formatting). You can even attach multiple external style sheets to a single page.

Types of Styles

Styles come in several different flavors. The two most common are *class* and *tag* styles.

A *class style* is one that you create, name, and attach manually to text or an HTML tag. Class styles work much like styles in word processing and page-layout programs. For example, if you want the name of your company to be displayed in bold and red wherever it appears in the text of a Web page, you can create a class style named *Company* with boldface and red text-color formatting. You would then select your company's name on the page and apply this style.

You may actually already be using class styles without even knowing it. The Property inspector's basic text-formatting controls, introduced in Chapter 3, generate basic style sheets whenever you use them. See page 98 for more details.

Note: Class styles are what previous versions of Dreamweaver called *custom styles.*

The other major type of CSS style is called a *tag style* and applies globally to HTML tags, as opposed to individual selections. For example, suppose you wanted to display every Heading 1 paragraph (see page 78) in the Arial font. Instead of creating a class style and applying it to every Heading 1 on the page, you could create an HTML tag style for the <h1> *tag*. In effect, you redefine the tag so that it's displayed in Arial. The main benefit of redefining an HTML tag in this way is that you don't have to apply the style by hand. Since the new style says that *all* <h1> tags must use Arial, wherever a Web browser encounters an <h1> tag, it displays the text in Arial, the specified font.

These HTML tag styles are the easiest way to format a page. For one thing, there's no need to select the tag and apply the style; the page only needs to contain an instance of the tag—<h1>, for example—that you've redefined.

Nevertheless, there are times when only a class style will do, such as when you want to apply different styles to various paragraphs on the same page. Simply redefining the <p> tag won't do the trick, since that would affect *all* paragraphs. Instead, you'd have to create a class style for each paragraph format, and then apply the styles by hand.

Note: In addition to classes and tag styles, other types of styles provide added control for particular situations. Dreamweaver considers these advanced styles, and you can read about them starting on page 186.

Creating Styles

You begin most CSS-related tasks in the CSS Styles panel, which is the command center for creating styles (see Figure 6-1). To open it, choose Window → CSS Styles (or press Shift+F11).

Note: Dreamweaver 8 introduces significant changes to how you create and use styles. The CSS Styles panel has two views ("All" as shown in Figure 6-1, and "Current," described on page 180). It also incorporates a Properties list with which you can quickly edit CSS styles. (This was called the "Rule Inspector" in Dreamweaver MX 2004.)

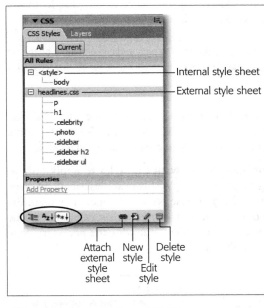

Figure 6-1:
With the "All" button selected, the CSS Styles panel lists the names of all styles available to the current page, including those in both external and internal style sheets. In this example, one external style sheet–headlines.css–contains seven styles. The first two styles are tag styles (notice that the names match various HTML tags), while the next five are class styles (note the period at the beginning). There's also one tag style defined in an internal style sheet–the one listed below "<style>." Click the minus (–) icon (arrow on Mac) to the left of the style sheet to collapse the list of styles, hiding them from view. The "Properties" list in the bottom half of the panel lets you edit a style as described on page 175; the three buttons at the bottom left of the panel (circled) control how the property list is displayed.

Internal style sheet

External style sheet

Attach external style sheet

New style

Edit style

Delete style

Phase 1: Set Up the CSS Type

To create a new style, click the New Style button on the CSS Styles panel (see Figure 6-1); right-click anywhere in the CSS Styles panel, and select New… from the menu that appears. Or choose Text → CSS Styles → New…. The New CSS Rule dialog box appears (Figure 6-2), where you begin the process of creating your new style:

- **Selector Type.** Click the appropriate radio button for the kind of style you're creating: *Class* (to create your own style from scratch) or *Tag* (to create an HTML tag style that Dreamweaver automatically applies to each occurrence of the tag). See the previous section ("Types of Styles") for a discussion of these two types.

  The third type offered here, Advanced, lets you create advanced style types such as IDs, pseudo-classes, and descendent selectors. (These are discussed beginning on page 186.)

- **Name.** If you clicked the Class button, type a name for the new style. All class styles begin with a period, according to standard Cascading Style Sheet convention.

Tip: If you're in a desperate hurry, you can leave the period out. Dreamweaver adds it automatically when it puts the style in the style sheet.

Class style names must *begin* with a letter, too, and can contain only letters and numbers. Dreamweaver lets you know if you use any invalid characters for the name.

If you chose Tag instead, select the HTML tag you want to redefine from the Tag pop-up menu (which appears when you click the Tag radio button).

Tip: If you're an HTML guru, you may find it faster to skip the Tag pop-up menu and just type the tag (minus the brackets) in the Name box. For example, if you want to create a style for all unordered (bulleted) lists, type *ul*.

If you clicked the Advanced button, Dreamweaver lets you type any valid CSS selector type in the Selector field (see page 187). You'll use this feature for some advanced CSS tricks, but you can also use it just to create a tag or class style.

- **Define in.** Click "This document only" if you want the styles to apply only to the current Web page (creating an *internal* style sheet, as described on page 163). To create a new *external* style sheet, choose New Style Sheet File from the "Define in" pop-up menu. This option not only creates a new external CSS file (which you can save anywhere in your site folder), but adds the necessary code in the current document to link it to that file.

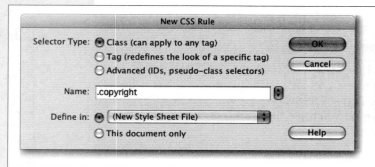

Figure 6-2:
In the New CSS Rule dialog box, you choose a type of style and give it a name. The label next to the naming box changes depending on the type of style you choose. In this example, since Class is selected, the Name label appears; if you choose the Tag option, it changes to Tag (or Selector, if you're using the Advanced option).

If you've previously linked this document to an external style sheet (see page 169), that style sheet's name appears in the pop-up menu, indicating that Dreamweaver is going to store the new style in this style sheet file.

Tip: If you create a bunch of internal styles in a particular page and later realize you'd like to turn them into an external style sheet that you can use in other pages, you're in luck. Dreamweaver has a command for this very task. Open the page containing the internal styles you want to reuse and choose File → Export → Export CSS Styles. A dialog box opens, letting you save the file as an external style sheet. Don't forget to add the .css extension to the end of the file name.

If you indicated that you want to create an external style sheet, clicking OK makes a Save Style Sheet As dialog box appear. Navigate to your site's folder and type a name for the new external CSS file. Just as HTML files end in .html, CSS files end in .css.

Tip: If you'll be using this style sheet for all of the pages in your site, you may want to save it in the root folder of your site, or in a folder specifically dedicated to style sheets, and give it a general name like *site_ styles.css* or *global.css*. (You don't have to type the .css file name extension, by the way. In this case, Dreamweaver adds it.)

No matter what "Define in" option you selected, clicking OK eventually brings you to the CSS Rule Definition window.

Phase 2: Defining the Style

The CSS Rule Definition window provides access to all of the formatting options available to you and your Web page text and graphics (see Figure 6-3). A blow-by-blow description of these various options begins on page 192.

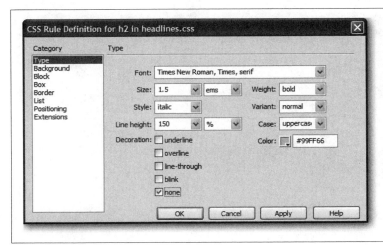

Figure 6-3:
For ultimate formatting control, Dreamweaver lets you set 67 different Cascading Style Sheet properties from the CSS Rule Definition window. To learn about these options, see page 192.

Once you've defined the style, click OK at the bottom of the Rule Definition window. Dreamweaver adds the style to the specified style sheet, and displays it in the CSS Styles panel (Figure 6-1).

The real trick to creating a style is mastering all of the different properties available, such as borders, margins, and background colors, and *then* learning which ones work reliably in the different browsers.

Using Styles

Once you've created styles, applying them is easy. In fact, if you created HTML tag styles, you needn't do anything to apply them, because their selectors (see the box below) automatically dictate which tags they affect.

Anatomy of a Style

Dreamweaver automatically handles the details of adding the proper CSS code to your pages, but if you're looking for something to read in bed, here's the behind-the-scenes scoop on how it works.

When you create an internal style sheet, Dreamweaver adds a pair of <style> tags to the head of the page (and a pair of HTML comment tags that hide the CSS from very old browsers). The opening <style> tag tells a Web browser that the following information isn't HTML—it's CSS code. When the Web browser encounters the closing </style> tag, it knows the CSS style information has ended.

Each line inside the <style> tag is a single style (in CSS-speak, styles are also called "rules"). An HTML tag style for the Heading 1 tag (<h1>), for example, might look like this:

```
h1 {
 font-size: 24px; color: #003399
}
```

The first part—h1—is called a *selector* (in CSS-speak) and indicates what the style applies to. In this case, wherever the <h1> (Heading 1) tag appears in the Web page's code, this style applies.

The information between the braces—{ }—states what formatting the browser should apply. For example, the code shown above contains two formatting instructions for the <h1> tag. Each one's called a *declaration* and is composed

of a *property* and a *value*. For example, *font-size: 24px* is one declaration with a property of *font-size* and a value of *24px*. In other words, this rule tells a Web browser that text inside an <h1> tag should be 24 pixels tall. The second declaration in the code makes the text of all <h1> tags show up in the color #003399.

A class style looks just like an HTML tag, except that instead of a tag, the selector is a name you've supplied, preceded by a dot, like this:

```
.company {
 font-size: 24px; color: #003399
}
```

Styles stored in an external style sheet look exactly the same; the only difference is that external style sheets don't include the <style> tags and shouldn't include any HTML code. You can open a page in Code view (choose View → Code) and edit an internal style sheet, just as you would the HTML of the page (see Chapter 9).

In Dreamweaver, you can also look at the raw style information of an external style sheet in several ways: open the .css file as you would a Web page (choose File → Open or double-click its name in the Files panel), or you can right-click (Control-click) on the style's name in the CSS Styles panel and choose "Go to code" from the pop-up menu; if you've changed Dreamweaver's preferences, double-clicking a style's name can also open the CSS file.

Linking to an External Style Sheet

Whenever you create an external style sheet, Dreamweaver automatically links it to the current document. To use its styles in a different Web page, however, you must *attach* it to the page.

To do so, open the Web page to which you wish to add the style sheet. Then click the Attach External Style Sheet button (see Figure 6-1) on the CSS Styles panel. (If the CSS Styles panel isn't open, choose Window → CSS Styles or press Shift-F11.)

Tip: You can also use the Property inspector to attach a style sheet. Just select "Attach Style Sheet…" from the Style menu.

The Attach External Style Sheet window appears (see Figure 6-4.) Click the Browse button. In the Select Style Sheet File dialog box that appears, navigate to and double-click the CSS (.css) file you wish to attach to the document. If Dreamweaver offers to copy the style sheet file into your site's root folder, click Yes.

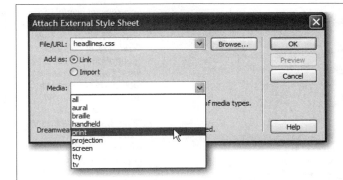

Figure 6-4:
Most of the options in the Media menu aren't very useful, since there aren't any devices programmed to work with them. However, "printer" and "screen" are handy ways to control how your page displays when viewed on a monitor and when printed on paper.

The Attach External Style Sheet window provides two other options: how to attach the style sheet and what type of "media" you want the styles to apply to. The "media" setting is optional.

When attaching an external style sheet you can either "link" it or "import" it. These two choices are nearly identical; they're simply two different methods of attaching an external style sheet to a Web page. The only real difference is that Netscape Navigator 4 doesn't understand the Import method. For greatest compatibility, use the Link option.

The Media menu defines which type of output device or display should use the style sheet. For example, selecting "printer" means that the style sheet applies *only* when the document is printed. Most of these options—such as TV for televisions or TTY for teletype machines—aren't of any use to the average Web designer. But the options "printer" and "screen" can come in handy. For example, you can create a set of styles that applies just to computer monitors by attaching a style sheet with the "screen" option—great for those moody white-text on black background designer sites—and another set—this time using printer-friendly black text on a white background—that applies only when printed. Then attach both sheets to the same page, and only styles in the "screen" style sheet appear when the page is viewed on a monitor, while those in the "printer" version appear only in the printed copy.

The "all" option in the Media menu is the same as not selecting anything—the style sheet applies when printed, viewed on a monitor, felt on a Braille reader, and so on. (Dreamweaver 8 also includes a helpful toolbar for controlling the display of style sheets aimed at different media—see Figure 6-5.) By using the Media menu, you can build one external style sheet that defines the basic look of all of your pages, and then create separate screen and printer style sheets that tweak that design for presentation on a monitor and on a piece of paper.

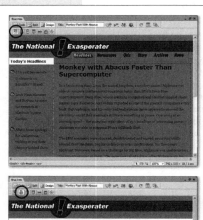

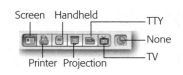

Figure 6-5:
Dreamweaver 8 adds a Style Rendering toolbar to its arsenal of helpful CSS tools. To turn it on, choose View → Toolbars → Style Rendering, or right-click (Control-click) on either the Insert bar or the document toolbar, and then choose Style Rendering. Click a button on the toolbar to show styles that match the media type you selected when you attached the page (see page 169). Screen (top left, circled) and Print (bottom left, circled) are the two most useful, though you can also hide all CSS styles by clicking the button on the far right of the toolbar (bottom right, circled).

Tip: You can preview the effect of the style sheet on your page by clicking the Preview button on the Attach External Style Sheet window.

After choosing your options, click OK, and Dreamweaver adds the necessary HTML code to the head of the Web page and automatically formats any tags in the document according to the style sheet's HTML tag styles. You'll see the formatting changes take place in the document window immediately after attaching the external style sheet.

If the style sheet contains *class* styles, on the other hand, you won't see their formatting effects until you apply them to an element on the page, as described next.

Applying a Class Style

You can apply class styles to any selection in the document window, whether it's a word, an image, or an entire paragraph. (You can apply any class style to any element, although doing so doesn't always make sense. If you format a graphic with a style that specifies bold, red Courier type, it won't look any different.)

For example, suppose your company's name appears in a paragraph of text on a Web page that includes (either in an internal style sheet or in a linked, external style sheet) a class style named *.company*. To format that text using the class style, you select the name in the document window and apply the style, as described below.

Similarly, to format larger selections, such as an entire paragraph, you'd select the paragraph and apply the class style. In fact, you can apply a class style to any HTML tag, such as the <p> (paragraph), <td> (table cell), or <body> tags.

When you apply a class style (*.company,* for example) to a tag, Dreamweaver adds a special *class* property to the page's code, like this: <p class="company">. On the other hand, if you apply a class to a selection that isn't a tag—a single word that you've double-clicked, for example—Dreamweaver wraps the selection within a <span> tag like this: <span class="company">The National Exasperator</span>. This tag, in other words, applies a style to a *span* of text that can't be identified by a single tag.

As you can see, it doesn't take much code to add a style to a Web page. A single application of a CSS style may add only 15 characters to your document (<p class="company">). When you compare that compact instruction with the equivalent HTML code required to produce the same formatted text (such as <font size="5" face="Georgia, Times New Roman, Times, serif" color="#999933">The National Exasperator</font>), class styles look downright petite.

To apply a class style to text, select some words. Then, from the Style menu in the Property inspector, select the style name (top image in Figure 6-6). To style an entire paragraph, you only need to place the cursor anywhere inside the paragraph (or heading) before using the Property inspector.

To apply a class style to an object like an image, select the object (as always, the tag selector in the bottom of the document window is a great way to select a tag). Then use the Class pop-up menu on the Property inspector (bottom image in Figure 6-6) to select the style name.

You can also apply a class style by selecting whatever element you wish to style, choosing Text → CSS Styles, selecting the style from the submenu, or by right-clicking

(Control-clicking) on the style's name in the CSS Styles panel, and then choosing "Apply" from the pop-up menu. Finally, you can also apply a class from the document window's tag selector, as shown in Figure 6-7.

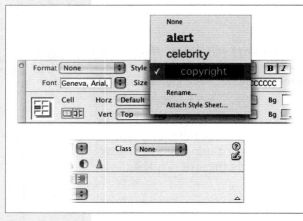

Figure 6-6:
The Property inspector provides the easiest method of applying a class style. Depending on what you've selected on the page (text, an image, or some other HTML tag) you'll encounter one of two different menus—the Style menu (top) or the Class menu (bottom). Either way, it's the same menu with the same options, and you use it to select the name of a style to apply it to whatever you've selected in the document window. You can also remove a style by selecting None from the menu.

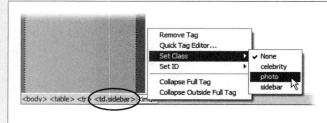

Figure 6-7:
You can apply a class style directly to a tag using the document window's tag selector. Just right-click (Control-click) the tag you wish to format, and then select the class style from the Set Class submenu. In addition, the tag selector lets you know if a tag has a class style applied to it. If so, the style's name is added at the end of the tag. For example, in this figure, a class style named .sidebar has been applied to a table cell (the <td> tag) on the page (circled).

Un-Applying a Class Style

To remove a style from an object on a Web page, simply select the element and then select None from the Property inspector's Style menu (see Figure 6-6). You can also choose Text → CSS Styles → None to remove a style from any selection (even nontext elements like images or tables).

Tip: If you've applied a class style to a selection of text, you don't actually have to select all of the text to remove the style. Just click anywhere inside it and select None from the Property inspector's Style menu (or choose Text → CSS Styles → None). Dreamweaver is smart enough to realize you want to remove the style applied to the text. (If you applied the style to a tag, Dreamweaver removes the Class property. If you applied the style using the <span> tag, Dreamweaver removes the span tag.)

You can't, however, remove *tag* styles from HTML tags. For example, suppose you've redefined the <h1> tag using the steps outlined on page 165. If your page has three Heading 1 (<h1>) paragraphs, and you want the third heading to have a different style than the other two, you can't simply "remove" the <h1> style from the third paragraph. Instead, what you need to do is create a new *class* style with all of the formatting options you want for that third heading and apply it directly to the <h1> tag (by the magic of CSS, the class formatting options override any existing tag style options—see page 182 for more on this sleight of hand).

FREQUENTLY ASKED QUESTION

When Formatting Disappears

Sometimes when I copy text from one Web page and paste it into another Web page, all of the formatting disappears. What's going on?

When you use Cascading Style Sheets, keep in mind that the actual style information is stored either in the <head> of the Web page (for internal style sheets) or in a separate CSS file (an external style sheet). If a page includes an internal style sheet, when you copy text, graphics, or other page elements, Dreamweaver copies those elements and any class style definitions used by that content. When you paste the HTML into another page, the styles are written into the <head> of that page. This feature, new in Dreamweaver 8, can save you some time, but won't solve all of your woes. It doesn't, for example, copy any tag styles you've *created* or most advanced styles you may create (see page 186). So if you copy and paste some text—say,

an <h1> tag styled with an h1 tag style—the <h1> tag and its contents will paste into another page, but not the tag style.

In addition, if a page uses an external style sheet, when you copy and paste text, the styles themselves don't go along for the ride. For example, if you copy a paragraph that has a class style applied to it and paste it into another document, the code in the paragraph is pasted (<p class="company"> for instance), but the actual "company" style, with all its formatting properties, isn't.

The best solution is to use a common external style sheet for all pages on your site. That way, when you copy and paste text, all the pages share the same styles and formatting. So in the example above, if you copy a paragraph that includes a class style—class="company"—into another page that shares the same style sheet, the paragraphs look the same on both pages.

Manipulating Styles

As with anything in Dreamweaver, styles are easy enough to edit, delete, or duplicate; all you need is a map of the terrain.

Editing Styles

While building a Web site, you continually refine your designs. That chartreuse color you assigned to the background of your pages may have looked great at 2 a.m., but it loses something in the light of day.

Fortunately, one of CSS's greatest selling points is how easy it makes updating the formatting on a Web site.

Note: Although this section focuses mainly on how to style your text, you can also use CSS styles to add background colors, background images, borders, and accurate positioning that can apply to images, table cells, and other page elements. For an example of a CSS style applied to an image, see the tutorial on page 216.

Dreamweaver 8 provides many ways to edit styles, some of which are new:

- Select a style in the CSS Styles panel (Figure 6-1) and click the Edit Style button to open the Rule Definition window (Figure 6-3). (This is the same window you used when first creating the style.) Make your changes and then click OK to return to the document window. Dreamweaver reformats the page to reflect any changes you made to styles used in the current document.

- Double-clicking the name of a style in the CSS panel also opens the Rule Definition window. This is a change from Dreamweaver MX 2004, which changed into Code view to edit the—ecck!—raw CSS code. If you liked this behavior you can turn it back on by opening the Preferences window (Ctrl+U [⌘-U]), clicking the CSS Styles category, and selecting the last button "Edit using Code View."

GEM IN THE ROUGH

A Time to Design

A Dreamweaver feature called *Design Time style sheets* lets you quickly "try out" different CSS style sheets while developing your Web page. Using the simple dialog box shown at bottom right, you can hide the (external) style sheets you've attached to a Web page and substitute in new ones.

Design Time style sheets come in handy when working on HTML that, later on, you intend to make part of a complete Web page. Dreamweaver Library items are a good example; this feature (discussed in Chapter 16) lets you create a chunk of HTML that can be used by any number of pages on your site. When you update the Library item, every page that uses it is updated. A time-saving feature, for sure, but since a Library item is only *part* of a page, it doesn't include the <head> portion needed to either store styles or attach an external style sheet. So when designing a Library item, you're working in the dark (or at least, without any style). But using Design Time style sheets, you can access all the styles in an external style sheet and even preview the effects directly in Design view.

You'll also turn to this feature when working with Dreamweaver 8's new XML tools, which let you add an "XSLT fragment" to a complete Web page—essentially letting you convert XML (like you'd find in an RSS news feed) into a chunk of HTML. But to accurately design these components, you'll need to use Design Time style sheets.

To apply a Design Time style sheet to your Web page, choose Text → CSS Styles → Design Time; the Design Time Style Sheets window appears. Click the top + button

to select an external style sheet to display in Dreamweaver. Note that clicking this button doesn't attach the style sheet to the page; it merely selects a .css file to use when viewing the page inside Dreamweaver.

To properly view your page with this new style sheet, you may need to get an attached external style sheet out of the way. To do that, use the bottom + button to add it to the Hide list.

Design Time style sheets apply only when you're working in Dreamweaver. They have no effect on how the page looks in an actual Web browser. That's both the good news and the bad news. Although Dreamweaver lets you apply class styles that you take from a Design Time style sheet to your Web page, it doesn't actually attach the external style sheet to the page. You have to attach it yourself when design time is over, or else your visitors will never see your intended result.

Note that this method works only with external style sheets; you can't use it to prevent Dreamweaver from displaying internal styles.

- Right-click (Control-click) the name of a style in the CSS Styles panel and choose Edit from the shortcut menu, which also opens the Rule Definition Window. Make your changes to the style, and then click OK to return to the document window.

- Select a style to edit in the CSS Styles panel, and then use the Properties list (see below) to edit the style's properties.

FREQUENTLY ASKED QUESTION

Help, My Styles Don't Work!

I've just edited a CSS style, but the changes I made don't appear when I preview the page. Why?

When you edit a style located in an external style sheet, Dreamweaver opens the .css file—in the background, where it then surreptitiously makes the change to the style. Unfortunately, the program doesn't save the file when it's done, so while the changes exist in the still-open .css file, the file safely saved on your hard drive doesn't yet contain the changes.

Therefore, if you preview a page on your site, and merrily click away to see how the newly edited styles look on your site's pages, you'll be sadly disappointed. Those pages are loading the .css file on your hard drive; they don't have access to the open file in Dreamweaver.

The method to this apparent madness: Dreamweaver is giving you a chance to undo changes you made to the external style sheet. Because the program hasn't closed the .css file, you can use the Edit → Undo command to undo edits to the file. To do so, you must have that file open in front of you—but where is it? Just pull it forward by choosing from the list of all open files at the bottom of the Window menu.

If you find this arrangement more a nuisance than a benefit, you can turn it off. Open the Preferences window by choosing Edit → Preferences (Dreamweaver → Preferences on the Mac). Select the CSS Styles category and turn off the "Open CSS files when modified" box. (Remember, if you turn this feature off, you won't be able to use Edit → Undo to undo edits you make to external style sheets.)

Editing Styles with the Properties Pane

The CSS Rule Definition window (Figure 6-3) can be a rather tedious way of editing CSS properties. It's easy to use, but the categories and menus may slow down experienced CSS jockeys. Dreamweaver 8 introduces a new tool—the Properties pane—to streamline the process of editing styles. The Properties pane, shown in Figure 6-8, displays a selected style's currently defined properties, as well as a list of other not-yet-set CSS properties.

MX 2004 Veterans: The Properties List pane is nearly identical to the Rule inspector, which has been spruced up a little and moved into the CSS panel.

Select the style you wish to edit in the CSS Styles panel, and the Properties pane displays CSS properties in one of three different views: a "set properties" view, which displays only the properties that have been defined for the selected style (Figure 6-8); a Category view, which groups the different CSS properties into the same seven categories used in the Rule Definition window (Figure 6-9, left); and a List view, which provides an alphabetical listing of *all* CSS properties (Figure 6-9, right). Clicking the view buttons at the bottom-left corner of the CSS Styles panel, switches between these three displays (see the circled buttons in Figures 6-8 and 6-9).

Note: What do all of these CSS properties do? Turn to page 192 for an explanation.

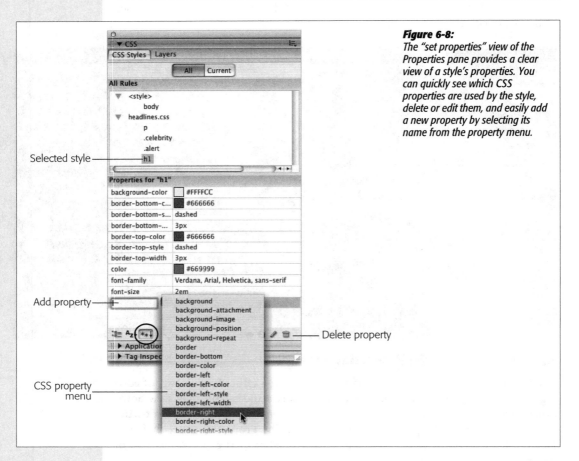

Selected style

Add property

CSS property menu

Figure 6-8:
The "set properties" view of the Properties pane provides a clear view of a style's properties. You can quickly see which CSS properties are used by the style, delete or edit them, and easily add a new property by selecting its name from the property menu.

Delete property

Property names are listed on the left, and their values are on the right. Figure 6-8 shows an example of a style for the <h1> tag, which lists 10 properties (for example, *background-color, font-family*) and their corresponding settings (#FFFFCC, "Arial, Helvetica, sans-serif," and so on).

To add a new property, click the "Add Property" link at the bottom of the list, and select the property name from the pop-up menu. You set (and can edit) the value of a particular property in the space to the right of the property name. Most of the time, you don't have to type in the value. Dreamweaver provides the tools you're likely to need for each property: the ubiquitous color box (see page 41) for any property that requires a color, like font color; a pop-up menu for properties that have a limited list of possible values, like "dashed" for the *border-top-style* property

---

shown in Figure 6-8; and the familiar Browse for File folder icon for properties that require a path to a file.

Some other properties, however, require you to know enough CSS to enter them manually, in the correct format. That's what makes the Properties pane a good advanced option for experienced CSS gurus. (If your goal is to become one, you can learn about the different CSS properties starting on page 192. Dreamweaver includes a built-in CSS reference so you can sharpen your knowledge of this exciting technology, as discussed on page 353).

Note: The Properties pane can only *edit* styles. You can add and remove properties with it, but you can't create, delete, or rename styles using it.

Even those not-so-experienced find the Properties pane helpful. First, it's the best way to get a bird's-eye view of a style's properties. Second, for really basic editing, such as changing the colors used in a style or assigning it a different font, the Properties pane is as fast as it gets.

To remove a property from a style, just delete its value in the right column. Dreamweaver then not only removes the value, but the property name as well from the style sheet. In addition, you can right-click (Control-click) a property name and select "delete" from the pop-up menu, or click a property name followed by the Trash can icon to banish it from your style sheet (see Figure 6-8).

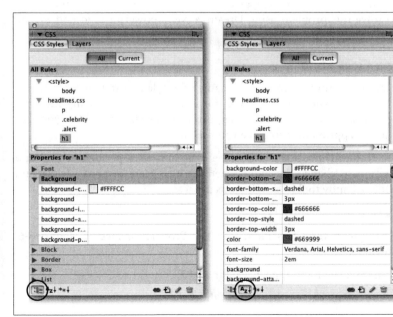

Figure 6-9:
The Properties pane's two other views are a holdover from MX 2004's Rule inspector, and aren't as streamlined or as easy to use as the "set properties" view pictured in Figure 6-8. Add new properties in these views by simply typing a value in the empty box to the right of the property name—in the left view, in the empty box to the right of "background," for example.

Deleting a Style

At some point, you may find you've created a style that you don't need after all. Maybe you redefined the HTML <code> tag, for example, and realize you haven't even used the tag in your site. There's no need to keep it around taking up precious space in the style sheet.

To delete a style, make sure the CSS Styles panel is open (Window → CSS Styles). Click the name of the style you wish to delete, and then click the Trash can at the bottom of the panel. You can also remove all of the styles in an internal style sheet (as well as the style sheet itself) by selecting the style sheet—indicated by "<style>" in the CSS Styles panel (see Figure 6-1)—and clicking the Trash can. If you "trash" an *external* style sheet, however, you merely unlink it from the current document without actually deleting the .css file.

Tip: A faster way to delete a style is to right-click (Control-click) the name of the style in the CSS Styles panel and choose Delete from the shortcut menu.

Unfortunately, deleting a class style *doesn't* delete any references to the style in the pages of your site. For example, if you've created a style called .company and applied it throughout your site, and you then delete that style from the style sheet, Dreamweaver doesn't remove the <span> tags or class properties that refer to the style. Your pages are still littered with orphaned code like this—<span class="company">The National Exasperator</span>—even though the text loses the styling. (See how to solve this problem using Dreamweaver's powerful Find and Replace tool on page 649.)

Renaming a Class Style

While there are many ways to change the name of a style in a style sheet (open the .css file in Code view and edit the name, for example), just changing the name doesn't do much good if you've already applied a class style throughout your site. The *old* name still appears in each place you used it.

What you really need to do is rename the style and *then* perform a find-and-replace operation to change the name wherever it appears in your site. Dreamweaver includes a handy tool to simplify this process.

To rename a class style:

1. **In the Style menu (or Class menu) on the Property inspector (Figure 6-6), choose Rename.**

   The Rename Style window appears (Figure 6-10).

2. **From the top menu, choose the name of the style you wish to rename.**

   This menu lists all class styles available on the current page, including external and internal styles.

3. **Type the new style name in the "New name" box.**

   You must follow the same rules for naming class styles described on page 166. But, just as when creating a new class, you don't need to precede the name with a period—Dreamweaver takes care of that.

4. **Click OK.**

   If the style whose name you're changing is an internal style, Dreamweaver makes the change. Your job's complete.

   However, if the style belongs to an external style sheet, Dreamweaver warns you that other pages on the site may also use this style. To successfully rename the style, Dreamweaver must use its Find and Replace tool to search the site and update all pages that use the old style name. In that case, continue to step 5.

5. **If you get cold feet, click Cancel to call off the name change, or click Yes to open the Find and Replace window, where you should click Replace All.**

   One last warning appears, reminding you that this action can't be undone.

Note: If you click No in the warning box that appears after step 4, Dreamweaver still renames the style in the external style sheet, but doesn't update your pages.

---

6. **Click Yes.**

   Dreamweaver goes through each page of your site, dutifully updating the name of the style in each place it appears. This hidden gem is a great tool and is particularly useful if you use the Property inspector to set font colors, types, and sizes (see Chapter 3). In that case, you can use this feature to rename the non-descriptive class names—Style1, Style2, and so on—that Dreamweaver starts you off with.

Figure 6-10:
The Rename Style tool is a fast and easy way to change the name of a class style even if you've already used the style hundreds of times throughout your site.

Duplicating a Style

Dreamweaver makes it easy to duplicate a CSS style, which is handy when you've created, say, an HTML tag style, and now decide you'd rather make it a class style. Or you may want to use the formatting options from one style as a starting-off point for a new style. Either way, you start by duplicating an existing style.

You can duplicate a style in two ways. The easiest method is to open the CSS Styles panel (Window → CSS Styles), right-click (Control-click) the name of the style you wish to duplicate, and then choose Duplicate from the shortcut menu.

The Duplicate CSS Rule window appears (Figure 6-11), where you can give the duplicated style a new name, reassign its Type setting, use the "Define in" menu to move it from an internal to an external style sheet, and so on.

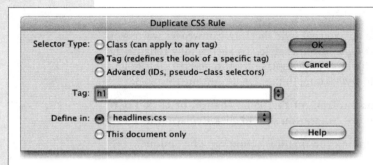

Figure 6-11:
The Duplicate CSS Style dialog box looks and acts just like the New CSS Rule box (Figure 6-2). You can select a new style type, name it, and add it to an external or internal style sheet. The only difference is that the duplicated style retains all of the CSS properties of the original style.

When you click OK, Dreamweaver adds the duplicate style to the page or external style sheet. You can then edit the new style just as you would any other, as described on page 173.

More about Styles

As you begin to pile styles onto your pages, you may notice some peculiar behaviors as styles start to interact. The rules governing these interactions can be complex, but they boil down to two main concepts: *inheritance* and *cascading*.

Inheritance

Imagine that you've created a new style by redefining the paragraph tag (<p>). This style has a font type of Arial, is red, and is 24 pixels tall. Then you select a single word in a paragraph and apply bold formatting to it. When you use the Property inspector's bold button to do this, Dreamweaver quietly wraps that word in a pair of <strong> HTML tags. (Dreamweaver doesn't use the <b> tag when making text bold—see page 91.)

When a browser loads the page, it formats all paragraphs in Arial, red, 24 pixels, because that's how you defined the <p> tag. But what happens when the browser suddenly encounters the <strong> tag? Since you didn't redefine the <strong> tag in red, Arial, 24 pixels, the browser scratches its little silicon head: should the browser just resort to the *default* font, size, and color when it gets to the <strong> tag?

No, of course not. The bolded word should look just like the rest of the paragraph— Arial, red, 24 pixels—but be bold, *too*. And indeed, that's how Cascading

Style Sheets work: the <strong> tag *inherits* the formatting of the surrounding <p> tag.

Just as human babies inherit traits—eye color, for example—from their biological parents, nested HTML tags inherit the properties of tags that surround them. A tag that's nested inside of another tag—that <strong> tag inside the <p> tag, for example—is called a *child*, while the enclosing tag is called the *parent*.

Note: In CSS-speak, a tag inside another tag is also called a *descendent*, while a tag that surrounds another tag is called an *ancestor*.

Inheritance passes from parent to child. So, in this example, the <p> tag (the parent) passes on the Arial font, red color, and 24 pixel size to the <strong> tag (the child). But just as children have their own unique qualities, the <strong> tag adds its own quality—boldness—to the properties of its parent.

Note: Inheritance applies to all styles, not just HTML tag styles. If you apply a class style, for example, to a <td> (table cell) tag, all tags inside the cell—paragraphs, images, and so on—inherit the properties of the class style.

Inheritance comes in quite handy at times. For instance, say you want to display *all* text on a page (paragraphs, headings, unordered lists, and links) using the Verdana font. You could, of course, knock off for the week and redefine *every* HTML tag used to format text—<h1>, <h2>, <p>, <a>, <ul>, and so on—or create a class style and then manually apply it to all text on the page.

Tip: For more information on inheritance, the Web offers some useful articles. For example, *www. creativepro.com/story/feature/14776.html?origin=story* takes you through the ins and outs of basic inheritance. The article at *www.brainjar.com/css/using/default3.asp* offers specific code examples. And *www. ddj.com/documents/s=2370/nam1011137269/index.html* is called "Style Inheritance: Friend *and* Foe," which speaks for itself.

However, a better and faster technique is to take advantage of inheritance. Every Web page contains a <body> tag, which contains all the elements of your page. The <body> tag, therefore, is the parent of *all* HTML you see in a page—images, paragraphs, headings, and so on. To quickly format all text, you could create an HTML tag style for the <body> tag using Verdana, or create a class style using that font and apply it to the <body> tag. Every bit of text inside the body—all children—then inherit the Verdana font property.

Note: Actually, not all CSS properties are inherited. For the most part, these are logical exclusions: For example, say you created a border around an unordered list to visually set it off in its own box. If the border property were inherited, then all the elements *inside* the unordered list—like list items, links, or bolded words—would each have their own box drawn around them as well. Use Dreamweaver's built-in CSS Reference to see which properties aren't inherited (see page 353).

Cascading

At times, styles can conflict. Let's say you redefine the <h1> tag in an external style sheet, so that all <h1> tags show up in red, using the Arial font. But now you attach this external style sheet to a Web page that already has an *internal* style sheet, whose <h1> tag style has been set to Times, 24 pixels.

When a Web browser has to display any text formatted as a Heading 1 paragraph, it runs into a little dilemma. The page has two different styles—two sets of formatting rules—for the *same tag*. So which does the browser choose: the style from the internal style sheet or the style from the external style sheet?

The answer is both. The browser merges the two styles into a sort of hybrid, following these rules:

- Properties that don't conflict are applied as usual. In the above example, the red color property exists only in the external style, while only the internal style specifies a font *size*. So far, the browser knows that, for this page, text inside <h1> tags should be both red *and* 24 pixels tall.

- When properties do conflict, a Web browser uses the property from the "closest" or more specific style. External styles (since they're in a separate file) aren't as specific as the internal styles, which were created specifically to style this one page. In this case, the font Times (specified in the <h1> tag style in the internal style sheet) wins.

To summarize this example, then: the Web browser determines that text inside an <h1> tag on this Web page should be Times, red, 24 pixels tall.

This cascading effect applies to all styles, including class styles and the advanced styles discussed on page 186. When there's a direct conflict between properties from a class style and an HTML tag style, the class style prevails. Because class styles must be applied directly to a tag—<h1 class="specialHeadline">—they are considered more specific than HTML tag styles. After all, you added the style to a specific instance of the <h1> tag on the page.

Note: In the CSS version of "rock, paper, scissors," HTML text formatting beats CSS formatting. So if you add new, improved CSS styles to old Web pages that include out-of-date HTML formatting, your CSS styles won't work. To eliminate this conflict, remove the <font> tag from the page's code using Dreamweaver's Search and Replace tool (see page 649) or the Clean Up HTML/XHTML command (page 518).

These same rules apply when child elements inherit properties from parent elements, as described on page 180. For example, if you apply a purple, Arial font class style to the body of a page, then the child elements (anything within the <body> tag) inherit those properties. If you then redefine the paragraph tag so that paragraph text is green, paragraph text inherits the Arial font from the body, but ignores the purple color in favor of the green you specified when redefining its own—paragraph—tag.

To learn more than you probably ever wanted to know about cascading, visit the following Web pages:

- *www.blooberry.com/indexdot/css/topics/cascade.htm*

- *http://nemesis1.f2o.org/aarchive?id=4*

- *www.w3.org/TR/REC-CSS2/cascade.html#cascade*

The Other Side of the CSS Style Panel

If you haven't yet set this book aside in hopes that the swelling in your brain will subside, you've probably absorbed the notion that the application of style properties is quite complex. With all this inheritance and cascading going on, it's very easy for styles to collide in unpredictable ways. To help you discern how styles interact and ferret out possible style conflicts, Dreamweaver 8 adds another view to the CSS Styles panel (see Figure 6-12). By clicking the Current button, the panel switches to Current Selection mode, which provides insight into how a selected item on a page—an image, a paragraph, or a table—is affected by inherited styles.

Tip: You can also switch the CSS Styles panel into Current Selection mode by selecting text on a page, and then clicking the new CSS button on the Property inspector. Doing so also opens the CSS panel, if it's closed—a nice shortcut. If the button's "grayed out," then the CSS panel is already opened in this mode.

Current Selection mode is really an incredible tool that's invaluable in diagnosing weird CSS behavior associated with inheritance and cascading. But like any incredible tool, it requires a good user's manual to learn how it works. The panel crams in a lot of information; here's a quick overview of what it provides:

- **A "summary" of style properties for the currently selected item in the "Summary for Selection" pane.** Remember that whole thing about how parents pass on attributes to child tags, and how as styles cascade through a page, they accumulate (which means, for example, it's possible to have an <h1> tag formatted by multiple styles from multiple style sheets)? The Summary for Selection section is like the grand total at the bottom of a spreadsheet. It tells you, in essence, what the selected element—a paragraph, a picture, and so on—looks like when a Web browser tallies up all of the styles and displays the page.

- **The origin of a particular property is displayed in the "About" pane** (Figure 6-12, top). If a headline is orange, but you never created an <h1> tag with an orange color, you can find out which style from which style sheet is passing its hideous orangeness to the heading.

- **A list of styles that apply to the current selection appears in the "Rules" pane** (Figure 6-12, bottom). Since any element can be on the receiving end of countless CSS properties handed down by parent tags, it's helpful to see a list of all the styles contributing to the current appearance of the selected object on the page.

• **The order of the cascade in the "Rules" pane** (Figure 6-12, bottom). Not only are styles that apply to the current selection listed, they're also listed in a particular order, with the most general style at the top and the most specific ones at the bottom. This means that when the same property exists in two (or more) styles, the style listed last (farthest down the list) wins.

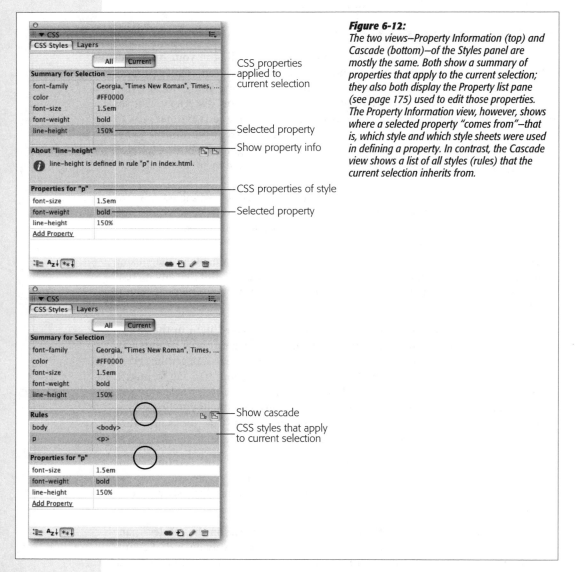

Figure 6-12:
The two views—Property Information (top) and Cascade (bottom)—of the Styles panel are mostly the same. Both show a summary of properties that apply to the current selection; they also both display the Property list pane (see page 175) used to edit those properties. The Property Information view, however, shows where a selected property "comes from"—that is, which style and which style sheets were used in defining a property. In contrast, the Cascade view shows a list of all styles (rules) that the current selection inherits from.

A few examples can help demonstrate how to read the CSS Style panel when it's in Current Selection mode. Figure 6-12 shows the CSS properties affecting a selection of text (in this case, a paragraph) on a Web page. The Summary for Selection pane lets you know that if you viewed this page in a Web browser, this paragraph would be displayed in bold using the Georgia typeface, at a font size of 1.5 ems, and with 150% line height (space between each line of text). When you select a property from the Summary for Selection pane, and then click the Show Property Information button (Figure 6-12, top), the About pane displays where the property comes from—in this case, that property belongs to the p tag style, which is defined in the internal style sheet of the file *index.html.*

You've seen the bottom part of this pane before. It's the Properties pane, and it's used to delete, add, and edit the properties of a style (see page 175). You simply click in the area to the right of the property's name to change its value, or click the Add Property link to select a new property for the style. Notice that in this example, the Properties pane contains fewer properties than the summary view. That's because it only displays properties of a single style (the <p> tag style), while the Summary view shows all properties inherited by the current selection.

Tip: Sometimes one or more of the three panes are too small for you to be able to see all the information displayed. You can use the gray bars containing the panes' names (circled in Figure 6-12, bottom) as handles and drag them up or down to reveal more or less of each pane.

Clicking the Show Cascade button (Figure 6-12, bottom) reveals a list of all styles that affect the current selection. In this case, you can see that two tag styles—one for the body tag and one for the p tag—contribute to styling the selected paragraph of text. In addition, as mentioned above, the order in which the styles are listed is important. The lower the name appears in the list, the more "specific" that style is—in other words, when several styles contain the same property, the property belonging to the style *lower* on the list wins out. (See page 182 for more on conflicts caused by cascading styles.)

The Properties pane provides even more information about conflicting properties. For example, Figure 6-13 shows that four styles are affecting the formatting of a single paragraph of text: three tag styles (<body>, <p>, and <p>) and one class style (.sidebar). Why two <p> tag styles? One is in an external style sheet, while the other belongs to the page's internal style sheet.

Clicking a style name in the Rules pane reveals that style's properties in the pane below. For example, in the bottom-left image in Figure 6-13, you can see that the *sidebar* class style has many properties, such as background color, text color, and so on. When a line appears through a property name (see the circled areas in Figure 6-13, bottom middle and bottom right), that property isn't applied to the current selection. Either it's overridden by a more specific style, or it's not an inherited property.

For example, the second-to-last style in the list in Figure 6-13 (bottom middle)—a <p> tag style—shows that it has a setting for the "font-family" property. In addition, there's a line through the property name, indicating that it doesn't apply to the current selection. Because the more specific ".sidebar" class style also has the

---

"font-family" property set (Figure 6-13, bottom left) in the battle of cascading style properties, ".sidebar" wins (see page 180 for more on inheritance and cascading).

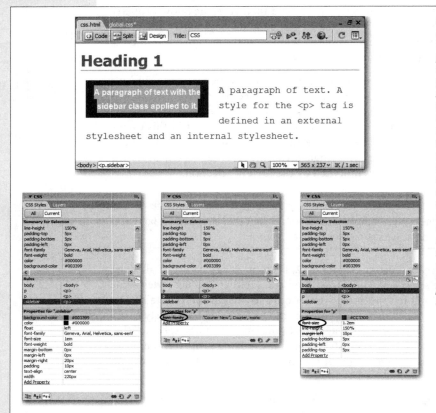

Figure 6-13:
Selecting the "Current" view of the CSS Styles panel lets you easily view all the properties for your Web page's styles. A line (circled in two of the panels below) strikes out properties from a style that don't apply to the selected paragraph (top). In this example, the font-family in the second <p> style is overridden by the font-family property in the more specific sidebar class style (bottom row, middle). Likewise, the sidebar class also overrides the font-size, color, and margin-left properties in the top <p> style (bottom row, right).

Tip: When you hover over a property name that's crossed out in the Properties pane, a pop-up window explains why the property doesn't apply. This is a big help when a certain property setting (such as a font color) from a style isn't being applied to your selection. The pop-up window explains which style it's in conflict with, providing you with the diagnostic information you need to go and fix the problem.

If your Web pages are elegantly simple and use only a couple of styles, you may not find much need for this aspect of the CSS Styles panel. But as you become more proficient (and adventurous) with CSS, you'll find that this panel is a great way to untangle masses of colliding and conflicting styles.

Advanced Styles

Tag and class styles are the most common types of styles, but they aren't the only ones available. There are many other style types with various functions and purposes, but Dreamweaver lumps them together under the term *advanced styles*. To be technically accurate, tag and class styles aren't really styles per se. In CSS lingo, they're known as different types of *selectors*.

A CSS selector is an instruction that tells a Web browser *what* it should apply the CSS formatting rules to. For example, a tag selector tells a browser to apply the formatting to *any* instance of a particular tag on the page. Thus, an *h1* tag style applies to *all* <h1> tags on a page. A class selector, on the other hand, applies only when the browser encounters the class name attached to an element on a page.

Note: For a detailed discussion of selectors, visit *http://css.maxdesign.com.au/selectutorial/*.

There are a variety of selectors in the CSS arsenal (a few of the most common and useful are mentioned below), but in Dreamweaver, you go about creating them all the same way: start by creating a CSS style, following the instructions on page 165. But when you get to the New CSS Rule window (Figure 6-2), instead of selecting the Tag or Class selector type, choose the Advanced option.

With the exception of four "pseudo-classes" (discussed next) in the advanced selector drop-down menu, you must type the selector name in the text field at the top of that window. As described in the following sections, each type of advanced selector has a different syntax. (The remainder of the process of creating the style is just like creating a tag or class style, and the process of editing or deleting these styles is also identical.)

Pseudo-Classes

When you select Advanced in the New CSS Rule menu, Dreamweaver lets you select one of four *pseudo-classes* from the Selector menu, as shown in Figure 6-14. These four options (a:link, a:active, a:visited, and a:hover) correspond to the types of links described in step 14 on page 40.

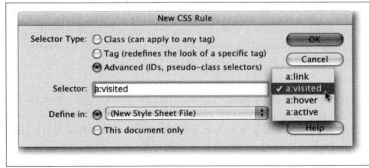

Figure 6-14:
Dreamweaver includes four advanced selector types in the Selector menu. These pseudo-classes affect how links appear.

For example, a:link represents the formatting state of an unvisited link on the page; a:active represents the look of the link as the visitor clicks it; a:visited represents the link's look after the visitor has already been to the linked page; and a:hover describes the look of the link as the mouse moves over it. This last option is particularly useful, since it works like a rollover image, but for text.

To use these pseudo-classes, select each in turn from the Selector menu and set its formatting characteristics (font color, size, underscore, and so on). You must, however, create these pseudo-classes in the order that they appear in the menu. (A helpful mnemonic for remembering this rule is LoVe HAte—that is, :link comes before :visited, which comes before :hover, which comes before :active.)

Using these styles, you could make your link text appear red and underscored before it's clicked, twice as large when the mouse moves over it, purple boldface when clicked, and pale pink after it's been visited. (All right, you might never be hired to do Martha Stewart's Web site, but you get the point.)

Note: When you use the Page Properties window to set colors for your links (see page 40), behind the scenes, Dreamweaver actually creates these pseudo-class styles in the page's internal style sheet.

These link pseudo-classes have one drawback: setting them affects *all* links on a page. In that respect, they're like tag styles, except they change the different *states* of a link (clicked, active, and so on).

If you want to use these styles for only certain links on a page, you could do the following: First, create a class style and apply it to each link you wish to have a special appearance. Then, create another new style, click the Advanced radio button, and type *a.className:link* (or *:active,* or *:hover,* or whichever state you wish to define), where *className* is the name of the class you applied to the link. (Alternatively, you could use contextual selectors to achieve the same goal, an advanced technique described on page 189.)

For example, say you have a set of five links that act as a navigation bar on the left side of a page. You want each of these text links to have a border and a background color, *and* you want the background color to change when a visitor moves her mouse over the link. Create a new class style named, say, *mainNav,* and then apply this style to each link (<a> tag). Then create your pseudo-classes for each of the different link states. For example, for the main link state, you could simply name the style *a.mainNav:link*; the visited link would be *a.mainNav:visited*; and so on.

IDs

An *ID* is a type of selector that lets you format a *unique* item on a page. You use an ID style to identify an object (or an area of a page) that appears only once—a banner, copyright notice, or main navigation bar, for example. IDs are frequently used with CSS-based layouts like those presented in Chapter 8.

An ID style is very similar to a class style, in that you supply the style's name and apply the style manually. However, while class styles begin with a period (.company, for example), ID styles must begin with the # symbol (#banner, for example).

Also, while you can apply a class style many times on a page, an ID style can appear only once per page.

Note: IDs are often assigned to a <div> tag. The <div> tag, which indicates a logical division of a page, is discussed on page 188.

To create an ID style, choose the Advanced option in the New CSS Rule window (see Figure 6-14), type the # symbol and then the style name—*#banner,* for example. Applying IDs can also be a little tricky, but the easiest method is to use the tag selector to apply an ID to a particular tag, as shown in Figure 6-15.

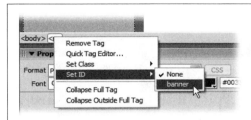

Figure 6-15:
You can use the contextual menu on the tag selector to apply an ID to a tag. Simply right-click (Control-click) a tag, choose Set ID, and then select the ID name from the menu. (Since an ID can be applied only once on a page, you won't see an already applied ID name in this list.)

Contextual Selectors (a.k.a. Descendent Selectors)

Tag styles have their drawbacks. While a tag style for the <p> tag makes simple work of formatting every paragraph on a page, it's also indiscriminate. You may not *want* every paragraph to look the same.

Maybe, for example, you want to divide a Web page into different sections—a sidebar and a main content area, for instance, using a smaller size text for paragraphs and headings in the sidebar. You *could* create two class styles—*sidebarText* and *mainText,* for example—and then apply them to the appropriate paragraphs in the respective parts of your design (<p class="sidebarText"> for sidebar paragraphs and <p class="mainText"> for body text). But who has that kind of time?

What you really need is a "smart" tag style, one that can adapt to its surroundings, like a chameleon, using the appropriate formatting depending on where it is in the page. Fortunately, CSS offers just such a type of style—*contextual selector.*

Note: "Contextual selector" is the name given in the original CSS standards. In the most recent incarnations of these rules, the name has been changed to "descendent selector." But because "contextual selector" is more descriptive, you'll see that term in this book.

A contextual selector lets you limit the application of a style to a certain context. For example, you can create a style that formats a <p> tag to be blue and 9 pixels tall, but *only* when that tag appears in a sidebar. How does a Web browser know the tag is in a sidebar? You tell it—usually by using another style.

For example, the Web page shown in Figure 6-16 has a common, table-based layout. The gray box on the left side of the page is a single table cell, while the white box to the right is another cell, containing the page's main content. By creating a class called .main and applying it to the <td> tag of the main cell, you set the context for all other HTML placed inside that cell. Now a heading tag (<h1>) that appears inside that cell is within the *context* of .main. Another way to think of it: Since the <h1> tag is nested inside of the table cell, the heading is a *descendent* of the cell—thus the newer name "descendent selector."

Note: The Cascading Style Sheets tutorial includes an example of the power of contextual selectors. See page 217.

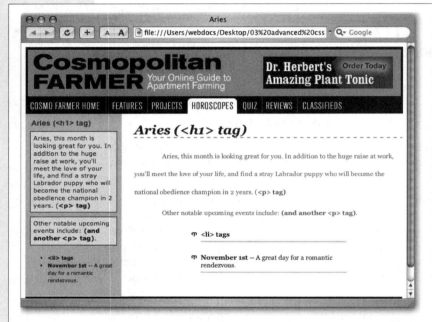

Figure 6-16:
Contextual selectors can reduce the amount of code used in a Web page. They also speed production by eliminating time-consuming formatting chores. In this example, the HTML code that appears within the left-side table cell is the same as the code in the right-side cell; only their contexts differ. The sidebar content is contained within a cell that's got a class style— .sidebar—applied to it. Thus the <h1>, <p>, and <li> tags are within the context of the .sidebar style.

Creating the "context"

There are a variety of ways that you can define the context of text, images, or other page content. Some are automatic, and some you'll craft yourself:

- HTML tags can automatically fall within the context of another tag, merely by being inside that tag. For example, if you want to emphasize a single word inside an <h1> tag, you can select the word and click the Bold button on the Property inspector. That step applies the <strong> tag to the word (see page 91). In essence, the context for this instance of the <strong> tag is the <h1> tag, since the <strong> tag is *inside* the <h1> tag.

Why would you care about this? Since headlines are already bold, the <strong> tag has no visual effect on the word inside the headline. However, you can create a contextual-selector style that could make the <strong> tag appear in italics, or red, or underlined, whenever it appears inside an <h1> tag.

- As in the example in Figure 6-16, applying a class style to a table cell—the <td> tag—makes everything *inside* that cell fall within the context of that class.

- Another common way to define an area of a page is to use an ID selector (described on page 188). You could apply an ID style to a table cell, or wrap an entire chunk of content inside a <div> tag and apply the ID to it. (See page 303 for more on the <div> tag.)

Creating contextual selectors

Creating contextual selectors is no more difficult than creating any other type of style. You follow the same process as described on page 165 for creating a style— but in the New CSS Rule window, select the Advanced option. You then type the contextual selector in the selector box. List the context for the style first, followed by a space and then a tag or other selector type. For example:

- To create a special look for the <strong> tag when it appears inside the <h1> tag, you would type *h1 strong* in the Selector box. The *h1* is the context in which the *strong* tag must appear for the formatting to apply.

- You use a similar naming scheme for tags that appear inside classes, too. Following the example in Figure 6-16, you could specify the look of paragraphs that appear inside another element with the class style .sidebar by typing *.sidebar p* into the Selector box. (Remember, classes begin with a period, so you must include one when creating the selector name.)

- Likewise, if you wanted to define the look of bulleted lists wherever they appear inside an ID Style named #banner, you'd type *#banner ul* in the Selector box.

- You can even create very complex contextual selectors that involve multiple elements. For example, to format anything inside an <li> tag that's inside a <td> tag that's inside a tag with the class style mainStory applied to it, you'd create a selector named *.mainStory td li*.

Tip: When working with contextual selectors, it may help you to read the selector name *backward*. Take, for example, the selector *.mainStory td li*. The *li* means "this style applies to the <li> tag"; the *td* means "but only when it's inside a <td> tag"; and the final *.mainStory* means "and only when that <td> tag is inside another tag that has the class .mainStory applied to it."

After you name the contextual selector, click OK in the New CSS Rule window. You're ready to start adding the CSS properties that define the formatting of your contextual-selector style. In other words, proceed as you normally would when creating *any* type of style.

Note: The type of selector used also affects the cascade (see page 182). ID selectors are considered more "specific" than class styles, which are more specific than tag styles. In general, this means that properties from an ID style override properties from a class style. Contextual selectors, which include combinations of tag, class, and ID names—for example *#banner h1,* or *.main p,* or *h1 b*—have even more force since the specificity adds up. For example, say you create a *p* tag style with a bright-red text color, and a contextual selector, *.sidebar p,* with purple text. Any paragraphs inside another element—a table cell, for example—with the .sidebar style is purple—*not* red.

Style Properties

Cascading Style Sheets are a powerful and complex technology, providing *many* more formatting options than HTML alone. In fact, Dreamweaver lets you set 67 different CSS properties using the Rule Definition window. The following pages cover each of the eight Rule Definition categories and the properties available from each. (If you'd prefer an online reference, don't miss the built-in CSS reference available from the Window → Reference command; it's described more completely on page 353.)

Note: As noted earlier, not all Web browsers can display the many different formatting options available through Cascading Style Sheets. Dreamweaver, in its zeal to give you access to as many options as possible, actually lets you set properties that don't work in many browsers, or that work differently in different browsers.

There's some hope, however. Here are two sites whose charts detail which CSS properties work on which browsers: *www.westciv.com/style_master/academy/browser_support/* and *http://macedition.com/cb/resources/abridgedcsssupport.html.*

Type Properties

As the name implies, the Type category of the Rule Definition window lets you set formatting options that affect text (see Figure 6-17). Here are the settings you can adjust:

- **Font.** You choose a font for the style from the Font menu. As when using the Property inspector to select a font (see page 91), you choose from *groups* of fonts rather than the specific one you have your heart set on. Unfortunately, your array of choices is no better than in HTML. Dreamweaver also lets you create your own "first-choice, second-choice..." font choices from this menu, exactly as described on page 94.

- **Size.** Unlike HTML, where font size is defined using a number from 1 to 7, CSS offers a dizzying array of size choices.

  If you want to make sure your text appears at the same size regardless of browser or platform, type a number in the Size box and select "pixels" from the unit menu to its right. Twelve pixels is a good size for regular type.

There's one downside to this approach: pixel values prevent Windows visitors using Internet Explorer from adjusting the size of text on the screen using their Web browsers' text size up/down controls. (Other Windows browsers and most Mac browsers let users resize pixel-sized text.)

Note: This isn't entirely true. Internet Explorer can be tweaked to allow resizing of pixel-sized text, but you have to change some of the default settings of the browser. That's something most people would never do.

Another option is to use *ems*. An em is a relative measurement that, when applied to text, works just like a percentage. One em starts out equal to a Web browser's default font size. In Internet Explorer for Windows, for example, the default font size is 16 pixels, so 1 em (or 100 percent of the default) equals 16 pixels. However, since an em is a relative measurement, if some visitor changed his default font size to 20 pixels, any text sized to 1 em would appear 20 pixels tall in his browser.

And to make things more complicated, when you use ems to define the size of text that's inside some other element with a fixed text size, the em is then determined relative to *that other element*. For example, say you created a style for the <body> tag that set the text size to .8 ems (in other words, 80 percent of the default text size). If the browser's default font size is 16 pixels, then all text in the body is 13 pixels tall. However, if you then define a *p* tag style that also has a text size of .8 ems, text modified by that *p* tag won't be 13 pixels tall. It's .8 ems of the *body's* .8 ems—in other words, 80 percent of 80 percent of 16 pixels, or roughly 10 pixels tall. If you find that your text is smaller than you think it should be, this cascading percentage effect may be the problem.

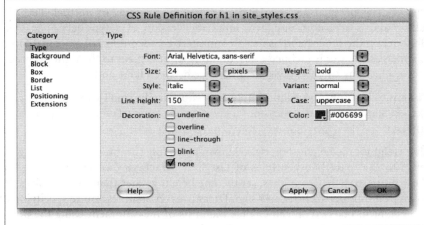

Figure 6-17:
You'll visit the Type category frequently while creating CSS styles. You can set many different properties for formatting text; it's the most common use of CSS. Rest assured that, unlike a lot of other CSS properties, type settings work well in almost all browsers that understand Cascading Style Sheets.

Note: Setting sizes for fonts is a hotly debated topic in CSS circles. For more in-depth discussion, check out the resources on this page: *http://css-discuss.incutio.com/?page=FontSize*.

- **Weight.** Weight refers to the thickness of the font. The Weight menu offers 13 different choices. Normal and bold are the most common, and they work in all browsers that understand CSS. See Figure 6-18 for details.

Figure 6-18:
The numeric values 100–900 are intended to work with fonts that have many different weights (ultrathin, thin, light, extra bold, and so on). 400 is normal; 700 is the same as bold. However, in today's browsers, you'll notice no difference between the values 100–500. Similarly, choosing any of the values from 600 to 900 just gets you bold text. You're better off keeping things simple and choosing either "normal" or "bold" when picking a font weight.

- **Style.** In this peculiar instance, Style means italic, oblique, or normal. Technically, italic is a custom-designed, emphatic version of a type face, *like this*. Oblique, on the other hand, is just a computerized adaptation of a normal font, in which each letter is inclined a certain number of degrees to the right. In practical application, there's no visible difference between italic and oblique.

- **Variant.** This pop-up menu simply lets you specify small-caps type, if you like—a slightly formal, fancy-looking type style much favored by attorneys' offices.

- **Line Height.** Line height, otherwise known as *leading* (pronounced "LED-ing"), refers to the space between lines of text in a paragraph (see Figure 6-19). To allow more space between lines, set the line height greater than the font size. (If you type a number without a % sign, Dreamweaver assumes you're specifying a line height in pixels. You can change the units of measurement using the pop-up menu to the right of the Line Height field.)

Tip: A good approach for line height is to type in a percentage measurement, such as *120%*, which is relative to the size of the text (see "Size," described earlier); if your text is 10 pixels tall, the space from the base of one line of text to the next is 12 pixels (120% of 10). Now, if you change the size of the text, the *relative* space between lines remains the same.

Normal, the default setting (top paragraph in Figure 6-19), uses a line height that's slightly larger than the height of the text. You don't get access to the pop-up menu of measurement units (pixels, points, %, and so on) unless you choose "value" from this menu.

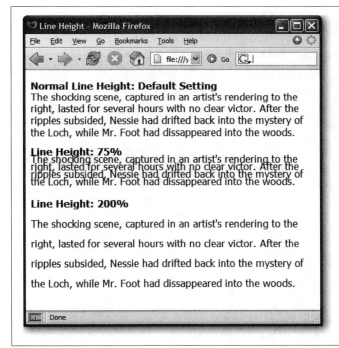

Figure 6-19:
Control the space between lines with the Line Height property (which you'll find in the CSS Rule Definition dialog box). In this example, each paragraph's text is set in 16-pixel Tahoma. With CSS, you can make lines bump into each other by setting a low line-height value (middle paragraph), or spread them far apart by using a larger value (bottom paragraph).

- **Case.** From this menu, you can set up automatic capitalization of the text in this style. To capitalize the first letter of each word, choose "capitalize." The "upper-case" option gives you all-capitals typing, while "lowercase" makes all letters lowercase. The factory setting is "none," which has no effect on the text.

- **Decoration.** This strange assortment of five checkboxes lets you dress up your text, mostly in unattractive ways. "Underline," "overline," and "line-through" add horizontal lines below, above, or directly through the affected text, respectively. Turning on "blink" makes affected text blink on and off (but only in some browsers); unless you want to appear on one of those "worst Web site of the week" lists, avoid it. You can apply any number of decorative types per style, except with "none," which, obviously, can't be chosen along with any of the other options.

Tip: On certain forward-thinking Web sites these days, text links don't appear underlined. Instead, they show up in a different color. You, too, can perform this trendy design stunt, just by redefining the <a> tag with Cascading Style Sheets, turning on the "none" option for the Decoration property, and voilà! No more underlines. Use this technique with care, however; most Web surfers have grown accustomed to associating underlines with clickable links. If you do remove an underline, use some other cue—bold and colorful text, for example—to indicate that the text is a link. In addition, using pseudo-classes (page 187), you can add or remove the underline for certain *states* of a link. For example, you can hide the line on a normal <a> tag but make it appear on the hover state (when a visitor's mouse moves over the link), or vice versa.

- **Color.** Set the color of the style's text using Dreamweaver's color box, which is described on page 41.

FREQUENTLY ASKED QUESTION

Pixels, Points, Picas, Oh My

When it comes to font size units, I never know which one to pick; which one should I use?

Specifying sizes, whether it's the size of a font on the page, or the width and height of a sidebar, is a common task when creating CSS styles. You'll notice that CSS lets you choose from a wide range of measuring systems—everything from the screen-dependent pixel to picas, points, and more. Most of these aren't relevant to designing pages that display on a computer screen. After all, a monitor doesn't really understand the concept of an inch—even if your display is set to 72 dots per inch, 72 dots may occupy a half-inch, an inch, or more depending on the screen's resolution (which you can change from 800 × 600 to 1600 × 1200 on the *same* monitor). The same goes for centimeters and millimeters. The bottom line? Skip 'em.

In general, stick to pixels, ems, and percentages. Pixel values are useful for dictating exact sizes on the screen, whereas ems and percentages are relative measurements. An em is a relative measurement based on the default text size of the browser viewing the page. Percentages are also a relative measurement and come in handy when your design needs to accommodate different sized monitors; for example, say you wanted a particular paragraph to always fill up half the screen, no matter how wide the Web browser window. Setting the width of that paragraph to 50

percent ensures that the paragraph resizes to fit exactly 50 percent of any browser window. This type of arrangement is useful for "liquid layouts," like those discussed in the next chapter on page 240.

Points and picas (two types of measurement used in typography and printed material) can also come in handy when you want your design to look just as good when it comes out of a laser printer. A point, in the computer world, is 1/72 of an inch; a pica is 12 points. You're probably used to "points" if you've used a word processor or a page-layout program; 12 points is a common size for type in these kinds of applications. Picas and points also are used by your inkjet or laser printer, which would be at a loss to understand what you meant by 12 pixels. Use this type of measurement when defining styles in an external style sheet that you attach using Dreamweaver's "printer media" option (see page 169). By doing so, you can create "printer-friendly" font styles that produce elegant looking copies from your printer.

Background Properties

While you're probably familiar with changing the background colors of Web pages, tables, and table cells, Cascading Style Sheets provide even more options for adding colors and images to the backgrounds of your styles (see Figure 6-20).

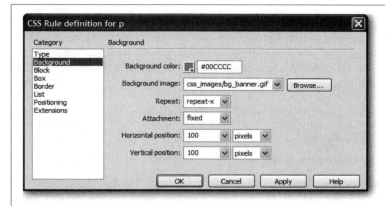

Figure 6-20:
The CSS Background category lets you specify a background color for a style; it also lets you control the placement of background images. Dreamweaver can't preview the "Fixed" option for the Attachment property (page 198), so to get an accurate view of what this property does, you need to preview it in a Web browser.

Background color

Any object can have a background color: a single word, a paragraph, or the Web page itself. Using this color box, you can redefine the <td> (table cell) tag, for example, using a light-blue background color (every table cell on the page gets filled with that light-blue color), or create a "reversed-out" text effect for headlines, by setting a dark background color behind a light text color; the background color looks like a box out of which jumps the light-colored headline.

Background image

Add a background image to the style by clicking the Browse button and selecting an image from your site. You can also type an absolute URL, starting with *http://*, to use an image off the Web.

To fill your entire page background with some repeating graphic, you could either redefine the <body> tag using this property, or create a class style with a Background Image property and apply it to the <body> tag as described on page 171.

You can even control how the image tiles (repeats) and where it's placed on the page (see the following sections). Furthermore, you can add background images to any *individual* element on your page: paragraphs, tables, layers, and so on.

Background images appear above any background color, so you can (and often will) combine the two. For example you may want to position an interesting graphic on top of a colorful background.

Tip: One common byte-saving technique is to create an image that looks like a button and then use it for the background image of navigation links on a page. The links themselves include text—"Home," "About Us," and so on—but the background of each link looks like a graphical button. The main benefit of this technique is that you don't need to create separate graphics for each button.

Background repeat

Background images—as the background of either a page (page 39) or of a table (page 253)—normally fill the available space by tiling (that is, repeating over and over again) across and down. A small image of a carrot added to the background of a page, for example, appears as a field of carrots—one next to another, row after row.

But with CSS, you can control how the background image repeats. You can select from the following options:

- **repeat** tiles the image horizontally and vertically. This is the factory setting.

- **repeat-x** and **repeat-y** display a horizontal and vertical band of images, respectively. So if you'd like to have a single row of images appear at the top of a page, use the repeat-x option; it's a good way to add a graphical background to a banner. repeat-y, on the other hand, is great for a graphical sidebar that appears down the left edge of a page.

- **no-repeat** displays the image one time only.

Background attachment

By default, the background image on a page scrolls with the rest of the page, so that as you scroll to read a long Web page, the image scrolls along with the text.

But using CSS, you can lock the image in place by choosing "fixed" from the Attachment menu. For example, say you added your company's logo to the background of a page and set the Repeat property (described above) to "no-repeat." The logo now appears only once in the upper-left corner of the page. If you use the "fixed" option for this property, when a visitor scrolls the page, the logo remains fixed in the upper-left corner. (Choosing "scroll" from the Attachment menu means, of course, that the background image scrolls with the page.)

Note: Internet Explorer for Windows supports the "fixed" setting only when it's applied to the <body> tag.

Horizontal and vertical position

Using these controls, you can specify a position for the affected text or other Web page element. The Horizontal Position options are: "left," "center," and "right." You can also choose "(value)," type an exact number in the box, and then select a unit of measurement from the menu to the right. Similarly, the Vertical Position options include "top," "center," and "bottom," or you can enter a specific value.

These positioning options refer to the position of the styled object. For example, suppose you created a class style that included a background image with Horizontal and Vertical Position both set to *center*. Then you applied that class style to a paragraph. The background image would appear in the center of that *paragraph,* not in the center of the Web page (see Figure 6-21).

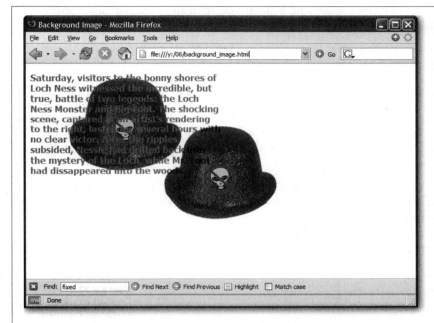

Figure 6-21:
Background images aren't just for the body of a Web page. You can apply styles that include background images to any selection, even a paragraph of text. Here, a class style with a background image is set to "no-repeat" (the image won't tile) and to center horizontally and vertically. The style was applied to the body of the page, resulting in the graphic appearing smack dab in the middle of the window. Meanwhile, the same style was applied to a paragraph; this time, the image floats right in the middle of the paragraph.

Likewise, if you set the horizontal position of the image to 10 pixels and the vertical position to 20 pixels, the image would start 10 pixels from the left edge of the paragraph and 20 pixels from the top edge.

And if you wanted to place an image in the exact middle of the page, you'd choose "center" from both the Horizontal and Vertical Position menus, set the Repeat property to "no-repeat," and apply the style to the page's <body> tag (see Figure 6-21).

Block Properties

The Block Properties panel is a hodgepodge of CSS settings that affect how letters and words are displayed (see Figure 6-22).

Despite this category's name, these properties don't just apply to block-level elements (paragraphs, headlines, and so on). You can apply a style with these properties to even a single word or two. (The one exception is the Text Align property, which can apply only to paragraphs and other block-level elements.)

- **Word spacing.** This property helps you clean up text by adding or removing space *between* words. The default value, "normal," leaves a normal, single space between words. If you want words in a sentence to be spaced   apart   like   this, then type a value of about 10 pixels. (Choose Value from the first pop-up menu, then the units you want from the second one.) The bigger the number, the larger the gap between words. You can also *remove* space between words by using a negative number—a great choice when you want to make your pages difficult to read.

- **Letter spacing.** This property works just like word spacing, but governs the space between *letters*. To add space l i k e t h i s, type a value of about 5 pixels. The result can make long passages of text hard to read, but a little space between letters can add a dramatic flair to short headlines and movie titles.

- **Vertical alignment.** With this property, you can control the alignment of an object —such as an image or movie—relative to other items around it. This feature works a lot like the image-alignment options discussed on page 133 (see Figure 5-7).

Two notable additions—"sub" and "super"—also let you create superscript and subscript styles when used on text. This property is a godsend when you want to properly format a trademark, copyright symbol, or footnote reference. For example, in the trademark symbol in *National Exasperator™*, the letters TM were selected and the "super" alignment was applied.

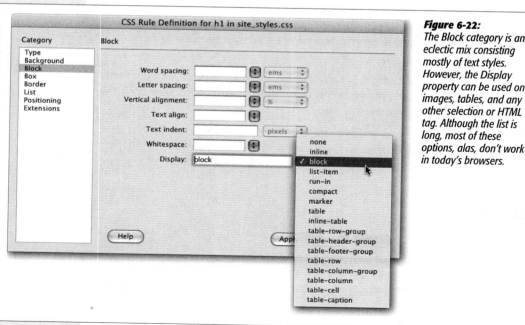

Figure 6-22:
The Block category is an eclectic mix consisting mostly of text styles. However, the Display property can be used on images, tables, and any other selection or HTML tag. Although the list is long, most of these options, alas, don't work in today's browsers.

Tip: The "sub" and "super" alignment options don't change the size of text. If you want to create true subscript or superscript (for chemical symbols, trademark or copyright symbols, and so on), you should also use a smaller font size in the style; 75 percent works great.

• **Text align.** This property controls the alignment of a block-level element like a paragraph or table. You can choose from among the usual suspects—"left," "center," "right," or even "justify." (Like the text in this paragraph, justified text has both the left and right edges of the text aligned.)

Avoid this option, however. Because Web browsers don't have the advanced controls that page-layout software does, they usually do an awful job of justifying text on a computer screen. The results are usually difficult to read and ugly.

• **Text indent.** This useful option lets you indent the first line of a paragraph. If you enter 15 pixels, you give each paragraph an attractive first-line indent, exactly as in a real word processor.

You can also use a *negative* number, which makes the first line extend past the *left* margin of the paragraph, creating a hanging indent (or *outdent*)—a nice effect for bulleted lists or glossary pages. (Beware: some browsers have trouble with negative values for this property.)

• **Whitespace.** This property controls how the browser displays extra white space (spaces, tabs, returns, and so on). Web browsers normally ignore extra spaces in the HTML of a page, reducing them to a single space character between words and other elements (see page 66). The "pre" option functions just like the HTML <pre> tag: extra white space (like tabs, multiple spaces, and carriage returns) *in the HTML code* appear in the document window (see page 79 for more on this option). The "nowrap" option prevents lines from breaking (and wrapping to the next line) when they reach the end of the browser window.

• **Display** defines how a Web browser should display a particular element like a paragraph or a link. You may be overwhelmed by the range of choices for this property—and you may be underwhelmed when you find out that most of these options aren't supported by most browsers.

Most CSS-capable browsers understand only three of the options: "none," "inline," and "block." The "block" option treats any item styled with this property as a block—separated from other content by space above and below it. This is how paragraphs and headings normally appear. But you can apply this value to a link (which normally appears inside of a block-level element like a paragraph) to turn it into its own block. In this way, you can transform links that appear next to each other into a series of links stacked one on top of the next.

The "inline" option treats the item like part of the current block or paragraph, so that any item styled with this property (like a picture) flows together with other items around it, as if it were part of the same paragraph. This property is frequently used to take a bulleted list of links and turn it into a horizontal navigation bar. For a good tutorial on this topic, visit *http://css.maxdesign.com. au/listutorial/horizontal_introduction.htm.*

The "none" option is the most fun: It *turns off* the display of an item. In other words, any text or item styled with this option doesn't appear on the page. You can use JavaScript programming to switch this property on and off, making items seem to appear and disappear. In fact, Dreamweaver's Change Property behavior provides one simple way to do this (see page 440).

Box Properties

CSS lets you control the space that appears around any affected Web page element. You work with those properties in the Box category of the CSS Rule Definition window (see Figure 6-23).

- **Width and Height.** You can specify a width and height for any styled object using these properties. Web designers use these settings most often to control layers, using Dreamweaver's Layer tools (see page 307), but they can also affect other Web elements. For example, if you want a paragraph to be 100 pixels wide, create a class style with the Width property set to 100 pixels and apply it to the paragraph. You'll often use the Width property in conjunction with the Float property (see the following paragraph) to do things like create a box with a set width that floats to either the left or right side of the page—a common format for pull-quotes, message boxes, and sidebars.

- **Float.** If you want to move an object to the left or right side of the page and have other content wrap around it, use the Float property. For example, if you want an image to appear at the right side of the page and have text flow around its left and bottom edges, choose "right" from the Float menu. The option behaves just like the right and left alignment options for images (page 132) and tables (page 251).

Note: The Float property has many uses, from aligning images to the right or left side of the page to creating drop caps and thumbnail photo galleries. For an excellent introduction and set of tutorials on this subject, visit *http://css.maxdesign.com.au/floatutorial/*.

- **Clear.** Clear *prevents* an element from wrapping around any object with a right or left Float property (see above). You may want, for example, all Heading 1 paragraphs to stand out on their own lines and not wrap around an image with a right float. In that case, you'd choose the "right" option from the Clear menu when you're styling the <h1> tag.

- **Padding.** Padding is the gap that separates the content of the style—such as a paragraph of text or an image—and its border (see page 205). For example, if you put a 1-pixel border around an image and want to add 10 pixels of space between the image and the border, type *10* into the top padding box and choose "pixels" from the pop-up menu. Turn off the "Same for all" box if you wish to set the padding around each edge separately; then, type values into each of the four boxes.

Warning: Unfortunately, Internet Explorer 5 for Windows doesn't handle the Box model correctly. If you set the padding or borders of a style, Internet Explorer displays the element smaller than other browsers, ruining the layout of your Web page. For more information on this problem and a clever workaround, visit *http://css-discuss.incutio.com/?page=BoxModelHack.*

- **Margin.** The margin is the outermost space surrounding an element (Figure 6-23). It surrounds the border and padding properties of the style and lets you add space between one element and another. Use any of the values—pixels, percentages, and so on—that CSS supports.

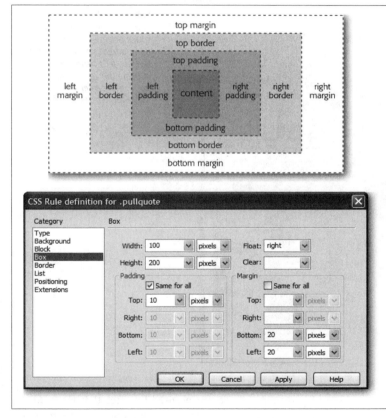

Figure 6-23:
Top: In the CSS Box model, every style is composed of multiple boxes, one inside the other. Each box controls certain display properties of the style. For example, the outermost box of a style is called the margin. It controls the space between the border of the style and any other objects around the styled object, such as images, paragraphs, or tables.

Bottom: This dialog box controls the margins and padding around a styled object that uses the Box category. Its fields correspond to the measurements shown in the top diagram. For a discussion of the Box model from the World Wide Web Consortium, visit: www.w3.org/TR/CSS21/box.html.

Tip: You can also use the Margin properties to *eliminate* a margin entirely, if, for example, you don't like the space that browsers automatically insert between paragraphs. Type *0* in the Top margin box and *0* in the Bottom margin box to create a style with no top or bottom margins.

CSS Layout Box Model

Margins and padding are invisible. They also have similar effects: 5 pixels of left padding adds 5 pixels of space to the left edge of a style, just like with a 5-pixel left margin. Because you can't see padding or margins (just the empty space they make), it's often difficult to know if the gap between, say, the banner at the top of your page and the main area of content is caused by the style applied to the banner or the main area. You also can't always tell if any extra space is caused by a padding or margin setting. Dreamweaver 8 adds a helpful diagnostic tool that lets you see these invisible properties clearly.

When you select a <div> tag (see page 303) that has margin or padding properties set, Dreamweaver draws a box around that div and adds slanting lines to indicate the space occupied by margins and padding (see Figure 6-24).

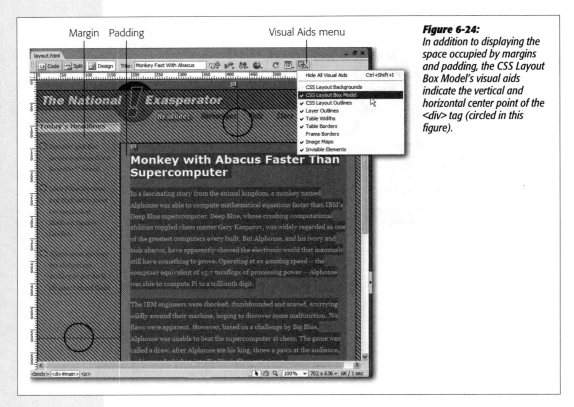

Figure 6-24:
In addition to displaying the space occupied by margins and padding, the CSS Layout Box Model's visual aids indicate the vertical and horizontal center point of the <div> tag (circled in this figure).

Margins appear outside of padding and are represented by lines that slant *downward* from left to right; padding appears inside of the margin and is represented by lines that go *upward* from left to right. For example, in Figure 6-24, the area that contains the main story is enclosed in a <div> tag with an ID style named *main* applied to it. When that div is selected (see the tag selector in the lower-left corner of the figure), Dreamweaver highlights the margins and padding values that are defined in that ID style. As you can see, there's a considerable amount of margin on both the top and left edges, and a smaller amount of padding (20 pixels) applied to both the left and right edges.

Note: Dreamweaver also displays visual aids for margins and padding values around any element with a style that has its display property set to "block" (see page 201) or that uses either "absolute" or "relative" positioning (these properties are described in Chapter 8 on page 297).

If you find these visual aids confusing, you can turn them off via the Visual Aids menu in the document window (see Figure 6-24) or by choosing View → Visual Aids → Layout Box Model. These same steps turn the margin and padding visual aids back on.

Border Properties

Only a few elements can have borders in HTML: tables, images, and cells. With CSS, however, you can add a border to any object, from an image to a paragraph to a single exclamation point (see Figure 6-25).

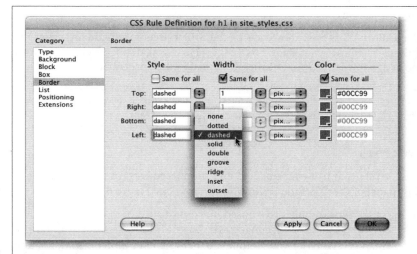

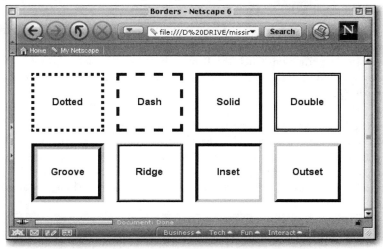

Figure 6-25:
Top: Add colorful and stylish borders to paragraphs, images, tables, and links with the CSS Border properties. Turning on only the bottom border for a paragraph is a great way to add a horizontal rule between paragraphs. While HTML's Horizontal Rule object also does this, only CSS lets you control the color.

Bottom: The eight different border styles provide interesting visual diversity to the otherwise plain border.

Even better, you can control each *side* of the border independently with its own width and color settings, or even turn *off* some parts of the border:

- **Style.** This menu lets you specify the type of line used for the border. Dreamweaver gives you more options than a frame shop: "none" (the default choice), "dotted," "dashed," "solid," "double," "groove," "ridge," "inset," and "outset." You can use a different style for each edge, or select a style from the top menu and turn on the "Same for all" box to apply the same style to all four borders.

- **Border Widths.** You can set the border around each side of a styled object separately. Choose one of the preset widths—"thin," "medium," "thick," or "auto"—or, if you choose "(value)" from the pop-up menu, you can type a value into the Width box and select a unit of measurement from the pop-up menu to the right. Again, you can choose from a wide range of types: "pixels," "percentage," "inches," and so on. If you want to eliminate the border on one side, type *0* into the appropriate box.

- **Border Colors.** You can color each of the four borders individually using the ubiquitous Dreamweaver color box (page 41). If you don't assign any colors, but do assign border *widths*, Dreamweaver makes the borders black.

Note: You have to select a style from the pop-up menu to see the borders. If you leave this option blank or select "none," you won't see the borders even if you set the width and color.

List Properties

To exercise greater control over bulleted and numbered lists, use the CSS options on the List panel of the CSS Rule Definition window (see Figure 6-26).

- **Type.** Select the type of bullet to be used in front of a list item. Options include: "disc," "circle," "square," "decimal" (1., 2., 3.), "lower-roman" (i, ii, iii), "upper-roman" (I, II, III), "lower-alpha" (a, b, c), "upper-alpha" (A, B, C), and "none" (no bullet at all).

- **Bullet image.** For the ultimate control of your bullet icon, skip the boring options preprogrammed into a Web browser (like disc, circle, square, or decimal) and supply your own. Click the Browse button and select a graphics file from your site folder. Make sure the graphic is appropriate bullet material—in other words, small.

Tip: A more versatile solution to adding bullet images to a list is the Background Image property (see page 197). Since you can accurately position a background image, you can easily tweak the placement of your bullets. Here's how to do it: Create a style for the <li> tag (or a class style that you apply to each <li> tag), make sure you set the List property type to "none" (this hides the bullet), set the background image to your graphical bullet, and play with the background position values (page 198). Playing with the padding values (page 202) helps position the text relative to the image.

- **Position.** This property controls how the bullet is placed relative to the list item's text. The "outside" option places the bullet outside of the margin of the text, exactly the way bulleted lists normally appear on a Web page. "Inside," on the other hand, displays the bullet within the text margin, so that the left edge of the *bullet* aligns with the left margin; Figure 6-26 should make the effect clearer.

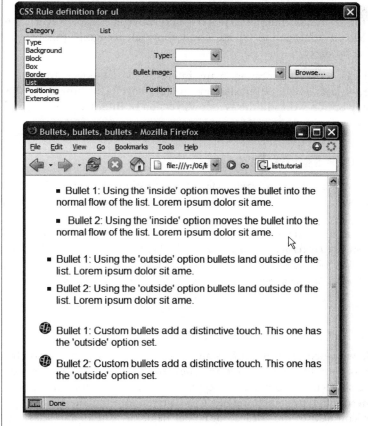

Figure 6-26:
Top: Take control of your bulleted and numbered lists using the CSS Rule Definition window's List panel. With Cascading Style Sheets, you can even supply your own graphic bullets.

Bottom: A bullet-crazed Web page, for illustration purposes. Parading down the screen, you can see "inside" bullets, "outside" bullets, and bullets made from graphics.

Positioning Properties

Cascading Style Sheets may be useful for formatting text and adding background colors and margins to objects, but this technology is also intended as a structural aid for laying out Web pages. You'll learn about these properties and how to set them on page 297.

Extensions

The final category in the CSS Rule Definition window is listed last for a good reason: not all Web browsers support its properties properly:

- **Page Break.** This property specifies, when your visitor makes a printout of your page, whether a page breaks before or after the styled object. You could apply this, for example, to the <h1> tag in order to make sure each printed page begins with a Heading 1 paragraph.

- **Cursor.** Of all the Extension properties, this one holds the most promise. When a visitor moves the mouse over an object with this style applied, this property changes the cursor shape to one of 15 different designs (a hand, an hourglass, or a crosshair, for example). Internet Explorer 4 and above, Netscape Navigator 6 and above, Mozilla, Safari, and Opera 5 and above all recognize this professional-looking property.

- **Filter.** The Filter property can apply many interesting visual effects to a page; for example, it can add a drop shadow to an image. Unfortunately, this Microsoft-only option works in the Windows version of Internet Explorer, and no other browsers.

Cascading Style Sheets Tutorial

In this tutorial, you'll create an external style sheet for a Web page on the *National Exasperator* Web site.

Note: As usual, this tutorial requires some half-finished starter documents from the Web. Using your Web browser, visit *www.sawmac.com/dw8/*. Click the Tutorials link to go to the tutorials page. Then, click the link for the Cascading Style Sheets Tutorial. When the files are downloaded and decompressed, you should have a folder named DWCSS on your computer, containing the Web pages and graphics for this tutorial.

Setting Up

Once you've downloaded the tutorial files and opened Dreamweaver, choose the DWCSS folder as your site folder, using the site-definition routine described on page 154. (For a shortcut, choose Site → New Site. In the Site Definition window, click the Advanced tab, type something like *CSS Tutorial* into the Site Name field, click the folder icon next to the Local Root Folder field, navigate to and select the DWCSS folder, and then click Choose or Select. Finally, click OK.)

To ensure that your files preview correctly, you'll need to make sure that a particular Dreamweaver preference is set:

1. **Press Ctrl+U (⌘-U) to open the Preferences window.**

   Alternatively, you can use Edit → Preferences (Dreamweaver → Preferences on Mac).

2. **Select the CSS Styles category and make sure the "Open CSS files when modified" checkbox is *not* turned on.**

   When this setting's turned on and you edit a CSS style in an external style sheet, Dreamweaver opens the CSS file. Unfortunately, when you preview your page, Dreamweaver doesn't *save* the CSS file, and since the browser is using the saved version of the file, it doesn't know about (or display) the styles you just created! For more on this dilemma and other solutions, see page 175.

3. **Click OK to close the window.**

Now you're ready to begin defining a style sheet.

Creating an External Style Sheet

In this example, you'll create a collection of styles for the headline news stories on the *National Exasperator* Web site.

1. **Choose File → Open; then navigate to, and double-click, the file in the DWCSS folder called *story1.html*.**

The Web page contains a headline news story from the *National Exasperator* (see Figure 6-27). The page's text is a bit boring looking, so you'll use CSS to spiff it up.

To start, you'll create a style for basic paragraphs and create an external style sheet at the same time.

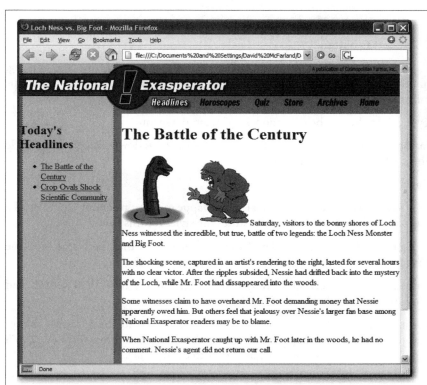

Figure 6-27:
Add style to this rather plain Web page using Cascading Style Sheets. In this tutorial, you'll improve the rather ho-hum appearance of the left sidebar and main section of this page—the white area in this figure. See Figure 6-37 for the completed page.

2. **If the CSS Styles panel isn't already open, choose Window → CSS Styles (or press Shift+F11).**

   The CSS Styles panel opens.

3. **At the bottom of the CSS Styles panel, click the New Style (+) button (see Figure 6-1).**

   The New CSS Rule window opens (see Figure 6-28). You'll first pick the type of style you wish to create.

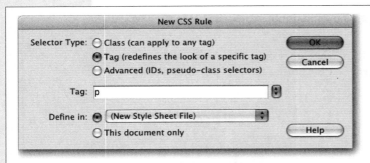

Figure 6-28:
If you've already attached an external style sheet to a page, you can select its name from the "Define in" menu. That way, the new style's added to that file. Your other option, which is what you're doing in this tutorial, is to create the new style sheet when you first create a style.

4. **Click the Tag button.**

   This lets you create a style for a particular HTML tag—in this case, the <p> tag. In other words, you're going to create a formatting rule that applies automatically to every basic paragraph.

5. **Type *p* into the Tag box, or choose "p" from the menu.**

   In the "Define in" section of the New CSS Rule window, click the New Style Sheet File button (see Figure 6-28).

6. **Click OK.**

   The Save Style Sheet File As dialog box appears. You're about to create the file—an external style sheet—that stores the styles for this page.

7. **Navigate to the DWCSS folder. Type *headlines.css* in the File Name box (the Save As field on the Mac), and then click Save to save the file.**

   Cascading Style Sheet files always end in .css; that's how Web servers and browsers can tell what kind of file they are.

   Having created the external style sheet, you can now create the first style, as suggested by the sudden appearance of the CSS Rule Definition window. You'll choose a font, set a size, and assign a color to the <p> tag.

8. From the Font menu, choose "Georgia, Times New Roman, Times, serif"; in the Size box, type *.8*; from the menu to the right, select "ems"; and in the Color field, type *#003366.*

Next, you'll add a little *leading* (space between lines of text) to the paragraph to make the page easier to read.

9. In the "Line height" box, type *150*, and from the menu to the right, select "%."

The CSS Rule Definition window should look like Figure 6-29.

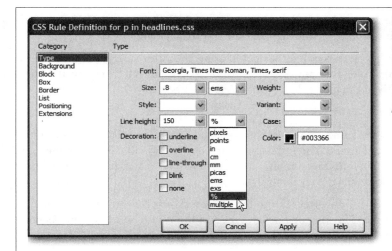

Figure 6-29:
You can set the CSS equivalents of HTML text formatting options from the Type category of the CSS Rule Definition window. (If Cadet Blue doesn't do anything for you, click the color box and choose a color you prefer.)

10. Click **Apply.**

You can actually preview the look of a tag style without closing the CSS Rule Definition window—just drag the window out of the way.

11. Click **OK.**

The CSS Rule Definition window closes and the paragraphs of text on the page are now formatted according to the style you just created. As you may have noticed, you didn't have to select the text to apply this style. Since it's an HTML tag style, it's applied *automatically* wherever the tag appears on the page.

Now, you'll create a style for the title of the story, which is an <h1> tag.

12. **On the CSS Styles panel, click the New Style button.**

The New CSS Rule window opens. The Tag button is already selected, and the menu in the "Define in" option lists the new external style sheet—*headlines.css.* In other words, Dreamweaver will add the new style to this external style sheet. All you need to do now is identify which tag you want to redefine.

13. **In the Tag box, type *h1*, or choose "h1" from the menu, and then click OK.**

    The CSS Rule Definition Window appears.

14. **From the Font menu, choose "Verdana, Arial, Helvetica, sans serif"; in the Size box, type *2*; from the menu to the right, choose "ems"; in the Color box, type *#669999*.**

    Click Apply again to preview the new headline style. What you've got so far isn't nearly sophisticated enough for the *National Exasperator,* so you'll add a background color and top and bottom borders to the tag.

15. **Choose Background from the category list on the left side of the CSS Rule Definition window. In the "Background color" box, type *#FFFFCC*.**

    Or, if you prefer, select another color using the color box. You've just set a background color that appears behind the text of any <h1> tag on the page. Next, you'll add snappy rules above and below the title.

16. **In the category list, click Border.**

    The CSS Rule Definition window now displays all the properties used to put a border around a style. You can control each border individually or use the same line style for all four edges. In this case, you'll add lines only to the top and bottom of the headline.

17. **Click to turn off all three "Same for all" checkboxes. From the Style menu, choose "dashed" for the top border, type *3* in the Width box, and type *#666666* in the color box. Do the same for the bottom border.**

    The window should now look like Figure 6-30.

18. **Click OK.**

    The window closes, and the title of the story appears with its new formatting. If there had been other Heading 1 headings on this page, you'd see all of them change, too.

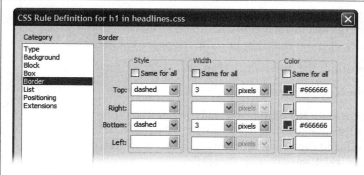

Figure 6-30:
Use the Border properties to add rules to any or all of the four edges of an object. You can give an image a stylish border or underline a heading with this property.

Editing a Style

The paragraph text is a tad too small, so you'll edit the <p> tag style you just created to make the text bigger:

1. **At the top of the CSS Styles panel, click the All button.**

   This displays all the styles in the page. You'll notice that in addition to the *headlines.css* file you created, there's an internal style sheet (whose styles are embedded in this page) with a previously defined style for the <body> tag.

2. **If it isn't already, expand the list of styles in the *headlines.css* style sheet by clicking the + icon (arrow on the Mac) to the left of "headlines.css."**

   This lists all of the styles you've added to the external style sheet.

3. **In the list, click "p," and Dreamweaver displays all of the properties for the <p> tag style (see Figure 6-31).**

   You can edit a CSS property directly in this panel.

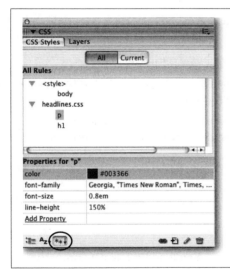

Figure 6-31:
The Properties section of the CSS Styles panel displays all the CSS properties for the style that's selected in the "All Rules" pane. Make sure the "Show only set properties" button is selected (circled in this figure). Otherwise, you'll also see a long list of every CSS property—both those that are set and those that aren't.

4. **In the "font-size" row, click "0.8" to highlight it. Type *1* and then hit Return or Enter.**

   The font size of the paragraph increases to 1 em. Another problem with the paragraphs is that there's no space between the text and the blue-gray sidebar at left. A little white space would provide some visual breathing room.

5. **Click the "Add Property" link at the bottom of the list of properties and select "margin-left" from the pop-up menu.**

   You'll have to scroll down the menu to find it. Another approach is to simply type *margin-left* in the box and press Return or Enter.

6. **Type *15*. Hit Return or Enter to apply the change.**

The text moves 15 pixels to the right, creating a nice space to the left of the text. You can also edit a style by selecting the style in the CSS Styles panel and clicking the Edit Style button (see Figure 6-1) or by double-clicking the style name. These alternate methods open the familiar CSS Rule Definition window—the same window you used to create the style in the first place. You should use whichever method you like best.

Creating a Class Style

Now you'll create a style to highlight the name of famous people mentioned in *National Exasperator* stories. This particular story deals with two well-known celebrities—notice their names in the first paragraph of Figure 6-27. But since the names consist of just a couple of words *within* the paragraph, you can't redefine an HTML tag to format them globally. Instead, you'll create a class style, which you can then apply to the names:

1. **On the CSS Styles panel, click the New CSS Style button (+).**

The New CSS Rule window opens. This time, you'll create a class style rather than an HTML tag style.

2. **Click the Class radio button. In the Name box, type *.celebrity*.**

Class styles always begin with a period. (If you forget to start with a period, don't worry. Dreamweaver's smart enough to do it for you.)

Since you want to add the style to the external style sheet, you don't need to do anything else in this dialog box; Dreamweaver already proposes storing it there.

Note: Some beginners think that whenever you create a new style, you also need to create a new external *style sheet.* On the contrary, you can—and should—store more than one style in a single external style sheet. In fact, if you're creating a set of styles for an entire site, put them all in the same external style sheet.

---

3. **Click OK.**

The CSS Rule Definition window appears. You'll add a few new properties to make this style stand out.

4. **From the Weight menu, choose "bold."**

To make this style even more prominent, you'll change its font color.

5. **In the Color box, type *#CC0000*.**

Or, if you don't normally dream in hexadecimal notation, you can select a color using the color box.

That's enough formatting for the .celebrity style. Now you'll return to the document and apply it.

6. **Click OK.**

   The Style definition window closes, but this time, nothing's changed in the document window. Unlike HTML tag styles, class styles don't show up anywhere until you apply them by hand.

7. **In the first paragraph, select "Loch Ness Monster."**

   This is the first star mentioned in the story.

8. **From the Property inspector's Style menu, choose "celebrity" (see Figure 6-32).**

   Boom—Dreamweaver formats the text with the bold, colored style. Now you'll style Big Foot's name.

9. **Select "Big Foot" in the first paragraph, and apply the *celebrity* style to it, too.**

   Your document text should look something like Figure 6-33.

Figure 6-32:
The Style menu in the Property inspector lists all class styles. It also displays the style name using the style's text formatting—in this case, bold and red text. Notice that only class styles are listed; tag styles don't appear in this menu since you don't need to apply them manually.

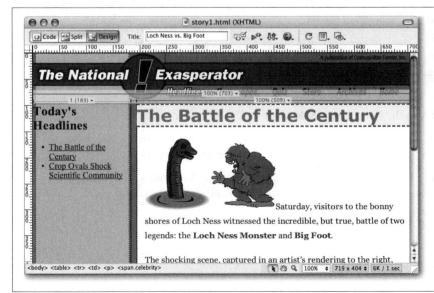

Figure 6-33:
At this point, the text in the page is coming along well. The headlines look distinctive, and you've achieved some effects (like the background color of the title) that only CSS can accomplish.

Formatting Images

CSS styles aren't just for text. You can create styles and apply them to anything on a page—tables, images, or links, for example. In this next section, you'll improve the appearance of the story image; specifically, you'll make it hug the right side of the page and add margins so it has some breathing room around it:

1. **On the CSS Styles panel, click the New CSS Style button (+).**

   The New CSS Rule window opens. You could redefine the <img> (image) tag, but this would affect *every* graphic on your page.

2. **Since you only want to create a style for the main story graphic, type *.photo* in the Name box, make sure the Class style button is selected, and then click OK.**

   The CSS Rule Definition window opens. You'll first make the image float to the right edge of the page.

3. **Click the Box category at the left side of the dialog box.**

   These properties affect margins, padding, and other attributes of a style (see Figure 6-34).

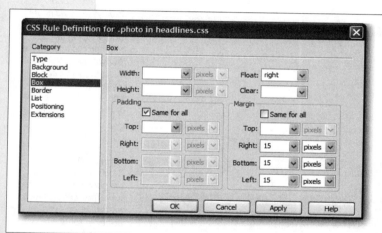

Figure 6-34:
Be careful not to confuse the Padding and Margin properties in the Box category. The Padding settings determine the amount of space between the styled object and its border. The Margins, by contrast, set the amount of space between the borders and other items around the object—in this case, the space between the photos and the text around them. See Figure 6-23 for a diagram of which margins are controlled by each setting.

4. **From the Float menu, select "right."**

   This option works like an image's Align Right property (see page 134); the graphic snaps against the right side of the browser window.

   But because text wraps around the sides of the photos, you should add a little space between the edges of the photo and any text around them. The Margin properties are just the ticket.

5. **Turn off the "Same for all" box for the Margin property and type *15* in the Right, Bottom, and Left margin boxes.**

   CSS lets you set different margin sizes for each edge of an object. Since browsers automatically add some empty space below the headline, there's no reason to add any margin to the top of the photo.

   The CSS Rule Definition window should look like Figure 6-34. You're done with the style; now it's time to apply it.

6. **Click OK to close the CSS Rule Definition window.**

   To apply this new class style, you'll start by selecting an image.

7. **Click to select the graphic—the battle between the Loch Ness Monster and Big Foot.**

   As you can see in the tag selector at the bottom of the window, clicking the photo automatically highlights the <img> (image) tag to which you'll apply the style.

8. **From the Class menu in the Property inspector, select "photo."**

   When applying a class style to text, the Property inspector includes the Style menu. For nontext objects, you use the Property inspector's Class menu, located to the far right of the inspector. (Aside from its name, this menu is identical to the Style menu.)

   The photo moves to the right edge of the page, and the rest of the text flows around it.

Tip: Although the image moves over to the right edge of the page, the actual position of the HTML code used to include the image—the <img> tag—appears *before* the word *Saturday.* Dreamweaver can provide visual clues—in the form of small gold shields—to indicate the position of the HTML for elements that actually *appear* in a different area of the page. Having those gold shields makes it easier to select the HTML the shields represent. To make these shields visible, see the Tip on page 59 and turn on the "Anchor points for aligned elements" checkbox.

---

9. **Choose File → Save. Press F12 (Option-F12 on Mac) to preview the page in a Web browser.**

   Depending on which browser you preview the page in, you may notice white space above the headline "Battle of the Century." Some browsers, like Mozilla and Safari, add extra space above headers. You can get rid of this space, if you wish, by editing the <h1> tag style and setting its Top margin property to *0*.

Creating Contextual Selectors

Now it's time to create a few styles for the left side of the page, which includes a heading and a list of links. You could create tag styles for the <h2> and <ul> tags

---

used in this part of the page, but those would then affect the same tags in the main area of the page, which would then look like the sidebar, which isn't what you want. Or you could use separate class styles, but then you'd have to apply them individually to each element.

A better option, as described in detail on page 189, is to use a type of CSS style known as a contextual selector (or descendent selector). First, you'll create a class style called .sidebar, which you'll apply to the tag containing all of the text in the sidebar region. Next, you'll create two contextual selectors to define how the <h2> and <ul> tags should look—but *only* when they appear inside the sidebar. Here's how to do it:

1. **On the CSS Styles panel, click the New CSS Style button (+).**

   The New CSS Rule window opens.

2. **Click the Class radio button. In the Name box, type *.sidebar*.**

   Dreamweaver adds the period before the style name if you forget.

   Dreamweaver also proposes storing it in an external style sheet, which is exactly what you want.

3. **Click OK.**

   The CSS Rule Definition window opens. In this case, you're creating a style that you'll apply to the tag that holds all of this content—a table cell. (Tables are a common technique for laying out pages. In the next chapter, you'll learn how to create them.)

4. **Click the Box category to view CSS options for Padding and Margins.**

   You'll add some padding to this style to create some space inside the cell, effectively indenting the text.

5. **Leaving the "Same for all" box turned on, in the Top box for the Padding property, type *10*. Click OK to create the style.**

   You've just added 10 pixels of space around the inside edges of the style. But since this is a class style, nothing happens until you apply it.

6. **Click anywhere inside the left sidebar, and using the tag selector, click the first <td> tag (see Figure 6-35).**

   Now that you've selected the table cell, you'll add the style to it.

7. **From the Style menu on the Property inspector, select "sidebar" (Figure 6-35).**

   The text indents 10 pixels, and in the tag selector, Dreamweaver now lists the table cell tag as "td.sidebar" to indicate that the sidebar class style is applied to it. Next, you'll create a contextual selector to format the headline.

8. **On the CSS Styles panel, click the New CSS Style button (+).**

   The New CSS Rule window opens.

9. **Click the Advanced radio button. In the Name box, type *.sidebar h2*.**

   This syntax for a contextual selector simply means that the style you're about to create applies to the <h2> tag (a tag style), but only when <h2> appears in the .sidebar style. In other words, it won't affect any <h2> tag outside of the sidebar.

   Note: The period before *sidebar* is **not** optional in this case. When creating Advanced styles, you must type the full class name, period and all.

   ---

10. **Click OK.**

    The CSS Rule Definition window appears. In this case, you'll just make a couple of style adjustments, but feel free to try other style properties while you're here.

11. **From the Font menu, choose "Verdana, Arial, Helvetica, sans-serif." Type *1* in the Size box and select "ems" from the menu to the right. Click OK to create the style.**

    The text "Today's Headlines" becomes smaller and changes to a different font. Next, you'll fix the list, which is indented too far.

12. **Once again, on the CSS Styles panel, click the New CSS Style button (+).**

    The now-familiar New CSS Rule window opens.

13. **Click the Advanced radio button. In the Name box, type *.sidebar ul*.**

    You're creating another contextual selector. It applies to every <ul> tag (meaning unordered, or bulleted, list) inside the *sidebar* style.

14. **Click OK.**

    The CSS Rule Definition window appears. In this case, you'll adjust the font and margins used to display the list items.

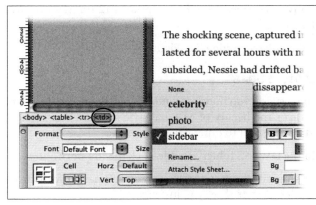

Figure 6-35:
For accuracy, use the tag selector to select an HTML tag—in this case, the <td> tag (circled). You can then apply a style to the tag from the Property inspector.

15. Select "Geneva, Arial, Helvetica, sans-serif" for the font and set the size to .8 ems.

Since the sidebar on this page is rather skinny, the standard indent that Web browsers add to bulleted lists is too broad for this list. You'll adjust that space using the Padding and Margin properties.

16. Click the Box category and turn off the "Same for all" box under both the Padding and Margin properties. Then type *10* in the Left box for both padding and margin (see Figure 6-36).

You'll make one more change to beautify the list: change the regular old circular bullets to square bullets.

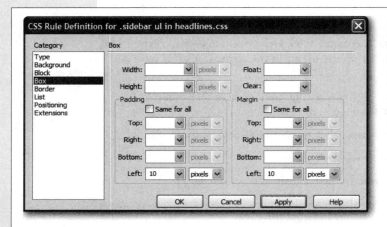

Figure 6-36:
Using the Margin property, strangely enough, doesn't adjust the margins for both bulleted (<ul>) and numbered (<ol>) list items for all browsers. To assure the most consistent experience across all browsers, set both the Padding and Margin properties.

17. Click the List category, and from the Type menu, select "square." Click OK to create the style.

The bulleted list changes font, the indent shrinks, and square bullets appear.

18. Choose File → Save to save the page. Press F12 (Option-F12 on Mac) to preview the page in a Web browser.

Your finished page should look something like Figure 6-37.

Attaching an External Style Sheet

Now that you've created these styles, you may be wondering how you can use them on other pages—after all, that's the beauty of external style sheets. Once created, it's a simple process to add a style sheet to other pages in the site.

1. Choose File → Open. In the DWCSS folder, double-click the file *story2.html*.

This is another headline story for the *National Exasperator*. It has no formatting yet, so you'll attach the external style sheet you just created.

2. **On the CSS Styles panel, click the Attach External Style Sheet button (see Figure 6-1).**

   The Link External Style Sheet window appears.

3. **Click the Browse button.**

   The Select Style Sheet dialog box appears. Navigate to the DWCSS folder and select the *headlines.css* file.

4. **Click OK to insert the path to the Link External Style Sheet window.**

   You can ignore the other settings (they're described in detail on page 169).

5. **Click OK to attach the style sheet to the page.**

   Dreamweaver instantly formats the top headline and main text of the story. Pretty cool—and very efficient. You only need to apply the *.sidebar* class style to the left table cell to format that text as well.

6. **Click anywhere inside the left sidebar, and in the tag selector, click to select the first <td> tag.**

   Next you'll add a style to the tag.

7. **From the Style menu on the Property inspector, select "sidebar" (Figure 6-35).**

   All of the text in the sidebar is instantly formatted.

8. **Press F12 (Option-F12 on Mac) to preview the page.**

   If you'd like to compare your finished product to the professionally completed version, visit *www.sawmac.com/dw8/tutorials.*

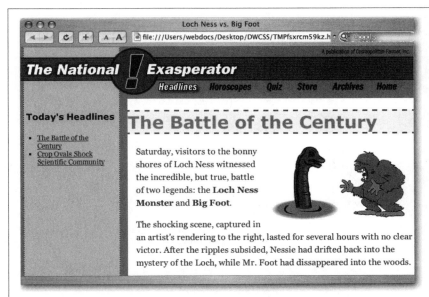

Figure 6-37:
Internet Explorer displays the headline "The Battle of the Century" without any space above, whereas other browsers like Safari (pictured here) and Firefox add a margin to all <h1> tags. To make the browsers perform similarly, you can edit the <h1> style and either remove the top margin (by setting it to 0) or make Internet Explorer display a margin, by setting the margin-top property to some value (10px, for example).

Page Layout 101

The Web was originally invented to help scientists exchange information, not to compete with the sophisticated design of newspapers, glossy magazines, or TV. Controlling a page's layout remains one of a Web designer's greatest challenges. The increasing expectations of Web surfers have forced designers to push HTML into new territories, and the primary weapon in this battle has been the HTML <table> tag.

Though originally intended to display tables of data, many Web designers use the <table> tag primarily for arranging elements on a Web page, as shown in Figure 7-1.

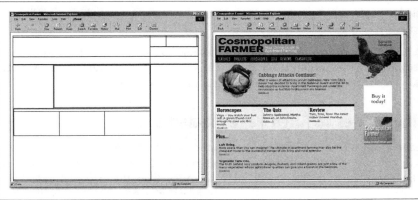

Figure 7-1:
Underneath many Web pages is an invisible skeleton that gives the page form and structure. HTML tables let you control the placement of graphics, text, and other elements on a Web page with accuracy. Without tables, Web contents would simply flow from top to bottom on a page—boring!

Of course, trying to force a round peg into a square hole isn't always easy, and for years, designers had to twist the <table> tag to their own ends, resulting in complex and byte-heavy code that was difficult to update. However, sophisticated browsers like Internet Explorer 5 and 6, Mozilla, Opera, and Safari give designers a wider variety of options. These days, three basic design approaches are the most popular:

- **Strict table-based layouts.** This method uses only tables to position elements on the page. Frequently, this old-school approach requires merging cells across rows and columns, nesting tables within tables (a cumbersome technique) and the excessive use of table elements just to create margins, gutters, and areas of white space.

- **Tables and Cascading Style Sheets.** This combination approach sticks with the seasoned and reliable <table> tag to create basic layout areas, but employs CSS for more sophisticated formatting like margins, white space, borders, and backgrounds. This type of design is easier to create and makes for smaller Web page files than the table-only method. It also overcomes some of the cross-browser problems you'll encounter with the next technique. (The tutorial on page 271 has an example of this method in action.)

- **Cascading Style Sheets.** CSS offers *absolute positioning* (discussed in Chapter 8), which means that, in theory, you can abandon tables completely and have total control over layout. Many sites now use CSS only. However, not all browsers display these designs correctly, and those that do don't always display them the same way. In fact, to get this type of design to work accurately, you may find yourself having to resort to as many tricks as you do with strict table-based layouts.

Fortunately, Dreamweaver provides the tools for creating any of these types of design. In this chapter, you'll learn about Dreamweaver's advanced table tools that let you build beautiful table-based layouts; in the next chapter, you'll learn how to maximize the power of CSS. With these tools—and this book—you'll soon be gliding along the path to attractive, effective Web pages. (If you can't wait to get started using Dreamweaver to create advanced layouts, see page 271 and follow the tutorial.)

But before you jump immediately into Dreamweaver's tools for creating table-based layouts, you should learn about a new addition to Dreamweaver 8, which makes creating sophisticated layouts substantially easier: guides.

Using Guides to Align Page Elements

Dreamweaver 8 adds a useful new design tool, one that's very common in graphic arts programs like Adobe Illustrator, InDesign, and Quark XPress. Guides are simply lines that you drag onto the document window from the top or left ruler. They provide alignment aids that make it easy to draw layout tables and cells, or (if you're using CSS positioning as discussed in the next chapter) to accurately position CSS-controlled <div> tags on a page.

To use guides, you must first turn on the document window's rulers by choosing View → Rulers → Show. A faster method is the keyboard shortcut Ctrl+Alt+R (⌘-Option-R on a Mac), which toggles the display of the rulers off and on. Finally, the View Options menu in the document toolbar also lets you show or hide rulers (see Figure 7-2).

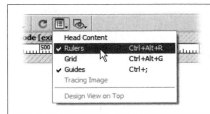

Figure 7-2:
The View Options menu lets you show or hide rulers as well as guides, head content (see Figure 1-2), a tracing image (see page 243), and a regularly spaced grid of lines.

You also need to make sure guides are turned on. Use the View Options menu (Figure 7-2), the View → Guides menu, or the keyboard shortcut Ctrl+; (⌘-;). After this initial setup, you just drag lines onto the page from either the top ruler (to create horizontal guides) or from the left ruler (to create vertical guides), as shown in Figure 7-3. As you drag a guide onto the page, a yellow box appears with a number indicating the distance (in pixels) between the guide and either the top ruler (if you're adding a horizontal guide) or the left ruler (if you're adding a vertical guide). Guides are a great way to lay down a pixel-accurate set of lines to help manage your design—sure to please the pickiest of designers who demand that the Web page look *exactly* like their Photoshop mock-up!

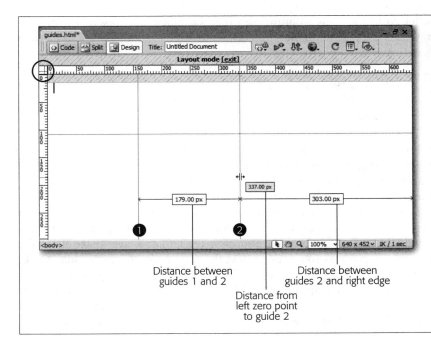

Figure 7-3:
Dreamweaver 8's new guides let you add helpful guidelines by dragging them from any point along the document window's top or left rulers. Guides let you accurately place page elements and also act like helpful measuring tapes that let you determine the distance between objects on a page.

Distance between guides 1 and 2

Distance between guides 2 and right edge

Distance from left zero point to guide 2

The number in the yellow box indicates the distance between the guide and the ruler's zero point. Normally the ruler starts at zero in the upper-left edge of the document window. However, you can drag the box at the edges of the rulers (circled in Figure 7-3) onto the document window to reset the zero point, placing it somewhere in the middle of the document. In earlier versions of Dreamweaver (before guides), this was a handy way to measure the distance from one object to another object on a page—just drag the zero point to the edge of one object and read on the ruler the distance to the next object. But now, guides can handle this function much more gracefully, as described next.

Tip: If you accidentally change the zero point, just double-click the ruler origin box (circled in Figure 7-3) to reset the zero point to the top-left corner of the document window.

If you hold down the Ctrl (⌘) key as you drag a guide onto the page, Dreamweaver provides other helpful information—the distance from one guide to another or, if there's no guide in the way, from the guide to the edge of the document (see Figure 7-3). The distance (in pixels) appears in a white box, and two blue lines appear, one with an arrow head that indicates where the measurement begins and another with an arrow head indicating where the measurement ends. These markers can come in very handy when you want to make sure two elements are separated by a specific distance. For example, say you want to begin the main area of a page exactly 23 pixels (dude, you're picky) below a page-topping banner and navigation bar. Drag one guide down from the top ruler until the guide covers the bottom edge of the banner; then, drag another guide below the first one while holding down the Ctrl (⌘) key. When the distance between the two guides is 23 pixels, let go of the mouse button, and the new guide is in position (note that Dreamweaver 8's new Zoom tool can help make this maneuver feel less like a game of Operation).

Tip: You can still see distances between guides and the edges of your document even after placing guides on a page. Just hold down the Ctrl (⌘) key and move your mouse over the guide whose distances you wish to know.

Once you've added a guide, to remove it, just drag it off any edge of the page, or, to reposition it, drag it to another part of the document window. You can temporarily hide the guides using one of the same methods discussed earlier for turning them on—for example, Ctrl+; (⌘-;). In addition, the View → Guides menu provides several other options for controlling guides (see Figure 7-4): you can lock guides so you don't accidentally move them; turn on "snap to" guides so that elements you draw on a page, like a layout cell (page 236) or a layer (page 307), snap to the edge of a guide as you draw or drag them; or make the guides snap to elements on the page, so if you've already built parts of a Web page, you can drag guides and have them snap into place right next to any element—an image, for example—on the page. This last maneuver's a good way to use guides to measure the distance between two objects on a page. (Holding down the Alt [Option] key temporarily turns off snapping.) And, if you're completely done with guides, you can choose Clear Guides to remove them permanently.

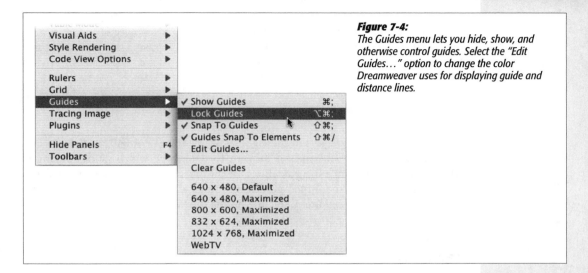

Figure 7-4:
The Guides menu lets you hide, show, and otherwise control guides. Select the "Edit Guides…" option to change the color Dreamweaver uses for displaying guide and distance lines.

Note: Dreamweaver remembers where you placed guides on a particular page, even if you quit and restart the program. It stores that information in a folder called _notes, which is stored in the same folder the page is in. If you delete the _notes folder, you lose all of the guide information for all pages in the same folder.

Checking the Fold

There's one final option provided by the new guides feature that helps Web designers see how their designs fit inside a variety of different size browser windows. One difficulty in designing Web pages is designing for a variety of different monitor sizes. People use a wide range of resolutions when using a computer—ranging from 640×480 pixel settings for small monitors up to the colossal 2560×1600 pixel resolution of Apple's 30" Cinema Display. It's all too easy, if you, Ms. Fancy-Pants Web Designer, have a big monitor, to create a page where all the important information won't appear to the average visitor unless he scrolls down or, even worse, scrolls to the right.

Note: Newspapers put the most important stories on the top half of the front page; stories of lesser importance appear "below the fold."

The Guides menu provides a quick way to slap down guides that mark the boundaries of the viewable area of most Web browsers at a variety of resolutions (see Figure 7-4). Just choose one of the resolutions—640×480, 800×600, and so on—and Dreamweaver displays green guides marking the bottom and right edge of the display area. If any of the page's content falls to the right of the vertical green line, a visitor viewing the page at the specified resolution needs to scroll right; anything below the horizontal green line appears only when the visitor scrolls down.

Note: The two 640×480 options are quickly become relics. Fewer and fewer people have monitors this small or set their monitors to this resolution. In addition, the default option's pretty much useless since browsers no longer open to a set or "default" size each time you open them. In this day and age, browsers open to whatever dimension the visitor last had the browser set at when she quit the browser. The "Maximized" option just means the browser window is expanded to fill as much area of the screen as possible.

You can turn on multiple sets of these guides at one time—for 640×480, 800×600, and so on. But doing so makes it difficult to determine which guides belong to which window size, since the guidelines are all the same color. It's even harder to tell which guides are the "fold" guides, if you've already dragged a lot of green guides onto the page. An alternative method is the Window Size menu in the bottom-right corner of the document window.

Table Basics

A table is a grid of rows and columns that intersect to form *cells,* as shown in Figure 7-5. A cell acts like a mini document window, in which you can place images, text, and even additional tables. And because a cell can have a fixed width and height, you can place these items with precision. For example, you can build a table with three cells in a row and fill each cell with a single column of text, thus simulating the column layout of a print publication such as a newspaper.

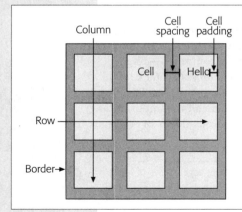

Figure 7-5:
Rows, columns, and cells make up a table. Cell spacing specifies how many pixels of space appear between cells. Cell padding, on the other hand, provides a space between the four sides of the cell and the cell's content, as described on page 20.

Tables are also the key to building more complex designs. For instance, you can merge cells together to create larger cells that span columns or rows, nest tables for added versatility, and create flexible designs that expand to fit the browser window.

(This should all sound familiar to anyone who's used, for example, the table tool in Microsoft Word.)

Since tables weren't originally intended for layout purposes, many people find working with them counterintuitive. For starters, creating tables usually involves thinking in terms of rows and columns—but having to determine the number of rows and columns you'll need just to place an image at a particular position on a page isn't a natural way to design.

That's why Dreamweaver offers two separate tools for achieving the same ends: *Standard view* and *Layout mode*. Both these tools are available from the Insert bar's Layout tab (see Figure 7-6). Layout mode and Standard view both produce the same results—an underlying grid of tables and cells that let you control the layout of a page (see Figure 7-1)—and nearly the same HTML code. (Layout mode adds a little extra code—in the form of HTML comments—that helps Dreamweaver display and manipulate tables.)

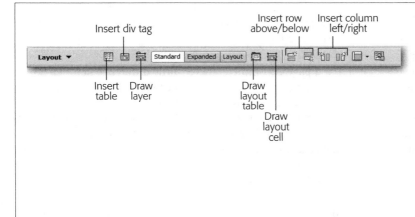

Figure 7-6:
You can switch between Standard view and Layout mode using the buttons in the Layout panel of the Insert bar. The Layout Table and Layout Cell tools work while in Layout mode only and are dimmed when Standard view is selected. Likewise, the standard Table tool, Insert Div object, and Draw Layer tool (described in Chapter 8) are available only while Standard view is selected. The standard Table tool and Insert Div object are available from the Common panel as well.

Note: Dreamweaver has a third mode, *Expanded Table*, which helps you see your table layout more clearly. It's discussed on page 249.

But although they produce the same table structures, the two views offer different approaches to building them.

Note: When you first enter Layout mode, the "Getting Started in Layout mode" window may appear, offering a quick overview of the layout tools. Turn on "Don't show me this message again" to prevent this window from opening every time you switch views; otherwise, it'll get old quick.

Standard view requires you to envision most of your design in advance, answering questions like: Where will items go on the page? How many table rows and columns will this require? What size should the table be? In essence, you need to know what the table will look like *before* beginning.

Layout mode, on the other hand, lets you work at either the smallest level—a table cell—or the largest—a table. If you use the Cell drawing tool to draw a cell in the document window, Dreamweaver creates the underlying table structure. If you move the cell, resize it, or delete it, Dreamweaver rewrites the code to create a table to fit your design.

This flexibility makes the Layout mode a very good place to start when creating a page's design. The changes that Dreamweaver can make to a table's HTML code in Layout mode take fractions of a second, while comparable modifications in Standard view could take you much longer. Though it's certainly possible to revise a table's structure in Standard view, it's more difficult.

Note: Even if you enjoy the ease of Layout mode, don't let it keep you from learning how HTML tables really work. If you plan to use Dreamweaver for more than just an occasional personal Web site, you'll do yourself a favor by learning everything you can about this important topic. Not only does the rest of this chapter steer you in the right direction, but you can find lots of additional tutorials and other helpful information at *www.dwfaq.com/Tutorials/Tables/*.

Once the basic design of a page is complete, there's little difference between a page viewed in Layout mode and a page viewed in Standard view. In fact, you may well switch to Standard view for good once the basic page design is complete. Standard view not only hides many of the visual aids included in Layout mode (because they sometimes obscure text, images, and other elements on a page), but also lets you access tools that are unavailable in Layout mode, such as the basic Table object and Draw Layer tool. Furthermore, you can set up some properties of a table, like the background image, *only* in Standard view.

Tip: If you're already familiar with using tables—perhaps from your hand-coding days—you may find Layout mode confusing. You can skip Layout mode and build tables the old-fashioned way (though still at a much faster pace than hand coding). Turn to page 245 for details.

The first part of this chapter introduces the Layout mode and its associated drawing tools; for a tour of Standard view and its techniques, see page 245. Just keep in mind that, whichever approach you take, you're still only creating basic HTML tables.

Layout Mode

In Layout mode, you can start creating a table-based design using either of the two drawing tools—the Layout Cell drawing tool or the Layout Table drawing tool. Both tools await you on the Layout tab of the Insert bar (see Figure 7-6).

How to Draw a Table in Layout Mode

Drawing a table is as simple as dragging. Click the Layout Table tool in the Insert bar's Layout tab (see Figure 7-6); the cursor changes to a + sign when you move it over the document window. Drag diagonally to create a rectangular box—the outline of the table. When you release the mouse button, a gray box appears, complete with green borders and a tab in the upper-left corner labeled Layout Table (see Figure 7-7).

A. Identifying tab   B. Cells

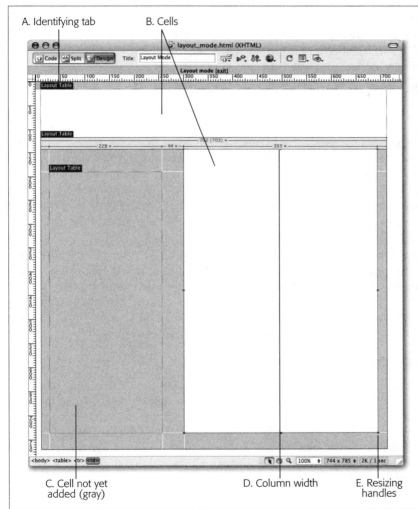

C. Cell not yet added (gray)   D. Column width   E. Resizing handles

Figure 7-7:
Dreamweaver's Layout mode may take some time to get used to. Tables are identified by small tabs on their top-left corners labeled Layout Table (A). You can include more than one table per page, and even put a table inside another table. Until you add cells to a table (white areas, B), you can't add text, graphics, or anything else. Areas of a table without cells have a gray background (C). The width of each column and the overall width of the table appear along the top or bottom of the table (D). When you select a cell (E), eight resizing handles appear, which you can drag to change the dimensions of that cell.

Note: Although Dreamweaver uses the words Layout Table and Layout Cell, they're still just HTML tables and cells. In other words, a Layout Table is simply a table viewed in Layout mode, and a Layout Cell is just a table cell viewed in Layout mode. In Standard view, the same items are just called tables and cells. In this book, you'll see the terms Layout Cell and Layout Table appear when referring to actions you perform while in Layout mode.

This Layout Table tool may be a bit confusing until you learn some of Dreamweaver's rules for drawing tables:

- If the document is blank when you draw a table, the table appears in the upper-left corner of the page.

- You can't draw a table over anything that's already on the page. If you move the Table tool over text, for example, the cursor changes to a forbidden symbol (a circle with a slash through it), and nothing happens when you drag. If there's anything on the page—text, images, tables, even an empty paragraph—you must move the cursor to the bottom of the page to draw a table. For this reason, it's usually best to start with a blank document, draw your tables and cells, and only at that point add content.

- Tables can't overlap. The Table tool won't create a table if you drag over the edge of an existing one.

- You can draw a Layout Table *inside* another Layout Table, a technique called *nesting tables* (see page 266). However, you can draw the second table only inside the gray area of the Layout Table. In other words, you can't draw a Layout *Table* inside a Layout *Cell*.

Tip: To draw a number of tables one after another, without having to keep reselecting the Table tool, hold down the Ctrl (⌘) key when drawing a table. The Table tool remains selected between drags.

Tables are made up of rows and columns, a structure Dreamweaver helps maintain by making the edges of tables snap against nearby tables or cells as you draw. If the cursor comes within eight pixels of the edge of a cell or another table, the table edge you're drawing snaps to the other table or cell's edge. This behavior helps you accurately align the borders of your tables. But if it bothers you, turn this snapping feature off by pressing the Alt (Option) key as you draw the table.

Layout Table Properties

After drawing a Layout Table, you'll see a rectangular gray square in the document window. A tab labeled Layout Table appears in the upper-left corner of the table, while information about the table's width appears at the bottom. (You won't see *any* of this helpful information if you've turned on Hide All Visual Aids. To see the measurements, choose View → Visual Aids → Hide All to remove the checkmark next to this option.) The Property inspector lists additional properties, such as table height, width, and background color (see Figure 7-8).

Table dimensions

The width and height of the table appear in the Property inspector. You can adjust these values by typing new pixel-measurement values in the Fixed and Height fields. Alternatively, to resize a table, you can drag one of the three handles that appear on the bottom edge, lower-right corner, and right edge of the table in the document window.

Instead of having a fixed width, a table can automatically adjust to fit the available space of your visitor's browser window. To activate this feature, click the Autostretch radio button in the Property inspector. (See page 240 for full details on flexible layouts.)

Tip: If you find the table tabs that appear at the bottom or top of a Layout Table distracting, you can turn them off. Choose View → Visual Aids and select the Hide All option. The keyboard shortcut Ctrl+Shift+I (⌘-Shift-I) also works.

Layout Mode

FREQUENTLY ASKED QUESTION

Dreamweaver Isn't PageMaker (or Quark XPress, or InDesign)

I'm used to graphic design programs like PageMaker and QuarkXPress. But when I use Dreamweaver's Layout mode, I constantly run into problems with my designs.

Even though Layout mode acts similarly to page-layout programs, you shouldn't attempt to emulate the kind of freedom available in print design. It's not Dreamweaver's fault. It's just how tables work.

Even though you can draw layout cells to create boxes anywhere on a page (as shown at bottom left), the resulting HTML is a nightmare (bottom right). If you don't have a background in building HTML tables, the temptation to create these kinds of layouts is very strong.

The best advice when using Layout mode (and even when building HTML tables in general) is to keep it simple. The

tutorial at the end of this chapter includes a good example of using Layout mode to create a well-crafted table.

In addition, always keep in mind that you're ultimately just building HTML tables, which isn't the most robust layout tool. So follow the tips on page 258, and review the helpful tutorials at *www.dwfaq.com/Tutorials/Tables/*.

Finally, remember that Cascading Style Sheets is quickly becoming the technique of choice among professional Web designers. CSS offers many of the design options that print designers are accustomed to, including exact placement of content on a page, freedom from the rigid grid pattern of tables, and the ability to overlap images, text, and other content. You can read more about that approach in the next chapter.

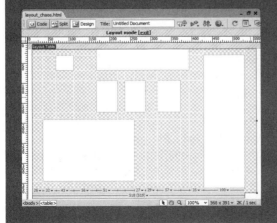
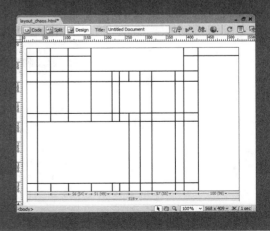

You'll also notice that the width information listed at the bottom of the Layout Table sometimes includes an additional number in parentheses. In Figure 7-8, for example the bottom table's width is listed (at the top of the pop-up menu) as 557 (558), and the nested table (left) is listed as 100% (154). Both numbers in parentheses indicate the actual width in pixels of the tables as they appear in Dreamweaver. The first number (the one not in parentheses), is the number defined in the underlying HTML.

These numbers don't jibe in several different instances: when a percentage value is set for a width—for example, 100%; when content inside the table forces it to be wider than you specified, which can happen when you insert an image that's wider than the table (a phenomenon that's discussed on page 259); or, if you've added a border, cell padding, or cell spacing to the table, in which case you've added more to the width—the thickness of the border lines, for example. The Make Cell Widths Consistent button on the Property inspector, also available from the Width menu (Figure 7-8), fixes this discrepancy by adjusting the widths of the cells and the table.

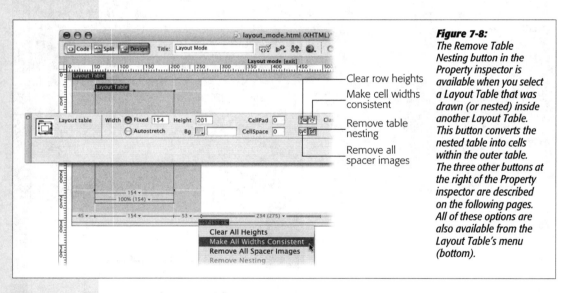

Figure 7-8:
The Remove Table Nesting button in the Property inspector is available when you select a Layout Table that was drawn (or nested) inside another Layout Table. This button converts the nested table into cells within the outer table. The three other buttons at the right of the Property inspector are described on the following pages. All of these options are also available from the Layout Table's menu (bottom).

Background color

You can give your table a background color that's independent of the page color. To pick a background color, click the Bg color box in the Property inspector and select from the pop-up palette. (You can actually select any color on your screen using the eyedropper; see page 41.)

Note: As with most properties that affect the look of an HTML element, CSS now offers an equivalent. You can use the Background Color property (page 197) to create a style that applies a background color to a table or table cell.

After you click, you may wonder whether Dreamweaver has gone color-blind; the table's color doesn't match the color you selected. Tables in Layout mode have a light-gray background to indicate empty areas of the table (places where no cells have yet been drawn). Dreamweaver *mixes* this gray with the color you selected, creating a muddy blend. That gray is just for showing you the table's boundaries in Dreamweaver and doesn't appear in a Web browser.

Tip: You can modify this gray background color. Choose Edit → Preferences (Dreamweaver → Preferences) and click the Layout Mode category (Figure 7-9). You can also modify colors for the table and cell outlines, as well as the cell-highlight and table-background colors.

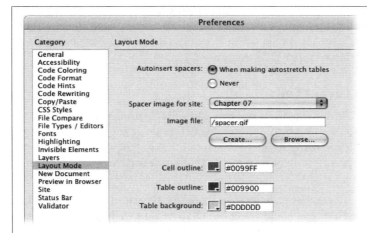

Figure 7-9:
Different colors identify Layout Tables and Cells. A cell outline is generally blue; when you move your mouse over it, the outline turns red. Table outlines are green, and a table's background is gray. You can change any of these colors in the Preferences box, as shown here.

Mac Note: Dreamweaver 8 doesn't always display the gray background color of Layout Tables, the area that you fill with Layout Cells. If the page has a background color (see page 39), sometimes the Layout Table is simply transparent. To get around this defect, change the table background color in the Preferences window (see note above) to a brighter color—#009900 works. Don't worry, this hideous color disappears as you start to add Layout Cells to the table.

Cell padding and cell spacing

When you add a background color to the cells in a table, you may sometimes want to create a visual gap between them, like the grout between tiles (but without the mold). To add this kind of space between cells in a table (see Figure 7-5), type a pixel value in the Property inspector's CellSpace field.

To add padding for all four edges inside a cell, type a pixel value in the CellPad field. This space keeps the text or graphics *inside* a cell from touching the edges of the cell. By default, both the CellSpace and CellPad values are set to 0, which is appropriate for a design that requires graphics to meet at the edges of cells.

Notice, for example, that the chicken in Figure 7-1 is actually made of four different graphics, each in its own cell. Chopping up a graphic in this way is a typical Web design trick that lends special flexibility. In Figure 7-1, for example, the chicken graphic appears to jut straight down into the text area of the Web page—a feat that would be impossible if the chicken were a single rectangular image. In this case, if either the CellSpace or CellPad were set above 0, there would be visible gaps between the segments of the image.

Note: There's no CSS equivalent for cell spacing. If you want space *between* each cell, stick with a table's cell-spacing properties.

However, CSS does provide a more flexible alternative to cell padding. You can use the CSS Padding property (see page 202) to control the padding on each edge of a table cell. In other words, you can indent the left edge 10 pixels, the top edge 20 pixels, and leave the other edges alone. You would create either a class style or a tag style (page 165) for the <table> or <td> tag, and set the Padding property to the dimension you wish. There's an example of this technique in the tutorial on page 287.

How to Draw a Layout Cell

With the Layout Cell drawing tool, you can add cells to any Layout Table on the page. However, you don't need to draw a table before using the Cell drawing tool. In fact, many people use the Cell tool to sketch out the content areas of their pages, drawing boxes freehand on the screen and letting Dreamweaver create the rest of the table to fit.

For example, suppose you have a banner ad that must be placed in the upper-right corner of the page. First, you could select the Draw Layout Cell tool in the Layout tab of the Insert bar (see Figure 7-6); the cursor changes to a + sign when it's over an empty area of a Layout Table or an empty area of the document window. You create a new cell just by dragging diagonally in the document window or inside an existing Layout Table. (If you draw a cell inside an existing Layout Table, Dreamweaver creates a rectangular cell. If you draw a cell in an empty document window, Dreamweaver creates a cell *and* a Layout Table that encloses it.)

Because tables are organized like a grid, Dreamweaver must organize cells in rows and columns. To indicate this underlying grid, Dreamweaver displays white lines projecting from the sides of a cell to indicate the rows and columns of the table (see Figure 7-7). In addition, as you add more cells to a table, the cursor snaps to these guidelines, as well as to table edges, when it's 8 pixels away or closer. This snapping feature helps you accurately align the edges of your cells; once again, you can temporarily override this feature, gaining complete dragging freedom, by pressing Alt (Option) as you draw the cell.

Tip: After drawing a cell, the insertion point blinks patiently inside the newly created cell, awaiting the text or graphics you're about to type, paste, or import. Creating another cell requires another click on the Layout Cell tool.

As mentioned in the tip on page 232, however, you can draw several cells in sequence, without having to re-click the Layout Cell tool after each, just by pressing the Ctrl (⌘) key while drawing a cell. The Layout Cell tool remains selected when you release the mouse, ready to draw another cell.

As with Layout Tables, there are some limitations to drawing Layout Cells:

- You can't draw a cell over already existing content. If you move the Cell tool over text, images, or other content on a page, the cursor changes to a symbol and won't draw over that area.

- Cells can't overlap one another.

- You can't draw a cell within a cell.

Layout Cell Properties

Like a table, a cell has its own width and height, and can have its own background color. You set these properties in the Property inspector.

To see the properties for a Layout Cell, first select it by clicking any highlighted edge of the cell (the edges appear highlighted in red when your cursor approaches). A faster approach: hold down the Ctrl (⌘) key and click inside the cell to select it. Resize handles appear around the cell, and the Property inspector displays its attributes (see Figure 7-10).

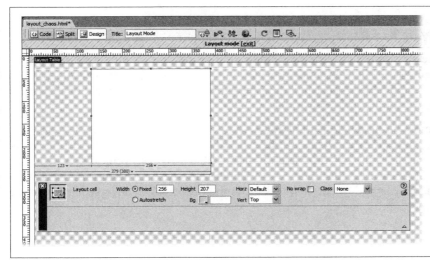

Figure 7-10:
When you select a Layout Cell, the Property inspector displays its size and cell alignment. Turning on No Wrap prevents a cell's contents from wrapping to the next line—usually with ugly results. Dreamweaver includes the ability to apply a CSS class style to the cell using the Class menu, which lists all class styles for this page.

Alignment

By default, content added to a Layout Cell aligns with the left side of the cell and rises to the top of the cell vertically. You can change either or both of these alignment options by setting the horizontal and vertical properties of the cell.

To align the content horizontally inside a cell (see Figure 7-11, top), select the cell and then choose an alignment option from the Horz (Horizontal) menu in the Property inspector (see Figure 7-10):

- The Left and Right options align a cell's contents with its left or right walls. (Since Left is the default, choosing Left here only adds unnecessary code to your page.)

- The Center option centers the cell contents between the left and right walls of the cell.

The vertical alignment property works the same way (see Figure 7-11, top); use the Vert (Vertical) menu of the Property inspector:

- The Top and Bottom options make the cell contents rest against the cell's top or bottom edge, respectively.

- The Middle option makes the cell contents float in the vertical center of the cell. (This is the default behavior of a cell. Choosing Default instead gives the same results without adding any additional code.)

- The Baseline option aligns the bottom of the first line of text in the cell with the baseline of text in all the other cells in the row (see Figure 7-11, bottom). Unfortunately, browser support for this feature is spotty: both Internet Explorer and Opera display the Baseline option correctly, but Firefox and Safari don't.

Moving and Resizing Layout Cells and Layout Tables

Once you've drawn cells and tables, you're not locked into that one design. Dreamweaver's Layout mode provides several ways to adjust the size and position of cells and tables. As usual, Dreamweaver makes a pleasant task out of a normally time-consuming and error-prone job.

To move a cell, drag one of its edges. (Avoid grabbing one of the eight resize handles, however, or you'll change the cell's size instead of moving it.) Dreamweaver lets you move the cell anywhere within the table. However, you can't move it outside of its Layout Table, into (or overlapping) another cell, or into another Layout Table. If you try, Dreamweaver displays the dreaded forbidden symbol—a circle with a slash through it.

Tip: You can nudge a selected cell by 1 pixel at a time by pressing the arrow keys. Hold down the Shift key, too, to nudge the cell 10 pixels per press of the arrow key.

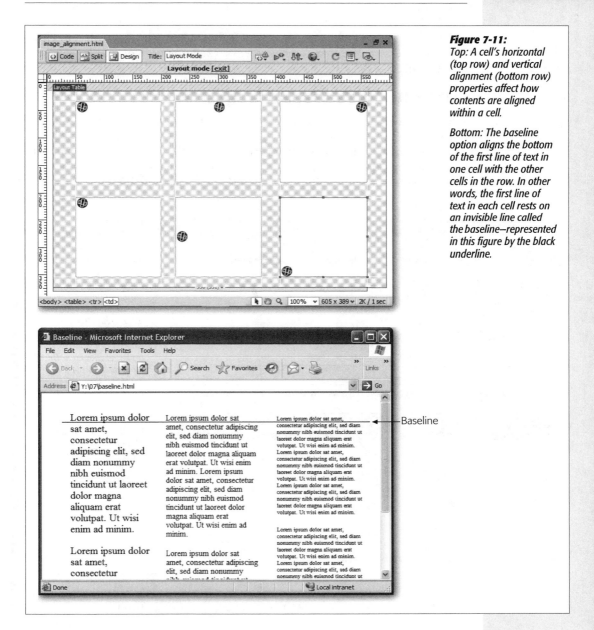

Figure 7-11:
Top: A cell's horizontal (top row) and vertical alignment (bottom row) properties affect how contents are aligned within a cell.

Bottom: The baseline option aligns the bottom of the first line of text in one cell with the other cells in the row. In other words, the first line of text in each cell rests on an invisible line called the baseline—represented in this figure by the black underline.

Once you've moved the cell, Dreamweaver redraws the underlying table to accommodate this change.

Resizing a table or cell is easy: For numerical precision, select the table or cell and use the Property inspector to adjust the Width and Height values. You can also resize a table or cell by dragging the handles that appear when you select it. However, since cells can't overlap one another or extend outside of a table, you can't drag the edge of a cell over another cell or out of a table.

Building Flexible Page Layouts in Layout Mode

When you set a fixed width for a Layout Table, as described on page 232, it remains the same width regardless of your visitor's browser window size. This level of certainty and control is great for making sure elements go where you want them. On the other hand, fixed-width designs leave large areas of empty space when viewed on larger monitors (see Figure 7-12 for an example).

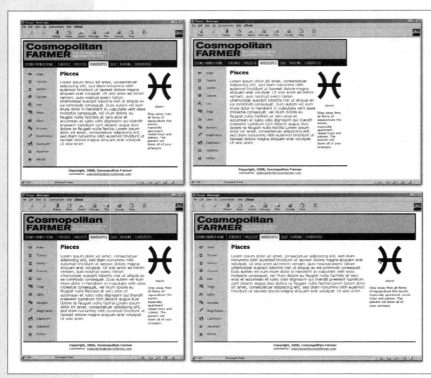

Figure 7-12:
Flexible table widths provide one solution to Web designers' greatest challenge: designing pages for different monitor and window sizes. A layout that uses a fixed width often has unwanted and distracting white space when viewed on larger monitors. The top two images, for example, show the same fixed-width table viewed on a small screen (left) and a wider one (right). Flexible tables, on the other hand, can shrink or grow to fit the browser window, as shown in the bottom two images.

One solution is to build flexible tables using Dreamweaver's Autostretch option. Flexible tables, sometimes called *liquid HTML,* expand or shrink to fit a browser window's available display area. In this way, your design can accommodate 15-inch *and* 21-inch monitors. (Imagine if newspapers grew or shrank to fit a reader's arm span!)

Creating a flexible-width table

Instead of being a certain number of pixels wide, a flexible table always fills the entire window. To achieve this effect, you must set *one* column in the table to Autostretch; that column expands to fill the page. For instance, in the example in Figure 7-12, the column containing the headline "Pisces" expands, while the left column, containing the navigation bar, remains a fixed width.

To create a flexible column, click the down-pointing triangle next to the pixel-width number in the column header (see Figure 7-13) and choose Make Column Autostretch from the contextual menu. You can also select the *cell* you wish to make flexible and click the Autostretch button on the Property inspector (Figure 7-10). (Although you can also create a flexible table by selecting the *table* and setting its width to Autostretch, it's not necessary to do so. Dreamweaver automatically sets it to Autostretch when you create a flexible column.)

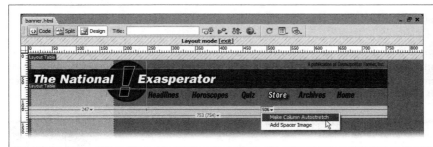

Figure 7-13:
Turning a fixed-width column into a flexible column is pretty easy. Just click on a column's width value and select Make Column Autostretch.

If you want to change the column back to a fixed-width size, use the same menu to choose Make Column Fixed Width.

Adding spacer images

For the Autostretch function to work, Dreamweaver uses a transparent image—an actual, see-through GIF file called a *spacer*—to control the spacing of the columns that *don't* stretch.

Understanding why Dreamweaver adds these invisible spacer images requires some understanding of the way the program thinks. When you ask it to make the autostretch column grow as necessary to fill a browser window, Dreamweaver uses a little trick. It sets the column's width to *100 percent*. In other words, the column attempts to take up *all* the space available, even space used by other columns. This greedy behavior, of course, would ordinarily squish the table's other columns into hyper-thinness. That's why Dreamweaver inserts a spacer image (and sets its width to the column width you've specified) into each *fixed-width* column. The image acts like a steel beam across the walls of the fixed-width column, reinforcing it and preventing it from shrinking smaller than the size of the spacer image (see "Do the math" on page 260).

The first time you make a column an autostretcher, Dreamweaver opens a Choose Spacer Image dialog box. It offers you three choices:

- **Create a spacer image file.** If you choose this option, Dreamweaver creates a 1-pixel by 1-pixel, transparent GIF image and prompt you to name the file and save it into any folder of your Web site.

- **Use an existing spacer image file.** If you're already using a 1-pixel by 1-pixel transparent GIF (a standard Web design tool), choose this option. Dreamweaver then lets you browse to and select the GIF file in your site folder.

- **Don't use spacer images for autostretch tables.** This isn't a wise choice if you want to use the Autostretch feature. Most likely, your fixed-width columns will appear much smaller than you intended.

Tip: After you've set the spacer image for the site, Dreamweaver continues to use that file whenever you need one. You can select a different file at any time from the Edit → Preferences → Layout mode tab (Dreamweaver 8 → Preferences → Layout mode), as shown in Figure 7-9.

While Dreamweaver automatically inserts spacer GIFs, you can also add them manually by choosing Add Spacer Image from the column-header menu (see Figure 7-13). This command is grayed out if you turned on the "Don't use spacer images" option in the Choose Spacer Image dialog box.

WORKAROUND WORKSHOP

Where Does the Spacer Image Go?

When inserting a transparent, 1-pixel-tall spacer image in a column, Dreamweaver creates a new table row at the bottom of the table. The spacer image is inserted in each fixed-width cell in that row.

Keep this behavior in mind if you try to place one table on top of another. If the two tables need to touch seamlessly—for example, if two cells in two separate tables share the same color and need to appear connected—that 1-pixel tall row created by the spacer images creates a 1-pixel gap between the two tables.

Unfortunately, you can't solve this dilemma in Dreamweaver's visually oriented Design view. You must delve into the HTML code; after consulting Chapter 9, choose View → Code to open Dreamweaver's Code view.

You'll need to locate the closing Table tag for the offending autostretch spacer image. Directly above that, you'll find a single table row composed of an opening <tr> tag, several lines of <td> (table data or cells) tags, and a closing </tr>

tag. Select the entire row, cut it, and paste it directly *after* the opening <table> tag. This maneuver essentially moves that bottom row (containing the spacer) to the top and allows the table to rest seamlessly on any table directly below it.

And what if you also want to prevent a gap at both the top and the bottom of an autostretch table? Go to the page's HTML source code and locate the last row of the table, the one containing only spacer images. Delete it. Then, back in Design view (View → Design), click inside one cell in each fixed-width column, insert a spacer image (see page 241), and set its width to match the desired width of that column. (These cells probably contain text or images. Insert the space image after any content in the cell.)

Removing spacer images

To remove a spacer image from a column, choose Remove Spacer Image from the column-header menu. You can also remove *all* of the spacer images on a page by choosing Remove All Spacer Images from the Layout Table menu, or by clicking the Remove All Spacer Images button on the Property inspector when a table is selected (see Figure 7-8).

Using a Tracing Image

Layout mode lets you draw your designs directly in the document window, which is a wonderful feature. However, unless you can visualize the layout you want, you may feel that you're just aimlessly drawing boxes on a blank canvas.

Dreamweaver's Tracing Image feature helps you find your way around the dreaded blank screen. With it, you can import a graphic representation of your finished page design—a sketch you've created in a more art-oriented program like, say, Fireworks or Photoshop, or even just something you've whipped up with a pen and paper and then scanned in—and use it as a pattern for tracing the table and cells of your page. In fact, it's very common in the Web-design biz to work up, in a program like Photoshop, a graphic that *looks* like a finished Web page—but that's just one giant image, without individual buttons, tables, or editable text.

To add a tracing image to your page, choose Modify → Page Properties (or choose View → Tracing Image → Load); the Page Properties dialog box opens (see Figure 7-14). Select the Tracing Image category and click the Browse button (next to the Tracing Image field); then, find and open a GIF, JPEG, or PNG file to use as the background image.

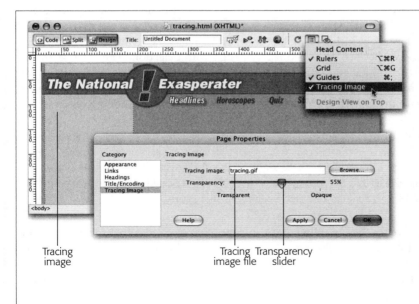

Tracing image

Tracing image file

Transparency slider

Figure 7-14:
Top: You can hide or show the tracing image using the View Options menu icon at the top of the document window.

Bottom: In addition to setting various properties for a Web page such as text color, margins, and background color, the Page Properties window lets you add a tracing image to your document and fade it into the background as much as you want. In this example, the tracing image represents a banner for the National Exasperator Web site. As shown by the Transparency slider, it's been faded to 55 percent opacity over the background of the page.

Now use the image Transparency slider shown in Figure 7-14. To fade the image into the background of the page, move the slider toward the transparent setting, making it easier to distinguish between the tracing image and the actual content on the Web page.

When you click OK, you return to your Web page with the tracing image in place. (The tracing image appears only in Dreamweaver, never on the Web.)

Hiding a tracing image

If you want to temporarily hide a tracing image, choose Tracing Image in the toolbar's View Options menu (shown at top in Figure 7-14); choose the same command again to show it. (The long way: choose View → Tracing Image and turn off the Show option.)

Moving a tracing image

When you first select a tracing image, it appears against the top and left margins, if you've specified them (see step 13 on page 40). If you didn't specify margins, Dreamweaver places the tracing image several pixels from the left and top edges of the document window—just where it would put text or graphics into a new Web page.

You can't just drag the tracing image elsewhere on the page. If you need it anywhere other than the upper-left corner, choose View → Tracing Image → Adjust Position. Type pixel values in the X and Y fields in the Adjust Tracing Image dialog box; the X value is the distance from the left edge, and the Y value is the distance from the top edge.

You can also align the tracing image to a selected object on the page, which comes in handy when you want to use a tracing image to create a portion of a Web page—a footer or sidebar element, for example. Select the element on the page and then choose View → Tracing Image → Align with Selection. The tracing image's upper-left corner aligns with the upper-left corner of the selected element. (In the case of a table cell, however, Dreamweaver isn't so smart. It aligns the tracing image with the top-left corner of the table containing the cell, not the cell itself.)

Tip: To reset the tracing image to the upper-left corner of the page, choose View → Tracing Image → Reset Position. Unfortunately, this command doesn't place the image in its original position, at the margins of the page; it merely places it at the very corner (the 0,0 position) of the document window. You'll probably need to adjust it by choosing View → Tracing Image → Adjust Position. (To restore the default values, use 10 pixels along the X axis and 15 pixels along the Y axis.)

Once you've finished building the Web page, it's a good idea to remove the tracing image. Not only is it distracting when you view the page in Dreamweaver, but Dreamweaver introduces extra lines of Dreamweaver-specific HTML to accommodate it. These extra bandwidth-consuming bytes are unnecessary once the page is complete.

To remove a tracing image from a page, open the Page Properties dialog box once again, and then select and delete the file name in the Tracing Image field.

Tip: Tracing images aren't just for the Layout mode. You can use a tracing image anytime—a handy feature when you're using Cascading Style Sheets to accurately position elements on a page (see Chapter 8).

Inserting a Table in Standard View

While the Layout mode is one way to lay out a page, it can't do everything. You can't, for instance, set a table cell's Background Image property in Layout mode. Nor can you add color to a row of cells, or even insert a simple table for displaying data. Likewise, if you're already comfortable visualizing table-based layouts in your head (or if you find the Layout tools cumbersome), you may prefer the basic approach offered by the Table object. In fact, even if you're sold on the Layout mode, it's a good idea to familiarize yourself with these steps so that you can troubleshoot tables more easily.

To insert a table, first switch to Standard view by clicking the Standard View button on the Layout tab of the Insert bar (see Figure 7-6) or by choosing View → Table Mode → Standard View. Then proceed as follows.

1. **Place the insertion point in the document window where you'd like to insert a table.**

   You can add a table anywhere you can add graphics or text. You can even add a table inside another table, by clicking inside a table cell.

Note: If you've never built HTML tables before, you may find them confusing. For an excellent set of tutorials, check out *www.dwfaq.com/Tutorials/Tables/*.

2. **Choose Insert → Table.**

   You can also click the Table button on the Insert bar. It appears under both the Common tab and the Layout tab. You can also press Ctrl+Alt+T (⌘-Option-T). Either way, the Insert Table dialog box opens (see Figure 7-15).

3. **Using the Rows and Columns fields, specify how many rows and columns you want your table to have.**

   If you're using the table for layout purposes, you may want only two or three columns. If you plan to create a spreadsheet, you could create many rows or columns. (Don't fret too much over your estimate, since you can always add or remove rows or columns later.)

4. **Type the amount of cell padding, in pixels, you want for the table.**

   Cell padding is the margin inside the cell—the space from the edge of a cell to its contents (see Figure 7-5). Unfortunately, this property applies to *every* cell in a table. You can't add this space to an individual cell in a table unless you use the Cascading Style Sheet Padding property as described in the Note on page 202.

5. **Type the amount of cell spacing, in pixels, you want for the table.**

Cell spacing specifies how many pixels of space separate one cell from another (see Figure 7-5). Again, this property applies to every cell in a table. (Note that leaving these fields empty isn't the same as setting them to zero; see Figure 7-15.)

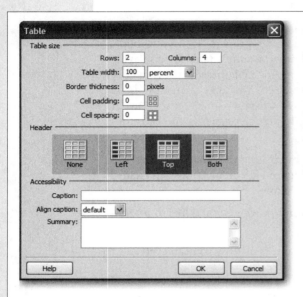

Figure 7-15:
The Insert Table dialog box lets you define the properties of the table. Leaving the Cell Padding and Cell Spacing fields empty isn't the same as setting them to 0. If these properties are empty, most Web browsers insert 1 pixel of cell padding and 2 pixels of cell spacing. If you notice unwanted gaps between cells in a table or between content in a table and the cell's edges, empty settings here are the most likely culprit. To truly leave zero space, set Cell Padding and Cell Spacing to 0. (Dreamweaver remembers the settings you use. When you use the Insert Table dialog box again, it starts with the same settings you entered previously.)

6. **Using the "Table width" field, specify how wide you want the table to be (in units that you specify using the pop-up menu).**

Tables can have either a specified, fixed minimum width, or they can take up a specified percentage of the space available on the page. To set a fixed width, choose Pixels as the unit of measurement and type a pixel amount in the "Table width" field. Fixed-width tables remain the same size regardless of the size of the browser window.

Percentage widths let tables grow or shrink relative to the space available. In other words, the size of a table that's 100 percent wide stretches all the way across your visitor's browser window, no matter how wide or narrow. (You achieve a similar effect with the Autostretch feature in Layout mode, as described on page 240.)

Note: Because of differences in the way browsers interpret HTML, the exact pixel dimensions of percentage-based tables may differ from browser to browser. In some cases, a Web browser leaves room at the right edge of the browser window for scroll bars—even if the page isn't long enough to require scroll bars!

7. **In the "Border thickness" box, type a number, in pixels, for the border.**

If you don't want a border, type *0*. Dreamweaver uses dotted lines to help you identify rows, columns, and cells whose border is 0. (The dotted lines won't appear on the finished Web page.) Again, CSS offers a much better method of adding borders (see page 205).

8. **Using the buttons in the middle of the dialog box, select a Header option.**

If you're actually using a table for its intended purpose—to display a grid of information—you'll find the Header property useful. It converts the HTML tag used for the cells (<td>) in the top row or right column into <th> tags—a table header tag—which indicates that a cell is a *headline* for a column or row of data. You'd use this, for example, to announce the purpose of the table ("UFO Sightings by City: 1980–2004") or to provide an explanation for the data in each column or row ("1980," "1981," "1982," and so on).

The only visible change is that, in most Web browsers, header cell text changes to bold type and gets center aligned. However, this option also makes the table more accessible by telling screen readers (used by the visually impaired) that the cell serves as a header for the information in the column. (You can always change the look of these cells using CSS; just create a style for the <th> tag as described on page 165.)

9. **In the bottom section of the Table dialog box, add any Accessibility settings you wish.**

Use this feature when creating full tables of data, spreadsheet-style, not when using tables to lay out the design of a page. Type information identifying the table in the Caption box; it appears above (centered, left, or right) or below the table, depending on what you select in the "Align caption" menu. Use the Summary box to provide a detailed explanation of the table. This information won't be displayed in a browser window; it's intended to be used by screen readers to provide detailed information about the table for the visually impaired.

For more information on these options and to get a complete rundown on table accessibility, visit *www.w3.org/TR/WCAG10-HTML-TECHS/#tables*.

10. **Click OK to insert the table.**

Once you've added a table to a page, you can begin filling the table's cells. A cell works like a small document window; you can click inside it and add text, images, and links using the techniques you've already learned. You can even insert a table inside of a cell (see page 266).

To move the insertion point from one cell to the next, press Tab. When you reach the last cell in a row, the Tab key moves the insertion point to the first cell in the row below. And if the insertion point is in the last *cell* of the last row, pressing Tab creates a new row at the bottom of the table.

Shift+Tab moves the cursor in the *opposite* direction—from the current cell to a cell to the left.

Selecting Parts of a Table in Standard View

Tables and their cells have independent properties. For example, a table and a cell can have different background colors. But before you can change any of these properties, you must first *select* the tables, rows, columns, or cells you want to affect.

Selecting a Table

There are a number of ways to select a table in the document window:

- Click the upper-left corner of the table, or anywhere on the bottom edge of the table. (Be careful using the latter technique, however. It's easy to accidentally *drag* the border, resetting the height of the table in the process.)

- Click anywhere inside the table, and then select the <table> tag in the document window's status bar (see page 21 to learn about the tag selector).

- Click anywhere inside the table, and then choose Modify → Table → Select Table.

- Right-click (Control-click) inside a table, and then choose Table → Select Table from the contextual menu.

- If the insertion point is in any cell inside the table, pressing Ctrl+A (⌘-A) twice selects the table.

Once selected, a table appears with a thick black border and three tiny, square resize handles—at the right edge, bottom edge, and lower-right corner.

Selecting Rows or Columns

You can also select an entire row or column of cells by doing one of the following:

- Move the cursor to the left edge of a row or the top edge of a column. When it changes to a right- or down-pointing arrow, click, as explained in Figure 7-16.

- Click a cell at either end of a row, or the first or last cell of a column, and then drag across the cells in the row or column to select them.

- Click any cell in the row you wish to select, and then click the <tr> tag in the tag selector. (The <tr> tag is how HTML indicates a table row.) This method doesn't work for columns.

When a cell is selected, it has a dark border around it. When multiple cells are selected, each cell has a dark border (see Figure 7-16).

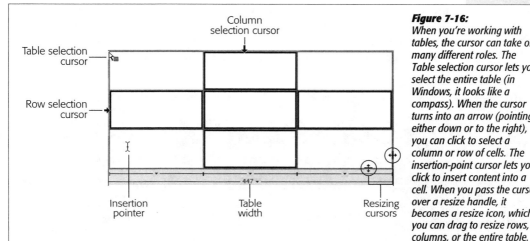

Column selection cursor

Table selection cursor

Row selection cursor

Insertion pointer

Table width

Resizing cursors

Figure 7-16:
When you're working with tables, the cursor can take on many different roles. The Table selection cursor lets you select the entire table (in Windows, it looks like a compass). When the cursor turns into an arrow (pointing either down or to the right), you can click to select a column or row of cells. The insertion-point cursor lets you click to insert content into a cell. When you pass the cursor over a resize handle, it becomes a resize icon, which you can drag to resize rows, columns, or the entire table.

Selecting Cells

To select one or more cells:

- Drag over adjoining cells. A solid black border appears around a cell when it's selected.

- To select several cells that aren't necessarily adjacent, Ctrl-click (⌘-click) them one at a time. (You can also Ctrl-click [⌘-click] an already selected cell to deselect it.)

- Click a cell, and then Shift-click another cell. Your two clicks form diagonally opposite corners of an imaginary rectangle; Dreamweaver highlights all cells within it.

- Use the tag selector (see page 21) to select a cell. Click inside the cell you wish to select, and then click the <td> tag in the tag selector. (The <td> tag stands for *table data*, which is how the HTML language refers to a cell.)

- If the insertion point is inside the cell you wish to select, press Ctrl+A (⌘-A).

Expanded Table Mode

When you use tables to lay out a Web page, you usually do things like hide table borders, use many small tables, and nest tables inside other tables. As you now know, these techniques conceal the actual table structure, creating an attractive Web page. But they can make it difficult for you to see how a table is put together, at least in Design view.

To make your task easier, Dreamweaver includes the Expanded Table mode. Clicking the Expanded button on the Layout tab of the Insert bar adds visible borders to every table and cell, and increases onscreen cell padding. As shown in Figure 7-17, now you can clearly see how many rows, columns, and cells your table has, making selecting and formatting that much easier. (Expanded Table mode never changes the actual page code; it merely affects how the page is displayed in Design view. The guideline borders and extra spacing don't appear in a Web browser.)

Figure 7-17:
Expanded Table mode lets you clearly view the structure of table-based layouts. In Standard view (top), it's difficult to distinguish tables, rows, columns, and cells. With Expanded Table mode turned on (bottom), Dreamweaver displays tables with extra borders and cell spacing to make selecting and working with tables and cells easier. (Expanded Table mode is just an extension of the Standard mode. You can't use any of the Layout mode tools—cell- or table-drawing tools, for example—in Expanded Table mode.)

To return to Standard view, click the Standard button on the Layout panel.

Formatting Tables

When you first insert a table, you set the number of rows and columns, as well as the table's cell padding, cell spacing, width, and borders. You're not stuck, however, with the properties you first give the table; you can change any or all of these properties, and set a few additional ones, using the Property inspector.

When you select a table in Standard view, the Property inspector changes to reflect that table's settings (see Figure 7-18). You can adjust the table by entering different values for height, width, rows, columns, and so on in the appropriate fields.

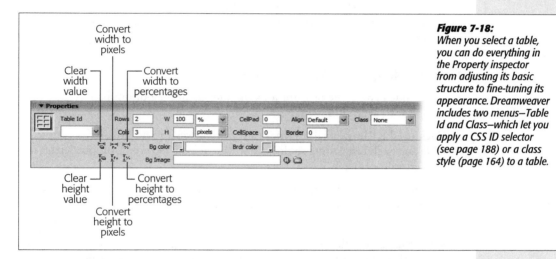

Figure 7-18:
When you select a table, you can do everything in the Property inspector from adjusting its basic structure to fine-tuning its appearance. Dreamweaver includes two menus—Table Id and Class—which let you apply a CSS ID selector (see page 188) or a class style (page 164) to a table.

In addition, the Property inspector lets you set alignment options and add colors or a background image, as described next.

Aligning Tables

In the normal flow of a Web page, a table acts like a paragraph, header, or any other HTML block-level element. It's aligned to the left of the page, with other elements placed either above it or below it.

But you can make several useful changes to the way a table interacts with the text and other elements around it. After selecting the table, use one of the three alignment options in the pop-up menu at the right of the Property inspector:

• The Left and Right options align the table with the left or right page margins. Anything you then add to the page—including paragraphs, images, or other tables—wraps around the right or left side of the table. You can also apply the CSS Float property to a table to achieve the same effect (see page 202).

- The Center option makes the table sit in the center of the page, interrupting the flow of the elements around it. Nothing wraps around the table.

Note: Some of the properties Dreamweaver lets you adjust to make tables look better aren't "valid" for some of the different HTML "document types" Dreamweaver can create. As you saw in the Tutorial in Chapter 1 (page 36), Dreamweaver can create HTML 4.01 Transitional, XHTML 1.0 Transitional, and (new in version 8) several other types of HTML documents. In general, HTML 4.01 Transitional and XHTML 1.0 Transitional are the most commonly used document types. However, the more "strict" types like HTML 4.01 Strict and XHTML 1.0 Strict don't support some table properties—the align property discussed above, for example. This discrepancy is more a technicality than a design nuisance; most Web browsers still display the alignment you select, even when used with these types of documents. The newer and recommended method is to use CSS properties to accomplish the same display goals; for example, using CSS to set the left and right margins of a table to "auto" centers the table on the page (see page 203), while applying a CSS Left Float and Right Float to a table is the same as the Left and Right align options (page 202). See page 506 for more on what "valid" HTML is.

Clearing Height and Width Values

Six tools hide behind the obscure-looking buttons in the bottom half of the Property inspector (see Figure 7-18).

- Clicking the Clear Height Values button removes the height properties of the table and each cell. Doing so doesn't set the heights to zero; it simply deletes the property altogether.

- Clicking the Clear Width Values button accomplishes the same purpose for the width properties of a table and its cells (see "Setting Cell Dimensions" on page 258).

When creating complex table designs, it's easy to get yourself into a situation where width and height measurements conflict and produce unreliable results. For example, it's possible to set one cell to 300 pixels wide, and later set another cell *in the same column* to 400 pixels wide. Since a Web browser can't do both (how can one column be both 300 *and* 400 pixels wide?), you'll get unpredictable results.

In tables with many cells, these kinds of problems are tough to ferret out. That's when you'll find these time-saving tools handy. You can delete the width and height measurements and start from scratch (see "Tips for Surviving Table Making" on page 258).

Four additional buttons let you convert pixel-based measurements to percentage measurements and vice versa. In other words, if a table is 600 pixels wide and you click the Convert Widths to Percentages button, Dreamweaver assigns percentages to the table and each cell whose width is specified using pixels.

These percentages depend on how much of the document window your table takes up when you click the button. If the document window is 1200 pixels wide, that 600-pixel-wide table changes to a 50-percent width. Because you'll rarely do this, don't waste your brain cells memorizing such tools. (See "Resizing a Table" below for more information.)

Decorating a Table

To spruce up a table, you can add color to its background and borders, and even add a background image. As usual in Dreamweaver, you make these changes in the Property inspector. First select the table (see page 248), and then click the appropriate box in the Property inspector—Bg color (background) or Brdr color (border)—and select a color from the color palette. (See page 41 for more on choosing colors in Dreamweaver.)

To add a graphic image to the background of a selected table, click the folder icon next to Bg Image in the Property inspector. Browse to and open an image in your Web site folder; it appears immediately as a background image for the selected table.

Note: Border color and background images aren't valid XHTML Transitional code (see the Note on the opposite page). In addition, neither HTML 4.01 Strict nor XHTML 1.0 Strict supports those properties or the background-color property.

The CSS background properties (see page 197) are a solution to this dilemma, and offer more control over setting background colors and images than the HTML equivalents described here. In addition, you can achieve more border effects—even different sizes, colors, and styles for each border—using the CSS Border properties described on page 205.

Resizing a Table

While you define the width of a table when you first insert it, you can always change your mind later. To do so, first select the table, and then take either of these steps:

- Type a value into the W (width) box on the Property inspector and choose a unit of measurement from the pop-up menu, either pixels or percentages.

- Drag one of the resize handles on the right edge or right corner of the table. (The corner handle adjusts the height and width of the table simultaneously.)

In theory, you can also convert a table from a fixed unit of measurement, such as pixels, to the stretchy, percentage-style width setting—or vice versa—using four buttons at the bottom of the Property inspector. What these buttons do depends on the size of the current document window in Dreamweaver. For example, suppose the document window is 700 pixels wide, and you've inserted a table that's 100 percent wide. Clicking the Convert Widths to Pixels button sets the table's width to around 700 pixels (the exact value depends on the margins of the page). However, if your document window were 500 pixels wide, clicking the same button would produce a fixed-width table around 500 pixels wide. Two buttons let you control this conversion separately for the height and width of the table and its cells (see Figure 7-18).

Note: The HTML <table> tag doesn't officially have a Height property. Dreamweaver, however, adds a Height property if you use the Property inspector or drag the bottom of the table to resize it. Most Web browsers understand this Height property and obey your wishes. But since it's not standard code, there's no guarantee that newer browsers will support this maneuver.

You have several alternatives: First, you could decide not to worry about height. After all, it's difficult to control the height of a table precisely, especially if there's text in it. Since text sizes appear differently on different operating systems and browsers, the table may grow taller if the text is larger, no matter where you set the height. Or you could use the CSS Height property (page 202) to set a height for a table. Finally, you can always insert a graphic in a table cell to pop it up to the height you want. (See "The contents take priority" on page 259.)

The Convert Width to Percentages buttons take the opposite tack. They set the width or height of a table and its cells to percentages based on the amount of the document window's width and height they cover at the moment. The bigger the window, the smaller the percentage.

Because the effects of these buttons depend upon the size of the document window, you'll find yourself rarely, if ever, using these two tools.

Modifying Cell and Row Properties in Standard View

Cells have their own properties, separate from the properties of the table itself. So do table *rows*—but not columns (see page 255).

When you click inside a cell, the top half of the Property inspector displays the cell's text formatting properties; the bottom half shows the properties for that particular cell (see Figure 7-19, top).

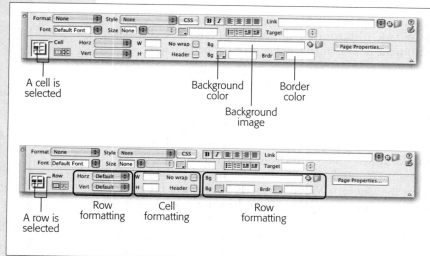

A cell is selected

Background color

Border color

Background image

A row is selected

Row formatting

Cell formatting

Row formatting

Figure 7-19:
The Property inspector displays the properties of a cell (top) or a row (bottom). Rows have distinct properties that you can set independently of a cell. For example, a row can have background and border colors that are different from the individual cells in that row. (Still, when a row is selected, the Width, Height, No Wrap, or Header options affect the individual cells in the row.)

Alignment Properties

At the outset, a cell's contents hug the left wall of the cell and float halfway between the top and bottom of the cell. After selecting a row, a cell, or several cells, you can change these alignments using the Property inspector. For example, the Horz (Horizontal) menu in the Property inspector (see Figure 7-19) offers Left, Center, Right, and Default alignment options. (Default produces the same effect as Center without adding any extra HTML code.)

Note that these options are distinct from the *paragraph* alignment options discussed in Chapter 3. In fact, you can mix and match the two. Suppose, for example, that you have a table cell containing four paragraphs. You want all but one paragraph to be center aligned; you want the last paragraph to be right aligned. To do so, you could set the alignment of the *cell* to Center, and then select just the last paragraph and set its alignment to Right. The paragraph's alignment overrides the alignment applied by the cell.

You can set the vertical alignment property in the same manner. Select the cells and then use one of the five options available in the Vert (Vertical) menu of the Property inspector: Default (the same as Middle), Top, Middle, Bottom, or Baseline.

(The Baseline option aligns the bottom of the first line of text in the cell to the baseline of text in all the other cells in the row. Internet Explorer and Opera display this correctly, but Firefox and Safari ignore the Baseline setting.)

Table Header

The Table Header option lets you convert a <td> tag to a <th> tag for specifying a table header. It's a similar scheme to the column or row headers available in the Insert Table dialog box, described on page 247.

POWER USERS' CLINIC

The Dawn of Columns

As far as the standard HTML language is concerned, there really isn't any such entity as a column. Tables are created with the <table> tag, rows with the <tr> tag, and cells with the <td> tag—but there's no column tag. Dreamweaver calculates the columns based on the number of cells in a row. If there are 7 rows in a table, each with 4 cells, then the table has 4 columns. In other words, the number of cells in each row determines the number of columns.

But times are changing. Two new tags introduced in HTML 4—the <colgroup> and <col> tags—let you control various attributes of columns in a table. At present, not all Web browsers understand these tags, and Dreamweaver provides no easy way to add them. You can find out more about them, however, in Dreamweaver's built-in HTML reference (see page 353).

You'll usually use this option for tables that include actual tabular data, like a spreadsheet, to indicate the meaning of the data that appears in the other cells in a row or column. For example, you may have a table containing data from different years; each cell in the top row may identify the year of the data in the cells below it.

While Dreamweaver lets you change a single cell into a header, you'll most likely apply this to a row of cells or the left column of cells.

A Property to Forget

The No Wrap option is of such little value that you'll probably go your entire Web career without using it.

But for the sake of thoroughness—and in case you may actually find a use for it— here's a description. The No Wrap property prevents a Web browser from wrapping a line of text within a cell onto multiple lines. The browser instead widens the cell so that it can include the line without line breaks. The result is almost never useful or attractive. Furthermore, if you specify a width for the cell, this property doesn't work at all!

FREQUENTLY ASKED QUESTION

Suddenly Jumbo Cells

When I added some text to a cell, it suddenly got much wider than the other cells in the row. What gives?

It isn't Dreamweaver's fault. This is how HTML works.

Web browsers (and Dreamweaver) display cells to match the content inside. In the example shown here, the first cell of the first row has a little text, the second cell is blank, and the third cell has a 125-pixel-wide image. Since the image is the biggest item, its cell is wider than the other two. The middle cell, with nothing in it, is given the least amount of space.

Usually, you won't want a Web browser making these kinds of decisions. By specifying a width for a cell (page 258), you can force a Web browser to display a cell with the dimension you want, but keep in mind that there are exceptions to this rule; see "The contents take priority" on page 259.

Cell Decoration

Cells needn't be drab. As with tables, you can give individual cells background colors, or even background graphics (see Figure 7-20).

Adding cell background colors

To set the background color of one or more selected table cells or rows, do one of the following:

- Click the Bg color box in the Property inspector, and then select a color from the pop-up palette.

- Type a hexadecimal color value into the Bg color field.

You also have the option to set a color for the cell's border using the color box or Brdr field in the Property inspector. However, only Internet Explorer recognizes this property, and, since it isn't officially part of HTML, it's unlikely that other browsers will ever support it.

Note: The same caveats about Table backgrounds (see the note on page 253) apply to cell backgrounds. Many Web developers have already abandoned the Cell Background and Border properties in favor of their more versatile CSS counterparts. See page 197 for more on CSS Background properties and page 205 for CSS Border properties.

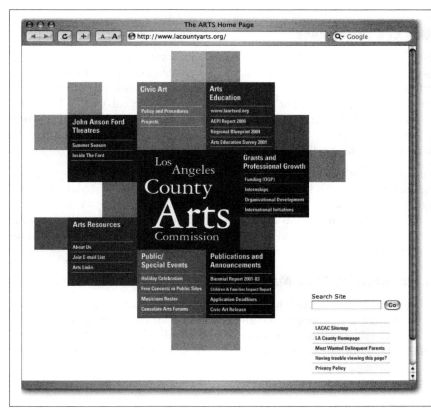

Figure 7-20:
Add impact with background color. The home page for the Los Angeles County Arts Commission (www.lacountyarts.org) makes a big visual statement without being a bandwidth hog. The trick? Instead of using graphics to add colorful squares to the page, they've simply applied background colors to the table cells.

Adding cell background images

You can also add an image to the background of a cell. In this scenario, the cell acts much like a miniature document window; the graphic tiles (repeats endlessly) within the cell to completely cover the cell's background.

To add a background image to selected cells, try either of these steps:

- Click the Browse for File icon (the folder icon) to the right of the Bg field in the Property inspector (see Figure 7-19). In the resulting dialog box, navigate to and open the graphics file you want.

- Type the file path or URL of the graphic you want in the Bg field in the Property inspector.

You can also set a background image for a table *row* (<tr> tag) using Dreamweaver, but it involves some coding that isn't officially part of HTML. In fact, Internet Explorer won't display a background image for a table row at all.

Note: Here's another instance where CSS outshines HTML. With CSS, you can control a background image's placement inside of a table or cell and how it tiles (if at all). See page 197.

Setting Cell Dimensions

Specifying the width or height of a particular cell works just as it does when you set the width or height of a table: select one or more cells, and type a value in the W (width) or H (height) field in the Property inspector. This value can be either specified in pixels or percentage. For instance, if you want a particular cell to be 50 pixels wide, type *50*. For a cell that you want to be 50 percent of the total table width, type *50%*. Read "Tips for Surviving Table Making" below for details on the tricky business of controlling cell and table dimensions.

You can also resize a column or row of cells by dragging a cell border. As your cursor approaches the cell's border, it changes shape to indicate that you can begin dragging. Dreamweaver also provides an interactive display of cell widths (Figure 7-21) when you use this method. This helpful feature lets you know exactly what width your cells are at all times so you can drag a cell to the exact width you're seeking.

Tips for Surviving Table Making

Nothing is more confounding than trying to get your tables laid out exactly as you want them. Many beginning Web designers throw their hands up in despair when working with tables, which often seem to have minds of their own. Layout mode eliminates many of the hassles associated with using tables for page layout, but here are a few problems that often confuse designers—and some tips to make working with tables more straightforward.

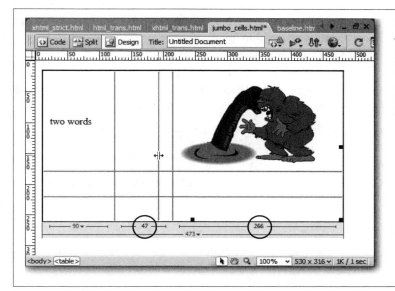

Figure 7-21:
As you drag the border between cells, Dreamweaver shows you the changing widths of the two adjacent cells in real time. The width values change to blue and update themselves as you move your mouse.

The contents take priority

Say you've created a 300-pixel-wide table and set each cell in the first row to 100 pixels wide. You insert a larger graphic into the first cell, and suddenly—Kablooie! Even though you set each cell to 100 pixels wide, as shown in Figure 7-22, the column with the graphic is much wider than the other two.

That's because a cell can't be smaller than the largest piece of content inside it. In this case, although you told the cell to be 100 pixels wide, the image is 155 pixels wide and forces the first column to grow (and the others to shrink) accordingly.

Figure 7-22:
Because a Web browser can't shrink the image or hide part of it, the cell has to grow to fit it. That first column of cells is now 155 pixels wide; the other two columns must shrink in order to keep the table 300 pixels wide. The numbers at the bottom of each cell indicate its width as set in the HTML—100—and the actual width as displayed in Dreamweaver in parentheses (155, 67, and 68).

There's no such thing as column width, only cell width

To set the width of a column of cells, you have to set the width of only *one* cell in that column. For example, say you have a table with three rows and three columns. You need only to set the width for the top row of cells; you can (and should) leave the cell widths for the remaining cells in the two bottom rows empty. (You can do this with any row of cells, not just the top row.)

This principle can save a lot of time and, because it reduces the amount of code on a Web page, makes your pages load and appear faster. For consistency, it's a good idea to pick either the first or last row of a table for width-setting.

The same holds true for the height of a row. You need only to set the height of a single cell to define the height for its entire row.

Fortunately, Dreamweaver is smart. When you resize one or more cells, it adds width and height values only where they're needed, without filling every cell with needless height and width values.

Do the math

Calculators are really useful when you're building tables. Although you *could* create a 400-pixel-wide table with three 700-pixel-wide columns, the results you'd get on the screen could be unpredictable ($700 + 700 + 700 \neq 400$).

As it turns out, Web browsers' loyalty is to *table* width first, and then column widths. If you make the widths of your columns add up to the width of your table, you'll save yourself a lot of headache.

You'll need to account for a few other factors if you add borders, cell padding, and cell spacing. For example, say you create a 500-pixel-wide table with two columns and 10 pixels of padding. If you want the first column to be 100 pixels wide, you would set the width value to 80 pixels: 10 pixels left padding + 80 pixels of cell space + 10 pixels of right padding = 100 pixels total width.

WORKAROUND WORKSHOP

Beware the Resize Handles

Dreamweaver provides several techniques for resizing tables and cells while in Standard view. Unfortunately, the easiest method—dragging a cell or table border—is also the easiest to do by mistake. Because moving the cursor over any border turns it into the Resize tool, almost every Dreamweaver practitioner drags a border accidentally at least once, overwriting carefully calculated table and cell widths and heights.

On occasions like these, don't forget the undo feature, Ctrl+Z (⌘-Z). And if all is lost, you can always clear the widths and heights of every cell in a table (using the buttons in the Property inspector) and start over by typing new cell dimensions (see Figure 7-18).

Spacer Image Revisited

Unfortunately, even if you explicitly set cell widths, some browsers still don't do a good job at controlling the width of cells. Remembering that a cell can't be smaller than the largest item inside it, as noted previously, is half the battle. For even more control, use a spacer image, just as Dreamweaver does when you use the Autostretch option in Layout mode (see page 240).

For example, suppose you want to create a table that's 580 pixels wide, with two rows and three columns. The widths of the columns will be 150 pixels, 20 pixels, and 410 pixels, respectively.

Specifying the widths of each cell in one of the rows would be a good start, but a more reliable approach would be to use a *transparent GIF image* to reinforce the column widths:

1. **In a graphics program, create a 1 × 1–pixel, transparent GIF graphic.**

   Dreamweaver can do this automatically if you use Layout mode. See page 230.

2. **Create a new row at the bottom of the table.**

   One easy way is to click the lower-right cell of the table, and then press Tab.

3. **Click in the first cell; insert the spacer image by choosing Insert → Image and selecting the spacer file in your site folder.**

   Dreamweaver inserts the image and selects it in the document window.

4. **Using the Property inspector, change the width of the GIF to 150 pixels.**

   Since the first column in the table is 150 pixels wide, this graphic keeps the column from shrinking any smaller—which, in some browsers, it might otherwise do, thanks to an all-too-common bug.

5. **In the second cell in the row, insert another spacer GIF. Set its width to 20 pixels.**

   Like the previous image, this one helps maintain the 20-pixel width of the column.

6. **Finally, move to the third cell in the row, insert another spacer, and set its width to 410 pixels.**

   Your table is now rock solid.

Now you can see the advantages of Dreamweaver's Layout mode, which eliminates the need for many of these workarounds. It takes care of a lot of the headaches of building table-based layouts.

Adding and Removing Cells

Even after inserting a table into a Web page, you can add and subtract rows and columns from your table. The text or images in the columns move right or down to accommodate their new next-door neighbor.

Adding One Row or Column

To add a single row to the table, you can use any of these approaches:

- Click inside a cell. Choose Modify → Table → Insert Row, or press Ctrl+M (⌘-M), to insert a new row of cells above the current row. Alternatively, you can right-click (Control-click) a cell and choose Table → Insert Row from the shortcut menu.

- To add a new row at the end of a table, click inside the last cell in the table and then press Tab.

The new rows inherit the properties (width, height, background color, and so on) of the row you originally clicked.

To add a single *column* of cells:

- Click inside a cell and then choose Modify → Table → Insert Column.

- Click inside a cell and then press Ctrl+Shift+A (⌘-Shift-A).

- Right-click (Control-click) a cell, and then choose Table → Insert Column from the shortcut menu that appears.

In each case, a new column appears to the right of the current column.

Adding Multiple Rows or Columns

When you need to expand your table more rapidly, you can use a special dialog box that lets you add many rows or columns at once.

1. **Click inside a cell. Choose Modify → Table → Insert Rows or Columns.**

   The Insert Rows or Columns dialog box appears (see Figure 7-23).

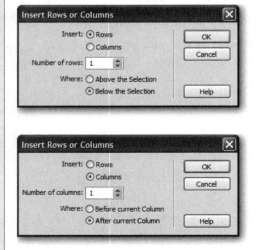

Figure 7-23:
The Insert Rows or Columns dialog box lets you add multiple rows or columns to a table. The wording of the options changes depending on whether you're inserting rows or columns. Note that the bottom dialog box offers the only way to add a column to the right edge of a table.

2. **Click either Rows or Columns. Type the number of rows or columns you wish to add.**

   You can also click the tiny up and down arrow buttons next to the "Number of rows" (or columns) field.

3. **Indicate where you wish the new rows or columns to appear, relative to the cell you selected, by clicking Above or Below (for rows) or Before or After (for columns). Click OK to insert them.**

Using the dialog box gives you the advantage of choosing whether you want the new row or column to come *before* or *after* the selected information in your table, as shown in Figure 7-23.

Deleting Rows and Columns

To delete a row from your table, you can use one of the following techniques.

Tip: When you remove a row or column, Dreamweaver also eliminates everything inside. So before you start hacking away, it's a good idea to save a copy of the page with the table.

- Select the row (see page 248); press Delete to delete all of the cells—and everything in them—for the selected row.
- Click a cell. Choose Modify → Table → Delete Row, or use the keyboard shortcut Ctrl+Shift+M (⌘-Shift-M).
- Right-click (Control-click) inside a cell, and then choose Table → Delete Row from the shortcut menu.

Deleting a column is equally straightforward.

- Select the column (page 248), and then press Delete. You've just eliminated all the selected cells and everything in them.
- Click inside a cell and choose Modify → Table → Delete Column, or use the keyboard shortcut Ctrl+Shift+Hyphen (⌘-Shift-Hyphen).
- Right-click (Control-click) inside a cell, and then choose Table → Delete Column from the shortcut menu.

Note: Dreamweaver doesn't let you delete a row if one of its cells is *merged* with a cell in another row. Nor can you delete a column if it contains a cell that's merged with a cell in an adjacent *column.* (Merged cells are discussed in the next section.)

Deleting a column in this way is actually quite a feat. Since there's no column tag in HTML, Dreamweaver, behind the scenes, has to select individual cells in multiple rows—a task you wouldn't wish on your worst enemy if you had to do it by editing the raw HTML code.

Merging and Splitting Cells

Cells are very basic creatures with some severe limitations. For example, all of the cells in a row share the same height. A cell can't be taller than the cell next to it, which can pose some serious design problems.

Consider Figure 7-24 at top, for example. In the top figure, the left cell (containing the gear graphic) is much taller than the top banner to its right. In fact, it's as tall as *both* banners to its right, as shown in the bottom figure. Ideally, you'd want the gear graphic cell to straddle the two cells to its right, as shown in the lower banner. In such situations, Dreamweaver provides several ways of persuading cells to work well together.

The trick is to *merge* cells—combine their area—to create a larger cell that spans two or more rows or columns. In Figure 7-24, the solution is to merge the two cells in the left column. This single cell holds the image of the gear, while perfectly aligning the two cells in the adjacent column. By using this technique, you can create some very complex designs. In fact, if you view tables created in Dreamweaver's Layout mode, you'll notice that Dreamweaver itself makes extensive use of this technique.

Note: It's easy to abuse this trick. Merging too many cells together can lead to complex and inflexible tables. In many cases, you can achieve the same effect by nesting simple tables; see page 266.

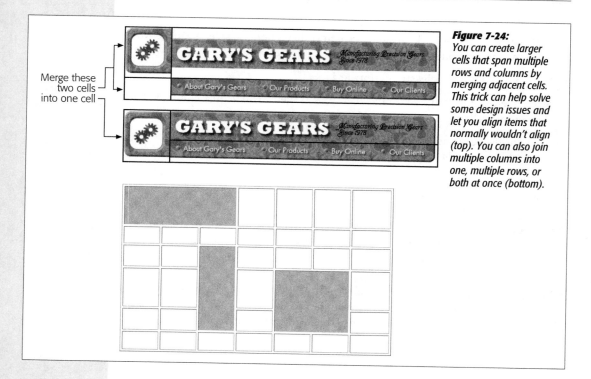

Merge these two cells into one cell

Figure 7-24:
You can create larger cells that span multiple rows and columns by merging adjacent cells. This trick can help solve some design issues and let you align items that normally wouldn't align (top). You can also join multiple columns into one, multiple rows, or both at once (bottom).

To merge cells, start by selecting the cells you wish to merge, using any of the methods described on page 249. (You can only merge cells that form a rectangle or square. You can't, for instance, select three cells in a column and only one in the adjacent row to create an L shape. Nor can you merge cells that aren't adjacent; in other words, you can't merge a cell in one corner of the table with a cell in the opposite corner.)

Then, on the Property inspector, click the Merge Cells button (Figure 7-25), or choose Modify → Table → Merge Cells.

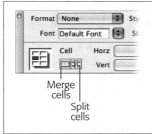

Figure 7-25:
The Merge Cells button is only active when you've selected multiple cells. The Split Cells button appears only when you select a single cell or have clicked inside a cell.

Merge
cells

Split
cells

Tip: Better yet, use this undocumented keyboard shortcut: the M key. Just select two or more cells and press M. It's much easier than the keyboard shortcut listed in the online help: Ctrl+Alt+M (⌘-Option-M).

Dreamweaver joins the selected cells, forming a single new super cell.

You may also find yourself in the opposite situation: you have one cell that you want to *divide* into multiple cells. To split a cell, click inside, or select, a single cell. Click the Split Cells button in the Property inspector. (Once again, you can trigger this command in several alternative ways. For example, you can choose Modify → Table → Split Cell. And if you prefer keyboard shortcuts, you can press Ctrl+Alt+S [Option-S]. You can even right-click [Control-click] the selected cell and then choose Table → Split Cell from the contextual menu.)

When the Split Cell dialog box opens (see Figure 7-26), click one of the buttons to indicate whether you want to split the cell into rows or columns. Then type the number of rows or columns you wish to create; click OK.

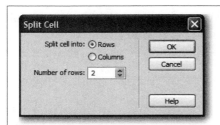

Figure 7-26:
The Split Cell dialog box lets you divide a single cell into multiple cells. You can choose whether to divide the cell into rows (multiple cells on top of one another) or columns (multiple cells side by side).

If you split a cell into columns, everything in the cell winds up in the right column, with the new, empty column or columns to the left. When you split a cell into rows, the contents end up in the top row.

Nesting Tables in Standard View

By merging cells, you can create complex tables that offer precise control over your layouts. If you use Layout mode to create a detailed, handcrafted design, you'll see how Dreamweaver can generate complex tables using this technique.

But on the Web, simpler is usually better. Sometimes, instead of spending time and effort chopping up and merging cells to create a certain look, the best solution is to *nest* tables—placing a table within a table—instead of creating one complex table (see Figure 7-27).

Since a table cell acts just like a mini document, you can put anything that you'd normally place on a page inside a cell—graphics, text, links and, yes, even tables. Simply click a cell and use one of the techniques described earlier to add and format the table.

You can even place *more* than one table in a single cell. In Figure 7-27, for example, three tables are nested in the right-side cell of the main table. They're in the flow of the cell contents, separated into individual paragraphs (it sounds complicated, but looking at the figure should makes things clear). By compartmentalizing and aligning information, nested tables make complex Web pages easier to both build and edit.

Be aware that there are some limits to nesting tables. For example, it's best not to nest more than three tables deep—in other words, a table inside of a table inside of a table. While most browsers can recognize and draw tables that are more deeply nested, such complexity is difficult to render, resulting in pages that are slow to load, especially on slower computers.

Tabular Data

So far, you've learned about using tables for complex Web page designs, using tricks like merging cells, invisible spacer images, and Dreamweaver's Layout mode. But what about the original purpose of a table—displaying data in an orderly manner? You can still do that, of course, and Dreamweaver provides a couple of tools to make the process of dealing with tabular data run smoothly.

Tip: You can directly import Excel files into Dreamweaver for Windows, which converts the data into a well-organized table. See page 67.

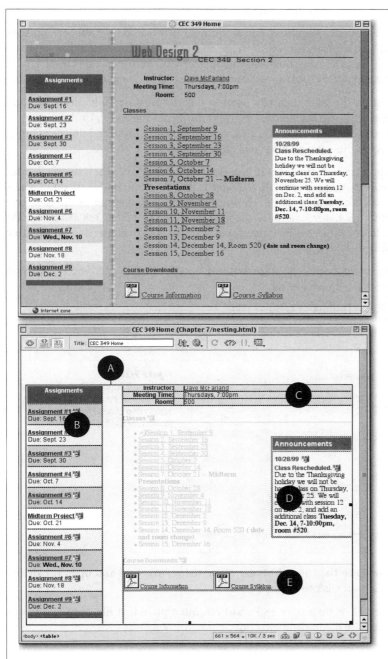

Figure 7-27:
The page at top looks complicated, but in Dreamweaver, it breaks down, as you can see in the HTML page below, to a series of simple tables. The outside table (A) is a one-row, three-column table with a series of nested tables (B, C, D, and E). The first cell contains another basic table (B), which has 12 rows and one column. (Using alternating colors for each cell helps set off the information inside.) The third column of the primary table holds the main content of the page; three tables (C, D, and E) are placed within the flow of the cell. One nice trick: Use the Align property of a table to create a "floating" sidebar within the normal flow of text. The Announcements table here, for instance, is aligned to the right, while text in the cell wraps around it. Note that aligning a table like this is only possible in Standard view.

Importing Data into a Table

Say your boss emails you your company's yearly sales information, which includes data on sales, profits, and expenses organized by quarter. She asks you to get this up on the Web for a board meeting she's having in half an hour.

This assignment could require a fair amount of work: building a table and then copying and pasting the correct information into each cell of the table, one at a time. Dreamweaver makes your task much easier, because you can create a table and import data into the table's rows and columns, all in one pass.

For this to work, the table data you want to display must begin life in a *delimited* format—a task that most spreadsheet programs, including Excel, or database programs, such as Access or FileMaker Pro, can do easily. (Choosing File → Export or File → Save As in these programs usually does it.)

In a delimited file, each line of text represents one table row. Each line is divided into smaller units using a special character called a delimiter—most often a tab, but possibly a comma or colon. Each unit represents a single cell in the row. In a colon-delimited file, for example, the line *Sales:$1,000,000:$2,000,000:$567,000: $12,500* would be converted by Dreamweaver into a row of five cells, with the first cell containing the word *Sales*.

Once you've saved your boss's spreadsheet as a delimited file, you're ready to import it into a Dreamweaver table:

1. **Choose File → Import → Tabular Data.**

   The Import Tabular Data dialog box appears (Figure 7-28).

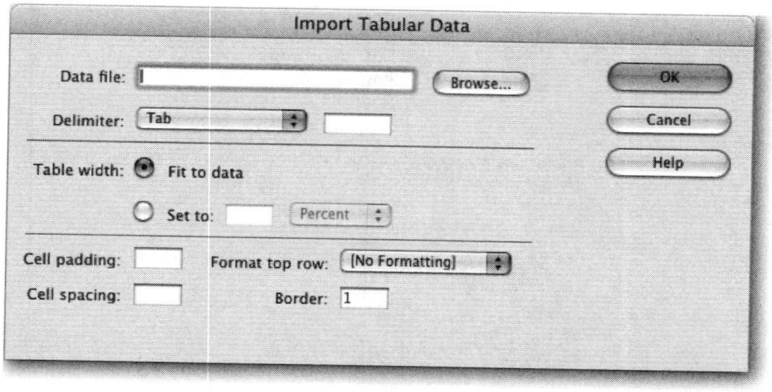

Figure 7-28:
The Import Tabular Data dialog box lets you select a text file of data to import and choose formatting options for the table.

2. **Click Browse. In the Insert Tabular Data dialog box, find and open the delimited text file you wish to import.**

   A delimited file is no longer a spreadsheet, but a plain text file. Navigate to and double-click the file in the dialog box.

3. **From the pop-up menu, select the delimiter that was used to separate the data in the text file.**

The choices are Tab, Comma, Colon, Semicolon, or Other. If you select Other, an additional field appears, where you can type the character you used as the delimiter.

4. **Select a table width.**

Choose "Fit to data" if you want the table to fit itself to the information you're importing—an excellent idea when you aren't completely sure how much information the file contains. (You can always modify the table, if necessary, after importing the data.)

On the other hand, if your Web page needs a table of a certain size, you can specify it by selecting the Set button and typing a value in the field next to it. Select pixel or percentage value (see page 246).

5. **Set Cell padding, Cell spacing, and Border, if you like.**

See page 245 for details.

6. **Select a formatting option for the top row of data.**

If the first line in the text file has column headings—Quarter 1 Sales, Quarter 2 Sales, and so on, for example—Dreamweaver lets you choose Bold, Italic, or Bold Italic to set this header row apart from the rest of the table. (No Formatting keeps the top row consistent with the rest of the table.)

7. **Click OK to import the data and create the table.**

If you'd like to jazz up your table a bit but are short on time, you can apply one of Dreamweaver's preinstalled table designs (see Figure 7-29).

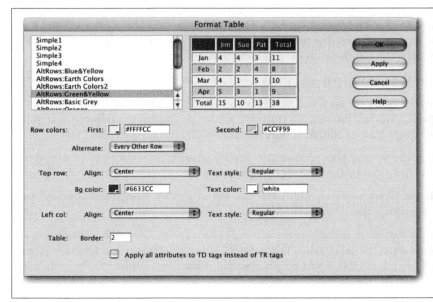

Figure 7-29:
Dreamweaver can apply canned designs to a table of data. Select a table in the document window, and choose Commands → Format Table. You can then select one of the 17 different designs from the list in the dialog box shown here. You can even create your own design using the option menus. Unfortunately, you can't save a design you create. While these designs aren't useful when you're using tables to lay out a page, as described earlier in this chapter, they are a quick way to spruce up a calendar or spreadsheet.

Sorting Data in a Table

If you have a table that lists employee names, you probably want to present that list in alphabetical order—or alphabetically *and* by department. Dreamweaver's Sort Table command takes a lot of the drudgery out of this task.

1. **Select the table you wish to sort.**

   See page 248 for some table-selection techniques.

2. **Choose Commands → Sort Table.**

   The Sort Table dialog box appears (Figure 7-30).

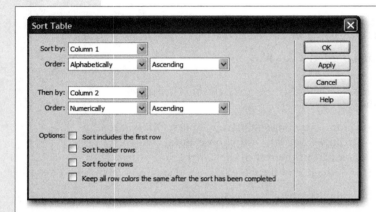

Figure 7-30:
The Sort Table command works well with Dreamweaver's Import Tabular Data feature. Imagine you're given a text file listing all of the employees in your company. You import the data into a table, but realize that the names aren't in any particular order.

3. **Using the "Sort by" pop-up menu, choose the column you wish to sort by.**

   You can choose any column in the table. For example, suppose you have a table listing a bunch of products. Each row has the product name, number, and price. If you want to see the products listed from least to most expensive, you could sort by the column with the product prices.

4. **Use the next two pop-up menus to specify how you want the data sorted.**

   Data can be sorted alphabetically or numerically. To order the product list by price, choose Numerically from the Order pop-up menu. However, if you're sorting a Name column, choose Alphabetically.

   Use the second pop-up menu to specify whether you want an Ascending sort (A–Z, 1–100) or Descending (Z–A, 100–1).

5. **If you like, choose an additional column to sort by, using the "Then by" pop-up menu.**

   This secondary sort can come in handy when several cells in the *first* sorting column have the same value. For example, if several items in your product list are all priced at $100, a sort by price would place them consecutively in the table;

you could then specify a secondary sort that would place the products in alphabetical order within each price group. In this way, all of the products would be listed from least to most expensive, *and* products that are the same price would be listed alphabetically within their group.

6. **If the first row of the table contains data to be sorted, turn on "Sort includes the first row."**

   If, however, the first row of the table contains *headings* for each column, don't turn on this box.

7. **Choose whether to sort header rows and footer rows as well.**

   The Sort Header Row option isn't referring to cells that have the "header" property set (see page 247). It, and the next option, refer to the <thead> (table header) and <tfoot> (table footer) tags, which are intended to allow you to turn one or more rows into repeating headers and footers for long tables. Since Dreamweaver doesn't insert these tags for you, you'll most likely never use these options.

8. **Choose whether to keep row colors with the sorted row.**

   One way to visually organize a table is to add color to alternate rows. This every-other-row pattern helps readers to stay focused on one row of information at a time. However, if you sort a table that you had formatted in this way, you'd wind up with some crazy pattern of colored and uncolored rows.

   The bottom line: If you've applied colors to your rows, and you'd like to keep those colors in the same order, leave this checkbox off.

9. **Click Apply to see the effect of the sort without closing the dialog box.**

   If the table meets with your satisfaction, click OK to sort the table and return to the document window. (Clicking Cancel, however, doesn't then undo the sort. If you want to return the table to its previous sort order, choose Edit → Undo Sort Table after closing the sort window.)

Exporting Table Data

Getting data out of a table in Dreamweaver is simple. Just select the table and choose File → Export → Table. In the Export Table dialog box that appears, select the type of delimiter (tab, comma, space, colon, or semicolon) and the operating system where the file will be used (Mac, Windows, or Unix), and then click OK. Give the file a name and save it on your computer. You can then import this delimited file into your spreadsheet or database program.

Tables Tutorial

In this tutorial, you'll learn how to use Dreamweaver's Layout mode to build a page for the *National Exasperator* Web site. You'll also practice adding tables using the Insert bar's Table object and gain experience with tracing images and Library elements.

Getting Started

Before you begin building the page, download the tutorial files. As always, you'll find them at *www.sawmac.com/dw8/*; click the Tutorials link to go to the tutorials page, and then click the Table Tutorial link to download a ZIP file containing all the files for this tutorial.

When the files have downloaded and decompressed, you should have a folder named DWTables on your computer, containing the Web pages and graphics needed for this tutorial. If you're having difficulties, the Web site contains detailed instructions for downloading the files you'll be using with this book.

For this tutorial, you'll build a "Headline Story" for the *National Exasperator* Web site. When you're done, it will look like Figure 7-43.

1. **In Dreamweaver, choose Site → New Site.**

   The Site Definition window appears. Make sure the Advanced tab is selected. (The Basic tab offers a simpler wizard-based approach to setting up sites, but once you've got the handle on setting up sites, it's just too slow. The Site Definition wizard is discussed on page 33.)

2. **Type *Tables Tutorial* in the Site Name field.**

   This is the name that Dreamweaver uses while you're working on this tutorial.

3. **Click the folder icon next to the label "Local root folder."**

   The Choose Local Root Folder window opens.

4. **Browse to and select the DWTables folder.**

   Windows and Macs handle this step slightly differently, as described on page 35. Selecting the DWTables folder makes it the local root folder—the folder that holds all the files, graphics, and other folders that are part of a single Web site (see page 29).

5. **Click the OK button.**

   Dreamweaver reads the files in the folder, and displays them in the Files panel.

Now you're all set to begin the tutorial.

Creating a New Page and Setting Its Properties

You'll first start by creating a new Web page and setting some of its basic properties.

1. **Choose File → New.**

   The New Document window opens. You'll be creating a basic Web page.

2. **Make sure the General tab is selected and, in the Category list, select the Basic Page option.**

    You'll be using HTML to create the page, but to keep in line with current standards, you'll use the more modern XHTML standard.

3. **Select HTML in the Basic Page list and, from the Document Type menu in the lower-right corner of the window, select XHTML 1.0 Transitional.**

    Dreamweaver 8 lets you create many different types of HTML files. They're all variations on the same theme, but some have stricter rules than others. Most Web sites these days use either HTML 4.01 Transitional or XHTML 1.0 Transitional.

4. **Click Create to close the window and create a new, blank document.**

    Dreamweaver generates all the XHTML code for the page. Always save a page immediately after creating it.

5. **Choose File → Save. Save the page as *battle.html* in the DWTables folder.**

    After saving a new file, it's wise to immediately name the page.

6. **Select the text "Untitled Document" in the Title field in the document toolbar; type *The Battle of the Century*.**

    If you don't see the Document toolbar (Figure 1-2), choose View → Toolbars → Document.

    Before you start adding tables to this page, you'll add a background image and color, and set a few other page properties.

7. **Choose Modify → Page Properties.**

    The Page Properties window opens (see Figure 7-31).

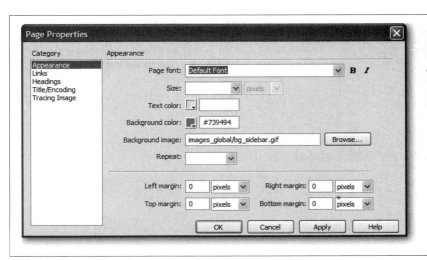

Figure 7-31:
The Page Properties window lets you set global properties for a page like link color, text color, background images, and margins.

8. **In the Background color box, type *#739494*; in each of the four margin boxes (Left, Top, Right, and Bottom), type *0*.**

This sets a background color for the page and eliminates the space that most Web browsers add around the content of a page. Next you'll add a background image that appears as a bar along the left edge of the page.

9. **Click the Browse button to the right of the "Background image" box; navigate to the *images_global* folder and select the file *bg_sidebar.gif*.**

The Page Properties window should now look like Figure 7-31.

10. **Click OK to close the Page Properties window and apply these changes.**

Whoops! Instead of a single bar along the left edge of the page, there are several vertical stripes filling the page. This isn't what you want. By default, a background image tiles repeatedly both vertically and horizontally. But with Cascading Style Sheets, you can overcome this limitation and control *how* a background image tiles. In this case, you want the image to tile *only* vertically (that is, just along the left edge) and *not* horizontally across the page. You can do this quickly with Dreamweaver's CSS Styles panel.

11. **Make sure the CSS Styles panel is open (Window → CSS Styles) and click the All button to display all of the styles available to this Web page. If the panel isn't already expanded, click the + (triangle) icon next to the label "<style>" in the All Rules pane. Click "body" to select the style (see Figure 7-32).**

Dreamweaver creates a CSS style whenever you apply properties to a page (unless you've turned off the Preferences setting discussed on page 30). This tag style (see page 164) redefines how the <body> tag is formatted. You can modify it as you would any other CSS style (see page 173 for more on editing CSS styles). You'll see the two background properties you set, listed at the top of the list (see Figure 7-32).

Figure 7-32:
The Properties pane lets you edit the properties of a selected style. To add a property, just click the Add Property link and select the new property name.

Tip: When you use the Page Properties window, Dreamweaver adds a new body tag style in an internal style sheet in the page. You may prefer to put all of your styles in an external style sheet (see page 163). If that's the case, you can skip the Page Properties window and just create a new tag style for the <body> tag in an external style sheet as described on page 165. You can also export the styles from a page into an external style sheet (see page 167).

12. **Make sure the "Show set properties" button is selected (circled in Figure 7-32). Click the Add Property link and, from the menu that appears, select "background-repeat."**

    If you know your CSS property names, you can also bypass the menu and just type the name. Next you'll set the value for that property.

13. **Click the menu in the column to the right of the newly added property and select "repeat-y."**

    Notice that the bar now tiles only on the left edge of the page, creating a nice continuous stripe exactly as planned.

14. **Choose File → Save to save your changes.**

    Now you're ready to start building your layout.

Using a Tracing Image and Guides

In this tutorial, you'll be building a news page for the *National Exasperator* Web site. To get a taste of the different table-building methods Dreamweaver offers, you'll use both the Layout mode and the Standard table mode. In this part of the tutorial, you'll use a tracing image and the Layout mode to draw the table design for the banner of the page. In addition, you'll see Dreamweaver 8's new guides feature in action:

1. **Choose Modify → Page Properties.**

    The Page Properties window opens.

2. **Select the Tracing Image category and click the Browse button.**

    The Select Image Source dialog box appears.

3. **In the DWTables folder, double-click the file called *tracing.gif*.**

    This file is a GIF image of the design for this page's banner.

4. **Move the Page Properties window so that you can see the document window underneath it, and then click Apply.**

    You should see the tracing-image graphic appear in the document window (see Figure 7-33).

5. **Move the Image Transparency slider to the middle—around 50%—and click OK to close the Page Properties dialog box.**

   The image fades into the background of the page. You've just inserted the *tracing image*—a GIF image that you prepared in some graphics program while brainstorming the design of your site, freed from the constraints of actually having to build the Web site while you played around with visual ideas.

   You'll use this graphic as a pattern for creating the layout of the banner. This image won't show up in a Web browser; it appears only in Dreamweaver. To help you create your layout, you'll next use page guides that help you place and align elements on a page.

6. **Choose View → Rulers → Show.**

   Rulers appear at the left and top sides of the Web page. You can drag guides from the rulers and drop them onto the page. Next, you'll add some guides, which help you lay out the banner area of the page.

7. **Drag from the top ruler down onto the page.**

   A green line appears—the new guide—as well as a number indicating how far away (in pixels) the guide is from the top of the page.

Note: Dreamweaver 8 comes shipped with guides turned on. But if you don't see a green guide as you drag from the ruler, they may somehow have gotten turned off. Look for checkmarks next to the Show Guides and Snap to Guides options in the View → Guides menu. If you don't see any checkmarks, then select each choice from the menu to turn them both on.

---

8. **Drag the line until the number reads 97px, and let go of the mouse button.**

   This drops the line in place. If you didn't get it to exactly 97px on your first try, grab the green line and drag again.

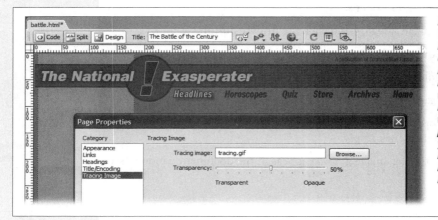

Figure 7-33:
You can use the Page Properties dialog box to change the page's background color, margins, link colors, as well as to apply a tracing image to a page. Call the window up quickly by pressing Ctrl+J (⌘-J). (If you think you may find rulers helpful, as shown here, choose View → Rulers → Show.)

You'll add a few more guides to indicate different areas where you will add table cells. As you'll see in the next section, what looks like a single unified banner is actually a series of images placed in individual table cells.

9. **Drag two more guides from the top ruler to the 19px mark and the 63px mark.**

   These new guides set off the area above the stripe in the National Exasperator logo and the space below it. You'll add a vertical guide next.

10. **From the left ruler, drag to add a vertical guide at 247px.**

    You've now set up guides that make it much easier to use Dreamweaver's table drawing tools.

11. **Choose File → Save.**

Congratulations! You're well on your way to creating a beautiful new Web site. Next, you'll start to add the details.

Building the Banner in Layout Mode

You'll use Dreamweaver's Layout mode to build one part of a table-based page design.

1. **In the Insert bar, click the Layout tab (see Figure 7-6).**

   This panel contains useful tools for controlling layout and switching between Dreamweaver's table-design views—Standard, Expanded, and Layout.

2. **Click the Layout button.**

   Dreamweaver switches to Layout mode.

   When you first switch to this view, the "Getting Started in Layout mode" window may appear. This window explains how to use the layout tools. If you don't need this wisdom, turn on "Don't show me this message again," and then click OK.

3. **On the Insert bar, click the Layout Table tool button (also shown in Figure 7-6).**

   The Layout Table tool lets you draw a table directly in the document window. Once you've drawn the table, you can add cells to it.

4. **Starting at the upper-left corner of the tracing image, drag diagonally down and to the right, creating a rectangle around the top banner of the tracing image—stop dragging when you've reached the bottom rule and the right edge of the red stripe in the tracing image.**

   A light gray box with a green outline appears over the tracing image. The green tab in the upper-left corner indicates that this is a Layout Table.

   Unfortunately, Dreamweaver inserts an annoying 15-pixel tall crosshatched area (a gray area on the Mac) that obscures the top part of the tracing image (see page 243) and also makes the table you just drew look like it's sitting about 15 pixels below the bottom of the banner. You'll temporarily hide that box next.

5. **Choose View → Visual Aids → Hide All.**

   This turns off visual aids that highlight normally invisible elements like image maps and table borders and widths, but that can get in the way of the Layout mode and tracing images. You'll still see the strip with the words Layout Mode at the top of the document, but the other area has disappeared.

6. **Select the Layout Cell tool (pictured in Figure 7-6).**

   You'll next add the cells that make up the table.

7. **Starting at the upper-left corner of the Layout Table, drag to the vertical and bottom guides, as shown in Figure 7-34.**

   This works best if you start just a few pixels down and to the right of the exact upper corner. The box you just created is outlined in blue.

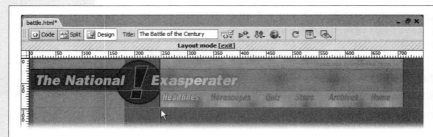

Figure 7-34:
Drag with the Layout Cell tool inside a Layout Table to add a table cell. The gray area to the right of the new cell indicates the area of the Layout Table that doesn't yet contain Layout Cells.

Tip: You can also drag from the bottom-right corner to the upper-left corner to add the cell. This sometimes works better.

Cells are indicated by a light-blue outline. When you release the mouse button, the insertion point blinks inside of the cell you just drew. You're ready to fill it up with text or graphics. This cell contains the site's logo.

You may wonder why the cell cuts off part of the *National Exasperator* name. Table designs often require dividing graphics into multiple rectangles to fit designs into the grid-like structure of tables. In this case, you couldn't use one large graphic for the *National Exasperator* logo, because the row of navigation buttons would have to overlap it—a feat not possible with tables alone.

Mac Note: You may not see a difference between an empty Layout Table (which should have a gray, semi-transparent background) and a Layout Cell (which shouldn't have any background). Sometimes there's no distinction between the two when the page itself has certain background colors set—including the background color of this tutorial page. For a solution, read the Note on page 235.

---

8. **Choose Insert → Image.**

Alternatively, select the Common tab of the Insert bar and then click the Insert Image button. Either way, the Select Image Source window appears.

You'll select a graphic to match part of the National Exasperator logo.

9. **Browse to the *images_global* folder inside of the DWTables folder. Then double-click the file called *logo_national1.gif.***

   If the "Image Tag Accessibility" window appears, type *The National Exasperator* in the Alternate text box and then click OK (for more on this feature, turn to page 130). For a refresher on inserting images, turn to Chapter 5. You've just inserted an actual graphic over the sketch you had made in your tracing image. In the event of an actual Web-creation experience, this is just what you would have done: placing actual graphics over the placeholders you had sketched in the tracing image.

10. **On the Insert bar, click the Layout Cell tool button again.**

    You'll next add three cells to the right of the one you just created: one to advertise the magazine's parent company, another for the rest of the magazine's logo, and a third one to hold the navigation bar.

11. **Holding down the Ctrl (⌘) key, drag from just to the right of the top-right corner of the first cell down to the right, just above the red stripe of the logo (see Figure 7-35).**

    Holding down the Ctrl (⌘) key when creating a cell keeps the Layout Cell tool active, so that you can continue drawing additional cells without clicking the Insert bar again.

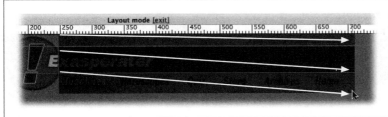

Figure 7-35:
Adding cells to a table is as simple as dragging. With guides added, the sides of a cell snap to other cells already in the table, making aligning the edges of cells…a snap.

12. **Create two more cells for the red stripe of the logo and the navigation bar, as shown in Figure 7-35.**

13. **Click inside the top cell you just added and choose Insert → Image.**

    The Select Image Source window appears.

14. **Browse to the *images_global* folder inside of the DWTables folder. Then double-click the file called *cosmo_pub.gif.***

    (If the Image Accessibility window appears, type *A publication of Cosmopolitan Farmer* in the Alternate text box.)

    You'll notice that the graphic doesn't appear at the right side of the page as it does in the tracing image.

15. **Move your mouse over the light-blue outline of the cell until it changes color; click to select the cell.**

    Selecting the correct cell is a bit tricky. Since you have several cells touching one another, when you move your mouse over a common border, you can easily select one cell *or* the other. Watch for an outline to appear around the cell you're about to select. The next step doesn't change the *cell's* alignment—its placement on the page—only the alignment of its contents.

16. **In the Property inspector, choose Right from the Horz Menu.**

    The graphic moves to the right edge of the cell.

    Next you'll add the rest of the logo.

17. **Click in the cell immediately below, and choose Insert → Image. Select the file** *logo_national2.gif* **in the** *images_global* **folder.**

    (If the Image Accessibility window appears, use the menu to select <empty>, and then click OK. Alternate text is meant only to provide a text equivalent of a graphic's meaning. Since this graphic doesn't contain any more meaning than the logo you placed in step 9, you don't need to add alternate text.)

    The graphic with the rest of the word *Exasperator* appears. However, the red stripe doesn't extend all the way across the page as it does in the tracing image. In fact, if you have a large monitor, the red stripe in the tracing image may not even extend all the way across the document window. Don't worry; you'll address that problem with a little Cascading Style Sheet magic in the next phase of this tutorial. For now, you'll finish the banner.

18. **Click in the bottom cell.**

    This cell contains the navigation bar for the site. When you release the mouse button, the insertion point blinks inside of the cell.

    In the next step, you'll insert a canned, ready-made navigation bar.

19. **Choose Window → Assets to open the Assets panel.**

    The Assets panel lets you quickly reuse elements contained in your site, including graphics, colors, Flash movies, and more. (The Assets panel is described in detail on page 492.)

20. **On the Assets panel, click the last icon on the left—the one that looks like an open book (circled in Figure 7-36).**

    This displays the site's Library. The Library lets you save and reuse frequently needed snippets of HTML (see Chapter 16 for much more detail).

21. **Select "navigation" from the list in the Library window; click Insert at the bottom of the panel.**

    Dreamweaver drops in a row of navigation buttons. Notice that the Property inspector indicates that this is a special type of object called a Library item.

You don't need the tracing image anymore, so you'll turn it off next.

22. **From the View Options menu in the toolbar at the top of your document window, choose Tracing Image (as shown in Figure 7-14).**

The tracing image disappears. If there's no checkmark next to Tracing Image in the menu, the tracing image is already hidden. (You can also show or hide a tracing image by choosing View → Tracing Image → Show.)

For the next steps, you need to show the visual aids you hid in step 5.

23. **Choose View → Visual Aids → Hide All Visual Aids to remove the checkmark.**

A checkmark next to Hide All Visual Aids in this menu means the visual aids are hidden; the keyboard shortcut Ctrl+Shift+I (⌘-Shift-I) is an even faster way to show and hide Dreamweaver's visual aids.

You'll notice that the guides you dragged onto the page no longer align with the cells you drew. Unfortunately, Dreamweaver isn't smart enough to move the guides when you show and hide the visual aids—that 15-pixel-tall crosshatched area (a gray area on the Mac) at the top of the document window. Since you're done designing the banner, you don't need those guides anyway.

24. **Choose View → Guides → Clear Guides.**

Dreamweaver erases the green guidelines.

Figure 7-36:
You can find and reuse Library items and other site elements, including colors and images, from Dreamweaver's Assets panel.

Improving the Banner

The banner is coming together, but it still has room for improvement. With a little help from CSS, and some advanced features of Layout mode, you'll make this banner stand out in the crowd. First, you'll address that issue of the logo's red stripe mentioned previously:

1. **Choose Window → CSS Styles to open the CSS Styles panel.**

You'll start by creating a new style.

2. **Click the New CSS Rule button (+) on the CSS Styles panel.**

   The New CSS Rule window opens. You'll create a class style that you can apply to the table cell with the second half of the red logo.

3. **Click the Class radio button. In the Name box, type .banner.**

   Class styles always begin with a period. (If you forget to start with a period, don't worry; Dreamweaver adds it.)

4. **Make sure the New Style Sheet File button is selected. Click OK.**

   The Save Style Sheet File As dialog box appears. You're about to create the file—an external style sheet—that stores the styles for this page.

5. **Navigate to the DWTables folder. In the File Name box, type styles.css (the Save As box on the Mac), and then click Save to save the file.**

   Cascading Style Sheet files always end in .css; that's how Web servers and browsers can tell what kind of file they are.

   Having created the external style sheet, you can now create the first style, as suggested by the sudden appearance of the CSS Rule Definition window.

6. **From the list of category names in the left side of the window, select Background.**

   You can add colors and images to the backgrounds of elements using these properties. In this case, you'll use a graphic that matches the red stripe in the logo.

7. **Click the Browse button and select the file bg_banner.gif from the images_global folder.**

   You should also set the way the graphic tiles so that it only continues horizontally across the page.

8. **Choose "repeat-x" from the Repeat menu.**

   The Rule Definition window should look like Figure 7-37.

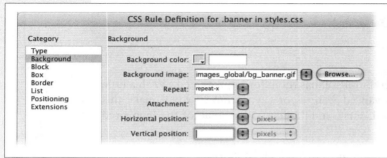

Figure 7-37:
The CSS Background properties offer a lot of control over how graphics are placed in the background of a page, table cell, or other page element. They're described in detail on page 197.

9. **Click OK to create the new style.**

   Since it's a class style, you must apply it by hand to the element you wish to format. In this case, it's the Layout Cell containing the second half of the *National Exasperator* logo.

10. **Move your mouse over the light blue outline of the cell until it changes color; click to select the cell.**

    You can use the Property inspector to apply a style to this cell.

Note: You can also Ctrl-click (⌘-click) inside a table cell to select it.

---

11. **On the Property inspector, select "banner" from the Class menu.**

    Notice that the red stripe fills the background of the cell. Since the background graphic matches the stripe in the logo graphic, they appear to form a single unified image.

12. **Now press F12 (Option-F12) to preview the page in your browser.**

    Maximize your browser window while viewing the page. If you have a high-resolution monitor, you'll notice that red stripe doesn't extend all the way across the browser window, and the *Cosmopolitan Farmer* graphic doesn't butt up against the right edge of the window. The page would look much better if the banner could automatically stretch to fill in the gap—a tricky bit of HTML programming, but an easy step in Dreamweaver.

Windows XP Note: If you preview this page in Internet Explorer, you may see an ominous looking "To help protect your security" message in a yellow box. This is IE's way of saying there's some JavaScript in this page (the navigation bar uses rollover images). To get rid of this message, just return to Dreamweaver and choose Commands → "Insert Mark of Web." This problem is discussed in detail on page 146.

---

13. **Return to Dreamweaver. Click the second column's header menu (Figure 7-38), and then choose Make Column Autostretch.**

    The Make Column Autostretch option makes one column in a table stretchy, as described on page 240, so that it can grow or shrink to fill the available space in a browser window.

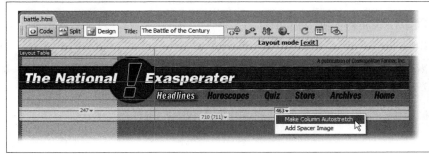

Figure 7-38:
The width of a column is listed at the bottom of the column in Layout mode. Clicking this number reveals a menu of options—including Make Column Autostretch, which is what you want here.

As soon as you choose this command, a dialog box appears asking if you're sure you want Dreamweaver to insert spacer graphics (page 241).

14. **In the dialog box, turn on "Create a spacer image file," and then click OK.**

    Dreamweaver uses a special trick for the Autostretch feature: it creates a tiny, 1-pixel, transparent GIF graphic. That's what Dreamweaver is prompting you to save now.

15. **In the Save Spacer Image window, navigate to the DWTables → *images_global* folder. Save the image with the name *spacer.gif*.**

    Dreamweaver adds a 1-pixel tall row at the bottom of the banner table, and inserts the graphic into the left cell. The right column can now stretch to fit the browser window, since the spacer prevents the left cell from collapsing down to nothing. (See page 240 for more on how this works.)

16. **Choose File → Save to save all your work so far.**

Press F12 (Option-F12) to view the final banner design in your default browser. Try resizing your browser window and notice how the stripe expands and contracts and the *Cosmopolitan Farmer* graphic always moves to the right edge of the window. The page is looking extremely promising.

Note: If, when you preview the page, the two images that make up the logo don't seem to align correctly, the culprit is most likely the height that Dreamweaver set for the Layout Cells (see page 236). To eliminate the height settings, choose Clear All Heights from the Layout Table's contextual menu (see Figure 7-8).

Building the Content Table

Now that you have the banner, it's time to turn to the actual contents of the page. This news page has two basic areas for content: a sidebar that runs along the left edge of the page and the large area to the right for the text of the news story. You'll start by adding another guide to the page.

1. **From the ruler on the left edge of the document window, drag a green vertical guide to the 200px mark.**

   You'll use this guide to help you draw a table cell.

2. **On the Layout tab of the Insert bar, make sure the Layout button is selected.**

   Figure 7-6 shows this button.

3. **Click the Layout Cell tool on the Insert bar.**

   You don't have to start with the Table tool when working in Layout mode. If you simply draw a cell, the program creates a Layout Table to fit.

4. **Starting just below the information for the first layout table (the gray area with numbers like 247), drag down a few inches and to the right until you've created a cell that touches the green guide (see Figure 7-39, left).**

This creates a new cell and a new Layout Table. But notice that the new cell doesn't butt up against the bottom of the first Layout Table. It's about 30 pixels below that first table. That's OK, but the page looks better if the sidebar content sits *directly* below the banner, so resize this cell in the next step.

Windows Fans: No matter what you do, you won't be able to draw a table cell that fits *exactly* below the first Layout Table. This is true even if you hide all visual aids. Dreamweaver doesn't always work logically! In fact, it's downright buggy. (Thank goodness you have this book.)

Mac Fans: You do have a way out of this dilemma. Actually two ways: If you hide all visual aids, you can (unlike your Windows counterparts) draw a cell starting just below the banner table that fits exactly below the first table. Another option is to draw the cell from the bottom right to the top left until the Layout Cell snaps into place at the left edge of the document window and right below the banner table.

---

5. **Select the cell by clicking carefully on its edge. Drag the resize handle at the top of the cell upward until it touches the bottom of the first table (Figure 7-39, right).**

Layout mode lets you draw table cells anywhere on the page, so that you can easily create gutters between blocks of text and add margins between the edge of the page and a table cell. Although it's a fast and easy way to control layout, it's not necessarily the best way to build a Web page that's fast-loading. Layout mode can lead to some complex tables that require lots of slow-loading HTML code. As a general rule, the simpler the table, the better the Web page.

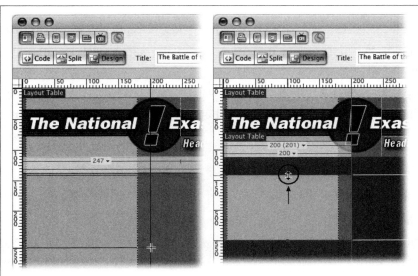

Figure 7-39:
Left: With the Draw Layout Cell tool, you just drag across the document window to create a cell.

Right: Adjusting the cell's size is a simple matter of dragging one of the cell's resize handles.

In this case, you're going to create a very simple table composed of just two columns, one for the sidebar and one for the main story text. To fine-tune the design and the placement of text *within* each cell, you'll use Cascading Style Sheets—today's professional method of choice.

6. **Select the Layout Cell tool one last time and draw a rectangle just to the right of the sidebar cell you added in the last step.**

   Since this cell holds the main text of the page, the cell should fill the rest of the space to the right of the sidebar. Next, add some already-created text to each cell.

7. **Choose File → Open. In the DWTables folder, double-click the file called *sidebar.html*.**

   This page holds the text for the sidebar. Instead of having to type all this information, you'll just copy and paste it from another Web page.

8. **Choose Edit → Select All to select all of the text on the page. Then choose Edit → Copy to copy it.**

   (Of course the keyboard shortcuts Ctrl+A [⌘-A] and Ctrl+C [⌘-C] are faster.) Now you'll switch back to your layout and paste the copied text.

9. **Switch back to the page you're working on by clicking its tab—*battle.html*—at the top of the document window.**

   This supremely easy way to switch between open documents has finally been added to the Mac version of Dreamweaver.

10. **Click inside the small sidebar cell. Choose Edit → Paste to paste the text into the cell.**

    (Ctrl+P [⌘-P] works for the keyboard fanatics.) The text doesn't fit perfectly inside the sidebar. That's OK. Momentarily, you'll create a CSS style to fix that.

11. **Choose File → Open. In the DWTables folder, double-click the file called *main_text.html*.**

    This page holds the text for the main story.

12. **Choose Edit → Select All to select all of the text on the page; choose Edit → Copy to copy it.**

    Now you'll switch back to your layout and paste the copied text.

13. **Click the *battle.html* tab.**

    Your Web page reappears.

14. **Click inside the larger cell in the middle of the page. Choose Edit → Paste.**

    The text doesn't fit perfectly here, either. It's a bit close to the navigation bar, and it nearly touches the sidebar text. Again, this is a problem easily fixed with

CSS. But first, you'll set the main content cell to autostretch, so, like the banner, it grows and shrinks to fit a visitor's browser window.

15. **From the column-header menu above the cell with the main story text, choose Make Column Autostretch.**

    This makes the cell flexible, as described in step 13 of the previous instructions. The cell now expands to fill the browser window so that you can see all the text.

16. **Choose File → Save. Press F12 (Option-F12) to preview your work in your browser.**

    It's a good idea to check your work in a browser every time you try something new, because Web pages can look slightly different in a browser window. The page is coming together, but you still need to deal with the text in the main part of the page. You'll do that next.

Using CSS to Control Table Cells

In the last chapter, you saw how Cascading Style Sheets can control the look of text. But you can apply CSS to all sorts of HTML elements. In this case, you'll build a couple of styles to enhance the look of the sidebar and main text cells:

1. **On the CSS Styles panel, click the New CSS Rule button (+). (If the CSS Styles panel isn't open, choose Window → CSS Styles.)**

    The New CSS Rule window opens. You'll create a class style that you can apply to the sidebar table cell.

2. **Click the Class radio button. In the Name box, type *.sidebar.***

    Class styles always begin with a period. This style controls the space around the text inside the sidebar.

3. **Click OK.**

    The CSS Rule Definition window opens. Since you've already created an external style sheet, Dreamweaver automatically adds this new style to it.

4. **Click the Box category.**

    With CSS, you can control the padding of each side of a table cell individually. This offers much more control than basic table properties.

5. **Turn off the "Same for all" box below the Padding settings; type *25* in the Right padding box and *10* in the Left padding box.**

    The window should look like Figure 7-40.

6. **Click OK to close the window and create the new style.**

    Since this is a class style, you must apply it manually to the table cell.

7. **Move your mouse over one of the edges of the sidebar cell. When the border around the cell changes color, click to select it.**

   Alternatively, you can hold down the Ctrl (⌘) key and click anywhere inside the cell to select it.

8. **From the Class menu on the Property inspector, select "sidebar."**

   The *sidebar* style indents the left and right margins of the text so that it fits neatly inside the cell. If the left and right margins still don't look right, you can edit the padding values for the style (see page 173 for information on how to edit a style).

   For the next part of this tutorial, you'll create a style for the main text.

9. **Follow steps 1–3 to create another new class style. Name the style *.story*.**

   Next, you'll format the new style to make the main story text easy to read on the Web.

10. **Click the Box category. This time, leave the Padding property's "Same for all" box turned on and type *15* in the top box.**

    This setting places 15 pixels of space all the way around the inside of the style.

11. **Click the Background category. Select white with the color picker (see page 41).**

    You can also simply type *#FFFFFF* (the hexadecimal code for white) in the Background color box. Either method sets the entire cell to white. But so it doesn't appear too boxy, you'll soften the design by rounding the top-left corner of the cell.

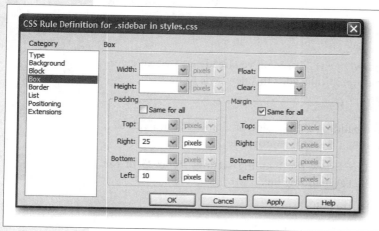

Figure 7-40:
The CSS Cell Padding property works much like the Table tag's Cell Padding property: it adds space between a border (an edge of a cell, for example) and what's inside. But using Cascading Style Sheets, you can control the amount of padding separately for each edge of a cell.

DREAMWEAVER 8: THE MISSING MANUAL

12. Click the Browse button to the right of the Background image box. Navigate to and select the file *content_corner.gif* in the *images_global* folder.

This file contains a graphic of a soft corner curve that matches the background color of the rest of the page. But since you don't want the graphic tiling over the entire cell, you need to set it to not repeat.

13. From the Repeat menu, select "no-repeat."

Because the graphic is going to appear in the upper-left corner, you can use the horizontal and vertical positioning properties to place it there.

14. From the Horizontal position menu, choose Left, and from the Vertical position menu, choose Top. The window should now look like Figure 7-41. Click OK.

That's all you need to do for this style. Now it's time to apply it to a table cell.

15. Follow steps 7–8 to apply the new style—*story*—to the cell containing the news story.

The text should indent from the edges of the cell, the cell's background should turn white, and a small curve should appear in the top-left corner of the cell.

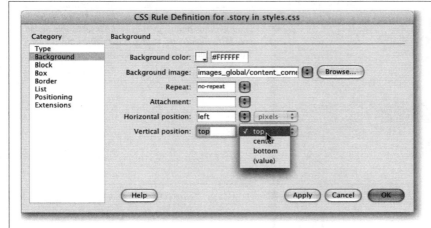

Figure 7-41:
CSS's background properties let you fine-tune the placement of background images. In this case, the image of a rounded corner appears once, in the top-left corner of a table cell, providing a gentle curve that softens the look of the page.

Using the Table Object

Like the Layout Table, the Table *object* is a useful tool for laying out Web pages; it's also the only way to achieve certain structures, like the nested table you'll create in the following steps. The Table object is available only in Standard view, not Layout mode.

For the next steps, you'll need the *battle.html* Web page you were working on in the previous steps. If it's not already on the screen, launch Dreamweaver and open the *battle.html* file.

Tip: Choose File → Open Recent to see a list of the 10 most recently viewed documents. Choose a file's name to open it.

1. **Click the Layout tab on the Insert bar. Then click the Standard view button to switch out of Layout mode.**

   The Layout Table tabs disappear, and the outlines of the tables and cells change to dotted lines. This is how Dreamweaver displays tables in Standard view.

2. **Click just before the T in the "The Battle of the Century" headline.**

   You've placed the insertion point at the beginning of the cell.

3. **Choose Insert → Table.**

   Or click the Insert Table button on the Insert bar. Either way, the Insert Table dialog box opens.

4. **Type the settings shown in Figure 7-42, pressing Tab to jump from box to box.**

   Don't forget to set the pop-up menu to "pixels."

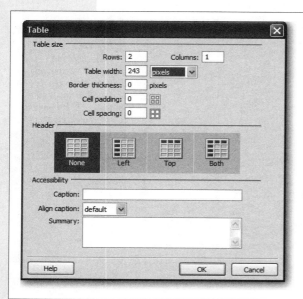

Figure 7-42:
Unlike Layout Tables, which you draw by dragging with the mouse, you create tables in Standard view by typing in dimensions and properties in the Insert Table dialog box. (This dialog box, in fact, is available only in Standard view.)

5. **Click OK.**

   The two-row, one-column Table object appears in your Web page, outlined by transparent (but now highlighted) borders.

6. **With the table selected, from the Align menu in the Property inspector, choose Right.**

   The table jumps to the right side of the main story area, and the text wraps around its left edge.

Tip: You can also use the CSS Float property to make the table (or any element) align to the right side of the page. See page 202 for more on how to do this.

---

7. **Ctrl-click (⌘-click) both cells in this new table, so that a black border surrounds both cells.**

   Both cells are now selected. The Property inspector changes to reflect the properties of these cells.

8. **In the Property inspector, choose Center from the Horz menu.**

   You've just center-aligned whatever you put into these cells. Now you're going to fill them up.

9. **Click the top cell; then, choose Insert → Image.**

   Of course, you can also click the Image button on the Insert bar's Common tab. Either way, the Select Image Source dialog box opens.

10. **Browse to the *images_global* folder in the DWTables folder; double-click the file called *fight.gif*.**

    (If the Image Accessibility window appears, type *Nessie vs. Big Foot* in the Alternate text box.)

    An artist's rendering of the story appears.

11. **Click the bottom cell, and then type *Artist's Rendering*.**

    Adding text to a cell is as simple as typing it, but there's much more you can do with text in Dreamweaver, as discussed in Chapter 3.

    There are also many things you could do to improve the look of this table. For example, try creating a CSS class style that adds a black border around the table and indents the text and image from the edges of the table.

    To polish off the design, you'll attach another external style sheet with some canned styles.

12. **On the CSS Styles panel, click the Attach External Style Sheet button (see Figure 6-1).**

    The Attach External Style Sheet window appears.

13. Click the Browse button; in the DWTables folder, select the file *more_styles.css*. Click OK to close the window and attach the external style sheet.

    The sidebar and main story text miraculously change—all thanks to the power of CSS contextual selectors (see page 189).

14. Choose File → Save. Press F12 (Option-F12) to preview your work in your default browser (see Figure 7-43).

Congratulations: You've built a page with a precise layout and flexible design. If you compare this page with the page you built in Chapter 1, you can see the greater control (and freedom) that tables offer the Web designer. In the next chapter, you'll explore another—newer—method of laying out Web pages using Cascading Style Sheets.

Feel free to compare with the finished Web page at *www.sawmac.com/dw8/*.

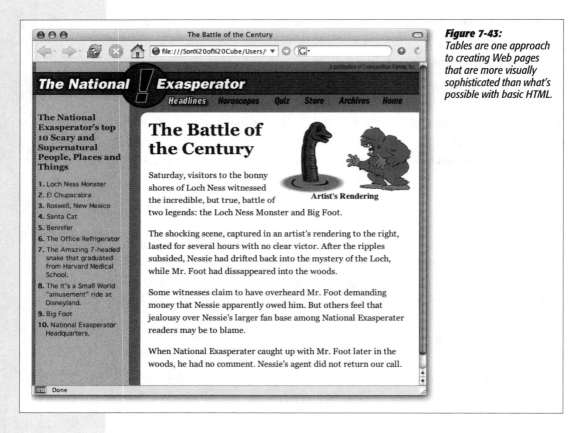

Figure 7-43:
Tables are one approach to creating Web pages that are more visually sophisticated than what's possible with basic HTML.

Advanced Page Layout

As you saw in the last chapter, table-based design gets the job done. With an admirable track record and great browser support, tables are still a good layout tool for Web designers. But tables have their disadvantages: Complex table designs download slowly, are difficult to update, and can't always be deciphered by assistive technologies, like the screen readers used by the visually impaired. In addition, newer devices that now surf the Web—cellphones, palmtops, and even game consoles—frequently choke on complex table layouts.

There's always more than one way to skin a Web page, however. Newer Web browsers can also take advantage of the golden child of Web page layout, Cascading Style Sheets. In Chapter 6, you saw how CSS provides powerful formatting options for text, images, and other page elements. In addition, a subset of CSS properties known as CSS-P (short for *CSS-Positioning*) lets you control the *placement* of elements on a page. Fortunately, Dreamweaver has many features that make building CSS-based layouts a breeze.

Introducing CSS Layout

If a picture's worth a thousand words, one Web site's worth at least several pages of explanation. To really grasp the power of CSS-based layout, point your favorite Web browser to *www.csszengarden.com* (Figure 8-1). Once there, click any of the designs listed in the "Select a Design" box.

Each design is an example of CSS-based layout. In fact, you may be surprised to realize that the HTML code for the page is the same in every one of these designs. The only difference is the style sheet used to format the page. The designers of major Web sites like ESPN.com, Wired.com, and Macworld.com have abandoned table designs in favor of CSS, because CSS offers easy format updates and smaller file sizes (which means faster downloads).

Figure 8-1:
CSS Zen Garden (www.csszengarden.com), the preeminent showcase for CSS-based layout, has caused many a Web designer to bow down and proclaim "I'm not worthy. I'm not worthy." The site's interesting not only for the great design work it showcases, but also because the only thing that's different between the three Web pages displayed here is the CSS. That's right: The exact same HTML is shared by these three pages—only the external style sheet and the graphics used in the style sheet differ.

CSS-positioning is akin to working with table cells—without the tables. You create styles that act like rectangular containers to hold other page material—images, text, form elements, and even other CSS-positioned elements. In this regard, CSS-P acts like a table cell: you can define the style's width and height, and give it a background color or image. But that's where the similarities end. What really sets CSS-positioned elements apart from other page elements is the way you can assign them an exact position on the page. Want an image to appear exactly 100 pixels from the top edge of the browser window and 200 pixels from the left? With CSS-P, no jury-rigged table scaffolding's required.

Note: CSS-P elements follow the *Box model* described on page 203. Each positioned element can have margins, borders, backgrounds, and padding.

Another property of CSS-P has no HTML equivalent—the third dimension. You can *layer* CSS-positioned elements on top of each other, making elements on a page overlap. For example, you can place HTML text on top of graphics, or vice versa. In this way, CSS-positioned elements act much like layers in graphic programs like Fireworks and Photoshop, and page-layout programs like Quark and InDesign. In fact, Dreamweaver refers to CSS-positioned elements as *layers* and includes a layer-drawing tool. Because the word "layer" is a lot friendlier than "CSS-positioned element" you'll see the term "layer" from this point on.

Note: While the word "layer" is a great catch-all for this complex concept, it isn't technically correct, nor is it commonly used in non-Dreamweaver Web design circles.

The Basics

Creating a CSS-based layout isn't much more involved than using CSS for text or images. It does require a little planning and a clear road map. The basic process requires three steps:

1. **Identify the building blocks of your page.**

   Start by determining how you want to organize your page. For example, you may want a banner that's 150 pixels tall and spans the entire top of the page, a 200-pixel-wide sidebar on the left edge of the page, and a main content area that fills the remaining space.

2. **Create styles for each layer.**

   The process is the same as creating any other CSS style, as described on page 165. However, to specify where the layer appears, you use CSS's positioning properties, described on page 297. In addition, instead of using a tag style or class style, you'll frequently create an advanced type of style known as an *ID selector,* described below. (Dreamweaver has its own layer-drawing tool as well. See page 307.)

3. **Wrap each building block with its style.**

Finally, you apply the style to all of the content that appears within the layer. With a normal style, you'd select the content and apply the style. However, since you may have lots of content—many paragraphs, images, lists, and so on—you wrap all of that content within another tag that acts as a container for your layer. This tag—the <div> tag—defines a logical "division" in a page, in other words, the new layer. Dreamweaver includes a Div tool that greatly simplifies this process.

Creating CSS Styles for Layers

After you've determined the size and position of a layer, your first step's to create a CSS Style. The process is the same as with any style, with just a few exceptions. First, create a new style. For example, click the New Style button on the CSS Styles panel (see Figure 6-1) or use one of the other methods described on page 165 to open the New CSS Rule window.

In the New CSS Rule window, choose a selector type. In most cases, you'll use an advanced type of style known as an ID, which is a special type of style that identifies a unique item on a page. For example, a Web page usually has only a single banner, a single left sidebar, or a single footer. Each of those elements would get its own ID style.

Unlike a class style, you can apply an ID style only *once* per page. Since an ID defines a layer with a specific position on the page, you probably wouldn't want to apply it to more than one element on a page anyway. Otherwise, both items would be *on top* of each other in the same place!

ID styles have another benefit as well: you can use them with JavaScript programming. ID styles (which *identify* layers) provide a method for JavaScript to "talk" to the layer. You can move layers with JavaScript, hide and show them, or even animate them across the screen. In this way, an ID style is like the name you give to an image so Dreamweaver's Rollover Image behavior can identify and manipulate it (page 144). In fact, Dreamweaver comes with several preprogrammed JavaScript routines for these kinds of effects (see page 428).

To create an ID style, choose Advanced from the Selector Type list in the New CSS Rule window (see Figure 8-2).

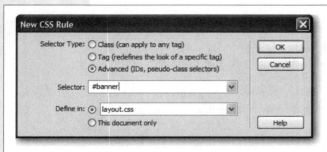

Figure 8-2:
Creating an ID style is as simple as creating any type of CSS style. But make sure you select the Advanced option and precede the name of the style with the # symbol. Unlike with class styles, Dreamweaver won't check to make sure you've used the correct syntax for the style's name.

Type a name for the style in the Selector box in the middle of the window. But to identify the style as an ID, you must precede the name with the pound symbol like this: *#banner*. From this point on, the process is the same as any other style: choose whether to include the style in an external or internal style sheet (page 163), and then click the OK button to open the CSS Rule Definition window and begin setting CSS properties (see Figure 8-3).

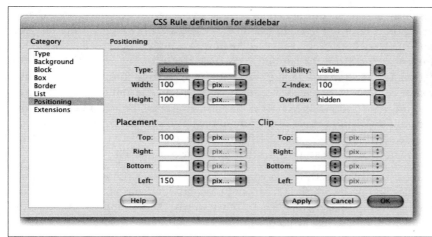

Figure 8-3:
The Positioning category of the CSS Rule Definition window lets you set the properties necessary to accurately place content on a Web page.

The CSS Positioning Properties

A layer can use any CSS-style property. For example, you can use the Background Color property to give the layer a background color, put a colorful border around the edges of the layer, or set the Font Family property to display all text inside that layer in Arial. (These properties are all described in Chapter 6.) But there are also some properties specific to positioning layers on a screen, found under the Positioning category of the CSS Rule Definition window (Figure 8-3).

Positioning type

There are four available position types: absolute, relative, static, and fixed. Each type affects how a layer is positioned on the screen.

- **Absolute** is the most common option. It lets you place a layer anywhere on a page, regardless of the location of the actual HTML code for the content inside the layer.

  For example, even as you polish off a Web page by adding some text at the bottom of the page, you can create a layer that moves that text to the top of the browser window. In other words, the normal flow of HTML content from top to bottom that you encounter with HTML doesn't apply when using absolutely positioned layers. The actual HTML code can go anywhere inside the <body> tag and appear anywhere on the page—its position has nothing to do with the positioning of the layer. After you select this option, use the Placement properties (see page 301) to specify a specific position on the page.

• The **relative** option lets you position a layer relative to its position in the HTML. For example, if you create a layer and specify that it should be 200 pixels from the top, if you use the "absolute" setting, that layer appears 200 pixels from the top of the page (or in the case of a nested layer, from the top of its parent layer—see page 312 for more on this). However, that same layer with a "relative" setting appears 200 pixels down from wherever the HTML code already appears on the page. Add more HTML at the top of the page (as long as it's not inside an absolutely positioned layer), and a relative layer moves down, whereas an absolute layer doesn't. For example, say you added two divs at the very bottom of a very long Web page. Perhaps you gave both divs the same positioning values—200px from the left and 10px from the top—but gave the first div an "absolute" position type, and the second div a "relative" position type. When a visitor comes to the page, he sees the first div 10 pixels from the top of the page and indented 200 pixels from the left edge. However, the second div isn't visible until the visitor scrolls all the way to the bottom of the page, where he finds it indented 200 pixels from the left edge of the page and 10 pixels lower than it would normally appear if no positioning were applied at all.

• **Static** is the default setting that you normally find in HTML. It keeps the style in its place in the flow of the HTML and prevents you from placing it at an exact position on the page with CSS. In other words, it's the opposite of what this chapter's about, so just avoid this option.

• **Fixed** is similar to the "fixed" value of the CSS "attachment" property used to lock a background image in place (see page 198). This option "fixes" the layer in place in the browser window. When you scroll down the page, the layer doesn't move but remains in an exact position in the browser window. It's a cool option with exciting possibilities and absolutely *no* support in Internet Explorer. You may want to experiment with the "fixed" option and the Firefox browser, but when building a Web site you actually want the whole world to see, skip it.

POWER USERS' CLINIC

A Wealth of Resources at Your Mouse Tip

CSS-based layouts can be complex, and the more complex your design, the more you may find yourself yanking handfuls of hair from your head as you struggle with your style sheets. The subject's worthy of an entire book (or two...or three). Fortunately, you can find lots of Web sites to help steer you in the right direction, including the following:

• Check out this list of **CSS Layout Resources** at: *http://css-discuss.incutio.com/?page=CssLayouts*.

• Bone up on **CSS Layout Techniques** at: *www.glish.com/css/*.

• Check out the design samples at **Little Boxes:** *www.thenoodleincident.com/tutorials/box_lesson/boxes.html.*

• Or dive into **The Layout Reservoir** at: *www.bluerobot.com/web/layouts/*.

And if you want to skip all this learnin' stuff, a Web site wizard called Layout-o-matic can generate the basic CSS and HTML code for a variety of simple layouts. Visit *www.inknoise.com/experimental/layoutomatic.php*. Just pick your desired layout options, and the site produces ready-to-use CSS and HTML code.

Width and Height

These properties, logically enough, set the width and height of the layer. You can use any of the available CSS measurement systems like pixels, ems, and percentages. In most cases, when you want precise control over the dimensions of your layers—that is, a layer that's *exactly* 200 pixels wide and won't change even if the visitor changes the size of her browser window—use pixels. However, if you want the layer to resize as the visitor resizes her browser window, you can use percentages. In this way you can make a layer that's 50 percent the width of the browser window, no matter the size of the window.

Tip: The Width and Height properties available under the Positioning category of the CSS Rule Definition window are identical to the options with the same name under the Box category. Also note that CSS calculates the total width of a style as this Width value *plus* any borders, margins, or padding (see the Warning on page 202 for more information).

Visibility

If left to its own devices, Dreamweaver makes the contents of all layers visible on the page, so you'll usually leave this property blank. But there are situations in which you may want to make a certain layer (and its contents) invisible in your visitors' Web browsers.

The power of the Visibility property is that, using Dreamweaver behaviors, you can later make the layer visible again, on cue. Imagine a Web page where you've superimposed many hidden layers on a diagram of a car engine. Moving the mouse over a part of the image makes a layer visible, revealing text that describes the corresponding engine part. (Page 436 shows you how to create this effect.)

The options for this property let you make the layer "visible" (which is how all layers start out); make it "hidden," so it won't appear until you make it visible; or make it "inherit" the visibility of another layer. (The only time you may use the inheritance option is with nested layers, as discussed on page 312.)

Z-Index

Welcome to the third dimension. Layers are unique in the world of Web elements, because they "float" above (or even behind) a Web page and can overlap each other, completely or partially.

If you were awake in high school algebra, you may remember the graphing system in which the X axis specified where a point was in space from left to right and the Y axis specified where the point was vertically. And if you were awake *and* paying attention, you may remember that the Z axis denoted a point's position in *front-to-back* space. When you draw a three-dimensional object on this type of graph, you need to use all three axes: X, Y, and Z.

The Z-Index of layers doesn't make your Web page *appear* three-dimensional; it simply specifies the "front-to-backness" of overlapping layers. In other words, the Z-Index, represented by a number in the Z-Index field, controls the stacking order of layers on a page.

> **Note:** The Z-Index setting doesn't always work when you try to overlap certain kinds of content, like pull-down menus, radio buttons, or other form elements. It also may not work with plug-in content like Flash or Java applets. This is because Web browsers let other programs control the display of these items.

In most cases, the page itself lies behind all layers, and the layers stack up from there. In other words, the higher the layer number, the higher the layer, so that a layer with a Z-Index of 4 appears *behind* an overlapping layer with a Z-Index of, say, 7.

However, you can also use a negative Z-Index (–1, for example) to place a layer *behind* the plane of the Web page. You could do that when, for example, you want an absolutely positioned layer to appear *below* a part of a page that isn't positioned. (These numbers have no relation to the actual number of layers on a page. You can have three layers with Z-Indexes of 2, 499, and 2000, if you choose. You'd still just have three layers, one on top of the other in ascending order. Spacing your Z-Index numbers in this manner is helpful, since it lets you add in layers as you develop your page without having to renumber everything.)

> **Note:** A negative Z-Index won't work if your visitors are using Firefox. Instead of displaying the layer below the content of a page, the layer won't be visible at all.

Overflow

Suppose you draw a square layer that's 100×100 pixels. Then you fill it with a graphic that's 150×162 pixels—that is, larger than the layer itself.

You've already seen how a table cell reacts to this situation: it simply grows to fit the content inside it. Layers, however, are more (or less) flexible, depending on your choice of Overflow option in the Property inspector. These choices let you decide how browsers handle the excess part of the image:

- **Visible** makes the layer grow to accommodate its contents. If you don't choose another setting, layers grow to fit automatically.

- **Hidden** chops off the excess. In the example above, only the top-left 100×100 pixels of the image would be visible.

- **Scroll** adds scroll bars to the layer, so that a visitor can scroll to see all of the layer's contents. It's like having a miniature browser window embedded in the page. This feature offers an interesting way to add a small, scrollable window within a Web page: Imagine a small "Latest Company News" box, which visitors can scroll to read the text inside without disturbing anything else on the page.

- **Auto** adds scroll bars to a layer *only* if necessary to accommodate its oversize contents.

Dreamweaver 8 displays these overflow settings differently than previous versions of the program. Now, in Design view, if you've selected any option besides "visible," you'll see the layer's set dimensions—for example, 100 pixels by 100 pixels. Any content outside that area—the overflow—won't be displayed.

You may have content you'd like to edit that's part of the overflow—the "Latest Company News" box example above, for example. Dreamweaver 8 does give you an easy way to edit any of that hidden content—just double-click the layer. Doing so expands the layer (just as if you'd selected the visible option) so you can edit it. To reset the layer back to its original dimensions, right-click (Control-click) the layer and, from the shortcut menu that appears, select Element View → Hidden.

Placement

These properties let you specify a layer's position, which is the whole point of layers. The four properties control where each of the four edges of the layer begin. For example, setting the Top box to 200 pixels places the top of the layer 200 pixels down the screen, whereas the Bottom option identifies where the bottom of the layer starts. And the Left and Right properties set where the left edge and right edge of the layer should appear.

Frequently, you'll use a combination of the Width property (page 299) with the Top and Left or Right properties. For example, to place a 150-pixel-wide sidebar 200 pixels from the top of the page and 15 pixels in from the left side of the page, you'd set the Width property to 150 pixels, the Top property to 200, and the left property to 15 pixels. The Right property is also handy. Say you want to put a 200-pixel-wide sidebar at the right side of the page. Since you don't know the exact width of a visitor's browser window—580 pixels, 1200 pixels?—you can't know ahead of time how far from the left edge of the window the layer needs to be. Instead, you can set the Right property to 0—if you want the sidebar to touch the right edge of the page. If you want to indent the layer 20 pixels from the right edge of the window, type *20*.

While it's technically possible to use Left and Right positioning simultaneously—say, placing a layer 300 pixels from the left edge and 20 from the right—Internet Explorer doesn't support this combination. Instead, use absolute positioning with one edge of the layer and a margin setting (see page 203) for the other edge.

Positioning isn't quite as straightforward as it may seem. The exact position of the layer is a combination of not only these position values but also what type of placement you choose for the layer—absolute or relative. As noted earlier, with relative positioning, the numbers you type for Top or Left, for example, are calculated based on where the layer already appears in the HTML code and on the screen. So setting the Top property to 100 pixels doesn't place the layer 100 pixels from the top of the browser window; it places it 100 pixels from where it would appear on the screen based on the HTML code.

Absolute positioning, however, lets you place a layer at an exact spot on a page. So setting the Top and Left properties for an absolutely positioned layer to 100 and 150 pixels *will* place that layer 100 pixels from the top of the browser window and 150 pixels from the left edge.

Note: There's one additional wrinkle to absolute positioning. For nested layers (page 312), the position values are calculated based on the position of the *parent* layer. For example, if you have one layer that's located 300 pixels from the top of the page, an absolutely positioned layer nested inside that layer with a Top position setting of 20 won't appear 20 pixels from the top of the page. Instead, it will appear 20 pixels from the top of the parent layer, or, in this example, 320 pixels from the top of the page.

Clip

The Clip property can hide all but a rectangular piece of a layer, as shown in Figure 8-4. In most cases, you should avoid this property, since it's rarely useful, and it's also a waste of precious bandwidth.

For example, say you put a large graphic into a layer, but only wanted to display one small area—like the monster's head shown in Figure 8-4. You *could* use the Clip property, but the Web browser still has to download the *entire* graphic, not just the clipped area. You're much better off just preparing the smaller graphic at the right size to begin with (see Chapter 5). The kilobytes you save may be your own.

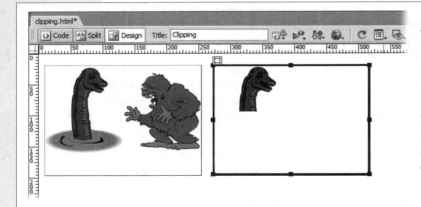

Figure 8-4:
A layer's Clip property lets you display only a selected section of the layer. In this example, the layer to the left has no clipping set, while the layer to the right has a clipping box that hides all but Nessie's head from sight. Notice that the layer itself remains the same size—as indicated by the black outline. Only the visible portion of that layer has changed.

You can use JavaScript to *move* the clipping area, creating an effect like a spotlight traveling across the layer. Although that may be a more useful purpose for the Clip property, Dreamweaver unfortunately offers no tools for performing this maneuver.

The four clipping settings—"top," "right," "bottom," and "left"—specify the positions of the clipping box's four edges. In other words, these indicate the borders of the visible area of the layer. Because understanding how this works is tricky and

---

can be confusing, you'll find a surefire technique for determining these four set-tings on page 311.

After setting the properties for the layer in the CSS Rule Definition window, just click the OK button to create the style. The next step's to apply the style to a chunk of HTML code to create the layer.

Applying the Layer Style

In most cases, a layer includes a variety of HTML elements—images, paragraphs, headlines, and so on. Unlike a normal style that you usually apply to a single tag or even a single word, all the elements inside a layer are *wrapped* inside a <div> tag. Dreamweaver includes a simple tool to make adding the <div> tag easy.

Available from the Layout tab of the Insert bar, the Insert Div Tag tool is a one-click tool for wrapping content in a CSS style (Figure 8-5). To use it, select all of the content you want to include in the layer and then click the button on the Insert bar (alternatively, you can choose Insert → Layout Objects → Div Tag). Either way, the Insert Div Tag window opens (see Figure 8-6).

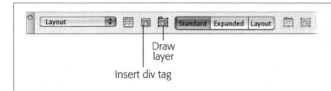

Figure 8-5:
The Insert Div and Draw Layer tools aren't available in Layout mode. If these tools are grayed out on the Insert bar, click the Standard button.

Figure 8-6:
Once you've applied an ID style to add a layer to the page, that ID's name no longer appears in the ID menu on subsequent visits to this dialog box. That's because you can use an ID only once per page.

You can select the name of a class or ID style from either the Class or ID menu. In the case of a layer, you'll most likely select the name of the layer style you created from the ID menu. Dreamweaver 8 adds a New CSS Style button to the Insert Div Tag window. Click it, and you go about the normal process of creating a style as described in Chapter 6; when you're done creating the style, the name appears in either the Class or ID box, depending on the type of style you created.

The Insert menu reads "Wrap around selection." Click OK to wrap the selected content in a <div> tag. The layer appears on the page with the ID style applied to it.

Note: The Insert menu includes a few other options as well. You can insert the <div> tag before or after a particular tag, and if you simply clicked in the document window, you can insert the <div> tag at the cursor position by selecting the "At insertion point" option. In addition, two options are available for nesting one layer inside of another, as discussed on page 312.

Alternatively, you might start with a blank page, create your layer styles, insert the layers, and *then* add content to each layer. The process is the same as above, except instead of selecting your page content and then wrapping it in a <div> tag, you place the cursor on the page where you want the HTML code for the layer to appear. Then use the Insert Div Tag tool and, from the Insert Div Tag window, select the ID name and choose the "At insertion point" option to insert the layer. Dreamweaver inserts the layer and adds a small amount of dummy text like this: "Content for id 'banner' Goes Here." Later, you can delete this text and then type or paste text, add graphics, and insert other HTML into the layer.

Unless you add a background color or border to your layer, it's difficult to identify its boundaries. And if you insert a layer without wrapping it around any content, it'll be invisible. To make working with layers easier, Dreamweaver provides visual cues in Design view, as shown in Figure 8-7.

- **Layer marker.** The gold shield with the letter C represents the position in the underlying HTML where the code for the layer actually appears.

  These markers aren't normally visible (unlike in previous versions of Dreamweaver). To see them, you must turn them on in the Preferences window: press Ctrl+U (⌘-U) to open the window, click the Invisible Elements category, and make sure the "Anchor points for layers" option's turned on.

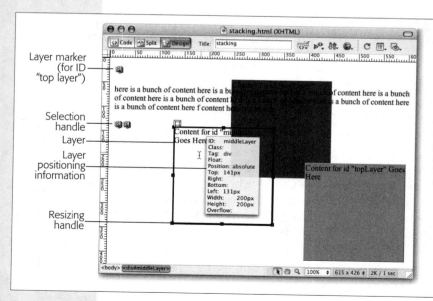

Figure 8-7:
Unlike other page elements, layers don't appear in the same place on the page as their HTML code. Here, the layer that appears in the bottom-right corner is actually the first bit of HTML on the page (and is therefore represented by the layer marker in the top-left corner of the page).

While HTML objects generally appear in the document window in a top-to-bottom sequence that mirrors their order in the HTML source code, the position of layers doesn't depend on where the layer-creating code appears in the page's HTML. In other words, it's possible to have a layer appear near the bottom of the final Web page, whose actual code may be the first line in the body of the HTML page (see Figure 8-7 for more detail).

Click the shield icon to select the layer. Note, however, the difference from the selection handle (described next): When you drag a Layer marker, you don't move the layer in the page layout. Instead, you reposition the layer's code in the HTML of the page.

That distinction can cause confusion. For instance, be careful not to drag a Layer marker (which represents the HTML code) into a table. Putting a layer inside a table can cause major display problems in some browsers.

That said, a layer can *overlap* a table, or even appear to be inside a cell; just make sure the gold Layer marker itself isn't inside a cell.

Tip: The Layer marker (shield icon) takes up room on the screen and can push text, graphics, and other items out of the way. In fact, even the thin borders that Dreamweaver adds to tables and layers take up space in the document window, and the space they occupy may make it difficult to place layers precisely. The keyboard shortcut Ctrl+Shift+I (⌘-Shift-I) hides or shows invisible items like Layer markers. The Hide All Visual Aids option from the Document toolbar does the same thing (see Figure 8-8).

- **Selection handle.** The selection handle provides a convenient handle to grab and move a layer around the page. The handle appears when you select the layer or when you click inside the layer to add material to it. The handle lets you move the position of the layer without changing the position of its code (see "Moving Layers" on page 310).

- **Layer outline.** A thin, gray, 3-D border outlines each layer. Like the Layer marker and selection handle, it's there only to help you see the boundaries of the layer and doesn't show up in Web browsers. You can turn it on and off, but to turn it off, you need to make sure two options in the View → Visual Aids menu don't have checkmarks next to their names: Layer Outlines and Layout Outlines. You can also use the Visual Aids menu in the Document window (see Figure 8-8).

Note: If one layer overlaps another, the top layer—the one with the higher Z-Index, as described on page 299—has a solid outline; the lower layer's outline appears as a dashed line where the top layer overlaps it.

- **Layer positioning summary.** If you select a layer and hover your mouse over that layer, Dreamweaver pops up a yellow box with information about how that layer is positioned (see Figure 8-7), including the name of the ID style or class style, what type of positioning is used, the dimensions of the layer, and so on. This box provides a quick summary of relevant positioning information and gives you a bird's-eye view of the CSS properties defining the layer's placement on the page.

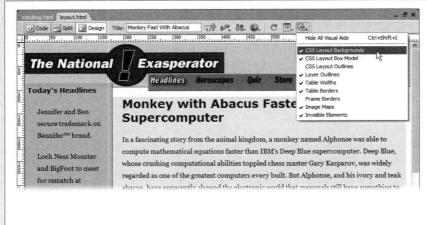

Figure 8-8:
The top four choices in the Visual Aids menu provide visual cues to help you with CSS layouts in Design view. The CSS Layout Backgrounds option—selected here—lights up each <div> tag on a page with a hideous, randomly selected background color. It also highlights any element whose display property is set to "block" (page 201) or that uses either absolute or relative positioning (page 298). Both the CSS Layout Outlines and Layer Outlines options draw a gray line around positioned elements. In addition, the Layout Outlines option draws a black border around <div> tags that aren't absolutely positioned. The CSS Box model option is discussed on page 203.

POWER USERS' CLINIC

Floats: An Alternative to Absolute Positioning

While CSS-Positioning uses precise measurements and absolute positioning to place elements on a page, many common design elements—like a left or right sidebar, or boxes with pullquotes—can also be achieved with the CSS Float property described on page 202.

Say you've got four paragraphs of text. You'd like the top two paragraphs to fit in a 200-pixel wide sidebar at the right edge of the page. You can create a CSS style with a width of 200 pixels and a Float property of Right. This moves those two paragraphs to the right edge of the page, letting the two bottom paragraphs move up and fill the empty space in the left side of the page. (For this kind of scheme to work, you should always set a width for the floated style. Otherwise, the style can span the entire width of the page, not providing any room for other content to appear next to the floated paragraphs.)

For excellent information on this technique, check out *www.complexspiral.com/publications/containing-floats/* or *http://css-discuss.incutio.com/?page=FloatLayouts*.

Drawing with the Layer Tool

Dreamweaver wouldn't be Dreamweaver if it didn't give you several ways to perform a certain task, like creating a layer. You can create a layer as described above or turn to two methods designed specifically for adding layers to a page: You can drag to create a layer freehand or use a menu command to insert a full-blown, complete layer. Your choices are:

- **Use the Layer tool.** The Draw Layer tool is in the Insert bar, on the Layout tab (see Figure 8-5). Click the Layer button and then drag the + cursor diagonally in the document window to create a box—the outline of the layer.

Tip: For accurate drawing, you should hide Dreamweaver's visual aids (like the layer border and selection handles), which take up space, moving layers slightly out of position in Design view. Ctrl+Shift+I (⌘-Shift-I) does the trick.

- **Use a menu command.** To insert a layer at the insertion point, choose Insert → Layout Objects → Layer.

  If you don't like the looks of the default layer that Dreamweaver inserts, choose Edit → Preferences (Dreamweaver → Preferences), select the Layers category, and then adjust the default layer's properties there. Add a background color, for example, or increase the layer's size. From then on, you can instantly create your favorite kind of layer using the Insert → Layer command.

However, Dreamweaver's layer tools have one drawback: they create internal styles with generic names like Layer1, Layer2, and so on. That means you don't get to take advantage of the byte-saving virtues of an external style sheet until you export the styles to an external style sheet, as described on page 167. In addition, you'll have to take a second to rename these layers to something a little more understandable—for example, changing Layer1 to *banner*. (Fortunately, the Layers panel makes this easy to do, as shown in Figure 8-9.)

So the Draw Layer tool provides ease of use up front, but you'll have to do a bit of work to turn the layers into logically named styles that can be shared by all of the pages in your site. You're better off taking the time to initially create a layer using the CSS Rule Definition window, as described on page 296. And as you'll see below, you can still take advantage of Dreamweaver's WYSIWYG tools for working with layers.

Note: When you draw a layer, Dreamweaver also inserts some JavaScript code to make the page work well in Netscape Navigator 4. For most designers, this is a needless precaution, since Navigator 4 has pretty much disappeared from the planet–although a museum in Copenhagen apparently has a copy. You can turn this feature off to prevent Dreamweaver from inserting this extra code: open the Preferences window (Ctrl+U [⌘-U]), click the Layers category, and turn off the "Add resize fix" box.

The Layers Panel

The Layers panel (Figure 8-9) helps you manage the layers in a document. To open it, choose Window → Layers, or press F2.

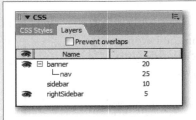

Figure 8-9:
The Layers panel lets you name, reorder, and change the visibility of layers. Turning on the "Prevent overlaps" checkbox makes sure you can't position or drag a layer on top of another. This feature is intended to make it easy to convert a layer layout to a table-based layout using the Modify → Convert → Layers to Table. Don't do it! This creates horribly bloated HTML that easily falls apart as you add, edit, and adjust content on the page.

The panel lists all layers in the document, and the three columns provide information on each layer:

- **Visibility.** To change a layer's visibility, click in the column with the eye icon next to the layer's name. An open eye indicates a layer is visible; a closed eye, hidden. No eye icon at all represents the factory setting (that is, visible).

- **Layer Name.** If you use Dreamweaver's Draw Layer tool, Dreamweaver gives the layer a generic name—Layer1, for example. If you created it yourself, you probably already came up with a pretty good name like *banner* or *navBar*. But if you want to change that name (or provide a more descriptive name for a Dreamweaver-created layer), double-click the layer name and type a new name. (Layer names must start with a letter and can contain only letters and numbers. As Dreamweaver's quick to remind you, spaces and other punctuation aren't allowed.)

  Clicking a layer name in the Layers panel, by the way, is another way to select a layer in the document window.

Tip: Don't rename a layer if you've already used it in a Dreamweaver behavior like the Show/Hide Layers action (see page 436). JavaScript uses your layer names to "talk to" the layers. If you change a layer's name in the Layers panel, Dreamweaver doesn't automatically update the name in the JavaScript code in your page. The behavior, therefore, no longer works. In that case, you'll need to edit the behavior using the new layer name.

- **Z-Index.** The Z-Index provides a third dimension to layers, letting them overlap one another (page 299). To change the Z-Index of a layer, click the number in the Z column and type another number. Software veterans will find that Dreamweaver's Layers panel works just as it does in Photoshop or Fireworks: you can drag a layer's name up or down the list to the desired position. The layer at the top of the list (highest number) is in front of all other layers, while the layer at the bottom of the list (lowest number) appears behind all other layers.

Modifying Layer Properties

Once you've added a layer, you don't need to go back to the CSS Rule Definition window to edit most of the layer's positioning properties. Using the Property inspector, you can rename it, resize it, move it, align it with other layers, and set many other properties.

But first, you must select the layer using one of these methods:

- Click the layer's name in the Layers panel (Figure 8-9).

- Click the layer's selection handle (Figure 8-7).

- Click the layer's border. The border turns red when you've moved your mouse into the proper position.

- Click the Layer marker that indicates the HTML code for the layer (Figure 8-7). (In Dreamweaver 8, the factory preset is to hide these markers, since they can get in the way of your design work; to show them, see page 304.)

And if those aren't enough ways to select a layer—Macromedia's programmers never sleep—you can also Shift-click a layer. This technique also lets you select multiple layers, so that you can set the properties of (or align) many layers at once. If you're working in a layer or have a layer selected, Shift-clicking another layer selects them both. You can continue to Shift-click to select additional layers. (Shift-click a second time to deselect a selected layer.)

Resizing Layers

When you select a layer, eight handles appear around the edges of the layer (see Figure 8-7). You can drag any of these handles to change the layer's dimensions. The corner handles resize both the width and height simultaneously.

You can also use the keyboard to resize a layer. First, select the layer, and then do one of the following:

- Press the Ctrl (⌘) key and press the arrow keys to change the layer's size by one pixel. The up and down arrow keys adjust the layer's height; the left and right arrows affect its width.

- To change the size *10* pixels at a time, press Ctrl+Shift (⌘-Shift) and press the arrow keys.

For better precision, use the Property inspector to set an exact width and height for the layer (see Figure 8-10). Type values in the W and H boxes to change the width and height of the layer, respectively. You can specify any unit of measurement that Cascading Style Sheets understands: px (pixels), pc (picas), pt (points), in (inches), mm (millimeters), cm (centimeters), em (height of the current font), ex (height of the current font's x character), or % (percentage)—see the box on page 196 for more on CSS measurement units. To pick your measurement unit, type a number *immediately* followed by the abbreviation for the unit. For example, type *100px* into the W box to make the layer 100 pixels wide. Don't leave out the measurement unit—px, em, or %, for example—or browsers won't display the correct dimensions of the layer.

Figure 8-10:
The Property inspector controls many layer properties (although some require editing CSS styles).

Another benefit of using the Property inspector is that Dreamweaver lets you resize multiple layers at once. Shift-click two or more layers to select them, and then type new widths and heights. Dreamweaver sets all selected layers to these same dimensions.

Tip: If the Prevent Overlaps feature's turned on (Figure 8-9), you can't drag any of a layer's resize handles over another layer. In other words, you can't resize layers so as to overlap other layers *when dragging*.

But if you use the Property inspector to change the dimensions of a layer, Dreamweaver *always* allows overlaps. Since the Prevent Overlaps feature is meant to be used with the not-very-useful Convert Layers to Tables command, you can safely leave this box turned off.

Moving Layers

Moving a layer is just as simple as resizing. Drag any border of the layer or the layer's selection handle (shown in Figure 8-7). (Avoid the eight resize handles, which change the size of the layer when dragged.)

For less speed but greater precision, you can move a layer using the keyboard. First select the layer and then do one of the following:

- To move a layer one pixel at a time, press the corresponding keyboard arrow key.

- Press Shift while using an arrow key to move a layer 10 pixels at a time.

As you'd guess, you can also control a layer's placement by using the Property inspector (see Figure 8-10). Dreamweaver measures a layer's position relative to the left and top edges of the page (or, for nested layers, from the left and top edges of the parent layer). The Property inspector provides two boxes for these values: L specifies the distance from the left edge of the page to the left edge of the selected layer; T specifies the distance from the top edge of the page to the top of the selected layer.

Note: You can't edit a layer's Right or Bottom positioning properties from the Property inspector. For these properties, edit the style using one of the methods discussed on page 173.

To position a layer using the Property inspector, select the layer (for example, by clicking the layer's border or selecting its name in the Layers panel) and type distances in the L and T boxes. You can use any of the units of measurement mentioned previously. You can even use negative values to move part or all of a layer off the page entirely (offstage, you might say), which is something you'd do if you intended a subsequent animation to bring it *onstage*, into the document window.

For example, if you draw a 100-pixel-tall and 50-pixel-wide layer, you can move it to the very top-left corner of the page by selecting it and typing *0* in both the L and T boxes. To position that same layer so that it's just off the left edge of the page, type *-50px* in the L box.

Note: You can't move a layer completely off the screen by dragging it. If you try, Dreamweaver rudely snaps the layer back to its previous position when you release the mouse. To completely move a layer out of sight, you must use the keyboard or Property inspector.

POWER USERS' CLINIC

The Simple Way to Create a Clipping Region

You can use Dreamweaver's Draw Layer tool and the program's WYSIWYG techniques for moving and resizing a layer to quickly determine the proper settings for creating a clipping region on a layer.

Click inside a layer whose contents you wish to clip. The layer should already contain an image.

Choose Insert → Layout Objects → Layer. Dreamweaver adds a nested layer. You'll use this layer to determine the coordinates of the clipping box.

Drag and resize the nested layer until it exactly covers the part of the layer you wish to show.

This is easy to do, because Dreamweaver lets you see the contents of the underlying layer. In Figure 8-4, a nested layer was positioned and sized so it precisely covered the head of the Loch Ness Monster. For better precision, hide all invisible elements in the page (View → Visual Aids → Hide All).

Select the nested layer and note its L, T, W, and H properties, which you can read in the Property inspector. (You

may find it helpful to jot these numbers down on a piece of scrap paper. These numbers let you calculate the exact dimensions of the clipping box.)

Delete the nested layer. (You needed it only to get the measurements in the previous step.)

Select the first layer and fill in the clip boxes in the Property inspector, using the numbers from the nested layer as a guide.

In the clip's L box, enter the nested layer's L value; in the T box type the T value you wrote down earlier. Add the nested layer's L and W values, and type the result in the R box. Finally, in the B box, type the total of the T and H values you wrote down.

You can't enter negative values in any of these boxes, which can happen, for example, if you drag one of the nested layer's edges outside the main layer. If you enter a negative value, Dreamweaver erases all values for the four clipping settings.

Only the area covered by the nested layer now appears.

Aligning Layers

At times, you may want to align several layers so that their left, top, bottom, or right edges line up with each other. Dreamweaver's Align command does just that; it can even make the width and height of selected layers the same.

Tip: Dreamweaver 8's new guides feature is another easy way to make sure layers line up. See page 224.

To use this feature, select two or more layers (by Shift-clicking them), choose Modify → Arrange, and then select one of the following options from the submenu:

- **Align Left** aligns the left edges of all selected layers. In other words, it gives each layer the same L property.

- **Align Right** aligns the right edges.

- **Align Top** aligns the top edges, so that the T properties are all set the same.

- **Align Bottom** aligns the bottom edges of the layers.

- **Make Same Width** sets the same width for all selected layers (in the W box in the Property inspector). **Make Same Height** does the same for the height of the layers.

The layer you select *last* dictates how Dreamweaver aligns the layers. For example, say you have three layers—A, B, and C—and select them in order from A to C. You then align them to Left. Dreamweaver uses the left edge of layer C (the last one you selected) as the value for the other layers.

Background Image and Color

You can set a layer's background in the same way you would for a table or table cell. To add a background image to the layer, click the folder icon next to the Bg Image field, and then select an image from your site folder. As usual, Dreamweaver tiles the image, if necessary, until the entire layer's filled with repeating copies of the graphic. (To adjust how or whether the image tiles, you'll need to edit the style using the normal CSS-style editing techniques; see page 173.)

Setting a background color is even easier. Just use the Bg Color box (see page 41) to select a color or sample a color off the screen.

Nesting Layers

Nesting doesn't necessarily mean that one layer appears inside another layer; rather, it means that the HTML for one layer is written inside the code for another layer. The nested layer itself can appear anywhere on the page (see Figure 8-11). The main benefit of nested layers is that the *parent* layer—the layer containing the HTML of one or more other layers—can control the behavior of its *child* layers.

For example, suppose you create one layer and nest two layers inside it. If you move the parent layer on the screen, the two child layers follow it, which gives you an easy way to move several layers in unison. Furthermore, the parent layer can control the visibility of its children. When you hide the parent layer (see page 299), the nested layers also disappear (unless you've specifically set the nested layers' visibility property to *visible*).

Tip: Dreamweaver 8's factory settings hide a useful visual cue—Layer markers (see Figure 8-7). These identify where in the code the HTML for the layer appears. Since a nested layer is a layer whose code appears inside the parent layer's code—for example, inside the <div> tag—a Layer marker appears inside the parent layer for each nested layer. To turn on the Layer marker feature, press Ctrl+U (⌘-U) to open the Preferences window; click the Invisible Elements category, and then turn on the Anchor Points for Layers checkbox. You also need to make sure visual aids are turned on (as explained in Figure 8-8).

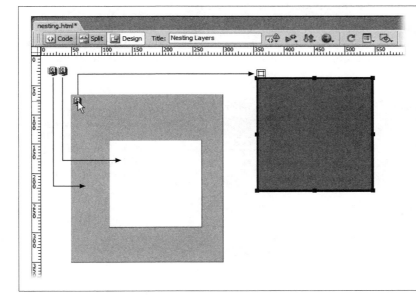

Figure 8-11:
An inner nested layer doesn't necessarily appear inside the outer layer. The HTML for the layer at far right, for example, is nested inside the large gray box layer. And a layer that appears on top of another layer isn't necessarily a nested layer, either; the white box here isn't nested at all. But the HTML for a nested layer does appear within the code for the outer layer. To identify a nested layer, click a Layer marker (the shield) within a layer; the nested layer's selection handle appears.

Here's how to create a nested layer:

- While pressing the Ctrl (⌘) key, drag one layer in the Layers panel (see Figure 8-9) onto another layer. The dragged layer becomes the child of the layer you drop it on, and its name appears indented in the Layers panel, also shown in Figure 8-9.

To un-nest a layer, drag it above or below the parent layer in the Layers panel. (Doing so places the code for the nested layer directly before the opening <div> tag of the parent layer.)

Tip: You can also un-nest a layer, and gain more control over where the HTML for that layer is written in the document, by dragging the Layer marker to a new spot in the document window. (This Layer marker isn't always immediately visible, however; see the Tip on page 304.)

- Use the Insert Div Tag button on either the Common or Layout tab of the Insert bar, or choose Insert → Layout Objects → Div Tag. In either case, the Insert Div Tag window appears (Figure 8-12). Select the name of the layer you wish to nest inside another layer; choose either "After start of tag" or "Before end of tag" from the first Insert menu; then choose the name of the parent layer from the second menu.

- Click inside a layer, and then choose Insert → Layout Objects → Layer. You get a new, nested layer inside it. This technique and the next one, however, create a new layer in an internal style sheet—the same as when drawing a layer. This isn't usually the best option, as described on page 307.

- Drag the Layer tool from the Layout tab of the Insert bar and drop it inside a layer on the page. (Note that this isn't the same procedure described on page 307, in which you click the Layer button and then drag in the document window.)

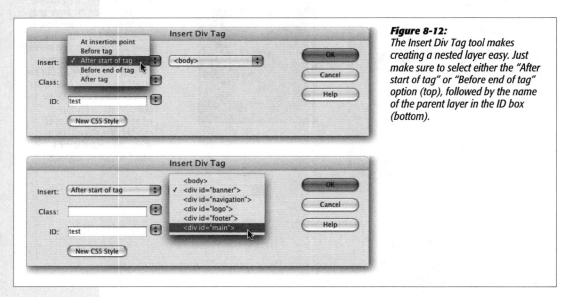

Figure 8-12:
The Insert Div Tag tool makes creating a nested layer easy. Just make sure to select either the "After start of tag" or "Before end of tag" option (top), followed by the name of the parent layer in the ID box (bottom).

CSS Layout Tutorial

In this tutorial, you'll build a basic two-column page design using nothing but Cascading Style Sheets (Figure 8-20 shows the final product). In the process, you'll use Dreamweaver 8's CSS tools, marvel at Dreamweaver's improved display, and learn how to use the program's layer tools.

Getting Started

Before you begin building the page, download the tutorial files. As always, you'll find them at *www.sawmac.com/dw8*. Click the Tutorials link to go to the tutorials page and then click the link to the Layout Tutorial.

When the files have downloaded and decompressed, you should have a folder named DWLayout on your computer, containing the Web pages and graphics needed for this tutorial. If you're having difficulties, the Web site contains detailed instructions for downloading the files you'll be using with this book.

1. **In Dreamweaver, choose Site → New Site.**

   The Site Definition window appears. Make sure the Advanced tab is selected. (The Basic tab offers a simpler, wizard-based approach to setting up sites, but once you've got the handle on setting up sites, it's just too slow. The Site Definition wizard's discussed on page 33.)

2. **In the Site Name field, type *Layout Tutorial*.**

   This is the name that Dreamweaver uses while you're working on this tutorial.

3. **Click the folder icon next to the label "Local root folder."**

   The Choose Local Root Folder window opens.

4. **Browse to and select the DWLayout folder.**

   Windows and Macs handle this step slightly differently, as described on page 35. Selecting the DWLayout folder makes it the local root folder—the folder that holds all the files, graphics, and other folders that are part of a single Web site (see page 29).

5. **Click the OK button.**

   Dreamweaver reads the files in the folder and displays them in the Files panel.

Now you're all set to begin the tutorial.

Adding a Banner Layer

So you can get right down to the fun of laying out a page with Cascading Style Sheets, you'll start with a partly finished page, complete with content and some basic CSS styles for text formatting. Now you'll add the layers that control the layout of the page:

1. **Choose File → Open and, in the DWLayout folder, select the file named *layout. html*.**

   Alternatively, open the Files panel (Windows → Files) and double-click the file *layout.html* to open it. This page is a headline story for the *National Exasperator* Web site. You'll notice that there's no layout, just content that runs from the top to the bottom of the page in the generic, ho-hum style of HTML. You'll create several CSS styles to position the banner, sidebar, and main content areas of the page.

2. **Make sure the CSS Styles panel's open (Window → CSS Styles) and click the New Style button (see Figure 6-1).**

   You'll start by creating a layer for the page's banner.

3. **Click the Advanced button and, in the Selector box, type *#banner*.**

   You're creating an ID style, an advanced style that always begins with a #. You'll also add this style to a new external style sheet file.

4. **From the "Define in" menu, select New Style Sheet File (see Figure 8-13).**

   There's already one external style sheet attached to this page, called *global_styles. css*. You could add these layer styles to that file, but for this tutorial, you'll see you can have multiple external style sheets attached to a single page.

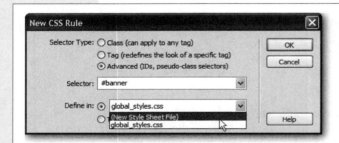

Figure 8-13:
You can have more than one external style sheet per page. For example, you can create a separate style sheet for form elements. That way, you only need to include that style sheet for pages that actually include forms.

5. **Click OK. In the Save Style Sheet File As box, type *layout.css* in the File Name field (Save As field on a Mac). Click Save.**

   Dreamweaver saves a new CSS file into your site and opens the CSS Rule Definition window. You'll start by adding a background property.

6. **Click the Background category, and then click the Browse button to the right of the Background Image box.**

   This opens the now-familiar Select Image Source window for selecting graphic files. You're going to add a red stripe (just like in last chapter's tutorial) that extends from the logo to the right edge of the page, giving the illusion of one really wide graphic.

7. **Navigate to the Images Global folder and double-click the *bg_banner.gif* file.**

   Because background images normally tile left to right and top to bottom, you're going to add instructions to this style so the stripe only tiles horizontally across the page.

8. **Choose "repeat-x" from the Repeat menu. Click Positioning in the Category list.**

   Dreamweaver displays all of the CSS Positioning properties—the heart of creating absolutely positioned elements. Here's where the magic is.

9. **From the Type menu, select "absolute."**

   This gives the layer an absolute position on the page. Because the banner stretches across the browser window—no matter what size that browser window is—you'll next give the layer a width that spreads across the page.

10. **Type *100* in the Width box and select % from the menu next to it.**

    You've just set the layer to 100 percent width, meaning it takes up 100 percent of the available space in the browser. Next, you'll position the layer in the top-left corner of the page.

Tip: There's a shortcut for typing values into a CSS box. Instead of typing a number in one box and then selecting a unit of measurement (pixels, percentages, or ems) from a menu, you can type the number and measurement together in the first box: *100%,* for example, or *1em,* or *20px.* Dreamweaver automatically adjusts the units menu.

Just don't put a space between the number and the measurement type. For example, *20 px* won't work.

---

11. **For the Placement options, type *0* in the Top box and *0* in the Left box.**

    The window should now look like Figure 8-14.

12. **Click OK to finish creating the style.**

    You've just created your first ID style. Congratulations. Applying it is a piece of cake.

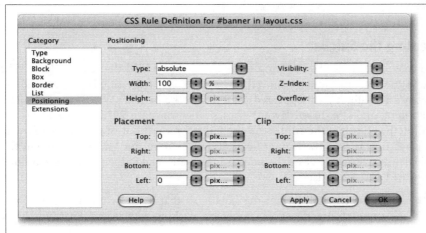

Figure 8-14:
The Positioning properties in the CSS Rule Definition window provide all the options you need to create absolutely positioned layers.

13. Select the National Exasperator logo graphic, and choose Insert → Layout Objects → Div Tag.

Alternatively you can click the Insert Div Tag object on the Layout tab of the Insert bar (see Figure 8-5). Either way, the Insert Div Tag window opens.

14. **From the ID menu, select "banner." Make sure the "Wrap around selection" option's turned on, and click OK.**

Dreamweaver wraps the new layer around the graphic. The banner moves to the top-left corner of the page, and the logo appears to extend the entire width of the window (see top image in Figure 8-15). In the next part of this tutorial, you'll create a layer to position the sidebar info on the left edge of the page below the banner.

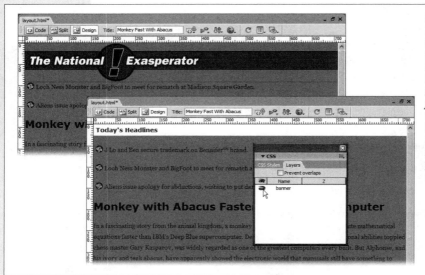

Figure 8-15:
The Layers panel can temporarily hide a layer that's getting in the way. It's easy to remove the National Exasperator banner in the top window; just click the eyeball icon on the Layers panel, and the banner disappears (bottom). When you're finished with your design, you can make the layer visible again.

Creating the Sidebar

You may have noticed something strange after you added that banner layer. The rest of the text on the page moved up, and much of the sidebar information—"Today's Headlines"—disappeared underneath the banner. Welcome to absolute positioning and CSS-based layout! As described on page 297, whenever you use absolute positioning, the content in the layer is moved out of the normal flow of the page. In this case, the banner floats above the page, and the other content fills in the leftover space. It's as if the sidebar information and other page content don't know the layer even exists.

In this next phase, you'll format the sidebar so that it fits below the banner, and you'll use some of Dreamweaver's tools for working with layers. First, you'll use the Layers panel to temporarily hide the banner as you format the other parts of the page:

1. **Choose Window → Layers to open the Layers panel.**

   The Layers panel lets you hide layers and change their layering (how a layer overlaps another layer). In this case, you'll temporarily make the banner invisible so you can work on the sidebar.

2. **In the Layers panel, click to the left of the word "banner" (see Figure 8-15, bottom).**

   You should see a closed eye appear in this column. This indicates that the layer is now invisible, and the banner should disappear from the page. If you still see the banner, keep clicking in the Layers panel until the closed eye appears. Now you can see all of the content for the sidebar. It's a simple process to create a layer for that.

3. **In the Design panel group—where the Layers panel is located—click the CSS Styles tab to bring that panel to the front.**

   Alternatively, you can choose Window → "CSS Styles panel" to open the panel.

4. **Click the New CSS Rule button to open the New CSS Rule window.**

   Again, you'll create an ID style.

5. **Click the Advanced selector button and, in the Selector name box, type #side-bar. The "Define in" menu should say layout.css. Click OK to begin creating the style.**

   This is another ID style that you'll store in the external style sheet you created earlier. You'll add some CSS properties to position this layer precisely on the screen.

6. **In the CSS Rule Definition window, click the Positioning category.**

   This is the same process you used when creating the banner; however, you'll position the sidebar in a different location on the screen.

7. **From the position menu, select "absolute."**

   The sidebar fills only a small part of the total width of the page, so set a pixel value for its width.

8. **In the width box, type 150.**

   Dreamweaver defaults to pixel values, so you don't have to do anything else with the width. However, you do want to position the layer so it's below the banner.

9. **For the Placement options, type *150* in the Top box and *0* in the Left box.**

   This places the sidebar 150 pixels down from the top of the page, but keeps it clinging to the left edge.

10. **Click OK to finish the style.**

    Next, you'll select the sidebar content and wrap it in the layer.

11. **Click just before the letter T in "Today's Headlines" and drag down and to the right until you've selected the headline and the three bulleted items below it.**

12. **Choose Insert → Layout Objects → Div Tag.**

    Alternatively, you can click the Insert Div Tag object on the Layout tab of the Insert bar (see Figure 8-5). Either way, the Insert Div Tag window opens.

13. **From the ID menu, select "sidebar." Make sure the "Wrap around selection" option is turned on, and click OK.**

    Dreamweaver wraps the new layer around the sidebar content. As with the banner, the sidebar is now taken out of the normal flow of the page, so the story text moves to the top of the page and flows under the sidebar. Don't worry; you'll fix that next.

Positioning the Main Content

The main content for this page—the story about the calculating monkey—should go below the banner and to the right of the sidebar. It won't have a set width, however. Like the banner, the content should be fluid, so that if someone resizes his browser window, the story grows or shrinks to fit the available space. (This is like the "liquid HTML" table designs described on page 240.)

Using absolute positioning, it's difficult to get that kind of fluid design to work across all of today's browsers. Fortunately, there's a simple trick you can use to achieve the same goal: Instead of absolutely positioning the story content, you'll use large top and left margins to actually *indent* the story area away from the banner and sidebar. This is a common trick used by many Web designers who employ CSS-based layout. Here's how it works:

1. **In the CSS Styles panel, click the New Rule button.**

   You'll create another ID style next.

2. **In the New CSS Rule window, create an ID style named *#main* for the *layout.css* style sheet. Click OK.**

   Refer to step 5 in the previous section for more detail on this process.

3. **In the CSS Rule Definition window, click the Box category.**

   You'll set the margin properties here.

4. **Turn off the "Same for all" box under the Margin heading; type *115* in the Top box, type *175* in the Left box, and type *10* in the Right box (see Figure 8-16).**

This indents the content 115 pixels from the top of the page and 175 pixels from the left edge. The 10 pixel value in the Right box moves the text away from the right edge so it doesn't collide with the edge of the browser window. Note that you're not using absolute positioning for this style. In other words, you're not creating a layer here, just indenting the text as you might with any CSS style you create. It just so happens that the margins you're adding are so large, they effectively position the text out of the way of the banner and sidebar.

You're also going to add a jazzy border along the left edge of the text, so you need to add a bit of padding to move the text away from the border.

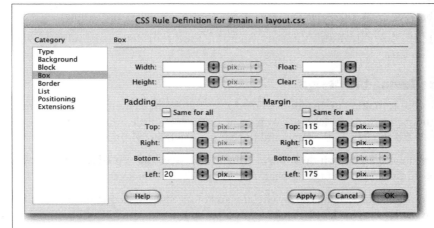

Figure 8-16:
Margin properties offer another way to place elements on a page by letting you indent content away from absolutely positioned elements on a page. This is particularly useful for parts of a page—like the main text—that need to change size based on the width of a visitor's browser window.

5. **Turn off the "Same for all" box underneath the Padding heading and, in the Left box, type *20*.**

The CSS Rule Definition window should look like Figure 8-16. Finally, you'll add a border to this style.

6. **In the Category list, click Border.**

You'll add a border only to the left edge of the text.

7. **Turn off all three "Same for all" boxes, and use the following three values for the Left border settings: dotted for the style, 2 pixels for the width, and a color of white (#FFFFFF).**

This creates a 2-pixel dotted white border along the left edge of the main content.

8. **Click OK to create the style.**

You apply this style just like all the others.

9. **Click before the letter "M" in Monkey and drag down and to the right to select all of the text for the story.**

You won't select the sidebar doing this. Even though the sidebar appears to be inside that text, its code is actually at the top of the page.

10. **Finally, repeat steps 12 and 13 on page 320 to wrap this text with the style you just created.**

The page is coming together nicely. You'll just make the banner visible again so you can see the page in all its glory.

11. **Choose Window → Layers to open the Layers panel. Click the closed eye icon to the left of the banner layer until the banner appears on the page again.**

You can either click until you see an open-eye icon—meaning the layer's visible—or until you see *no* icon (the default setting, which is also visible).

In the last part of this tutorial, you'll fine-tune your design and add a navigation bar.

Fine-Tuning the Design

The page is looking pretty good. You've placed different elements in different parts of the page—without tables! However, it could use a little adjustment. The sidebar's a tad too low on the page, and the banner needs a navigation bar:

1. **In the document window, move your mouse over the top edge of the sidebar until the cursor changes appearance. Click to select the layer.**

You can also select a layer by clicking any of its edges, selecting the layer's name in the Layers panel, or by clicking the layer's selection handle (see Figure 8-7).

2. **Grab anywhere on the top edge of the layer, except any of the resize handles, and drag up until the top of the layer overlaps the banner by a couple of pixels (see Figure 8-17).**

Notice that you can actually put this layer on top of the banner—something you can't do with normal HTML. The exact placement isn't important—whatever looks good to you. After testing the design in a browser, you can always return and change its placement.

Dragging either the top or bottom resize handle sets a height for the layer. In this case, you don't want to do that. Since you don't know how many headlines you may have listed at a time, you'll never know the exact height. Better to let the Web browser just resize the layer automatically based on the content inside it.

Note: You may notice that if you make a mistake—drag the layer off the left edge of the page, for example—you can't use Edit → Undo to get the layer back to its original position. That's because you're not actually changing the Web page; you're altering the CSS in the external stylesheet: *layout.css.* That file has to be opened, and you have to switch to it, to undo any changes you make to a layer by dragging it around the page.

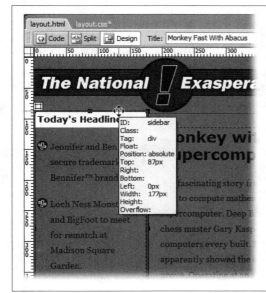

Figure 8-17:
You can use Dreamweaver's WYSIWYG layer-editing tools to change the position, width, height, and other layer properties. When you resize a layer by dragging one of the resize handles, Dreamweaver updates the CSS style for the layer—even if the CSS information is in an external style sheet! Also, if you hover over a selected layer, Dreamweaver 8 provides a quick overview of the style name and any relevant positioning properties in a yellow pop-up box, as shown here.

3. **With the layer still selected, type *177px* into the Width box in the Property inspector.**

   This makes the layer 177 pixels wide—just wide enough to touch the white border on the left edge of the main content. Of course, you could have used the right resize handle to make this layer wider. Dreamweaver provides many ways to do the same thing.

Note: You may notice that resize handles never appear around the main content of this page. Dreamweaver includes resize handles only for absolutely positioned elements—what Dreamweaver calls *layers.* Because you used a little trick to position the main content—setting the Margin properties—you can't resize this part of the page like you can the layers. If you want to move the main content higher on the page, or farther to the right, you have to adjust the Margin properties of its style.

In the last part of this tutorial, you'll add a navigation bar to the banner.

4. **Choose Window → CSS Styles to open the CSS Styles panel. Click the New CSS Rule button.**

   You'll create another layer to hold the site's navigation buttons.

5. **As with the previous layers, create an ID style named *#nav* in the *layout.css* style sheet. Click OK.**

   This process is detailed in steps 4 and 5 on page 319.

6. **In the CSS Rule Definition window, click the Positioning category and enter the values shown in Figure 8-18.**

   In essence, you're creating an absolutely positioned layer that's 455 pixels wide and appears 65 pixels from the top and 251 pixels from the left.

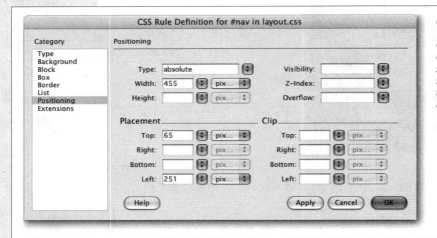

Figure 8-18:
To accurately place an element on a page, you only need two placement settings—Top and Left—to specify where the layer's top and left edges appear on the page.

7. **Click OK to create the style.**

   This time, instead of wrapping already existing content with a layer, you'll insert the layer and then add content to it.

8. **Choose Insert → Layout Objects → Div Tag.**

   Again, you can also use the Insert Div Tag object on the Layout tab of the Insert bar. Either way, the Insert Div Tag window appears (see Figure 8-19).

9. **Select "Before end of tag" and <div id="banner"> from the two Insert menus. Select "nav" from the ID menu (see Figure 8-19).**

   This series of steps inserts the new layer. However, instead of wrapping it around something, or even just dropping the layer on the page, you're inserting the layer *inside* the banner layer. This is called nesting a layer and has the benefit of making the navigation-bar layer a part of the banner. If you move the banner layer—say, you want it a few pixels farther down on the screen—the navigation bar moves along with it.

Note: This example demonstrates the flexible nature of absolutely positioned elements. When an absolutely positioned layer is nested inside another absolutely positioned layer (in this example, the nav layer is inside the banner layer), its position isn't relative to the top and left edges of the page. Instead, a nested layer's positioning is in relation to the edges of its *parent* layer. In this case, the navigation layer appears 65 pixels down from the top edge of the banner *no matter where* the banner's placed on the page. Nested layers are discussed on page 312.

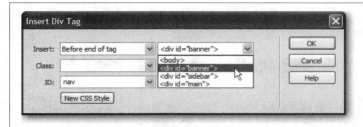

Figure 8-19:
You can use the Insert Div Tag dialog box to nest one layer inside another.

10. **Click OK to insert the new layer.**

    Dreamweaver adds a layer with the text "Content for id 'nav' Goes Here." You'll put the navigation bar here.

11. **Choose File → Open. Navigate to and open the file *navigation.html* in the DWLayout folder.**

    You can also double-click the file in the Files panel to open it.

12. **Select the navigation bar on the page and copy it.**

    For example, click inside the page, choose Edit → Select All and then Edit → Copy.

13. **Click the *layout.html* tab at the top of the document window to switch back to the page you're designing.**

14. **Triple-click anywhere inside the navigation layer.**

    That is, anywhere inside the text "Content for id 'nav' Goes Here." This selects that paragraph of text. You can also click inside and choose Edit → Select All to select the contents of the <div>.

15. **Choose Edit → Paste.**

    The navigation bar is dumped into the layer. The page is looking great. Just one last change. The banner's too close to the top of the window. It would look better if it were just a few pixels lower.

16. **In the document window, move your mouse to the top edge of the banner area. When the cursor changes to a cross with four arrows, click to select the layer.**

    Again, you can use any of the techniques listed in step 1 on page 309.

17. **Press the down arrow key three times.**

    This step moves the banner down 3 pixels—the perfect amount. Notice that the navigation bar moves also. Because it's nested inside the banner, it always goes where the banner layer goes.

18. **Press F12 (Option-F12) to preview your design in a Web browser (see Figure 8-20).**

    Congratulations! You've had your first taste of CSS-based layout.

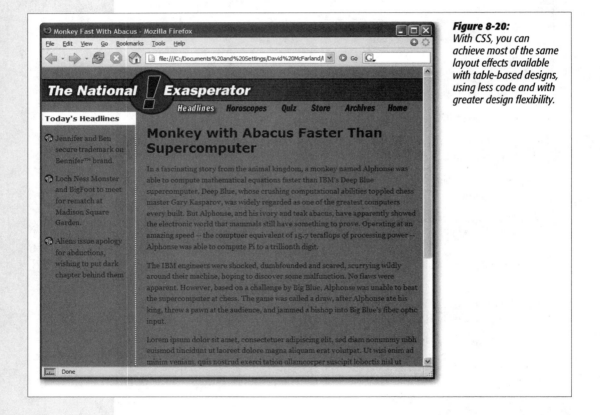

Figure 8-20:
With CSS, you can achieve most of the same layout effects available with table-based designs, using less code and with greater design flexibility.

Under the Hood: HTML

While Dreamweaver started life primarily as a visual Web page editor, each new version has brought enhancements to its text-editing features. Dreamweaver 8 continues that trend, by adding several new and powerful code-editing tools that let you work on your pages' HTML, CSS, and JavaScript code directly. In fact, in recognition of the ever-multiplying types of files used on the Web, Dreamweaver lets you edit all text-based files, including XML, Java, ActionScript, and just plain text files. The code editor includes professional features like customizable syntax highlighting, auto indenting, line numbering, and code hints; tantalizing new features like code collapse, so you can concentrate on just the code you want; and the Code view toolbar, which provides one-click access to frequent hand-coding tasks. Now, Dreamweaver may be the only Web page creation program even hard-core code junkies ever need.

Roundtrip HTML

Unlike many other visual HTML editors, Dreamweaver has always graciously accepted HTML written by hand (and even by other programs). In fact, Dreamweaver has always made it easy to jump between itself and text-editing programs like the much loved, but retired, HomeSite (for Windows) and BBEdit (for the Mac).

This ability, which Macromedia calls *Roundtrip HTML*, lets Web developers write code the way they want, without worrying that Dreamweaver will change it. For example, suppose you have a particular way of formatting your handwritten code. Maybe you insert an extra carriage return for spacing after every <td> (table cell) tag or like to use multiple tabs to indent nested tags. In such cases, Dreamweaver won't try to rewrite that to fit its own style—unless you ask it to.

Auto-Fixing Your Code

That's not to say that Dreamweaver doesn't *ever* change your code. In fact, the program can automatically fix errors when you open a page that was created in another program, including:

- **Overlapping tags.** Take a look at this example:

```
<p><strong>Fix your tags!</p></strong>
```

This HTML is invalid, because the opening and closing <strong> tags should appear *inside* the <p> tag. Dreamweaver rewrites this snippet correctly:

```
<p><strong>Fix your tags!</strong></p>
```

- **Unclosed tags.** Tags usually come in pairs, like this:

```
<em>This text is in italics</em>
```

But if a page is missing the ending tag (<em>*This text is in italics*), Dreamweaver adds the closing tag.

- **Extra closing tags.** If a page has an *extra* closing tag (<strong>bold text</strong> </strong>), Dreamweaver helpfully removes it.

This feature comes turned *off* in Dreamweaver 8. If you're working on a site that was hand coded or created by another, less capable Web-editing program, it's wise to turn this feature on, since all of those errors are improper HTML that can cause problems for browsers. (Once upon a time, some Web developers, for example, deliberately omitted closing tags just to save a few kilobytes in file size. While most browsers can still interpret this kind of sloppy code, it's poor practice.)

You can turn auto-fixing on in the Preferences window (see Figure 9-1); just turn on "Fix invalidly nested and unclosed tags" and "Remove extra closing tags."

Note: The "Warn when fixing or removing tags" option isn't really a warning as much as it is a report. By the time you see the "Warning" message, Dreamweaver's already rewritten the code in your page and saved it—without the possibility of undoing it.

Dreamweaver can also change the capitalization (case) of HTML tags and properties, if you want. For example, if you prefer lowercase letters for tags and properties, like this:

```
<a href="nextpage.html">Click here</a>
```

Dreamweaver can convert uppercase tags (<A HREF="next.html">) to lowercase, or vice versa, when it finds them in pages created by other programs. (You can turn on this feature as described on page 341.)

Note: If you're creating XHTML pages (see page 6), you don't get the option to choose between cases—tags always must be lowercase in XHTML files.

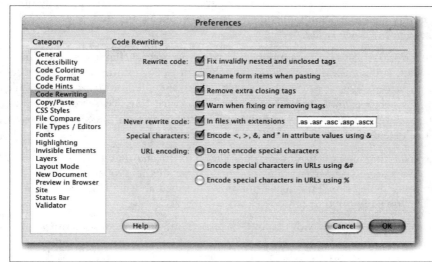

Figure 9-1:
To specify a file name extension whose code you never want Dreamweaver to touch, choose Edit → Preferences. Then, in the Category list, choose Code Rewriting and type a new extension in the extensions field. (Make sure the "Never rewrite code" checkbox is turned on, as well.)

Web Application Server Pages

Dreamweaver can leave pages with certain file name extensions untouched—pages created for *Web application servers,* for example. Web application servers process Web pages that access databases and other dynamic services like shopping cart programs and form-processing applications. You'll read about this capability in Part Six of this book. Many of these systems rely on special code within the HTML of a page—code that Dreamweaver might "fix," interpreting the portions as HTML errors.

Unless you change its settings, Dreamweaver doesn't rewrite code in pages that are designed for the leading application-server technologies—that is, files whose names end in .asp (Active Server Pages that run on Microsoft's IIS Web Server), .aspx (Microsoft's next-generation ASP pages, called .NET), .cfm and .cfml (ColdFusion Markup Language pages that run on Macromedia's ColdFusion Server), .jsp (Java Server Pages that run on any Java Server), or .php (PHP pages), among others. To add an extension to this list, see Figure 9-1.

Special Characters and Encoding

The Code Rewriting Preferences window also lets you control how Dreamweaver handles special characters like <, >, and ", whenever you enter them into the Property inspector or a dialog box. Some characters have special meaning; the "less than" symbol (<), for example, indicates the beginning of an HTML tag, so you can't just link to a page named *bob<zero.html*. If you did, a Web browser would think a new HTML tag (called *zero*) was starting after the < symbol.

There are several ways to avoid this problem. The simplest and wisest method: avoid strange characters when you name pages, graphics, CSS styles, or any other object in your site. Sticking to letters, numbers, hyphens, and underscores (_) will make your life much easier.

Another option is to let Dreamweaver *encode* those special characters. Encoding a character simply means using a code to represent it. For example, you can represent a space as *%20*, or a < symbol as *%3C*. Thus, the infamous *bob<zero.html* file becomes *bob%3C.html*, and your link will work just fine. To set up encoding, choose Edit → Preferences (Dreamweaver → Preferences on the Mac) and select the Code Rewriting category. Your options are as follows:

• **Special characters.** Turning on this checkbox means that Dreamweaver will convert any special character you might type in the Property inspector, or another dialog box, into the % notation described above. (This feature has no effect on code you type in Code view.)

Dreamweaver comes with this option turned off, since it can sometimes interfere with *server-side* code (see Part Six of this book). If you stick to the simple rule "Don't use strange characters in your file names," you'll probably never notice the difference.

• **Do not encode special characters.** Selecting this option, the first of three under "URL encoding," tells Dreamweaver not to touch any Web addresses you enter (in the Link box of the Property inspector, say). (Again, selecting this option has no effect on any links you type in Code view.)

• **Encode special characters in URLs using &#** is the safest choice. It's especially helpful if you use a language that has a non-Latin alphabet. If you name your files using Japanese characters, for example, choosing this option can translate them into code that successfully transmits over the Internet.

• **Encode special characters in URLs using %** is intended for use with older browsers (and we're talking *old*, as in pre-4.0).

Tip: If you're developing (or want to develop) pages in languages other than English, you'll find some helpful information at *www.macromedia.com/support/dreamweaver/ts/documents/font_encoding.htm*.

Code View

Dreamweaver provides several different ways to view a page's HTML code:

• **Code view.** In Code view, Dreamweaver displays your page's raw code.

• **Split view.** This shows the HTML code and the "regular" Design view simultaneously (Figure 9-2).

- **Code inspector.** The Code inspector is a floating code window that lets you use Design view in its full glory (not cut in half as in Split view), while still providing access to the code. (To open the Code inspector, choose Window → Code Inspector, or press F10.) Code warriors who are into serious multitasking can also use the Code inspector to look at one area of code, while using the main document window to work on another area of code.

The rest of this chapter assumes that you're using Code view for HTML editing.

To move between Dreamweaver's different views, use the buttons in the Document toolbar (Figure 9-2) or choose a name from the View menu: Code, Design (the "regular" visual mode), or Code and Design (Split view).

Figure 9-2:
In Split view (also called Code and Design view), the top half shows your page's HTML; the bottom half shows the WYSIWYG Design view. Selecting an object in the visual half (circled) also selects the corresponding HTML in the code half (the highlighted paragraph tag)— a great way to identify an object in your HTML. As you work in one half of the Split view, Dreamweaver updates the other half. Use the buttons (labeled) in the Document toolbar to jump between the different views. (Notice that the tag selector at the bottom of the document window [circled] also identifies the selected tag.)

Tip: You can quickly jump between Code and Design view by pressing Control+` (on both Windows and the Mac). In Split view, this shortcut jumps between the two views, so you could insert an image in the design half of Split view and then press Control+` to jump right into the HTML for that image in the Code half of the window.

Code view functions just like a text editor. You can click anywhere inside the window and start typing HTML, JavaScript, Cascading Style Sheet, or other programming code (such as ASP, ColdFusion, or PHP).

That doesn't mean you have to type out *everything* by hand; the Insert bar, Insert menu, and Property inspector also function in Code view. Using these sources of canned HTML blobs, you can combine hands-on HTML work with the easy-to-use, rapid action of Dreamweaver's objects. This trick can be a real time-saver when you need to add a table, which would otherwise be a multiline exercise in typing accuracy. You can also select a tag (an image's <img> tag, for example) in Code view and use the Property inspector to modify it.

Tip: When you add HTML to Code view, Dreamweaver doesn't automatically update Design view, which can be disconcerting when you're working in Split view. (After all, how would Dreamweaver display a half-finished tag like this: *<table border*="*"?*) Click the Refresh button in the Property inspector (see Figure 9-3), or press F5, to update the visual display.

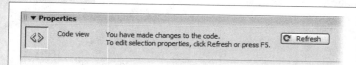

Figure 9-3:
After changing code in Split view, click Refresh on the Property inspector to update Dreamweaver's visual display.

To help you navigate your code, Code view provides several visual cues. They include:

- **Syntax coloring.** Dreamweaver displays different elements in different colors. Comments, for example, are gray. Text is black, HTML tags appear in dark blue, and HTML properties show up in bright blue. You can change any of these colors, and even specify unique colors for different types of tags, using the Preferences window (see Figure 9-4).

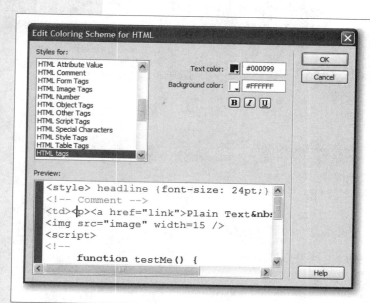

Figure 9-4:
From the Preferences window, you can control the color Dreamweaver uses to display HTML and script code while in Code view. To do so, select the Code Coloring Category. Then select the type of document—HTML, ASP, CSS, or whatever—and click Edit Coloring Scheme. In the Edit Coloring Scheme window (shown here), select an item whose color you wish to change—Library Item or HTML Form Tags, for example—and set a text and/or background color using the color boxes. You can also make the code bold, italic, or underlined using the appropriate formatting buttons.

To really make a tag stand out, you can underline it, make it bold, italicize it, and even give it a background color. Dreamweaver has separate color schemes for 24 different types of documents, such as ASP, CSS, and XML files. (But do you really need different colors for HTML forms in ASP pages, HTML pages, and PHP pages? You be the judge.)

- **Bad code highlighting.** When you type incorrect code (an opening tag without a closing tag, say), it's highlighted in yellow (see Figure 9-5).

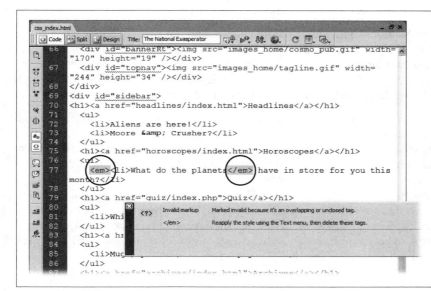

Figure 9-5:
Dreamweaver highlights incorrect HTML code with bright yellow highlighting in Code view (circled). If you click inside the yellow area, the Property inspector reveals the mistake. In this case, a tag is improperly nested—part of it is outside the <li> tag. (In Design view, on the other hand, Dreamweaver indicates mistakes by showing the HTML tag—the characters <, e, m, and >, for example—in front of a bright yellow background.)

- **Browser error highlighting.** Not all browsers understand all the HTML tags and properties available in Dreamweaver, especially since older browsers may not be aware of current standards. This feature, which is part of the Check Browser Support tool described on page 501, lets Dreamweaver identify code that doesn't work with certain browsers.

Here's how you use it: In Code view, a squiggly red underline appears under code that doesn't work with the browsers you've told Dreamweaver to check (see page 505). Mousing over the squiggly line produces a pop-up dialog box with a description of the problem.

For example, in Figure 9-5, the code <div id="sidebar"> displays with a squiggly line under *id="sidebar"*; mousing over the *id* attribute generates a message saying that it isn't supported by Navigator 3.0. (In other words, that old Windows 95 machine in the Museum of Ancient Computing might have trouble displaying this page.)

- **Library Items.** Library items and uneditable regions in pages built from templates appear in light gray. You can't actually change this code in Code view. This coloring scheme is a little confusing since HTML comments (see page 336) are also displayed in gray, and you *can* edit those. (For more on templates and the Library, see Chapters 16 and 17.)

You can also control Code view display by using the View Options pop-up menu in the toolbar (see Figure 9-6), or by using the View → Code Options submenu:

- **Word Wrap.** This option makes long lines of code wrap (at the window's edge) to the next line, so you don't have to scroll horizontally to see it all. This option affects only how Dreamweaver displays the line in the document window; it doesn't actually change your code by introducing line breaks.

- **Line Numbers.** This automatic line numbering can come in handy when you're using Dreamweaver's Check Target Browser tool (see page 501), or when you encounter an error in a page containing server-side code (such as the code you create in Part Six of this book). You can also click a line number in Code view to select the entire line, which is a great way to delete or cut a line of code.

- **Hidden Characters.** Some characters you can type on the keyboard aren't visible on the screen: the end of a line, created by hitting the Enter or Return key, for example. Sometimes, these hidden characters can cause big trouble. For example, when working with dynamic, server-side Web pages (described in Part Six), you might find some cool code on the Web and copy it to your own page. Sometimes copying and pasting code from a Web page introduces hidden characters that prevent the code from working. Turning on the "Hidden Characters" option can help you ferret out these problem characters and eliminate them. Spaces appear as dots, tabs as a set of greater than signs (>>), and paragraphs as a paragraph symbol (¶) (see Figure 9-6).

Figure 9-6:
Code view provides easy access to common code-writing tasks with the new Coding toolbar (left edge) and the View Options menu (top right), which let you modify how Dreamweaver displays the code. The Word Wrap option, for example, forces all code to fit inside the width of the window. If a line of code extends off the page, Dreamweaver wraps it to the next line (as in the highlighted code in this illustration). Your only clue that you're looking at one long line is that the entire glob of text has only a single line number.

- **Highlight Invalid Code.** This is the on/off switch for Dreamweaver's friendly tendency to highlight bad HTML in Code view (see Figure 9-5).

- **Syntax Coloring.** This option turns tags, comments, and text into colorful (and informative) text (see Figure 9-4).

- **Auto Indent.** When you're working with nested HTML tags, it's often helpful to press the Tab key to indent each level of nested tags, making it easier to identify large blocks of HTML (a table and all its contents, for example). The Auto Indent option carries the same size indent onto the next line when you hit the Return or Enter key. For example, suppose you hit the Tab key twice, type a line of code, and then hit Return. Dreamweaver would place the insertion point on the next line, indented using two tabs. To un-indent, just press the Backspace key.

Coding Toolbar

Dreamweaver 8 introduces a handy toolbar that makes many basic hand-coding tasks go much more quickly. While working in Code view, the Coding toolbar appears on the left edge of the document window (see Figure 9-6). If you don't see it, you can turn it on by choosing View → Toolbars → Coding, or by right-clicking (Control-clicking) on another toolbar such as the Insert or Document toolbar, and turning on the Coding option in the pop-up menu. Use the same technique to close the toolbar, if you don't use it.

The toolbar contains buttons that duplicate tasks and preference settings that you can control from other parts of Dreamweaver. Here's a quick rundown of the buttons listed in Figure 9-6, with a quick explanation of what they do and, when applicable, a cross-reference to a more detailed description of the tool or action:

- **Open Documents.** This is just a pull-down menu, displaying all open documents. It lets you switch among the different documents you're currently working on, but it's actually more work than just clicking a document's tab at the top of the document window (see page 19), so you'll probably want to skip it.

- **Collapse Full Tag/Collapse Selection/Expand All.** These three buttons work with Dreamweaver 8's Code Collapse feature described on page 338. They let you collapse (and expand) multiple lines of code, essentially keeping it out of the way, letting you concentrate on the code you're currently working on.

- **Select Parent Tag.** This handy feature lets you quickly select the tag that surrounds your current selection. For example, say you've selected the text inside of a link (<a>) tag, or just clicked inside that tag, and your cursor's blinking happily. Click this button, and the entire <a> tag is selected. Click it again, and that link's parent tag is selected. This button provides a quick way to select the tag you're currently working on. If you really want to be productive, the keyboard shortcut Ctrl-[(⌘-[) is quicker.

- **Balance Braces.** If you do a lot of programming using JavaScript or one of the server languages like PHP, ColdFusion, or ASP, this button can help you find the matching brace ({ or }) character in a chunk of programming code. Just click to the right of an opening brace ({) and then click this button to find the closing brace. To find a closing brace's mate, click to the left of the brace, and then click this button. The button also finds matching parentheses characters. The keyboard shortcut—Ctrl+' (⌘-')—is even faster.

- **Apply/Remove Comments.** Comments are a way of including helpful notes in your code that don't appear on the page when it's displayed in a browser. You may want to leave some explanatory notes in your HTML page to help future generations of Web developers understand what you were doing. For example, you might put a comment before a <div> tag (see page 303) that explains what should go inside it—"For corporate logo and navigation bar." Comments are also frequently used to mark the end of a section of the page—"End of navigation bar." These buttons let you add or remove comments to HTML, CSS, Java-Script, PHP, and VBScript code, as demonstrated in Figure 9-7.

Tip: Comments are very useful with Cascading Style Sheets (see Chapter 6). You can open a CSS file, select a property inside a style, and stick a pair of comment tags around this property. When you preview a page that uses the style, you'll see the style minus the property you've commented (or commented out, as some programmers say). This maneuver lets you preview a style, temporarily hiding the effect of one or more styling properties without permanently deleting the property. It's a great help in debugging problematic styles.

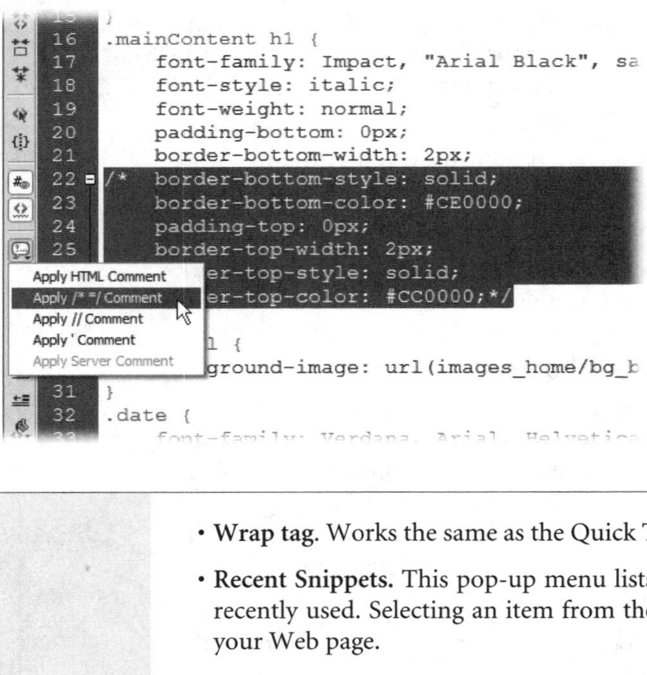

Figure 9-7:
The Coding toolbar lets you wrap HTML, CSS, JavaScript, or other programming code within comment characters. Just select the code you wish to turn into comments, click the Add comment button, and select the type of comment you wish to add. Use the HTML comment option to hide HTML code; the /* */ option to hide multiple lines of CSS, JavaScript, or PHP code; the // option to hide each line of CSS, JavaScript, or PHP code; the ' option to hide VBScript code; and, if you're working on a server-side page as described in Part Six, use the last option to hide code in those pages. To remove a comment, select all of the code (including the comment) and click the Remove comment button (just below the Apply comment button).

- **Wrap tag.** Works the same as the Quick Tag editor described on page 344.

- **Recent Snippets.** This pop-up menu lists all the snippets (see page 573) you've recently used. Selecting an item from the menu inserts that snippet's code into your Web page.

- **Indent/Outdent.** These buttons will indent or outdent lines of selected code using the settings you've defined in the Code Formatting preferences (see page 341).

- **Apply Source formatting.** This button lets you apply specific formatting to an entire Web page, or just a selection of code, using the code-formatting options you've set up in the Code Formatting preferences window (see page 341) and the rules defined in the type-A-über-geek-what-a-lot-of-work Tag Library described in the box on page 343.

Code Hints

Typing code can be a chore, which is why even longtime hand coders take advantage of anything that helps speed up the process. A perfect example is Dreamweaver's Code Hints feature (shown in Figure 9-8). It lets you select tags, attributes, and even Cascading Style Sheet styles from a pop-up menu as you type.

Tip: Code Hints work with other tags as well as scripting languages like ASP.NET, ColdFusion, and PHP. In addition, Dreamweaver includes CSS Code Hints, so if you write your style sheets by hand, you can take advantage of the auto-completion features of Code Hints to quickly type out CSS style properties.

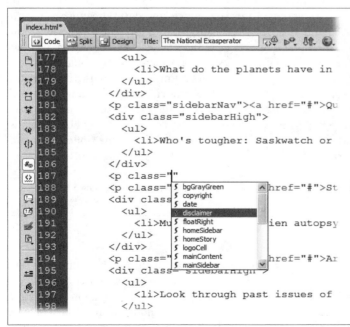

Figure 9-8:
The Code Hints feature saves your tired fingers from typing tags and tag properties. Just select the appropriate item from a pop-up list and let Dreamweaver type it for you. Dreamweaver's even thoughtful enough to show you all available CSS styles when you insert a class attribute in a tag.

Here's how it works. After you begin a new tag by typing an opening bracket (<), a menu pops up, listing all available HTML tags. Use your mouse or arrow keys to select a tag, or type the first few letters of the tag and let Dreamweaver select the closest matching item. When you press Enter (Return), Dreamweaver automatically fills in the tag name. Even better, a second menu now pops up, listing all the properties of that tag.

Tip: You can also open the Code Hints menu by pressing Ctrl+Space bar (in both Mac and Windows). This shortcut's very useful when you're editing code and want to add a property or edit a property of a tag you've already created. For example, you could click inside the name of a class style applied to a tag—click inside the word "copyright" in this code *class="copyright"*, for instance—and then press Ctrl+Space bar. This not only selects the name so you can change it, but also opens a menu listing all of the classes available to the page. Then you could use the up and down arrow keys (or even your mouse) to select a different CSS style.

If the feature annoys you, you can get it out of your way. You can turn off Code Hints completely, rein it in by setting a delay (so that pop-up lists don't appear immediately), or turn off Code Hints for only selected types of elements (such as tag properties). To make any of these adjustments, open the Preferences window by pressing Ctrl+U (⌘-U) and then select the Code Hints category. Make your desired changes to the Code Hints preferences, and then click OK.

Dreamweaver 8 also adds a subtle change to the Code Hints feature. After you've typed an opening tag—<p>, for instance—and the content that goes inside this new paragraph tag, Dreamweaver simplifies the writing of the closing tag: as soon as you type </ (the first two characters for any closing tag), Dreamweaver automatically finishes off your thought by closing the tag for you. In this example, you'd end up with </p>. For a longer tag like the <table> tag, this feature will save your fingers a lot of work. (Previous versions of Dreamweaver would automatically insert the closing tag immediately after you finished typing the opening tag. This was a pain if you were going to follow your opening tag with a whole bunch of HTML, since the opening and closing tags in this case were not next to each other but separated by many lines of code. If you like the old way better, or just can't stand the feature at all, you can make your wishes felt in the Code Hints category of the Preferences window mentioned in the previous paragraph.)

Tip: If you like Code Hints, you'll love the Snippets panel, which makes reusing code a snap. See page 573 for details.

Code Collapse

One problem with raw HTML is, well, it's raw—a bunch of letters, numbers, and symbols that tend to blend together into a mind-numbing sea of code. This can make locating a particular bit of code needle-in-a-haystack tough. On large pages, with lots of code, it's easy to get lost as you scroll up and down to make a change. In many cases, you don't need to see all of the code, because you're not likely to change it—for example, the top portion of a page containing the *DOCTYPE* and *html* declarations (see page 6)—or because you can't change it—like the HTML embedded in template-based pages (Chapter 17) or containing Dreamweaver Library items (Chapter 16).

Fortunately, Dreamweaver 8 introduces a new feature that lets you get that in-your-way code out of your face. The Code Collapse feature condenses multiple lines of code into a single highlighted box of 10 characters (Figure 9-9). The basic process is simple: select the code you want to collapse—all of the code above the <body> tag, for example—and click the icon (circled in Figure 9-9, top) that appears just to the left of both the first and last line you wish to collapse. On Windows, this icon is a small box with a minus sign (–); on Mac, it's a down-pointing arrow (at the beginning of the selection) and an up-pointing arrow (at the end). The code collapses into a gray outlined box. To expand the code, just select it and then click the icon (a plus sign [+] in Windows, a right-pointing arrow on the Mac).

Figure 9-9:
Now you see it, now you don't. You can collapse a multiline selection of HTML code (top) into a compact little gray box (circled in the bottom image). The collapsed code is still there in your page—you haven't deleted it—but now it's conveniently tucked out of sight. If you need a reminder of what code you've collapsed, move your mouse over the gray box, and a yellow tooltip window appears displaying the HTML code.

Tip: To quickly select multiple lines of HTML, click in the blue, line-number area to the left of the code, indicating where you wish to begin the selection, and then drag to the line where you want to end the selection.

Dreamweaver includes a few more nuanced methods of collapsing code. You can:

- **Collapse an individual tag.** For example, say you want to hide a long paragraph of text. Instead of selecting it, just click anywhere inside the paragraph (<p>) tag and either click the Collapse Tag button on the Coding toolbar (Figure 9-6), choose Edit → Code Collapse → Collapse Full Tag, or press Ctrl+Shift+J (⌘-Shift-J).

  This feature works on the tag the cursor is nearest. For example, say you have a paragraph of text and, inside it, a link. If you click inside the <a> tag and use this feature, the <a> tag collapses. But if you click anywhere else inside the paragraph, the paragraph or <p> tag collapses. This behavior is a little confusing, but it can be really useful. Say you want to hide everything inside a page's <head> tags. Instead of having to select all the lines inside the <head> tag, just click anywhere between the two <head> tags (but make sure you're not inside *another* tag like the <title> tag) and use any of the commands mentioned in the last paragraph.

- **Collapse the code *outside* an individual tag.** This is a quick way to hide everything *except* the code you want to work on. For example, say you wanted to see only the code inside of the body tag. Click immediately after the <body> tag (to make sure you're not inside another tag that's inside the <body> tag) and either press the Alt (Option) key and click the Collapse Tag button on the Coding toolbar (Figure 9-6), choose Edit → Code Collapse → Collapse Outside Full Tag, or press Ctrl+Alt+J (⌘-Option-J).

- **Collapse the code *outside* the current selection.** This is another way to view only the code you wish to work on. Select the code and either press the Alt (Option) key and click the Collapse Selection button on the Coding toolbar (Figure 9-6), choose Edit → Code Collapse → Collapse Outside Selection, or press Ctrl+Alt+C (⌘-Option-C).

- **Expand All.** If you miss all that hidden code, you can quickly restore it to its full glory by clicking the Expand All button in the Coding toolbar (Figure 9-6), choosing Edit → Code Collapse → Expand All, or pressing Ctrl+Alt+E (⌘-Option-E).

You can hide any number of regions in a page—for example, the top portion of a page, a navigation sidebar that never gets edited, and the copyright notice at the bottom of the page—so you can easily identify the code that you're really interested in working on. Dreamweaver even remembers the state of these sections, so if you close a document and then reopen it, the collapsed sections are still collapsed, so you don't have to continually hide code in a page each time you open it for editing.

Setting Code Formatting

Whenever you use the Insert bar, Dreamweaver adds a chunk of HTML that's pre-formatted for easier reading. The code for table rows, for instance, comes indented using two spaces; the code for table *cells,* meanwhile, is indented four spaces. If you're particular about how your HTML is written, Dreamweaver gives you plenty of control over these settings.

Note: If you don't work in Code view frequently, you may not care a whit how your HTML is formatted in the file—and that's fine. As long as the underlying HTML is valid (and Dreamweaver always writes valid HTML), Web browsers can display HTML formatted in many different ways. In fact, Web browsers simply ignore multiple spaces, empty lines, and other "white space" characters used to make HTML code more readable.

Dreamweaver provides several ways to control the formatting of the code it produces. Basic settings are available in the Preferences window; advanced settings for obsessive coders even let you control the formatting of individual tags (see the box "Take Control of Code Formatting" on page 343). For basic formatting settings, open the Preferences window (Edit → Preferences or Ctrl+U [⌘-U]) and click the Code Format category (see Figure 9-10). While Dreamweaver's standard settings work fine, you can still configure a number of options.

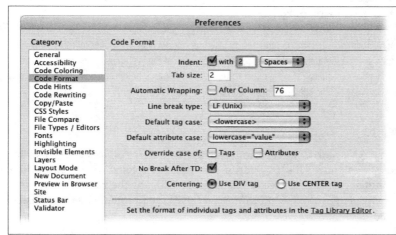

Figure 9-10:
For general control of HTML code, Dreamweaver offers the Code Format category in the Preferences window. For most people, this degree of control is overkill, but if the way HTML code appears in a page's file matters to you, go wild. (These settings don't affect how the page looks in a Web browser—only how the code appears when viewed in Dreamweaver's Code view or another text editor.)

Indents

To make your code easier to read, it helps to indent nested tags and other block-level elements. But if you'd prefer that Dreamweaver quit auto-indenting such elements, turn off the Indent checkbox. This is also your opportunity to request tabs instead of spaces for indenting lines of code; just choose Tabs from the pop-up menu.

You can also set the amount of indentation, like this:

- If Spaces is selected in the Indent menu, type the number of spaces you want into the Indent size field. The default setting is two, meaning each indent will be two spaces in the code.

- If you selected Tabs in the Indent menu, the number in the "Tab size" field indicates the size of each tab, measured in spaces. (The size you specify here affects only the display in Code view. In the code itself, Dreamweaver simply inserts a plain tab character.)

Text wrapping

When a line gets long, Dreamweaver can break it into two or more lines by inserting a hard return. This can make your HTML more readable in Code view and free you from having to scroll to see all of your code. If that's the way you like it, turn on Automatic Wrapping and type a number in the After Column field. The number specifies how many characters long a line must be before Dreamweaver attempts to break it up.

This option doesn't affect how the page will look to your visitors, only how it looks in a text editor. But unlike Code view's simulated word-wrap option shown in Figure 9-6, this option adds real line-break characters to split your code into multiple, shorter lines. If you use the Code view's word wrap, you can skip this more intrusive form of text wrapping.

Note: Although Dreamweaver can shorten lines by inserting returns after a specified number of characters, it never does so if the final effect will change the appearance of the Web page. The program is smart enough not to sacrifice the quality of a page just to make the code look better in Code view. That's why some lines of HTML may be considerably longer than the limit you specify here.

Line breaks

Windows, Mac OS, and Unix each look for a different invisible character at the end of each line of code. This expectation can cause problems when you use one kind of computer to create a page, while another OS runs the remote server that dishes out the page. Fortunately, Dreamweaver fixes the problem when it transfers a file to a Web server.

If you plan to use another text editor to edit your Dreamweaver pages, you should select your operating system from the "Line break type" pop-up menu. Doing so assures that the program on the receiving end will properly read the line breaks in Dreamweaver-produced pages.

Case for tags and attributes

You can write tag and property names using either uppercase letters (<B>bold</B>) or lowercase (bold); Web browsers don't care. However, *you* may care how they appear in your HTML display. If so, choose your preference from the two Case pop-up menus. Select either the lowercase or uppercase option from the two menus.

Note: HTML may treat capital and lowercase letters in its tags identically, but XML does not. Both it and the hybrid language *XHTML* require all-lowercase tag and property names.

That's why many Web developers now strictly use lowercase characters, even in their HTML. And that's why, if you select the XHTML option when creating a new page (see page 36), Dreamweaver will ignore an uppercase setting in the Preferences panel—even if you turn on either of the "Override case of" checkboxes.

If you also turn on the "Override case of" checkboxes, you can make Dreamweaver scan tags and properties when opening a page created by someone else (or some other program). If the case doesn't match your preferences, Dreamweaver will rewrite the code to fit the wishes of you, its master.

Take Control of Code Formatting

For ultimate control over tag formatting, Dreamweaver includes the Tag Library Editor. Not only does it let you control *exactly* how Dreamweaver formats every HTML tag it inserts into a page, it also lets you dictate the formatting for nine other Tag Libraries such as ASP, PHP, JSP, and Cold-Fusion tags.

Even if you're using some new bleeding-edge tag language unfamiliar to Dreamweaver, you're not out of luck. You can create additional Tag Libraries, and even import custom ASP.NET and JSP tags, as well as DTD Schemas for XML. You can also add additional tags to any Library; so if the HTML standard suddenly changes, you can add new or remove obsolete tags.

To control the formatting of tags in a Library, choose Edit → Tag Libraries to open the Tag Library Editor window. A list of all Tag Libraries appears. Click the + symbol to the left of a Tag Library name to see a list of tags for that Library. Select a tag, and then select formatting options from the Tag Format area in the bottom half of the window. A shortcut for quickly reformatting a particular tag already present on a page is to select the tag in the tag selector first, and then choose Edit → Tag Libraries; that tag will then be preselected for you.

You can control where a line breaks in relation to the tag, choosing: no line breaks after the tag; no breaks before and after the tag; or no breaks before, inside, *and* after the tag. In addition, you can choose whether any formatting rules are applied to the contents of a tag and choose the case—upper, lower, mixed—to be used when Dreamweaver adds the tags to the code.

No break after TD

Even though adding a line break after an opening <td> (table cell) tag may look good in Code view, in some browsers, it adds an unwanted extra space character in the table cell. Because the extra space can wreak havoc on your design, make sure this box is always turned on.

Centering

The Centering buttons let you specify which HTML tag you want Dreamweaver to use when centering block-level elements (like paragraphs) on the page. Leave "Use DIV tag" turned on. The center tag won't work in future browser versions.

Quick Tag Editor

Code view is great when you really need (or want) to dig into the trenches and fine-tune your HTML. But if a text editor is all you wanted, you wouldn't have bought Dreamweaver in the first place. Most of the time, you'll be working in Dreamweaver's Design view, enjoying the pleasures of its visual authoring environment.

Occasionally, however, you'll want to dip momentarily into the HTML pond, especially when you need to use some HTML that's not available from the Insert bar. You might wish you could type out a quick HTML tag on the spot, right there in Design view, without having to make the mental and visual shift required for a switch into Code view.

That's what the Quick Tag Editor is all about (see Figure 9-11).

To access the Quick Tag Editor, press Ctrl+T (⌘-T)—or, if you're feeling especially mouse-driven, click the Quick Tag editor button in the Property inspector (see Figure 9-12). Depending on what you've selected in the document window, the Quick Tag Editor opens in one of the following three modes (see Figure 9-12):

- **Insert new tag.** Inserts a new tag in the page. You get this mode if nothing is currently selected in your document window.

- **Edit tag.** Lets you edit the tag for whatever is selected in the document window (a graphic, for example), and all its properties.

- **Wrap tag.** If you've selected a swath of text or other objects (two images, for example), the editor opens in this mode, which makes it easy to wrap a new tag around the current selection.

Tip: You can cycle through the modes by repeatedly pressing Ctrl+T (⌘-T).

Using the Quick Tag Editor

You can type tag names, properties, and property values directly into the Quick Tag Editor window. If you're editing a selected tag, you can change any of the properties listed and even add new ones. When you're done, press Enter (Return). The Quick Tag Editor closes, and the changes take effect.

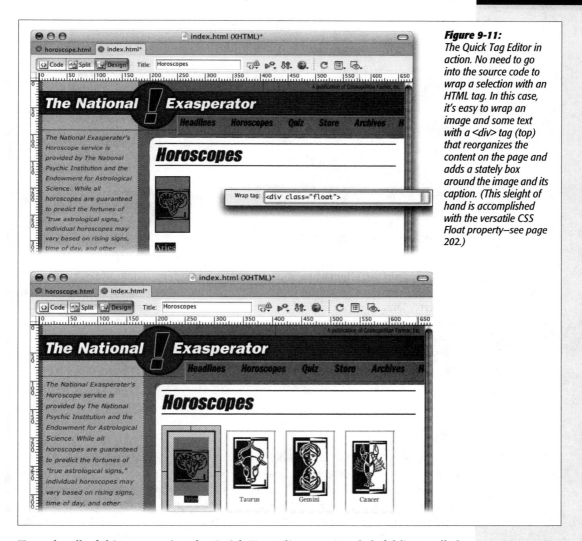

Figure 9-11:
The Quick Tag Editor in action. No need to go into the source code to wrap a selection with an HTML tag. In this case, it's easy to wrap an image and some text with a <div> tag (top) that reorganizes the content on the page and adds a stately box around the image and its caption. (This sleight of hand is accomplished with the versatile CSS Float property—see page 202.)

To make all of this even easier, the Quick Tag Editor sports a helpful list—called *Tag Hints*—of HTML tags and properties, for your selection pleasure. It's much like Code view's Code Hints feature (in fact, the Code Hints category in the Preferences window also controls Tag Hints). When you insert a tag, for example, a menu of available tags appears (top right in Figure 9-12). Use the up and down arrow keys or the scroll bar to move through the list. And when you type the first few letters of a tag or property, Dreamweaver jumps to the nearest match in the list.

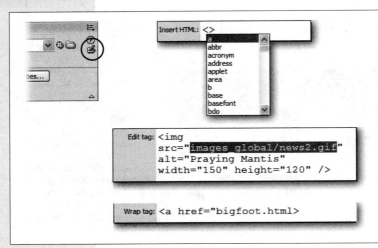

Figure 9-12:
Left: You can open the Quick Tag Editor by clicking the corresponding button in the upper-right corner of the Property inspector (circled). (This button is visible only in Design view.)

Right: The three modes of the Quick Tag Editor let you insert new tags, edit old tags, or wrap a new tag around a selection. The Quick Tag Editor is mobile: drag the window by its handle (the mode name) anywhere on the screen—ideal when you want to see the part of the page you're modifying.

To choose the highlighted name, press Enter or Return. Dreamweaver adds that tag or property name to the Quick Tag Editor window. If you've selected a tag property, Dreamweaver adds the proper punctuation (href=" ", for example). The insertion point appears between the quotation marks, waiting for you to type the property's value.

Tip: When editing an existing tag in the Quick Tag Editor, press Tab to select the next property or property value. You can then type a new property or value. Shift+Tab selects the *previous* property or value.

Tag Inspector

The Property inspector is a handy tool. With it, you can adjust properties for all sorts of HTML tags, like a table's width or a paragraph's font. But even the Property inspector doesn't tell the whole story: Some HTML tags have additional properties that don't appear there, such as the *tabindex* property of the <a> tag, which lets you control the order in which links are highlighted as the Tab key is pressed. You can set this property with the Tag inspector. As with *tabindex,* the properties listed in the Tag inspector are less frequently used, but you don't have to go into Code view to add or edit them.

For these hard-to-reach properties, turn to the *Tag inspector* (see Figure 9-13). Think of it as the über–Property inspector. For hard-core HTML fanatics, it's the best way to set properties for every HTML tag. To display it, press the F9 key, or choose Window → Tag inspector (the same procedure also hides this panel).

When you select a tag on the page (in either Code or Design view), *all* of its properties appear in the panel. You can choose one of two views for displaying these properties: one long list, or grouped into tidy categories (see Figure 9-13). You can edit any of these properties by clicking in the space to the right of the property name. You can type a new value or, for certain properties, use a pop-up menu to choose from a list of property values. For color properties, use Dreamweaver's ubiquitous color box to select just the right shade.

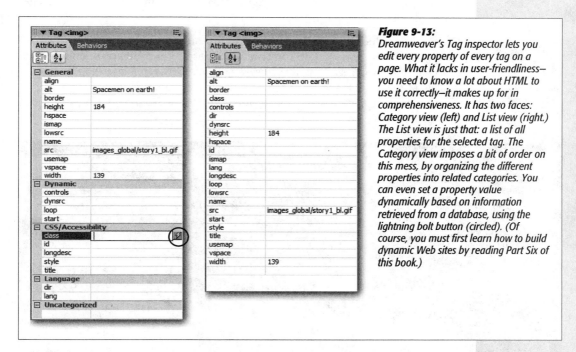

Figure 9-13:
Dreamweaver's Tag inspector lets you edit every property of every tag on a page. What it lacks in user-friendliness—you need to know a lot about HTML to use it correctly—it makes up for in comprehensiveness. It has two faces: Category view (left) and List view (right.) The List view is just that: a list of all properties for the selected tag. The Category view imposes a bit of order on this mess, by organizing the different properties into related categories. You can even set a property value dynamically based on information retrieved from a database, using the lightning bolt button (circled). (Of course, you must first learn how to build dynamic Web sites by reading Part Six of this book.)

Unfortunately, you need to understand HTML fairly well to set the correct values; Dreamweaver doesn't make the process foolproof, leaving open the possibility that you could enter an invalid property. (To learn more about HTML tags and their properties, turn to Dreamweaver's built-in HTML reference, described on page 353.)

Comparing Versions of a Web Page

Sometimes you'll make a change to a page, save it, preview it, close it, and move along to the next assignment for the day. Only later, when you're previewing your day's changes, just before moving them up to the Web server, you notice that one of the pages you changed has some problem you didn't notice at first: perhaps the left sidebar is suddenly wider than it was before. Since you've already closed the file, you can't use the Undo feature to remove whatever wacky mistake you made. You could, of course, retrieve the current version of the page from the Web server (see page 546), thus overwriting your changes. But what if you did a lot of good work on the page—adding text, graphics, and links—that you don't want to lose? Ideally, you'd like to see all of the changes you made to the page, and selectively undo the mistake you accidentally introduced to the sidebar.

Enter the Compare File command. Dreamweaver 8 introduces this new command that lets you compare two files and see what lines of code are different between the two. This tool is a perfect solution for problems like the unintentionally botched sidebar. With it, you can compare the local file (the one with the messed-up sidebar) with the remote file (the live version of the Web site that works, but is missing the fine new pictures and words you added). You can then identify any changes you made and undo your mistake.

Dreamweaver doesn't actually have this tool built into it. Instead, Dreamweaver just passes the files you wish to compare to a separate file-comparison utility (often called a "diff" tool, since it identifies *differences* between files). You'll need to download this utility, and there are a lot of different ones to choose from. Fortunately, there are several free utilities for both Windows and Mac that you can download (see the boxes below).

WINDOWS ONLY

Getting Your Hands on the Goodies

There are lots of file-comparison tools for Windows. Beyond Compare from Scooter Software (*www.scootersoftware.com/*) is a commercial product ($30) that offers a wide range of comparison options. For a free alternative, check out WinMerge (*www.winmerge.org*). This open source software provides all the basic options you'll need. But, of course, in typical open source style, directions for identifying and downloading the software aren't really clear. So here's how you get it. Go to *www.winmerge.org*. Click the "WinMerge" link in the Downloads section of the left sidebar. This link takes you to a different site—Source Forge.net, a kind of warehouse for open source software. Here's where things get a little weird: You'll see a list of around eight different downloads.

Click the one labeled *Download WinMerge-2.2.4-Setup.exe*—the number 2.2.4 in this example may be different, as they often release newer versions. At any rate, this link takes you to another page, where you select a download location from a long list of Web sites. Just click any of the file icons that appear under the "Download" category.

The file should then start downloading onto your computer. Once completed, the process for installing the program is like most other Windows programs. Just double-click the file to launch an installer, and follow the step-by-step installation instructions. Once it's installed, you're ready to proceed as described on page 350.

MACS ONLY

What Difference Does It Make?

The Mac version of Dreamweaver supports only three file-comparison tools: File Merge (which is a Mac developer program that comes with the XCode tools on your Mac OS X installation disc), BBEdit (the powerful, $199 commercial text editor), and Text Wrangler (the free little brother of BBEdit). Bare Bones Software (*www.barebones.com*) produces both BBEdit and Text Wrangler, but since Text Wrangler's free, it's the best place to begin.

Point your Web browser to *www.barebones.com/products/textwrangler/download.shtml* and click any of the download links to download the program to your computer. As with many Mac programs, this download opens a disk image—just like a folder—with the application inside it. Just drag it to your Applications folder to install it. Once installed, you're ready to proceed as described on page 352.

After downloading and installing the file-comparison utility (see the boxes on the opposite page), you need to tell Dreamweaver where to find your new helper:

1. **Open the Preferences panel, by choosing Edit → Preferences (Dreamweaver → Preferences on the Mac), or pressing Ctrl+U (⌘-U), and click the File Compare category.**

    There's not much to this Preferences category, just a single box and a Browse button.

2. **Click the Browse button and navigate to and select the file-comparison utility.**

    For example, on Windows you might find your utility here: *C:\Program Files\ WinMerge\WinMerge.exe.*

    On the Mac, it's slightly different. Instead of selecting the text-editing program Text Wrangler or BBEdit, you need to specify the proper "diff" tool, which is stored in a special location on your computer. Navigate to the */usr/bin* folder— something like this: *Macintosh HD:usr:bin*—and select the correct file. For Text Wrangler, it's *twdiff;* for BBEdit, it's *bbdiff;* and for FileMerge, it's *opendiff.*

3. **Click OK to close the Preferences window.**

    Dreamweaver's been notified of the location of the utility, so you're ready to begin comparing files.

The Compare File command works with a local file and a remote file, so you'll need to have already defined a site with both local and remote root folders (see Chapter 15 for details on how to do this). In addition, since you're comparing two files, you'll need to make sure you've got two versions of the same file on your local computer and your remote site—for example, your home page, or one of the other pages in your site. To compare the files, follow these steps:

1. **In the Files panel, locate the file you wish to compare.**

    This can be either a file listed in the "Local View" or "Remote View" of the Files panel (see page 479).

2. **Right-click (Control-click) the file, and from the pop-up menu that appears, select "Compare with Remote."**

    This menu will say "Compare with Local" if you're in the Remote view of the files panel.

    Dreamweaver does a little behind-the-scenes trickery before passing the files off to the file comparison program. It first creates a folder (if it's not already created) named *_compareTemp* in the local root folder of your site. Dreamweaver then creates a temporary file with all of the code from the remote-site file, and stores that in the new folder. In other words, you don't actually compare the file on the live Web server with the local file on your computer; you compare a copy of the remote file with the local file. This distinction is important to keep in mind if you want to incorporate changes between the files, as described in step 3.

At any rate, your selected file-comparison program—for example, WinMerge or Text Wrangler—will start and compare the two files. If there are no differences—they're *exactly* the same files—then you'll most likely get a message saying something to the effect of "The Selected Files are Identical." So if no differences are found between the files, your work is done. If there is a difference, the file-comparison program will display the two files and identify the code that differs between the two files (see Figures 9-14 and 9-15).

3. **Evaluate the differences and incorporate any changes into your local file.**

   File-comparison programs work generally the same way. When comparing two files, you'll see the code for the two files side by side. In addition, the program will have some way of notifying you of any differences. You can then review the differences in the code, and merge the changes into one file or the other. For example, say you accidentally deleted a table from your local file; a comparison of this file with the remote file will show the table intact in the remote file and indicate that it's missing in the local file. You can then copy the table code from the remote file into the local file. If, however, you deleted the table purposefully, then do nothing and move on to evaluate the next difference.

   Here's where Dreamweaver's little bait-and-switch mentioned in step 2 becomes important. You're not actually comparing the remote file with the local file; you're comparing a *copy* of the remote file saved locally in the *_compareTemp* folder. As a result, you'll want to move changes only in one direction—from the temporary file to your local file. Changes in the temporary file will have no effect on the actual live file on your Web server. So how do you update the remote file? Move any changes you want made *from* the temporary file *to* your local file. Once you're satisfied with the changes, you can save them, return to Dreamweaver, and then upload them to your remote site folder. Then pour yourself a cup of tea and be thankful you don't have to do *that* very often.

4. **Save any changes, return to Dreamweaver, and then move your newly updated local file to your Web server.**

   The exact process varies from program to program, but see the next two sections for examples using WinMerge and Text Wrangler.

Using WinMerge to Compare Files

If you've got a Windows PC and you're interested in taking Dreamweaver 8's new Compare Files command for a test drive, see the box on page 348 for instructions on how to download WinMerge, and then follow these steps:

1. **Once you've downloaded and installed WinMerge, follow the steps on page 349 to set up Dreamweaver's preferences for working with WinMerge.**

   First you need to make sure Dreamweaver knows to use WinMerge for file comparison.

2. **Follow steps 1 and 2 at the bottom of page 349 to select a file and tell Dreamweaver to compare it with its sibling on the remote Web server.**

WinMerge launches, and if there are any differences between the files, the program shows the code for the two files side by side with all differences highlighted (see Figure 9-14).

In WinMerge, differences are highlighted by one or more yellow bars in the left-side "Location" pane (circled in Figure 9-14), and the code is either highlighted in yellow (meaning there's content present in one file that's missing in the other file) or gray (meaning there's content missing in one file that's present in the other file).

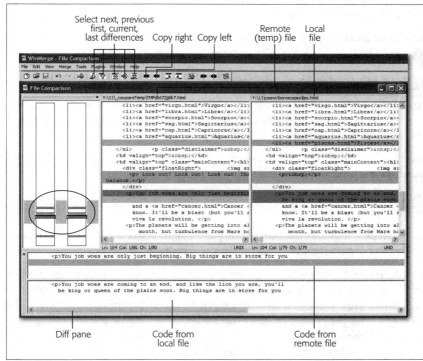

Figure 9-14:
WinMerge includes a kind of bird's-eye view of code differences in the far-left Location pane. Click near any yellow bands (circled) to jump to code that differs between the two files. You can also tell which file is the temp (remote) file, by looking at the file path just above the page's code and locating the file with _compareTemp in the name. In this example, the left page's path is Y:\11_compareTemp\TMPdbt72jj6k7.htm; it's the code from the remote file.

3. **Click anywhere in the page and click any of the "diff" navigation buttons—next diff, previous diff, first diff, or last diff (see Figure 9-14).**

"Diff" stands for difference, so clicking these buttons takes you to the locations in the files where the code differs. Doing so also selects the differing code and highlights it in red. You can now see which code you wish to keep.

4. **If the code in the remote file looks correct, click the Copy Right or Copy Left button.**

Which button you click depends on whether the remote file is in the left or right side of the window (see Figure 9-14 for instructions on figuring this out).

If the remote code is on the left, click the Copy Right button. This button moves the code over to the page on the right—your local file.

You don't need to do anything if the code in the local file looks okay.

Tip: The "diff" pane gives a clear picture of how the code differs between the files. To view it, choose View → Diff Pane.

---

5. **Continue with steps 3 and 4 until you've evaluated all of the differing code in the two pages.**

   At this point, the "perfect" copy is your local file. It has all of the correct code from the remote file and all of the correct code from the local file. You just need to move it to your Web server.

6. **Move your local file to your Web server, using one of the techniques described on page 542.**

Using Text Wrangler to Compare Files

Mac owners can download the free Text Wrangler if they want to compare files (see the box on page 348). Fortunately, since BBEdit is a more powerful version of Text Wrangler, these steps will work for that program as well:

1. **Once you've installed Text Wrangler, follow the steps on page 349 to set up Dreamweaver's preferences.**

   First you need to make sure Dreamweaver knows to use Text Wrangler for file comparison.

2. **Follow steps 1 and 2 at the bottom of page 349 to select a file and tell Dreamweaver to compare it with its sibling on the remote Web server.**

   Text Wrangler launches, and if there are any differences between the files, it shows the code for the two files side by side (see Figure 9-15). Where lines of code differ, Text Wrangler identifies them in the Differences panel below the two pages. The program also gives some indication of how the lines differ: for example, "Nonmatching lines" means the lines are similar (some of the code is the same) but not identical, while "Extra lines before line xx" means that completely different lines of code are in one file but not the other.

   If the files are identical, Dreamweaver pops up a "No difference found between these files" message.

3. **In the Differences panel, double-click the difference you wish to inspect.**

   It's a good strategy to just start at the top of the list and work your way down.

4. **If the code in the remote file looks correct, click one of the Apply buttons in the Differences panel.**

   Which button you click depends on whether the remote file is in the left or right side of the window (see Figure 9-15 for instructions on figuring this out).

If the remote code is on the left, click the "Apply to Old" button. Doing so moves the code over to the page on the right, your local file.

You don't need to do anything if the code in the local file looks OK.

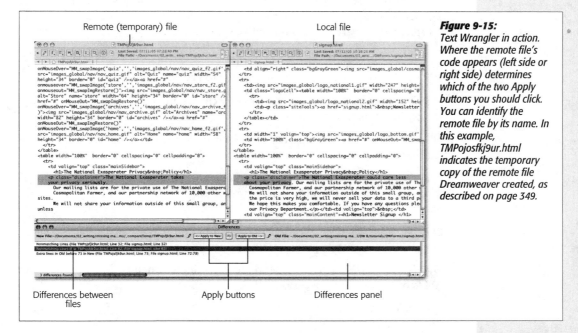

Remote (temporary) file   Local file

Differences between files   Apply buttons   Differences panel

5. **Continue with steps 3 and 4 until you've evaluated all of the differing code in the two pages.**

   At this point, the "perfect" copy is your local file. It has all of the correct code from the remote file and all of the correct code from the local file. You just need to move it to your Web server.

6. **Move your local file to your Web server, using one of the techniques described on page 542.**

Comparing a local file to a remote file with Dreamweaver is quick and easy. You can also access the file-compare feature to compare two local files, or two remote files, but the steps are so convoluted that it's a lot easier just to bypass Dreamweaver and go directly to WinMerge, Text Wrangler, or the file-comparison utility of your choice. In the case of two remote files, download them first and then conduct the comparison.

Reference Panel

When it comes to building Web sites, there's a lot to know. After all, Cascading Style Sheets, HTML, and JavaScript are filled with cryptic terms and subtle nuances. Fortunately, Dreamweaver's Reference panel makes your search for knowledge a little bit easier. It gives you quick access to reference excerpts on 13 Web topics from a variety of authoritative sources, including:

- *O'Reilly CSS Reference.* In-depth information on Cascading Style Sheets.

- *O'Reilly HTML Reference.* Complete guide to HTML tags and properties.

- *O'Reilly JavaScript Reference.* A not-so-well-organized reference to JavaScript topics, concepts, and commands.

- *O'Reilly PHP Pocket Reference.* A less-than-user-friendly reference to PHP. For seasoned programmers.

- *O'Reilly SQL Language Reference.* If you plan to go deeper into database-driven Web development, this great reference can help you figure out how to write the perfect database query.

- *O'Reilly ASP Reference.* Look up commands for Active Server Pages, one of Microsoft's server-side programming technologies.

- *O'Reilly ASP.NET Reference.* More server-side commands, but this time for ASP's more powerful successor, .NET.

- *UsableNet Accessibility Reference.* Guidelines for making Web pages more accessible to the disabled.

- *Macromedia CFML Reference.* Complete reference to tags used in the Cold-Fusion Markup Language (used with Macromedia's ColdFusion application server).

- *Macromedia CF Function Reference.* A reference of different functions (commands) built into ColdFusion functions. Includes helpful examples of how to use each function.

- *O'Reilly JSP Reference.* Java got you down? Quickly look up Java Server Page commands here.

- *O'Reilly XML Reference.* Dreamweaver 8 introduces some interesting XML features (see Chapter 24), but this general dictionary of XML terms and properties isn't the place to start your education.

- *O'Reilly XSLT Reference.* To turn XML into readable XHTML, you'll turn to XSLT (and Chapter 24, where you'll learn how to use it). This reference describes the various XSLT functions.

To open the Reference panel, choose Window → Reference, or press Shift+F1. Thankfully, the Dreamweaver 8 designers moved the Reference panel to a place where there's a little more reading room: you'll now find the Reference panel docked at the bottom of the screen with the Results panel group (see Figure 9-16). The first menu at the top of the panel lets you choose the "book" you want. Once you've selected a reference, choose a particular HTML tag, CSS style, JavaScript object, or appropriate reference topic from the menu to the right of the Book menu. A description of that item appears in the main window. Depending on the reference, there may be sample usage and browser-support details. A secondary menu to the right lets you access additional information about a particular property or details of the selected tag, style, object, or topic. For example, in Figure 9-16, to display information about the <a> tag's *tabindex* property, you'd choose "a" from the Tag menu and "tabindex" from the Attribute menu.

Tip: You can quickly see reference information for a tag by either clicking a tag or selecting a tag and pressing Shift+F1. The Reference panel opens, and information for that particular tag appears.

While you won't spend every waking minute in the Reference panel, it's a good way to keep your HTML, CSS, and JavaScript chops sharp.

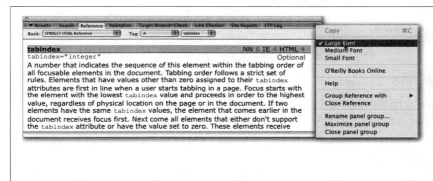

Figure 9-16:
If the print in the Reference panel is too small or too large, use the panel's shortcut menu (click the arrow in the upper-right corner of the panel), as shown here, and select a different size. When perusing the reference panel, Dreamweaver lets you copy examples of tags and code, so you can paste them into a page, but it won't let you copy the reference information that explains the tag or code. Oh well. You'll just have to hand-type your "Plagiarist's Guide to the Web."

Inserting JavaScript

As Chapter 11 makes clear, Dreamweaver's *behaviors* (prewritten JavaScript programs) let you add exciting interactive effects—mouse rollovers, pop-up windows, animated layers, and so on—with very little effort. But they can't do everything: When you, the native JavaScript speaker, need to wade into the depths of JavaScript programming yourself, you'll find two entrances within Dreamweaver.

The most straightforward approach, especially if you're already familiar with Java-Script programming, is to simply switch into Code view (Ctrl+` [Option-`]) and type away. Or, if you prefer, you can use Dreamweaver's Insert Script window to add your JavaScript code (see Figure 9-17).

To add your JavaScript code, click in either the head or body section of the page, and then choose Insert → HTML → Script Objects → Script (alternatively, you can access this option from the Script menu on the HTML tab of the Insert bar). In the Insert Script window (Figure 9-17), choose a language from the menu: JavaScript, JavaScript1.1, JavaScript1.2, or VBScript. (The JavaScript option works with all browsers that understand JavaScript, while JavaScript 1.2 works only in 4+ version browsers. VBScript, on the other hand, works only in the Windows version of Internet Explorer.)

Tip: You can use the Insert Script command in Design view also, but to add a script to the <head> of the page, first chose View → Head Content, which opens a small bar below the Document toolbar that lists all of the different tags like <title>, <script>, and <meta> that appear in the head of a page. Click here, and then follow the above recipe for inserting a script.

Just type your script into the Content section (no need to include <script> tags, as Dreamweaver handles that part) and then click OK. If you inserted the script in the body of the document, you'll see a small gold icon (indicating an invisible element on the page) to mark its location.

You can edit your script in Code view, of course. In Design view, select the script icon and then click Edit in the Property inspector.

Dreamweaver 8 adds a useful new feature to the Insert Script window. If you use external JavaScript files, you can link to them directly in this box (see Figure 9-17). Instead of typing any code, click the familiar Browse for File icon (to the right of the Source box), locate the external JavaScript file, and then click OK. Dreamweaver adds the appropriate code to link the script file to the Web page. (You'll find an example of this technique on page 441.)

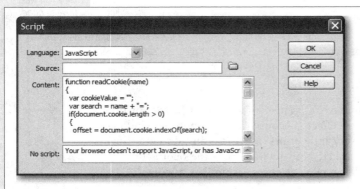

Figure 9-17:
Unlike the Code view, the Insert Script window doesn't respond to the Tab key; if you're accustomed to indenting your code, you'll need to use spaces. You can also insert "No script information"—text that appears if the Web browser doesn't understand JavaScript.

Dreamweaver also lets you open and work on external JavaScript files (.js files) right in Code view. The program doesn't try to interpret the file as an HTML page; it won't attempt to make any of the changes described on page 328. But you can just use the built-in text-editing capabilities of Code view to write your JavaScript programs.

Note: JavaScript programming is no walk in the park. While it's certainly easier to learn than full-featured languages like Java or C++, it can still be challenging. If you want to get your feet wet, here's a great resource for basic tutorials and information on JavaScript: *www.w3schools.com/js/*.

Part Three: Bringing Your Pages to Life

3

Forms

A Web site is a great way for you to broadcast a message, announce a new product, post late-breaking news, or just rant about the state of the world. But that's all *one-way* communication, which you may find a bit limiting. You may be curious to get some feedback from your audience. Or you may want to build your business by selling your product online, and you need a way to gather vital stats from your customers. If you want to receive information as well as deliver it, it's time to add *forms* to your Web design repertoire (see Figure 10-1 for a simple example). Whatever type of information you need to collect on your site, Dreamweaver's *form objects* make the task easy.

Figure 10-1:
A form can be as simple as a single empty text box (a field) and a button, or as complex as a 100-question survey composed of fill-in-the-blank and multiple-choice questions.

Form Basics

A form begins and ends with the HTML <form> tag. The opening <form> tag indicates the beginning of the form and sets its properties; the closing </form> tag, of course, marks the form's end.

In between these tags, different objects provide the basic user-interface elements—the design—of the form. Radio buttons, text fields, and pull-down menus are just a few of the ways you can gather input. It's perfectly okay to include other HTML elements inside a form, too. In fact, your site's visitors would be lost if you couldn't also add (and format) text that explains the purpose of each form object. And if you don't use a table or Cascading Style Sheets to lay out a form in an organized way, it can quickly become an unreadable mess (see the box on page 376).

Every form element, whether it's a text field or a checkbox, has a *name* and a *value*. The name indicates what information the element is intended to collect. For example, if you want your visitors to type their email address into a text field, the name of that field might be *email*. The value, on the other hand, is the person's input—what your visitors type into the text field, for example, or the selections they make from a pull-down menu.

After your visitors fill out the form and click the Submit button to transmit their responses, each form element is transmitted as a name/value pair like this: *email=bob@bobville.com.* Submitting both pieces of information helps the program that processes the form figure out what the input means. After all, without a name, a value of 39 doesn't mean much (39 what? Potatoes, steps, days until Christmas?). The name/value pair (age=39) provides context for a visitor's input.

The Code Backstage

Creating a form is just the first step in collecting information from your Web site's visitors. You also need to connect the form to a computer program that actually *does* something with the information. The program may simply take the data from the form and email it to you. However, it could do something as complex as contacting a bank, processing a credit card payment, creating an invoice item, or notifying a shipping department to deliver the latest Stephen King novel to someone in Nova Scotia. A form is pretty useless without a program like this running on the Web server. These information-crunching programs come in a variety of languages—Perl, C, C#, Visual Basic, VBScript, JavaScript, Java, ColdFusion Markup Language, PHP—and may be part of a dedicated application server like Macromedia's ColdFusion Server or Microsoft's Active Server Pages technology.

Writing the necessary behind-the-scenes processing software can be complex, but the concepts behind forms are straightforward:

- First, someone fills out a form on your Web page and clicks the Submit button.

- Next, the form data is transmitted over the Internet to a program on your Web server.

- The program collects the data and does something with it—whatever you and the programmer decide it should do.

- Finally, the Web server returns a page to the Web visitor. It may be a standard Web page with a message like "Thanks for the info," or a page dynamically generated by the program itself—a detailed invoice page, for example.

So how do you create the processing half of the forms equation if you're not a programmer? You can use Dreamweaver, of course. Part Six of this book describes Dreamweaver's dynamic Web building tools for creating pages that use information collected from forms in a database. If your Web server accommodates Active Server Pages, ASP.NET, ColdFusion, Java Server Pages, or PHP, Dreamweaver can create form-processing programs for you.

If you're part of a Web development team in a company, you may already have in-house programmers who can help you create the processing program.

Furthermore, even if your Web hosting company doesn't tolerate any of the application servers that work with Dreamweaver, they probably offer free form-processing programs as part of their services. Contact your Web host and ask about this. If so, the company will provide instructions on how to use these programs.

Finally, if you feel adventurous, many form-processing programs are available for free on the Web. For a thorough sampling, see the CGI Resource Index at *http://cgi.resourceindex.com*. Using these free programs can be tricky, however, because you need to download the appropriate program and install it on your Web server. Your Web hosting company may not even permit you to do so.

Creating a Form

In Dreamweaver, you can build forms with one-click ease using the Forms tab of the Insert bar (see Figure 10-2).

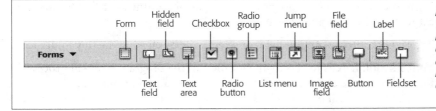

Figure 10-2:
The Forms tab on the Insert bar gives you one-click access to all of the different form elements—buttons, text fields, checkboxes, and more.

To begin, you need to insert a <form> tag to indicate the boundaries of a form:

1. **In the document window, click where you wish to insert the form.**

   You might decide to place it after a regular paragraph of introductory text, for example.

2. **Select the Forms tab on the Insert bar.**

   The tab reveals 14 form-building tool icons.

3. **Click the Form icon on the Insert bar (the far-left square).**

   Alternatively, if you're a menu-driven person, choose Insert → Form → Form instead.

   Either way, a red, dashed-line rectangle appears in the document window, indicating the boundaries of the form. (If you don't see it, choose View → Visual Aids → Invisible Elements.) The top line represents the opening <form> tag; the bottom represents the closing tag. Make sure you always insert form objects, like buttons and menus, *inside* these lines. Otherwise, Dreamweaver will think you're trying to create a second form on the page. (It's perfectly valid to include more than one form per page, but your visitor can submit only one form—and its data—at a time.)

   Since you can place so many other HTML elements inside of a form, it's often easier to insert the form first, adding tables, graphics, text, and form objects later.

4. **If it isn't already selected, click anywhere on the dotted red line to select the form.**

   Unlike other objects, like images, the red line of the form doesn't change its appearance when selected. The only way you know you've selected the form is by checking the Property inspector. If it displays the "Form name" label at the upper-left corner, as shown in Figure 10-3, you've done it correctly.

Figure 10-3:
You'll generally want the POST method of sending data to the server.

5. **If you like, type a name for your form into the "Form name" field.**

   This step is optional. A form doesn't need a name to work, but a name is useful if you use JavaScript or a Dreamweaver behavior (see the next chapter) to interact with the form or any of its fields.

6. **Type a URL into the Action field, or select a file by clicking the tiny folder icon.**

   Your mission here is to specify the location of the program that will process the form. If someone else is responsible for the programming, ask that person what to enter here. It will be a standard Web path—either an absolute URL (one that begins with *http://*) or just the path to the server's form-processing program. (See page 104 for more on these different kinds of links.) If you're using Dreamweaver's dynamic page-building tools, you'll most often leave this field blank. When you apply a server behavior—the programming code that makes the page "dynamic"—Dreamweaver inserts the correct URL.

   Either way, the file name *doesn't* end in .html. The path might be, for example, *../cgi-bin/forms.pl.* In this case, .pl is the extension used to indicate a program written in the Perl programming language. Other common file extensions for

Web programs include .asp (for Active Server Pages), .cfm (for ColdFusion Markup Language pages), .jsp (for Java Server Pages), .php (for PHP pages), or .cgi (for CGI programs).

7. **Using the Method pop-up menu, specify how you want the form data transmitted to the processing program (see Figure 10-3).**

Basically, forms can transmit data to a Web server in either of two ways. The more common method, called POST, is the one you'll use most often. (It's what browsers use unless you tell them otherwise.) It sends the form data in two steps: first, the browser contacts the form program at the URL you specified in the previous step; then, it sends the data to the server. This method gives a bit more security to your data, and it can easily handle forms with lots of information.

The GET method, on the other hand, transmits the form data in the URL, like this: *http://search.yahoo.com/bin/search?p=dogs*. The characters following the ? in the address represent the form data. This code submits a single form field—named *p*, with the value *dogs*—to the server. As you can see, such a URL could get extremely long. Because some servers can't handle very long URLs, the GET method is inappropriate for forms that collect a lot of data.

8. **If you're using frames, select a Target option.**

The Target option lets you specify a particular frame for displaying the results of the form submission. You can also choose the "_blank" option to open a new browser window to display the results. (See page 112 for more on the Target property.)

9. **Select an encoding type, if you like.**

You usually don't have to select anything from the Enctype menu. The default value—*empty*—is almost always correct and is the same as selecting the much more long-winded "application/x-www-form-urlencoded" option.

But if you're using the File Field button (see page 108) to let visitors upload files to your site, you should use the "multipart/form-data" option. In fact, Dreamweaver automatically selects this option when you add a File Field to a form.

Note: In some cases, you may find that the server generates errors or doesn't process your forms correctly.

One cause may be the form's encoding method. If you add a File Field button to a form (page 377), Dreamweaver sets the form's encoding method to "multipart/form-data." For this method to work, the Web server must be set up to receive files, and many Web servers have this option turned off for security reasons. So when your visitors attempt to submit a form—even one without a file attachment—and you've used this encoding method, the Web server spits back a nasty error.

Now then: If you delete this File Field button from your form, Dreamweaver doesn't reset the encoding method to the original setting of "application/x-www-form-urlencoded." If your Web server is programmed to not allow form submissions using the "multipart/form-data" setting, you'll receive a nasty "Method not allowed" error. You must remedy the situation manually by selecting the form and using the Property inspector to change the encoding method back to "application/x-www-form-urlencoded."

You've laid the foundation for your form. Now you're ready to add the input controls to it—menus, checkboxes, and so on—as described in the next section.

Adding Form Elements

Unless you've never used a computer before, the different user-interface elements available for HTML forms should look familiar (Figure 10-4): text fields where people can type in information (their names, addresses, phone numbers, and so on); checkboxes for making multiple-choice selections; and menus for picking items from a list. The Forms tab of the Insert bar lets you create all of these elements and more (see Figure 10-2).

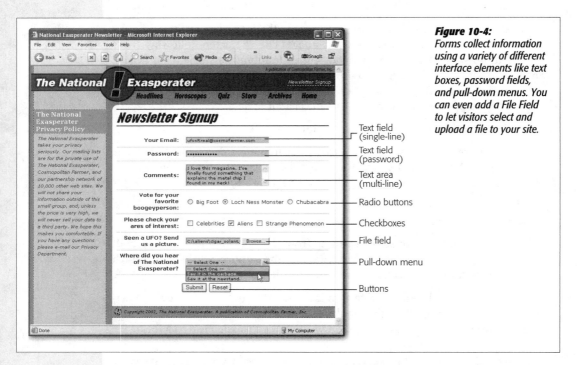

Figure 10-4:
Forms collect information using a variety of different interface elements like text boxes, password fields, and pull-down menus. You can even add a File Field to let visitors select and upload a file to your site.

What All Form Elements Have in Common

Adding form elements to your document always follows the same pattern:

1. **In the document window, insert a form (see page 363).**

   Or, if the page already has a form, click inside its red border.

Tip: If a text field is the first element of the form, you can skip this step. As soon as you add a form element, like a field, checkbox, or pop-up menu, to a page that doesn't yet have a form, Dreamweaver asks if you'd like to add the proper form tag. Click the Yes button, and Dreamweaver automatically creates the red, dotted-line form boundaries (and, behind the scenes, the corresponding <form> tags). You should *always* click the Yes button. A form field that isn't surrounded by the proper form tag won't work.

---

2. **Click the appropriate button on the Insert bar (see Figure 10-2).**

   Alternatively, use the Insert → Form submenu. You'll soon discover that every form object on the Insert bar is also represented by a command on the Insert menu (for example, Insert → Form Objects → Text Field).

Tip: Instead of just clicking a form-element button on the Insert bar, you may prefer to drag it off the tab and into a specific position on your Web page. This trick works with any of the user controls on the Insert bar, not just text fields.

---

3. **Type a label and select label options from the Input Tag Accessibility Attributes window (see Figure 10-5).**

   These accessibility options are intended to add information and tools for the benefit of those surfing your site using "assistive technologies"—for example, screen readers for those with poor vision—or those who don't use mice to jump from form field to form field.

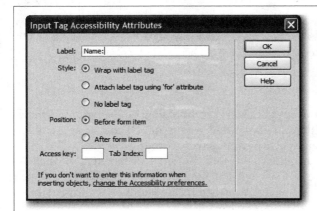

Figure 10-5:
This window appears when you're inserting a form element. If you don't see it, you or someone else has turned off Dreamweaver's factory setting to automatically launch this window. To summon it, choose Edit → Preferences (Dreamweaver → Preferences), click the Accessibility category, and then turn on the Form Objects checkbox. You can also turn off this option by clicking the "change the Accessibility preferences" link at the bottom of this window.

The label option lets you add text that identifies the form element's purpose (see page 381 for a description of the Label tag). For example, if you add a text field to collect someone's name, the label might be *Name:*. It's always a good idea to add a label. In addition, Dreamweaver wraps the text you type inside an HTML tag created just to indicate a form's purpose: the <label> tag.

Tip: Sometimes you won't need or want a label. For example, buttons already have a label—Submit or Reset, for example—so you don't need to add another. In this case, either click the Cancel button, which just adds the form field without any of these *accessibility* properties, or leave the label box empty and select the "No label tag" radio button.

There are a two ways to attach a label to a form element. The first method, indicated by the radio button labeled "Wrap with label tag" (as shown in Figure 10-5) wraps the <label> tag around both the text you type and the form element itself. This method keeps the two together and easily identifies which label goes with each form field. This is the easiest approach.

The second method, "Attach label tag using the 'for' attribute," also wraps the text you type inside a <label> tag. However, it places the form field *outside* of the label tag. This method is useful if the label and form field don't appear directly next to each other in the HTML code. For example, it's common to use a table to visually organize forms (see the box on page 376). By placing text labels in one table column and form fields in an adjacent column, you can neatly align the labels and their corresponding fields. However, organizing your page like this puts the labels and form fields into separate table cells and "breaks" the connection between the label and the field. Those visitors who use a screen reader, for example, to read your form may not understand which label applies to which form field. Fortunately, Dreamweaver can add a *for* property to the label tag, which tells a Web browser which form element the label is "for."

Unfortunately, Dreamweaver kind of drops the ball with this feature, and you have to go into Code view to make it work correctly. Here's what the HTML looks like after you insert a text field and a label using the *for* property:

```
<label for="textfield">Name:</label>
<input type="text" name="textfield" id="textfield" />
```

The actual *name, id,* and *for* values will vary depending on the type of form field you add—textfield, textarea, radio button, and so on. Of course, as mentioned in step 5, you should always change the generic names—*textfield,* in this example—that Dreamweaver initially adds to form fields. Unfortunately, when you use the Property inspector to change the name of the form field—for example, from *textfield* to *name*—Dreamweaver doesn't update the *for* property of the <label> tag, so you end up with code like this:

```
<label for="textfield">Name:</label>
<input type="text" name="name" id="name" />
```

Now the *for* property is pointing to a field that doesn't exist on the page. To fix this, you need to go into Code view (see page 330) and manually change the *for* property to the new name you supplied for the form field. Another solution is to click anywhere inside the label tag, choose Window → Tag Inspector, click the Attributes tab, and then change the *for* property that appears in the panel.

If you just want to skip this whole <label> tag thing, select the "No label tag" radio button, and Dreamweaver will just insert the label text you've typed without the <label> tag.

Finally, you can tell Dreamweaver if you wish the text to appear before or after the form field by selecting one of the *position* radio buttons.

4. **Type an "Access key" and a Tab Index number, and then press OK.**

These are optional steps that let visitors access the form field using the keyboard. The "Access key" option lets visitors use a keyboard shortcut to jump immediately into or select a field. For example, if you type *M* for a form element's access key, visitors will be able to jump to that element using Alt+M (Windows) or Control-M (Mac). While this feature seems to be a great way to make your forms more usable, there are a couple of drawbacks. First, not all browsers support this feature. In addition, since it's not at all obvious to your site's visitors what keyboard shortcuts you've added to your form, you'll need to list the shortcut next to the form element or create a "user's manual" of sorts that explains the shortcuts used in your forms.

The Tab Index is more commonly supported by browsers than the "Access key" property. It lets you number each form field and, in the process, set the order in which the fields will be selected as a visitor presses the Tab key. Number 1 indicates the first field to be selected when a visitor presses the Tab key, and each number after that—2, 3, 4, and so on—dictates the order of selection when the Tab key is pressed. You won't usually need to go to this extreme, since most browsers will jump to the next form field when you press the Tab key, but it sometimes comes in handy when you have a particularly complex form and use either tables or CSS to lay it out. For example, in some cases, the order the fields are selected by default doesn't match the visual presentation of the form (in other words, when you press the Tab key, you actually jump to a different field than the one you expect). If this is the case, setting the Tab Index lets you correctly specify the tab order.

5. **Select the freshly minted form element and type a name into the Property inspector's name box (see Figure 10-6).**

Dreamweaver automatically names the field—for example, it might propose *textfield, textfield1,* and so on. It's a good idea, however, to give the field a new, unique name, because this name will be submitted with the visitor's input as the *name* part of a name/value pair. (The name box is directly below the form element's name on the Property inspector.)

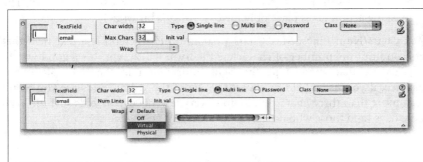

Figure 10-6:
The Property inspector looks slightly different depending on the type of text field you choose. The Class menu (available to all form elements) lets you apply a Cascading Style Sheet class style (see page 164) to the selected form field.

6. **Set the form element's properties.**

For example, you may be able to specify its width, height, and other variables. The following descriptions indicate the options available for each form element.

Text Fields

When you need to collect a specific piece of information like a person's name, phone number, or address, you'll use a text field (shown in Figure 10-4). Text fields accept typed responses and are great for open-ended questions. They come in three different flavors: *single-line* fields for short responses, *password* fields to hide user input from snooping eyes, and *multi-line* fields for longer typed replies.

Once you've inserted the text field, you can adjust the following settings in the Property inspector (see Figure 10-6):

- **Char Width.** The width of a text field is measured in characters; so if you type *20* for the Char Width (character width), the text field will be as wide as necessary to hold 20 typed letters. Be aware that the exact size can vary from browser to browser. (You can use Cascading Style Sheets to set an exact width. You'll find an example of this in the tutorial on page 388.)

- **Type.** There are three different types of text fields to choose from.

  — A **single-line** text field, of course, holds just one line of text. This is the most common kind of text field; use it for collecting small pieces of information, like a last name, Social Security number, or credit card number.

  — **Multiline** fields provide a larger area for adding multiple lines of text. You'll need to use this kind of text field when offering a place to type longer comments, such as in a "Let us know what you think!" or "Nature of problem:" field.

Tip: Dreamweaver includes a separate button for adding a multiline text field–called *Textarea* in HTML (see Figure 10-2).

  — **Password** fields hide a password being typed from the prying eyes of passing spies. Whatever your Web visitor types appears as asterisks *** (Windows) or bullets •••• (Mac) on the screen. (Of course, the information in the password field is still transmitted as plain text, just like any other form field. The masking action takes place only in your visitor's browser.)

- **Max Chars/Num Lines.** Max Chars (maximum characters) is a text field that lets you limit the number of characters the form will accept. It's a good way to help ensure that guests type the right information in the right place. For instance, if you use a field to collect the age of the visitor, odds are you won't need more than three characters to do it; very few 1,000-year-olds surf the Web these days (and those who do don't like to reveal their ages).

When you've specified a multiline text field, the Max Chars box morphs into the Num Lines box. In this case, you can't limit the amount of text someone types into the field. Instead, this field lets you specify the height of the text field on the screen.

Note: The limit you specify here affects only how tall the field will be *onscreen.* Your visitors can type as many lines of information as they want. (A scroll bar will appear if the typing exceeds the size of the box you've specified with the Num Lines option.)

- **Wrap.** The Wrap property is meant to specify what happens when your visitor types right to the edge of the text box. Although most browsers recognize this property, it isn't officially part of the HTML or XHTML standard. In general, the "Default" option is your best bet. It leaves this nonstandard property out of your HTML and lets the text box behave as most people would expect: when the typing reaches the edge of the box, it automatically wraps to the next line. The Off setting completely prevents sentences from wrapping inside the text field. When the typed text exceeds the width of the field, a horizontal scroll bar appears at the bottom of the field, and the text scrolls to the left. The text remains on a single line until the visitor hits Enter or Return. You'll almost never want to use this option, because it forces your visitor to scroll not only up and down, but left and right, too, to see everything she's typed. And the last two options—Virtual and Physical—have no effect in most browsers.

- **Init Val.** Here, you can specify the Initial Value of the field—starter text that automatically appears in the field, so that it won't be empty when the visitor begins completing the form. You can use this feature to include explanatory text inside the field itself, such as "Type your name in this box" or "Example: (212) 555-1212."

FREQUENTLY ASKED QUESTION

Using the Password Field for Credit Card Numbers

Can I use the Password field type for credit card numbers and other sensitive information?

Yes, but it won't give the information any extra security.

The Password field does one thing: it hides user input on the screen. Someone looking over your visitor's shoulder won't be able to read what's being typed—it'll look like a bunch of dots—but once that information is submitted over the Internet, it's just as visible as a regular text field.

To provide real security for form information, you need an encrypted connection between the Web server and the visitor's computer. Most Web site creators use SSL (Secure Socket Layer) technology for this purpose.

Most Web browsers understand this technology, but your Web server must be specially configured to work in this mode. Contact your Web host to see if you can use SSL on your server (the answer is usually yes). If so, they'll be able to tell you how to set it up.

Note: If the page is one of the dynamic file types Dreamweaver works with—ASP, ASP.NET, PHP, Cold-Fusion, or JSP—you'll also see a small lightning bolt to the right of this box. This button lets you add *dynamic data*—information drawn from a database—to the text field. (In-depth coverage of this feature starts on page 776.)

Checkboxes

Checkboxes (see Figure 10-4) are simple and to the point; they're either selected or not. They're great for questions in which your visitor is allowed to select more than one item in a group. For example, suppose you produce three different email newsletters that you send out each month. In your form, you might include some text—"Check the boxes for the newsletters you'd like to receive"—and three corresponding checkboxes, so that each visitor can sign up for only the newsletters he wants.

Once you've added a checkbox to a form, you can set up these options for it in the Property inspector (Figure 10-7):

- **Checked value.** You're specifying here the information that, if your visitor turns on this checkbox, will be submitted when the form data is sent to your processing program. It doesn't necessarily have to match the checkbox's label (which you'll create in a subsequent step); it could, instead, transmit some special coded response to your processing application. Your visitors will never actually see this information.

- **Initial state.** If you like, your checkbox can be already checked when your Web page first appears. You may have seen this setup on sites that require you to sign up for some service. Usually there's a checkbox—already checked—down near the bottom of the form, with fine print like this: "Check here if you want to get daily, unsolicited email from our marketing department."

Note: As with many form elements, your checkbox can respond to information it retrieves from a database. The Dynamic button on the Property inspector—available only when you're working on a dynamic page (ASP, PHP, and so on)—lets you set the checkbox state (Checked or Unchecked) based on data in a database. (See page 779 for details.)

After adjusting the Property inspector, if you don't use Dreamweaver's accessibility options discussed on page 367, make sure you return to the document window to add a text label next to the field. Let people know what the checkbox is for: "Yes, sign me up!" for example. Finally, you may want to insert another checkbox. Checkboxes don't have to come in groups, but they often do.

Figure 10-7:
The actual value of a checkbox is defined by the "Checked value" property.

Radio Buttons and Radio Groups

Radio buttons, like checkboxes, are very simple (see Figure 10-4); they're either selected (represented on screen as a solid circle) or not (an empty circle).

But unlike checkboxes, radio buttons restrict your visitor to making only one choice from a group, just like the radio buttons on an old-style automobile dashboard (or, if you're too young to remember those car radios, like the buttons on a blender). Radio buttons are ideal for multiple-choice questions. For example, "What is your income: A. $10–35,000, B. $35–70,000, C. $70–100,000, D. None of your business."

You can set up these options for a radio button in the Property inspector (Figure 10-8):

- **Checked value.** This is the information that the form will submit when your visitor selects this button. Once again, it doesn't necessarily have to match the radio button's onscreen label.

- **Initial State.** Often, when a form page first loads, one radio button in each set is preselected. To do your visitors this time-saving courtesy, turn on Checked for the button that holds the default value—the one they'll choose most often.

  Of course, if making a choice here is optional, then you can leave all of the buttons unselected by setting their initial states to Unchecked. However, once somebody *does* select a radio button, only the Reset button (if you add one) can make them *all* unselected again (see page 379 for information on creating a Reset button).

Figure 10-8:
Radio buttons offer answers to a single multiple-choice question.

Radio buttons come in groups; only one button in the group can be selected at the same time. To achieve this effect, every button in the same group shares the same name (although they should have different Checked values). If, when testing your page, you notice that you can select more than one radio button at a time, you must have given them different names. (Consider using Dreamweaver's Radio Group object, described next. It acts as a wizard that simplifies the process of creating a group of radio buttons.)

The final step in creating radio buttons is to add text labels for the entire group. If you have the accessibility features turned on (see page 367) you'll have already added labels to each button. If not, simply click in the document window and type, just as you'd add any text to the page. Your whole-group-of-buttons label may take the form of a question ("How would you like to pay?"); the labels for the individual buttons might say, for example, "Visa," "MasterCard," and "I.O.U."

Radio Group

Although creating a group of radio buttons using the Radio Button object is easy, Dreamweaver includes the Radio Group object to make it even simpler. The Radio Group object provides a single dialog box for creating a group of radio buttons and their labels in one fell swoop. To use it:

1. **On the Insert bar, click the Radio Group button.**

   The Radio Group window appears (see Figure 10-9).

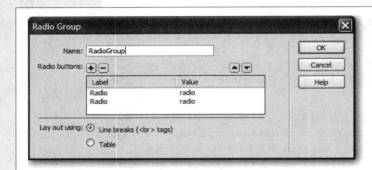

Figure 10-9:
The Radio Group dialog box lets you quickly add multiple radio buttons to a page. The buttons form a single group that lets visitors select one of a group of options.

2. **Type a name in the Name field.**

   This name covers all radio buttons in the group, saving you the trouble of typing the name for each button yourself.

3. **In the Label column, click the top Radio label. Type a label for the first button.**

   This label will appear next to the button onscreen.

4. **Hit the Tab key to jump to the Value column for that button and type a value for the first button.**

   This is the "checked value" of the button. Type what you want to be passed to the Web server when somebody selects this button and submits the form.

5. **Repeat steps 3 and 4 for the second button in the group.**

   You can create additional radio buttons by clicking the + button. Follow steps 3 and 4 for each additional button you add in this way.

6. **Select a layout option for the group.**

   Dreamweaver puts each radio button in the group on its own line. You can choose whether Dreamweaver uses a line break (
 tag) to separate each line, or whether it uses a table—one radio button per row.

   Don't care for either of these options? Pick one anyway. You can always redesign the layout later.

7. **Click OK to add the radio group to your page.**

The radio buttons and their labels are essentially text and buttons on the screen. You can move the buttons around, change their labels, and alter each button's properties in the Property inspector.

Pull-Down Menus and Lists

While checkboxes and radio buttons both provide ways to offer multiple choices, you should consider them only when there are relatively few choices. A form can quickly become overcrowded with buttons and boxes if there are too many options to choose from. The beauty of lists and pull-down menus (usually called *pop-up menus* on the Macintosh) is that they offer many choices without taking up a lot of screen space. (Figure 10-10, top, shows an example.)

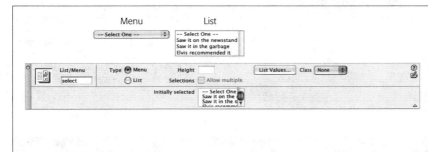

Figure 10-10:
Top: A menu is a single compact line; a list can take up any number of lines on the page.

Bottom: Use the first menu or list item to instruct visitors what to do. For example, "Select the state you live in" or "–Select One–."

Once you've inserted a menu or list object into your document window, here's how to adjust the Property inspector settings:

• **Type.** Menus and lists differ both in appearance (see Figure 10-10) and in function, as described in a moment. Click the one you want (Menu or List).

• **Height.** A list can be a single line tall (in which case you may as well use a menu) or many lines (allowing your visitors to see a number of choices at once). The number you type into the Height box (available for lists only) should reflect the amount of space you wish the list to take up on the page. A vertical scroll bar will appear automatically if the height you specify here is smaller than the number of items in the list.

• **Allow multiple.** Here's a key difference between menus and lists: If you turn on this option, a visitor can select more than one item from a list, just by pressing the Ctrl (⌘) key while clicking different options in the list.

• **List Values.** This button opens the List Values dialog box (see Figure 10-11), where you build the list of options in your list or menu. Each item is composed of two parts: a *label* (the text that actually appears in the menu or list on the Web page) and the *value* (the information that gets submitted with the form, which isn't necessarily the same thing as the label).

To use this dialog box, type an item label. Press Tab (or click in the Value column) and then type the value, if you like. (See Figure 10-11 for details.)

Including a value is optional; if you don't specify one, your form will submit the item's label *as* the value. Still, setting up a separate value is often useful. Imagine that you've designed a pull-down menu on an e-commerce site so that your visitors can select the month of their credit card's expiration. Figure 10-11 shows what the items for such a pull-down menu might look like: the names of the months would appear on the menu, but when a visitor selected, say, April, the number 4 is what the form would actually transmit to your form-processing program.

Add/remove items   Change item order

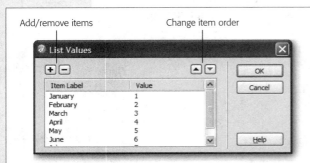

Figure 10-11:
Using the + button, you can add an item to the end of a list; when you click in the Value column of the last item of the list, pressing Tab creates a new list item. To delete an item, select it and click the minus sign (–) button. You can move an item higher or lower in the list of options by selecting the option and then clicking the up or down arrow buttons. Like radio buttons, pop-up menu and list items always flock together—nobody ever creates just one.

POWER USERS' CLINIC

Giving Order to Your Forms

If you're not careful, creating forms can quickly lead to visual chaos. The different shapes and sizes of text boxes, radio buttons, and other form objects don't naturally align well with text. One solution: Use tables to get a handle on the appearance of your forms.

In the picture on the left, form elements were added next to the text on each line, forcing your eye to follow an ungainly zigzag pattern created by the form's text boxes. The result is not only ugly, but also hard to read.

In the second picture, a table made of 2 columns and 13 rows (one row for each question) organizes the text and form elements into two columns. Notice that the text next to each form element aligns to the right, creating a clean edge that effectively mirrors the edge created by the form fields.

To make this table-based solution work most effectively, set each text field to the same width using the Char Width property or Cascading Style Sheets (see page 388 for an example of this).

When using this technique, add the <form> tag first, insert the table inside the form's dotted red boundaries, and then add form elements inside the table. If you make a table first and then try to insert a form, Dreamweaver will only let you add it to a single cell of the table.

See Chapter 7 for more on creating tables.

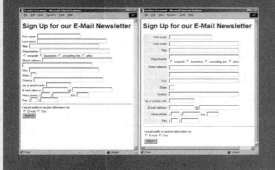

Since computer programs are often more comfortable with numbers than names—and humans often the exact opposite—it makes more sense to use numbers for list values in this case.

Another example: When offering your visitors a pop-up menu of products from which to choose, the label might be the human-friendly name of the product, like "Blue Wool Cap." The value would be the model number that your form-processing program can understand, like XSD1278.

• **Dynamic values.** Dreamweaver can also create a *dynamic menu,* where the labels and values of the menu come from a database. This option—available only when you insert a menu into one of the dynamic page types, as described in Part Six of this book—is great when the menu items change frequently, as they would in a list of employee names, for example. This feature is described on page 781.

Click OK when you're finished building your menu or list. You can always return to this screen and edit the list of options. To do so, click the menu or list in the document window and then click the List Values button on the Property inspector. You return to the dialog box shown in Figure 10-11.

As with other form elements, you can, and probably should, add some explanatory text alongside the list or menu in the document window. One easy method: You can automatically add a label to a menu or list using Dreamweaver's accessibility features as described on page 367.

File Field

Receiving responses to checkboxes, radio buttons, and pull-down menus is all well and good, but what if you'd like your visitors to submit something a little more meaty—like an entire file? Imagine a bulletin-board system, for example, that allows guests to post JPEG images of themselves or upload word processing documents to share with others. They can do just that, thanks to the File Field field (see Figure 10-4)—and a little magic from your Web server.

Before you get carried away with the possibilities the File Field offers, you'll need to do a little research to see whether you can use it on your Web site. Although Dreamweaver makes it easy to *add* a field for uploading image files, text files, and other documents, you'll need to check with the administrator of your Web server to see if anonymous file uploads are permitted (some servers don't allow this kind of activity for fear of receiving viruses or overly large files). Then, of course, you'll have to ensure that the program that processes the form is programmed to *do* something with the incoming file—store it somewhere on the server, for instance. Dreamweaver doesn't have anything built in that helps with this, but you can enlist some third-party solutions as described in the box on page 378.

When you click the File Field button on the Insert bar (or choose Insert → Form Objects → File Field), Dreamweaver inserts a text field *and* a Browse button; together, they constitute a single File Field. When you click either one, you highlight both.

The Browse button, once it's posted on the Web and visible in somebody's browser, opens up the standard Windows or Macintosh Open File dialog box, permitting your visitor to navigate to and select a file for uploading.

The Property inspector offers only two settings to change (other than specifying a more creative name):

- **Char Width.** The width of a text field is measured in characters; if you type *20* for the character width, the field will be 20 characters wide.

- **Max Char.** Leave this blank, as shown in Figure 10-12.

Your File Field isn't finished until you've added a label to it in the document window, something like "Click the Browse button to select a file for uploading" (again, a task that Dreamweaver simplifies with the Label option in the forms Accessibility window described on page 367).

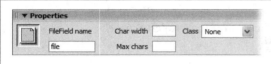

Figure 10-12:
Avoid the "Max chars" field. It's intended to limit the number of characters that the field will accept, but doesn't have any effect on the File Field, which selects the full path to the file regardless of how many characters long it is.

EXTENSION ALERT

Adding File Upload Ability to Your Site

Imagine adding a "Job Application" page to your site, where applicants could upload their resumes for review. Or a Web-based way for clients to submit their graphic files and word processing documents.

Dreamweaver lets you add a File Field to a form, but doesn't provide the tools to make this useful feature function on your Web site. To compensate for that glaring omission, you can turn to *extensions* that add this missing power to Dreamweaver when building a dynamic Web site (as described in Part Six of this book). DMXZone (*www. dmxzone.com*) offers three fee-based extensions for ASP,

ASP.NET, and PHP. The Pure Upload extension offers many different settings to manage the process of uploading files to a Web site, including the ability to rename duplicate files and add file information to databases.

For ColdFusion as well as ASP and PHP, Interakt (*www. interaktonline.com*) also sells an extension, MX File Upload. This extension not only uploads graphic files, but it can also resize them on the server, so that they take up less room and will fit the particular dimensions you require—for example, so all the photos fit nicely in a Web photo album.

Hidden Field

Most form elements are designed to accommodate interaction from your visitors: clicking radio buttons, typing into text fields, and making choices from menus, for example. But there's one kind of field that your visitors won't even know about and will never see: the *hidden* field.

Why, you're probably asking, would you need to submit a value you already know? Hidden fields are intended to supply information to the programs that process forms—information that the program has no other way of knowing. For example, most Web hosting services offer a generic form-processing program that collects information submitted with a form and emails it to a selected person. But how does the program know who to email the data to? After all, it's a *generic* program that's used by hundreds of other people. The solution: a hidden field that stores the information required for the program to properly process the form—*email=me@mydomain.com,* for example.

To insert a hidden field, click the Hidden Field button on the Insert bar, or choose Insert → Form → Hidden Field. A gold shield icon appears on the page (this is Dreamweaver's symbol for HTML that won't be visible in Web browsers). Use the Property inspector to give the field a name and a *value*—that is, the value that will get submitted to your form-processing program (in the example above, your email address).

Note: The gold shield indicating a hidden field appears only if the Hidden Form Fields box is turned on in the Invisible Elements category of the Preferences window (see page 59) and if Invisible Elements is turned on in the View menu (View → Visual Aids → Invisible Elements).

Buttons

No form is complete without a Submit button for your Web visitors to click as a final step (see Figure 10-4). Only then do their responses set out on their way to your form-processing application. Another button that's sometimes added to a form is a Reset button, which your visitors can click when they've filled out a form and realize they've made an error. The Reset button clears all of the form entries and resets all of the form fields to their original values.

Use the Forms tabs of the Insert bar (see Figure 10-2) or choose Insert → Form → Button. If the Accessibility window appears (see page 367), you don't need to add a label, since the button itself will have "Submit," "Reset," or whatever text you wish emblazoned across its face.

The Property inspector controls (Figure 10-13) for a freshly inserted button are:

- **Button Name.** The button's name provides the first half of the "name/value" pair that's sent when the form is submitted (see page 362).

- **Value.** The value is the label that appears on the button. Dreamweaver proposes *Submit,* but you're free to substitute *Do It, Make It So,* or *Send my data on its merry way.*

  So what your visitors see printed on the button—"Click Me"—is also the value that's transmitted along with the button's name when the form is submitted. This opens up some interesting possibilities. You could, for example, include *several* Submit buttons, each with a different label. Maybe you're creating a form for a database application; one button might say Delete, while another says Edit. Depending on which button your visitor clicks, the program processing the form either deletes the record from the database or modifies it.

- **Action.** These three buttons govern what happens when somebody clicks your button. A "Submit form" button transmits the form data over the Internet to the form-processing program. A "Reset form" button sets all the fields back to their original values. (This doesn't mean that the fields, checkboxes, or menu items are left blank, unchecked, or unselected. Instead, they return to their *initial* values, which you specified when creating these various controls. For example, if you set the Initial State property of a checkbox to Checked, and your visitor unchecks the box and then clicks the Reset button, a checkmark will reappear in the box.)

The Reset button used to appear on nearly every form on the Web; these days it's used far less frequently, mainly because it's unlikely that anyone would want to *completely* erase *everything* they've typed into the form. In addition, its presence offers the unfortunate possibility that a visitor, after painstakingly filling out a form, will mistake the Reset button for the Submit button, and click it—erasing everything they've typed. If you do add a Reset button, make sure you don't put it right next to a Submit button.

Setting the button's action to None means that clicking on the button has no effect on the form. "Gee *that's* useful," you're probably thinking. But although the button doesn't submit the data or reset the form's fields, you'll need to choose the None option if you want to add interactivity to the button using Dreamweaver's built-in behaviors (see the next chapter). In this way, you can use a common user-interface element—the 3-D beveled look of a form button—to trigger any of many different actions, like opening a new browser window, starting or stopping a Flash movie, or popping up a message on the screen. If you're a JavaScript programmer, you can use the button to activate your own programs.

Tip: You can also use a graphic as a Submit button, thanks to something called an Image Field, thus freeing you to be more creative with the look of the button itself. Click the Image Field button on the Insert bar, or choose Insert → Form Objects → Image Field, to select a graphic you want to use as a button. When a Web visitor clicks the image, it submits the form and all its data. (Unfortunately, Image Fields only do one thing: submit form data. They can't be used as form Reset buttons.)

Figure 10-13:
Buttons have just three properties: Name, Value, and Action. Like other form elements and HTML tags, Dreamweaver also lets you apply a CSS class style to improve the design of your forms.

Label Tag

The Label tag lets you associate a label with a particular form element—a checkbox or text field, for example. Of course, you can always do that by placing plain text next to a form element on the page. But because a Label tag is "attached" to a particular form element, it's more helpful in explaining the function and layout of your form to people who use assistive technologies like screen-reading software for the blind.

The Label tag button on the Forms tab of the Insert bar (see Figure 10-2) doesn't do much more than switch you into Code view and drop the <label> tag into your HTML. A far better way to insert labels is to use Dreamweaver's form accessibility option, as described on page 367. However, there are some cases where you won't want to put the label directly next to the form field; for example, when using tables to lay out a form, you'll usually put the label in one table cell and the form element in another. In this case, you'll need to jump into Code view to add a label anyway, and this button can save you a little typing. This process is described in the tutorial on page 389.

FREQUENTLY ASKED QUESTION

Emailing the Results of a Form

I don't want to store form submissions in a database or anything fancy like that. I just want to receive an email with the information from each form submitted on my site. How do I do that?

This common function—available on countless Web sites—may seem like an easy task, but Dreamweaver doesn't supply a tool for automating the process. Basically, you need a program to collect the data and send it off in an email. Most Web hosting companies provide just such programs. They generally work like this: you build a form, set the form's Action property (see page 364) to point to the URL of the form-emailing program, and add one or more hidden fields. The hidden fields contain information for the program to use—such as the email address the results should go to and the page the visitor should end up at after she submits the form. Since this form-emailing program varies from server to server, you need to contact your Web hosting company for details.

There are, however, a few free extensions, and some commercial ones, that let you set up this emailing scheme without leaving the friendly confines of Dreamweaver. On the free side, check out Kaosweaver Kaosmailer (*www.kaosweaver.com/extensions/details.php?id=69&cid=18*), which works for ASP, ColdFusion, and PHP server models (see page 685 for more on server models). Dan Short's SOS Basic CDO Emailer (*www.dwfaq.com/Store/detail/?id=wsBasicCDO*) offers similar features for Windows Web servers.

There are also many commercial extensions. For basic form mailing, the Mail Form extension for ASP and PHP is available from Felix One (*www.felixone.it/extensions/dwextensionsen.asp*). Two other extensions offer much more advanced emailing features, including the ability to mass-email newsletters to email addresses stored in a database: WA Universal Email from WebAssist (*www.webassist.com*) works for ASP and ColdFusion pages, and DMXZone (*www.dmxzone.com*) sells both an ASP and a PHP version of its Smart Mailer extension.

Fieldset Tag

The Fieldset tag is a form organization tool, intended to let you group related form fields. For example, if you're creating an online ordering form, you can organize all of the "ship to" information—address, city, state, Zip code, and so on—into a single set. Again, this arrangement can help those using assistive technology to understand the organization and intent of a form.

In most of the latest browsers, the Fieldset tag also has a visual benefit. Internet Explorer 4 and above, Firefox, Safari, Opera, and other newer browsers display an attractive border around fieldsets and add a useful label to identify the fields.

To use this tag, select the related form fields. They must be next to each other on screen, and can be organized within other HTML elements like a table. Then click the Fieldset button on the Insert bar (see Figure 10-2). Type a label (called, somewhat dramatically, a "Legend") for the fieldset in the Label window that appears, and then click OK.

Previous versions of Dreamweaver didn't display a fieldset's border. Dreamweaver 8, in addition to displaying the label you typed, displays a simple border around all of the fields you selected. Because different browsers display this border differently, make sure to preview the page (F12 or Option-F12 on a Mac) in a recent version of Internet Explorer, Mozilla, Opera, or Safari to see both the label and the border surrounding the form elements in the set.

Validating Forms

It can be frustrating to look over feedback that's been submitted via a form on your Web page, only to notice that your visitor failed to provide a name, email address, or some other piece of critical information. That's why, depending on the type of form you create, you might want to make certain information *mandatory*.

For instance, a form used for subscribing to an email newsletter isn't much use if the would-be reader doesn't type in an email address for receiving it. Likewise, if you need a shipping address to deliver a brochure or product, you'll want to be sure that the visitor included his address on the form.

Luckily, Dreamweaver provides a behavior—a ready-made JavaScript program—that accomplishes this exact task. Called Validate Form, this Dreamweaver behavior alerts visitors when they haven't filled out a form properly. You can specify that a particular field can't be left blank, or that it must contain numbers only, or that it must contain a proper email address. If someone attempts to submit the form without the correct information, a small dialog box pops up identifying the mistake. No more blank forms!

Unfortunately there's a built-in limitation to this Dreamweaver behavior: you can only validate *text fields*. In other words, you can't check to see whether someone clicked a particular checkbox or made a selection from a pull-down menu. Nor can you see if she chose a file to upload or clicked a radio button. (For some more advanced solutions, see the box on page 384.)

Nonetheless, the Validate Form behavior is a great tool for making sure you get the right information from your site's visitors. (Dreamweaver behaviors are discussed in depth in Chapter 11.)

To validate a form:

1. **Select the form or a text field you wish to validate.**

   You can validate form fields in two ways: one field at a time or all fields at once.

   The first option involves adding the Validate Form behavior to each text field you wish to validate. The form will check to see if the field contents are valid (using one or more of the criteria you set using the subsequent steps), after the visitor exits the field either by tabbing out of it or by clicking anywhere else on the page. In this way, you can validate a particular field immediately, as soon as your visitor has finished entering information into it. (Of course, if the visitor never clicks into the field to type, the validation never occurs, so it's usually a good idea to combine this with the option described in the next paragraph.)

   If you choose to validate the entire form, no checking takes place until your visitor clicks the Submit button. At that moment, the browser checks all the fields you specified; an error message appears if any of them don't meet the criteria you've specified. To select a form, click its red dashed border or click <form> in the document window's tag selector.

2. **Choose Window → Behaviors.**

   The Behaviors panel appears.

3. **On the Behaviors panel, click the + button; choose Validate Form from the menu.**

   The Validate Form dialog box appears, showing the names of all text fields in the form. In this box, you can set up validation criteria for any text fields in a form. For example, in Figure 10-14, the text field "name" must have a value in it; the field "email" is not required, but if the visitor does fill out this field, it must contain an email address.

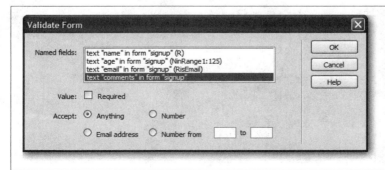

Figure 10-14:
If a form can be left blank—the Comments field, in this example—there's no need to validate it. Don't turn on the Required checkbox, and make sure the Anything radio button is selected.

4. **Select the field you wish to validate from the list.**

   You can click it with the mouse, or press the up and down arrow keys to highlight the one you want.

5. **Turn on the Required checkbox if completing a certain field is mandatory.**

6. **Using the Accept radio buttons, choose one of the four validation types.**

   Anything accepts any value—numbers, letters, or symbols.

   Number means that only numbers will be accepted in the field. You might turn this option on, for example, for text fields labeled "How old are you?" or "How much do you weigh?"

   "Email address" is for fields that require an email address. Note that this feature checks for the correct email address *format,* not for a *valid* email address—it can't go out on the Internet and determine whether or not your visitor is trying to fool you by typing in a bogus address. In fact, this feature only checks to see if an @ symbol was used in the field.

   You can also specify a range of acceptable numbers using the "Number from" option by entering starting and ending numbers. Use this for questions on your form that run along the lines of, "Rate this service from 1 to 10."

   As you go, Dreamweaver helps you remember your selections by adding a letter in parentheses after each field name in the dialog box. *R* means that a value is required; *N* means that the field can be left blank; *isEmail* means that the field should contain an email address; *isNum* means that the value should be a number; and *inRange1:10* means the value must be a number within a certain range (in this example, 1 to 10).

EXTENSION ALERT

Advanced Form Validation

The Validation options Dreamweaver offers are rather rudimentary. The email validation option, for example, doesn't even really check for a correctly formatted email address; it just looks for at least one character followed by an @ symbol followed by one more character.

You'll find many form-related extensions on the Macromedia Exchange Web site (see page 670). Once you're on the Dreamweaver exchange page, perform a search for the word "validate." For example, you'll find three extensions by developer Massimo Foti. With these add-ons to Dreamweaver, you can check your form fields for Zip codes, phone numbers, Social Security numbers, and much more. You can also validate a form on the server, after your visitor has submitted it. This type of validation isn't instantaneous

like JavaScript-based validation, but it's another common way to validate a form. It has the advantage of being more secure—turning off JavaScript is one way to bypass Dreamweaver's built-in Validation behavior—and it lets you add error messages directly into the Web page. For example, it can be more elegant to return the form page to the visitor with all missing form information highlighted in red, bold letters. Page 768 lists some extensions for adding server-side form validation.

And if you're willing to spend some money, you can have both JavaScript and server-side validation with WebAssist's WA Validation Toolkit, available at *www.webassist.com/ Products/ProductDetails.asp?PID=33,* which works with ASP, PHP, and ColdFusion Web pages.

If you're validating the entire form, select additional fields and add validation criteria, if you like.

7. **Click OK to apply the behavior.**

   You return to your document window, where your fields are now ready to use and equipped to check themselves for accurate entries. To see if they work, press F12 (Option-F12) to preview the page in a Web browser. Try clicking the Submit button without filling out any of the text fields.

Forms Tutorial

In this tutorial, you'll build a simple newsletter sign-up form for *The National Exasperator* Web site.

Note: Before you begin building the page, you'll need to download the tutorial files from this book's Web site (*www.sawmac.com/dw8*). Once there, click the Tutorials link; then, click the link to the Forms Tutorial. The files download to your computer.

When the files have downloaded and uncompressed, you should have a folder named DWForms on your hard drive, containing the Web pages and graphics needed for this tutorial. (If you're having difficulties, the Web site contains detailed instructions for downloading.)

Getting Started

You need to direct Dreamweaver's attention to the new Web site folder you've just downloaded. Full details of this process begin on page 472, but here's the *Reader's Digest* version:

1. **In Dreamweaver, choose Site → New Site.**

   The Site Definition window opens. Make sure the Advanced tab is selected.

2. **In the Site Name field, type *Forms*.**

   This is the name that Dreamweaver will use while you're working on this tutorial.

3. **Click the folder icon next to the Local Root Folder field; browse to and single-click the folder *DWForms*, and click Choose. Click OK.**

   You've just defined the site you'll be working on in this tutorial. Defining Web sites and using Dreamweaver's site management features are discussed in depth in Part Four of this book.

Inserting a Form and Creating a Structure

The first step to building a form is inserting a <form> tag. This tag encloses all of the different fields in the form and indicates where the form begins and ends. As noted earlier in this chapter, you can also insert other HTML elements, like text and tables, within the form. In fact, you'll be using a table to make this form look better:

1. **Choose File → Open. Double-click the file called** *signup.html* **in the DWForms folder.**

   (If you have the Files panel open [Window → Files], you can also just double-click the *signup.html* file in the panel to open it.) The page is partly designed already with a banner, sidebar, and footer.

2. **Click in the empty white space below the headline Newsletter Signup. On the Insert bar, select the Forms option (see Figure 10-2).**

   The Insert bar now shows you the Forms icons you'll need.

3. **Click the Form button on the Insert bar (see Figure 10-2), or choose Insert → Form → Form.**

   A red, dashed rectangle appears in the document window, indicating the boundaries of the form.

4. **In the Property inspector, type** *signup* **in the "Form name" field (Figure 10-15).**

   You've just named your form.

5. **In the Action field, type** *http://www.nationalexasperator.com/signup.php.*

   (Leave off the final period, as shown in Figure 10-15.)

Figure 10-15:
The Action property of a form is simply the URL for the program that processes it.

A form's Action property identifies the address of the program that will process the form's submitted data. In this case, you've been spared the effort of writing (or hiring a programmer to write) the required form-processing software. Such a program already exists on the Web site whose address you've just specified, and it's waiting to process the form you're about to design.

You may be creating your own form-processing programs if you're using Dreamweaver's dynamic Web-building tools described in Part Six. See the tutorial on page 788 for an example.

6. **Make sure POST is selected in the Method menu. Leave the Target and Enctype fields blank.**

   The Method indicates how the form sends information to the form-processing program (see page 365).

Now you're ready to begin building a table to design your form.

7. **In the document window, click inside the form—anywhere inside the red, dashed lines. Choose Insert → Table.**

   The Insert Table dialog box opens. (See Chapter 7 for the full story on tables.)

8. **Use the following settings for this table: 6 rows, 2 columns, width 100%, Border thickness 0, Cell padding 5, Cell spacing 0 (see Figure 10-16). Select None for Header, and leave the Accessibility information blank. Click OK.**

   Dreamweaver pops your empty table onto the screen. Next, you'll add the labels and form elements to the table, and then add a little Cascading Style Sheet information to make it look beautiful.

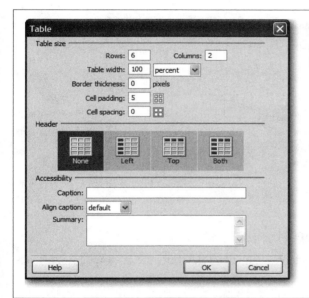

Figure 10-16:
Tables are an excellent way to organize form elements of various shapes. Also, see the box on page 376, which describes how tables can bring order to an unruly form.

Adding Labels and Form Elements

Now that your table is in place, it's time to start adding the different parts of the form. Since text fields, radio buttons, menus, and other form elements aren't always self-explanatory, it's a good idea to add labels explaining the purpose of each element.

1. **Click the top-left cell, and then type** *What is your Name?*

   This text identifies what your visitors should type into the text field you'll add in the next step.

2. **Press Tab to move the insertion point to the next cell, and then click the Text Field button on the Insert bar (Figure 10-17).**

   Alternatively, you can choose Insert → Form → Text Field. If Dreamweaver's Form Accessibility feature is on, the Input Tag Accessibility Attributes window appears. Because you've already added a label, you don't need to use this window. So click Cancel to close the Accessibility window (if it's shown up) and just insert the text field.

Note: Dreamweaver doesn't make it easy to add a label to a form field in situations where the label and form field aren't next to each other. That's the case here where the labels and form fields reside in separate table cells (see the discussion regarding this problem on page 367). Although you *could* click the "change the Accessibility preferences" link and turn off the "Form Objects" checkbox to make sure this window doesn't appear again, don't. You'll use this option to add a label to radio buttons in a few steps. If you want, you can add the HTML label tag another way, following a few additional steps as described in the Note on page 389.

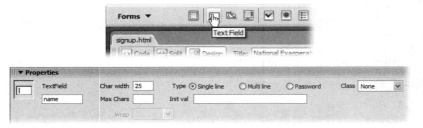

Figure 10-17:
Top: The Text Field button inserts, of course, a text field into your form.

Bottom: The Property inspector as it looks when you've selected a text field.

3. **Type *name* into the TextField box (Figure 10-17, lower left).**

   Every form element must have a name that describes the information it collects.

Note: Most programs that process forms won't work correctly if the name of the form element differs from its programming. In other words, if you mistyped "name" in step 3 as "mame," the form-processing program won't work correctly. If, when you've finished this tutorial, the form response isn't what you expected, first check to make sure you named each form field *exactly* as described here.

---

4. **Type *25* into the Char Width (character width) field.**

   You've just specified, in characters, how wide the field will be. Setting a width does not limit the amount of text someone can type into it; it only controls the display of the field in the browser. You can also use CSS to set the width of a form field, which you'll do later in the tutorial.

Note: Using a Label tag to indicate which text–for example, "Please enter your name"–goes with which form field is often considered good practice. It isn't absolutely necessary, since your forms will still work without them, but the Label tag can help Web browsers identify the purpose of a particular form field and can help those who use special browsers such as screen readers to connect a label with a text field. Unfortunately, when using tables to put labels in one cell and form elements in another, Dreamweaver doesn't offer much help. Here's how you can do it yourself:

First, add the text in one cell (as in step 1 earlier); next, add a form element, name it, and set any other properties using the Property inspector (steps 2, 3, and 4 earlier); then:

1. Select the text you wish to turn into a label.

2. Click the Label tag in the Forms tab of the Insert bar (see Figure 10-2). Dreamweaver switches into Split view (see page 330), displaying both Design view and Code view. You'll see the text is now surrounded by the <label> tag like this: <label>What is your name?</label>. To indicate which form element this label applies to, you need to do one last step.

3. Click just before the closing bracket (>) in the opening <label> tag and press the Space bar.

4. Type *for="name_of_field"*, where *name_of_field* is the name you gave to the form field. In step 3 above, that's *name*. So in this example, the code would look like this:

    ```
    <label for="name">What is your name?</label>
    ```

That's all there is to it. You can click the Design button in the Document window to leave the code and continue with your form building.

5. **In the left column of the table, click the second cell from the top and type** *What is your Email Address?* **Press Tab, and then click the Text Field button on the Insert bar.**

    Alternatively, choose Insert → Form → Text Field. If the Input Tag Accessibility Attributes window appears, click Cancel to dismiss it.

6. **In the Property inspector, type** *email* **into the TextField box. Type** *25* **in the Char Width field.**

    You've just specified the name and width of your email address field.

7. **Click the cell just below the "email" question. Type** *Vote for your favorite boogeyperson.* **Press Tab; in the Insert bar, click the Radio Button button.**

    Alternatively, choose Insert → Form → Radio Button. The Input Tag Accessibility Attributes window appears (if it doesn't, you can turn this feature on as described on page 368).

8. **In the Label box, type** *Big Foot.* **Click the "wrap with label tag" button, and select the "After form item" option. Click OK to insert the radio button and label.**

    In this cell, you'll be adding three grouped radio buttons. Your visitors will be able to choose only one of the three options.

9. Select the newly inserted radio button. In the Property inspector, type *vote* in the Radio Button field and *Big Foot* in the "Checked value" field (Figure 10-18).

Figure 10-18:
You can save time by copying the first button and then changing only the "Checked value" field.

10. Click to the right of the text "Big Foot." In the Insert bar, click the Radio Button object to insert a second button. In the Accessibility window that appears, type *Loch Ness Monster* in the Label box. The other options should already be set as in step 8, so click the OK button to insert the radio button.

The button's added; you just need to tweak its settings.

11. Select the radio button and, in the Property inspector, type *vote* in the Radio Button field and *Loch Ness Monster* in the "Checked value" field.

Radio buttons in the same group share the same Radio Button name; this is what prevents a visitor from selecting more than one button at a time.

12. Click to the right of the text "Loch Ness Monster." On the Insert bar, click the Radio Button button to insert the last button. Type *El Chupacabra* as the label, and then click OK to insert the button.

13. Select the radio button and, in the Property inspector, type *vote* in the Radio Button field and *El Chupacabra* in the "Checked value" field.

Your three radio buttons are all set.

14. Choose File → Save. Press F12 (Option-F12) to preview your page.

Once in your browser, try out the radio buttons. Check to make sure you can only select one at a time. If you're able to select two or more buttons, you've probably typed slightly different names.

Adding a Menu and Submit Button

Only a few more elements are required to produce a fully functional form:

1. Return to Dreamweaver. Click in the left column cell just below the "Vote for your favorite boogeyperson" question. Type *Where did you hear about the National Exasperator?*

In the next step, you'll build a pull-down menu from which visitors can select a response.

2. **Press Tab to jump to the next cell. On the Insert bar, click the List/Menu button (or choose Insert → Form → List/Menu). (Click the Cancel button on the Accessibility window.)**

   Dreamweaver inserts a small box with a selection arrow—a menu—into the cell.

3. **In the Property inspector, type *referral* in the name field. Click the List Values button.**

   The List Values dialog box appears (Figure 10-19). You'll use this box to add items to your menu.

Figure 10-19:
As you build your list of menu options, press Tab twice after each entry—a shortcut that saves you from having to click the + button.

4. **Type -- *Select One* -- .**

   The first item on the list is actually an instruction, which lets your readers know what they need to do with the menu.

5. **Press Tab.**

   The cursor jumps to the Value column. As noted earlier, list items *can* have separate labels and values. If you don't specify a value, your form will simply send the selected *label* to the form-processing program. For this tutorial, you won't add a value.

6. **Press Tab again to add an additional list item.**

   You can click the + button in the dialog box, if you prefer.

7. **Type *Saw it on the newsstand,* and then press Tab twice. Complete the list as shown in Figure 10-19.**

8. **Click OK.**

   You've just built a working menu. You'll find that it doesn't operate in Dreamweaver, however. You must preview the form in a Web browser to see the menu in action. All in good time.

9. Click in the left table cell, below the last question you added. Type *Add any comments here.*

You'll add one last text field to the form, so that your visitors can submit their comments and suggestions.

10. Press Tab. On the Insert bar, click the Textarea button (see Figure 10-2). (Again, click Cancel on the Accessibility window.)

Alternatively, you can choose Insert → Form → Textarea. Either way, Dreamweaver inserts a text box.

11. In the Property inspector, type *comments* into the TextField field. Type *25* in the Char Width field (Figure 10-20).

Doing so establishes the width of the text box, in characters.

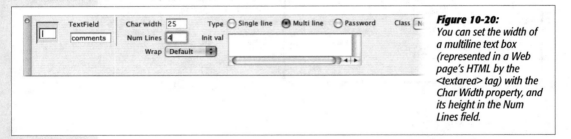

Figure 10-20:
You can set the width of a multiline text box (represented in a Web page's HTML by the <textarea> tag) with the Char Width property, and its height in the Num Lines field.

12. In the Num Lines (number of lines) field, type *4.*

This setting controls how tall the text box appears on the Web page. It doesn't limit the amount of text that can be typed into it, however.

13. Click in the cell directly below this new text field. On the Insert bar, click the Button button. (Once again, dismiss the Accessibility window by clicking Cancel.)

Don't confuse the Button button with a Radio Button; they're two different beasts (see Figure 10-2).

14. In the Property inspector, change the button's value to Sign Up (Figure 10-21).

The default value is *Submit,* but since the value is also the label that appears on the button, you should add a more accurate description. (You *don't* need to change what Dreamweaver here calls "Button name," which also says "Submit." It doesn't show up on your Web page and isn't used by the form-processing program.)

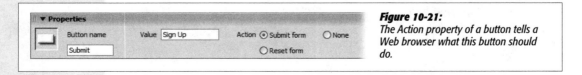

Figure 10-21:
The Action property of a button tells a Web browser what this button should do.

15. **Choose File → Save.**

Congratulations. You've just created a fully functional Web form!

16. **Press the F12 (Option-F12) key to preview the form.**

Go ahead—fill it out (with bogus information, if you like). Click the Submit button when you're finished to see what happens. If you're online, your Web page sends the form information to the waiting form-processing program specified at the beginning of the form creation process. The program sends you back a Web page reflecting your entries, exactly as though you had built a professional, working Web site.

If nothing happens, make sure the Action property of the Form is set correctly (see page 386).

Styling the Form

At this point, the form is rather plain-looking. It would be nice if the text labels were a bit bolder and lined up with the form elements. Also, a few graphical touches—like a line dividing the questions and some text formatting for the form elements—would add a lot. You'll use Cascading Style Sheets to do this:

1. **Make sure the CSS Styles panel is open (choose Window → CSS Styles); click the + button on the Styles panel to create a new style.**

Alternatively, you can choose Text → CSS Styles → New Style. Either way, the New CSS Style window opens. (For a refresher on creating styles, see page 165.)

2. **Make sure the Class radio button is selected and, in the Name box, type .formLabels (see Figure 10-22).**

You'll create a class style that will define the look of each table cell containing a form label. This page already has an external style sheet attached to it, filled with styles used to format the page. You'll add a couple more styles to it.

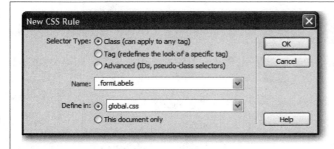

Figure 10-22:
In CSS, all class styles begin with a period like this: .formLabels. If you choose the Class type and enter a name without a period, Dreamweaver will add it for you. Dreamweaver is forgiving that way.

3. **In the "Define in" menu, make sure global.css is selected, and then click OK.**

The CSS Style Definition window opens, ready for you to set formatting properties for the new style.

4. **Under the Type category, set the font to "Verdana, Arial, Helvetica, sans-serif," the size to .8 ems, and the weight to "bold" (see Figure 10-23).**

This sets the basic text-formatting options for the labels. Next, you'll make the text align to the right, so that the labels sit next to the form elements they describe.

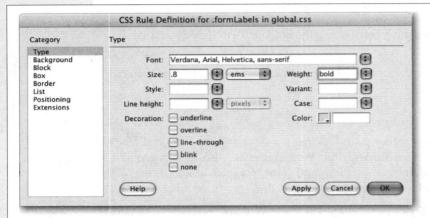

Figure 10-23:
You can use CSS to set the font face, size, color, and other type properties for text that appears inside of a form field. When a visitor enters text into a field, the Web browser formats the text using those settings. This also applies to text as it appears inside menus and lists.

5. **Click the Block category and choose "right" from the Text align menu.**

As things are now, the column of cells containing the labels takes up half the table. That's too much. You'll shrink that down to make the form fields more prominent.

6. **Click the Box category, and in the Width box, type *200*.**

You'll apply this style to the table cells containing the labels. You can use CSS to set properties of table cells—including their width. In addition, you can use CSS to add a decorative border to the bottom of each of these cells.

7. **Click the Border category and turn off the three "Same for all" boxes.**

You won't add a border to all sides of the cell, just the bottom.

8. **For the bottom border properties, set the style to solid, the width to 1 pixel, and the color to #CCCCCC. Click OK to finish creating the style.**

You're finished with this style. Now it's time to apply it.

9. **Select the five table cells containing the labels.**

Click in the top cell and drag to the last cell with a label, for example. (See page 249 for more cell-selection techniques.)

10. From the Style menu in the Property inspector, choose *formLabels* (the style you just created).

    The column of cells should get thinner; the text should become bold and should align to the right of the cell. In addition, though it's hard to see if the table outline is visible, a light gray line should appear at the bottom of each cell. The cells with the form elements could use a little help, too, so you'll apply an already created style to them.

11. **Select the five table cells to the right of the column of labels, and from the Style menu in the Property inspector, select the *formCell* style.**

    A light gray line appears under these cells as well, and the text in those cells changes to another font. Finally, you'll create a new style to add some pizzazz to the form elements themselves. You can style form elements just as you would text or other parts of a Web page. You'll change the font used *inside* of these form elements, as well as set their width and background colors.

12. **Repeat steps 1–3 from earlier to create a new class style called *formElement*.**

13. **In the Type category, set the font to "Verdana, Arial, Helvetica, sans-serif."**

    To make all the little boxes in your form a uniform width (they'll look more consistent that way), you'll set a specific width.

14. **Click the Box category, and in the width box, type *200*.**

    Now every form element to which you apply this style will be 200 pixels wide. Finally, you'll add a background color to make the form really jump out.

15. **Click the Background category and set the Background Color property to #CCCCCC. Click OK to close the window and complete the style.**

    Applying this groovy new style to your form is just a matter of selecting the form element and using the Property inspector.

16. **Select the first text field, and from the Class menu in the Property inspector, select the *formElement* style.**

    The text field grows to 200 pixels, takes on a gray background, and (although you can't see this in Dreamweaver) when you preview the page and type something in the field, you'll notice that the font has changed as well.

Note: Mac owners previewing the page using Safari (version 1) won't see the background color. Only Safari 2 supports background colors for form elements. However, Firefox on the Mac and Internet Explorer 5 for the Mac will display the form field correctly.

---

17. **Repeat step 16 for the email field, pull-down menu, and comment box.**

    When you're done, preview the page in a Web browser (press F12 [Option-F12]) and see all the changes you just made.

Validating the Form

Now that you have a working form, you'll add the finishing touches. Since this form will be used by visitors to sign up for an email newsletter, a couple of pieces of information are crucial, including the name and email address of the person who's subscribing. Using one of Dreamweaver's behaviors, you can make sure that no one submits a form without these two important pieces of information:

1. **Return to Dreamweaver. Click anywhere on the form's red line boundary to select it.**

   Check to make sure the Property inspector says Form Name in the upper-left corner. Alternatively, you can click anywhere inside the table and then use the tag selector at the bottom of the document window to select the form—just click the tag labeled <form#signup>.

2. **Choose Window → Behaviors.**

   This opens Dreamweaver's Behaviors panel, which you can use to add interactive effects to a Web page. You'll probably find it in the lower-left corner of your screen.

3. **From the + menu, choose Validate Form.**

   The Validate Form window opens, listing the three text fields in your form.

4. **Click the first item in the list (name). Turn on the Required checkbox (see Figure 10-24).**

   "Required" means that your visitors can't submit the form unless they type something into this field.

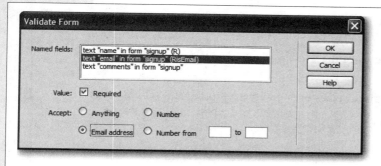

Figure 10-24:
Use Dreamweaver's Validate Form behavior to make sure your visitors don't submit empty forms. You can require visitors to fill out specific text fields and even check to see if the information is in an appropriate format—a number or email address, for example.

5. **Click the second item in the list (email).**

   For the email field, you'll not only specify that it's mandatory, but also that its contents must look like an email address, complete with an @ symbol.

6. **Turn on the Required checkbox. Then, from the Accept group of radio buttons, select "Email address." Click OK.**

7. **Choose File → Save. Press F12 (Option-F12) to preview and test the page.**

See Figure 10-25 for the results.

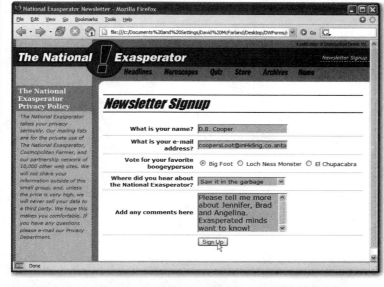

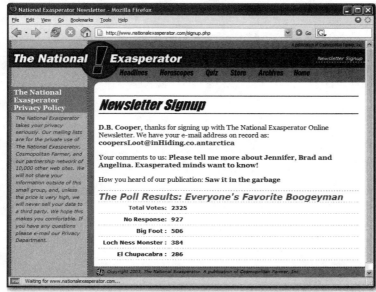

Figure 10-25:
Once again, test your form (top). Pretend you're a particularly clueless or malevolent Web visitor—leave the Name or Email address empty, for example, and then click Sign Up to see what happens. Then, once you enter some valid info, see what happens when you submit the form. If all goes well, the page that appears after you submit the form should look like the illustration at bottom. If you like, you can compare your work with the finished page online at www.sawmac.com/dw8/tutorials/.

Dreamweaver Behaviors

Chapter 5 makes clear how easy it is to add mouse rollover effects using Dreamweaver's Rollover Image object. That and other interactive features rely on *scripts* (small programs) written in the JavaScript programming language.

You *could* create the same effects without Dreamweaver, but you'd need to take a few extra steps: buy a book on JavaScript; read it from cover to cover; learn about concepts like arrays, functions, and document object models; and spend weeks discovering the eccentric rules governing how different browsers interpret JavaScript code differently.

With behaviors, however, Dreamweaver lets you add these dynamic JavaScript programs to your Web pages without doing a lick of programming.

Note: Unfortunately, Macromedia hasn't added any new behaviors or improved the current crop since Dreamweaver MX. However, if you're an intrepid programmer, you can use Dreamweaver Extensions (see Chapter 19) to whip up your own behaviors.

Understanding Behaviors

Dreamweaver behaviors are prepackaged JavaScript programs that let you add interactivity to your Web pages with ease, even if you don't know the first thing about JavaScript. By adding behaviors, you can make your Web pages do things like:

- Make layers appear and disappear.
- Require visitors to fill out certain fields in a form (Chapter 10)—when, for example, you want to make sure that visitors enter an email address or name before submitting the form.

• Open a new browser window to a specified size, with or without scroll bars, status bar, location bar, and other Web browser "chrome."

• Let your visitors navigate a Web site using a pop-up menu.

• Give feedback to the visitor in a dialog box or in the browser's status bar.

Tip: Try it yourself. See examples of all of Dreamweaver's behaviors on the companion Web site for this book: *www.sawmac.com/dw8/behaviors/*.

Behavior Elements

To use a behavior, you bring together three elements: an action, an event, and an HTML tag:

• The **action** is whatever the behavior is supposed to *do*—open a new browser window or display a message in the browser's status bar, for instance.

• The **event** is the *trigger* that causes the action to happen. It's usually something your visitor does, like clicking a Submit button on a form, moving the mouse over a link, or even simply loading a Web page into the browser.

• Finally, you apply the event and the action to an **HTML tag** to bring interactivity to your Web page.

Let's say you want to let visitors access different Web pages on your site by using a pop-up menu (also known, ironically, as a drop-down menu)—a common forms element. This menu lists the different pages of your site—*About This Company, Contact Us, See Our Products,* and so on.

FREQUENTLY ASKED QUESTION

Behaviors and Added Code

I hear the JavaScript that Dreamweaver produces adds excessive lines of code, unnecessarily adding to a page's file size. Is this a reason not to use behaviors?

In some cases, it's true that a JavaScript programmer could write a program that does what a Dreamweaver behavior does using less code.

However, Dreamweaver behaviors were created to work in as many browsers as possible without producing errors in older browsers. The hitch is that JavaScript doesn't work the same in all browsers or even in all versions of browsers.

Indeed, many browsers have until recently understood JavaScript so differently that programmers have resorted to elaborate workarounds, requiring a lot of experience, practice, and patience.

Accordingly, the engineers at Macromedia use their vast understanding of JavaScript, HTML, and Web browsers to ensure that Dreamweaver behaviors work in as many browsers as possible. At times, this compatibility may lead to larger files with more lines of code, but it also assures that your Web pages will work for the broadest audience possible.

When someone selects one of the options from the menu, his browser opens the Web page for that section of the site. In this case, the HTML tag is the pop-up menu itself—a <select> tag; the *action* is opening another Web page in the site; and the *event* brings the two together so that when your visitor makes a selection from the pop-up menu, his browser goes to the selected Web page. Voilà—interactivity!

More about Events

When people visit a Web page, they do more than just read it—they interact with it. You already know that when someone clicks a link, the browser reacts by loading a new Web page or jumping to a named anchor (page 116).

But visitors can also interact with a Web page in a variety of other ways. They may resize the browser window, move the mouse around the screen, make a selection from a pop-up menu, click an image, type inside a form field, or click a form's Reset button. Web browsers "listen to" and react to these triggering events with actions.

GEM IN THE ROUGH

Link Events Without Loading a New Web Page

As you start to use behaviors, you'll quickly notice that there are an awful lot of useful events associated with links. Links can respond to interactions of all sorts, like moving the mouse over the link, moving it away from the link, or clicking the link.

Clicking a link usually opens a different Web page. But there are times when you may want to use the onClick event to trigger an action without leaving the current Web page.

For instance, you may have a Web page with lots of unusual or technical words. It would be great to program the page so that when someone clicks an unfamiliar word, a dialog box displaying its definition pops up on the screen (using the Popup Message action, described on page 429). Unfortunately, a Web browser doesn't know when you click a word, since there's no event associated with regular text. However, browsers do know when you click a link and can respond to this action accordingly.

But in this case, you don't want to use a real link; that would force a new page to load. You just want to use a link's onClick event.

The secret is, instead of using a real URL or path for the link, you use a "dummy" link—a link that goes nowhere. This way, you can still take advantage of all of the great events links have to offer without adding links that take you away from the page.

There are two types of "dummy" (also called "null") links. The first uses the pound symbol (#). Select the text or graphic to which you want to add the behavior, and then, in the Property inspector, instead of adding a URL in the Link field, type in #. (You can also create a dummy link by typing *javascript:;* into the Link field. Be sure to include both the colon and semicolon.) This dummy link doesn't load a new Web page, but provides a link to which you can apply behaviors.

The advantage of the second method is that some browsers (including Internet Explorer for Windows) scroll to the top of the page when a visitor clicks a link that uses the # symbol, which could be disconcerting if you attached a behavior that appears far down a page.

In JavaScript and Dreamweaver, the names of events always begin with the word "on," which essentially means "when." For example, the onLoad event refers to the moment when an object fully loads into the browser—like when a Web page, its images, and other linked files have downloaded. Events also include the various ways someone can interact with a particular HTML tag (element). For instance, when someone moves the mouse over a link or clicks a link, the corresponding events are called onMouseOver and onClick.

Note: Traditionally, JavaScript programmers have capitalized the second word in a JavaScript event—onMouseOver, for instance. Trouble is, XHTML doesn't allow uppercase letters for tags or their properties. So if you're creating XHTML pages, events should always be lowercased, like this: onmouseover. (Dreamweaver converts such terms to lowercase automatically as you create XHTML pages.)

Applying Behaviors

Dreamweaver makes adding behaviors as easy as selecting a tag and choosing an action from a drop-down menu in the Behaviors panel.

The Behaviors Panel

The Behaviors panel is mission control for Dreamweaver's behaviors (Figure 11-1). On it, you can see any behaviors that are applied to a tag, add more behaviors, and edit behaviors that are already applied.

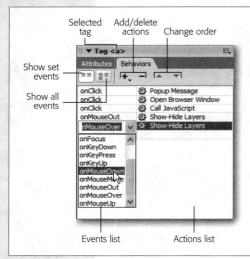

Figure 11-1:
Behaviors are grouped by event and listed in the order in which they occur on the Behaviors panel. You can change the type of event by clicking the event name and selecting another event. For actions with different events, the order is irrelevant, since the event determines when the action takes place, not the order. However, as you see here, it's possible to have one event—onClick—trigger multiple actions. When one event triggers several behaviors, you can change the order in which they occur with the up and down pointing arrows

You can open the Behaviors panel in any of three ways:

- Choose Window → Behaviors.
- Press Shift+F4.
- If the Tag inspector is open, click the Behaviors tab.

In any case, the panel appears on your screen.

Note: Dreamweaver includes two different types of behaviors, and it's important not to get them confused. This chapter describes JavaScript programs that run in your audience's Web browsers—these are called "client-side" programs. The *server behaviors* listed in the Application panel group, on the other hand, run on the Web *server* to let you access information from a database. These are described in Part Six.

The currently selected tag is indicated at the top of the Behaviors panel, and a list of all of the behaviors applied to that tag, if any, appears below. Each behavior is listed in two parts: Events and Actions, as described earlier.

The Behaviors panel offers two different views (Figure 11-1). You switch between them using the buttons at the upper left of the panel:

- **Show set events** (pictured in Figure 11-1) gets down to the specifics: which behaviors you've applied to the tag and which events trigger them. When you're working on a Web page, this view moves extraneous information out of your way.

- **Show all events** lists all of the events *available* to a particular tag. Someday, should you decide to *memorize* which events apply to which tags (see page 406), you may no longer need this view.

Applying Behaviors, Step by Step

Open the Behaviors panel, and then proceed as follows:

1. **Select the object or tag.**

   You must attach a behavior to an HTML tag, such as a link (indicated by the <a> tag) or the page's body (<body> tag). Take care, however: It's easy to apply a behavior accidentally to the wrong tag. Form elements, like checkboxes and text fields, are easy—just click one to select it. For other kinds of tags, consider using the tag selector, as described on page 21, for more precision.

Tip: You can be sure which tag the behavior is applied to by looking at the Tag inspector's header (above the Behaviors tab). For example in Figure 11-1, "Tag <a>" indicates that the behaviors listed are applied to an <a>, or link tag.

2. **In the Behaviors panel, add an action.**

   Click the + button in the Behaviors panel and, from the Add Action menu, select the action you wish to add (see Figure 11-2). You'll find a complete list of these behaviors and what they do beginning on page 411.

   Some actions are dimmed in the menu because your Web page doesn't have elements necessary for the behavior to work. For instance, if you haven't included a form in your Web page, the Validate Form behavior is grayed out. Others are dimmed because they must be applied to a particular page element. For example, Jump Menu is off limits until you've added a list/menu field to the page and selected it.

3. **In the dialog box that opens, set options for the action.**

Each action has properties that pertain specifically to it, and you set them to your liking in the dialog box that now appears. For instance, when you choose the Go To URL action, Dreamweaver asks what Web page you want to load. (Once again, the following pages describe each of these actions.)

4. **Click OK to apply the action.**

At this point, Dreamweaver adds, to the underlying code of your page, the HTML and JavaScript required to make the behavior work. Your behavior's name appears in the Behaviors panel.

Unlike HTML objects, behaviors usually add code to two different places in a document. For behaviors, Dreamweaver usually adds JavaScript code to the head of the document *and* to the body of the page.

5. **Change the event, if desired.**

When your newly created action shows up in the Behaviors panel, Dreamweaver displays, in the Events column of the panel, a default event (trigger) for the selected tag and action. For example, if you add a Set Text of Status Bar behavior to a link, Dreamweaver suggests the onMouseOver event.

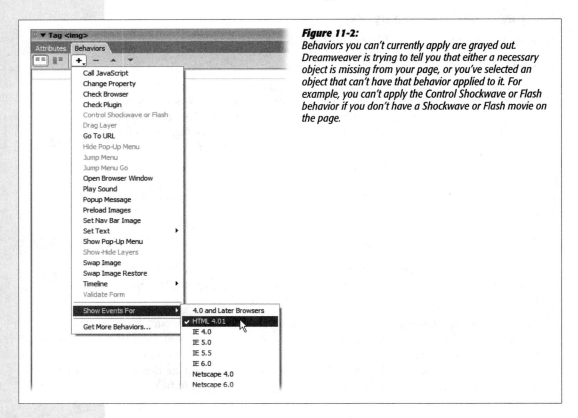

Figure 11-2:
Behaviors you can't currently apply are grayed out. Dreamweaver is trying to tell you that either a necessary object is missing from your page, or you've selected an object that can't have that behavior applied to it. For example, you can't apply the Control Shockwave or Flash behavior if you don't have a Shockwave or Flash movie on the page.

However, this default event may not be the only event available. Links, for instance, can handle many different events. An action could begin when your visitor's cursor moves *over* the link (the onMouseOver event), *clicks* the link (the onClick event), and so on.

To change the event for a particular behavior, click the event's name, and the Events pop-up menu appears (see Figure 11-1). Select the event you want from the list of available events that appears for that particular tag. (See page 406 for a list of all available events in current versions of the most popular browsers.)

When you're done, you can leave the Behaviors panel open to add more behaviors to the tag, or to other tags. Select another tag, using the document window or tag selector, and repeat steps 2 through 5.

Adding Multiple Behaviors

You're not limited to a single behavior per HTML tag. You can, and often will, apply several behaviors to the same tag. For instance, when a page loads—the onLoad event of the <body> tag—it can preload images to be used in rollover effects, open a small browser window displaying a pop-up advertisement, *and* put a small text message in the browser's status bar.

Nor are you limited to a single *event* per tag. For instance, you can add to a link any number of actions that are triggered by different events, such as onMouse-Over, onMouseOut, and onClick.

For example, if you set things up for a link as shown in Figure 11-1, when you click the selected link in the browser window, a pop-up message appears first, and then a new browser window opens, and finally a custom JavaScript program is run. The link also responds to other events, like moving the mouse over it—in this example, making an invisible layer appear on the page.

Editing Behaviors

Once you've applied a behavior, you can edit it anytime. Double-click the behavior in the Behaviors panel to reopen the Settings dialog box, as described in step 3 of the previous instructions. Make any changes you like, and then click OK.

To remove a behavior from your Web page, select it in the Behaviors panel and click the minus sign (–) button or press Delete. (If you *accidentally* delete a behavior, just choose Edit → Undo Remove Behavior.)

A Quick Example

This brief example is designed to give you a clear overview of the behavior-creation process. In it, you'll use a behavior that makes an important message appear automatically when the Web page opens.

1. **Choose File → New to create a new untitled document.**

    You'll start with a new page.

2. **Choose File → Save and save the file to your computer.**

It doesn't matter where you save the page, since you won't be including any graphics or linking to any pages.

You'll start the process of adding a behavior by selecting a specific tag—in this case, the page's <body> tag.

3. **In the tag selector at the lower-left corner of the document window, click <body>.**

Once the tag is selected, you can apply one or more behaviors to it. But first, make sure the Behaviors panel is open. If you don't see it, choose Window → Behaviors or press Shift+F4.

4. **Click the + button on the Behaviors panel. From the Add Action menu, choose Popup Message (see Figure 11-2).**

The Popup Message dialog box appears.

5. **In the message box, type *Visit our store for great gifts!* Then click OK.**

Dreamweaver adds the required JavaScript code to the page. Notice that the Behaviors panel lists the *action* called Popup Message next to the *event* called onLoad. The onLoad event triggers an action *after* a page and everything on it—graphics and so on—have downloaded.

To see the page in action, preview it in a Web browser.

6. **Press the F12 (Option-F12) key to preview the page.**

See page 48 for more on using this preview function.

Note: Dreamweaver behaviors rely on little JavaScript programs running inside the Web browser. If you've got Windows XP and have Service Pack 2 installed, whenever you preview a behavior-using page in Internet Explorer, you'll run into the same problems you encountered with rollover images in Chapter 5. For a solution, turn to page 146.

Events

Unfortunately, JavaScript works differently not only in different browsers, but in different *versions* of browsers. Older versions of Netscape Navigator and Internet Explorer don't recognize the same range of events as newer versions. Moreover, the most recent crop of browsers—including Firefox, Safari, Opera, and Internet Explorer 6—differ significantly when it comes to JavaScript. (The events available in Netscape Navigator 6 are far fewer than those in Internet Explorer 6.) These incompatibilities can make a chore out of developing interactive Web pages that work for the largest possible audience.

If you hope to build successful interactive Web sites, you can't avoid learning which tag/event combinations work in which browsers. Over 95 percent of Web surfers today, however, use versions 4 or greater of Netscape Navigator or Internet Explorer, so this book concentrates on behaviors that work with those browsers. Fortunately, these behaviors also work with most other modern browsers like Safari or Firefox.

Refer to the following pages, which list and explain the most common and useful HTML tags and events that work in these browsers, whenever you apply a behavior.

Each entry shows you the name of the event as you'll see it listed in the Behaviors panel, a plain-English description of what that event really means, and the list of tags to which this event is most commonly applied. See Figure 11-3 for the visual representations of those HTML tags. For example, you'll find out that the <select> tag represents a pop-up menu.

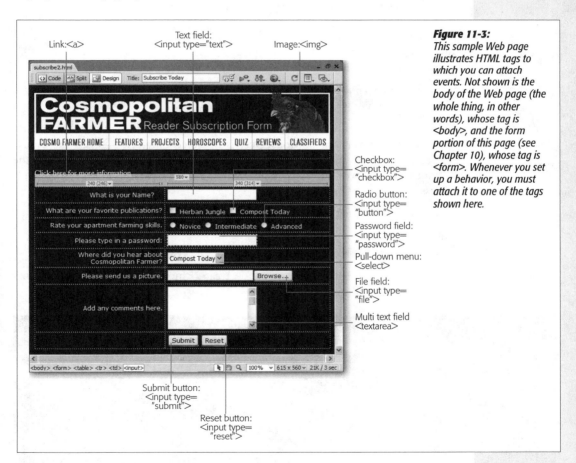

Figure 11-3:
This sample Web page illustrates HTML tags to which you can attach events. Not shown is the body of the Web page (the whole thing, in other words), whose tag is <body>, and the form portion of this page (see Chapter 10), whose tag is <form>. Whenever you set up a behavior, you must attach it to one of the tags shown here.

Mouse Events

Web designers most often use mouse *movement* events to trigger actions (like the familiar rollover image). But mouse *clicks*—on checkboxes, radio buttons, and other clickable form elements—can be mouse events, too.

Note: In the following list, the many different types of *input* form elements are listed like this: <input type="button | checkbox | radio | reset | submit">. This notation simply means that *any* of these form elements—buttons, checkboxes, radio buttons, reset buttons, or submit buttons—react to the listed event. Also, when you see an <area> tag, it refers to the hotspots on an image map (see page 142).

Most current browsers—Firefox, Safari, Internet Explorer 6—support a wide range of events for many HTML tags. In most cases, you'll find that any of the events in the following list work with all of the tags pictured in Figure 11-3 (and even a few more tags). The list presents the most commonly used combinations. Of course you could, if you wanted to, make a window pop up with a message whenever a visitor moves her mouse across a text field in a form. But would you want to?

onMouseOver

Gets triggered: When the cursor moves over the tag.

Commonly used with these tags: <a>, <area>, <img>

onMouseout

Gets triggered: When the cursor moves off of the tag.

Commonly used with these tags: <a>, <area>, <img>

onMouseMove

Gets triggered: When the cursor moves anywhere inside the tag. Works similarly to onMouseOver, but onMouseOver is triggered only once—when the mouse first moves over the tag. onMouseMove is triggered continually, whenever the mouse moves over the tag. The possibilities for an annoying Web page are endless.

Commonly used with this tag: <body>

onClick

Gets triggered: When a visitor clicks the tag and releases the mouse button.

Commonly used with these tags: <a>, <area>, <input type="button | checkbox | radio | reset | submit">

FREQUENTLY ASKED QUESTION

The Vanishing Events List

I applied a behavior to a link, but the only event available is onMouseOver. What happened to all the other events?

To make sure your behavior works in as many browsers as possible, check out the Show Events For submenu (also shown in Figure 11-2). The earlier the browser version you choose here, the fewer events you'll see listed. On the other hand, choosing an earlier browser version ensures that your behavior will work for more of your visitors. If you're developing your site with modern, standards-compliant browsers in mind, you can safely pick the HTML 4.01 specification listed on the Show Events For submenu. Your site will then work with the vast majority of Web browsers in use today.

---

onDblClick

Gets triggered: When a visitor double-clicks the tag.

Commonly used with these tags: <a>, <area>, <input type="button | checkbox | radio | reset | submit">

onMouseDown

Gets triggered: When a visitor clicks the tag. The mouse button doesn't need to be released for this event to occur (note the contrast with onClick).

Commonly used with these tags: <a>, <img>, <input type="button | checkbox | radio | reset | submit">

onMouseUp

Gets triggered: When a visitor releases the mouse button while cursor is over the tag. The effect is the same as the onClick event.

Commonly used with these tags: <a>, <img>, <input type="button | checkbox | radio | reset | submit">

Keyboard Events

Keyboard events respond to key presses and releases. Most Web designers use them in association with form elements that accept text, such as password or text fields. (See Chapter 10 for more on forms.)

onKeyPress

Gets triggered: When a visitor presses and releases a key while the tag is selected.

Commonly used with these tags: <textarea>, <input type="file | password | text">, <a>

onKeyDown

Gets triggered: When a visitor presses a key while the tag is selected. The key doesn't need to be released for this event to occur.

Commonly used with these tags: <textarea>, <input type="file | password | text">, <a>

onKeyUp

Gets triggered: When a visitor releases a key while the tag is selected.

Commonly used with these tags: <textarea>, <input type="file | password | text">, <a>

Body and Frameset Events

Several events relate to actions involving an entire Web page or frameset.

onLoad

Gets triggered: When a Web page *and* any embedded elements—like images and Flash and QuickTime movies—load. Very often used for triggering actions when a visitor first loads the Web page; can also be used with an image tag to signal when that particular image has finished loading.

Commonly used with these tags: <body>, <frameset>, <image>

onUnload

Gets triggered: When the Web page is about to be replaced by a new Web page—for instance, just before the Web browser loads a new Web page after a visitor clicks a link.

Commonly used with these tags: <body>, <frameset>

onResize

Gets triggered: When a visitor resizes the Web browser window.

Commonly used with these tags: <body>, <frameset>

onError

Gets triggered: When an error occurs while a Web page or an image loads.

Commonly used with these tags: <body>, <img>

Note: The onFocus and onBlur events described in the following section also apply to the <body> and <frameset> tags.

Selection and Highlighting Events

Some events occur when the visitor focuses on different parts of a Web page, selects text, or chooses from a menu.

onSelect

Gets triggered: When a visitor selects text in a form field.

Commonly used with these tags: <textarea>, <input type="text">

onChange

Gets triggered: When a visitor changes the text in a form field.

Commonly used with these tags: <textarea>, <input type="file | password | text">, <select>

onFocus

Gets triggered: When an element becomes the focus of the visitor's attention. For instance, clicking in a form text field or tabbing to it gives the text field focus.

Commonly used with these tags: <body>, <frameset>, <textarea>, <input type="button | checkbox | file | password | radio | reset | submit | text">, <select>

onBlur

> *Gets triggered:* When an element loses the focus. For instance, if the visitor is typing into a form text field and then clicks outside of that field, the onBlur event occurs. The onBlur event is also triggered when the surfer sends a window to the background. For example, suppose your visitor is reading your Web site in one window and has another open in the background. If he clicks the background window, the current page loses focus and an onBlur event occurs.
>
> *Commonly used with these tags:* <body>, <frameset>, <textarea>, <input type="button | checkbox | file | password | radio | reset | submit | text">, <select>

Form Events

While each element of a form—radio button, text field, checkbox—can respond to a variety of events, the whole form—the entire collection of elements—can respond to only two events:

onSubmit

> *Gets triggered:* When a visitor clicks the Submit button on a form.
>
> *Commonly used with this tag:* <form>

onReset

> *Gets triggered:* When a visitor clicks the Reset button on a form.
>
> *Commonly used with this tag:* <form>

The Actions, One by One

While events get the ball rolling, actions are, yes, where the action is. Whether it's opening a 200×200 pixel browser window or using HTML to control the playback of a Flash movie, you'll find an action for almost every interactivity need.

In some cases, alas, the actions aren't very good. Macromedia hasn't added many behaviors since version 4, and, unfortunately, they haven't gone through and weeded out the behaviors that aren't very useful or that don't work well. In those cases, this book makes clear which are the rotten eggs to steer clear of.

After you complete the steps required to set up an action, the new action appears in the Behaviors panel, and your Web page is ready to test. At that point, you can click the behavior's name in the Behaviors panel, where—by clicking the Events pop-up menu, as shown in Figure 11-1—you can change the event that triggers it.

Note: Although Macromedia hasn't added any new behaviors to Dreamweaver 8, *you* can add an almost unlimited number of new behaviors—if you know where to look. You can find loads of behaviors (written by non-Macromedia programmers) at the Dreamweaver Exchange or at one of the many extension Web sites listed on page 673.

Navigation Actions

Many of Dreamweaver's actions are useful for adding creative navigational choices to your Web sites, giving you the opportunity to go beyond the simple click-and-load approach of a basic Web page.

Pop-Up Menu

As the appetites of Web surfers grow, Web sites are getting bigger and more complex, sometimes making it harder to navigate them. Instead of a handful of links cleanly placed on the home page, you may have hundreds of links that could easily overwhelm your visitors. To maintain order, use Dreamweaver's Show Pop-Up Menu behavior to add navigation menus that appear only when the mouse moves over related links (see Figure 11-4).

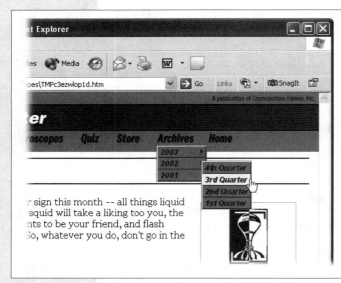

Figure 11-4:
Dreamweaver's Show Pop-Up Menu behavior adds complex navigation menus to a page. You can even add nested menus, as in this example, where moving the mouse over the Archives button pops up a menu with three options. Moving the mouse over the second option pops up yet another menu with four additional choices. The only limit to the number of submenus you can create is the width of your monitor: if there are too many submenus, they'll disappear off the right edge of the screen.

The pop-up menu is composed of invisible *layers* (see page 299) that become visible when you move your mouse over a link. Aside from the wow factor of making things appear out of nowhere, the main benefit of this behavior is that you can provide lots of navigation options without squandering valuable screen space. One drawback is that you can only use *text* in these menus, not cool graphic buttons to match your main navigation elements. Another drawback—one that fills the Macromedia Dreamweaver Forums with hand-wringing anguish—is that, unlike all other aspects of the program, Dreamweaver doesn't update the links in the pop-up menus; so if you move the page into a subfolder of your site, all document-relative links in the menu break. And unfortunately, there are a few additional problems with pop-up menus (see the box on page 413).

If you aren't scared off and still want to give the Show Pop-Up Menu behavior a try, here's what you do: Start by selecting a link on the page. The menu pops up when the visitor's mouse passes over this link, so pick a link that's related to the menu you're creating. For example, if you want to create a menu that lets visitors select one of the five products you sell, using a link labeled Products would make sense.

Tip: Pop-up menus don't work if the visitor doesn't have JavaScript turned on in her Web browser. In addition, search engines can't access the links on your pop-up menus. For this reason, it's a good idea to make the top-level links (the ones you mouse over to make the pop-up menus appear) link to a main page—one for each top-level link, representing each section of your site. On each of *those* pages you'll also want to include links to the other pages listed on each pop-up menu.

WORKAROUND WORKSHOP

Are Pop-Up Menus All Pooped Out?

There are several problems with Dreamweaver's Show Pop-Up Menu behavior. First, the JavaScript code is rather bulky—around 30 KB of extra data stored in an external JavaScript file—meaning the page first needs to download that file, taking longer to load. In addition, the code used isn't accessible by browsers with JavaScript turned off, or by search engines; so if you want to make your Google rank soar, you should steer clear of pop-up menus, or provide other (non-pop-up) links to the same pages.

But the most glaring error in the Show Pop-Up Menu behavior is that Dreamweaver doesn't update links you create with it.

In other words, if you add a pop-up menu to a page in the root folder of your site and then save the page into another folder, Dreamweaver doesn't automatically update the links in the pop-up menu. If you've used document-relative links, your beautiful pop-up menu is now filled with broken links. You're faced with two solutions. You could use root-relative links, which has the unfortunate side effect that you can't actually see if the links work until you move your site onto a Web server; or, if you're using document-relative links, you could keep all of your files in a single folder. You

won't be able to add subfolders to organize your site, since that would require the paths of the links to change. In addition, if you plan to use template pages (Chapter 17), add the pop-up menu before saving the file as a template. If you add the pop-up menus later, the links won't work. (For more on the difference between document- and site-root-relative links see page 104.)

There's one other solution: just don't use Dreamweaver's pop-up menus. You'll find a more advanced pop-up menu system in Fireworks 8, the graphics companion program to Dreamweaver. You can use Fireworks to build a much more functional pop-up menu, and then export it for use in Dreamweaver.

In addition, you'll find many extension developers who provide a variety of interesting, reliable, and powerful pop-up menu systems. Here are a few:

- Menu Magic Extensions from Project Seven (*www.projectseven.com*)

- MiniMenus from 4LevelWebs (*www.fourlevel.com*)

- MX CSS Dynamic Menus from InteraktOnline (*www.interaktonline.com*)

Once you've selected Show Pop-Up Menu from the + (Add Action) menu in the Behaviors panel, you see the dialog box shown in Figure 11-5. If you simply want to create a quick pop-up menu, you only have to use the first tab, Contents, which lets you create and arrange menu items. The other three tabs control the appearance and placement of menu items:

- **Adding menu items.** To add a menu item, click the + button on the Contents tab. Next, in the Text field, type the words you'd like to appear for one of your menu items. You can then type a link into the Link field or click the folder icon and select a file in your site.

  If you're using frames, you can direct the link to open in a specific frame by choosing its name from the Target menu. Alternatively, to open the link in a new blank window, choose "_blank." Continue, as shown in Figure 11-5, until you've covered all your menu items.

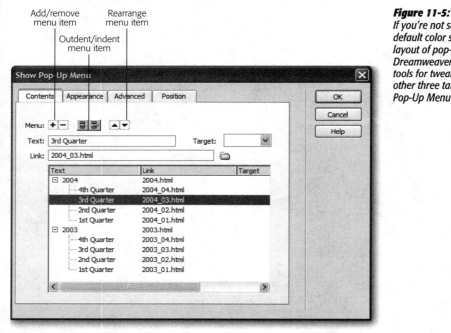

Figure 11-5:
If you're not satisfied with the default color scheme, font, or layout of pop-up menus, Dreamweaver offers plenty of tools for tweaking them in the other three tabs of the Show Pop-Up Menu dialog box.

- **Deleting menu items.** To delete a menu item, select it from the list on the Contents tab and click the minus sign (–) button.

- **Changing the order of menu items.** To rearrange the menu you've built, select a menu command from the list on the Contents tab, and press the up or down arrow buttons. The order in which the items are listed in the dialog box is the order they'll take in the onscreen pop-up menu.

- **Creating a submenu.** You can also create submenus—additional menus that appear when you move your mouse over an item in the main pop-up menu. For example, in Figure 11-4, moving the mouse over the "2002" link opens another menu with four additional items.

  To create a submenu, select a menu item and then click the Indent button (Figure 11-5) on the Contents tab. The link becomes the first item of the submenu. As you add additional items using the + button, they become other members of the submenu. (You can't indent the top item in a menu in this way.)

- **Removing an item from a submenu.** To move a submenu item back into the main menu, select it and then click the Outdent button (Figure 11-5).

The Appearance tab offers some useful options of its own:

- **Orientation.** Select either vertical (stacked) or horizontal (side-by-side) menu items. Be careful with the horizontal option—it's easy to build a menu that extends off the right edge of the browser window, where no one can click it!

- **Font options.** Choose a font, font size, and formatting (bold or italic) for menu items. You can even set the alignment of text within each menu item—left, center, or right. These settings apply to *all* text in the pop-up menu.

- **Colors.** These menu items have two different sets of colors: one for a menu item's *up state* (its appearance when the menu appears) and one for its *over state* (its appearance when the mouse is on a menu command). Use the color boxes to select contrasting colors for the background color of the menu item and the color of the text inside the menu.

Tip: After you add the pop-up menu behavior to a page, Dreamweaver puts a file called *mm_menu.js* in the folder containing that page. It's a JavaScript file containing most of the complex programming required to make the pop-up menu feature work. Don't delete this file! Doing so breaks your pop-up menus and causes JavaScript errors in your page. Also, remember to upload this new file to the Web site (Chapter 15) when you're ready to make your site "live." If you do happen to delete it, just add another Pop-Up Menu behavior to another page in that folder. (If you add a submenu to a menu item, Dreamweaver also adds a graphic file called *arrows.gif.* Don't delete this, either.)

For more detailed design of a pop-up menu, click the Advanced tab (see Figure 11-6):

- **Cell width.** Each item in a pop-up menu acts like a cell in a table (see page 228), with a background color, content (text of the menu item), width and height, and other properties. You can set the width to an exact pixel size by selecting Pixels from the pull-down menu and typing a number in the "Cell width" box. Setting an exact width is a good option if you're adding several pop-up menus to a page—one for each of the buttons of the main navigation bar, for example—and you want each menu to be the same width for visual consistency. (You can set only one pixel setting, which applies to both the menu and any submenus. Dreamweaver won't let you set this smaller than the space taken up by the text in a button.)

If you accept the proposed setting, Automatic, Dreamweaver determines the width of the menu based on the longest menu item, and determines separate widths for the submenus. For example, in Figure 11-4, Dreamweaver calculated the width of the submenu with its three short items—4th Quarter, 3rd Quarter, and so on—automatically.

- **Cell height.** You can change the height of menu items in the same manner.

- **Cell padding.** To adjust the space from the edge of a menu to the text inside the menu, type a pixel value in this box. Cell padding here works exactly like cell padding in a table, as described on page 228.

- **Cell spacing.** You can also adjust the space between menu items, as you would the space between cells in a table, as described on page 228.

- **Text indent.** To add space between the left edge of the menu and text, type a pixel value in the "Text indent" box. You'll probably find that the "Cell padding" option adds enough spacing to the menu, and you won't need this one.

- **Menu delay.** When you move your mouse off a menu, you may notice a slight delay before the menu disappears. This delay is controlled by the "Menu delay" property. It's specified in milliseconds, so a delay of 1000 means the menu takes 1 second to disappear.

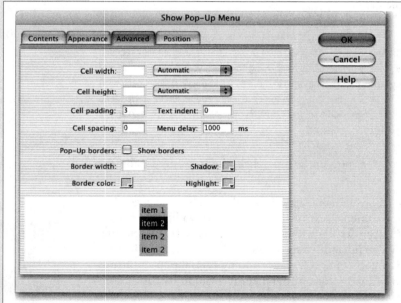

Figure 11-6:
You can tweak the appearance of pop-up menus using the Advanced tab of the Show Pop-Up Menu dialog box. Bear in mind that the preview in the bottom half of the window isn't very accurate. It doesn't show shadow and highlight colors, or any text indents. To get an accurate view, you'll need to close this box and press the F12 key (Option-F12 on the Mac) to preview your new menu in an actual Web browser.

Of course, your first reaction might be: "I don't want no stinkin' delay! Just make the menu disappear when I move my mouse off!"

Unfortunately, if you set the delay *too* low, the pop-up menu won't appear at all. Without any delay, the menu would disappear the instant your mouse moved off the triggering link (the link you originally attached the behavior to), making the menu disappear before you could click your choice. You need some delay to allow enough time to choose from the menu; 500 ms is a good compromise.

- **Borders.** Here's where you get to decide whether any borders appear around each menu item. To turn off borders entirely, turn off the "Show borders" checkbox.

Dreamweaver even lets you specify colors for three different border elements. The Border color affects the outside border—a line that encloses the entire menu. The Shadow color applies to a menu's shadow lines, which appear along the right and bottom edges of the menu, just inside of the outer border. (It's also the color of the lines that separate each menu item.) The Highlight color applies to the borders at the top and left edge of the menu. Together, these colors give a menu a 3-D appearance.

Tip: Web browsers hide any menu items that aren't visible within the available space of a frame. If your page uses frames, therefore, make sure your frame is deep enough to accommodate the expanded menu. (That's a particular concern if you create a nifty navigation bar that sits in a frame at the top of the window.)

POWER USERS' CLINIC

Taking Control of Submenus

Although Dreamweaver lets you set the position of the main pop-up menu, it doesn't offer any controls for positioning submenus. They always appear in the same place: 5 pixels in from the right edge of the menu item that triggers the submenu and 7 pixels below the top.

But you're not stuck with these settings—if you're willing to dig into the HTML of the page.

When you create a pop-up menu, Dreamweaver adds a chunk of JavaScript code to the page. You need to locate a particular line of code, located in the <head> section of the page that looks something like this:

```
window.mm_menu_0514155110_0 = new Menu
("root",188,18,"Arial, Helvetica,
sansserif",
12,"#FFFFFF","#000000","#000000","#FFFFFF
","left","middle",3,0,500,
-5,7,true,true,true,0,true,true);
```

Zero in on the two numbers near the end: –5 and 7. These represent the position for any submenus added to items in the menu. However, in this case, the submenu position is relative to the upper-right corner of the menu. So the –5 means 5 pixels in from the right edge of the menu item, and the 7 means 7 pixels down from the top edge.

Two other useful numbers appear near the beginning of line, right after "new Menu." In this example, they're 188 and 18, but these numbers vary from menu to menu. The 188 stands for the width of each item in the menu, and the 18 is the height. Thus, if you want submenus to appear directly below an item in this menu, replace the –5 with –188 and the 7 with 18.

If you decide to delve into the HTML code in this way, remember that every menu you add—and this includes submenus—adds a line like the one above to your Web page. So make sure you're working on the correct line.

By default, a pop-up menu is positioned to the right of its triggering link, and 10 pixels below. The Position tab lets you change the following:

- **Positioning options.** The Position tab offers four preset positioning options, represented by four buttons. The first button is the default position. The second button places the menu directly *below* the triggering link. The third button places the menu directly *above* the triggering link (good if you're adding the pop-up menu to a link near the bottom of a page). And the fourth button places the menu directly to the *right* of the triggering link.

- **Pixel location.** If none of those four options suits your taste, you can use these controls to pinpoint a location for the menu, expressed in pixels measured from the top-left corner of the triggering link.

  For example, if you enter 0 in the X box (the horizontal measurement), the menu lines up with the left edge of the triggering link. Typing 0 in the Y box (the vertical dimension) produces a menu whose top aligns with the top of the triggering link. Using 0 in *both* boxes places the menu smack-dab on top of the trigger.

  Submenus are unaffected by these settings; they always overlap the right edge of the corresponding main-menu item (Figure 11-4). (If you're up for it, there's an HTML workaround in the box "Taking Control of Submenus" on page 417.)

- **Hide Menu checkbox.** Keep the "Hide Menu on onMouseOut" event turned on. It ensures that the menu disappears when you move your mouse off it.

Open Browser Window

No matter how carefully you design your Web page, chances are it won't look good in every size window. Depending on the resolution of your visitor's monitor and the dimensions of his browser window, your Web page may be forced to squeeze into a window that's 400 pixels wide, or it could be dwarfed by one that's 1200 pixels wide. Designing your Web pages so they look good at a variety of different window sizes is challenging.

It's the Open Browser Window action to the rescue (Figure 11-7). Using this behavior, you can instruct your visitor's browser to open a new window to whatever height and width *you* desire. In fact, you can even dictate what elements the browser window includes. Don't want the toolbar, location bar, or status bar visible? No problem; this action lets you include or exclude any such window chrome.

To open a new browser window, you start, as always, by selecting the tag to which you wish to attach the behavior. You can attach it to any of the tags discussed on pages 408–411, but you'll usually want to add this action to a link with an onClick event, or to the <body> tag with the onLoad event.

Note: Most new browsers have "pop-up blockers." This nifty feature prevents the browser from opening a new browser window unless the visitor initiates the request. In other words, browser windows that are meant to open when a new page is loaded won't, but browser windows that open based on a visitor's action—like clicking a link—will.

Figure 11-7:
You, too, can annoy your friends, neighbors, and Web site customers with these unruly pop-up browser windows. Just add the Open Browser Window action to the <body> tag of your document. Now, when that page loads, a new browser window opens with the ad, announcement, or picture you specify. To be even more annoying, use the onUnload event of the <body> tag to open a new browser window—with the same Web page—when your visitors try to exit the page. They won't be able to get to a different page, and may even encounter system crashes. Now that's annoying! Most current Web browsers, however, prevent these kinds of automatic window-opening tricks.

Once you've selected this action's name from the + menu in the Behaviors panel, you'll see the dialog box shown in Figure 11-8. You have the following settings to make:

- **URL to display.** In this box, type in the URL or path of the Web page, or click Browse and find the Web page on your computer (the latter option is a more foolproof method of ensuring functional links.) If you're loading a Web page on somebody else's site, don't forget to type an *absolute* URL, beginning with *http://* (see page 104).

- **Window width, Window height.** Next, type in the width and height of the new window. These values are measured in pixels; in most browsers, 100×100 pixels is the minimum size. Also, strange visual anomalies may result on your visitors' screens if the width and height you specify here are larger than the available space on their monitors.

- **Attributes.** Turn on the checkboxes for the window elements you want to include in the new window. Figure 11-9 shows the different pieces of a standard browser window.

- **Window name box.** Give the new window a name here (letters and numbers only). If you include spaces or other symbols, Dreamweaver displays an error message and lets you correct the mistake. This name won't actually appear on your Web page, but it's useful for targeting links or actions from the original window.

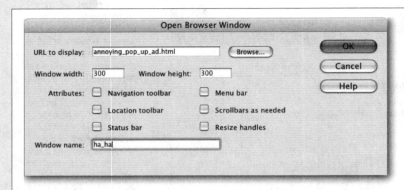

Figure 11-8:
Here, you can define the properties of the new window, including what Web page loads into it, its dimensions, and so on. If you leave the "Window width" and "Window height" properties blank, the new window is the same size as the window it opens from.

Figure 11-9:
The parts of a browser window. Note: The menu bar only appears as part of the browser window on Windows machines. On Macintosh systems, the menu bar appears at the top of the screen and can't be hidden; in addition, the Safari browser won't hide the resize handle or the scroll bars (if they're needed).

Once a new window is open, you can load other Web pages into it from the original page that opened the window; simply use the name you give to the new window as the target of the link. For example, you could add this behavior to the <body> tag of a page so that when the page opens, a small new window also appears, showcasing a photo. You could add links to the main page, that, when clicked, load additional photos into the small window.

If you use more than one Open Browser Window behavior on a single page, make sure to give each new window a unique name. If you don't, you may not get a new window for each Open Browser Window action.

When you click OK, your newly created behavior appears in the Actions list in the Behaviors panel.

Go to URL

The Go to URL action works just like a link, in that it loads a new Web page. However, while links work only when you click them, this action can load a page based on an event *other than* clicking. For instance, you may want to load a Web page when your visitor's cursor merely moves over an image, or when she clicks a particular radio button.

Once you've selected a tag and chosen this action's name from the + menu in the Behaviors panel, you can make these settings in the resulting dialog box:

- **Open in.** If you aren't using frames, only Main Window is listed here. But if you're working in a *frameset* file and have named each of your frames, they're listed in the "Open in" list box. Click the name of the frame where you want the new page to appear.

    URL. Fill in the URL of the page you wish to load. You can use any of the link-specifying tricks described on page 108: type in an absolute URL starting with *http://*, type in a path, or click the Browse button and then select a page from your site.

Jump Menu and Jump Menu Go

Conserving precious visual space on a Web page is a constant challenge for a Web designer. Putting too many buttons, icons, and navigation controls on a page can quickly clutter your presentation and muddle a page's meaning. As sites get larger, so do navigation bars, which can engulf a page in a long column of buttons.

The Pop-Up Menu behavior (see page 412) is one solution. But it requires lengthy JavaScript code and has a few problems of its own (see the box on page 413). A simpler way to add detailed navigation to a site without wasting pixels is to use Dreamweaver's Jump Menu behavior. A *jump menu* is a pop-up menu that lets visitors navigate by choosing from a list of links.

The Jump Menu behavior is listed in the Behaviors panel, but for a simpler, happier life, don't insert it onto your page that way. Instead, use the Insert bar or Insert menu, like this:

1. **Click where you want the jump menu to appear on your Web page.**

   It could be in a table cell at the top of the page, or along the left edge, for example.

2. **Under the Forms tab on the Insert bar, click the Jump Menu icon (see Figure 10-2 on page 363). Or choose Insert → Form → Jump Menu.**

   If you use the Behaviors panel instead, you first have to add a form and insert a menu into it. The Insert Jump Menu object saves you those steps.

Tip: Even though the jump menu uses a pop-up menu, which is a component of a *form*, you don't have to create a form first, as described in Chapter 10. Dreamweaver creates one automatically when you insert a jump menu.

The Jump Menu dialog box opens, as shown in Figure 11-10.

3. **Type an instructive label, like *Select a Destination,* in the text box.**

   What you enter in the text box sets the menu's default choice—the first item listed in the menu when the page loads. Dreamweaver provides two methods for triggering the jump-menu behavior: when the visitor makes a selection from the list—which is an onChange event, since the visitor changes the menu by selecting a new option—or when the user clicks an added Go menu button after making his selection. The second method requires extra effort from the visitor—making a selection *and* clicking a button. The first method, therefore, offers a better visitor experience. But it does mean that you can't include an actual link in the first item in the menu; after all, the behavior is triggered only when a visitor selects an item other than the one currently listed.

   If you do intend to add a Go button, you can skip this step and the next two.

4. **Leave the "When selected, go to URL" box empty.**

   Since the first item in the list is just an instruction, you don't link it to any page.

5. **To add a link, click the + button.**

   Doing so adds another item to the menu.

6. **Type the name of the link in the text field.**

   You're specifying the first link in your pop-up menu.

   The name you type here doesn't have to match the page's title or anchor's name; it's whatever you want your menu to say to represent it. For instance, you can call a menu choice *Home* even if the title of your home page is "Welcome to XYZ Corp."

7. **Enter a URL for this link in the "When selected, go to URL" field.**

   Use any of the usual methods for specifying a link (see page 108).

8. **To add the next link in your pop-up menu, click the + button and repeat steps 6 and 7. Continue until you've added all of the links for this menu.**

   If you want to remove one of the links, select it from the Menu Items list and then click the minus sign (–) button. You can also reorder the list by clicking one of the link names and then clicking the up and down arrow buttons.

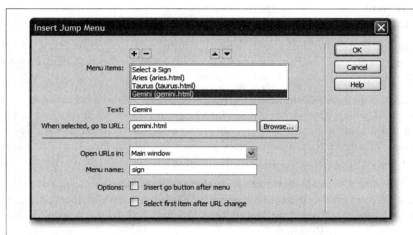

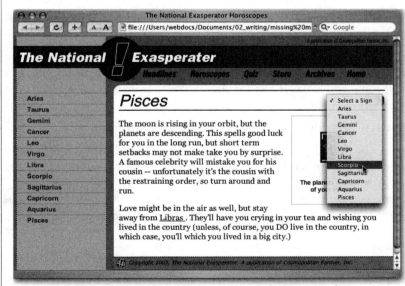

Figure 11-10:
Top: The Insert Jump Menu dialog box shown here is set up so that the onChange event of the <select> tag triggers the Jump Menu action. That is, the Jump Menu behavior works when your visitor selects an item other than the one currently listed.

Bottom: Unless you include the "Insert go button after menu" option, the first item of a jump menu should never be used as a link. Instead, use some descriptive text—such as "Select a Sign"—to let visitors know what the menu does. Then leave the URL blank in the Insert Jump Menu dialog box. When placed on a page, the resulting menu is very compact, but it can offer a long list of pages.

9. **If you're using frames, use the "Open URLs in" pop-up menu to specify a frame in which the indicated Web page should appear.**

    Otherwise, the Main Window option loads links into the entire browser window.

10. **In the "Menu name" box, give the menu a name.**

    This step is optional; you can also just accept the name Dreamweaver proposes. Since Dreamweaver uses this name only for the internal purposes of the Java-Script that drives this behavior, it doesn't appear anywhere on the page.

11. **If you want a Go button to appear beside your jump menu, turn on "Insert go button after menu."**

    You need to use this option only when the jump menu is in one frame and is loading pages into another, or when you want to make the first item in your jump menu a link instead of an instruction.

    When you include a Go button, Dreamweaver adds a small form button next to the menu, which your visitor can click to jump to whatever link is listed in the menu. But most of the time, your visitors will never get a chance to use this Go button. Whenever they make a selection from the menu, their browsers automatically jump to the new page without waiting for a click on the Go button.

    The Go button's handy, however, when there's no selection to make. For example, if the first item in the menu is a link, your visitors won't be able to select it; it's *already* selected when the page with the menu loads. In this case, a Go button is the only way to trigger the "jump."

12. **If you want to reset the menu after each jump (so that it once again shows the first menu command), turn on "Select first item after URL change."**

    Here's another option that's useful only when the jump menu is in one frame, loading pages into another frame. Resetting the menu so that it shows its default command makes it easy for your visitor to make another selection when ready.

13. **Click OK to apply the action and close the Jump Menu dialog box.**

    Your newly created pop-up menu appears on your Web page, and the newly created behavior appears in the Actions list in the Behaviors panel.

Tip: To edit a jump menu, click the menu in your document and then, in the Behaviors panel, double-click the Jump Menu action in the Actions list. The settings dialog box reappears. At this point, you can change any of the options described in the previous steps, except you can't add a Go button to a jump menu that didn't have one to begin with. Click OK when you're finished.

The Jump Menu Go action (available on the Behaviors panel) is useful only if you didn't add a Go menu in step 11 earlier. In this case, if there's a jump menu on the page and you wish to add a Go button to it, click next to the menu, add a form button, and then attach this behavior to it. (For more on working with forms, see Chapter 10.)

Check Browser

Dinosaur alert! This behavior was once useful. As noted earlier, not all Web browsers work the same way. The Check Browser behavior lets you shuffle visitors off to different pages based on the type of browser they have. For example, you could send a Netscape Navigator 4 browser off to a simplified version of your site, letting it bypass pages that included more complex code that Navigator 4 simply didn't understand.

But since this behavior was put into Dreamweaver, the browser landscape has changed significantly. Netscape Navigator 4 is dead (except for one lone computer locked in a fallout shelter in Appalachia), and many new browsers—Firefox, Opera, Safari, to name a few—are in use. Check Browser only sniffs out Netscape and Internet Explorer, and just doesn't work in today's multibrowser world. You're better off skipping this one.

Image Actions

Images make Web pages stand out. But adding Dreamweaver behaviors can make those same images come to life.

Preload Images

It takes time for images to load over the Internet. A 16 KB image, for instance, takes about 4 seconds to download over a standard dial-up modem. However, once a Web browser loads an image, it stores the image in its *cache,* as described on page 529, so that it loads extremely quickly if a page requires the same graphic again. The Preload Images action takes advantage of this fact by downloading an image or images and storing them in the browser's cache, *even before* they're actually needed.

Preloading is especially important when using mouse rollover effects on a Web page (see page 144). When a visitor moves the mouse over a particular button, it may, for example, appear to light up. If you couldn't preload the image, then the lit up graphic wouldn't even begin to download until the cursor rolled over the button. The resulting delay would make your button feel less like a rollover than a layover.

In general, you won't need to apply this action by hand, since Dreamweaver adds it automatically when you use the Insert Rollover Image command (see page 144). But there are exceptions, such as when you use the Preload Images action to load graphics that appear on *other* pages in your site.

For example, suppose you build a graphics-heavy Web site. People hate to wait too long for a Web page to load, but they're slightly more patient when waiting for the *first* page of a site to load. You could capitalize on that fact by adding a Preload

Images action to the body of a home page (or even a page that says "Loading Web Site") that preloads most of the site's graphics. Be careful, though: if any page preloads too many images, even the most patient Web surfer may not stay around to watch the show. Remember to refer to the download stats listed in the document's status bar for the size of your Web page, as discussed on page 528.

Tip: If you use background images in your style sheets, the Preload Images behavior may also come in handy. If you swap a background image using the CSS Hover property (see page 187), you'll notice a delay when the graphic loads the first time. Use the Preload Image behavior to rid you pages of that disorienting delay.

To add the Preload Images action, select the tag to which you want the behavior attached. Most often you'll use the <body> tag with an onLoad event.

If you've added rollover images or a navigation bar to your page, this behavior may already be in the <body> of the page. In this case, just double-click the Preload Images action that's already listed in the Behaviors panel. If not, just choose this action's name from the + menu in the Behaviors panel. Either way, you're now offered the Preload Images dialog box.

Click the Browse button and navigate to the *graphics* file that you wish to use for preloading purposes, or type in the path or (if the graphic is on the Web already) the absolute URL of the graphic. Dreamweaver adds the image to the Preload Images list. If you want to preload another image, click the + button and repeat the previous step. Continue until you've added all the images you want to preload.

You can also remove an image from the list by selecting it and then clicking the minus sign (–) button. (Be careful not to delete any of the images that may be required for a rollover effect you've already created—the Undo command doesn't work here.)

When you click OK, you return to your document; your new action appears in the Behaviors panel. Here you can edit it, if you like, by changing the event that triggers it. But unless you're trying to achieve some special effect, you'll usually use the onLoad event of the <body> tag.

That's all there is to it. When your page loads in somebody's browser, the browser continues to load and store those graphics quietly in the background. They'll appear almost instantly when they're required by a rollover or even a shift to another Web page on your site that incorporates the graphics you specified.

Swap Image

The Swap Image action exchanges one image on your page for another. (See the end of this section for detail on Swap Image's sibling behavior, Swap Image Restore.)

Simple as that process may sound, swapping images is one of the most visually exciting things you can do on a Web page. Swapping images works something like rollover images, except that a mouse click or mouse pass isn't required to trigger them. In fact, you can use *any* tag and event combination to trigger the Swap Image action. For instance, you can create a mini slide show by listing the names of pictures down the left side of a Web page and inserting an image in the middle of the page. Add a Swap Image action to each slide name, so that the appropriate picture swaps in when your visitor clicks any one of the names.

To make this behavior work, your Web page must already contain a starter image, and the images to be swapped in must be the same width and height as the original graphic. If they aren't, the browser resizes and distorts the subsequent pictures to fit the "frame" dictated by the original.

To add the Swap Image behavior, start by choosing the *starter image* file that you want to include on the page. (Choose Insert → Image, or use any of the other techniques described in Chapter 5.) Give your image a name in the Property inspector, so that JavaScript knows which image to swap out. (JavaScript doesn't really care about the original graphic image itself, but rather about the space that it occupies on the page.)

Tip: You can swap more than one image using a single Swap Image behavior (Figure 11-11). Using this trick, not only can a button change to another graphic when you mouse over it, but also any number of other graphics on the page can change at the same time. An asterisk (*) next to the name of an image in the Swap Image dialog box (see Figure 11-12) indicates that the behavior will swap in a new image for that particular graphic. In the example in Figure 11-12, you can see that two images—*horoscope* and *ad*, both marked by asterisks—swap with a single action.

Now select the tag to which you want the Swap Image behavior attached. When you choose this action's name from the Behaviors panel, the Swap Image dialog box appears, as shown in Figure 11-12:

- **Images.** From the list, click the name of the starter image.

- **Set source to.** Here's where you specify the *image* file that you want to swap in. If it's a graphics file in your site folder, click Browse to find and open it. You can also specify a path or an absolute URL to another Web site, as described on page 112.

- **Preload images.** Preloading ensures that the swap action isn't slowed down while the graphic downloads from the Internet.

- **Restore images onMouseOut.** You get this option only when you've applied this behavior to a link. When you turn this checkbox on, moving the mouse *off* the link makes the previous image reappear.

Swap Image Restore

The Swap Image Restore action returns the last set of swapped images to its original state. Most designers use it in conjunction with a rollover button, so that the button returns to its original appearance when the visitor rolls the cursor off the button.

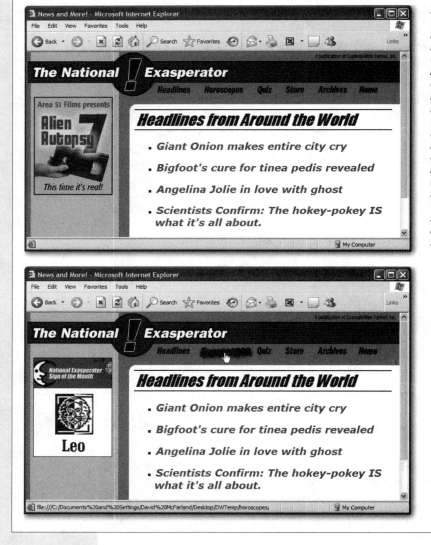

Figure 11-11:
You can use the swap image behavior to make multiple graphics change with a single mouse-over. A humble Web page (top) comes to life when the mouse is moved over the Horoscopes button (bottom). Not only does the graphic for the Horoscopes button change, but the ad on the left sidebar is also replaced with a tantalizing look at the "Sign of the Month." This type of effect, sometimes called a disjoint rollover, is easy with the Swap Image action.

You'll probably never find a need to add this behavior yourself. Dreamweaver automatically adds it when you insert a rollover image and when you choose the Restore Images onMouseOut option when setting up a regular Swap Image behavior (see

Figure 11-12). But, if you prefer, you can add the Swap Restore Image behavior to other tag and event combinations, using the general routine described on page 403. (The Swap Image Restore dialog box offers no options to set.)

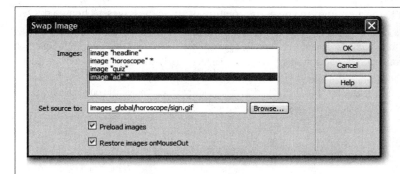

Figure 11-12:
Some actions, like the Swap Image action, can automatically add behaviors to a Web page. In this case, the "Preload images" and "Restore images onMouseOut" options actually add a Swap Image Restore action to the onMouseOut event of the currently selected tag, and a Preload Images action to the onLoad event of the <body> tag.

Set Navigation Bar Image

The Navigation Bar object's enticing name tricks many people into thinking that they can quickly and easily build a useful navigation bar for their sites. They can, sort of, but the object adds lots of additional JavaScript code that's easily avoided by simply using Dreamweaver's "Rollover image" feature. The Navigation Bar is really a tool for those outdated dinosaurs—frames-based Web sites (see the box on page 112).

You're better off avoiding the Navigation Bar object and its companion behavior.

Message Behaviors

Communication is why we build Web sites: to tell a story, sell a product, or provide useful information that can entertain and inform our visitors. Dreamweaver can enhance this communication process with actions that provide dynamic feedback. From subtle messages in a browser's status bar to dialog boxes that command a visitor's attention, Dreamweaver offers numerous ways to respond, in words, to the things your visitors are doing on your Web pages.

Popup Message

Use the Popup Message behavior to send important messages to your visitors, as shown in Figure 11-13. Your visitor must click OK to close the dialog box. Because a pop-up message demands immediate attention, reserve this behavior for important announcements.

To create a pop-up message, select the tag to which you want the behavior attached. For example, adding this action to the <body> tag with an onLoad event causes a message to appear when a visitor first loads the page; adding the same behavior to a link with an onClick event makes the message appear when the visitor clicks the link. (You've seen an example of the pop-up message used with the form-validation behavior on page 382.)

From the Add Action menu (+ button) in the Behaviors panel, choose Popup Message. In the Popup Message dialog box, type the message that you want to appear in the dialog box. (Check the spelling and punctuation carefully; nothing says "amateur" like poorly written error messages, and Dreamweaver's spell-checking feature isn't smart enough to check the spelling of these messages.) Then click OK.

Tip: A note to JavaScript programmers: Your message can also include any valid JavaScript expression. To embed JavaScript code into a message, place it inside braces ({ }). If you want to include the current time and date in a message, for example, add this: {*new Date( )*}. If you just want to display a brace in the message, add a backslash, like this: \{. The backslash lets Dreamweaver know that you *really* do want a { character, and not just a bunch of JavaScript, to appear in the dialog box.

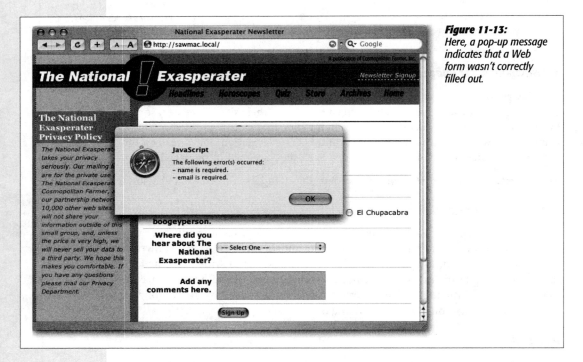

Figure 11-13:
Here, a pop-up message indicates that a Web form wasn't correctly filled out.

Set Text of Status Bar

Pop-up messages, like those described above, require your visitors to drop everything and read them. For less urgent messages, consider the Set Text of Status Bar behavior. It displays a message in the status bar of a browser window—the strip at the bottom of the window. You can add a message to a link, for example, that lets surfers know where the link takes them. Or you could set things up so that when a visitor moves the cursor over a photograph, copyright information appears in the window's status bar.

Note: The Set Text of Status Bar effect was common in the early days of the Web, but its popularity has waned for several reasons: People don't always notice their status bars. The bar is down at the bottom of the browser window and doesn't change dramatically—flash, blink, or sing, for example—when text appears. What's worse, visitors can hide the status bar and *never* see your message. And finally, your message is likely to be missed for another reason: the behavior doesn't work in many newer browsers like Opera, Safari, and Firefox.

To apply the Set Text of Status bar action, select a tag (a very common example is a link [<a>] tag with the onMouseOver event); choose this behavior's name from the Add Action menu (+ button) in the Behaviors panel; and then, in the Set Text of Status Bar dialog box, type your message. Keep the message short, since browsers cut off any words that don't fit in the status bar. Your message can also include any valid JavaScript expression, exactly as described in the Tip on page 430.

Set Text of Text Field

Normally, a text field in a form (see page 370) is blank. It sits on the page and waits for someone to type into it. The Set Text of Text Field behavior, by contrast, can save your visitors time by filling in form fields automatically with answers that have become obvious.

For instance, imagine you've created a Web survey that has a series of questions. The first question might require a yes or no answer, along the lines of "Do you own a computer?" And you've provided radio buttons for Yes or No. The second question might be "What brand is it?" followed by a text field where your visitors can type in the computer brand.

But if someone answers "No" to question 1, there's no point in her typing a response to the second question. To help keep things moving along, you can set the second question's text field so that it says, "Please skip to Question 3." To do so, simply add the Set Text of Text Field action to the onClick event of the No radio button of Question 1.

To apply the Set Text of Text Field action, make sure your page includes a form and at least one text field. Because this behavior changes the text in a form text field, you won't get very far without the proper HTML on the page.

Select the tag to which you want the behavior attached. In the example above, you'd attach the behavior to the form's No radio button with an onClick event. However, you aren't limited to just form elements. Any of the tags discussed on pages 408–411 work.

Tip: You can also use this behavior to *erase* text in a field. This way, you can present your visitor with a text field that's already filled out with explanatory text like "Please type your name in this box." When someone clicks in the field, triggering the field's onFocus event, the box empties itself in readiness to accept input.

When you choose Set Text of Text Field from the + menu in the Behaviors panel, the Set Text of Text Field dialog box opens. Make the following changes:

- **Text field.** The menu lists the names of every text field in the form; choose the name of the text field whose default text you'll want to change. (See Chapter 10 for the full story on building online forms in Dreamweaver.)

- **New text.** Type the text you want that field to display. Make sure you don't make the message longer than the space available in the field.

    (Once again, your message can include a JavaScript expression, as described in the Tip on page 430.)

Set Text of Layer

Another way to get your message across is to change the text that appears in a layer (see Chapter 7). This action has an added benefit: it lets you use HTML code to *format* the message that appears in the layer. (Actually, the "Set Text" part of this action's name is a bit misleading, since this action also lets you include HTML code, images, forms, and other objects in the layer—not just text.)

As always, you start by selecting a tag. In this case, you could select a link, for example, so that moving the mouse over the link changes the text in the layer to read, "Click here to see our exclusive photos of unexplained phenomena."

When you choose this action's name from the + menu in the Behaviors panel, you get these controls in a dialog box:

- **Layer.** The menu lists the names of every layer on the Web page (Chapter 8); choose the name of the layer whose text you want to set. (This list includes not just layers created using Dreamweaver's Layer tool but *any* CSS style that uses absolute positioning and an ID selector, as described on page 296.)

- **New HTML.** In this field, type the text you wish to add to the layer. You can type in a plain-text message, for example, or use HTML source code to control the content's formatting.

    For instance, if you want a word to appear bold in the layer, place the word inside a pair of strong tags like this: important. Or if you'd rather not mess around with HTML code, you can also design the content using Dreamweaver's visual Design view—that is, right out there in your document window. Copy the HTML source from the Code view (Chapter 9), and then paste it into this action's New HTML field.

Tip: To create a similar effect to a rollover button, you could add another "Set Text of Layer" behavior to the same link, include the HTML that originally appears inside the layer, and change the event to onMouse-Out. So when the visitor mouses over the link, the layer changes to one message, but when he mouses off, it reverts back to the original message.

Text of Frame

Like the Set Text of Layer action, the Set Text of Frame action replaces the content of a specified frame with HTML you specify. It's like loading a new Web page into a frame, only faster. Since the HTML is already part of the page that contains this action, your visitors don't have to wait for the code to arrive from the Internet.

To apply the Set Text of Frame action, create frameset and frame pages (for more about frames, see the online chapter about frames, which you can find at *www. sawmac.com/dw8/frames.pdf*). When you select a tag in any of the frames—even the one whose content you intend to replace—and then choose this action from the + menu in the Behaviors panel, the Set Text of Frame dialog box opens:

- **Frame.** The menu lists the names of every available frame. Choose the name of the frame where you want the text to appear.

- **New HTML.** Type the text you want the frame to show. You can type in a plain-text message, or use HTML source code to control the content's formatting: <strong> like this </strong> for bold, for example.

  You can also copy the HTML currently in the frame by clicking the Get Current HTML button, which copies the HTML source into the New HTML Field. Once it's there, you can modify it as you see fit. Use this technique if, for example, you want to keep much of the formatting and HTML of the original page. Be careful, however. This action can only update the *body* of the frame; any code in the <head> of the frame is lost. You can't add behaviors, meta tags, or other <head> content to the frame.

- **Preserve Background Color.** This option ensures that the background color of the frame won't change when the new text appears.

Multimedia Actions

Multimedia, from background sounds to fully interactive Flash movies, can add a depth of experience that goes well beyond basic HTML. Several Dreamweaver actions let you play sounds, Flash movies, and Shockwave movies. (For more information on incorporating multimedia elements into your Web pages, see Chapter 12.)

Control Shockwave or Flash

Flash and Shockwave have become standard elements of many Web sites, and as more and more sites combine Flash and Shockwave movies with regular HTML, it becomes increasingly useful to be able to control how those movies play. With the Control Shockwave or Flash action, regular HTML objects can control the playback of a movie. For example, you could add a set of small, VCR-like control buttons—Play, Stop, and Rewind—to a page. These graphics—regular HTML on the page—could control the playback of a Flash or Shockwave movie:

1. **Add a Flash or Shockwave movie to the page.**

   See Chapter 12 for details.

2. **Select the movie and name it in the Property inspector (see page 449).**

   Dreamweaver uses this name to identify the movie in the JavaScript that runs the behavior.

3. **Select the tag to which you want the behavior attached.**

   This tag can be a dummy link (see page 401) attached to a button graphic. Using the onClick event would help simulate the function of a button.

4. **From the + menu in the Behaviors panel, choose Control Shockwave or Flash.**

   The Control Shockwave or Flash dialog box opens, as shown in Figure 11-14.

Figure 11-14:
The Control Shockwave or Flash action can only choose one type of control per action. So if you want to play a movie from a particular frame, you would need to add two actions: the first would use the "Go to frame" option, and the second would use the Play option to start the movie.

5. **Choose how you want this action to control the movie.**

   You have four options for controlling a movie: Play (starts the movie from the current frame), Stop, Rewind (to the first frame), or Go to Frame (jumps to a frame you specify by typing its number into the "Go to frame" field).

6. **Click OK.**

Play Sound

The Play Sound action lets you embed a *sound* file in a Web page and trigger its playback using any available event.

That's the theory, anyway. Here's another behavior you should avoid. Because browsers don't have a built-in sound feature, they rely on plug-ins to play *sound* files. But JavaScript (that is, Dreamweaver behaviors) can't control some plug-ins, and some plug-ins can handle only certain types of *sound* files. The bottom line is that in all likelihood, you may wind up with a silent Web page.

If sound is absolutely essential for your Web page, you're better off using a Flash or Shockwave movie (see Chapter 12) and including a Control Shockwave or Flash Movie behavior (described in the previous section).

Check Plugin

Flash animations, QuickTime movies, and Shockwave games can add a lot of excitement to any Web site. Unfortunately, they don't work unless your visitors have downloaded and installed the corresponding browser plug-ins (see page 147 for more on this topic).

The Check Plugin behavior can detect whether or not your visitor's browser has the required plug-in installed (Flash, Shockwave, LiveAudio, Netscape Media Player, or QuickTime)—and if not, it can redirect your visitor to a special page for such less-fortunate Web surfers. Again, this behavior works in theory. In reality, this behavior doesn't work with Internet Explorer—the most popular Web browser—except in the case of the Flash and Shockwave players. That's because Internet Explorer doesn't have an easy way to determine which plug-ins are installed. In the case of Flash and Shockwave, however, Dreamweaver adds some additional code in VBScript, a language understood by Internet Explorer.

Because of this limitation, it's really best to use this behavior just for determining if the plug-ins for these Macromedia technologies are installed, and skip the other plug-in options.

You can attach this behavior to the <body> tag and trigger it with the onLoad event. For example, you may want to include this behavior on your home page to immediately detect if the Flash plug-in is installed in your visitor's browser; if it is, you can either send visitors off to your crazy Flash page, or keep them on the home page. Alternatively, you could add this behavior to a link with an onClick event. That way, when your visitors click the link, they see one page if they have the plug-in, and another if they don't.

When you choose Check Plugin from the + menu in the Behaviors panel, a dialog box (Figure 11-15) lets you make the following settings:

- **Plugin.** From the pop-up menu, choose the plug-in's name, or type its name in the Enter field.

  The plug-in options in the menu are Flash, Shockwave, LiveAudio, Netscape Media Player, and QuickTime. Only the Flash and Shockwave options work with Internet Explorer, and some don't work with other browsers. In Safari, for example, this behavior doesn't work for detecting Apple's QuickTime player.

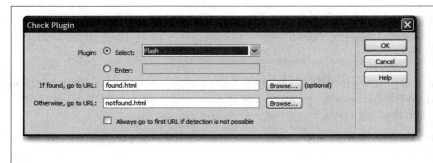

Figure 11-15:
If you leave the "If found, go to URL" field empty, the visitor who has the correct plug-in installed stays right there on the same page. Use this arrangement when you apply the action to a <body> tag with an onLoad event and the page contains the plug-in object.

- **If found, go to URL/Otherwise, go to URL.** Using these text fields, specify the Web pages to which your visitor is directed if the plug-in is, or isn't, installed.

  You can indicate these pages just as you would any link (see page 108). For example, if the Web page is part of the site you're working on, click Browse to locate and open the Web page document.

  The "Otherwise, go to URL" page could let visitors know that they need a plug-in to view the site. Furthermore, it should offer a link to the site where the plug-in can be found.

- **Always go to first URL if detection isn't possible.** Remember that Internet Explorer can't detect all plug-ins. It wouldn't make sense to send Internet Explorer people to a "You don't have the correct plug-in" page when they may very well have the plug-in installed. If you turn on this checkbox, your Web page assumes that the plug-in is installed if it can't determine otherwise.

Tip: However you plan to use this action, always make sure that you give visitors who don't have the plug-in a way to quickly and easily download and install it, so they can return to your site to bask in the glorious multimedia experience you've created for them.

Layer Actions

Dreamweaver layers (called "absolute positioned divs" in CSS-speak) let you place Web page elements with absolute precision. Since you can control layers using JavaScript, Dreamweaver includes several behaviors for manipulating layers.

Show-Hide Layers

Do you ever stare in awe when a magician makes a handkerchief disappear into thin air? Now you, too, can perform sleight of hand on your own Web pages, making layers disappear and reappear with ease. Dreamweaver's Show-Hide Layers behavior is a piece of JavaScript programming that lets you make your own magic.

Show-Hide Layers takes advantage of the Visibility property. You can use it for things like adding pop-up tooltips to your Web page, so that when a visitor's mouse moves over a link, a layer appears offering a detailed explanation of where the link goes (see Figure 11-16).

The following steps show how to create this effect:

1. **Add layers to your Web page using the techniques described in Chapter 8. Use the Visibility setting (page 299) to specify how you want each layer to look when the page loads.**

   If you want a layer to be visible at first and then disappear when your visitor performs a specific action, set the layer to Visible. If you want it to appear only *after* some specific event, set it to Hidden.

Note: You don't have to use Dreamweaver's Layer tool to take advantage of this behavior; any CSS *ID type* style that uses absolute positioning works. (See page 188 for more on IDs and page 296 for more on absolute positioning.)

2. **In the tag selector, click the tag to which you want the behavior attached.**

   Web designers often attach behaviors to link (<a>) tags. But you can also attach them to images or, as in Figure 11-16, to an image map, which defines hotspots on a single graphic.

Figure 11-16:
Using Dreamweaver's Show-Hide Layers behavior, you can make layers appear and disappear. In this example at www. safetreekids.net/ awesome/parts.html, several layers lay hidden on the page. When a visitor moves the mouse over different parts of the tree cross-section, informative graphics (each placed in a hidden layer) suddenly appear. Moving the mouse away returns the layer to its hidden state. Notice how the information bubble overlaps the tree image and the text above it—a dead giveaway that this page uses layers.

   To create this effect, attach two behaviors to each hotspot in the document window (that is, to each <area> tag in HTML): one to show the layer, using the onMouseOver event, and one to hide the layer, using the onMouseOut event.

Note: If this is all Greek to you, see page 142 for more on image maps and hotspots.

3. **If it isn't already open, choose Window → Behaviors to open the Behaviors panel.**

   The Behaviors panel (as pictured in Figure 11-1) appears. It lets you add, remove, and modify behaviors.

4. **Click the + button on the panel. Select Show-Hide Layers from the menu.**

The Show-Hide Layers dialog box appears (see Figure 11-17). You'll use this box to tell Dreamweaver what layer you intend to work with first.

5. **Click a layer in the list of named layers.**

Here's an example of why it's useful to give your layers descriptive names. It's difficult to remember which layer is which when all have the Dreamweaver default names (Layer1, Layer2, and so on).

6. **Choose a Visibility setting for the layer by clicking one of the three buttons: Show, Hide, or Default.**

You're now determining what happens to the layer when someone interacts with the tag you selected in step 2. Show makes the layer visible, Hide hides the layer, and Default sets the layer's Visibility property to the browser's default value (usually the same as the Inherit value described on page 294).

The choice you selected appears in parentheses next to the layer's name, as shown in Figure 11-17.

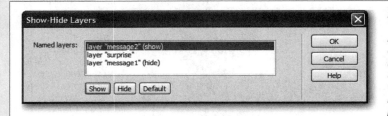

Figure 11-17:
This box lets you hide or show any layer on the page. In fact, you can control multiple layers at once. Here, the "message2" layer appears, while the layer "message1" disappears, when the behavior is triggered. The layer "surprise" is unaffected by this particular action.

7. **If you like, select another layer and then apply another visibility option.**

A single Show-Hide Layers action can affect several layers at once. A single action can even make some visible and others invisible. (If you apply an action to a layer by mistake, select the same option again to remove it from the layer.)

8. **Click OK to apply the behavior.**

The Show-Hide Layers action is now listed in the Behaviors panel, as is the event that triggers it.

Once you've added Show-Hide Layers, you can preview the behavior in a Web browser (Dreamweaver can't display behaviors by itself). Like other Dreamweaver behaviors, you can edit or delete this action; see page 405.

Draggable and Animated Layers

Dreamweaver includes a few other behaviors for working with layers: one—the Drag Layer behavior—lets you create pages with layers that you can freely position anywhere on the Web page (think interactive jigsaw puzzle), and another—the Timeline—lets you create animations—letting your layers travel freely around a page. Both of these were cool behaviors in their day, but they haven't been updated for years. Not only do they add lots and lots of JavaScript code that really weighs down your Web page, but they're also based on really old code that isn't guaranteed to work in any new browser. In fact, Macromedia even recognized that the code was so old; when they first released Dreamweaver MX 2004, they temporarily removed the animation features. (The few, die-hard fans of the animation tools raised such a ruckus that Macromedia put them back in.)

At any rate, the tools still sort of work. If you're interested in them, you'll find instructions on how to use them online at *www.sawmac.com/dw8/*.

Advanced Actions

Dreamweaver has two advanced behaviors that let you call custom JavaScript functions and change the properties of various HTML elements. Both of these actions require familiarity with JavaScript and HTML (Chapter 9). Unlike the other Dreamweaver behaviors, these two can easily generate browser errors if used incorrectly.

Call JavaScript

You can use the Call JavaScript behavior to execute a single line of JavaScript code or to call a JavaScript function that you've added to the <head> section of your Web page.

When you select a tag and choose this behavior's name from the Behaviors panel, the Call JavaScript dialog box opens. If you want to execute a single line of JavaScript code, simply type it in. For instance, if you wanted to make the browser window close, you would type *window.close( )*. If you want to call a JavaScript function, type the function name, like this: *myFunction( )*.

POWER USERS' CLINIC

Closing Browser Windows with the Call JavaScript Behavior

Suppose you've added an Open Browser Window behavior to your home page, so that when visitors come to your site, a small window opens, displaying a Web page that advertises some new feature of your site.

After they've read the ad, your visitors will want to close the window and continue visiting your site. Why not make it easy for them by adding a "Close this Window" button?

To do so, simply add a graphic button—text works fine, too—and then add a dummy (null) link to it (that is, in the

Property inspector, type *javascript:;* into the Link field). Next, add the Call JavaScript behavior; in the Call JavaScript window that appears, type the following line of JavaScript code: *window.close( )*.

Finally, after you click OK, make sure that the event is set to onClick in the Behaviors panel.

That's all there is to it. The link you've added to the pop-up window offers a working Close button.

Change Property

The Change Property action can dynamically alter the value of a property or change the style of any of the following HTML tags: <div>, <span>, <img>, <form>, <textarea>, or <select>. It can also change properties for radio buttons, checkboxes, text fields, and password fields on forms (see Chapter 10). As with the previous behavior, this one requires a good knowledge of HTML, CSS, and Java-Script. Dreamweaver's built-in HTML, CSS, and JavaScript references (see page 353) can help you get up to speed.

Select a tag, choose this behavior's name from the + menu in the Behaviors panel, and then fill in the following parts of the Change Property dialog box (see Figure 11-18):

- **Type of object.** This pop-up menu lists the 11 HTML tags that this behavior can control. Choose the type of object whose property you wish to change.

Note: Ignore the <layer> option in the "Type of object" menu. It's a really old tag that was only ever supported in Netscape 4.

- **Named object.** From this pop-up menu, choose the name of the object you want to modify. Names are more common for form elements. You'll more often use an ID (see page 188) to identify a <div> tag.

- **Property.** Choose the property you want to change (or, if you know enough about JavaScript and CSS, just type the property's name in the Enter field). Any of the options in the menu that begin with "style" refer to CSS style properties. For example, "style.fontFamily" refers to the Font-family property discussed on page 192.

    Ignore all but the IE 4 option in the right-side menu—the other browsers listed are uncommon, and incompatible with current browsers. The IE 4 option actually works with IE 5 and IE 6 as well as Firefox and Safari, so it's really more versatile than its name suggests.

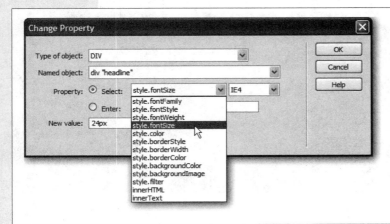

Figure 11-18:
Caution: The Change Property behavior requires a bit of knowledge about HTML, JavaScript, and CSS. You'll find that modern browsers like Firefox, Safari, and Opera understand all but the style.filter property, which works only in Internet Explorer. In addition, Firefox doesn't understand the innerText option. The options beginning with the word "style" refer to CSS properties. For example, style.backgroundImage is the same as the Background Image property discussed on page 197.

- **New value.** Type the new value you wish to set for this property. This value should be appropriate to the type of property you'll be changing. For example, if you're changing a background color, the value should be a color, like #FF0066. Many of the options in the Property menu refer to CSS properties, so you'll find that the different possible values listed for the different CSS properties in Chapter 6 should work. For example, the *style.fontWeight* property is the CSS Font Weight property (page 194), so you could enter a value of "bold" to change text in an object (inside a <div> tag, for instance) to bold.

Creating an External JavaScript Library

You'll use some Dreamweaver behaviors constantly. The basic rollover image, for example, is so useful for navigation bars, you may end up putting it on every page of your site.

Unfortunately, each time you add a behavior to a page, Dreamweaver adds lines of JavaScript code as well—and more code means slower downloads.

One way to decrease download time is to put frequently used JavaScript programs into a separate file containing nothing but JavaScript, and then link that file to each page that uses the script. Once your visitors' Web browsers load and cache this *JavaScript library* file, they don't have to waste time loading it again. Every page in your site that uses, say, Dreamweaver's Swap Image behavior needs just a single line linking it to the JavaScript file, instead of lines and lines of code.

Dreamweaver doesn't create external JavaScript library files automatically, but you can create your own for any Dreamweaver behavior you use frequently. The following steps demonstrate the process of creating a JavaScript file containing all the code Dreamweaver inserts for rollover images.

Note: In this context, *library* simply refers to a file of frequently used programming code. A JavaScript library file isn't related to Dreamweaver's Library tool, described in Chapter 16.

---

1. **Create a new, blank Web page.**

   Since you're going to copy and paste chunks of code, you can see what you're doing better if you start fresh with a new page.

2. **Insert a rollover image.**

   (For a refresher on these steps, see page 144.)

   Dreamweaver adds a bunch of JavaScript code to the page.

3. **Choose View → Code.**

   Dreamweaver shifts into Code view, where you'll locate and copy the JavaScript for the *library* file.

4. **Scroll to the top of the page and look for the following code: <script language="JavaScript" type="text/JavaScript">.**

   This code marks the beginning of the JavaScript. Everything between this tag and the closing </script> tag is the JavaScript code you want.

5. **Select and copy all of the code between the script tags.**

   You should be copying four different *functions* (commands): MM_swapImg-Restore, MM_preloadImages, MM_findObj, and MM_swapImage. (Skip the HTML comments, <!-- and -->. They're HTML, not JavaScript, and don't belong in a JavaScript file like the one you'll create next.)

Note: The names of Macromedia's JavaScript programs begin with MM—for example, MM_swapImage.

---

6. **Choose File → New and click the General tab.**

   The New Document window appears with a list of possible document types.

7. **From the Category list, select Basic Page; from the Basic Page list, choose Java-Script. Click Create.**

   You've just created a blank new "JavaScript" file (technically, it's just an empty text document).

8. **Paste the Code you copied in step 5 into the document.**

   There isn't any HTML in this file (and don't add any) because it's a JavaScript file.

9. **Save the file to your site.**

   Name your JavaScript library anything you want—*rollover.js* or *shared.js,* for example. You can go on to paste other JavaScript functions into the file as well. If you use, say, the Popup Message behavior on most pages of your site as well, by all means, include code for that in the library, too.

Even though Dreamweaver can't create external JavaScript libraries itself, it *does* recognize Dreamweaver behaviors inside of any JavaScript file you create. This is a great feature, because once you link the JavaScript file to a page, you can add a behavior to the page and—as long as the behavior's code is in the file—Dreamweaver doesn't add any additional programming code to the page.

Note: This tactic works only with *Dreamweaver* behaviors. If you use a third-party behavior (see page 670), Dreamweaver adds that behavior's code to the page even if the exact code is in a linked external JavaScript file.

Once you've created your JavaScript library file, it's time to link your Web pages to it. Here's how:

1. **Open a page you want to add the behavior to.**

   For example, open a page that will contain rollover images whose code is stored in the JavaScript file.

2. **Make sure you're in Design view (View → Design). Choose View → Head Content.**

   Dreamweaver displays everything that appears in the <head> portion of the page.

3. **Choose Insert → HTML → Script Objects → Script.**

   The Insert Script window opens. This window lets you add your own Java-Script commands to a page, or link to an external JavaScript file.

4. **Click the folder icon, to the right of the Source box, and then locate and select the JavaScript file you created earlier.**

   This is the familiar "browse to file" technique you use throughout Dreamweaver to link to Web pages, graphics, style sheets and, yes, JavaScript files.

5. **Click OK to close the Insert Script window.**

   Dreamweaver links the file to the page. Whenever the page is loaded into a Web browser, all of the JavaScript commands in the external file also load.

Now you can add rollovers to your page without adding any additional JavaScript code, resulting in slimmer files and faster downloads.

Adding More Behaviors

Dreamweaver's behaviors can open a new world of interactivity. Even if you don't understand the complexities of JavaScript and cross-browser programming, you can easily add powerful and interesting effects that add spice to your Web visitors' experience.

Dreamweaver comes with the preprogrammed behaviors described in this chapter, but you can download many additional behaviors from Macromedia's Exchange Web site (*www.macromedia.com/exchange*) or any of the Web sites mentioned on page 673. Once you've downloaded them, you can easily add them to Dreamweaver, as described in Chapter 19.

Flash, Shockwave, and Other Multimedia

With Cascading Style Sheets (Chapter 6), Dreamweaver behaviors (Chapter 11), and images (Chapter 5), you can bring your Web pages to life with interactivity and animation. But as you may have noticed, more and more Web pages these days blink, sing, and dance with sound, video, and advanced animation.

You can create these effects too, but you'll need outside help from programs like Flash (see Figure 12-1), Director, or Java, all of which are designed to create complex multimedia presentations. Dreamweaver provides powerful tools for adding these external media files and embedding them within your Web pages.

Four warnings, however. First, while all of the technologies discussed in this chapter let you expand your Web pages into new and exciting territory, they also require that your site visitors have external applications (not just a Web browser). These programs, usually called *plug-ins,* are controversial in the Web development community, mainly because they limit your audience. Not all Web site visitors have the necessary plug-ins installed on their computers. Those guests must choose from three equally unpalatable options: go to a different Web site to download the plug-in, skip the multimedia show (if you've built a second, plug-in–free version of your site), or skip your Web site entirely. All media types in this chapter require a plug-in of some kind; see each section for more detail.

Second, it's worth noting that these effects can bulk up your Web site considerably, making it slower to load and making it still more likely that some of your visitors (especially those using dial-up modems) won't bother sticking around.

Third, these flashy multimedia effects are easy to overuse. Blink and flash too much, and you'll find your audience beating a hasty retreat for the cyber-exits.

Finally, creating external movies, animations, or applications is an art (and a book or two) unto itself. This chapter is a guide to *inserting* such add-on goodies into your Web page and assumes that a cheerful programmer near you has already *created* them.

Figure 12-1:
External multimedia files like this Flash movie can add a dimension of sound, animation, and interactivity that brings new life to a site, making possible a complexity that's difficult to emulate using HTML alone. In this case, clicking the man on the ladder affects your score and lets you play for bonus points.

Flash

Flash is the standard for Web animation, complex visual interaction, and what has become known as "Rich Internet Applications" (just a fancy way of saying you can make a Web page work a lot like a desktop program). Macromedia's Flash technology produces high-quality animated images—known as Flash movies—at a relatively small file size. Its drawings and animations are *vector graphics,* which means that they use mathematical formulas to describe objects on the screen. By contrast, *bitmap* technology like GIF and JPEG include data for every pixel of an image, gobbling up precious bytes and adding download time. Flash's vector graphics, on the other hand, save file size with their compact mathematical expressions.

Flash can also handle MP3 audio and advanced programming features, providing an added dimension of sound and interactivity that can make a plain HTML page look dull by comparison. For example, sophisticated Flash gurus can build automatic score tracking into an online game or add a cannon-firing animation each time the player clicks the mouse. While Dynamic HTML (see Chapter 11) can do some of these things, Flash movies are easier to create. An intriguing advantage of Flash movies is that they look and work exactly the same on every browser, whether on Windows or Mac. (Don't try *that* with HTML.)

Of course, all of this power comes at a price. Although Dreamweaver has some limited Flash-creation abilities (such as the Flash elements feature, discussed on page 452), you need another program, such as Macromedia Flash or Swish (*www. swishzone.com*) to produce full-fledged movies. These programs aren't difficult to learn, but they're more programs to buy and more technologies to get under your belt.

Furthermore, your visitors can't play Flash movies without the Flash Player plug-in (see page 147). If they don't have it, they'll need to download and install it—a sure spontaneity killer. Fortunately, chances are your visitors already have Flash Player, since all major browsers (even Opera) now come with the Flash plug-in installed. In fact, Macromedia says that (insert grain of salt here) over 98 percent of Web browsers in use now have some version of the Flash Player (a much smaller percentage has the *latest* version of the player).

Inserting a Flash Movie

To insert a Flash movie into a Web page, click where you want to insert the movie, and then choose Insert → Media → Flash (or, on the Common tab of the Insert bar, choose Flash from the Media menu). Either way, a Select File dialog box appears. Navigate to the Flash movie file (look for an .swf extension) and double-click it. Dreamweaver automatically determines the width and height of the movie and generates the appropriate HTML to embed it into the page. The movie appears as a gray rectangle with the Flash logo in the center; you can adjust its settings as described in the next section.

Tip: You can also drag a Flash movie file from the Files panel (see page 479) into the document window. Dreamweaver automatically adds the correct code.

POWER USERS' CLINIC

The <object> and <embed> Tags

If you choose View → Code after inserting a Flash movie, you may be surprised by the amount of HTML Dreamweaver deposits in your page. You may also encounter some HTML tags you've never heard of, including <object>, <embed>, and <param>. These tags provide browsers with the information they need to launch Flash Player and play a Flash movie. Other embedded media (Shockwave, for example) make use of these tags, too.

The <object> and <embed> tags do the same thing in different browsers. Some browsers (including Netscape, Opera, Internet Explorer for Mac, and Mozilla) use <embed> to insert movies and other plug-in media, while Internet Explorer for Windows uses the <object> tag to insert ActiveX controls (Microsoft's own kind of plug-in technology). For maximum browser compatibility, Dreamweaver adds both tags. Browsers ignore HTML tags that they don't understand, so this method doesn't cause problems.

To preview Flash files directly in Dreamweaver, just select the movie and then click the Play button on the Property inspector (see Figure 12-2). To stop the movie, click the same button, which has now become a Stop button.

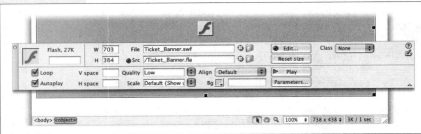

Figure 12-2:
When you insert a Flash movie into a page, Dreamweaver tracks the original Flash file. When you click the Edit button here, the file opens in Flash for you to edit.

Note: When inserting a Flash movie, an "Object Tag Accessibility Options" window appears. This dialog box lets you set options that are intended to make accessing the Flash content easier, but they don't really work in most browsers. If you don't want to set these options, just click Cancel, and Dreamweaver still inserts the Flash movie. To permanently turn off this window, open the Preferences window—Edit → Preferences (Dreamweaver → Preferences on Mac)—click the Accessibility category, and then turn of the Media checkbox.

If your page has lots of Flash movies—numerous animated buttons, perhaps—you can play all of them at once by pressing Ctrl+Shift+Alt+P (⌘-Shift-Option-P). Then sit back and watch the show. To stop all running movies, press Ctrl+Shift+Alt+X (⌘-Shift-Option-X). You can also preview Shockwave movies in Dreamweaver (see page 448). (And no wonder: Macromedia makes Shockwave, too.)

EXTENSION ALERT

Who's Got Flash?

One tricky thing about using Flash movies is that you never know whether the people visiting your site even have the correct version of Flash Player. For example, say you create a snappy new Flash-based program for translating text into different languages using Flash 8 Professional. This cool Flash movie will have people across the globe communicating in each other's language–but, unfortunately, only if they have the latest version of Flash Player. Earlier versions don't understand some of Flash 8's complex features.

Instead of letting your visitors scratch their heads and curse your name when they can't get this cool movie to work, you can advise them they need a newer version of the player. Macromedia offers a Flash Detection kit that includes an extension for Dreamweaver. This kit (a collection of instructions, sample files, and, most importantly, a Dreamweaver behavior) lets you build pages that can tell whether visitors have Flash Player and, if so, which version they have. For information and downloads, visit *www.macromedia.com/ devnet/logged_in/fsharples_detectionkit.html*.

Flash Movie Properties

You'll rarely have to change the default properties Dreamweaver assigns to a Flash movie. But if you ever want to change the margin of space around a movie, restore it to original size after resizing it, or swap in a different movie, the Property inspector is the place to do it.

Naming a Flash movie

As with images and navigation buttons, you can use JavaScript to control Flash movies. For example, Dreamweaver's built-in Control Shockwave or Flash behavior lets you start, stop, or jump to a specific frame in a Flash movie (see page 433).

As noted on page 434, however, if you plan to use JavaScript with your Flash movie, you need to give the Flash element a name. To do so, type the name you wish to use in the Name field (the box directly below Flash in the Property inspector). JavaScript uses this name to identify the movie in its code.

The movie file

The File field specifies the path to the Flash movie file on your hard drive. To select a different file, type a new path into the File field, or click the folder icon to access your site folder's contents.

Src property

As with Fireworks files (see page 140), Dreamweaver can keep track of the original Flash file you used when creating a Flash movie. That's fortunate because, once again, Flash movies start off in the program's native format (as .fla files) and then must be exported as .swf (Flash movie) files, which are viewable on the Web.

The Src property field indicates where the original Flash file is stored. Clicking the Property inspector's Edit button launches Flash and opens the original Flash file. You can then make any changes you wish to the movie and, in Flash, click Done. Flash exports the updated .swf file into your site, replacing the previous version of the file.

Movie size

Although dragging to enlarge a GIF or JPEG image can turn it into a pixellated mess, you can usually resize Flash movies without problems, since their vector-based images are based on mathematical formulas that scale nicely. (The exception is when you've included bitmap images, such as GIFs or JPEGs, in your Flash movie. Then, as when resizing an image in a Web page, you'll see distortion and pixellation in the movie.)

To resize a movie, do one of the following:

- Select the movie in the document window; drag one of the three resizing handles that appear at the edges of the movie. To avoid changing the movie's proportions in the process, press Shift as you drag the lower-right corner handle.

- Select the movie in the document window; type new width and height values into the W and H boxes in the Property inspector. You can also use percentage values, in which case Web browsers scale your movie to fit the window.

If you make a complete mess of your page by resizing the movie beyond recognition, just click Reset Size in the Property inspector.

Play options

The Loop and Autoplay checkboxes control how the Flash movie plays back. When you turn on Loop, the Flash movie plays over and over again in an endless loop, an approach advertisers often choose for use in animated banner ads.

The Autoplay checkbox instructs the Flash movie to start playing when the page loads.

Note that neither of these options overrides specific programming instructions in the Flash movie. For instance, if you've added a Stop action to the final frame of a movie—an action that stops the movie at that frame—then the Loop option has no effect.

Margins

Flash-movie *margins* are especially useful if you've wrapped text around the movie on the page; they determine how much buffer space falls between the movie and the text.

To add space above and below a selected movie, type a number of pixels into the V space field in the Property inspector (note that you need to type only a number; don't add *px* to specify pixels). Press Enter to see the results of your change. To add space to the left and right, type a pixel measurement in the H space field; 10 or 20 pixels usually provides an attractive amount of space. Unfortunately, you can't specify independent values for each of the four margins—only top/bottom and side/side. (You can, however, accomplish this setting using Cascading Style Sheets; see page 203.)

Quality settings

If your Flash movie's heavy data requirements overwhelm a visitor's computer, it may run slowly and appear choppy, especially if the animation is action-packed and complex. Not every computer on earth already has at least a three-gigahertz processor and two gigabytes of RAM. Until then, you may need to adjust the quality settings of your Flash movies to help them look better on all computers, from the sluggish to the speedy.

By default, Dreamweaver sets the quality to High, but you can choose any of the following four settings from the Quality menu in the Property inspector:

- **High** provides the greatest quality, but the movie may run slowly on older computers.

- **Low** looks terrible. This setting sacrifices quality by eliminating all *antialiasing* (edge smoothing) in the movie, leaving harsh, jaggy lines on the edges of every image. Movies set to Low quality look bad on *all* computers; to accommodate both the fast and the slow, use Auto High or Auto Low.

- **Auto Low** forces the movie to start in Low quality mode, but to switch automatically to High if the visitor's computer is fast enough.

- **Auto High** makes the movie switch to Low quality mode only if the visitor's computer requires it. In this way, you can deliver a high-quality image to most visitors, while still letting those with slow computers view the movie. This mode is the best choice if you want to provide a high-quality image but still make your movie accessible to those with older computers.

Scaling

When you resize a Flash movie (see page 449), changing its original proportions, your visitors' Web browsers scale or distort the movie to fit the newly specified dimensions. Scaling becomes an issue particularly when, for example, you give a Flash movie *relative* dimensions (setting it to, say, 90 percent of the browser window's width), so that it grows or shrinks as your visitor's browser window grows or shrinks.

The Scale property lets you determine *how* the Flash Player plug-in scales your movie. For example, in Figure 12-3, the top movie's original size is 200×50 pixels. But if you resize the movie so that it's *300×50* pixels, one of three things may happen, depending on your choice of Scale setting:

- **Show All.** This setting, the default, maintains the original aspect ratio (proportions) of the movie (second from top in Figure 12-3). In other words, although the overall size of the movie may go up or down, the movie's width-to-height proportion remains the same. This setting keeps the movie from distorting, but it may also cause borders to appear on the top, bottom, or either side of the movie. (To hide the borders, match the movie's background color to the color on the page.)

- **No Border.** This setting resizes the movie according to your specifications *and* maintains its aspect ratio, but may also crop the sides of the movie. Notice how the top and bottom of "Cosmopolitan Farmer" are chopped off (third from top in Figure 12-3).

• **Exact Fit.** This option may stretch your movie's picture either horizontally or vertically. In Figure 12-3 (bottom), "Cosmopolitan Farmer" is stretched wider.

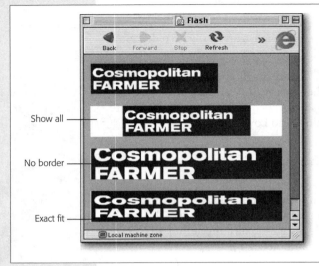

Show all

No border

Exact fit

Figure 12-3:
This browser window shows the results of your different choices in the Scale menu on the Property inspector. A Flash movie's Scale property specifies how a movie should be scaled when its Width and Height properties are set differently than the original movie. If you've resized a movie, press F12 to see how it looks in a Web browser, and then, if necessary, choose a different setting from the Scale pop-up menu in the Property inspector.

Alignment

You can align Flash movies relative to the paragraphs around them, just as you do with images. In fact, the alignment options in the Property inspector work exactly the same as the *image-alignment* properties discussed on page 132. For example, choosing Right from the Align menu positions the movie at the right of the screen and wraps text around its left side. (If the movie is inside a cell, Align Right moves it all the way to the right of the cell.)

Background color

To set a background color for a Flash movie, use the Bg color box in the Property inspector. This color overrides any background color set in the movie itself; it fills the space where the movie appears when the page first loads (and the movie hasn't).

Flash Elements

Flash elements are essentially prebuilt Flash movies that you can customize within Dreamweaver. Dreamweaver comes with only one Flash element (Image Viewer), but the Insert bar has an entire tab dedicated to this feature.

Note: If you'd like to build your own Flash elements, check out this useful tutorial: *www.macromedia. com/devnet/mx/dreamweaver/articles/flash_elements.html*.

Image Viewer is essentially a Flash slideshow. You can add your own photos to the Flash movie; add titles, captions, and links; and choose from a variety of groovy transition effects to make the change from photo to photo more entertaining (see Figure 12-4). Sorry to say, unlike most aspects of Dreamweaver, Flash Elements don't have a user-friendly dialog box. You have to use Dreamweaver's Tag inspector to set the various properties of the Image Viewer, as shown in Figure 12-5:

1. **Click the page where you'd like to insert the Flash slideshow.**

   The viewer's factory-set size is 400 pixels wide by 325 pixels tall, so you should place it in an open space like a table cell. Alternatively, you could dedicate an entire page to the slideshow and adjust the size settings. Since the Image Viewer is just a Flash movie, you can use the Property inspector to change any of its basic Flash properties as described on page 449.

2. **Choose Insert → Media → Image Viewer.**

   Or, from the Flash Elements tab of the Insert bar, select Image Viewer (it's the only button there).

   The Save Flash Element dialog box appears. You'll create a new Flash movie in the next step, so you need to provide a name and choose where you'd like to save this new movie.

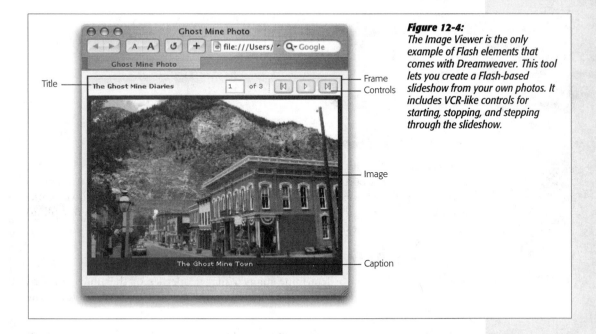

Figure 12-4:
The Image Viewer is the only example of Flash elements that comes with Dreamweaver. This tool lets you create a Flash-based slideshow from your own photos. It includes VCR-like controls for starting, stopping, and stepping through the slideshow.

3. **Navigate to the folder in your site where you'd like to save this file, enter a name, and then click Save.**

This process is just like creating any new file in Dreamweaver, like an external CSS file. (Although the names of Flash movie files end in .swf, you don't have to type the extension: Dreamweaver adds it automatically.)

After you save the file, you'll see a gray rectangle with the Flash logo in the center—the generic "Flash on your page" icon.

4. **Set the properties of the Image Viewer using the Tag inspector (Figure 12-5).**

There are a variety of options for controlling the display of the Image Viewer, as described next.

Figure 12-5:
The Tag inspector temporarily turns into the "Flash element" panel whenever you select a Flash element on the page. It's the only way to set properties for Flash elements. The property names appear in the left column, while the values you give those properties are on the right. You can directly edit any text in this column (type a hexadecimal color code, like #333333 in this example) or use the basic widgets provided (like color boxes and pop-up menus).

Image Viewer Properties

You can control many aspects of the Image Viewer, not just the photos you want to display. The properties fall into three basic categories, and you set them using a variety of methods. Some options have familiar pop-up menus or color boxes; others use pop-up boxes that accept multiple entries (for adding more than one photo to the slideshow, for example).

General Image Viewer properties

You have the power to determine many *visual* properties of the Image Viewer, including background color, whether it has a frame around it, and the color of the frame. Here's the rundown:

- **bgColor** lets you set a background color for the areas of the slideshow outside of the photo. Click the color box to the right and select a color, just as you would elsewhere in Dreamweaver (see page 41).

- **frameShow** offers a simple yes or no choice. Choose Yes if you want a frame around the viewer, No if you don't.

- **frameThickness** is the thickness of the frame, in pixels. Just click in the box to the right of the property name and type a number. This property (and the next one) works only if **frameShow** is set to Yes.

- **frameColor** works just like the bgColor option, except it sets the color for the frame.

- **title** lets you give your slideshow a name, which appears in the upper-left corner of the viewer (see Figure 12-4). Just click in the box and type a name. Some of the title may get cut off in your final presentation, depending on how long the title is and what font and size you use.

- **titleColor, titleFont,** and **titleSize** all have to do with the format of the title. With the titleColor box, you can use any of Dreamweaver's color tools to choose a text color. The titleFont pop-up menu lists all the fonts installed on your computer. Since Flash movies can embed fonts, you can use any of these fonts—not just the select handful normally used on Web pages. For titleSize, specify one in pixels.

Image options

Of course, the heart of Image Viewer consists of the pictures you add to it. You can choose which JPEG images to use, add captions below each image, and even add individual links to each photo. The viewer comes sized to 400 pixels wide by 325 pixels tall; however, not all of this space is available to your images. Because a small border appears on all four edges of the image, each picture gets only 386 × 259 pixels' worth of space. If your image is wider than this, the viewer shrinks it to fit the available width, and extra space is added to the top and bottom of the view screen. If the photo is taller than 259 pixels, extra space appears on each side of the shrunken image.

Tip: Although the Image Viewer can't use GIF images or "Progressive" JPEG files (a special JPEG that most Web graphics programs can create), you can include Flash movies (.swf files). You could even build a portfolio viewer to display your most interesting Flash animations one by one.

You're not stuck with the default size of 400 × 325, however. You can resize the Image Viewer using the Property inspector just as you would any Flash movie (see page 449) and give yourself the freedom to include larger images if you want. Note, however, that while the Image Viewer shrinks an image to fit its screen, it won't scale an image up beyond its original dimensions. In other words, if you scale the Image Viewer up to 600 × 400 pixels and include a 100 × 100 pixel image in your slideshow, you won't get an enlarged image filling the larger available space. That's a good thing, since scaling the image larger would cause it to distort and pixellate.

Note: If you plan to keep the Image Viewer at its dainty 400×325 pixel size, make sure your images aren't any bigger than that. Although the Image Viewer shrinks larger images to fit, Web browsers still have to download those images, causing unnecessary delays.

There are a variety of settings for adding and controlling images:

- **imageURLs** specify the paths to the images (JPEG or .swf files). Here's where you specify which images to display. To add images, click the area to the right of the imageURLs label; the Edit Array Values button appears (circled in Figure 12-5). Click this button to open the Edit 'imageURLs' Array window (Figure 12-6). To add an image, click the + button, and then click the folder icon. When the Select File window appears, navigate to and select a JPEG or .swf file, and then click OK. The path to the file appears in the window. You can add more photos by repeating this procedure. To remove a picture or movie from the list, select a URL and click the minus sign (–) button. To later edit the list of images, just click the Edit Array Values button again.

- **imageLinks** let you add a link to each image in the slideshow. This feature is optional but could be useful if, for instance, you're a Web designer and use the Image Viewer to display images of your clients' sites. You could link each image to the actual site on the Internet, creating a live "portfolio."

You add links the same way you add images: click to the right of the imageLinks label, and then click the Edit Array Values button; the Edit 'imageLinks' Array window opens. You can add, edit, and delete links just as you did images. But how do you know which link goes with which image? The order of the links in the list corresponds to the order of the images in the imageURLs list. For example, say the second link you add is *http://www.myclients_site.com/* and your list of images matches the one in Figure 12-6; in this case, the link would go with the first image—*summer_vacation.jpg*.

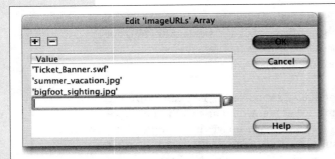

Figure 12-6:
The Edit 'imageURLs' Array window lets you specify which images to add to the Image Viewer. Click the folder icon to open the now familiar Select File dialog box and navigate to the image file on your computer. You can also specify an image using an absolute path like this: http://www.somewebserver.com/somepicture.jpg. Unfortunately, there are no controls for changing the order of the images, so plan carefully.

Unfortunately, there are no controls for rearranging these lists. Accordingly, if you want to move an image's position in the slideshow or move its link, you pretty much have to *rebuild both lists*.

Tip: You can edit the list directly in the Tag inspector, without using the Edit Array Values window. Just click in the area to the right of the property label to highlight the text so that you can edit it.

- **imageLinkTarget** lets you specify *where* links open. For example, you can make it so that when a visitor clicks on an image, the link (which you specified in the *imageLinks* property) opens in a new browser window. The options are the same as those described on page 112.

- **imageCaptions** lets you add text descriptions that appear below each image (see Figure 12-4). Like imageLinks and imageURLs, imageCaptions are stored in a list, the order of which must match the order of the images. You add captions by clicking in the area to the right of the imageCaptions label and then clicking the Edit Array Values button. You can then add, edit, and remove captions.

- **captionColor, captionFont,** and **captionSize** work just like their title counterparts, as described on page 455.

Playback options

You can also specify different options for playing back your slideshow:

- **showControls** lets you show or hide the VCR-like controls that appear at the top of the Image Viewer by choosing Yes or No from the pop-up menu. If you choose No here, the viewer's title (see page 455) won't appear either.

- **slideAutoPlay** determines whether the slideshow begins automatically or whether the visitor must push the Play button (see showControls, above) to start it. Yes means the show starts immediately; No means your audience must start it.

Note: If you hide the controls in the showControls setting, you should set the slideAutoPlay option to Yes; otherwise, visitors won't see beyond the first image.

- **slideDelay** specifies how long in seconds each slide remains on the viewer screen before the next image appears.

- **slideLoop** lets the show *loop*—that is, return to the first slide after it reaches the last slide. If you set this option to No, the slideshow simply stops at the last slide.

- **transitionsType** indicates what kind of transition effect governs the change from image to image. If you're familiar with PowerPoint presentations or basic film-editing software, you've probably encountered such favorites as Wipe, Zoom, and Fade. Try different settings until you find a transition that suits your presentation, or choose Random to have the Image Viewer apply a different transition at random as each slide changes to the next.

The Image Viewer is simply a Flash movie. Once you've inserted it, you can change any of its generic *Flash* properties (see page 449) using the Property inspector. To delete an Image Viewer, simply select it in the document window and then press the Delete key.

Flash Video

Dreamweaver 8 includes an exciting new feature: the ability to insert video directly into a Web page, including VCR-like controls (or maybe that's now DVD-like controls) for start, stop, pause, and volume control. Unfortunately, Dreamweaver doesn't actually create the video, and you can't use just any video format like MPEG or AVI. You need a special type of file, called a Flash Video file. Flash video files end in the extension .flv and are created using one of several Macromedia products. If you bought Studio 8, you're in business; it includes the Flash 8 Video Encoder for creating these types of files. Otherwise, you need Flash MX 2004 Pro, Flash 8 Pro, or the Macromedia Video Kit with Sorenson Squeeze, a $99 product (*www.macromedia.com/software/studio/flashvideokit/*). In addition, Flash MX 2004 Pro doesn't actually export the video (thought the Video Kit does). You'll also need a pro, or semi-pro, video product like Final Cut Pro or Avid Xpress Pro (for a complete list of supported products, see *www.macromedia.com/devnet/mx/flash/ articles/video_primer_02.html#thirdparty*).

Note: For a quick intro to creating Flash videos, visit *www.macromedia.com/devnet/mx/flash/articles/ flv_howto.html*. Macromedia also provides a more comprehensive reference on their Web site: *www. macromedia.com/devnet/mx/flash/video.html*.

If that long list of requirements doesn't get you down, or you already have some Flash Video files you'd like to add to your site, Dreamweaver makes the process of adding the video easy:

1. **Click the page where you'd like to insert the Flash video.**

   Like other Flash movies, you'll want an open area of your page to place the video.

2. **Choose Insert → Media → Flash video.**

   Or, from the Common tab of the Insert bar, select Flash Video from the Media menu (see page 148). The Insert Flash Video window appears (see Figure 12-7).

3. **Select Progressive Download from the "Video type" menu.**

   Dreamweaver provides two options, but the second one, Streaming Video, requires some expensive software (the Flash Server) or a Flash video streaming service like Vital Stream (*www.vitalstream.com*), which starts at nearly $100 a month...ouch.

   Progressive Download means that the video doesn't have to download completely before it begins playing, so visitors to your site don't have to wait 30 minutes while your 40 MB movie downloads. Instead, they just wait until they've got enough movie so there won't be any delays in playback as the rest of the movie downloads.

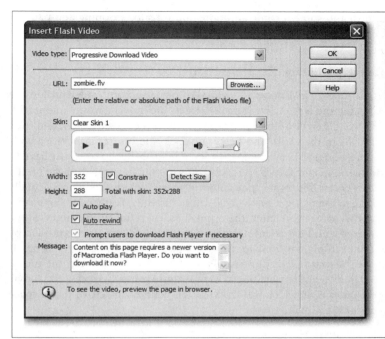

Figure 12-7:
The new Insert Flash Video command is probably the easiest way to add video to your Web site. All that your visitors need is the Flash player, which in most cases comes preinstalled in their browser.

4. **Click the Browse button and select the Flash Video (.flv) file you wish to add to the page.**

   Due to some differences in how operating systems work, you're better off putting your Flash Video files in the same folder as the Web page. If you want to put your Flash video files elsewhere (even on a different Web server), use absolute links (see page 104) to make sure your video appears.

5. **Select a Skin.**

   The really useful part of this feature is the ability to add controls to your video: buttons for starting, pausing, and stopping the video; a progress bar; and various volume-adjustment controls (see Figure 12-8).

Movie

"skin"

Pause/play/stop   Progress bar   Volume control

Figure 12-8:
The "Clear" skin controls lie directly over the movie ("Clear Skin 3" is shown here). They disappear if the mouse isn't anywhere inside the movie, but they reappear the moment you mouse back over the video. Try each skin to see which fits your taste.

These controls are added to your video, and they're offered as nine different "skins"—actually, three different types of controllers, each with three different graphical styles. Each skin includes controls for starting the video and controlling the sounds, and some include additional buttons for stopping and pausing the video, or a progress bar that lets you see how far into the video you are as you watch it.

6. **Click the Detect Size button.**

Flash Videos contain *meta-data,* additional information embedded inside the *video* file. Clicking the Detect Size button extracts the movie's width and height, adds the width and height of the various elements of the selected skin, and then automatically fills in the width and height boxes in the Insert Flash Video window (see Figure 12-7.) If your file doesn't include meta-data, you'll just have to type the width and height values yourself—these define how much space on the page the Flash video fills. Note that entering these dimensions won't actually distort your video—making it really, really thin, or really, really wide, for example. No matter what size you enter, the original aspect ratio (proportions) of the movie is preserved, and extra, empty space is added to fill any area not filled by the movie. For example, say your movie is 352 pixels wide and 288 pixels tall. If you entered width and height dimensions of 100×288, respectively, the movie wouldn't stretch like you're watching it in fun-house mirror. Instead, the movie would appear 100 pixels wide and 82 pixels tall, with 53 pixels of blank space above and below the movie.

7. **If you want, turn on the "Auto play" checkbox.**

Doing so makes the movie play as soon as enough video data has downloaded from the Web. Otherwise, your site's visitors need to press the play button to begin the video.

8. **If you want, turn on the "Auto rewind" checkbox.**

If you want the movie to automatically rewind to the beginning after the movie is done, turn on this checkbox. Your movie will then return to the first frame of the video after it's played through. But you may not always want to abide by the video-store credo "Be Kind, Rewind." If your movie ends with a dramatic message—"Stay tuned for the next exciting installment of Blind Mole Rats from Mars. Appearing soon in the bargain bin of a video store near you!"—you might prefer to leave the movie on its last frame when it's complete.

9. **Turn on the "Prompt users to download Flash player if necessary" checkbox.**

Flash Video is a relatively new and advanced technology. It requires your visitors to have at least version 7 of the Flash player. Many computer owners out there don't have this player installed, so turning on this checkbox provides them with a helpful message—and a link to the Macromedia site where they can download and install the latest Flash Player. If you want to customize the message those viewers see, type a new message in the Message box.

10. **Click OK to add the Flash Video to your page.**

This step installs the necessary code not only for the video, but for the "Flash detection" message from step 9 as well. You can check out the newly inserted video by pressing F12 (Option-F12) to preview the page in a Web browser.

Note: When you upload your Web page and Flash Video to your site (see Chapter 15), you also need to upload two additional files that Dreamweaver secretly added to your site behind your back: FLVPlayer_progressive.swf and the .swf (Flash movie) file for the skin you selected. It's named after the skin you choose—for example, Clear_Skin_1.swf, or Halo_Skin_1.swf. If you choose to include "dependent files" when uploading, as described on page 544, Dreamweaver handles this task for you.

FlashPaper

Dreamweaver's Insert FlashPaper command is another exercise in Macromedia cross-marketing. FlashPaper is a PDF-like technology that lets you print out a document into a format that's readable by the Flash player; it's one easy way to get a Word document or Excel spreadsheet into a Web-ready format (see Figure 12-9).

Visitors can zoom in on a FlashPaper document, scroll through it, and print it out. Unfortunately, Dreamweaver doesn't create these documents. Studio 8 includes FlashPaper and Contribute 3 (as well as Flash and Fireworks). But if you bought the standalone version of Dreamweaver, you'll have to buy Contribute 3 or shell out a little moola for the Windows-only FlashPaper program (*www.macromedia. com/software/flashpaper/*).

Since FlashPaper documents are just Flash movies—.swf files—the Insert Flash-Paper command is nothing more than the Insert Flash command with a couple of extra options. To insert a FlashPaper document, choose Insert → Media → Flash-Paper or choose FlashPaper from the Media menu on the Common tab of the Insert bar. When the Insert FlashPaper window opens, click the browse button and select the FlashPaper document (an .swf file), type a height and width, and then click OK. The height and width you specify determine the size of the "window" that contains the FlashPaper document. Viewers of your page can use the Flash-Paper controls to zoom, scroll, and print the document.

After inserting the FlashPaper document into the page, it acts like a regular Flash movie. You can select it and use the Property inspector to set any of the normal Flash movie properties discussed on page 449. However, don't turn off the "Autoplay" checkbox (see page 450); if you do, the FlashPaper document won't appear on the page.

Shockwave

As the Internet-ready form of movies created with Macromedia's Director, Shockwave is an older brother to Flash. Director has a longer history as a tool for developing complex interactive presentations. It began life as a program for creating

---

CD-ROMs. But when the Web exploded onto the scene, Director quickly morphed into a Web authoring tool. As a result of its CD background, Shockwave offers complex programming possibilities, which makes it ideal for detailed interactive presentations.

Like Flash, Shockwave requires a plug-in, but unlike the Flash plug-in, this one doesn't generally come preinstalled with Web browsers. If you include Shockwave animation in your Web site, many of your visitors will need to download the Shockwave player—a 2.5 MB download!

That annoying requirement is a good argument against using Shockwave for general-audience Web sites (and why it's not commonly used except for specialty Web sites like online game sites). Some of your visitors—especially the ones that don't have cable modems or DSL—may not put in the time and effort required to allow their browsers to view your masterpiece.

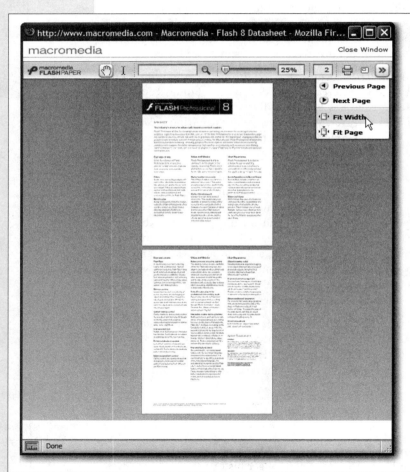

Figure 12-9:
FlashPaper is like PDF-lite. You can view documents produced in a program like Word directly in your Web browser, with a few helpful controls like a search box and tools for zooming in and out of the document.

But if you just can't do without Shockwave, you can insert a Shockwave movie into a Web page just as you would any multimedia format. Click where you want to insert the movie, and then choose Insert → Media → Shockwave (or choose Shockwave from the Media menu on the Common tab of the Insert bar). Either way, a Select File dialog box appears. Find and double-click the Shockwave movie file (look for the .dcr extension).

The Shockwave movie appears as a gray rectangle with the Shockwave logo in the center. But Dreamweaver can't automatically calculate the dimensions of Shockwave movies, so you need to type the width and height of the movie in the W and H fields of the Property inspector. Use the same dimensions you specified when creating the file in Director.

You can preview Shockwave files directly in Dreamweaver by selecting the movie and clicking Play on the Property inspector. To stop the movie, click the same button (which is now a Stop button).

You resize a Shockwave movie just like a Flash movie, as described on page 449.

Shockwave Movie Properties

The only Shockwave movie properties you have to set by hand are the width and height of the movie. Most of the time, you won't need to bother changing the default properties. The Property inspector does, however, let you change the movie's name (a requirement for using JavaScript to control its playback), substitute a different movie, choose the movie's alignment relative to the text around it, specify a background color, select an ActiveX ID, or specify top/bottom or side/side margins. All of these options work just as they do for Flash movies (see page 449).

EXTENSION ALERT

Plug-In Support at Macromedia Exchange

The Plug-In object is a simple way to embed code for plug-in files. Unfortunately, because it's designed as a generic method of adding files for any and all plug-ins, it's not pre-tailored for any one plug-in, such as the Real Media Player.

That's not to say that you can't add ready-to-use plug-in objects to your Web pages—you can. If you visit Macromedia's Dreamweaver Exchange (*www.macromedia.com/exchange/dreamweaver/*), you can find extensions (see page 670) that help you insert media in a variety of different plug-in formats. These extensions help you put the proper code in your page to make the plug-in work.

Once on the Exchange Web site, choose Rich Media from the Browse Extensions menu. You'll find extensions that help you add QuickTime, Real Video and Audio, and other plug-in–dependent media. For example, an extension creatively named "Insert a QuickTime Movie" does just that. For more on using the Dreamweaver Exchange, see Appendix A.

Other Multimedia Controls

Dreamweaver also includes tools for inserting other *multimedia* and *plug-in* files. In fact, these tools have been around since much earlier incarnations of Dreamweaver, when there really were *other* media types like Java applets, ActiveX controls, and other plug-in technology. However, Java applets never really took off (their performance never quite lived up to the hype), and ActiveX controls are limited to Internet Explorer for Windows.

Part Four:
Building a Web Site

4

Introducing Site Management

As the dull-sounding name *site management* implies, organizing and tracking your Web site's files is one of the least glamorous, most time-consuming, and error-prone aspects of being a Web designer. On the Web, your site may look beautiful, run smoothly, and appear to be a gloriously unified whole, but behind the scenes, it's nothing more than a collection of varied files—HTML, images, Cascading Style Sheets, Flash movies, and so on—that must all work together. The more files you have to keep track of, the more apt you are to misplace one. A single broken link or missing graphic can interfere with the operation of your entire site, causing personal—even professional—embarrassment.

Fortunately, computers excel at tedious organizational tasks. Dreamweaver's site management features take care of the complexities of dealing with a Web site's many files, freeing you to concentrate on the creative aspects of design. In fact, even if you're a hand-coding HTML junkie and you turn your nose up at all visual Web page editors, you may find Dreamweaver worth its weight in gold just for the features described in this chapter and the next two.

Where the first three parts of this book describe how to create, lay out, and embellish a Web site, this part offers a bird's-eye view of the Web production process as you see your site through to completion and, ultimately, upload it to the Internet.

To get the most out of Dreamweaver's site management features, you need to be familiar with some basic principles for organizing Web files, as discussed in the next section.

Structuring a Web Site

When you build a Web site, you probably spend hours providing your visitors with carefully planned links, helpful labels, and clear, informative navigation tools. You want your *site architecture* to make it easy for visitors to understand where they are, where they can go, and how to return to where they came from (see Figure 13-1). Behind the scenes, it's equally important to organize your site's files with just as much clarity and care, so that you can find *your* way around when updating or modifying the site later. And, as on your home computer, a Web site's main organizational tool is the *humble* folder.

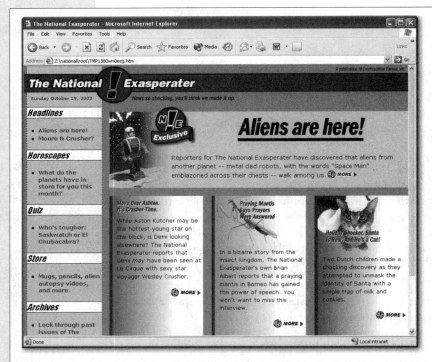

Figure 13-1:
A good site has an easy-to-understand structure. Content is divided into logical sections, and a prominent navigation bar—the column of white buttons on the left side of this image—gives visitors quick access to the site's information. When building a site, this "information architecture" provides a useful model for naming and creating the folders that hold the site's files.

You organize files on your computer every day, creating, say, a folder called Personal, within which are folders called Financial Planning and Vacation Pictures. Inside the Vacation Pictures folder, you have separate folders for your memories of Maui, Yosemite, and the Mall of America.

The same principle applies to the folders that make up a Web site: All Web sites have one primary folder—the *root folder*—that holds all of the site's Web pages, graphics, and other files used in the site. The root folder usually contains additional folders for further subdividing and organizing the site's files.

A good structure (see Figure 13-2) speeds up the production and maintenance of your site by providing quick access to whatever graphic, style sheet, or Flash movie you're looking for. But don't fall into the trap of becoming so obsessed that you put every graphic or Web page you create in its own separate folder; creating a structure for the files in a site should make your job easier, not harder.

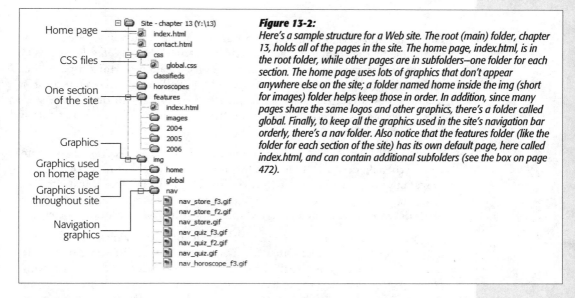

Figure 13-2:
Here's a sample structure for a Web site. The root (main) folder, chapter 13, holds all of the pages in the site. The home page, index.html, is in the root folder, while other pages are in subfolders—one folder for each section. The home page uses lots of graphics that don't appear anywhere else on the site; a folder named home inside the img (short for images) folder helps keep those in order. In addition, since many pages share the same logos and other graphics, there's a folder called global. Finally, to keep all the graphics used in the site's navigation bar orderly, there's a nav folder. Also notice that the features folder (like the folder for each section of the site) has its own default page, here called index.html, and can contain additional subfolders (see the box on page 472).

Tip: If you already have a Web site that suffers from lack of organization, it's not too late. Dreamweaver can help you reorganize your files quickly and accurately. Take the following rules to heart and then turn to "Organizing Site Files" on page 479 to learn how Dreamweaver can whip your current site into shape.

Here, then, are some guidelines for effective site organization:

• **Plan for future growth.** Like ever-spreading grapevines, Web sites grow. Today you may have only enough words and pictures for 10 Web pages, but tomorrow you'll put the finishing touches on your new 1,000-page online catalog. It may seem like overkill to create a lot of folders for a small site, but better to start with a solid structure today than find yourself knee-deep in files tomorrow.

For instance, it's useful to create additional folders for *graphics* files that appear within each section of the site. If a section of your site is dedicated to promoting your company's products, create a folder called *products* for storing product Web pages. Create an additional folder called *images* to store the pictures of those products. Then, when you add more products or images, you know right where to put them.

Note: While you can start with no organization plan and later use Dreamweaver to bring it all into shape (see page 479), you may run into unforeseen problems if your site is already on the Internet. If your site's been up and running for a while, search engines may have indexed your site, and other Web sites may have linked to your pages. If you suddenly rearrange the pages of your site, those cherished links from the outside world may no longer work, and people who try to access your site from a search engine may be foiled.

- **Follow the site's architecture.** Take advantage of the work you've already done in organizing the content on your site. For instance, the *National Exasperator's* site content is divided into five main sections: Headlines, Horoscopes, Quiz, Store, and Archives, as shown in Figure 13-1. Following this architecture, it makes sense to create folders—*headlines, horoscopes,* and so on—in the site's root folder for each section's respective Web pages. If one section is particularly large, add subfolders.

- **Organize files by type.** After you create folders for each section of your site, you'll probably need to add folders for storing other types of files like graphics, Cascading Style Sheets, external JavaScript files, and PDF files. Most sites, for instance, make extensive use of graphics, with several graphics on each page. If that's the case for you, then you need to file those images neatly and efficiently.

  One way to organize your graphics is to create a folder for images that appear on your home page and another for images that appear elsewhere in the site. Often, the home page is visually distinct from other pages on the site and contains graphics that are unique to it. You can create a folder—*images_home,* for example—in the root folder for images that appear only on the home page. Create another folder—*images_global,* for example—to store graphics that all or most of the pages use, such as the company logo, navigation buttons, and other frequently used icons. When you add these images to other pages of your site, you'll know to look for them in this folder. Alternatively, you could create an *images* folder in the root of your site and add subfolders such as *home, global,* and *nav* (see Figure 13-2). The choice of an organizational system is yours; just make sure you have one.

- **Use understandable names.** While file names like *1a.gif, zDS.html,* and *f.css* are compact, they aren't very explanatory. Make sure file names mean something. Clear, descriptive names like *site_logo.gif* or *directions.html* make it a lot easier for you to locate files and update pages.

  This principle is especially important if you work as part of a team. If you're constantly explaining to your coworkers that *345g.gif* is the banner for the home page, changing the file name to *home_banner.gif* could save you some aggravation. There's a tradeoff here, however, as long file names can waste precious bytes. For instance, a name like *this_is_the_image_that_goes_in_the_upper_ right_corner_of_the_home_page.gif* is probably not a good idea.

Note: You may have noticed that Dreamweaver 8 no longer uses .htm as the extension for file names. Instead Dreamweaver now employs the more industry-standard .html extension—as in *index.html*. It doesn't really matter which you use, and if you like the old way, you can now easily change it in the Properties window (another neat new feature). Just choose Edit → Properties to open the Properties window, select the New Document category, and type *.htm* in the default extension box.

It's also helpful to add a prefix to related files. For example, use *nav_* at the beginning of a graphic name to indicate that it's a navigation button. In this way, you can quickly identify *nav_projects.gif, nav_quiz.gif,* and *nav_horoscopes. gif* as graphics used in a page's navigation bar. As a bonus, when you view the files on your computer or in Dreamweaver's Files panel (see Figure 13-6), they'll appear neatly sorted by name; in other words, all the *nav_* files cluster together in the file list. Likewise, if you have rollover versions of your navigation graphics (see page 144), give them names like *nav_projects_over.gif* or *nav_ horoscopes_high.gif* to indicate that they're the highlighted (or over) state of the navigation button. (If you use Fireworks, its button-creation tools automatically use names like *nav_projects_f1.gif* and *nav_projects_f2.gif* to indicate two different versions of the same button.)

• **Be consistent.** Once you've come up with a system that works for you, follow it. Always. If you name one folder *images,* for instance, don't name another *graphics* and a third *pretty_pictures.* And certainly don't put Web pages in a folder named *images* or Flash movies in a folder named *style_sheets.*

In fact, if you work on more than one Web site, you may want to use a single naming convention and folder structure for all of your sites, so that switching among them goes more smoothly. If you name all your graphics folders *images,* then no matter what site you're working on, you already know where to look for GIFs and JPEGs.

UP TO SPEED

Naming Your Files

The rules for naming files in Windows and Macintosh are fairly flexible. You can use letters, numbers, spaces, and even symbols like $, #, and ! when naming folders and files on these operating systems.

Web servers, on the other hand, are far less accommodating. Because many symbols—such as &, @, and ?—have special significance on the Web, using them in file names can confuse Web servers and cause errors.

The precise list of no-no's varies from Web server to Web server, but you'll be safe if you stick to letters, numbers, the

hyphen (-), and the underscore (_) character when naming files and folders. Stay away from spaces. File names like *company logo.gif* or *This company's president.html* probably won't work on most Web servers. Replace spaces with underscores or inner caps—*company_logo.gif* or *companyLogo.gif*—and remove all punctuation marks.

Sure, some operating systems and Web servers permit strange naming conventions, but why take the chance? Someday you may need to move your site to another, less forgiving Web server. Play it safe: keep your file names simple.

Tip: Put only files that go on your Web site in the root folder and its subfolders. Keep your source files—the original Photoshop, Fireworks, Flash, or Word documents where you created your content—stored elsewhere on your computer. This way, you're much less likely to accidentally transfer a 14.5 MB Photoshop file to your Web server (a move that would *not* gain you friends in the IT department). But if you insist on keeping all those files together with your Web site files, check out Dreamweaver's *cloaking* feature (described on page 549). Using it, you can prevent certain file types from being transferred to your Web server when using Dreamweaver's FTP feature.

FREQUENTLY ASKED QUESTION

All Those Index Pages

Why are so many Web pages named index.html *(or* index.htm*)?*

If you type a URL like *www.missingmanuals.com* into a Web browser, the Missing Manuals home page opens on your screen. But how did the Web server know which page from the site to send to your browser? After all, you didn't ask for a particular Web page, like *www.missingmanuals.com/about.html*.

When a Web server gets a request that doesn't specify a particular Web page, it looks for a default Web page—often named *index.html* or *index.htm*. It does the same thing even when the URL you've typed specifies (with a slash) a folder inside the site root, like this: *www.missingmanuals.com/cds/*. In this case, the Web server looks for a file called *index.html* inside the *cds* folder and—if it finds the file—sends it to your Web browser.

If the Web server doesn't find an *index.html* file, two things can happen, both undesirable: the Web browser may display either an ugly error message or a listing of all the files inside the folder. Neither result is helpful to your visitors.

While your site still functions without this step, it's good form to give the main Web page inside each folder in your site the proper default page name. Web servers use different names for these default pages—*index.html* or *default.html*, for example—so check with your Web server's administrator or help desk. In fact, you can name any page as a default page, as long as you set up your Web server to look for the correct default name. So if you're creating a dynamic site like those discussed in Part Six, you can set up a server to look for a dynamic page like *index.asp* or *index.php* as the default page. On many Web servers, multiple default page names are specified, so if it doesn't find a file named *index.html*, it may then look for a file called *index.php*.

Defining a Site

Organizing and maintaining a Web site—creating new folders and Web pages; moving, renaming, and deleting files and folders; and transferring pages to a Web server—can require going back and forth between a couple of different programs. With Dreamweaver's site management features, however, you can do it all from within one program. But to take advantage of these features, you must first *define* the site; in other words, give Dreamweaver some basic information about it.

Defining the site involves showing Dreamweaver which folder contains your Web site files (the *root folder*) and setting up a few other options. You've already learned how to do this site building using Dreamweaver's Site Definition Wizard (see page 33). But for fine-tuning your settings, it's time to get to know the advanced Site Definition window.

Start by choosing Site → New Site. This opens the Site Definition window (see Figure 13-3). Click the Advanced tab to access Dreamweaver's advanced settings. There are eight categories of information for your site, but to get up and running, you need to provide information only for the first category: Local Info. (The remaining categories are discussed in Chapters 14 and 15.)

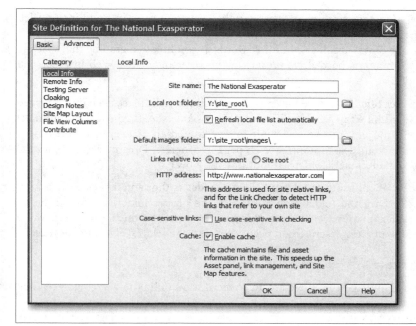

Figure 13-3:
The Basic tab of the Site Definition window provides a simple method for new users to set up a Web site. But Dreamweaver pros can take advantage of the greater options available under the Advanced tab shown here. The eight categories listed on the left side of the window are discussed in this and the next two chapters.

Here are the options on the Local Info tab.

Site name

Into the Site Name field, type a name that briefly identifies the site for you—and Dreamweaver. This is the name that appears, among other places, on the Site pop-up menu on the Files panel (Figures 13-6 and 13-7), so that you can tell what site you're working on. It's just for identifying your site while working in Dreamweaver and doesn't have any effect on the actual pages of your site.

Local root folder

Identify your site's local root folder—the folder that contains all files belonging to your site—by clicking the folder icon to the right of the "Local root folder" field. The procedure is described on page 35. (Also see the box on page 476 for more information on local root folders.)

All of Dreamweaver's tools for managing your sites' files rely on the local root folder. Once you've defined a site, you see all of its files listed in the Files panel.

Make sure to turn on the "Refresh local file list automatically" checkbox so that new files—graphics, Web pages, and so on—automatically appear in the Files panel as you add them. Alternatively, click the Refresh button (Figure 13-13) each time you want to see your recent changes in the site's files list.

Default images folder

For a graphic image to work properly on the Web, you can't just add it to a Web page (Chapter 5); you also have to store a copy of the *graphics* file in the local root folder or one of its subfolders. In other words, if you link to a graphic that's sitting on your computer's hard drive *outside* of the root folder, the Web browser will never find it.

Dreamweaver offers a feature that puts images in the right place even if you forget. When you add a stray *graphics* file to a page in your site, the program automatically copies the file into your default images folder. In fact, even if you drag a graphic from your desktop onto a Web page in progress, Dreamweaver copies the file to the default images folder without missing a beat.

The process of choosing the default images folder is the same as selecting a local root folder. Click the folder icon and select the proper folder, which can be an existing folder in your local root or a new one you create on the spot. (If you're following the process described on page 468, select the *images_global* folder here.)

Links relative to

As discussed on page 108, there are a variety of ways to link to a Web page. When linking to another page in your site, Dreamweaver lets you create document-relative or root-relative links. Document-relative is often the easiest way to go (see page 104), but Dreamweaver offers you the flexibility to choose. Click either the Document or Site Root radio button. Dreamweaver then uses that method when adding links between pages of your site.

> **Tip:** You can override this setting and use whichever type of link you wish, site root–relative or document-relative, when actually creating the link, as described in step 4 on page 109.

FREQUENTLY ASKED QUESTION

Bringing Your Own Web Site

I already have a Web site. Will Dreamweaver work with it?

Yes. In fact, Dreamweaver's site management features are an invaluable aid in organizing the files of an existing site. As you can read in "Organizing Site Files" on page 479, you can use Dreamweaver to rearrange, rename, and reorganize files—tasks that are extremely difficult and time-consuming to do by hand.

Furthermore, Dreamweaver lets you clean up and reorganize a site without breaking links. So Dreamweaver is just as useful for working with a completed site as it is for creating one from scratch.

To work on an existing site, first save a copy of all site files on your computer, all in one folder. When defining the site (see page 472), choose this folder for the local root folder.

HTTP address

This option serves two functions: first, if you use absolute URLs to link to pages within your site (see page 104), you must fill out the "HTTP address" field for Dreamweaver's link-management features to work properly. Type your site's full URL beginning with *http://*. Dreamweaver uses this address to check for broken links within your site and to correctly rewrite links if you move pages around. For example, maybe your Webmaster has told you to link a form to *http://www.your-domain.com/cgi/formscript.php* instead of using a document-relative link. In this case, you'd type *http://www.yourdomain.com/* in the "HTTP address" box. Now, if you move or rename the *formscript.php* page from within Dreamweaver, the program's smart enough to update the link on the page with the form.

Dreamweaver 8 introduces another use for this setting—one that's of incredible valuable for one particular situation: if you're using site root–relative links, but the site you're working on isn't actually located in the site root on the Web server. For example, maybe you're running the marketing department at International ToolCo. You manage just the Web pages for the marketing department, and they're located in a folder called *marketing* on the Web server. In essence you manage a sub-site, which acts as an independent site within the larger International ToolCo site. Maybe your Webmaster demands that you use site root–relative links—man is that guy bossy.

In older versions of Dreamweaver, you'd be totally out of luck. Here's why: site root–relative links always begin with a /, indicating the root folder on the Web server (for a refresher on this concept, see page 106). In Dreamweaver MX 2004 and earlier, if you added a root-relative link, say to the main page in a folder named *personnel* located inside the local root folder, Dreamweaver would write the link like this: */personnel/index.html.* But in this case, that wouldn't work. The *personnel* folder is actually located (on the Web server) inside the *marketing* folder. So the link should be */marketing/personnel/index.html.* In other words, older versions of Dreamweaver think that the local root folder maps exactly to the Web server's root folder.

Dreamweaver 8 solves this common dilemma. In this example, you'd type *http://www.intltoolco.com/marketing/* in the HTTP address box. Then, whenever you add a site root–relative link, Dreamweaver 8 begins with */marketing/* and then adds the rest of the path to the URL. In summary, *if* you use site root–relative links *and* you're working solely on pages located inside a subdirectory on the actual Web server, *then* fill out the absolute URL to that subdirectory. Finally, add this whole rigmarole to the list of reasons why document-relative links are easier to manage in Dreamweaver.

Case-sensitive links

Some Web servers (namely, those of the Unix and Linux variety) are sensitive to the case used in a file name. For example, INDEX.html is a different file than *index.html.* In this case, you can turn on the "Use case-sensitive link checking" box to make sure Dreamweaver doesn't mistake one file for another when checking links. For example, say you link to a file named INDEX.html, but change the name of another file named *index.html* to *contact.html*. Without this option turned on, Dreamweaver may mistakenly update any links to INDEX.html.

In real-world use, you probably won't need this option. First, it's not possible to have two files with the same name but using different combinations of upper- and lowercase letters in the same folder on a Mac or Windows machine. So if your local root folder is located on your Mac or Windows computer, you'll never be able to get into this situation. In addition, it's confusing (and just plain weird) to use the same name but different cases to name your files. Revisit the rules of file naming (see page 471) if you find yourself tempted to do this.

Cache

The cache is a small database of information about the files in your site. It helps Dreamweaver's site management features work more efficiently; leave this checkbox turned on.

Once you've provided the local information for your site, click OK to close the Site Definition window and begin working.

Editing or Removing Defined Sites

Sometimes you need to edit the information associated with a site. Perhaps you want to rename the site, or you've reorganized your hard drive and moved the local root folder to a different location, and you need to let Dreamweaver know what you've done.

UP TO SPEED

Local vs. Remote Root Folders

A root folder is the main, hold-everything folder for your site. It contains every piece of the site: all Web page documents, graphic images, CSS style sheets, flash movies, and so on.

The word "root" implies that this is the master, outer, main folder, in which there may be plenty of subfolders. Remember that, in most cases, your Web site exists in two locations: on your computer as you work on it, and on the Internet where people can enjoy the fruits of your labor. In fact, most Web sites in the universe live in two places at once—one copy on the Internet, the original copy on some Web designer's hard drive.

The copy on your own computer is called the *local site* or the *development site*. Think of the local site as a sort of staging ground, where you build your site, test it, and modify it.

Because the local site isn't on a Web server, and the public can't see it, you can freely edit and add to a local site without affecting the pages your visitors are viewing, meanwhile, on the remote site. The root folder for the version of the site on your computer, therefore, is called the *local root folder*.

When you've added or updated a file, you move it from the local site to the *remote site*. The remote, or live, site mirrors the local site. Because you create it by uploading your local site, it has the same organizational folder structure as the local site and contains the same polished, fully functional Web pages. However, you leave the half-finished, typo-ridden drafts on your local site until you've perfected them. Chapter 15 explains how to use Dreamweaver's FTP features to define and work with a remote site.

To edit a site, open the Manage Sites dialog box (choose Site → Manage Sites or, in the Files panel, choose Manage Sites from the Site pop-up menu) and double-click the name of the site you want to edit. The Site Definition window opens (Figure 13-3). Now you can type a new name in the Site Name box, choose a new local root folder, or make any other changes. Click OK to close the dialog box when you're done.

Tip: If you want to edit the current site's information, there's a shortcut. In the Files panel (Figure 13-6), just double-click the name of the site in the Sites menu. (Mac owners need to click once to select the name in the menu, and then click again to open the Site Definition window.)

Once you've finished a site and are no longer working on it, you may wish to remove it from Dreamweaver's list of sites. To delete a site from the list, open the Manage Sites dialog box as described above, click to select the site you wish to delete, and click Remove.

A warning appears telling you that this action can't be undone. Don't worry; deleting the site here doesn't actually *delete* the site's images, Web pages, and other files from your computer. It merely removes the site from Dreamweaver's list of defined sites. (You can always go back and define the site again, if you need to, by following the steps on page 472.) Click Done to close the Manage Sites window.

Tip: If you do, in fact, want to delete the actual Web pages, graphics, and other site components, you can either switch to the desktop (Windows Explorer or the Finder, for example) and delete them manually, or delete them from within Dreamweaver's Files panel, described on page 479.

Exporting and Importing Sites

When you define a site, Dreamweaver stores that site's information in its own private files. If you want to work on your site using a different computer, therefore, you must define the site again for *that* copy of Dreamweaver. In a design firm where several people are working together on many different sites, that's a lot of extra setup. In fact, even if there's just one of you working on two computers, duplicating your efforts is a pain.

So that you can put your time to better use, Dreamweaver lets you import and export site definitions. For example, you can back up your *site definition* files—in case you have to reinstall Dreamweaver—or export a site definition for others to use.

To export a site definition:

1. **Choose Site → Manage Sites.**

   The Manage Sites window appears, listing all the sites you've defined (Figure 13-4).

2. **Select a site from the list, and then click Export.**

If the site definition includes remote site information (see page 532), you'll see a dialog box called "Exporting site" (Figure 13-5). If you're simply making a backup of your site definition because you need to reinstall Dreamweaver, select the "Back up my settings" radio button. (The other option, "Share settings," is useful when, for example, your local root folder is on the C: drive, but the root folder's on the E: drive on someone else's computer, so your setup information doesn't apply to them. It's also handy when you don't want to give someone else your user name and password to the Web server.)

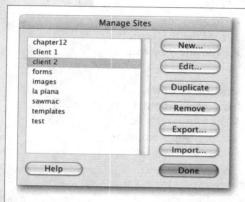

Figure 13-4:
The Manage Sites window is the control center for managing your sites. Add new sites, edit old sites, duplicate a site definition, and even export site definitions for use on another computer, or as a precautionary backup.

Figure 13-5:
This dialog box lets you back up your settings, or share them (minus your login information) with other people.

3. **Click OK.**

The Export Site panel appears.

Tip: Unfortunately, you can import or export only one site at a time. So if you have a lot of sites you need to import, grab some coffee and get clicking. (Windows people have another option; see the Note on page 479.) You can, however, save a few steps when exporting. You can Ctrl-click (⌘-click) multiple sites in the Manage Sites window and click Export. You still need to save each file individually, but at least you don't have to click the Export button multiple times.

---

4. **In the Export Site panel, specify where you want to save the file and give it a name.**

If you're merely making a backup, saving the file to that site's local root folder is a good choice.

Note: If you use Windows, a helpful utility called DW-Exporter can let you export all of your site definitions at once–a great time-saver when backing up your site. In fact, this utility can back up lots of important data, including serial numbers and Dreamweaver's configuration folder. As of this writing, a version for Dreamweaver 8 isn't available, but the developer usually updates the program quickly so that it works with the latest Macromedia products. For more information, visit *http://mm-exporter.joexx.de/index_en.php*.

Once you have a *site definition* file, you can import it into any version of Dreamweaver as follows:

1. **Choose Site → Manage Sites.**

   The Manage Sites panel appears.

2. **Click Import.**

   The Import Site panel appears. Navigate to a *site definition* file—look for a file ending in .ste. Select it, and then click OK.

If you're importing the site definition to a computer other than the one you used to export the site, you may need to perform a few more steps. If Dreamweaver can't locate the local root folder in the *site definition* file, it asks you to select a local root folder on the new computer, as well as a new default images folder.

Organizing Site Files

Once you've defined your local site, Dreamweaver helps you organize your files, create folders, and add new Web pages to your site, using the Files panel as your command center. To open the Files panel, choose Window → Files, or just press F8.

In its most basic incarnation, the Files panel displays the files in the current site's local root folder (see Figure 13-6). This list looks and acts just like Windows Explorer or the Macintosh Finder; you see names, file sizes, and folders. You can view the files inside a folder by clicking the + (▶) symbol next to the folder (or simply by double-clicking the folder). Double-click a Web page to open it in Dreamweaver.

Tip: You can open certain types of files in an outside program of your choice by defining an external editor for that file type. For example, you can tell Dreamweaver to open GIF files in Fireworks, Photoshop, or another image editor. (See "Setting Up an External Editor" on page 138 for more on this feature.)

You can view your site's files in four different ways using the View pop-up menu (shown in Figure 13-6):

• **Local view** shows the files in your local root folder. Folders in this view are green.

• **Map view** shows a map of your site (see page 487).

- **Remote view** shows files on the Web server in the remote root folder (see page 476). Of course, before you've posted your site on the Web, this list is empty. Information appears here only after you've set up a connection to a remote root folder (see page 532) and connected to a Web server. Folders in this view are blue.

- **Testing Server view** is useful when you're creating the dynamic, database-driven sites discussed in Part Six of this book. No files appear in this view until you've set up a testing server (see page 689) and connected to it. Folders in this view are red.

Tip: In Windows, you can quickly hide and show the panel groups by clicking the Show/Hide Panels button at the left edge of the panel groups (see Figure 13-6). On small monitors, hiding panels can give you breathing room to work on your Web pages. You can also resize the panel groups by dragging this button left or right. And pressing F4 hides (or shows) all panels, including the Property inspector and Insert bar.

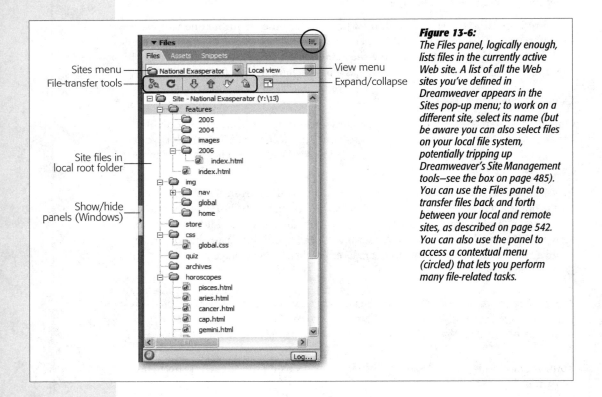

Figure 13-6:
The Files panel, logically enough, lists files in the currently active Web site. A list of all the Web sites you've defined in Dreamweaver appears in the Sites pop-up menu; to work on a different site, select its name (but be aware you can also select files on your local file system, potentially tripping up Dreamweaver's Site Management tools—see the box on page 485). You can use the Files panel to transfer files back and forth between your local and remote sites, as described on page 542. You can also use the panel to access a contextual menu (circled) that lets you perform many file-related tasks.

Sites menu
File-transfer tools
View menu
Expand/collapse
Site files in local root folder
Show/hide panels (Windows)

Adding New Folders and Files

The Files panel provides a fast way of adding blank Web pages to your site. With one click, you can create a new page in any folder you like, saving several steps you'd otherwise have to perform using the File menu.

FOR WINDOWS PCS

The Windows Files Panel

If you'd like to expand the Files panel, so you can see a side-by-side view of both the *remote site* files and *local site* files, click the Expand/Collapse button. The Files panel fills the screen (see Figure 13-7). The obvious drawback is that you can't work on a Web page while the Site window is maximized, because you can't even see it. Click the Expand/Collapse button again to minimize the Files panel and gain access to your document window.

To get around this limitation, you can undock the Files panel before clicking the Expand button: Grab the Files panel group by its grip—the tiny column of dots to the left of the *word* Files—and drag it toward the middle of the screen. (Stay away from the edges of the screen when performing this maneuver; touching there may simply redock the panel group.) The panel group then becomes a floating panel. Now press the Expand button to get the side-by-side files view. You're now free to resize the Files panel even after expanding it.

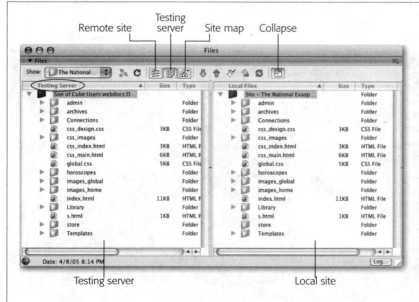

Figure 13-7:
Clicking the Expand/ Collapse button (shown in Figure 13-6) maximizes the Files panel and lets you display two views simultaneously. This way, you can view both the remote and local sites at the same time. Local files always appear on the right (unless you change the preference setting located in the Site category of the Preferences window—Ctrl+U (⌘-U). The view that appears on the left side— Remote, Testing, or Site Map—depends on which view you selected before clicking the Expand button. To change views, click a different view button— remote, testing or Site Map.

Adding files

To create a new, blank Web page, open the Files panel using one of the methods described on page 479, and then right-click (Control-click) a file or folder in the Files panel.

In the shortcut menu that appears, choose New File. Dreamweaver creates a new, empty Web page. (Actually, the page doesn't have to be empty; you can edit the file Dreamweaver uses as its default new page, as described in the box below.)

Note: The type of file Dreamweaver creates depends on the type of site you're creating. For a plain HTML site, Dreamweaver creates a blank HTML page. However, if you're building a dynamic, database-driven site like those described in Part Six, Dreamweaver creates a blank page based on the type of server model you've selected. For example, if you're building a site using PHP and MySQL, the page is a blank PHP page (named *untitled.php*).

The new file appears in the Files panel with a highlighted naming rectangle next to it; type a name for the page here. Don't forget to add the appropriate extension (.htm or .html) to the end of its name.

Tip: If you rename the new file immediately after creating it and add a new extension, the contents of the file update to reflect the new file type. For example, changing *untitled.html* file to *global.css* erases all of the HTML code in the file and turns it into an empty CSS file.

POWER USERS' CLINIC

Changing the Default New Page

Whenever you make a new Web page—for example, by choosing File → New or by right-clicking (Control-clicking) an existing file in the Files panel—Dreamweaver gives you a blank, white document window. But what if you always want your pages to have gray backgrounds, or you always want to include a link to the same external style sheet?

Every new Web page you create is actually an untitled copy of a default template document called Default.html (found in the Macromedia Dreamweaver 8 → Configuration → DocumentTypes → NewDocuments folder). You can open this file within Dreamweaver and edit it however you like: change its background color, margins, text color, or whatever, so that all subsequent new pages you create inherit its settings. Consider making a backup of this file before editing it, however, so that you can return

to the factory settings if you accidentally make a mess of it. (Also, make sure you don't touch an HTML fragment that probably appears to you to be incorrect: namely, the *charset="* snippet, which appears at the end of the <meta> tag. This fragment of HTML is indeed incomplete, but when you create a new page, Dreamweaver correctly completes this code according to the alphabet—Chinese, Korean, or Western European, for example—that your page uses.)

You'll also notice lots of other files in this folder. Since Dreamweaver can create lots of different file types—Cascading Style Sheets, Active Server Pages, and so on—you'll find a default blank file for each. You can edit any of these—but don't, unless you're sure of what you're doing. You can easily damage some of the more complex file types, especially those that involve dynamic Web sites.

Adding folders

You can add folders to your site directly in Dreamweaver using the Files panel. Just right-click (Control-click) a file or folder in the local files list. From the shortcut menu, choose New Folder. If you clicked a file, Dreamweaver creates the new folder in the same folder as that file; if you clicked a folder, you get a new folder inside it.

If you crave variety, you can add a folder another way. Select a file or folder in the Files panel and then click the contextual menu button (circled in Figure 13-6) and select File → New Folder.

Finally, in the naming rectangle that appears in the Files panel, type a name for the new folder.

Moving files and folders

Because the Dreamweaver Files panel looks and acts so much like the Windows Explorer and the Macintosh Finder, you may think it does nothing more than let you move and rename files and folders on your computer. You may even be tempted to work with your site files directly on the Mac or Windows desktop, thinking that you're saving time. However, when it comes to moving the files and folders in your site, Dreamweaver does more than your computer's desktop ever could.

In your Web travels, you've probably encountered the dreaded "404: File Not Found" error. This "broken link" message doesn't necessarily mean that the page doesn't exist, just that your Web browser didn't find the page at the location (URL) specified by the link you just clicked. In short, someone working on that Web site probably moved or renamed a file without updating the link. Because Web site files are interrelated in such complex ways—pages link to other pages, which include paths to graphics, which in turn appear on other pages—an action as simple as moving one file can wreak havoc on an entire Web site. That's why you shouldn't drag Web site files around on your desktop or rename them in Windows Explorer or the Macintosh Finder.

In fact, moving and reorganizing Web site files is so headache-ridden and error-prone that some Web designers avoid it altogether, leaving their sites straining under the weight of thousands of poorly organized files. But you don't have to be one of them: Dreamweaver makes reorganizing a site easy and error-free. When you use the Files panel to move files, Dreamweaver looks for actions that could break your site's links and automatically rewrites paths of links, images, and other media (see the cautionary box on page 485).

Note to programmers: If your custom JavaScript programs include paths to images, Web pages, or other files in your site, Dreamweaver can't help you. When you reorganize your site with the Files panel, the program updates *links* it created, but not *paths* you've included in your JavaScript programs.

Just be sure to do your moving from within Dreamweaver, like this: In the Files panel, drag the folder or file into its new folder (see Figure 13-8). To move multiple files, Ctrl-click (⌘-click) each of the ones you want to move, and then drag them as a group; to deselect a selected file, Ctrl-click or ⌘-click it again. You can also select one folder or file and Shift-click another to select all files and folders in the list between the two.

Note: Close *all* of your Web documents *before* reorganizing your files in this way. Dreamweaver has been known to not always correctly update links in open files. But if you do end up with malfunctioning links, you can always use Dreamweaver's Find Broken Links tool (see page 510) to ferret out and fix any broken links.

When you release the mouse button, the Update Files dialog box appears (Figure 13-8); just click Update. Dreamweaver updates all the links for you.

Tip: If you accidentally dragged the file or folder to the wrong location, click Don't Update. Then drag the file back to its original location and, if Dreamweaver asks, click Don't Update once again.

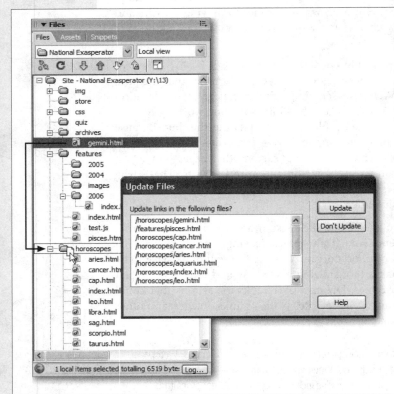

Figure 13-8:
Left: You can move files and folders within the Files panel just as you would in Windows Explorer or the Macintosh Finder. Simply drag the file into (or out of) a folder. But unlike your computer's file system, Dreamweaver constantly monitors the links between Web pages, graphics, and other files.

Right: If you move a file using Windows Explorer or the Finder, you'll most likely end up breaking links to that file or, if it's a Web page, links in that file. By contrast, Dreamweaver's smart enough to know when moving files will cause problems. The Update Files dialog box lets you update links to and from the file you're moving, so that your site keeps working.

Renaming files and folders

Renaming files and folders poses the same problems as moving them. Because links include file and folder names, altering a file or folder name can break a link just as easily as moving or deleting the file or folder.

For example, say you've created a new site with a home page named *home.html*. You cheerfully continued building the other pages of your site, linking them to *home.html* as you went along. But after reading this chapter and checking to find out what default file name your Web server requires (see page 472), you found that you need to rename your home page file *index.html*. If you were to rename the file *index.html* using Windows Explorer or the Macintosh Finder, every link to *home. html* would result in a "File not found" error.

FREQUENTLY ASKED QUESTION

Beware "Site-less" Web Design

Why doesn't Dreamweaver warn me when I delete or move a file?

Dreamweaver's site management tools are always watching your back—unless you're not working in a site. Dreamweaver tries to be a flexible tool for use in all situations. Some developers don't like the whole notion of sites and prefer to just work on their pages in the old (unmonitored) way of most programs. And in cases where you just want to edit a single page, but don't want to go through the whole business of defining a site, Dreamweaver's Files panel lets you browse your files, just like the regular Windows Explorer or Mac Finder. If you click the Sites menu (where you'd normally switch between defined sites) and scroll to the top of the menu, you'll see a list of hard drives and other networked storage devices. For example, you could select your main drive (C:, or Macintosh HD, for example). The Files panel then displays all of the files on that drive. Unfortunately, this flexibility can also cause a lot of trouble.

Sometimes people accidentally select their hard drive instead of their site in the Sites menu, and *then* navigate to the folder holding their site's files. They then begin working, blissfully unaware that they're working without Dreamweaver's safety net. When looking at your files in this way, changes you make to your existing site files—like moving, deleting, or renaming—aren't monitored by Dreamweaver

(it figures you know better). Similarly, all of Dreamweaver's other site management features like Libraries (Chapter 16), templates (Chapter 17), and file transfers (Chapter 15) don't work when you're off in un-site-managed-land. In other words, it's best to always define a site, and always make sure you've selected the site's name in the Files panel, as you work on your Web site.

Dreamweaver, on the other hand, handles this potential disaster effortlessly, as long as you rename the file in the Files panel instead. To do so, just click the file or folder in the Files panel. Pause a moment, and click the *name* of the file or folder. (The pause ensures that Dreamweaver won't think you just double-clicked the file for editing.)

A renaming rectangle appears; type the new name. Be sure to include the proper extension for the type of file you're renaming. For example, GIFs end with .gif and Cascading Style Sheets end with .css. Although Dreamweaver lets you name files without using an extension, the extensionless files won't work when you move them to a Web server.

Finally, in the Update Files dialog box (Figure 13-8), click Update. Dreamweaver updates all the links to this file or folder to reflect the new name.

Warning: It bears repeating: never rename or move files and folders *outside* of Dreamweaver. If you use Windows Explorer or the Macintosh Finder to reorganize the files in your site, links will break, images will disappear from your pages, and the earth will open underneath your feet. (Well, actually, that last thing won't happen, but it can *feel* that way when your boss comes in and says, "What's happened to our Web site? Nothing works!")

If you've edited files outside of Dreamweaver by accident, see page 510 to learn how to find and fix broken links.

Deleting files and folders

It's a good idea to clean up your site from time to time by deleting old and unused files. Just as with moving and renaming files, you delete files from the Files panel.

To delete a file or folder, just click to select it in the Files panel and press Backspace or Delete. (To select multiple files or folders, Ctrl-click [⌘-click] them as described on page 484.) If the doomed file or folder isn't referenced by any other page on the site, a simple "Are you sure you want to delete this file?" warning appears; click Yes.

However, if other files link to the file—or to files within the folder—that you're deleting, then a warning dialog box (Figure 13-9) appears informing you that you're about to break links on one or more pages in your site.

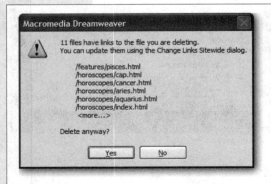

Figure 13-9:
When you delete files in the Files panel, Dreamweaver warns you if other pages reference (link to) the file. If you click Yes, you'll need to go back and repair the links. Dreamweaver gives you a convenient way to do so—the Change Links Sitewide command (see page 510)—and reminds you of it in this dialog box.

The message even lists the first few pages that use the file. If you've made a mistake, click No to leave your site untouched.

If you're sure you wish to delete the file, click Yes. And yes, this move does *break links* in all the pages listed. Repairing those links, which usually means linking them to a new page, requires a separate step: using the Site → Change Links Sitewide command, as described on page 516.

Viewing a Site Map

While the Files panel's list of files and folders is a great aid in managing those files, it doesn't give you a picture of how your site's Web pages are linked together. You can see that the *index.html* file in the root folder is the site's home page, for instance, but you can't see how it relates to the other pages in the site. In other words, you can't tell which pages link to or from it. To see those relationships, you need Dreamweaver's Site Map view.

The Site Map is a visual guide to the links in a site (see Figure 13-10). An icon representing the home page appears at the top of the map, and arrows connect the home page to icons, representing each of the links it contains. As shown in Figure 13-10, special icons clearly mark external, broken, and email links.

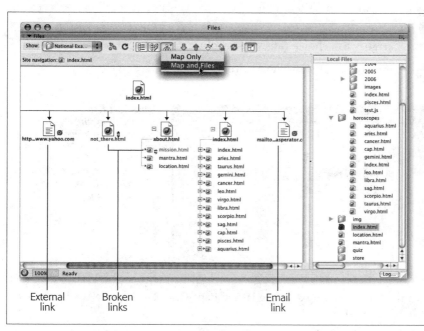

Figure 13-10:
The Site Map displays icons for each link in a Web site. Symbols provide added information about the pages: The globe icon indicates an external link, such as http://www.yahoo.com. The broken-link icon indicates that the file either doesn't exist or has been misfiled, so that the link won't work. Dreamweaver also highlights the name of the missing file in red. For more on finding and fixing broken links, see page 510.

The best way to view these links is by expanding the Files panel (see page 481), which spreads the links out into easy-to-read columns. In regular collapsed view, all the links in the map are put into a single column, so you need to scroll down to see each one. Furthermore, the Site Map does more than just provide a visual overview; it also gives you an easy way to rename files and even retitle Web pages.

Note: Web designers often create site maps to show the organization of a site. These neatly formatted, hierarchical charts demonstrate the structure of the site by indicating the logical sections in which the site's content has been divided. Warning: Dreamweaver's Site Map doesn't show this kind of organization. It treats *every* link on the page the same, whether it links to a major section of the site, or just to an insignificant side note; so just by looking at the Dreamweaver's Site Map, you won't necessarily get a good idea of the *logical* structure of the site.

Setting Up Site Map View

To view a Site Map, you'll first need to do a little preparation:

1. **Choose Site → Manage Sites (or, from the Site menu in the Files panel, choose Manage Sites).**

   The Manage Sites window appears, listing all of your sites.

2. **Click a site name and click Edit (or just double-click the site name).**

   The Site Definition window opens.

   If you're defining this site for the first time, you can also follow the steps on page 472.

3. **In the Category list, choose Site Map Layout.**

   You see the dialog box shown in Figure 13-11.

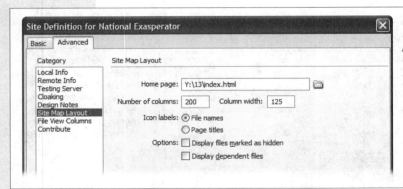

Figure 13-11:
Here, you define the site's home page and set preferences for Dreamweaver's Site Map view. If your home page file is named anything other than index.html or index.htm, you must specify it in the Home Page field.

4. **Click the folder icon next to the Home Page field. Navigate to the home page file in the site's root folder.**

   Click Select (Windows) or Open (Mac) to set this page as the home page.

   Remember that your home page must be in the root folder. Technically, you *can* choose a file that's buried several folders deep in your site folder, but don't do it—unless, of course, you really want to tell people to visit your company's home page at *www.mycompany.com/about_us/about_me/my_dog/ralphie.html*. By specifying a home page in the outer level of your root folder, you ensure the home page is at *www.mycompany.com*.

5. **Set any other Site Map preferences you wish.**

The "Number of columns" field determines how many links are displayed in a single row of the Site Map. For instance, if you set the number of columns to five, but the home page has 10 links on it, the Site Map has only enough columns for the first five links; the remaining five icons get bumped down to a second row directly below the first. Displaying more than one row of links from the home page is confusing, so it's best to use a number of columns that's at least equal to the number of links on the home page. Dreamweaver's default value of 200 is just fine.

The "Column width" represents the width, in pixels, of each column. As you can see in the box on page 490, file names and page titles may not fully appear if the column width is too small. Again, stick with Dreamweaver's default value of 125.

Note: The column width and number settings have no effect except when the Files panel is in expanded view (Figure 13-7).

Using the "Icon labels" buttons, choose whether you want the Site Map to display the file name (*index.html*) or page title ("Welcome to The National Exasperator") next to each page's icon. Ctrl+Shift+T (⌘-Shift-T) toggles between the two views when viewing the Site Map.

Once you've got your Site Map on display, you can hide certain files for the sake of clutter reduction by marking them as hidden. To make sure they stay hidden, leave "Display files marked as hidden" turned off. You can always make the hidden files reappear using the steps described on page 491.

The "Display dependent files" option makes GIF, JPEG, CSS, Flash, and all other non-HTML files show up in the Site Map. Since this can make the Site Map a confusing jumble of files, it's best to leave this option turned off.

6. **Click OK.**

You return to the Files panel.

Viewing and Customizing Site Map View

Once you've set up Site Map view as described above, you can see it by choosing Map View from the Files panel's unlabeled View menu (identified in Figure 13-6). Because the Files panel is narrow, click the Expand/Collapse View button (also shown in Figure 13-6) to maximize the map area.

When you first view the Site Map, only the first two levels—the home page and all of the pages linked from it—appear. A + symbol next to a page indicates that there are additional links on that page; clicking the + expands the list of links on that page. If those pages in turn have links, additional + symbols appear. You can continue to follow the links by expanding each page, but viewing too many levels at once can produce a confusing complication; see the box below for advice.

As in the Site file list, you can open a page by double-clicking its icon in the Site Map. In fact, if the Files panel is expanded (so that both the Site Map and Local Site file listings appear), selecting a page in the Site Map highlights the corresponding page in the File list, and vice versa.

Identifying pages in the Site Map

The Site Map view starts out displaying the file name of each Web page, which is less than informative. If you've structured your site (as recommended on page 468) so that the main page for each section of the site is stored in a different folder and is named *index.html*, the Site Map is an unhelpful sea of *index.html* labels (see Figure 13-10).

A better approach: use each page's *title* as the icon label. You can do this either when you first set up the site, as described on page 488, or choose View → Site Map Options → Show Page Titles from the Files panel's contextual menu. Repeat the same command to see the file names again. The keyboard shortcut Ctrl+Shift+T (⌘-Shift-T) is a fast way to toggle between the two views.

TROUBLESHOOTING MOMENT

Don't Get Lost in the Site Map

The Site Map clearly displays links between pages, but if you're not careful, you may end up chasing your tail. Very often, Web pages link back and forth to each other. For example, the home page may link to a page in the site that, in turn, links back to the home page.

In the example illustrated here, the horoscopes main page ("Horoscopes") has a link to the home page ("The National Exasperator"), which links to the horoscopes page, which links back to the home page, which links to the horoscopes page—and so on. All three of the pages indicated by arrows are, in fact, the same page! As shown here, the Site Map shows the horoscope page, which is a link from the home page. When you then click the + sign to expand the horoscopes page, you see a duplicate icon for the home page (whose original icon appears at the top of the Site Map). When you click the + sign next to the home page icon under the horoscopes page, you don't get a new level of site links, even though the Site Map displays it that way.

What you've done is "re-expand" the home page to display more duplicate icons.

Note: In Windows, if the Files panel is expanded, you'll see a menu across the top of the panel. This menu offers the same options as the contextual menu visible in the collapsed panel, circled in Figure 13-6.

Viewing just part of a Web site

When viewing large Web sites, you may find the Site Map awkward. Perhaps you're working on just a single section and don't want to be bothered with the extraneous details of the rest of the site. No problem: You can isolate a particular page when viewing the Site Map. Right-click (Control-click) the page and select View as Root from the menu that appears. The page you selected appears as the top-level page in the Site Map (see Figure 13-12).

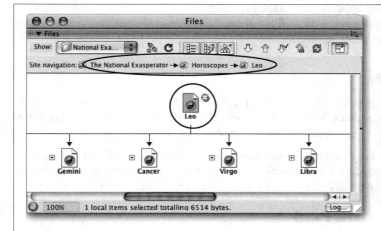

Figure 13-12:
This Site Map is zoomed in on a single page (Leo), which appears at the top level of the Site Map where the home page normally would be. The path from the home page to this file appears above the map in the Site Navigation bar. The home page is titled "The National Exasperator." A link from the home page leads to a page titled "Horoscopes," which in turn links to the "Leo" horoscope page. To once again view the home page as the top level of the Site Map, click its name in the Site Navigation bar.

Hiding extraneous links

Like some people you may know, the Site Map loves detail; it includes *all* links from your pages, including external links and email links. At times, this may be a bit more information than you need. Suppose you provide 200 email addresses on a single page; you probably don't need to see all of those listed in the Site Map.

Fortunately, Dreamweaver lets you hide any links you wish. All you have to do is select the files you want to hide (Shift-click them, or drag across a group of them) and then choose View → Show/Hide Link from the Files panel's contextual menu, or right-click (Control-click) the selected files and choose Show/Hide Link from the menu that appears; Dreamweaver makes them disappear.

To show hidden files again, choose View → Map Options → Show Files Marked as Hidden from the Files panel's contextual menu. Dreamweaver makes all hidden files appear with their names italicized, indicating that you've marked them as hidden.

You can turn off a file's "hidden" status by selecting it and choosing View → Show/Hide Link, or right-clicking (Control-clicking) the file and choosing Show/Hide link.

Renaming Pages in the Site Map

You can rename files in Site Map view, which works similarly to renaming them in the File List view. However, only the Site Map lets you easily change the *titles* of your site's Web pages. In fact, this is one of the best features of the Site Map. While displaying the page titles, you can quickly scan your site for missing or incorrect page titles and fix them without having to open the documents.

You rename a file in the Site Map just as you do in the Files panel; the steps appear on page 485. In this case, just be sure you're looking at the right kind of data— either page titles or file names—before you begin. Press Ctrl+Shift+T (⌘-Shift-T) to switch back and forth when viewing the Site Map.

When you're finished, Dreamweaver rewrites the title in the HTML of the page. The new title also appears next to the page icon. Or, if you've changed the name of the file, Dreamweaver's Update Files dialog box appears, letting you fix any links that point to the newly named file.

Site Assets

Web pages integrate lots of different elements: GIFs, JPEGs, links, colors, and Flash and Shockwave movies, to name just a few. In a large site with lots of files, it's a challenge to locate a particular image or remember an exact color.

To simplify the process, Dreamweaver provides the Assets panel. For want of a better generic term, Macromedia defines the term *asset* to mean any element you use on a Web page, such as a GIF file, a link, or even an individual color.

Viewing the Assets Panel

Dreamweaver lists your site's assets on the nine category "pages" of the Assets panel (Figure 13-13). To open the panel, choose Window → Assets, or press F11.

You select an asset in the list by clicking its name; a miniature preview appears above the Assets list. To preview a movie, click the green arrow that appears in the preview window.

The Assets panel highlights nine different categories of site elements. To view the assets in a particular category, click its icon at the left of the Assets panel:

- ▣ The **Images** category lists all of the GIF, JPEG, and PNG files in your site. Dreamweaver 8 lists the dimensions of each image next to its name, so you can quickly identify whether *logo1.gif,* or *logo2.gif* is your 728 × 90 pixel banner logo. You can also see the images' sizes, types, and where they're located in the site (you may need to scroll to the right to see all of this information).

- ▦ The **Colors** category shows all of the colors specified in the Web pages and embedded style sheets of your site. These include link colors, background colors, and text colors.

- **The URLs** category lists all external links—not just standard *http://* links, but also email links, FTP addresses, and JavaScript links. (For an example of a JavaScript link, see the box on page 401.)

- **The multimedia** categories—Flash, Shockwave, and Movies—are roughly equivalent. They each display *movie* files with their corresponding extensions: .swf (Flash), .dcr (Shockwave), .flv (Flash video), and .mov or .mpg (QuickTime and MPEG).

- **The Scripts** category lists JavaScript or VBScript files. This category only includes external *script* files that Web pages link to. Scripts that are embedded *into* a Web page—like those created using Dreamweaver behaviors—aren't listed.

- **The last two categories—templates** and **Library**—are advanced assets that streamline Web site production. They're discussed in Chapters 16 and 17.

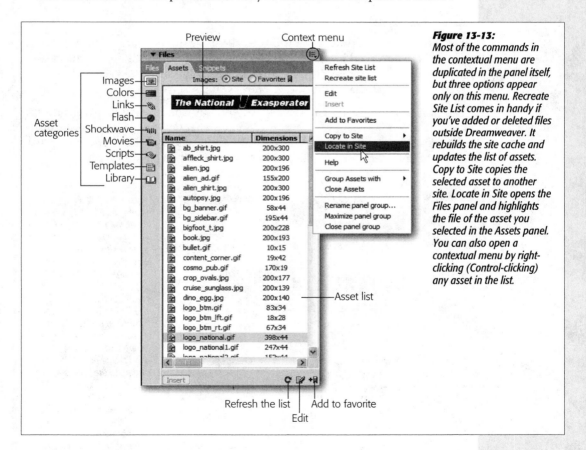

Figure 13-13:
Most of the commands in the contextual menu are duplicated in the panel itself, but three options appear only on this menu. Recreate Site List comes in handy if you've added or deleted files outside Dreamweaver. It rebuilds the site cache and updates the list of assets. Copy to Site copies the selected asset to another site. Locate in Site opens the Files panel and highlights the file of the asset you selected in the Assets panel. You can also open a contextual menu by right-clicking (Control-clicking) any asset in the list.

You can switch between two different views for each asset category—Site and Favorites—by clicking the radio buttons near the top of the Assets panel. The Site option lists all the assets that appear in the Site for the chosen category. Favorites lets you create a select list of your most important and frequently used assets (see page 495).

Note: Dreamweaver's cloaking feature lets you hide files from many site-wide tasks, including the Assets panel. So, if you have a folder with thousands of *image* files that you'd rather not display on the Assets panel, you can hide that folder and its files. See page 549 for more on this feature.

If, as you're working on a site, you add additional assets—for example, you create a new GIF image in Fireworks and import it to the site—you'll need to update the Assets panel. Click the Refresh Site List button (see Figure 13-13) to update the list of assets.

Inserting Assets

The Assets panel's prime mission is to make using assets easier. From the Assets list, you can add graphics, colors, and links to your pages with a click of the mouse. Most of the categories on the panel refer to external files that you can include on a Web page: images, Flash, Shockwave, movies, and scripts.

The easiest way to insert an asset file is to drag it from the Assets panel into the document window. You can drag the asset anywhere on the page you'd normally insert an object—in a table cell, at the beginning or end of a page, or within a paragraph. Script assets can go in the head of a Web page (see Figure 13-14).

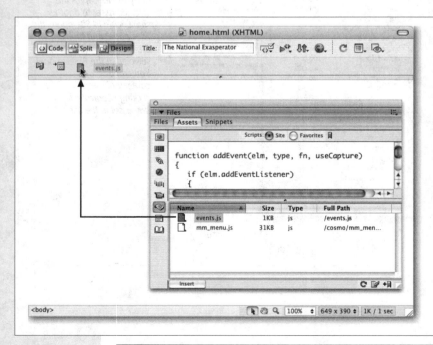

Figure 13-14:
While you'll insert most assets into the body of a Web page, you can (and usually should) place script files in the head of the page. To do this, first choose View → Show Head Content. Then drag the script from the Assets panel into the head pane, as shown here. (Adding a script asset doesn't copy the JavaScript or VBScript code into the Web page. Instead, just as with external style sheets, Dreamweaver links to the script file so that when a Web browser loads the page, it looks for and then loads the file from the Web site.)

(If you're billing by the hour, you may prefer the long way: click in the document window to plant the insertion point, click the asset's name, and then click Insert at the bottom of the Assets panel.)

The Return of Root-Relative Paths

Chapter 4 explains the different types of link paths—absolute, document-relative, and root-relative—that Dreamweaver understands (see page 104). While it's best to use document-relative paths for linking to pages within your own site, or for adding images and other media to a page, you may notice that Dreamweaver frequently displays root-relative paths in its site management tools.

For instance, the list in the Assets panel includes the full root-relative path of each asset–*/images_home/banner.gif*, for example. The initial "/" indicates the root folder of the site, and the information that follows indicates the rest

of the path to that asset. In this example, the graphic asset *banner.gif* is in a folder called *images_home*, which is itself in the site's root folder. Dreamweaver needs to look no further than the root folder to find the asset in question.

Root-relative paths indicate a precise location within a site and let Dreamweaver know where to find a file. This doesn't mean, however, that when you use the Assets panel to insert an image or other file, that Dreamweaver uses site-root-relative links. Dreamweaver uses the type of link you specified for the site as described on page 474.

Adding color and link assets

Color and link assets work a bit differently than other asset files. Instead of standing on their own, they *add* color or a link to images or text you've selected in the document window. (You can add colors to any text selection, or add links to images and text.) In this way, you can quickly add a frequently used link—the URL to download the Flash player or Adobe Reader, for example.

To do so, start by highlighting the text (to change its color or turn it into a link) or image (to turn it into a link). In the Assets panel, click the appropriate category button—Colors or Links. Click the color or link you want, and then click Apply. Alternatively, you can drag the color or link asset from the panel to the selection.

Note: Applying color to text using the Assets panel either creates a new CSS style or wraps the selected text in a <font> tag. The actual result depends on the Preferences setting described on page 30.

Favorite Assets

On a large site, you may have thousands of *image* files, *movie* files, colors, and external links. Because scrolling through long lists of assets is a chore, Dreamweaver lets you create a compact list of your favorite, frequently used assets.

For example, you might come up with five main colors that define your site's color scheme, which you'll use much more often than the other miscellaneous colors on the Assets list. Add them to your list of *favorite* colors. Likewise, adding *graphics* files you use over and over—logos, for example—to a list of favorites makes it easy to locate and insert those files into your pages. (Don't forget that you can also use

Dreamweaver's Library and template features for this function. They're similar, but more powerful tools for keeping frequently used items at the ready. Turn to Chapter 16 for the details.)

Identifying your Favorites

If the color, graphic, or other element to be added to your Favorites list already appears on your Assets panel, highlight it in the list and then click the Add to Favorites button (see Figure 13-13).

Even quicker, you can also add Favorites as you go, snagging them right from your Web page in progress. If you're working on your site's home page and you insert a company logo, for example, that's a perfect time to make the logo a favorite asset.

Simply right-click (Control-click) the image. From the shortcut menu, choose Add Image to Favorites; Dreamweaver instantly adds the graphic to your list of favorites. You can do the same with Flash, Shockwave, and QuickTime files, as well as with links. (Unfortunately, this shortcut doesn't work for *colors* and *script* files.)

When it comes to colors and links, there's another way to turn them into Favorites. In the Assets panel, select the Color or URLs category, click the Favorites radio button, and then click the New Asset button (see Figure 13-15). Then:

- If you're adding a favorite color, the Dreamweaver color box appears. Select a color using the eyedropper (see page 41).

GEM IN THE ROUGH

Better Use of Color Assets

Although color assets are meant only for coloring text, you can use them any time Dreamweaver's eyedropper tool appears, such as when you're creating a CSS style and wish to add text color, background color, or border color. In other words, any time you need a frequently used color, you can hop right to the Assets panel rather than pecking around on the color palette or trying to find another occurrence of the color on your screen.

Whenever you click a color box—in the Page Properties window, Property inspector, or Style Definition window, for example—a color palette appears and the cursor changes to an eyedropper. You could, of course, use this eyedropper to pick a color from the palette or to sample a color from the screen. But if you've already used the color in your site—or saved it in the Favorites list—just grab

it from the Assets panel. To do so, move the eyedropper to the colored swatch in the Assets list and click.

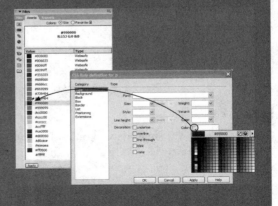

- If you're adding a favorite link, the Add URL window opens. Type an absolute URL in the first field, either a Web address starting with *http://* or an *email* link (for instance, *mailto:subscriptions@nationalexasperator.com*). Next, type a name for the link in the Nickname field—*Acrobat Download* or *Subscription Email,* for instance—and then click OK.

Your new color or link appears in the Favorites list.

Using your Favorites

You insert assets from the Favorites list into your Web pages just as you would any other assets; see page 494.

Removing Favorites

Removing assets from the Favorites list is just as straightforward as adding them: just select one in the Favorites list of your Assets panel and then press Delete. The Remove from Favorites button (see Figure 13-15) on the Assets panel does the same thing. Yet another approach is to use the contextual menu (Figure 13-13).

Don't worry; removing an asset from the Favorites list *doesn't* delete that asset from the Assets panel (or your site)—only from the Favorites list. You can still find it listed if you click the Site radio button.

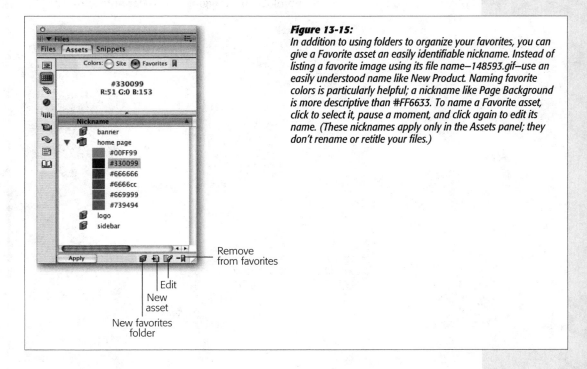

Figure 13-15:
In addition to using folders to organize your favorites, you can give a Favorite asset an easily identifiable nickname. Instead of listing a favorite image using its file name—148593.gif—use an easily understood name like New Product. Naming favorite colors is particularly helpful; a nickname like Page Background is more descriptive than #FF6633. To name a Favorite asset, click to select it, pause a moment, and click again to edit its name. (These nicknames apply only in the Assets panel; they don't rename or retitle your files.)

Remove from favorites

Edit

New asset

New favorites folder

Organizing Favorite assets

On a large site with lots of important assets, even a Favorites list can get unwieldy. That's why you can set up folders within the Assets panel to organize your assets. For example, if you use lots of ads on a site, create a folder in the Image assets Favorites called Ads or, for even greater precision, create multiple folders for different types of ads: Banner Ads, Half Banner Ads, and so on.

You can then drag assets into the appropriate folders, and you can expand or contract the folder to show or hide the assets inside (see Figure 13-15). These folders simply help you organize your Assets panel; they don't actually appear anywhere within the structure of your site. Moving a Favorite asset into a folder in the Assets panel doesn't change the location of files within your site.

To create a Favorites folder, click the appropriate category button at the left edge of the Assets panel (any except the bottom two, since, alas, you can't create folders for templates and Library items). Click Favorites at the top of the Assets panel (you can't create folders in Site view). Finally, click the New Favorites Folder button (see Figure 13-15) at the bottom of the Assets panel. When the new folder appears with its naming rectangle highlighted, type a new name for the folder and then press Enter. (Don't use the same name for more than one folder.)

To put an asset into a folder, just drag it there from the list. And if you're really obsessive, you can even create subfolders by dragging one folder onto another.

Testing Your Site

As you've no doubt realized by now, there are quite a few steps involved in building a Web site. At any point in the process, it's easy to introduce errors that affect the performance of your pages. Both small mistakes, like typos, and site-shattering errors, like broken links, occur frequently in the Web development cycle.

Unfortunately, Web designers often don't develop a good procedure for testing their sites. This chapter offers some helpful techniques for testing your site, including using Dreamweaver's wide array of site-testing tools.

Site Launch Checklist

Don't wait until you've finished your site before embarking on a thorough strategy of testing. By that time, serious design errors may have so completely infested your site's pages that you may have to start over, or at least spend many hours fixing problems that could have been prevented early on.

- **Preview early and often.** The single best way to make sure a page looks and functions the way you want is to preview it in as many Web browsers as possible. Use Dreamweaver's Preview command (see page 48) to preview your page in every browser you can get your hands on. Make sure the graphics look right, that your layout remains the same, and that Cascading Style Sheets, Dreamweaver behaviors, and complex layout methods work as you intended.

Tip: If you don't have every browser ever created installed on your Mac, Windows, and Linux machines (you *do* have all three, don't you?), consider the commercial Web site *www.browsercam.com*. This service lets you view screenshots of your site using a wide variety of browsers and operating systems to make sure your site is working. The downside: $40 a month (ouch).

Free alternatives include iCapture (*www.danvine.com/icapture*) for getting screen captures of your Web pages using the Macintosh Safari browser, and Browsershots (*www.browsershots.org/*), which provides a wide-range of Linux screenshots plus IE 6 on Windows, and Safari 2 on the Mac.

Alternatively, you can download and install the real thing from *browsers.evolt.org/*. This site has archived versions of nearly every Web browser created.

For a thorough evaluation, however, you should preview your pages using every combination of browser *and* operating system you think your site's visitors may use. Enroll co-workers, family members, and household pets, if necessary, in this effort. At the very least, test your pages using Internet Explorer 5 and 6 on Windows, Firefox on Windows and the Mac, and Safari on the Mac. According to several sources, including TheCounter.com (*www.thecounter.com/stats/*) and BrowserNews (*www.upsdell.com/BrowserNews/stat.htm*), Internet Explorer 6 for Windows is installed on upwards of 80 percent of all computers surfing the Web, followed by Internet Explorer 5, Firefox, Safari, and others. If you have access to an AOL account—like 22 million other people around the world—use it. And as the population of Opera browsers grows, add this browser to your test schedule, too.

Tip: If you already have a site up and running, you can find useful browser information in your site's log files. These files track information about visits to your site, including which browsers and platforms your visitors are using. Most Web hosting companies provide access to these files, as well as software to analyze the confusing code inside them. You can use this information, for example, to see whether *anyone* who visits your site still uses Netscape 4. If no one does, that's one less browser you have to design for.

Unfortunately, you'll discover that what works on one browser/operating system combination may not work on another. That's why you should preview your designs *early* in the process of constructing your site. If you design a page that doesn't work well in Internet Explorer 6 on Windows, for example, it's better to catch and fix that problem immediately than discover it after you've built 100 pages based on that design.

• **Check pages in a range of browsers.** Dreamweaver's Check Browser Support command (see page 501) is a helpful diagnostic tool; it analyzes the code of your Web pages and checks for compatibility with various versions of a handful of Web browsers.

Once again, take this step early in the process of building your site. After completing a preliminary design for your home page, for example, use this tool to see if the code works in the browsers you're aiming for.

- **Validate your pages.** Dreamweaver includes a tool that lets you compare your Web pages against agreed-upon standards for HTML and other Web languages. It checks to make sure your pages are *valid* (that they conform to these standards).

  Valid pages are more likely to work in a predictable way on all Web browsers—not just Internet Explorer. And if you envision your site on mobile devices such as cellphones and palmtops, valid pages are again a better bet. In fact, you can even validate your Web pages to see if they conform to Wireless Markup Language (WML)—a tag-based language like HTML used for creating content for mobile phone Web browsers.

- **Check for accessibility.** Not everyone experiences the Web in the same way. People with poor vision, for example, will miss out on the beautiful, full-color banner and navigation buttons you've created. To help you build Web sites that don't shut out people with disabilities, Dreamweaver can check your Web site to make sure it conforms to Section 508 (a Federal regulation mandating that Web sites built by or for the Federal Government are accessible to those with disabilities).

Some troubleshooting steps should come at the end of the process, when a page (or entire site) is ready to be moved to a Web server:

- **Check spelling on your pages.** Amazingly, this simple step is often overlooked. As a result, it's easy to find otherwise professional-looking Web pages on the Internet that are undermined by sloppy spelling. To learn how to use Dreamweaver's built-in spell checker, see page 70.

- **Check your links.** As the name indicates, a Web site can be a complex and twisted collection of interconnected files. Web pages, graphics, Flash movies, and other types of files all work together. Unfortunately, if one file is moved or deleted, problems can ripple through the entire site. Use Dreamweaver's Check Links command to identify and fix broken links (see page 510).

- **Run site reports.** It's always the little things. When building a Web site, small errors inevitably creep into your pages. While not necessarily life-threatening, forgetting to title a Web page or to add an Alt property to an image does diminish the quality and professionalism of a site. Use Dreamweaver's site-reporting feature to quickly identify these problems (see page 521).

Check Browser Support

As noted early in this book, different browsers don't always display HTML in the same way. What's worse, really old browsers don't even *understand* some of the code that Dreamweaver can produce, because Dreamweaver may conform to HTML or CSS standards that were developed only in recent years.

The best way to ensure that visitors see your site the way you intend it is to frequently preview your pages in as many browsers on as many computers as possible. In this way, you can identify and fix problems early.

But if you don't happen to have old computers with old browsers lying around your basement, Dreamweaver can identify elements of a page that won't work in older browsers, or that may be supported by only a single browser. For example, the <layer> tag works *only* in Netscape 4.

Note: The Netscape <layer> tag is *not* the same as Dreamweaver layers (Chapter 8).

Dreamweaver's Check Browser Support feature checks the HTML and CSS code of pages you've selected and tells you if you've used code that doesn't work in various browsers: Internet Explorer, Firefox, Safari, Netscape Navigator, Mozilla, and Opera.

You can even specify which *versions* of the browsers you'd like to test, all the way back to the 3.0 version of Internet Explorer for Windows (which is still being used by Jason P. O'Gillicuddy of Muddy Ditch, Kansas).

In fact, you can have Dreamweaver automatically check browser support each time you open a file. If the program detects an error, it displays a yellow warning sign on the Browser Check menu on the Document toolbar (Figure 14-1). You can choose Show All Errors from this menu to see the errors listed in the Target Browser Check panel shown in Figure 14-2. Alternatively, you can choose File → Check Page → Check Target Browsers to check the page and open the reports panel.

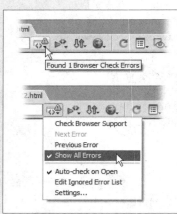

Figure 14-1:
If a page has any code that a particular browser can't understand, the Browser Check menu lets you know with a yellow warning icon.

Top: Place your cursor over the menu button to see how many errors Dreamweaver found.

Bottom: To see a list of all errors, choose Show All Errors from the menu. (You can check an external style sheet the same way.)

Keep in mind that Dreamweaver doesn't actually *test* your pages in these different browsers. It merely compares the HTML in your page against a series of files—called *browser profiles*—that identify which HTML tags the various browsers understand. In other words, don't count on this feature to help you with the subtle differences between browsers—such as the way different browsers display CSS-based layouts, as discussed in Chapter 8. Just because a browser can interpret a particular piece of HTML doesn't mean it always does the job correctly. Throughout this book, you'll find information on these kinds of problems, but there's no substitute for thoroughly testing your pages in as many browsers as you can find.

Once you've identified any errors, you can either choose to remove the offending code—perhaps by getting rid of a rollover effect or abandoning CSS-positioning (see page 296)—or live with the fact that not everyone on earth will be able to view your site exactly as you intended. In many cases, the errors have minimal or no effect. For example, Internet Explorer 5 doesn't support dotted lines for CSS borders (see page 205); oh well, those visitors will just have to suffer with solid lines. *Quel dommage!*

If your Web site absolutely must work with (really) old versions of browsers, you'll need to steer clear of most CSS-based layout and other new technologies, and use the Check Browser Support command. But before abandoning such useful and advanced features, keep in mind that well over 90 percent of the Web-surfing public uses version 5 or later of Internet Explorer, or one of the newer upstarts such as Firefox, Safari, or Opera.

You can check an open page by choosing Show All Errors from the Check Browser Support menu in the Document toolbar (see Figure 14-1), or you can check any or all pages in a site by following these steps:

1. **Choose Window → Results and click the Target Browser Check tab.**

   The keyboard shortcut is F7. Either way, you open the Results panel to the Target Browser Check tab (see Figure 14-2).

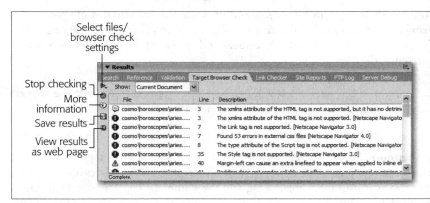

Figure 14-2:
As you may suspect, the older the browser you check support for, the more errors Dreamweaver is likely to find.

2. **Using the green arrow in the Target Browser Check panel, select which files to check.**

   Clicking the green arrow provides a menu with three options for checking pages (plus two preference settings described on page 505). The first checks the page you're currently working on. The second option checks all pages in your site, and the final option checks only files (or folders of files) you've selected in the Files panel. (For tips on selecting files in the Files panel, see the box on page 512.)

Tip: Dreamweaver can also generate a Web page listing the errors: click the globe icon in the Target Browser Check panel (see Figure 14-2). To save a file with the results, click the floppy disk icon. But because this option saves all of the error information into an almost indecipherable XML file, you probably won't find much use for it.

---

3. **Review the results.**

The results list displays four columns of information: an icon indicating the severity of the error, the name of the file with the error, the line number the error occurs on, and a description of the error, including which browser won't work with the code. (The line numbers refer to lines in the HTML code of your page. See Chapter 9 for details on Code view.)

An error appears when a browser doesn't understand a particular HTML tag or property. For example, Internet Explorer 3 has a very limited understanding of JavaScript; therefore, you'll see an error listed for every page where you used an *image rollover* effect (see page 144). The error indicates that IE 3 doesn't understand the JavaScript code, and the rollover won't work.

Note: Of course, this is an extreme example; realistically, no one uses Internet Explorer 3.0 anymore. Fortunately, Dreamweaver gives you a way to specify which browsers to check against, so you don't have to wade through line after line of errors that apply to some Web browser not available since the Paleolithic era (you know, the browser that the dinosaurs in *Jurassic Park* used to sell fossils on eBay).

Don't panic if you run this command on your site and see lots of errors. The errors don't mean that *you* made mistakes. They simply indicate that one of the browsers you selected doesn't understand some of the tags Dreamweaver inserted.

Note: If you work in Code view or Split view (see page 330), Dreamweaver also underlines browser-check errors with a squiggly red line. To read a tooltip describing the error, move your mouse over the red line.

Furthermore, Dreamweaver is often smart enough to use *two* tags to overcome browser limitations. For example, when inserting Flash movies into a page, Dreamweaver uses the <object> tag and the <embed> tag. The <embed> tag is intended to allow Netscape Navigator 4 browsers to correctly view the Flash movie, while the <object> tag works with Internet Explorer and later versions of Navigator. Because Navigator 4 doesn't understand the <object> tag, you'll still get an error if you check your page against that browser, even though the <embed> tag Dreamweaver inserted means the Flash movie works in Netscape 4.

In other words, an error reported by Dreamweaver doesn't necessarily mean that your page won't work in a specified browser. Since your site's visitors may not even be using Netscape 4, this is another reason to make sure you check *only* for the browsers that actually visit your site, as described in the next section.

The Check Browser Support command is a good way to quickly learn about the different HTML tags each browser recognizes. In time, you'll probably know enough to avoid using elements that don't work for the browsers your visitors use, and you'll find this command unnecessary.

Editing the List of Browsers to Check Against

You probably won't need to check *all* of the browsers and *all* of their versions. Few (if any) people still use Internet Explorer 3 for Windows, for example. As mentioned earlier, the most important consideration is making sure you meet the needs of your site's audience: if they're all on Windows machines, check Internet Explorer for Windows. A site that includes a lot of Macintosh visitors had better be prepared for Safari (Apple's Web browser).

To customize the list of browsers you want to check against, choose the Settings option from one of two places:

- The green-arrow menu in the Target Browser Check tab of the Results panel (see Figure 14-2).

- The Check Browser Support menu in the Document toolbar (see Figure 14-1).

In either case, the Target Browsers window appears (Figure 14-3). The window lists seven different browsers and includes a submenu where you can select a version number. Dreamweaver checks the support of any browsers whose checkbox is turned on.

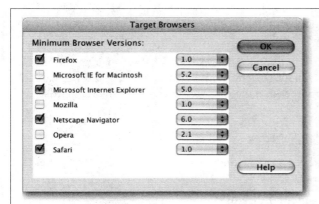

Figure 14-3:
You can check the HTML of your pages against the capabilities of any or all of the browsers listed here. Use the menu next to each browser name to select which version of that browser you want to check against. Try to limit your choices to the browsers your visitors are likely using. If you choose an old, little-used browser like Netscape Navigator 3.0, Dreamweaver generates an unnecessarily long list of errors, since much of the HTML code Dreamweaver generates wasn't even around back when Navigator 3.0 was written.

In addition, you can specify a *minimum* version number from the menu to the right of the browser name. For example, if your site doesn't have any visitors using version 4 of Internet Explorer (a likely scenario), choose 5.0 from the menu. Dreamweaver checks for compatibility only with versions of Internet Explorer that are 5.0 or greater.

Validating Web Pages

The Web is a far-flung collection of technologies, scripting and programming languages, and people all working together. When you think about it, it's pretty amazing that an 11-year-old in Fargo, North Dakota, can create a Web site viewable by millions of people around the world, or even that hundreds of different browsers, from Internet Explorer to cellphones, can browse the same Web site. This kind of global communication owes its success in large part to the World Wide Web Consortium (the W3C), an organization composed of representatives from universities, research institutions, corporations, and government agencies dedicated to creating standards for different Internet-related technologies.

The W3C developed standards for HTML, XHTML, CSS, XML, and other Web languages, and continues to create new standards as technologies evolve. Thanks to these standards, companies have a guide to follow when creating new Web browsers.

It sure would be great if all companies followed the standards when building Web browsers, and all Web designers followed the standards when building Web pages. Then anyone with any Web browser could view any Web page. What a wonderful world *that* would be—you'd never have to test your Web pages in different browsers.

Of course, this kind of utopian thinking hasn't always been applied by the major browser makers. As a result, Web developers have been forced to come up with techniques to deal with the way different browsers display HTML. (The Check Browser Support command mentioned in the previous section is great for helping you figure out where browsers fail.)

Fortunately, the situation is improving; browser makers are making more of an effort these days to stick to the W3C's recommended standards. And you can, too: Dreamweaver includes a tool for making sure your pages meet the standards set by the W3C.

Steps for Validating Web Pages

You can check either an open page or any pages selected in the Files panel (see page 479) by following these steps:

1. **Choose Window → Results and click the Validation tab.**

    The keyboard shortcut for the Results panel is F7. Either way, the Results panel opens, showing the Validation tab (Figure 14-4).

Tip: If you want to validate just the page you're working on, choose File → Check Page → Validate Markup.

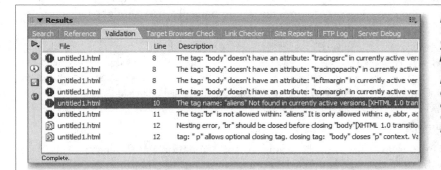

Figure 14-4:
The Validation panel lets you check your Web pages against various W3C standards. The buttons along the left edge work like the ones on the Target Browser Check panel (see Figure 14-2).

2. **In the Validation panel, click the green arrow and select which files to check.**

   The green arrow reveals a menu with four options. The first checks the page you're currently working on. The second option checks all pages in your site, and the third option checks just those files selected in the Files panel.

POWER USERS' CLINIC

Cut Down on Error Messages

As you go about creating Web pages, you may use some code that always generates errors during browser checks. For example, the Leftmargin property of the <body> tag always spits up errors for Navigator, Mozilla, and Opera, because only Internet Explorer uses that property (to set the left margin of a page). None of those other browsers understand it.

If you get annoyed seeing these red warning errors for tags or properties that you need to use so that all browsers get the same experience, you can tell Dreamweaver to exclude certain errors from its report. To do so, right-click (Control-click) the error message (red error icons only) in the Results panel. From the menu that appears, select Ignore Error.

Unfortunately, Dreamweaver doesn't actually "ignore" these errors. It simply demotes them from "errors" to "cautions" (the yellow warning icon). There's no way to remove these warnings completely from the results panel.

Behind the scenes, Dreamweaver adds code to a special file called Exceptions.xml, located in the program's configuration folder. This file contains a collection of the tags, attributes, CSS properties, or CSS values Dreamweaver should ignore. For example, to hide the <body> tag's Leftmargin property from the browser checker, the code looks like this: <attribute tag="body" attribute="leftmargin"/>. Accordingly, if you want to bring back the Leftmargin property error that you excluded previously, you must open the XML file and delete this line of code (or the relevant line of code for whichever property or tag you want Dreamweaver to start checking again). You can open the file quickly from the Browser Support menu in the document toolbar (see Figure 14-1). Choose Edit Ignored Error List and, once the XML file opens, make your changes and save the file. (Unfortunately, this list has no effect on browser-check warnings—the ones marked with a yellow icon in the Results panel.)

The fourth option—Settings—opens the Validator Preferences window, which lets you select which type of standard to validate against if no *doctype* is specified. A doctype (see page 6) is just a line of code that goes in the head of a document and tells a Web browser which standard the particular page is attempting to adhere to. Because Dreamweaver automatically inserts a doctype, you won't need to change any of these settings.

Note: You can also validate the file as an XML file by choosing File → Check Page → Validate as XML. (To the technically inclined: you can not only check whether your XML is "well-formed," but you can also check it against the Document Type Definition [DTD] specified in your document.)

---

3. **Review the results.**

Dreamweaver displays the results in the Validation panel (Figure 14-4). Each validation message is divided into four columns: the first includes an icon that indicates the severity of the error, the second lists the file, the thirds lists which line in the code the message applies to, and the fourth describes the validation error or message.

The icon at the beginning of the message helps you determine which errors are important. A red stop sign identifies a violation of the standards for the particular doctype (HTML 4.01 Transitional, XTHML 1.0 Transitional, and so on) the page is attempting to follow. In some cases, this warning can indicate that a tag is missing or incorrectly closed—a serious problem.

Other stop-sign errors aren't necessarily fatal. For example, when you insert a Flash movie, Dreamweaver uses the <embed> tag to insert information needed by Netscape to play the movie—a tag that's deprecated (set for retirement) in the HTML standards. You'll get all manner of errors if you validate a page containing this tag, even though it's necessary for viewing the Flash movie in Netscape.

GEM IN THE ROUGH

Is the Validator Valid?

Dreamweaver's validation feature is a big help in seeing where your code fails to match the standards set by the W3C, but it's an imperfect tool. For example, it doesn't provide very good explanations for errors, it doesn't always catch invalid code, and it can't validate CSS.

For the best source of validation information and tools, turn to the W3C's free validation services and information resources. You can find the HTML (or XHTML) validator at *http://validator.w3.org/*. For CSS validation, visit *http://jigsaw.w3.org/css-validator/*. With these tools, you can validate files already online or upload a Web page or CSS file for analysis. It's free, and it provides detailed information about the meaning of any errors.

Because Dreamweaver's validator is faster (you don't need to upload files to the Internet or wait for the W3C validator to download files over the Web), it's a good approach to start with it. Find and fix errors Dreamweaver identifies, and then try out the W3C validator for the finishing touches.

You may also get the red stop-sign error when you use some of Dreamweaver's own tools. For example, if you use a tracing image (see page 243), Dreamweaver adds some code to the <body> tag that isn't "real" HTML. You'll get an error every time you check a page with a tracing image (or at least until you remove the tracing image, as described on page 244).

Less serious problems are flagged with little message balloons. These may inform you that the page has *no* problems, or point out optional fixes. (See the following section for a list of common errors and messages.)

You may also encounter an icon that looks like two pieces of paper placed one on top of the other (who comes up with these things?). These usually occur when you validate against any of the HTML standards and have incorrectly written code—an unclosed <p> tag, for example.

4. **Fix the errors.**

Alas, Dreamweaver can't fix all of these validation errors. For errors related to improperly written code (see the last paragraph of step 3), you can usually run the Clean Up HTML/XHTML command (see page 518).

For the other errors, it's up to you and your knowledge of HTML to go into the code and fix any problems. For assistance, check out the online HTML reference (see page 353).

To get started, double-click an error in the Validation results panel. The Web page opens in Split view, with the invalid HTML code selected. You can then delete or modify the offending code. Keep in mind, though, that the code Dreamweaver produces is the result of many thousands of hours of engineering and testing. Unless you're sure you know how to fix a problem, you may just want to trust the code Dreamweaver produces.

Common Validation Errors

Although a complete reference for creating valid Web sites would fill a book of its own, here are some errors you'll encounter frequently when using Dreamweaver's validator:

- **In HTML 4.0, FONT is deprecated.** You encounter this message in pages you've built with earlier versions of Dreamweaver, or if you set your preferences to work with the old style <font> tag. Since version MX 2004, Dreamweaver has used Cascading Style Sheets when formatting text with the Property inspector, so you probably won't encounter this error on any pages you build using Dreamweaver 8 (unless you've changed Dreamweaver's factory presets as described on page 30).

- **The tag name: "embed" not found in currently active versions.** This error appears when you insert Flash movies (including Flash buttons and Flash text), as described on page 146. Other errors related to the <embed> tag may also appear, including "The tag: 'embed' doesn't have an attribute: 'quality' in currently active versions." Ignore them.

- **In tag: 'script' the following required attributes are missing: 'type'.** This message indicates that the <script> tag used to insert JavaScript programs is missing the following Type property. Dreamweaver now inserts this property correctly, but it didn't always. If you used Dreamweaver 4 to build your site, for example, you'll get this error message for any page that uses a Dreamweaver behavior. To fix it, add *type="text/JavaScript"* to the <script> tag.

- **The tag: 'body' doesn't have an attribute: 'marginwidth' in currently active versions.** (Similar messages for *marginheight* may also appear.) If you set the left and top margin of a page in the <body> tag (in a previous version of Dreamweaver, for example), you'll encounter this message. Dreamweaver's Page Properties window (see page 40) uses CSS to set margins instead. Marginwidth is a Netscape-specific property and not part of any HTML standard. Internet Explorer's Leftmargin and Topmargin properties are similarly browser-specific. Although using these properties poses no real problems—other browsers ignore them—the recommended solution is to use Cascading Style Sheets to set the margins of a page.

Find and Fix Broken Links

Broken links are inevitable. If you delete a file from your site, move a page or graphic outside of Dreamweaver, or simply type an incorrect path to a file, broken links and missing graphics may result. In the B.D. era (Before Dreamweaver), the only way to fix such problems was to methodically examine every link on every page in your site. Fortunately, Dreamweaver's link-checking features can automate the process of tracking down broken-link problems.

Note: In this context, a *link* doesn't only mean a hyperlink connecting one page to another. Dreamweaver also uses the term to include the paths that identify external files incorporated in your Web page, such as GIFs, JPEGs, external CSS style sheets, and Flash movies. For example, if a graphic is missing or isn't in the place specified by the Web page, Dreamweaver reports a broken *link.*

Finding Broken Links

The Check Links Sitewide command scans an entire site's worth of files and reports all links and paths that don't lead to a file. (It's one of Dreamweaver's site management features, meaning that you have to define a local site before using this command; see page 472.) Note that Dreamweaver checks only links and paths *within* the local site folder; it doesn't check links that lead to other people's Web sites.

Note: If your local site contains a lot of pages, you may not want to check links in one or more folders whose pages *you know* have no broken links. You can exclude files from the Check Links Sitewide operation using the Cloaking feature described on page 549. Doing so also makes the link-checking operation go faster.

Checking just one page

To check links on an open page, save it in your local site folder. Then choose File → Check Page → Check Links (or press Shift+F8). Dreamweaver scans the page and opens the Link Checker window, which lists files containing broken links (see Figure 14-5). If Dreamweaver doesn't find any broken links—you HTML god, you—the window comes up empty.

Tip: Although Dreamweaver can't check links to the outside world, a free tool from the W3C can. You can find its link checker at *http://validator.w3.org/checklink*. This tool checks both internal links (between pages on the same site) and external links (to other sites). The only possible downside: the pages you wish to check must already be up on the Web.

Checking specific pages

You can also check links just on specific pages of your site from the Link Checker panel:

1. **Choose Window → Results to open the Results panel and click the Link Checker tab.**

   The Link Checker panel opens.

2. **Use the Files panel to select the site you wish to check (see page 480).**

   If you're already working on the site you want to check, you can skip this step.

3. **In the Files panel, select the files you'd like to check.**

   For techniques on selecting files and folders in the Files panel, see the box on page 512.

Tip: Selecting a folder makes Dreamweaver scan all files in that folder.

---

4. **Click the green-arrow icon in the Link Checker panel. From the menu that appears, choose Check Links for Selected Files/Folders in Site.**

   Alternatively, you can right-click (Control-click) the selected files, and then choose Check Links → Selected Files/Folders from the shortcut menu.

   Either way, Dreamweaver scans the pages and opens the Link Checker panel (Figure 14-5).

Checking the entire Web site

You can check all the links on all pages of your Web site in any of three ways:

- Open the Web site you want to check (press F8 to open the Files panel and use the panel's menu to select the site), and then choose Site → Check Links Site-wide. Or use the keyboard shortcut, Ctrl+F8 (⌘-F8).

- Open the Files panel and right-click (Control-click) any file. Choose Check Links → Entire Local Site from the shortcut menu.

- Open the Link Checker panel (Window → Results to open the Results panel, and then click the Link Checker tab), click the green-arrow icon, and, from its menu, choose Check Links for Entire Current Local Site.

Once again, Dreamweaver scans your site and opens the Link Checker panel, which lists files containing broken links (Figure 14-5).

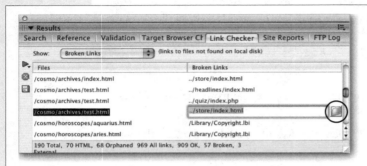

Figure 14-5:
The Check Links Sitewide command generates a list of all external links and orphaned files (files with no links to them). If you wish, click the Save (floppy disk) button to save all of this information into a tab-delimited text file. You can also fix a broken link directly inside this panel using the Browse for File button (circled) as described on page 513.

Selection Shortcuts for the Files Panel

You'll often want to use the tools in the Results panel on more than one page in your Web site. Fortunately, most of these tools can work on multiple pages in the Files panel.

You probably can figure out that you should click a file to select it. But you can also select several files that are listed consecutively: click the first one, scroll if necessary, and then Shift-click the last one. Dreamweaver highlights all the files between your first and final clicks.

If you want to select several files that aren't consecutive in the list, the trick is to click each one while pressing the Ctrl (⌘) key.

Once you've selected one or more files, you can deselect one by Ctrl-clicking (⌘-clicking) it once again.

Dreamweaver also includes a snazzy command for selecting recently modified files in the Files panel. Suppose you want to select all the files you created or changed today (to see if the links work or to upload them to your Web server, as described on page 542). To use this command, you need

to click the Files panel's contextual-menu button in the upper-right corner of the panel. From the menu that appears, select Edit → Select Recently Modified.

The Select Recently Modified window appears. You can either specify a range of dates (for example, files you created or changed between January 1, 2005, and January 7, 2005) or a number of days (to specify all modified files in, say, the last 30 days). (The last option—Modified By—works only with Macromedia's Contribute program.) Set the options, click OK, and Dreamweaver selects the appropriate files in the Files panel.

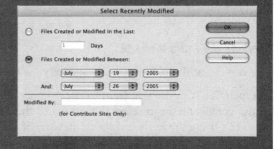

Fixing Broken Links

Of course, simply finding broken links is only half the battle. You also need to *fix* them. The Link Checker panel provides a quick and easy way to do this:

1. **In the Link Checker panel, click a path in the Broken Links column.**

   The path is highlighted, and a tiny folder icon appears to the right (circled in Figure 14-5).

Tip: The Link Checker panel shows you which pages *contain* broken links, but doesn't show you the text or images of the broken links themselves, which can make it difficult to figure out how you're supposed to fix them ("Was that a button that links to the home page?"). In such a case, *double-click* the file name in the Link Checker panel. Dreamweaver opens the Web page and, even better, highlights the link on the page.

Once you've determined where the link should lead ("Oh yeah. That's the button to the haggis buffet menu"), you can fix the link on the page (see page 120) or go back to the Link Checker panel and make the change as described in the next step.

---

2. **Click the tiny folder icon.**

   The Select File dialog box opens. From here, you can navigate to and (in the next step) select the correct page—the one that *should* have been opened by that link.

   If you prefer, you can type a path directly in the Link Checker panel. Doing so usually isn't a good idea, however, since it's difficult to understand the path from one page to another by just looking at the Link Checker panel. Searching for the proper page using the Select File dialog box is a much more accurate and trouble-free method.

3. **Double-click a Web page in the Select File dialog box.**

   The dialog box disappears, and Dreamweaver fixes the link.

   If your Web site contains other links pointing to the same missing file, Dreamweaver asks if you'd like to fix the same broken link on those pages, too—an amazing time-saver that can quickly repair broken links on dozens of pages.

Tip: Dreamweaver's behavior is a bit odd in this regard, however. Once you fix one link, it remains selected in the Link Checker panel. You must click another broken link, or one of the buttons in the window, before Dreamweaver asks if you'd like to fix that same broken link on other pages.

---

4. **Continue to fix broken links, following steps 1 through 3.**

   When you've repaired all the broken links, click the close button.

Listing External Links

Although Dreamweaver doesn't verify links to other Web sites on your pages, it does show you a list of such *external links* when you run the link checker. To see this list, choose External Links from the Show menu of the Link Checker panel (see Figure 14-6). The list includes absolute URLs leading to other sites (like *http:// www.yahoo.com*) as well as email links (like *mailto:alien_sightings@nationalexasper- ator.com*).

Figure 14-6:
Although Dreamweaver can't check external links, you can use this window to change the URL of an external link.

This window is especially useful if you've created a link to a certain external Web site several times throughout your Web site and you've decided to change the link. For example, you discovered through testing (or through the W3C Link Checker mentioned on page 508) that an external link that you've peppered throughout your site no longer works:

1. **Choose Site → Check Links Sitewide (or press Ctrl+F8 [⌘-F8]).**

   Dreamweaver scans your site and opens the Link Checker panel.

2. **From the Show pop-up menu, choose External Links.**

   The window lists links you've created to sites outside your own.

3. **Click the external link you want to change.**

   Dreamweaver highlights the link, indicating that you can now edit it.

4. **Type the new URL; press Enter (Return).**

   If other pages contain the old URL, Dreamweaver asks if you would like to fix them as well. If so, click Yes; the deed is done.

Orphaned Files

The Link Checker panel also provides a list of files that aren't used by any Web page in the site—*orphaned files,* as they're called. You wind up with an *orphaned* graphic file when, for example, you save a GIF into your site folder but then never use it on a Web page. Or suppose you eliminate the only link to an old page that you don't need anymore, making it an *orphaned* file. Unless you think you may link to it in the future, you can delete it to clean up unnecessary clutter in your site.

In fact, that's the primary purpose of this feature: to locate old and unused files and delete them. Here's how it works:

1. **Choose Site → Check Links Sitewide, or press Ctrl+F8 (⌘-F8).**

   Dreamweaver opens the Link Checker panel.

2. **From the Show menu, choose Orphaned Files.**

   The list of *orphaned* files appears (see Figure 14-7).

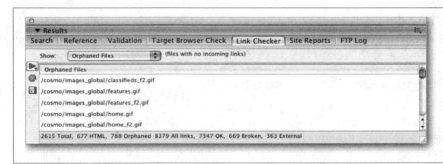

Figure 14-7:
Identify (and delete) unused files using Dreamweaver's Link Checker panel. This panel lists external links and orphaned files as well as broken links; use the Show menu to isolate the different types of link.

3. **Select the files you want to delete.**

   For example, by Ctrl- (⌘-) clicking the files.

4. **Press Delete.**

   Dreamweaver asks if you really want to delete the files. Click OK if you do, Cancel if you suddenly get cold feet.

5. **Click the Close button when you're finished.**

Before you get spring-cleaning fever and delete all *orphaned* files in your site, however, keep a few pointers in mind:

- Just because a file isn't *currently* in use doesn't mean you won't need it again later. For example, say you have an employee-of-the-month page. In March, you included a photo of Robin Albert, your best salesperson. In April, someone else got the award, so you removed Robin's photo. You're not using that photo now—rendering it an *orphaned* file—but next month you may need it again, when Robin develops a spurt of motivation. Make sure a file is really useless before deleting it.

- More important, Dreamweaver may flag files your site actually needs as *orphaned*. For example, some sites include what's called a *splash page*: an introductory page that first appears when someone comes to the site. It can be a page with a bold graphic and the text "Click here to enter the site." Or it may be a fancy Flash movie intended to make a big impact on your visitors. Usually, this page is nothing more than a welcome mat that leads to the *real* home page. Since it's simply an introductory page, no other page in the site links to it. Unfortunately, that's precisely what Dreamweaver considers an *orphaned* file.

- If you write your own JavaScript code, you may reference graphic files and Web pages. Dreamweaver doesn't keep track of these references, and identifies those files as orphans (unless they're inserted or linked to elsewhere in the page or site).

  On the other hand, Dreamweaver is somewhat smarter when it comes to behaviors. It can track files referenced as part of its own JavaScript programs—for example, graphic files you use in a rollover effect—and doesn't list them as *orphaned* files.

The bottom line is that while this report is useful, use it cautiously when deleting files.

Changing a Link Throughout a Site

Suppose you've created a page on your site to teach your visitors about the basics of the HTML language. You think this page would be really, really helpful to your visitors, so you create links to it from every page on your site. After a while, you realize you just don't have the time to keep this page up to date, but you still want to help your visitors get this information. Why not change the link so it points to a more current and informative source? Using Dreamweaver's Change Link Sitewide command, you can do just that:

1. **Choose Site → Change Link Sitewide.**

   The Change Link Sitewide dialog box opens (see Figure 14-8).

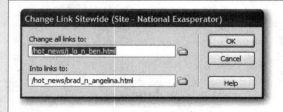

Figure 14-8:
Dreamweaver uses a root-relative link to specify the page, as indicated by the slash (/). Don't worry: this doesn't mean Dreamweaver makes the link root-relative. It's just how Dreamweaver identifies the location of the page in the site. See page 105 for more on root-relative links.

This dialog box offers two different fields: "Change all links to" and "Into links to." Understanding what you're supposed to do at this point is easier if you imagine that the first label is actually "Change All Links That *Currently* Point To." In other words, first you'll indicate where those links point now; then you'll indicate where you'd like them to go instead.

At this point, you can type the new Web address into the "Change all links to" field. For example, if your aim is to round up every link that now points to

Yahoo! and redirect them to Google, you could start by typing *http://www. yahoo.com* here.

If the links you're trying to change refer to a page in your own site, however, proceed to step 2.

2. **Click the folder icon to the right of the "Change all links to" field.**

   The Select Link to Change dialog box opens. You're about to specify the file that the links point to *now*.

3. **Select a file in the local site folder; click OK (Windows) or Choose (Mac).**

   In the following steps, Dreamweaver will change every link that leads to *this file*, whether it's a graphic, Cascading Style Sheet file, or any other external file that can be part of a Web page.

Tip: As a shortcut to following steps 1, 2, and 3, you can select a file in the Files panel, and *then* choose Site → Change Link Sitewide. Dreamweaver automatically adds the selected file's path to the "Change all links to" field.

Now it's time to substitute the new URL or file—the one to which all of those links will be redirected. If you're reassigning them to a different Web site, you can type its URL directly into the "Change all links to" field. For example, in the previous example, you can type *http://www.google.com*.

Tip: For another way to change one external link into another, see Figure 14-6.

If you'd like the changed links to point to a file on your own Web site instead, proceed to step 4.

4. **Click the folder icon to the right of the "Into links to" field.**

   The Select Link to Change dialog box opens.

5. **Select a file in the local site, and then click OK (Windows) or Choose (Mac).**

   You've just selected the new file you wish to link to. In other words, every link that once led to the file you selected in step 3 now links to this file. You can select graphics, Cascading Style Sheet files, and any other external files you can include in a Web page.

   You'll get unpredictable results, however, if you change a link that points to a graphic file into, say, a link that points to a Web page, or vice versa. Make sure the "before" and "after" links share the same file type: Web page, style sheet, or graphic.

6. **Click OK to make the change.**

   The same Update Files dialog box you encountered in the last chapter appears, listing every page that will be affected.

7. **Click Update to update the pages.**

Dreamweaver scans your site and updates the pages.

Cleaning Up HTML (and XHTML)

You've been reading about what great HTML code Dreamweaver writes, and how all you hand coders need to get on the WYSIWYG bandwagon. But there are exceptions to every rule. In the process of formatting text, deleting elements, and—in general—building a Web page, it's quite possible to end up with less-than-optimal HTML coding. While Dreamweaver usually catches potentially sloppy HTML, you may nonetheless run across instances of empty tags, redundant tags, and nested tags in your Dreamweaver pages.

For example, in the normal course of adding, editing, and deleting content on a page (either by hand or even in Dreamweaver's Design view), you can occasionally end up with code like this:

```
<div align="center"> </div>
```

This empty tag doesn't serve any purpose and only adds unnecessary code to your page. Remember, the less code your page uses, the faster it loads. Eliminating redundant tags can improve the download speed of your site.

Another possible source of errors is you. When you type HTML in Code view or open pages created by another program, you may introduce errors that you'll need to clean up later.

Note: If you're creating XHTML documents (see page 6) and using Dreamweaver behaviors (Chapter 11), it's a good idea to run the Clean Up XHTML command. Dreamweaver occasionally inserts uppercase letters in the names of JavaScript events—onLoad or onClick, for example—a no-no in the land of all lowercase XHTML.

Aware of its own limitations (and yours), Dreamweaver comes with a command that's designed to streamline the code in your pages: Clean Up HTML (if you're using Dreamweaver's XHTML mode, the command is called Clean Up XHTML). This command not only improves the HTML in your page, it can also strip out other nonessential code such as comments and special Dreamweaver markup code, and it can eliminate a specific tag or tags.

Tip: The Clean Up HTML command is extremely useful. Once you've tried it a few times, you'll probably want to use it on all your pages. Unfortunately, it doesn't come with a keyboard shortcut. This is a classic case when Dreamweaver's *keyboard-shortcut editor* is just the white knight you need; using it, you can add a key combination to trigger this command from the keyboard. See page 665 for details.

To use this command:

1. **Open a Web page to clean up.**

   Unfortunately, this great feature works only on one page at a time. No cleaning up a site's worth of pages in one fell swoop! Accordingly, it's best to first use the Site Reports feature (see page 521) to identify problem pages. *Then* open them in Dreamweaver and run this command.

2. **Choose Commands → Clean Up HTML (or Clean Up XHTML).**

   The Clean Up HTML/XHTML window appears (see Figure 14-9).

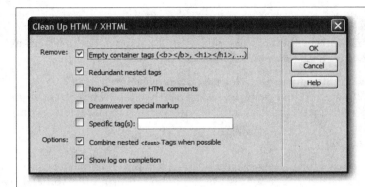

Figure 14-9:
The Clean Up HTML/XHTML command lets you improve the quality and speed of a Web page by stripping out redundant and useless code. You can even use it to strip out useful tags by specifying a tag in the "Specific tag(s)" field (although the Find and Replace command provides a much more powerful method of identifying and removing HTML tags; see page 649).

3. **Turn on the checkboxes for the options you want.**

   Here's a rundown:

   - **Empty Container Tags** deletes any tags that don't actually contain anything. For example, you may delete some text that had been set in boldface, leaving behind opening and closing bold tags without any text in between: <b></b>. Or you may delete an image within a link, leaving behind a useless pair of <a> tags. It's always a good idea to turn on this option.

   - **Redundant Nested Tags** deletes tags that appear within other tags of the same type, like this: <b>You can't get any <b>bolder</b> than bold</b>. The second set of bold tags does no good, so choosing this option would produce this: <b>You can't get any bolder than bold</b>. This is an extremely useful option.

   - **Non-Dreamweaver HTML Comments** deletes any comments *not* inserted by someone using Dreamweaver. Web designers place notes within code to give directions or explain parts of the code. (These comments are invisible in a Web browser. They appear only in the Code view, or as a gold comment icon in Dreamweaver's document window.) Since comments are often added as an aid for maintaining a Web page, you may not want to choose this option.

However, if the page is finished, and you doubt you'll need the information the comments contain, you can decrease the file size of a page by using this option.

- **Dreamweaver Special Markup** deletes any special code Dreamweaver inserts. Dreamweaver relies on certain code in some of its features, including tracing images (Chapter 7), templates (Chapter 17), and Libraries (Chapter 16). Choosing this option also eliminates the special code that makes those features work, so use this option with care. (Since the template feature adds a great deal of this specialized code, Dreamweaver includes a Template Export command that lets you export an entire site with all template code removed. See page 629.)

- **Specific Tag(s)** deletes HTML tags you specify. Type the name of the tag (without brackets) in the field like this: *font*. To remove multiple tags at once, separate each tag name by a comma like this: *font, blink*.

  Be careful with this option. Since it lets you remove *any* tag from a page, it's easy to delete an important and necessary tag (like the <body> tag) from your page by accident. Furthermore, Dreamweaver's Find and Replace command provides much more powerful tools for performing this kind of surgery (see page 649).

- **Combine Nested <font> Tags when Possible** combines multiple *font* properties into a single tag. This, too, is a useful option to turn on if you aren't using Cascading Style Sheets to format your text.

- If you want to see a report of all the changes Dreamweaver makes to a page, turn on **Show Log on Completion.**

4. **Click OK to clean up the page.**

   If you selected Show Log on Completion, a dialog box then appears, listing the types of changes and the number of changes that Dreamweaver made to the page.

Note: When running this command on an XHTML page, Dreamweaver also checks to make sure the syntax of the page matches the requirements of an XHTML document (see page 6). Among other concerns, in XHTML, all tags must be lowercase, and any empty tags must be terminated correctly—
 for the line break tag, for example. Dreamweaver fixes such problems.

As long as you keep the page open, you can undo changes Dreamweaver made. Suppose you asked Dreamweaver to remove any comments, and suddenly realized you really did need them. Ctrl+Z (⌘-Z) does the trick. You can also use the History panel, which lists this step as Clean Up HTML/XHTML (see page 518).

Site Reporting

The Clean Up HTML command is a great way to make sure your code is well written. But what if you forget about it until after you've built all 500 pages of your site? Do you have to open each page and run the command—whether there's a problem or not?

Fortunately, no. Dreamweaver's Site Reports feature makes identifying problems throughout a site a snap. As well as locating the problems fixed by the Clean Up HTML command, it makes Dreamweaver check your pages for other problems, such as missing titles, empty Alt properties for images, and other problems that can make your Web site less accessible to disabled Web surfers.

Tip: To save time when running a report, you can exclude select folders from a Site Report operation using the cloaking feature described on page 549.

After running a report, Dreamweaver displays a list of pages with problems. Unfortunately, the Site Reports feature only finds problems; it doesn't fix them. You have to open and fix each page individually.

To run a report on one or more Web pages, proceed like this:

1. **Choose Site → Reports.**

   The Reports window opens (see Figure 14-10).

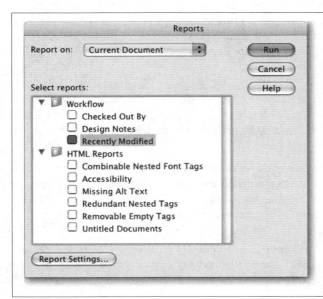

Figure 14-10:
Dreamweaver's Site Reports feature makes quick work of finding common page errors. It's also one of Dreamweaver's many customizable features. You can download additional types of reports from the Macromedia Exchange Web site or even program your own. For more information on customizing Dreamweaver and using Macromedia Exchange, see page 670.

2. **From the "Report on" menu, select the files to analyze.**

   Dreamweaver can report on a single Web page, multiple pages, or even an entire site. Choose **Current Document** to check the Web page that's open at the moment. **Entire Current Local Site** checks every Web page in the local site folder, including folders inside it. This option is great when you want to check your entire site prior to uploading it to a Web server and making it "live" (more on that in Chapter 15).

   Selected Files in Site checks only the files you choose in the Files panel. You need to open the Files panel and select files in the local file list for this option to work. See the box on page 512 for methods on selecting files in the Files panel. Choose this option when you've modified or added pages to a site, and are ready to move them to the Web server.

   Folder checks all Web pages in a selected folder. After you choose this option, an empty field and a folder icon appear. Click the folder icon; a dialog box gives you the opportunity to locate and select the folder you wish to check, including any folders inside it. You can also use this option when you wish to check pages that aren't actually part of the current site.

3. **Select the types of reports you want Dreamweaver to generate.**

   The Reports window is divided into two types of reports. The first set, Work-flow reports, mostly deals with features that facilitate working with others as part of a production team (see the following chapter). The last option in this group—Recently Modified—generates a list of files that have either been created or modified within a certain number of days or within a range of dates (February 1 of last year to the present, say). When you run this type of report, Dreamweaver lists the files in the Site Reports panel *and* opens a Web page listing the files in your browser.

Note: The Recently Modified site report looks for files created or changed in the last seven days, but you can adjust that time frame. Select Recently Modified in the Reports window and click the Report Settings button (Figure 14-10). A window appears like the one pictured in the box on page 512, where you can change the range of dates to check.

In fact, you'll probably find the technique described on page 512 more useful. It not only identifies recently modified files, but also selects them in the Files panel, giving you a lot more options for acting on this information. For example, with those files selected, you can upload them to your Web server, run Find and Replace operations on just those files, or access many other tools.

The second type, HTML Reports, are useful for locating common errors, such as forgetting to title a Web page or forgetting to add an Alt property to an image.

Three of the HTML Report options—**Combinable Nested Font Tags, Redundant Nested Tags,** and **Removable Empty Tags**—search for pages with common code mistakes. These are the same problems fixed by the Clean Up HTML command (see page 518).

The **Accessibility** report lets you see how usable your site is to people with disabilities. This sophisticated command checks to see how well your pages conform to Web accessibility guidelines mandated by the U.S. Government and recommended by the W3C (see page 525). This option produces detailed reports, so it's usually best to run it separately.

Turn on **Missing Alt Text** to search for pages with images that are missing an alternate text description (see page 128). If you turn on the Accessibility option, you can leave this option turned off; the Accessibility analyzer already includes missing Alt text.

Finally, turn on **Untitled Documents** to identify pages that are either missing a title or still have Dreamweaver's default title ("Untitled Document").

Note: The Site Report command won't identify XHTML syntax errors like those fixed by the Clean Up XHTML command (see page 518).

4. **Click Run.**

   Dreamweaver analyzes the pages you specified. It then produces a report that lists pages that match your report settings (see Figure 14-11). Each line in the Results window displays the name of the file, the line number where the error occurs, and a description of the error.

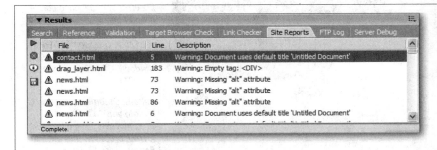

Figure 14-11:
If you decide that the report is taking too long, you can always stop it by clicking the icon in the left-hand toolbar of the Results panel. It looks like a red stop sign with an X through it.

5. **In the Results panel, double-click the file to open it (see Figure 14-12).**

   Dreamweaver opens the file and automatically highlights the offending code.

6. **Fix the problem according to its type.**

   For a page containing **Combinable Nested Font Tags, Redundant Nested Tags,** or **Removable Empty Tags** errors, use the Clean Up HTML command as described on page 518.

   For pages missing a title, add one using the technique described on page 656.

For Accessibility problems, read the detailed discussion starting on page 525.

You can add **Missing** Alt properties using the Property inspector, as described on page 128, but you may find it faster to use Dreamweaver's powerful Find and Replace command (page 661).

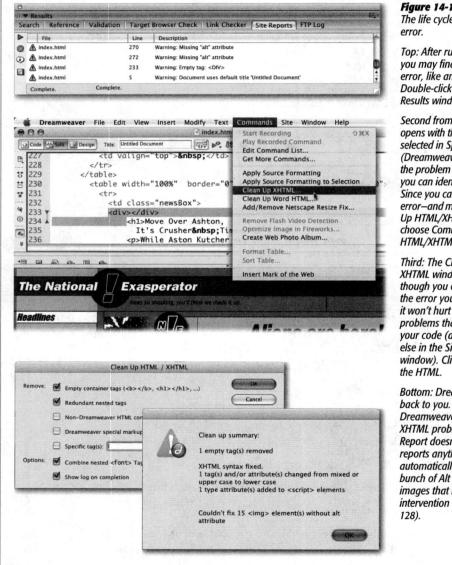

Figure 14-12:
The life cycle of a typical HTML error.

Top: After running a report, you may find a common HTML error, like an empty div tag. Double-click the page in the Results window to open it.

Second from top: The page opens with the offending code selected in Split Code view. (Dreamweaver often highlights the problem HTML code so that you can identify the problem.) Since you can fix this particular error—and more—with the Clean Up HTML/XHTML command, choose Commands → Clean Up HTML/XHTML.

Third: The Clean Up HTML/ XHTML window opens. Even though you can just clean up the error you identified earlier, it won't hurt to clean up other problems that may appear in your code (and somewhere else in the Site Report Results window). Click OK to clean up the HTML.

Bottom: Dreamweaver reports back to you. In this case, Dreamweaver fixes a few other XHTML problems that the Site Report doesn't catch and reports anything it can't automatically fix—in this case, a bunch of Alt properties for images that require human intervention to fix (see page 128).

7. Continue opening files from the Results window and fixing them until you've corrected each mistake.

   Unfortunately, Dreamweaver doesn't provide a quick, one-step method to fix any of these problems. Except when using the Find and Replace tip for adding missing Alt text, you must open and fix each page individually.

If you want to save the results of your report, click the Save Report button. Dreamweaver opens a Save As dialog box and lets you save the report as an XML file (so you can file it in the "Files I don't really need" folder on your desktop).

Accessibility

Even the clearest, most well-planned Web sites can pose a real challenge to people with vision problems. Likewise, people with motor skill problems may be unable to use a mouse and have to rely on keyboard shortcuts to navigate a Web page.

To make Web sites more accessible to those with a variety of disabilities, the Web Accessibility Initiative (WAI)—a part of the World Wide Web Consortium—has proposed guidelines for the design of Web sites. In fact, the U.S. government has mandated its own set of guidelines (Section 508 of the U.S. Rehabilitation Act) for all Web sites built by and for the government. Some states have even more stringent guidelines, and countries throughout the world are in the process of developing similar requirements. Following the WAI guidelines improves your site by making it accessible to a larger audience.

Dreamweaver provides several tools for meeting these guidelines and helping Web designers build more accessible sites (see page 527). But for comprehensive analysis of your site, use the Accessibility site report. With it, you can evaluate your Web pages to make sure they comply with W3C guidelines and the requirements of Section 508.

Checking your site against accessibility standards is similar to running any other report. Follow steps 1–4 on page 521, taking care to turn on the Accessibility checkbox.

Once the report is complete—which may take awhile for an entire site—the process of identifying and fixing the errors is a little different than with other reports:

1. Select an error in the Results panel (see Figure 14-13).

   Accessibility errors come with one of two designations: *Failed* and *Manual*. A failure (marked by a red X in the Results panel) indicates that some item on the page fails to meet one of the prescribed guidelines. The most common failure is missing Alt text for graphics.

   "Manual" errors are those that Dreamweaver's not sure about. Check them manually and make corrections, if you deem them necessary.

   In both cases, fixing the problems is up to you; Dreamweaver doesn't do any auto-fixing here.

Tip: You can set up the Insert Image command to help you with missing Alt tags; see page 128. In addition, you'll find some guidance in the accessibility guide built into the Reference panel (see page 353).

2. **Click the More Information (i) button in the Results panel.**

The Reference panel shows a description of the problem and techniques for fixing it (see Figure 14-13).

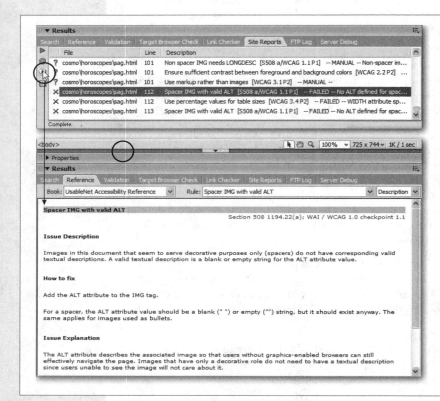

Figure 14-13:
The UsableNet Accessibility Reference provides diagnosis and recommendations for all accessibility problems encountered by Dreamweaver's Accessibility reporting command. Since Dreamweaver 8 has moved the Reference panel to the Results panel group, Windows owners will probably have to stretch the panel to a taller height to read this information: drag the dark bar (circled in the bottom figure) between the document window and the Property inspector upward to make the Reference panel taller.

3. **Double-click the name of the file in the Results panel.**

As with other reports, Dreamweaver opens the file and automatically highlights the offending code. You can then make the recommended changes and save the page.

Accessibility Priorities

As you'll quickly learn, there are a *lot* of different guidelines for creating accessible sites. The whole issue can be confusing (some helpful resources are listed in the box on page 527).

To get you started, here are a few of the priority items recommended by the WAI:

- **Images, animations.** Use the Alt property to describe the function of each visual element on a page (see page 128).

- **Image maps.** Provide Alt descriptions for each link in an image map (see page 142).

- **Hypertext links.** Use understandable text for all links. Try reading it aloud to make sure the text clearly indicates where the link goes. Avoid "click here" links.

- **Organizing page content.** Use headings, lists, and consistent structure. Avoid the <font> tag; instead, use Cascading Style Sheets for text styling.

- **Graphs, charts.** Summarize information contained in informational graphics.

- **Scripts, applets, plug-ins.** Provide alternative content, in case active features are inaccessible or unsupported.

- **Frames.** Use the *noframes* element and title each frame page. You can learn more about frames by consulting the online Dreamweaver frames guide that accompanies this book, available at *www.sawmac.com/dw8/frames.pdf*.

POWER USERS' CLINIC

Making Accessible Web Sites

Building Web sites that meet everyone's requirements is a daunting task. Unless you have screen-reader software to simulate the experience of a visually impaired visitor, or a crew of people with a variety of impairments (from color-blindness to repetitive stress injury) to test your site, how do you know what it takes to build a fully accessible Web site?

Fortunately, there are plenty of resources to get you started. The best place to start is at the Web Accessibility Initiative's Web site, especially their accessibility resources page: *www. w3.org/WAI/Resources/*.

Here you'll find lots of information, including examples of different disabilities some Web surfers face, plus tips, checklists, and techniques for making sites accessible. And if you do want to see how screen readers work with your site, you can download a demo of JAWS, one of the most popular screen readers, at *www.freedomscientific.com/fs_ downloads/jaws.asp*.

Finally, Macromedia dedicates an entire section of its site to accessibility issues: *www.macromedia.com/macromedia/ accessibility/*. Here, you'll find explanations of the issues, tips for using Macromedia products, and a showcase of accessible Web sites.

Accessibility Options

Dreamweaver's accessibility report covers all the WAI recommendations and Section 508 requirements; Dreamweaver 8 adds support for the WAI's latest set of accessibility recommendations: WCAG Priority 2. This thoroughness is commendable, but it may be more than you need. By all means, pare down the report to include just the guidelines that apply to your site. To do so, choose Site → Reports and turn on the Accessibility box. Click the Report Options button to open the window shown in Figure 14-14.

You can disable any rules Dreamweaver uses to evaluate your pages. To turn off an entire category—forms, frames, or tables, for example—click the name and then click Disable. If you'd like to get more specific, click the + button next to a category name to expand a list of individual rules for that category. You can select and disable one or more rules. For example, if your site doesn't use frames, you'll save time and Dreamweaver's energy by turning off the frames category.

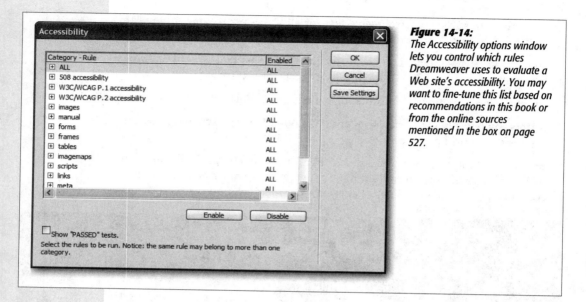

Figure 14-14:
The Accessibility options window lets you control which rules Dreamweaver uses to evaluate a Web site's accessibility. You may want to fine-tune this list based on recommendations in this book or from the online sources mentioned in the box on page 527.

Download Statistics

Remember the joke that WWW really stands for "World Wide Wait"? Even as more and more people upgrade to speedy DSL and cable modems, file size is the constant foe of the Web designer. What takes only a moment to load from your computer's hard drive could take minutes to travel across the Internet. The more information you put into a Web page, the more time it takes to load.

You can judge how big your page is, and therefore how long it will take to download, by looking at the download stats in the status bar at the bottom of the document window. You'll see something like this: *5k/2 sec.* This term indicates the file size of the Web page and how long it will take a visitor to download the page using a 56 Kbps modem.

Unfortunately, the behavior of this once helpful feature has changed. In previous versions of Dreamweaver, the file size and download time took into account linked files like images, external CSS style sheets, and Flash movies. This information provided a realistic picture of download speed, since not only does a page have to download, but any files that page uses (like a photo) also need to travel across the Internet to a visitor's browser. Dreamweaver 8 now shows only the actual size of the HTML file, which frequently is much smaller than bandwidth-hogging graphics or Flash movies. In other words, the statistic's pretty much useless, so don't bother paying attention to it (though file this bit of information away for your next Dreamweaver Trivia Challenge night—you're sure to win).

Note: People hate to wait. You may think that the graphic design of your Web site is so compelling that even if it takes a full minute to download that zippy new Flash home page, people will stick around.

Think again. Research shows that 10 seconds is the maximum amount of time that someone stays focused on a task while waiting. That means if you're designing a Web site for people with 56 Kbps modems, keep your pages below about 45 KB.

GEM IN THE ROUGH

Caching In

Behind the scenes, Web browsers store the graphics they download onto the computer's hard drive. This is a speed trick. If you click your Back button to return to a Web page whose graphics files the browser has already downloaded, the browser simply pulls them out of the cache—off the hard drive, in other words—instead of re-downloading them. This arrangement makes the page load more quickly, since the hard drive is generally much faster than the modem.

As a Web designer, you can capitalize on this standard Web browser feature by reusing the same graphics files on more than one page of your site. For instance, you can create a navigation bar composed of small graphic buttons (Home, Contact Us, Products, and so on). If you reuse those buttons on other pages of the site, those pages appear to download more quickly.

This same trick works for external CSS style sheets. A browser needs to download a complete style sheet with hundreds of formatting commands only once for any page on a site to reuse it. By putting all of your formatting into one or more external files, you can keep your Web pages mean and lean.

Moving Your Site to the Internet

Building Web pages on your computer is a big accomplishment, but it's not the whole job. Your beautifully designed and informative Web site will simply languish in obscurity on your hard drive unless you move it to a Web server.

Fortunately, once your Web site is ready for prime time, you can put it on a server without ever leaving the comfort of Dreamweaver. The program includes simple commands for transferring files back and forth between the Web server and your desktop.

Depending on how you operate, choose one of these two methods for transferring your files:

- If you're the sole Web developer for a site, Dreamweaver's Get and Put commands are the easiest way to go.

- If, on the other hand, there's a group of people working on your site, Dreamweaver's Check Out and Check In tools let you move files at will without wiping out others' hard work. In addition, this group feature integrates seamlessly with two other industrial-strength Web collaboration tools: Microsoft's Visual SourceSafe and WebDAV, an open source file management tool.

Either way, you begin by defining a remote site.

Note: Dreamweaver 8 introduces some major changes to how Dreamweaver moves files back and forth from your computer to your Web server. The changes include faster performance, better synchronization tools, and, best of all, background FTP, which lets you keep working in Dreamweaver as it transfers hundred of files to your Web site.

Defining a Remote Site

As you create your Web site on your computer, you keep it in a *local site folder* (see page 476), often called a *local site* for short. You can think of a local site as a work-in-progress. As your site is under construction—whether you're building it from scratch or adding and modifying pages—you'll routinely have partially finished documents sitting on your computer.

Then, when you've perfected and tested your pages using the techniques described in Chapter 14, you're ready to transfer them to a Web server that's connected to the Internet. Dreamweaver calls the Web server copy of your files the *remote site,* and the program provides five methods for transferring files between it and your local site:

- **FTP.** By far, the most common method is *FTP,* or File Transfer Protocol. Just as HTTP is the process by which Web pages are transferred from servers to Web browsers, FTP is the traditional method of transferring files over the Internet, and it's the one to use if a Web hosting company or Internet Service Provider (ISP) provides the home for your Web pages.

- **Over the local area network.** If you're working on an intranet, or if your company's Web server is connected to the company network, you may also be able to transfer files just as you would any files on your office network (using the Network Neighborhood, My Network Places, or Connect to Server command, depending on your operating system), without even connecting to the Internet.

- The last three options—**RDS, SourceSafe, and WebDAV**—are advanced file management systems used for collaborative Web development. They're discussed on page 538.

Setting Up a Remote Site with FTP

You can set up a remote site only if you've first set up a *local* site on your computer. Even if you're just putting up a temporary site while working on your *real* Web site, you must at least have the temporary site constructed and defined in Dreamweaver (see page 472).

FREQUENTLY ASKED QUESTION

Beyond Dreamweaver

Do I have to use Dreamweaver to move my files to the Web server?

No. If you're used to using another program for this purpose, such as CuteFTP (Windows) or RBrowser (Mac), you can continue to use it and ignore Dreamweaver's Remote Site feature.

However, if you've never before used Dreamweaver to move files to a server, you may want to at least try it; you'll

find that Dreamweaver simplifies much of the process. For example, when you want to move a file from your computer to the Web server using a regular FTP program, you must first locate the file on your local machine and then navigate to the proper folder on the Web server. Dreamweaver saves you both steps; when you select the file in the Files panel and click the Put button, Dreamweaver automatically locates the file on your computer and transfers it to the correct folder on the Web server.

Note: Dreamweaver lets you edit *directly* on pages located on a Web server, using an FTP connection (or if you're working with ColdFusion files, an RDS connection). This feature isn't always the best way to go: it's slow and leaves your works-in-progress open for the world to see on the Internet.

Once that's done, here's how you go about creating an Internet-based mirror of your local site folder:

1. **Choose Site → Manage Sites.**

   The Manage Sites dialog box opens, listing all sites that you've defined so far. You're about to create a living, Internet-based *copy* of one of these hard drive–based local sites.

2. **Click the name of the site you want to post on the Internet, and then click Edit.**

   Alternatively, just double-click the site name in the list. The Site Definition window appears for the selected site, as shown in Figure 15-1.

Note: You can also define the remote site and the local site simultaneously, when you first begin creating a Web site (as described on page 472). Even then, however, Dreamweaver requires that you first give the site a name and choose a local root folder. At that point, you rejoin the steps described here.

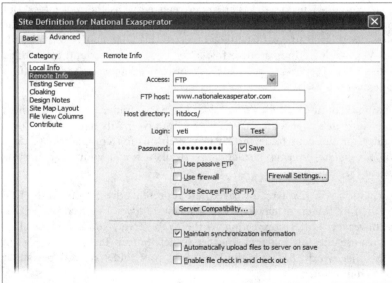

Figure 15-1:
If a Web hosting company or ISP hosts your Web site, you'll most likely use FTP to put your site on the Web. To make sure you have all the information you need to connect to the Web server, ask your ISP for these four pieces of information: (1) the FTP host name of the server, (2) the path to the root directory for your site, (3) your login name, and (4) your password. (If the Web server comes with your email account, your login and password may be the same for both.)

3. **Click the Advanced tab.**

   You can also use the Site Definition Wizard (Basic tab) to set up a remote site. However, since the wizard requires you to step through screen after screen of setup information—even after you've already supplied most of it—the Advanced tab is faster.

4. **In the Category panel, click Remote Info. From the Access pop-up menu, choose FTP.**

The Site Definition window now shows menus and fields for collecting your connection information (see Figure 15-1).

5. **Fill in the "FTP host" field.**

Your *FTP host name* may be a name like *www.nationalexasperator.com* or *ftp. nationalexasperator.com*. It never includes directories, folders, or slashes (like *www.nationalexasperator.com/home*); never includes codes for the FTP protocol (*ftp://ftp.nationalexasperator.com*); and is never only a domain name, such as *nationalexasperator.com*. It can also be an IP address, like *64.226.43.116*. In most cases, it's the address you would enter into a Web browser (minus the *http://*) to get to your site's home page.

If you don't know the host name, there's only one way to find out: call or email your Web hosting company or ISP, or check its Web site.

6. **In the Host Directory field, type the path to the root directory.**

You're specifying which *folder* within your Web hosting account will contain your Web page files and serve as the root folder for your site.

Just as on your own hard drive, all the files of your Web site on the Web are completely contained inside a master folder referred to as the *root folder*. But when you connect to your Web server using FTP, you're rarely connected to the root folder itself. Instead, you usually connect to a folder that isn't accessible over the Web—some administrative folder for your Web account, often filled with folders for log reports of your site's Web traffic, databases, and other files not visible over the Web.

Your hosting account's root directory folder (or even a folder within it) is where you place your *site's* root folder; that's why you're typing its name here. Common names for the root folder at ISPs or Web hosting companies are *docs, www, htdocs, public_html, or virtual_html*. (Call or email your Web hosting company or ISP to find out.)

The information you give Dreamweaver here represents the path from the FTP folder to the root folder. It may look like this: *www/htdocs*. In effect, you're telling Dreamweaver: "After connecting to the Web server, you'll find a folder named *www*. Inside *this* folder is another folder, *htdocs*. Put my site files in there." In other words, *htdocs* is the Web site's root folder on this particular remote hosting account.

7. **In the Login field, type your user name; type your password in the Password field.**

Dreamweaver uses bullets (•••) to display your password so that passing evil-doers in your office can't see what you're typing.

If you want Dreamweaver to remember your password each time you use the program, turn on the Save checkbox. This way, you won't have to type your password each time you connect to the Web server.

Warning: For security reasons, don't turn on the Save box if you access the Web using computers at, say, your local library, or anywhere else where people you don't trust may use the machine. Otherwise, you might just awaken one morning to find the following splattered across your home page: "Hi there! Welcome to Jack's house of illegally acquired and unlawfully distributed music, featuring Metallica's greatest hits."

---

8. **Turn on the "Use passive FTP" or "Use firewall" boxes, if necessary.**

If you're building sites from your home, home office, or small company, you may never need to use these technical options.

Many corporations, however, use *firewalls*: hardware- or software-based gateways that control incoming and outgoing traffic through a network. Firewalls protect the company network from outside hackers; unfortunately, they also limit how computers inside the network—*behind the firewall*—can connect to the outside world.

If your company's system administrator confirms that you have a firewall, you'll need to also get the name of the firewall host computer and its port number. Click the Firewall Settings button, which opens the Site Preferences dialog box). Your firewall configuration may also require *passive FTP*—a method of connecting using your local software, rather than the firewall server. Check with your administrator to see if this is the case, and, if so, turn on the "Use passive FTP" checkbox.

9. **If your Web server uses SFTP (a secure, encrypted form of FTP), turn on the Use Secure FTP (SFTP) box.**

Secure FTP encrypts *all* of your data, not just your user name and password, so information transferred in this way is unintelligible to Internet snoops. It's ideal if your site isn't open to the public (password-protected) and contains sensitive information like personnel records. Unfortunately, not all Web hosting companies offer this advanced option.

By the way, leave "Automatically upload files to server on save" turned off. Because it makes Dreamweaver upload the file each time you save, it slows you down and runs the risk of putting half-finished Web pages on your server for all the world to see. It's better to just upload the page after you're completely finished with it.

10. **Leave the Server Compatibility options alone.**

That big Server Compatibility button is useful when you're having trouble connecting to the server or moving files to the server. Dreamweaver, out of the box, is tuned to make FTP run as fast as possible, so leave these options alone, unless you're having trouble. If you are having trouble connecting to your server, click this button and turn off the "Use FTP performance optimization" box.

If everything's okay when you're connecting to your server, but you're getting errors when moving files between your computer and the server, you should turn on the "Use alternative FTP move method" box. This method is slower but more reliable. It's also handy if you use Macromedia's Contribute program and are taking advantage of the "rollback" feature (to learn more about Contribute, visit *www.macromedia.com/contribute*).

11. **If you don't want to synchronize files, turn off the "Maintain synchronization information" box.**

Dreamweaver's synchronization feature has been greatly improved in Dreamweaver 8. It helps you maintain the most recent versions of a file on the remote server, by keeping track of when you've changed a file on your computer. When you synchronize a site, Dreamweaver can move the more recent files onto the Web server. This feature is described in detail on page 557. If you don't use synchronization, definitely turn off this checkbox. When this feature is on, Dreamweaver inserts little files named *dwsync.xml* throughout your site in folders named *_notes*. These items keep track of synchronization information about each file in your site, but there's no need to clutter things up with these files if you don't use synchronization.

12. **Turn on "Enable file check in and check out," if you like.**

Turn it on if, for example, you and your team of Web developers all use Dreamweaver. Then fill in the corresponding options as explained in Figure 15-2.

If you do wind up using the "checking out" feature (see page 551), you can save yourself some clicks by turning on "Check out files when opening." (Fill in your name and email address, too, as shown in Figure 15-2.) Now you can "check out" a file from the remote server just by double-clicking its name in the Site Files list.

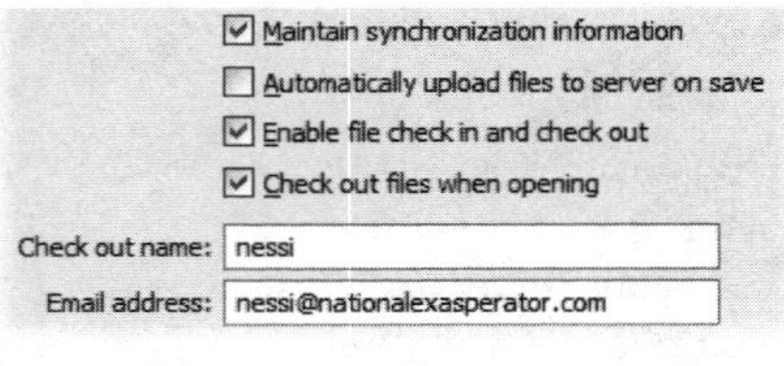

Figure 15-2:
If you're using Dreamweaver's Check In/Check out feature and you work on your site in several different locations (for example, from home and your office), use a different name for each location (BobAtHome and BobAtWork, for example). In this way, you can identify which files you've checked out to your home computer and which to your computer at work.

13. **Click the Test button to see if Dreamweaver can connect to the Web server.**

If everything goes according to plan, you'll see a "Dreamweaver connected to your Web server successfully" message. If not, you'll get an "FTP error" message with some additional information that can help you determine the problem (see the box on page 548).

14. **Click OK to return to the Manage Sites dialog box; click Done.**

The Manage Sites dialog box closes, and the Files panel opens.

At this point, you're ready to connect to the Web server and transfer files. If you're the only person working on the site, Dreamweaver's Get and Put commands will do the trick (page 542). If, however, you're part of a development team, use Dreamweaver's Check In and Check Out feature, described on page 551.

FREQUENTLY ASKED QUESTION

When Your Remote Site Is Too Remote

Help! I can't connect to my Web server. What should I do?

Things don't always go smoothly. That's doubly true when trying to connect to a Web server, since you depend on a variety of things—your Internet connection, the networks connecting you to your Web server, the Web server itself, and the FTP software—working together in harmony. Dreamweaver presents an error message if you can't successfully establish an FTP connection with your Web server. The error box frequently contains useful information that can help you determine the problem. Here are some of the most common:

- **Remote host cannot be found** usually means you typed an incorrect FTP Host address (step 5 on page 534).

- **Your login or password is incorrect** means just that—you've typed the wrong user name or password (step 7 on page 534.).

- **Cannot open remote folder** usually means you mistyped or input the wrong Host directory (step 6 on page 534).

Unfortunately, there are lots of reasons Dreamweaver may not be able to connect, so sometimes the error message isn't particularly helpful. Here are a few other suggestions for troubleshooting: make sure you're connected to the Internet (open a Web browser and see if you can visit a site on the Web); return to the Remote Info category of the Site Definition window, click the Server Compatibility button, and then turn off the "Use FTP performance optimization" box; turn on the "Use passive FTP" option (sometimes this just makes things work); and if you have another FTP program like CuteFTP or RBrowser, see if you can connect to your Web server using the same settings you gave Dreamweaver. If all these steps fail, you can visit this page on the Macromedia Web site for additional troubleshooting tips: *www.macromedia.com/support/dreamweaver/ts/documents/troubleshooting_ftp.htm.*

Setting Up a Remote Site over a Local Network

If you're working on an intranet, or if your company's Web server is connected to the company network, you may also be able to transfer your Web files just as you'd move any files from machine to machine. Dreamweaver provides the same file-transfer functions as with FTP, but setup is simpler.

Follow steps 1 and 2 of the previous instructions, but in step 4, click the Remote Info category and then choose Local/Network from the Access pop-up menu. Menus and fields for collecting your connection information appear in the Site Definition box (see Figure 15-3).

Now click the folder icon next to the "Remote folder" field. In the resulting dialog box, navigate to and select your site's remote root folder. On a local network, this folder functions as the root folder on your company's Web server (see page 476),

---

even though it's actually still within the walls of your building. (For differences on selecting root folders on Windows and Macs, see page 35.)

Wrap up with steps 10, 11, 12, and 14 of the previous instructions. At this point, you're ready to connect to the Web server and transfer files.

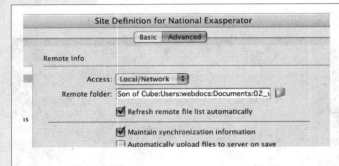

Figure 15-3:
Turning on the "Refresh remote file list automatically" box updates the list of files in the Files panel. Changes to the remote site, such as when someone adds a file, are then listed automatically. Because automatic updating slows down the process of moving files to the remote site, however, you may want to turn off this option when you begin a session of moving many files. You can always refresh the file list manually by clicking the Refresh button on the Files panel (see Figure 13-13 on page 493).

Setting Up a Remote Site with RDS

RDS (Remote Development Services) is a feature of Macromedia's ColdFusion Server. It lets designers work on Web files and databases in conjunction with a ColdFusion application server. If you aren't using ColdFusion, then this option isn't for you.

To create a remote site in Dreamweaver that works with RDS, follow steps 1 through 3 on page 533. In step 4, click the Remote Info category, and then choose RDS from the Access pop-up menu.

The Site Definition window displays a version number, a short description, and a Settings button. Click Settings to open the Configure RDS Server window, shown in Figure 15-4. Fill in the dialog box as directed by your server administrator or help desk.

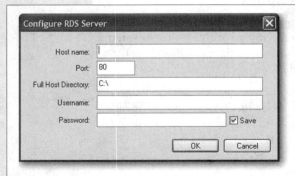

Figure 15-4:
Remote Development Services is a feature of the ColdFusion application server. However, even if you use ColdFusion, you may not be able to use RDS, since most Web hosting companies that offer ColdFusion servers turn off RDS due to potential security problems.

Setting Up a Remote Site with WebDAV

Dreamweaver also allows access to a remote site using *WebDAV*, short for Web-based Distributed Authoring and Versioning. Like FTP, it's a method, or protocol, for transferring files. Like SFTP, it lets you use a secure connection (SSL or Secure Socket Layer) so that all of your data is encrypted as it passes back and forth between your computer and the Web server. But unlike both of those technologies, WebDAV also addresses the kinds of problems you encounter when collaborating on a Web site with other people.

Note: WebDAV isn't a very common option at most Web hosting companies, where FTP is still the norm. So you may not be able to take advantage of this exciting technology. However, if you're a Mac fan and have an Apple .Mac account, your iDisk actually works using WebDAV, so you can connect to your .Mac Homepage files using Dreamweaver. (Even Windows owners can use Dreamweaver to work on a Web-DAV .Mac Web site.)

For instance, all kinds of havoc can result if two people edit a page simultaneously; whoever uploads the page to the Web server *second* winds up wiping out the changes made by the first person. WebDAV supports a check-in and check-out system that works similarly to Dreamweaver's Check In/Check Out tool (see page 551) to make sure only one person works on a file at a time and no one tramples on anyone else's files. In fact, Dreamweaver's Check In and Check Out tools work seamlessly with WebDAV.

Both Microsoft Internet Information Server (IIS) and Apache Web Server can work with WebDAV. To find out if your Web server can handle WebDAV (and to find out the necessary connection information), consult your Web server's administrator (for example, call or email your Web hosting company).

Setting up WebDAV access to a remote site is very similar to setting up FTP access. Follow steps 1 through 3 on page 533, and then follow these steps:

1. **Click the Remote Info category, and then choose WebDAV from the Access pop-up menu.**

   The Site Definition window displays the WebDAV settings (Figure 15-5).

2. **In the URL box, type in the URL of the WebDAV server.**

   In most cases, this is the URL of the Web site, so it begins with either *http://* or *https://*. The *s* in *https* means you'll connect securely to the Web server using SSL. The normal *http://* method doesn't use any encryption, which means that, just like with regular FTP, your user name, password, and all data are sent "in the open" across the Internet. Note that just adding an *s* won't suddenly make your file transfers secure; the Web server needs to be set up to accept https connections (a technically challenging task).

Note: .Mac account holders who want to connect to their Homepage Web site should type *https://idisk. mac.com/UserName/Sites* where "UserName" is your .Mac account name.

---

3. **In the Login field, type your user name; type your password in the Password field.**

   Turn on the Save checkbox if you want to save yourself the hassle of having to type in your password each time you move files to your Web server (but heed the Warning on page 535).

4. **Click the Test button to see if your connection works.**

   If Dreamweaver succeeds, it proudly tells you. Unfortunately, if it fails, you'll get an error message that isn't exactly helpful. WebDAV isn't nearly as finicky as FTP, so if there's an error, you most likely just typed the URL, password, or login incorrectly, or WebDAV just isn't available for the server.

5. **Turn off the "Refresh remote file list automatically" option.**

   This option works just like the one for local networks described in Figure 15-3.

6. **Leave the "Automatically upload files to server on save" box turned off.**

   This option makes Dreamweaver upload the file each time you save; it slows you down and runs the risk of putting half-finished Web pages on your server for all the world to see. It's better to just upload the page after you're completely finished with it.

The rest of the process is identical to the FTP setup process, so follow steps 11, 12, and 14, starting on page 536. You're ready to connect to the Web server and transfer files, as described on page 542.

Note: You can find more information on WebDAV at *www.webdav.org/*.

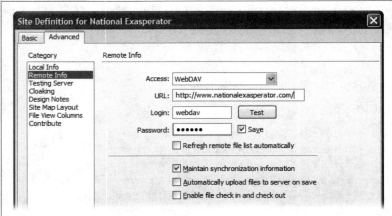

Figure 15-5:
WebDAV, short for Web-based Distributed Authoring and Versioning, is a powerful tool for working on a site with other people. It's built into several Web server packages but, unfortunately, isn't a very common option at most Web hosting companies.

Setting Up a Remote Site with SourceSafe

Microsoft originally created Visual SourceSafe for managing team software development. Like WebDAV, SourceSafe makes sure you don't accidentally stomp on someone else's hard work by overwriting a Web page they just modified. In addition, this sophisticated program tracks different versions of files and lets an administrator "roll back" to previous versions of a Web page, or even an entire site; it's the granddaddy of Undos.

To take advantage of this power, however, you need a Visual SourceSafe (VSS) server and VSS database already setup. In addition, Windows people need to install Microsoft Visual SourceSafe Client version 6 on their PCs.

Note: The Visual SourceSafe option isn't available in the Mac version of Dreamweaver 8.

Once you've installed the VSS Client software, and you've created and defined a local site (see page 472), you're ready to configure Dreamweaver for SourceSafe using the Site Definition window. Basically, you tell Dreamweaver where to find the SourceSafe database and how to sign on to the server.

Once again, follow steps 1 though 3 on page 533. But in step 4, click the Remote Info category, and then choose Microsoft® Visual SourceSafe® from the Access pop-up menu. In the resulting dialog box, click Settings to reveal the Open Microsoft® Visual SourceSafe® Database dialog box, shown in Figure 15-6.

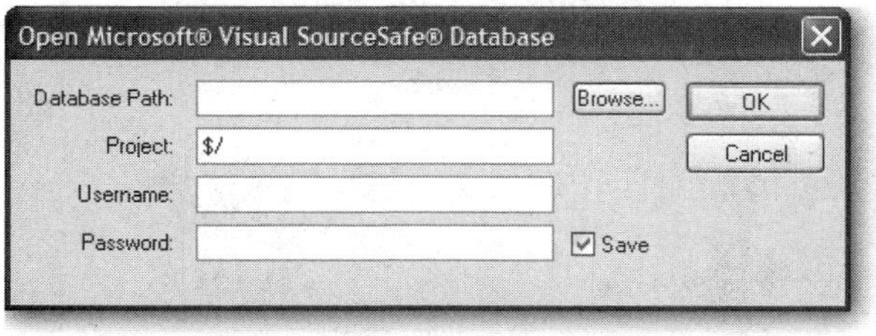

Figure 15-6:
*This window, sometimes called the "Microsoft's®
Lawyers Are Everywhere®" dialog box, lets you set
up Dreamweaver for use with Microsoft's Visual
SourceSafe system. Many corporations use this
powerful file-control system to control access to
files in large projects involving many people.*

Click Browse to select the Visual SourceSafe (VSS) database file on your computer (or type in the file path, if you know it, into the Database Path field)—the *srcsafe.ini* file that Dreamweaver uses to initialize SourceSafe.

Then, in the Project field, fill in the name of the *project* within the VSS database that you wish to use as the remote root folder. (A VSS database can have many projects and Web sites listed in it. Make sure you enter the correct project name for this site. If in doubt, contact the administrator of the Visual SourceSafe database.) Type your user name and password into the appropriate fields; again, ask the administrator for guidance.

Click OK. But before dismissing the Site Definition dialog box, turn on Check Out Files when Opening, so that Dreamweaver's Check In and Check Out features (see page 551) work with the VSS system. Click OK, and then click Done.

Transferring Files

Once you've told Dreamweaver *how* you plan to ship off your Web page files to the Net, you can set about *doing* it. Thanks to Dreamweaver's Files panel, the whole process takes only a few steps.

Note: Dreamweaver 8 adds "Background FTP" to the file-transfer process, so you can keep working on a Web page while Dreamweaver transfers files in the background. See the box on page 545 for more information.

Moving Files to the Web Server

To transfer files to your Web server:

1. **Open the Files panel (Figure 15-7).**

   Choose Window → Files (keyboard shortcut: F8).

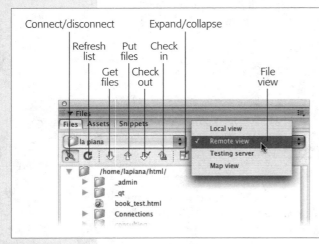

Connect/disconnect   Expand/collapse

Refresh   Put   Check
list   files   in

Get   Check   File
files   out   view

Figure 15-7:
The Files panel offers toolbar buttons for uploading and downloading your Web files to and from the actual Web server that dishes them out to your site's adoring public. (See Chapter 13 for much more on this important window.)

Local view
✓ Remote view
Testing server
Map view

/home/lapiana/html/
_admin
_qt
book_test.html
Connections

2. **From the Site menu, choose the name of the site whose files you wish to move (if it isn't already selected).**

   The Files panel displays files for the selected site. You can use the File View pop-up menu to access either a list of the local files or the remote files on the Web server (see Figure 15-7). You can also see both local and remote files side by side if you first choose "Remote view" from the File View pop-up menu and then click the Expand button on the Files panel, as described on page 481.

Tip: The color of the folders in the Site panel lets you know which view you're currently in: green folders mean Local view (your computer), beige (blue on the Mac) folders mean Remote view, and red folders indicating the Testing view described on page 690.

3. **From the file list in the Files panel, select the files you wish to upload to the Web server.**

   To move a folder and every file inside it, just select the folder. (In other words, you can transfer your *entire* Web site to the server by simply selecting the local root folder—the folder listed at the very top of the Local Folder file list.) When only a few files have changed, you can also select only certain files or folders for uploading, using any of the techniques described on page 512.

Tip: If you don't see the files you wish to upload in the Site Files list, you may have Remote view selected. Select Local view to see only those site files on your computer.

When you use do-it-yourself FTP programs like WS_FTP or Fetch, you have to specify a folder location for every file you transfer to the Web server. But here's one of the great advantages of letting Dreamweaver do your file shuffling; it already knows where the files should go on the remote site. The local and remote sites are, after all, mirror images, so Dreamweaver simply puts files in the corresponding folders on the remote site.

For example, suppose you select the file *mayo.html,* which is in a folder called Condiments, which is itself stored in the local root folder. When you transfer the file, Dreamweaver knows to put this file in the Condiments folder in the root folder on the remote site. In fact, if the folder Condiments doesn't exist on the remote site, Dreamweaver creates it and *then* puts the file into it. Now that's service.

A hush falls over the audience; you're ready to go live with your Web page.

4. **Click the "Put files" button—the up-arrow icon identified in Figure 15-7—on the Files panel.**

   Alternatively, you can use the keyboard shortcut Ctrl+Shift+U (⌘-Shift-U).

   Several things happen when you do this: First, if you're using an FTP connection, Dreamweaver attempts to connect to your Web server, dialing your modem if necessary. As you can see in the status window that opens, it may take a minute or so to establish a connection; the Connect button (see Figure 15-7) displays a bright green light when Dreamweaver is connected.

   Next, if any of the files you're transferring are currently open and have unsaved changes, Dreamweaver asks if you want to save the files before transferring them to the server. Click Yes to save the file, or, if there are multiple unsaved files, click the Yes To All button to save all of them before posting them online.

In addition, Dreamweaver asks if you wish to transfer any *dependent files* (see Figure 15-8). Dependent files are graphics, frame pages in a frameset, or external Cascading Style Sheets files that you've placed onto a page.

This feature can save you considerable time and hassle; no need to hunt for and upload each graphic file or external style sheet yourself. On the other hand, if all the dependent files are *already* on the server, having Dreamweaver transfer the same files again is a waste of time. Fortunately, Dreamweaver 8 helps stop this wasted effort as described in the next step.

Tip: If you turn on the "Don't show me this message again" box and then click Yes, Dreamweaver copies dependent files without asking. On the other hand, if you turn on the "Don't show me this message again" box and click No, Dreamweaver *never* copies dependent files.

If you want the Dependent Files dialog box to appear again after you've turned it off, hold down the Alt (Option) key when you transfer a file (using any method *except* a keyboard shortcut). Or choose Edit → Preferences → Site Category (Dreamweaver → Preferences → Site Category) to turn this feature on or off.

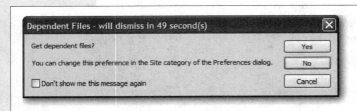

Figure 15-8:
The Dependent Files feature of Dreamweaver's File Transfer command makes sure all necessary files—graphics, Flash movies, and so on—are copied to the Web server along with your Web pages. Dreamweaver 8 adds a countdown—a "will dismiss in xx seconds" message. If you don't click a button within 60 seconds, Dreamweaver assumes you mean "No" and just uploads the selected files.

5. **Click Yes to transfer dependent files, or No to transfer only the files you selected.**

Dreamweaver copies the files to the Web server. If you're copying a file that's inside a folder that isn't already on the remote site, Dreamweaver creates the folder as well. In fact, Dreamweaver creates as many subfolders as necessary to make sure every file is transferred to the same folder location on the remote site as it is in the local site. (Try doing *that* with a regular FTP program.)

If you've chosen to transfer dependent files as well, Dreamweaver may or may not put the dependent file on the Web server. If you've turned on the "Maintain Synchronization Information" checkbox when defining your remote site (see step 11 on page 536), Dreamweaver 8 determines if the dependent file is already on the Web server and, if it is, whether your local copy of the file is a newer version. If the dependent file doesn't exist on the server *or* your local copy is newer (meaning you've made some changes to it locally but haven't yet moved it onto the Web), Dreamweaver puts it on the remote site when you tell it to transfer dependent files.

However, if Dreamweaver thinks that it's the same file, or that the copy of the file on the Web server is newer, it won't transfer the dependent file. This behavior is a huge time-saver, since you won't have to repeatedly upload the same 50 navigation buttons each time you say "Yes" to transferring dependent files; but, best of all, Dreamweaver still transfers those dependent files that really *are* new.

Note: Dreamweaver's ability to correctly determine whether a dependent file on your computer is the same as the file on the remote site depends on its Site Synchronization feature, described on page 557. While Dreamweaver 8 greatly improves on the accuracy of this tool, it has been known to get it wrong. If Dreamweaver isn't moving a dependent file that you want moved to the remote server, you can just select that file and upload it manually (for example, select it in the Files panel and click the Put button). Dreamweaver always obeys a direct order to move a selected file to the remote site.

6. **Continue using the Put button to transfer all files in your Web site to the remote site.**

   Depending on the number of files transferred, this operation can take some time. Transferring files over the Internet using FTP isn't nearly as fast as copying files from one hard drive to another (see the box below).

A Little More Background on File Transfers

Dreamweaver 8 introduces a productivity-boosting enhancement to its FTP feature. In earlier versions, Dreamweaver would essentially "lock up" as it moved files to or from the remote site; you couldn't do anything else—edit a Web page, create a new style sheet, or complete any other Dreamweaver task—while the program concentrated on transferring files. If you had to move hundreds of files over a slow Internet connection, this lock-up became a real productivity sink.

Fortunately, now you can continue to work in Dreamweaver as it dutifully moves files in the background. However, there are some things you can't do while Dreamweaver is transferring files. These are mostly logical restrictions: you can't edit the site definition (since this could affect how you connect to the remote server); you can't put or get other files (since Dreamweaver's already busy doing that); you can't delete a file on the local or remote server (since you may be transferring that file). Dreamweaver lets you know if you try to do one of these forbidden actions while it's working with the server.

If you find the background activity window (pictured here) a nuisance, click the Hide button and it temporarily disappears. In addition, if you accidentally start uploading a 10,000 page Web site, you probably won't want to wait until Dreamweaver is finished. Click the Cancel button to stop the process.

Once Dreamweaver's finished moving files around, you can see a record of Dreamweaver's actions by clicking the Log button that appears at the bottom-right corner of the Files panel. This log is a different record than the raw FTP log discussed in the box on page 548. This plain-language window lets you know what Dreamweaver did—"Put successful," "Get successful," and so on. If you see a "not transferred" message, this means that you tried to Get or Put a file, but both the local and remote copies were identical, so Dreamweaver didn't do anything. See the above Note for more information.

Other ways to move files to the Web server

In the Files panel, you can also *drag* a file from the Local Folder list into the Remote Site list. (You first must expand the Files panel, as described on page 481.) But don't do it: it's too easy to drag a file into the wrong place. If you drag a file to the wrong folder on the remote site, for example, you'll probably break all the links on the page. It's much better to let Dreamweaver keep track of where files should go in the organization of your site. (However, if you're already in this mess, see "Find and Fix Broken Links" on page 510.)

You can also copy your current document to the Web server without using the Files panel at all. You can go directly to the Put command when, say, you finish building or modifying a Web page and want to immediately move it to the Web server. Just choose Site → Put or press Ctrl+Shift+U (⌘-Shift-U); Dreamweaver automatically copies the fresh page to the proper folder online.

The toolbar also provides a quick menu shortcut for this operation, as shown in Figure 15-9.

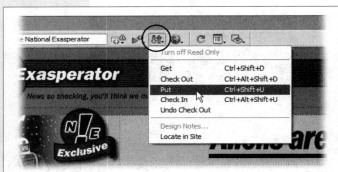

Figure 15-9:
Click the File Status button (circled) and choose Put to quickly move a file to your Web server. You can also use this menu to retrieve a copy of this file from the server (Get), use Check In and Out features (page 551), or review Design Notes (page 561) for the page. To select this file in the Files panel, choose Locate in Site.

Getting Files from the Web Server

So far, this chapter has described getting your hard drive–based Web pages *to* the Internet. Sometimes, however, you'll want to download one or more files *from* the Web server. Perhaps you've made a horrible (and irreversible) mistake on the local copy of a file, and you want to retrieve the last version from the Web server, using the remote site as a last-ditch backup system. Or perhaps someone else uploaded some files to the site, and you want to download a copy to your own computer (although the Synchronize feature described on page 557 would also work).

To get files from the remote site, open the Files panel (press F8) and proceed as follows:

1. **From the Site pop-up menu, choose the site whose files you wish to retrieve.**

   From the Files panel's View menu (see page 480), choose Remote View.

2. **Click the Connect button.**

Dreamweaver tells you that it's attempting to connect to the Web server. Once the connection has been made, a list of files and folders appears in the Remote Site list, and the Connect button displays a bright green dot. (Dreamweaver automatically disconnects you after 30 minutes of inactivity, and the green dot turns black. It's usually a good idea not to stay connected to a server indefinitely, since doing so takes processing power away from the server and poses a security risk.)

Tip: Dreamweaver disconnects from the Remote site after 30 minutes of inactivity. If you'd like to change this setting, press Ctrl+U (⌘-U) to open the Preferences window. Click the Site category and change the number listed in the Minutes Idle box. Be aware, however, that some Web servers have their own settings and may disconnect you sooner than you've specified.

If you're connected to the Web server over a local network as described on page 537, the Connect button is dimmed, and you can skip this step. You use the Connect button only when connecting to the Web server via FTP, RDS, or Visual SourceSafe.

TROUBLESHOOTING MOMENT

Don't Replace the Wrong File

One strange feature of the Files panel's Get and Put commands may get you in trouble. Suppose, having just added new information to the home page (*index.html*), you want to transfer it to the Web server. You select it in the Local Folder list—but then you accidentally click Get instead of Put.

Not knowing your true intention, Dreamweaver dutifully retrieves the file from the Web server and prepares to replace (wipe out) the newly updated home page on your computer.

Fortunately, Dreamweaver also opens a warning message asking if you really want to overwrite the local file. Click No or Cancel to save your hard work.

There may be times when you *do* want to wipe out your local copy—for example, if your cat walks across your keyboard, types illegible code, presses Ctrl+S to save the ruined page, and Ctrl+Q to quit Dreamweaver (keeping

you from using Undo to fix the mistakes). In this common situation, you'll want to replace your local copy with the remote copy. To do so, press the Yes key to wipe out your cat's errors. Oh yeah, this is also a useful trick if *you* ever make a mistake on a page you can't fix and want to return to the working copy on your Web server.

Dreamweaver 8 adds a useful "Compare" button. Clicking it lets you compare the local and remote copies of the page, so you can identify which changes you made. In this way, you can salvage changes you made to the local copy and discard errors you (or your cat) may have introduced to the page. This feature is described on page 347.

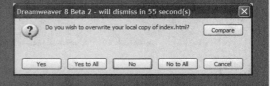

---

3. **From the Remote Site file list, select the files you wish to download from the Web server.**

   For techniques on selecting files in the Files panel, see page 512. To download a folder and every file inside it, just click the folder. This technique also lets you get your *entire* Web site from the server; just click the remote root folder, which appears at the very top of the Remote Site file list.

4. **Click the Get files button—the down arrow.**

   Alternatively, you can use the keyboard shortcut Ctrl+Shift+D (⌘-Shift-D).

   If the *local* version of any file you are getting from the remote site is currently opened and has unsaved changes, Dreamweaver warns you that you'll lose those changes. (No surprise there; copying a file from the remote site automatically replaces the same file in the local site, whether it's open or not.) Dreamweaver also warns you if you're about to replace a local file that's *newer* than the remote one.

   In addition, Dreamweaver offers to transfer any dependent files, as described in Figure 15-8.

5. **Click Yes to transfer dependent files, or No to transfer only the files you selected.**

   Dreamweaver copies the files to the local site folder, creating any folders necessary to replicate the structure of the remote site.

POWER USERS' CLINIC

Troubleshoot with the FTP Log

If you're having problems moving files using Dreamweaver's FTP command, you may be able to find some clues in the records Dreamweaver keeps when transferring files. If you've used other FTP programs, you may have seen little messages that are sent back and forth between the Web server and the FTP program like this:

```
200 PORT command successful. LIST 150
Opening ASCII mode data connection for
/bin/ls.
```

Dreamweaver also sends and receives this information, but it keeps it hidden. In order to see the FTP log, choose Window → Results, and then click the FTP Log tab. Any errors appear in this log.

For example, if you encounter a "cannot put file" error, it may mean that you're out of space on your Web server. Contact your ISP or the administrator of your Web server for help. WebDAV connections also produce a log of file-transfer activity, but it's not very easy to decipher.

And Secure FTP (SFTP) produces no log in Dreamweaver—hush, hush, it's a secret.

Cloaking Files

You may not want *all* files transferred to and from the Remote site. For example, as part of its Library and Template tools, Dreamweaver creates folders inside your local root folder. The Library and Templates folders don't do you any good on the Web server; their sole purpose is to help you build the site on your computer. Likewise, you may have Photoshop (.psd), Flash (.fla), or Fireworks (.png) files in your local root folder. They're inaccessible from a Web browser and take up a lot of disk space, so they shouldn't be transferred to the Web server when you move your site online.

Note: If you work on a Web site with other people, you probably *will* want to have the Library and templates folders on the server. This way, others who work on the site can access them as well.

To meet such challenges, Dreamweaver includes a feature called *cloaking*. It lets you hide folders and specific file types from many file-transfer operations, including Get/Put files, the Check In/Check Out feature (page 557), and site synchronization (page 557). In fact, you can even hide files from many site-wide Dreamweaver actions, including reports (see page 521), search and replace (page 649), check and change links sitewide (page 510), and the Assets panel (page 492). There's one exception: files that are linked to Library items (see Chapter 16) or templates (Chapter 17) can still "see" items in cloaked Library and template folders.

Dreamweaver lets you cloak specific folders in your site or particular file types (those that end with a specific extension such as .fla or .png). Each type of cloak requires a different technique.

To hide specific types of files:

1. **Choose Site → Manage Sites.**

   The Manage Sites window opens, listing all sites you've defined in Dreamweaver.

2. **Select the site you wish to use cloaking on and click Edit.**

   That site's Site Definition window opens.

3. **Click the Cloaking category.**

   The cloaking settings appear (see Figure 15-10). The factory setting is On for every site you define. (If you want to turn it off, just turn off the "Enable cloaking" box.)

Tip: You can quickly turn cloaking on and off by right-clicking (Control-clicking) any file or folder in the Files panel and selecting Cloaking → Enable Cloaking from the context menu. A checkmark next to Enable Cloaking means cloaking is turned on.

---

4. **Turn on the "Cloak files ending with" checkbox.**

   Dreamweaver identifies file types by their extensions—.png for Fireworks files, for example.

   Note: Mac programs don't always add these file name suffixes, but without them, Dreamweaver can't cloak.

5. **In the text box, type the extensions you wish to cloak.**

   Each extension should start with a period followed by three or four letters. To type multiple extensions in the box, separate them with a space.

6. **Click OK twice to close this window and the Manage Sites window.**

   All cloaked files have a red slash through them in the Files panel.

You can also cloak a folder using the Files panel like this:

1. **Open the Files panel by pressing F8.**

   Alternatively, choose Window → Files.

2. **Right-click (Control-click) a folder in Local Files view.**

   A shortcut menu appears with many site-related options.

3. **Select Cloaking → Cloak.**

   Dreamweaver adds a red slash through the folder's icon in the Files panel. All files and folders inside the cloaked folder are hidden as well, as indicated by the red slashes through their icons.

   Note: You can't hide individual files in the Files panel—only *folders* and *file types*.

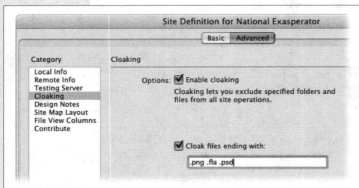

Figure 15-10:
The Cloaking category of the Site Definition window lets you turn cloaking on and off—a feature that lets you hide specific file types and folders from site-wide operations like transferring files to a Web server or searching and replacing text. In this window, you can specify which types of files to hide by listing their extensions (.psd for Photoshop files, for example).

Once you've cloaked a folder, it and any folders inside it disappear from Dreamweaver's file-transfer functions. Files with specific extensions that you specified in the Preferences window are also hidden.

However, there are exceptions. You can override the cloaking, for example, by selecting a cloaked folder or file and then using the Get or Put file buttons as described on page 542. Dreamweaver assumes that since you specifically selected that file or folder, you intend to override the cloaking feature.

Dreamweaver also ignores cloaking if you answer Yes in the Include Dependent Files message box (Figure 15-8) when you put or get files. In that case, Dreamweaver transfers all dependent files, even if they're cloaked (this applies to Library and template files as well).

Check In and Check Out

If you're the sole developer for a Web site, the Files panel's Get and Put buttons are fine for transferring your files. But if you're on a team of developers, these simple tools can get you in trouble.

For example, suppose your boss emails you an important announcement that she wants posted on the home page immediately. So you download the home page from the Web server and start to edit it. At the same time, your co-worker Bob notices a typo on the home page. He downloads it, too.

You're a much faster worker than Bob, so you've added the critical news to the home page and moved it back to the Web server. But now Bob transfers his corrected home page to the Web server, *overwriting* your edits and eliminating that urgent notice you just uploaded. (An hour later, your phone rings. It's the boss.)

Without some kind of system to monitor who has what file, and to prevent people from overwriting each other's work, collaborative Web development is a chaotic mess. Fortunately, Dreamweaver's Check In and Check Out system provides a civilized answer to this problem. It works like your local public library: When you check a file out, no one else can have it. When you're finished, you check the file back in, releasing control of it, and allowing someone else on the team to check it out and work on it.

To use the Check In/Check Out feature effectively, it helps to keep a few things in mind:

- When you're developing a Web site solo, your local site usually contains the most recent versions of your files. You make any modifications or additions to the pages on your computer first and *then* transfer them to the Web server.

  But in a collaborative environment where many people are working on the site at once, the files on your hard drive may not be the latest ones. After all, your co-workers, like you, have been updating pages and transferring them to the Web server. The home page file sitting in the local site folder on your computer may be several days older than the file on the remote site, which is why checking out a file from the *remote* site, rather than editing from the copy on your computer, is so important. It guarantees that you have the latest version of the file.

• In a collaborative environment, nobody should post files to the Web server using any method except Dreamweaver's Check In and Check Out system.

The reason is technical, but worth slogging through: When Dreamweaver checks out a file, it doesn't actually *lock* the file. Instead, it places a small, invisible text file (with the three-letter suffix .lck) on both the remote server and in your local site folder. This text file indicates who has checked out the file. When Dreamweaver connects to a remote site, it uses these files to know which Web files are in use by others.

But only Dreamweaver understands these *.lck* files. Other FTP programs, like WSFTP (Windows) or Fetch (Mac), gladly ignore them and can easily overwrite any checked-out files. This risk also applies when you simply copy files back and forth over the office network.

Note: Dreamweaver's word processor–like Web page editing program, Contribute, also takes advantage of this Check In/Check Out feature, so you can use the two programs on the same site.

• All Dreamweaver people must configure their remote site to use Check In and Check Out (see page 551). If just one person doesn't do it, you risk overwritten files.

Note: Visual SourceSafe and WebDAV people are free of these last two constraints. As long as everyone working on the site uses programs that support the Visual SourceSafe client or the WebDAV protocol, they can work seamlessly with Dreamweaver people. And vice versa.

Checking Out Files

When you want to work on a file in a collaborative site, you check it out from the Web server. Doing so makes sure that *you* have the latest version of the file, and that nobody else can make changes to the file.

If you're used to creating sites by yourself, this business may feel a little strange; after all, your local site (the files on your computer) contains the latest versions of all files. When working with a group, however, you should consider the *remote* site—where everyone can access, edit, and add new Web pages—to be the master copy of your site's files.

Note: There's nothing to check out when you're creating a *new* page for the site. Since the only version of the file in the universe is on your computer, there's no fear that someone else may work on it at the same time as you. In this case, you only need to check the file *into* the site when you're done (see page 556).

You check out a file using the Files panel; if it's not open, press F8 or use any of the methods described on page 479. Then choose the remote site you wish to work on from the Site pop-up menu (shown at top in Figure 15-11).

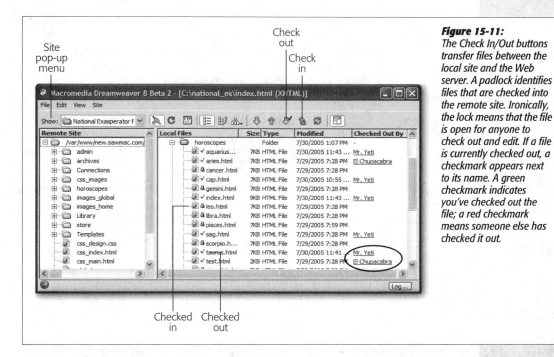

Figure 15-11:
The Check In/Out buttons transfer files between the local site and the Web server. A padlock identifies files that are checked into the remote site. Ironically, the lock means that the file is open for anyone to check out and edit. If a file is currently checked out, a checkmark appears next to its name. A green checkmark indicates you've checked out the file; a red checkmark means someone else has checked it out.

Now you're ready to begin. From the Local Folder file list in the Files panel, click to select the files you wish to check out from the Web server—or, to check out an entire folder and every file inside it, just select the folder.

You may in some instances want to select a file from the Remote Site list as well. For example, maybe you need to modify a page that you didn't create, and which you've never before checked out. In this case, the file isn't *in* your local folder, so you must select it from the Remote Site list. First, connect to the Web server by clicking the Connect button (see Figure 15-7). After Dreamweaver connects to the server, the remote files appear in the Remote Site list. Select the ones you wish to check out.

Tip: If, when you define the remote site (page 532), you select the Check Out File when Opening option, you can also check out (and open) a file by double-clicking it in the Files panel. This is a quick way to open a page for editing while still using Dreamweaver's Check Out feature.

In any case, now just click the Check Out files button on the Files panel (see Figure 15-11), or use the keyboard shortcut Ctrl+Alt+Shift+D (⌘-Option-Shift-D). (Not enough fingers? See page 665 to learn how to change Dreamweaver's shortcuts.)

Dreamweaver asks if you wish to also check out any dependent files. Click Yes if you think the page you're checking out uses files you haven't yet downloaded. Dreamweaver 8 acts differently (and more intelligently) than previous versions of Dreamweaver, which used to *also* check out the dependent files, locking them so nobody else could modify them on the server. Now Dreamweaver 8 simply copies the dependent files to your computer, so the page you've checked out and are working on displays the current images, CSS style sheets, and other linked files correctly. If you do want to edit a dependent file—for example, you need to also edit styles on a linked external style sheet that's used by the page you checked out—you must also check out that file.

When you check out files, Dreamweaver copies them to your computer and marks them as checked out so others can't change them. As when uploading and downloading files, checking out files can take time, depending upon the speed of your Internet connection.

After you've checked out a file, a green "checked-out" checkmark appears next to its name in the Files panel (see Figure 15-11). You can now open and edit it, and (when you're done) check the file back in.

If you attempt to check out a file someone else has already checked out, Dreamweaver tells you as much. It also gives you the option to override the person's checkout—but unless you're the boss, resist the temptation, for two reasons. First, your colleagues may have made some important changes to the page, which you'll wipe out with your shenanigans. Second, because you so rudely stole the file, they may decide to stop talking to you.

WORKAROUND WORKSHOP

Manual Checkout Override

Occasionally, you may wish to erase the checked-out status of a file. Suppose, for example, someone who's checked out a lot of files suddenly catches the plague and can't continue working on the site. To free those files so others can work on them, you should undo his checkout (and quarantine his cubicle).

To do this, make sure the Files panel is in Remote view (this trick won't work when looking at the Local Files). Then, right-click (Control-click) the checked-out file in the Files panel and select Undo Checkout from the menu that appears.

You'll get two warnings. First, Dreamweaver informs you that whoever checked out the file won't be able to check it back in. (This is, in fact, false. That person can still check in the file, overwriting whatever's on the Web server. So you can see why you should override the check-out only when the person who checked it out is very unlikely to check it back in. Stranded on a deserted island, perhaps.)

Second, Dreamweaver warns you that overriding a check-out also copies the remote site version of the file to your local site. You can stop the process, if necessary, by clicking No in either of these warning boxes.

When complete, a padlock icon appears next to the file.

You can also use this technique if, after checking out a file, you've made a horrible mistake on the page and wish to revert to the copy on the Web server.

A better way to work with someone who's checked out a file you need is to use Dreamweaver's email feature. You can see who checked out a file by consulting the Checked Out By column (only visible when you've expanded the Files panel; see the circled entries in Figure 15-11). Even better, if you click the name, Dreamweaver opens your email program and addresses an email to that person, so you can say: "Hey Bob, you've had the home page checked out for two days! I need to work on it, so check it back in!"

Note: Dreamweaver 8 starts with the Checked Out By column turned off. To make it appear in the expanded view of the Files panel, see "Organizing the Columns in the Files Panel" on page 565.

The name and email address Dreamweaver uses depends on the information your co-workers provided, just as you did when you configured your computer for remote site use (see page 532).

FREQUENTLY ASKED QUESTION

Get and Put, In and Out

I'm using Dreamweaver's Check In and Check Out buttons to transfer my files. What do the Get and Put buttons do when the Check In/Out feature is in use?

If you're using Check In and Out, the Get and Put commands function slightly differently than described on page 542. Get copies the selected file or files to your local site. However, Dreamweaver draws a small lock icon next to each of these "gotten" files in your Local Folder list. The files are locked, and you shouldn't edit them. Remember, checking out a file is the only way to prevent others from working on it. If you edit a locked file on your computer, nothing is stopping someone else from checking the page out from the Remote site, editing it, and checking it back in.

But using the Get command in such a situation can still be useful. For example, suppose someone just updated the site's external style sheet. Pages you're editing use this style sheet, so you'd like to get the latest version. You don't want to edit the style sheet itself, so you don't need to check it out. If you use Get instead of checking out the

pages, you can keep a reference copy on your computer without locking it for anyone else and without having to check it back in later.

Put, on the other hand, simply transfers the file on your local site to the remote site. If you're using the Check In/Check Out feature and you haven't also checked out the file, using Put is a bad idea. The remote site should be your reference copy; several rounds of revisions may have been made to a file since you last checked it out. Your local copy will be hopelessly out of date, and moving it to the server using Put destroys the most recent version of the file.

However, if you do have the file checked out, you can use Put to transfer your local copy to the server so it can be viewed by your site's visitors. For example, say you're updating the home page with 20 new news items. To keep your site "up-to-the-minute" fresh, you can Put the home page after you add each news item. Then the whole world will see each news item as soon as possible. When you're completely finished editing the home page, check it in.

Checking In Files

When you're ready to move a page you've edited back onto the server, you check it in. (You also check in *new* files you've created.)

To check in files, open the Files panel (press F8), choose the site you're checking into from the Site pop-up menu, and (using the Local Folder file list in the Files panel) select the files you wish to check in to the Web server. As always, you can click a folder to check it in, along with every file inside it.

The files you select should be files you've checked out, or brand-new files that have never been on the Web server. If you attempt to check in a file that someone else has checked out, Dreamweaver warns you with a message box. Click Cancel to stop the check-in procedure, so that you won't overwrite the checked-out file on the server. Dreamweaver also warns you if you try to check in a file that's older than the server copy. Again, unless you're sure this is what you want to do, click Cancel.

Tip: If you want to check the page you're currently working on into the remote site, use the toolbar in the document window (see Figure 15-9).

You can check in the selected files in any of the usual ways:

- Click the Check In files button on the Files panel (see Figure 15-11).
- Use the keyboard shortcut Ctrl+Alt+Shift+U (⌘-Option-Shift-U). (See page 665 to learn how to change the Dreamweaver shortcut to something less cumbersome.)

Note: The Site → Check In menu option checks in only the document you're currently working on, not any files you've selected in the Files panel.

Dreamweaver asks if you wish to also check in any dependent files (see Figure 15-8). You should transfer dependent files only if you first checked them out, or if the dependent files are new and have never been uploaded to the server. If you attempt to check in a dependent file that someone else has checked out, Dreamweaver warns you with a message box.

After you've clicked through all message boxes, Dreamweaver copies the files to the remote site. Once you've checked in a file, a padlock icon appears next to its name in the Files panel (see Figure 15-11); checking in locks the file so that you don't accidentally change the local copy. If you wish to modify the file in some way, check it out again (see page 552).

Generating a Report on Checked-Out Files

As described in Chapter 14, Dreamweaver can generate a series of reports on the files in your site. One of those reports lets you see which files a specific person has checked out. In this way, for instance, you can identify all the files you've checked out, or all the files that have been checked out by your co-worker Bob (who has since left the company).

To generate a report, follow the steps described on page 521. Turn on the Checked Out By option when specifying the type of report to run. Then click Report Settings. In the dialog box that appears, type the person's name as it appears in the Checked Out By column (Figure 15-11). (To find *all* checked-out files, leave the box blank.) Click OK, and then click Run to generate the report.

Unfortunately, a couple of issues undermine the usefulness of the "Checked Out By" report. First, if you're connected to the remote server using FTP, you'll wait a while; Dreamweaver needs to download a lot of information, which, even on a small site, can take several minutes.

Note: If you find the report is taking too long, you can stop it in its tracks by clicking the Stop button (the red stop sign icon) in the Site Reports panel (see Figure 15-12).

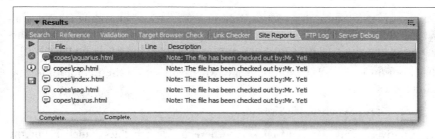

Figure 15-12:
Running a report to see who has checked out which file is a great idea. Unfortunately, this feature may not produce very useful results.

Second, the report you finally get isn't very useful (see Figure 15-12). The operations you're most likely to perform on checked-out files—checking them back in, undoing their check-out status, or contacting the person who checked them out—require you to switch to the Files panel. Because there's no link between the report and the Files panel, you can't, for example, make Dreamweaver highlight the reported files in the Files panel.

Synchronizing Site Files

As you may suspect, when you keep two sets of files—Local Folder and Remote Site—it's easy to lose track of which files are the most recent. For example, say you finish your Web site and move all the files to the Web server. The next day, you notice mistakes on a bunch of Web pages, so you make corrections on the copies in your local site. But in your rush to fix the pages, you didn't keep track of which ones you corrected. So although you're ready to move the corrected pages to the Web server, you're not sure *which* ones you need to transfer.

Note: Dreamweaver 8 introduces an entirely new method for synchronizing files. With some remote server setups, earlier versions of Dreamweaver often failed to synchronize correctly. The new method is much more reliable.

When you use the Check In/Check Out feature described on page 551, you avoid this problem altogether. Using that system, the version on the Web server is *always* considered the latest and most definitive copy—*unless* you or someone else has checked out that file. In that case, whoever checked out the file has the most recent version.

But if you're operating solo, for example, and don't use the Check In/Check Out feature, you may get good mileage from the Synchronize command, which lets you compare the remote and local sites and transfer only the newer files in either direction. (In fact, since the Synchronize command uses the Get and Put methods of transferring files, you may not get the results you expect if you synchronize your site while also using Check In and Check Out [as described in the box on page 555].)

To synchronize your sites:

1. **Make sure the "Maintain synchronization information" checkbox is turned on in the Remote Info category of the Site Definition window (you'll make this choice when you're setting up a new site, as described in step 11 on page 536).**

   This option is turned on automatically when you set up the Remote information for a site (see Figure 15-1).

2. **Choose Site → Synchronize Sitewide.**

   Alternatively, you can right-click anywhere inside the Files panel. From the shortcut menu that appears, select Synchronize. In either case, the Synchronize Files dialog box appears (see Figure 15-13).

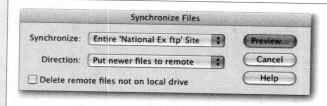

Figure 15-13:
Using the Synchronization command, you can copy newer files from your computer to the Web server, or get newer files from the remote site. (The Synchronization command isn't available if you're using Visual SourceSafe.)

3. **Using the Synchronize menu, specify the files to update.**

   You can either synchronize all files in the current Web site, or just files you've selected in the Local Folder list. This last option is good when you have a really big site and you want to limit this operation to just a single section of the site— one folder, for example. For site file-selection techniques, see page 512.

4. **Using the Direction pop-up menu, choose where you'd like to copy newer files.**

   You have three choices. **Put newer files to remote** updates the Web server with any newer files from your local site folder. It also copies any *new* files on the local site to the remote site. Use this option when you've done heavy editing to the local site and you want to move all new or modified pages to the Web server.

Get newer files from remote does just the reverse: it updates your local site folder with any newer (or new) files from the remote site. Here's one instance where the synchronize feature comes in handy in team-design situations. If you've been out of the office for a while, click this option to download copies of the latest site files. (Note that this doesn't check any files out; it merely makes sure you have the latest files for your own reference. This is one example where synchronization works well with Check In/Check Out, since it refreshes your local copy of the site with the latest files, including graphics and external CSS style sheets that your checked-out pages may depend on.)

Get and put newer files is a two-way synchronization. Any new files on the local site are transferred to the remote site and vice versa. The result is that both "sides" contain the latest files.

5. **Turn on the Delete checkbox, if desired.**

   The wording of this option reflects the option you selected in the previous step. If you're moving newer files to the remote site, it says "Delete remote files not on local drive." It's a useful option when, for example, you've spent the afternoon cleaning up the local copy of your site, deleting old, orphaned graphics files and Web pages, for example, and you want Dreamweaver to update the Web server to match.

   If you chose to transfer newer files *from* the remote site, Dreamweaver lets you "Delete local files not on remote server." Use this feature when your local site is hopelessly out of date with the remote site. Perhaps you're working on the site with a team, but you've been on vacation for two months (this is, of course, a hypothetical example). The site may have changed so significantly that you want to get your local copy in line with the Web site.

Note: Of course, you should proceed with caution when using *any* command that automatically deletes files. There's no Undo for these delete operations, and you don't want to accidentally delete the only copy of a particular page, graphic, or external Cascading Style Sheet.

   If you chose the "Get and put new files" option in step 4, the Delete checkbox is dimmed and unavailable. This option truly synchronizes the two; Dreamweaver copies newer files on the remote site (including files that exist on the Web server but not on your computer) to your local site, and vice versa.

6. **Click Preview to begin the synchronization process.**

   Dreamweaver connects to the remote site and compares the two sets of files—if your site is large, this comparison is a time-consuming process. When it finishes, the Synchronize preview window appears (Figure 15-14), listing which

---

files Dreamweaver will delete and which it will transfer, and providing an additional set of options for working with the listed files.

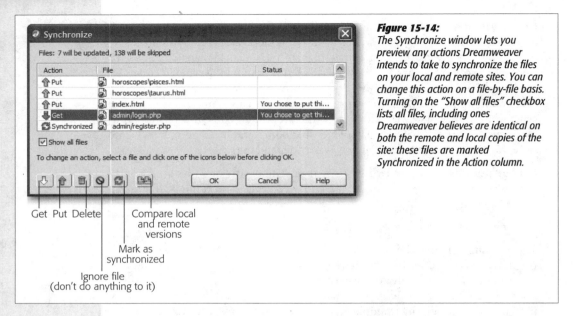

Figure 15-14:
The Synchronize window lets you preview any actions Dreamweaver intends to take to synchronize the files on your local and remote sites. You can change this action on a file-by-file basis. Turning on the "Show all files" checkbox lists all files, including ones Dreamweaver believes are identical on both the remote and local copies of the site: these files are marked Synchronized in the Action column.

7. **Change the action Dreamweaver takes on the listed files.**

   The preview box tells you what Dreamweaver plans to do with a file—get it, put it, or delete it. You can override these actions by selecting a file from the list and clicking one of the action buttons at the bottom of the window. For example, if you realize that Dreamweaver is going to delete a file that you *know* you need, select the file in the list and click the "Ignore file" button (the red circle with a line through it).

   Most of these options are useful only if you know Dreamweaver made a mistake: for example, when the program says you should get a file, but you know your local copy is identical to the server's copy. In that case, you could select the file and click the "Mark as synchronized" button, to tell Dreamweaver that they're identical. However, if you knew exactly which files were identical and which ones needed updating, you wouldn't need to use the synchronize feature in the first place, right?

   One option can come in quite handy. The "Compare local and remote versions" button lets you compare the code in the local file to the code in the remote file so you can identify exactly what differs between the two. You can use this, for example, to see exactly what changes someone else may have made to the remote copy of the file. This feature is described in detail on page 347.

8. **Click OK to proceed, or Cancel to stop the synchronization.**

If you click OK, Dreamweaver commences copying and deleting the chosen files. If you want to stop this process after clicking OK, click the Cancel button in the Background File Activity window (see the box on page 545).

9. **Click Close.**

Tip: If you just want to *identify* newer files on the local site without synchronizing them (to run a report on them, for example), choose Edit → Select Newer Local in the Files panel menu bar (Windows) or choose Site → Site Files View → Select Newer Local (Mac). Dreamweaver connects to the remote site and compares the files, and then, in the Files panel's Local Folder list, highlights files on the Local site that are newer than their remote counterparts.

You can also identify newer files on the remote site: Choose Edit → Select Newer Remote from the Files panel menu bar (Windows) or choose Site → Site Files View → Select Newer Remote (Mac). As with the Synchronization command, these options are unavailable if you're using Visual SourceSafe (page 541).

You can also identify files on your computer that you've either created or modified within a given date range, using the new Select Recently Modified command described on page 512.

Communicating with Design Notes

Lots of questions arise when a team works on a Web site: Has this page been proofread? Who is the author of the page? Where did this graphic come from? Usually, you must rely on a flurry of emails to ferret out the answers.

But Dreamweaver's Design Notes dialog box (Figure 15-15) eliminates much of that hassle by letting you attach information, such as a Web page's status or author, to a file.

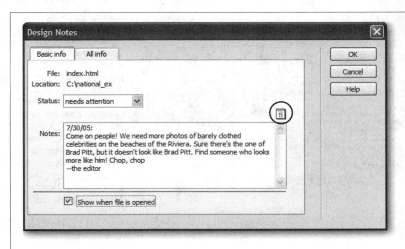

Figure 15-15:
If you want the Design Notes window to open whenever someone opens the page, turn on "Show when file is opened." This option makes sure no one misses an important note attached to a Web page. When the page is opened in Dreamweaver, the Design Notes window appears automatically. (This option has no effect when adding notes to GIFs, JPEGs, Flash movies, or anything other than a file that Dreamweaver can open and edit, such as a Web page or an external CSS style sheet.)

You can open these notes (from the Files panel or from a currently open document), edit them, and even share them with others. In this way, it's easy to leave notes for other people—such as, "Hey Bob, can you make sure that this is the most recent photo of Brad and Angelina?" You can even add notes to files other than Web pages, including folders, images, Flash movies, and external Cascading Style Sheets—anything, in fact, that appears in the Files panel.

Setting Up Design Notes

You can't use Design Notes unless the feature itself is turned on. To find out if it is, open the Site Definition dialog box by double-clicking the site's name in the Manage Sites dialog box (choose Manage Sites from the Site menu or the pop-up menu in the Files panel). In the Category list, click Design Notes; as shown in Figure 15-16, two checkboxes pertain to the notes feature:

- **Maintain Design Notes.** This checkbox lets you create and read notes using Dreamweaver's File → Design Notes command (see the opposite page).

- **Upload Design Notes for sharing.** If you're using Design Notes as part of a team, turn on this checkbox, which makes Dreamweaver upload design notes to the remote site, so that your fellow team members can read them.

Note: Design Notes are especially useful for keeping track of pages that are built and maintained by a team of developers. But if you're a solo operator and still want to use them—maybe you're the type with a hundred Post-it notes taped to the edges of your monitor—then turn off "Upload Design Notes for sharing." You'll save time and server space by preventing Dreamweaver from transferring note files to the Web server.

Click OK to close the Site Definition dialog box. You can double-click another site in the Manage Sites dialog box to turn on its Design Notes feature, or click Done.

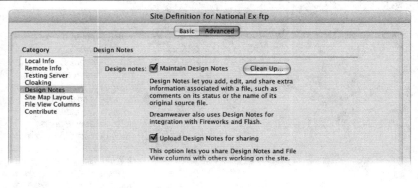

Figure 15-16:
The Clean Up button deletes any notes that were attached to now-deleted files. (To avoid stray notes files in the first place, always delete pages in Dreamweaver's Files panel, instead of on your desktop.) If you turn off the Maintain Design Notes checkbox, clicking Clean Up removes all Design Notes files for the site.

Adding Design Notes to a File

To add a Design Note to a document you're working on, choose your favorite method:

- Choose File → Design Notes.

- From the File Status menu in the toolbar, choose Design Notes (see Figure 15-9).

- Right-click (Control-click) a file in the Files panel (or an external object, such as a graphic or Flash movie, in the document window), and choose Design Notes from the shortcut menu.

In any case, the Design Notes window now opens (Figure 15-15). If you like, you can use the Status pop-up menu to let your team members know where the file stands. For example, is it ready to move to the Web server? Is it just a draft version? Or is there something wrong with it that requires specific attention? Dreamweaver provides eight different options: "draft," "revision1," "revision2," "revision3," "alpha," "beta," "final," and "needs attention." If these categories don't match your workflow—for example, you want a "needs proofing" flag—you can change them; see the box below.

The note itself, which you type into the Note box, could be a simple question you have for the author of the page ("Are you sure 'Coldplay: Defining a New Musical Language for the Modern Age' is an appropriate title for this article?") or more information about the status of the page ("Still need studio shot of foil-wrapped cigar hanging from a string").

POWER USERS' CLINIC

Create Your Own Status Menu

The Status pop-up menu in Design Notes is a great feature. With a flick of the mouse, you can assign a status to a page or file, letting others know if a page is finished or just a rough draft. But the preset status options may not exactly fit your process. Your team may not use the terms "alpha" or "beta." Instead, you may have other stages you'd like to add, such as "copy edit," to signify that a page is ready to be proofread and tested.

With a little sly hacking, you can change the status categories to suit your needs. The file Design Notes.htm, in the Dreamweaver 8 → Configuration → Commands folder, holds the key to this puzzle. Start by making a safety copy of the file; you can always return to it if something goes wrong.

Then open this file in a text editor like NotePad or TextEdit, or even within Dreamweaver's Code view (page 330).

Find line 28 in the file, which looks like this:

```
STATUS_ITEMS = new
Array("","draft","revision1","revision2",
"revision3","alpha","beta","final","needs
attention");
```

The words between the double-quotes are the choices that appear in the Status menu. You can change or delete them as you see fit (if you delete one, be sure to delete the word, both sets of quotation marks, and the following comma). Then, after saving changes to the file, quit and restart Dreamweaver, where you'll see your new, improved Status pop-up menu ready for action.

To make sure you and your co-workers see the same choices, give each of them the modified Design Notes.htm file, and advise them to put it in their own Dreamweaver 8 → Configuration → Commands folders.

Tip: Click the calendar icon (circled in Figure 15-15) to pop the date into your note—a great way to keep a running tally of notes and the dates they were made.

When you click OK, Dreamweaver creates a file with all the note information in it. This file ends with the extension .mno and begins with the name of the file; for the file *index.html,* for example, the note would be called *index.html.mno.*

Dreamweaver stores notes in a folder called *_notes* that it keeps in the same folder as the page or file. For example, if you add notes to the home page, Dreamweaver stores the notes file in the *_notes* folder inside the root folder.

Viewing Design Notes

You can view Design Notes in a number of ways. If the note's author turned on "Show when file is opened" (see Figure 15-15), of course, the Design Notes window opens automatically when you open that page.

Otherwise, to look at a note, you have any number of options:

- Choose File → Design Notes.

- Choose Design Notes from the File Status drop-down menu in the document window's toolbar (see Figure 15-9).

- Double-click the small yellow balloon icon in the Notes column of the Files panel (see Figure 15-17). (This column is visible only when the Files panel is expanded, as described on page 481.)

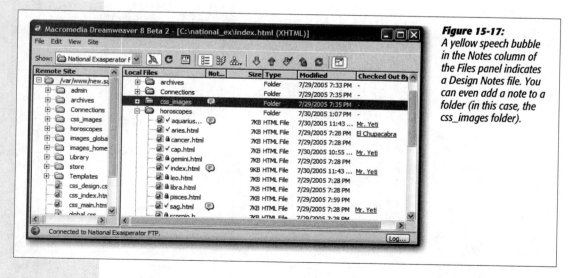

Figure 15-17:
A yellow speech bubble in the Notes column of the Files panel indicates a Design Notes file. You can even add a note to a folder (in this case, the css_images folder).

- Right-click (Control-click) an embedded object, like a graphic or Flash movie, right in the document window, and choose Design Notes from the shortcut menu.

- Right-click (Control-click) a file in the Files panel and choose Design Notes from the shortcut menu.

Organizing the Columns in the Files Panel

When the Files panel is fully expanded (see page 481), the columns identify a file's name, file size, modification date, type, and so on.

This may be more information than you're interested in—or it may not be enough. So remember that Dreamweaver lets you show or hide these various columns, change their order, or even create new columns with information retrieved from a file's Design Notes (page 561).

Tip: You can adjust the relative widths of these columns by dragging the dividing line between the column names. You can also sort all the pages listed in this window by clicking the relevant column's name. Clicking Modified, for example, sorts the files so that the newest appear first. Click a second time to reverse the sort, placing oldest files first.

When you're setting up a Web site in the Site Definition window (page 472), you can view the column setup by clicking the File View Columns category (Figure 15-18).

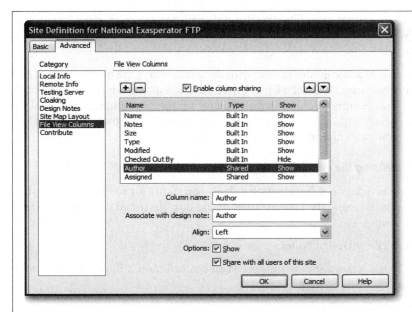

Figure 15-18:
If you're working with others, you'll probably want to share any columns you add. Turn on the "Enable column sharing" checkbox; then, you'll be able to see columns that others on your team have added, and they'll be able to see columns you've added (if you've turned on "Share with all users of this site" for each column, of course).

Once you're looking at the display shown in Figure 15-18, you can perform any of these stunts:

- **Reorder columns.** Click a column name in the Site Definition window to select it. Then click the up and down arrow buttons to move the column one spot to the left or right, respectively, in the Files panel.

- **Hide columns.** You may not care what date a file was last modified or whether it's a folder or Web page. If that's the case, hide the column by clicking its name in the Site Definition window and then turning off the Show checkbox (see Figure 15-18). (You can always return to the Site Definition window and turn the column back on.)

- **Share a column.** If you work with a team of designers, you may want to make newly added columns visible to them, too. (See Figure 15-18 for details.)

- **Adding Columns.** You can add informational columns of your own, as described next.

- **Deleting columns.** Click the column name, and then click the minus (–) button to delete the column. (Dreamweaver doesn't let you delete the built-in columns: Name, Notes, Type, Modified, and so on.)

"All Info" Design Notes in Column Views

Your Files panel offers columns for all the usual information bits: Name, Checked Out, and so on. But you may someday wish there were a column that showed each page's status, so that your Files panel could show you which files need proofreading, or who wrote each article, or which pages are being held until a certain blackout date.

You can indeed add columns of your own design, although the process isn't streamlined by any means. It involves two broad efforts: First, using an offshoot of the Design Notes feature described earlier, you set up the new columns you want displayed. Then, using the column-manipulation dialog box shown in Figure 15-18, you make the new columns visible in the Files panel.

Phase 1: Defining the new information types

You create new kinds of informational flags—primarily for use as new columns in the Files panel—using the Design Notes dialog box, described on page 561. Here's the rundown:

1. **Choose File → Design Notes.**

   The Design Notes window appears. (You can summon it in various other ways, too, as described on page 563.)

2. **Click the "All info" tab.**

   This peculiar window shows the programmery underbelly of the Dreamweaver Notes feature (see Figure 15-19). It turns out that it stores every kind of note as a name/value pair. If you used the main Notes screen (Figure 15-15) to choose Beta from the Status pop-up menu, for example, you'll see a notation here that says "status=beta." (*Status* is the name of the info nugget; *beta* is the value.) If you turned on the option called "Show when file is opened," you'll see "showOnOpen=true." And if you typed *Badly needs updating* as the note itself, you'll see "notes=Badly needs updating" on this screen.

But those are just the built-in info types; you're free to create your own.

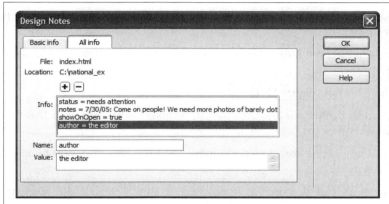

Figure 15-19:
Dreamweaver lets you create your own types of notes in the "All info" tab of the Design Notes window. This lets you add more information to a page, such as its author or designer. If you want to delete a note you've added, it's a simple matter of clicking on the note in the Info box and then clicking the minus (–) button.

3. **Click the + button.**

   You may wonder why you'd do this; after all, you can type a lot of information in the Notes box under the Basic Info tab. The primary benefit of creating new types of notes is that you can display that information in the Files panel.

4. **Type the name of the new note in the Name field.**

   It may be Author, for example, so that you can note who wrote the text of each page. Or it could be Artist, if you wish to add a note to each image specifying who created it. Maybe you need a column called Hold Until, which lets you know when certain information is OK to publish online.

5. **Press Tab (to jump to the Value field); type the contents of the note.**

   You can enter the actual name of the author or artist—Jane Stevens, for example—or the actual "Hold Until" date.

   Repeat steps 3–5 if you want to add more notes to the page or file.

Tip: Keep the value short—one or two words. Otherwise, the narrow Files panel column chops off the latter part of it. If you've got enough screen real estate, you can resize the columns by dragging the divider bars between column names.

---

6. Click OK.

The dialog box closes.

Phase 2: Adding the column

Just creating a new note type gets you only halfway home; now you have to tell Dreamweaver that you want to see that information in the Files panel.

To add a column:

1. **Open the Site Definition window for the particular site and select the File Views category.**

   See page 476 for a reminder of how to edit a site definition. The File Views dialog box appears.

2. **Click the + button (Figure 15-18).**

   A new, untitled column is added to the list, complete with three fields that need filling in (they now say "untitled").

3. **In the Column Name box, type the column-heading name you want to appear in the Files panel.**

   Make it short and descriptive. If possible, it should match the note type (Author, Artist, Hold Until, or whatever).

4. **Press Tab. Type the name of the Design Note you wish to use for this column.**

   This is the name part of the name/value pair described in step 4 of the previous instructions. For example, if you added a note named Author to a file, you would type *Author* here. Capitalization matters; so if you named the Design Note *Author*, type it with a capital A.

   There's a pop-up menu here, too, but it always lists the same four options: Status, Assigned, Due, and Priority. If you choose Status, you'll get a column that reflects your choice from the Status pop-up menu. The other three options do nothing *unless* you created a matching note type in step 4 of the previous instructions. (It would be nice if this pop-up menu listed *all* of the note names you've created, so that you didn't have to remember them.)

   Before you wrap up the column-adding procedure, you can, if you wish, choose an alignment option for the text in the column (left, right, or center). Check to make sure that the Show checkbox is turned on (otherwise, your new column won't appear, and you've just defeated the purpose of this whole exercise). Finally, turn on "Share with all users of this site," if you like.

The Share feature works like this. The next time you connect to the remote site, Dreamweaver uploads a file containing your newly defined column information. The next time another member of the team connects to the remote site, *his* copy of Dreamweaver downloads this file, so that his Files panel shows the same columns yours does.

Note: The column-sharing feature is very handy; it lets everyone working on a site share the same note information. But it works properly only if everyone on the team has the "Enable column sharing" checkbox turned on (see Figure 15-18).

5. **Click OK.**

   You should now see the new information column in your Files panel, as shown in Figure 15-20. (If not, you may need to expand the Files panel view and widen the window to reveal the additional column.)

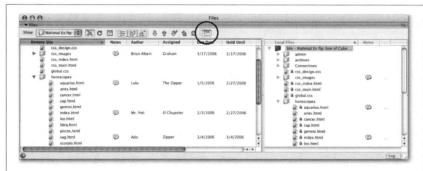

Figure 15-20:
The Files panel can show newly created kinds of status information, but only if you've expanded the Files panel view by clicking the Expand/ Collapse button, circled here. Each piece of information (Author, Assigned, and so on) is actually a Design Note you've invented. To sort the list, click the gray column heading.

Part Five:
Dreamweaver Power

5

Snippets and Libraries

You've finished the design for your company's new Web site. It looks great and your boss is ecstatic. But you've really only just begun. There are hundreds of pages to build before you launch. And once the site's online, you'll need to make endless updates to keep it fresh and inviting.

This is where Dreamweaver's Snippet and Library features come in, streamlining the sometimes tedious work of building and updating Web pages.

As you build more and more Web pages (and more and more Web sites), you may find yourself creating the same Web page elements over and over again. Many pages of a site may share certain common elements that are always the same: a copyright notice, a navigation bar, or a logo, for example. And you may find yourself frequently using more complex items, such as a pull-down menu listing the twelve months of the year, or a particular table design you use for photos and their captions.

Recreating the same page elements time after time is tiresome and—thanks to Dreamweaver—unnecessary. Dreamweaver provides two subtly different tools for reusing common page elements: *Snippets* and *Library items*.

Snippets Basics

Snippets aren't fancy or complex, but they sure save time. A snippet is simply a chunk of code that you store away and then plunk into other Web pages. It could be HTML, JavaScript, or any of the other programming languages you may encounter. Dreamweaver comes with hundreds of snippets organized into different folders, like Footers (canned footer designs), Form Elements (useful form parts like pull-down menus), and JavaScript code (programming code for interesting effects like adding a random image to a page).

For example, say you always use the same table design to create a sidebar on a page. Each time you want to create a similar table, you could go through all the same steps to build it—or you could turn that table into a snippet and then, with a simple double-click, add it to page after page of your site.

You keep these code chunks in the Snippets tab of the Files panel (see Figure 16-1). You get to them in any of several ways:

- Choose Window → Snippets.
- Windows people can press Shift-F9. (There's no Mac keyboard shortcut for opening the Snippets tab, but you can create your own if you want, as described on page 665).
- Click the Snippets tab on the Files panel.

Above and beyond Dreamweaver's preinstalled snippets, you can quickly build a collection of your own.

Dreamweaver MX 2004 users: Note that the Snippets panel has moved. It's now grouped with the Files and Assets panels.

Using Snippets

Snippets come in two varieties: those that are a simple block of code and those that wrap around whatever you've currently selected in the document. For example, in the Text folder of the Snippets tab, you'll find a snippet called Service Mark. Adding this snippet to a page instantly inserts the code *^{sm}*, creating a superscript service mark (sm) symbol.

But on occasion you may want to wrap code around something you've already typed. You may want to add an HTML comment to your page (a message that won't appear in a Web browser, but that you can use for helpful notes to yourself or other Web designers). The "Comment, multi-line" snippet (in the Comments folder) can help you quickly add such comments. It wraps whatever you've selected with opening (<!--) and closing HTML comments (-->). Adding an HTML comment is as easy as typing the comment, selecting it, and then inserting this snippet. (This may sound a lot like the Apply Comment button in the Coding toolbar described on page 336. The cool thing about this snippet is that it works in Design view, too, not just Code view.)

Note: Unfortunately, unless the snippet's description (visible in the Snippet Panel's *Description* column) specifies that the snippet wraps, there's no way to tell whether a snippet is intended to wrap around a selection. You either have to try the snippet or open the snippet in editing mode (see page 577) to find out. (While you've got the snippet open, you can add a note to its description indicating its ability, or inability, to wrap.)

To add a snippet to a Web page, click in the document where you want the item to go, or select the object you wish to wrap with a snippet. Then do one of the following:

- Double-click the name of the snippet on the Snippets tab of the Files panel.

- Select the snippet on the Snippets tab, and then click the panel's Insert button.

- Drag the snippet from the panel into the document window. (If the snippet's supposed to wrap a selection, drag the snippet *onto* the selected object.)

Snippets can be used in either Design or Code view (see page 330), but some snippets make sense only in Code view. For example, the JavaScript snippets that come with Dreamweaver typically have to be inserted in the <head> of a page, inside <script> tags. To use them, you must switch to Code view, insert the script tags, and then put the snippets inside.

Tip: Dreamweaver 8 provides a fast way to add a snippet you've recently used. Select the snippet from the Insert → Recent Snippets menu. Better yet, create a keyboard shortcut for your favorite snippets and insert them with a quick keystroke as described on page 665.

Snippets simply dump their contents into a document; Dreamweaver doesn't step in to make sure that you're adding the code correctly. Unless you're careful—and have some knowledge of HTML—you may end up adding snippets that make your Web page unviewable. (For advice on how to avoid such pitfalls, see the box on page 579.)

Creating Snippets

Dreamweaver comes with a lot of snippets, and you many have no use for many of them. No problem—it's simple to create snippets of your own. Here's how:

1. **Create and select the code you wish to turn into a snippet.**

   You could, for instance, select a table in Design view, or select the opening and closing <table> tags (as well as all the code between them) in Code view.

   If you make a snippet out of code that isn't visible in Design view, such as a JavaScript program or content that appears in the <head> of the page, you need to switch into Code view first and then select the code.

2. **Click the New Snippet button on the Snippets tab (Figure 16-1).**

   The Snippet window appears (Figure 16-2), displaying the code you selected in the Insert field.

Note: If you skip step 1 and just click the New Snippet button, you can either type the code or paste a previously copied selection into the Insert box (see step 6).

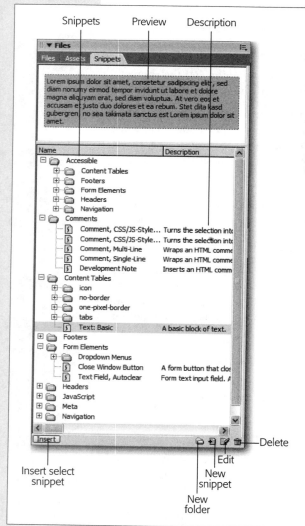

Snippets   Preview   Description

Insert select snippet

New folder

New snippet

Edit

Delete

Figure 16-1:
The Snippets tab on the Files panel contains reusable chunks of code—snippets—which you can organize into folders. After selecting a snippet from the list, a preview appears in the Preview pane. In this example, you can see a preview of the snippet: a simple table with a colored background and dummy text. Snippets can have either a graphic preview (as in this example), called design preview, or a code preview, which is the raw code. Code previews are useful for snippets that aren't visible in Design view, such as JavaScript code. (When you create your own snippets, you specify the preview type.)

3. **Title the snippet.**

   The name you type in the Name field appears in the Snippet tab. Make sure to give it an easily understood name.

4. **In the Description field, type identifying details.**

   This step's optional, but useful. Use this field to provide a description of when and how to use the snippet and whether or not the snippet wraps a selection.

5. **Select a Snippet type.**

   "Wrap selection" makes the code wrap around a selection when you use the snippet in your Web pages. The "Insert block" option is for a snippet that's a single block of code inserted into the document—for example, a simple copyright notice.

6. **If necessary, add the code for the snippet.**

   If you initially selected code in the document window, it already appears in the "Insert before" or "Insert after" field. If you're creating a wrapping snippet, then some code goes in the "before" field and some in the "after" field.

   For example, say you wanted to create a snippet that would let you set off a paragraph of text by adding a horizontal rule at the beginning of the paragraph and one at the end. In both the "Insert before" and "Insert after" fields, you'd type *<hr>*—the HTML code for a horizontal rule. (If you're creating XHTML pages as described on page 6, you'd type *<hr />* in both fields.)

7. **Select a "Preview type."**

   The preview type determines how the snippet appears in the Preview pane of the Snippets tab (see Figure 16-1). *Design* means the snippet looks as it would in Design view—a snippet of a table appears as a table, for instance. *Code* means the code itself appears in the Preview pane (in that case, a snippet for a horizontal rule would preview like this: <hr>). Use Code preview for snippets that aren't visible in Design view, such as JavaScript code.

8. **Click OK.**

   Dreamweaver adds the snippet to the Snippets tab, and you can then drop it in your Web pages using any of the techniques described on page 574.

If you need to go back and edit a snippet—change the code, type, description, or name—select the snippet in the Snippets tab and click Edit Snippet (Figure 16-1). You can also right-click (Control-click) the snippet name and then select Edit from the shortcut menu.

Whichever method you chose, the Snippet window (Figure 16-2) appears. Make your changes, and then click OK.

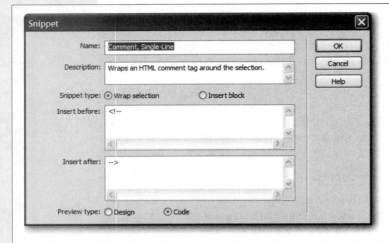

Figure 16-2:
The Snippet window lets you create reusable chunks of HTML called snippets. For snippets that wrap around a currently selected object on the page—for example, a snippet that adds a link to any selected text or graphic—you put code in the two insert boxes. The code that appears before the selected object goes in the top box, and the code that goes after the object appears in the bottom box. In this example, the snippet wraps the current selection in HTML comments.

Organizing Snippets

To keep snippets organized, you can create new folders to store them by category. To add a folder to the Snippets tab, click the New Folder button (see Figure 16-1). An untitled folder appears; type a name for it. If you select a folder before clicking New Folder, Dreamweaver creates the new folder *inside* that folder. You can move folders around by dragging them into other folders.

Note: To drag a folder or snippet to the top level of the Snippets list, you have to drag it all the way to the *bottom* of the tab, below any other folders. If you try to drag it to the top, Dreamweaver puts the folder or snippet inside the top folder in the list.

To move a snippet into or out of its folder, simply drag it. If you drag a snippet over a closed folder without releasing the mouse, that folder expands to reveal the folders inside, if any.

To delete a snippet, select it from the Snippets tab and then click the Delete Snippet (Trash can) button (see Figure 16-1). Quicker yet, press Delete.

Note: Having lots of snippets can slow down the Snippets panel, so it's best to remove any snippets you don't use (like a lot of the ones that came with the program, for example). If you don't want to permanently delete them, you can move them out of the main Macromedia Dreamweaver 8 → Configuration → Snippets folder and store them in a separate folder on your hard drive. (For more on the configuration folder and how to find it, see the box on page 677.)

Built-in Snippets

Many of the snippets that come with Dreamweaver offer solutions to specific problems you may never encounter, like a page footer containing two lists of links and a copyright notice. However, some of them are useful for most Web developers. Here are some examples:

- **Close Window Button.** When you create a pop-up window (page 418), this snippet lets you add a Close button to let people dismiss the window. The "Close Window Button" snippet (in the Form Elements folder) places a form button with the words Close Window on the window page, complete with the JavaScript necessary to close the window when your visitor clicks the button.

Note: Some browsers don't recognize a Form button without the <form> tag. To play it safe, first insert a form (see page 363), and then insert the Close Window Button snippet inside it.

- **Dropdown Menus.** If you create a lot of forms for your sites (see Chapter 10), you'll find some useful snippets in the Form Elements folder, especially in the Dropdown Menus subfolder. For example, the "Numbers 1-12" snippet inserts a menu with the numbers 1–12 already coded into it—great for capturing credit card expiration dates on an e-commerce site. (To create an even more useful drop-down snippet, see the tutorial on page 587.)

TROUBLESHOOTING MOMENT

A Snippet of Caution

Snippets aren't as smart as other Dreamweaver features. Dreamweaver's usually good about warning you before you make a mistake, but it doesn't make a peep if you're incorrectly adding a snippet.

For instance, when you use one of the program's form snippets to add, say, a text field to a page, Dreamweaver doesn't check to see if you're really putting the snippet into a form. Dreamweaver doesn't let you know if the required <form> tag is missing, and certainly doesn't add it itself. Furthermore, if you're working in Code view, Dreamweaver lets you add snippets to the <head> or even outside the <html> tags altogether, which is useful when creating dynamic Web pages that include server-side programming code, but just creates messy and invalid HTML on normal Web pages.

Furthermore, snippets don't take advantage of Dreamweaver's site management features to keep track of links or paths to images. Suppose you create a snippet that includes

an image. If you insert that snippet into another page, the image may not show up correctly. If you create a snippet that includes a link from one page to another on your site, that link's also unlikely to work in another page.

So it's best to create snippets without images or links—but there are workarounds. For instance, you can create snippets with fake links—use nothing but the # symbol for the link, for example—and update the link after you insert the snippet into a page. For images, you can use Dreamweaver's Image Placeholder object to simulate a graphic in a snippet (choose Insert → Image Objects → Image Placeholder). After adding the snippet to the page, update the placeholder with your real image file.

If you want to create reusable content that can keep track of links and images, see Dreamweaver's Library feature, described on page 580.

• **Autoclear Textfield.** Ever seen a Web form with a text field that has some help-ful instructions *inside* the field ("Type your name here," for example)? This text magically disappears when you click in the field, leaving you free to type as instructed. A snippet called "Textfield, Autoclear" (also in the Form Elements folder) supplies both the text field and the bit of JavaScript that perform this lit-tle trick.

Library Basics

Imagine this situation: You manage a relatively large Web site consisting of thou-sands of Web pages. At the bottom of each page is a simple copyright notice: "Copyright MyBigCompany. We reserve all rights—national, international, com-mercial, noncommercial, and mineral—to the content contained on these pages."

Each time you add another page to the site, you *could* retype the copyright mes-sage, but this approach invites both typographic errors and carpal tunnel syn-drome. And if you must *format* this text too, then you're in for quite a bit of work.

Fortunately, Dreamweaver's Library can turn any selection in the document win-dow (a paragraph, an image, a table) into a reusable chunk of HTML that you can easily drop into any Dreamweaver document. The Library, in other words, is a great place to store copyright notices, navigation bars, or any other chunks of HTML you use frequently.

But this is only half of the Library's power. Each Library item that you add to a Web page is actually only a copy, which remains linked to the original. Thanks to this link, whenever you update the original Library item, you get a chance to update every page that uses that item.

Suppose your company is bought, for example, and the legal department orders you to change the copyright notice to "Copyright MyBigCompany, a subsidiary of aMuchBiggerCompany" on each of the Web site's *10,000 pages*. If you had cleverly inserted the original copyright notice as a Library item, you could take care of this task in the blink of an eye. Just open the item in the Library, make the required changes, save it, and let Dreamweaver update all the pages for you (see Figure 16-3).

Compared to Snippets, Library items are much smarter. They possess the unique ability to update the same material on an entire site's worth of files in seconds, and can successfully deal with links and images. Unlike Snippets, however, Dream-weaver's Library feature is site-specific. In other words, each site that you've defined in Dreamweaver has its own Library. You can't use a Library item from one site on a page from a different site.

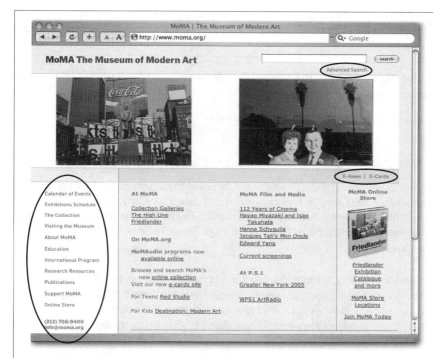

Figure 16-3:
The Museum of Modern Art's home page, which was created with Dreamweaver, takes advantage of Library elements. Many of the navigation options on the page (circled) are Library items. If the Museum decides to add or remove a navigation link, it can update the Library item to change every page on the site in one simple step (see page 583). In fact, since a Library item is a chunk of HTML, the Museum could decide to replace the left-hand navigation bar with a Flash movie, plain-text links (instead of graphics), or any other valid HTML code.

Creating and Using Library Items

To create a Library item, start by opening the Library window. Choose Window → Assets, and click the Library Items button (it looks like an open book, circled in Figure 16-4) to reveal the Library category.

Now select the part of your document that you wish to save as a Library item: a blob of text, a graphic, or whatever.

Note, however, that Library items can contain only page elements that appear in the document window—in other words, only HTML from the <body> of a Web page. You can't include anything that appears in the <head> of a page, like Cascading Style Sheets, Dreamweaver Behaviors (Chapter 11), or meta tags. Furthermore, Library items must include a complete set of HTML tags—both an opening and closing tag—as well as all tags necessary to complete the original object. For example, Dreamweaver doesn't let you turn just a single cell, row, or column of a table into a Library item. If you try, Dreamweaver adds the *entire* table to the Library.

Tip: Use the tag selector (see page 21) to make sure you select the precise tag information you want. To select *all* of the contents of a cell, click at the beginning of the content and drag until you've selected everything in the cell.

Next, add the selection to the Library. As you may expect, Dreamweaver provides several ways to do this:

- Drag the highlighted selection into the list of Library items.

- Click the New Item button (Figure 16-4).

- Choose Modify → Library → Add Object to Library.

The new item appears in the Assets panel, bearing the jaunty name "Untitled." Just type to replace that with a more useful name, such as *Copyright notice* or *Logo*. (Avoid hyphens in your Library item's name. These tend to trip up the Firefox Web browser, as described in the box on page 585.) Your new Library element is ready to use.

Note: Even though you can't turn a CSS style into a Library item, you *can* turn HTML that has been styled with CSS into a Library item. For example, you can add to the Library a paragraph that has a custom CSS style applied to it. When you attempt to add this paragraph to the Library, Dreamweaver warns you that the item may not look the same when you place it in other documents—because the style sheet information doesn't come along for the ride. To make sure the Library item appears correctly, make sure that you attach the same style sheet to any page where you use that item. External style sheets (see page 163) make this easy.

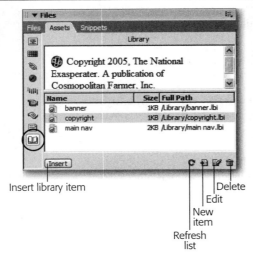

Figure 16-4:
The Assets panel's Library category lists the name, file size, and location of each Library item in the currently opened site. When you select a Library item from the list, you see a small preview. In this example, the Library item "copyright" is a copyright notice.

Insert library item
Delete
Edit
New item
Refresh list

Adding Library Items to a Page

To add a Library item to a Web page, drag it directly out of the Assets panel's Library items listing onto your page. (The long way: Click to plant your insertion point in the Web page, click the Library item you want in the Assets panel, and then click the Insert button on the Assets panel, shown in Figure 16-4.)

Note: Library items (*.lbi* files) also appear in the Files panel in a site's Library folder. Dragging a Library item from the Files panel to a page, however, *doesn't* insert it into the page. It merely opens the Library item for editing.

When you insert a Library item into a Web page (or turn a selected item *into* a Library item), it sprouts a light-yellow background color. The highlighting indicates that Dreamweaver intends to treat the Library item as a single object, even though it may be made of many different HTML elements. You can select it or drag it around, but you can't change it. (Unfortunately, if you turn a nontransparent graphic into a Library item—like a logo, for example—Dreamweaver doesn't give you this helpful visual cue.)

Remember, too, that the placed Library item is linked to the original copy in the Library. The copy in your document automatically changes to reflect any changes you make to the copy in the Library, using the technique described next.

Tip: Sometimes you may want to sever the connection between the Library and a Library item you've already placed onto a Web page—to modify a copyright notice on a particular page, for example. Select the item on the page and then click "Detach from original" in the Property inspector (Figure 16-5). Dreamweaver removes the comment tags (see the box on page 585), thus breaking the link to the Library.

You can also insert the HTML of a Library item *without* maintaining a link to the Library by pressing the Ctrl (⌘) key when you add it to your document. Now Dreamweaver doesn't update the HTML on this page when you change the original Library file.

Don't use this method if the Library item contains images or document-relative links, however. Dreamweaver doesn't update the links with paths appropriate to the document's location when you insert the Library item in this way. In this case, first insert the Library item normally and then unlink it using the method described in this tip's first paragraph.

Editing Library Items

You'll appreciate the real power of Library items when it's time to make a change. When you update the file in the Library, all pages that you've graced with that item update themselves, too.

Start by opening the Library, as described on page 581. Then:

1. **Open the Library item that you want to edit.**

   You can do this by double-clicking the Library item in the Assets panel, by highlighting it and then clicking the Edit button (Figure 16-4), or by highlighting a

Library item on a Web page and then clicking the Open button on the Property inspector (Figure 16-5). (You can also open the Library item file—an *.lbi* file—in the Library folder of your site's root directly from the Files panel.)

Dreamweaver opens what looks like a miniature Web page document, containing nothing but the text, graphics, or other elements of the Library file.

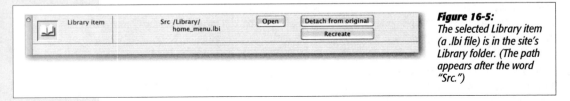

Figure 16-5:
The selected Library item (a .lbi file) is in the site's Library folder. (The path appears after the word "Src.")

2. **Edit away.**

   A Library item is only a selection of HTML; it's not a complete Web page. That means you can't edit *page* properties like the title or background color. Also, you can insert Library items only in the body of a Web page, so stick with objects that would normally appear in the document window, such as links, images, tables, and text. Don't add any code that appears in the head of a Web page, such as Cascading Style Sheets, meta tags, behaviors, or timelines.

   And since a Library item can't contain a style sheet, if the HTML in your Library item relies on a CSS, you'll have trouble previewing it correctly. Dreamweaver's Design Time Style Sheet tool comes in handy here. It lets you temporarily "add" a style sheet while designing a page, without actually adding the CSS code to the page. For more on this cool feature, turn to page 174.

Tip: Even though you can't *add* a Dreamweaver behavior to a Library item, you can include HTML code that uses Dreamweaver behaviors in a Library item.

For example, suppose you create a navigation bar with rollover graphics. You could select the navigation bar and turn it into a Library item. Even though Dreamweaver doesn't actually put the JavaScript programming into the Library item, whenever you add the Library item to a page, Dreamweaver's smart enough to add the necessary JavaScript code to the Head of the Web page.

---

3. **Choose File → Save.**

   Dreamweaver checks to see if there are any pages that use the Library item, and, if there are, it opens the Update Library Items window. A list of pages in the site that use that Library item appears.

4. **Click Update.**

   Dreamweaver opens the Update Pages window, updates the HTML in all the pages that use the Library item, and then lists all of the files that it changed.

On the other hand, you don't necessarily have to click Update. Perhaps you have a lot of changes to make to the Library item, and you just want to save the work you've done so far. You're not done editing it yet, so you don't want to waste time updating pages you'll just have to update again. You can always update later (see the box on page 628); in that case, click Don't Update. (Once you're finished with the changes and save the file for the final time, *then* update the site.)

5. **Click Done.**

As you can see, the Library is an incredible time-saver that greatly simplifies the process of changing common page elements.

Renaming Library Elements

To rename something in your Library, click its name on the Assets panel (Figure 16-4). Pause briefly, then click again, and the name highlights, ready to be edited. Type the new name and press Enter (Return).

If you've already added the item to your Web pages, Dreamweaver prompts you to update those pages. Click Update. Otherwise, the link between those pages and the Library breaks.

Tip: If you accidentally click Don't Update, don't panic. Simply change the Library item back to its original name and then *re*-rename it. Don't forget to click Update this time!

POWER USERS' CLINIC

Under the Hood of Library Items

Behind the scenes, Dreamweaver stores the HTML for Library items in basic text files. Those files' names end with the extension .lbi, and they stay in the Library folder inside your local site folder (see page 476).

When you insert a Library item into a Web page, Dreamweaver inserts the item's HTML and adds a set of comment tags. These tags refer to the original Library file and help Dreamweaver remember where the Library item begins and ends. For instance, if you turned the text "Copyright 2004" into a Library item called *copyright* and inserted it into a Web page, Dreamweaver would add the following HTML to the page:

```
<!-- #BeginLibraryItem "/Library/
copyright. lbi" -->Copyright 2003<!--
#EndLibraryItem-->
```

It's important to avoid the use of hyphens when naming Library items. Why? Since HTML comments use hyphens, <!-- -->, some browsers, most notably Firefox, get tripped up by additional hyphens and respond by hiding the contents of a Library item, or displaying raw HTML code instead.

In addition, although you can't edit a Library item on a page in Design view, you can muck around with the code in Code view. In the example above, you could change 2003 to 2005 in Code view. Don't do it! Dreamweaver obliterates any changes you make the next time you update the original Library item. If you want to make a change to a Library item, edit the original Library item, or detach the item from the Library (as described in the Tip on page 583) and then edit it.

Deleting Library Elements

You can delete unnecessary elements from your Library at any time, but do so with caution. When you delete something from the Library, Dreamweaver leaves behind every copy of it that you've already placed onto your Web pages—complete with links to the now-deleted Library item.

In other words, you won't be able to edit the copies on your Web pages until you break those links. If you do indeed want to edit them, you have to break the links manually on each page where the Library item appears by selecting the item and then clicking the "Detach from original" button (see Figure 16-5).

Now that you've been warned, here are the instructions. To get rid of a Library item, click it in the Assets panel and then do one of the following:

- Click the Trash can icon in the Assets panel.
- Press Delete.
- Right-click (Control-click) the item's name, and then choose Delete from the shortcut menu.

Tip: If you ever accidentally delete an item from the Library, you can recreate it, provided you've used it somewhere on one of the Web pages in the site.

Open the page containing the Library item, and then click the Library item to select it. Click Recreate on the Property inspector (Figure 16-5) to make it anew. A new Library item appears in the Library, using the name and HTML from the item you selected.

Snippets and Library Tutorial

In this tutorial, you'll do two things: first, you'll create a useful form pull-down menu snippet, and then you'll turn the *National Exasperator* copyright notice into a reusable Library item and add it to several pages in the site.

Note: The tutorial in this chapter requires the example files from this book's Web site, *www.sawmac. com/dw8/*. Click the Tutorials link to go to the tutorials page. Then click the link under Snippets and Library Tutorial to download the files.

After your browser downloads and decompresses the files, you should have a DWSnipLib (short for Dreamweaver Snippets and Libraries) folder on your computer, containing the Web pages and graphics you need for this tutorial. If you're having difficulties, the Web site contains detailed instructions for downloading the files you'll be using with this book.

To begin, you need to define a new site in Dreamweaver, using the folder you just downloaded as the local root folder. You can use Dreamweaver's Site Wizard by following the steps on page 33, or you can use the alternate setup method described on page 472. In either case, name the site *Snippets and Library* and specify the DWSnipLib folder as the local root folder. Defining sites is discussed in more detail on page 472.

Creating a Snippet

1. **With your site freshly defined, make sure the Files panel's open.**

   If the panel isn't open, press the F8 key or choose Window → Files.

2. **In the Files panel, double-click the file, *snippet.html*.**

   A page with several form pull-down menus opens. The page includes menus for the months of the year, names of U.S. states, and the numbers 1–31. These menus are very useful for specifying dates when something needs to be done, states for shipping orders to, or simply for selecting a month for one's astrological sign. Dreamweaver's own Snippets don't include these useful menus, but, fortunately, you can add them yourself.

3. **Click the first form menu at the top of the page.**

   This menu appears to the right of the words "Months of the Year." You've selected the menu (and its underlying HTML code.). To add this as a snippet you need to open the Snippets panel.

4. **Click the Snippets panel tab to the right of the Files panel, or choose Window → Snippets.**

   The Snippets panel (Figure 16-1) is your control center for adding, editing, and deleting Snippets.

5. **Click the New Snippet button at the bottom of the panel (Figure 16-1).**

   The Snippet window opens. Dreamweaver automatically copies the code for the menu into the window. You just need to name the snippet and add a few more details.

6. **Type *Month Menu* in the Name box, and *A list of month names, with numeric values* in the description box, as pictured in Figure 16-6.**

   The name and description appear in the Snippets panel. In this case, the description identifies what appears in the menu on the page (a list of month names) and what value someone submits when selecting a month from the list and submitting the form—in other words, the name/value pair for this form field. (See page 362 for more information on how forms work.)

7. **Select the "Insert block" radio button.**

   This button identifies the snippet as a chunk of HTML that's simply plopped down on a page, as opposed to HTML that wraps around a selected graphic or text like a link or table cell might (if you wanted to do that, you'd select the "Wrap selection" button).

8. **Select the Design button at the bottom of the window.**

You've just told Dreamweaver to display the snippet visually when it's selected in the Snippets panel. In other words, when you select this snippet in the panel, you see a preview of the form menu, not a bunch of HTML code.

9. **The window should now look like Figure 16-6. Click the OK button to create your new snippet.**

The snippet should now appear in the Snippets panel, ready to be inserted into a page.

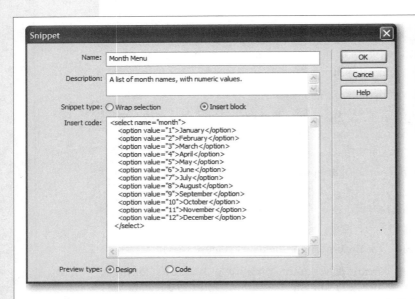

Figure 16-6:
The HTML code for the snippet appears in the "Insert code" box. You can edit it, adding or removing HTML, or you can create code that wraps around anything selected on the page by choosing the "Wrap selection" button.

10. **Select the Files panel by clicking the Files tab or pressing the F8 key; then double-click the file *form.html*.**

This opens a blank Web page, the empty canvas for your latest and greatest form. Remember that snippets don't have smarts; that is, when you insert a snippet, Dreamweaver doesn't make sure the HTML is correct. In this case, the snippet's just a menu—for it to really function, it has to be part of a form, so you first need to insert a form field.

11. **Choose Insert → Form → Form.**

A dashed red line appears on the page, indicating the outline of the form. Inside this area you can insert any form element you want, including your new snippet.

12. **Return to the Snippet panel once again by clicking the Snippets tab or choosing Window → Snippets.**

    Now for the moment of truth.

13. **Drag your new snippet—Month Menu—from the Snippets panel to anywhere inside the form's red outline.**

    Ta-da, Dreamweaver adds the new menu. Now, whenever you need to add a menu listing the months of the year, don't bother creating it from scratch. Just use the snippet! If you wish, you can create more snippets using the other menus on the *snippet.html* page.

Creating a Library Item

Now you'll see one way in which Dreamweaver's powerful Site Management tools can help you create and update your Web sites more effectively:

1. **In the Files panel, double-click the file *index.html*.**

   The *National Exasperator's* home page opens.

2. **Scroll to the bottom of the page and select the copyright notice.**

   Copyright information should be on every page of the site, so it makes a perfect candidate for a Library item. Notice that the copyright information is more than just text; it's actually a paragraph including a small image. The best way to select it is to click inside the text and then click the <p.copyright> tag in the status bar of the document window (Figure 16-7).

Figure 16-7:
Click <p.copyright> to select the paragraph containing the site's copyright notice.

3. **Choose Window → Assets, and then click the Library button.**

   The Assets panel opens and displays the Library category.

4. **Click the New Library Item button on the Assets panel (Figure 16-4).**

   A warning message appears, saying that the Library item may not look the same in other pages. Dreamweaver's trying to tell you that Library items can contain only HTML from the body of a Web page—not Cascading Style Sheets. (You can still include HTML, such as this paragraph, that's had a style applied to it, as long as you make sure that any *pages* to which you add the Library item have the appropriate style sheets.)

The text in this example *is* formatted using a style sheet, so, sure enough, it won't look the same in pages that don't have the same style sheet. In this exercise, however, this formatting isn't a problem, since all the pages in the site share the same linked external style sheet (see page 163).

Click OK to dismiss the warning. The copyright notice item appears in the Library list, with an "Untitled" naming rectangle next to it.

5. **Type *copyright* next to the new item on the Assets panel, and then press Enter.**

You've just checked this standard blob of text into your Library. It's ready to use anywhere else on your site.

6. **In the Files panel, double-click the file called *index.html* that's inside the *horoscopes* folder.**

Notice that this page is missing a copyright notice at the bottom of the page.

You'll frequently jump between the Files panel and the Assets panel, so these keyboard shortcuts come in handy: the F8 key to open the Files panel, and the F11 key to switch to the Assets panel.

7. **Switch back to the Assets panel, and drag the copyright Library item to the bottom of the page, as shown in Figure 16-8.**

You can recognize the newly inserted Library item by its yellow background. Click the text in the item and notice that you can't edit it; Dreamweaver treats it like a single object.

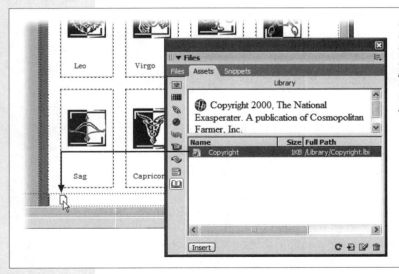

Figure 16-8:
In addition to dragging a Library item into the document window, you can also insert the item by placing the insertion point in the document window and then clicking the Insert button on the Assets panel.

8. **Add the footer Library item to the other pages in the *horoscopes* folder.**

There are 12 other pages in this folder. Open each page (by double-clicking its name in the Site window) and repeat step 7. All right, you don't have to do *all* of the pages, but at least do three or four to experience the full impact of what's next.

(You can close and save the pages as you go, or leave them open. Leave at least one open at the end and go on to step 9.)

9. **Notice the mistake!**

The copyright notice has the wrong date. The year 2000 is long gone! Oh, great—you'll have to change the date on every page. Fortunately, you've used a Library item, so you can easily make the change.

10. **Double-click the copyright item's icon (not its name) in the Assets panel.**

The Library item opens up, ready for editing.

11. **Change 2000 to the current year. Choose File → Save.**

The Update Library Items dialog box appears, listing all of the pages in the site that use the footer item.

12. **Click Update.**

Dreamweaver opens the Update Pages dialog box and updates all the Web pages that use the footer item.

13. **Click Close to close the Update Pages dialog box.**

And *now* if you open a file in the *horoscopes* folder, you'll find that the copyright date is correct.

Now imagine that you just used this auto-update feature on a 10,000-page site. Sit back and smile.

Templates

Some Web designers handcraft sites with loving care, changing layouts, colors, fonts, banners, and navigation from page to page. But that approach isn't always practical—or desirable. Consistency is a good thing. Web pages that look and act similarly reassure visitors; when only important material changes from page to page, readers can concentrate on finding the information they want. Even more importantly, a handcrafted approach is often unrealistic when you're designing on a deadline.

Here's where *templates* come in. Frequently, the underlying design of many pages on many Web sites is identical (see Figure 17-1). For instance, a company Web site with an employee directory may dedicate a single Web page to each employee. Each employee page probably has the same navigation bar, banner, footer, and layout. Only a few particulars differ, like the employee name, photo, and contact information.

Template Basics

Templates let you build pages that share a similar structure and graphic identity, quickly and without having to worry about accidentally deleting or changing elements. Templates come in very handy when you're designing a site for which other, less Dreamweaver-savvy individuals are responsible for adding new pages. If you use a template, these underlings can modify only the areas of a page that you, the godlike Dreamweaver guru, define.

Tip: Macromedia Contribute, a simple, word processor–like program for updating Web sites, works very well with sites built using Dreamweaver templates. If you build sites that are updated by people who don't know the first thing about Dreamweaver or building Web pages, Contribute can help. You can find more information about this program at Macromedia's Web site: *www.macromedia.com/contribute/*.

A new page based on a template—also called a template *instance,* or *child page*—looks just like the template, except that you can edit only certain areas of the page, called, logically enough, *editable regions.* In the example shown in Figure 17-1, one editable region includes the question-and-answer text area; the rest of the page remains untouched and is, in fact, locked.

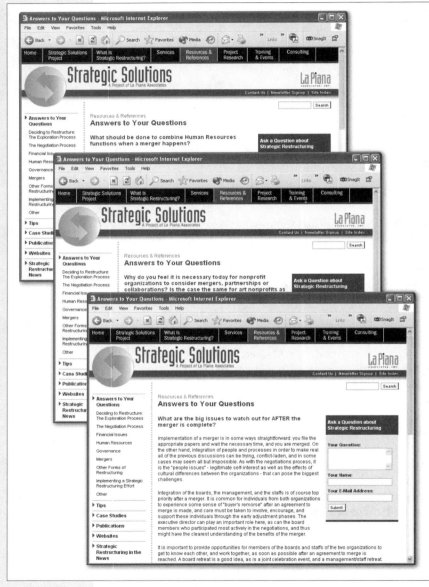

Figure 17-1:
These three Web pages are part of a section of a Web site dedicated to answering frequently asked questions. The pages each provide the answer to a different question, but are otherwise identical, sharing the same banner, navigation buttons, sidebar, and footer. This is a common scenario for Web sites that include news stories, employee profiles, product pages, or press releases. In fact, it's so common that Dreamweaver has a special feature—Templates—to help you build such pages.

A Dreamweaver template can be very basic: one or more areas of a page (the editable regions) can be changed, others can't (*locked regions*). But Dreamweaver also includes many subtle ways for controlling template instances. Here's an overview of the features you'll encounter when creating and using templates:

- **Editable regions.** These are the basic building blocks of a template. An editable region is a part of a page—a paragraph, table cell, or headline, for example—that people can change on each template instance. A template page can have multiple editable regions—for example, one in a sidebar area and another in the main content section of a page.

- **Editable tag attributes.** There may be times when you want to make a particular *tag* property editable. For instance, if you want to specify a different background color for each page, you'll want to permit changes to the <body> tag's *Bgcolor* property, or let people set the tag's *class* property to a particular CSS class style.

  Or perhaps you've built a template that includes a photo with some complex formatting (left-aligned by a Cascading Style Sheet, perhaps). Turning the entire image into an editable region could pose problems: When someone creates a new page from the template and then inserts a new photo, all of the formatting information can get lost. Instead, you could make just the image's *Src* property editable. People would then be able to insert new images for each page without inadvertently ruining the photo's formatting. (If the *Width* and *Height* properties vary from image to image, you could also make those attributes editable.)

- **Repeating regions and repeating tables.** Some Web pages include *lists* of items: catalogs of products, lists of news articles, albums of photos, and so on. Dreamweaver lets you define *repeatable* regions for pages like this.

  For example, a page of product listings can include a picture, name, and price for each product in a catalog, organized using a table with multiple rows (Chapter 7).

  As template builder, you may not know in advance how many products the page will eventually list, so you can't fully design the page. However, you can use Dreamweaver to define a row—or any selection of HTML—as a repeating region, so that page authors can add new rows of product information when needed.

- **Optional regions and editable optional regions.** *Optional regions* make templates even more flexible. They let you show or hide content on a page-by-page basis.

  Suppose you create a template for your company's products. When some products go on sale (but others remain full price), you could add an *optional* region on the template that displays a big "On Sale!" logo. When you create a new product page, you could *show* the optional region for products that are on sale and keep it *hidden* for the others.

  Editable optional regions are similar, but they have the added benefit of being editable. Maybe you're creating a template for an employee directory, giving each employee a separate Web page with contact information. Some employees also want their picture displayed on the page, while others don't (you know the type). Solution: Add an editable optional region that would let you show the space for a photo and add a different photo for each page. For the shyer types, you would simply hide the photo area entirely.

Furthermore, Dreamweaver can create *nested* templates, which inherit design elements from a master template. In this way, you can create a general unified design that's shared by other templates; this feature is described on page 617.

But facilitating page creation is only one of the benefits of templates. You'll also find that templates can greatly simplify the process of updating a Web site's design. Like Library items, pages based on templates retain a reference to the original template file. Any changes made to the template pass on to all pages created from it, which can save you hours of time and trouble when it comes time to update the look or structure of your site. Imagine how much time you'll save when your boss asks you to add "just one more" button to the site's navigation bar. Instead of updating thousands of pages by hand, you need to update only a few template files.

Creating a Template

The first step in creating a template requires building a basic Web page and telling Dreamweaver you'd like to use it as a template. You can go about this in two ways: build a Web page and turn it into a template, or create a blank, empty template file and add text, graphics, tables, and other content to it.

Turning a Web Page into a Template

The easiest way to create a template is simply to base it on a Web page in your current site folder. Although you can create templates based on Web pages that *aren't* part of the current local site, you may run into problems with links and paths to images, as described in a moment.

Once you've opened the Web page, just choose File → Save As Template or, on the Common tab of the Insert bar (see Figure 17-2), click the Templates button and then select Make Template from the menu. In the Save As Template window (Figure 17-3), the name of the current local site appears in the Site pop-up menu; meanwhile, all templates for that site show up in the Existing Templates field.

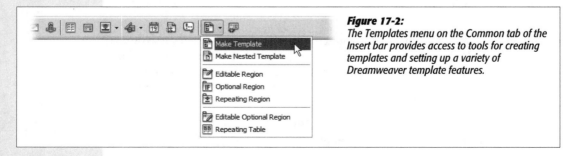

Figure 17-2:
The Templates menu on the Common tab of the Insert bar provides access to tools for creating templates and setting up a variety of Dreamweaver template features.

Note: At this point, you could theoretically use the Site menu to save a template into any local site folder you've defined (see Chapter 13 for a discussion of local sites), but be careful with this option. If your page contains images and links and you save it as a template for another local site, Dreamweaver doesn't copy the images from the first site folder into the other one. As a result, the paths to the image files and links don't work correctly.

If you must use a page from one site as a template for another, copy the Web page *and graphics* into the new site's root folder, open the page from there, and then create a template as described here.

Figure 17-3:
The Save As Template dialog box lets you save your template into any of the local site folders you've defined in Dreamweaver. Stick to your current local site to avoid broken links and similar problems.

Dreamweaver 8 adds a Description field for adding a brief note describing the template. This description appears when you're selecting a template as the basis for a new page you're creating. The description is very useful when *other* people are building a site using your templates and aren't sure whether templateA1, templateA2, or templateA3 is the correct choice; a simple "use this template for all FAQ pages" is much clearer.

Finally, type a name for the new template, and then click Save. Choose Yes when Dreamweaver asks if you want to Update Links for the page. If you choose No, all page-relative links break, and all the images on the page appear as broken-image icons.

Note: Avoid double hyphens in the names of your templates—for example, "Store -- Product." Since Dreamweaver uses HTML comments like this <!-- --> (see the box on page 601) to identify what template was used on a particular page, the extra hyphens trip up the Firefox Web browser, which mistakes them for other HTML comments.

Dreamweaver saves the page in the Templates folder of your local site root folder. It adds the extension .dwt to the file to indicate that it's a Dreamweaver template. (For dynamic Web pages, Dreamweaver adds the .dwt *before* the file's extension. For example, an Active Server Page template may have a name like *maintemplate.dwt.asp*.)

Building a Template from Scratch

It's easiest to create a Web page first and then save it as a template, but you can also build one from scratch. Open the Asset panel's Templates category by choosing Window → Assets and then clicking the Template assets icon (see Figure 17-4). Then click the New Template button at the bottom of the Assets panel. Once Dreamweaver adds a new, untitled template to the list, type a new name for it. Something descriptive like "press release" or "employee page" helps you keep track of your templates.

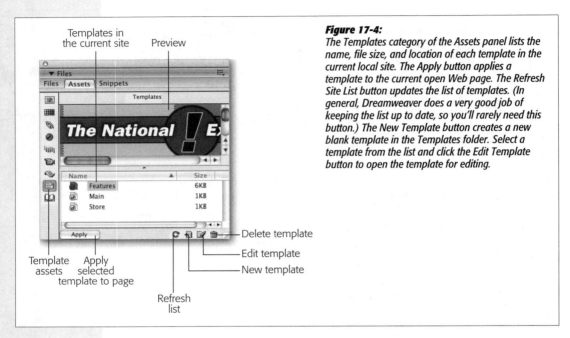

Templates in the current site   Preview

Template assets   Apply selected template to page

Refresh list

Delete template
Edit template
New template

Figure 17-4:
The Templates category of the Assets panel lists the name, file size, and location of each template in the current local site. The Apply button applies a template to the current open Web page. The Refresh Site List button updates the list of templates. (In general, Dreamweaver does a very good job of keeping the list up to date, so you'll rarely need this button.) The New Template button creates a new blank template in the Templates folder. Select a template from the list and click the Edit Template button to open the template for editing.

After you've created a blank template for the site, you can open it by double-clicking its name in the Assets panel (or selecting its name and then clicking the Edit button at the bottom of the Assets panel). It opens just like any Web page, so that you can get busy designing it.

Defining Editable Regions

Your next task is to specify which parts of your template are locked and which are editable. By default, *everything* on a page is locked. After all, the main reason to use templates is to maintain a consistent, unchanging design and structure among pages. To make a template usable, you must define the area or areas you *can* change.

Adding a Basic Editable Region

To add an editable region to a template, start by selecting the part of the page you want to make changeable. You can designate as editable anything in the document window (that is, any HTML between the <body> tags).

Note: You can always add Cascading Style Sheets, JavaScript code, and meta tag information to the <head> of a template-based page. Any <head> content in the original template files stays put, however. For example, you can't remove an external style sheet applied to the template file from a page based on that template.

The Broken-Link Blues

Why aren't the links in my templates working?

When you created the link, you probably typed a path into the Property inspector's Link field—a recipe for heartbreak. Instead, always select the target Web page for a link by clicking the folder icon in the Property inspector, or by pressing Ctrl+L (⌘-L). In other words, when adding links to a template, always link to pages within the site by browsing to the desired file.

Dreamweaver saves templates in the Templates folder inside the local root folder; all relative links need to be relative to this location. (Absolute links, like those to other Web sites, aren't a problem; see page 104 to learn the difference.) The reason you should browse to, rather than type in, your links is so that Dreamweaver can create a proper relative link.

Imagine this situation: You create a template for your classified ads. You store all classified ads for April 2001 inside a series of folders like this: classifieds → 2001 → april, as shown in the site diagram here.

A link from a page in the *april* folder to the home page would follow the path marked 1 here. So when you create a link in your template, you can create a link to the home page by typing the path *../../../index.html.*

That choice is logical if you're thinking about the page (in the *april* folder) you'll create from the template—but

it won't work. Dreamweaver stores templates in the Templates folder, so the correct path would be path 2, or *../index.html.* When you create a new page based on the template and save it in the *april* folder, Dreamweaver, in its wisdom, automatically rewrites all paths in the page so that the links function correctly.

The beauty of Dreamweaver is that you don't have to understand how all this works. Just remember to use relative links in your templates and create them by clicking the folder icon in the Property inspector.

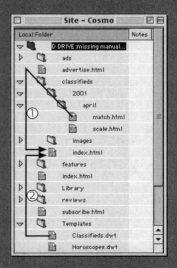

Drag across your page to select the elements you wish to make editable, or, for greater precision, use the tag selector (see page 21) to make sure you select the exact HTML you want.

Now tell Dreamweaver that the selected elements are to be editable. You can use any of these techniques:

- In the Common tab of the Insert bar (Figure 17-2), select Editable Region from the Template menu.

- Choose Insert → Template Objects → Editable Region.

- Press Ctrl+Alt+V (⌘-Option-V).

- Right-click (Control-click) the selection and then choose Templates → New Editable Region from the shortcut menu.

FREQUENTLY ASKED QUESTION

When Save Won't Behave

I keep getting an error message when I save my template. What's going on?

If you add an editable region *inside* certain block-level elements like a paragraph, or a heading, Dreamweaver pops up a warning message when you save the template, explaining that you can't create additional paragraphs or headings inside this region on any pages you build from this template. This just means that you didn't select the <p> or heading tag when you made the region editable. Dreamweaver considers anything outside of the editable region locked, so you can't change those tags. Since it's improper HTML to have a paragraph, heading, or other block-level elements inside *another* paragraph, or heading, Dreamweaver doesn't let you add other block-level elements to the selection.

This characteristic may not be such a bad thing, however. Imagine you're creating a template that's to be used by other people building a Web site. You have a heading 1, maybe the title of the page you applied a style to, and you want to make sure it looks the same on every page. You wouldn't want anyone changing the heading tag, and possibly erasing the style. In addition, you don't want them to be able to change the heading 1 to a heading 2, or a heading 3; nor do you want them to completely erase the h1 tag

and type paragraph after paragraph of their random thoughts. You just want them to type in new text for the page title. Selecting just the text inside the heading and turning it into an editable region does just that. Viva micromanagement!

If this is in fact what you want to do, you can save yourself the bother of having to constantly see the warning box shown here each time you save the template by simply turning on the "Don't show me this message again" checkbox. However, if you made a mistake and *do* want to allow people to change the heading, or add more headings and paragraphs in this region, you need to do two things: First, unlock the editable region you created (see page 602); then, select the text *and* tag (the tag selector [page 21] is the best way to make sure you've selected a tag) and turn that into an editable region.

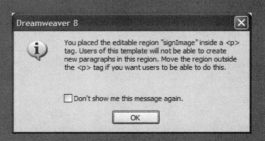

When the New Editable Region dialog box appears, type a name for the region (you can't use the same name twice) and then click OK—avoid hyphens in the name (see the Note on page 585). You return to your template, where the name you gave the region appears in a small blue tab above the editable region (see Figure 17-5).

Tip: If you use tables to lay out your pages (see Chapter 7), you'll often assign one table cell as the main area to hold the primary content of the page. For example, in the pages shown in Figure 17-1, the Frequently Asked Question and its answer appear in a single cell on the page. This cell makes a perfect editable region for a template. In the tag selector, just click the <td> tag associated with that cell and use any of the techniques discussed here to convert the contents of that cell into an editable region.

If you use CSS, on the other hand, you can create a separate <div> tag (see page 303) for the main content area. In this case, select just the contents of the <div> tag, not the tag itself. Here's one instance where you want to avoid the tag selector (page 21), which selects the entire <div>, tags and all. If you turn the <div> tag into an editable region, it's possible for someone modifying the page later to delete the tag entirely, which could wreak untold havoc on your CSS-based layout.

Fortunately, Dreamweaver 8 has introduced a handy shortcut for selecting just the contents of a <div> tag. Click anywhere inside the <div> tag, and press Ctrl-A (⌘-A) or choose Edit → Select All. Next, turn this selection into an editable region, and the <div> tags will remain *outside* of the editable region, so no one can inadvertently delete a <div> tag that helps define the basic structure of a page.

POWER USERS' CLINIC

Under the Hood of Templates

Dreamweaver saves templates as HTML files in the Templates folder inside your current local site folder (see Chapter 14 for information on local sites). Each template bears the file name extension .dwt to distinguish it from regular Web pages.

The program treats files in the Templates folder differently from normal Web pages, so don't save anything but .dwt files there. In addition, since Dreamweaver expects the Templates folder to be in the local root folder of your site, don't move the Templates folder or change its name in any way (don't even change the capital T in Templates, even if you're a low-key type of person). If you do, your templates won't work.

As with Library items, Dreamweaver uses HTML comment tags to indicate the name of the template. If you inspect the HTML code of a template-based document (see Chapter 9),

you'll see that, immediately following the opening <html> tag, Dreamweaver inserts a comment tag with the text "InstanceBegin" followed by the location and name of the template. Additional comment tags indicate areas of the page that you can modify, plus special template features like template parameters used for optional regions. For instance, the title of a page based on a template is always editable; its comment tag might look like this:

```
<!-- InstanceBeginEditable
    name="doctitle" -->
<title>My New Page</title>
<!-- InstanceEndEditable -->
```

The first comment indicates the editable region's beginning and also includes the editable region's name. When editing pages based on the template, you can change only the HTML between these comment tags. Everything else on the page is locked, even when you're working in Code view.

You may find that a single editable region is all you need—for example, a single area of the page (a table cell, or section of a page enclosed by a <div> tag, for example) containing the text for a product review. However, if you need to edit *multiple* areas of a Web page, just add more editable regions to the template. For instance, when you create a template for an employee page, you can create editable regions for the employee's name, telephone number, and photo. If you change your mind and want to lock a region again, select the editable region and then choose Modify → Templates → Remove Template Markup. Dreamweaver removes the code that makes the region editable. You can do the same thing with other types of template regions, like repeating and optional regions.

Warning: You can rename an editable region by clicking the blue tab on the template page and typing a new name into the Property inspector. However, if you've already built pages based on this template, it's not a good idea. Because template-based pages use the name to identify editable regions, Dreamweaver can lose track of where content should go when you rename a region. See Figure 17-18 for a workaround.

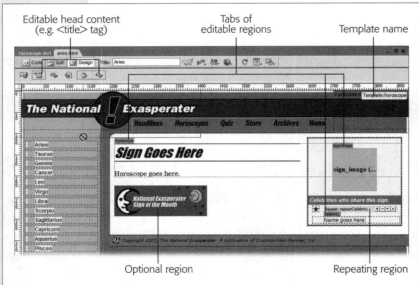

Editable head content (e.g. <title> tag)

Tabs of editable regions

Template name

Optional region

Repeating region

Figure 17-5:
This page is based on a template called Horoscope, as you can tell from the little tab in the document window's upper-right corner. You can modify editable regions, which are labeled with small tabs. In this example, two editable regions are called horoscope and signImage. An additional editable region—named celebrity—appears within a repeating region—labeled repeatCelebrity—which lets you duplicate editable regions to form a list of items. Optional regions don't have any clear identifier on the page; you can identify them only in the Template properties window, as described on page 623. The title of any page created from a template is also editable. All other parts of the page are locked; you can only make changes to the original template file.

Adding a Repeating Region

Some Web pages contain lists of items. A catalog page may display row after row of product information—picture, name, price, and description. An index of Frequently Asked Questions may provide a list of questions and the dates they were posted.

If you were to make a template for either of these pages, you would add an editable region to the area of the page where these lists appear. Just creating an editable region, however, wouldn't give you any ability to enforce (or easily update) the design of these lists, because *everything* within an editable region can be changed.

Fortunately, Dreamweaver provides a pair of template tools to overcome this problem: *repeating regions* and *repeating tables*. Both let you create areas of a page that include editable (and uneditable) regions that can be repeated any number of times (see Figure 17-6).

FREQUENTLY ASKED QUESTION

Hindered by Highlighting

I'm distracted by the tabs and background colors that Dreamweaver uses to indicate Library items and Templates. How do I get rid of them?

When you use Library items or Templates, you see blue tabs and yellow backgrounds to indicate editable regions and Library items. Although these visual cues don't appear in a Web browser, they can still make your page harder to read while you work in Dreamweaver. Fortunately, you can alter the background color of these items and even turn highlighting off altogether.

Choose Edit → Preferences, or press Ctrl+U (⌘-U). In the Preferences Category list, click Highlighting. To change the background color for editable regions, locked regions, and Library items, use the color box (see page 41) or type in a hexadecimal color value. To remove the highlighting, turn off the Show box next to the appropriate item.

Oftentimes, it's useful to keep highlighting on to help you keep track of Library items and editable regions. If you want

to turn off highlighting temporarily, simply choose View → Visual Aids → Invisible Elements, or use the keyboard shortcut Ctrl+Shift+I (⌘-Shift-I) to toggle these visual cues off and on. This technique has the added benefit of hiding table borders, layer borders, and image maps, as well as other invisible elements.

Adding a repeating region is similar to adding an editable region. Select the area of the template page you wish to make repeatable, which usually contains at least one editable region. Most often, this area's a table row, so you could select the row (<tr> tag) with the information to be repeated. You could also just as easily select a paragraph or a list item (<li> tag).

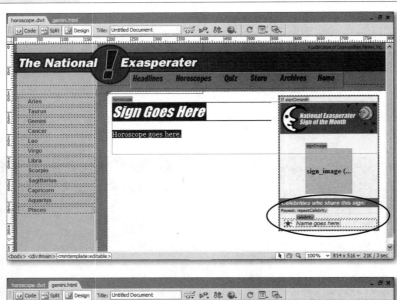

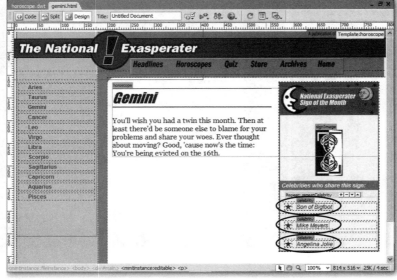

Figure 17-6:
A repeating region lets page authors add multiple selections of repeating information.

Top: In this example, the template has one repeating region, labeled repeatCelebrity (circled).

Bottom: A complete page based on this template includes three repeated editable regions (circled in the lower-right corner of the page). If another page requires more celebrity listings, you could easily add additional rows to each list. However, the template still controls the basic design. Changing the star graphic of the repeating region (an uneditable part of the region) in the template page automatically changes the same elements in all pages created from the template. From a design perspective, this strategy also means that page authors can't tamper with the design of a repeating region—just the content marked as editable.

Tip: You can make a repeating region that *doesn't* include an editable region. For example, a template for a movie review Web page could include a repeating region that's simply a graphic of a star. A page author adding a new movie review could repeat the star graphic to match the movie's rating—four stars, for example. (There's just one caveat—see the Warning on page 622.)

Next, tell Dreamweaver that the selected elements are part of a repeating region. You can use any of these techniques:

- On the Common tab of the Insert bar (Figure 17-2), select the Repeating Region option from the Templates menu.

- Choose Insert → Template Objects → Repeating Region.

- Right-click (Control-click) the selection and choose Templates → New Repeating Region from the shortcut menu.

When the New Repeating Region dialog box appears, type a name for the region and then click OK. You return to your template, where the name you gave the region appears in a small blue tab above the editable region (see Figure 17-6). (See page 622 for a discussion of using a repeating region when building a new template-based page.)

Warning: Dreamweaver lets you name a repeating region with a name already in use by an editable region. But don't—multiple template areas with the same name make Dreamweaver act unpredictably.

Repeating Tables

The *repeating table* tool is essentially a shortcut to creating a table with one or more repeating rows. If you had a lot of time on your hands, you could achieve the same effect by adding a table to a page, selecting one or more rows, and applying a repeating region to the selection. To use the repeating table tool:

1. **Click the template page where you wish to insert the table.**

    You can't insert a repeating table into an already defined editable, repeating, or optional region, as explained in the box on page 607. You must be in an empty, locked area of the template.

2. **On the Common tab of the Insert bar (Figure 17-2), select the Repeating Table option from the Templates menu.**

    Alternatively, you can choose Insert → Template Objects → Repeating Table. Either way, the Insert Repeating Table window appears (Figure 17-7).

3. **Fill out the basic properties of the table.**

    The top part of the window lets you set up the basic structure of the table: rows, columns, cell padding, cell spacing, width, and border. Basically, it's the same information you'd provide when creating any table, as described on page 245.

You usually start a repeating table with two rows—one for a heading, and another to contain the information you wish to repeat.

4. **In the "Starting row" box, type the number of the row where the repeating region should begin.**

Often you'll have just one repeating row: one row of product information, for example. You may want to use the top row for labels indicating the information contained in the rows below. If that's the case, enter *2* at this step, leaving the first row as an uneditable part of the template.

It's conceivable, however, that you may want each entry to take up *two* rows. The first would list Name and Description; the second would contain a cell for a photo and a cell for the price. You set up this effect in this step and the next.

5. **In the "Ending row" box, type the number of the last repeating row.**

If you wish to repeat only a single row, enter the same number you provided for step 4. If you're creating a double repeating row, add 1 to the number you provided in step 4. For example, if you need three rows for each repeating entry, add 2 to the number from step 4.

6. **Type a name for this repeating region.**

Don't use the same name as another template region. You'll run the risk of unpredictable results on template-based pages.

7. **Click OK.**

Dreamweaver inserts a table into the page. A blue tab with the name of the repeating region appears (see Figure 17-6), as do blue tabs in each cell of each repeated row. These tabs indicate new editable regions—one per cell.

Since these new editable regions have uninformative names like EditRegion4, you may want to rename them. Click the blue tab and type a new name in the Property inspector. (But do so *before* you create any pages based on the template—see the Warning on page 605.)

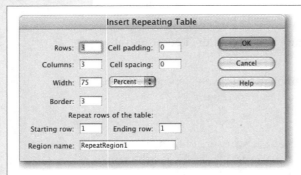

Figure 17-7:
The Insert Repeating Table dialog box lets you kill three birds with one stone: it adds a table to a page, turns one or more rows into a repeating region, and adds editable regions into each table cell inside the repeating region.

To remove a repeating region, select it by clicking the blue Repeat tab, and then choose Modify → Templates → Remove Template Markup. A more accurate way to select a repeating region is to click anywhere inside the region and then click <mmtemplate: repeat> in the tag selector (see page 21 for more on the tag selector). Note that removing a repeating region doesn't remove any editable regions you added inside the repeating region. If you want to rename a repeating region, heed the Warning on page 605.

Making a Tag Attribute Editable

An editable region lets you change areas of HTML—like a paragraph, image, or entire table—on new pages you create from a template. However, when you're creating a template for others to make pages from down the line, you may want to limit these page authors' editing abilities. You may want to allow budding Web designers to change the color of a table cell without changing other properties like *cell width* or *paragraph alignment*. You can use Dreamweaver's Editable Tag Attribute to specify which *tag* properties your successors can change.

Note: Before making a tag attribute editable, first set that property to a default value in the template. Doing so inserts a default value and makes the attribute appear in the Editable Tag Attribute window (see steps 3 and 7 in the following instructions).

FREQUENTLY ASKED QUESTION

Editable Regions, Repeating Regions, and Errors

When I try to insert an editable region inside a repeating region, I get the following error: "The selection is already in an editable, repeating, or optional region." What's that about?

This error message essentially means you're trying to add a template region where it doesn't belong. It most commonly appears when you attempt to put a repeating or optional region inside an editable region. That kind of nesting is a no-no; anything inside an editable region can be changed on template-based pages, and as such, Dreamweaver can't touch it.

However, you may get this error message seemingly in error. For instance, it's perfectly OK to add an editable region inside a repeating region, and it's even OK to add a

repeating region inside an optional region, and vice versa. But one day you select text inside a repeating region and try to turn it into an editable region, and boom—error message. What probably happened was, when you selected the text, Dreamweaver actually selected part of the hidden code used to define a template region (see the box "Under the Hood of Templates" on page 601) and thought you were trying to put an editable region inside it. To avoid confusion, use the tag selector to select the tag you wish to turn into an editable region. For example, click <p> in the tag selector to select the paragraph inside the repeating region. Alternatively, go into Code view (see page 330) and select whatever part of the code inside the repeating region you wish to make editable.

To make a tag attribute editable:

1. **Select the tag whose property you wish to make editable.**

   Using the tag selector (see page 21) is the most accurate way.

2. **Choose Modify → Templates → Make Attribute Editable.**

   The Editable Tag Attributes window opens (Figure 17-8).

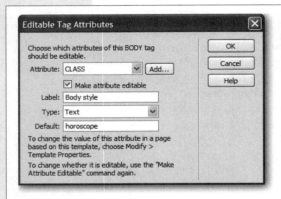

Figure 17-8:
Dreamweaver provides detailed control for template pages. To make just a single property of a single tag editable when pages are later based on your template, turn on the "Make attribute editable" checkbox. In this case, the "class" attribute of the body tag is editable, allowing page designers the freedom to apply different CSS styles to the body of each template-based page.

3. **Select an attribute from the menu or add a new attribute with the Add button.**

   Only properties you've already set for the selected tag appear in the Attribute menu. In other words, if you've selected an image, you probably see the *Src, Width,* and *Height* properties listed. But unless you've set the image's border, the *Border* property doesn't appear.

   To add a property, click the Add button. In the window that appears, type the appropriate property name. For example, to make the path to a graphics file editable, you'd set the <img> tag's *Src* attribute by typing *src* here. (If you're not sure of the property's name, check out Dreamweaver's built-in HTML reference, described on page 353.)

Note: If you want page editors to be able to change a CSS class applied to the <body> tag on template-based pages—to apply different fonts, background colors, or any of the many CSS formatting options to each template-based page—you *have* to make the Class attribute editable. (See page 164 for more on CSS classes.)

---

4. **Make sure the "Make attribute editable" box is turned on.**

   If you decide that you no longer want to allow editing of this property, you can return to this dialog box and turn off editing, as described on page 609.

5. **Type a name in the Label field.**

What you type here should be a simple description of the editable tag and property, which helps page authors correctly identify editable properties. For example, you could use *Product Image* if you're making a particular image's *source* (Src) property editable.

6. **Choose a value type from the menu.**

Your choices are:

- **Text.** Use this option when a property's value is a word. For example, you can change the image tag's *Align* property to *top, middle, baseline*, and so on. Or, when using Cascading Style Sheets, you could make a tag's *Class* property editable to allow page authors to apply a particular custom style to the tag—*content, footer*, and so on.

- **URL.** Use this option when the editable property is a path to a file, like an image's *Src* property or a link's *Href* property. Using its site management tools, Dreamweaver keeps track of these paths and updates them when you move your pages around your site.

- **Color.** If the property requires a Web color, like a page's background color, select this option. This option makes Dreamweaver's color box available to people who build pages from the template.

- **True/False.** You shouldn't use this option. It's intended for Dreamweaver's Optional Regions feature (discussed on page 610), and it doesn't apply to *HTML* properties.

- **Number.** Use this choice for properties that require a numeric value, like an image's *Height* and *Width* properties.

7. **Type a default value into the Default field.**

This step is optional. The default value defines the initial value for this property, when people first create a page based on the template. They can then modify this value for that particular page. If you've already set this property in the template, its value automatically appears in this box.

8. **Click OK to close the window.**

Dreamweaver adds code to the template page that allows page authors control of the attribute. Setting this attribute on pages created from the template is described on page 623.

If you later decide that you *don't* want a particular tag's property to be editable, Dreamweaver can help. Open the template file, select the tag with the editable attribute, and choose Modify → Templates → Make Attribute Editable. In the window that appears, turn off the "Make attribute editable" checkbox (Figure 17-8). Unfortunately, doing so doesn't remove *all* of the template code Dreamweaver added. Even after you turn off editing for an attribute, Dreamweaver leaves behind the parameter used to control the tag's property. To eliminate *this* extra code, see the box on page 616.

Adding Optional Regions

Templates provide consistent design. While consistency's generally a good thing, it can also get boring. Furthermore, there may be times when you'd like the flexibility to include information on some template-based pages but not on others.

Dreamweaver provides a fairly foolproof way to vary page design: *optional regions*. An optional region is simply part of a template page that you can hide or display on each template-based page (see Figure 17-9). When creating a new page based on the template, a page author can turn the region on or off.

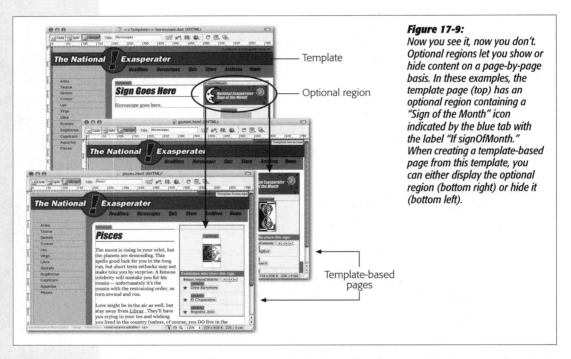

Figure 17-9:
Now you see it, now you don't. Optional regions let you show or hide content on a page-by-page basis. In these examples, the template page (top) has an optional region containing a "Sign of the Month" icon indicated by the blue tab with the label "If signOfMonth." When creating a template-based page from this template, you can either display the optional region (bottom right) or hide it (bottom left).

Creating an optional region is a snap. Just select the HTML code you wish to make optional, and then do one of the following:

- On the Common tab of the Insert bar (Figure 17-2), select the Optional Region option from the Templates menu.

- Choose Insert → Template Objects → Optional Region.

- Right-click (Control-click) the selection and choose Templates → New Optional Region from the shortcut menu.

In the New Optional Region window, type a name (Figure 17-10). Make sure not to use the same name as any other region on the page, and—although Dreamweaver allows it—don't use spaces or other punctuation marks. (Following the rules for naming files as described on page 471 is the best method, and ensures that the optional region works properly.) Click OK to close the window and create the new optional region. Dreamweaver adds a light blue tab with the word "If," followed by the name you gave the region (Figure 17-9).

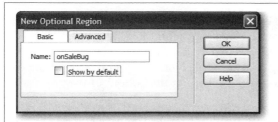

Figure 17-10:
The Optional Regions feature lets you show or hide specific content on template-based pages. Turning on "Show by default" tells Dreamweaver to display the region when a page author first creates a template-based page. Turn this box on if the optional region needs to show on most pages. You'll save someone the effort of turning the region on each time she creates a new template-based page.

Locking Optional Regions

An optional region can include editable and repeating regions, *and* locked regions. For example, if you simply want to allow a page author to turn on or off a graphic ("This item on sale!!!!"), insert the graphic outside an editable region on the page, and then make it an optional region as described above. Since anything not inside an editable region is locked, a page author can't change the graphic or ruin its formatting—he can only make it visible or hidden.

Repeating Optional Regions

An optional region can also include repeating regions. For example, suppose you create a repeating region (see page 603) that lets a page author add row after row of links to a list of related articles. You could then turn this repeating region into an optional region, as described above, so that if a particular page had no related articles, the author could simply hide the entire "related articles" section of the page.

Optional Editable Regions

Dreamweaver's Optional Editable Region command inserts an optional region with an editable region *inside* it. To use it, click in the template at the spot where you'd like to add it, and then choose Insert → Template Objects → Optional Editable Region (alternatively, you can choose this option from the Templates menu on the Common tab of the Insert bar). The New Optional Region window appears; give it a name, and then follow the same steps outlined previously for an optional region.

This technique doesn't offer a lot of control; it's hard to insert HTML *outside* the editable region, for example. So if you want to have an image or table that's optional but *not* editable, it's usually better to just create the editable region as described on page 598 and turn it (and any other HTML you wish to include) into an optional region.

Note: The Optional Editable Region command doesn't let you name the editable region; instead you get a generic name like *EditRegion7*. You can select the editable region and change its name in the Property inspector, but do so *before* you build any pages based on this template (see the Warning on page 605).

Advanced Optional Regions

A basic optional region is a rather simple affair: It either appears or it doesn't. But Dreamweaver offers more complex logic for controlling optional regions. For example, maybe you want several different areas of a page to be either hidden or visible at the same time—perhaps an "On Sale Now!" icon at the top of the page *and* a "Call 1-800-SHIZZLE to order" message at the bottom of the page. When one appears, so does the other.

Because these objects are in different areas of the page, you have to create two separate optional regions. Fortunately, using Dreamweaver's advanced settings for optional regions, you can easily have a single region control the display of one or more additional areas of a page. Here's how to do it:

1. **Create the first optional region using the steps on page 610.**

   Give the region a name using the Basic tab of the New Optional Region window (Figure 17-10).

2. **Select the part of the page—an image, paragraph, or table—that you wish to turn into a second optional region.**

   In this case, you make the display of this region dependent on the optional region added in step 1. If the first region is visible on the page, this second region also shows.

3. **On the Common tab of the Insert bar (Figure 17-2), choose the Optional Region item from the Templates menu.**

   The New Optional Region window appears.

4. **Click the Advanced tab.**

   The optional region's advanced options appear (see Figure 17-11). In this case, you want the first optional region you created to control the display of this new region. So instead of giving this region a name, you'll simply select the name of the first optional region in the next step.

5. **Click the "Use parameter" button and select the name of the first optional region from the menu.**

   This step is what makes the first optional region control this region. If a page author displays the first region, this second region also appears.

---

6. **Click OK to close the window and create the new optional region.**

You can continue adding optional regions in this way, using the Advanced tab and selecting the name of the first optional region from the menu. This way, a single region can control the display of many other areas of the page.

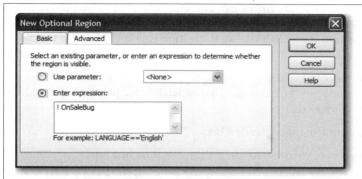

Figure 17-11:
The New Optional Region box lets you more precisely control the display of an optional region. You can make the region appear only when another region's visible, or use Dreamweaver's template expression language to create a more complex behavior. In this case, the selected region appears only when another region—named OnSaleBug—is not visible (the ! is a programming equivalent to "is not").

Even fancier tricks

You can use these advanced controls for even more elaborate Web page stunts. For example, say your site is composed of several sections. When a visitor is in one section of the site, its navigation button is attractively highlighted and a secondary navigation bar miraculously appears, offering links to other pages in that section.

Using a template, you can add an optional region containing the highlighted section button. When you add the secondary navigation bar to the page, you make *it* an optional region controlled by the highlighted navigation button. Then, when you add a page to that section of the site, you simply show the optional region containing the highlighted button, causing the secondary navigation bar to appear as well (see Figure 17-12 for a look at how this works).

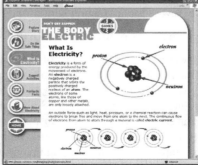

Figure 17-12:
An optional region on the page at left highlights the top navigation button. By turning on a different optional region (right), the navigation system can highlight the site's current section—"What is Electricity?" (the third button from the top).

Controlling regions with expressions

You can program even more complex behaviors using a basic *expression language*, loosely based on JavaScript, that Dreamweaver understands. For example, instead of having an optional region appear when another optional region is visible (as in the above example), suppose you want to have a region appear when another region is invisible. This arrangement can come in handy when you're creating a navigation bar. When a page is in a particular section, for instance, the navigation button for that section is highlighted, but the button isn't highlighted if the page is in another section.

In other words, you can build a single template for all the sections of a site, but control the appearance of the navigation bar separately for pages in each individual section (see Figure 17-12).

Here's how you'd control the navigation bar:

1. **Click the page where you wish to insert the navigation buttons.**

2. **Insert the highlighted ("You are in this section") navigation button.**

   This button could be a rollover image (see page 144) or just a single graphic. If you have multiple pages in the section, you probably also want to link this graphic to the main page for that section.

3. **Click next to the highlighted button and insert the plain ("You can go here") navigation button.**

   The button could also be a rollover image with a link to the main page for this section (for example, the main Products page).

4. **In the Property inspector, select the highlighted navigation button and link (if it has one).**

   This button appears on any template-based page for this section.

5. **On the Common tab of the Insert bar (Figure 17-2), choose Optional Region from the Template menu.**

   The New Optional Region window appears. Make sure the Basic tab is selected.

6. **Type the name of the section into the Name field. Click OK.**

   For example, if this section of your site advertises your company's products, you can call it *products*. Don't use any spaces or punctuation other than hyphens (-) or underscores (_) for the name. Also make sure the "Show by default" box is *not* turned on. Since you'll be building template-based pages for all the sections of your site, most pages you build will be in other sections of the site. Your work goes faster if this highlighted button starts out hidden. In the next steps, you'll make the plain navigation button appear by default.

7. **Use the Property inspector to select the plain button and link, and then click the Optional Region button on the Insert bar.**

The New Optional Region window appears again, but this time you'll use the advanced options.

8. **Click the Advanced tab; select "Enter expression." (Figure 17-11)**

You're going to type an *expression* in the Expression field. An expression is a programming statement that is either true or false. (For an obvious example, the statement 2=2 is true, but the statement 2=4 is false.) The important thing to remember here is that when an expression's true, the optional region is visible; when it's false, it's hidden.

9. **Type an exclamation point (!) followed by the name you entered in step 6—** *!products,* **for example.**

Dreamweaver's template expression language is based on the JavaScript programming language. An exclamation mark means "not," so this code means *"not products."* Translation into non-caveman language: when the *products* region (remember, that's the highlighted button) is *not* displayed, this region (button) appears on the page.

The logic gets a little complicated, but have faith. When you add a new page based on this template, the optional region you added in step 6 is *not* visible (because you turned off the "Show by default" box). In other words, because the region—products in this example—is *not* showing, this region, the one with the plain navigation button, by default appears on the page. Turning the *products* region on (as described on page 623), *hides* the plain navigation button. In other words, the first optional region works like a light switch, alternately turning on one or the other navigation button.

10. **Click OK to close the window and add the additional optional region.**

Repeat this process for each button in the navigation bar. Now your template is perfectly suited for displaying customized navigation bars for each section of your site. When you create a new template-based page, simply turn on the region for the particular section in which the page is located. (Hiding and showing optional regions is described on page 623.)

As you can see, optional regions are very powerful—and potentially confusing. But using even basic optional regions, you can exert a great deal of control over your template-based pages. For more information on template expressions and optional regions, take a look in Dreamweaver's built-in Help system. (Press F1; then, in the window that appears, click the *Search* tab. Type *template expressions* in the box, and then click the List Topic buttons. The Dreamweaver Help system then lists several articles related to templates and template expressions.)

Editing and Removing Optional Regions

After inserting an optional region, you can always return to the New Optional Region dialog box to change the region's name, alter its default settings, or use advanced options. To edit an optional region, first select it using one of these techniques:

- Click the region's blue tab in the document window (Figure 17-9).

- Click anywhere inside the optional region in the document window; click the <mmtemplate:if> tag in the tag selector (see page 21 for details on the tag selector).

When you select an optional region, an Edit button appears in the Property inspector. Click it to reopen the New Optional Region window. You can then change the region's properties.

POWER USERS' CLINIC

Understanding Template Parameters

When you insert an optional region, Dreamweaver adds special code to the head of the Web page. Called a *template parameter*, this code is responsible for showing or hiding an optional region.

In fact, Dreamweaver uses parameters when you make a tag attribute editable, too. A typical parameter for an optional region might look like this:

```
<!-- TemplateParam name="SaleBug"
type="boolean" value="true" -->
```

The <!-- and --> are HTML comments that hide this code from a Web browser. TemplateParam tells Dreamweaver that the comment is actually part of the program's Template features—specifically, a template parameter.

A parameter is composed of three parts: name, type, and value. The name is the name you gave the editable region. The type—Boolean—indicates that the value of this parameter can be only one of two options: true or false. In this example, the value is "true," which simply means that the optional region called SaleBug is visible. (Don't worry; you don't have to actually edit this code by hand to turn optional regions on and off, as you'll see on page 623.)

In programming jargon, a template parameter is known as a *variable*. In simpler terms, it's just a way to store information

that can vary. Dreamweaver reacts differently depending on this value: show the region if the parameter's true, or hide it if the parameter's false.

Editable tag attributes also use parameters to store the values you enter for the tag attribute. For example:

```
<!-- TemplateParam name="PageColor"
type="color" value="#FFFFFF" -->
```

On template-based pages, you can change the value of a parameter used for an editable tag attribute to change that tag's property (see page 623).

Unfortunately, when you delete an optional region from a template, or remove the ability to edit a tag attribute, Dreamweaver always leaves these parameter tags hanging around in the head of the template document. Keeping in mind that Dreamweaver adds these parameter tags directly before the closing </head> tag, you can find and remove unused parameter tags in Code view (see Chapter 9).

For an excellent discussion of template parameters, in particular, and Dreamweaver templates, in general, check out the book *Dreamweaver MX Templates* (New Riders Press) by Murray Summers and Brad Halstead.

To remove an optional region, select it using one of the techniques listed previously and choose Modify → Templates → Remove Template Markup. Dreamweaver removes most of the code associated with the optional region (but see the box "Understanding Template Parameters" on the previous page).

Nested Templates

Large sites may have many different sections or types of pages. Each section of the site or type of page may have its own unique look. A Frequently Asked Questions page may have distinct areas for a question, an answer, and links to further resources, while a product page may have a picture, a product description, and ordering information. You could create different templates for each type of page, but even that may be more work than necessary.

While many pages in a site may have subtle differences, they usually share very basic design features. The overall structure of every page, for example, may be the same: same logo, banner, and navigation bar. Even the basic layout may be the same. And there lies the problem with creating individual templates for each section: if you need to make a very basic site-wide change, like adding a new button to the site's overall navigation system or altering the banner, you need to edit *each* template individually, adding extra time, effort, and risk of making a mistake.

Fortunately, Dreamweaver offers a tool to solve just this problem: nested templates. A *nested template* is a template you make from another template, which then becomes the *master* template (see Figure 17-13).

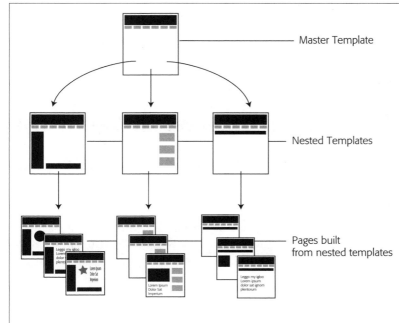

Figure 17-13:
Nested Templates (middle row) let you build templates that share common site-wide design elements while providing precise control for particular types of pages or sections of a Web site. A page built from a nested template (bottom row) contains both elements from a master template (top row)—like a banner and a site-wide navigation bar—in addition to elements specific to its nested template—like a section-specific secondary navigation bar. Changes you make to the master template are passed on to all pages of the site, including nested templates. Changes to a nested template, by contrast, pass on only to pages based on the nested template.

Master Template

Nested Templates

Pages built
from nested templates

Imagine a basic software company Web site with three sections: Support, Our Products, and Downloads. Each section has its own brand of information and specific layout needs. However, all three sections share the same banner and navigation.

To create a template system for this site, you must first create a very basic template that includes elements (including editable regions) shared by all pages—the master template. You can then create a nested template based on the master. On the nested template, you can add further design refinements and additional editable regions for the areas that can be changed on pages created from the nested template.

Yes, this process sounds complex—and yes, it is. But when the alternative is hours or days of manual template updating, you can see why serious Web designers are willing to spend the time to master any shortcut they can get.

To create a nested template:

1. **Build a template as described on page 596.**

   This page acts as the master template and controls all nested templates. It should include the basic elements shared by all nested template pages, like your logo and email links. Now is also the time to add editable regions in the areas the nested templates can change, like table cells to hold blocks of text and images.

2. **Name and save this template (File → Save as Template), and then close it.**

   Your template is safe on the hard drive.

3. **Choose File → New.**

   The window for creating new documents and template-based pages opens (see Figure 17-14).

4. **Click the Templates tab. In the "Templates for" list, select the Web site on which you're working.**

   You can open templates from any site you've defined in Dreamweaver.

5. **From the list of templates, select the name of the master template file you created in step 1.**

   Make sure the "Update page when template changes" box is turned on. Otherwise, the nested template doesn't update when you edit the master template.

6. **Click OK.**

   Dreamweaver creates a new template-based page. At this point, it's simply a basic Web page based on the original template. Next, you'll turn it into a *nested template*.

7. Choose File → Save as Template. Or, on the Common tab of the Insert bar (Figure 17-2), select Make Nested Template from the Templates menu.

The Save As Template window appears (see Figure 17-3).

8. Type a name for the template and click the Save button.

Voilà! A nested template.

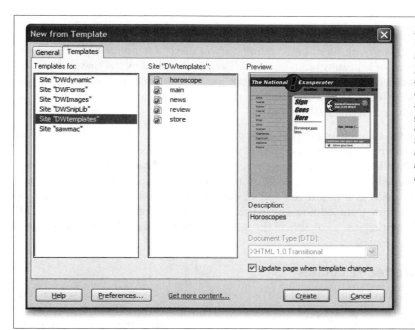

Figure 17-14:
You can use the "Templates for" list to choose another site you've defined and reveal the list of templates it uses. However, choosing a template stored in a different site isn't a good idea. Dreamweaver doesn't copy any images on the template to the current site and can't translate relative links correctly. The result is broken links aplenty.

Customizing Nested Templates

When you first create a nested template, there's no difference between it and the master template. They share the same design, content, and template regions.

The next step is adding the design elements that are specific to pages built from that template. For example, you can add a special type of table for displaying a product photo, description, price, and other information. This table appears only in pages built from this nested template, not from the master template or any other nested template.

There are a few things you should keep in mind when planning your template development strategy:

• When creating pages from templates, you can add content only to an editable region. That's true not only for template-based pages, but for nested templates, too. If the master template has *no* editable regions, you won't be able to change anything on the nested template created from it.

- When working on a nested template, you can insert an editable region only into an editable region supplied by the master template. For example, say you've created a master template to provide a consistent banner and navigation bar to the site, all in a locked region of the master template. Then you add a large empty area at the bottom of the page and turn it into an editable region that you can customize to make specific layouts for each nested template. After creating a nested template from the master template, you can then add new editable regions to this open area. In fact, you can add any template region—repeating, optional, or editable—to this area.

- If, when working on a nested template, you insert a template region (editable, optional, or repeating) into an editable region supplied by the master template, pages based on the nested template can modify *only* those new regions. The rest of the editable region supplied by the master template isn't editable on the pages based on the nested template.

Using the example in the previous paragraph, let's say you next add a repeating table to your nested template (see page 605 for more detail about repeating tables). When you create a page based on this nested template, you can change *only* the editable areas marked out in the repeating table. Of course, the other side of the coin is that if you add an editable region to the master template and then refrain from adding any particular template regions, all of the HTML inside that region is editable in the nested template *and* in all pages based on the nested template.

Using Nested Templates

Here's an example of how you can use nested templates. Suppose you want to create a uniform design for your site where every page of the site has a logo as well as a site-wide navigation bar. Each page within one section of the site also has a sidebar containing a *secondary* navigation bar with navigation buttons for just that section. Finally, every page has a large content area to hold the information specific to that page.

Using nested templates, creating a Web site like this couldn't be easier. Create a master template containing the site banner and navigation bar. This template also includes editable regions for the sidebar and main content area.

Next, create a nested template for one *section* of the site, leaving the content area as it is. Since each page has its own content in this area, you don't need to do anything to this region. Then add the secondary navigation bar to the sidebar area. To lock this region so no one can tinker with the sidebar (in pages built from the nested template), add an empty editable region, or see the Tip on the next page. If you want, you can build similar nested templates for the other sections of the site.

Now you're ready to start building the pages of your site. Create a new page based on one of the section templates. Add text or graphics to the editable content area of the page. Should you need to change the site logo or add a button to the site-wide navigation bar, open the master template, make the changes, save the file, and let Dreamweaver update all the pages of your site with the new look. If you simply need to change the secondary navigation for one section of the site, then open the appropriate nested template, change the sidebar, save the template, and let Dreamweaver update all the section pages.

Tip: You can lock an editable region passed from a master template to a nested template, so that pages based on the nested template can't be changed in this region. In the nested template, go into Code view, and then locate the beginning of the editable region, which looks something like, <!-- InstanceBeginEditable name="regionName" -->. Then insert the text @@("")@@ directly after the -->.

If you find yourself typing this code often, think about creating a snippet (see page 575) containing the text @@("")@@.

Building Pages Based on a Template

Building a template is only a prelude to the actual work of building your site. Once you finish your template, it's time to produce pages.

To create a new document based on a template, choose File → New to open the "New from Template" window (see Figure 17-14). Click the Templates tab and select the current site you're working on from the "Templates for" list. All templates for the selected site appear in the right column. Select the template you wish to use, and then click Create.

Tip: If you don't want your new Web page linked to the template (so that changes to the template also affect the Web page), turn off the "Update page when template changes" checkbox. The result is a new page that looks just like the template, but has no locked regions; you can edit the entire page. This method is useful, for example, when you want to start with the general design and structure of a certain template when creating a brand-new design for another template. (Be aware that Dreamweaver remembers this choice the next time you create a new template-based page. In other words, future pages you create from a template will *also* be unlinked—unless you remember to turn the "Update page" box back on.)

A new Web page document opens, based on the template, bearing a tab in the upper-right corner that identifies the underlying template name. Dreamweaver outlines any editable regions in blue; a small blue tab displays each region's name (Figure 17-5).

Dreamweaver makes it painfully obvious which areas you aren't allowed to edit; your cursor changes to a "forbidden" symbol (a circle with a line through it) when it ventures into a locked area.

To add content to an editable region, click anywhere inside the editable region. You can type inside it, add graphics, or add any other objects or HTML you can normally add to a document. You can also change the document's title and add Behaviors (see Chapter 11), Cascading Style Sheets (see Chapter 6), and meta tag information (items that go in the <head> of an HTML document).

Note: Dreamweaver doesn't let you use the Layer tool to draw a layer in an editable region. It stops you because when using this method, Dreamweaver tries to add the code for the layer at the very beginning of the page, which is usually a *non*-editable region. Instead, you're better off creating a CSS style using absolute positioning (page 296) and then using the Insert Div Tag tool (page 303) to place a layer inside an editable region.

Working with Repeating Regions

Repeating regions work a bit differently than editable regions. In most cases, a repeating region includes one or more editable regions (which you can edit using the instructions above). However, Dreamweaver provides special controls to let you add, remove, and rearrange repeating entries (see Figure 17-15).

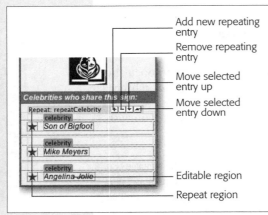

Add new repeating entry

Remove repeating entry

Move selected entry up

Move selected entry down

Editable region

Repeat region

Figure 17-15:
Repeating regions are a great way to quickly add lists to your Web pages. In this example, there's a list of celebrities who share the same astrological sign. Clicking the + button adds another row to this table, complete with an icon (in a region locked by the template) and an editable region for adding a celebrity name.

These regions are intended to let a page author add repeated page elements—like rows of product information in a list of products. To add a repeating entry, click the + button that appears to the right of the Repeat region's blue tab. You can then edit any editable regions within the entry. Click inside an editable region inside a repeating entry and click + again to add a new entry *after* it.

Deleting a repeating entry is just as easy. Click inside an editable region within the entry you wish to delete and click the - sign button.

Note: You can create repeating regions that don't have any editable regions—for example, repeating a star several times to indicate the rating for a product. Although you can use the + button to repeat such regions, you can't delete those regions with the minus sign (-) button. In other words, you're stuck with any extras you've added. The only workaround is to add an editable region to the repeating region. Then Dreamweaver lets you remove any repeating regions you wish.

To rearrange entries in the list, click inside an entry's editable region. Click the up or down arrows to move the entry up or down in the list (to alphabetize it, for example).

Changing Properties of Editable Tag Attributes

Unlike editable or repeating regions, an editable tag attribute isn't immediately apparent on template-based pages. There's no blue tab to represent it, as there are for editable regions; in fact, nothing appears in Design view to indicate that there are *any* editable *tag* properties on the page. The only way to find out is to choose Modify → Template Properties to open the Template Properties dialog box (see Figure 17-16).

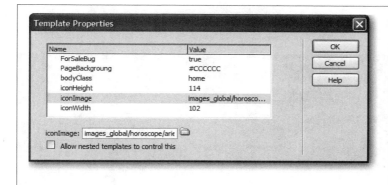

Figure 17-16:
The Template Properties window lets you control editable tag attributes and other parameters for optional regions. Depending on which parameter you select, the options at the bottom of the window change. In this case, the SRC property of an image tag has been made editable. You can click Dreamweaver's familiar Browse for File button to change the image tag's SRC property by selecting a new graphic file to display on the page.

All editable tag attributes for this page appear in this window. In addition, all parameters defined for this page, including optional regions, appear here, as discussed in the box on page 616.

To change the value of a *template* property—in other words, to edit the property of an editable tag—select its name from the list and fill out the option that appears at the bottom of the window. For example, in the case of *color* properties, use the color box to pick a Web-compatible color. If the property is a path (like a link or an image's *source* property indicating the graphic file's location in the site), click the "select a file" folder icon to browse to select the file.

Once you've finished setting the editable properties for the page, click OK to close the window.

Hiding and Showing Optional Regions

As with Editable Tag Attributes, you use the Template Properties window to control the display of optional regions. On template-based pages, you can show or hide an optional region by choosing Modify → Template Properties to open this dialog box (see Figure 17-17). Next, select the name of the optional region. To make all page elements in the region appear, turn on the "Show" checkbox at the bottom of the window. To hide the optional region, turn off this box.

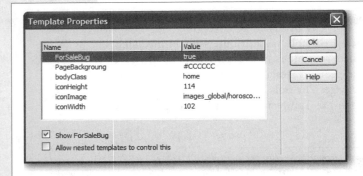

FREQUENTLY ASKED QUESTION

Controlling the Nest

The Template Properties dialog box includes a checkbox labeled "Allow nested templates to control this." What does it do?

Imagine that you create a template and add several optional regions and editable tag attributes to it. You then use this template as a basic design for more refined templates for each section of your site. When you create one of these nested templates based on the master template, it has access to the Template Properties window, where page authors can modify any of the *template* properties created by the original, master template.

For example, to better identify each section of a site, you can add a different background color to each section's pages: blue for the products section, orange for the support section, and so on. In the master template, you make the <body> tag's *Bgcolor* property editable. Now, when you create a nested template for the products section, you simply open the Template Properties dialog box and set the property to the blue color you desire. For the support section's nested template, set the property to orange. Now when you create a template-based page for the support section, its background is orange, while a page for the products section has a blue background.

However, to let your site's color palette go really wild, you may want every page in the site to have its own unique background color. (Disclaimer: Don't try this at home.) In this case, you'd want to let every page based on a nested template have an editable *Bgcolor* property.

To do so, open the nested template, open the Template Properties window, select the property that should be editable in pages built from this template (*color* in this case), and turn on the "Allow nested templates to control this" checkbox. Now this property is uneditable in the nested template, but editable in all pages created from it.

You've probably realized by now that the phrase "Allow nested templates to control this" doesn't make much sense. Turning it on actually prevents the nested template from controlling the property. A better way to think of it is "Allow pages created from this template to control this property."

The bottom line: Turning on this box makes the attribute uneditable on that page. If it's a nested template, it lets the *Template* property "pass through" to all pages based on this template. In other words, you can't set the background color in the template, but page authors can change it in pages created from the template.

Applying a Template to a Page You Already Made

What happens if you create a Web page and *then* decide you want it to share the look of a template? No problem. Dreamweaver lets you apply a template to any Web page in your site. You can even swap one template for another by applying a template to a page that's already based on a different template

To apply a template to a page you've already created:

1. **Choose File → Open to open the page you want to alter.**

   The Web page opens.

2. **Choose Window → Assets. Click the Asset panel's Templates button (see Figure 17-4).**

   The Assets panel appears and reveals a list of the site's templates.

Tip: You can also apply a template to a page by choosing Modify → Templates → Apply Template to Page. Select the name of the template from the window that appears and skip to step 5.

---

3. **Click a template in the list on the Assets panel, and then click Apply.**

   The Inconsistent Region Names dialog box opens (Figure 17-18).

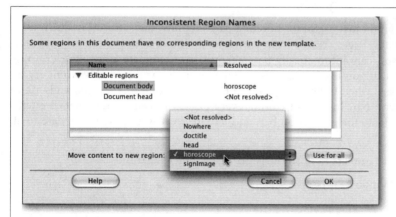

Figure 17-18:
When you apply a template to a page you've already created, you must tell Dreamweaver what to do with the material that's already on the page. Tell it what to do by selecting one of the template's editable regions from a pop-up menu, which takes charge of all editable regions in your page.

4. **In the list under "Editable regions," choose "Document body."**

   To the right, in the Resolved column, you see <Not resolved>. This is Dreamweaver's way of saying it doesn't know what to do with the contents of the current page. You need to pick one of the template's editable regions.

5. **From the "Move content to new region" menu, select an editable region.**

   If you want to keep the material, select the name of an editable region in which to place it from the list; otherwise, choose Nowhere, which, in effect, creates a new blank page based on the template.

Unfortunately, you can only select a single editable region. If there're several content regions in the original, Dreamweaver merges them all into a single editable region.

6. **If "Document head" also appears in the window, select it and choose "head" from the "Move content to new region" menu.**

This step preserves any special information you added to the head of your page, like Cascading Style Sheets, meta tags, custom JavaScript programs, and other information that goes in the <head> of the document. Unfortunately, the title of your original page is always replaced with the default title of the template. You have to reenter the title (see page 20) after you apply the template.

Warning: If you apply a template to a page that has Dreamweaver Behaviors (Chapter 11) applied to it, be careful when you select this option. If the same behaviors already exist in the template code, Dreamweaver actually makes a duplicate copy of the JavaScript code in the <head> of the page. To get rid of the extra code, you need to go into Code view (Chapter 9) and manually remove it.

---

7. **Click OK.**

Your new page appears.

Updating a Template

Templates aren't just useful for building pages rapidly; they also make quick work of site updates. Pages created from templates maintain a link to the original template file; you can automatically pass changes to a template along to every page built from it. If you used templates to build your site, you probably won't cry on your keyboard when the boss says you must add an additional button and link to the navigation bar. Instead of editing every page, you can simply open the template file, update the navigation bar, and let Dreamweaver apply the update to all the pages.

You update a template (and all the pages based on it) like this:

1. **Choose Window → Assets.**

The Assets panel appears.

2. **Click the Templates button (see Figure 17-4).**

A list of the site's templates appears.

3. **Double-click the template's name to open it.**

Alternatively, you can select the template in the Assets panel, and then click the Edit button to open the original template (.dwt) file (see Figure 17-4).

The template opens.

Tip: You can also open a template by double-clicking the appropriate template (.dwt) file located in the Templates folder in the Files panel.

4. **Edit the template as you would any Web page.**

   Since this is the original template file, you can edit any of the HTML in the document, including Cascading Style Sheets, meta tags, and layers. You can also add or remove editable regions (see page 599).

   Take care, however, to edit *only* the areas that you did *not* mark as editable regions. The reason: When you update your pages, any region marked as editable in a template file isn't passed on to pages based on that template. After all, the template is supposed to dictate only the design of those pages' *non*-editable regions.

Note: Be careful when you remove editable regions from a template. If you've already built some pages based on the template, Dreamweaver warns you when you save the template. As described below, you can either *delete* the content that was added to that region in each of the pages you created, or move it to another editable region in the page.

5. **Choose File → Save.**

   If you've already created pages based on this template, Dreamweaver opens the Update Template Files dialog box. It lists all the files that use the template.

6. **Click Update to update all files based on the template.**

   Dreamweaver automatically applies the changes you made to the pages based on the template. Then, the Update Pages dialog box opens. If you want to see a list of all files Dreamweaver changed while updating your site, turn on the "Show log" box.

   On a large site, this automatic update feature can be an incredible time-saver, but you may *not* want to click Update, at least not right now. Perhaps you're just saving some of your hard work on the template but aren't quite finished perfecting it—why waste your time updating all those pages more than once? In such a scenario, click the Don't Update button. Remember, you can always update the pages later (see the box on page 628).

7. **Click Close.**

   The Update Pages dialog box closes.

You need to update all your files even if you make a simple change to the template, like changing its name.

Updating Nested Templates

When you build a Web site using nested templates, you have multiple templates affecting your pages. The master template controls design elements of a nested template, which in turn controls pages based on the nested template. (You can even make nested templates *out of* nested templates, but for sanity's sake, you'd better not.) With this level of complexity, updates to nested templates can get confusing fast.

In a nutshell, here's how it works:

- If you edit a locked region in a master template and then update your site, not only does a nested template update, but so do all pages built from it.

- If you edit a locked region in a nested template and then update, those changes pass on to pages built from that nested template.

However, changes you make to an *editable* region of a master template don't pass on to any page. Neither do changes you make in editable regions of a nested template.

Note: Sometimes after making changes to a master template, Dreamweaver doesn't update pages based on nested templates. The surefire way to verify that all template updates are correctly done is to first recreate the Site Cache (Site → Advanced → Recreate Site Cache), choose Modify → Templates → Update Pages, and then select the "Entire Site" option.

Wait to Update

Whenever you modify and save a Library item or a template, Dreamweaver gives you the option of updating any pages in the site that are descended from it. Very often, you'll say Yes.

But there are times when you'll want to wait to update the site. If you're making a lot of changes to multiple Library items or templates, for example, you may wish to wait until you've finished all your edits before letting the changes ripple through your pages. After all, it can take some time to update large sites with lots of pages.

Dreamweaver lets you update pages that use Library items and templates at any time. Just choose Modify → Library → Update Pages, or Modify → Templates → Update Pages. Both menu options open the same dialog box, as shown here.

At this point, you can update pages that use a specific Library item or template by choosing "Files that Use" from the "Look in" menu and then selecting the appropriate name from the pop-up menu. If you would like to update

all pages in the site, choose Entire Site, and then select the name of the local site from the pop-up menu. Turn on both the "Library items" and Templates checkboxes to update all pages.

To see the results of Dreamweaver's work, check the "Show log" box. This presents a list of all files Dreamweaver changed as it updated the site.

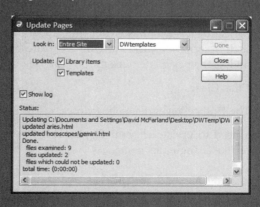

DREAMWEAVER 8: THE MISSING MANUAL

Unlinking a Page from a Template

If you're confident that you won't be making any further changes to a page's template, and you'd like to be able to edit the page's locked regions, you can break the link between a page and its template choosing Modify → Templates → Detach from Template.

All the HTML in the page is now editable, just as on a regular Web page—which is what it is now. You've removed all references to the original template, so changes to the template will no longer have any effect on this page.

Note: If you unlink a nested template from its master template, Dreamweaver removes only the code provided by the original master template. Any editable regions you added to the nested template remain.

Exporting a Template-Based Site

The good news about Dreamweaver's sophisticated templating features is that they let you build complex Web pages that are easy to create and update. The bad news is that some behind-the-scenes code is necessary to achieve this ease of use. Dreamweaver's template features rely on HTML comment tags to identify editable, optional, and repeating regions, as well as nested template and editable tag attributes (see the box on page 601). Although this code is only for Dreamweaver's use and has no effect on how a Web browser displays the page, it does add a small amount to the size of your Web pages.

Fortunately, Dreamweaver includes a feature that lets you export an entire site into a new folder on your computer *without* any template markup code. It's a good last step before transferring a freshly completed Web site to a Web server.

1. **Choose Modify → Templates → Export Without Markup.**

   Dreamweaver uses the currently active site, so make sure you've got the site you wish to export selected in the Files panel (see page 480). The Export Site Without Template Markup window appears (see Figure 17-19).

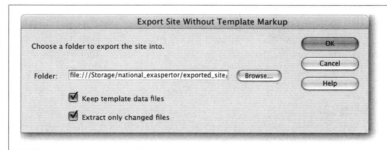

Figure 17-19:
Dreamweaver lets you strip out template code from template-based pages with the Export Site Without Template Markup command.

2. **Click the Browse button and select a folder for the exported site.**

   Select a folder *other* than the current local site folder. You always want to keep the original files in the local folder, since they're the ones that keep the template markup, making future updates possible.

3. **Turn on the export options you want.**

   The Export window includes two options. The first, "Keep template data files," creates an XML file for each template-based page. In other words, when you export the site, there's one HTML page (without any special template code) and an XML file (which includes all the template code as well as the page content).

   Theoretically, you could then go back and choose the File → Import → XML into Template to recreate the page, complete with the original template information. However, in practice, you probably won't. For one thing, this process creates lots of additional files that you wouldn't want to move to the Web site. Also, when you want to work on the site to update and edit it, you should use the original files in the site's local folder anyway, since they still have the useful template code in them.

   The "Extract only changed files" option speeds up the process of exporting a large template-based site. This option forces Dreamweaver to export only pages that you've changed since the last export. Unfortunately, it doesn't tell you *which* files it exported until after the fact. So, to make sure you get those newly exported files to the Web server, you need to keep track of changes by hand.

4. **Click OK to export the site.**

   Dreamweaver goes through each page of the site, stripping out template code and exporting it to the folder you specified.

It's a fine idea to perform an export after you've completed your Web site and are ready to move it to the Internet. You can then move the lean, clean exported files to the Web server.

You can use Dreamweaver's FTP feature to do the uploading (see page 542), but you need to create a new site and define the folder with the *exported* files as a local root folder. Whenever you need to add or update template-based pages, use the original site files, and then export the changed files. You can then switch to the site containing the exported files and transfer the new or updated files to the Web server.

Template Tutorial

In this tutorial, you'll create a template for the Horoscopes section of the *National Exasperator* site. Then you'll build a page based on that template and enjoy an easy site-wide update courtesy of Dreamweaver's templates feature.

Note: The tutorial in this chapter requires the example files from this book's Web site, *www.sawmac. com/dw8/*. Click the Tutorials link to go to the tutorials page. Then click the "Chapter 17: Templates Tutorial" link to download the files.

After your browser downloads and decompresses the files, you should have a DWTemp (short for Dreamweaver Templates) folder on your computer, containing the Web pages and graphics you need for this tutorial. If you're having difficulties, the Web site contains detailed instructions for downloading the files you'll be using with this book.

Creating a Template

This tutorial guides you through the creation of a template, the creation of a page *based* on that template, and then an editing and auto-update procedure.

These instructions assume that you've downloaded the necessary tutorial files, as described in the previous note, and defined a site using the DWTemp folder as your local root folder (for information on defining a site, see page 33 and page 472):

1. **Open the Site window by pressing the F8 key.**

   Of course, if it was already open, you just closed it. Press F8 again.

2. **In the Site window, find and double-click the page *horoscope.html*.**

   It's usually easier to start with an already-designed Web page and then save it as a template. For the purposes of getting to bed before midnight tonight, pretend that you've just designed this beautiful, half-finished Web page.

3. **Choose File → Save As Template.**

   The Save As Template dialog box opens.

4. **In the description field, type *Template for horoscope pages.***

   This description appears in the New Template window when you create a page based on this template.

5. **Name the template *Horoscope*; click Save. In the Update Links window, click Yes.**

   Behind the scenes, Dreamweaver creates a new folder—Templates—in the site's root folder and saves the file as Horoscope.dwt inside it. A new template is born. You can see it in the Templates page of the Assets panel, as well as the new Template folder in the Site window.

   The template is a model for other pages. But although they'll be *based* on its design, they won't be identical. The next step is to identify those areas of the design that'll change from page to page—the editable regions.

6. **Click the gray square labeled *sign_image*.**

   For placement purposes, you've put a dummy graphic on the page. When you add new horoscopes to the site, you can replace this graphic with a real astrological sign. To make it possible to replace it with a real image in the result-ing Web pages, you need to mark this graphic as editable, as follows.

7. **Choose Insert → Template Objects → Editable Region.**

   The New Editable Region dialog box appears. Here, as in the following steps, you can also choose the Editable Region option from the Templates menu on the Common tab of the Insert bar (Figure 17-2) or press Ctrl+Alt+V (⌘-Option-V).

8. **Type *signImage*; click OK.**

   A small tab, labeled *signImage*, appears on the placeholder graphic. There is one more thing you'll want to replace every time you create a Web page based on this template: the horoscope text.

9. **Click before the "S" in the heading Sign Goes Here and drag down and to the right until you've selected the two lines of text.**

   At this point, the heading and the paragraph marked "Horoscope goes here" should be selected.

10. **Choose Insert → Template Objects → Editable Region, type *horoscope*, and then click OK.**

    So far, you've added two editable regions—the most basic type of template region. Next, you'll explore some of the advanced templating features Dream-weaver offers.

11. **Select the "Sign of the Month" image.**

    Of course, only one sign each month can be the Sign of the Month, so you'll want this graphic to appear only on a single page each month. An image like this is the perfect opportunity to use an optional region—an area of the page that you can hide or show on a page-by-page basis.

Note: If you're a conscientious computer veteran, you've probably already saved this template by now, and may have noticed a couple of things. First, an annoying box pops up warning you that the *signImage* region is inside a <p> tag. This is the same warning discussed on page 600, and below in step 22. Don't worry about it, it's OK. If it bugs you, just turn on the "Don't show me this message again" checkbox. Second, Dreamweaver may have opened another window telling you you've updated a template and asking you if you want to update your site. Since you haven't built any pages from this template, there's nothing yet to update, so just cancel this window by clicking the "Don't Update" button.

---

12. **Choose Insert → Template Objects → Optional Region.**

    The New Optional Region window appears.

13. **Type *SignOfMonth* in the name field, turn off the Show by Default checkbox, and then click OK.**

    Since most pages *won't* display this graphic, you'll speed up your work by hid-ing it by default, and making it visible just on the one "Sign of the Month" page.

Next, you'll add a repeating region to the box on the right side of the page to accommodate multiple names of "Celebrities who share this sign." You'll then make the text editable, so that you can type the list of individual celebrity names.

14. **In the yellow box at the right side of the page, click anywhere inside the text "Name goes here."**

    This text is enclosed inside a <div> tag, which is itself wrapped by another <div> tag that has a Cascading Style Sheet class called "celebrity" applied to it (see page 303 for more detail on the use of the <div> tag). Each time you want to add a celebrity name, you need to duplicate this tag. To do so, turn it into a repeating region, as follows.

15. **In the tag selector at the bottom of the window, click the <div.celebrity> tag.**

    You've just selected the <div> tag and everything inside it. This <div> tag contains a little graphic and a space for typing a celebrity's name. Because many celebrities share the same sign, you'll want to list multiple names per page (maybe more on some pages and less on others). So this spot's a perfect place for a repeating region.

16. **Choose Insert → Template Objects → Repeating Region. In the window that appears, type *repeatCelebrity*. Click OK.**

    Dreamweaver inserts a new repeating region with the familiar blue tab. The tab reads "Repeat: repeatCelebrity," indicating that it isn't any ordinary template region—it's a repeating region. However, turning a part of the page into a repeating region doesn't automatically make it editable. Since you want to edit the text and add new names to each page, you need to add an editable region *inside* this repeating region.

17. **Select the text "Name goes here," and choose Insert → Template Objects → Editable Region. In the Name field, type *celebrity*, and then click OK.**

    Another blue tab, labeled "celebrity," appears inside the repeating region. On template-based pages, you can now change this text, plus add additional celebrity names easily.

    There's one last item for this page—the ad. The current ad you see is just a placeholder. Because all ads that go in that location are the same size and require the same formatting, you don't need to make the entire graphic editable. You'll use Dreamweaver's Editable Tag Attribute feature instead.

18. **At the left side of the page, click the graphic labeled Dummy Ad. Choose Modify → Templates → Make Attribute Editable.**

    The Editable Tag Attributes window appears.

19. **Choose SRC from the Attribute menu. Turn on "Make attribute editable."**

    The other fields in the window become active (see Figure 17-20).

20. In the Label field, type *adSrc*. Choose URL from the Type menu, and leave the Default value as it is.

The window should look like Figure 17-20. The label helps you identify which property of which page element you're editing. *URL* in the Type menu informs Dreamweaver that this attribute is a path, enabling Dreamweaver's site management tools to accurately update links and paths to graphics files as you move template-based pages around your site.

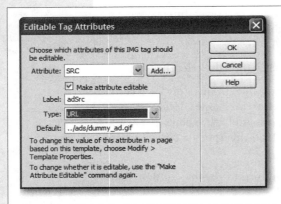

Figure 17-20:
The Editable Tag Attributes window lets you make a specific property of a selected tag editable on template-based pages—in this case, an image's source property, which indicates which graphic file should appear on the page.

21. **Click OK to close the window.**

The graphic suddenly changes into Dreamweaver's broken-image icon. Don't worry; everything is just fine, as you'll see in the next section. (Note that in the real world, you'd also want to make the image's *Alt* property editable as well, so that you can add different alternate text for each ad on each page.)

22. **Choose File → Save.**

Dreamweaver pops up an annoying message informing you that the editable region *signImage* (the region containing the gray placeholder graphic for each sign's astrological symbol) is inside a <p> tag, and that anyone who uses this template can't create new paragraphs. When building a page from this template, page authors can only change this image; they can't delete the image and, say, type a 40-page treatise instead (thank goodness!). This irritating error is Dreamweaver's way of "helping" by pointing out what must be an error on your part. To make it go away, turn on the "Don't show me this message again, you annoying program" box.

23. **Click OK to close the dialog box. Close this file.**

Congratulations! You've created your first template.

Creating a Page Based on a Template

Now it's time to get down to business and build some Web pages. Look at the Files panel and make sure you've selected the site that you defined in step 1 at the beginning of this tutorial (page 631). Then proceed as follows:

1. **Choose File → New.**

   The New Document window opens.

2. **Click the Templates tab.**

   A list of all defined sites appears in the "Templates for" box at left.

3. **Make sure the site you defined for this tutorial is selected; also make sure the "Update page when template changes" checkbox is turned on.**

   If you don't turn on the "Update page" box, the new page won't link to the original template file—and won't update when you make changes to the template.

4. **Select Horoscope from the templates list and click Create.**

   And lo, a new, untitled Web page document appears, one that looks (almost) exactly like the template (Figure 17-21).

5. **Choose File → Save. Save the file as *gemini.html* in the *horoscopes* folder.**

   To indicate that it's the offspring of your template, the document window has a yellow tab in the upper-right corner that reads Template: Horoscope. You can see your editable and repeating regions indicated by blue tabs.

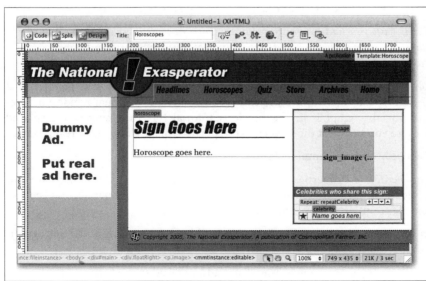

Figure 17-21:
In template-based pages, blue tabs identify editable areas of the page, and the yellow tab at the top right lists the template's name. Notice that the repeating region has small control buttons (+, -, and up and down arrows) and the optional region—the moon graphic—is invisible. (Remember, you deselected the "Show by Default" option for this graphic.)

6. **Make sure the document window's toolbar is visible (by choosing View →**
   Toolbars → Document); type _Gemini_ into the Title field.

   You've just named your page, saving you from the ignominy of showing up in
   search engines as "Untitled." Next stop: replacing the dummy astrological sign
   image with a real one.

7. **Click the gray "sign_image" box to select it. Press Delete or Backspace.**

   It's useful to include placeholders for your text and graphics, like this image
   placeholder, in your templates to give your page shape and make clear what the
   content should look like. You'll now replace this placeholder with a Gemini sign
   image.

8. **Insert the Gemini image.**

   Choose Insert → Image, for example. Navigate to the _images_global_ → _horoscope_
   folder; double-click the file called _gemini.gif_. If Dreamweaver's accessibility features are turned on (see page 130), the "Image Tag Accessibility Attributes"
   window appears.

9. **Type _Gemini symbol_ and press OK.**

   When you return to your document, you'll discover that Dreamweaver has
   replaced the placeholder image with Gemini's "twins" astrological symbol.

   Now you'll add a proper horoscope.

10. **Select the words Sign Goes Here, and type _Gemini_.**

    You also want to add Gemini's unfortunate astrological forecast.

11. **Select the text "Horoscope goes here" and type the following:**

    You'll wish you had a twin this month. Then at least there'd be someone else to
    blame for your problems and share your woes. Ever thought about moving? Good,
    'cause now's the time: You're being evicted on the 16th.

    Oh, well—there'll be other months for Gemini. However, it just so happens that
    Gemini is the "Sign of the Month." (Remember the optional region you cre-
    ated for this graphic in the previous tutorial?) It isn't currently displayed
    because you turned it off. In the next step, you'll magically make it reappear.

12. **Choose Modify → Template Properties.**

    The Template Properties window appears (see Figure 17-22). There are two
    items listed: the first is the editable tag attribute for the banner ad, and the sec-
    ond is the optional region you wish to make visible.

13. **In the properties list, select "signOfMonth" and turn on the "Show signOf-**
    Month" checkbox.

    While you're here, you may as well also add a real ad to the page.

14. **Select "adSrc" in the Template Properties window. A field for adding the path to an image file appears, as does the ubiquitous folder button. Click the Folder icon at the bottom of the window. Browse to and select the file** *alien_ad.gif* **in the** *ads* **folder.**

    As when selecting any file in Dreamweaver, the helpful "select file" button makes supplying the proper path to a file a snap.

15. **Click OK to close the window.**

    The "Sign of the Month" button appears, as does an ad for the amazing and historically accurate video, *Alien Autopsy 7*. You're nearly done building this new page. The last task is adding a list of celebrities who share this unfortunate horoscope.

Note: This tutorial would like to apologize to those who have a true belief in and understanding of the zodiac. The astrological predictions included herein are purely fictitious and intended for entertainment purposes only.

---

16. **At the bottom right of the page, click the blue tab labeled "celebrity."**

    You've just selected the text in that editable region.

17. **Type** *Mike Myers.*

    There are a lot of Gemini celebrities out there. Fortunately, you can add more entries using the repeating region controls.

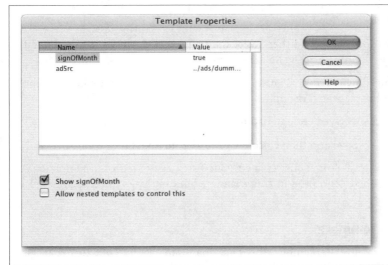

Figure 17-22:
The Template Properties window does double duty. Not only does it let you hide or show optional regions, but it's also the place to set values for editable tag attributes.

18. **Click the + button just to the right of the blue "Repeat: repeatCelebrity" tab.**

    You've added another row to the page, as shown in Figure 17-23.

Tip: If a page has a lot of elements crowded together—tables, images, text—Dreamweaver sometimes can't display the small buttons that let you add and remove repeating entries. In this case, you can also use the Modify menu. Click inside a repeating region and choose Modify → Templates → Repeating Entries, and then select an action from the submenu, such as New Entry After Selection, to add another editable entry.

Figure 17-23:
The control buttons to the right of repeating regions (circled) let you add, remove, and rearrange repeating entries. In this example, clicking the + button adds another table row for inputting an additional celebrity name.

---

19. **Click the blue tab of the newly added "celebrity" editable region and type *Angelina Jolie*.**

    For now, you'll add just one more celebrity to the list, though you can actually add as many as you want.

20. **Repeat steps 18 and 19 to add one last celebrity name: Son of Bigfoot.**

    But since Son of Bigfoot is a corporate spokesperson for the *National Exasperator*, he'd better get top billing.

21. **Select "Son of Bigfoot" (either select the text, or click the blue tab above the name), and double-click the up arrow button next to the repeating region.**

    The up and down arrows (Figure 17-23) let you move a repeated region above or below other repeated regions.

    OK. Gemini's received enough bad news for one month. This page is done.

22. **Choose File → Save and then close the *gemini.html* document window.**

    Congratulations! You've just created your first page based on a template. You could, of course, continue in this manner, building page after page based on this template.

Updating a Template

Now the fun begins. Remember, this page maintains a reference to the original template. In the final phase, you're going to make a few changes to the template. Choose Window → Assets to open the Assets panel, and then click the Template button to reveal the templates for this site (see Figure 17-4):

---

1. **In the Assets panel, double-click the Horoscope template to open it.**

   The original template, the Horoscope.dwt file, opens. It would be nice to add a navigation bar to the left side of this page, so that visitors can quickly jump to a particular horoscope. Fortunately, there's a Library item already created for doing so. (See Chapter 16 for more on Dreamweaver's Library tool.)

2. **Click the Library icon in the Assets panel (directly below the Template icon).**

   There's one Library item listed: Horoscope Nav.

3. **Drag the Library item from the Assets panel and drop it into the empty space just above the broken-image icon for the ad on the left edge of the template.**

   Alternatively, you can click inside this area in the document window, select the Library item in the Assets panel, and then click the Insert button at the bottom of the Assets panel. Either way, a fresh new navigation system appears on the page.

   It would also be nice if the "Sign of the Month" graphic were a little more prominent—inside the box on the right side of the page, for example.

4. **Click the blue tab labeled "If Sign of Month."**

   You've just selected the optional region you created earlier. Now you need to move it to the box on the right side of the page.

5. **Remove the region from the page by choosing Edit → Cut.**

   Don't worry—you'll add it back next. What you really want to do is place it at the top of the box, before the astrological symbol for the particular sign. The tag selector makes your task easier.

6. **Click just below the top of the yellow box and to the left of the "sign image" region.**

   The cursor is now just to the left of the sign image, but not at the top of the box. It's also inside the editable region for the sign image. You can't add regions *inside* editable regions (after all, those areas can be freely changed from page to page). You'll need to put the cursor outside of the editable region. At this point, you need to know a little bit about the HTML code used here; the placeholder graphic is actually inside a paragraph tag. To put the "Sign of the Month" optional region above it, you need to place the cursor *before* this paragraph. Unfortunately, you can't do it by clicking in the document window, but you can use the tag selector to help you.

7. **Click the <p> tag in the tag selector at the bottom of the document window and press your keyboard's left arrow key.**

   Now you're probably thinking, "But everything looks the same!" After all, the cursor still appears just to the left of the image.

However, even though Dreamweaver doesn't show it, you've just moved the cursor to the outside of the <p> tag. You've just learned one of the most valuable tips for using Dreamweaver to edit HTML code. If you understand your code, you can navigate around it easily using the tag selector and your keyboard's arrow keys.

8. **Choose Edit → Paste.**

    Dreamweaver drops the optional region into its new location.

9. **Choose File → Save.**

    Once again that annoying message appears (see the note on page 632); just click OK. The Update Template Pages dialog box appears, listing all the pages in the site based on this template (in this case, just the lone *gemini.html* file).

10. **Click Update.**

    Dreamweaver opens the Update Pages dialog box and updates the appropriate Web pages, adding the new sidebar navigation to each one. In this case, you based only one page on the template, so Dreamweaver updates only one page—as indicated by the list of changes Dreamweaver shows when it's finished.

11. **Click Close to close the Update Pages dialog box. Finally, open the file *gemini. html,* and press F12 (Option-F12) to preview it in a Web browser.**

    Notice that the horoscope navigation bar now appears in the *gemini.html* document and the "Sign of the Month" graphic has moved (see Figure 17-24). This series of events happened because you changed the template to which the page was genetically linked. Ah, the power!

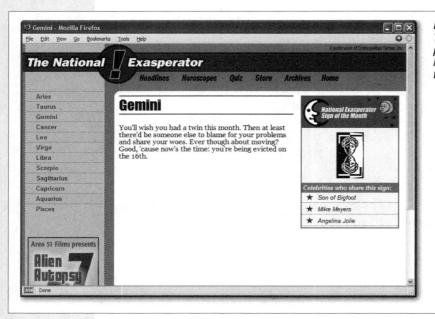

Figure 17-24:
The finished tutorial page, complete with ad, horoscope, and "Sign of the Month" logo.

Automating Dreamweaver

One of Dreamweaver's greatest selling points is that it makes you more productive. You've experienced this firsthand if you ever labored over tables in an HTML text editor. What once took many keystrokes now takes one click of the Insert bar's Table object.

If you're looking for even more ways to cut time off your day, Dreamweaver doesn't disappoint. In addition to its Snippets, Library, and Template features (see Chapters 16 and 17), the program offers two tools that let you automate common and time-consuming tasks—the History panel and the Find/Replace command— as well as one tool that makes creating graphic photo albums a snap.

The History Panel Revisited

As you work on a Web page, Dreamweaver keeps track of everything you do. You can see a list of your actions—your *history*—in the History panel. Each document has a separate history, which Dreamweaver discards when you close the document or quit the program.

You can use the History panel to quickly undo or redo multiple actions (see page 72), but that's only the tip of the iceberg. You can also use it to replay and record a series of actions you wish to repeat. If you've ever used macros in Microsoft Word or actions in Adobe Photoshop, you'll probably quickly get the hang of this feature.

To open the History panel, choose Window → History, or press Shift+F10 (see Figure 18-1).

Replay Your Steps

To replay a step in the History panel, click the step's name to highlight it. You can also select multiple steps by using one of these methods:

- To select a group of consecutive steps, drag over them. You can drag your cursor across either the labels or icons. Take special care not to move your cursor onto the History slider on the left edge of the window, as clicking there undoes or redoes steps (page 73).

- You can also select consecutive steps by holding down the Shift key as you click down the list.

- To select steps that aren't consecutive, Ctrl-click (⌘-click) only the ones you want. For example, say you hit Return, typed *hello*, and then inserted a horizontal rule. If you wanted to omit the step where you typed *hello*, you could Ctrl-click (⌘-click) the other two. Dreamweaver ignores unselected steps.

Now, when you click Replay (see Figure 18-1), Dreamweaver replays the selected steps in an encore performance. For example, if you insert an image using the Common tab of the Insert bar (see page 124), that's recorded as one step. You could then add that image to your page again, later, simply by clicking where you want the image to appear and then replaying the "insert image" step. Unfortunately, you can't reorder the steps; they always play from the top of the list to the bottom.

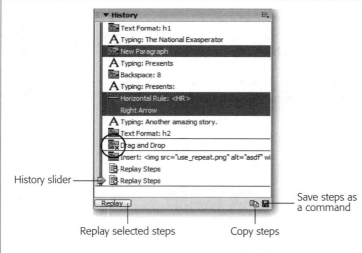

History slider

Replay selected steps

Replay

Copy steps

Save steps as a command

Figure 18-1:
The History panel lists every little step you've taken while working on the current document—even typos. You can replay one or more actions on the list, copy them for use in another document, or save them as a command in the Commands menu. If Dreamweaver can't replay an action, such as a mouse click, it appears with a red X next to it (circled). Furthermore, you can't replay two consecutive steps if you clicked or dragged in the document in between them (you'll see a solid line in the History list separating such steps). Dreamweaver merely replays the first selected step. The History slider indicates where you are in the document's history.

Once you've created a series of steps, you can reuse it. For example, say you format a paragraph as a bulleted list and apply a custom style to it. Once Dreamweaver records these steps in the History panel, you can select more text and replay those steps to format it the same way. Now imagine that, instead of a two-step process, you have a 10-step chore that involves not only keystrokes, but multiple visits to the Insert bar and Property inspector—you can begin to see the power of this feature.

Tip: You probably know that you can repeat your last action by pressing Ctrl+Y (⌘-Y) or choosing Edit → Repeat. For example, if you type the word *hello* in the document window, pressing Ctrl+Y (⌘-Y) will type the word *hello* again. Unless you're Jack Nicholson's character in *The Shining*, this feature may sound less than useful, but used in combination with the History panel's Replay feature, it can be a real time-saver. When you use the History panel to replay several steps, you'll notice the last item in the History list becomes Replay Steps. Dreamweaver treats the replaying of all these steps as a *single action*. Now if you press Ctrl+Y (⌘-Y), you replay all of the steps again.

Exceptions and Errors

Unfortunately, Dreamweaver can't record and play back everything. The exceptions generally involve making changes in certain dialog boxes or moving objects with the mouse. For example, you can't record tasks you perform in the Modify Page Properties dialog box. And you're left to your own devices when you want to click, drag, or drop a graphic in the document window.

On the other hand, not everything you do with the mouse is off-limits to the History panel. It can track most common tasks, like clicking the Insert bar, choosing a menu item, or clicking in the Property inspector to set a property. Also, you can avoid using many mouse movements by using the equivalent keystrokes, which Dreamweaver *can* record. (See the box "Keyboard to the Rescue" below.)

If you take a step, such as a mouse drag, that Dreamweaver *can't* replay, a red X appears next to it in the History panel. A line between two actions also indicates a step that can't be repeated. This problem usually arises when you've clicked in the document window (to deselect a selected image, for example). One way you can avoid these non-recordable actions is to get into the habit of deselecting an object in the document window by pressing the keyboard's arrow keys instead.

FREQUENTLY ASKED QUESTION

Keyboard to the Rescue

If Dreamweaver can't track mouse movements, how can I replay an action that involves selecting something?

It's easy to use the mouse to make selections and move items around the screen, but you can do much of the same with the humble keyboard. That's a good thing, because if you can type it, Dreamweaver can record it.

To move up one line, for instance, press the up arrow key; to move down a line, press the down arrow. You can move to the top or bottom of the document window with the Page Up and Page Down keys, or move to the beginning or end of a line by pressing Home or End. Press Shift while pressing the right or left arrow key to select the object or letter to the right or left of the insertion point. Add the Ctrl

(⌘) key to that combination to select one word at a time. Unfortunately, Dreamweaver doesn't record the keystrokes you use for moving between table cells (Tab and Shift-Tab). However, there's a workaround: to move from one cell to the cell on its right, press End, followed by the right arrow key. To move to the cell to the left, press Home, followed by the left arrow key. Arrow keys not only move the cursor but are also a helpful way to deselect an object that's currently highlighted on the page. Best of all, the History panel can track all of these keystrokes.

(You don't have to memorize all of this. You can print out a complete list of keyboard shortcuts, as described on page 665.)

Copying and Pasting Actions

Each document has its own history. Thus, if you work on one page and then switch to another, the History panel changes to reflect only the actions you performed on the new document. The biggest drawback of this quirk is that you can't immediately replicate a series of steps you've made in one document by replaying them in another document.

For example, while working on your home page, you might click the Date object in the Insert bar to insert the current date (see page 61), and then choose a format for the date in the dialog box. Then, say you want to place the date on another page using the same format. But when you switch to that page and click Replay on the History panel, your steps aren't there!

Fortunately, there's a workaround: ye olde copy/paste routine. Select the steps you want to copy (see "Replay Your Steps" on the opposite page for selection techniques), and then click the "Copy selected steps" button (see Figure 18-1) on the History panel. (The regular copy shortcut, Ctrl+C or ⌘-C, *doesn't* work in this situation.) Now switch to the new document, select an object (or click to place the insertion point), and then choose Edit → Paste or press Ctrl+V (⌘-V).

Dreamweaver responds by playing the copied steps.

Save Steps as Commands

It's quick and easy to replay and copy steps to automate repetitive tasks, but if you close the document or quit Dreamweaver, your recorded actions disappear—and with them, any chance you had of replaying them in the future. What if you come up with a great sequence of steps that you'd like to use over and over again?

POWER USERS' CLINIC

Copy (and Study) Actions

Dreamweaver is relatively easy to customize, because the objects that appear in the Insert bar, the behaviors available from the Behaviors panel, and even the Property inspector are all, behind the scenes, combinations of HTML pages and JavaScript programs. If you understand JavaScript, you can add your own commands, behaviors, and objects.

When learning JavaScript, however, you may need all the help you can get. The History panel's Copy Steps feature is a good place to start.

To study how Dreamweaver's built-in commands, behaviors, and objects have been programmed, copy one or more actions using the method that's described above.

Switch to a text editor like Notepad or TextEdit (Word will work, too), and then choose Edit → Paste.

What you see is the JavaScript code that Dreamweaver uses to carry out those actions. You'll find out, for example, that while you perceive adding a new paragraph to your Web page as a matter of hitting Enter, to Dreamweaver it looks like this: *dw.getDocumentDOM( ).newBlock( )*.

The History panel also has a secret shortcut that lets you view the JavaScript code for each step, right inside the panel: Ctrl+Shift+click (⌘-Shift-click) anywhere inside the History panel (Ctrl+Shift+click [⌘-Shift-click] again to return to the normal, human-readable description for each step).

The solution: Before it disappears forever, turn it into a *custom command*. That way, Dreamweaver adds your command to the bottom of the Commands menu, and you can choose it whenever you want from there.

To save steps as a command, select the steps you want to copy (see "Replay Your Steps" on page 642 for selection techniques), and then click the Save Steps button (its icon looks like a little floppy disk) on the History panel.

The Save as Command dialog box pops open. (If you've selected steps that Dreamweaver can't replay, such as mouse movements, a warning appears. Click Yes to continue without those steps; the valid steps work just fine.) Type a short, descriptive name, and then click OK. Now take a look at the Commands menu—sure enough, your command now appears at the bottom.

To use your custom command, simply select its name from the Commands menu.

Note: If you decide you want to delete your command or change its name, choose Commands → Edit Command List. In the dialog box that appears, click the command's name to select it. Type a new name or click Delete.

Recording Commands

You can also create a command by telling Dreamweaver to watch and record your actions. This time, Dreamweaver doesn't *let* you perform mouse movements while you're recording, so you can be sure recorded commands will play back properly.

To record a command, make sure the relevant Web page document is frontmost, and then choose Commands → Start Recording, or press Ctrl+Shift+X (⌘-Shift-X). The cursor turns into a cassette-tape icon to indicate the command is recording. Now's your chance to do whatever you want Dreamweaver to memorize. (If you try to use the mouse to move or select anything in the document window, Dreamweaver complains with a dialog box.)

When you're finished, choose Commands → Stop Recording, or press Ctrl+Shift+X (⌘-Shift-X). Your cursor returns to normal, and Dreamweaver saves the sequence as a command, which you can replay by choosing Commands → Play Recorded Command.

Note, however, that this command disappears when you quit Dreamweaver or record another command. (Dreamweaver can only save one recorded command at a time.) If you want to preserve it for posterity, you have to save it to the Commands menu, like this:

1. **Choose Commands → Play Recorded Command.**

   The History panel lists this action as Run Command.

2. **Click the Run Command step in the History panel.**

   The step is highlighted to indicate you've selected it.

---

3. **Click the Save Steps button (its icon looks like a little floppy disk).**

The Save as Command dialog box appears.

4. **Type a name for the command; click OK.**

Dreamweaver adds your new command to the Commands menu, where it's ready for action in this or any future Dreamweaver session.

Creating a Web Photo Album

So you took your digital camera to your nephew's wedding. Your phone's ringing off the hook with family members wanting to see those pictures. Using Dreamweaver's Create Web Photo Album command, you can quickly generate a simple showcase for your digital masterpieces (see Figure 18-2). (This command works only if you have Macromedia Fireworks on your computer.)

To create a photo album, put all the graphics you want featured into a single folder. (It doesn't have to be in your site folder.) Then choose Commands → Create Web Photo Album. The dialog box that appears (Figure 18-3) offers these controls:

- **Photo album title, Subheading info.** The title you type appears in a gray box on the thumbnail page, and at the top of each photo page (Figure 18-2). If you type a subheading, it appears in smaller type on the thumbnail page, below the title.

- **Other info.** Use this optional box to provide a short description of the photos. This text appears as plain paragraph type below the subhead.

- **Browse.** Click the top Browse button (next to the "Source images folder" box) to find and select your folder of graphics files. The graphics files themselves don't have to be in a Web-ready format (GIF, JPEG, or PNG). Fireworks can take GIF, JPEG, PNG, Photoshop (.psd), or TIFF files and convert them into a Web-friendly graphics file format. (That's why you need Fireworks in order to generate Web photo albums.)

  Click the lower Browse button (next to the "Destination folder" box) to find and highlight the folder where you want to store the converted graphics (and the album Web pages). This should be an empty folder in your site folder.

  Dreamweaver creates a new *index.htm* page for the album's thumbnail page, as well as additional folders for the thumbnail images, larger images, and photo pages.

- **Size pop-up menu.** You can choose from five preset sizes for the thumbnail images: 36×36, 72×72, 100×100, 144×144, or 200×200 pixels. These sizes represent the *maximum* width and height of the thumbnail image. For example, if a photo in its original format is 785 pixels wide and 405 pixels tall, the 100×100 option will create a miniature image that's 100 pixels wide by 52 pixels tall (Fireworks doesn't distort the image by turning it into a 100×100 pixel square; instead, it preserves the picture's proportions).

- **Columns.** Specify the number of columns you want for the thumbnail page layout. If you have nine photos, for example, type *3* in the column box. Dreamweaver produces a page that displays your images 3 across and 3 down.

Figure 18-2:
Use Dreamweaver's built-in Create Web Photo Album command to whip up a set of Web pages that showcases your photos. The command creates a simple index for your photo album (top), including clickable thumbnail images. When clicked, each opens up an individual page that showcases a larger version of the photo (bottom).

- **Thumbnail Format.** Choose the graphics format for the thumbnail. (You can choose separate formats for thumbnails and the larger photo images.) Fireworks converts the photos in the folder you've specified into either JPEG or GIF images. (JPEG is best for photographic images, while GIF is best with illustrations, logos, and images with large areas of solid color and text.)

- **Photo Format.** You can choose a separate file format for the larger photo images. If your original images are photos, choose JPEG. For line art like logos and illustrations, choose GIF.

- **Scale.** Here, you can type a percentage for scaling the original images. If the original photos are very large, for example, you might want to create smaller versions that fit on a Web page better and are small enough to download quickly. For example, say your original digital photos are 1000 pixels wide—really huge for a Web page—you might type *40* (percent) to bring the images on the resulting Web pages down to a reasonable size.

- **Create Navigation Page for Each Photo.** This useful option creates a separate page for each photo, complete with its title, file name, and previous/next links (Figure 18-2, bottom). If you turn off this box, Dreamweaver merely links the thumbnail images directly to each larger photo. When a visitor clicks the thumbnail, the full-size image still appears, but without the title or navigation controls.

When you click OK, Fireworks opens and creates the thumbnail and larger photo images. This may take a few minutes, depending on how many image files Fireworks must process and how big they are. When it's done, Dreamweaver steps in and creates the pages themselves. An "Album Created" message appears when your new photo gallery is ready to preview; Press F12 (Option F12) to open it in your Web browser.

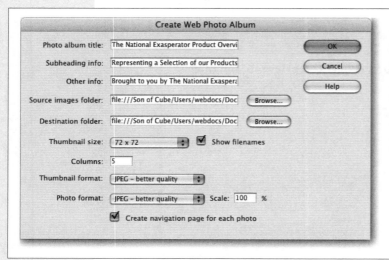

Figure 18-3:
The Create Web Photo Album dialog box lets you define the properties of your photo album. The "Show filenames" box tells Dreamweaver to add the actual file name of the image under each thumbnail. If your images are from a photo CD or stock image disc, you'll probably get uninformative names such as DS3746F7.jpg.

Note: Macromedia offers a free extension called Web Photo Album 2.2. It works similarly to the built-in command described above (you also need Fireworks to use it), but it includes professionally designed templates to jazz up the otherwise humdrum album pages with backgrounds and graphics. You can find it on the Macromedia Exchange Web site at this Web page: *www.macromedia.com/cfusion/exchange/index.cfm?view=sn121&extID=1009904*. (See page 670 for more information on Dreamweaver extensions and the Macromedia Exchange.)

Find and Replace

You've probably encountered find-and-replace tools in word processing programs and even some graphics programs. As the name implies, the command finds a piece of text (*Webmaster*, for example) and then *replaces* it with something else (*Webmistress*). Like Microsoft Word, Dreamweaver can search and replace text in the body of your Web pages. But it also offers variations on this feature that enhance your ability to work within the tag-based world of HTML.

What's more, Dreamweaver lets you find and replace text on *every* page of your Web site, not just the current, open document. In addition, you can *remove* every appearance of a particular HTML tag, or search and replace text that matches very specific criteria. For example, you can find every instance of the word "Aardvark" that appears within a center-aligned paragraph. These advanced find-and-replace options are some of the most powerful—and underappreciated—tools in Dreamweaver's toolbox. If you learn how to use them, you can make changes to your pages in a fraction of the time it would take using other methods.

Tip: You can use Find and Replace to search an entire site's worth of files. This is powerful, but can also be slow, especially if some folders hold files you don't want to search—old archives, for example. You can use Dreamweaver's cloaking feature to hide files from find-and-replace operations. See page 549 for more details.

Find and Replace Basics

To start a search, press Ctrl+F (⌘-F), or choose Edit → Find and Replace. The Find and Replace window opens (see Figure 18-4). Now all you have to do is fill in the blanks and set up the search.

Whether you perform a simple text search or a complex, tag-based search and replace, the procedure for using the Find and Replace command is basically the same. First, you need to tell Dreamweaver *where* to search (within text you've selected on the page, in a file, a folder, or an entire Web site). Next, tell it *what* to search for (text, HTML, or a particular tag with a specific attribute). Finally, you can decide what to replace the item with. This last step is optional; you can use the Find and Replace window as a way to locate an item on the page, or in your site, without actually changing it to anything.

Tip: After you've entered the Find and Replace criteria, click the Save Query button (see Figure 18-4). A Save dialog box appears; you can type in a name for your query, which Dreamweaver saves as a *.dwr* (Dreamweaver replace query) file. You can save this file anywhere on your computer. If it's a query you'll use for a particular site, you might want to save it with those files. To reuse a query, click the Load Query button and locate the *.dwr* file. After the search-and-replace criteria load, you can click any of the four action buttons—Find Next, Find All, Replace, or Replace All.

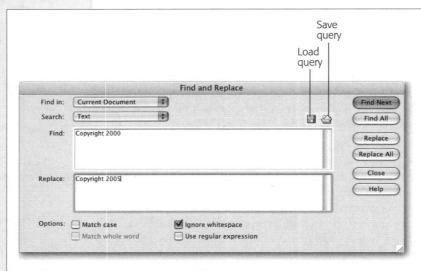

Figure 18-4:
Dreamweaver's Find and Replace feature lets you replace text and HTML quickly and accurately. By using the Load Query and Save Query buttons, you can even save complex searches to use in the future.

Basic Text and HTML Searches

Dreamweaver can either search all of the source code in a page or simply focus on text that appears in the document window. You'll choose one of these in Phase 2 on page 652.

- A **source code** search lets you find and replace any character in the code of a page, including words, letters, and symbols. This means *anything* you see in Code view, such as HTML, CSS, or server-side programming code used to create the dynamic database-driven sites described in Part Six of this book.

- **Text** searches are more refined. They look only for text that appears within the body of a page. That is, Dreamweaver ignores HTML tags, properties, and comments when searching—in short, it ignores anything that doesn't appear as actual words in the document window. By using a text search when you want to change the word "center" to "middle," for example, you won't accidentally alter the center *alignment* option of a table cell—<td align="center">—by setting the alignment value of its HTML tag to "middle" (an invalid value that Web browsers would just ignore).

If you've used Find and Replace in other programs, the following routine will seem familiar:

Phase 1: Determine the scope of your search

Using the "Find in" menu (see Figure 18-5), choose any of these options:

- **Selected Text.** Searches only the current selection of the Web page you're working on. This can be useful if you're working in Code view and you want to search the code in just a certain section of the page, such as the head of the document. It's also great when you're writing your own server-side programs (like those described in Part Six of this book) and you want to search only one part of the code.

- **Current Document.** Searches the Web page you're working on.

- **Open Documents.** Searches all currently open Dreamweaver documents. This option's great if you're working on a bunch of pages at the same time and realize you've made the same typo on each page.

- **Folder.** Search all Web pages in a particular folder. Dreamweaver also searches Web pages in all folders *within* the selected folder. You can use this option to search pages that aren't part of the current site.

- **Selected Files in Site.** To use this option, open the Site window and select files that you want to search in the local file list. (See page 512 for details.)

- **Entire Current Local Site.** Searches every Web page in the current site folder, including pages in folders *inside* the site folder. This option is invaluable when some basic piece of information changes throughout your site. For instance, use this when your boss's sex-change operation requires you to replace every instance of "Mark Jones" with "Mary Jones" throughout your company's site.

Warning: Using the Find and Replace command is one of the best ways to quickly make changes to an entire site, but it's also one of the easiest ways to *wreck* a site's worth of Web pages. Dreamweaver can't undo changes made by the Find and Replace command to files that aren't open on your computer. So be careful. If you plan on making extensive changes, make a backup copy of your files first!

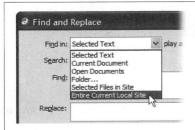

Figure 18-5:
The Find and Replace command is not limited to the current document. You can also search multiple Web pages, or even an entire site.

Phase 2: Specify what to search for

For your next trick, you'll tell Dreamweaver what you want to search for. Use the Search pop-up menu to choose one of these two options:

- **Text.** This makes Dreamweaver search for a certain word or phrase of text that appears in the *body* of the documents you've specified. Type the text you want to find into the Search field. If you're searching for a pattern in your text, enter a *regular expression* here and turn on "Use regular expression." (See the box on page 655 for more on regular expressions.)

- **Source Code.** Basic text searches are very useful, but they're limited to text that appears in the body of the page (what you see in the document window). If you want to search and replace code, you need the Source Code option.

  Source-code searches work identically to text searches. The only difference is that Dreamweaver searches *everything* within the file—text, HTML, JavaScript, Cascading Style Sheets (CSS), and so on—and replaces any part of the file. Using this option, you could search for any instance of the tag <img src="mark_jones_photo.jpg">, for example, and then replace it with <img src="mary_jones_photo.jpg">.

  (If you're in Code view, Dreamweaver automatically selects the Source Code option.)

  As you fill in the Search field, be aware that some plain English words are also special words in HTML, JavaScript, or CSS. If you try to replace *table* with *desk* using a source-code find and replace, you'll completely destroy any <table> tags on the page.

  You can also enter a regular expression to search for patterns in your HTML source code (see the box on page 655).

Phase 3: Provide the replacement text

If you want to change the text that Dreamweaver finds, type the replacement text into the Replace box. It may be the word or words you'd like to swap in (for a Text search), or actual HTML code if you're performing a source-code search.

If you want to only find the text without replacing it, then skip this step.

Tip: If you want to find the specified text and replace it with *nothing* (that is, deleting every occurrence of the text), leave the Replace field blank and perform a replace operation, described in Phase 5.

Phase 4: Choose the search settings

Dreamweaver gives you three options that govern its search and replace; some of them are quite complex:

- The **Match Case** option limits the Find command to text that exactly matches the capitalization you use in the Search field. If you search for the text *The End* with the Match Case box turned on, Dreamweaver finds a match in "The End is near," but not in "You're almost at the end." Use this trick to find every instance of *web* and replace it with *Web*.

- **Match Whole Word** searches for an entire word—not a portion of a larger word. For example, if you turn this option on, a search for *Rob* matches only "Rob," and not any parts of "Robert," "robbery," or "problem." If you don't select this option, Dreamweaver stops on "rob" in all four instances, and could cause serious problems if you also *replace* "rob" with something else. (Note that if you selected the Match Case option, Dreamweaver would match *Rob* in "Rob" and "Robert," but *not* in "robbery" and "problem," since they don't include a capital R.)

- The **Ignore Whitespace Differences** option treats multiple spaces, tabs, non-breaking spaces, and carriage returns as a single space when searching. For instance, if you search for *the dog* and turn on this option, Dreamweaver matches "the   dog" as well as "the dog"—even if the multiple spaces are actually the HTML nonbreaking space character * * (see page 60).

  Unless you have a good reason, always leave this option turned on. The HTML of a page can contain lots of extra spaces, line breaks, and tabs that don't appear in a Web browser or in Dreamweaver's document window. For example, in the HTML of a document, it's possible to have two lines of code that look like this:

  ```
  <p>This sentence will appear on one
  line in a Web browser</p>
  ```

  Even though this text would appear on a single line in the document window, a search for "one line" *without* the Ignore Whitespace Differences would find no match. The carriage return at the end of "one" is not an exact match for the space character in "one line."

- The **Use Regular Expression option** is used for matching patterns in text. For a discussion of this advanced technique, see the box on page 655.

Phase 5: Take action

Finally, you're ready to set the search in motion by clicking one of the four action buttons in the Find and Replace window (see Figure 18-4):

- **Find Next** locates the next instance of the search term. If you're searching the current document, Dreamweaver highlights the matching text. If you're searching an entire Web site or a folder of pages, Dreamweaver opens the file *and* highlights the match. You can cycle through each instance of the search term by repeatedly clicking this button.

- **Find All** locates every instance of the search terms, all at once, and shows them to you in a list in the Search tab of the Results panel (Figure 18-6). The name and location of each file (if multiple files are searched) appear to the left, and the matched text appears to the right. Dreamweaver displays part of the sentence in which the matched word or words appear. The exact match is underlined with a squiggly red line, so that you can see the search in context and identify text you may *not* want to replace.

  Unlike the Find Next action, Find All doesn't automatically open any of the Web pages containing matches. Instead, to open a matched page, double-click its name in the results list. Only then does Dreamweaver open the Web page and highlight the match.

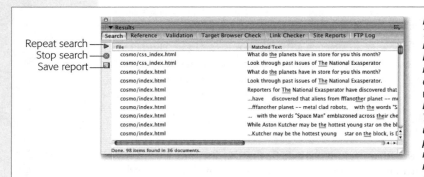

Repeat search
Stop search
Save report

Figure 18-6:
The green-arrow button reopens the Find and Replace window. Click the red Stop button to abort the current search (for example, when you inadvertently begin a search for "the"). You can also save a rather useless XML file that provides a report of the results of the find-and-replace command (remember the old adage: Just because you can doesn't mean you should).

- **Replace** locates the next instance of the search term *and* replaces it with the text in the Replace field, leaving the replaced text highlighted for your inspection.

  You can use this button in combination with Find Next to selectively replace text. First, click Find Next. Dreamweaver locates and highlights the next match. If you want to replace the text, click Replace. If not, click Find Next to search for the next match, and repeat the cycle. This cautious approach lets you supervise the replacement process and avoid making changes you didn't intend.

- **Replace All** is the ultimate power tool. It finds every instance of the search term and replaces it with the text entered in the Replace field. Coupled with the Find in Entire Local Site option, you can quickly make site-wide changes (and mistakes—so back up all your files before you Replace All!).

When you click this button, Dreamweaver warns that you can't undo this operation on any closed files. You can erase mistakes you make with the Find and Replace in *open* documents, by choosing Edit → Undo, but Dreamweaver *permanently* alters closed files that you search and replace. So be careful! (On the other hand, changes to open documents aren't permanent until you save those files.)

Tip: Before you take the plunge and click the "Replace All" button, it's a good precautionary step to click Find All first. This way you can really be sure that you're going to change exactly what you *want* to change.

If you use the Find All or Replace All commands, the Find and Replace window closes, and the results of the search appear in the Search tab (see Figure 18-6). You can reopen the Find and Replace window (with all of your previous search criteria still in place) by clicking the green arrow on the Search tab—called the Find and Replace button—but only if you haven't selected anything else—like text on a page, or even a file in the Files panel—first.

POWER USERS' CLINIC

Turbocharge Your Searches

If you want to find the phone number 555-123-5473, no problem; just type *555-123-5473* into the search field. But what if you wanted to find any and every phone number—555-987-0938, 555-102-8870, and so on—on a Web page or in a site?

In such a case, you need to use *regular expressions*, the geeky name for a delightfully flexible searching language, carried over from early UNIX days, consisting of wildcard characters that let you search for patterns of text instead of actual letters or numbers. Each phone number above follows a simple pattern: three numbers, a dash, three more numbers, another dash, and four more numbers.

To search for a pattern, you use a variety of symbols combined with regular text characters to tell Dreamweaver what to find. For example, in the world of regular expressions, \d stands for "any number." To find three numbers in a row, you could search for \d\d\d, which would find 555, 747, 007, and so on. There's even shorthand for this: \d{3}. The number between the braces ({}) indicates how many times in a row the preceding character must appear to match. To finish up the example of the phone numbers, you could use a regular expression like this: \d{3}-\d{3}-\d{4}. The \d{3} finds three numbers, while the hyphen (-) following it is just the hyphen in the phone number.

Here are some of the other symbols you'll encounter when using regular expressions:

- . (period) stands for any character, letter, number, space, and so on.

- \w stands for any letter or number.

- * (asterisk) represents the preceding character, zero or more times (and is always used after another character). This is best explained with an example: The regular expression colou*r, for instance, matches both colour and color—the * following the u indicates that the u is optional (it can appear zero times). This would also match colouuuuur (handy for those times when you've fallen asleep at the keyboard).

To see a complete list of the regular-expression characters Dreamweaver understands, launch the Dreamweaver online Help system (press F1) and search for the topic "Regular Expressions." A full-length discussion of regular expressions could—and does—fill a book of its own; check out *Mastering Regular Expressions* (O'Reilly) by Jeffrey E. F. Friedl or, for made-to-order regular expressions, check out *Regular Expression Recipes* (Apress) by Nathan Good.

For a complete example of using regular expressions in Dreamweaver see page 661.

Advanced Text Searches

If you want greater control over a text search, you can use the Find and Replace command's *advanced* text search option, which lets you confine a search to text either inside or outside a specific tag.

For example, when Dreamweaver creates a new blank document, it sets the page's *Title* property to *Untitled*. Unfortunately, if you forget to change it, a site can quickly fill up with untitled Web pages. A basic text search doesn't identify this problem, because it searches only the body of a page; titles appear in the head. And a source-code search for *Untitled* would turn up the word "untitled" *wherever* it appeared in the page, not just inside the <title> tag.

In cases like this, an advanced text search is your best choice. Simply set the Find and Replace command to search for *Untitled* whenever it appears within the <title> tag.

To use the advanced text search, use the same general routine as described on the previous pages. But before using one of the action buttons, you make a few additional setup changes to the dialog box.

Limiting the search by tag

Choose Text (Advanced) from the Search pop-up menu to make the expanded, new controls appear (see Figure 18-7).

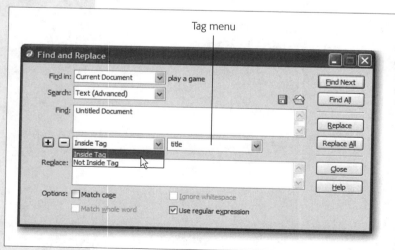

Tag menu

Figure 18-7:
Use an advanced text search to limit your search to text that appears within a particular HTML tag. Or, conversely, use it to search for text that doesn't appear in a particular tag.

Now, from the menu next to the + and - buttons, choose either Inside Tag or Not Inside Tag. For example, consider this line of code: "Stupid is as <strong>stupid</strong> does." The first instance of "stupid" isn't inside the <strong> tag, but the second one is.

Note: A more descriptive name for the first option would be *"Enclosed* By Tag"; Dreamweaver actually searches for text that's between *opening and closing* tags. In fact, an advanced text search using this option doesn't identify text that's literally inside a tag. For example, it won't find "aliens" in this line of code: <img src="ufo.jpg" alt="Aliens live among us.">, but it would find "aliens" in this one: <strong> Aliens live among us.</strong>. In the first example, *aliens* appears as part of the <img> tag, while in the second, *aliens* is enclosed by the opening and closing <strong> tags.

Once you've specified whether you're looking for text inside or outside tags, you can choose a specific HTML tag from the Tag menu identified in Figure 18-7.

The menu lists all HTML tags—not just those with both an opening and closing tag. So the image tag (<img>) still appears, even though Dreamweaver doesn't identify text inside it.

Tip: A great way to search for text in both the title and body of a Web page is to choose the Inside Tag option and then select HTM from the Tag menu. That way, you can search for any text that appears within the opening <html> and closing </html> of the page—which, since those tags start and end any Web document, is *all* text on a page. This trick is handy when you want to change text that might appear in the body *and* the title of a page (for example, a company name).

Limiting the search by attribute

To limit the search further, click the + button (see Figure 18-8); yet another new set of fields appears.

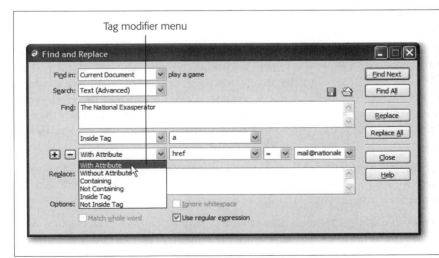

Tag modifier menu

Figure 18-8:
When you click the + button on the Find and Replace window, a new set of fields appears. Use these options to carefully hone your Find and Replace commands, and zero in on text that matches precise criteria.

Using the Tag Modifier menu—next to the + and - buttons (Figure 18-8)—you can choose from any of six options that break down into three groups:

- **With Attribute/Without Attribute.** To limit the search, you can specify that a tag must either have (With Attribute) or not have (Without Attribute) a specific property.

  For example, say the following line of code appears throughout a Web site:

  ```
  <p>For assistance, please email
  <a href="mailto:mail@nationalexasperator.com">
  The National Exasperator.</a></p>
  ```

  Now, for the sake of argument, say you need to change it to read "For assistance, please email Customer Service." A basic text find-and-replace would incorrectly change the words "The National Exasperator" to "Customer Service" *everywhere* on the site.

  However, an advanced text search using the With Attribute option would let you specifically target the text "The National Exasperator" wherever it appears inside an <a> tag whose *Href* attribute is set to *mailto:mail@nationalexasperator. com.* You could then just change that text to "Customer Service" while leaving all other instances of "National Exasperator" alone. (To learn about the different HTML tags and attributes, use Dreamweaver's built-in code reference; see page 353.)

  After you choose With Attribute, use the menu on the right to select *which* of the tag's properties you want to find. (Dreamweaver automatically lists properties that are appropriate for the tag you've specified.) For example, if you search inside a <table> tag, the menu lists such properties as *align, background, bgcolor,* and so on.

  Advance to the next pop-up menu to choose a type of comparison: = (equal to), != (not equal to), > (greater than), or < (less than). These options are useful only when the property's value is a numeric amount, such as the *Width* property of an image. In this way, you could locate all images that are wider than 100 pixels (width > 100). (This setting has no effect on values that are words, such as *center* in this example: <td align="center">.)

  Finally, type the value of the property in the last field. For instance, if you were searching for a black-colored background, the value would be #000000 (the hex value for black; see page 41 for more on working with colors).

  You can also click the menu and choose "[any value]"—a useful option when you want to find tags that have a certain property, but you're not interested in the property's value. For example, if you want to find all <table> tags with a background color (no matter whether the color's #336699, #000000, or #FFFFFF), choose the *Bgcolor* attribute and "[any value]."

- **Containing/Not Containing.** These options let you specify whether the tag contains, or does not contain, specific text or a particular tag.

When you choose this option, a different set of fields appears. Choose either Text or Specific Tag from the menu to the right, and then either enter some text or select a tag in the last field in the row.

For example, another solution to the problem above would be to search for the text "The National Exasperator" wherever it appears inside a <p> (paragraph) tag that *also contains* the text "please email."

- **Inside Tag/Not Inside Tag.** These last two choices are identical to those described on page 656. They let you specify whether the tag is inside or not inside a specific tag. Use these to limit a search, for example, to text that appears only within a <span> tag that's *inside* a Heading 1 (<h1>) tag.

If you like, you can add even more restrictions to your search, adding new rules by clicking the + button and repeating the setup just described. When you're really on a roll, it's even possible to add so many modifiers that the Find and Replace window actually grows past the bottom of your monitor. To remove a modifier, click the minus sign (-) button.

Advanced Tag Searches

If you find the number of options an advanced text search offers overwhelming, you haven't seen anything yet. Dreamweaver's tag search adds more choices to help you quickly search for, and modify, HTML tags. You can use a tag search to strip out unwanted HTML tags (for example, if you're migrating an old site to CSS, you could remove the <font> tag), transform one tag into another (you could turn old style *bold* [<b>] into the more widely accepted *strong* [<strong>] tag), and perform a host of other powerful actions.

In its basic outline, a tag search is much like the regular text search described on page 650. But this time, from the Search menu, you should choose Specific Tag.

Now a Tag menu appears next to the Search menu, and the dialog box expands to display a new set of fields (see Figure 18-9). Some of them are the same as the controls you see when performing an advanced text search (page 656), such as the Tag Modifier menu and the + button that lets you add additional restrictions to the search.

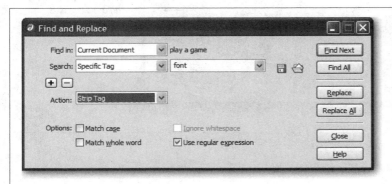

Figure 18-9:
It's a snap to remove tags when you use the Specific Tag option in Dreamweaver's Find and Replace command. This option is handy if you're replacing old-style text formatting with Cascading Style Sheets. Use it to strip out unwanted <font> tags, for example.

But a key difference here is the Actions menu (Figure 18-10), which lets you specify the action Dreamweaver will perform on tags that match the search criteria when you click Replace or Replace All (if you intend to search, but not replace, these options don't apply):

- **Replace Tag & Contents** replaces the tag, and anything enclosed by the tag (including other tags), with whatever you put into the With box to the right of this menu. You can either type or paste text or HTML here.

- **Replace Contents Only** replaces everything enclosed by the tag with text or HTML that you specify. The tag itself remains untouched.

Note: Depending on which tag you're searching for, you might not see all the actions listed here. For example, the <img> tag doesn't have both an opening and closing tag like the <p> tag, which surrounds text inside a paragraph, so you won't see any of the options such as "Replace Contents Only" that affect the content between an opening and closing tag.

- **Remove Tag and Contents** deletes the tag and *everything* inside.

- **Strip Tag** deletes the tag from the page, but leaves anything enclosed by the tag untouched. The outmoded <font> tag is a perfect candidate for this action.

- **Set Attribute** *adds* an attribute to the tag. For example, you could set the *Alt* property of an image this way (see the example in the next section).

- **Remove Attribute** removes an attribute from a tag. For example, you could remove the not-so-useful *Lowsrc* attribute from all image tags on your pages.

- **Add Before (After) Start (End) Tag.** The last four actions in the menu simply offer variations on the same theme. They each let you place content in a Web page just before or after the tag for which you're searching.

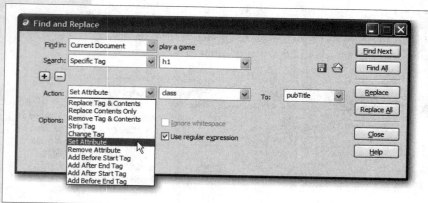

Figure 18-10:
Once Dreamweaver finds a specific tag, it can perform any of 11 different actions on the tag or its contents.

To understand how these actions work, remember that most HTML tags come in pairs. The paragraph tag, for example, has an opening tag (<p>) and a closing tag (</p>). Say you searched for a paragraph tag; you could add text or HTML *before* or *after* the start tag (<p>), or *before* or *after* the end tag (</p>). (For an example of this action at work, see the box "Convenient Copyright Notices" on page 662.)

A Powerful Example: Adding Alt Text Fast

You've just put the finishing touches on the last page of your brand-new, 1,000-page site. You sit back and smile—and then snap bolt upright when you notice you forgot to add an Alt description for the site's banner graphic (see page 128). This graphic, called *site_banner.gif*, appears on every single one of the 1,000 pages. With rising dread, you realize that you'll have to open each page, select the graphic, and add the *Alt* property by hand.

And then you remember Dreamweaver's advanced tag-based find-and-replace.

Here's what you do. Press Ctrl+F (⌘-F) to open the Find and Replace window. Set up the dialog box like this:

1. **From the "Find in" menu, choose Entire Current Local Site.**

   You want to fix *every* page on your site.

2. **From the Search pop-up menu, choose Specific Tag; from the pop-up menu to its right, choose "img."**

   You'll start by identifying every image (the <img> tag).

3. **On the next row, use the three pop-up menus to choose With Attribute, "src," and the equals sign (=).**

   This tells Dreamweaver to look for specific images—in this case, images with a *Src* attribute (the path that tells a Web browser where to find the image file on the Web server) with a specific value.

4. **Type** .**site_banner\.gif* **in the box next to the = sign.**

   For this exercise, assume the graphic file is stored in a folder called *images* located in the root folder of the site. The name *site_banner.gif* is the name of the image file. The .* is the magic, and it'll be explained in a moment (as will the backslash hanging out before the second period).

5. **Click the + button.**

   Another row of Tag Modifier menus appears.

6. **From the new row of menus, choose Without Attribute and "alt."**

   You've further limited Dreamweaver's search to only those images that don't already have the *Alt* attribute. (After all, why bother setting the *Alt* property on an image that already has it?)

7. **From the Action menu, choose Set Attribute; from the Tag menu, choose "alt."**

You've just told Dreamweaver what to do when you click the Replace or Replace All button. When Dreamweaver finds an <img> tag that matches the search criteria, it will then *add* an *Alt* property to that tag.

In this example, you might type *The National Exasperator* in the To field; you've just specified the Alt text for Dreamweaver to add to the image.

8. **Turn on "Use regular expressions."**

Regular expressions, described on page 655, let you search for specific patterns of characters and, in this case, help you accurately identify the banner graphic file everywhere it appears.

You know you're looking for the file *site_banner.gif*, wherever it appears in the site. Unfortunately, if you just type *site_banner.gif* as the value of the *Src* property of step 3, Dreamweaver can't succeed in its task. That's because the *Src* attribute, the part of the <img> tag that includes the name of the file, varies from page to page. Depending on where a page is relative to the graphic, the Src might be *site_banner.gif*, *images/site_banner.gif*, or even *../../../images/site_banner.gif*. What you need is a way to match every *Src* attribute that *ends* in *site_banner.gif*.

A simple regular expression, *.*site_banner\.gif*, does the trick. The period stands for *any* character (6, g, or even %, for example), while the * (asterisk) means "zero or more times." When you add these codes to the graphic name, *site_banner.gif*, you instruct Dreamweaver to find every *src* value that ends in *site_banner.gif*.

Note the backslash before the last period: *\.gif*. Since in the world of regular expressions, a period means "any character," simply using *site_banner.gif* would not only match *site_banner.gif*, but also *site_banner1gif*, *site_bannerZgif*, and so on—in other words, any character between *site_banner* and *gif*. The backslash means treat the next character literally; it's just a period with no special regular-expression power.

The dialog box should look like the one in Figure 18-11.

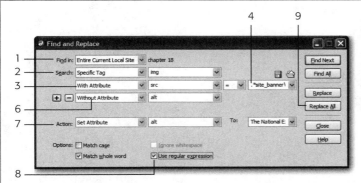

Figure 18-11:
The numbers shown here correspond to the steps in this fictional example, in which you want to add an <alt> tag— for the benefit of people who can't, or don't want to, see graphics in their browsers—to every occurrence of the banner logo.

9. **Click the Replace All button and sit back.**

In a matter of moments, Dreamweaver updates all 1,000 pages.

To test this out first, you might try a more cautious approach: Click the Find Next button to locate the first instance of the missing *Alt* property; verify that it's correct by looking in the Search box (see Figure 18-6); then click the Replace button to add the proper Alt value. Double-check the newly updated page to make sure everything worked as planned. You can continue updating pages one at a time this way, or, once you're sure it works correctly, press Replace All.

Customizing Dreamweaver

Whether you're a hard-core HTML jockey who prefers to be knee-deep in Code view, or a visually oriented, drag-and-drop type who never strays from the document window, Dreamweaver lets you work your way.

By now, you're probably already using the Favorites tab on the Insert bar to store your most frequently used objects in one place, as discussed on page 118. But don't stop there. Dreamweaver also gives you the power to add, change, and share keyboard shortcuts—a simple way to tailor the program to your needs. If that's not enough of an efficiency boost, you can add features that even Macromedia's engineers never imagined, from new Flash button designs to additional behaviors. Dreamweaver's design allows amateur and professional programmers alike to write new features and functions using HTML, JavaScript, and XML (Extensible Markup Language). There are hundreds of these extras, called *extensions*, for you to explore. Best of all, you can try many of them for free.

Keyboard Shortcuts

As you use Dreamweaver, you'll hit the same keyboard shortcuts and travel to the same palettes and menus time and again. Perhaps your site uses a lot of graphics and Flash movies, and you're constantly using the keyboard shortcuts to insert them. But you may find that, after the 1,000th time, Ctrl+Alt+F (⌘-Option-F) hurts your pinkie and uses too many keys to be efficient. On the other hand, the things you do all the time (inserting text fields into forms or adding rollover images, for instance) may not have shortcuts at all, so you're forced to go to a menu.

To speed up your work and save your tendons, Dreamweaver comes with a keyboard-shortcut editor that lets you define or redefine shortcuts for most of the program's commands.

Dreamweaver stores keyboard shortcuts in sets. It's easy to switch between them—a useful feat when you share your computer with someone who likes different keystrokes.

Four sets come with the program:

- **Macromedia Standard.** When you first fire up Dreamweaver, this is the set that's turned on. The latest versions of Macromedia products, including Fireworks and Flash, share these shortcuts, meaning that you can switch between Macromedia programs without missing a keystroke.

- **Dreamweaver MX 2004.** Some keyboard shortcuts have changed since Dreamweaver MX 2004—for example, Shift-F5 instead of Ctrl-F5 now opens the Tag Editor window. But the changes are so minor, it's not really necessary to use this set.

- **BBEdit.** If you're a Mac user with a code-editing past, you may have spent a lot of time learning shortcuts for Bare Bones Software's popular BBEdit. If so, choose this set.

- **HomeSite.** Likewise, if you're adept at the Windows HTML text editor HomeSite, you may want to use its keyboard shortcuts.

You can access the shortcut sets from the Keyboard Shortcuts window. Choose Edit → Keyboard Shortcuts. Be patient; the sets can take some time to load. Once the dialog box appears, you can switch sets by choosing a new one from the Current Set menu (see Figure 19-1).

Make Your Own Shortcut Set

What if you want a set that *combines* BBEdit shortcuts with your most-used Dreamweaver ones? Or, you're a radical individualist who wants to remap *every* command to the keys of your liking? You can easily create keyboard shortcut sets that fit the way you work. Dreamweaver doesn't let you alter any of the four standard sets, so if you want to create your own, the first step is to make a copy of an existing one.

To do so, choose Edit → Keyboard Shortcuts (on the Mac, it's Dreamweaver → Keyboard Shortcuts). In the Keyboard Shortcuts window, use the Current Set pop-up menu to choose the set you wish to copy, and then click the Duplicate Set button (see Figure 19-1). Dreamweaver asks you to name the new set; do so, and then click OK.

You can delete or rename any set you create—once you figure out that the button in the Shortcuts window with the cryptic icon is the Rename Set button (see Figure 19-1). The Trash Can button, of course, lets you delete a set.

Note: Dreamweaver lets you delete the four main keyboard shortcut sets. If you want one of them back, don't worry. The actual file isn't gone. You just need to edit a file called *mm_deleted_files.xml* in the Dreamweaver 8 → Configuration folder. Remove the line that lists the keyboard shortcut set you want to get back and save the file. Then quit and restart Dreamweaver. (Note that each account holder on Windows XP, 2000, and NT, and on Mac OS X, maintains a separate Configuration folder. See the box on page 677 for more.)

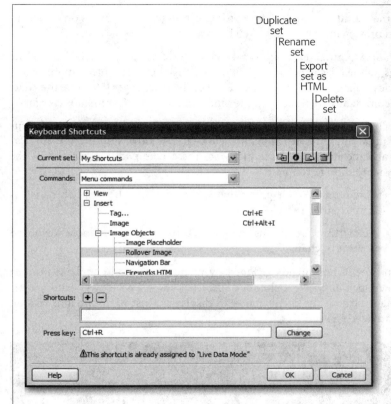

Duplicate
set
Rename
set
Export
set as
HTML
Delete
set

Figure 19-1:
The Keyboard Shortcuts window lets you select or duplicate a shortcut set, as well as add and remove keyboard shortcuts for every menu item in Dreamweaver. You can also create keyboard shortcuts for Snippets (see page 573). When you attempt to create a shortcut that another command's already using, Dreamweaver warns you. If you wish, you can ignore the warning and reassign the keys to the new command.

Changing Keyboard Shortcuts

Once you've created a new set, you can select any command and alter its shortcut. Start by choosing Edit → Keyboard Shortcuts (Dreamweaver → Keyboard Shortcuts) to open the Shortcuts window, if it's not already open. Then:

1. **From the Commands pop-up menu, choose the command type.**

   Dreamweaver organizes shortcuts into four (Macintosh) or six (Windows) primary categories. These categories don't always make sense: for example, Copy and Paste appear under the Code Editing category, even though you use them at least as frequently while editing a document in the visual Design view. Browse to see which commands have (or could have) keyboard shortcuts associated with them:

- **Menu Commands** are the commands in Dreamweaver's menus, such as Insert → Image.

- You might presumably use the **Code Editing** commands when editing HTML code. However, you could just as easily use them in Design view. They include Cut, Paste, and Move to Top of Page, to name a few.

- **Document Editing** commands are for selecting text and objects on a page, as well as previewing a page in a Web browser.

- **Site Panel Commands** (Windows only) are the commands available from the menus on the Files panel, such as Site → Change Link Sitewide, but only when the Files panel is fully expanded, as described on page 480. (On the Mac, these commands are listed with the others in the Menu Commands category.)

- **Site Window Commands** (Windows only) are an odd assortment of commands that apply to situations like closing a window, quitting the application, or canceling FTP. (On the Mac, these commands are listed in the Document Editing group.)

- **Snippets** are reusable code pieces that you select from the Snippets panel, as discussed in Chapter 16.

2. **In the list below the Commands menu, click the command whose keyboard shortcut you want to change.**

    You'll find menu commands grouped by menu name: commands in the File menu, like Open and Save, fall under File. Click the + (Windows) or flippy triangle (Mac) next to the menu name to display the list of commands hidden underneath (see Figure 19-1).

FREQUENTLY ASKED QUESTION

Sharing Shortcuts

How do I share my keyboard set with other people?

Dreamweaver stores your keyboard shortcuts as XML files— but in Dreamweaver 8, finding them can be tricky. These files are in different locations depending on your operating system. Each keyboard set lives in an XML file; the file's name ends with the extension .xml.

In Windows XP, 2000, or NT, you'll find the custom keyboard set on your main hard drive in Documents and Settings → [Your Name] → Application Data → Macromedia → Dreamweaver 8 → Configuration → Menus → Custom

Sets. In Mac OS X, these files are squirreled away in your Home folder → Library → Application Support → Macromedia → Dreamweaver 8 → Configuration → Menus → Custom Sets.

You can copy these files and place them in the Custom Sets folder on other computers. Once you've done so, Dreamweaver users on those machines can use the Keyboard Shortcuts window (Edit → Keyboard Shortcuts or, on the Mac, Dreamweaver → Keyboard Shortcuts) to select the new set, just as though it had been created in that copy of Dreamweaver.

If the command already has a keyboard shortcut, it appears in the right-hand column. If it doesn't have a shortcut, you see an empty space.

3. **Click inside the "Press key" field, and then press the new keystroke.**

Unless you're assigning the shortcut to an F-key or the Esc key, you must begin your shortcut with the Ctrl key (⌘-key). For example, the F8 key is a valid shortcut, but the letter R isn't. Press Ctrl+R (⌘-R) instead.

Note: Some keyboard shortcuts may already be in use by your operating system, so assigning them in Dreamweaver may have no effect. For example, in Windows XP, Ctrl+Esc opens the Start Menu, while in Mac OS 10.4 (Tiger), Dashboard uses the F12 key.

Of course, many commands already have shortcuts. If you choose a key combination that's in use, Dreamweaver tells you which command has dibs. You can pick a different key combination, or simply click the Change button to reassign the shortcut to your command.

4. **Click the Change button.**

Dreamweaver saves the new shortcut in your custom set.

Repeat from step 1 if you want to make other keystroke reassignments; when you're finished, click OK to close the dialog box.

What if a command you use often doesn't have a shortcut at all? It's no problem to create one. As a matter of fact, Dreamweaver lets you assign *two* keyboard shortcuts to every command—one for you, and one for your left-handed spouse, for example.

To give a command an additional shortcut (or its first):

1. **Choose the command.**

Follow the first two steps of the preceding instructions.

2. **Click the + button next to the word Shortcuts.**

The cursor automatically pops into the "Press key" field.

3. **Press the keys of your additional shortcut, and then click the Change button again.**

Repeat from step 1 if you want to make other keystroke reassignments; when you're finished, click OK.

Deleting shortcuts is just as easy. Simply click the command in the list, and then click the minus sign (-) button next to the word Shortcuts.

Create a Shortcut Cheat Sheet

Unless your brain is equipped with a 400-gig hard drive, you'll probably find it hard to remember all of Dreamweaver's keyboard shortcuts.

Fortunately, Dreamweaver offers a printable cheat sheet for your reference. At the top of the Shortcuts window, there's a handy Export Set as HTML button. (It's labeled with a cryptic icon; see Figure 19-1.) Click this button to name and save a simple HTML page that lists all of the commands and keyboard shortcuts for the currently selected set. Once you've saved the file, print it out or use it as an online reference—a great way to keep a record of your shortcuts for yourself or a team of Web page designers (see the box on page 668).

Dreamweaver Extensions

While keyboard shortcuts give you an easy way to access frequently used commands, they're not much help if the command you want doesn't exist. Suppose, for example, that you use the Validate Form behavior to make sure visitors to your site properly fill out your forms (see page 382). However, you wish that in addition to just checking for an email address or number, it could check for phone numbers, Zip codes, and Social Security numbers. What's a Web designer to do? You could dash off a quick email to *wish-dreamweaver@macromedia.com*, asking the bustling team of programmers to add the command to the next version. But you'd have to wait (and there's no guarantee that Macromedia would do it).

The legions of hard-core Dreamweaver fans have taken this feature wish-list issue into their own hands. As it turns out, amateur (and pro) programmers can enhance Dreamweaver relatively easily by writing new feature modules using the basic languages of the Web: HTML, JavaScript, and XML. (In fact, HTML forms, JavaScript programs, and XML documents constitute much of the program. The objects in the Insert bar, for example, are actually HTML pages stored within Dreamweaver's Configuration folder, and all of Dreamweaver's menus have actually been written as an XML file.)

Because of this "open architecture," you can add new functions and commands, called *extensions*, to Dreamweaver by downloading the work of all of those programmers. A Dreamweaver extension can take many forms and work in a variety of ways to change the way the program works. It can be an icon on the Insert bar, a behavior listed on the Behaviors panel, or a command in the Commands menu. It might even be an entirely new floating window, like the Property inspector, that you use to alter some aspect of your page.

Best of all, whereas programming ability may be required to *create* extensions, none at all is necessary to use them. You can download hundreds of extensions from the Web and install them on your computer for free. In addition, many sophisticated extensions, like those for creating e-commerce sites, are commercially available.

Note: Extensions have been around for many versions of Dreamweaver. Unfortunately, each version of Dreamweaver added a few kinks for extension developers, so not all extensions out there work with Dreamweaver 8. (Many extensions that were compatible with Dreamweaver MX 2004 *do* work with Dreamweaver 8.) Most extension developers list which versions of Dreamweaver their extensions work with, and you can also check for version compatibility on the Dreamweaver Exchange (see Figure 19-2).

Browse the Exchange

The largest collection of extensions waits at the Macromedia Exchange Web site. Here, you'll find hundreds of free and commercial extensions. Although some come from Macromedia itself, the vast majority are written by an army of talented Dreamweaver users.

Using the Exchange is a straightforward process:

1. **In your Web browser, go to *www.macromedia.com/exchange/dreamweaver/*.**

   You can also get there from within Dreamweaver by choosing Commands → Get More Commands.

2. **Log in (see Figure 19-2).**

   You can *browse* the site without logging in, but to *download* any of the extensions, you need to get a free Macromedia ID and sign in, using the Exchange Sign In form.

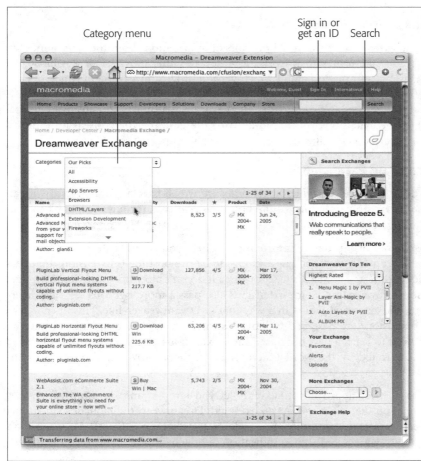

Category menu   Sign in or   Search
                 get an ID

Figure 19-2:
You can peruse the Dreamweaver Exchange freely, check out the offerings, and even buy commercial third-party extensions. However, if you want to download one of the free extensions, you must get a Macromedia ID and log into the site. Unfortunately, the marketing machine must be appeased, so you'll need to provide personal information and face a (fortunately optional) survey of your Web development habits.

3. **Browse the extensions.**

Once you've logged into the site, the home page highlights new and popular extensions. Overall, however, you may find the Exchange site a bit confusing and difficult to use. (For example, the entire site is in Flash, so Mac visitors can't even use their browser's Back button to travel back to earlier screens.)

Near the top of each page, you'll see a pop-up menu that lists different categories of extensions: Accessibility, DHTML/Layers, Navigation, Productivity, Flash media, Scripting, Tables, Text, eCommerce, and so on. When you choose a category, you go to a page listing all of the extensions within that category (see Figure 19-2).

If you're looking for a *particular* extension, the Search command is your best bet. Click the Search Exchanges button (see Figure 19-2). On the Search page, type the extension's name, or a few descriptive words, into the Search Extensions field; select Dreamweaver Exchange from the exchange menu (Macromedia has exchanges for several products, including Flash and ColdFusion); and then click Search.

4. **Click an extension's name to go to its Web page.**

On an extension's page, you'll find lots of information about the extension, such as a description of how it works, a button to either purchase or download the extension, information about which version of Dreamweaver and which operating system (Windows or Mac) it's compatible with, and buttons to add the extension to Favorites and Alerts lists. The Favorites option lets you create a personal list of the extensions you've found to be the best; the Alerts list feature means you'll receive an email whenever the extension is updated (see Figure 19-3).

Find a Good Extension

How do you figure out which extensions are worth checking out? First, you can find some recommendations of the best ones scattered through this book in special boxes labeled Extension Alert (see page 114 and page 378, for example).

The Exchange also provides information to help you separate the wheat from the chaff. Macromedia tests each new extension before posting it. Extensions that pass a basic set of tests—it installs OK, it works, it doesn't blow up your computer—get a Basic approval rating. Some extensions also pass a more rigorous test that determines if the extension works in a way that's "Dreamweaver-like." In other words, these extensions are designed to look, feel, and act like the program, so that you won't need to learn a new interface. These extensions get a Macromedia Approved rating, indicated by the word Macromedia in the approval section of an extension's details page.

Of course, these approval ratings only let you know if an extension works; they don't tell you that it's *useful*. As an extra aid, Dreamweaver aficionados (including you) can rate each extension on a scale of 1 (worst) to 5 (best). An extension's average rating gives you a good indication of how handy it is. When you're browsing the Exchange, look for the column labeled with a star to the right (see Figure 19-2). Click the header to organize the extensions from most to least recommended.

Other Extension Sources

Unfortunately, the glory days of totally free extensions are over. You can still find plenty of extensions offered free of charge, but many developers have realized they can't survive by giving away their work. The upside is that there are more excellent, polished, well-documented commercial extensions than ever—many even with customer support. Here are a few highlights:

- The **DMXZone** (*www.dmxzone.com*) has a large selection of free and commercial extensions, including a collection of extensions for PHP, ASP, and ASP.NET that let you add file-uploading features to your site.

- **Project Seven** (*www.projectseven.com/extensions/*) offers free extensions and several excellent commercial extensions for creating animated Dynamic HTML and CSS menus, scrolling text areas, CSS-based page layouts, and more.

Figure 19-3:
Each extension has its own page in Macromedia Exchange that provides information about the extension and its developer. A helpful voting mechanism (1–5 stars) lets you know what other people think of the extension.

- **Tom Muck** (*www.tom-muck.com/extensions/*) is a longtime extension programmer and has a good selection of extensions for dynamic, database-driven Web sites. He offers many free extensions in addition to his excellent commercial products.

- If PHP (see page 687) is your bag, then you'll find an impressive collection of extensions at **Felix One** (*www.felixone.it/extensions/dwextensionsen.asp*).

- And if Dreamweaver's PHP/MySQL tools don't cut the mustard, you can turn to the well-respected development company **InterAKT** (*www.interaktonline.com*). This company sells a powerful extension set that replaces Dreamweaver's PHP tools for creating dynamic Web sites. They've also increased their line of extensions with e-commerce offerings, menu systems, and more.

- **WebAssist** (*www.webassist.com*) is one of the newer extension developers, but with a former Dreamweaver product manager at the helm, they've quickly produced a wide variety of high quality extensions.

- **Trent Pastrana** (*www.fourlevel.com*) sells extensions for building photo galleries, whiz-bang DHTML effects (like menus that slide onto the page), or scrollers that move text up and down (or left and right) across a Web page.

You can find a much longer list of extension developers at *www.sawmac.com/resources/index.php?cat=4*.

Download and Install Extensions

Once you've found a great extension, download it to your computer. You can save the resulting downloaded file anywhere on your computer, but you might want to create a special folder. That way, if you ever need to reinstall Dreamweaver, you can quickly find and add your collection of extensions.

A downloaded extension file's name ends with .mxp, which stands for Macromedia Exchange Package. That's a special file format that works with the Extension Manager—the program, described next, that actually installs the extension into Dreamweaver.

Extension Manager

To add or remove a Dreamweaver extension, you use the Extension Manager, a standalone program that's integrated with Dreamweaver. It's designed to manage extensions for many Macromedia programs (not just Dreamweaver): you can install extensions, turn them on and off, and remove them. This feature can be quite handy if you also use Macromedia's Flash or Fireworks programs; you have a single access point for managing all your extensions.

You can launch the Extension Manager from within Dreamweaver by choosing Help → Manage Extensions or Commands → Manage Extensions (see Figure 19-4).

Install
extension

Delete
extension

Go to
Exchange Help

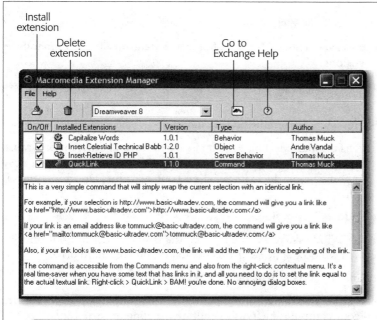

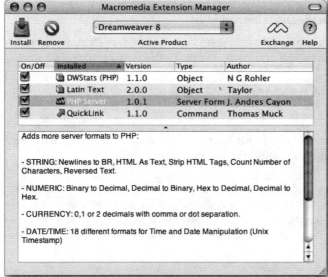

Figure 19-4:
The Extension Manager window lists each extension you've installed, along with its version number, type, and author. If you select an extension from the list, a description displays in the bottom half of the window. The Windows and Macintosh versions differ slightly. The Windows version (top) includes four buttons for easy access to common tasks; you can perform the same tasks on the Mac (bottom) from the File and Help menus.

To add an extension:

1. **Download an extension package (.mxp file) from the Exchange or another Web site.**

   See instructions on page 674.

2. **From Dreamweaver, choose Help → Manage Extensions (or Commands → Manage Extensions).**

   The Extension Manager launches. It lists all currently installed extensions (see Figure 19-4).

3. **Choose Dreamweaver 8 from the pop-up menu.**

   Since the Extension Manager handles extensions for several different programs, you need to specify which program you're using. Of course, if you don't have any other Macromedia products installed on your machine, Dreamweaver 8 is the only option.

4. **Choose File → Install Extension.**

   If you're using Windows, you can also click the Install Extension button. The Select Extension window appears, listing the folders on your hard drive.

5. **Navigate to and select the extension package (.mxp file) you wish to add.**

   A disclaimer appears with a lot of legal text. In brief, it holds Macromedia free of liability if your computer melts as a result of installing the extension.

6. **Click Accept in the Disclaimer window.**

   A message may appear that asks you to quit and restart Dreamweaver. If so, follow the directions.

Tip: You can also install an extension simply by double-clicking the .mxp file after you download it, which saves you a few steps.

To remove an extension, select it from the list and choose File → Remove Extension (or, in Windows, click the Trash Can button).

Tip: If you install a lot of extensions, Dreamweaver may take longer than usual to load; it needs to process every extension file as it opens. If you want to temporarily turn off an extension (as opposed to deleting it), open the Extension Manager and turn off the box next to the extension's name. To turn it back on again, simply turn on the box again. You may need to restart Dreamweaver to make the extension available again.

Make Your Own Extensions

The Exchange is a great resource for finding useful extensions. But what if you can't find the extension you need? Create your own.

Writing extensions requires in-depth knowledge of JavaScript and HTML. But when you create a command that lets you complete a weekly task in a fraction of the time it previously took, the effort may just be worth it. For more information, the Extensions menu available from the Help menu provides two electronic references that can help. The Macromedia Web site also offers help at the Dreamweaver support center: *www.macromedia.com/support/dreamweaver/extend.html*.

POWER USERS' CLINIC

The Secret Life of Extensions

Where do extensions go? The basic answer is: inside the Dreamweaver 8 → Configuration folder. (This folder's location varies by operating system, as described on page 668.)

But Dreamweaver actually supplies you with multiple configuration folders: the main folder located with the program itself, and account-specific folders for each user account on a computer. Windows and Mac let multiple users have an account on a single computer—one for you, your spouse, and pet ferret, for example. Of course, you may be the only one using your computer, so in that case there'd be just one additional configuration folder.

The main configuration folder is located, on a Windows machine, in *C:\Program Files\Macromedia\Dreamweaver 8* (assuming the C:\ drive is your main drive). On a Mac, you can find it here: *Mac Volume Name:Applications:Macromedia:Dreamweaver 8*. The individual account configuration folders are located in folders dedicated to each user. In Windows: *C:\Documents and Settings\User Name\Application Data\Macromedia\Dreamweaver 8*. On a Mac: *Volume Name:Users:User Name:Library:Application Support:Macromedia:Dreamweaver 8*.

Some changes you make to Dreamweaver are recorded in your personal configuration folder, such as when you add

an extension, delete a keyboard shortcut set (see page 669), or save a workspace layout (see page 26).

The main Configuration folder holds many of the files that control the look and operation of the program. For instance, the entire menu structure, including menu items and submenus, is described in a file called *menus.xml*. When Dreamweaver starts, it reads this file and uses the information inside it to draw the menus on the screen.

The Configuration folder holds many subfolders, each with a special purpose. For instance, the Objects folder contains files that tell Dreamweaver which icon buttons appear on the Insert bar and how each one works.

Depending on the type of extension you've downloaded—command, object, behavior, or whatever—the extension manager stores the file (or files) required by the extension in one or more folders inside the Configuration folder. Because all of the files inside the Configuration folder are crucial to the way Dreamweaver works, don't delete the folder or any of the files inside it. In fact, because the Extension Manager automatically makes any required changes to the Configuration folder, there's no reason for you to even look inside it.

(The only exception is when you want to copy your keyboard shortcut set to another computer. See page 668.)

Part Six:
Dynamic Dreamweaver

6

Getting Started with Dynamic Web Sites

So far in this book, you've learned to build and maintain Web sites using Dreamweaver's powerful design, coding, and site management tools. The pages you've created are straightforward HTML, which you can immediately preview in a Web browser to see a finished design. These kinds of pages are often called *static*, since they don't change once you've finished creating them. For many Web sites, especially ones where you carefully handcraft the design and content on a page-by-page basis, static Web pages are the way to go.

But imagine landing a contract to build an online catalog of 10,000 products. After the initial excitement disappears (along with your plans for that trip to Hawaii), you realize that even using Dreamweaver's Template tool (Chapter 17), building 10,000 pages is a lot of work!

Fortunately, Dreamweaver offers a better and faster way to deal with this problem. Its *dynamic Web site creation tools* let you take advantage of a variety of powerful techniques that would be difficult or impossible to use with plain HTML pages. With Dreamweaver, you can build pages that:

- Display listings of products or other items like your record collection, your company's staff directory, or your mother's library of prized recipes.

- Search through a database of information and display the results.

- Require login so you can hide particular areas from prying eyes.

- Collect and store information from visitors to your site.

- Personalize your visitors' experience: "Hello Dave, it's been a while since you've visited. Did you miss us?—Hal."

Visit Amazon.com, for example, and you'll find more books than you could read in a lifetime. In fact, you'll find more products—DVDs, CDs, and even outdoor lawn furniture—than could fit inside a Wal-Mart. In just an hour, you could browse through hundreds of products, each with its own Web page. Do you really think Amazon hired an army of Web developers to create each Web page for every product they sell? Not a chance.

Note: Luckily you aren't limited to *either* "static" *or* "dynamic" Web pages. Web sites frequently contain both—static pages for custom designs and handcrafted content, and dynamic pages for mass production of a thousand catalog pages.

Instead, when you search for a book on Amazon.com, your search triggers a computer program, running on what's called an application server, which searches a large database of products. When the program finds products that match what you're searching for, it merges that information with the HTML elements that make up the page (banner, navigation buttons, copyright notice, and so on). You see a new Web page that's been created on the spot—perhaps for the first time ever (Figure 20-1).

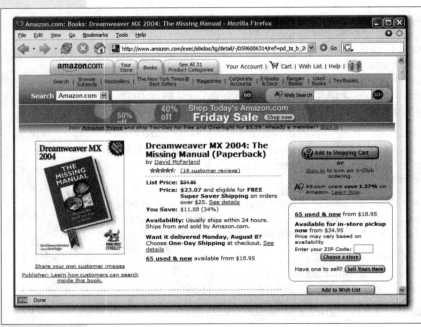

Figure 20-1:
An infinite number of monkeys couldn't create all the Web pages for all the products Amazon sells. A dynamic Web site where pages are created by accessing information from a database is often the best choice for sites that present lots of similar information.

Dynamic Web sites are usually the realm of professional programmers, but Dreamweaver can simplify routine tasks like viewing information from a database and adding, updating, and deleting data. Even if you don't have a programmer's bone in your body, this chapter and the next few give you the basics.

Pieces of the Puzzle

You may be thinking, "Yeah, that sounds fantastic, but so did that time-share in the Bahamas. What's the catch?"

The catch is that dynamic Web sites are more complex and require more technologies to get off the ground. Simple static Web sites require only the computer you use to build them and a Web server to dish them out. In fact, as you can see by previewing your site from your own computer with a Web browser, you don't even need a Web server to effectively view a static Web site.

Dynamic Web pages, by contrast, require more (see Figure 20-2). Not only is there a Web server that handles requests for Web pages, there are also two other types of servers: an *application server* and a *database server*.

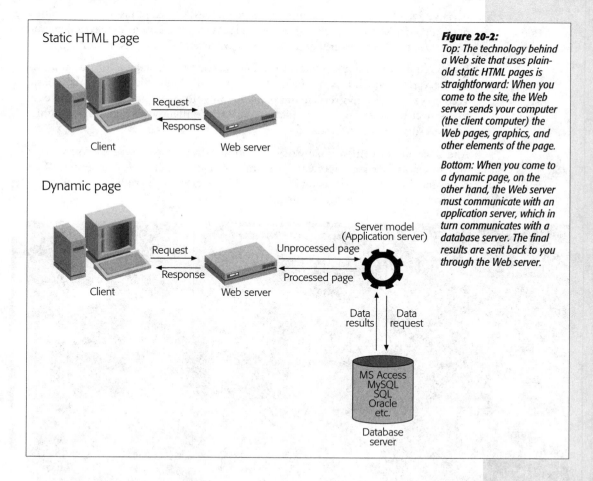

Figure 20-2:
Top: The technology behind a Web site that uses plain-old static HTML pages is straightforward: When you come to the site, the Web server sends your computer (the client computer) the Web pages, graphics, and other elements of the page.

Bottom: When you come to a dynamic page, on the other hand, the Web server must communicate with an application server, which in turn communicates with a database server. The final results are sent back to you through the Web server.

You'll still be using a lot of HTML (and CSS) to build a dynamic site—for example, to provide the layout, add banner graphics and navigation bars. But you'll augment this mix with some form of programming code. The application server processes this code and sends a complete HTML page to the Web server, which, in turn, sends that on to the visitor. In many cases, the programming code requires the application server to retrieve information from a database and then merge it with the HTML of a page.

Note: In this context, a *server* is software that dishes out particular types of information—Web pages, database queries, or the output of a program. It doesn't necessarily mean a separate computer; you can (and frequently do) have Web, database, and application servers all running happily together on a single machine.

Because dynamic Web sites require more technology, you can't just open a dynamic page in your Web browser as you can a regular Web page. You must view a dynamic page through a Web server that has an appropriate application server running.

It also requires setting up a database and connecting that database to your application server. Although this can be quite complex, it's not difficult to set up a basic Web server, application server, and database on your own computer. It's also easy to connect to other computers that are already configured to serve up dynamic, database-driven Web pages.

And once you or your company's system administrator have set up the Web server and other assorted components, Dreamweaver can easily create complex Web pages that access databases and let you build powerful Web applications, all without ever learning any programming.

FREQUENTLY ASKED QUESTION

The Dynamic Duo

How does a dynamic Web site differ from dynamic HTML?

Dynamic is a word that's thrown around a lot in Web circles, and it has a variety of uses.

For starters, *dynamic* sometimes refers to the power of JavaScript. For example, the Show Pop-Up Menu behavior discussed on page 412 uses a combination of JavaScript and CSS to make menus appear and disappear. The result is often called "Dynamic HTML," because the elements on the page *change*.

However, in this section of the book, *dynamic* refers to any Web page that's processed by an application server—pages that undergo some form of transformation on the

Web server's side of the Internet, like connecting to a database or collecting information from a form.

What's important to remember is that JavaScript, used for dynamic HTML and Dreamweaver Behaviors, is a *client-side* programming language. It runs in someone's Web browser and is limited to only a handful of actions, like mouse rollovers or any of Dreamweaver's Behaviors (Chapter 11).

Dynamic Web sites, on the other hand, use *server-side* programs—those that run on an application server, out there on the Web somewhere. The visitors to your site never see the code, and their computers never have to run the program. They merely enjoy the results of the application server's hard work: a finished HTML page.

Even so, there are literally hundreds of combinations of Web, application, and database servers, and Dreamweaver doesn't work with all of them. However, it is capable of working with five of the most popular and powerful combinations, using seven different programming languages!

Note: The term *Web application* refers to Web pages that work together to complete a task. For example, code that builds pages that let visitors do things like search a database of products, view individual product pages, or add products to a shopping cart would be considered a Web application.

Understanding Server Models

In Dreamweaver lingo, the different application servers combine with a programming language to create a *server model*. Dreamweaver recognizes several server models, including ASP and ASP.NET (pronounced "a-s-p" and "a-s-p dot net"), ColdFusion, PHP, and JSP. Each server model has its own set of unique requirements and its own methods of performing identical tasks.

Each server model also works with one or more programming languages. For example, you can create an ASP page using either VBScript or JScript. In some cases, the server model understands only a single programming language: JSP pages, for instance, use the Java programming language, while PHP can refer both to a programming language named PHP *and* to the application server. Likewise, CFML, or ColdFusion Markup Language, is a programming language, and Cold-Fusion server is an application server. Essentially, an application server processes programming code and carries out various actions, like talking to a database or spitting out a Web page.

Which server model you use depends on which resources you have available: which type of Web server hosts your site, the operating system it uses, and which application server is available. For example, if you're hosting on Linux or Unix, you'll most likely end up using PHP; if you're hosting on Windows NT or 2000, meanwhile, you've already got access to ASP and possibly ASP.NET. It all comes down to what you have on your computer, what your company uses, or (if you're using a Web hosting service) what the host computer understands. Here's a brief description of each.

ASP

ASP (Active Server Pages) is one of the most common ways to start building database-driven Web sites. This Microsoft technology is well established, so you'll find numerous resources (for example, books and Web sites) to help you along. In addition, if you're working on Windows 2000 or XP Professional, you already have the software you need to get started: Internet Information Server (IIS).

Note: Windows XP Home Edition can't run IIS. Microsoft, of course, recommends upgrading to Windows XP Professional (ka-*ching!*).

IIS is a Web server that has a built-in application server—the part that understands ASP code. In fact, it understands two different programming languages: VBScript and server-side JavaScript, both of which Dreamweaver speaks fluently. (Although you don't need to know either of these programming languages to get started—just pick one and let Dreamweaver take care of the rest—you'll find many more resources for using VBScript with ASP pages. So if you plan to expand your knowledge of ASP beyond what Dreamweaver can do, you might want to use VBScript.)

If you don't have IIS software already set up on your computer, you'll find it on the installation CDs that come with Windows 2000 and Windows XP Professional.

ASP can work with a variety of databases. For small projects, you can use Microsoft Access (the database program that comes with some versions of Microsoft Office), since it's fairly easy to use. For more demanding projects where lots of data needs to be stored and many users will access it, Microsoft's SQL Server's a better choice.

.NET

.NET is a newer Microsoft server technology. It's actually an entire suite of technologies intended to integrate many activities over the Internet.

ASP.NET is more advanced and more powerful than ASP, but also more difficult to learn. It hasn't taken off quite as rapidly as Microsoft expected, so you'll find fewer teaching resources available to get started. ASP.NET can be programmed in numerous languages, including Microsoft's VB.NET, C# (pronounced "see sharp"), and JScript.NET, as well as more than 20 other languages. Dreamweaver recognizes only the C# and VB languages.

Like regular ASP, ASP.NET runs in conjunction with Microsoft's IIS Web server. You need to be running Windows 2000 or Windows XP Professional, and have IIS installed. You also need to install the *.NET Framework*, downloadable from *www. asp.net*.

Like ASP, ASP.NET works with many different databases.

ColdFusion

ColdFusion is a server application from Macromedia (the maker of Dreamweaver) that's programmed using CFML (ColdFusion Markup Language). ColdFusion works in conjunction with several different Web servers, including IIS and Apache, and uses its own programming language, which resembles HTML. For this reason, some Web designers find it easier to learn than other programming languages.

The downside is that this application isn't free. You *can* download a developer's edition—a free version that runs on your computer—so you can build and test ColdFusion Web pages. But if you want to host the Web site on the Internet, you have to either buy the ColdFusion Server package (which isn't cheap) or find a Web hosting company that offers ColdFusion hosting. Fortunately, in recent years, more and more Web hosting companies have started offering ColdFusion as an option, at rates that are close to or match regular hosting plans.

The Developer Edition of ColdFusion comes with the Macromedia Studio package and is available for download at *www.macromedia.com/downloads/*.

Like ASP and ASP.NET, ColdFusion works with many different databases.

JSP

JSP (Java Server Pages) is based on Sun's popular Java programming language. It requires a Java application server, like Macromedia's JRun server.

This approach is not for the faint of heart, however, since setting up a Java Server and connecting it to a database can be tricky. Java is one of the more difficult languages to learn, too. If you don't have a knowledgeable guide, you're better off starting with a simpler technology like ASP or PHP.

A widely used version of JSP is Tomcat, available at *http://jakarta.apache.org/*. It's open source (that is, polished by a worldwide population of volunteer programmers), free, and it works with the Apache Web server and many different databases.

PHP

PHP (PHP Hypertext Preprocessor) is a programming language that was created specifically for building dynamic Web pages. The PHP interpreter—that's the application server—works in conjunction with a variety of Web servers including IIS, but was initially created for the Apache Web server. Like Apache itself, it's available as a free download for Windows, Mac OS X, or any flavor of Unix or Linux. Download it from *www.php.net*.

While PHP can work with a variety of different database servers, Dreamweaver only understands MySQL—another free product available at *www.mysql.com*.

Note: PHP and MySQL are often coupled with Apache, the most popular Web server in the world. You can get this free Web server at *www.apache.org*. But to make installation of all of these technologies easier, XAMPP (*www.apachefriends.org/en/xampp.html*) provides a program for Windows, Mac and Linux that installs all of this software on your computer. This way, you can easily set up a testing environment on your desktop computer, so you can build PHP and MySQL-driven Web sites.

Picking a Server Model

With so many choices, you're probably wondering which server model to choose. If you've never built a dynamic Web site before, are on Windows, and want to be operational as quickly as possible, your best bet is to start with ASP, using a Microsoft Access database. You can create a database using Access (a relatively inexpensive program) and take advantage of IIS to serve ASP pages.

In fact, since this is the easiest method, this book's tutorials will concentrate on building ASP pages. Once you get the hang of Dreamweaver's dynamic Web-building tools, you can always try any of the other server models to build your sites. (However, switching a single site from one server model to another is difficult and not recommended.)

Note: This section's tutorials are also available for the PHP/MySQL server model; you can find them at *www.sawmac.com/dw8/*.

However, when you're building a real-world Web site, this decision may be out of your hands. You may be working for a company that's already using ColdFusion for its Web site. Or, if you've already got a Web site up and running but want to add some database-driven content, you have to use what's installed on that server. For instance, if your site is currently hosted at a Web hosting company, you should contact them to find out which operating system, Web server, and databases it uses. If they're Windows-based, odds are that they use IIS, meaning that you can use ASP and either Access or SQL Server databases. On the other hand, if they're a Unix operation, you'll most likely find the Apache Web server, PHP, and MySQL database.

Fortunately, the tools Dreamweaver provides for the different server models are largely the same. Essentially, you build dynamic Web pages using the same techniques you've learned in the earlier sections of this book. For the heavy lifting (for example, retrieving data from a database or password protecting a Web page), you'll turn to Dreamweaver's menu-driven database tools to add the programming code necessary to make an application server do all the server-side magic needed to work with databases and generate dynamic Web pages. Once you learn Dreamweaver, you'll be able to build pages for any of the server models it works with.

FOR MACS ONLY

Mac OS X and PHP

When it comes to dynamic Web site production, Mac folks have often had to rely on others for help, because ASP, ASP.NET, and ColdFusion don't run on the Mac operating system. But since OS X is based on Unix, it can run many Unix-based programs, including the Apache Web Server, the PHP application server, and the MySQL database. In fact, Apache and PHP come supplied with Mac OS X; you can download the MySQL server for free from *www.mysql.com/downloads/mysql-4.0.html*.

If the very thought of Unix makes you squeamish, you can opt for an easier way to get up and running: XAMPP is a complete package for installing Apache, MySQL, PHP and a bunch of other cool stuff (see *www.apachefriends.org/en/xampp.html*). As of this writing, the Mac version's still in beta, so it may have a few hiccups.

You'll also find helpful instructions for setting up MySQL, PHP and Apache for Mac at the following sites:

- *www.macromedia.com/devnet/mx/dreamweaver/articles/php_macintosh.html*

- *www.entropy.ch/software/macosx/*

- *www.phpmac.com*

Dynamic Web Sites: The Setup

Now that your head is spinning, and you're considering some noble career alternative like farmer, firefighter, or carpenter, it's time to set up Dreamweaver to work with an application server and database.

You can go about it in several different ways. One involves using what Dreamweaver calls a *testing server*. Remember how you can create a Web site on your own computer (the *local site*) before posting it online for all to see (the *remote site*)? Here, the concept is similar. When building Web applications, it's again a good idea to keep all the "work in progress" pages on your own computer. After all, you don't want to fill up an active online database with test data, or put half-finished product pages on the Internet. But because dynamic Web sites require an application server and database, it's a good idea to create a *testing server* for storing and previewing dynamic pages in progress: a real Web server, application server, and database running on your own computer.

Then, when you've finished the site, you can transfer the pages to the remote site using Dreamweaver's built-in FTP feature (see page 542). If you're working in a group setting with other Web developers, the testing server can be set up on a machine that's part of your group's local network. Each developer can then connect to the testing server and retrieve files to work on. (Using Dreamweaver's Check-In/Check-Out feature [see page 551] is a good idea when you're working with a group of people on the same site.)

Note: You can always use your remote site as a testing server, as long as it has one of the application servers and databases that Dreamweaver works with. While this is an easy way to get started, you must contact your Web host to see what application server it uses and whether it can handle databases. In addition, you should have a fast Internet connection to the server. Otherwise, testing your dynamic pages may just test your patience.

Finally, whenever you work on dynamic files directly on a live Web server, be aware that mistakes you make along the way may affect a database that's used by *other* dynamic pages. For example, if, while hurriedly trying to complete your Web site, you accidentally create a page that deletes records from your database, important information may no longer be available on your Web site. So whenever possible, the testing server should be separate from the server where the finished and perfected site resides.

In the next four chapters, you'll be building a dynamic Web site using ASP and an Access database. The concepts you learn will work for all of the other server models as well, though some of the details may be different. Significant differences among various server models will be mentioned where applicable.

Setting Up a Testing Server

You can browse static HTML files on your computer without any special software. But for dynamic data, you need a Web server and database server.

If you're using Windows 2000 or Windows XP Professional, you must install IIS on your PC. To do so, insert your Windows 2000 or Windows XP Setup CD. If the setup program doesn't start automatically, browse to the CD and then double-click *setup.exe*.

After rebooting, open a Web browser and type *http://localhost/* into the Address bar. You see the default page for the Web server—a generic IIS welcome page. Voilà! A functioning Web server. But where are those Web pages kept? The root folder for your new Web server is *C:\Inetpub\wwwroot* on your PC.

If you're on a Mac, you must connect, via a network, to a Windows machine that has been set up as described above. You can use the Mac's built-in file-sharing command (Go → Connect to Server) to do so. (Alternatively, you can follow along with the PHP/MySQL tutorial online at *www.sawmac.com/dw8/*.)

Setting Up Dreamweaver

To learn Dreamweaver's dynamic features, you'll be building a small Web application for the *National Exasperator* (see Figure 20-3). In fact, you'll turn the site's online store into dynamic Web pages that retrieve information from a database and merge it with already-created HTML code.

Before you begin building the page, download the *tutorial* files. As always, you can find them at *www.sawmac.com/dw8/*; click the Tutorials link to go to the tutorials page. Then click the appropriate link under the "Chapters 20-24: Dynamic Dreamweaver Tutorials" heading.

When the files have downloaded and decompressed, you should have a folder named DWDynamic on your computer, containing a folder called *nationalEx_root* (the root folder for this Web site) and a file called *nationalEx.mdb* (the Access database containing the *National Exasperator's* online store data). If you're having trouble, the Web site offers detailed instructions for downloading the files you'll be using with this tutorial.

Note: Microsoft Access doesn't actually have to be installed on your computer for this procedure to work. Windows is clever enough to read, understand, edit, and save an Access file without the database program itself.

To begin, move the *nationalEx_root* folder into the newly installed Web server's root folder. If you followed the directions above, the root folder should be located at *C:\Inetpub\wwwroot*. (If your Windows computer's main drive is not the C:\ drive, the root folder might be located on another drive—D:\, for instance.) Place *nationalEx_root* inside the *wwwroot* folder. To make sure you've set this up right, open a Web browser and type *http://localhost/nationalEx_root/index.asp* in the Address bar. If a Web page appears, your Web server is set up correctly.

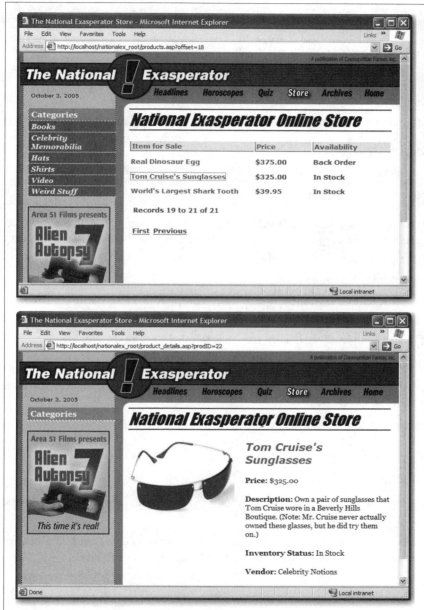

Figure 20-3:
Whenever you need to display lots of similar information, dynamic Web pages may be the answer. Dynamic pages at the National Exasperator online store list many different products. Because all the product information is stored in a database, the dynamic pages can display a list of products (top) and then individual product pages (bottom) by using the power of Dreamweaver's dynamic Web page building tools.

Note: Unless you've changed the original setup of the Web server, you'll notice that if you just enter *http://localhost/nationalEx_root* into a Web browser, you don't see a Web page. That's because, without specifying *index.asp*, the Web server doesn't know which page to display. If you'd like to make *index.asp* a default page (see page 472), you can do so by following these steps:

1. Choose Start → Control Panels to open the Windows control panel.

2. Double-click the Administrative Tools icon. This action opens a window displaying different tools used to make your computer run.

3. Double-click the Internet Information Services icon. This action opens a control panel for managing IIS.

4. Click the + sign next to the local computer icon to display two options—Web Sites and Default SMTP Virtual Server.

5. Right-click on the Web Sites folder, and select Properties from the menu.

6. Click the documents tab and click the Add button. The window that appears lets you add another default page name.

7. Type *index.asp* and press the OK button. Click the OK button again, and you get a window, cryptically named "Inheritance Overrides." Just click the Select All button, and then click the OK button. Doing so applies the changes you made to all of the folders in the site.

The first step in working on this dynamic Web application is to define a new site. The process of defining a dynamic site, as outlined below, is slightly different than for static sites, but not any harder:

1. **Choose Site → New Site.**

   The Site Definition window opens. Use Dreamweaver's Site Wizard to help you set up this new site.

2. **If it isn't already selected, click the Basic tab at the top of the window.**

   The first step is to give this new site a name.

3. **Type *Exasperator Store* in the first box and *http://www.nationalExasperator. com* in the second box.**

   You've just told Dreamweaver the name you want to use while working on this site, and the URL of the Web site. In a real-world scenario, you'd type the address of your Web site.

4. **Click Next.**

   The next screen lets you choose whether you're building a static or dynamic Web site.

5. **Select "Yes, I want to use a server technology," and then choose ASP VBScript from the pop-up menu (see Figure 20-4). Click Next to proceed.**

In the next step, you'll tell Dreamweaver where your local files are and where you intend to put the files for the testing server.

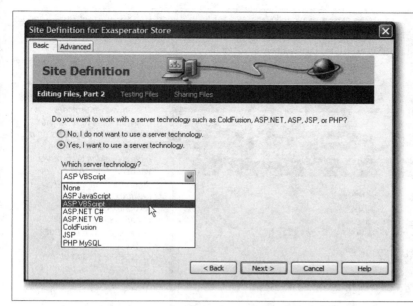

Figure 20-4:
When building a dynamic site, you must choose one of seven different server models. There are actually only five different application servers, but since Dreamweaver lets you use two different languages for both ASP and ASP.NET, there are two server models for each of those application servers.

6. **Select "Edit and test locally." (See Figure 20-5.)**

Dreamweaver provides three ways to work with dynamic Web page files and a testing server.

"Edit and test locally" is a good choice when you've set up a Web and application server on your computer (as you've done in this tutorial). Essentially, this means that you're working on a Web site located on a functioning Web server. In this way, you preview the pages running on a real Web server, so you can immediately test out all the nifty dynamic stuff.

Use the other two options when the testing server is located on another computer. This may be a computer on your local network or a full-fledged Web server running on the Internet that you connect to using FTP.

"Edit locally, then upload to remote testing server" is a good option when you can't run a testing server on your computer—for example, if you're building ASP pages but you're on a Mac (see Figure 20-5).

You should use the last option when the testing server is on another computer, but you're the only developer working on the files. Since the files are available on your local network, anyone in your company or office who has access to the computer with the testing server can also edit those files. Your Web pages can end up in an unrecoverable mess if you and someone else are simultaneously editing and saving the exact same file.

Note: If you're a Mac person who's following along with this tutorial, and you've set up a Windows machine to act as a testing server, choose "Edit directly on remote testing server using local network." Your Mac must be networked to the Windows server for this to work.

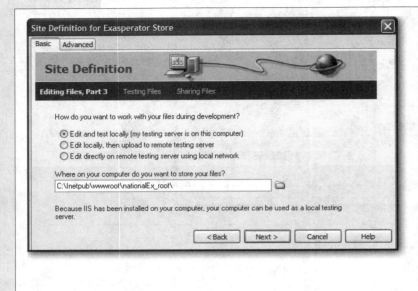

Figure 20-5:
Dreamweaver provides different ways to work with dynamic Web page files on a testing server. If you don't have a working Web server on your computer, but do have an account with a Web hosting company that recognizes one of Dreamweaver's server models, you can use that server to test your files. Choose the second option: "Edit locally, then upload to remote testing server." This method is a bit laborious—you edit the pages on your computer; then, when you test them (a simple F12 [⌘ F12] to see if they'll work), Dreamweaver connects to your Web server, uploads the file, launches your Web browser, and loads the page from your Web site. But it's one way to get started building dynamic Web sites.

The next step involves telling Dreamweaver where to find the files for the Web site.

7. **Click the folder at the right side of the middle of the window; navigate to and select the *nationalEx_root* folder on the Web server. Click Next.**

The *nationalEx_root* folder is probably at *C:\Inetpub\wwwroot\nationalEx_root*. You've nearly completed the setup.

8. **Type the URL of the test server in the box, and then click Test.**

Dreamweaver may have already filled in this box. If the test server's running on your computer, the URL begins with *http://localhost/* and ends with the folder that contains the Web pages. In this case, the URL is probably *http://localhost/nationalEx_root/*.

If you get an error message when you click Test, you've probably entered the wrong URL. You can make this mistake when the folder following *localhost* in the URL is not actually on the Web server.

9. **Click Next.**

You may get a warning box squawking about how the URL doesn't match the testing server. This just means that in step 3 previously, you didn't specify any folder, but in step 7 you said the site was in a folder named *nationalEx_root*. This means site-root-relative links (see page 105) won't work. In a real-world case, you'd probably have your site's files in *C:\inetpub\wwwroot*—the real root folder of your local Web server—so you wouldn't run into this error. But since this is a made-up example, and you're using document-relative links (see page 104), you're safe. So click OK to close the warning box.

10. **Click No, and then click Next one more time.**

If you were planning to move this site onto a Web server connected to the Internet, you would select Yes at this stage and provide all of the information needed to move your site files to the Internet as described in Chapter 15. But since this tutorial is just an exercise, you won't be putting it up on a live Web server.

11. **Click Done.**

Dreamweaver has successfully set up your site. You're now ready to learn about databases and connect Dreamweaver to the *National Exasperator* online store database. (You may encounter the same warning from step 9; just click OK to dismiss it.)

Databases: A Quick Introduction

Simply put, databases store information. You encounter them every day in one way or another, whether charging a dinner on a credit card or calling Moviefone to get local movie listings.

A database is like an electronic filing cabinet that stores related information. At home, you might have a filing cabinet to store the bits and pieces of your life. For instance, you might have a filing folder labeled Insurance, in which you keep information about the various insurance policies you carry. Other folders might contain information on phone bills, car service records, and so on.

Tables and Records

Databases have an electronic equivalent to filing folders: tables. A *table* is a container for information about a set of similar items. For example, in the *Exasperator's* online store database, a table stores information on all of the products for sale on the site.

The Products table tracks certain information—the name of the product for sale, its price, a short description, and a few other items. Each piece of information, like price, is stored in a column. All the information for each product (all the columns taken together, in other words) makes up a single *record*, which is stored in a row (see Figure 20-6).

Column							
prodID	prodName	prodPrice	prodDesc	vendorID	categoryID	imagePath	
1	Alien Autopsy VII Video	29.95	The final film ...	1	1	images/alien.jpg	
2	Big Foot T-Shirt	20.00	Bigfoot Lives!!!	5	5	images/foot.jpg	
3	Tom Cruise's Sunglasses	375.00	Own a pair of ...	2	3	images/sg.jpg	
4	My Son, The Oyster	4.50	A touching story.	2	2	images/book.jpg	

Row ——

Figure 20-6:
This diagram shows the structure of the Products table, in which four records are stored. Each row in a table represents a single record or item, while each piece of information for a record is stored in a single field, or cell.

If you were designing a database, you'd try to model a table on some real-world item you needed to track. If your database was used for generating invoices for your business, you might have a table called Invoices in which you'd store information such as the invoice number, date, and so on. Since your customers are another source of data that needs tracking, you'd also create a table called Customers to store the information about them.

Tip: If you're designing a database to track a business process that you already track on paper, a good place to start is with the forms you use. For example, if your company uses a personnel form for collecting information on each employee in the business, you've got a ready-made table. Each box on the form is the equivalent to a category column in a table.

In addition to the Products table, the *National Exasperator* also tracks the vendors who manufactured the products. (After all, after they run out of inventory, the online store staff will need to order more products from their vendors.) Because a product and a vendor are really two different things, the database has a *second* table, called Vendors, that lists all the companies that make the products for sale on the Web site.

Warning: Some databases are extremely picky about the names you give your tables and database columns (also called fields). For example, you can't have a database column named Date in an Access database.

You might think, "Hey, let's just put all that information into the first table." After all, you could consider the vendor's information as part of the information for each product. While it seems like this might simplify things (because you'd have one table instead of two), it can actually create a lot of problems.

Imagine this scenario: The *National Exasperator* begins selling a hot new item, *Alien Autopsy VII*, produced by Area 51 Films. All the product information, including the name and price of the film, as well as the phone number and mailing address for Area 51 Films, are stored in a single table row. Next month, Area 51 Films releases another film. But, in the meantime, having to stay one step ahead of certain government agencies, Area 51 has changed its phone number and moved to another state. So when someone at the *National Exasperator* adds the new film to the Products database, she adds the new phone number and address as part of the new film's record.

Now the database contains *two* sets of contact information for Area 51 Films—one for each film. Not only does this redundant data take up extra space, but the contact information in one record is now wrong.

You could run into an even worse problem when deleting a record. Suppose that the online store decides to discontinue the two videos from Area 51 Films. If an *Exasperator* staffer removes those two records from the database, she also deletes any contact information for Area 51 Films. If the *Exasperator* staff ever decide to stock up on videos again, they have no way of contacting the vendor.

Now you can see why it's prudent to keep separate classes of information in different tables. With two tables, when Area 51 Films moves, you have to update only the information in the Vendors table, without touching the Products table at all. This way, if the staff deletes a product, they'll still have a way of contacting the vendor to learn about new products.

You may be wondering, with a setup like this, how to tell which vendor makes which product. All you have are two distinct tables—one with just product information and one with just vendor information. How do you make the connection?

Note: For a great book on database design, check out *Database Design for Mere Mortals* (Addison-Wesley Professional) by Michael J. Hernandez.

Relational Databases

To connect information between tables, you create a *relationship* between them. In fact, databases that use multiple related tables are called *relational databases*.

The most common way to connect tables is by using what's called a *primary key*—a serial number or some other unique identifying flag for each record in the table. In the case of the *Exasperator* database, the Products table includes a field named *prodID*, the product's ID (see Figure 20-7). Whenever a product is added to the database, it's assigned a new number. If you're building a database that contains a table about employees, for example, you might use an employee's Social Security number as a primary key.

The Vendors table has a primary key named, not so creatively, *vendorID*. This key, too, is generated automatically whenever a new vendor is added to the database.

To join these two tables, you'd add another column called vendorID to the Products table (see Figure 20-7). Instead of storing *all* the contact information for a

---

vendor within the Products table, you simply store the vendor's ID number. To find out which vendor makes which product, you can look up the product in the Products table, find the vendor's ID number in the vendorID column, and use *that* information to look up the vendor in the Vendors table.

While this hopscotch approach of accessing database tables is a bit confusing at first, it has many benefits. Not only does it prevent the kinds of errors mentioned earlier, it also simplifies the process of adding a new product from a vendor. For example, when Area 51 Films adds yet a third title to their video collection, a store staff person determines if any of Area 51 Films' info has changed (by checking it against the Vendors table). If not, she simply adds the information for the new product and leaves the vendor's contact info untouched. Thus, relational databases not only prevent errors, they also make data entry faster.

Databases, of course, can be much more complicated than this simple example. It can take many tables to accurately hold the data needed to run a complex e-commerce site such as Amazon.com. In some cases, you may already be working with a previously created database, so you won't have to worry about creating one or even learning more than what's described above. For the tutorials in this section of the book, you'll use the already created *National Exasperator* Database.

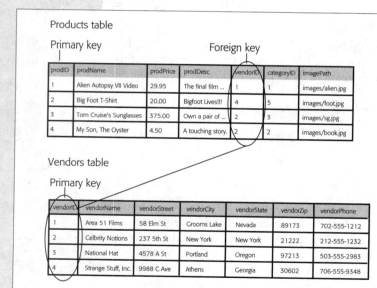

Figure 20-7:
Each table should have a primary key—a column that contains a unique identifier for each record in a table. To relate information from one table to another, it's common to add an additional column with information pertaining to another table. In this case, a column called vendorID in the Products table contains a primary key from the Vendors table. To determine which vendor produces the Big Foot T-Shirt, say, look at the fifth column in the Products table, which identifies the vendor's ID number as 4. When you check the Vendors table, you see that vendor 4 is Strange Stuff, Inc. A column that contains the primary key of another table is called a foreign key.

Creating a Dynamic Page

Once you've set up an application server and a database server, you're ready to connect to the database, retrieve information, and display it on a Web page.

You already know the first step: Design an HTML page to display the database information. You can do this in any number of ways:

- Choose File → New to open the New Document window. Click the Dynamic Page category and double-click the appropriate dynamic page type: ASP VBScript, ColdFusion, PHP, or whatever. When you save the file, Dreamweaver automatically adds the proper extension: .asp for ASP pages, .aspx for ASP.NET, .cfm for ColdFusion, .jsp for JSP, or .php for PHP pages.

- Right-click (Control-click) in the Site panel; choose New File from the shortcut menu. Dreamweaver creates a file in the correct server model format, with the proper extension.

Note: Just renaming a file in the Sites panel (from *about.html* to *about.asp*, for example) does *not* give the file the code necessary to apply the correct server model to the page. This is true for ASP, .NET, and JSP pages. (However, PHP and ColdFusion pages don't start life within any special code, so you could start with an .html page, change the extension to .php, and then add PHP programming.) More importantly, changing the file's extension (from .asp to .php, for example) doesn't change the page to the new server model, either, and probably "breaks" the page.

You can then use any of the page-building tools described in this book—tables, Cascading Style Sheets, Library items, or whatever—to design the page. Even though the file's officially an ASP page, it still contains lots of HTML. Unlike a plain-vanilla HTML page, though, this one also contains the server-side programming code that lets the page communicate with a database.

You can edit the newly created page using either Design view or Code view. But before you can add dynamic content to a page, you must create a connection to a database.

Connecting to a Database

Dreamweaver works with a variety of different databases, from simple Microsoft Access files to corporate mainstays like Oracle 10g. Depending on the server model you've chosen, Dreamweaver connects to those databases in a variety of ways. For the PHP server model, for instance, Dreamweaver works using only the MySQL database and must connect directly to the MySQL server. For this tutorial, you'll use the Access database you downloaded earlier.

Note: The online PHP/MySQL tutorial at *www.sawmac.com/dw8* shows you how to make a MySQL connection.

Databases, like server models, come in many shapes and sizes. Access is different from SQL Server, which is different from Oracle, FoxPro, or MySQL. Fortunately, there's a common language that lets operating systems and programs communicate with all of these databases and more—a protocol called *ODBC* (Open Database Connectivity). Each database company creates its own ODBC driver software.

The ODBC drivers for most popular databases are preinstalled on most Windows machines. To further simplify the process, Windows computers let you assign a *data source name*, a "nickname" that points to a particular database through a specific ODBC driver. A data source name (DSN) is one of the most common methods of connecting to a database on Windows. Instead of having to remember a long, complex series of codes to access your data, you simply use a short name—the DSN. Many Web hosting companies that provide Windows-based Web hosting services let you set up DSNs on their computers, making database connections easy.

However, DSN connections tend to be slower than the other option available in the ASP server model: connection strings. A *connection string* is simply a line of information that informs the Web server how to connect to the database and where the database is located on the system. It's a bit trickier to set up than a DSN connection, since each database requires its own set of instructions for the connection, but it's more reliable and quicker than a DSN connection.

Note to Mac users: Follow these steps on a networked Windows machine. Copy the database file—*nationalEx.mdb*—onto the Windows server and use the following instructions to create a DSN. You can then connect to it from your Mac. Or follow the PHP version of this tutorial located at *www.sawmac.com/dw8/*.

---

1. **Open the Databases panel by choosing Window → Databases.**

   The Application panel group opens.

2. **Click the + sign button at the top right of the panel. From the pop-up menu, choose the appropriate database connection.**

   The options you see depend on which server model you've selected. For example, if you're using ColdFusion, you get a list of all *data sources* (databases) defined in the ColdFusion server. If you're using JSP, you see a long list of different database options. In PHP, you see only one listing: MySQL Connection.

   For the purposes of this tutorial using ASP, your options are Custom Connection String and Data Source Name (DSN). Select Custom Connection String. The window shown in Figure 20-8 opens.

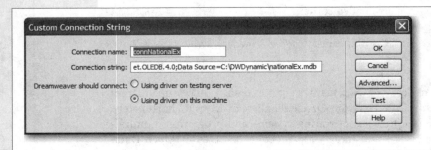

Figure 20-8:
A custom connection string specifies where the database file is and how the Web server should connect to that database. In this example, the file is located on the C:\ drive in a folder named DWDynamic.

Tip: Dreamweaver won't let you set up a connection to a database unless a dynamic page is already open. You need to either open an existing page (*index.asp*, for example) or create a new dynamic page, as described on page 698.

3. **In the Connection Name box, type *connNationalEx*.**

   You can use any name you want, as long as it doesn't start with a number and doesn't contain any characters other than letters, numbers, and the underscore character. In this case, *conn* is a helpful indicator that this is a database connection and makes identifying it easier if you ever need to look into the underlying code of the page.

   Next, you'll add the connection string that tells the Web server where the database is and how to connect to it.

4. **In the connection string box, type *Provider=Microsoft.Jet.OLEDB.4.0;Data Source=C:\DWDynamic\nationalEx.mdb*.**

   This should all be typed on a single line—don't press Return, for example. This piece of information breaks down into two parts. The first part—Provider=Microsoft.Jet.OLEDB.4.0;—explains how to connect to the database (in this case, using a Microsoft method known as OLE DB). The second part—Data Source=C:\DWDynamic\nationalEx.mdb—identifies the location of the Access database file on your computer. For this to work properly, make sure the *nationalEx.mdb* file is in fact inside the DWDynamic folder and located directly on your C:\ drive. If it's not, you need to change this filepath so that it matches your setup. For example, if your computer's main drive is D:\ and you've put the *nationalEx.mdb* file in your Documents folder, you would change *C:\ DWDynamic\nationalEx.mdb* to *D:\Documents and Settings\Your Name\My Documents\nationalEx.mdb*.

5. **Make sure the Using Driver on this Machine button is selected, and then click the Test button.**

   If all goes well, a message reading "Connection made successfully" appears.

6. **Click OK to close the dialog box.**

   Behind the scenes, Dreamweaver creates a small file in the selected server model's programming language, stores it in a folder called Connections in your site's root folder, and adds it to every page on your site that communicates with the database. (The file's name reflects the connection name you typed in step 3—here it's *connNationalEx.asp*.)

Note: Don't delete the Connections folder. This folder holds scripts that let your pages connect to one or more databases. If, while cleaning your site, you throw this folder away, you break the database connection for all pages.

You're not limited to a single database connection. You can repeat the steps above to connect to as many databases as you like. Once you've created a database connection, Dreamweaver attaches it to all the pages within your site; you don't have to recreate the connection for each page.

Exploring the Databases Panel

The Databases panel (Figure 20-9) lets you do more than just connect databases to your site. It also lets you explore a database's structure and data. By clicking the + sign buttons (flippy triangles on Macs), you can view any of three lists:

- **Tables.** Lists all the tables in the database (see page 695). Expanding a table displays all the columns for that table (as shown way back in Figure 20-6). You'll use this option most often.

- **Views.** Lists all *views* stored in the database. A view is a selection of data in the database—a slice of its data. Unless you've created views using the database systems tools, this list is empty.

- **Stored Procedures.** Lists programs that access and manipulate information in the database. Since they're stored right in the database, they run faster than similar code in a Web page. (Some database systems—Access and MySQL, for example—don't recognize this feature.)

Tip: To get a quick peek at the data in a database table, right-click (Control-click) the table's name in the Databases panel. From the shortcut menu, choose View Data. A window appears, displaying a table of data extracted directly from the database!

Figure 20-9:
The Application panel group contains four panels for working with dynamic database-driven Web sites. The Components tab contains advanced features for use with ColdFusion, JSP, and ASP.NET Web sites. (It doesn't have any effect for the ASP or PHP server models.)

In this chapter, you've laid the foundation for a dynamic Web site. In the next chapter, you'll start adding data from a database to the page you created in the preceding tutorial—and building a real, dynamic Web application.

FREQUENTLY ASKED QUESTION

Parenthetical Puzzler

In the Databases panel, I see some weird information in parentheses next to the column names—Integer 4 Required, for example. What's that about?

You're right—there's a notation next to each column name. For example, Figure 20-9 shows a column called *prodID*, which is followed by (*Integer 4 Required*).

The information in parentheses denotes the *type* of data in that column. In this instance, it's an *integer* (a whole number like 1, 3, or 5), it's *4* bytes of data long (meaning it can be a very, very large number), and it's *required* (meaning that every new record *must* have a value stored in this field). Within each of these categories, there can be sub-types like time stamp, decimal number, and so on. Different databases recognize different data types, so there's quite a

long list of possible data types for all the server models Dreamweaver supports.

These notations may appear cryptic, but they can come in handy. For example, if you're creating a form for updating or inserting a record in a database (as described in the next chapter), the data type and length can help you figure out what kind of information you're looking for and how long it should be.

For example, the prodName column pictured in Figure 20-9 contains text (that's what "Char" stands for, as in "characters") and is only 50 characters long. So if you're creating a form element, you'll probably want to create a text field that accepts at most 50 characters (see page 370 for details on form elements).

Adding Dynamic Data to Your Pages

What sets a database apart from a mere pile of facts is its ability to selectively retrieve information. After all, when you visit Amazon.com, you don't want to see every piece of information on every single book and product they sell. You probably want to see just a list of books on a certain subject or by a particular author, and then view more detail about the books that pique your interest.

This chapter shows you how to use Dreamweaver to display database information on your Web pages. Because these concepts can be tricky, you may prefer to get some hands-on experience by completing the tutorial on page 744 before reading the rest of the chapter.

Retrieving Information

Since databases can contain lots of information, you need a way to find just the data you need. Even though your company keeps information about its products, customers, suppliers, and so on in one database, you may be interested only in, say, an alphabetical list of all your customers. After securing that list, you might want to look at a particular customer's contact information, or perhaps the list of products that person bought.

Understanding Recordsets

To retrieve specific information from a database, you start by creating what's called a recordset. A *recordset*—also called a *database query*—is a command issued to a database asking for particular information: "Hey Database, show me all the customers listed in the Customers table." It's the heart of many database operations you'll perform in Dreamweaver (and a piece of jargon you can't escape in the dynamic Web page business).

Recordsets let you retrieve specified columns in a database. They can also sort records alphabetically or in numerical order, as when viewing a list of products from least to most expensive. In addition, a recordset can zero in on a specific record based on information submitted by a visitor to the site or on information provided in a URL. In essence, recordsets let you winnow down massive amounts of database information in a fraction of a second—a powerful benefit, indeed.

ASP.NET note: Dreamweaver uses the term DataSet instead of recordset to refer to database queries in ASP.NET.

Creating Recordsets

Querying a database can be quite simple or extremely complex. Dreamweaver provides tools to get the novice database developer up and running quickly, while also supplying what's necessary to create more advanced recordsets. Whatever your level of expertise, you start by opening the Recordset dialog box using one of these methods (each of which assumes you've set up a server model, as described in Chapter 20):

- Click the Recordset button on the Application tab of the Insert bar (see Figure 21-1).

- Choose Insert → Application Objects → Recordset.

- Click the + sign button on either the Bindings or Server Behaviors panels in the Application panel group (see Figure 20-9), and then select Recordset from the menu that appears.

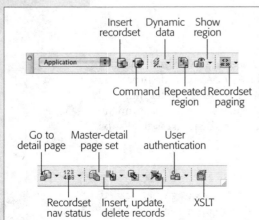

Figure 21-1:
The Application tab of the Insert bar (shown here split in half to fit on the page) provides one-click access to many powerful application objects, which automate common dynamic Web page-building tasks. (The Insert, Update, and Delete records buttons are discussed in the next chapter; the User Authentication features are discussed in Chapter 23; and the last option, XSL Transformation, is presented in Chapter 24.)

Whichever technique you choose, the Recordset dialog box opens (Figure 21-2). This box lets you create a database query or recordset, and provides both simple and advanced modes of operation.

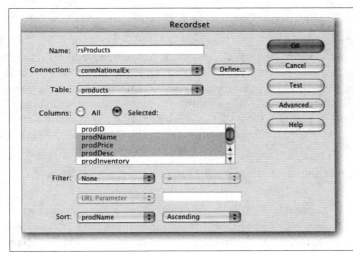

Figure 21-2:
The Recordset window lets you retrieve data from a database. The main window (pictured here) lets beginners search and sort databases for specific information. Advanced options let even seasoned database programmers take advantage of Dreamweaver's dynamic page-building abilities.

To create a simple query, make sure you're in the *Simple* mode. (If a button labeled Simple appears at the right edge of the dialog box, click it to make it say Advanced. Now you're in Simple mode.)

1. **In the Name field, type a name for the recordset.**

   You can use any name you want, as long as it doesn't start with a number and doesn't contain any characters other than letters, numbers, and underscores (_).

Tip: A common technique is to begin the name with *rs* (*rsProducts*, for example). The *rs* helps identify the recordset when you're working in Code view.

---

2. **From the Connection menu, select a database connection.**

   The menu lists all of the database connections you've defined for the site. If you haven't yet created a connection, you can do so now by clicking Define and following the instructions for creating database connections on page 699.

3. **From the Table menu, select the table that'll supply the data.**

   Information in a relational database is usually distributed among different tables, each of which holds information about a particular type of item, such as customer data or product data (see page 697). For example, to get a list of customers from a database, you'd select the Customers table (or whatever its name happens to be).

Note: To retrieve data from more than one table at a time, you need to create an *advanced* recordset (see page 717).

4. **To select columns from which you want to extract data, click the All or Selected button. If you choose Selected, then click the columns you wish to select.**

   By default, Dreamweaver highlights the All button, but you may not want to get data from *all* columns. For example, suppose your table contains lots of detailed information for each product your company sells. You may want to create a basic index of all your products that simply lists names, prices, and descriptions. For this index, you don't need all of the details like SKU number, sizes, inventory status, and so on. Therefore, just select the three columns you're interested in.

   To select multiple columns, Ctrl-click (⌘-click) their names in the list in the Recordset dialog box.

   It's always best to limit your recordset to just those columns whose information you need. The more data you retrieve, the more you make the application and database servers work, and the more you slow down your site, especially when the database is large.

5. **Choose a Filter option, if you like.**

   In many cases, you don't want to retrieve *every* record in a table. For example, if you were looking for a phone number of a particular customer in your database, you wouldn't want the details on every one of your customers. *Filters* let you limit the records retrieved by a recordset. (Details on page 709.)

6. **Choose a Sort option, if desired.**

   Data from a database may not appear in any particular order. Dreamweaver's sort options let you sort information based on a particular column. For example, maybe you're creating a recordset that gathers the title and release date for every CD you own. You might want to sort the results in alphabetical order by the title of the album, or chronologically by the date they were released.

   To sort database records, choose a column to sort by from the first Sort menu (Figure 21-2). Then select the sort order: either Ascending (A–Z, 0–10, earliest to latest) or Descending (Z–A, 10–0, latest to earliest).

   The simple recordset mode lets you sort by only one column. So, continuing with the above example, if you want to sort records by date (so the most recent CDs appear first) and *then* by name (so CDs with the same date are then listed in alphabetical order), you have to use the *advanced* mode (see page 717).

   To view the results of the recordset, click Test to open the Test SQL Statement window, which contains all records that match that query. If there are more than 25 matches, you can see the next group of results by clicking Next 25 at the bottom of the window. When you're done looking at the test results, click OK to return to the Recordset window.

If the test results look right, click OK to close the Recordset window and add the code into the currently opened page.

Note: Unlike a database connection, which is listed in the Databases panel and is available to every page on the site, a recordset is specific to a particular page. (See page 721 to learn how to reuse recordsets on other pages.)

Filtering Information

Although you may have selected a limited number of columns when creating a basic recordset, the final results of the recordset still include *all* of the records within the table. That's fine when you want a list of all items in a database, like when you're creating an index of all your company's products. But it's not so useful when you want a particular subset of those records, like a list of just the red toupees your company sells, or when you want details on a *single* record—the "Flaming Inferno 78B toupee," for example.

To search a database table for specific records, use the Filter option in the Recordset window (see Figure 21-3). A *filter* lets you compare the information in one database column with a particular value and then select records that match. Suppose, for example, that your products database table contains a column named *prodPrice* that contains a product's price. To find all products that cost less than $35, you could create a filter that looks for all records where the price column holds a value of less than 35.

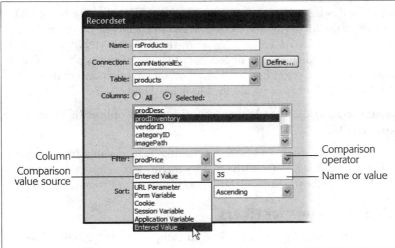

Figure 21-3:
Filters let you limit the number of records retrieved by a recordset using information supplied in a URL, in a form submitted by a visitor to the site, or simply based on what you type into the recordset. Using a filter, a recordset can identify and retrieve data for a single record in the database.

Using the Filter feature in the Recordset dialog box takes only a few steps:

1. **Create a recordset as described on page 706.**

   To create a filter, you must fill out the four form fields of the Recordset window's Filter options—three menus and one text field.

2. **From the first Filter menu, select a column name.**

   This is the column that Dreamweaver compares to a particular value. In the example above, you would select "prodPrice" from the menu to indicate the table's price column (see Figure 21-3).

3. **From the next menu, choose a comparison operator (< or >, for example).**

   To find products whose prices are less than $35, for example, you would use the < (less than) operator. To find an exact value (all products that are exactly $35), use the = sign. Comparison operators are described below.

4. **Using the third Filter pop-up menu, select a source for the comparison value.**

   A filter compares the information in a table column against some other value. There are many different sources for such a comparison value. For example, on a Search page, you could create a form that allows visitors to type in a search term and click a Search button. In this case, the comparison value would come from a form. To set up this arrangement, you, the designer, would select Form Variable from this menu.

   For complete information on selecting a source for a comparison value, see the section "Getting Comparison Values" on the opposite page.

5. **Into the lower-right Filter box, type a name or value.**

   The value for this field depends on the source you selected in the last step; type in the name of the form variable, cookie, session variable, or whatever. The one exception: If you selected Entered Value in the previous step, type a specific value in this field. For instance, to compare the "prodPrice" column to a specific value, you would select Entered Value and then type a number into the text field. The Recordset window would then look like Figure 21-3.

6. **Complete the Recordset window by choosing a sort option (if desired) and then clicking OK.**

   You can test the recordset and filter by clicking Test. If you selected anything other than Entered Value from the source menu, a message prompts you to type in a test value for the source—URL parameter, form variable, and so on.

Comparison Operators for Filters

Dreamweaver provides many different ways to compare information from a database column with information from another source, such as a form, cookie, or simply a value you type into the Recordset window. The type of comparison you choose also depends on the type of data you're comparing: text or numbers.

Comparing text values

You'll often want to create recordsets that find database matches to particular words. For example, a recordset could filter a list of products to find only those records whose descriptions contain the word "green," or you could filter a database of clients to search for a record for "Craig McCord." Dreamweaver provides the following types of text comparisons:

- **Equality.** To check whether the information in a column is *exactly* the same as another value, select the = sign from the comparison menu.

- **Inequality.** To find records that don't match a particular piece of text, select the <> (doesn't match) operator from the menu. You would use this, say, if you wanted to search a database of clothing for items that do *not* match a particular phrase (like "winter" in the Season column).

- **Begins With, Ends With, and Contains.** The last three comparison operators are ideal for locating one or more words within text. For example, a database of movies might have a column containing a short review of each movie. To locate reviews that included the words "horrible acting," you could choose the Contains option, which will find any movie that includes the phrase "horrible acting" anywhere in its review.

  The Begins With and Ends With options are more selective. The former finds records only when the text at the very beginning of a particular record matches; the latter works only when the text appears at the end. You probably won't use these options very often, but they could come in handy if you wanted to search a database for people whose names are Bob or Bobby, but not Joe-Bob. In this example, you'd use the "Begins With" option, and use Bob as the comparison value.

The other comparison operators (<, >, <=, >=) aren't very useful for searching text in a database. They're intended for comparing numbers, as described next.

Comparing numbers

Filters are particularly useful for numbers: finding products that cost less than $35, albums that were released in 1967, products with more than 3,000 items in stock. If you've taken basic algebra, these options for comparing numbers should be familiar: = (equal to), <> (not equal to), < (less than), > (greater than), <= (less than or equal to), or >= (greater than or equal to).

Getting Comparison Values

By now it should be clear that the Filter option of the Recordset window lets you compare data from one column with some other value. But you're probably wondering where this "some other value" comes from. It depends on which option you selected from the third drop-down menu—the Comparison Value Source menu (see Figure 21-3).

The most straightforward option is the last item in the menu: Entered Value. After selecting it, you simply type the value into the field to the right of the menu. This could be a number, a letter, or one or more words. So, to create a recordset that will find a product whose price is more than $50, you'd select the price column, the > (greater than) comparison symbol, and the Entered Value source option, and then type *50* into the value field.

Unfortunately, this kind of recordset is rather limited. The comparison value you specify (50) is hardwired into the recordset, making it very inflexible. What if a visitor wanted to see products that cost more than $15, $30, or $100? No joy. This recordset is limited to what you, the designer, entered as a value.

You're better off creating the filter on the fly from information you get when the visitor's Web browser requests the recordset. In this way, you can create very flexible recordsets that are capable of searching databases for a variety of different pieces of information, not just the *one* value selected by a programmer. (After all, how good a search engine would Yahoo! be if the *programmers* determined what the search criteria were? No matter what you searched for—*Web design, Used cars*—it would always find Web sites about Java, Burning Man, and Diet Coke.)

Dreamweaver can also draw a filter value from a form, cookie, or even a link's URL. The process is always the same: From the filter's Comparison Value Source menu (Figure 21-3), select the source you want, and then type the name of the appropriate source item. For example, if you select Form Variable from the source menu, type the name of the form field in the box to the right.

In most cases, you must depend on an additional Web page to provide the source of these values. For example, a search function on a Web site usually requires more than a single page: one (or more) pages containing a Search field and a Submit button to send the information, and another that displays the results of the search. In this example, the form on one page sends information (the search terms) to another page (the results page), which uses the form information to search the database. In essence, Dreamweaver uses the words typed into the search form on one page to create the recordset on another page.

The two most common ways to pass information from one page to another are forms and URLs. (Three advanced sources—cookies, session variables, and application variables—are discussed on page 818.)

Form variables

A *form variable* is simply the information that a visitor types into a form field (or the value of a selected radio button, menu item, or checkbox). Forms are discussed in depth in Chapter 10, but their use in recordset filters is straightforward:

1. **Create a form page.**

   It can include a text field, pop-up menu, or some other form element. Make sure you *name* the form element. For use in a *simple* recordset filter, you're limited to a single form variable. Using an *advanced* recordset (see page 717), you can use information from more than one form field to filter the data in a recordset.

If you wanted to give your site's visitors a chance to look at differently priced products, for example, you could create a menu that included the values 10, 50, 100, 500, and so on. People could then choose one of those options to look at products below the selected price. (Also be sure to give the menu a name, such as "price," as described on page 362.)

2. **Set the *Action* property of the form (page 364).**

    You'll want it to point to the results page.

Note: For these steps to work, the form's method must be set to *Post* in the Property inspector (see page 365). If *Get* is selected, the form information appears in the URL when the form is submitted. What's more, form information isn't sent as a form variable. (You can, however, use the Get method in conjunction with the URL parameters option discussed next.)

---

3. **Open (or create) the results page.**

    This page displays the results of the recordset that's created using information from the form. This page needs to be a dynamic page using the server model you've chosen—ASP, PHP, and so on. (See page 698 for information on how to create a new dynamic page.)

4. **Add a recordset to the page, using the directions on page 706.**

    You'll also create a filter using a form variable.

5. **From the Filter menu, select a database column. Then choose a type of comparison, as described on page 710.**

    All of this is the standard filter-creation routine.

6. **From the source pop-up menu, select Form Variable. In the box to the right of the source menu, type the name of the form field that contains the value for comparison.**

    In keeping with the above example, you would type *prodPrice* into the box, since that's the name of the menu on the form page.

7. **Add a sort option, if you like, and then click OK to create the recordset.**

    Remember that this kind of recordset's results depend upon information sent from a form. If a visitor just stumbles across the results page without using a form, the recordset most likely produces no results. That's why you should link to this kind of page only by using a form's *Action* property (see page 364).

URL parameters

In your Web travels, you've probably encountered URLs that look kind of strange, along the lines of *www.nationalExasperator.com/shopping.asp?prodID=34&quantity=4*. Everything up to the *?* looks fine, but you're probably wondering what the *?prodID=34&quantity=4* means.

Forms aren't the only way to pass information to a dynamic Web page; URLs can do it, too, thanks to information tidbits called *parameters*. Dynamic Web sites can read parameters and use them to create a recordset, among other things. (In fact, using the Get method for a form puts the form's information into the URL.)

By using the Recordset window's Filter option, you can use one of these parameters to search a database. To identify a single record in a database, for instance, the URL could contain a number identifying the record's *primary key* (see page 697 for a definition). You'll find an example of this trick in the tutorial on page 752.

The steps for using URL parameters to filter recordsets are similar to those for form variables. You need two pages, one with a link containing the URL parameter and another containing the recordset.

TROUBLESHOOTING MOMENT

The Default Value for a Filter Source

There's a problem with using a variable source of information for a filter. If the filter requires information from a form or URL parameter, what happens if someone comes to the page without first filling out the form or clicking a link with a URL parameter? In most cases, the recordset's empty, and the page displays no records. You can, however, set a *default* value for the form variable or URL parameter, so that at least some records always appear.

Using the steps outlined on page 706, create a basic recordset; include a filter using a form variable or URL parameter. Then click the Advanced button in the Recordset window.

Now you get a more complex view of the recordset. In the Variables list, there's a single entry: the selected filter source (Form or URL). Click in the Default Value column and change the 1 to something that matches records in your database.

You could type a value that matches *all* the records in the database. For example, if the recordset's used to find products under a certain price, type a value (price) that's larger than the most expensive product in the database. This way,

the recordset retrieves all items under that price—in other words, all the products. (This trick also works for the other sources discussed on page 818: cookies, application variables, and session variables.)

One last word of warning. If you switch back to the basic recordset view by clicking the Simple button, Dreamweaver resets the recordset variable to the default value of 1. In other words, if you change the default value in the advanced view, *don't* switch back to the basic recordset view.

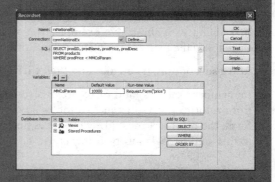

Note: It's possible to add a link with a URL parameter on the *same* page as the recordset. For example, you could have several text links like "Products under $10" and "Products under $100" that link to the same page but have different URL parameters.

Creating a link with a URL parameter

Dreamweaver provides several ways to create a link that contains a URL parameter. The simplest way is to highlight the item you wish to turn into a link—usually text or a graphic. Then, in the Property inspector's link box, type the link followed by a ?, a parameter name, an =, and the value (for example: *products.asp?category=7*).

However, you'll probably find it easier to browse for the file and let Dreamweaver write all the complex stuff. To do so, proceed as follows:

1. **Highlight the item you wish to turn into a link.**

   In other words, select a graphic or text on the page.

2. **Click the folder icon (browse button) on the Property inspector.**

   The Select File window appears. (For more on creating links, see Chapter 4.)

3. **Browse to and select the page containing the recordset.**

   This is the page that displays the results of the database search.

4. **Click the Parameters box in the lower-right corner of the Select File window.**

   The Parameters window appears (see Figure 21-4).

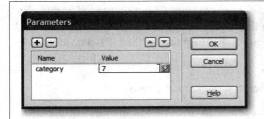

Figure 21-4:
The Parameters window lets you add URL parameters to a link. Recordsets can use these pieces of information to filter a database query, as discussed on page 709.

5. **Click in the space below the Name column and type the name of the URL parameter.**

   Avoid spaces and any punctuation characters for the name, since you're likely to run into troubles when you try to use such a name in the recordset filter.

6. **Click in the space below the Value column and type the value for the URL parameter.**

   This is the value that the filter in the recordset uses to match records in the database.

Usually this is a simple value like *17, blue,* or *yes.* But you can also use spaces and punctuation marks in the value—for example, *Bob Jones,* in order to search for "Bob Jones" in the database. However, you need to make sure Dreamweaver's Preferences are set accordingly: choose Edit → Preferences (Dreamweaver → Preferences); click the Code Rewriting category and make sure one of the "Encode special characters" buttons is selected (the &# option supports a wider range of characters and is the choice suggested by Dreamweaver). Either of these options rewrites invalid characters in a form that works in a URL. For example, a space is converted to %20.

Note: Forms using the Post method don't suffer from any of these problems and can accept all types of punctuation and space characters.

7. **Click OK to close the Parameters window. Click OK to close the Select File window and apply the link.**

Creating the recordset for the Results page

Once you've created the link, you need to create an appropriate recordset for the results page. Here's how:

1. **Open (or create) the results page.**

   This page displays the results of the recordset created using information from the form.

2. **Add a recordset to the page, using the directions on page 706.**

   You'll also create a filter using a URL parameter.

3. **From the Filter menu, select a database column. Choose a type of comparison, as described on page 710. From the source menu, select URL Parameter. In the box to the right of the source menu, type the name of the URL parameter.**

   This is the name supplied in step 5 of the previous instructions.

4. **Add a sort option, if you like; click OK to create the recordset.**

Like form variables, this recordset depends on information included in the URL of a link. If a visitor just stumbles across the results page without using a link with a URL parameter, the recordset most probably produces no results. Because of this, make sure you link to this kind of page only via a link with a parameter. Otherwise, modify the default value for the URL parameter in the recordset, as described in the box on page 714.

Tip: Using URL parameters (as opposed to form variables) for retrieving records has an added benefit: since the parameter is embedded in the URL—*www.nationalexasperator.com/products.php?category=5*, for example—you can bookmark or email a link that matches a particular results page. In this way, you could bookmark, say, a page displaying all the products under $50. Then when you want to see if any new products (under $50) have been added to a site, you don't have to search the site again; merely revisit the bookmarked page.

Advanced Recordsets and SQL

Sometimes you'll need more power than Dreamweaver's simple recordset tool gives you. For example, say you're building an online classified ads system. On one page, you want to present various pieces of information: the name of the sale item, its price, who's selling it, and how to contact the seller, for example. In order to store this kind of information, your database has two tables—one for products and one for sellers.

To present all this information, you must simultaneously access both tables. In addition, you need to connect the records of those two tables so that each product is associated with the correct seller—John Smith is selling the Whirligig 2003, for example. There's only one way to create this kind of complex query: using the advanced options of the Recordset window.

To display these options, insert a recordset using the steps described on page 706. Then, in the Recordset window, click the Advanced button. The Advanced Recordset window should appear (see Figure 21-5). (If you see a Simple button, then you're in the advanced options.)

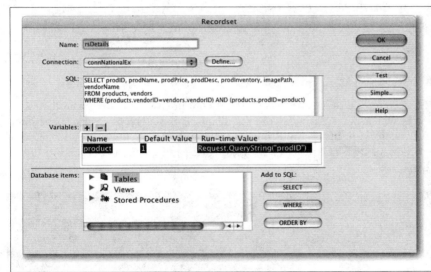

Figure 21-5:
The Recordset window's advanced options aren't for the uninitiated. You need to have a good grasp of SQL—the standard database program language—to make complex recordsets.

Unfortunately, putting together advanced database queries is not as easy as most other operations in Dreamweaver. The Advanced Recordset window is basically just a way of typing in commands, using a database programming language called *SQL* (Structured Query Language, pronounced "ess-cue-ell"). SQL is a standard language that many database servers use to access, update, delete, and add information to a database.

To create an advanced recordset, type an SQL statement in the window's SQL box.

SQL: The very basics

SQL lets you communicate with a database in order to add, update, and delete records. SQL even lets you do more advanced database work, such as adding new tables to a database and even deleting tables and databases. In the context of the Advanced Recordset window, you need to understand only how SQL *retrieves* information. After all, a recordset is just a selection of data pulled from the database.

To make an SQL query (called an SQL statement), you must first specify:

- **Which columns of data you want to retrieve.** For example, product prices, product names, seller name, and seller contact information.

- **Which tables will supply this data.** In the earlier example, the information is stored in two tables: Ads and Sellers.

- **How the search should be limited.** You might just want products that are less than $10 or whose seller is Zachariah Smith.

- **The sort order.** You could sort items using the Price column to view a list of products from least to most expensive, for example.

Only the first two pieces of information are absolutely necessary. A very basic SQL statement would look like this:

```
SELECT prodPrice, prodName
FROM products
```

SELECT is an SQL keyword that specifies columns of data for retrieval; FROM indicates which database table contains them. This statement instructs the database server to look inside the Products table and retrieve the price and name of each product listed. The result's a list of the price and the name of each product in the database.

UP TO SPEED

Getting Your Feet Wet in SQL

SQL isn't difficult to pick up. While you can create very complex SQL queries, a basic SQL statement is straightforward. Once you've reached the limits of Dreamweaver's basic recordset, you may want to expand your skills beyond this simple tool.

A great place to start learning how to write SQL statements is in Dreamweaver itself. After you create a simple recordset (see page 706), click the Advanced button. The SQL statement for the simple query appears in the SQL box.

This chapter introduces the very basics of SQL. For a more complete introduction, check out SQLCourse.com (*www.sqlcourse.com*). Or pick up a book like *SQL Queries for Mere Mortals* (Addison-Wesley Professional) by Michael Hernandez or *SQL in a Nutshell, 2nd Edition* (O'Reilly) by Kevin Kline.

> **Note:** SQL keywords are usually written in all caps–SELECT, for example. This is just a convention, not a hard-and-fast rule. "select" would also work. But since it's easier to identify the keywords if they're capitalized, it's best to stick with this convention.

Of course, you may not always want *every* record in a table. You may want to limit the search to a select number of items, such as products under $10. The WHERE keyword lets you do just that:

```
SELECT prodPrice, prodName
FROM products
WHERE prodPrice < 10
```

Now the SQL statement retrieves only the price and the name of products that cost less than $10. Finally, SQL can sort records into order. In this example, you could also sort all the results from least to most expensive, like this:

```
SELECT prodPrice, prodName
FROM products
WHERE prodPrice < 10
ORDER BY prodPrice ASC
```

The ORDER BY keywords indicate which column Dreamweaver should use to sort the records. Specifying the prodPrice column sorts the items by price. ASC is short for *ascending*, meaning that the records appear in low-to-high price order. (DESC sorts records into *descending* order, Z–A, or high-to-low.) You can even sort by multiple columns. If, for example, you wanted a list of all products sorted by price and *then* alphabetically by product name, you would simply change the above ORDER BY keyword to read like this:

```
ORDER BY prodPrice ASC, prodName ASC
```

In this way, all the products that were the same price (for example, $10) would then be presented in alphabetical order (A–Z).

Using the Data Tree view

Although you need to know SQL to use the Recordset window's advanced options, you can get a little help from the data tree in the "Database items" list at the bottom of the window (see Figure 21-5). This area of the window functions just like the Databases panel and lets you view the tables, columns, views, and stored procedures in the database (see page 702).

Click the + (arrow) button next to the word Tables to see a list of all tables in the database. Click the + (arrow) next to a table name to see all the columns within that table. This technique's very helpful when you're building an SQL statement, because you may not remember the exact names of every table and column in your database.

To build an SQL statement, you can select a column name and click one of the three buttons—SELECT, WHERE, or ORDER BY. The SQL command and column name then appear in the SQL box.

Suppose, for example, you wanted to create the following SQL statement:

```
SELECT prodPrice, prodName
FROM products
```

To build this statement using the data tree, click the + button next to the table named Products, which expands to show a list of all columns. Then click the column named prodPrice and click SELECT. Next, click the prodName column, and then click SELECT again.

Although these buttons can save you time, they don't check whether the SQL statement is valid. Unless you've got some grasp of SQL, you can easily create a statement that generates errors when the test server runs it.

Tip: Be careful when using multiple database tables that contain the same column name. For example, it's possible to have two tables—*products* and *sellers*, for example—that contain columns with the same name, such as sellerID. Dreamweaver doesn't make any distinction when inserting columns with the same name using the Database Items tools (though it does pop up a warning if you attempt to test your SQL statement). To correctly differentiate like-named columns in the Advanced Recordset's SQL box, you must begin the column name with the name of the table, like this: *products.sellerID* or *sellers.sellerID*.

Creating variables for filtering data

Variables let you filter data using information from sources such as forms, URLs, cookies, session variables, and application variables. If you use the filtering option in the basic Recordset window, Dreamweaver creates the variables for you—but in the Advanced Recordset window, you must create them yourself.

To add a variable for use in an SQL query, follow these steps:

1. **In the Recordset window, click the + button above the Variables box (see Figure 21-5). Click the empty space below the Name column and type a name for the variable.**

   The name shouldn't include spaces or other punctuation marks.

Tip: As with database connections and recordsets, it's a good idea to prefix the name of the variable so you can more easily identify it in the code. For example, you could begin the variable name with *var*—varPrice, for instance—just as you'd begin a recordset name with *rs* (rsProducts, for example).

---

2. **Press Tab to jump to the Default Value column. Type a default value for the variable.**

   A default value comes in handy when the form, URL, cookie, session variable, or application variable's empty. The recordset uses the default value to filter the database records.

---

3. **Press Tab to jump to the Run-time Value column; type the appropriate code.**

The exact code depends on the server model you selected. For example, in ASP-speak, you'd type *Request.Form("price")* to retrieve the value of a form field named *price*. To do the same thing in PHP-land, you'd type *$_POST['price']*. The best way to learn how to create variables is to use Dreamweaver's filter tool in the Recordset window (see instructions on page 709), and then switch to the Advanced Recordset window. The proper code for collecting information from forms, URLs, cookies, and so on appears in the variables' Run-time Value column.

Note: Keep in mind that if you add more than one SQL variable in the Advanced Recordset window, you can't switch back to the simple view.

Once you create a variable, you can include it in your SQL statement. Since variables help filter information, you'll often add them to the SQL *WHERE* keyword. For example, if you create a variable named *FormPrice* that retrieves information from a form, you can add it to the SQL statement like this:

```
SELECT prodPrice, prodName
FROM products
WHERE prodPrice < formPrice
```

In this example, whatever information is passed from the form is stored in the *FormPrice* variable and compared to the price stored in the *prodPrice* column of the database.

Reusing Recordsets

Recordsets are created on a page-by-page basis. In other words, when you create a recordset, it's added only to the current document. If you create another Web page that requires the same recordset, you must add the proper code to the new page. You can do this either by recreating the recordset—a potentially laborious process—or by simply copying the recordset from one page and pasting it into another.

Here's how:

1. **Open the Server Behaviors panel by choosing Window → Server Behaviors.**

   Ctrl+F9 (⌘-F9) also works. You can also copy and paste from the Bindings Panel.

2. **Right-click (Control-click) the name of the recordset you wish to copy; choose Copy from the shortcut menu that appears.**

   In the Server Behaviors panel, recordsets appear like this: *Recordset (rsName)*, with the name of the recordset inside the parentheses.

Now switch to the document that'll receive the pasted recordset. Right-click (Control-click) in the Server Behaviors (or Bindings) panel, and then choose Paste from the shortcut menu.

Tip: If you need a recordset that's similar to a recordset you've already created—but not identical—you can copy the original recordset, paste it into a new document, and then edit it, following the instructions in the next section.

Editing Recordsets

What if you have to edit a recordset? Maybe you forgot an important column of information when you originally created the recordset, or perhaps you want to modify a recordset you copied from another page. The process is easy: simply open either the Bindings panel (Ctrl+F10 [⌘-F10]) or Server Behaviors panel (Ctrl+F9 [⌘-F9]) and double-click the name of the recordset you wish to edit.

The Recordset window appears, looking just as it did when you first created the recordset (see Figure 21-2). Make any changes to the recordset, and then click OK.

Tip: If you change the name of a recordset while editing it, Dreamweaver displays a message indicating that you need to use Find and Replace (page 649) to locate and update every instance of the recordset's name. Dreamweaver opens the Find and Replace window for you when you click OK, but it's up to you to make sure the changes are correct.

This is another reason why beginning a recordset with "rs" (*rsProducts*, for example) is a good idea. If you've named a recordset simply "products," you could end up finding and replacing not only the name of the recordset, but also any other cases where the word "products" appears in the page.

The safest (although slowest) way to change a recordset's name is to recreate it. Of course, that's extra effort—a good argument for making sure you're satisfied with a recordset's name when you *first* create it.

Deleting Recordsets

If you add a recordset to a page and later realize that the page isn't using any of the information retrieved by the recordset, you should delete it. Each recordset forces the database server to do some work. Unnecessary recordsets only make your Web pages work harder and more slowly.

You can delete a recordset using either the Bindings or Server Behaviors panel. Just select the name of the recordset in either panel and click the minus sign (-) button at the top of the panel (pressing Delete on your keyboard has the same effect).

Adding Dynamic Information

Once a recordset is created, it's a snap to add dynamic information to a Web page. In fact, Dreamweaver provides several ways to add information. Start in the document window by clicking the spot where you wish to add the dynamic information. Then do one of the following:

- Choose Insert → Application Objects → Dynamic Data → Dynamic Text.

- Click the Dynamic Data button in the Application tab of the Insert bar and select Dynamic Text from the menu (see Figure 21-6).

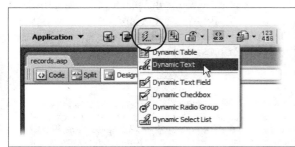

Figure 21-6:
The Dynamic Data button (circled) on the Insert bar's Application tab lets you insert a variety of dynamic data—from form fields filled in with information retrieved from a database, to a complete table based on a recordset.

Either way, the Dynamic Text window appears (see Figure 21-7), listing the recordsets on the current page. Click the + sign button next to the recordset from which you wish to get information from. This expands to show all columns retrieved in that recordset. Pick the database column (also called Field) containing the information you wish to add to the page. You can pick only one column at a time, but you can repeat this process to add multiple columns to the page.

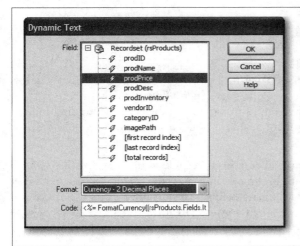

Figure 21-7:
After you select a database field to add to a page, Dreamweaver displays the necessary code in the Code field. This is the programming code that makes the data appear on the page. It's written in the programming language specified by the current server model.

Note: *Dynamic Text* is a bit of a misnomer. This tool can also insert dates, numbers, and dollar values—not just text.

The format menu lets you format the data, like making a date appear as *January 17, 2005*. Formatting is discussed in depth in the "Formatting Dynamic Information" section below.

The Bindings Panel

The Bindings panel (Figure 21-8) provides two other ways to put data from a recordset onto a page. (It's called Bindings because the panel provides a mechanism to "bind" or attach data from a database to a particular spot on a Web page.) Recordsets appear in the Bindings panel of the Application panel group. To open this panel, choose Window → Bindings or press Ctrl+F10 (⌘-F10).

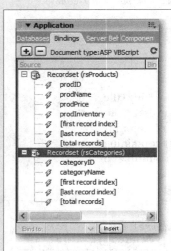

Figure 21-8:
A recordset listing in the Bindings panel includes the name of each column, plus three additional items: first record index, last record index, and total records. Dreamweaver uses these as part of the Recordset Navigation Status server behavior (see page 730) to display just a handful of results from a much larger recordset, so you can display a message like "items 11–20 out of 149 items."

To add data from the Bindings panel to a page, click in the document window where you wish to insert the dynamic data. Then select the column you wish to add, and click Insert. Or, faster yet, just drag a column's name from the Bindings panel directly into the document window—into a paragraph or table cell, for example.

After adding dynamic information to a page, it looks something like *{rsProducts. prodName}*. The information in braces indicates the name of the recordset (rsProducts) and the name of the data column (prodName). (You can make real data appear instead of this code when you use Dreamweaver's Live Data view, as described on page 734.)

Formatting Dynamic Information

Suppose a database includes a column for a product price, storing it as 8 or 10.99. But on your Web page, you want prices properly formatted with a dollar sign and two decimal places, like $8.00 or $10.99.

Dreamweaver includes many different formatting options for numbers, dates, and text. You can choose a formatting option when using the Insert Dynamic Text window (Figure 21-7). You can also apply, remove, or change a formatting option using the Bindings panel.

To set a format using the Bindings panel (Ctrl+F10 [⌘-F10]), proceed as follows:

1. **In the document window, click the dynamic item you wish to format.**

    A down-pointing arrow appears under the Format column in the panel.

2. **In the Bindings panel, click the down-pointing arrow under the Format column and select a formatting option from the menu (Figure 21-9).**

    Pick an option that's appropriate to the selected piece of data: Currency formatting for the price of a product, for example. If you try to apply a formatting option that isn't appropriate for the selected item (Currency to a text description, say), the page may produce an error when previewed on the testing server.

PHP users' tip: Dreamweaver doesn't include date, currency, or number formatting options for the PHP/MySQL server model. You can, however, find a free extension called *PHP Server Formats* at *http://dmxzone.com/ShowDetail.asp?NewsId=4138*, which adds formatting options for dates, currency, and text.

You can also format selected dynamic data just as you would other text on a page by applying CSS styles, headings, bulleted lists, and so on.

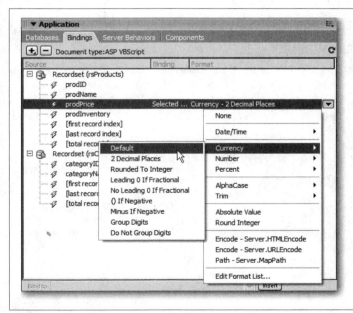

Figure 21-9:
The options shown here (for the ASP/VBScript server model) include a dizzying array of choices, including 19 date and time formats. One of them, "Encode – Server.HTMLEncode," may come in handy if your database stores HTML code. For example, maybe you've created a bulletin board whose messages are stored in a database. When you're adding one of those messages to a page, applying the Encode – Server.HTMLEncode format ensures that Web browsers don't render any code in a message as part of your page. Instead, any HTML in that dynamic text appears to visitors as code. Similarly, if there's any chance a data field might store a bracket like this <, the Encode formatting option prevents a Web browser from thinking that the opening bracket is the start of an HTML tag—a situation that could make your page not appear at all!

Deleting Dynamic Information

Dynamic information added to a page behaves like a single object. Just click to select it. You can also drag it to another location on the page, copy and paste it, remove it from a page by selecting it and pressing Delete, and so on.

If you remove all the dynamic information from a page, and don't plan on using any information from the recordset, make sure you delete the recordset, too, as described on page 722. Even though you may not display any dynamic information on the page, if a page contains a recordset, it must still communicate with the database server, slowing down your pages.

Displaying Multiple Records

Often, you'll want to create a Web page that displays multiple records, such as a page that lists all the products in your company's catalog.

So far, you've learned how to insert dynamic data only from a single record. Fortunately, Dreamweaver provides two tools for displaying multiple records: the Dynamic Table and Repeat Region objects.

Creating a Repeating Table

People initially created HTML tables (see Chapter 7) to display data. The columns and rows of tables provide tidy compartments for individual pieces of information. It's not surprising, then, that in database terminology, *row* often refers to a single record in a database, and *column* indicates a single type of information in a record. Where a row and column meet, they form a "cell" that holds one piece of data from a single record.

Dreamweaver's Dynamic Table tool lets you display the results of a recordset in an HTML table. The top row of the table includes the name of each database column to identify the data in the rows below. The bottom row includes dynamic data—one database column per table column (Figure 21-10).

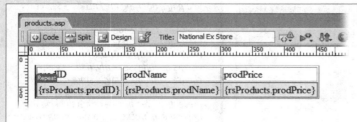

Figure 21-10:
Although the Dynamic Table tool creates a table that displays multiple records, you see only one table row's worth of dynamic data. The Repeat tab that appears above the row indicates that this row will repeat, once for each record in the recordset. To see the effect, use Live Data view (see Figure 21-15).

The magic of this tool is that it can duplicate a row for each record in the record-set. In other words, the table displays multiple records, one per table row. Here's how to use it:

1. **Create a recordset (see page 706). In the Application tab of the Insert bar, select Dynamic Table from the Dynamic Data button menu (see Figure 21-6).**

   You can also choose Insert → Application Objects → Dynamic Data → Dynamic Table. Either way, the Dynamic Table window opens (see Figure 21-11).

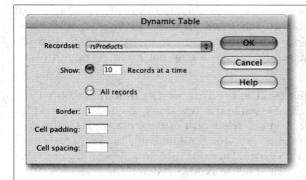

Figure 21-11:
The Dynamic Table tool lets you quickly create a table to display all or some of the records in a recordset. This easy-to-use tool isn't available if you're using either of the ASP.NET server models. Instead, you use an ASP.NET datagrid—a more complex, but more versatile tool. For more information, check out www.macromedia.com/ devnet/mx/dreamweaver/articles/data_grids.html.

2. **From the Recordset menu, choose the recordset you'd like to use.**

   Since a page can contain more than one recordset, you have to indicate which records you want to display.

3. **Using the Show radio buttons, specify the number of records you wish to display.**

   You can show all of the records on a single page by clicking the All Records but-ton. However, if your recordset is huge—if your company has 10,000 employ-ees, say—a single page with all of that information could be very large and difficult to navigate. In this case, you should display only a handful of items at a time.

   If you type *10* in this box, you see at most 10 records when previewing the page. (If you choose this method, make sure to add a Recordset Navigation bar, as described on page 730, to let visitors page through the list of results.)

4. **Set the Border, Cell Padding, and Cell Spacing values for the table.**

   These HTML *table* properties are described on page 245. All you're creating here is a plain old HTML table. You can dress it up later in Design view by changing the border, cell padding, cell spacing, background cell color, and other *table* properties.

Note: If you insert a repeating table and then later alter the recordset used in this table—for example, by adding a column of information to your query—Dreamweaver doesn't update the repeating table as a result of this change. In fact, if you remove a column of information from a query, you get an error when you try to preview the repeating table. If you edit the recordset and change the number of columns it retrieves (see page 722), it's usually best to delete the current repeating table and then replace it with a new repeating table.

5. **Click OK.**

Dreamweaver inserts a table into the page. The top row contains the names of each column from the recordset—one name per table cell. You can, and probably should, edit these names to make them more understandable. After all, *prodNameprodID, prodName*, and *prodPrice* may not mean anything to your visitors.

The bottom row of the table contains the dynamic data from the recordset and represents one record. Each table cell in that row simply holds dynamic text for each field in the recordset. You can select each of these placeholders and style them as you would any dynamic text—for example, using the Property inspector's style menu to apply a CSS style. The table row has a Repeat Region object applied to it, which you can edit or delete as described in the next section.

Creating a Repeat Region

While the Repeating Table is easy to use, it doesn't provide the flexibility you might require. For example, what if your dynamic information needs to be presented in a bulleted list (one record per bulleted item) or in individual paragraphs (one paragraph per record)? In these cases, you must create a *repeating region*—a chunk of HTML that repeats once for each record in a recordset.

Here's an example that can help you understand how to use the Repeat Region object. Imagine you're creating a directory to list your company's staff. This page would include the name, telephone number, email address, and department of each employee. Of course, all of this information's stored in a table in a database—one column for each piece of information, and one record for each employee.

In Dreamweaver, you create the basic design of the page, and then add a recordset that retrieves the required information about each employee in the company. The page layout presents each employee's information in a single paragraph, so the finalized page has many paragraphs—one for each employee.

Since this is a dynamic page, you can't predict how many paragraphs you'll need. After all, your company may hire many new employees, which would add records to the database. To allow for this uncertainty, create a single paragraph by adding the dynamic information you want in it, following the steps on page 722. Then tell Dreamweaver to *repeat* that paragraph using information from each record the recordset retrieves.

Just follow these steps:

1. **Using the Bindings panel or one of the techniques described on page 722, insert dynamic text onto the page.**

   You should put these items together on the page, maybe in a single paragraph or in a bulleted or numbered list. Select the dynamic text and any HTML code you wish to repeat.

   For example, select the paragraph (click the <p> in the document window's tag selector) containing the dynamic data. If you're using a bulleted list to present this information, select the list item (<li> tag) containing the dynamic data. For data in a table row, select the table row (<tr> tag).

2. **In the Application tab of the Insert bar, click the Repeated Region button (see Figure 21-1).**

   You can also choose Insert → Application Objects → Repeated Region. Either way, the Repeat Region window appears (Figure 21-12).

Figure 21-12:
In a Repeated Region that reveals only a limited number of records at a time (in this case, 10), add a Recordset Navigation bar (see page 730). Otherwise, visitors to the page see the first 10 records of a recordset, but have no way to view additional records.

3. **From the Recordset menu, choose the recordset you want the page to work with.**

   Since it's possible to have more than one recordset per page, be sure to select the recordset whose data is included in the area you're going to repeat.

4. **Choose the number of records you wish to display.**

   If you decide not to use the "All records" option, make sure that you add a Recordset Navigation bar, as described on page 730, to let visitors page through the list of results.

5. **Click OK.**

   Dreamweaver adds the proper programming code to the Web page.

Editing and Removing a Repeat Region

If you selected the wrong recordset, or you want to increase the number of records displayed at a time, you can easily change a repeating region. Simply open the Server Behaviors panel (Ctrl+F9 [⌘-F9] or Window → Server Behaviors) and double-click Repeat Region from the list. In the Repeat Region window (Figure 21-12), make any changes and then click OK.

To remove a Repeat Region, open the Server Behaviors panel. Select Repeat Region from the list and click the minus sign (–) button (or press the Delete key).

Recordset Navigation

Dreamweaver's Repeating Region tool lets you display multiple database records on a single Web page. But a recordset with large amounts of data—like 1,000 employee records—can quickly choke a Web page. A large amount of information takes a long time to download and forces visitors to scroll for many screens to see it all.

Fortunately, the tool also lets you limit the number of records displayed at once. Of course, this limit presents its own set of problems: how do visitors see additional records, and how do you let them know where they are among all the records in the recordset?

To solve this dilemma, Dreamweaver comes with two handy commands for adding navigation to a recordset—and providing useful feedback about the recordset.

FREQUENTLY ASKED QUESTION

A Little Less Repetition

I applied the Repeat Region object, and when I preview the page, the same record's repeated over and over. That's not what I wanted to do! What's going on?

This can happen when you apply a Repeat Region object and inadvertently select the wrong recordset from the Repeat Region window (see Figure 21-12)—a mistake that's easy to make if you've included more than one recordset on a page.

The Repeat Region object adds programming code that steps through each record of a recordset. So, in practice, the Repeat Region object should get the information from the first record in a recordset and write it to the Web page, then go to the second record and add *its* info to the page. This process should continue until it's either gone through

all the records in the recordset or reached the limit specified in the "Records at a Time" box.

However, if the information you want repeated is retrieved by a different recordset from the one selected in the Repeat Region window, this system breaks down. Instead, the code continues to cycle through each record from the selected recordset, but doesn't cycle through each record from the recordset containing the dynamic information you want repeated. The result: you get the same information over and over again. The first record of the recordset (the one you want repeated) is repeated for each record in the *other* recordset (the one you don't want repeated).

In other words, to ensure that Repeat Region works, select the recordset whose data is contained in the area you want *repeated*.

Recordset Navigation Bar

Suppose a page contains a recordset that retrieves 100 records from a database, but the repeating region on the page limits the display to 10 records at a time. In this case, you should insert a Recordset Navigation Bar to add either text links or graphic buttons to a page. These navigation bars let your audience view the next 10 records in the recordset, jump to the last records in the recordset (see Figure 21-13), jump back to the first record, or move to previous records in the recordset.

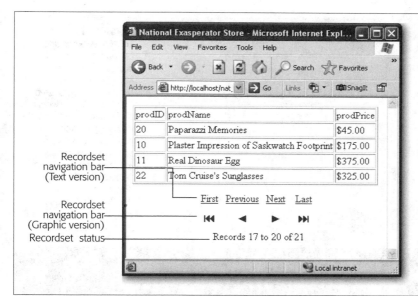

Recordset navigation bar (Text version)
Recordset navigation bar (Graphic version)
Recordset status

Figure 21-13:
Dreamweaver's Recordset Navigation Bar object prevents information overload by letting Web page visitors step through easily digested pages of information. The Recordset Status message also keeps visitors informed about how many records are available.

EXTENSION ALERT

Repeating Regions Left to Right and Top to Bottom

When you use the repeating region on a table row, you end up stacking each record on top of the next. While this successfully displays your records, it lacks pizzazz. Wouldn't it be great if you could list, say, a couple of records per row?

For example, say you've got a database of books. You could display titles and covers for *three* books from left to right across the page, and then add another row of three books below that one, and so on.

Dreamweaver can't do this out of the box, but you can turn to the creative army of programmers who write *extensions*—add-on commands and functions (see Chapter 19 for more information on extensions). For the ASP, JSP, and PHP server models, download the free Horizontal Looper from *www.tom-muck.com/extensions/help/HorizontalLooper/*. A commercial product, MX Looper, provides support for ASP, ColdFusion, and PHP, as well as several cool ways of displaying repeating regions: *www.interaktonline.com/Products/Dreamweaver-Extensions/MXLooper*.

To add a Recordset Navigation bar, follow these steps:

1. **Click in the document window at the location where you want to insert the navigation bar. In the Application tab of the Insert bar, click the Recordset Paging button (see Figure 21-1) and then select Recordset Navigation Bar from the menu (see Figure 21-14).**

   You can also choose Insert → Application Objects → Recordset Paging → Recordset Navigation Bar. In either case, the Recordset Navigation Bar window appears.

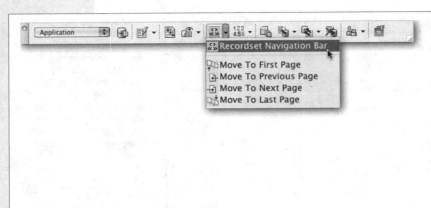

Figure 21-14:
The Recordset Paging button lets you insert a navigation bar for navigating the records returned in a recordset. In addition, if you want to build your own recordset navigation system, you can individually apply server behaviors like Move to First Record and Move to Next Record. These server behaviors are discussed on page 826.

FREQUENTLY ASKED QUESTION

Behaviors That Serve You Well

What's the difference between Dreamweaver Behaviors (Chapter 11) and a server behavior?

Both are prewritten programs created by Dreamweaver's engineers. They differ mainly in where the programs run and what they attempt to accomplish.

A Dreamweaver Behavior is a JavaScript program that runs in a Web browser. It usually affects the interaction between a visitor and a Web page. For instance, the Swap Image behavior makes the Web browser exchange one image for another when a visitor mouses over a link. The behavior itself runs in the visitor's Web browser, and anyone can see the program by looking at the page's source code in the browser.

A server behavior, on the other hand, always runs on the *application* server—that is, on the Web-server side of the

Internet. Instead of JavaScript, server behaviors can be written in a variety of different languages—VBScript, PHP, C#, Java, and so on, depending on the server model your site uses. Server behaviors specifically let you create connections to databases and display, edit, and delete information from databases. Furthermore, since these programs run on the application server, your site's visitors never see the actual programming code. All they see if they look at the source of the page is plain-old HTML (the results of the server program).

In a nutshell, Dreamweaver Behaviors add interactive elements to a Web page, like rollovers and JavaScript alert boxes. Server behaviors supply the programming code you need to build sophisticated database-driven Web sites.

2. **From the Recordset menu, select the recordset to navigate.**

   If the page contains more than one recordset, select the one that you used when you made the dynamic table or added the repeating region.

3. **Select whether to use text or graphic buttons for the navigation bar.**

   If you select Text, Dreamweaver proposes the words First, Previous, Next, and Last to indicate the navigation controls. (You can edit them later.) The graphic buttons resemble standard VCR controls, representing forward and backward. If you select this option, Dreamweaver copies the four GIF files into the folder with the dynamic Web page. Later, you can replace these graphics with ones you create.

4. **Click OK to insert the navigation bar.**

   Dreamweaver inserts a table, consisting of one row and four columns, into the document window. Each cell contains one text or graphic navigation button. You can change the alignment and any other property of the table to fit your design.

Tip: If you use the Recordset Navigation bar frequently, you may long to replace the VCR-control graphics that Dreamweaver displays. Just create your own graphics and name them FIRST.gif, LAST.gif, PREVIOUS.gif, and NEXT.gif, and place them in the Dreamweaver 8 → Configuration → Shared → UltraDev → Images folder.

Recordset Navigation Status

When you're viewing hundreds of records, it's nice to know where you are and how many records there are in all. The Recordset Navigation Status tool adds just such information to your pages, as shown in Figure 21-13. Dreamweaver presents the status message in the form of "Records 1 to 10 of 18," indicating which records the visitor is currently viewing and the total number of records.

Here's how to add a Recordset Navigation Status message:

1. **Click in the document window at the location you want to insert the status message. In the Application tab of the Insert bar, click the Recordset Navigation Status button (see Figure 21-1).**

   You can also choose Insert → Application Objects → Display Record Count → Recordset Navigation Status. In either case, the Recordset Navigation Status window appears.

2. **Select a Recordset from the menu.**

   If the page contains more than one recordset, select the one that you used when you inserted the Recordset Navigation bar.

3. **Click OK to close the window and insert the status message.**

The Recordset Navigation Status message is simply text with the three dynamic text items (see page 724 for more on dynamic text). Change the words "Records," "to," and "of" to anything you like, such as in "Products 1-10. 149 total products retrieved."

Viewing Live Data

After you add dynamic information to a Web page, you see something like this in the document window: *{rsProducts.prodID}*. It gives you an idea of what the information is—in this example, the database column prodID from a recordset named rsProduct—but it doesn't show any real database information, which can make designing a page more difficult. You're especially far from seeing the actual result when a page contains a repeating region: what appears as a single row of dynamic text actually shows up as multiple rows or records when someone views it in a Web browser.

Fortunately, you can preview a page with real database records directly in Dreamweaver. In addition to Design view and Code view, Dreamweaver includes a view for working with dynamic information: Live Data view. When viewing a dynamic page in Live Data view, Dreamweaver contacts the testing server, retrieves recordset data from the database, and displays it in the document window, as shown in Figure 21-15.

To turn the Live Data view on or off, click the Live Data View button on the toolbar, choose View → Live Data, or press Ctrl+Shift+R (⌘-Shift-R). It may take a few seconds for the document window to change, since Dreamweaver must contact the testing server and retrieve information from the database. After a moment, the Live Data toolbar appears (see Figure 21-15), complete with tools for refreshing the displayed data, changing settings for the Live Data view, and adding URL parameters to test recordset filters.

Note: If you're using Microsoft's IIS Web Server, you may get an error when you turn on Live Data view. This means there's a permissions problem that prevents IIS from controlling the database. You can find instructions for fixing this problem on Windows 2000 at *www.webwizguide.info/asp/faq/server_permissions.asp*. Windows XP users can find instructions at *www.sawmac.com/dw8*.

With the Live Data view turned on, it's much easier to see what your page looks like when viewed on the Web. You can continue to work on a Web page in this view just as you would in Design view. You can add text and graphics, modify page properties, and even format dynamic data, as described on page 724.

However, when you're working with a repeating region, you can only select, delete, or format the *first set* of dynamic data items. For instance, as you can see in Figure 21-15, a dynamic table displays repeating rows of database records. If you wanted to apply a Cascading Style Sheet style to the name of each product listed, you would click the item in the first row of dynamic data—in this example, "Crop

Ovals and Other Lesser-Known Alien Visitations"—and apply the style to it. To see the style applied to the other records, click the Refresh button in the Live Data View toolbar.

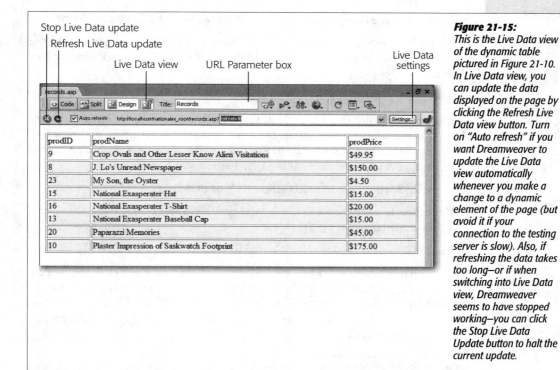

Figure 21-15:
This is the Live Data view of the dynamic table pictured in Figure 21-10. In Live Data view, you can update the data displayed on the page by clicking the Refresh Live Data view button. Turn on "Auto refresh" if you want Dreamweaver to update the Live Data view automatically whenever you make a change to a dynamic element of the page (but avoid it if your connection to the testing server is slow). Also, if refreshing the data takes too long—or if when switching into Live Data view, Dreamweaver seems to have stopped working—you can click the Stop Live Data Update button to halt the current update.

Live Data View Settings

Some recordsets depend on information provided by a form or URL. Often when you use the filter option, for instance, a recordset searches a database for records that match information from a form or URL.

This feature can come in handy for pages that provide detailed information about a single record. Frequently, for these types of pages, the URL might appear something like this: *details.asp?prodID=38*, where the name of the page (*details.asp*) is followed by a URL that includes a name (*prodID*) and value (*38*). The recordset then looks for the product whose ID (*prodID*) matches 38.

Because pages like this can't show up properly without a little outside help, you need to provide extra information in the Live Data View Setting window, like this:

1. **In the Live Data toolbar, click the Settings button (see Figure 21-15).**

   You can also choose View → Live Data Settings. Either way, the Live Data Settings window appears (Figure 21-16).

2. **Click the + button to add a new name and value pair.**

   Dreamweaver refers to this as a "URL request," but essentially it means either a form variable (see page 712) or a URL parameter (see page 714).

3. **Click the Name column and type a name for the new "URL request" item.**

   If the "URL request" is being used to filter data in a recordset, you would use the name you used when you created the filter in the Recordset window (see step 5 on page 710).

4. **Click the Value column and type a value.**

   This may be a number or text, but the value must retrieve at least one record from the database, according to the filter options you set up in the recordset. For example, if you created a filter to find products under a certain price, you might type *price* as the name of the URL request and *10* as its value.

5. **From the Method menu, select either GET or POST.**

   If the filter in your recordset uses a form variable, select POST; if the filter uses a URL parameter, select GET.

6. **Click OK to close the Live Data Setting window.**

   If you haven't turned on the Auto Refresh button, you must click the Refresh button in the Live Data toolbar (see Figure 21-15) to see the new results. In addition, if you selected the GET method in step 5, a URL Parameter box appears in the Live Data toolbar. You can change the values of the URL parameter directly in this box.

Note: The Recordset Navigation Bar and Status message objects react differently, depending on which records in a recordset are displayed. To see this effect in action, add a new URL request item named *offset* in the Live Data Settings window. Set the value to something other than 1. Click OK to return to the Live Data view. You can change this value directly in the URL parameter box in the Live Data View toolbar (see Figure 21-15) to see how the page reacts with different offset values.

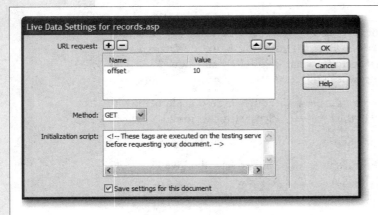

Figure 21-16:
The Live Data Settings window lets you define information that the dynamic page needs to operate correctly. For example, the page may include a recordset that uses information contained in the URL to search records in a database. The Initialization Script section of the window stores temporary code that the application server executes before viewing the page in Live Data view. Use this advanced option for setting the session and application variables that the application server uses to process the page (see page 823).

Master Detail Page Set

When you build a database-driven Web site, you often want to give your visitors both an overview and a detailed view of information. Usually, it takes two separate Web pages to do the job: one that lists limited information about all the records in a recordset, and one that links to a second page with detailed information about a single record. Dreamweaver calls these *master* and *detail* pages and gives you a tool for making quick work of this task. Figure 21-17 shows you how these pages work together.

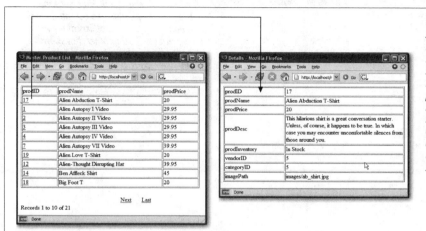

Figure 21-17:
An example of Dreamweaver's Master Detail Page Set. The screen on the left represents a master page—a list of items retrieved from a recordset. Clicking a link on this page opens a detail page (right), which displays the details of a single record.

The Master Detail Page Set object automates the process of creating dynamic tables and recordset navigation bars, as well as adding many different server behaviors to your pages. In fact, there's nothing this tool does that you can't do (albeit more slowly) with the other tools you've learned about in this chapter.

Note: The Master Detail Page Set object isn't available for the ASP.NET server model.

To create a Master Detail Page set, follow these steps:

1. **Create two Web pages—one for the master page and another for the detail page.**

   They can be new, blank pages or existing pages that require the dynamic information from the database. It helps to use descriptive names for these pages, such as *productIndex.asp* and *productDetails.asp*. (Save each page with an extension appropriate for the server model you're using: .asp, .cfm, .php, or .jsp.)

2. **Open the master page—the one listing all the records—and add a recordset to it.**

   This recordset must include not only all the columns to be displayed on the master page, but also all the columns to appear on the detail page. Both pages use the same recordset, so this one recordset must retrieve *all the* information you want on both pages.

3. **In the Application tab of the Insert bar, click the Master Detail Page Set button (see Figure 21-1).**

   You can also choose Insert → Application Objects → Master Detail Page Set. Either method opens the Insert Master-Detail Page Set window (see Figure 21-18).

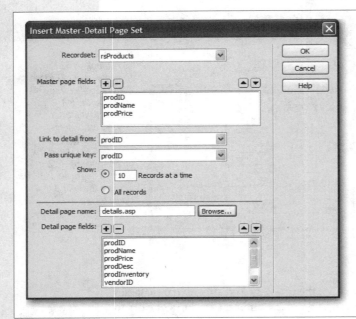

Figure 21-18:
The Insert Master-Detail Page Set window lets you quickly create two common types of dynamic pages: one that lists many records in a database, and another that shows detailed information about a single database record. Unfortunately, this tool is not available in the ASP.NET server model in Dreamweaver.

4. **From the Recordset pop-up menu, chose the name of the recordset you created in step 2.**

5. **Select the fields (database columns) you wish to appear on the master page.**

   You'll probably remove a bunch of columns from the "Master page fields" box, since most of the information's reserved for the detail page. To remove a column, click its name to select it and then click the – button. (If you accidentally delete a column, click the + button to add it back.) You can also change the order of the columns by selecting a column name and then clicking the up or down arrow buttons. The order the fields are listed in the box dictates the order in which they appear on the master page.

6. **From the "Link to detail from" pop-up menu, choose a column.**

   Here you're determining which item on the master page is linked to the detail page. In Figure 21-17, each product's ID number has a link to the detail page. If you're creating a staff directory, you might select the column that contains each staff member's name. In this way, visitors can click a name to see a page with that staff person's details.

7. **Using the "Pass unique key" field, select a column.**

   Choose a column that uniquely identifies a single record in the database, such as a product identification number or Social Security number. In most cases, this is the *primary key* in a database table (see page 697 for more on primary keys).

8. **Select how many records you wish to show.**

   You can either type a number into the "Records at a time" box or select "All records."

9. **Click Browse. Select the detail page you created in step 1.**

   In this step and the next, you're defining the detail page and what information appears on it.

10. **Select the fields you wish to display on the detail page.**

    The process is the same as step 5, but in this case, you'll probably include most, if not all, of the columns. After all, the detail page is where most of the information for an individual record shows up.

11. **Click OK to close the window and create the pages.**

    It may take a few moments for Dreamweaver to complete this step. It's adding a lot of code to both the master and detail pages.

Once completed, you can (and should) modify the tables, format the dynamic items, and design the page to your liking. Because the Master Detail Page Set tool just automates the process of adding repeating regions, recordset navigation bars, and other server behaviors, you must edit those items individually on the page. In other words, you can't return to the Insert Master-Detail Page Set window (Figure 21-18) to alter items on either page. For example, if you decide to remove a piece of dynamic information from the detail page, you must make this change on the detail page itself.

While the Master Detail Page Set tool makes building these types of pages a snap, it does have its drawbacks. The primary problem is that Dreamweaver uses the same recordset for both the master and detail pages. This can slow down the works, because even though you may want to display only a few columns of data on the master page (the prodName, prodID, and prodPrice fields in Figure 21-17), the recordset added to the page must retrieve *all* of the information the detail page needs. The database server is doing a lot of extra work retrieving unused data. However, there is a workaround: after creating the master and details pages, return to the *master page*, edit the recordset, and then select *only* the fields that that page uses. (Editing recordsets is described on page 722.)

Although the Master Detail Page Set makes quick work of creating these types of pages, you can do all the same tasks using the tools you've already learned—repeating regions, recordset navigation bars, and so on—with the added benefit of greater design flexibility. For an example of creating a more complex master and detail page set by hand, complete the tutorial at the end of this chapter.

Passing Information Between Pages

Every now and then, you'll want to pass a piece of information from one page to another. The master-detail page set described in the previous section uses this concept: a link on the master page not only points to the detail page, but also passes along a unique ID used to create a filtered recordset on the detail page. In other words, the master page lists a bunch of records from a database. Each record not only links to the detail page, but also passes along its unique ID. The link might be something like *prodDetails.asp?prodID=7*.

The information after the ? in the URL is a *URL parameter*, which the detail page uses to build a recordset. In this example, the detail page would find only one record—the one whose *prodID* is 7—and display its details on the page. The key to the success of the master-detail page set, then, is the ability to pass information to another page and then use that information to filter a recordset (see page 709 for details on filtering database records).

Dreamweaver can pass information to other dynamic pages using either of two tools: the Go To Detail Page and Go To Related Page server behaviors.

Note: These two tools are available only for the ASP and JSP server models. For the other server models, several developers have created extensions to fill the gap. The PHP Missing Tools extension by Felix One (*www.felixone.it*) includes both the Go To Detail Page and Go To Related page server behaviors for PHP. In addition, Deng Jie has created Go To Detail page extensions for ColdFusion, ASP.NET, and PHP. You can find these at the Macromedia Exchange (page 670)—just search for "Go To Detail Page." (These extensions work identically to the ones that come with Dreamweaver, so the following instructions still work.)

Go To Detail Page

A detail page, logically enough, is intended to provide more details on a single database record. To retrieve details on only one record, the detail page must include a recordset that filters the records of a database table based on some unique identifier, usually a record's primary key. For example, if every ad in a database of advertisements had its own unique ad ID, then a recordset could filter the data based on that ID number.

Note: The tutorial that starts on page 744 includes an example of this server behavior in action.

The Go To Detail Page server behavior provides a way to pass information to a detail page in the URL of a link—for example, *productDetails.asp?productID=4*. In this way, when the detail page loads, it can use this URL variable—productID, in this example—to filter the database to retrieve the requested record (see page 714 for tips on using a URL variable to filter recordsets).

In many cases, you use this server behavior in conjunction with a repeating region (page 728) on a page that lists multiple database records. In other words, you use this behavior on a master page. Then you link each record in the list to the same page—the detail page—but pass along a different, unique ID for each record.

To use this server behavior, first add a recordset to the page. The recordset provides the information that's passed to the detail page (usually a record's primary key). Frequently, you'll also add a repeating region, or use Dreamweaver's Repeating Table command (page 726). Here's the whole process:

1. **Select an item on the page (graphic or text) to serve as a link to a detailed page.**

   Since you frequently use this server behavior in conjunction with a repeating region, you could select a piece of dynamic text within the repeating region. For example, on a page that lists many products, you could select the name of the product.

2. **Make sure the Server Behaviors panel is open (Ctrl+F9 [⌘-F9]). Click the + button; from the pop-up menu, choose Go To Detail Page.**

   The Go To Detail Page window appears (Figure 21-19). Skip the Link pop-up menu. (You can also use either the Go To Detail Page button on the Application tab of the Insert bar [see Figure 21-20] or choose Insert → Application Objects → Go To → Detail Page to reach the Go To Detail Page window.)

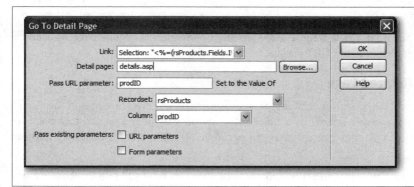

Figure 21-19:
The Go To Detail Page server behavior can pass information from a recordset to another page by adding a URL parameter to a link.

Figure 21-20:
You can also apply the Go To Detail Page and Go To Related Page server behaviors from the Application tab of the Insert bar.

3. **Click Browse and select the detail page.**

   You're choosing a dynamic page, of course.

   Keep in mind that this server behavior doesn't actually *do* anything to the detail page, like adding a recordset to it. This behavior merely links to that page, passing along some additional information in the URL. In other words, to take advantage of the data passed along in the link, you need to add a recordset to the detail page that uses the URL variable. (You can also use the URL variable in other ways, as described on page 820.)

4. **Type a name into the "Pass URL parameter" box.**

   Often, your best bet is to use the same name as the database column whose value you're using. But at the very least, the name should contain only letters and numbers, without spaces or other punctuation (because it's transmitted in the URL).

5. **From the Recordset pop-up menu, choose a recordset.**

   This is the recordset containing the information to be included in the URL.

6. **From the Column pop-up menu, select a database column.**

   This should be a primary-key field.

7. **If you want to pass on URL variables and form variables already present on the page, turn on the "URL parameters" and "Forms parameters" boxes.**

   For a discussion of these options, read the following section.

8. **Click OK to close the window and add the link.**

   Dreamweaver adds a link with all the programming that your site's server model needs.

Once you've completed these steps, open (or create) the detail page and add a recordset that uses the URL variable.

Go To Related Page

The other Dreamweaver tool for passing information between pages is the *Go To Related Page* server behavior. It takes information that's been passed to a page (in the form of URL parameters or Form parameters) and passes it on to yet another page.

Here's how you might use this feature. Suppose your Web site sells expensive manufacturing equipment. On a detail page, which lists the specifications for a particular machine, you include a link to a page with a larger photo of the machine. When the visitor clicks the "click for larger photo" link, the photo page retrieves and displays the proper photo.

But how does the photo page know which photo to display? An easy way would be to pass along the ID for the product, information that's included in the URL on the detail page.

The Go To Related Page server behavior is ideal for this situation. It simply links to another page, passing along any URL parameters or form information already processed by the page. To use it:

1. **Select the graphic or text that will serve as the link to another page.**

   This could be text like "Click for larger photo," or "See a related review." Make sure the Server Behaviors panel is open (Ctrl+F9 [⌘-F9]).

2. **Click the panel's + button; from the pop-up menu, choose Go To Related Page.**

   The Go To Related Page window appears (Figure 21-21). Ignore the Link pop-up menu.

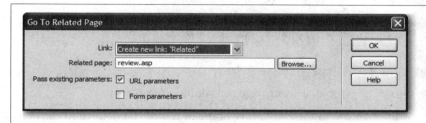

Figure 21-21:
This server behavior links from one page to another and passes along information contained in the URL, or data that was already sent to the first page as a form.

3. **Click Browse. Select the page to which you want to pass the URL or form variables.**

   In order for the linked page to take advantage of these variables, you need to add a recordset and use the variables to filter the results. You can also add these variables to your Bindings panel, as described on page 818, and use them as dynamic text elements on the page, or even bind them to form elements.

4. **Turn on the appropriate boxes.**

   The "URL parameters" box passes along any URL variables to the linked page. For example, suppose you add this behavior to a Details page, creating a link to page named *moreInfo.asp*. When someone comes to the detail page, the URL might be *productDetails.asp?prodID=9* (depending on which record they're viewing). When the visitor clicks the link, the URL becomes *moreInfo. asp?prodID=9*. In other words, the *prodID=9* from the detail page is sent along to the *moreInfo.asp* page.

   The "Form parameters" box does the same thing for form variables. For example, when someone fills out and submits a Search form, the information travels to a Results page, which displays the results of that search. You could then preserve the form information submitted to the results page and pass it along to another page.

5. **Click OK to close the window and apply the server behavior.**

To edit one of these behaviors, double-click its name in the Server Behaviors panel; to delete one, select it in the panel and press the – button or Delete.

Tutorial: Displaying Database Info

In this tutorial, you'll continue the work you started in the last chapter. The *National Exasperator's* online store requires two dynamic pages. The first displays a list of all products available on the site. From that page, visitors can jump to a detailed description of an item for sale by clicking its name. You'll learn how to create both basic and advanced recordsets, and take advantage of some of Dreamweaver's built-in application objects.

To get started, download the files and complete the tutorial in Chapter 20. If you haven't yet done this, turn to page 689 and follow the instructions for preparing the application server, database, and Dreamweaver for this project.

Note: A PHP/MySQL version of this tutorial is available at *www.sawmac.com/dw8/*.

Creating a Recordset

You'll start by opening an existing page and adding a recordset to it:

1. **Open *products.asp* in the root folder of the local site you defined in the previous chapter.**

   Either choose File → Open and navigate to and select *products.asp*, or double-click the file name in the Site Files panel.

   The basic structure of this page is already complete. It was built using tables, image rollovers, Cascading Style Sheets, and the other HTML features you've already learned. There's nothing dynamic about this page yet, so you'll need to create a recordset and insert database information into the page.

2. **Choose Insert → Application Objects → Recordset.**

   You can also click the Insert Recordset button on the Application tab of the Insert bar (see Figure 21-1), or click the + button on either the Bindings panel or Server Behaviors panel, and select a recordset from the menu that appears. In any case, the Recordset box should now be on the screen. (Make sure you're using the *simple* mode—you should see a button labeled Advanced—as described on page 707.)

   Next, select the information you want to retrieve.

3. **Type *rsProducts* into the Name box.**

   Since Dreamweaver lets you connect to more than one database, you must now indicate *which* database connection it should use.

4. **From the Connections pop-up menu, select "connNationalEx."**

   This is the name of the connection you created in the last chapter.

   The *National Exasperator* database contains several tables. At this point, you're interested in the Products table and the Vendors table. For this page, you'll create an index of all products for sale. That information is in the Products table.

5. **From the Tables menu, choose "products." Click Selected.**

   You don't need to retrieve *all* the information from the Products table. Since this dynamic page will present a listing of all of the products, you need only basic information, like the name of the product, its price, and its inventory status. More details about each product will appear on a second page, to be created later in this tutorial.

6. **In the Columns list, Ctrl-click (⌘-click) "prodName," "prodPrice," and "prod-Inventory."**

   These are the columns of data you want to get from the database.

   You don't have to filter this recordset—you can ignore these controls in the dialog box—but it would be nice if the product names appeared in alphabetical order.

7. **From the first Sort pop-up menu, choose "prodName." From the second one, choose Ascending.**

   The Ascending option makes certain the records start with products whose names begin with A and end with names that begin with Z.

8. **Click OK to close the Recordset dialog box. In the Bindings panel (Ctrl+F10 or ⌘-F10), click the + icon next to the Recordset icon.**

   The Bindings panel should look like Figure 21-22.

9. **In the document window, click inside the table cell directly below the one labeled Item for Sale.**

   In this cell, you'll add the name of the item for sale.

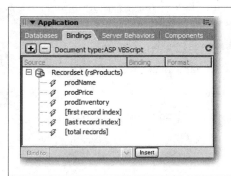

Figure 21-22:
The Bindings panel provides a list of a page's recordsets and data fields. You can use these fields to add dynamic text to a page.

10. In the Bindings panel, click "prodName" and then click Insert.

You've just added dynamic data to the page. For the moment, it looks like {rsProducts.prodName}.

11. **Repeat steps 9 and 10, this time inserting "prodPrice" and "prodInventory" into the remaining two cells.**

You can also drag an item from the Bindings panel onto the page.

At this point, your page should look like Figure 21-23.

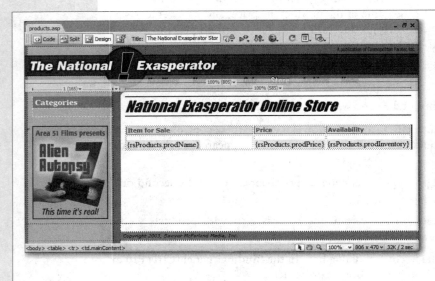

Figure 21-23:
After you add dynamic information to a page, it appears with a blue background. Here, three pieces of dynamic data are added to the page from the rsProducts recordset: rsProducts.prodName, rsProducts.prodPrice, and rsProducts.prodInventory. To change this background color, choose Edit → Preferences (Dreamweaver → Preferences). Click the Highlighting category and change the Live Data View colors at the bottom of the window.

Formatting Dynamic Information

Once you've added dynamic data to a page, you can format it so it looks like other text on your page. Dreamweaver lets you apply all the available formatting options that you can to regular text, including Cascading Style Sheets. In addition, Dreamweaver includes some formatting options specific to dynamic information, such as multiple formatting options for dates, currency, and numbers.

You'll start by adding some CSS formatting to the page:

1. **In the document window, click the product name data ({rsProducts.prodName}).**

You've just selected the data you want to format.

2. **In the Property inspector, select ProductInfo from the Style menu.**

The text is formatted in bold green.

3. **Repeat steps 1 and 2 for the other two data items, using the ProductInfo style in the Property inspector.**

   Dreamweaver also includes special dynamic-text formatting options for dollar amounts, percentages, and more. That comes in handy now.

4. **Click the price data ({rsProducts.prodPrice}) on the Web page.**

   Before you proceed, make sure that the Bindings panel is open (Ctrl+F10 or ⌘-F10). Notice that the price is highlighted under the recordset.

5. **In the Bindings panel, click the down-pointing arrow in the Format column. In the shortcut menu that appears, choose Currency → 2 Decimal Places (see Figure 21-24).**

   You've just added a $ sign to the beginning of the price, and ensured that the price always appears with two decimals, like this: $100.00. You can also pick from a variety of different formats for presenting dates.

   Unfortunately, you can't see the effect of this formatting choice; you see only that cryptic {rsProducts.prodPrice} on the page. You'll get to see the actual formatted price in the next section.

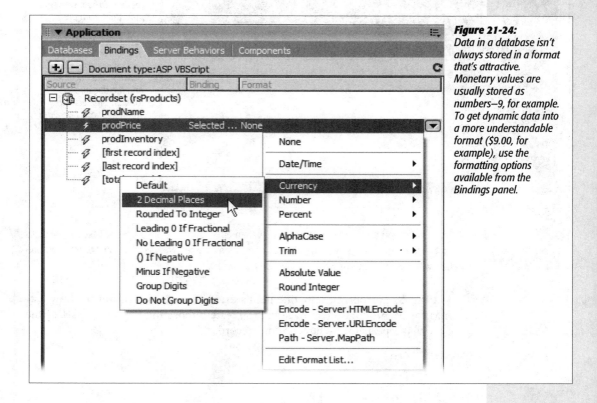

Figure 21-24:
Data in a database isn't always stored in a format that's attractive. Monetary values are usually stored as numbers—9, for example. To get dynamic data into a more understandable format ($9.00, for example), use the formatting options available from the Bindings panel.

Live Data View and Creating Repeating Regions

When you add dynamic data to a page, it doesn't look like much. All you see is the recordset and column name between braces ({rsProducts.prodName}, for example). Not only can this interfere with your design, it certainly doesn't give you a clear picture of what your page looks like.

Thank goodness for Dreamweaver's Live Data view:

1. **Click the Live Data View button in the document window's toolbar (circled in Figure 21-25).**

   Dreamweaver connects to the testing server and database to retrieve the data requested by the recordset (this may take a few seconds). For the first time, you get to see the page as it will appear on the Web (Figure 21-25). Notice the price formatting; it's just what you specified.

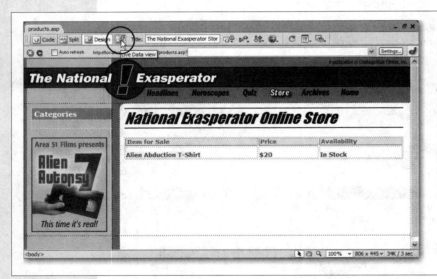

Figure 21-25:
When you click the Live Data View button (circled) in the document toolbar, Dreamweaver pulls data from the database and displays it in the document window. In addition, a second toolbar appears, between the document and the document toolbar, that lets you control various Live Data view settings.

Note: If, when you try the Live Data view, you get an error saying that the page can't be displayed, it's probably because the Web server doesn't have permission to access the database file. For troubleshooting help with this problem, visit *www.sawmac.com/dw8/trouble*.

But there's a problem: only one item's listed. This page is meant to show listings for *all* products. You have yet to create a repeating region—a part of the page that repeats for each record in a recordset.

2. **Move your cursor to the left of Alien Abduction T-Shirt until the right-pointing arrow appears, and then click.**

   That's how you select the bottom row of the table. (For other methods of selecting a table row, see page 248.) Since this row displays the info for a single product, it's a perfect candidate for a repeating region, where an additional row appears in the table for each product.

3. **On the Application tab of the Insert bar, click the Repeated Region button (see Figure 21-1).**

   The Repeat Region dialog box (Figure 21-12) appears, so that you can select which recordset to use (if the page has more than one) and how many records to display. In this case, since you have only one recordset, you just have to tell Dreamweaver how many records to show.

4. **In the Records at a Time box, type 9. Click OK.**

   You don't know how many products the *National Exasperator* offers at any time. If it were a lot, you wouldn't want to show them all on a single page—a thousand listings would make a pretty long Web page. In this case, just list nine records at a time.

   If the database has more than nine products, you need to provide a way for people to see the other items. You'll do that next.

5. **Click to the right of the table that lists the products and press Enter to create a new paragraph. Then, in the Application tab of the Insert bar, click the Recordset Paging button and select Recordset Navigation Bar from the menu (see Figure 21-14).**

   The Recordset Navigation dialog box appears. There's only one thing to do here.

6. **Make sure the Text button is selected; click OK.**

   Dreamweaver plops a table containing four columns onto the page. The columns contain links that let visitors navigate the product listings.

   The table will look better if it's aligned to the left side of the page.

7. **In the document window, select the table. From the Align pop-up menu in the Property inspector, choose Default. Set the width of the table to 200 pixels.**

   For techniques on selecting a table, see page 248. (Tables *are* left-aligned by default, which is why you chose Default.)

8. **Click directly above the new table Dreamweaver just inserted; click the Recordset Navigation Status button (see Figure 21-1).**

   Dreamweaver inserts something that looks like this: *Records {rsProducts_first} to {rsProducts_last} of {rsProducts_total}*. That's placeholder code for this notation: "Records 1 to 9 of 21."

Now for a touch of formatting.

9. **Select the paragraph Dreamweaver just inserted. In the Property inspector, select ProductInfo from the Style Menu.**

   You've just formatted the paragraph with the ProductInfo CSS style. (While you're at it, apply the same style to the four parts of the Recordset Navigation Bar—First, Previous, Next, and Last, if you like.)

10. **Press F12 to preview the page in your Web browser.**

   The page opens in a Web browser displaying nine records (see Figure 21-26).

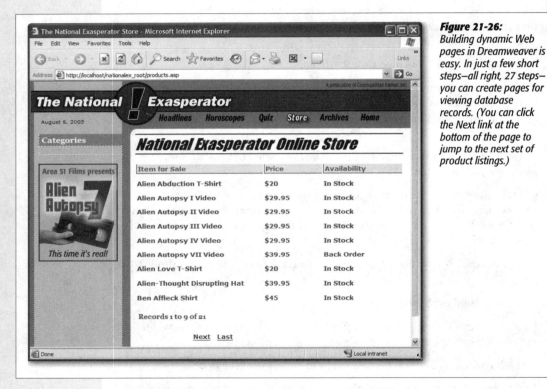

Figure 21-26:
Building dynamic Web pages in Dreamweaver is easy. In just a few short steps—all right, 27 steps—you can create pages for viewing database records. (You can click the Next link at the bottom of the page to jump to the next set of product listings.)

Editing a Recordset and Linking to a Detail Page

Now that the main Products listings page is complete, you need to create a link to the name of each product that, when clicked, opens a page with the details for that item:

1. **Open the Server Behaviors panel by pressing Ctrl+F9 (⌘-F9), or clicking the Server Behaviors tab in the Application panel group.**

   A list of all the different *server behaviors* appears; these were added when you created a recordset, put dynamic text on the page, and used Dreamweaver's other dynamic-page-creation tools. (Server behaviors are discussed in depth in Chapter 23.)

Instead of adding another server behavior at this point, you can edit one you've already created: the recordset. When you first added this recordset, an important piece of information was missing—the product's ID number. (Actually, it was omitted from the tutorial intentionally, so that you'd now have this engaging educational opportunity to learn how to edit a recordset.)

Each product has its own ID number, which you'll use to tell the Details page which item to display.

2. **Double-click "Recordset (rsProducts)" in the Server Behaviors panel to open the Recordset dialog box.**

3. **Ctrl-click (⌘-click) "prodID" in the columns list, and then click OK.**

    You've just added one additional column (prodID) to the recordset. Now the recordset not only retrieves the name, price, and posted dates for each product, but also its unique ID number.

4. **In the document window, select the dynamic data containing the product's name: "{rsProducts.prodName}."**

    A simple link to an already created Web page doesn't work here. Since the page containing a product's details is dynamic—it changes based on which product is being viewed—you need one of Dreamweaver's server behaviors.

5. **From the Application tab of the Insert bar, choose Go To Detail Page (see Figure 21-1).**

    The Go To Detail Page dialog box appears (Figure 21-27). This window lets you create a special link to a dynamic page. Although each item listed on the main products page links to the same Details page, each link includes additional information telling that page which product to display.

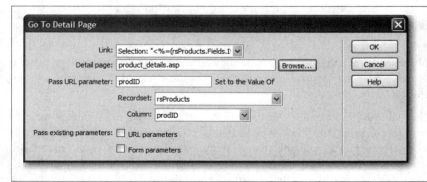

Figure 21-27:
The Go To Detail Page server behavior makes it easy to create a link that passes URL parameters, Form data, and other necessary information to a detail page. This behavior is discussed in depth in Chapter 23.

6. **Click the Browse button. Select the file *product_details.asp*.**

   This is the page that displays the detailed records of each product. All the other settings should already be filled out and should resemble Figure 21-27.

7. **Click OK to close this window.**

   And now to make sure everything works:

8. **Press the F12 key to preview the page in your Web browser. Click the Alien Thought-Disrupting Hat link.**

   The detail page loads...without any details! You'll get to that step in a moment. In the meantime, look at the URL in the Web browser's Address bar. It should look something like this: *http://localhost/nationalex_root/product_details. asp?prodID=12*. Notice the *?prodID=12* tagged onto the page *product_details.asp*. That's the information the details page needs to retrieve the proper product information. The two pieces of information—prodID and 12—are what's called a key/value pair. The key, prodID, tells the details page which field to look in, while the value, 12, identifies a particular product with a product ID of 12.

9. **Save and close this page.**

Building the Detailed Product Page

In this part of the tutorial, you'll build a detail page that displays all the details for a particular product. In addition, you'll create an advanced recordset that combines information from two separate database tables:

1. **Open the file called *product_details.asp* in the root folder of the site.**

   Either choose File → Open and navigate to and select *product_details.asp*, or double-click the file name in the Files panel.

   Since this page displays the details for a product, it must retrieve data from the database. To set this up, start by creating a recordset.

2. **Click the Insert Recordset button on the Application tab of the Insert bar (see Figure 21-1).**

   You can also choose Insert → Application Objects → Recordset. Or click the + button on either the Bindings panel or Server Behaviors panel, and then select *recordset* from the pop-up menu. In any case, the Recordset dialog box should now be open.

   The *National Exasperator* database contains several database tables—one for product information, one for vendor information, one that lists the different product categories, and one that contains user information (user names and passwords). The detail page incorporates information from the Products table and the Vendors table, so that it can reveal both the description of the product and information about its manufacturer. Because the basic panel of the Recordset dialog box doesn't let you retrieve information from more than a single database table, you must use the advanced setting.

3. **Click the Advanced button on the right side of the Recordset window.**

The Advanced Recordset dialog box appears.

Unfortunately, this isn't one of the areas in which Dreamweaver is particularly user-friendly. It helps to understand SQL (see page 718)—or you can just take the following steps.

4. **In the Name field, type *rsDetails*. From the Connection menu, choose "connNationalEx."**

In the next few steps, you'll create an SQL query—essentially a line of programming code that asks the database for particular information that matches specific criteria. In this case, it's the information for a particular product.

5. **Click the + icon (flippy triangle) next to the word Tables in the Database Items list (at the bottom of the dialog box).**

It expands to reveal the four tables of the database: Category, Products, Users, and Vendors.

6. **Click the + icon (flippy triangle) to expand the Products table.**

Your job is to select the information from this table that you want to display on the page.

7. **Select "prodID"; click the Select button to the right.**

Notice that Dreamweaver writes *SELECT prodID FROM products* in the SQL box. This is SQL code for selecting a particular column of data from a table. You can now choose the other pieces of information.

8. **Repeat step 7 for the following items in the Products table: prodName, prodPrice, prodInventory, prodDesc, imagePath.**

These are all the items you need to retrieve from the Products table. Now you can choose data from the Vendors table.

Note: Once you understand SQL, you can bypass this point-and-click approach and simply write a SQL query directly in the SQL box.

---

9. **Click the + icon (flippy triangle) to expand the Vendors table. Repeat step 7 for the vendorName item in that table.**

The dialog box should now look like Figure 21-28. Congratulations, you've just created a basic SQL query.

But there's a problem here: Because of this query's structure, it retrieves *all* the records for both tables. To remedy the situation, you must do two things: first, combine information from two tables so that you get the vendor information for the corresponding product; and second, retrieve only the information for the particular product specified by the link you created in the last part of this tutorial.

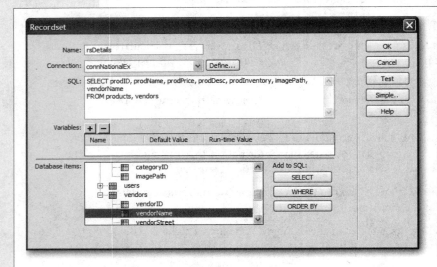

Figure 21-28:
The Advanced option of the Recordset window lets you use a data tree to build an SQL statement. By selecting a column name and clicking either the SELECT, WHERE, or ORDER BY buttons, you can get Dreamweaver to do some of the heavy lifting. Unfortunately, you still need to understand a little bit of SQL to create functioning database queries using these advanced options. See page 718 for a brief introduction to SQL.

10. **Click inside the SQL box after the word "vendors." Press Enter or Return.**

    You'll have to dive into typing out SQL code.

11. **Type *WHERE (products.vendorID = vendors.vendorID).***

    This little bit of code is called a *WHERE clause*, and it helps filter information in a database. In this instance, you've created what's called a *join*—a statement that joins two or more tables together. When you retrieve product information, you also want to retrieve the name of the vendor who manufactures that product. By matching the vendor ID from the Products table to the identical vendor ID in the Vendors table, the database can produce the proper vendor name.

    If your eyes are glazing over, go get a cup of coffee before plunging ahead.

12. **Click the + button to the right of the word Variables.**

    You've just created a new SQL variable.

    You're about to expand on the WHERE clause you just wrote. Not only do you need to get the details of a product (plus the vendor's name), you also want to retrieve just a single record—the particular product whose details the visitor wants to review.

13. **Click in the Name column and type *product.* Type *1* for Default Value. And, type *Request.QueryString("prodID")* for the Runtime Value.**

    Look back to step 8 in "Editing a Recordset and Linking to a Detail Page" (see page 752). Remember that the ID number for the product is embedded in the

URL. In other words, when someone clicks a link on the main product listings page, the ID number for the product is passed along like this: *product_details. asp?prodID=12*.

In this step, you're retrieving that information from the URL—that's the *Request. QueryString("prodID")* part—and storing it in a variable that you'll use in the rest of the SQL query.

14. **Return to the SQL box. At the end of the WHERE clause (after the closing parenthesis), type *AND (products.prodID = product)*.**

The Recordset window should now look like Figure 21-29.

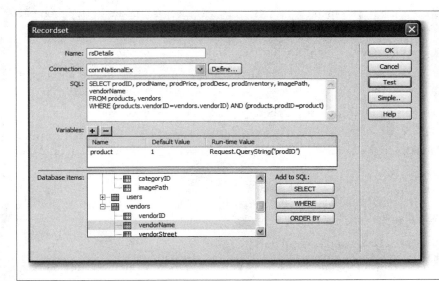

Figure 21-29:
In the Advanced settings of the Recordset window, you can create more detailed SQL queries that can retrieve and merge information from multiple database tables.

15. **Click the Test button.**

A Test SQL Statement window opens, containing a single record. Hallelujah: It includes not only product details but also the vendor's name.

16. **Click OK to close the window. Choose File → Save to save your changes.**

Filling in the Details

Now all you need to do is add the information retrieved in the recordset to the page:

1. **In the document window, click in the empty space directly above the word Price.**

You'll add the name of the "for sale" item here.

2. **Open the Bindings panel.**

   Either press Ctrl+F10 or click the Bindings tab in the Application panel group.

3. **In the Bindings panel, click the + icon (flippy triangle) next to the recordset to display all the columns retrieved in the recordset. Select "prodName," and then click Insert.**

   That data appears in the document window. Next, you'll try the drag-and-drop method of inserting dynamic data.

4. **In the Bindings panel, drag "prodPrice" into the document window, just to the right of the text Price:**

   At this point, you might want to format the price, as you did in step 5 on page 747.

5. **Continue adding content to this page using these same steps.**

   Add the description, inventory status, and vendor name in the appropriate places in the document window.

   To finish off this page, add a photo in the area to the left of the product info.

6. **Click in the empty table cell that's to the left of the cell with the product information. In the Common tab of the Insert bar, click the Image button or choose Insert → Image.**

   The Insert Image window appears. You've encountered this dialog box many times before when you inserted a graphic (see Chapter 5). However, in this case, you'll retrieve the path to the image from the database.

7. **Select the Data Sources radio button.**

   The window should now look like Figure 21-30. A list of all of the different data items from the recordset appears. See the item labeled "imagePath?" The database stores the path to an image for each product in the database. This is the path that the page uses when it displays the graphic.

8. **Select "imagePath"; click OK. (If the Image Tag Accessibility Attributes window appears, just click OK to dismiss it.)**

   A little square icon appears in the document window.

9. **Click the Live Document View button. If everything looks good (Figure 21-31), choose File → Save.**

To see the results of your hard work, open the *products.asp* page in Dreamweaver and press the F12 key (option-F12) to preview the page in a browser. Now click a link to see the details for that product.

Note: If your local root folder isn't the same as your testing server, you need to move your files *from* the root folder *to* the testing server to preview these dynamic pages. See page 542 for more details on transferring files.

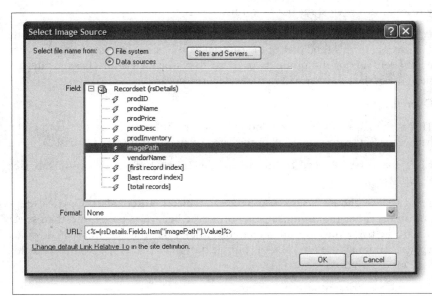

Figure 21-30:
Paths for links and images needn't be hardwired into a Web page. You can retrieve paths for images and links from a database source. In this case, depending on which product's currently on display, a different product image appears on the page.

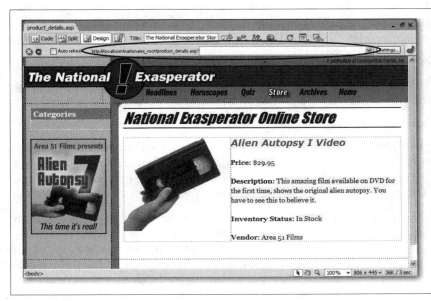

Figure 21-31:
You can preview additional records by modifying the URL that appears just below the document toolbar (circled). In the box just to the right of product_details.asp?, type: prodID=12. The information for the product with ID number 12 appears. Try other numbers to view other products.

Operators Standing By

One final touch would make the products page perfect. Each product sold at the *National Exasperator* online store belongs to a category—shirts, videos, books, weird stuff, and so on. Shoppers might find it useful to view a list of just what they're looking for—just the books, for instance.

Since category information is stored in the database, you can use this info to create such a feature. In this final part of the tutorial, you'll add a category navigation bar along the left side of the products page, so that when a visitor clicks a category name, a list of the products within that category appears:

1. **Open the *products.asp* page.**

   This is the page to which you add the category links. The first step is to add a new recordset that retrieves all of the category names from the database.

2. **Click the Insert Recordset button on the Insert bar's Application tab (see Figure 21-1).**

   You can also choose Insert → Application Objects → Recordset. Or click the + button on either the Bindings panel or Server Behaviors panel, and then select Recordset from the pop-up menu. In either case, the Recordset dialog box opens. (You may need to click the Simple button to switch the Recordset dialog box out of advanced mode.)

3. **Type *rsCategories* into the Name box.**

   The *National Exasperator* database includes a table with the names of each category of product sold. You'll use this table to dynamically generate the list of category names.

4. **From the Connections pop-up menu, select "connNationalEx."**

   This is the same connection you've used throughout this tutorial. In this case, you're going to retrieve information from a different table in that database.

5. **Select Category from the Table menu.**

   The Category table is very basic: just a name and ID number. The Products table identifies a category by using a Category ID number—the table's categoryID field. You may wonder why a separate table's even necessary. Why not just store the category name with the product information?

   This design has two advantages. First, because the table's just a list of category names, you can easily retrieve an alphabetized list of those names by creating a recordset. That ability's useful, for example, when you want to add a list of categories to a page—as in these tutorial steps. In addition, the separate category table makes changes to categories easier. If you decide you want to change a name—say "Strange stuff" to "Rare and unique"—you need to update it only in one record in the Category table. If "Strange stuff" were stored in the Products table, you would then have to change the name to "Rare and unique" in potentially hundreds of records.

6. **Make sure the All radio button is selected, and then choose "categoryName" from the Sort box.**

At this point, the dialog box should look like Figure 21-32.

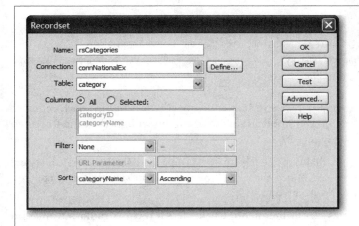

Figure 21-32:
By storing all the product category names in a single table, you can build a dynamic category navigation bar with the help of a simple recordset.

7. **Click OK to apply the recordset to the page.**

Now the page has two recordsets—one to retrieve product info, the other to retrieve the list of categories. You'll add the category name to the page next. The Bindings panel should look like Figure 21-33 (if the Bindings panel isn't open, press Ctrl+F10 (⌘-F10).

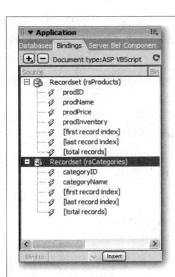

Figure 21-33:
The Bindings panel displays all recordsets currently applied to a page. To hide the recordset's field names, click the – sign (arrow on the Mac) to the left of the recordset icon.

8. **From the Bindings panel, drag "categoryName" to the empty space just below the word "Categories" in the Document window.**

   This adds the dynamic text for the category name to the page. Next, you'll add a repeating region so that *all* the category names appear.

Note: You'll probably notice that step 8 makes the sidebar bump out into the main area of the page. This happens because Dreamweaver is currently using the long-winded placeholder name *rsCategories. categoryName.* When the real category names (which are much shorter) appear on the real Web page, the sidebar returns to its normal width.

---

9. **Make sure the dynamic text you just added is still selected in the Document window, and then, on the Application tab of the Insert bar, click the Repeated Region button (see Figure 21-1).**

   The Repeat Region dialog box (Figure 21-12) appears, so that you can select which recordset to use. Since there are now two recordsets on this page, you need to pick the appropriate one.

10. **Select "rsCategories" from the menu. Click the All records radio button, and then click the OK button to create the repeating region.**

    If you preview the page at this point, you see a list of categories along the left side of the page. To make this list a functional navigation bar, you'll add a Go To Detail Page server behavior.

11. **If the dynamic text you added in step 8 isn't still selected in the document window, click to select it.**

    You'll add a link to this text using the Go To Detail Page server behavior.

12. **From the Application tab of the Insert bar, choose Go To Detail Page (see Figure 21-19).**

    The Go To Detail Page dialog box appears. This window lets you create a special link to another dynamic page—in this case a page that lists all the products in a particular category.

13. **Click the Browse button. Select the file *categories.asp*, and then select "rsCategories" from the Recordset menu.**

    Dreamweaver fills out all the other settings (Figure 21-34).

14. **Click OK to close this window.**

    And now you'll preview the page to make sure everything's working.

15. **Press F12 (Option-F12). When the page opens, click any of the category names at the left side of the page.**

A new page should open, listing all of the products within a particular category, as shown in Figure 21-35.

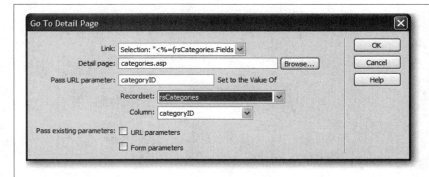

Figure 21-34:
The categories.asp page, linked to in this case, is a dynamic page that's already been created. Essentially it's built just like the products.asp page—the only difference is that the products recordset has an added filter that only retrieves records that match a particular category ID.

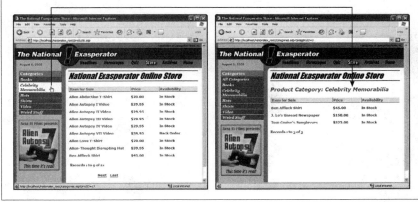

Figure 21-35:
The Go To Detail Page server behavior isn't limited to linking a page that lists just one record. It can provide the information necessary to retrieve any number of database records that meet certain requirements—in this case, all records that match a particular category.

Congratulations! You've just built two powerful, complex, dynamic Web pages (and probably watched three presidential administrations pass). As you can see, Dreamweaver has an impressive array of tools for building dynamic pages. And even though there were some twists and turns to negotiate, you never once had to resort to the dreaded Code view.

Web Pages that Manipulate Database Records

Just displaying database information on a Web page is useful, but you may be more interested in using the Web to *collect* information from your site's visitors (see Figure 22-1). Maybe something as simple as an online registration form will do the trick. Other times, you may have something more ambitious in mind—a full-fledged e-commerce system, for example, which doesn't pay the bills unless it provides a way to collect product orders and credit card numbers.

Once you've got data in the database, clearly you'll need a way to update and delete that information. After all, prices change, products are discontinued, and you may suddenly want to remove any record of "Harvey the Wise Guy" from your site's online guestbook. Thankfully, Dreamweaver makes changing information in a database simple and painless.

Tip: You may feel more comfortable learning these concepts by *doing* them. If so, turn to the tutorial on page 788 before reading this next section.

Adding Data

As noted in Chapter 9, the primary method of collecting information over the Internet is the *HTML form*. Its basic elements—text boxes, radio buttons, pop-up menus, and so on—can collect a wide assortment of data. But to put this information into a database, you need to either write your own program or simply use Dreamweaver's built-in tools. With its Record Insertion Form wizard and Insert Record server behavior, Dreamweaver makes adding data a simple process.

Warning: You might not want just anyone adding, editing, or deleting database information. To control access to these types of pages—or any page, for that matter—use Dreamweaver's User Authentication server behaviors, as discussed on page 807.

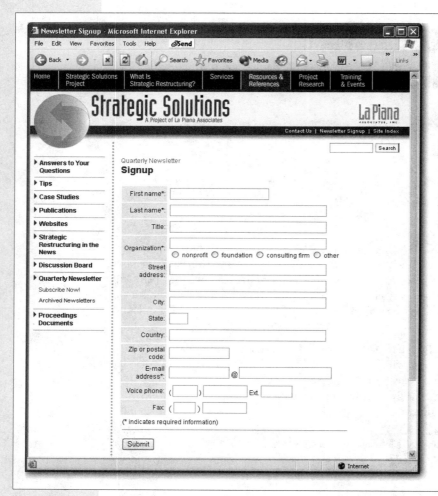

Figure 22-1:
Whether you're collecting credit card information for an e-commerce site or gathering sign-up information for an online newsletter, Dreamweaver simplifies the process of collecting information from a Web page and storing it in a database.

Dreamweaver's Record Insertion Form Wizard

Dreamweaver's Record Insertion Form wizard is the quickest way to build a page for adding records to a database. It builds a form, creates a table, and adds all of the necessary programming code in just a couple of steps. To use it:

1. **Create a new Web page and save it to your site (or open a dynamic Web page that you've already created).**

   Make sure the page uses the extension (.asp, .aspx, .cfm, .php, .jsp) that matches the server model (page 685) of your site. (See page 698 for info on creating new dynamic pages.)

2. **In the document window, click where you want the insertion form to appear. Choose Insert → Application Objects → Insert Record → Record Insertion Form Wizard.**

   You can also select Record Insertion Form Wizard from the Insert Record menu on the Application tab of the Insert bar. Either way, the Record Insertion Form window opens (Figure 22-2).

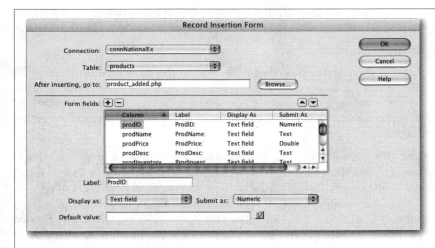

Figure 22-2:
When creating a form, it's a good idea to remove columns the database creates for its own use, such as record ID numbers. Here, the column prodID is a unique ID number created by the database. Whenever someone adds a new record, the database creates a new, unique product ID number. You wouldn't want anyone to tamper with this number, so leave it off the form.

3. **From the Connection menu, select the database connection.**

   Dreamweaver needs a place to put the data your forms are collecting. If your site works with several databases, select the connection for the database that this form will add information to. (Database connections are described on page 699.)

4. **Choose a table from the Table menu.**

   A list of all tables available in the database appears in this menu. You can insert data only into a single table, and one page can hold only one Insert Record behavior. This means if you need to add records to multiple tables, you must create multiple Web pages, each with its own Record Insertion form.

   If you have a table for customers and another for products, you'll need separate Add Customers and Add Products pages. You could then create a main Administration page that provides links to each of these table-updating pages.

5. **Click the Browse button. Navigate to and select a file from your Web site.**

Choose the page your visitors will see after adding a record to the database. It could simply be a page saying, "Thanks for signing up with our Web site." Or if the insertion form adds a new employee to your company's employee database, you could choose the page that lists all of the employees (including the one just added to the database).

ASP.NET note: On ASP.NET pages, you also have the option of specifying an "error page," which appears when the addition to the database fails for some reason.

You can also change how the menu item for each database column is formatted on the page, as follows.

6. **In the "Form fields" box, select a database column and change its settings, if you like.**

Your options include:

- **Label** is the text Dreamweaver adds next to the form field on the page. It identifies what someone should type in the field, like First Name. Dreamweaver just uses the name of the column in the database—fName, for instance—so it's usually best to change this text to something more understandable.

- **The "Display as" menu** lets you select the *type* of form element you want to use to collect the column's information. For example, if the column is someone's first name, select Text Field. This selection will add a text box to the form, where visitors can type their names. On the other hand, if people are supposed to choose from a limited number of choices (U.S. Postal Service, FedEx–2 day, and FedEx–next morning, for example), you might select Radio Group instead.

  Radio buttons or pop-up menus can also ensure consistency and rule out typos. On a form that asks visitors to indicate the state they live in, you could offer a pop-up menu that lists the 50 states. If you provided a text box instead, your visitors would be able to type in every conceivable abbreviation and misspelling. (For a description of the different types of form elements, see page 366.)

Note: Dreamweaver can also create *dynamic* menus, which display data taken from a database. See page 781.

- **The "Submit as" menu** is automatically determined according to how you've set up your database. It tells Dreamweaver what kind of data the field contains: text, number, date, and so on. In most cases, Dreamweaver figures this information out correctly, so you won't need to change anything.

- The **"Default value" text box** lets you preload a form field with information. It's actually the same as a text field's *initial value*, as described on page 371. You can also add a dynamic value generated by your server model's programming language. If you had a field called *date*, for example, you could add today's date to the field automatically by typing <%= *date* %> (in the ASP/VBScript server model).

Depending on what type of field you selected from the "Submit as" menu, the Default value text box might be replaced with one of three different types of controls: for a checkbox, radio buttons provide the simple choice of either checked or not checked; if you selected Menu or Radio Group, a properties button appears that lets you set the options that appear in the drop-down menu or radio group on the insert form—the process is the same as adding a dynamic menu or dynamic radio button group, as described on page 781.

PHP note: To generate the current date (year, month, and day) in a format that can be stored in a MySQL date field, use this code: <?php echo date("Y-m-d") ?>. MySQL stores dates in a special format, so a date like 1/15/2005 is stored in a MySQL date field as 2005-01-15.

In most cases, you'll change the label of every column. But for now, leave the other options alone.

7. **Click OK to close the window and create the form.**

Dreamweaver inserts a table, form, and all of the form elements you specified. At this point, the page is complete and ready to accept information. Unfortunately, Dreamweaver doesn't let you return to this window to make any changes. (If you quickly realize that you made a mistake, you can always use Ctrl+Z [⌘-Z] to undo the operation and then reapply Insert Record Form.)

To ensure your form works correctly and doesn't produce any errors when it's submitted, add form validation (see the box "Validate That Form" on page 768).

Warning: Once you've added the form, don't rename any form fields. You'll break the script responsible for inserting the record. If that happens, see page 770 for information on updating the Insert Record server behavior.

Using the Insert Record Behavior

Dreamweaver's Record Insertion Form wizard makes quick work of adding the table, form, and programming code required to create a Web page for adding data to a table. At times, though, you might want a more customized approach. Perhaps you've already designed a form that you'd like to use or created a beautiful table design for your form. Rather than relying on Dreamweaver's rather pedestrian table and form design, you can supercharge your own design with the Insert Record server behavior.

To build a page for adding database records, start by creating a Web page for your server model (ASP, PHP, ASP.NET, or whatever). Add a form to the page (see Chapter 10). Make sure it has one form field for every column you wish to add data to. Every time a visitor fills out the form, the database acquires a new record.

In some cases, you won't include certain form fields. For example, a database table's primary key (a unique identifier for each record) is usually generated automatically by the database for each new record. In this case, you wouldn't add a field for this column.

TROUBLESHOOTING MOMENT

Validate That Form

You never know what someone might type into a Web form and try to submit to a database. Maybe the form field asks for the visitor's age. Aside from the fact you probably won't get an honest answer, the visitor may make an honest mistake by typing the wrong keys—ew instead of 32, for example. If you set up the database to accept only numbers for the age column, the person submitting the form will receive a stern error message.

In another situation, you may require a name and email address. However, someone could easily overlook or ignore these form fields. Dealing with missing and incorrect data is the bane of all database developers.

To circumvent these problems, it's a good idea to turn to *form validation*. You've already encountered Dreamweaver's Form Validation behavior on page 382. It prevents a form from being submitted if information is missing or in the wrong format—if the information in a field is not a number, for instance.

Better still, you can download the ultimate extension for validating forms from renowned extension developer Jaro Von Flocken: the Check Form MX extension. It can validate not just text fields but menus, checkboxes, and radio buttons.

You can also make sure a value typed into a field is a date, or that two fields have the same value. (You'd want to check that two fields match, for example, in situations where you require visitors to register and make up a password before using your site. To rule out typos, you might require two Password fields—one labeled Password and another called Confirm Password.) To download the Check

Form MX extension, point your Web browser to *www.yaromat.com/dw/?t=Behavior&r=validation*.

Both Dreamweaver's built-in validation tool and Check Form MX are client-side JavaScript programs. That is, when someone submits the form containing a validation error, a JavaScript alert window pops up with the error message. Dreamweaver doesn't include any server-side validation features—programs that check the form after it's submitted to the Web server, and then return a Web page listing the errors. This latter option is usually more attractive and professional-looking, but it requires knowledge of programming in VBScript, PHP, or whatever server language your site uses.

If you don't know how to do the programming, there's free help, at least for the PHP/MySQL and ASP.NET server models. X-Code.com offers the VDaemon Extension (*www.x-code.com/vdaemon_web_form_validation.php*) to simplify server-side form validation for PHP. You have a choice of either a basic, free extension, or a souped-up commercial product. ASP.NET aficionados can download WWWeb Concepts' free ASP.NET Form Validation Tool Kit v1.1.5 (*www.ebconcepts.com/asp/extension_details.asp?MXP_ID=4*).

If you're willing to spend some money, WebAssist offers a commercial extension for server-side *and* client-side JavaScript validation that works with PHP, ASP, and ColdFusion (*www.webassist.com/Products/ProductDetails.asp?PID=33*).

In other cases, you might add *hidden* fields (page 378) that aren't set by someone filling out the form. Suppose someone signs up for your online newsletter, and you want to store the date of registration. Instead of letting the visitor fill out the date, add a hidden form field with the current date.

Once you've created the form, add the Insert Record server behavior like this:

1. **Choose Window → Server Behaviors to open the Server Behaviors panel.**

   The keyboard shortcut is Ctrl+F9 (⌘-F9). You can also use the Insert Record menu (see Figure 22-3).

Figure 22-3:
The Insert Record menu (found on the Application tab of the Insert bar) lets you use either an automated wizard (Record Insertion Form Wizard) or a basic server behavior (Insert Record) to add a record to a database.

2. **Click the + button on the panel and select Insert Record.**

   The Insert Record window opens (see Figure 22-4). It's very similar to the Insert Record Form window, but one key difference is that you must manually associate a form element with the correct database column. (Another difference is that you can't define default values for each form element in this window. You can, however, still apply default values to a form field using the Property inspector, as described on page 371.)

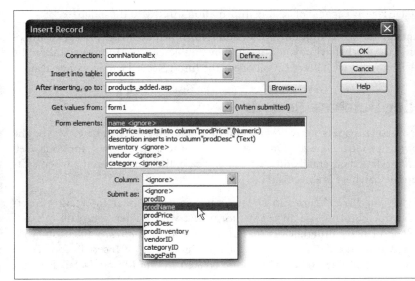

Figure 22-4:
In this example, the form contains a field named "name." To ensure that data typed into this field goes into the proper place in the database, you must select prodName from the Column menu. This tells Dreamweaver to store whatever visitors type into the "name" field in the "prodName" column. (You may not have to worry about selecting anything; see the Tip on page 770.)

3. **Make your selections from the first three options.**

   They're the same options described in steps 3–5 for the Insert Record Form tool (see page 765). You're telling Dreamweaver which database to use, which table to add data to, and which page to go to once the information is added to the database.

4. **Using the "Get values from" pop-up menu, select the name of the form.**

   Even though you can have only one Insert Record behavior per page, it's still possible to have multiple forms on a single page—a form for adding a record and a form for searching the site, for example. Select the name of the form used for adding data to the database.

5. **Select a form element from the list. Choose the matching database column from the Column menu.**

   For the form's information to end up in the proper columns of the database, you must tell Dreamweaver which database column will store the selected form field's information. You can let Dreamweaver choose the proper type from the Submit As pop-up menu. As with step 6 on page 766, this choice depends on how your database is set up (which Dreamweaver can figure out).

Tip: You need to perform step 5 only if the names of the form fields *differ* from the names of the columns in the database. If you name a form field *prodName,* for example, and there's also a database column named *prodName,* Dreamweaver automatically connects the two in the Insert Record window.

---

6. **Click OK to close the window and apply the server behavior.**

   The page is now capable of adding information directly to the database.

If you change the name of a form field, add a form field, or wish to change any of the settings for this behavior, you can edit it by double-clicking Insert Record on the Server Behaviors panel. This selection opens the Insert Record window once again.

Updating Database Records

Maybe someone made an error while entering data into the database. Maybe the price of your product changes. Or maybe you want to provide a way for your Web visitors to update their email addresses. In any case, the time will come when editing an online database is a necessity.

Creating *Update Record Forms* in Dreamweaver is very similar to creating Insert Record Forms. Both require an HTML form that your audience can fill out and submit. The primary difference is that an update form is *already* filled out with information from the database. It's like a combination of an Insert Record Form and a record detail page (such as the one created by the Master Detail Page set described on page 737).

The first step in creating an update form is to add a *recordset* to the update page (page 706). The recordset will retrieve the data that appears in each field of the update form.

The recordset should contain only a single record—the one to be updated. Therefore, you must use a form or URL parameter to filter the recordset (see page 709 for more on filtering). For example, on a page listing company employees, you could add an Edit button that would link to the page containing the update form. If you added a Go To Detail Page server behavior (see page 740) to the employee listing page, you could then pass the ID for a specific employee to the update page. In turn, the update page would use that ID to filter the database for a single record and display the employee information in the form. (If all of this sounds confusing on paper, try the tutorial starting on page 788, which takes you step by step through the process.) After you add the recordset to the update-form page, you have two options for building an update form. You can either let Dreamweaver automate the process with its Insert Update Record Form wizard, or build a form yourself and add the Update Record server behavior. The following pages cover both methods.

The Update Record Form Wizard

Dreamweaver can automate most of the steps involved in creating an update form:

1. **Open a dynamic page with a recordset already added.**

   Remember, the recordset should contain only a single record—the one to be updated. So you must add a filter when you create the recordset (see page 709 for more on filtering recordsets).

Warning: Make sure the recordset used to retrieve the information for the update form is the *first* recordset added to the page. If it isn't, Dreamweaver won't automatically fill out the Default Value field for each form element (see Figure 22-5).

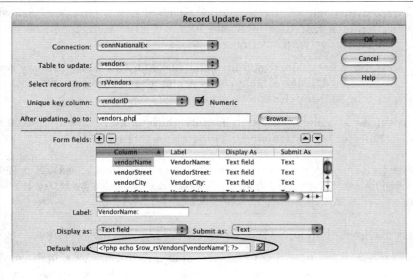

Figure 22-5:
A form field's default value is the information visible when the form first appears on the page. In the case of an update form, each form element will already be filled out with information from the database. After all, this page is meant for editing data that already exists, not for adding a new record. When using the Update Record Form wizard, Dreamweaver is smart enough to fill out the default value for each form field with the proper information from the database (circled in this image). (See the previous Warning above, however.)

2. **In the document window, click where you wish the insertion form to appear. Choose Insert → Application Objects → Update Record → Record Update Form Wizard.**

You can also select Record Update Form Wizard from the Update Record menu on the Application tab of the Insert bar (Figure 22-6). Either way, the Record Update Form window opens (Figure 22-5).

Figure 22-6:
The Update Record menu's wizard can create a no-frills Update Record Form.

3. **From the Connection menu, select the database connection.**

If your site works with several databases, select the connection for the database that this form will add information to. (Database connections are described on page 699.)

4. **From the "Table to update" menu, choose a table to work with.**

A list of all tables available in the database appears in this menu. You can edit data only from a single table, and a page can hold only one Update Record behavior. (In fact, a single page can contain only one record-editing server behavior. Therefore, you can't use a single page to add, edit, and delete records; you must create a separate page for each operation.)

5. **Make sure the recordset you created earlier is selected in the "Select record from" menu.**

The recordset should be selected already. If it's not, you must have created another recordset first. As a result, the Record Update Form command may function incorrectly (see the Warning on page 771).

6. **In the "Unique key column" pop-up menu, make sure the table's primary key column is selected. If the column contains a number—and it usually does—verify that the Numeric checkbox is turned on.**

The "Unique key column" is used to identify which record to change during the update process. (For a description of primary keys, see page 697.)

Tip: If you get the following error—"Please choose a unique key from the selected Recordset, or Click Cancel"—then the recordset you added to the page did not include the table's primary key. Edit the recordset and click the "All" button next to the word Columns.

7. **Click the Browse button; navigate to and select a file from the Web site.**

This represents the page that will appear after a record has been updated. A good technique is to select a page that lists the details of the record that's being edited (like the detail page in the master/detail pages discussed on page 737).

Then, after updating the page, the visitor will immediately see a page showing the changes.

8. **If you like, change a column's settings.**

   After clicking a row in the Form fields list, you can change the Label, Display As menu, and Submit As properties of the database column, the same as when inserting a record as described on page 766. For example, if the table includes a Description column that might hold a fair amount of text, then select Text Area from the Display As menu. This way, the form will include a larger text box that can display all of the description.

   You usually don't change the Submit As option, which determines what kind of data to submit—text, a number, and so on—because Dreamweaver automatically gets this information from the database. In addition, you would rarely change the Default Value property. Since this represents the data pulled out of the database for a particular record, modifying the default value will *always* change that information in the database.

Tip: Sometimes you want to change the Default Value for a column. For example, say a table includes a column to track the date a record was last updated. In this case, you would make the Default Value show the current date (instead of the date already stored in the database). When someone updates a record, the database automatically records the current date in the "last update" field. You can find the ASP and PHP code needed to do just that on page 767.

   To delete a field so it doesn't appear in the form, click the Remove (minus sign [–]) button. You should *always* take this opportunity to remove the table's primary key—the column you selected in step 5. Since the key identifies the record, allowing someone to edit this could cause problems to your database, such as overwriting data for another record.

9. **Click OK to close the window.**

   Dreamweaver inserts a table, form, and all of the form elements you specified.

Once you click OK to close the Record Update Form dialog box, you can never again return to it. From now on, you make any changes by editing the Update Record Server behavior, as described next. You're also free to use any of Dreamweaver's editing tools to format the table, labels, and form elements any way you wish.

Note: After using the Update wizard, don't change the name of the form or its fields. Because the program that updates the database relies on these names, changing them will stop the update code from working.

The Update Record Server Behavior

Dreamweaver's Record Update Form wizard makes it delightfully easy to add the table, form, and programming code required to create a Web page for editing

---

database records. But when you need more flexibility—if you've already designed a form that you'd like to use or created a table design for your form—the Update Record server behavior lets you keep your own beautiful design and give it the power to update a database.

You must start with a page that has a filtered recordset, as described on pages 770–771. Then add a form to the page (see Chapter 10). Make sure the form has one form field for every database column that is to be edited. Don't include a form field for the database table's primary key. (Allowing anyone to change the primary key could have disastrous effects on your database.)

Tip: Giving your form fields the same names used for the database table's columns will speed up the process of adding the Update Record server behavior.

At this point, the form is full of empty fields. If you preview the page, none of the data you retrieved from the recordset appears. To fill the form with data, you must *bind* data from the recordset to each form field, as follows:

1. **In the document window, select the form field.**

   Just click the form field to select it.

Note: These instructions apply to text and hidden fields. Information on binding data to radio buttons, checkboxes, and menus appears on page 779.

---

2. **In the Property inspector, click the dynamic data button (the lightning bolt) to the right of the Init Val box.**

   The Dynamic Data window appears (Figure 22-7).

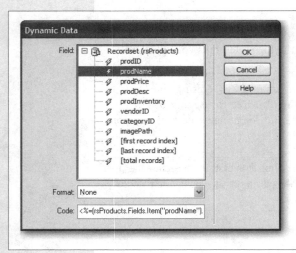

Figure 22-7:
The Dynamic Data window lets you add information from a recordset to form fields, so parts of a form can be pre-filled out. This is exactly what you want to do when updating information already in the database. In fact, the Dynamic Data window will display and let you use additional data sources (like URL variables) that you've added to the page (see page 818).

Tip: You can also bind data from a recordset to a form field by dragging the database column from the Bindings panel (page 724) and dropping it onto the form field.

3. **Click the + button next to the recordset used for the update page.**

A list of all columns retrieved by the recordset appears.

4. **Select the name of the table column you wish to bind to the form field. Click OK.**

You should ignore the Format menu and Code box. The form field is now set to display information from the recordset.

Once you've created the form and added recordset information to each field, add the Update Record server behavior:

1. **Choose Window → Server Behaviors to open the Server Behaviors panel.**

The keyboard shortcut is Ctrl+F9 (⌘-F9).

2. **Click the + button on the panel and select Update Record.**

The Update Record window opens (see Figure 22-8).

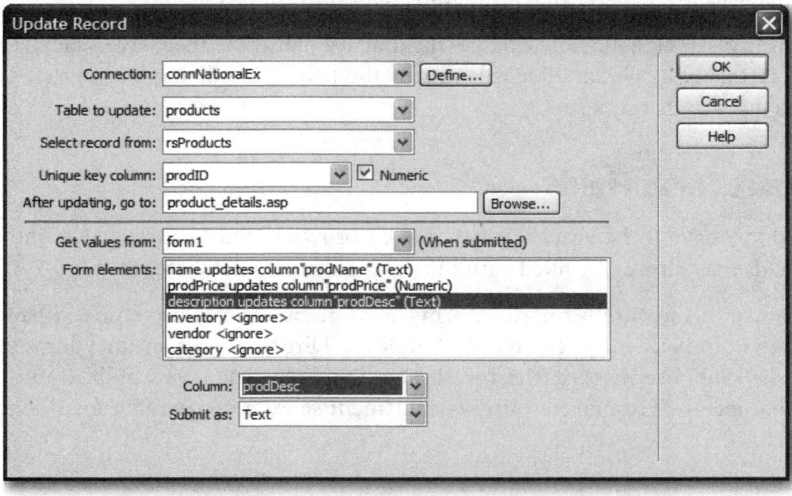

Figure 22-8:
The Update Record window is very similar to the Record Update Form window (Figure 22-5). The main difference is that here you must manually associate a form element with the correct database column.

3. **Change the first five options, if you like.**

They're the same as described in steps 3–7 for the Record Update Form tool on page 772. They tell Dreamweaver which database to use, which table to update data to, which recordset the record information is coming from, the table's primary key, and which page to go to once the edited information is added to the database.

---

4. **From the "Get values from" menu, select the name of the form.**

   Even though you can have only one Update Record behavior per page, it's still possible to have multiple forms on a single page: a form for editing a record and a form for searching the site, for example. Select the name of the form used for editing data.

5. **Select a form element from the list, and then select the matching database column from the Column menu.**

   For the form's information to end up in the proper database columns, you must tell Dreamweaver which database column you want to store the selected form field's information.

Tip: If you use the name of your database columns to name the form fields too, Dreamweaver automatically associates the two, so you can skip this step.

   Let Dreamweaver choose the proper type from the Submit As menu. As with step 6 on page 766, this choice depends on how your database is set up (which Dreamweaver can figure out).

6. **Click OK to close the window and apply the server behavior.**

   The page is now capable of editing information from the database.

As with any server behavior, double-clicking its name on the Server Behaviors panel—in this case, Update Record—opens the behavior's dialog box so you can make changes to its properties.

Dynamic Form Fields

Forms don't have to be empty. When a Web browser loads a form page, one or more fields may already be filled with information from a database.

You can use this feature for update forms on your site. It can also come in handy when, for example, you've created an Employee Directory section for your company's site. Suppose that, on the Insert New Employee page, you built a pop-up menu that lets the Human Resources department select a department for the new employee.

Note: Dreamweaver 8 adds some advanced form features for ASP.NET and ColdFusion 7. When working on a .NET page, an ASP.NET tab appears on the Insert bar. This advanced feature requires a good understanding of ASP.NET to use. You can find information on .NET here: *http://asp.net/Tutorials/quickstart.aspx* and a specific discussion of .NET form controls at *www.macromedia.com/devnet/dreamweaver/articles/dotnet_webform2.html*.

Additionally, Dreamweaver 8 now includes commands (available under the CFForm tab of the Insert bar) for adding special ColdFusion forms. For more information on how these work, visit *www.macromedia.com/devnet/dreamweaver/articles/cf_extensions.html*.

You, the designer, *could* create a menu like this department list by manually typing the name of each department. But what if the names of the departments change, or new departments are added? You'd have to reopen the page and edit the form field each time. But if you opted for a dynamic menu instead, the page would build the Departments pop-up menu automatically by retrieving the current list of departments from the database (see Figure 22-9).

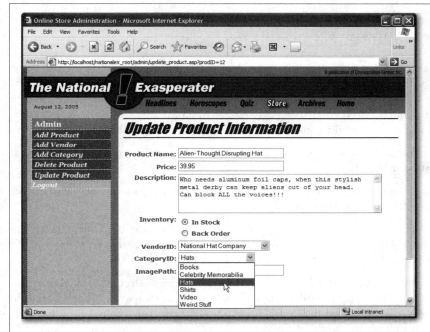

Figure 22-9:
Dynamic form fields come in handy with update forms. Form fields are already filled out with database information that's ready to be edited. Menus can also be dynamically generated from records in a recordset. In this case, the menu (shown open) lists records retrieved directly from a database table containing the product categories for the National Exasperator online store.

Dreamweaver's Record Update Form wizard creates these kinds of dynamic form fields automatically. In essence, a dynamic form field is a form element whose value comes from dynamic data in the Bindings panel. The dynamic data can come from a recordset (as with an update form), a form or URL parameter, or even a cookie or session variable (see page 818).

Whenever you wish to use a dynamic form field, start by creating a form. Add all form fields that might include dynamic content. (Not all the fields have to be dynamic, however. In the employee directory example discussed earlier, only the Department menu on the Insert New Employee form would be dynamic. The other fields for entering an employee's information would be empty.)

Next, add a recordset, request variable, session variable, or application variable to the Bindings panel (see page 724). Then, finally, attach the dynamic data to the form field. The process for binding dynamic data depends on the type of form field.

Dynamic Text Form Fields

Any form field that accepts typing—text, text area, and password fields—can be dynamic. For example, if a site requires a user login, you could include a "remember me" feature, so that when a visitor who's previously signed in returns to the site, the user name and password will already be filled out.

Tip: If you like the idea of a "remember me" feature for password-protected pages, try the free Save Password Login Form extension, which works with ASP, ASP.NET, PHP, and ColdFusion. You can find it on the Macromedia Exchange Web site (see page 670).

You can add dynamic data to a text field (also called *binding* data to the field) using any of the methods described below. (Remember, you must first have added the form field to the page and added the dynamic data to the Bindings panel, which means adding a recordset to a page, as described on page 706, or creating additional data sources [like cookies or session variables], as described on page 818.)

- In Design view, drag the dynamic data item from the Bindings panel and drop it onto the form field.

- In Design view, select the text field. In the Bindings panel, select the dynamic data item and click the Bind button.

- Select the text field. In the Property inspector, click the dynamic data button (the lightning bolt). The Dynamic Data window appears (see Figure 22-7); select the dynamic data item from the list and click OK.

- In the Server Behaviors panel, click the + button and select Dynamic Form Elements → Dynamic Text Field. In the window that appears, you'll see a Text field menu. Select the text field you wish to add dynamic data to; then click the lightning bolt button to open the dynamic data window. Select the dynamic data item from the list and then click OK. (Insert → Application Objects → Dynamic Data → Dynamic Text Field works, too.)

Tip: You can bind dynamic data to a *hidden* field using the same steps.

After binding the data to the field, the name of the data item appears inside the field—{rsDetails.adName}, for example. If you're using Live Data view (page 734), the actual data from the database appears inside the field.

Warning: Dreamweaver lets you format dynamic data in a form field just like dynamic text you add to a page, as described on page 724. Be careful with this option, though. If the form is submitting to a database, data may sometimes have to be in a certain format.

For example, prices are often stored as numbers inside a database. But using Dreamweaver's currency format, you can make a price appear as $34.00 in a form field. When your visitor submits the form, the $ sign goes along for the ride, causing the database to spit out a horrible error message upon encountering this nonnumeric character.

To remove dynamic data from a text field, just select the field and then click the Unbind button in the Bindings panel. (Deleting the contents of the field's Init Value box in the Property inspector also works.)

Dynamic Checkboxes and Radio Buttons

With a text field, you can dynamically change the *value* of the field. With checkboxes and radio buttons, however, you can control only their status (checked or unchecked) dynamically.

You can use this value to select one radio button in a group based on a value in the database. For example, as part of a product ordering system, shoppers could select a particular shipping option: USPS, FedEx, or UPS. But after reviewing their orders, what if they change their minds and choose a different shipping option? When they return to the order page, you'd want the Shipping Option radio button to reflect the choice the shopper had made earlier. In other words, you want the page to read the shipping option for the order from the database and highlight the radio button that matches. (You'll find an example of this in the "Building a Page for Editing Database Records" section of the tutorial starting on page 796.)

Dynamic radio buttons

You add dynamic radio buttons like this:

1. **Add a group of radio buttons to the page.**

   You should have as many radio buttons as there are possible values stored in the database column. Remember, if you wish to create a group of related radio buttons, you must give every button in the group the same name (see page 373).

   Note, too, that the value of each radio button must also exactly match the values stored in the database. For example, if a Shipping column in the database stores *USPS, FedEx,* or *UPS,* then the radio group should have three buttons. Each button would share the same name—*shipping,* for instance—but their checked values would match the different values stored in the database: USPS, FedEx, and UPS.

2. **Open the Server Behaviors panel (Window → Server Behaviors). Click the + button and select Dynamic Form Elements → Dynamic Radio Buttons.**

   The Dynamic Radio Buttons window appears (see Figure 22-10).

3. **From the first menu, choose the radio button group.**

   If your form has more than one group of radio buttons, select the one you wish to be dynamic.

4. **Click the dynamic data button (the lightning bolt) to the right of the "Select value equal to" field.**

   The Dynamic Data window opens (see Figure 22-7). Select the dynamic data item for this radio group. In a nutshell, the radio button whose value matches the dynamic data will be selected. If no radio buttons contain the same value, then no buttons will be selected.

Note: You only set the "Select value equal to" field once per radio group (not once per button in the group).

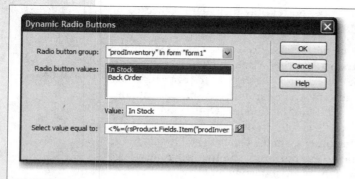

Figure 22-10:
The Dynamic Radio Buttons window lists the values of each button in the group. By selecting a button from the list, you can change its value in the Value field.

5. **Click OK to close the window.**

   Dreamweaver adds a Dynamic Radio Buttons server behavior to the page.

Dynamic checkboxes

Dynamic checkboxes work almost the same way:

1. **Add a checkbox to the page.**

   This process is described on page 372.

2. **Open the Server Behaviors panel (Window → Server Behaviors); click the + button and select Dynamic Form Elements → Dynamic CheckBox.**

   The Dynamic CheckBox window appears (Figure 22-11).

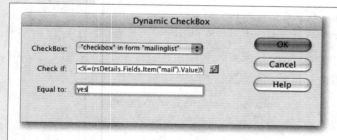

Figure 22-11:
The Dynamic CheckBox server behavior lets you control whether a checkbox is turned on or not, based on information from a database, cookie, URL parameter, or other piece of dynamic data.

3. **If the form has more than one checkbox, select a checkbox from the first menu.**

   Select the checkbox you wish to control dynamically.

4. **Click the dynamic data button (the lightning bolt) to the right of the "Check if" field.**

   The Dynamic Data window opens (see Figure 22-7). Select the dynamic data item for this checkbox.

5. **Type a value into the "Equal to" box.**

   If the value from the dynamic data (previous step) matches the value you provide here, the checkbox will be turned on. (If the checkbox is part of an update form, this should match the value you gave the checkbox from step 1.)

6. **Click OK to close the window.**

   Dreamweaver adds a Dynamic CheckBox server behavior to the page.

To *remove* the dynamic properties from a group of radio buttons or a checkbox, open the Server Behaviors panel (Window → Server Behaviors). Among the list of server behaviors, you'll see the dynamic radio button or checkbox behavior. It looks something like "Dynamic Radio Buttons(group_name)" or "Dynamic Check Box(checkbox_name)"—where *group_name* or *checkbox_name* will be replaced with whatever name you gave the buttons or checkbox. Select it from the list and click the Remove (minus sign [–]) button. (Pressing the Delete key does the same thing.)

Dynamic Menus and Lists

Dynamic menus and lists are among the most used form elements. They save you the effort of having to rebuild traditional menus or lists every time your company opens a store in a new state, adds a new employee department, or adds a new category to their product line.

To create a dynamic menu or list, proceed as follows:

1. **Create a form and add a menu or list to the page.**

   For example, choose Insert → Form, and then Insert → Form Objects → List/Menu. This is the same process as adding a menu or list, as described on page 375. Don't add any items to the list, though. That's the whole point of this exercise: Dreamweaver will build the menu or list automatically.

Note: Dreamweaver doesn't provide an automated way to create a dynamic list or menu for the ASP.NET server model. However, it can create one when you use the Update Record Form wizard (see page 771), and you can build one manually by following the instructions at *www.macromedia.com/support/dreamweaver/ts/documents/how_to_create_dynamic_list.htm*.

Alternatively, you can use the new ASP.NET insert bar to add special .NET form controls. See the Note on page 776.

---

2. **Add a recordset to the page that includes the information you wish to appear
in the menu or list.**

Perhaps you want to create a menu listing the different categories of products
your company sells—books, DVDs, CDs, lederhosen, clogs, and so on. If the
database has a table containing the categories, you could then create a recordset
that retrieves the name of each category. (In most cases, you'll also retrieve a
primary key, like the category ID field. The name of the category will appear in
the menu, while the primary key will be the value submitted with the form.)

3. **In the document window, select the menu or list, and then click the Dynamic
button on the Property inspector.**

The Dynamic List/Menu window opens (see Figure 22-12). The name of the
menu or list you selected appears in the Menu box.

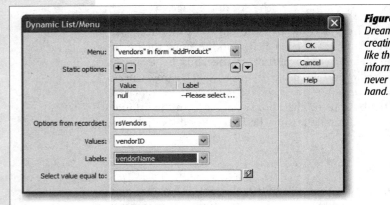

Figure 22-12:
*Dreamweaver simplifies the process of
creating automatically generated menus
like the one pictured in Figure 22-9. Using
information pulled from a database, you
never have to create another menu by
hand.*

4. **If you like, add some static options to the menu or list.**

A *static option* is simply a value and a label that you enter by hand—menu or
list items, appearing at the top of the list, that won't change. It doesn't come
from the recordset you created.

You could use this feature for options not likely to change—Amazon.com may
begin to sell electronics, hors d'oeuvres, and dermatology services, but chances
are good that books will always be among its categories. You can also use it to
provide clear instructions about operating this menu: "Pick a state," or "Choose
an option from this list," for example. Of course, this step is optional. (Adding
static options works just like it does in a regular menu's List Values box, as
described on page 375.)

5. **From the Options From Recordset menu, choose the recordset you created in
step 2.**

You've just told Dreamweaver where the items to be listed in the menu are
coming from.

6. **Choose a table column from the Values menu; choose another column from the Labels menu.**

   Menu and list items consist of a *label* (what the user actually sees in the menu) and a *value* (the information that's transmitted when the form is submitted). Using the example in step 1, you would select *categoryID* (or whatever the name of the recordset's primary key is) from the Value menu, and *categoryName* from the Label menu. If the label and value are the same, choose the same table column from both menus.

7. **If you want your menu to have one item preselected, then click the Dynamic data button (the lightning bolt). In the Dynamic Data window (Figure 22-7), select a dynamic data item.**

   This step is optional and most frequently used for an update form. For example, suppose you create a form for updating information on your catalog of products. When the update page loads, all of the form fields would already be filled out with information about a particular product. The menu that lets you specify the product's category, therefore, should have the name of the category that matches the database record displayed and preselected.

8. **Click the OK button.**

   Dreamweaver adds a Dynamic List/Menu server behavior to the page.

You can remove the dynamic menu or list by selecting and deleting it. To leave the menu but remove its *dynamic* properties, open the Server Behaviors panel (Window → Server Behaviors). Here, you'll see the dynamic list/menu behavior; it will be listed as "Dynamic List/Menu(menu_name)," where *menu_name* is the name you gave the menu or list. Select it from the server behavior list and click the Remove (minus sign [–]) button or press the Delete key.

To edit the behavior, just select the menu in the document window, and once again click the Dynamic button in the Property inspector.

Deleting Records

Dreamweaver's Delete Record server behavior lets you build pages for removing records from a database. Depending on which server model you use, the method of adding this server behavior varies. The Dreamweaver server behavior for ASP and JSP is the same, while the server behavior for PHP, ASP.NET, and ColdFusion offers a bit more flexibility.

Deleting Records for ASP and JSP

The setup is similar to using the Update Record server behavior, in that you must create a page with a recordset that retrieves a single record—the item to delete. This is just like a detail page, as described on page 737. Another page must link to the delete page and provide the proper key for filtering to a single record on the delete page.

One way to go about this is to add a link—Delete This Record, perhaps—on a record detail page. The link should pass the primary key for the condemned record to another page (the Go to Detail Page server behavior described on page 740 can help with this). This page—the delete page—would include a recordset that retrieves the file to be deleted. To confirm the deletion, the page might say something like, "Are you sure you wish to delete this record?" (Adding some dynamic text from the recordset, such as a name column, will help identify the record.)

What makes a delete page differ from a regular detail page is that it also includes a form with a single Submit button and a Delete Record server behavior.

To create a delete page, proceed as follows:

1. **Create a dynamic page containing a filtered recordset.**

   As noted above, the recordset should retrieve a single record—the one to be deleted. However, you don't need to retrieve *all* of the columns for the record. At a minimum, the recordset must retrieve the record's primary key, since the Delete Record server behavior needs it to know which record to remove. But beyond that, you should probably include some identifying information on the delete page, so that your visitor can make sure she's really deleting the right record. For example, if the page deletes an employee from the database, consider putting the employee's name on the page as one final check.

2. **Add a form to the page with a single Submit button (see page 379).**

   Change the label of the button so that it reflects the action it will perform—Delete This Record, for example.

3. **Open the Server Behaviors panel (Window → Server Behaviors). Click the + button and select Delete Record.**

   The Delete Record window appears (see Figure 22-13).

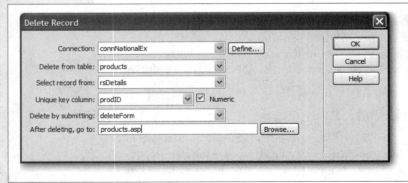

Figure 22-13:
Dreamweaver's Delete Record server behavior simplifies the process of removing information from a database.

4. Select a database from the Connection menu. From the "Delete from table" menu, select the table with the record to be deleted.

These steps should be familiar by now; the table you select should be the same one you used when creating the detail recordset for this page.

5. From the "Select record from" menu, select the recordset you added to this page.

This specifies the recordset on the page (if there's more than one) that Dreamweaver should use for specifying the record to be deleted.

6. Choose the table's primary key from the "Unique key column" menu. If it's a number, make sure the Numeric box is also turned on.

The "Unique key column" identifies which record to delete. (For a description of primary keys, see page 697.) Make sure you retrieved this primary-key information when you created the recordset, or the server behavior won't work.

7. Select the name of the form that contains the Delete button.

Unless the page has more than one form, the name of the form you created in step 2 should appear here automatically.

8. Click the Browse button; navigate to and select a file from the Web site.

This represents the page that will appear after a record has been deleted. This could either be a page with a confirmation message—"The Record has been successfully deleted"—or a page that lists the records of the database—a master page.

9. Click the OK button.

Dreamweaver inserts the code necessary to delete a record from the database.

Deleting Records for PHP, ASP.NET, and ColdFusion

Deleting a record using ASP or JSP is straightforward. For the other server models, the Delete Record server behavior offers a bit more flexibility and can be implemented in a variety of ways. You do not have to add a recordset to a page to delete a record, nor do you have to add a form with a delete button.

The main requirement: the page with the Delete Record server behavior must have some way to retrieve the primary key for the record you wish to delete. This can be a form, a URL, a cookie, a session variable, or any of the other data sources discussed on page 818.

For example, on a page that lists the details of a particular record, you could include a link to a delete page and pass the ID of that record in the URL (see "Passing Information Between Pages" on page 740). The delete page could then use the ID number in the URL to delete the record and then send the visitor off to another page—perhaps a page verifying that the record was successfully deleted.

Note: Because of this flexibility, under the PHP, ASP.NET, and ColdFusion server models, you could place a Delete Record server behavior on a blank dynamic page. All the page would do is delete the specified record and then go to another page on the site.

There are many ways, therefore, that you could delete a record in this server model. Here is a method that would provide the same experience as the ASP and JSP models discussed above—that is, a delete page that lets people confirm the item they wish to delete by clicking a button on a form:

1. **On one of the pages in your site, add a link to the delete page.**

   For example, on a page that provides the details of a single record, you could add a link to the delete page—maybe the word "Delete" or a button with a picture of a trash can.

   Alternatively, you could add a "delete this record" link as part of a repeating region (see page 728). In this way, you would have multiple records on a single page, each with its own link to the delete page. In both cases, you'd attach the record's primary key to the link, as described on page 740.

2. **Create a dynamic page—the delete page—containing a filtered recordset.**

   This recordset should retrieve a single record—the one to be deleted. As mentioned for the ASP and JSP models, you don't need to retrieve *all* of the columns for the record. At a minimum, the recordset must retrieve the record's primary key, since the Delete Record server behavior needs it to know which record to remove. You may want to include some identifying information, such as the name of the item to be deleted, so that your visitors can see what they're about to delete.

3. **Add to the page a form consisting of a single Submit button (as described on page 379).**

   When you create the button, change its label to reflect what it does—Delete This Record, for example.

4. **Select the form. Then, in the Action box in the Property inspector, type the page's file name.**

   For example, if the page is called *delete.php*, type *delete.php*.

   The *Action* property indicates where the form should be sent (see page 364). In this case, when the visitor clicks the Submit button, the form information goes *back* to the same page.

   This kind of trickery is common in dynamic pages. When your visitor clicks the Delete button, the form is sent to the same page—but this time the form doesn't show up. Instead, the Delete Record server behavior (which you're going to add in step 6) deletes the record and sends the visitor off to another page.

5. **Add a hidden field to the form (page 378). Name this field whatever you wish, but bind (attach) to it the primary key from the recordset you created in step 2.**

   This hidden field is what tells the Delete Record server behavior which record to delete. (For instructions on binding dynamic data to a form field, see page 776.)

6. **Open the Server Behaviors panel (Window → Server Behaviors). Click the + button and select Delete Record from the list of server behaviors.**

   The Delete Record window appears (Figure 22-14). This window differs slightly among ASP.NET, PHP, and ColdFusion. However, the basic steps described here are the same.

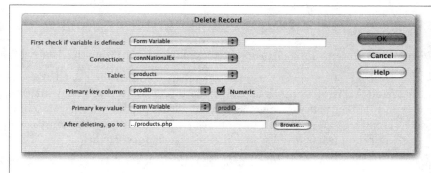

Figure 22-14:
The Delete Record window for PHP differs slightly from its .NET and ColdFusion counterparts. .NET lets you specify an error page so that visitors will see a different page if the delete action fails; ColdFusion lets you specify a user name and password for the database.

7. **From the "First check if variable is defined" menu, choose Primary Key Value.**

   This may seem like putting the cart before the horse, because you won't define the primary key value until step 10 below. However, this option lets you control *when* the record is deleted, by making sure the proper variable is defined *before* the server behavior deletes the record. In this case, the record won't go away until the visitor clicks the Delete button, causing the server to send a form variable containing the record's primary key.

   This is a necessary precaution; without this option, the record would be deleted whenever the page loads. Since the page really serves two functions—allowing visitors to confirm that they wish to delete the record, and actually deleting the record from the database—you need to make sure the visitor has first visited the page and *then* clicked the Submit button you added in step 3.

8. **From the Connection menu, select a database. From the Table menu, select the table with the record to be deleted.**

   These steps should be familiar by now. The table you select should be the same one you used when creating the detail recordset for this page.

9. **From the "Primary key column" menu, select the table's primary key.**

   This tells Dreamweaver which database field contains the unique key that identifies which record to zap from the table.

10. From the "Primary key value" menu, select Form Variable. In the box just to the right of that menu, type the name of the hidden field you added in step 5.

This is the final piece of the puzzle. It tells the server behavior where to find the ID number for the doomed record. In this case, the form with its hidden field will supply the ID number.

11. Click the Browse button; navigate to and select your confirmation page from the Web site.

The confirmation page will appear after a record has been deleted. It's a page you've created in advance—either a page with a confirmation message ("The Record has been successfully deleted"), or a page that lists the records of the database—a *master* page.

12. Click OK.

Dreamweaver inserts the code necessary to remove a record from the database.

As with any of the other server behaviors that change content in a database, you should carefully control who has access to the delete page. Going to work one morning and finding that someone has deleted all the products from your company's e-commerce site is enough to ruin your whole morning. Dreamweaver's User Authentication behaviors, discussed in the next chapter, can help.

If you ever need to change any of the properties of the Record Delete action, such as picking a different page to go to after a record is deleted, you can double-click Delete Record on the Server Behaviors panel. The Delete Record window opens; make any changes and click OK.

Tutorial: Inserting and Updating Data

In this tutorial, you'll continue working on the *National Exasperator's* online store. You'll work on two administrative pages that allow employees of the *National Exasperator* to add new products to the database, and to edit products already in the database.

This tutorial assumes you've already completed the tutorials for Chapters 20 and 21. If not, turn to page 689, follow the instructions for preparing the application server, database, and Dreamweaver for this project. Then turn to page 744 and build the product catalog pages.

Adding an Insert Product Page

Start by opening a page that's already been created:

1. Open the file named *add_product.asp* in the *admin* folder of the local site you defined in Chapter 20.

Pages for adding and editing the online store's products shouldn't be accessible to the public; you wouldn't want just anyone adding products—"The Electric

Whoopee Cushion, by Mr. Hacker," for example—to the store. Accordingly, these pages are kept in a folder reserved for administrators of the Web site. (In the next chapter, you'll learn how to password-protect these pages.)

One piece of information required for each new product is an ID number for the vendor who manufactures the product. The database for these products actually contains several tables: Products, Vendors, and Category. Information about each vendor (name and contact info) is in the Vendors table, while information on each product (price, description, and so on) is in the Products table. A third table contains a list of product categories, which you used in the last tutorial to create the category navigation bar.

To keep the Vendors and Products tables connected, so that you know which vendor manufactures which product, the Products table includes a field containing the vendor's ID number. Whenever you add an item to the Products table, then, you also need to insert the vendor's ID number.

To make the process of selecting a vendor easier, you should add a pop-up menu that lists all of the vendors in the database. To make this kind of dynamic menu, start by creating a recordset.

2. **Choose Insert → Application Objects → Recordset.**

Or use any of the methods described on page 706 to add a new recordset; for example, clicking the + button in either the Bindings or Server Behaviors panel and choosing Recordset (Query). The Recordset window opens. Make sure that the simple recordset options show up (see Figure 22-15). Next, you'll define the properties of this recordset.

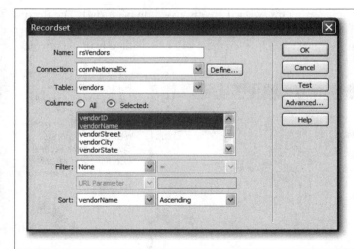

Figure 22-15:
When creating this recordset, make sure you're using the window's Simple options. If you see a button labeled Advanced, you're in the right place. (If that button's missing, click the Simple button to access the basic recordset options.)

3. **In the Name box, type *rsVendors*. Select connNationalEx from the Connection menu. Select "vendors" from the Table menu.**

    These three steps set up the name, database, and table required for the record-set. For a recap of creating recordsets, turn to page 706.

4. **Click the Selected radio button; select vendorID and vendorName from the Columns list.**

    You can do this by holding down the Ctrl (Option) key while clicking the name of each column. Finally, pick an order for sorting the list of vendors.

5. **Choose vendorName from the Sort menu. Make sure Ascending is selected in the Order menu.**

    The Recordset window should now look like Figure 22-15.

6. **Click OK to close the window and insert the recordset in the page.**

    Since the database also contains a list of product categories, next you'll create a dynamic menu for them as well.

7. **Add another recordset to the page by following steps 2–6: name the recordset *rsCategories*, select the "category" table, choose the All columns radio button, and sort by CategoryName.**

    You've just added a second recordset to this page. Now you're ready to add a form for inserting a new record.

8. **Click in the area directly below the headline "Add a Product." Choose Insert → Application Objects → Insert Record → Record Insertion Form Wizard.**

    (Other methods of inserting this wizard are discussed on page 764). The Record Insertion Form window opens (Figure 22-16). Next, you'll tell Dreamweaver which database to connect to and which table will receive data from the form.

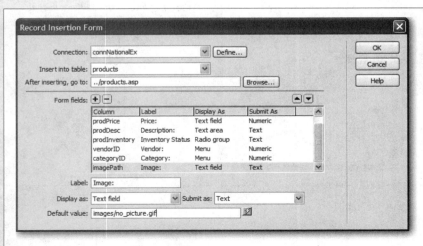

Figure 22-16:
While you can manually create a form and program it to insert a new record in a database, Dreamweaver's Record Insertion Form wizard makes the task a snap to complete.

9. **From the Connection menu, choose "connNationalEx." From the "Insert into table" menu, choose "products."**

   You can insert data into only one table at a time. In this case, you've selected the Products table because it holds all of the information for each item at the store. After information is added to the database, the visitor will be redirected to another page. You'll set this up next.

10. **Click the Browse button. Select the file *products.asp*.**

    After adding a new product to the database, your staff will be taken to the Products page (the one you created in the previous chapter). Since the newly added product is part of the database, browsing the products catalog will reveal the newly added item.

11. **In the "Form fields" list, select "prodID." Click the Remove (minus sign [–]) button to remove this field.**

    In some cases, the database itself fills in certain fields. For instance, every product in the database has its own unique ID—the table's primary key, which is generated by the database. When a new record is added, the database creates a new, unique number and stores it in the prodID column. Since you don't want anyone entering the wrong information here, you should remove it from the form Dreamweaver is about to create.

12. **Select the prodName column. Change the label in the Label field to *Product Name:*.**

    The label you type here doesn't affect your database in any way. It's just the text that visitors will see next to the form field. (You'll do the same thing with each field, to make the labels reader-friendly.)

    You don't need to change any of the other options such as "Display As" or "Submit As." You'll often change the "Display As" option, which changes what type of form element—like a checkbox or menu—Dreamweaver will display (you'll see this in step 14). However, you'll probably never change the "Submit As" option, which determines how Dreamweaver submits the data to the database. Dreamweaver figures this out correctly based on the design of your database.

13. **Select the prodPrice column and change the label in the Label field to *Price:*.**

    The next field, ProdDesc contains a product description, so it might contain a fair amount of text. The one-line Text Field form element, then, is just too small. You'll change that to the more spacious Text Area next.

14. **Select the prodDesc column and change the label to *Description:*. From the Display As menu, choose Text Area.**

    The database also tracks a product's inventory status: whether the product is in the warehouse or on back order with the manufacturer. You could let a store administrator type in the correct status, but that would take time, and, besides, he might make a mistake. (It wouldn't do for shoppers to see that the "Big Foot T-Shirt" is on "Gack Order.") So you'll simplify the process by adding radio buttons.

15. **Select the prodInventory column and change the label to *Inventory Status:*. From the Display As menu, choose Radio Group, and click the Radio Group Properties button.**

    The Radio Group Properties window appears (Figure 22-17). Here you're going to add the radio buttons you want to appear on the form. Remember, the value of each button must match the data stored in the database (see page 779).

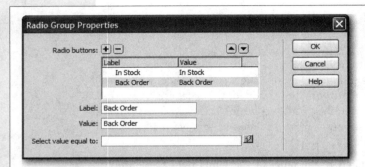

Figure 22-17:
Use the Radio Group Properties window to add radio buttons to a form. Radio buttons make data entry faster and less error-prone.

16. **In the Label field, replace "button1" with *In Stock*. Type *In Stock* in the Value field as well.**

    The label is what appears on the page, while the value is the information that gets stored in the database. You need to add one more button.

17. **Click the + button to add another radio button; repeat step 16 but type *Back Order* for the label and value of the second button.**

    The window should look like Figure 22-17. You're almost done with the form.

18. **Click OK to close the Radio Group Properties window.**

    Again, in an effort to speed up data entry and make sure the form is filled out correctly, the next two fields will be pull-down menus. First, you'll create a dynamic menu to display the list of vendors, as follows.

19. **Select the vendorID column, and then change its label to *Vendor:*.**

    This column only stores a number; the vendor's name and contact information is stored in a different table. To make entering this information easier, you'll make a dynamic menu that lists all of the vendors' names. When somebody chooses a name from the menu, the appropriate *vendorID* number will be submitted to the database.

20. **From the Display As menu, choose Menu. Then click the Menu Properties button.**

The Menu Properties window opens (see Figure 22-18). Use this window to build the menu.

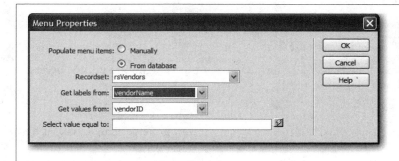

Figure 22-18:
Dreamweaver can create dynamic menus—pull-down menus (also known as pop-up menus) that get their labels and values from a database.

21. **Click the "From database" radio button. Make sure "rsVendors" is selected in the Recordset menu.**

You're telling Dreamweaver that the items to be listed in the menu are actually coming from a database query. In fact, they come from the recordset you created at the beginning of this tutorial—rsVendors.

22. **From the "Get labels from" menu, choose "vendorName." Then, from the "Get values from" menu, choose "vendorID."**

The labels—the text that appears in the menu—will be the names of each vendor. The value that's submitted with the form, meanwhile, will be the vendor's ID number.

You can skip the "Select value equal to" field. It's useful if you want a particular value to be preselected when the form loads, which is usually the case when you're *updating* a record in the database, since you need to display the current database information in order to update it.

23. **Click OK to close the window.**

The product category is another instance where a pull-down menu makes sense. You'll follow the same procedure to add a pop-up menu listing the names of all the categories available at the store.

24. **Select the categoryID column, and then change its label to *Category:*.**

The next few steps should feel familiar.

25. **Repeat steps 20–23; use the "rsCategories" recordset, retrieve the label from the "categoryName" field, and set the value to "categoryID."**

For the final field, you'll change the label and manually enter a default value.

26. Select the imagePath column, and change its label to *Image Path:*.

Because not every product has an image, you'll change the default value to point to a graphic that's already been created—one used to indicate that no graphic is available.

27. In the "Default value" box, type *images/no_picture.gif*.

At this point, the Record Insertion Form window should resemble Figure 22-16.

28. Click OK again to insert the form.

Dreamweaver adds a table, a form, and all of the programming code necessary to add a new product to the database.

29. Choose File → Save.

You're nearly finished. All that's left is to finish up the design and take it for a test drive.

Finishing the Insert Form

To make your form ready for primetime, you'll spruce up its appearance and prevent users from submitting bad data:

1. Select the table containing the form fields.

   The fastest method is to click anywhere inside the table and then, in the tag selector, click the <table> tag (the one farthest to the right in the tag selector). For other table-selection techniques, see page 248.

2. In the Property inspector, from the Align pop-up menu, choose Default.

   The Default option aligns the table to the left without adding bandwidth-hogging HTML code.

   It would be nice if the text looked more like the rest of the site, too; in the next step, you'll update the style of the text.

3. In the Property inspector, from the Class menu, choose productInfo.

   The text inside the table should now be formatted to better match the site's style.

   Next, add form validation so that users can't submit the wrong kind of information.

4. Select the form by clicking the <form> tag in the tag selector.

   You can also click the red, dashed line to select the form.

5. Open the Behaviors panel by choosing Window → Behaviors.

   Shift+F4 does the same thing.

6. **Click the + button and select Validate Form.**

   The Validate Form window appears. In this case, you want to make sure that when this form is submitted, both a product name and a price have been entered. It wouldn't make sense to have a product without a name or price. In addition, you need to make sure that the person types a *number* (not alphabetic text) into the price field. Since the database expects a number for the price, you'll receive a nasty error if anything but a number is submitted.

7. **From the listing in the "Named fields" box, select "prodName."**

   This is the field used for collecting the name of the item for sale. There should be something in this box when the form is submitted.

8. **Turn on the Required box.**

   Notice that (R) appears next to the "prodName" item. It tells you that a value is required for this field. Set up the price field next.

9. **In the "Named fields" box, select the text "prodPrice" item. Turn on the Required box and the Number radio button.**

   The window should now look like Figure 22-19.

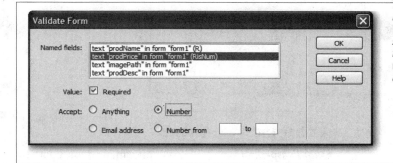

Figure 22-19:
The Validate Form behavior is a simple way to ensure your Web forms don't generate any errors when you're attempting to insert data into a database.

10. **Click OK to close the window and apply the behavior. Choose File → Save; press F12 (Option-F12) to preview the page in your Web browser.**

    The finished page should resemble Figure 22-20.

11. **Type information into each of the fields and click the "Insert record" button.**

    If you filled out all of the fields correctly, you should see the product page you built in the last chapter. Click the category name of the new product you just added, or navigate through the product pages until you find the newly added item. Try filling out the form, except for the name and price, to see how the Validate Form behavior prevents you from submitting the form.

There are many ways to enhance this page. For example, there's currently no way to *add a vendor* to the database. When you add a product to the database using the form you just created, you're stuck selecting one of the names listed in the pop-up menu. To make this application more useful, you could add a button or link to the right of the Vendor menu, call the link Add New Vendor, and link it to another insert record page that would include form fields for inserting a new record into the Vendors table. With the steps you've learned in this tutorial, you could even make that form return you to the Add Product page after you've added the vendor to the database.

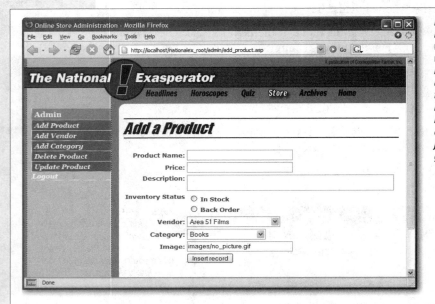

Figure 22-20:
No database-driven site would be complete without a way to add new records to the database. Use forms like this one to collect newsletter sign-up information, collect order and payment details, or just create an online guest book.

Building a Page for Editing Database Records

If employees at the *National Exasperator* type the wrong information for a particular product and have no way to correct it, they could be in a lot of trouble. After all, they'd be losing money hand over fist if the site were selling those $15.00 Loch Ness Monster keychains for only $1.50. That said, here's how to add an update-record page to the site.

Linking to the update page

An update page is very much like an insert-record page; the only difference is that the form is already filled out with information about a particular record. The first step is to tell the update page which product it's supposed to update. To do so, you must add a link to the product-details page you built in the last chapter.

1. **Open the file named *product_details.asp* in the root folder of the local site.**

   This page lists details for a particular product. As you may recall from last chapter, this page is itself accessed from the *products.asp* page, which displays a listing of all products in the database. By clicking the name of a product on that page, the *product_details.asp* page retrieves and displays information on just that product.

Now you need to create a link on this page that, when clicked, takes a visitor to an update page for the particular product.

2. **Click in the empty space under the table with the product information and type *Edit This Information*. Select the text you just typed and click the Browse For File button (the little folder icon) next to the Link field in the Property inspector.**

    The standard Open File dialog box appears. (The Go To Detail Page, described on page 740, is another way to create this link.)

3. **Navigate to and select the file in the *admin* folder called *update_product.asp*, but don't close the window yet.**

    You need to add some additional information, which identifies the product that needs updating, to the end of the URL.

4. **Click the Parameters button to open the Parameters window. Click in the name column and type *prodID*.**

    The Parameters button lets you add a URL parameter to the end of a link, allowing you to pass information on to another page. In this case, you're passing on a dynamic piece of data—the product ID number for the item currently displayed on the Product Details page.

5. **Press Tab twice to hop to the Value column. Click the dynamic data button (the lightning bolt).**

    The Dynamic Data window opens. Here you can select data that you've already added to the Bindings panel, such as columns from a recordset.

6. **From the rsDetails recordset, select the item "prodID" and then click OK.**

    (You may need to click the + button to the left of the word Recordset to see this option.) The link is nearly complete.

7. **Click OK to close the Parameters window. Click OK once again to close the Select File window and apply the link.**

    When you're all done, the link box in the Property inspector should look like this:

    ```
    admin/update_product.asp?prodID=<%=(rsDetails.Fields.Item("prodID").Value)%>
    ```

8. **Choose File → Save.**

    That was a lot of work, and you haven't started building the update page yet.

Note: You probably wouldn't want a link like this to appear for the average visitor to your site. After all, customers shouldn't be changing information on the products you sell. In the next chapter on page 837, you'll learn how to hide this link from unauthorized eyes.

Creating the update page

Now that the initial legwork is out of the way, you're ready to build the actual Record Update Form. To start, you'll add a filtered recordset to retrieve information for the product to be updated:

1. **Open the file *update_product.asp* in the *admin* folder.**

2. **Add a recordset, using any of the methods described on page 706. For example, choose Insert → Application Objects → Recordset.**

   The Recordset window opens. Make sure the simple options are displayed, as shown in Figure 22-21.

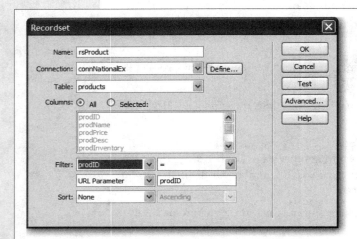

Figure 22-21:
When you filter on a table's primary key (prodID, in this case) using the = operator, the recordset never retrieves more than one record.

3. **In the Name field, type *rsProduct*; choose "connNationalEx" from the Connection menu, and select "products" from the Tables menu. Leave the All button selected.**

   Next, add a filter to the recordset. This will ensure that the recordset retrieves only a single record—the product you wish to update.

4. **From the Filter menu, select prodID. From the Comparison menu, select =. From the Source menu, choose URL Parameter. Finally, in the last field in the Filter area of the window, type *prodID*.**

   The Recordset window should now look like Figure 22-21. In essence, it instructs the recordset to retrieve only the record whose prodID matches the number passed in the URL parameter prodID.

5. **Click OK to close the window and add the recordset to the page.**

   Next, you'll create two more recordsets—a listing all of the vendors and a listing of product categories. You'll use them to create dynamic menus, just as you did on the insert form.

6. **Follow steps 2–7 from the "Adding an Insert Product Page" part of this tutorial (see page 788) to create new rsVendors and rsCategories recordsets.**

(You can also copy those recordsets from the insert-product page as described on page 721). The hard part's behind you. You can now use Dreamweaver's Update Record Form tool to finish the page.

7. **Click in the empty area directly below the "Update Product Information" headline. Choose Insert → Application Objects → Update Record → Record Update Form Wizard.**

The Record Update Form window opens (see Figure 22-22). Next, you'll specify the recordset and fields the form should update.

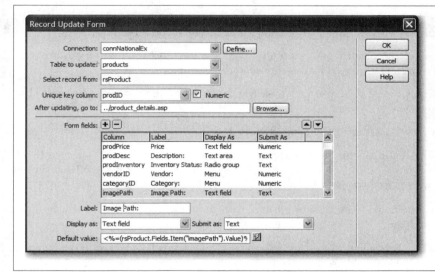

Figure 22-22:
Dreamweaver's Record Update Form makes very quick work of creating pages to update records in a database. But for it to work properly, you must make sure that the recordset selected in the "Select record from" menu was the first recordset added to the page (see page 771).

8. **From the Connection menu, select connNationalEx. Make these selections for the next three menus: "products" in the "Table to update" menu, rsProduct in the "Select record from" menu, and prodID in the "Unique key column."**

Next, you need to specify which page will appear after someone updates the record. Since the update page lets you edit a single product, it makes sense that after submitting any changes, you should see the newly updated information on that product's detail page.

9. **Click the Browse button. In the Select File window, navigate to and select the file *product_details.asp*. Click OK to choose the file.**

Now you must specify which fields will appear in the form. You also need to change which type of form element they should use, and edit their labels. This process is very similar to the Insert Record form; it's summarized in the following steps.

10. In the "Form fields" list, select "prodID"; click the Remove (minus sign [–]) button to remove this field from the list.

    Since prodID is a primary key generated by the database, no one should be allowed to change it.

    Next, you'll change the text label that will appear next to a couple of the fields.

11. Select the "prodName" form field and change its label to *Product Name:*. Select the "prodPrice" form field and change its label to *Price:*.

    Next, you'll provide some more room for lengthy descriptions of each product.

12. Select the "prodDesc" column. Change the label to *Description:*, and from the Display As menu, choose Text Area.

    As with the insert product page, inventory status information is better displayed with a simple pair of radio buttons. You'll add those now.

13. Select the prodInventory column. Change the label to *Inventory Status:*, and from the Display As menu, choose Radio Group.

    You now need to give Dreamweaver a bit of information about the radio buttons you wish to add to the page.

14. Click the Radio Group Properties button.

    The Radio Group Properties window appears (Figure 22-17). You need to add the radio buttons you want to appear on the form. The value of each button must match the data stored in the database.

15. In the Label field, replace *button1* with *In Stock*. Type *In Stock* into the Value field, too.

    The label will appear on the page, while the value will be stored in the database. You need to add one more button.

16. Click the + button to add another radio button; repeat step 15, but type *Back Order* for the label and value of the second button.

    The window should look like Figure 22-17, except that the "Select value equal to" box will be filled with the programming code necessary to select the correct button. After all, since this is an update form, one of the buttons should *already* be selected when the page loads.

17. Click OK to close the Radio Group Properties window.

    Again, in an effort to speed up data entry and make sure the form is filled out correctly, the next two fields will be pull-down menus. First, you'll create a dynamic menu to display the list of vendors.

18. Select the vendorID column, and then change the label to *Vendor:*. From the Display As menu, choose Menu; click the Menu Properties button.

    The Menu Properties window opens (see Figure 22-18).

19. Click the "From database" radio button, make sure "rsVendors" is selected in the Recordset menu, and then choose "vendorName" from the "Get labels from" menu. Now, from the "Get values from" menu, choose "vendorID."

    Leave the "Select value equal to" field as is. Dreamweaver automatically selects the appropriate choice, based on which vendor manufactures the product.

20. Click OK to close the Menu Properties window.

    You need to repeat the process for the product categories menu.

21. Select the categoryID column, and then change the label to *Category:*. From the Display As menu, choose Menu; click the Menu Properties button.

    The Menu Properties window opens (see Figure 22-18).

22. Click the "From database" radio button, make sure "rsCategories" is selected in the Recordset menu, and then choose "categoryName" from the "Get labels from" menu. Now, from the "Get values from" menu, choose "categoryID." Click OK to close the Menu Properties window.

    As with the previous menu, Dreamweaver automatically added the correct code to make sure the category for the product being edited is correctly selected when this update page loads.

23. Select the imagePath form field and change its label to *Image Path:*.

    At this point, the Record Update Form window should look like Figure 22-22.

24. Click OK to close the Record Update Form window.

    Dreamweaver inserts a table, form, form fields, and programming code to the update page. All that's left are some final cosmetic touches.

25. Repeat steps 1–10 from the "Finishing the Insert Form" part of this tutorial (page 794).

    Doing so properly formats the form and adds the necessary form validation behavior. Your finished page should resemble Figure 22-23.

26. Save this page and close it.

    To get a feel for what you've done, it's time to test your application.

27. Open the *products.asp* page. Press F12 (Option-F12) to preview it in a browser.

    The page lists the products in the database. Take a close look at one product in particular.

28. Click the name of any product in the list.

    A details page for that product appears.

29. Click the Edit This Information link near the bottom.

    The Update Product page appears, with the form already completed.

---

30. Change some of the information on the form and then click the "Update record" button.

Voilà! You're taken back to the details page for this product listing, which proudly displays the freshly edited content.

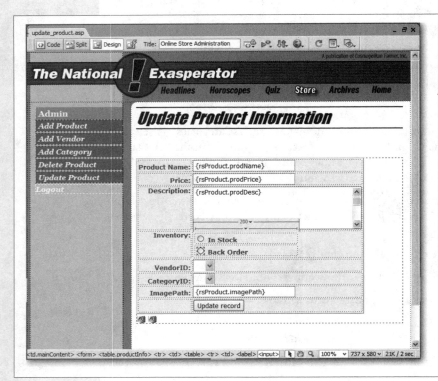

Figure 22-23:
When you're working in Design view, Dreamweaver highlights dynamic areas of the page—like this update form—in light blue. In Live Data view (see page 734), the same areas change to yellow. If you'd like to hide this coloring, open the Preferences window (Edit → Preferences [Dreamweaver → Preferences]), select the Highlighting category, and turn off the two Live Data checkboxes.

Creating and Linking to the Delete Page

Obviously, if a vendor stops manufacturing a product, or the staff at the *National Exasperator* decides to discontinue an item, they need a way to remove a product listing from the database.

Adding a link on the details page

To begin, you must provide a link to delete the product. A good place for this would be on the details page of each product. Since you've already added an Edit This Information link to this page, you must now add a Delete This Product link:

1. Open the file *product_details.asp.*

   Add a link that leads to a delete page.

2. **Near the bottom of the page, click to the right of the text you added earlier: Edit This Information. Press the Space bar, followed by the | character and another space; type *Delete This Product.***

   Now you'll link this phrase to the delete page.

Note: It's easy to accidentally click into the "Edit This Information" link. Doing so will make any text you type a part of that link. If this happens, just delete the new text you typed, click the <a> in the tag selector at the bottom of the document window, and then press the right arrow key. This moves the insertion point to the right of the link.

---

3. **Select the text "Delete This Product" and click the Browse for File button in the Property inspector (the little folder icon). Navigate to and select the file *delete_ product.asp* in the *admin* folder, but don't close the window yet.**

   You need to add the information that will let the delete-page form know which product it should delete. (ASP pages can also use the Go To Detail Page server behavior to accomplish the same thing; see page 740.)

4. **Follow steps 4–7 in the "Linking to the update page" part of this tutorial (page 796).**

   Doing so creates a link that not only goes to the delete page, but also passes along the ID number of the product to be deleted.

   There's one final step for this page: copying a recordset to use on the delete page.

5. **Open the Bindings panel. Select "Recordset (rsDetail)," right-click (Control-click) it, and choose Copy from the shortcut menu.**

   You've just copied the recordset information so you can use it on another page. (You can also copy a recordset from the Server Behaviors panel in this way.)

6. **Save and close this page.**

Creating the delete page

You've just created a link to the delete page; now you need to make the delete page do its stuff:

1. **Open the file *delete_product.asp.***

   This is where you'll paste the recordset that you copied a moment ago.

2. **Make sure the Bindings panel is open. Right-click (Control-click) in the empty area of the panel; from the shortcut menu, choose Paste.**

   Dreamweaver pastes all the programming code to create a recordset from the Details page. This is a fast way to reuse a recordset.

3. **In the Bindings panel, expand the recordset listing by clicking the small + button to the left of the recordset.**

Don't click the *large* + button, which lets you add additional recordsets. You just want to see an expanded listing of recordset columns so you can add some dynamic data to the page.

4. **Drag the prodName column from the Bindings panel and drop it onto the document window, just to the right of the text "Product to Delete."**

This inserts dynamic data into the page. When this page appears in a Web browser, the name of a product will appear in bold type.

5. **Click in the empty space just below the name of the product. Choose Insert → Form → Form.**

A red, dotted line—the boundaries of the form—appears on the page. Now you need to add a Delete button to the form.

6. **Choose Insert → Form → Button. (If the "Input Tag Accessibility Attributes" window appears, click Cancel to close it). In the Property inspector, change the value to Delete.**

This button, when clicked, removes one product from the database.

Note: If you have the form accessibility settings turned on (see page 367), then you'll see the Input Tag Accessibility Attributes window. Click Cancel to close this window.

---

7. **Open the Server Behaviors panel (Window → Server Behaviors). Click the + button and select Delete Record.**

The Delete Record window appears (see Figure 22-24).

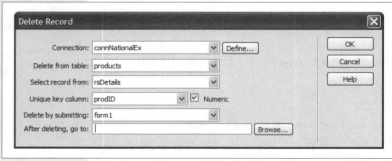

Figure 22-24:
The Delete Record behavior adds all the necessary programming code to remove a record from the database. All that's needed to make it work is a recordset that retrieves a single record— and a form with a Delete button.

8. **From the Connection pop-up menu, choose connNationalEx.**

Now tell Dreamweaver which table the record belongs to.

9. **From the "Delete from table" menu, choose "products."**

    This menu indicates the table containing the record that is to be deleted. The next box, the "Select record from" box will already be filled out with the name of the recordset you added in step 2. This recordset retrieves only a single record: the record that is to be deleted from the "products" table.

    You next have to specify the primary key (see page 697) of the record to be deleted.

10. **Select "prodID" from the "Unique Key Column" menu and make sure the Numeric box is checked.**

    The Delete Record window should now look like Figure 22-24. To finish filling out this window, you'll just tell Dreamweaver which page should appear after someone deletes the record.

11. **Click the Browse for File button in the Property inspector. Navigate to and select the file *products.asp*.**

12. **Click OK.**

    Dreamweaver adds the Delete Record server behavior to the page. You've done it! Now you need to test it out.

13. **Save and close this page. Open the *products.asp* page. Press the F12 key (Option-F12) to preview it in a browser.**

    The page lists the products in the database. Take a closer look now at a specific item.

14. **Click the name of any product in the list.**

    A details page for that product appears.

15. **Click the Delete This Product link near the bottom.**

    The Delete Product page appears (see Figure 22-25). Notice that both the product name and a Delete button appear.

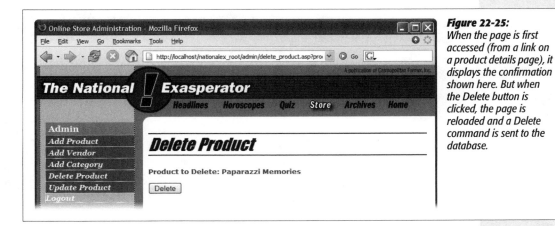

Figure 22-25:
When the page is first accessed (from a link on a product details page), it displays the confirmation shown here. But when the Delete button is clicked, the page is reloaded and a Delete command is sent to the database.

16. **Click the Delete button to remove the item.**

    Don't worry, you can always insert more products later!

    In any case, you'll note that that the product is no longer listed in the Product listings.

Of course, in the real world, you wouldn't want just anybody deleting, adding, or editing products on an e-commerce Web site. So in the next chapter, you'll learn how to keep prying eyes and mischievous fingers away from your coveted insert, update, and delete pages.

Advanced Dynamic Site Features

Dreamweaver's basic database capabilities are impressive. But there may come a time when you need to dig deeper into the program to build successful Web applications. Dreamweaver's advanced features let you, the mere mortal, do things that the pros do every day, like password-protect pages; display (or hide) content based on database results; and access information from forms, cookies, and URLs.

Password-Protecting Web Pages

Although Dreamweaver lets you create Web pages that can add, edit, and delete records from a database, your e-business wouldn't last very long if just *anyone* could remove orders from your online ordering system or view credit card information stored in your customers' records. And certainly your company's executives wouldn't be happy if someone accessed the staff directory database and changed the boss's title from, for example, CEO to Chief Bozo. For these and other reasons, Dreamweaver provides a simple set of tools for locking your pages away from prying eyes.

The User Authentication server behaviors can password-protect any page on your site. With this feature, you can limit areas of your site to registered users only, allow customers to access and update their contact information, create maintenance pages accessible only to administrators, or personalize Web pages with customized messages ("Welcome back, Dave").

ASP.NET note: Dreamweaver doesn't provide any User Authentication behaviors for ASP.NET. If you want to add these to your ASP.NET pages, you'll have to program them yourself or try a commercial extension like ASP.NET Authentication Suite from WebXcel (*www.webxel-dw.co.uk*).

To password-protect pages on your site, you'll need to get several elements in order:

- A database table containing visitors' login information.

- A registration form for adding new visitors. (This is an optional step, but it's frequently useful when you want to automate the process of adding user login information to the database.)

- A login form.

- One or more pages that need to be password-protected.

The Users Table

Your database must hold several pieces of information. For example, each visitor must have a user name and password to type in when he attempts to log into your site. If the name and password match a record in the database, then he's logged into the site and can access password-protected pages.

You might also need to include a field in the record for assigning an *access level* to each person. This way, your site can have multiple sections, accessible by different groups of people. Dreamweaver provides tools not only to require a proper name and password, but also to allow access to only those with the proper clearance level.

For example, if your site has a members-only section that affords registered visitors extra content or special features, you could assign the level of "member" to everyone who registers and give them access to these pages. However, you want only your site's administrators and staff to be able to update a product database or retrieve sales records, so you would give these users a level of "administrator" for access to these areas.

At a minimum, then, your database needs a users table with three fields (user name, password, and access level). You can either use a standalone table or incorporate this information into another table. For example, if you require people to provide their names, addresses, email addresses, and so on when registering with your site, you could include the three login fields in this table. For an e-commerce system, login information could be stored in the table holding customer information.

Tip: Most database systems let you assign a *default* (automatically proposed) value to a column. That way, when someone creates a new record and supplies no information for the column, the application enters the default value instead.

For starters, it's a good idea to assign a default value for the access-level field. You can set your database to assign the lowest access level–"guest," say–whenever someone creates a new user record. In this way, if you use a Web form for collecting and creating a new member, you can omit a form field for assigning an access level. This method is a good security precaution, as adept (and malicious) Web surfers could submit a fake form with a higher access level, potentially granting them access to sensitive areas of your site.

Creating a Registration Form

Once you've added a users table to your database, you'll need a way to add new members. If you plan to use password protection for sensitive pages that only your site's staff should access, you probably *shouldn't* create a Web form for adding new administrative members. You'd run the risk of someone finding the form and adding herself to the list of administrators. In such cases, you're better off adding the proper login records in the database system itself—using Microsoft Access, SQL Server, or MySQL Monitor, for example.

Note: If you do create a Web form for adding new members with a high access level, password-protect this form! Otherwise, anyone stumbling upon it could add new administrative members–and from there, Pandora's box would be open.

On the other hand, if you want to let *lots* of people sign up as members of your site, you might want to add a registration form that adds them to the list of the site's members *automatically*. This setup would free you from the headache of manually assigning user names and passwords for everyone who wants to become a member.

If the site already includes a form for collecting visitor information, you can simply add the proper user fields to this form. Say your site includes a "Sign up for our email newsletter" page that collects a visitor's name, email address, and other contact information. You could add a field called *user name* and another called *password.*

Tip: It's common to use an email address as a person's user name for password-protected pages. If you're already collecting an email address, exclude the user name field from the form.

When the visitor submits the form, the Web application adds all of these fields to the database. (To add records to a database using a Web form, see page 763.) While the process of creating a new member for password-protected pages is basically the same as adding a new record to a database, there's one additional step: you must make sure that every visitor has a unique user name.

Dreamweaver's Check New User Name server behavior ensures that each user name submitted in the form is unique. If the name already exists, the server won't add the new record to the database and will redirect the visitor to another page. To apply this server behavior, follow these steps:

1. **Add an insert-record form to a dynamic page.**

   The form should include fields for a user name and password. You might also add a field for an access level, if that's how you've structured your site. However, for a form that's accessible to the public, it's best to use the database to set a default value for this; see the Tip on page 809. (You'll need to use Dreamweaver's Insert Record server behavior. Creating insert-record forms is described on page 767.)

2. **Make sure the Server Behaviors panel is open (Window → Server Behaviors). Click the Add (+) button and, from the pop-up menu, choose User Authentication → Check New Username.**

   You can also use the User Authentication menu on the Application tab of the Insert Bar (see Figure 23-1).

   Either way, the Check New Username window appears (see Figure 23-2).

Figure 23-1:
Dreamweaver provides access to all user-authentication server behaviors from the Application tab of the Insert bar.

Figure 23-2:
When adding a new person to your database, the Check New Username server behavior lets you verify that the user name isn't already in use by another person.

3. **Select the name of the database field that stores each user name.**

   Note that this is the name of the column in the *database*, not the name of the form field on the Web page. This field doesn't necessarily need to be named "userName." It could be "login" or something else.

4. **Click Browse and select a Web page.**

Here, choose the page that will open if the user name is already assigned to someone else. This page (which you should create before applying this behavior) should include a note to your visitor, clearly spelling out the problem (the user name just supplied is already in use and therefore unavailable). To make re-entering information easier for your guest, you should include the insert form on this page as well, or provide a link back to the registration-form page.

5. **Click OK to close the window and add the server behavior to the page.**

Now when someone fills out the registration form, this behavior will kick in and make sure that no one else has the same user name.

Note: Unfortunately, registering a new member doesn't automatically log him into the site. He'll still need to go to a login page (described next).

After inserting the server behavior, Dreamweaver lists it in the Server Behaviors panel. If you wish to change any of its properties, double-click its name in the panel to reopen the Check New Username window (Figure 23-2). To delete the behavior, select it in the Server Behaviors panel, and then click the Remove (minus sign [–]) button.

Creating the Login Page

To access a password-protected page, your visitor must first log into the site using a Web form. This simple Web form should contain just two fields—a user name field and a password field—and a Submit button.

When someone attempts to log in, the values she types into the form are compared with the user name and password columns in the database. If there's a match, then she's transported to another page—often the main page of a password-protected area of the site. If there is no matching record, then the visitor is carted away to a page of your creation—an "Access Denied!" page or maybe just the original login page.

To create a login page:

1. **Add a Web form to a dynamic Web page.**

If your site includes password-protected pages aimed at a general audience of Web visitors, you could place this form on your home page. Or you could create a dedicated login page (remembering to provide links to this page throughout your site). However, if you're creating a login for administrators, you might want to put the login form out of the way, so that it doesn't get in the way of the average visitor.

Either way, the form should contain only a user name field, a password field, and a single Submit button. Naming the fields "username" and "password" (rather than keeping Dreamweaver's factory-set field names) will help with step 3.

---

2. **Open the Server Behaviors panel (Window → Server Behaviors). Click the + button and choose User Authentication → Log In User.**

   You can also use the Application tab of the Insert bar (see Figure 23-1) or choose Insert → Application Objects → User Authentication → Log In User to open the Log In User window (see Figure 23-3).

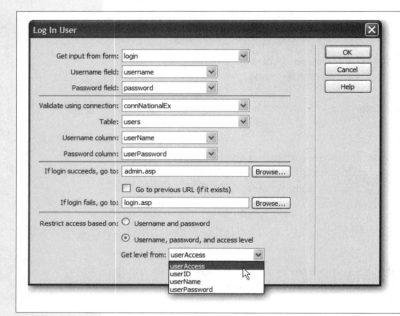

Figure 23-3:
Dreamweaver's Log In User server behavior gives visitors a way to log into your Web site, so they can visit password-protected pages. There are quite a few items to fill out here, but they're all straightforward. The last option lets you use access levels to limit pages of the site to particular groups of visitors—administrators, for example.

3. **From the first three menus, select the names of the login form, the form field for collecting the user name, and the password field, respectively.**

   You're telling Dreamweaver which form (if the page has more than one) and which fields to use for comparison to the users table in the database.

Tip: Dreamweaver automatically makes these first three menu selections for you if you've got just one form on the page. The first field on that form is the user name field, and the second field is the password field.

---

4. **From the "Validate using connection" menu, choose the name of the database connection.**

   This should be the database that contains the table with user login information.

5. **From the Table menu, choose the name of the users table.**

6. **From the "Username column" menu, select the database column that stores names. From the "Password column" menu, choose the database column for passwords.**

   The User Authentication server behavior will search these two database columns for a record that matches the values your visitor types into the form.

7. **To the right of the "If login succeeds" field, click the Browse button; navigate to and select a page from your site.**

   Most of the time, this will be the main page for a password-protected area of the site. If the site contains a members-only section, then, after logging in, the visitor would arrive at the Members page. If you're adding features for administering the site—adding, deleting, and editing database info, for example—create a main Administrators page with links to all of the database administration pages.

8. **Turn on the "Go to previous URL" checkbox.**

   This option is a little confusing, but very convenient. Imagine a visitor stumbling across a password-protected page (you'll learn how to protect pages in the next section). He simply comes across a link to a password-protected page and clicks it. Of course, since he hasn't logged in, he's denied access to the page and sent to another page. At this point, you're probably redirecting him to the login page, so he can log in and continue clicking his way through your site.

   That's where this feature comes in handy. By turning on this box, you permit the login form to take the visitor *back* to the page he couldn't get past at the outset. In other words, the visitor tries to access a password-protected page (*any* password-protected page in the site); he's not logged in, so he's sent to the login page. After successfully logging in, he's taken directly to the page he first tried to access (*not* the page you specified in step 7). This is very convenient for visitors who bookmark password-protected pages in your site, since it saves them the hassle of having to log in and then navigate to the page they wanted in the first place!

9. **To the right of the "If login fails" field, click Browse; navigate to and select a page from your site.**

   This page, which you need to create in advance, should explain that the user name and password were not correct. Since the visitor may have just made a typo, it's polite to either include another login form on this page or a link back to the login page.

10. **If the database includes a column for storing an access level, select the "Username, password, and access level" radio button.**

    This option not only lets folks log into the site, but also tracks their access levels. In this way, you can limit areas of your site to people with the proper access level—administrators, for example.

11. **From the "Get level from" pop-up menu, select the name of the database column that contains visitors' access levels.**

    Dreamweaver lists all of the columns in the table you selected in step 5. If the table doesn't have a column for this information, go to your database application and add it, or deselect the Access Level radio button. (Even if you don't currently have plans for offering different levels of access, it's a good idea to keep this option in mind. In the future, you may very well want to add special pages for administrators or Super Premium Members. Without an access level, anyone who has a user name and password will be able to visit those pages.)

12. **Click OK to close the window and apply the behavior to the page.**

    You can edit or delete this behavior by double-clicking its name in the Server Behaviors panel.

The Log Out User Behavior

Dreamweaver's Log *Out* User server behavior lets someone log out by clicking a link. Thereafter, her Web browser won't be able to load any password-protected pages in the site until she logs back in.

POWER USERS' CLINIC

Logging In: Behind the Scenes

The Log In User server behavior checks to see if the user name and password submitted by a form matches a user name and password in the database. If it does, the behavior generates two session variables (see page 823): MM_Username and MM_UserAuthorization (in the PHP/MySQL server model, these are MM_Username and MM_UserGroup). The first one stores the user name of the logged-in visitor; the second stores the visitor's access level. (The MM stands for Macromedia, since programs written by Dreamweaver engineers create these session variables.) The variables follow visitors from page to page of the site, until they log out, close the browser, or don't do anything on the Web site for at least 20 minutes.

The password-protection scripts use these session variables to allow or deny access to a page. But you can take advantage of these variables in other ways. You can add MM_Username to the Bindings panel (see page 818), for example.

You can then add it to your pages, like other dynamic data, for customized pages: "Welcome back Kotter176@aol.com."

Furthermore, since each user name is unique—just like a primary key—you can use the session variable to filter records in a recordset (see page 709). You could use this technique, for instance, when a logged-in visitor wishes to see all of his contact information. Create a recordset that filters the user table by the session variable.

You can also use the MM_UserAuthorization variable (MM_UserGroup for PHP) to control the display of certain areas of a page. For example, while regular members of your Web site might see a simple listing of products on a dynamic catalog page, administrators might see additional items like "Edit this product" and "Delete this product" buttons. The tutorial at the end of this chapter has an example of this scheme in action (see page 837).

This setup is useful when a visitor shares her computer with others, maybe at the library or at school, because it provides a sense of security that she has the ability to log out. (It's not absolutely necessary, though; her computer destroys the cookie used to identify the session variable used to keep track of her login status, anyway, as soon as she quits her browser. Furthermore, if a certain amount of time passes without any activity—usually 20 minutes—the Web server automatically destroys the session variable, effectively logging out the visitor. Again, though, a logout link can be reassuring to your audience.)

To add a Log Out server behavior:

1. **Open a dynamic page.**

   Note that since this adds programming code to the page, it works only on dynamic pages. You can't add a logout link to a static HTML page. So if you want to provide this option on all pages of your site, you'll have to save each page in your site as an ASP, PHP, JSP, or other dynamic page that matches your server model.

2. **Click the page where you'd like to add a logout link.**

3. **Open the Server Behaviors panel (Window → Server Behaviors). Click the + button and, from the pop-up menu, choose User Authentication → Log Out User.**

   Alternatively you can use the Application tab of the Insert bar (see Figure 23-1) or choose Insert → Application Objects → User Authentication → Log Out User. In any case, the Log Out User window appears (see Figure 23-4).

Figure 23-4:
To add a logout function to text or an image that's already on a page, simply select it and then apply the Log Out User server behavior.

4. **Select one of the two radio buttons.**

   There are two ways a visitor can be logged out. You can log her out when a page loads or when she clicks a link. You'd use the first method when you want to automatically log someone out when she reaches a specific page. For example, say you create an online testing application, where students would sit at a computer and answer page after page of questions. When students reach the last page of the quiz—maybe a page summarizing their results—you could automatically log them out. The next student sitting down at the same computer would have to log in, preventing the testing application from thinking the new test taker is the same person as the previous student.

The second method lets visitors log themselves out by clicking a link, so the menu starts out reading, "Create new link: 'Log out'," which adds a new link with the words "Log out" to the page. After adding the behavior, you can then edit the page and change *Log out* to any text you like, or even add a graphic button to the link.

Tip: You can also first add some text like "Quit system," select it, and then apply the Log Out User server behavior. Dreamweaver will automatically use that text, instead of its standard "Log Out" text, when creating the link.

---

5. **Click Browse; navigate to and select a page from your site.**

   Good choices for this page are the login page—so the next visitor can log in—or the home page.

6. **Click OK.**

   You've just applied the link and server behavior.

Protecting Individual Pages

To password-protect a Web page, apply the Restrict Access to Page server behavior. You have to do this for each page you wish to protect, and you can only apply it to dynamic Web pages. In other words, you can't password-protect regular HTML files, text files, graphics, or any other file that isn't first processed by the application server.

Note: Although some Web servers let you password-protect an entire folder's worth of files, Dreamweaver doesn't provide any tools to do so. (If your site runs on an Apache Web server, however, you can use .htaccess files to password-protect an entire folder. You'll find a quick tutorial at *www.freewebmasterhelp.com/tutorials/htaccess/3*, and a free online tool for creating these files at *www.webmaster-toolkit.com/htaccess-generator.shtml*. Visit *http://apache.org/docs/howto/htaccess.html* for more information.)

The Restrict Access to Page behavior works like this: When someone attempts to load a password-protected page, programming code in the page determines whether he's already logged in. If the page also requires a particular access level—administrators only, for instance—it checks to see whether the visitor has the proper clearance; if so, the browser displays the page. If the visitor isn't logged in, however, or doesn't have the proper access level, then he's redirected to another page—like an "Access Denied" page or the login page.

To apply this server behavior, follow these steps:

1. **Open the dynamic page you wish to protect.**

   It must be a dynamic page that uses the site's server model (see page 685).

2. **Open the Server Behaviors panel (Window → Server Behaviors). Click the + button and choose User Authentication → Restrict Access to Page.**

   The Restrict Access to Page window appears (see Figure 23-5).

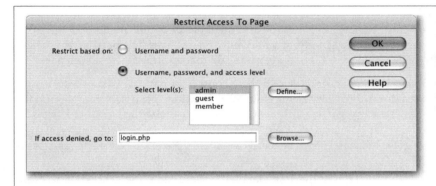

Figure 23-5:
If you want to give access to more than one group, you can Ctrl-click (⌘-click) more than one level in the Select Levels list to highlight them simultaneously.

3. **Turn on one of the two radio buttons.**

   If you want to allow access to anyone in the users table, then select the Username and Password button. However, if you want to limit the page to visitors with a particular access level, then turn on the second button.

   The first time you use this behavior, you'll have to define the different access levels, so click Define. You must type in each access level exactly as it appears in the database—*admin, member,* and *guest,* for example. Capitalization counts.

   You need to define these access levels only once. Dreamweaver will remember these settings for other dynamic pages in the same site.

4. **Click Browse; navigate to and select the page people will see if they aren't logged in.**

   It's often a good idea to simply dump unregistered visitors onto the login page. That way, if they're legitimate customers, they can simply log in and return to the page. (Dreamweaver can help with this. See step 9 on page 813.)

5. **Click OK to apply the link and server behavior.**

Like the other server behaviors, Dreamweaver lists the Restrict Access to Page behavior in the Server Behaviors panel after it's applied. If you wish to change any of its properties, double-click its name in the panel. To delete the behavior, select it in the Server Behaviors panel and then click the minus (–) button.

Additional Data Sources

So far, you've been using Dreamweaver's dynamic page-building features to retrieve information from databases to build catalog pages, product detail pages, and other pages that require database-generated content. But at times, you'll want to collect data from other sources and add them to your page. For example, when someone logs into a site (see the Log In User server behavior on page 833), her user name travels along with her from page to page in what's called a *session variable*. Using the Bindings panel, you can capture this session name and then use it on a Web page.

Similarly, you can create *cookies* to store small pieces of information on a person's computer—such as a counter tracking how many times he's been to your site—and use Dreamweaver's Bindings panel to add that information to a Web page.

The Bindings panel lets you access these sources of data, as well as information submitted from form fields and embedded in URLs. Each server model understands different types of dynamic data, but most recognize the ones listed below.

ASP.NET note: Dreamweaver doesn't let you add any of these additional data sources to the Bindings panel.

Regardless of the type of dynamic data you wish to add, the process of accessing these data sources is essentially the same. It differs only among server models.

For ASP

1. **Click the + button in the Bindings panel. Depending on the type of dynamic data you're interested in, select either Request Variable, Session Variable, or Application Variable.**

   In ASP, Request Variable covers a wide range of data sources, including form variables, URL variables, cookies, and server variables, so there's an extra step you must perform. After selecting Request Variable to open the Request Variable window (see Figure 23-6), choose a type of variable from the Type menu.

Figure 23-6:
The Request Variable window (for the ASP server model only) lets you add a wide variety of variable types for use in an ASP page. "Request.QueryString" is ASP's way of referring to a URL variable.

2. **Type the name of the variable into the Name field.**

   Capitalization doesn't matter. To ASP, *username, UserName,* and *USERNAME* are all the same.

3. **Click OK.**

Dreamweaver adds the variable to the Bindings panel.

Note: These steps don't actually *create* the variable; they only let you find out what's stored in a variable that's already been created, and then use it on a Web page. For example, adding a cookie variable in the Bindings panel doesn't actually create a cookie on a visitor's system. (For information on creating cookies, see page 822.)

For PHP and ColdFusion

1. **Click the + button in the Bindings panel and then select the proper variable type: URL, Form, Cookie, or whatever.**

   A window appears for the particular type of data source.

2. **Type the name of the variable in the Name field.**

   This time, capitalization matters; *username, UserName,* and *USERNAME* are all different variables. Find a system you're comfortable with (all lowercase, all uppercase, or mixed case) and stick with it.

3. **Click OK.**

   Dreamweaver adds the variable to the Bindings panel.

For JSP

For JSP pages, Dreamweaver supplies tools for adding only form, URL, and session variables:

1. **Click the + button in the Bindings panel and then select either Request Variable or Session Variable.**

   Depending on the choice, either the Request Variable or Session Variable dialog box appears.

2. **Type the name of the variable into the Name field.**

   Here again, capitalization matters, so *username, UserName,* and *USERNAME* are all different variables.

3. **Click OK.**

   Dreamweaver adds the variable to the Bindings panel.

After you add the variable to the Bindings panel, you can drag it to your Web page; any of the techniques for adding recordset data to a page also work (see page 706), and you can use them whenever the Dynamic Data window appears (see Figure 22-7), for example, as the content of a form field.

Tip: You can drag data sources listed in the Bindings panel into Code view, as well. Once you've got your programming chops sharpened, this trick is helpful for quickly adding data to your own server-side programs.

URL Variables

Some URLs include information tagged onto the end of the name of a Web page, like this: *www.nationalExasperator.com/catalog.asp?prodID=4*. The information following the ? is known as a *query string*, and it provides additional information to a dynamic page.

In most cases, this information comes in the form of one or more name/value pairs, which Dreamweaver refers to as *URL variables*. In this example, the name of the URL variable is *prodID*, and its value is *4*. URL variables are often used to transfer specific information for use in a recordset. You saw an example of this in the tutorial in Chapter 21: the number of a particular product was passed in a URL to the product details page, which used this number to retrieve details on a particular item.

You can also add a URL variable to the Bindings panel, and then include it in a Web page or use it anywhere you'd use a dynamic data source. For example, you can use it as a parameter added onto the end of a link to hand off the information to another page.

Keep in mind that a page that links *to* the page using the URL variable must include the proper query string in the link. For example, say you add a URL variable named "username" to the page *crop_circles.html*; the page uses the query string to personalize the page: "Welcome, [username]". For this to work, you then need to link to the *crop_circles.html* page with the query string attached to the URL, like this: *crop_circles.html?username=bob*.

You can add a URL variable to a link using the methods described on page 715.

Note: Don't use this method for accessing private or sensitive data. For example, suppose you used a URL variable as a method for accessing the personal data of one of your customers, like this: *customer_data.asp?customerID=78*. A nefarious visitor could just change the number in the URL to, say, 79 to view all of the personal data for customer number 79.

Form Variables

You can also add information from *forms* to the Bindings panel and use them on your page. If you add a form on one page, you can then collect that information on the page the form submits to (the same page specified in the form's *Action* property, as described on page 364). In other words, the page receiving the form data can display that information on the page *or* use it in some other fashion—such as inserting the information into the database, or creating a cookie or session variable.

If you're mainly using forms in conjunction with Dreamweaver's Insert Record and Update Record server behaviors, you won't generally take advantage of form variables. Those two behaviors work by collecting data from a form, adding or updating a database record, and then redirecting the Web browser to another page. The page the visitor finally sees never has access to the form information, so you can't add any form variables to that page.

However, adding a form variable to the Bindings panel can come in handy when you create a search page. For example, suppose you've created a page for searching a database. The search form lets the visitor type in a name—of an author or musician, for instance. You could then create a search *results* page that looks in the database for any records that match the search term. On that page, along with the database results, you could add text like "Search Results for: [search_term]", where *search_term* would be the word the visitor typed into the form. Just add the form variable to the Bindings panel and then drag it to the spot in the search page where you wish it to appear.

Note: If you use the GET method for submitting a form, the names and values of each form field are included in the URL. In this case, they're considered URL variables, so if you wish to add any of these fields to the Bindings panel, use the URL variable method instead. (For the difference between GET and POST, see page 365.)

Cookies

One problem with Web servers is that they have no memory.

Suppose, for example, that a site has a particularly long and annoying Flash movie that welcomes visitors with an ear-pounding, seizure-inducing multimedia display. Even if the designer was kind enough to include a "Skip this nauseating display" button, the Web server won't remember that you clicked it the *last* time you were there.

To overcome this limitation, most Web browsers store *cookies*—small text files containing specific information—that Web servers can create and read. In the example above, the Web server could drop a cookie onto your computer when you click the "Skip intro" button. The next time you visit the site, the Web server reads the cookie and kindly ushers you past the Flash movie and directly to the home page.

You can use cookies to store information on visitors' computers, too. They're a great way to store customer ID numbers, the number of visits to a particular page, and other bits of identifying information.

Cookies play by a few rules:

- A single cookie is stored on just one browser and one computer at a time. If you log onto a site that adds a cookie to your computer, and then log on again later from the public library, that computer won't have access to the cookie. In fact, if you use a different Web browser on the *same computer,* the Web server won't be able to read the original cookie from the other browser. (A variation: In some corporations, a Web browser stores cookies on a network server. This kind of cookie *can* be accessed by a particular browser—Internet Explorer, for example—on different computers on the network.)

- Only the domain that created the cookie can read it. *You* can't create dynamic pages that read a cookie set by Amazon.com, for example. Fortunately, that means other Web sites can't read the cookies you set on your visitors' computers, either.

- Web browsers can only store 300 cookies total, and each cookie can be no larger than 4 KB in size, so that hard drives won't crumble under their weight.

POWER USERS' CLINIC

Adding and Deleting Cookies Using ASP Pages

While Dreamweaver doesn't provide a tool for adding the scripts necessary to create and delete cookies with ASP pages, it isn't difficult to add the code yourself. (Dreamweaver can easily retrieve cookie information, as described on page 818.)

First, decide which page should add the cookie. The script will run when a visitor's browser requests the page, sending the cookie to the browser before the page content. Thus, you could add a script like this at the beginning of a form processing page. For example, if someone registers at your site, your script can store the name he enters in the registration form as a cookie on his computer. When he returns to the site, the home page can then read the cookie and display "Welcome back, Bob"—assuming, of course, that his name is Bob.

To add a cookie, use this code:

```
<%
Response.Cookies("name_of_cookie")=
"value_of_cookie"
Response.Cookies("name_of_cookie").Expires
= Date + 30
%>
```

Remember to include the opening <% and closing %>, which tell the application server that everything in between is programming code and not HTML. Replace *name_of_cookie* with whatever name you wish to give the cookie: *username,* for example. Also replace *value_of_cookie* with whatever you want to store in the cookie. In many cases, this will be a dynamic value—information from a recordset,

a URL variable, or a form variable, for example. Using the steps described on page 818, add the appropriate dynamic data to the Bindings panel, and then drag it into the code directly after the = sign (omit the quote marks [""]).

The next line of code sets an expiration date. In this case, "Date + 30" means 30 days from today. You must set an expiration date; if you don't, the cookie will last only as long as the visitor's browser remains open.

One thing to keep in mind: where you place the code will effect when the cookie is set. For example, if you put the cookie-setting code below the first line of code in Code view, then the server will deliver the cookie before doing anything else. However, if you want to set the value of a cookie using information retrieved from a recordset, then you need to place the cookie code *after* the recordset code.

You may also want to delete a cookie at some point. For example, on an e-commerce site, you could use a cookie to store items a visitor adds to her shopping cart. When she wants to empty her cart—after she purchases everything in it, for example—you could simply delete the cookie. Just assign no value to the cookie you wish to delete, like this:

```
<%
Response.Cookies("name_of_cookie")= ""
%>
```

If you find yourself typing this code a lot, you can save yourself some time by turning the programming code into Snippets (see page 573).

You can add a cookie to the Bindings panel using the method described on page 818. Unfortunately, Dreamweaver doesn't provide any tools for creating cookies (send your feature requests for the next version of Dreamweaver to: *wish-dreamweaver@macromedia.com*). Several third-party developers have risen to the occasion, however:

- **PHP developers.** Dreamweaver Extension developer Felice Di Stefano has developed a free cookie extension for the PHP server model. It includes server behaviors for adding and deleting cookies from a PHP page. In addition, it can set a cookie to the value of a form field, or redirect a visitor to another page if a specific cookie doesn't exist, or if it matches a particular value. You can find it at the Macromedia Exchange or at *www.felixone.it*.

- **ColdFusion developers.** Basic UltraDev distributes a free extension called CF_ Cookie. You'll find it in the extensions section of their site: *www.basic-ultradev. com/extensions/index.asp*.

- **JavaScript cookies.** You can also use JavaScript to set cookies. This technique works with any type of page—even nondynamic pages. The only catch is that the visitor's browser must both understand JavaScript and have JavaScript enabled (most do). Dreamweaver comes with two Snippets for setting and reading cookies using JavaScript. They're in the cookies folder of the JavaScript folder in the Snippets panel. See Chapter 16 to learn about Snippets. For the king of JavaScript cookie creators, check out WebAssist's Cookies extension at *www.webassist.com/Products/ProductDetails.asp?PID=6*.

ASP note: See the box on page 822 for information on how to add cookies yourself.

Session Variables

Web servers don't know or care whether the person requesting your company's home page just placed a $10 million order or is a first-time visitor. Of course, *you* probably care, and so do most Web applications, which need to follow visitors as they travel through a site. For example, in a typical e-commerce site, people use a "shopping cart" to store items they're interested in purchasing. For this to work, however, you need to track each shopper's movement from page to page.

To make this possible, most Web servers recognize what are called *session variables*. A session variable is created by the Web developer (or, more accurately, by a dynamic Web page that creates the variable) and follows the visitor from page to page. This type of variable lasts, logically enough, for a single *session*: if the visitor closes the browser, the session ends and the variable disappears. Most Web servers also add a limited time that the variable sticks around—usually 20 minutes. In other words, if the visitor doesn't hit any page in the site for 20 minutes, the Web server assumes that he's no longer around and destroys the session variable.

Note: Session variables take up resources from the Web server. That's why a Web server gets rid of them as soon as it can. Creating lots of session variables for a busy Web site can slow down the server.

When it creates a session variable, the Web server sends a cookie to the visitor's machine. The cookie contains a unique number (not the actual data contained in the variable), which the server uses to keep track of each visitor. When that person requests a page, the Web server reads the cookie with the unique ID. It can then retrieve session variables for that individual. For this reason, session variables won't work if the visitor's Web browser doesn't accept cookies. (PHP, however, has a built-in method for maintaining session information even when cookies aren't turned on.)

Note: Dreamweaver itself creates session variables when you use the User Authentication server behaviors. See page 814 for a discussion of these session variables and how you can use them.

You may be wondering how cookies and session variables differ, and when you'd want to use one over the other. The difference is that cookies can last between visits. If you want access to a piece of information when a visitor comes back tomorrow, or next week, or next month, use a cookie. For example, you'd use a cookie to remember a selection someone made from a previous visit, such as "Skip this crazy Flash Intro."

POWER USERS' CLINIC

Adding and Deleting Session Variables Using ASP Pages

While Dreamweaver doesn't provide a simple wizard for adding the code necessary to create and delete session variables with ASP pages, it isn't difficult to add it yourself. (Dreamweaver does, however, make quick work of retrieving session variables; see page 818.)

The procedure is much like the one for adding cookies (see the box on page 822)—for example, here again, the script will run when a visitor requests the page. When people register at your site, therefore, the email address they enter in the registration form could be stored as a session variable.

To add a session variable, use this code:

```
<%
Session("name_of_variable") = "value_of_
variable"
%>
```

Replace *name of variable* with whatever name you wish to give the session variable: *email,* for example. Also replace *value of variable* with whatever you want to store in the session variable. In many cases, this will be a dynamic value, like information from a recordset, a URL variable, or a form variable. Using the steps described on page 818, add

the appropriate dynamic data to the Bindings panel, and then drag it into the spot in the code in the previous column just after the = sign (in this case, omit the set of double quote marks: ""). As with cookies, *where* you place the session-creating code determines *when* it kicks in. So if you want to set a session with a value from a recordset, place the session code after the code that creates the recordset.

You may also want to delete a session variable to conserve server resources. (Dreamweaver's Log Out User server behavior uses this method to log a visitor out of a site.) To delete a server variable, add this code to the beginning of a page:

```
<%
Session.Contents.Remove("name_of_
variable")
%>
```

To delete all session variables for a particular individual in one fell swoop, use this code:

```
<%
Session.Abandon
%>
```

Session variables, on the other hand, provide better security. The actual information stored in the session variable stays on the Web server, while cookies exist as text files on a computer and can be opened and read by anyone with access to the computer. Accordingly, if you need to keep track of a confidential piece of information (someone's bank-account password, for example), you'd use a session variable.

You can add a session variable to the Bindings panel using the method described on page 818.

Unfortunately, as with cookies, Dreamweaver doesn't provide any tools for creating or destroying session variables. To find third-party extensions that work with session variables, try the Macromedia Exchange (*www.macromedia.com/exchange/*). Click the Dreamweaver link, and search using the term *session*.

PHP note: Felice Di Stefano has developed a free session extension for the PHP server model. It includes server behaviors for adding and deleting session variables from a PHP page. You can find it at the Macromedia Exchange or *www.felixone.it*.

Server Variables

Web servers collect and produce lots of information, much of which is hidden from the everyday Web surfer (and even the everyday Webmaster). Some of that information is obscure, but some can come in handy. For example, you can find out which Web browser the visitor is using, or which language the browser uses. While the exact list of server variables differs by Web server, here are some useful variables that work on many Web servers:

• **HTTP_USER_AGENT.** Information about the browser visiting the page. Unfortunately, you don't get a neat little summary like *Microsoft Internet Explorer 6 for Windows.* Instead, browser info is usually rather long-winded, like: *Mozilla/4.0 (compatible; MSIE 6.0; Windows NT 5.1; Q312461; .NET CLR 1.0.3705).* For a discussion on how to decipher this confusing jumble of information, visit *http://perl.about.com/od/cgiprogramminginperl/a/020905.htm*.

• **REMOTE_ADDR.** The IP address of the computer requesting the Web page. It'll look something like 65.57.83.12. Depending on the visitor's setup, this could be the exact address of the computer. (Big Brother, where art thou?)

Knowing this address has its uses. If someone frequently causes problems on your site—posts phony information to registration forms, say, or submits offensive messages to a message board—one potential solution is to prevent submissions to your database from that particular IP address. (However, since many users' IP addresses frequently change, this isn't a foolproof solution.)

• **HTTP_REFERER.** This is the URL of the page that *leads* to the current page. For example, say you click a link on page A to get to page B. Page B's HTTP_REFERER server variable would be A.

You could use this knowledge to create the ultimate Back button. Simply add the HTTP_REFERER server variable to the Bindings panel. Then add a link to whatever you wish to be the Back button—graphic or text—and use the server variable as the link. When visitors click this link, it will take them back to whichever page brought them there in the first place.

For a list of server variables supported by Microsoft's IIS Web server, visit the Microsoft Developer's Network site at *http://msdn.microsoft.com/library/* and search for *IIS Server Variables*. For a list of server variables for use with the Apache Web server, visit *http://hoohoo.ncsa.uiuc.edu/cgi/env.html*.

Advanced Server Behaviors

In addition to the server behaviors described already, you'll find two other sets of behaviors that come in handy on dynamic Web pages.

Tip: You can download many more third-party server behaviors from the Macromedia Exchange. Click the + button in the Server Behaviors panel and choose Get More Server Behaviors. Dreamweaver launches your Web browser and connects to the Dreamweaver Exchange site.

Not all extensions listed here work with Dreamweaver 8. On the other hand, many of the server behaviors for MX 2004 also work with Dreamweaver 8.

Recordset Paging

This set of five different behaviors lets you add links for jumping to different records in a recordset (straight to the last record, for example). In fact, Dreamweaver makes use of these same behaviors as part of its Recordset Navigation Bar object (page 730). You'll use these for moving through a long list of records, like a complete listing of products in a database.

To begin, add a recordset to a page. It should contain multiple records, since jumping to the *next* record when there's only one doesn't make much sense. The page could also contain a repeating region, so that several records appear.

You can add the recordset-paging server behaviors from the Server Behaviors panel, or from the recordset-paging menu on the Application tab of the Insert bar (see Figure 23-7):

• **Move to First Record** adds a link that jumps to the first record in the recordset.

Note: In ColdFusion, ASP.NET, and PHP, you'll see the word Page instead of Record in this example and the following ones. For example, you'll see Move to First Page instead of Move to First Record.

• **Move to Previous Record** adds a link that jumps to the record before the current record. If you use a repeating region, it jumps to the previous *set* of records. For example, say you create a repeating region that displays five records at a time. If the page currently displays records 6–10, clicking a link with this server behavior applied to it causes records 1–5 to appear.

- **Move to Next Record** adds a link that jumps to the next record in the record-set. If you use a repeating region, it jumps to the next *set* of records.

- **Move to Last Record** adds a link that goes to the last record in the recordset.

- **Move to Specific Record** adds a link that goes to a single record based on information passed in the URL. (This option is available only in the ASP and JSP server models.)

Figure 23-7:
You can create your own recordset navigation controls using the recordset-paging server behaviors.

Using any of the first four behaviors involves the same steps:

1. **Create a recordset and add dynamic content to the page.**

   For example, you could create a list of all the products your company sells. The recordset should contain at least enough records to span several pages. (You wouldn't use any of these behaviors if you displayed *all* of the records on a single page.)

2. **Click the page where you wish to insert the link.**

   You can also select an item on the page—text or a graphic—that you'd like to turn into a link.

3. **From the Server Behaviors panel, click the + button. Select Recordset Paging, and then choose a behavior from the submenu.**

   The window for the particular server behavior appears (see Figure 23-8).

Figure 23-8:
The recordset-paging behaviors can add a new link, or add a link to text or an image you've selected on the page. You can also use the menu to select any link already on the page. That's usually not a good idea, however, since Dreamweaver will erase whatever link was previously applied.

4. **Choose a recordset from the Recordset menu.**

This is the recordset the behavior will move through.

5. **Click OK.**

Dreamweaver adds the server behavior to the page and adds its name to the Server Behaviors panel.

The Move to Specific Record behavior works a bit differently. It doesn't add a link to the page; it simply forces the page to display a particular record when the page is requested. It does this by looking for a URL parameter that specifies a particular record in the recordset. In general, this isn't a good approach, since it requires the database server to retrieve many records just to display a single item from the database, which is a waste of server resources. On a busy site, that could mean a slow-down. You're better off creating a detail page (see page 737), which simply retrieves one record from the database.

Show Region Server Behaviors

At times, you'll want to display different information on a page based on the results of a recordset. For example, if a visitor searches your site's database of products for a product you don't sell, the search results page should say something like, "Sorry, we don't carry alligator skin bicycle seats." But if someone searches for a product you do sell, then the page should present the relevant details for that product. The Web page displays different text depending upon whether the search item was in the recordset.

Dreamweaver provides three sets of server behaviors that let you display any selection of HTML based on the results of a recordset (Figure 23-9):

- **Show If Recordset Empty.** If the recordset retrieves no records, this behavior will make the selected HTML appear in the browser window.

  This behavior comes in handy for a search page. On the search results page, apply it to some text like "We're sorry, your search retrieved no results," and you've got yourself a friendly solution for searches that turn up empty.

- **Show If Recordset Not Empty.** If the recordset retrieves *any* records, this behavior will cause the selected HTML to appear in the browser window: a list of search results or details on a specific database record, for example.

- **Show If First Page.** This server behavior, like the next three, works in conjunction with recordset-paging behaviors. It makes the selected HTML appear when the page displays the *first* record of a recordset, which comes in handy when you want to let people step through several pages of records.

- **Show If Not First Page** is the opposite of the previous one. If the page *does not* contain the first record in a recordset, then the selected HTML appears.

Dreamweaver makes use of this behavior in its Recordset Navigation Bar (see page 730). In that case, if the page displays anything *except* the first item in a recordset, the First Item and Previous Page links appear. If the page *does* display the first item in a recordset, those links are hidden. (After all, you can't very well view the Previous Page if you're on Page 1.)

- **Show If Last Page** functions just like the Show If First Page behavior, but for the last record in a recordset.

- **Show If Not Last Page** functions just like the Show If Not First Page behavior, but for the last record in a recordset. Dreamweaver uses this behavior to hide or show the Next Page and Last Item links in the Recordset navigation bar on the last page of records (page 730).

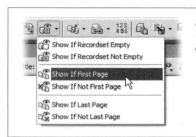

Figure 23-9:
The Show Region server behaviors are available on both the Application tab of the Insert bar and the Server Behaviors panel.

You can use these behaviors to show any selected object on the page—a paragraph of text, an image, a table, and so on. Your page can contain any combinations of these behaviors, and you can use any behavior two or more times to display multiple areas of a page. For example, maybe you'd like two things to appear when the recordset successfully retrieves a record: a graphic in the page's sidebar and a message in the main area of the page. You'd apply a Show If Recordset Is Not Empty server behavior to both selections of HTML (the graphic and the message).

You'll often use these behaviors in pairs. For example, a search results page should include both the Show If Recordset Empty behavior to display a "no results" message, and a Show If Recordset Not Empty behavior to display the search results.

To apply any of these behaviors:

1. **Create a dynamic page containing a recordset.**

    This could be a search results page or a master page that lists many records from the database.

2. **Select the HTML you wish to show based on a recordset outcome.**

    For example, when applying a Show If Recordset Is Empty server behavior to a search result page, select the message that should appear if the search returns no results.

3. **Open the Server Behaviors panel (Window → Server Behaviors). Click the + button, select Show Region, and choose one of the six behaviors from the submenu.**

A window looking like Figure 23-10 appears. While the title of the window varies depending on which behavior you selected, each of the six behaviors has just this one option.

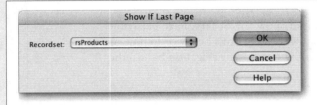

Figure 23-10:
Regardless of which of the Show Region server behaviors you apply, there's only one option to choose: the recordset whose results control the display of the region.

Note: The last four behaviors—Show If First Page, Show If Not First Page, Show If Last Page, and Show If Not Last Page—work only on pages that also have one of the recordset-paging server behaviors (discussed on page 826) applied.

---

4. **Select the name of the recordset from the menu and then click OK.**

The recordset you select should be the one whose results you're interested in. For example, on a search results page, you'd select the recordset you created to perform the search.

After applying one of these behaviors to a selection of HTML, a gray line appears around the selection, and a gray tab appears bearing the words "Show If." That's the area that will appear if the given recordset condition is met (for example, if the page is displaying the last record of the recordset).

To remove a Show Region server behavior, select its name in the Server Behaviors panel and click the minus (–) button (or press the Delete key). Doing so removes the gray tab and outline. Now the affected HTML will appear regardless of the recordset results.

PHP note: An extension called PHP Show If Recordset Field Condition Is True (available for free on the Macromedia Exchange site, *www.macromedia.com/exchange/*) lets you display part of a page when a field from a recordset matches a certain condition. Suppose, for example, that you have a products database with a field that records whether a particular item is for sale. If the item is indeed for sale, then you can use this behavior to display a large "For Sale" graphic on the product's detail page.

Tutorial: Authentication

In the tutorial at the end of Chapter 22, you created Web pages that could add, delete, and update records in the *National Exasperator* database. But you wouldn't want to allow just anyone who visits the Web site to access these pages, let alone delete products from the site. So in this tutorial, you're going to learn how to password-protect these sensitive, mission-critical Web pages.

The following steps assume that you've worked through the tutorial in Chapter 22 and have all of the completed files ready to go. You'll build on them in the following steps.

Building a Login Page

The first step is to create a login page—a simple form with fields for a user name and password. After a successful login from this page, an administrator will be able to access the administration pages:

1. **Open the file *login.asp* in the *admin* folder of the site.**

    This page will contain the form for typing in an administrator's user name and password. You'll add the form next.

2. **Click in the empty space directly below the headline "Administrator Login." Choose Insert → Form → Form.**

    Dreamweaver adds a red dashed line to the page, indicating the beginning and ending <form> tags.

3. **In the Property inspector, type *login* as the name of the form.**

    While this step isn't required, it's good to get into the habit of assigning your forms descriptive names. Next, you'll add a box for entering a user name.

Note: The next steps assume you have the Form Accessibility feature turned on (see page 367). To make sure this is in fact the case, open the Preferences window by choosing Edit → Preferences (Dreamweaver → Preferences), select the Accessibility category, and make sure the "Form Objects" checkbox is turned on.

---

4. **Choose Insert → Form → Text Field.**

    The Input Tag Accessibility Attributes window appears (Figure 23-11). You'll add a label that will appear next to the form field on the page.

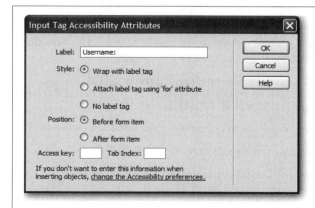

Figure 23-11:
Dreamweaver's Accessibility features let you add helpful controls—including a descriptive label—to form elements.

Note: You can also use the Forms tab of the Insert bar to add forms and form objects to your page, as described on page 363.

---

5. **In the Label box, type *Username:*; select the "Wrap with label tag" and "Before form item" buttons, and then click OK.**

   Dreamweaver inserts a form field with a descriptive label.

6. **In the Property inspector, choose Paragraph from the Formatting menu.**

   This wraps a paragraph tag around the label and form field. Next, you'll provide a descriptive name for this form field.

7. **Click the newly inserted form field and, in the Property inspector, name this field *username.***

   Next, because a login requires both a user name and password, you need to also add a form field for capturing a password.

8. **Click to the right of the form field you just inserted and press the Enter (Return) key to add a new paragraph.**

   The routine for adding the next form field is the same.

9. **Choose Insert → Form → Text Field. In the window that appears, type *Password:* in the label box and then click OK.**

   This inserts another form field and label.

10. **Select the new form field and, in the Property inspector, name this field *password* and select the Password radio button.**

    By turning this form element into a password field, anything your visitors type in the field will be displayed like this **** or this ••••, hiding the secret password from nosy passersby watching over their shoulders.

    To complete the form, you'll add a Submit button.

11. **In the document window, click to the right of the password field and press the Enter (Return) key. Choose Insert → Form → Button.**

    The Accessibility window appears yet again. In this case, however, you don't need to add a label, since text will appear directly on the button.

12. **Click Cancel to close the Accessibility window and insert a Submit button.**

    The form is complete. Now it's time to let Dreamweaver do its magic.

13. **Choose Window → Server Behaviors to open the Server Behaviors window.**

    Alternatively, you can use the keyboard shortcut Ctrl+F9 (⌘-F9).

14. **Click the + button and choose User Authentication → Log In User.**

    The Log In User window appears (see Figure 23-12). The first three items should already be filled out: the name of the form, the name of the user name field, and the name of the password field. If you had more than one form on the page, or additional fields inside the one form, you'd have to tell Dreamweaver which form and which fields to use for collecting the login information.

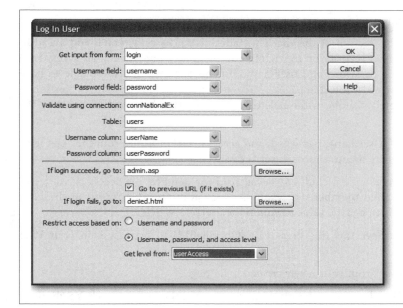

Figure 23-12:
Before visitors can access password-protected pages, they first need to log into the site. Dreamweaver's Log In User server behavior makes adding this feature a snap.

15. **From the "Validate using connection" pop-up menu, select "connNationalEx."**

    This indicates which database contains the login information. You also need to specify which table and columns contain the user name and password.

16. **From the Table menu, select Users. From the "Username column" pop-up menu, choose "userName." From the "Password column" pop-up menu, choose "userPassword."**

    You've just established the basic logic of the login behavior: Whatever a visitor types into the two form fields is compared with data stored inside the Users table in the *National Exasperator* database.

    Next, you need to specify what happens when there's a match—when your visitor types a valid user name and password into the form—and what happens when the visitor types in an invalid user name or password.

17. **Click the Browse button to the right of the "If login succeeds, go to" field. In the Select File window, navigate to and select the file *admin.asp* inside the *admin* folder. Click OK.**

    You've just chosen the page that will appear if the login is successful; your visitor's browser will display an administration page. (For the purposes of this tutorial, it doesn't matter if the "Go to previous URL" checkbox [see step 8 on page 813] is turned on.)

18. Click the Browse button to the right of the "If login fails, go to" field. In the Select File window, navigate to and select the file *denied.html* inside the *admin* folder. Click OK.

This, of course, is the "access denied" page that will appear when somebody types in an invalid user name or password.

Because this section of the site is for administrators only, you'll add an additional layer of security by restricting administrative pages using an access level as well as a password and user name. In this way, you'll also be able to have other password-protected pages—such as a special "paid subscribers" section— for registered visitors, without letting them access administrative areas of the site.

19. Select the "Username, password, and access level" button. From the "Get level from" pop-up menu, choose "userAccess."

The database table includes a special field for defining the access privileges of each registered member. For example, each administrator record in the *users* table also includes the value *admin* in the userAccess field.

20. Click OK. Save this file. Press F12 (Option-F12) to preview it in your Web browser.

You'll now try out your newly created login page.

21. In your Web browser, type anything you want in the two fields; click Submit.

Unless you've just made an incredible guess, you just typed in a user name and password that doesn't exist in the database. If the technology gods are smiling, an "Access Denied" page appears.

Now try it again.

22. Click the "Try logging in again" link to return to the login page. Type *big-cheese* in the Username field and *sesame* in the Password field; submit the form.

This time, you're in; the browser takes you to the main administration page. Here, you can jump to the pages you created earlier for adding, updating, and deleting products.

Tip: *sesame* is simply an awful password. Don't ever use it, or any word you can find in a dictionary, as a password. The reason? Web vandals often launch so-called "Dictionary attacks," in which they run through different terms pulled from a dictionary until they find a match.

The login script works just fine—you end up at the right page when you type in a valid user name and password. However, none of those other pages are protected yet. You can go to any of them, even if you haven't logged in. In the next part of this tutorial, you'll lock down each admin page, so only logged-in administrators can access them.

Password-Protecting the Administration Pages

The password-protection features offered by Dreamweaver require you to add a server behavior to each page you wish to protect:

1. **Open the file *admin.asp* in the *admin* folder.**

   This page is the main jumping-off point for adding, deleting, and updating products. It should be accessible only to administrators, so you'll add password protection to it.

2. **Make sure the Server Behaviors window is open (Window → Server Behaviors). Click the + button and choose User Authentication → Restrict Access To Page.**

   (Alternatively, you can use the User Authentication menu in the Insert bar, as pictured in Figure 23-1.)

   The Restrict Access To Page window appears (see Figure 23-13). Since you want to limit access to administrators only, make sure the page is restricted to those with the proper access level.

Figure 23-13:
Administrative pages can be reserved for those with the access level "admin," while regular subscribers of the National Exasperator would have access to pages intended for subscribers.

3. **Select the "Username, password, and access level" radio button.**

   You want to specify which type of user has access to this page, but first you must tell Dreamweaver what the different levels *are*.

4. **Click Define to open the Define Access Levels window. In the Name field, type *admin*. Next, click OK to close the window.**

   The word *admin* appears in the "Select levels" box. If you had other areas of the site with different access privileges, such as a subscriber area of the site only paying subscribers could access, you could continue to add levels by repeating this step.

5. **Click Browse; select the *denied.html* file in the *admin* folder and then click OK. Click OK again to close the Restrict Access To Page window.**

   To finish this page, you'll add a "Log out" link.

6. **Select Logout (the last link in the left navigation bar on the page).**

   You'll turn this text into a "Log out" link.

7. **On the Server Behaviors panel, click the + button and then select User Authentication → Log Out User.**

   Again, this option is also available from the Insert bar, as pictured in Figure 23-1. In any case, the Log Out User window appears (see Figure 23-14). The first radio button should already be selected. The text *Selection: "Logout"* appears in the menu.

   These are the proper settings; you're simply adding the logout script to the words you selected on the page.

   Next, you'll tell Dreamweaver which page to go to after the visitor logs out.

8. **Click the Browse button; navigate to and select the file *products.asp* in the root folder of the site, and click OK.**

   When people log out, they'll simply end up at the main products page. Since they're no longer logged in as administrators, they won't be able to access any of the administrative pages without logging back in. The Log Out User window should now look like Figure 23-14.

Figure 23-14:
This server behavior lets you offer visitors the polite option of logging out from your site. It destroys the session variables that track the login status of a visitor.

9. **Click OK to close the Log Out User window.**

   Now it's time to test the result.

10. **Choose File → Save; press F12 (Option-F12) to preview the page in your browser.**

    One of two things will happen: either you'll end up on the Access Denied page, or you'll see the *National Exasperator's* administration page.

    If you quit your Web browser after the previous section of this tutorial, or never logged in to begin with, the Restrict Access To Page server behavior is working: It doesn't recognize you as a registered administrator and denies you access to this page. Click the "Try logging in again" link to go to the login page. Type *big-cheese* in the Username field and *sesame* in the Password field, and submit the form. You're now logged in and are taken to the admin page.

    However, if you logged in following the instructions from the previous section in this tutorial, and you haven't quit your Web browser in the meantime, you're still logged in. In this case, the Restrict Access To Page server behavior is again doing its job. You're allowed onto this admin page, because you *are* a registered administrator.

11. **Click Log Out.**

The site logs you out and takes you to the main products page. To make sure you really are logged out, you'll open the administration page again.

12. **Return to Dreamweaver and the *admin.asp* page. Press F12 (Option-F12) to preview the page again.**

You're immediately redirected to the Access Denied page. You're not logged in, so you can't see the administration page. Hooray! The page is successfully protected from snoops.

Note: Some browsers will "cache," or store, the previously viewed administration page, so you might not actually see the Access Denied page. In this case, reload the page by clicking your browser's refresh button.

Of course, the most vulnerable pages (the update-, delete-, and add-product pages) are still accessible to everyone. You need to lock down those pages as well.

13. **Open the *add_product.asp* page and repeat steps 2–5 on page 835.**

Repeat this step for all other dynamic pages (*delete_product.asp* and *update_ product.asp*) in the *admin* folder, with the exception of *login.asp*. (After all, *that page* should be visible to those who haven't yet logged in.)

If you want, you can also add a Log Out link to each of these pages by repeating steps 6–9.

Now all of the administrative pages in the site are password protected. Only authorized administrators who log into the site can add, edit, or delete records from the database.

Displaying a Portion of a Page to Logged-In Users

Even though unauthorized users can't access any of the pages that can change the database, they can still see the links you added to the Product Details page in the last chapter—"Edit this Information" and "Delete this Product." Nothing particularly earth-shattering will happen if they click them—unauthorized users will just end up at the Access Denied page—but even that's not very elegant. Wouldn't it be tidier if those links didn't even *show up* except to people logged in as administrators?

You'll set that up next:

1. **Open the *productDetails* page.**

You'll be doing a little painless programming in the Code view at this point.

---

2. **In the document window, click inside the text "Edit this Information"; in the tag selector, click the <p>.**

You've just selected the paragraph containing the two links. This paragraph should appear only to administrators.

3. **Choose View → Code.**

The document window switches into Code view (see Figure 23-15).

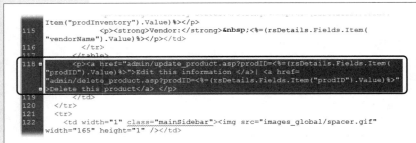

```
      Item("prodInventory").Value)%></p>
115           <p><strong>Vendor:</strong> <%=(rsDetails.Fields.Item(
      "vendorName").Value)%></p></td>
116        </tr>
117       </table>
118       <p><a href="admin/update_product.asp?prodID=<%=(rsDetails.Fields.Item(
      "prodID").Value)%>">Edit this information </a>| <a href=
      "admin/delete_product.asp?prodID=<%=(rsDetails.Fields.Item("prodID").Value)%>"
      >Delete this product</a> </p>
119      </td>
120    </tr>
121    <tr>
122      <td width="1" class="mainSidebar"><img src="images_global/spacer.gif"
      width="165" height="1" /></td>
```

Figure 23-15:
When you enter Code view, whatever you had selected in the document window is highlighted in the code. The HTML code outlined here includes the Edit and Delete product links you wish to hide from unregistered visitors.

4. **Click at the beginning of the selection, just before the opening <p>.**

The insertion point is now at the start of the paragraph. You'll add some programming code here.

5. **Type <% IF Session("MM_UserAuthorization") = "admin" THEN %>.**

The opening <% tells the application server that some ASP code is coming. In other words, this isn't HTML—it's a program that the application server must process. The IF and THEN parts of this code indicate what's called a *conditional statement*. In this case, it means, "*if* this person is logged in with an access level of 'admin,' *then* the paragraph will appear on the page."

To determine if the visitor is logged in with the proper access level, the code sneaks a peak at a session variable called MM_UserAuthorization. As mentioned on page 814, when someone logs into the site, the server behavior creates a session variable called MM_UserAuthorization. This bit of code follows the visitor around the site and contains a word that indicates what level of access he has. In this case, if the authorization is "admin," then he's logged on as an administrator, and the paragraph appears.

6. **Click to the right of the closing </p> tag (just after "Delete this product") and type <% END IF %>.**

This code concludes the conditional statement. In other words, all of the HTML between the first line of code you added in the previous step and this final <% END IF %> code will appear *only* if the user is logged in as an administrator.

The code should now look like Figure 23-16.

```
116        "vendorName").Value)%></p></td>
117            </tr>
118          </table>
           <%IF Session("MM_UserAuthorization")="admin" THEN %><p><a href=
       "admin/update_product.asp?prodID=<%=(rsDetails.Fields.Item("prodID").Value)%>"
       >Edit this information </a>| <a href="admin/delete_product.asp?prodID=<%=(
       rsDetails.Fields.Item("prodID").Value)%>">Delete this product</a> </p> <% END
       IF %>
119          </td>
120        </tr>
121        <tr>
```

Figure 23-16:
*Here's the finished code
that hides the "Delete
this Product" paragraph
from unregistered users.*

7. **Choose File → Save; press F12 (Option-F12) to preview the page.**

   Because you logged out earlier, the links should now be invisible. To see them, you must log in and return to the product details page.

8. **Go back to Dreamweaver, and open the *login.asp* page. Press F12 (Option-F12) to preview the page. Type *bigcheese* in the Username field and *sesame* in the Password field. Click Submit.**

   You're now logged in and taken to the main administration page. If you return to a product details page, the links will miraculously return.

9. **Click the Store button in the top navigation bar on the page to go to the product listings page. Click the name of any product to see its details.**

   Voilà! The links are back. You can freely edit or delete any product in the database. If you return to the administration page and click the Log Out button, you won't see these links until you log back in.

You could also use this trick to show the "Log out" link only if the visitor is logged in. With very little programming experience, you can use Dreamweaver's server behaviors together (and perhaps bring in server behaviors from extension developers) to build sophisticated database-driven Web sites.

Now go forth and electrify your sites!

XML and XSLT

XML is everywhere. You'll find it used in countless files on your computer—for everything from tracking what's in your iTunes music library to providing the structure and options in Dreamweaver's menus. In addition, Microsoft has announced that the document format for the next versions of Word, Excel, and PowerPoint will be XML-based. On the Web, XML is used to broadcast news and information, and provide product, pricing, and availability information from Amazon.com and eBay using a technology known as Web Services.

So what exactly is XML? XML, or Extensible Markup Language, is a tag-based language, somewhat like HTML, used to organize data in a clear, easy to understand way so that different computers, operating systems, and programs can quickly and easily exchange data.

Dreamweaver 8 introduces new tools that let you work with and format XML files for presentation on the Web. In this way, you can retrieve news supplied by others in an XML format like RSS or Atom and display it on your own home page. Imagine adding headlines from CNN.com or technology news from Wired.com directly to your site. Or building a page that keeps you up to date with your favorite bloggers' words of wisdom. And if your company uses XML files to store data like calendar events, contact lists, and so on, you can build Web pages that automatically display this information, without having to copy and paste that data from an XML file into a Dreamweaver document.

Note: RSS and Atom are simply two different XML-based formats used to identify document informa-tion—like an author's name, a title, a brief description, and so on—and provide a link to a complete article on a Web site. These formats are commonly used on news sites and blogs to provide readers with a syn-dicated news feed. RSS stands for "Rich Site Summary" or "Really Simple Syndication" (depending on whom you ask). Atom is a newer standard that competes with RSS but pretty much does the same thing. For more information on RSS, see *www.w3schools.com/rss/default.asp*, and for Atom, see *www. atomenabled.org/developers/syndication/*.

What Is XML?

XML, or Extensible Markup Language, has many similarities to HTML. Like HTML, it's a tag-based language used to identify different pieces of information and to structure data into a meaningful document. For example, HTML has the <h1> tag to identify the most important headline, or the <ul> tag to denote a bul-leted list. But HTML has only a handful of tags, and, in many cases, they don't always meaningfully identify the information you're presenting. For example, you can format a news title like "Bigfoot to Wed Super Model" with an <h1> tag, but you could also use the <h1> tag to format the name of a product you're selling, the title of a book, or an event on a calendar. In these cases, you're using the same tag to identify different types of information; it would be more informative to use a tag that accurately identifies the type of information, like <product>, <title>, or <event>.

That's where the "X" in XML comes in. XML is not really a markup language like HTML, as much as it's a set of guidelines for creating your own markup lan-guages. The X, or *extensible*, part of XML lets you define your own types of tags— or "extend" the language to fit your needs. In this way, you can create very specific tags to describe different types of information like invoices, books, personnel, and so on.

Note: To learn more about XML check out *www.w3schools.com/xml*, grab a copy of *Learning XML* (O'Reilly) by Erik T. Ray, or visit the XMLTopic Center on the Macromedia Web site: *www.macromedia. com/devnet/topics/xml.html*.

For example, say the *National Exasperator* wanted to come up with a way of stor-ing a list of headlines, publication dates, and summaries for its news stories. In HTML, this might look something like:

```
<h1>Praying Mantis Says Prayers Were Answered</h1>
<p>10-30-2005<br/>In a bizarre story from the insect kingdom, The National
Exasperator's own Brian Albert reports that a praying mantis in Borneo has
gained the power of speech. You won't want to miss this interview.</p>
```

This is all well and good for display in a Web browser, but it doesn't give any sense of what kind of information is being presented. This is particularly important when you keep in mind that XML was invented as a way of exchanging data between computers. So if another computer encountered this HTML, it wouldn't understand the purpose of the text inside the <h1> tag. In fact, even a human viewing this code might not easily discern what the "10-30-2005" means; it looks like a date, but maybe it's an ID number or some secret code used at *National Exasperator* headquarters. XML provides a much clearer way of defining the structure and meaning of content. For example, the *National Exasperator's* IT staff could decide to come up with their own XML format to store this information. In this case, the same information might be written in XML like this:

```
<news>
<title>Praying Mantis Says Prayers Were Answered</title>
<pubdate>10-30-2005</pubdate>
<summary>In a bizarre story from the insect kingdom, The National
Exasperator's own Brian Albert reports that a praying mantis in Borneo has
gained the power of speech. You won't want to miss this interview.</summary>
</news>
```

Kind of like HTML, right? But with a completely different set of tags. This new markup makes the meaning of each chunk of information clearer: you can easily tell that this data is a news item and that it has a title, a publication date, and a summary. In a nutshell, that's what XML is about: creating tags that meaningfully identify the information inside them.

Rules of the Road

Because XML is intended to be an easy way to exchange data between different computers, operating systems, programs, institutions, and people, there are some fairly strict requirements to ensure that everyone's playing by the same rules. If you've done your fair share of writing raw HTML code, much of this will be familiar to you (see page 3). In fact, if you've written XHTML code (see page 6), you've already been writing XML. XHTML is an XML version of HTML that just has a few more rules than plain-old HTML.

- **Every XML document must have a single "root" element.** A root element is a tag that surrounds all other tags in a document and appears only once in a document. In an XHTML (and an HTML) document, for example, this is the <html> tag. In the *National Exasperator* news XML format introduced above, this tag is <news>. If you're creating your own XML-formatted file, you could make this root element whatever you wanted: <calendar>, <invoice>, and so on. It makes sense for this tag to be descriptive of whatever content you're storing inside the file.

- **All tags must be nested properly, with no overlapping tags.** This rule works just as it does in HTML. You can't have code like this: <b><i>Bold and italics</b></i>. Since the opening <i> tag appears after the opening <b> tag, its closing tag—</i>—must appear before (or inside of) the closing <b> tag, like this: <b><i>Bold and italics</i></b>.

- **All tags must have both an opening and closing tag, or be self-closing.** For example, in HTML a paragraph of text is indicated by both an opening <p> and a closing </p>. Some HTML tags, however, don't hold content, like the <img> tag or the line break (<br>) tag. The XML version of these tags include a forward slash at the end of the tag, like this: <br/>. This type of tag is called an *empty element.*

- **The property values of all tags must be quoted.** For example, in HTML, the <a> tag is used to add a link to a page, using the "href" property. In non-XML HTML you could get away with this: <a href=index.html>Home</a>. In XML, this doesn't fly. You need to quote the href property's value like this <a href="index.html">Home</a>. You're probably used to doing this already, and if you've been using Dreamweaver, the program always does this for you. But when writing your own XML files, make sure to include quotes around a tag's property values.

If your XML file meets these conditions, it's known as (to use the official XML designation) "well-formed." In other words, your XML code is written properly. If you write more complex XML documents, there are additional rules you'll need to follow, but these are the basic requirements.

In many cases, you'll also include what's called a *prolog*—an introduction of sorts, that appears at the very top of the document and announces what kind of document it is. In its most basic form the prolog looks like this:

```
<?xml version="1.0"?>
```

The prolog can also include the type of encoding (useful for indicating different characters for different languages) used in the document.

Here, then, is a basic, complete, and well-formed XML document:

```
<?xml version="1.0" encoding="ISO-8859-1"?>
<news>
<pub>National Exasperator News</pub>
<rights>Copyright 2005, The National Exasperator</rights>
<entry id="284">
<title>Battle of the Century</title>
<link>http://www.nationalexasperator.com/headlines/battle.html</link>
<summary>The terrifying true story of the battle between two of the most
feared legends of all time: Bigfoot vs. the Loch Ness Monster.</summary>
<pubdate>10-30-2005</pubdate>
</entry>

<entry id="295">
<title>Aliens are Here!</title>
<link>http://www.nationalexasperator.com/headlines/aliens.html</link>
<summary>Reporters for The National Exasperator have discovered that aliens
from another planet--metal clad robots, with the words "Space Man" emblazoned
```

```
across their chests--walk among us.</summary>
<pubdate>10-30-2005</pubdate>
</entry>
</news>
```

Tip: Dreamweaver can verify whether an XML file is well formed. Open the file in Dreamweaver and then choose File → Check Page → Validate as XML. The Results panel group will open. If nothing appears inside the Validation panel, the file is OK. If there's an error, a message explaining the problem will appear. Fix the error and try to validate the document again. Dreamweaver can even validate XML using a DTD file (see the box below).

UP TO SPEED

Taming the Tower of Babel: DTDs and XML Schemas

You may be wondering: if anyone can make up her own tags to create her own types of XML files, how can XML help computers, people, and organizations exchange data. After all, if you come up with one way of formatting invoices using XML, and your buddy in accounting uses his own set of tags to create invoices, you'll end up with two different and incompatible types of files for tracking the same information. It's like the Tower of Babel—everyone speaking their own language and unable to talk to each other. Fortunately, XML provides two solutions to this problem: *DTDs* (or Document Type Definitions) and XML Schemas. Both are methods of creating a common vocabulary, so everyone can use the same language to talk about the same things.

In fact, you've already been using a DTD when building Web pages in Dreamweaver. When you create a new Web page, Dreamweaver adds a line of code at the beginning of the page, like this:

```
<!DOCTYPE html PUBLIC "-//W3C//DTD XHTML
1.0 Transitional//EN" "http://www.w3.org/
TR/xhtml1/DTD/xhtml1-transitional.dtd">
```

This line will vary depending on the type of HTML or XHTML you use (see page 6). But the concept is the same. The line defines the document type for the page—in this example, XHTML 1.0 Transitional—and points to a URL where the DTD can be found—here, it's *http://www.w3.org/TR/xhtml1/DTD/xhtml1-transitional.dtd*.

Essentially, the DTD for each type of HTML or XHTML defines what tags are allowed and how they should be

written. If you don't follow the rules, the page is considered invalid. In fact, Dreamweaver's validator, discussed on page 506, is doing just that—making sure your code follows the rules of a particular DTD.

XML Schemas are just another method of enforcing a language for a particular XML format, with a few bells and whistles that DTDs lack. DTDs have been around a long time and are more common; schemas are a newer concept, but will probably eventually replace DTDs. Both XML Schemas and DTDs are very confusing beasts—difficult to read and difficult to create. There are many DTDs and Schemas available for describing a wide range of different types of information. They're often created by a consortium of businesses that agree to a single way of describing information, so that they can easily share data with each other. You probably won't be creating your own anytime soon, but just keep in mind that they exist and are a common way to make sure everyone's speaking the same tongue.

Dreamweaver 8 includes a nice feature related to both DTDs and Schemas: If you include a DTD or Schema in an XML file, and then edit that XML file in Code view, Dreamweaver will display Code Hints for the various XML tags as you type. Code Hints are shortcuts for typing an entire tag or tag property; as you begin to type a tag, Dreamweaver pops up a small window displaying any tags that match what you've typed so far. At that point, you can just select the correct tag, instead of having to type it all out. This feature is also available when working with HTML in Code view and is described on page 330.

If all this sounds like a lot of work, you're right. XML is a big topic, full of complex nooks and crannies. If you're just a busy Web designer making sure you get your client's latest press release up on the Web, you may not find yourself needing to create a *brand-new XML format* for your client's documents, or learn the ins and outs of creating XML files. And you may never have to. However, there are already a lot of XML files in existence and even more on their way. One of the reasons XML is so popular is that, although it may be a bit tedious for humans to write, computers are whizzes at following the detailed rules needed to create and read XML files. XML has become a kind of *lingua franca* for computer communication; different computers, operating systems, and programs can easily exchange information using an agreed-upon XML-based type of document.

XML lets programmers access Amazon.com's vast databases of information without understanding anything about how Amazon's computers are set up or what programs Amazon uses. This is also what lets any number of programs know what to expect when they retrieve an RSS feed from a blogger or Wired.com. Because XML makes it easy to exchange data, you'll find it becoming more and more common as you continue your career as a Web designer.

Looking at the sample code on page 844, you can see that XML doesn't have much going for it in the looks department. There's nothing but text and tags. To turn that information into an attractive display, you need to use two other XML-related technologies: XSLT and XPath.

XSLT and XPath

Although XML is very much like HTML in many ways, it doesn't have any inherent formatting capabilities. Unlike with HTML, where an <h1> tag is at least displayed differently—bolder and bigger—than other text, a Web browser doesn't know how to display an XML tag. For example, should the <news> tag be black, blue, or red all over? XSLT and XPath are two complementary (and very complex) languages that let you define how XML tags should look. Fortunately, even though these languages are hard to master, Dreamweaver takes care of the entire process. All you need to know is how to use Dreamweaver's Design view to create cool-looking Web pages.

But just so you can show off to your co-workers and pad your resume, here's a brief explanation of these technologies.

XSLT is the magic dust that transforms an XML document into an HTML document. In fact, it's used to create any number of different types of documents for Web browsers, palmtops, printers, and so on, out of a single XML file. XSLT stands for Extensible Style Language Transformations, which is just a really weird name for a programming language that converts XML tags—<event>Halloween Social</event>, for example—into something else, like the code a Web browser understands—<h1>Halloween Social</h1>. In a nutshell, that's what Dreamweaver's XML tools do: they use XSLT to transform XML into HTML.

Note: Because XSLT adds formatting to XML, much like Cascading Style Sheets add formatting to HTML, you'll often see an XSLT file referred to as an *XSLT style sheet*.

But XSLT can't do the job on its own. Another technology, XPath, is needed to tell XSLT which tags to transform. XPath (yet another language!) provides the means to identify particular elements or tags in an XML file. You use XPath to create what's called an "XPath expression," which is kind of like a trail of cookie crumbs that leads from one part of the document (frequently the beginning tag, or "root element") to the particular "node"—tag or tag property—you wish to select. In its most basic form, XPath works very much like the document window's tag selector: it pinpoints a tag nested in any number of other tags. For instance, using the XML code on page 844 as an example, the XPath expression to the title of one of the news items is */news/entry/title*.

Think of it this way: XPath is used to identify the XML tags that XSLT transforms into HTML. XSLT does the actual conversion to HTML, but XPath tells XSLT which tags to convert. They work hand in hand to get the job done. And, fortunately, that's all you need to know. In fact, it's more than you need to know to use Dreamweaver to turn XML into cool-looking Web pages.

Note: Dreamweaver 8 adds built-in reference material covering XML and XSLT. See page 353 for more on Dreamweaver's Reference panel.

Building a Static Page from an XML File

Dreamweaver 8 provides two methods for converting XML files into Web browser–friendly pages: server-side and client-side approaches. With the server-side approach (discussed on page 857), all the XML-related files are read on the application server and processed by a program Dreamweaver creates. The result— regular HTML—is spit back across the Internet to a visitor's Web browser. The client-side approach is very different: the transformation of the XML file happens directly within a visitor's Web browser (which is known as the "client"). Most modern browsers—like Internet Explorer 6, Safari, and Firefox—can actually read XML and XSL files (that's the file containing the XSLT style sheet), apply the XSLT instructions, and then generate a display that looks just like a Web page. You'll learn about this approach next.

Note: XSL files hold the XSLT and XPath code that transform XML into another format like HTML.

Presenting XML using a client-side approach requires two files—the XML file and an XSLT style sheet. The XSLT style sheet is created in Dreamweaver very much like you'd create a Web page. In fact, when working in Design view, you won't really notice any difference between creating XSLT and creating a regular HTML Web page; you can add design elements like logos and other graphics, use table-based or

CSS-based layout techniques, and even format the XML content much like you'd format dynamic text from a recordset (see page 724).

The first thing you need to do is add an XML file to your site. This could be a file supplied by your client, one you've created yourself, or one produced by a computer program. Dreamweaver's client-side XSLT tools work *only* with XML files located in your site.

Note: Dreamweaver's server-side XSLT tools let you retrieve XML files from *anywhere* on the Web. This capability's useful for grabbing news feeds from other Web sites, for example. See page 851 for details.

Once you have an XML file that you're ready to "transform" into a good-looking Web page, you create an XSLT file in one of two ways: by creating a new, blank XSLT document or by converting an already created HTML page into an XSLT file.

To start with a fresh, blank canvas:

1. **Choose File → New.**

   The New Document window opens.

2. **Make sure the General tab is selected; click the Basic Page category, select XSLT (Entire Page), and click the Create button.**

   The Locate XML Source window appears (Figure 24-1). Because XSLT is meant to make an XML file look great, you need to tell Dreamweaver which XML file to use.

Note: Don't choose the XSLT (Fragment) option. This is used only with dynamic Web pages, as discussed on page 852.

Figure 24-1:
Only the first option—"Attach a local file…"—works with a static, client-side page. By contrast, dynamic, server-side pages (page 851) can use either an XML file stored on your site or from any other site on the Web.

3. **Click the Browse button and locate the XML file in your site. Click OK.**

   Dreamweaver finds the file in your local site, reads its contents, and displays the file's tags and properties in the Bindings panel. At this point, jump to page 855 to learn how to add XML data to the page.

4. **Save the new XSLT style sheet.**

   Make sure the file ends in the extension .xsl. In addition, you must save the file in the same folder as your XML file. If you don't and the XSLT file contains links, graphics, and other linked elements, they may not show up when the XML file is viewed.

It may be easier to create your page design—logo, banner, navigation, copyright, layout, and so on—first. Or, you may have an already completed Web page design that you'd like to use for displaying the information from your XML file. In either case, you can convert the HTML to XSLT by following these steps:

1. **Open the HTML page.**

   Don't use a dynamic page. In most cases, you'll run into trouble with the programming code in these types of pages. It's best to start with a plain vanilla HTML design.

2. **Choose File → Convert → XSLT 1.0.**

   Dreamweaver makes a copy of the HTML page, converts it to XSLT, and then saves it into the same directory as the Web page, with a file extension of .xsl. So, for example, if you converted a file named *products.html* into XSLT, Dreamweaver would create a new document named *products.xsl* and save it in the same folder in your site.

   You next have to "attach" an XML file to the XSLT file. This step, which is automatically taken care of when you create a new, blank XSLT file (see page 848), is required so that Dreamweaver knows which XML file you plan on formatting.

3. **Open the Bindings Panel (Window → Bindings) and click either the "Source.."** **or the XML link (see Figure 24-2).**

   The Locate XML Source window appears (Figure 24-1). The process, at this point, is the same as when creating a new XSLT document (page 848)—that is, click the Browse button, locate the XML file in your site, and then click OK.

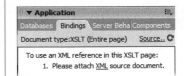

Figure 24-2:
Both the "Source.." and the XML links in the Bindings panel let you select the XML file you wish to format.

Whichever method you choose to create the XSLT file, it behaves just like a Web page in Dreamweaver. In other words, you can use Design view to add tables, graphics, text, and so on. You can even use CSS styles to format elements on the page. But behind the scenes, Dreamweaver adds some pretty weird-looking code: if you delve into Code view in one of these pages, you'll see things like <xsl:template match="/"> and <!ENTITY nbsp " ">. So unless you understand XSLT well, it's best to stick to Design view as much as possible. Accidentally deleting or changing any of the XSLT code may break the page.

Note: Although Dreamweaver claims that it's "attaching" the XML file to the XSLT document, it's really just adding a comment tag to the XSLT file, like this: <!-- DWXMLSource="feed.xml" -->. This comment helps Dreamweaver know which XML file to use with the XSLT document—so don't delete it. Technically, you actually attach an XSL file to an XML file to make this whole process work (as described below).

You use the Bindings panel to insert XML elements into your Web page. The process is very much like working with recordsets on dynamic pages (see page 724). The only difference is that instead of the data coming from a database, it comes from an XML file. You can apply CSS to the XML data and format the page as you would any Web page, with tables or CSS for layout, background images, and so on. You can also add various cool options like repeat regions and conditional statements. This process is the same for client-side and server-side processed XSLT files, and is discussed in depth starting on page 855.

The final piece required to transform an XML file into a presentation for a Web browser is to attach the XSLT style sheet to your XML file. In this client-side scenario, the Web browser reads the XML file, loads the attached XSLT style sheet, and formats the XML according to the instructions in the XSL file—pretty much the same as when displaying a Web page with an external CSS style sheet. To attach the XSL file to the XML, follow these steps:

1. **Open the XML file and choose Commands → Attach an XSLT Stylesheet.**

   The Attach XSLT Stylesheet window appears. It just has a single option: select the XSLT style sheet.

2. **Click the Browse button and select the XSLT style sheet (the file ending in .xsl) you created earlier, and then click OK.**

   This step writes code into the XML file that links the XSL file (that's the XSLT style sheet) to the XML file.

Note: Make sure the XSLT and XML files are in the same folder in your site. If they're not, links may not work and graphics may not appear.

---

3. **Press F12 (Option-F12) to preview the XML file in a Web browser.**

   The Web browser loads the XML file and the XSLT style sheet and transforms the whole mess into a display that looks just like a Web page.

This client-side approach is (relatively speaking) easy: You don't need to bother setting up an application server or any of the other components required for a dynamic Web site. It does have some big drawbacks, however. For example, not all Web browsers can view XML files. Most of the latest and greatest can: Internet

Explorer 5 and 6, Firefox, and Safari, for example. But this means that if you're attempting to reach a large audience, this client-side method may not be the answer. It also means visitors need to download both the XML and XSL files. In some cases, you'll display only part of an XML file; if the file's large, your visitors will need to wait longer than they should have to in order to download all of the data (even the stuff you never intend to display) from the XML file. Finally, you can't take advantage of one of Dreamweaver's new XSLT feature's greatest uses: including news, blogs, and other Web site feeds in your Web pages.

Fortunately, Dreamweaver's server-side approach overcomes all of these limitations. Its XSLT server behavior produces regular HTML out of XML and XSLT style sheets. And, fortunately, since Dreamweaver handles all of the complex programming required to make this happen, it's no more difficult than building a dynamic Web page.

Creating Dynamic Pages with XSLT and XML

The most effective way to use XML in your site is with Dreamweaver's XSLT server behavior. It processes all of those "X" files and produces nothing but clean HTML for your visitors. To take advantage of this feature, you'll need to set up an application server, as described in Chapter 20, so that you can run ASP, PHP, JSP, .NET, or ColdFusion pages with the necessary programming code.

Next, you need to either have an XML file in your site, or know the URL of an XML file out on the Web that you'd like to use—for example, *http://www.nationalexasperator.com/news.xml*. Then you create an XSLT style sheet—either by creating a new, blank XSLT style sheet or by converting an already created HTML file into a XSL file, as explained starting on page 849.

FREQUENTLY ASKED QUESTION

Finding XML Files

XML sounds great. But, where do I get these XML files?

XML files have to be written either by hand or, very frequently, by a computer program. Dreamweaver lets you create your own XML files, but since XML is just a bunch of code, and isn't a "visual" language like HTML, you have to use Dreamweaver's Code view and type everything yourself. Dreamweaver 8's new tools don't make creating XML files much easier; they just let you convert an already existing XML file into something nice to look at in a Web browser.

While you may already be writing your own XML files, or plan on doing so, you'll more likely find them as part of your company's documents—more and more information is saved as XML these days—or as the output from a computer program. In fact, XML is most commonly encountered on the Web in the form of a "feed" like RSS or Atom, containing summaries of Web articles, blog entries, or news stories. You'll usually find these listed as "RSS," "Feeds," or "XML" on a Web site. The tutorial on page 872 demonstrates how you can use Dreamweaver 8 to incorporate these types of XML files into your Web site.

PHP note: For server-side XSLT to work, the version of PHP you're using must have XSLT support. PHP 5 has this capability built in, but PHP 4 requires extra work to get this going. Unfortunately, most Web hosting companies still use PHP 4, and most of those don't offer XSLT support. So before moving ahead with your XML-fueled dynamic-page-creation efforts, call or email your Web hosting company to see if their PHP installation supports XSLT.

In addition, you can create what's called an *XSLT fragment,* which lets you add a "chunk" of formatted XML to just one part of a dynamic page. For example, say you want to list the top 10 headlines from CNN.com's RSS feed (see the note on page 842) on your home page. Using Dreamweaver, you can transform the news feed from XML into HTML code. Of course, that won't be the only thing you want on your home page. Most of the page will consist of information related to your site. In this case, you only need to dedicate a fragment of the page—a sidebar on the right edge of the page, for example—to these headlines.

The process for creating and inserting an XSLT fragment is simple: create the fragment, add and format XML information, open a dynamic page, and then insert the XSLT fragment into it. When your visitors view the dynamic page, the application server will process the XSLT fragment and add its contents to the rest of the page.

Here's how to create and use an XSLT fragment:

1. **Choose File → New.**

   The New Document window appears.

2. **Make sure the General tab is selected; click the Basic Page category, select XSLT (Fragment), and click the Create button.**

   The Locate XML Source window appears (Figure 24-1). Because XSLT is meant to make an XML file look great, you need to tell Dreamweaver which XML file to use. You have two choices when working with server-side XSLT: select a local file or type the URL of an XML file out on the Web.

3. **Select either "Attach a local file…" or "Attach a remote file on the Internet."**

   If the XML file is on your site, choose the first option. Select the second option if the XML file is on another Web site.

4. **If you're using an XML file on your site, click the Browse button to locate the file. Otherwise, type an absolute URL—*http://www.the_site.com/xml_file.xml,* for example—in the box. Click OK.**

   If you're pointing to a file out on the Internet, you *must* use a full, absolute URL including the *http://* part. Dreamweaver finds the file in your local site (or looks for the file out on the Internet), reads its contents, and displays the file's tags and properties in the Bindings panel. At this point, jump to page 855 to learn how to add XML data to the page.

Note: If you want to try this out for fun, you can load an XML file from Wired.com. Use this URL: *http:// www.wired.com/news/feeds/rss2/0,2610,,00.xml.*

5. **Save the new XSLT style sheet fragment.**

   Make sure the file ends in the extension .xsl. In addition, make sure you save it in the same folder as the dynamic page you wish to attach the XSLT style sheet fragment to. Otherwise, if the style sheet contains links, graphics, and other linked elements, they may not show up when the XML file is viewed.

Tip: One way to get around this limitation of needing to store everything in the same folder is to use root-relative or absolute URLs (see page 104) for links, and to add graphics and external CSS files to your XSLT style sheet. Of course, taking these steps is probably more work than simply saving the XSL file in the same folder as your dynamic Web page.

6. **Add XML elements to the XSLT style sheet as described on page 855.**

   You can also add regular Web page content—like images, tables, CSS styles, and so on—to the page, and format the XML just as you would text on any other dynamically generated page. Once you've finished the design of your XSLT fragment, you then add it to your dynamic Web page.

Note: Because the XSLT fragment will be part of a larger Web page, you won't be able to see the effects of that page's CSS styles as you format your XML data. Fortunately, if you're using external CSS style sheets, you can use Dreamweaver's Design Time Stylesheets feature to temporarily attach, preview, and use the same CSS styles you're using on your final Web page. See page 174 for instructions.

7. **Open the dynamic page that you wish to add the XSLT fragment to.**

   This must be a dynamic page using the same server model as your site—for example ASP, PHP, or ColdFusion. Because the XML transformation magic occurs via programming that Dreamweaver inserts in the page, you can't add an XSLT fragment to a regular Web page—an .html file.

8. **Click where you wish to insert the XSLT fragment.**

   The spot you pick could be inside a table cell or within another layout region—such as a sidebar—on your page. The XSLT fragment will be added to this spot, just like a Dreamweaver Library item (see page 580)—that is, it will just be a chunk of HTML inside your page.

9. **Make sure the Server Behaviors panel is open (Window → Server Behaviors), click the + button, and then select XSL Transformation.**

   The XSL Transformation window appears (see Figure 24-3). Next, you select the XSL file you created earlier.

10. Click the top Browse button to open the Select XSLT File window. Navigate to and select the XSL file you created; click the OK (Choose, on the Mac) button to choose the file, and then close the Select XSLT File window.

This tells Dreamweaver which fragment to use. In addition, Dreamweaver should automatically fill out the path to the XML file (it reads the comment inserted in the XSLT file identifying which XML file to use—see the Note on page 850). If the XML file path doesn't appear, you can click the Browse button next to the XML file box and select the proper XML file yourself. In addition, if you're using XML from another Web site, you'll see the URL of that file, and the Browse button will disappear.

The "XSLT parameters" option lets you pass information to the XSL file that can be used to alter how the XML file is displayed. This advanced feature is discussed on page 868.

11. Click the OK button to close the window and insert the fragment.

Dreamweaver displays the XSLT fragment in your Web page. If you've set up a testing server (see page 690), you can preview the effect by pressing F12 (Option-F12).

You can't directly edit the fragment inside the dynamic Web page. Dreamweaver treats it like a single element on the page. To make changes to the fragment—for instance, to add graphics, changes links, or reformat the XML—you must open the XSL file and make changes directly to it.

Note: Dreamweaver adds additional folders and files to your site when you use the XSLT server behavior. These additions contain the necessary programming code to successfully embed XML data into a Web page. That means when you're moving everything—the dynamic page, the XSLT fragment file, and the XML file—to your Web server, you also need to upload these files, which you'll find stored in a folder named *includes* in your site's local root folder. Upload this folder to your Web server. (See page 532 for instructions on using Dreamweaver's FTP tool.)

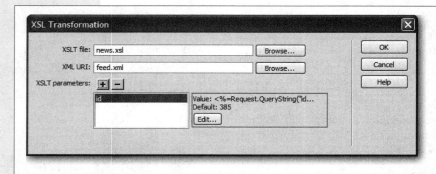

Figure 24-3:
The XSL transformation window lets you attach an XSLT style sheet to a dynamic page. You can also send special information—XSLT parameters—to the style sheet that affects the display of the page (this process is described on page 868).

Inserting and Formatting XML

Now you know the basics of creating and using XSLT style sheets. But how do you actually add and format XML data? Dreamweaver makes this process easy, and if you've used the program's database tools, you already know how to do it: just use the Bindings panel. Once you create an XSL file and attach the XML file to it, Dreamweaver reads all of the tags in the XML file and adds them to the Bindings panel (see Figure 24-4).

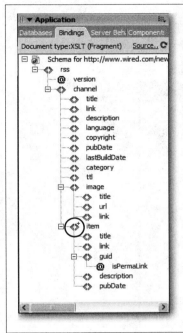

Figure 24-4:
When using Dreamweaver's XSLT tools, the Bindings panel lists all of the tags and properties in the XML file you're formatting. Dreamweaver includes a few visual clues about the XML file: ◇ represents an XML tag and is the most common icon you'll encounter; the @ icon represents a tag property (also called an attribute; for example, in the tag <item id="154" >, "id" is an attribute); and next to some tags, you'll see a small + sign (circled in this image) or a ? symbol. The + indicates that the tag is repeated multiple times; in the National Exasperator XML file on page 844, for example, the "entry" tag is repeated multiple times (once for each news headline in the file). The ? symbol (not shown here) means the tag is optional, and it appears next to tags inside of other repeated tags (the one with the + symbol).

You can drag any element in the Bindings panel into your XSLT style sheet page, just as you'd drag information from a database recordset. That means you can place XML information in a table cell, in a footer, in a banner—in short, anywhere you can place regular HTML elements on a page.

You should keep a couple things in mind when inserting XML by using this dragging method:

- Only the contents of the XML tags and properties are inserted, not the tags or property names themselves. For example, in Figure 24-4, dragging the <title> tag that appears inside the <channel> tag onto a document just prints the text inside this tag, not the tag itself. This is a good thing: you don't usually want to include the tags—<title>An Important Story</title>. Instead, you just want the text: An Important Story.

• Dragging a tag that includes *other* tags often results in a hard-to-read mess. That's because Dreamweaver includes text from each of the nested tags, as well. For example, Figure 24-5 shows what happens when the root element—"rss"— is dragged from the Bindings panel pictured in Figure 24-4. Text from all of the other tags—the channel, the title, the description, and so on, as well as each of the repeated "item" tags—is included as one long paragraph. Dreamweaver treats this as a single big blob. To get around this, drag tags that don't include other nested tags. (Nested tags are called *child* tags.) For example, in Figure 24-4, the title tag that appears directly inside the channel tag doesn't have any tags inside it. Likewise, a repeating tag—item, for example—includes tags that don't have any children: "title," "link," "description," "pubDate." These are all good candidates for adding to a document.

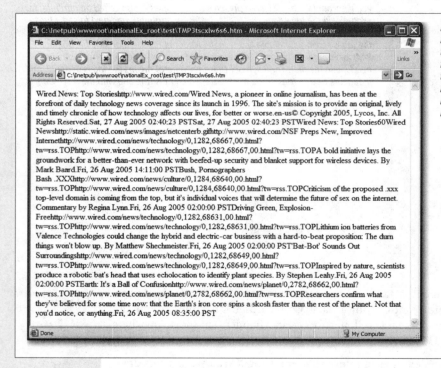

Figure 24-5:
If you use an XML tag that's too high up on the food chain—that is, other tags are nested inside of it—you can end up with a large chunk of hard-to-read text.

You can also insert XML into a Web page by choosing Insert → XSLT Objects → Dynamic Text or by clicking the Dynamic Text button on the XSLT panel of the Insert bar (see Figure 24-6). Either method opens the XPath Expression Builder window (Figure 24-7). An XPath Expression is just a way of identifying a particular element—called a node—inside an XML file (see page 846).

To add the dynamic text, select the XML tag or property you wish to insert. In the Expression box in the bottom half of the window, you'll see the XPath code required to locate your selection. For example, in Figure 24-7, the expression is *rss/channel/description.* This is shorthand for: Find the "description" tag, which is inside the "channel" tag, which is located inside the "rss" tag. In other words, this expression lists the order in which the tags are nested (in this sense, it's very much like the document window's tag selector [see page 21]).

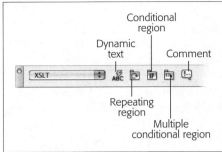

Figure 24-6:
Dreamweaver's XSLT tab includes five buttons for adding XSLT objects. The comment object just inserts an XSL comment—like an HTML comment (see page 336)—so you probably won't use it much, if ever.

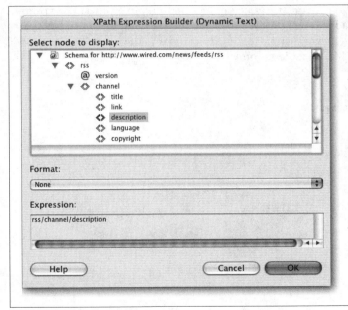

Figure 24-7:
Use the Format drop-down menu to apply a format to the XML data. Unfortunately, the formats are aimed almost entirely at formatting numbers—adding a $ sign to currency data, for example—so they won't do anything for text-only XML data.

Dreamweaver also lets you apply some formatting options to the selected text using the Format menu. Almost all of the options have to do with formatting numbers, so if you're inserting text that's actually a numeric value, these formatting controls can come in handy. For example, say you add a tag that's used to indicate a price—<price>3.25</price>. Selecting any of the currency options will add a $ sign in front of the number when it's displayed on the page. If you're dealing with big sums of money—<price id="Trump Tower">34589585</price>—then the "Currency group to 3 digits, 2 decimal places" is a good option. Then, the output would be something like this: $34,589,585.00. Again, all but two of the options are for formatting numbers, and the two that help format text aren't very useful.

After selecting a tag and setting a formatting option (if desired), click OK to insert the dynamic text. Dreamweaver adds a placeholder to the page: it has a blue background and displays the XPath expression inside of curly brackets (for example, {rss/channel/title}).

Tip: You can summon the XPath Expression Builder window again by double-clicking any dynamic XML text placeholder on the page.

Click an XML text placeholder to select it. You can then apply a CSS style to it, format it as a header or paragraph, or drag it to another spot on the page, just as you would any other HTML element.

Inserting a Repeat Region

XML files frequently contain the same tag repeated multiple times. For example, an XML file that's a list of employees might use the tag <employee> to begin each employee listing. For every employee in the company, the <employee> tag will appear once. The XML might look something like this:

```
<companyInfo>
<company>
<name>Big Co.</name>
    <phone>555-3333</phone>
</company>
<employeeList>
<employee id="485734">
<name>Mark</name>
<phone>555-3333 x405</phone>
</employee>
<employee id="38753">
<name>Jane</name>
<phone>555-3333 x406</phone>
</employee>
</employeeList>
</companyInfo>
```

If you added the <name> tag inside the first <employee> tag to an XSLT style sheet, attached that XSL file to a dynamic page, and then previewed it in a Web browser, you would see just a single name: the first employee name in the XML file. But just as with recordsets, you'll usually want to display multiple XML records. The answer is Dreamweaver 8's XSLT Repeat Region object. To use it:

1. **Insert elements that appear within a tag that is repeated multiple times. (Use any of the methods described on page 855.)**

   The Bindings panel lets you know if an XML tag is repeated multiple times: check for a + sign to the right of the <> icon in the panel (see Figure 24-4).

   So, in the above employee-list example, you wouldn't insert the <name> tag that appears inside the <company> tag, since <company> appears only once in the file. You would, however, insert the <name> tag and perhaps the <phone> tag inside the <employee> tag, since these are both "children" of a tag that's repeated twice in the document.

Note: This example points out a sometimes confusing aspect of XML: tags with the same name may appear as children within different kinds of tags. The <name> tag, for instance, appears both within the <company> and <employee> tags, but obviously refers to two different things–the name of a business and the name of a person.

   Articles in a Web feed are another case. For example, the RSS standard (see page 842) requires that each news item delivered in an RSS XML document be surrounded by an <item> tag with the following children: <title>, <link>, and <description>. Therefore, for an RSS feed, the elements you'd want to add to the page (and repeat once for each news item) would be <title>, <link>, and <description>.

2. **Select (by dragging, for example) the XML placeholders and any other content that you want to be repeated once for each instance in the XML file.**

   This would at least include the XML placeholders you inserted in step 1, but may also include other HTML elements, such as a graphic that's repeated once for each item, or a <div> tag that contains the XML data you're repeating. You can select only elements that are together: you can't, for instance, select an XML element at the top of the page and another at the bottom of the page, and use the same Repeat Region object.

Tip: You can, however, include multiple repeat regions on a page, so you could repeat the same XML data in several locations on a page, by adding multiple Repeat Region objects.

---

3. **Choose Insert → XML Objects → Repeat Region, or click the Repeat Region button on the XSLT tab (see Figure 24-6).**

   The XPath Expression Builder window appears (see Figure 24-8). This is a similar window to the one that appears when you insert dynamic text (Figure 24-7). However, instead of a format menu, the window includes a "Build Filter" option.

4. **Select the repeating tag.**

This tag will always have a + to the right of its <> icon and is usually the parent tag of the tags you inserted in step 1. So, in the employee list example above, you would select the <employee> tag; in the case of an RSS feed, it would be the <item> tag.

5. **Build a filter to limit the information retrieved from the XML file.**

An XSLT filter works similarly to filters on recordsets (see page 709). It's a way to select only certain information from the XML file. For example, you might want to select only employees whose last name is Smith, or product tags that have only an <instock> XML tag containing the word "true." Filters are discussed on page 861.

6. **Click OK to insert the repeat region.**

Dreamweaver adds a gray border around the repeating elements and adds a gray tab labeled "xsl: for-each." (If you don't see these, make sure invisible elements are turned on: View → Visual Aids → Invisible Elements or using the Visual Aids menu on the document window (see Figure 6-24 on page 204).

You can see the effect by pressing F12 (Option-F12): Dreamweaver translates all of that XSLT gobbledy-gook into a temporary HTML file. But to see the final presentation, you need to attach the XSLT style sheet to a dynamic page (steps 8–11 on page 853) or XML file (steps 1–2 on page 850), and preview it in a browser.

If you want to edit the repeat region, click the gray tab to select it and, in the Property inspector, click the lightning-bolt icon to open the Repeat Region window again (Figure 24-8).

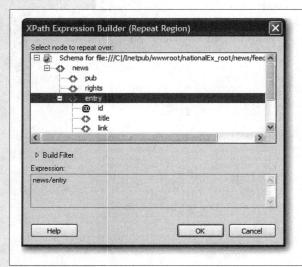

Figure 24-8:
Display repeating XML data using the XPath Expression Builder for repeat regions.

To remove a repeat region, right-click (Control-click) on the gray "xsl: for-each" tab, and select "Remove Tag: <xsl:for-each>." You can also click anywhere inside the repeat region, right-click (Control-click) on "xsl: for-each" in the tag selector (see page 21), and then choose Remove Tag. Don't try to remove the tag by hand in Code view: The code used to specify the tags inside the region also must be changed; Dreamweaver does this automatically and accurately.

Inserting and Formatting XML

Building a repeat-region filter

If the XML file you're using has lots and lots of repeating items, or you just want to home in on a single item, you can build an XSLT filter that lets you search and select XML elements that match certain criteria. For example, you might want to display only employee tags with a "department" property whose value is "marketing." Dreamweaver 8 lets you create very complex filters. In a nutshell, to filter a repeat region:

1. **Follow steps 1–4 on page 859 to insert a repeat region.**

2. **In the XPath Expression Builder (Repeat Region) window, click Build Filter to display the filter tools (see Figure 24-9), and then click the + button to add a filter.**

   You build a filter by first selecting a tag that contains the information you wish to compare to a certain value.

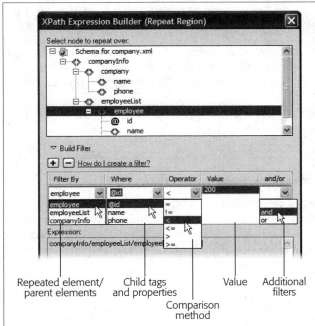

Figure 24-9:
Limit the XML data displayed by creating a filter that includes only XML tags that match certain criteria. Here's an example using the "employee list" XML code on page 858.

3. **Click in the Filter By column and, from the pop-up menu, select a tag.**

   This menu lists the repeating tag, its parent tag, its parent's parent tag, and so on, up the food chain, until it reaches the top (root) element. You'll just leave it as the repeating tag you selected in step 4 on page 860 (finish reading these steps and then read the following note to understand why this is the case).

Note (hold onto your thinking caps): A filter lets you select criteria that each repeated region is tested against. If it passes the test, the XML data is displayed. For example, the "id" property of the <employee> tag will vary with each employee listing. In a repeated region, the only elements that change are either a property of the tag that's repeated or the contents of other tags inside the repeated tag. That's why you should always select the repeated tag from the "Filter By" menu; the parent (and grandparent, and so on) of the repeated tag doesn't change with each region that repeats. If the parent has a property named "version," that property value will be the same whenever the filter is applied to a repeat region. In other words, the filter will either always be true or never be true, and you'll either get all of the XML data or none of the XML data from the repeated tags. Dreamweaver 8 includes a more flexible tool for displaying or hiding information based on some "test" or condition: conditional regions (see page 863).

---

4. **Click in the Where column, and select an option from the pop-up menu.**

   This menu will list any properties of the repeated tag, and all the repeated tag's child tags. In the employee-list code (page 858), for example, each <employee> tag has a property named "id" and children tags called <name> and <phone>. So in this case, those options would be listed in the "Where" menu. Tag properties begin with a @ symbol, so in this example, the "id" property would be listed as "@id" in the menu (see Figure 24-9).

   To continue with the employee-list example, if you wanted to display only employees whose employee id number was less than a certain number (perhaps to list the company's first 200 employees), you'd choose "@id" from the menu.

Note to Power Users: If you're up on your XPath expressions (and who isn't?), you can actually click in the Where column and type your own path to identify tags and properties located deeper in the tag structure.

---

5. **Select a comparison method from the Operator menu.**

   Your options are = (equal to), != (not equal to), < (less than), <= (less than or equal to), > (greater than), and >= (greater than or equal to). If the property or tag you selected in step 4 contains a number, you can use any of these comparison operators (as they're called). So if you wanted to find employees whose id number was less than 200, you'd select <.

   For properties and tags that contain text (<department>marketing</department>, for example) stick to either the = or != options. That way, a repeat region would show only employees who are either in the "marketing" department (use the = sign) or not in it (use the != operator).

---

6. **Type a comparison value in the value box.**

   The value is what you're testing against. For example, if you're looking for employee IDs that are less than 200, type *200*; for <department> tags that contain the word "marketing" type *marketing*.

7. **If you want to add more filters, select either "and" or "or" from the "and/or" menu, click the + button to add another filter, and then repeat steps 4–7.**

   This lets you add additional conditions that must be met in order to select XML data to include in the repeat region. For example, maybe you want to display employees who are *both* in the marketing department *and* are one of the first 200 employees. In this case, select the "and" option and add another filter. Or, you may want to display a list of employees who are *either* in the marketing department *or* the finance department: Select "or" and add a filter where the <department> tag is equal to "finance" as well.

   The ability to add multiple filters lets you build up complex filters that either let you continually narrow the number of regions that are repeated (by adding more and more *and* options) or that include more and more data from the XML file (by using additional *or* filters).

8. **After adding one or more filters, click the Close button to create a filtered repeat region.**

   Dreamweaver inserts the repeat region into the XSLT style sheet. You can edit or remove this region as described on page 861.

Inserting a Conditional Region

At times, you may want to display a part of a page only if certain conditions are met. The "Filter" feature of the Repeat Region tool (see page 858) offers some help, since it can display select XML data when a tag's property or contents pass a particular test: an *id* property that's less than 200, for example. But there are other occasions when the filter doesn't help. For example, say you want to display only the last item in a repeat region; there's no tag or property containing this information, so a filter won't work.

Note: If you use Dreamweaver templates, this problem may sound familiar. It's the same concept as a template optional region (see page 610).

Or maybe you want to display a graphic or another part of a page only when a certain XML property appears. For example, perhaps an XML document listing products has a tag like this: <product stock="in">. The "stock" property serves to indicate whether a product's available (in which case, it's value is "in") or when it's not ("out"). In such cases, you could use a conditional region to display an "out of stock" button next to each product that's not available.

To use a conditional region:

1. **Select the part of the page—either the XSLT file, or XSLT fragment—you want to display if a condition is true.**

   A simple example is an "out of stock" or "on sale" graphic. But you could also select XML data placeholders: maybe you want to display just the first five items inside a repeat region. In this case, select all the XML placeholders inside the repeat region (you need to add the repeat region first).

   Note: Many Web designers find it useful to place conditional regions inside of repeat regions, since this lets them fine-tune the display of information on a per-item basis. For example, in a repeating list of products, showing an "on sale" graphic for only those products that are actually on sale.

2. **Choose Insert → XSLT Objects → Conditional Region or click the Conditional Region button in the XSLT tab (see Figure 24-6).**

   The Conditional Region window opens (see Figure 24-10).

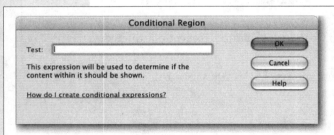

Figure 24-10:
The Conditional Region window lets you show or hide content on your page based upon certain conditions in the XML or XSL files.

3. **Type a test condition in the Test box.**

   Duh! "But what am I supposed to type?" you're asking. This is the tricky part, since Dreamweaver doesn't really give you much help. Your test condition can actually be a number of different things, many of which can be quite complex. Here are a few examples:

   • **An XPath expression followed by some kind of comparison.** For example, say you're working with the XML document on page 858. You've created a repeat region listing all of your company's employees, and you want an "employee of the month" graphic to appear in the listing, but only next to the employee whose ID is, say, 38753. To make that happen, the condition you'd type would be *@id=38753*. @id refers to the "id" property (@ is used before a property name) of the repeated tag (<employee>, in this example.) Likewise, if you wanted to highlight all employees whose name is Jane (that is, the text inside the <name> tag is 'Jane'), the condition would be *name='Jane'*. (Note that whenever you're testing whether a tag has text inside it—as opposed to just numbers—you must place quotes around the word, like this: 'Jane'.)

- **The position of an item in a repeated region.** When applying conditions to content that comes from a repeat region, you can access an item's position using position( ). So, for example, if you wanted to have the selected page elements inside a repeat region appear only when the first item is displayed, you could type *position( )=first( )*; for the last item, the condition would be *position( )=last( )*. And if you wanted to limit the repeat region to just 5 items (for example, if you want to show only the first 5 headlines from a news feed), you could use this expression: *position( )<=5*.

- **An XPath expression to determine if a tag or property exists.** You can also just enter an XPath expression for a particular *node* (page 846) in the document. If the node exists, then the selected element is displayed; otherwise, it's hidden. For example, say you have a repeat region that contains some optional tags. Again, using the employee list example, imagine if some employees had their own offices. For those employees, you might add an XML tag called <office> that includes the office number, like so: <office> Room 222</office>. You'd like to include the text "Office:" followed by the actual office number in your final Web page. However, if someone doesn't have an office (meaning that her entry in the XML file has no <office> tag), you don't want the word "Office:" to appear. To make that happen with a conditional region, type *"Office:"* somewhere inside the repeat region (perhaps on a line below the employee phone number); next, drag the <office> tag from the Bindings panel to the page, and then select both the text and the XML placeholder. Finally, add a conditional region as described on page 863, and simply type *office* as the condition. Now "Office:" and the office number will appear only for <employee> tags that have an <office> tag inside them.

- **Tag or property values that begin with one or more particular characters.** Say you want to display only those employees whose names begin with 'M.' You can do this easily with the starts-with( ) function. In the Conditional Region box, you would type *starts-with(name, 'M')*. Translated from XSLT-speak, this means any <name> tag whose contents start with the letter M will appear on the final Web page; so <name>Mark</name> and <name>Mary</name> would match, but <name>Andrea</name> wouldn't.

4. **Click OK to insert the conditional region.**

   Dreamweaver adds a gray border around the page elements you selected in step 1 and adds a gray tab labeled "xsl:if" to indicate the conditional region. (If you don't see these, make sure invisible elements are turned on by choosing View → Visual Aids → Invisible Elements or by using the Visual Aids menu on the document window (see page 204).

You can still edit the page elements inside the conditional region's gray border: you can edit, add, or remove text, images, and XML placeholders.

If you want to edit the conditional test, click the gray "xsl:if" tab to select the conditional region, and change the test listed in the Property inspector.

CHAPTER 24: XML AND XSLT

To remove a conditional region, right-click (Control-click) the gray "xsl:if" tab, and then select "Remove Tag <xsl:if>." You can also click anywhere inside the conditional region, right-click "xsl:if" in the tag selector (see page 21), and then choose "Remove Tag."

Using Multiple Conditional Regions

A conditional region is pretty straightforward: it either shows or hides part of the page based on the results of a simple test. But what if you wanted to display one thing if the condition is true, but show different stuff if the condition is false. For example, say you had two graphics called "In Stock" and "Out of Stock" that need to appear next to each product name in a repeat region. You could use two conditional regions: the first to display the "In Stock" image if the product tag's stock property was set to "in" (<product stock="in">) and another for out-of-stock products (<product stock="out").

Note: If you've ever done any computer programming, you'll recognize the upcoming maneuver as a variation on the venerable "if-then-else" statement.

But using conditional regions in that way requires far too much work on your part. Fortunately, Dreamweaver's Multiple Conditional Region tool makes it easy to deal with these "either/or" situations. Here's how to use it:

1. **Select the part of the page you want to display if a condition is true.**

   For instance, this might be a graphical button with the text "In Stock" printed across it. This step is the same as a conditional region described on page 864. In fact, most of the steps are the same.

2. **Choose Insert → XSLT Objects → Multiple Conditional Region or click the Multiple Conditional Region button in the XSLT tab (see Figure 24-6).**

   The Multiple Conditional Region window opens. Except for its title, the window's identical to the Conditional Region window (see Figure 24-10.)

3. **Type a test condition in the Test box.**

   For example, @stock="in" would cause the region to display if the value of the repeating tag's *stock* property was "in." For more examples, see page 864.

4. **Click OK.**

   Dreamweaver inserts three different sections of XSL code, each marked with their own gray tab: XSL:choose, XSL:when, and XSL:otherwise. The XSL:when section contains the actual condition or test you set in step 3.

   The XSL:otherwise section is the part of the page that will display if the test *isn't* true. Dreamweaver adds "Contents goes here" to that area.

5. **Select and delete "Contents goes here" and then add the page elements you wish to display if the test from step 3 isn't true.**

This would be the alternative to the content selected in step 1—for example, an "Out of Stock" icon.

You can edit the contents of either the XSL:when or XSL:otherwise sections. To edit the test, either click the gray XSL:when tab or click anywhere inside the XSL:when section and use the tag selector (see page 21) to select the <xsl:when> tag. The Property inspector displays the test condition: edit it, and press Enter or Return.

Removing a multiple conditional region is a bit trickier. You can't just right-click (Control-click) the gray "xsl:choose" tab and then select "Remove Tag <xsl:choose>" to remove all of the multiple conditional region code. You must remove each of the three sections separately. To do so, follow the same process as required when removing a conditional tag, as described on page 866.

Advanced XSLT Tricks

XSLT is a complex language with lots of bell and whistles—and just as many pitfalls. It's all too easy to head ambitiously into Code view and, with just a few keystrokes, completely break your XSLT style sheet. But since Dreamweaver's XSLT tools take you only so far, you'll undoubtedly find yourself wanting to dip into the code. Here are a couple of examples to help your explorations go a little more smoothly.

Sorting Data in a Repeat Region

The Repeat Region feature normally works by spitting out data that it retrieves from an XML document in the order it appears in the XML file. But what if you want that information sorted in a particular way—employees listed in alphabetical order, for example. Dreamweaver doesn't have a visual tool to let you accomplish this common goal. Fortunately, adding the code yourself is pretty easy:

1. **Click inside a repeat region and then click the "Code" or "Split" buttons in the document window's toolbar.**

Alternatively you can choose View → Code or View → Code and Design. Doing so drops you into the scary world of XSLT code; don't look too hard—you might go blind.

2. **Locate the beginning of the repeat region.**

What you're looking for is something like this: <xsl:for-each select="companyInfo/employeeList/employee">, where the stuff in quotes after "select" is the XPath expression pointing to the repeating tag. You need to add your new code directly after this tag.

3. Click immediately after the closing bracket (>), hit Enter, and then type <*xsl: sort select="xml_tag_to_sort_on" data-type="text" order="ascending" />*.

Replace *xml_tag_to_sort_on* with the XML tag inside the repeat region that you wish to use as the basis for sorting. For example, pick a tag used for a name or a tag used for a price.

Note: Don't forget the forward slash at the end of the sort tag: />. The tag you're adding is an empty tag (meaning there's no accompanying closing tag). In XML, these types of tags must be "self closed" using the forward slash (see page 844 for details).

The value for *data-type* can be either "text" or "number." Use the one that matches the type of data contained in the XML tag you're using as a sorting key. For example, use "text" if you're sorting names and "number" if you're sorting prices.

Depending on how you want to sort the data—smallest number to largest or largest number to smallest, type either *ascending* or *descending,* respectively, for the *order* property. "Ascending" gets you smallest number to largest, or A–Z; "descending" results in largest number to smallest, or Z–A.

Using XSLT Parameters

The Repeat Region's filter feature is very useful. With it, you can winnow down a mass of XML data to a smaller collection of useful facts. But what if you wanted the data retrieved from the XML file to *change* based on information from a database or information submitted by a visitor? For example, say you've already created an employee-list page, and now you want to create separate pages for each employee (kind of like the master-detail pages described on page 737). You could create an XSLT style sheet for each employee, thereby filtering the XML file based on the employee's ID number. But that's a lot of work. A better approach is to use an *XSLT parameter.*

Note: This solution applies only to server-side XSL Transformations, not the client-side approach described on page 847.

XSLT parameters provide a way of passing information from an outside source to the XSLT style sheet; the parameters can affect how the XSLT style sheet processes and displays the XML file. You've already encountered one way to pass a parameter to an XSLT style sheet—the XSL Transformation server behavior (see Figure 24-3). You can use the server behavior to pass either a value you manually enter, a dynamic value pulled from a database, or any of the other sources of data accessible in dynamic Web pages (see page 818). In this way, you could present a separate page for each employee simply by passing the employee's ID number to the XSLT style sheet (instead of manually creating separate XSLT files for each employee).

For this maneuver to work, you need to string together several different concepts involving both dynamic pages and XSLT files that you've already learned in this book. Here's an example of how to use XSLT parameters to dynamically filter XML data:

1. **Create an XSLT fragment as described on page 852.**

   You'll eventually include this fragment on a dynamic page (ASP, PHP, or whichever server method you're using) to display the final, filtered data.

2. **Follow steps 1–5 on page 859 to insert a repeat region and create a filter.**

   With this technique, all the steps in creating a filter are the same as those on page 861, except for entering the value in the "value" box, as explained in the next step.

3. **In the filter's Value box type *$your_param* (see Figure 24-11).**

   Change "your_param" to a name you'd like to use for the parameter. For example, if you want to filter for an ID that matches a particular value, you might type *$id*. You must include the $ sign, but you can come up with whatever name you like. It helps if it's descriptive, like $id, $name, or $price. It also must follow a few rules: use only numbers and letters, always start the name with a letter (not a number), don't use spaces, and stay away from punctuation marks, except for hyphens and underlines.

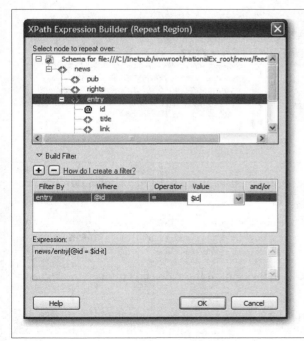

Figure 24-11:
You can use an XSLT parameter as a filter value. The parameter always begins with the $ sign and can let you dynamically filter the contents of an XML file.

Unlike a static value that you type into the Value box, like "38," "Dave," or "marketing," a parameter can be different each time the XSLT style sheet does its magic. But to get it to work, you do need to dip (just a bit) into Code view.

4. **Click the "Code" or "Split" button to view the XSLT code. Locate the line <xsl: template match="/">, and then click just before the opening bracket (<).**

   In XSLT, you first need to tell the style sheet that you'll be using a parameter.

5. **Type <xsl:param name="your_param"/>.**

   Replace "your_param" with the text you typed in step 3. Note that you leave off the $ sign. Also make sure you include the forward slash before the final bracket, like this: />

   You're done with the XSLT style sheet. It's all primed to have dynamic data sent to it. The next steps involve adding the XSLT fragment to a dynamic page.

6. **Repeat steps 8–10 on page 853.**

   This step is the same process as adding any XSLT fragment to a dynamic page—that is, using the XSL Transformation server behavior.

   In the next step, you add the XSLT parameter.

7. **In the XSL Transformation window, click the + button next to the label XSLT Parameters (see Figure 24-3).**

   The Add Parameter window opens (Figure 24-12).

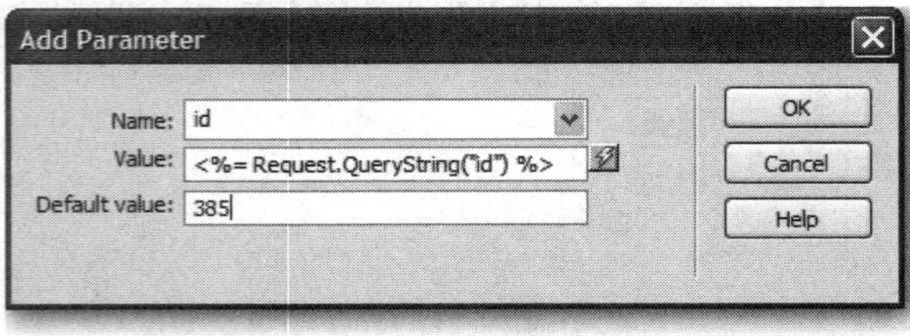

Figure 24-12:
While inserting the XSLT server behavior, you can add one or more parameters that let you pass information to the XSLT fragment–that way, you can control which data from the XML file is displayed on the Web page.

8. **In the Name box, type the name you used in steps 3 and 5 above (don't include the $ sign).**

   The value you enter here defines the name of the parameter that the dynamic page will pass off to the XSLT style sheet. Next (and this is the magic part), you'll add the value.

9. **Click the lightning-bolt icon to the right of the Value box to open the Dynamic Data window.**

   This is the same Dynamic Data window you've encountered with dynamic pages (see Figure 22-7). Don't get it confused with the XSLT Dynamic Text box

(Figure 24-7). Here, "dynamic" refers to any of the many sources of dynamic information you've used when creating database-driven pages—recordsets, URL variables, form variables, cookies, session variables, and so on. (For a recap on creating recordsets, see page 706; the other types of dynamic data can be added to the Dynamic Data window as described on page 818.)

10. **Select a source from the Field list and then click OK.**

   What you select here is the crucial part of the puzzle. You're telling the dynamic page where to get the information that will be passed off to the XSLT style sheet. To use the employee-list example again, you would need to identify where the "id" number used to select just a single employee comes from. Here are a few examples:

   • **Recordsets.** You could use the value from a field in a recordset. For this to work, you'll need to add a recordset (page 706) to the dynamic page first.

   • **Form fields.** One way to pass a value to a page is via a form. For example, you could add a form to a separate Web page. The form submits to this dynamic page (the one with the XSL Transformation) and includes a form menu that lists every employee's name (and includes the employee ID in the menu's value column—see page 375 for more on form menus). When a visitor selects a name from the menu, the employee ID is submitted to the dynamic page, which turns it into an XLST parameter and hands it off to the XSLT style sheet for use in the repeat region filter. (Turn to page 820 to see how to add a form field name to the dynamic data window.)

   • **URL variables.** You can apply the same idea to URL variables, but instead of getting the employee id from a menu, you'd attach it to a link to the dynamic page. For example, you might use a URL variable that looks something like this: *employee.php?id=15*. (Turn to page 820 to see how to add a URL variable to the Dynamic Data window.)

   These are just a few examples. You can use dynamic data from any dynamic source: cookies, session variables, and so on.

11. **Type a value in the "Default value" box.**

   This is the value the dynamic page will use if the source you picked in step 10 doesn't come through—for example, if the dynamic page is accessed without adding a URL variable (in which case you'd be passing just *employee.php*, instead of *employee.php?id=15*). Entering a default value will ensure that the XSLT style sheet has some value to work with. If, as in this example, you're using this technique to dynamically control XML filtering, the default value should match at least one record in the XML file.

12. **Click OK to close the Add Parameter box, and then click OK once again to close the XSL Transformation window.**

   Dreamweaver adds the new server behavior and the new parameter to your page.

Note: If you want to remove or change the XSLT parameter, just re-open the XSL Transformation window by double-clicking its name in the Server Behaviors panel.

13. **Provide a way to pass the dynamic data to the page.**

    For example, if you selected a URL variable as the data source for step 10, you would add links to other pages on your site that would point to the page with the XSL Transformation—*products.php?sku=10294* or *employee.asp?id=15,* for example.

Hopefully, by this point, your brain hasn't completely melted. As you can see, XML, XSLT, and all of the other x's can be pretty "X"-hausting. Take a breath, go have a cup of tea (or a bottle of Jolt cola), and when you're ready for some hands-on experience with Dreamweaver's exciting new XML tools, move on to the tutorial.

XML and XSLT Tutorial

In this tutorial, you'll learn how to create an XSLT fragment that formats news headlines from the *National Exasperator*. The headlines are contained in an XML file. You'll add the XSLT fragment to a dynamic page on the same site you've been working on in tutorials throughout this book. To get started, you need to grab the dynamic site files from *www.sawmac.com/dw8/tutorials*, and you'll have to have set up a Web server and application server as described in Chapter 20. However, you don't need to have finished any of the tutorials for Chapters 21, 22, or 23 to complete this tutorial.

Start by creating a new XSLT fragment:

1. **Choose File → New.**

   The New Document window appears.

2. **Make sure the Basic tab is selected. Choose Basic Page from the category list and XSLT (fragment) from the basic page list. Click Create.**

   The Locate XML Source window appears (see Figure 24-1), from which you can tell Dreamweaver which XML file to use. This can be either the XML file located with the tutorial files (*feed.xml*) or, if you're connected to the Internet, you can try the online version of the file located on the National Exasperator Web site at *http://www.nationalexasperator.com/feed.xml*. Using the online file lets you simulate what it's like to access an RSS feed from a news site like CNN.com or Wired.com.

3. **To use the local XML file, click the Browse button, navigate to the *news* folder in the site's root folder, and then select the *feed.xml* file. To use an XML file from some online source, select the "Attach a remote file on the Internet" button and then type *http://www.nationalexasperator.com/feed.xml*.**

In this particular case, both files are identical, so after this step, everything else in the tutorial will be the same.

4. **Whichever method you use, click the OK button to close the Locate XML Source window.**

If you have the Bindings panel open (Window → Panel), you'll see it fill with the tags from the XML file (see Figure 24-13).

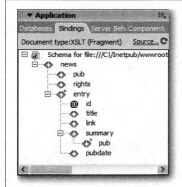

Figure 24-13:
When working with an XML file, the Bindings panel displays all of the XML tags contained in the file. See page 724 for more on how the Bindings panel works.

5. **Choose File → Save, and save this file as *news.xsl* in the *news* folder.**

You've just created an XSLT style sheet! Next, you'll add XML data to it.

6. **Drag the *title* tag from the Bindings panel into the Document window.**

You'll see {news/entry/title} with a blue background on the page. The blue background indicates that this is dynamic data—just as you see when adding recordset information to database-driven pages. The "news/entry/title" is an XPath expression, which, translated, means: use the "title" tag, which is located inside the "entry" tag, which is located inside the "news" tag. (The "news" tag is the *root*, or top-level element, in the XML file.) The XPath expression is much like the nesting of HTML tags that you see listed in the document window's tag selector (see page 21).

7. **In the Property inspector, choose Heading 3 from the Format menu.**

Alternatively, you can use the keyboard shortcut Ctrl+3 (⌘-3) to format the newly inserted chunk of XML as a header. One problem with designing just a fragment of a larger page is that you don't really know what the design will look like once it's included in your final dynamic Web page. Remember, an XSLT fragment will appear as just *one* chunk of code within the larger canvas of a dynamic Web page. The page probably will use its own set of CSS styles—so a Heading 3 on that page may already be formatted with a particular style.

Fortunately, Dreamweaver includes a great feature that lets you design an XSLT fragment using the styles from the dynamic page on which the fragment will ultimately be displayed: it's called Design Time Style Sheets. (Yep, this feature works just like the Design Time feature you learned about on page 174.)

8. **Choose Text → CSS Styles → Design Time….**

The Design Time Style Sheets window appears. Here, you'll tell Dreamweaver which external style sheet to use while you design the page.

9. **Click the + button. In the Window that appears, navigate to the local root folder of the site, select the *global.css* file, and then click OK.**

The file is now listed in the Design Time Style Sheets window, which means that you can apply any of the already-created styles from the site to the XML data on this page.

10. **Click OK to close the Design Time Style Sheets window.**

National Exasperator's distinctive gray sidebar strip appears in the background of the page. But there are a couple of things wrong here. First, the headline overlaps the sidebar; on the final page, it will actually go inside a table cell that holds the page's main content. Second, the Heading 3 isn't displaying as it will in the final page, since there, it will be inside a table cell that has a CSS class style named *mainContent* applied to it. A Heading 3 (or h3 tag) looks different when placed inside that class style, thanks to the power of *descendent selectors* (see page 189).

At any rate, you need to take a couple of extra steps to make it easier to use Dreamweaver's visual design tools (thereby saving yourself from having to muck around in Code view). First, you need to wrap the h3 tag in a temporary <div> tag.

11. **In the document window, click the XML tag you added in step 6 and then choose Insert → Layout Objects → Div Tag.**

The Insert Div Tag window appears.

12. **Make sure "Wrap Around Selection" is selected in the first menu, and select *mainContent* from the Class menu. Click OK.**

The design suddenly changes. The newly added *mainContent* div tag shows how the fragment will ultimately look. Since the tag will ultimately be placed inside a table cell with the class *mainContent* applied, you're now seeing the tag's true "context" within the page. In addition, due to a descendent selector that specially formats h3 tags that appear inside any tag with the class *mainContent* applied, the heading also changes appearance.

As brain-churning as all these details can sometimes seem, you'll find that using Design Time Style Sheets will make designing XSLT fragments a lot easier.

13. **Click to the right of the XML data ({news/entry/title}) and press the Space bar.**

You'll add the date the headline was published next.

14. **Drag the *pubdate* tag from the Bindings panel to the right of {news/entry/title} to add it to the page. From the Style menu in the Property inspector, choose "date."**

You can apply CSS styles to any of the XML data you add to a page. In this case, the style is from the Design Time Style Sheet you added earlier.

15. **Click to the right of the *pubdate* tag, and press Enter (Return) to create a new paragraph.**

You're almost done adding information from the XML file. You'll add the story summary, and then the *National Exasperator* copyright notice.

16. **Drag the summary tag from the Bindings panel to the new paragraph.**

And, finally, you'll add the copyright notice.

17. **Click to the right of the *summary* tag, press Enter (Return), and then drag the *rights* tag from the Binding panel to the page. In the Property inspector, choose "copyright" from the Style menu.**

You're done with the basics. You've added XML and all the formatting you'll need to make the page look pretty. Next, you'll learn how to add a link from an XML file.

Adding a Repeat Region and a Link

The XSLT fragment you created in the previous section is nearly complete. However, if you used it as is, only one headline, publication date, and summary would be displayed. Many XML files include multiple versions of the same set of tags (just like a recordset from a database often includes multiple records). The XML file you're using actually lists several headlines (the *National Exasperator* is a busy publication). To display multiple sets of the same tags from an XML file, you need to use a repeat region:

1. **In the document window, click to the right of the story summary ({/news/entry/summary}) and drag up and to the left until you've selected the summary, publication date, and headline.**

You'll turn this selection into a repeat region, so that all of this information will be displayed one time for each story in the XML file.

2. **Choose Insert → XSLT Objects → Repeat Region.**

The XPath Expression Builder window appears (see Figure 24-14). You simply have to select the tag that represents a story in the XML file—in this case, the tag's name is *entry*.

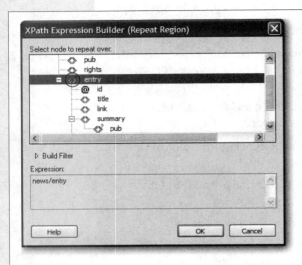

Figure 24-14:
To repeat a region, you must select a tag that appears multiple times and that contains the tags you want to repeat. The + sign (circled) next to the tag icon indicates that the tag repeats multiple times in the XML file. In this example, you can see that the tags you want to repeat—title and summary, for example—are nested inside the entry tag.

3. **Select the *entry* tag, and then click OK.**

A gray box appears around the selection, and a gray tab with the label "xsl:for-each" appears in the top-left corner of the box. The box represents the repeating region. In addition, you'll notice that those long-winded names—{/news/entry/summary}, and so on—have changed to shorter and simpler labels: title, pub-date, and summary.

The headline and news summary are just teasers for the real content. Fortunately, the XML file you're using contains a link to a Web page with the juicy story behind the headlines. Linking headlines and summaries to full stories is a common practice with feeds from news Web sites and blogs. The feed usually contains just a brief description of the story or blog posting, and then a link pointing to the whole story. Next, you'll add a link to the headlines.

4. **In the document window, click the XML tag labeled {title} to select it.**

You'll add a link to this tag.

5. **In the Property inspector, click the Browse for File folder button.**

The Select File window opens. (For a refresher on creating links, see page 108.)

6. **Click the Data Source radio button.**

The tags from the XML file appear in the Select File window (see Figure 24-15). Most of these tags wouldn't make sense as a link, since they contain just text or other tags, but the XML file happens to include a URL to a Web page in the <link> tag.

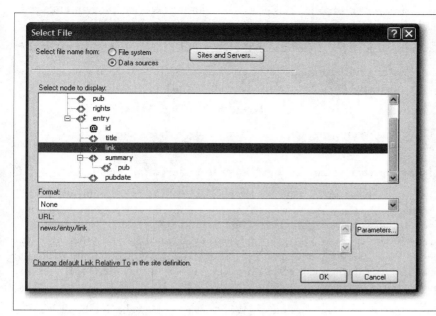

Figure 24-15:
The "Select node to display" box let's you use the content of an XML tag as a link. In XML-speak, a node is one of the discrete parts of an XML document, such as a tag, a property, a comment, or even just plain text. In this case, node refers to either the contents of the tags, or the contents of the attribute of a tag.

7. **Select the link tag, and then click the OK button.**

   Dreamweaver turns the headline into a link.

Note: You need to add the repeat region *before* the link, due to a bug in Dreamweaver 8. If you add the link first and then select all of the text you wish to repeat (as in step 1, earlier), Dreamweaver doesn't actually select the entire link tag. The link then won't work after you convert this partial selection to a repeat region. This problem happens only when the link is added to the first part of the information you wish to repeat, and then again only in some unusual circumstances. But since you might run into this nuisance, it's best to add the repeat region first, and then the link.

Believe it or not, that's all there is to creating the XSLT file. You just need to do one last thing to get the XSLT file ready to insert into a dynamic page.

8. **In the tag selector (in the bottom-left corner of the document window), right-click (Control-click) the tag <div.mainContent>. From the shortcut menu that appears, select Remove Tag.**

   Remember you placed that <div> tag temporarily in the file so you could accurately format the XML data using Cascading Style Sheets? You no longer need that tag, since the design is done and the dynamic page you're adding this XSLT fragment to already has that tag in place.

9. **Save and close the XSL file.**

Adding the XSLT Fragment to a Dynamic Page

The last piece of the puzzle is adding the XSLT fragment to a dynamic page using a Dreamweaver server behavior. This procedure adds the necessary programming code to magically transform the XML, XSLT, and so on, into browser-readable HTML:

1. **Open the page** *index.asp* **located in the** *news* **folder in the root folder of the site.**

   Use your favorite technique; for example, choose File → Open and select the file, or open the Files panel and double-click the file to open it.

2. **Click in the empty space directly below the headline "Latest Headlines."**

   This spot is where you'll place the XSLT fragment, but due to a small bug in Dreamweaver 8, you need to do one thing first.

3. **In the Property inspector choose "None" from the Format menu.**

   The empty space was actually an empty paragraph complete with the HTML <p> tags. Changing the format to "none" removes the <p> tags, which is a good thing. Otherwise, all the HTML from the XSLT style sheet would be placed *inside* of this <p> tag, meaning you'd have <h3> and other <p> tags nested inside of the paragraph. That arrangement would not only make the page look weird when viewed in a browser, but it's also invalid HTML—shame on you, Dreamweaver.

4. **Open the Server Behaviors panel (Window → Server Behaviors). Click the + button and then select XSL Transformation.**

   You can also click the XSLT button on the Application tab of the Insert bar— it's the last button on the right side of the tab. The XSL Transformation window opens (see Figure 24-16). Here, you select the XSLT file you created earlier.

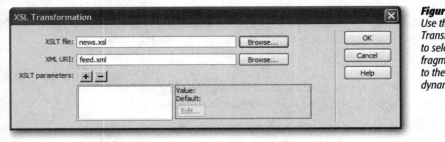

Figure 24-16:
Use the XSL Transformation window to select the XSLT fragment you wish to add to the currently opened dynamic Web page.

5. **Click the first Browse button, select the** *news.xsl* **file, and then click the OK button in the Select XSLT File window.**

   The XSL Transformation window should now look like Figure 24-16. The XML file is automatically entered in the XML URI box. It will read either *feed.xml* (if you used the local file) or *http://www.nationalexasperator.com/feed.xml* (if you grabbed the XML file from the National Exasperator Web site.)

6. **Click OK to apply the server behavior to the page.**

The document window should look like the top image in Figure 24-17.

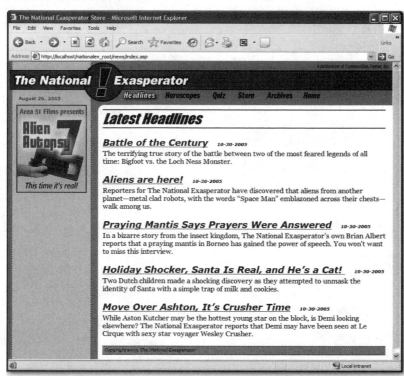

Figure 24-17:
Although the XSLT fragment might not look like much in Dreamweaver, when viewed through a Web browser, the page is magically transformed into a finished Web page, complete with headlines, summaries, links, and a copyright notice.

7. **Save the file and press F12 (Option-F12) to see the results (Figure 24-17, bottom).**

That's all there is to it. Expand on the steps in this tutorial using a real news feed from your favorite news site. (You can usually find these as links on the home page labeled "Feed," "RSS," or "XML.") If you can't find any feeds, try this one from Wired.com: *http://www.wired.com/news/feeds/rss2/0,2610,,00.xml*.

Part Seven: Appendixes

7

Getting Help

Hard as it may be to believe, even this book may not answer all your questions about Dreamweaver. Fortunately, a wide range of other resources awaits when a particular feature doesn't work for you.

Getting Help from Dreamweaver

There's plenty of assistance built right into the program, from beginner tutorials to a complete browser-based help system. You can also access Dreamweaver's electronic help system and online support center from the Help menu.

What's New

If you want a comprehensive overview of Dreamweaver 8's new features, select the "What's New in Dreamweaver 8" option from the Help menu. A categorized list of new features includes short descriptions and links to more detailed discussion in the electronic help system. Unfortunately, they neglected to put references to the appropriate pages in this *Missing Manual*.

Getting Started

If you're brand new to Dreamweaver, see the Getting Started with Dreamweaver materials (Help → Getting Started with Dreamweaver) and follow the step-by-step tutorials that cover specific Web-creation tasks. These range from setting up a Web site to using Dreamweaver's dynamic page-building tools. You'll find them fairly basic (this book's tutorials cover most of the same ground more thoroughly), but you can never have too much practice.

Detailed Assistance

For detailed information on specific features of the program, turn to the Using Dreamweaver reference. This electronic help system includes information on all the program's features, although its coverage, alas, can be spotty and lacking in detail. Choose Help → Using Dreamweaver or press F1 to open this help system (the Dreamweaver Help option in the same menu opens the same help documents).

Macromedia has also introduced a new, more interactive version of their help system. Called LiveDocs, this Web-based reference includes much of the same content you'll find in the program's Using Dreamweaver reference, with one notable exception: the ability to leave comments. This feature's new, so you may not find much on the site yet, but it promises to be a great way for Dreamweaver users to point out problems in the documentation, clarify confusing explanations, and share undocumented tips and tricks. To get to this tool from within Dreamweaver, choose Help → Dreamweaver LiveDocs. This action opens a browser window and connects to Macromedia's Web site, so you need to be connected to the Internet to view the LiveDocs.

If you're interested in writing your own Web code, Dreamweaver's Reference window (select Help → Reference or Window → Reference, or press Shift-F1) provides in-depth information on HTML, CSS, JavaScript, ASP, JSP, ColdFusion, and Web accessibility.

Getting Help from Macromedia

You can also get more up-to-date and personalized support from Macromedia, ranging from technical notes on the Macromedia Web site to pay-as-you-play support plans.

Free Help by Email

www.macromedia.com/support/email/complimentary/

As a registered owner of Dreamweaver, you're entitled to free help by email for two problems within 90 days. In other words, you get help with only two problems (can you say "cheapskates"?) and only if you make both requests within 90 days. The clock starts ticking when you make your first request for help. It's available only if you've registered your copy of the software first by choosing Help → Online Registration to register via the Web or Help → Print Registration to print out a paper registration form (those still exist?) that you can fill out and mail to Macromedia.

To post a question, go to the Web site whose address appears above, where you'll find a Web-based support form to fill out. Macromedia says it'll usually send you an answer within one business day.

For phone assistance, call this *not* toll-free number: (415) 252-9080. Expect to wait on hold, but the support staff is usually very helpful and knowledgeable.

Note: Dreamweaver users outside the United States should visit Macromedia's International Support page at *www.macromedia.com/international/support/*.

Paid Support

www.macromedia.com/support/programs/

Once your free email help expires, you can turn to four levels of personalized fee-based support, ranging from $99 for a single incident to the whole-hog luxury of the $3,000 Gold Support program. For more information on these programs, go to the Web page whose address appears above. Each program has its own phone number, so read the Web site to determine the type of support (Incident to Gold) that you need. If you have just a single nagging question, the single-incident help program gets you a Macromedia technician who will work with you until the issue is resolved. But at $99, make sure you've tried to answer the question yourself first using one of the free resources listed in this appendix. Customers in the U.S. and Canada should call (800) 470-7211 to order this service. (More information on this option, as well as choices for international customers, is at *www.macromedia.com/support/programs/singlesupp.html.*)

Macromedia Web Site

www.macromedia.com

If you don't mind hunting around for the right answers, you'll find plenty of good, free information on Macromedia's Web site; select Dreamweaver Support Center from the Help menu to open a Web browser and load the main page for Dreamweaver's support. If you've got a question or problem, this is the best place to start. Here, you'll find useful tips, techniques, and tutorials, along with a searchable archive of tech notes (short articles on specific, tweaky problems) that just may hold the answer you're seeking.

For tutorials and in-depth articles on using Dreamweaver, turn to Macromedia's Developer Center—choose Dreamweaver Developer Center from the Help menu. This site includes sample database applications, video tutorials, and in-depth articles. It's worth checking out frequently.

Online Documentation

You can also find all the documentation for the program on the Macromedia Web site at *www.macromedia.com/support/documentation/en/dreamweaver/*, or just choose Dreamweaver Documentation Resource Center from the Help menu. On this Web page, you'll find not only a downloadable version of the electronic documentation, but other helpful reference material such as a Quick Reference Guide—a concise Dreamweaver cheat sheet.

The Forums

Macromedia provides both online forums that you get to with a browser and newsgroups that require newsgroup-reading software like the software built into Outlook Express. To get to either of these, choose Help → Online Forums or visit *www.macromedia.com/cfusion/knowledgebase/index.cfm?id=tn_12606*. The forums are a terrific source of information, offering almost real-time answers on Dreamweaver and related Web design techniques. Macromedia sponsors several forums and newsgroups. Of most interest to average Dreamweaver users are the General Discussion forum for basic questions and the Application Development forum, where people discuss Dreamweaver's dynamic Web page features. Odds are one of the many knowledgeable experts who always seem to be hanging around will come back with an answer, sometimes within minutes. (If you're new to forums, *www. macromedia.com/support/forums/using.html* explains how to use them.)

If you're a little late to the party, you can search previous forum questions as well, since these forums are all indexed at Google Groups—see *http://groups.google.com/ advanced_group_search?q=+group:macromedia.dreamweaver*.

Help from the Real World

If Macromedia doesn't have the answer, there's probably a Web site somewhere that does. In fact, you're likely to find more honest critiques of the program at some of these sites. Here are two of the best non-Macromedia sites for answers.

DMX Zone

www.dmxzone.com

The DMX Zone includes tutorials, extensions, and Macromedia-related news. It also offers "Premium Content," a subscription-based service that provides more in-depth information on Dreamweaver.

Community MX

www.communitymx.com/

Another subscription service (it's so hard to find free help these days). This site has lots of material for all things MX (the two previous versions of Dreamweaver were part of Macromedia's "MX" family of products), including Flash and other Macromedia programs. It does have some free content as well, and it's updated regularly.

Help Creating Your Own Extensions

If you're excited by the possibilities of the Dreamweaver extensions (discussed in Chapter 19), you may want to have a go at creating your own. You should be well versed in JavaScript and have an interest in programming. To help you out, Dreamweaver includes a *detailed* electronic help system covering every aspect of extension development. Choose Help → Extending Dreamweaver, which launches an electronic help system. You can view its table of contents or use a search feature.

In addition, you'll need to learn Dreamweaver's advanced programming interface (API). An API lets you use JavaScript to communicate with and control Dreamweaver. It's not for the faint of heart, however; take a look by choosing Help → API Reference.

Finally, after creating your extension masterpiece, you can submit it to the Dreamweaver Exchange to show off your masterful programming talent to the world. This Web page has more information on how to do that: *www.macromedia.com/ cfusion/exchange/upload/index.cfm*.

Dreamweaver 8, Menu by Menu

Dreamweaver 8: The Missing Manual is quite complete; in its pages, you'll find descriptions of every major Dreamweaver function (and most minor ones). In the interests of completeness, however, here's a quick reference to every command in every menu—and the answer to the occasional "What does that mean?" mystery.

File Menu

The commands in the File menu control the open Dreamweaver document as a whole. They also include basic file functions like saving and quitting:

- **New.** Opens the New Document window, which lets you select a new, blank document of many different types, from basic HTML pages to dynamic pages like ASP or PHP. This window also lets you access templates you've created for your site.

- **Open.** Opens the standard Open File dialog box so you can choose an existing Dreamweaver document to open. You can set the Show pop-up menu to show only specific types of documents—only HTML or style sheets, for example. The Preview button displays a thumbnail image of the document, if one's available.

- **Open Recent.** Displays a submenu that lists the 10 most recently opened documents. Selecting a document from the list opens it. The last option in this menu, "Reopen Documents on Startup," is kind of cool. If you quit Dreamweaver when any documents are still open (and this option is checked), those documents will automatically reopen the next time you start up Dreamweaver.

- **Open in Frame.** Opens an existing HTML page within one frame of a frameset. To make this command available, you must first click inside a frame to select it—not just in the Frameset document. The Select HTML file dialog box opens and lets you navigate to the file you wish to insert into the Frame. You can also choose to make the file's URL relative to the document or the root folder, as described in Chapter 4. (See note about frames in the box on page 112.)

- **Close.** Closes the open Dreamweaver document. If you have unsaved changes, Dreamweaver gives you the opportunity to save them.

- **Close All.** Closes *all* currently open documents. If you have unsaved changes, Dreamweaver gives you the opportunity to save them.

- **Save (Save Frameset/Save Frame).** Saves any changes you've made to your document. The Save command is dimmed if you haven't made any changes to the document since the last time you saved it.

Note: If you're working on a frames-based document, this command may say Save Frameset or Save Frame, depending on what's selected.

- **Save As (Save Frameset As/Save Frame As).** Saves a copy of the current document under a new name, closing the original version and leaving the new version onscreen. Here again, if you're working on a frames-based document, this command says either Save Frameset As or Save Frame As, depending on what's selected.

- **Save All.** Saves changes to all the open documents.

- **Save to Remote Server.** Lets you save the current file to *any* site for which you've defined a remote site. In other words, if you use Dreamweaver's FTP feature to move your files to a Web server (see Chapter 15), this option lets you access that Web server directly. In fact, it lets you access any Web server for any Web site you've defined in Dreamweaver. Because of this behavior, this option can be risky. You can accidentally save a file into the wrong Web site, or in the wrong folder of the right Web site. Therefore, it's generally better to use the Files panel and its "Put Files" button—see page 542.

- **Save as Template.** Saves the current document as a template file with the suffix .dwt. The Save as Template dialog box appears, so that you can specify the template's file name and indicate which site it belongs to. Dreamweaver automatically saves all template documents in a Templates folder in the selected site's folder. Templates are discussed in Chapter 17.

- **Revert.** Undoes any changes you've made to the document since the last time you saved it. Edit → Undo can often be a better choice; it might take a few more steps to undo all the changes you've made, but it can actually undo changes *past* your last save. So if you're one of those gotta-save-it-every-five-seconds types, the Undo command is for you.

- **Print Code.** Prints the code (that is, what you see in Code view) of the current document.

- **Import.** Allows you to import data from other sources into your Dreamweaver document, such as XML data into a Template document, HTML generated by Microsoft Word, or tabular data from a spreadsheet program like Microsoft Excel. (Use the submenu to specify which.)

- **Export.** Extracts tabular data, Cascading Style Sheet styles, or template data as XML from your Dreamweaver document, for use in other applications.

- **Convert.** Converts more modern technologies such as Cascading Style Sheets into code that's understandable by older browsers. In addition, you can convert older HTML pages into a variety of more modern formats like HTML 4.01 Strict and two forms of XHTML—the current standard for HTML Web pages. Unfortunately, it's kind of hit-or-miss: this feature can't always update older files to more modern standards.

- **Preview in Browser.** Opens the current document in your Web browser. (You have to save your framesets before you can preview them.) By selecting Edit Browser List, you can add new browsers to, or delete browsers from, your browser list, or specify a preferred browser.

- **Check Page.** Checks the current page for a variety of problems, such as broken links, code that's incompatible with various browsers, accessibility limitations, and invalid HTML or XML code. These same tools are available from the Results panel for checking an entire site's worth of files—choose Window → Results and click an appropriate tab—for example, the Link Checker to check links.

- **Compare with Remote/Compare with Testing.** Lets you use a third-party code-comparison tool to see how a local copy of a page differs from either the remote copy (on the Web server) or a copy on your testing server. This lets you see exactly what code differs between two copies of the same page. This feature is discussed on page 347.

- **Design Notes.** Opens the Design Notes window (Chapter 15), where you can add additional information about the document, set the status, and choose to have the design note appear whenever the document is opened.

Note: To use Design Notes on your site, you must make sure the Maintain Design Notes option is selected in the "Design notes" section of the Site Definition window.

- **Exit/Quit.** Exits Dreamweaver. If any of your open Dreamweaver documents have unsaved changes, the program prompts you to save them before quitting.

Edit Menu

The Edit menu applies common document changes like copying and pasting:

- **Undo.** Undoes the most recent change made to your document. You can choose this command repeatedly to move progressively backwards through your changes, even *after* you've saved the document.

- **Redo (Repeat).** Restores whatever changes you just made by using the Undo command. Selecting Redo multiple times moves you progressively forward through changes you've undone. If you've just performed an operation other than Undo, Repeat instead of Redo will appear. This lets you repeat the last action. For example, if you just pressed Delete, the Repeat command presses it again.

- **Cut.** Deletes the selected text or objects from the document and copies them to the invisible Macintosh or Windows Clipboard so they can be pasted elsewhere. (The Clipboard holds only one selection at a time.)

- **Copy.** Copies the selected text or object to the Clipboard so it can be pasted elsewhere—without disturbing the original.

- **Paste.** Places the most recent selection from the Clipboard into your document at the insertion point.

- **Paste Special.** Opens the Paste Special window, which lets you choose how you wish to paste the Clipboard into your document. Options range from Text Only for just plain text to increasingly more elaborate options, which force Dreamweaver to attempt to preserve various levels of formatting. For example, preserving styles, bold, italics, bulleted lists, and so on.

- **Clear.** Deletes the selected text or objects from the document without placing it on the Clipboard.

- **Select All.** Selects everything in the document so you can make document-wide changes in one fell swoop.

- **Select Parent Tag.** Increases the current selection to include everything within the *parent tag,* including its content. For example, if you had a table cell selected, this command would increase the selection to the entire table *row.* Choosing the command a second time would increase the selection to include the entire table. In short, this command ensures that any changes you make apply to the entire tag.

- **Select Child.** Decreases the current selection to include everything within the child tag, including its contents. If you selected a table row, choosing this command would decrease that selection to include only the first table *cell* and its contents.

- **Find and Replace.** Opens the Find and Replace window, which you can use to search the document—or entire site—for a specific word, tag, or source code and replace it with something different (see page 649). This command lets you make such changes either en masse or one instance at a time.

- **Find Selection.** This command lets you find another instance of the current selection. For example, say you've selected the word "Mothball" on the page. Choosing this command will search the page for another example of "Mothball."

- **Find Next.** Uses the most recent search settings from the Find and Replace window to search the current document, highlighting the next instance of the requested search item.

- **Go to Line.** Opens the Go To line dialog box. Type a number, and Dreamweaver positions the cursor at the beginning of the specified line of code. (Available only in Code view.)

- **Show Code Hints.** Immediately displays any code hints (overriding the delay set in the Preferences window) available for the current tag. Code Hints, described in Chapter 9, provide a pop-up menu of tag properties appropriate for the current tag. (Available only in Code view.)

- **Code Hint Tool.** When working in Code view, lets you access Dreamweaver's color picker, Browse for File button, and list of fonts so you don't have to type things like *#FF6633, ../../images/dog.gif,* or *Arial, Helvetica, sans-serif,* every time you use a color, link to a file, or want to use a font.

- **Indent Code.** Adds one indent before the selected line of code. (Available only in Code view.)

- **Outdent Code.** Removes one indent from the selected line of code. (Available only in Code view.)

- **Balance Braces.** When you're editing a script in Code view, this command helps you check for unbalanced braces (that is, an introductory { without a closing }) by highlighting the matching tags enclosing the selected code. It doesn't do anything for plain HTML, but if you're writing a JavaScript program or using a dynamic programming language like PHP or ASP, it can help identify missing braces—a common source of programming errors. Works with ( ) as well.

- **Repeating Entries.** Lets you cut, copy, paste, and delete repeating regions in templates. Repeating regions are described in Chapter 17.

- **Edit with External Editor.** If you haven't already specified an external HTML code editor, such as BBEdit or Notepad, to use when editing large amounts of source code, this command opens the Preferences window so that you can find and select one on your hard drive. Once you've specified an editor, this command opens the current document in that editor.

- **Tag Libraries.** Lets you modify the way Dreamweaver writes code for various types of tags: HTML, ColdFusion, ASP, and so on. You can create new tag libraries for working with other types of tag-based languages, or modify the ones that ship with Dreamweaver.

- **Keyboard Shortcuts.** Opens the Keyboard Shortcuts window and shows you all the current keyboard shortcuts for Dreamweaver. You can create a new set of shortcuts for specific sites or programs, or export the settings to HTML to share with others. (You must duplicate the factory settings before you can add or delete your own shortcuts.) Details are in Chapter 19. (In Mac OS X, this option appears under the Dreamweaver 8 menu.)

- **Preferences.** Opens the Preference window, which is full of options that customize the way Dreamweaver works. There are 16 categories of preferences, including the color and format of different HTML tags, shorthand for CSS styles, and the order in which panels appear on the screen. (In Mac OS X, this option appears under the Dreamweaver 8 menu.)

View Menu

The View menu controls the appearance of the document window. A checkmark in the menu lets you know which view you're in:

- **Zoom In.** Zooms in on the document in 50% increments. For example, if you're looking at a document at normal size (100%), selecting this option zooms to 150%; selecting it again zooms to 200%.

- **Zoom Out.** Zooms out from the document in 50% increments.

- **Magnification.** Lets you choose from a list of magnification levels from the absurdly small and illegible 6% all the way to a ridiculously large, land-of-the-giant-pixels 6400%.

- **Fit Selection, Fit All, Fit Width.** Additional magnification options that either zoom in or zoom out depending of the size of the document or selected element.

- **Code.** Displays the file's source code.

- **Design.** Displays the file's visual design.

- **Code and Design.** Splits the document window into two panes: source code on top, visual design at the bottom. You can adjust how much of each pane is visible by dragging the center divider up or down.

- **Switch Views.** Switches between the Code and Design views.

- **Refresh Design View.** Updates the Design view to reflect changes you've made directly to the source code in either Code view or split (Code and Design) view.

- **Head Content.** Opens a new menu bar in the main document window that contains shortcuts to accessing the file's Head contents. You can use these menu items to highlight your document's Title tags, meta tags, and scripts, and then edit their content in the Property inspector.

- **Noscript Content.** When inserting JavaScript code into the document window, you can also include what's called "Noscript" tags—information that appears in browsers that don't understand JavaScript (of which there are very few), or which have their JavaScript turned off. After selecting this option, all information inside of noscript tags appears in the document window. To hide this information, select this menu option again.

- **Table Mode.** Lets you switch between the standard table view, Expanded Tables view and the Layout Table view (Chapter 7). When in the Layout Table view, you can also choose to have your tables display helpful tabs (by choosing the Show Layout Table Tabs subcommand), which make it easy to adjust the table's dimensions, make columns autostretch, or add spacer images.

- **Visual Aids.** Lets you summon onscreen symbols that represent typically invisible page elements like image maps, anchors, and borders.

- **Style Rendering.** Lets you hide or show the effect of all style sheets on a page, or selectively display the formatting changes caused by a style sheet that's applied for a particular media—for example, for screen-only or printer-only.

- **Code View Options.** Lets you adjust the appearance of your HTML code in Code view. You can turn on (or off) options that wrap lines of text to fit in the document window, add line numbers, highlight invalid HTML, turn on syntax coloring, or indent lines of code.

- **Rulers.** When you choose Show, Dreamweaver displays rulers along the top and left sides of the document window. Using the options you find here, you can choose your ruler units: pixels, inches, or centimeters. You can also reset the orientation of the two rulers so that both start from zero in the upper-left corner of the screen.

- **Grid.** Places a grid of vertical and horizontal lines over the document window to use as a guide when building your layouts. Selecting Edit Grid opens the Grid Setting dialog box, where you can adjust your grid's colors, spacing, behaviors, and line appearance.

- **Guides.** Shows, hides, locks, and erases user-added guidelines that have been dragged from a ruler onto the page. Also controls options for guides, and displays guidelines that mark the visible area of a Web browser window on monitors of different resolutions.

- **Tracing Image.** Adjusts the document's background tracing image. You can load a new tracing image, make a current one visible, or adjust its position.

- **Plugins.** Lets you "play" browser plug-ins within the document window to test embedded media. You can choose to play a document's plug-ins one at a time, or all at once, to simulate how the page will look to your viewers.

- **Hide Panels (Show Panels).** Hides all open panels. If panels are already hidden, the command says Show Panels instead and restores the panels to their original positions.

- **Toolbars.** Displays toolbars for use with Dreamweaver. Select Document from the submenu to display the Toolbar menu at the top of the document window. This menu offers common commands like the document's View settings, page title, file management options, code navigation options, and browser preview. The Standard toolbar option displays a toolbar with common buttons for common commands, such as opening files; closing files; and cutting, copying, and pasting content. The Style Rendering toolbar lets you toggle style sheets off and on like the Style Rendering menu described earlier in this section.

Insert Menu

The Insert menu adds selected page elements to the document at the insertion point's position. The commands listed here correspond to the buttons on the Objects panel:

- **Tag.** Opens the Tag Chooser window, which provides access to all the tags—not only HTML, but any tag Dreamweaver has stored in its Tag Library (see entry under the Edit menu on page 893). You can insert any tag and set any of its properties from this window. However, Dreamweaver doesn't make sure you're inserting the tag correctly, so you should understand HTML (or the tag language you're using) before trying this option.

- **Image.** Inserts an image file, such as a JPEG or GIF, into the document. The Select Image Source window appears and lets you navigate to the file you want on your hard drive. You can choose to make the URL for the file relative to either the document or the Site Root.

- **Image Object.** Lets you insert placeholder graphics, rollover images, navigation bars, or HTML from Fireworks. These options are discussed in Chapter 5.

- **Media.** Inserts other types of media files, including Flash, Shockwave, Generator Applets, Plug-ins, and Active X. In most cases, the standard Select File window appears, which you can use to navigate to the desired file. This menu also lets you insert Flash text, Flash buttons, and the Image Viewer Flash element described on page 452.

- **Table.** Inserts a new table into the document. The Insert Table dialog box appears and lets you format the table by specifying the number of rows and columns; the table width; measurements for cell padding, cell spacing, and the table border; and whether or not and where to include table headers.

- **Table Objects.** Provides methods to insert tabular data (see the Import entry under the File menu on page 891) and add other table-related tags such as the <th>—table header—tag into the page. The tag options listed under this menu item assume you understand HTML and just insert the tags, without making sure you're doing it correctly.

- **Layout Object.** Lets you insert layers, divs, table layout cells, and table layout tables—in other words, different objects for designing and laying out a page as described in Chapters 7 and 8.

- **Form.** Inserts Form Objects—the <form> tag, text fields, buttons, checkboxes, or lists—into the document. (If you have not already inserted the <form> tag, Dreamweaver prompts you to do so.)

- **Hyperlink.** Inserts a link. The Insert Hyperlink dialog box lets you specify the text that should appear inside the link, the file to link to, as well as many other link options such as target and tab index.

- **Email Link.** Creates a new email link at the insertion point. The Insert Email Link dialog box appears; specify both the email address and the link's text (such as "Click to email me").

- **Named anchor.** Inserts a named anchor for adding links *within* a page. See page 116.

- **Date.** Inserts the current date into the document. The Insert Date dialog box lets you format the appearance of the day of the week, the date, and the time. You can also elect to have the date automatically updated each time the document's saved.

- **Server-Side Include.** Opens a Find File window, from which you select a file that's dynamically added to the content of your page. Works only with special server setup, such as the dynamic server-driven pages discussed in Part Six of this book.

- **Comment.** Inserts an HTML comment into your page. This comment isn't viewable in Web browsers, but in Dreamweaver's design view appears as a little gold shield. Use these to leave notes for yourself and others about specific information about a page. For example, a comment indicating where an ad should be placed can help someone updating the page know what to do.

- **HTML.** Menu including lots of specific HTML tags, such as a horizontal rule, frames, text objects (many of which are also available under the Text menu), script objects for JavaScript, and head tags that go in the *head* portion of a Web page—including meta tags such as keywords and descriptions used by some search engines.

- **Template Objects.** When working on a template file, this menu option lets you insert many of Dreamweaver's template features such as optional, editable, and repeating regions.

- **Recent Snippets.** Lists the most recently inserted snippets. Selecting a snippet from the list inserts it into the document. Snippets are discussed in Chapter 16.

• **XSLT Objects (only visible when working on an XSL file).** Inserts various objects for converting XML data into a Web browser–readable format. This feature is discussed in Chapter 24.

• **Customize Favorites.** Lets you add your favorite objects from the Insert panel into a special "favorites" tag, so your most common objects, images, divs, rollovers, tables, can be just one click away. See page 118 for more information.

• **Get More Objects.** Opens the Macromedia Exchange for Dreamweaver Web site in your browser. There you can search for and download new extensions and objects to add new features to your copy of Dreamweaver. Use the Commands → Manage Extensions command to add downloaded extensions to Dreamweaver.

Modify Menu

You can use the commands in the Modify menu to adjust the properties of common document objects: links, tables, and layers, for example:

• **Page Properties.** Opens the Page Properties window, where you can specify document-wide attributes—such as the page title, background and link colors, page margins, and background image—or select a *tracing image* to use as a reference for designing the page.

• **Template Properties.** Opens the Template Properties window, where you can modify settings for various template features, such as controlling the visibility of optional regions, the properties of editable attributes, and the values of any template expressions you've created. Only available when working on a template-based page, as described in Chapter 17.

• **Selection Properties.** When this item is selected (as indicated by a checkmark in the menu), the Properties Inspector palette's on the screen; you use it to edit the current settings for selected page elements. The list of options displayed in the Properties window changes according to what type of page element is selected. This item has the same effect as choosing Properties from the Window menu.

• **CSS Styles.** Controls the display of the CSS Styles Panel. A checkmark tells you that the panel's open. This item has the same effect as choosing CSS Styles from the Window menu.

• **Edit Tag.** Opens a dialog box with detailed options for the HTML tag that's active in the current document. This advanced feature is for the true HTML geek—it gives access to *all* the properties for a specific tag (not just the ones Dreamweaver displays in the Property inspector).

• **Quick Tag Editor.** Lets you edit an HTML tag without leaving the Design view. If nothing on the page is selected, the Quick Tag editor prompts you to enter a new HTML tag at the insertion point (by choosing from the alphabetical menu). But if text or an object is already selected when the Quick Tag Editor is opened, the window displays the selection's HTML tags for editing.

- **Make Link.** Turns a highlighted page element (graphic or text) into a link. The standard Select File dialog box appears; choose the document you want to open when someone clicks the link.

- **Remove Link.** This command is available only when a link is selected or the insertion point is inside a link. It deletes hyperlinks by removing the <a href> tag from the selected text or image.

- **Open Linked Page.** Opens the linked page in a new document window. This command is available only when a link is selected or the insertion point is inside a link. (You can, however, hold down the Ctrl key [⌘] and double-click a link to open the page to which it's linked.)

- **Link Target.** Sets a link's target and defines whether the linked page appears in the same browser window or a new one. You can choose from blank, parent, self, or top targets, or manually define the target in the Set Target dialog box. This command's only available when a link is selected or the insertion point is inside a link. (See Chapter 4 for details on links.)

- **Table.** Opens a list of options for modifying a selected table. You can adjust the number of rows and columns, add row or column spans, or completely clear cells' defined heights and widths (see Chapter 7).

- **Image.** Opens a list of options for modifying a selected image, including optimizing it in Fireworks or using one of the new built-in image-editing tools, such as the crop, resample, and sharpen tools. See page 134.

- **Frameset.** Offers options for splitting the current page into *frames*. Or choose the Edit No Frames Content command to create alternative Web-page material that can be read by older browsers that don't support frames.

- **Arrange.** Lets you change the Z-Index (the front-to-back order) of overlapping CSS layers. You can choose to send a layer in front of other layers, send it to the back, and so on. You can also tell Dreamweaver to prevent overlapping layers altogether. If two or more layers are selected, you can also choose from one of this menu's alignment options to align, for example, the tops of two layers.

- **Convert.** Because some older Web browsers don't support CSS layers, you can choose to convert a layer-based layout into a single, large table. (Note that you cannot convert *overlapping* layers into a table.) You can also reverse the process by breaking up an HTML table into separate CSS layers. In this case, every table cell becomes a unique layer.

- **Navigation Bar.** If you inserted an interactive navigation bar from the Insert menu, you can use this command to edit its settings or add new navigation elements.

- **Library.** Lets you add selected document objects to the site's Library file (Chapter 16). You can also update the current document, or multiple documents, to reflect any changes you've made to a Library object.

- **Templates.** These commands affect *template* documents (Chapter 17). Using these commands, you can apply a pre-existing template to the current page, separate the page from its template, or update the page to reflect changes made to its template. If the open document is a template file, you can use this menu to create or delete editable regions (remove template markup) and update all site files based on that template. You can also use this menu to add repeating template regions and editable tag attributes.

- **Timeline.** The submenu provides options for adding or deleting timelines, animation frames, objects, or behaviors. This feature is a bit archaic and adds lots of JavaScript code to your page. If you're still interested, you can download a chapter from an earlier edition of this book, which discusses how to use this feature: *www.sawmac.com/dwmx2004/DWmx_Ch12.pdf*.

Text Menu

As you could guess, the commands in the Text menu format and modify the document's text:

- **Indent.** Adds one level of indentation to everything within the current block-level element (paragraph, headline, bulleted list).

- **Outdent.** Removes one level of indentation from everything within the current block-level element.

- **Paragraph Format.** Applies a paragraph format, such as Heading 1, Heading 2, or preformatted text, to all the text in the current block-level element. You can also choose None from the submenu to remove the paragraph formatting.

- **Align.** Aligns text in the selected paragraph to the left margin, center, or right margin of the document. If the paragraph is inside a table cell or layer, Dreamweaver aligns it with the left, center, or right of that cell or layer.

- **List.** Turns the selected paragraph into an ordered, unordered, or definition *list*. You can edit the list's format by selecting the Properties option from the submenu.

- **Font.** Lets you choose from a list of common font combinations for application to the selected text. When displaying text, your visitor's browser moves down the list of assigned paragraph fonts until it finds one installed on its system (Chapter 3). You can create your own combination of paragraph fonts by choosing Edit Font List from the submenu.

- **Style.** Applies predefined text styles—such as Bold, Italic, or Strikethrough—to the selected text.

- **CSS Styles.** Lets you create new CSS (Cascading Style Sheet) styles and apply them to selected text (Chapter 6). You can also choose to attach an existing style sheet to the current document, or export the document's own style sheet for use in other sites.

- **Size.** Applies a new size to the selected text. Sizes range from 1 (the smallest) to 7 (the largest); as described in Chapter 3, HTML sizes are relative, and they change depending on your visitors' browser preferences. CSS offers a much better alternative to sizing text that is not only more flexible, but also uses less code and is more in line with current Web standards and techniques (see Chapter 6).

- **Size Change.** Increases or decreases the selected text's size relative to the document's base font size (which is set to 3 by default). The same note about CSS mentioned in the previous item applies here, too.

- **Color.** Opens the standard Mac or Windows color-picker dialog box, so that you can choose a color to apply to the selected text. *Macintosh*: You can choose from a variety of color palettes, including CMYK, RGB, HTML (Web safe), HSV, and HLS. *Windows*: In general, the Property inspector's Color box is a better way to assign Web colors to text.

- **Check Spelling.** Checks the current document for possible spelling errors (see page 70).

Commands Menu

You can use the Commands menu to apply advanced features to your Dreamweaver document. Some menu items, such as the Record commands, eliminate repetitive tasks; others, such as the Clean Up HTML command, fix common problems in a single sweep:

- **Start/Stop Recording.** Records a series of actions that can then be reapplied to other parts of the document (Chapter 18). When you select the Start Recording command, Dreamweaver records each of your actions until you choose Stop Recording. Note that Dreamweaver only retains one recorded command at a time.

- **Play Recorded Command.** Reapplies the most recently recorded command.

- **Edit Command List.** Opens a list of all saved commands. You can rename the commands or delete them permanently.

- **Get More Commands.** Opens the Macromedia Exchange for Dreamweaver Web site in a new browser window so that you can search for and download new extensions or commands. Extensions are downloaded to your Extension Manager (see Chapter 19).

- **Manage Extensions.** Opens the Extension Manager, a program that lets you manage extensions you download from the Macromedia Exchange Web site

(Chapter 19). The Extension Manager helps you install, delete, and selectively disable extensions.

- **Apply Source Formatting.** Changes you make to Dreamweaver's HTML source formatting (which is defined in the Preferences window and the SourceFormat. txt file) apply only to newly created documents. This command, on the other hand, offers a way to apply these formatting preferences to existing HTML documents.

- **Apply Source Formatting to Selection.** Same as the previous command, "Apply Source Formatting," but applies only to whatever you've selected. In this way, you can make sure the HTML for a <table> is nicely formatted (by selecting it and applying this command), while the rest of your finely crafted HTML is left alone.

- **Clean Up HTML/XHTML.** Opens a list of options for correcting common HTML problems, such as empty tags or redundant nested tags. Once you've selected what you'd like to fix, Dreamweaver applies those changes to the current document and, if requested, provides a log of the number and type of changes made. (See Chapter 15.)

- **Clean Up Word HTML.** If you import HTML that was generated by Microsoft Word, you often end up with unnecessary or cluttered HTML tags that can affect your site's performance. This command opens a list of options that can correct formatting problems common in Microsoft Word's HTML. Dreamweaver applies your selected changes to the document and, if requested, displays a log of the number and type of changes it made.

- **Add/Remove Netscape Resize Fix.** This command lets you insert JavaScript code into your document that counteracts a bug in version 4 of Netscape Navigator (the bug causes pages that use layers to display incorrectly when the browser window is resized). The inserted code makes the page reload every time a browser window is resized. Does anyone still use Netscape 4?

- **Remove Flash Video Detection.** If you've added Flash Video to your page as described on page 458, Dreamweaver inserts some JavaScript code used to help make sure your site's visitors can view the video. Unfortunately, if you just delete the movie from your page, the JavaScript code is left in the page. This command removes it.

- **Optimize Image in Fireworks.** Opens the selected image in Macromedia Fireworks' Optimization window, where you can experiment with different compression settings to find the best balance between file size and image quality. If you used Fireworks to create the image in the first place, you can choose to use the original Fireworks PNG file or the selected image (GIF or JPEG file) as the source image. Dreamweaver then replaces the selected image with the newly optimized image.

- **Create Web Photo Album.** Lets you turn a folder of images into a Web-based photo album. The Create Web Photo Album window appears; specify a title for your album, the source folder, and so on (see Chapter 18).

Note: This command requires Macromedia's Fireworks image-editing program, which creates thumbnail and full-size versions of each image. Dreamweaver then creates a Web site with one page displaying all of the thumbnail images. The thumbnails are linked to individual HTML pages containing the full-size images.

- **Format Table.** Opens a list of preset formatting options for your HTML table, including color schemes, text alignment and style, and border measurements. (Unavailable when a table is in Layout mode.)

- **Sort Table.** Sorts the information in a selected table. You can choose to sort alphabetically or numerically, in ascending or descending order. This command cannot be applied to tables that include *rowspans* or *colspans*.

- **Insert Mark of the Web.** This is applicable only to Windows XP with Service Pack 2. This software update inserted code into Internet Explorer to "protect" it from malicious Web page code. Unfortunately, this also had the effect of preventing you from previewing JavaScript effects—like the image rollovers discussed in Chapter 5—or Flash movies. Strangely, this happens only when you preview a local page, not when you view a page on the Internet. This menu option lets you overcome that peculiar problem.

- **Attach an XSLT Stylesheet.** This menu option, available only when working on a XML file, lets you attach an XSL file, which miraculously transforms cryptic XML into a beautiful, browser-viewable page. This feature is discussed in Chapter 24.

Site Menu

As its name suggests, the commands in this menu apply to your entire Web site, rather than to one document at a time. These commands can help keep your Web site organized and promote collaboration between large workgroups:

- **New Site.** Opens the New Site window, where you can set up a site for working in Dreamweaver.

- **Manage Sites.** Opens the Manage Sites Panel where you can create, delete, or edit site definitions. See Chapter 13.

Note: The next five menu commands let you transfer files between your computer (the *local* site) and a Web server (the *remote* site). These commands, in other words, don't work unless you've first defined a remote site in the Site Definition window. In addition, these operations work only on files that you've *selected* in the Site window.

- **Get.** Copies files (those you've selected in the Site window) from the remote server to the local site folder for editing. Note that if the File Check In and Check Out feature's active, the downloaded files aren't editable.

- **Check Out.** Copies files (those you've selected in the Site window) from the remote server to your local site and marks them on the remote server as *checked out*. No one else can make changes to the document until you upload it back onto the remote server.

- **Put.** Uploads files (those you've selected in the Site window) from the local site to the remote site. The uploaded file replaces the previous version of the document.

- **Check In.** Uploads checked-out files from the local site to the remote site and makes them available for others to edit. Once a file's checked in, the version on your local site becomes read-only (openable, but not editable).

- **Undo Check Out.** Removes the checked-out status of selected files. The file isn't uploaded back to the remote server, so any changes you made to the file aren't transmitted to the Web server. Your local copy of the file becomes read-only.

- **Show Checked Out By.** Lets you see who's checked out a particular file.

- **Locate in Site.** When working on a document, selecting this option opens the Site window and highlights that document's file in the site's local folder.

Note: See Chapter 15 for the full scoop on remote sites, local sites, and checking files in and out.

- **Reports.** Opens the Reports window and lists options for generating new reports (Chapter 14). Reports can monitor workflow (such as design notes and checkout status) and common HTML problems (such as Missing Alt text, empty tags, untitled documents, and redundant nested tags). You can generate a report on just the open document, on multiple documents, or on the entire site.

- **Synchronize Sitewide.** Opens the Synchronization window, which lets you compare all your local files with all the files on your Web server. Use this to make sure all the most recent files you've updated locally are transferred to the Web server, or vice versa.

- **Check Links Sitewide.** Analyzes the current site for broken links, external links, and orphaned pages. Dreamweaver then generates a report listing all the found problems. You can fix problematic links directly in the Report window—or click the file name to open the errant file in a new document window with the link highlighted and ready to repair.

- **Change Link Sitewide.** In one step, replaces a broken link that appears multiple times throughout your site. In the Change Link dialog box, you first specify the incorrect link; below it, enter the link with which you'd like to replace it. Dreamweaver searches your site, replacing every instance of the old link.

- **Advanced.** Provides access to advanced site options, such as FTP Log, which opens the *FTP log*—a record of all FTP file transfer activity; "Recreate Site Cache," which forces Dreamweaver to rescan the site's files and update its cache file to reflect any changes to the files or links in the site; "Remove Connection Scripts" for removing the script files Dreamweaver creates to work with dynamic, database-driven Web sites; and "Deploy Supporting Files" to move necessary programming files to the Web server when using Dreamweaver's ASP.NET server model to build dynamic pages.

Window Menu

This menu controls which panels and windows are visible or hidden at the moment. (A checkmark in the menu denotes open panels.)

- **Insert.** Opens the Insert bar, from which you can insert various types of objects (such as images, layers, or forms) into your document. The Insert bar also contains options for switching between Layout and Standard table views, and accessing options for dynamic Web pages.

- **Properties.** Opens the Property inspector, where you can edit the relevant properties for a selected object. The options in the Property inspector depend on which page element's selected.

- **CSS Styles.** Opens the CSS (Cascading Style Sheet) Styles panel, from which you can define and edit CSS styles, or apply existing ones to selected text.

- **Layers.** Opens the Layers panel, which lists all the layers created using Dreamweaver's layer tool, or all *absolutely positioned elements*. See Chapter 8 for more details.

- **Behaviors.** Opens the Behaviors panel, which lets you associate *behaviors* (such as swapping images in a rollover or checking for needed plug-ins) to selected page elements (see Chapter 11).

- **Databases.** Opens the Databases panel for working with dynamic Web sites. This panel lets you connect your site to a database, view the structure of a database, and even preview data currently stored in the database.

- **Bindings.** Opens the Bindings panel, which lets you create database queries for working with dynamic sites. In addition, the panel displays and lets you add dynamic data to a Web page.

- **Server Behaviors.** Opens the Server Behaviors panel, the control panel for viewing, editing, and adding advanced functionality to dynamic Web pages.

- **Components.** Opens the Components panel, for use with ColdFusion MX and JSP sites, as well as Web Services. This advanced feature lets ColdFusion and JSP developers take advantage of prewritten, self-contained programs, which makes building complex dynamic sites easier.

- **Files.** Opens the Files panel. From this window, you can open any file and transfer files between your computer and the remote server.

- **Assets.** Opens the Assets panel, which conveniently groups and lists all of the assets (such as colors, links, scripts, or graphics) you've used in your site.

- **Snippets.** Opens the Snippets panel, which contains snippets of HTML, Java-Script, and other types of programming code. You can create your own snippets to save your fingers from having to retype frequently repeated code.

- **Tag Inspector.** Opens the Tag Inspector panel, which provides a listing of *all* properties available for the currently selected HTML tag. This über-geek option is like the Property inspector on steroids.

- **Results.** Lets you open Dreamweaver's many site tools, such as the Find and Replace command, Link Checker, and Reports command. Pick the type of site-wide action you'd like to perform using the submenu.

- **Reference.** Opens the Reference panel, a searchable guide to HTML tags, Cascading Style Sheets, and JavaScript commands. The guides are culled from the popular O'Reilly reference books and include an explanation of what specific tags do, when you can use them, and what additional components are required, as well as tips for getting the most out of them.

- **History.** Displays the history panel for viewing a record of actions performed in the current document.

- **Frames.** Displays the frames panel for selecting frames and framesets for editing.

- **Code Inspector.** A window displaying the HTML code for the current document. You can edit the code directly in the window, while still looking at the Design view. It's often easier to just use Dreamweaver's "Code and Design" view (View → Code and Design).

- **Timelines.** Opens the Timelines panel, in which you can set up and refine animations within Dreamweaver. This feature was added in Dreamweaver MX and then removed in Dreamweaver MX 2004…and *then* put *back in* with the Dreamweaver 7.01 updater (available from the Macromedia Web site). This feature's a bit archaic and adds lots of JavaScript code to your page, so this edition doesn't include details on how to use it. You can, however, download the chapter from an earlier edition of this book that describes how timelines work: *www.sawmac.com/dwmx2004/DWmx_Ch12.pdf*.

- **Workspace Layout.** Lets you save the position and size of Dreamweaver's panels and windows in any arrangement you like.

- **Hide Panels.** Closes all currently open panels. Choosing Show Panels reopens only those panels that were displayed before you selected Hide Panels.

- **Cascade.** By default, when there are multiple documents open, you switch from page to page by clicking on tabs that appear at the top of the document area. If you prefer to have all open documents floating and resizable within this space, this and the next two options let you "undock" the current documents. The cascade option resizes each open document and places them one on top of the next. Windows users can redock pages by clicking the Maximize button on any currently opened document. Mac users can select the Combine As Tabs option.

- **Tile Horizontally (Windows Only).** Places all open documents one on top of the other. The documents don't float on top of each other; rather, they fill the available document area as row upon row of thin, horizontal windows. With more than a few documents open, this option displays so little of each page that it's difficult to work on any one page.

- **Tile Vertically (Windows Only).** Just like the previous command, except that documents are placed vertically like stripes going across the screen.

- **Tile (Mac Only).** This has the same effect as Tile Vertically above.

- **Combine As Tabs (Mac Only).** Returns documents that either tile or cascade (see those options above) on the screen into the single, unified tab interface.

- **Next document, Previous document (Mac Only).** This pair of commands let you step through all your open documents, bringing each document in turn to the front of the screen for editing.

- **List of Currently Open Documents.** All the documents that are currently open are listed at the bottom of this menu. Selecting a document brings it to the front for editing. But with the easy document tabs, why bother?

Help Menu

The Help menu offers useful links and references for more information about using, troubleshooting, and extending Dreamweaver:

- **Dreamweaver Help.** The electronic help system that includes a handful of tutorials, background information on Web publishing, and documentation on Dreamweaver's many features.

- **Getting Started With Dreamweaver.** Opens the same Help system as above but "turns the page" directly to the introduction and tutorial section.

- **Dreamweaver LiveDocs.** An online version of the help system, with the added benefit that it hosts reader comments—if the help system doesn't have the answer you're looking for, perhaps someone has provided it on this Web site. (Hey, but look in this book first!)

- **What's New In Dreamweaver 8.** An overview of the new features introduced in Dreamweaver 8.

- **Using Dreamweaver.** Alright, enough is enough! Opens the same help system as the previous Dreamweaver Help and Getting Started With Dreamweaver menu options.

- **Extending Dreamweaver.** An electronic help system for those interested in writing their own "extensions" to Dreamweaver. Extensions are discussed in Chapter 19.

- **Dreamweaver API Reference.** Even more in-depth information for the Extension developer. Über-geeky information on how to communicate directly with Dreamweaver. Programmers only; all others continue, move along, there's nothing to see here.

- **Using ColdFusion.** A reference guide for setting up and using ColdFusion, Macromedia's dynamic server application. Includes information for creating ColdFusion Web pages.

- **Reference.** Opens the Reference panel, a searchable guide to HTML tags, Cascading Style Sheets, and JavaScript, as described on page 353.

- **Dreamweaver Support Center.** Opens Macromedia's online Dreamweaver Support Center Web page in your browser. This Web site offers technical support for known bugs or common questions, downloadable updates to the program, and a link to online forums.

- **Dreamweaver Developer Center.** Open Macromedia's Dev Center—a Web site with tips, tricks, and in-depth articles aimed at Dreamweaver users of all levels.

- **Dreamweaver Documentation Resource Center.** A Web page on Macromedia's site that offers downloadable versions of the electronic documentation provided with Dreamweaver. Also offers supplemental information, like a Dreamweaver cheat sheet and errata—corrections to the documentation.

- **Macromedia Online Forums.** Opens an index of available online forums from Macromedia's Web site (in your Web browser). You can use the forums to interact with other Macromedia customers, post questions, share techniques, or answer questions posted by others. Requires Internet access and a newsgroup reader.

- **Macromedia Training.** Opens Macromedia's Training Web page, where you can spend even more money learning how to use the program. Cool! Advertising, built right into Dreamweaver.

- **Online Registration.** Goes to the online registration system, where you can register your copy of Dreamweaver. You must do this in order to receive any free technical support (see page 884).

- **Print Registration.** For those Web developers who don't have an Internet connection, or who just don't trust sending their information over the Internet. Doesn't actually print anything—just opens a browser window with an HTML form in it that you then print, fill out, and mail or fax to Macromedia.

- **About Dreamweaver (Windows Only).** Opens an About Dreamweaver window, showing your software's version number. (On the Macintosh, this command is in the Dreamweaver 8 menu.)

Index

Colophon

Sanders Kleinfeld was the production editor and proofreader for *Dreamweaver 8: The Missing Manual*. Marlowe Shaeffer and Genevieve d'Entremont provided quality control. Lucie Haskins wrote the index.

The cover of this book is based on a series design by David Freedman. Karen Montgomery produced the cover layout with Adobe InDesign CS using Adobe's Minion and Gill Sans fonts.

David Futato designed the interior layout, based on a series design by Phil Simpson. This book was converted by Keith Fahlgren from Microsoft Word to Adobe FrameMaker 5.5.6 using Open Source XML technologies. The text font is Adobe Minion; the heading font is Adobe Formata Condensed; and the code font is LucasFont's TheSans Mono Condensed. The illustrations that appear in the book were produced by Robert Romano, Jessamyn Read, and Lesley Borash using Macromedia FreeHand MX and Adobe Photoshop CS.

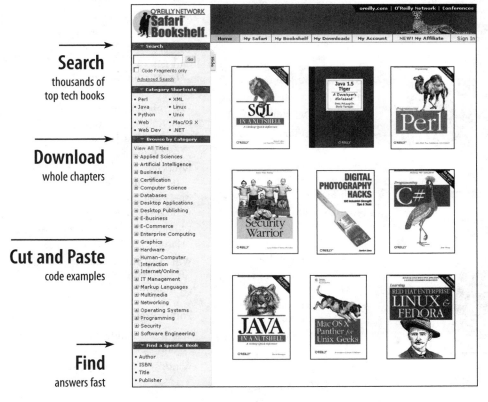

Related Titles from O'Reilly

Missing Manuals

Access 2003 for Starters:
The Missing Manual

AppleScript:
The Missing Manual

AppleWorks 6: The Missing
Manual

Creating Web Sites:
The Missing Manual

Dreamweaver 8: The Missing
Manual

Dreamweaver MX 2004:
The Missing Manual

eBay: The Missing Manual

Excel: The Missing Manual

Excel for Starters:
The Missing Manual

FileMaker Pro 8:
The Missing Manual

Flash 8: The Missing Manual

FrontPage 2003:
The Missing Manual

GarageBand 2:
The Missing Manual

Google: The Missing Manual,
2nd Edition

Home Networking:
The Missing Manual

iLife '05: The Missing Manual

iMovie HD & iDVD 5:
The Missing Manual

iPhoto 5: The Missing Manual

iPod & iTunes: The Missing
Manual, *3rd Edition*

iWork '05: The Missing
Manual

Mac OS X: The Missing
Manual, *Tiger Edition*

Office 2004 for Macintosh:
The Missing Manual

PCs: The Missing Manual

Photoshop Elements 4:
The Missing Manual

QuickBooks 2006:
The Missing Manual

Quicken 2006 for Starters:
The Missing Manual

Switching to the Mac:
The Missing Manual,
Tiger Edition

Windows 2000 Pro:
The Missing Manual

Windows XP for Starters:
The Missing Manual

Windows XP Pro: The Missing
Manual, *2nd Edition*

Windows XP Home Edition:
The Missing Manual,
2nd Edition

Pogue Press

Mac OS X Panther Power
Hound

Windows XP Power Hound

O'REILLY®

Our books are available at most retail and online bookstores.

To order direct: 1-800-998-9938 • *order@oreilly.com* • *www.oreilly.com*

Online editions of most O'Reilly titles are available by subscription at *safari.oreilly.com*